THE CONTINENTAL EDITION

OF

World Masterpieces

VOLUME 1

THIRD EDITION

Uniform with this volume,
and also under the General Editorship of
Maynard Mack

THE TWO-VOLUME EDITION OF
World Masterpieces, Third Edition

VOLUME 1

Literature of Western Culture through the Renaissance

VOLUME 2

Literature of Western Culture since the Renaissance

THE CONTINENTAL EDITION OF
World Masterpieces, Third Edition

IN ONE VOLUME

Masterpieces of the Orient
Edited by G. L. Anderson
UNIVERSITY OF HAWAII

THE CONTINENTAL EDITION
OF
World Masterpieces
THIRD EDITION

Maynard Mack, *General Editor*
YALE UNIVERSITY

Bernard M. W. Knox
CENTER FOR HELLENIC STUDIES

John C. McGalliard
THE UNIVERSITY OF IOWA

P. M. Pasinetti
UNIVERSITY OF CALIFORNIA, LOS ANGELES

Howard E. Hugo
UNIVERSITY OF CALIFORNIA, BERKELEY

René Wellek
YALE UNIVERSITY

Kenneth Douglas
FORMERLY OF YALE UNIVERSITY

VOLUME 1
Continental Literature through the Renaissance

W · W · NORTON & COMPANY · INC · *New York*

Library of Congress Cataloging in Publication Data

Mack, Maynard, 1909–   ed.
  The continental edition of World masterpieces.

  Includes bibliographical references.
  CONTENTS: v.1. Continental literature through the Renaissance.—
v.2. Continental literature since the Renaissance.
    1. Literature—Translations into English.
    2. English literature—Translations from foreign literature. I. Title.
PN6019.M2 1974   808.8   73-16390
ISBN 0-393-09319-0 (v.l)

Book design by John Woodlock

PRINTED IN THE UNITED STATES OF AMERICA

4 5 6 7 8 9 0

Contents

Masterpieces of the Middle Ages

Masterpieces of the Renaissance

Preface to the Third Edition

The Continental Edition of *World Masterpieces* is an anthology of Western literature containing only writings from the ancient and the modern foreign languages.

It reaches in time from Homer and the Old Testament writers to Isaac Singer and Alexander Solzhenitsyn, and the literatures represented in it include French, German, Gaelic, Greek, Hebrew, Italian, Latin, Norwegian, Russian, Spanish, Swedish, and Yiddish.

In modes and genres, its range is similarly comprehensive. Epic poetry appears liberally in large selections from works as different as *The Iliad, The Odyssey, The Aeneid, The Song of Roland, The Divine Comedy* (the *Inferno* is given complete in the sensitive new translation by Mark Musa), and *Faust* (Part I is given complete in the spirited English of Louis MacNeice. Prose fiction also appears in a dazzling variety of styles and moods. Selections are drawn from Petronius, Boccaccio, Rabelais, Cervantes, Voltaire, Flaubert, Dostoevsky, Tolstoy, Proust, Mann, Gide, Kafka, Camus, Sartre, and Solzhenitsyn. Four novels or seminovels are represented complete—*Candide, Madame Bovary, Notes from Underground,* and *Felix Krull*—along with a number of the finest "long-stories" of modern times: *The Death of Iván Ilyich, The Return of the Prodigal Son, The Metamorphosis, The Renegade,* and *Matryona's House.* In addition, the anthology contains fifteen full-length plays. Seven of these come from the ancient world (*Agamemnon, Prometheus Bound, Oedipus Tyrannus, Antigone, Medea, The Trojan Women, Lysistrata*); one is from Golden-Age Spain (*Life Is a Dream*); two are from the French Classical Theater (*Tartuffe* and *Phaedra*); and the remainder exemplify currents in the main stream of modern drama (*The Wild Duck, The Ghost Sonata, The Cherry Orchard,* Pirandello's *Henry IV,* and *The Caucasian Chalk Circle*).

All this, thanks to the generosity of our publisher, we have been able to bring together in the Continental Edition without scanting either the lyric vein in poetry (represented by Archilochus, Tyrtaeus, Mimnermus, Sappho, Alcaeus, Solon, Anacreon, Xenophanes, Theognis, Catullus, Ovid, Petrarch, La Fontaine, Hölderlin, Novalis, Heine, Pushkin, Lamartine, Hugo, Nerval, Leopardi, Baudelaire, Rimbaud, Rilke) or the philosophic discursive vein in prose (Thucydides, Plato, Cicero, St. Augustine, Erasmus, Castiglione, Machiavelli, Cellini, Aretino, Montaigne, La Rochefoucauld, Diderot, Rousseau, Chateaubriand). Those who have already used the Continental Edition of *World Masterpieces* in either of its two forms, one-volume or two-volume, will rejoice with us, we feel sure, at the many hundreds of pages of new selections now added to both formats. Though the one-volume version is necessarily more compact, its survey of some twenty-eight hundred years of human experience as expressed in literature remains remarkably full. It affords, in fact—as Dryden said of Chaucer's poetry—"God's plenty."

Teachers and students making the acquaintance of this anthology for the first time in the new edition will perhaps find it helpful to know the principles by which its editors have been guided:

(1) Like all versions of *World Masterpieces*, the Continental Edition is an anthology of *Western* literature. Eastern literatures (apart from the Old Testament) have been excluded, on the ground that the principal aim of a course in world literature is to bring American students into live contact with their own tradition, and that this aim cannot be adequately realized in a single course if they must also be introduced to a very different tradition, one requiring extended treatment to be correctly understood.

(2) The emphasis of all editions of *World Masterpieces* is decidedly on imaginative literature. We have not tried to cover the entire history of the West in print, and have avoided filling our pages with philosophy, political theory, theology, historiography, and the like. This principle was adopted not because we disapprove of coming at the history of an epoch by way of literature, but because imaginative literature, in our view, itself best defines the character of its epoch: Great monuments of art, we would be inclined to say, furnish the best documents for history. They lead us deeper into the meaning of a past age than other modes of writing do, because they convey its unformulated aspirations and intuitions as well as its conscious theorems and ideals; and yet, being timeless, they have also an unmatched appeal to our own age. For this reason, we have admitted into *World Masterpieces* only works which have something important to say to modern readers, and we have made it a point to interpret them with reference not only to their time but to ours.

(3) We believe that effective understanding of any author depends upon studying an autonomous and substantial piece of his

work: a whole drama, a whole story, at least a whole canto or book of a long poem. Our anthology therefore contains no snippets. Where it has been necessary to represent a long work by extracts, they are large extracts, forming a coherent whole. These considerations have also affected our treatment of lyric poems. Our conviction that the value of reading poems in translation diminishes in proportion as the poetry assumes the intensive iconic character of lyric is set forth clearly and, we hope, persuasively, in the Note on Translation with which all volumes of *World Masterpieces* close. We are aware, nevertheless, that there are readers from whom lyric poetry, even when seriously impaired by translation, offers a more satisfying glimpse of the self-hood of an age than any other genre. We have consequently sought to meet this problem by selecting (upon the whole) longer rather than shorter lyrics and by choosing them from periods in which, as in the Romantic period notably, they are a dominant form of expression; or, as in the Greek sixth and seventh centuries B.C., the chief surviving form; or, as with, say, Ovid, Petrarch, and La Fontaine, indicative of attitudes and values not found elsewhere in our selections from that period.

(4) Since nothing has so deterred students from enjoying the great masterpieces of the classical and modern foreign languages as translations in an English idiom that is no longer alive, we have taken special pains in all editions of *World Masterpieces* to use translations that show a powerful feeling for the English language as it is written and spoken today. In the current editions, we believe we have fulfilled our obligation in this matter with some distinction. Fresh renderings of *Oedipus Tyrannus* (Theodore Brunner and Luci Berkowitz), "Dinner with Trimalchio" (J. P. Sullivan), *The Song of Roland* (Dorothy Sayers), *The Inferno* (Mark Musa), and *Candide* (R. M. Adams), now join forces with works translated by Roy Campbell, Robert Fitzgerald, Richmond Lattimore, C. Day Lewis, Robert Lowell, Louis MacNeice, Edwin Muir, Charles Murphy, Samuel Putnam, Rex Warner, and Richard Wilbur, among the selections held over from the last edition, and with work by Thomas Chubb, Wallace Fowlie, Horace Gregory, Guy Lee, Elizabeth Sprigge, Marianne Moore, Vernon Watkins, and Avraham Yarmolinsky, among those now presented for the first time. A more dignified company of translators we are sure this world has not, and we indicate here with pleasure our gratitude to them and to their publishers for permission to reprint their work.

(5) Our introductions—in consonance with the scheme of the book—emphasize criticism rather than history. While providing all that seems to us necessary in the way of historical background (and supplying biographical summaries in the appendix following

each introduction), we aim to give the student primarily a critical and analytical discussion of the works themselves. We try to suggest what these works have to say to us in our own time and generation, and why they should be valued now. With the same ends in view, we give exceptional space to seminal writers of our own century, feeling that this is the best way to help students grasp the continuity of literature and realize that all of it, however remote at first glance, is in one way or other about us.

> Though grave diggers' toil is long,
> Sharp their spades, their muscles strong,
> They but thrust their buried men
> Back in the human mind again.

The Editors

THE CONTINENTAL EDITION

OF

World Masterpieces

VOLUME 1

THIRD EDITION

Masterpieces of the Ancient World

EDITED BY

BERNARD M. W. KNOX

Director of the Center for Hellenic Studies

This section represents, not the ancient world as a whole, but the most significant area and period of ancient man's development. The area is the Mediterranean basin, and the period the twelve hundred years from, roughly, 800 B.C. to A.D. 400. In this place and time ancient man laid the intellectual and religious foundations of the modern Western outlook.

The literature of the ancient world, which, whether or not we are acquainted with it, is still the background of our institutions, attitudes, and thought, was written in three languages —Hebrew, Greek, and Latin. The peoples who spoke these languages created their civilizations independently in place and time, but the development of the Mediterranean area into one economic and political unit brought these civilizations into contact with each other and

produced a fusion of their typical attitudes which is the basis of all subsequent Western thought. This process of independent development, interaction, and final fusion is represented in the arrangement of this section: In the last part of it the three separate lines converge, and they finally meet in the figure of St. Augustine, who had the intellectual honesty and curiosity of the Greek at his best, the social seriousness and sense of order of the Roman, and the Hebrew's feeling of man's inadequacy and God's omnipotent justice.

PALESTINE

The territory of the Hebrews was of no particular strategic importance, and their record is not that of an imperial people. In their period of independence, from their beginnings as a pastoral tribe to their high point as

1

a kingdom with a splendid capital in Jerusalem, they accomplished little of note in the political or military spheres; their later history was a bitter and unsuccessful struggle for freedom against a series of foreign masters—Babylonian, Greek, and Roman. They left no painting or sculpture behind them, no drama, no epic poetry. What they did leave is a religious literature, probably written down between the eighth and second centuries B.C., which is informed by an attitude different from that of all the peoples surrounding them, a conception of divine power and of the government of the universe so simple that to us, who have inherited it from them, it seems obvious, yet in its time so revolutionary that it made them a nation apart, sometimes laughed at, sometimes feared, but always alien.

THE CREATION—THE FALL

The typical attitudes of the Hebrews appear in the story which they told of the creation of the world and of man. This creation is the work of one God, who is omnipotent and omniscient, and who creates a perfect and harmonious order. The disorder which we see all around us, physical and moral, is not God's creation but Adam's; it is the consequence of man's disobedience. The story not only reconciles the undeniable existence of evil and disorder in the world with the conception of God's infinite justice, it also attributes to man himself an independence of God, free will, which in this case he has used for evil. The Hebrew God is not limited in His power by other deities, who oppose His will (as in the Greek stories of Zeus and his undisciplined family); His power over inanimate nature is infinite; in all the range of His creation there is only one being able to resist Him—man.

Since God is all-powerful, even this resistance on Adam's part is in some mysterious way a manifestation of God's will; how this can be is not explained by the story, and we are left with the mystery that still eludes us, the coexistence of God's prescient power and man's unrestricted free will.

The story of the Fall of Man ends with a situation in which Adam has earned for himself and his descendants a short life of sorrow relieved only by death. It was the achievement of later Hebrew teachers to carry the story on and develop a concept of a God who is as merciful as He is just, who watches tenderly over the destinies of the creatures who have rebelled against Him, and brings about the possibility of atonement and full reconciliation.

Adam's son Cain is the first man to shed human blood, but though God drives him out to be a wanderer on the face of the earth, He does not kill him, and the brand on Cain's forehead, while it marks him as a murderer, also protects his life—no man is to touch him. Later when the descendants of Adam grow so wicked that God is sorry He has created the human race, He decides to destroy it by sending a universal flood. But He spares one man, Noah, with his family, to beget a new human race, on which God pins His hopes. His rainbow in the sky reminds men of His promise that He will never again let loose the waters. But men do not learn their lesson: they start to build a tower high enough to reach to Heaven, and God is afraid that if they succeed they will then recognize no limit to their ambitions. Yet He does not destroy them; He merely frustrates their purpose by depriving them of their common language.

And yet Man must eventually atone for Adam's act; human guilt must be wiped out by sacrifice. The development of this idea was extended over centuries of thought and suffering; it reached its highest expression in the figure of Christ, the Son of God, who as a man pays the full measure due in human suffering and human death. Before this event, the idea of the one who suffers for all was a major theme in Hebrew literature; not only did there emerge slowly a concept of the Hebrews as a chosen nation which suffers for the rest, but individual figures of Hebrew history and imagination embodied this theme in the form of the story of the suffering servant whose suffering brings relief to his fellow men and ultimate glory to himself. This is the idea behind the story of Joseph.

JOSEPH

Joseph, his father's favorite son, has a sense of his own great destiny, confirmed by his dreams, which represent him as the first of all his race. He is indeed to be the first, but to become so he must also be the last. He is sold into slavery by his brothers; the savior is rejected by those whom he is to save, as the Hebrews were rejected by their neighbors and as they rejected their own prophets.

With the loss of his liberty, Joseph's trials have only begun.

In Egypt after making a new and successful life for himself, he is thrown into prison on a false accusation. He interprets the dream of Pharaoh's butler, who promises, if his interpretation is correct, to secure his release; the butler is restored to freedom and royal favor, but, as is the way of the world, forgets his promise and leaves his comforter in jail. Joseph stays in prison two more years but finally obtains his freedom and becomes Pharaoh's most trusted adviser. When his brothers come from starving Palestine and bow down before him asking for help, he saves them; not only does he give them grain but he also provides a home for his people in Egypt. "I am Joseph your brother, whom ye sold into Egypt," he says to them when he reveals his identity. "God sent me before you to preserve you a posterity in the earth, and to save your lives by a great deliverance."

One of the essential points of this story, and the whole conception of the suffering servant, is the distinction which it emphasizes between an external, secular standard of good and a spiritual, religious standard. In the eyes of the average man, prosperity and righteousness are connected, if not identified; he tends to think of the sufferer as one whose misfortune must be explained as a punishment for his wickedness. This feeling is strong in ancient (especially in Greek) literature, but modern man should not be unduly complacent about his superiority to the ancients in this respect, for the attitude is still with us. It is in fact a basic assumption of the competitive society—the view, seldom expressed but strongly rooted, that the plight of the unfortunate is the result of their own laziness, the wealth of the rich the reward of superior virtue.

The writer of the Joseph story sees in the unfortunate sufferer the savior who is the instrument of God's will; it is because of what he suffers that the sun and the moon and the eleven stars will bow down to Joseph. Yet the story does not emphasize the sufferings of Joseph; he is pictured rather as the man of action who through native ability and divine protection turns the injuries done him into advantages. We are not made to feel the torment in his soul; when he weeps it is because of the memory of what he has suffered and his yearning for his youngest brother, and he is in full control of the situation. And his reward in the things of this world is great. Not only does he reveal himself as the savior of his nation, but he becomes rich and powerful beyond his brothers' dreams, and in a greater kingdom. The spiritual and secular standards are at the end of the story combined; Joseph's suffering is neatly balanced by his worldly reward.

JOB

Later Hebrew writers developed a sadder and profounder view. The greatest literary masterpiece of the Old Testament, the Book of Job, is also concerned with the inadequacy of worldly standards of happiness and righteousness, but the suffering of Job is so overwhelming and so magnificently expressed, that even with our knowledge of its purpose and its meaning it seems excessive. Joseph suffered slavery, exile, and imprisonment, but turned them all to account; Job loses his family and wealth in a series of calamities, which strike one on the other like hammer blows, and is then plagued with a loathsome disease. Unlike Joseph, he is old; he cannot adapt himself and rise above adverse circumstances, and he no longer wishes to live. Except for one thing. He wishes to understand the reason for his suffering.

For his friends the explanation is simple. With the blindness of men who know no standards other than those of this world, they are sure that Job's misfortune must be the result of some wickedness on his part. But Job is confident in his righteousness; his torture is as much mental as physical; he cannot reconcile the fact of his innocence with the calamities that have come upon him with all the decisive suddenness of the hand of God.

The full explanation is never given to him, but it is given to the reader in the two opening chapters of the book. This prologue to the dramatic section of the work gives us the knowledge which is hidden from the participants in the ensuing dialogue; the writer uses the method characteristic of Greek tragedy—irony, the deeper understanding of the dramatic spoken word which is based on the superior knowledge of the audience. The prologue explains God's motive in allowing Job to suffer. It is an important one: God intends to use Job as a demonstration to His skeptical subordinate, Satan, of the fact that a human being can retain faith in God's justice in the face of the greatest imaginable suffering. This motive, which Job does not know and which is never revealed to him, gives to the dialogue between Job and his friends its suspense and its importance; God has rested His case, that humanity is capable of keeping faith in divine justice, against all appearances to the contrary, on this one man.

The arguments of Job's friends are based on the worldly equation, success = virtue. They attempt to undermine Job's faith, not in God, but in himself. ". . . who ever perished, being innocent?" asks Eliphaz, "or where were the righteous cut off?" Job's misfortune is a proof that he must have sinned; all he has to do is to admit his guilt and ask God for pardon, which he will surely receive. He refuses to accept this easy way out, and we know that he is right. In fact, we know from the prologue that he has been selected for misfortune not because he has sinned, but precisely because of his outstanding virtue. "There is none like him in the earth," God says, "a perfect and an upright man, one that feareth God, and escheweth evil." What Job must do is to persevere not only in his faith in God's justice but also in the conviction of his own innocence. He must believe the illogical, accept a paradox. His friends are offering him an easy way out, one which seems to be the way of humility and submission. But it is a false way. And God finally tells them so. "The Lord said to Eliphaz the Temanite, My wrath is kindled against thee, and against thy two friends: for ye have not spoken of me the thing that is right, as my servant Job hath."

Job's confidence in his own righteousness is not pride, but intellectual honesty. He sees that the problem is much harder than his friends imagine; to let them persuade him of his own guilt would lighten his mental burden by answering the question which tortures him, but his intelligence will not let him yield. Like Oedipus, he refuses to stop short of the truth; he even uses the same words: "let me alone, that I may speak, and let come on me what will." He finally expresses his understanding and acceptance of the paradox involved in the combination of his suffering with his innocence, but he does so with a human independence and dignity. "Though he slay me, yet will I trust in him: but I will maintain mine own ways before him." He sums up his case with a detailed account of the righteousness of his ways, and it is clear that this account is addressed not only to his three friends but also to God. "My desire is, that the Almighty would answer me," he says. His friends are silenced by the majesty and firmness of his statement, they "ceased to answer Job, because he was righteous in his own eyes," but God is moved to reply.

The magnificent poetry of that reply, the voice out of the whirlwind, still does not give Job the full explanation, God's motive in putting him to the torture. It is a triumphant proclamation of God's power and also of His justice, and it silences Job, who accepts it as a sufficient answer. That God does not reveal the key to the riddle even to the man who has victoriously stood the test and vindicated His faith in humanity is perhaps the most significant point in the poem. It suggests that there is not and never will be an explanation of human suffering that man's intelligence can comprehend. The sufferer must, like Job, cling to his faith in himself and in God; he must accept the inexplicable fact that his own undeserved suffering is the working of God's justice.

ECCLESIASTES

But there were some whose questions about the justice of God were not satisfied by a voice from the whirlwind. In the book known as Ecclesiastes (which claims it is the work of King Solomon but almost certainly comes from a much later time) the impermanence of all things human, the certainty of death, and the prevalence of injustice on earth produce in the writer a mood which at first sight seems a philosophy of despair: life is short, rewards transient—best to enjoy each moment for what it offers, enjoy one's work for the doing of it, without thought of results. But the book is informed throughout by a profoundly religious spirit; the moral that man "should make his soul enjoy good in his labour" is "from the hand of God" and the somberly magnificent evocation of old age and death, with which the book concludes, opens with the words: "Remember now thy Creator in the days of thy youth . . ."

THE PROPHETS

In the last days of Israel's independence, before conquerors overran the land and transported the population to captivity in the East (an exile mourned in Psalm 137—"By the rivers of Babylon . . ."), a series of prophets reproved the children of Israel for their transgressions and foretold the wrath to come, the end of the kingdom of Israel, and, beyond that, the overthrow of the neighboring kingdoms. The prophet was a man who believed himself to be the spokesman of God, the messenger of a terrifying vision. The horror of the vision of destruction was often too heavy a load for the human mind, and the disbelief and mockery of his hearers tipped the precarious balance so that what might have been merely a strange urgency came often close to madness. The vision of things to come was expressed in magnificent but disconnected images which to the workaday mind of the man in the street seemed only to confirm the suspicion that the prophet was deranged. Amos, Nahum, Jeremiah, and many another poured out their charged and clotted imagery of catastrophe to an unbelieving people.

But the story of Jonah shows us a prophet who *was* believed. When they heard his message, the people and ruler of Nineveh repented of their sins and made amends to God. They were spared, but Jonah objected and God had to rebuke him; God was more forgiving to sinners than the human prophet to his fellow man.

The prophets were not always messengers of doom; it is in the words of an unnamed prophet (whose writings are included in the Book of Isaiah) that the theme of the one who suffers for others finds its most profound and moving expression. In the earlier versions the sufferer has it all made up to him in the end: Job, like Joseph, has his reward. Job's suffering is greater than Joseph's and it is clear that the writer of the Book of Job shows, alike in the speeches and in the ironic framework of the whole, a profounder understanding of the nature and meaning of suffering than the narrator of the story of Joseph, but like Joseph, Job lives to see the end of his troubles and has his material reward. "The Lord gave Job twice as much as he had before. . . . After this lived Job an hundred and forty years, and saw his sons, and his sons' sons, even four generations."

But in the Song of the Suffering Servant there is no recompense in this life: the suffering ends in death. In this deeper vision there is no reconciliation between the standards of this world and the standards of the higher authority behind the suffering. The one who is to save Israel and the world is not well favored like Joseph: "he hath no form nor comeliness." Nor is he, like Job, "the greatest of all the men of the east"; he is "despised and rejected of men." He suffers for his fellow men: "the Lord hath laid on him the iniquity of us all." His suffering knows no limit but death; he is oppressed and afflicted, imprisoned and executed. "He was cut off out of the land of the living" and "he made his grave with the wicked."

The circumstances described here are familiar from other cultures than the Hebrew; they are found in the primitive ritual of many peoples, and ceremonial relics of them still existed in civilized fifth-century Athens. In certain primitive societies, to rid the group of guilt a scapegoat was chosen, who was declared responsible for the misdeeds of all, and who was then mocked, beaten, driven out of the community, and killed. The scapegoat was hated and despised as the embodiment of the guilt of the whole community; his death was the most ignominious imaginable. The memory of some such primitive ritual is unmistakable in the Hebrew song; but its meaning has been utterly changed. It is precisely in the figure of the hated and suffering scapegoat that the Hebrew prophet sees the savior of mankind—an innocent sufferer, "he had done no violence, neither was any deceit in his mouth"— and he sees this without visible confirmation; there is no recognition by the brothers, no vindication by a voice out of the whirlwind. It is the highest expression of the Hebrew vision at its saddest and most profound, this portrayal of the savior who comes not in pomp and power but in suffering and meekness, who dies rejected and despised, and who atones for human sin and makes "intercession for the transgressors." It implies the complete rejection of all worldly standards, a rejection which is to be made explicit later in the words of Christ, the embodiment of the suffering servant: "No man can serve two masters . . . God and Mammon."

GREECE

HOMER

Greek literature begins with two masterpieces, the *Iliad* and the *Odyssey*, which cannot be accurately dated (the conjectural dates range over three centuries), and which are attributed to a poet, Homer, about whom nothing is known except his name. They were probably fixed in something like their present form before the art of writing was in general use in Greece; it is certain that they were intended not for reading but for oral recitation. Until quite recently it was generally believed that the poems as we now have them were an amalgam of the work of many different minstrels, composing at different times and in different places, adopting and adapting the lines of their predecessors while adding their own; much of the Homeric criticism of the nineteenth century was an attempt to distinguish the early material from the late according to the canons of linguistics, history, and archaeology. But the poetic organization of each of the two epics, the subtle interrelationship of the parts which creates their structural and emotional unity, is now for most critics ample assurance that these poems owe their present form to the shaping hand of a single poet, the architect who selected from the enormous wealth of the oral tradition and fused what he took with original material to create the two magnificently ordered poems known as the *Iliad* and the *Odyssey*.

Of these two the *Iliad* is per-haps the earlier; it is generally agreed that it is the greater poem. Its subject is war; its characters are men in battle and women whose fate depends on the outcome. The war is fought by the Achaeans against the Trojans for the recovery of Helen, the wife of the Achaean chieftain Menelaus; the combatants are heroes who in their chariots engage in individual duels before the supporting lines of infantry and archers. This romantic war aim and the outmoded military technique suggest to the modern reader a comparison with chivalrous engagements between medieval knights —a vision of individual prowess in combat which the nostalgia of our mechanized age contrasts sentimentally with the mass slaughter of modern war. But there is no sentimentality in Homer's description of battle. "Patroclus went up to him and drove a spear into his right jaw; he thus hooked him by the teeth and the spear pulled him over the rim of his car. As one who sits at the end of some jutting rock and draws a strong fish out of the sea with a hook and line —even so with his spear did he pull Thestor all gaping from his chariot; he threw him down on his face and he died while falling." This is meticulously accurate; there is no attempt to suppress the ugliness of Thestor's death. The bare, careful description creates the true nightmare quality of battle, in which men perform monstrous actions with the same matter-of-fact efficiency they display in their normal occupations; and the simile reproduces the grotesque appearance of violent death—the simple spear thrust takes away Thestor's dignity as a human being even before it takes his life. He is gaping, like a fish on the hook.

The simile does something else too. The comparison of Patroclus to an angler emphasizes another aspect of battle, its excitement. Homer's lines here combine two contrary emotions, the human revulsion from the horror of violent death and the human attraction to the excitement of violent action. This passage is typical of the poem as a whole. Everywhere in it we are conscious of these two poles, of war's ugly brutality and its "terrible beauty." The poet accepts violence as a basic factor in human life, and accepts it without sentimentality; for it is equally sentimental to pretend that war is not ugly and to pretend that it does not have its beauty. Three thousand years have not changed the human condition in this respect; we are still both lovers and victims of the will to violence, and as long as we are, Homer will be read as its greatest interpreter.

The *Iliad* describes the events of a few weeks in the ten-year siege of Troy. The particular subject of the poem, as its first line announces, is the anger of Achilles, the bravest of the Achaean chieftains encamped outside the city. Achilles is a man who lives by and for violence, who is creative and alive only in violent action. He knows that he will be killed if he stays before Troy, but rather than decay, as he would decay, in peace, he accepts that certainty. His

inadequacy for peace is shown by the fact that even in war the violence of his temper makes him a man apart and alone. His anger cuts him off from his commander and his fellow princes; to spite them he withdraws from the fighting, the only context in which his life has any meaning. He is brought back into it at last by the death of his one real friend, Patroclus; the consequences of his wrath and withdrawal fall heavily on the Achaeans, but most heavily on himself.

The great champion of the Trojans, Hector, fights bravely, but reluctantly; war, for him, is a necessary evil, and he regrets the peaceful past, though he has little hope of peace to come. His pre-eminence in peace is emphasized by the tenderness of his relations with his wife and child and also by his kindness to Helen, the cause of the war which he knows in his heart will bring his city to destruction. We see Hector always against the background of the patterns of civilized life—the rich city with its temples and palaces, the continuity of the family. Achilles' background is the discord of the armed camp on the shore, his loneliness, and his certainty of early death. The duel between these two men is the inevitable crisis of the poem, and just as inevitable is Hector's defeat and death. For against Achilles in his native element of violence nothing can stand.

At the climactic moment of Hector's death, as everywhere in the poem, Homer's firm control of his material preserves the balance in which our contrary emotions are held; pity for Hector does not entirely rob us of sympathy for Achilles. His brutal words to the dying Hector and the insults he inflicts on his corpse are the mark of the savage, but we are never allowed to forget that this inflexible hatred is the expression of his love for Patroclus. And the final book of the poem shows us an Achilles whose iron heart is moved at last; he is touched by the sight of Hector's father clasping in suppliance the terrible hands that have killed so many of his sons. He remembers that he has a father, and that he will never see him again; Achilles and Priam, the slayer and the father of the slain, weep together:

. . . the two remembered, as Priam
    sat huddled
at the feet of Achilleus and wept
    close   for   manslaughtering
    Hektor
and Achilleus wept now for his
    own father, now again
    for Patroklos.*

Achilles gives Hector's body to Priam for honorable burial. His anger has run its full course and been appeased; it has brought death, first to the Achaeans and then to the Trojans, to Patroclus and to Hector, and so to Achilles himself, for his death is fated to come "soon after Hektor's." The violence to which he is dedicated will finally destroy him too.

This tragic action is the center of the poem, but it is surrounded by scenes which remind us that the organized destruction

of war, though an integral part of human life, is only a part of it. Except for Achilles, whose worship of violence falters only in the final moment of pity for his enemy's father and his own, the yearning for peace and its creative possibilities is never far below the surface. This is most poignantly expressed by the scenes which take place in Troy, especially the farewell between Hector and Andromache; but it is made clear that the Achaeans too are conscious of what they have sacrificed. Early in the poem, when Agamemnon, the Achaean commander, tests the morale of his troops by suggesting that the war be abandoned, they rush for the ships so eagerly and with such heartfelt relief that their commanders are hard put to it to stop them. These two poles of the human condition, war and peace, with their corresponding aspects of human nature, the destructive and the creative, are implicit in every situation and statement of the poem, and they are put before us, in symbolic form, on the shield which the god Hephaestus makes for Achilles. Its emblem is an image of human life as a whole. Here are two cities, one at peace and one at war. In one a marriage is celebrated and a quarrel settled by process of law; the other is besieged by a hostile army and fights for its existence. Scenes of violence—peaceful shepherds slaughtered in an ambush, Death dragging away a corpse by its foot—are balanced by scenes of plowing,

---

* The translator has transliterated the original Greek names, rather than use the more familiar Latin forms. Thus we find "Patroklos" rather than "Patroclus," "Achilleus" instead of "Achilles," and so on.

harvesting, work in the vineyard and on the pasture, a green on which youths and maidens dance. And around the outermost rim of the shield runs "the great strength of the Ocean River," a river which is at once the frontier of the known and the imagined world and the barrier between the quick and the dead. The shield of Achilles is the total background for the tragic violence of the central figures; it provides a frame which gives the wrath of Achilles and the death of Hector their just proportion and true significance.

THE ODYSSEY

The other Homeric epic, the *Odyssey*, is concerned with the peace which followed the war, and in particular with the return of the heroes who survived. Its subject is the long drawn out return of one of the heroes, Odysseus of Ithaca, who had come farther than most (all the way from western Greece) and who was destined to spend ten years wandering in unknown seas before he returned to his rocky kingdom. When Odysseus' wanderings began, Achilles had already received, at the hands of Apollo, the death which he had chosen, and which was the only appropriate end for his fatal and magnificent violence. Odysseus chose life, and his outstanding quality is a probing and versatile intelligence, which, combined with long experience, keeps him safe and alive through the trials and dangers of twenty years of war and seafaring. To stay alive he has to do things that Achilles would never have done, and use an ingenuity and experience that Achilles did not

possess; but his life is just as much a struggle. Troy has fallen, but "there is no discharge in the war." The way back is as perilous as the ten-year siege.

The opening lines of the poem state the theme:

Sing, Muse, of that versatile man, who wandered far, after sacking Troy's holy citadel. He saw the cities of many men, and knew their mind; he suffered much on the deep sea, and in his heart, struggling for a prize, to save his life. . . .

In this world it is a struggle even to stay alive, and it is a struggle for which Odysseus is naturally endowed. But his objective is not life at any price. Where honor demands, he can be soberly courageous in the face of death (as on Circe's island, where he goes alone and against his mate's advice to save his sailors), and he can even be led into foolhardiness by his insatiable curiosity (as in the expedition to see the island of the Cyclops). Much as he clings to life, it must be life with honor; what he is trying to preserve is not just existence but a worldwide reputation. His name has become a byword for successful courage and intelligence, and he must not betray it. When he reveals his identity at the palace of the Phaeacians, he speaks of his fame in an objective manner, as if it were something apart from himself.

I am Laertes' son, Odysseus.
          Men hold me
formidable for guile in peace and
    war:
this fame has gone abroad to the
    sky's rim.

This is not boasting, but a calm

recognition of the qualities and achievements for which he stands, and to which he must be true.

Ironically enough, to be true to his reputation, he is twice forced to conceal his name. In the Cyclops' cave, he calls himself "Nobody," in order to assure his escape, and it is clear how hard he finds this denial of his reputation when, out of the cave and on board ship, he insists on telling Polyphemus his name. Not only does this reassertion of his identity bring himself, his ship, and his crew back within reach of Polyphemus' arm, but it also enables the blinded giant to call down on his enemy the wrath of his father Poseidon, who, from this point on, musters the full might of the sea against Odysseus' return. And when the hero finally returns home, to a palace full of violent suitors for his wife's hand who think that he is dead and who have presumed so far that they will kill him if they now find out that he is alive, he has to become Nobody again; he disguises himself as an old dirty beggar, to flatter and fawn on his enemies for bread in his own house.

The trials of the voyage home are not just physical obstacles to his return, they are also temptations Odysseus is tempted, time after time, to forget his identity, to secede from the life of struggle and constant vigilance for which his name stands. The lotus flower which makes a man forget home and family is the most obvious form of temptation; it occurs early in the voyage and is easily resisted. But he is offered more attractive bait. Circe gives him a life of ease and self-indulgence on an enchanted island; his resistance has by this time been lowered, and he stays a full year before his sailors remonstrate with him and remind him of his home. At the Phaeacian palace where he tells the story of his voyages, he is offered the love of a young princess, Nausicaa, and her hand in marriage by her father Alcinous —a new life in a richer kingdom than his rocky Ithaca. The Sirens tempt him to live in the memory of the glorious past. "Come here, famous Odysseus," they sing, "great glory of the Achaeans, and hear our song. . . . For we know all that at broad Troy the Argives and the Trojans suffered by the will of the gods." If he had not been bound to the mast, he would have gone to hear and join the dead men whose bones rot on the Sirens' island. Calypso, the goddess with whom he spent seven years, longing all the time to escape, offers him the greatest temptation of all, immortality. If he will stay as her husband, he will live forever, a life of ease and tranquility, like that of the gods. Odysseus refuses this too; he prefers the human condition, with all its struggle, its disappointments, and its inevitable end. And the end, death, is an ever-present temptation. It is always near him; at the slightest slackening of effort, the smallest failure of intelligence, the first weakness of will, death will bring him release from his trials. But he hangs on tenaciously, and, toward the end of his ordeals, he is sent living to the world of the dead to see for himself what death means. It is dark and comfortless; Homer's land of the dead is the most frightening picture of the afterlife in European literature. Odysseus talks to the dead and any illusion he had about death as repose is shattered when he talks to the shade of Achilles and hears him reply.

Let me hear no smooth talk
of death from you, Odysseus, light
of councils.
Better, I say, to break sod as a farm
hand
for some poor country man, on iron
rations,
than lord it over all the exhausted
dead.

When he hears these words Odysseus does not yet understand their full significance (that he, the living man, will taste the depths of degradation, not as a serf, but as a despised beggar, mocked and manhandled in his own palace), but he is prepared now to face everything that may be necessary, to push on without another look behind.

In this scene Homer brings his two great prototypes face to face, and poses the tragic fury of Achilles against the mature intelligence of Odysseus. There can be little doubt where his sympathy lies. Against the dark background of Achilles' regret for life lost the figure of Odysseus shines more warmly: a man dedicated to life, accepting its limitations and making full use of its possibilities, a man who is destined to endure to the end and be saved. He finds in the end the home and the peace he fought for, his wife faithful, a son worthy of his name ready

to succeed him, and the knowledge that the death which must come at last will be gentle.

Then a seaborne death
soft as this hand of mist will come
upon you
when you are wearied out with rich
old age,
your country folk in blessed peace
around you.

THE HOMERIC GODS

The Homeric poems played in the subsequent development of Greek civilization the same role that the Old Testament writings had played in Palestine: they became the basis of an education and therefore of a whole culture. Not only did the great characters of the epic serve as models of conduct for later generations of Greeks, but the figures of the Olympian gods retained, in the prayers, poems, and sculpture of the succeeding centuries, the shapes and attributes set down by Homer. The difference between the Greek and the Hebrew hero, between Achilles and Joseph, for example, is remarkable, but the difference between "the God of Abraham and of Isaac" and the Olympians who interfere capriciously in the lives of Hector and Achilles is an unbridgeable chasm. The two conceptions of the power which governs the universe are irreconcilable; and in fact the struggle between them ended, not in synthesis, but in the complete victory of the one and the disappearance of the other. The Greek conception of the nature of the gods and of their relation to man is so alien to us that it is difficult for the modern reader to take it seriously. The Hebrew basis of European Christianity has made it almost impossible for us to imagine a god who can be feared and laughed at, blamed and admired, and still sincerely worshiped. Yet all these are proper attitudes toward the gods on Olympus; they are all implicit in Homer's poem.

The Hebrew conception of God is clearly an expression of an emphasis on those aspects of the universe which imply a harmonious order. The elements of disorder in the universe are, in the story of Creation, blamed on man, and in all Hebrew literature the evidences of disorder are something the writer tries to reconcile with an *a priori* assumption of an all-powerful, just God; he never tampers with the fundamental datum. Just as clearly, the Greeks conceived their gods as an expression of the disorder of the world in which they lived; the Olympian gods, like the natural forces of sea and sky, follow their own will even to the extreme of conflict with each other, and always with a sublime disregard for the human beings who may be affected by the results of their actions. It is true that they are all subjects of a single more powerful god, Zeus, but his authority over them is based only on superior strength; though he cannot be openly resisted, he can be temporarily deceived (as he is, in comic circumstances, in the fourteenth book of the *Iliad*). And Zeus, although in virtue of his superior power his will is finally accomplished in the matter of Achilles' wrath, knows limits to his power too;

he cannot save the life of his son, the Lycian hero Sarpedon. Behind Zeus stands the mysterious power of Fate, to which even he must bow.

Such gods as these, representing as they do the blind forces of the universe which man cannot control, are not thought of as connected with morality. Morality is a human creation, and though the gods may approve of it, they are not bound by it. And violent as they are, they cannot feel the ultimate consequence of violence; death is a human fear, just as the courage to face it is a human quality. There is a double standard, one for gods, one for men, and the inevitable consequence is that our real admiration and sympathy is directed not toward the gods but toward the men. With Hector, and even with Achilles at his worst, we can sympathize; but the gods, though they may excite terror or laughter, can never have our sympathy; we could as easily sympathize with the blizzard or the force of gravity. Homer imposed on Greek literature the anthropocentric emphasis which is its distinguishing mark and its great contribution to the Western mind; though the gods are ever-present characters in the incidents of his poem, his true concern, first and last, is with men.

THE CITY-STATES OF GREECE—
LYRIC POETS

The stories told in the Homeric poems are set in the age of the Trojan War, which archaeologists (those, that is, who believe that it happened at all) date to the twelfth century B.C. Though the poems do perhaps preserve some blurred and faded memory of that time (the Mycenaean period, as it has been known since archaeologists uncovered the golden treasures in the royal tombs at Mycenae) there is no doubt that the poems as we have them are the creation of later centuries, the ninth to the seventh, the so-called Dark Age which succeeded the collapse (or destruction) of Mycenaean civilization. This was the time of the final settlement of the Greek peoples, an age of invasion and migration, which saw the foundation and growth of many small independent cities. The geography of the Greek peninsula and its scattered islands encouraged this fragmentation: the Greek cities never lost sight of their common Hellenic heritage but it was not enough to unite them except in the face of unmistakable and overwhelming danger, and even then only partially and for a short time. They differed from each other in custom, political constitution, and even dialect: their relations with each other were those of rivals and fierce competitors.

In these cities, constantly at war with each other in the pursuit of more productive land for growing populations, the kings of Homeric society gave way to aristocratic oligarchies, which maintained a strangle hold on the land and the economy of which it was the base. An important safety valve was colonization; in the eighth and seventh centuries B.C. landless men founded new cities (always near the sea and generally owing little or no allegiance to the home base) all over the Mediterranean coasts—

in Spain, southern France (Marseilles, Nice, and Antibes were all Greek cities), in South Italy (Naples), Sicily (Syracuse), North Africa (Cyrene), all along the coast of Asia Minor (Smyrna, Miletus), and even on the Black Sea as far as Russian Crimea. Many of these new outposts of Greek civilization experienced a faster economic and cultural development than the older cities of the mainland. It was in the cities founded on the Asian coast that the Greeks adapted to their own language the Phoenician system of writing (adding signs for the vowels to create the first efficient alphabet); its first use was probably for commercial records and transactions, but as literacy became a general condition all over the Greek world in the course of the seventh century B.C. treaties and political decrees were inscribed on stone and literary works written on rolls of paper made from the Egyptian papyrus plant.

This literature, all of it poetry (literary prose was a later development), was very different from the Homeric poems. Homer, too, was first written down at this time, but the Homeric poems had been composed before the alphabet was invented. The oral poet had at his disposal not reading and writing, but a vast and intricate system of metrical formulas—phrases which would fit in at different places in the line—and a repertoire of standard scenes (the arming of the warrior, the battle of two champions) as well as the known outline of the story. Of course he could and did invent new phrases and scenes as he recited

—and this is especially true of the culminating oral poet we call Homer, who gave the poems their magnificent architecture—but his base was the immense poetic reserve created by many generations of singers before him. When he told again for his hearers the old story of Achilles and his wrath, he was recreating a traditional story which had been recited, with differences, additions, and improvements, by a long line of predecessors: the poem was not, in the modern sense, his creation, still less an expression of his personality. Consequently there is no trace of his identity to be found in it. Homer remains as hidden behind the action and speech of his characters as if he were a dramatist.

The new poets, however, dealt with themes less traditional or not traditional at all and their own personalities, prejudices, and emotions show clearly in their work. This is partly due to the social evolution of the Greek peoples: in the colonies where sea-borne trade was as common a way of life as work on the land the individual broke free of the solid tribal group, and in the mainland cities economic stagnation led to the gradual polarization of class conflicts and eventual revolution. But it seems likely, too, that this new phenomenon, the appearance of the "I" in literature, has some connection with the spread of literacy. For writing could now preserve for future ages poetry which, far from being traditional in form and outlook, was highly individual, concerned with private passions, even critical of social or religious norms.

The personal note struck in these early lyric poems marks the beginning of a new age: even the small selection in this book gives a vivid impression of the intense concern these poets feel for themselves, their own opinions and feelings. Archilochus, the professional soldier, sings of the joys and dangers of the soldier's life (and also his personal preference in the matter of commanding officers); Mimnermus, of the sweetness of young love and the gloomy prospect of old age; Sappho gives us some of the most frank and passionate love poems ever written (though she can be humorous about love, too); Alcaeus, the factious aristocrat, conveys to us his joyous fascination with the new weapons he and his party are about to put to use in civil war; Solon defends his reforms at Athens; Anacreon sings of love with a light touch that reminds us of Sappho in her playful mood and a ground swell of melancholy that recalls Mimnermus; Xenophanes attacks the Greek idolatry of successful athletes; and Theognis pours out his bitter complaints against the democratic revolutionaries who had driven him into exile and had taken away his lands. In these poems we can feel the excitement, passion, and vigor that marked the life of the emergent Greek city-states as they pursued their different and often conflicting ways to political and intellectual maturity.

ATHENS AND SPARTA

By the beginning of the fifth century B.C. the two most prominent of these city-states were Athens and Sparta; these two cities led the combined Greek resistance to the Persian invasion of Europe in the years 490 to 479 B.C. The defeat of the solid Persian power by the divided and insignificant Greek cities surprised the world and inspired in Greece, and particularly in Athens, a confidence that knew no bounds.

Athens was at this time a democracy, the first in Western history. It was a direct, not a representative, democracy, for the citizen body was small enough to permit the exercise of power by a meeting of the citizens in assembly. Athens' power lay in the fleet with which she had played her decisive part in the struggle against Persia, and with this fleet she rapidly became the leader of a naval alliance which included most of the islands of the Aegean Sea and many Greek cities on the coast of Asia Minor. Sparta, on the other hand, was a totalitarian state, rigidly conservative in government and policy, in which the individual citizen was reared and trained by the state for the state's business, war. (The Spartan ideal is vividly expressed in the poem of Tyrtaeus, p. 259) The Spartan land army was consequently superior to any other in Greece, and the Spartans controlled, by direct rule or by alliance, the majority of the city-states of the Peloponnese.

These two cities, allies for the war of liberation against Persia, became enemies when the external danger was eliminated. The middle years of the fifth century were disturbed by indecisive hostilities between them and haunted by the probability of full-scale war to come; as the years went by this war came to be accepted as "inevitable" by both sides, and in 431 B.C. it began. It was to end in 404 B.C. with the total defeat of Athens.

Before the beginning of this disastrous war, Athenian democracy provided its citizens with a cultural and political environment which was without precedent in the ancient world. The institutions of Athens encouraged the maximum development of the individual's capacities and at the same time inspired the maximum devotion to the interests of the community. It was a moment in history of delicate and precarious balance between the freedom of the individual and the demands of the state. Its uniqueness was emphasized by the complete lack of balance in Sparta, where the necessities of the state annihilated the individual as a creative and independent being. It was the proud boast of the Athenians that without sacrificing the cultural amenities of civilized life they could yet when called upon surpass ·in policy and war their adversary, whose citizen body was an army in constant training. The Athenians were, in this respect as in others, a nation of amateurs. "The individual Athenian," said Pericles in the speech which is at once the panegyric of Athenian democracy and its epitaph, "in his own person seems to have the power of adapting himself to the most varied forms of action with the utmost versatility and grace." But the freedom of the individual did not, in Athens' great days, produce anarchy. "While we are . . . unconstrained in our private intercourse," Pericles had observed earlier in his speech, "a spirit of reverence pervades our public acts."

This balance of individual freedom and communal unity was not destined to outlast the century. It went down, with Athens, in the war. The process of disintegration, and the forces behind it, are described and analyzed in the tragic pages of the Athenian historian of the Peloponnesian War, Thucydides. With an apparent dispassionateness which increases the somber effect of his writing, he shows how his countrymen, under the mounting pressure of the long conflict, lost the "spirit of reverence" which Pericles saw as the stabilizing factor in Athenian democracy. They subordinated all considerations to the immediate interest of the city and surpassed their enemy in the logical ferocity of their actions; they finally fell victims to leaders who carried the process one step further and subordinated all considerations to their own private interest. The most brilliant and dangerous of these new statesmen, Alcibiades, carried his personal freedom to the point of betraying his own city in her critical hour. His career is symptomatic of the decay of the freedom in unity described in Pericles' speech; by the end of the fifth century Athens was divided internally as well as defeated externally. The individual citizen no longer thought of himself and Athens as one and the same; the balance was gone forever.

While it lasted, it provided an atmosphere for the artist which has rarely, if ever, existed since. The dramatic poet, whose play was performed at a religious festival attended by most of the citizen body, addressed an audience of quick-thinking and keenly critical minds which were yet culturally and politically homogeneous; he spoke to the whole city, at a city festival, and in the city's name. Shakespeare had to please the groundlings as well as the court wits, but the Athenian dramatist speaks with the same emphasis and in the same tone to the entire audience.

THE DRAMA

European drama begins in Athens in the fifth century B.C. Its origins are shrouded in obscurity into which the researches of many scholars, especially those who have drawn on comparative anthropology, have brought a certain amount of light, though what has been illuminated is the general nature of the development rather than any particular aspects of it. What no one has explained (and it is perhaps inexplicable) is why the religious dances which are to be found in practically all primitive cultures, gave rise in Greece, and in Greece alone, to what we know as tragedy and comedy.

TRAGEDY—AESCHYLUS

Tragedy developed from the dance and song of a chorus performing on a circular dancing floor. An actor, whose medium was speech, not song, and who performed outside the circle, was introduced by some unknown innovator (his name was probably Thespis), and as the number of actors was increased to two and then to three, the spoken part of the performance grew in importance. In the *Agamemnon* of Aeschylus, produced in 458 B.C., an equilibrium between the two elements of the performance has been established; the actors, with their speeches, create the dramatic situation and its movement, the plot; the chorus, while contributing to dramatic suspense and illusion, ranges free of the immediate situation in its odes, which extend and amplify the significance of the action.

The *Agamemnon* is the first play of a trilogy; that is, it was followed at its performance by two more plays, the *Choephoroe* and the *Eumenides*, which carried on its story and its theme to a conclusion. The theme of the trilogy is justice; and its story, like that of almost all Greek tragedies, is a legend which was already well-known to the audience which saw the first performance of the play. This particular legend, the story of the house of Atreus, was rich in dramatic potential, for it deals with a series of retributive murders which stained the hands of three generations of a royal family, and it has also a larger, a social and historical significance, of which Aeschylus took full advantage. The legend preserves the memory of an important historical process through which the Greeks had passed, the transition from tribal institutions of justice to communal justice, from a tradition which demanded that a murdered man's next of kin avenge his death, to a system requiring settlement of the private quarrel by the court of law, the typical institution of

the city-state which replaced the primitive tribe. When Agamemnon returns victorious from Troy, he is killed by his wife, Clytemnestra, and her lover, Aegisthus, who is Agamemnon's cousin. Clytemnestra kills her husband to avenge her daughter Iphigenia, whom Agamemnon sacrificed to the goddess Artemis when he had to choose between his daughter's life and his ambition to conquer Troy. Aegisthus avenges the crime of a previous generation, the hideous murder of his brothers by Agamemnon's father, Atreus. The killing of Agamemnon is, by the standards of the old system, justice; but it is the nature of this justice that the process can never be arrested, one act of violence must give rise to another. Agamemnon's murder must be avenged too, as it is in the second play of the trilogy by Orestes, his son, who kills both Aegisthus and his own mother, Clytemnestra. Orestes has acted justly according to the code of tribal society based on blood relationship, but in doing so he has violated the most sacred blood relationship of all, the bond between mother and son. The old system of justice has produced an insoluble dilemma; it can be surmounted only by the institution of a new system, and this is accomplished in the final play of the trilogy, in which a court of law is set up by the goddess Athene to try the case of Orestes. He is acquitted, but more important than the decision is the nature of the body which makes it. This is the end of an old era and the beginning of a new. The existence of the court is a guarantee that the tragic series of events which drove Orestes to the murder of his mother will never be repeated. The system of communal justice, which allows consideration of circumstance and motive, and which punishes impersonally, has at last replaced the inconclusive anarchy of individual revenge.

But the play is concerned with much more than the history of human institutions, with more even than the general problem of violence between man and man for which the particular instances of the trilogy stand. It is also a religious statement. The whole sequence of events, stretching over many generations, is presented as the working out of the will of Zeus. The tragic action of the *Iliad* was also the expression of the will of Zeus (though it is characteristic of Homer that Achilles was at least equally responsible), but for Aeschylus the will of Zeus means something new. In this trilogy the working out of Zeus's will proceeds intricately through three generations of bloodshed to the creation of a human institution which will prevent any repetition of the cycle of murder that produced it. Agamemnon dies, and Clytemnestra dies in her turn, and Orestes is hounded over land and sea to his trial, but out of all this suffering comes an important advance in human understanding and civilization. The chorus of the *Agamemnon*, celebrating the power of Zeus, tells how he

...setting us on the road
Made this a valid law—
"That men must learn by suffering."

From the suffering comes wis-

dom, whereas in the *Iliad* nothing at all comes out of the suffering, except the certainty of more. ". . . far from the land of my fathers," says Achilles to Priam, "I sit here in Troy, and bring nothing but sorrow to you and your children"; but his last words to Priam are a reminder that this interval of sympathy is only temporary. After Hector's burial the war will go on as before. This is Zeus's will; Homer does not attempt to explain it. But the Aeschylean trilogy is nothing less than an attempt to justify the ways of God to man; the suffering is shown to us as the fulfillment of a purpose we can understand, a purpose beneficent to man.

The full scope of Zeus's will is apparent only to the audience, which follows the pattern of its execution through the three plays of the trilogy; as in the Book of Job, the characters who act and suffer are in the dark. They claim a knowledge of Zeus's will and boast that their actions are its fulfillment (it is in these terms that Agamemnon speaks of the sack of Troy, and Clytemnestra of Agamemnon's murder), and they are, of course, in one sense, right. But their knowledge is limited; Agamemnon does not realize that Zeus's will includes his death at the hands of Clytemnestra, nor Clytemnestra that it demands her death at the hands of her son. The chorus has, at times, a deeper understanding; in its opening ode it announces the law of Zeus, that men must learn by suffering, and at the end it recognizes the responsibility of Zeus in the death of Agamemnon—"Brought by

Zeus, by Zeus, / Cause and worker of all." But the chorus cannot interpret the event in any way it can accept, for it can see no further than the immediate present; its knowledge of Zeus's law is an abstraction which it cannot relate to the terrible fact.

In this murky atmosphere (made all the more terrible by the beacon fire of the opening lines, which brings not light, but deeper darkness), one human being sees clear; she possesses the concrete vision of the future which complements the chorus' abstract knowledge of the law. This is the prophet Cassandra, Priam's daughter, brought from Troy as Agamemnon's share of the spoils. She has been given the power of true prophecy by the god Apollo, but the gift is nullified by the condition that her prophecies will never be believed. Like the Hebrew prophets, she sees reality—past, present, and future—so clearly that she is cut off from ordinary human beings by the clarity of her vision and the terrible burden of her knowledge; like them she expresses herself in poetic figures, and like them she is rejected by her hearers. To the everyday world, represented by the chorus, she appears to be mad, the fate of prophets in all ages; and it is only as she goes into the palace to the death she foresees that the old men of the chorus begin to accept, fearfully and hesitantly, the truth which she has been telling them.

The great scene in which she mouths her hysterical prophecies at them delays the action for which everything has been prepared—the death of Agamem-non. Before we hear his famous cry off stage, Cassandra presents us with a mysterious vision in which she combines cause, effect, and result: the murders which have led to this terrible moment, the death of Agamemnon (which will not take place until she leaves the stage), and the murders which will follow. We do not see Agamemnon's death—we see much more. The past, present, and future of Clytemnestra's action and Agamemnon's suffering are fused into a timeless unity in Cassandra's great lines, an unearthly unity which is dissolved only when Agamemnon, in the real world of time and space, screams in mortal agony.

The tremendous statement of the trilogy is made in a style which for magnificence and richness of suggestion can be compared only with the style of Shakespeare at the height of his poetic power, the Shakespeare of *King Lear* and *Antony and Cleopatra*. The language of the *Agamemnon* is an oriental carpet of imagery in which combinations of metaphor, which at first seem bombastic in their violence, take their place in the ordered pattern of the poem as a whole. An image, once introduced, recurs, and reappears again, to run its course verbally and visually through the whole length of the trilogy, richer in meaning with each fresh appearance. In the second choral ode, for example, the chorus, welcoming the news of Agamemnon's victory at Troy, sings of the net which Zeus and Night threw over the city, trapping the inhabitants like animals. The net is here an image of

Zeus's justice, a retributive justice, since Troy is paying for the crime of taking Helen, and the image identifies Zeus's justice with Agamemnon's action in sacking the city. This image occurs again, with a different emphasis, in the hypocritical speech of welcome which Clytemnestra makes to her husband on his return. She tells how she feared for his safety at Troy, how she trembled at the rumors of his death:

...If Agamemnon
Had had so many wounds as those
    reported...
Then he would be gashed fuller
    than a net has holes!

This vision of Agamemnon dead she speaks of as her fear, but we know that it represents her deepest desire, and more, the purpose which she is now preparing to execute. When, later, she stands in triumph over her husband's corpse, she uses the same image to describe the robe which she threw over his limbs to blind and baffle him before she stabbed him—"Inextricable like a net for fishes/I cast about him a vicious wealth of raiment" —and this time the image materializes into an object visible on stage. We can see the net, the gashed robe still folded round Agamemnon's body. We shall see it again, for in the second play Orestes, standing over his mother's body as she now stands over his father's, will display the robe before us, with its holes and bloodstains, as a justification for what he has just done. Elsewhere in the *Agamemnon* the chorus compares Cassandra to a wild animal caught in the net, and later

Aegisthus exults to see Agamemnon's body lying "in the nets of Justice." For each speaker the image has a different meaning, but not one realizes the terrible sense in which it applies to them all. They are all caught in the net, the system of justice by vengeance which only binds tighter the more its captives struggle to free themselves. Clytemnestra attempts to escape, to arrest the process of the chain of murders and the working out of the will of Zeus. "I am ready to make a contract/With the Evil Genius of the House of Atreus," she says, but Agamemnon's body and the net she threw over him are there on the stage to remind us that her appeal will not be heard; one more generation must act and suffer before the net will vanish, never to be seen again.

PROMETHEUS BOUND

The *Prometheus Bound*, the only surviving play of a trilogy, or perhaps—for this like everything else about the play is a matter of dispute among scholars—the first of two plays (the second entitled *Prometheus Unbound*), has given the modern world one of its most powerful symbolic figures. The champion of human progress, chained and tortured by a tyrannical Zeus, has appealed to man's imagination wherever and whenever revolutionary forces faced the harsh repression of established authority. In Shelley's famous poem Prometheus stands for the democratic movement of nineteenth-century Europe in its struggle against the Holy Alliance of king, emperor, and tsar. In later nineteenth-century writers he is presented as a symbol of science harassed by ignorance and reaction. It is characteristic of great creations of the imagination that they assume fresh significance and renewed force for later generations. Sometimes, in fact, their significance for later times is very far removed from anything envisaged by their creator; it would surely have been very difficult for Milton to understand Blake's influential judgement of *Paradise Lost*, that Satan was the hero of the poem. Something similar has happened to Prometheus, for though Aeschylus has spared no pains to make him and his defiance of Zeus magnificent, there can be no doubt that the play we have was the prelude to a full reconciliation of the two great adversaries. This emerges clearly from the few fragments which have been preserved of the second play of the trilogy. The chorus consists of Titans, brothers of Prometheus, who have been released from the imprisonment Zeus inflicted on them. And later in the play Heracles, the son of Zeus, kills the vulture which feeds on Prometheus' flesh and releases him. "Dearest son of the father my enemy" Prometheus calls him; the reconciliation of Zeus and Prometheus is not far away. It has to come, for in these two figures, Zeus and Prometheus, the two fundamental attributes of divinity, omnipotence and omniscience, are separated and in fact at war with each other. But without each other they are not themselves. All-power without all-knowledge will destroy itself (as Zeus will marry Thetis and beget his own destroyer) and all-knowledge without power can do nothing but suffer and threaten. The problem of reconciliation betwen two figures neither of whom can surrender is neatly solved by the appearance of Heracles. He is Zeus's son and so his liberation of Prometheus stems from Zeus; but his action is independent and Zeus cannot be thought of as giving way to Prometheus. He is also a descendant of Io, so that even the cruel persecution of an innocent girl turns out, after the lapse of many generations, to have its meaning and its beneficent result. This play was part of an over-all pattern of suffering and struggle which ended, like the great trilogy of the *Oresteia*, in reconciliation.

THE INTELLECTUAL REVOLUTION OF THE FIFTH CENTURY

Aeschylus belonged to the generation which fought at Marathon; his manhood and his old age were passed in the heroic period of the Persian defeat on Greek soil and the war which Athens fought to liberate her kinsmen in the islands of the Aegean and on the Asiatic coast. Sophocles, his younger contemporary, lived to see an Athens which had advanced in power and prosperity far beyond the city that Aeschylus knew, but it was an Athens in which it became clearer every year that something had gone wrong. The league of free Greek cities against Persia which Athens had led to victory in the Aegean had become an empire, in which Athens taxed and coerced the subject cities that had once been her allies; and inside the city a new and dangerous spirit was abroad. Democratic institutions had created a demand for an education which would prepare men for public life, especially by training them in the art of public speaking. The demand was met by the appearance of the professional teacher, the Sophist, as he was called, who taught, for a handsome fee, not only the techniques of public speaking but also the subjects which gave a man something to talk about —government, ethics, literary criticism, even astronomy. The curriculum of the Sophists, in fact, marks the first appearance in European civilization of the liberal education, just as they themselves were the first professors.

The Sophists were great teachers, but like most teachers they had little or no control over the results of their teaching. Their methods placed an inevitable emphasis on effective presentation of a point of view, to the detriment, and if necessary the exclusion, of anything which might make it less convincing and produced a generation which had been trained to see both sides of any question and to argue the weaker side as effectively as the stronger, the false as effectively as the true; to argue inferentially from probability in the absence of concrete evidence; to appeal to the audience's sense of its own advantage rather than to accepted moral standards; and to justify individual defiance of general prejudice and even of law by the distinction between "nature" and "convention." These methods dominated the thinking of the Athenians of the last half of the century. The emphasis on the technique of effective presentation of both sides of any case encouraged a relativistic point of view and finally produced a cynical mood which denied the existence of any absolute standards. The canon of probability (which implies an appeal to human reason as the supreme authority) became a critical weapon for an attack on myth and on traditional conceptions of the gods; it had its constructive aspect too, for it is the basis of Thucydides' magnificent guesswork about early Greek history. The appeal to the self-interest of the audience, to expediency, became the method of new political leaders and the fundamental doctrine of a new school of political theory; this theory and its practice, stripped to their terrifying essentials, are set down as an example to future ages in Thucydides' account of the negotiations between Athens and Melos. The distinction between "nature" and "convention" is the source of the doctrine of the superman, who breaks free of the conventional restraints of society and acts according to the law of his own "nature," as Alcibiades did when he betrayed his country in the Peloponnesian War. The new spirit in Athens has magnificent achievements to its credit, but it brought disaster. At its roots was a supreme confidence in the human intelligence and a secular view of man's position in the universe that is best expressed in the statement of Protagoras, the most famous of the Sophists: "Man is the measure of all things."

TRAGEDY—SOPHOCLES

It was in this atmosphere of critical re-evaluation of accepted standards that Sophocles produced his masterpiece, *Oedipus Tyrannus*, probably performed for the first time in the opening years of the Peloponnesian War, which began in 431 B.C. This tragedy of a man of high principles and probing intelligence who follows the prompting of that intelligence to the final consequence of true self-knowledge, which makes him put out his eyes, was as full of significance for Sophocles' contemporaries as it is for us. Unlike a modern dramatist, Sophocles used for his tragedy a story well known to the audience and as old as their own history, a legend told by father to son, handed down from generation to generation because of its implicit wealth of meaning, learned in childhood and rooted deep in the consciousness of every member of the community. Such a story the Greeks called a *myth*, and the use of it presented Sophocles, as it did Aeschylus in his trilogy, with material which, apart from its great inherent dramatic potential, already possessed the significance and authority which the modern dramatist must create for himself. It had the authority of history, for the history of ages which leave no records is myth —that is to say, the significant event of the past, stripped of irrelevancies and imaginatively shaped by the oral tradition. It had a religious authority, for the Oedipus story, like the story of the house of Atreus, is concerned with the relation between man and god. Lastly, and this is especially true of the Oedipus myth, it had the power, because of its subject matter, to arouse the irrational hopes and fears which lie deep and secret in the human consciousness.

The use of the familiar myth enabled the dramatist to draw on all its wealth of unformulated meaning, but it did not prevent him from striking a contemporary note. Oedipus, in Sophocles' play, is at one and the same time the mysterious figure of the past who broke the most fundamental human taboos and a typical fifth-century Athenian. His character contains all the virtues for which the Athenians were famous and the vices for which they were notorious. The best commentary on Oedipus' character is the speech which Thucydides put into the mouth of the Corinthian spokesman at Sparta, a hostile but admiring assessment of the Athenian genius. "Athenians . . . [are] equally quick in the conception and in the execution of every new plan . . ."—so Oedipus has already sent to Delphi when the priest advises him to do so, and has already sent for Tiresias when the chorus suggests this course of action. "They are bold beyond their strength; they run risks which prudence would condemn . . ."—as Oedipus risked his life to answer the riddle of the Sphinx and later, in spite of the oracle about his marriage, accepted the hand of the queen. ". . . in the midst of misfortune they are full of hope. . . ."—so Oedipus, when he is told that he is not the son of Polybus and Merope, and Jocasta has already realized whose son he is, claims that he is the "child of Fortune." "When they do not carry out an intention which they have formed, they seem to have sustained a personal bereavement . . ."—so Oedipus, shamed by Jocasta and the chorus into sparing Creon's life, yields sullenly and petulantly.

The Athenian devotion to the city, which received the main emphasis in Pericles' praise of Athens, is strong in Oedipus; his answer to the priest at the beginning of the play shows that he is a conscientious and patriotic ruler. His sudden unreasoning rage is the characteristic fault of Athenian democracy, which in 406 B.C., to give only one instance, condemned and executed the generals who had failed, in the stress of weather and battle, to pick up the drowned bodies of their own men killed in the naval engagement at Arginusae. Oedipus is like the fifth-century Athenian most of all in his confidence in the human intelligence, especially his own. This confidence takes him in the play through the whole cycle of the critical, rationalist movement of the century, from the piety and orthodoxy he displays in the opening scene, through his taunts at oracles when he hears that Polybus is dead, to the despairing courage with which he accepts the consequences when he sees the abyss opening at his feet. "Ah master, do I *have* to speak?" asks the herdsman from whom he is dragging the truth. "You have to," Oedipus replies. "And I *have* to hear." And hear he does. He learns that the oracle he had first fought against and then laughed at has been fulfilled; that every step his intelligence prompted was one step nearer to

disaster; that his knowledge was ignorance, his clear vision blindness. Faced with the reality which his determined probing finally reveals, he puts out his eyes.

The relation of Oedipus' character to the development of the action is the basis of the most famous attempt to define the nature of the tragic process, Aristotle's theory that pity and terror are aroused most effectively by the spectacle of a man who is "not eminently good and just, yet whose misfortune is brought about not by vice or depravity, but by some error or frailty. He must be one who is highly renowned and prosperous —a personage like Oedipus. . . ." Other references by Aristotle to this play make it clear that this influential critical canon is based particularly on Sophocles' masterpiece, and the canon has been universally applied to the play. But the great influence (and validity) of the Aristotelian theory should not be allowed to obscure the fact that Sophocles' *Oedipus Tyrannus* is more highly organized and economical than Aristotle implies. The fact that the critics have differed about the nature of Oedipus' error or frailty (his errors are many and his frailties include anger, impiety and self-confidence) is a clue to the real situation. Oedipus falls not through "some vicious mole of nature" or some "particular fault," but because he is the man he is, because of all aspects of his character, good and bad alike; and the development of the action right through to the catastrophe shows us every aspect of his character at work in the process of self-revelation and self-destruction. His first decision in the play, to hear Creon's message from Delphi in public rather than, as Creon suggests, in private, is evidence of his kingly solicitude for his people and his trust in them, but it makes certain the full publication of the truth. His impetuous proclamation of a curse on the murderer of Laius, an unnecessary step prompted by his civic zeal, makes his final situation worse than it need have been. His anger at Tiresias forces a revelation which drives him on to accuse Creon; this in turn provokes Jocasta's revelations. And throughout the play his confidence in the efficacy of his own action, his hopefulness as the situation darkens, and his passion for discovering the truth, guide the steps of the investigation which is to reveal the detective as the criminal. All aspects of his character, good and bad alike, are equally involved; it is no frailty or error that leads him to the terrible truth, but his total personality.

The character of Oedipus as revealed in the play does something more than explain the present action, it also explains his past. In Oedipus' speeches and actions on stage we can see the man who, given the circumstances in which Oedipus was involved, would inevitably do just what Oedipus has done. Each action on stage shows us the mood in which he committed some action in the past; his angry death sentence on Creon reveals the man who killed Laius because of an insult on the high-

way; his impulsive proclamation of total excommunication for the unknown murderer shows us the man who, without forethought, accepted the hand of Jocasta; his intelligent, persistent search for the truth shows us the brain and the courage which solved the riddle of the Sphinx. The revelation of his character in the play is at once a re-creation of his past and an interpretation of the oracle which predicted his future. His character is his fate.

This organization of the material is what makes it possible for us to accept the story as tragedy at all, for it emphasizes Oedipus' independence of the oracle. When we first see Oedipus, he has already committed the actions for which he is to suffer, actions prophesied, before his birth, by Apollo. But the dramatist's emphasis on Oedipus' character suggests that although Apollo has predicted what Oedipus will do, he does not determine it; Oedipus determines his own conduct, by being the man he is. Milton's explanation of a similar situation, Adam's fall and God's foreknowledge of it, may be applied to Oedipus; foreknowledge had no influence on his fault. The relationship between Apollo's prophecy and Oedipus' actions is not that of cause and effect. It is the relationship of two independent entities which are equated.

This correspondence between his character and his fate removes the obstacle to our full acceptance of the play which an external fate governing his action would set up. Nevertheless, we feel that he suffers more than he deserves. He has served as an example of the inadequacy of the human intellect and a warning that there is a power in the universe which humanity cannot control, nor even fully understand, but Oedipus the man still has our sympathy. Sophocles felt this too, and in a later play, his last, the *Oedipus at Colonus*, he dealt with the reward which finally balanced Oedipus' suffering. In *Oedipus Tyrannus* itself there is a foreshadowing of this final development; the last scene shows us a man already beginning to recover from the shock of the catastrophe and reasserting a natural superiority. "I shall go—on this condition," he says to Creon when ordered back into the house, and a few lines later Creon has to say bluntly to him, "Do not presume that you are still in power." This renewed imperiousness is the first expression of a feeling on his part that he is not entirely guilty, a beginning of the reconstitution of the magnificent man of the opening scenes; it reaches its fulfillment in the final Oedipus play, the *Oedipus at Colonus*, in which he is a titanic figure, confident of his innocence and more masterful than he has ever been.

ANTIGONE

Oedipus was expelled from Thebes, to wander as a blind beggar, accompanied only by his daughter Antigone. His sons, Eteocles and Polynices, raised no hand to help him and after he died at Athens (where, in death, he became a guardian spirit of the Attic soil), they fought each other for the throne of Thebes. Eteocles expelled his

brother, who recruited supporters in Argos; seven champions attacked the seven gates of Thebes. The assault was beaten off; but Polynices and Eteocles killed each other in the battle. The rule of Thebes fell to Creon, the same Creon we have seen in *Oedipus Tyrannus*. His first decision is to forbid burial to the corpse of Polynices, the traitor who brought foreign troops against his own city. Antigone disobeys the decree by scattering dust on the body; captured and brought before Creon, she defies him in the name of the eternal unwritten laws. In the struggle between them it is the king who in the end surrenders; he buries the body of Polynices and orders Antigone's release. But she has already killed herself in her underground prison, thus bringing about the two deaths which crush her enemy, the suicides of his son Haemon and of his wife Eurydice. In this

Antigone, as a heroine of the resistance to tyrannical power, has deservedly become one of the Western world's great symbolic figures; she is clearly presented, in her famous speech, as a champion of a higher morality against the overriding claims of state necessity, which the Sophist intellectuals of Sophocles' time had begun to formulate in philosophical terms. But Creon, too, is given his due; he is no mere melodramatic tyrant but a ruler whose action stems from political and religious attitudes which were probably shared by many of the audience. Antigone and Creon clash not only as individuals, shaped with all Sophocles dramatic genius (the ancient life of Sophocles says truly that he could "match the moment with the action so as to create a whole character out of half a line or even a single word"), but also as representatives of two irreconcilable social and religious positions.

Antigone's chief loyalty is clearly to the family. She makes no distinction between the brothers though one was a patriot and the other a traitor, and when her sister Ismene refuses to help her defy the state to bury a brother she harshly disowns her. The denial of burial to Polynices strikes directly at her family loyalty, for it was the immemorial privilege and duty of the women of the house to mourn the dead man in unrestrained sorrow, sing his praises, wash his body, and consign him to the earth. Creon, on the other hand, sees loyalty to the state as the only valid criterion, and in his opening speech expressly repudiates "one whose friend has stronger claims upon him than his country" (the Greek word translated "friend" also means "relative"). This inaugural address of Creon repeats many concepts and even phrases that are to be found in the speeches of the democratic leader Pericles; and in fact, there was an ancient antagonism between the new democratic institutions which stressed the equal rights and obligations of all citizens and the old powerful families which through their wide influence had acted as separate factions in the body politic. The nature of Creon's assertion of state against family, refusal of burial to a corpse, is repellent, but the principle behind it was one most Athenians would have accepted as valid.

These opposing social viewpoints have their corresponding religious sanctions. For Antigone, the gods, especially the gods below, demand equality for all the dead, the common inalienable right of burial. But Creon's gods are the gods who protect the city; how, he asks, could those gods have any feeling for Polynices, a traitor who raised and led a foreign army against the city they protect and which contains their temples? Here again, there must have been many in the audience who saw merit in this argument.

But as the action develops whatever validity Creon's initial position may have had is destroyed, and by Creon himself. For like all holders of absolute power, he proceeds, when challenged, to equate loyalty to the community with loyalty to himself—"the city is the King's" he tells his son Haemon. And in the end the prophet Tiresias tells him plainly that Antigone was right— the gods are on her side. He swallows his pride and surrenders, but too late. Antigone's suicide brings him to disaster in that institution, the family, which he subordinated to reasons of state; his son spits in his face before killing himself, and his wife dies cursing him as the murderer of his son.

Creon is punished, but Antigone is dead. "Wisdom we learn at last, when we are old" the chorus sings as the play ends, but the price of wisdom is high: the *Antigone*, like so many of the Shakespearean tragedies, leaves us with a poignant sense of loss.

TRAGEDY—EURIPIDES

Euripides' *Medea*, produced in 431 B.C., the year that brought the beginning of the Peloponnesian War, appeared earlier than the *Oedipus Tyrannus* of Sophocles, but it has a bitterness that is more in keeping with the spirit of a later age. If the *Oedipus* is, in one sense, a warning to a generation which has embarked on an intellectual revolution, the *Medea* is the ironic expression of the disillusion that comes after the shipwreck. In this play we are conscious for the first time of an attitude characteristic of modern literature, the artist's feeling of separation from his audience, the isolation of the poet. "Often previously," says Medea to the king,

Through being considered clever
    I have suffered much....
If you put new ideas before the eyes
    of fools
They'll think you foolish and
    worthless into the bargain;
And if you are thought superior to
    those who have
Some reputation for learning, you
    will become hated.

The common background of audience and poet is disappearing, the old certainties are being undermined, the city divided. Euripides is the first Greek poet to suffer the fate of so many of the great modern writers: rejected by most of his contemporaries, he became universally loved and admired after his death.

The change in atmosphere is clear even in Euripides' choice of subject and central character. He still dramatizes myth, but the myth he chooses is exotic and disturbing, and the protagonist is not a man but a woman. Medea is both woman and foreigner; that is to say, in terms of the audience's prejudice and practice she is a representative of the two free-born groups in Athenian society which had almost no rights at all (though the male foreign resident had more rights than the native woman). The tragic hero is no longer a king, "one who is highly renowned and prosperous—a personage like Oedipus," but a woman, who, because she finds no redress for her wrongs in society, is driven by her passion to violate that society's most sacred laws in a rebellion against its typical representative, Jason, her husband. She is not just a woman and a foreigner; she is also a person of great intellectual power. Compared to her the credulous king and her complacent husband are children, and once her mind is made up, she moves them like pawns to their proper places in her barbaric game. The myth is used for new purposes, to shock the members of the audience, attack their deepest prejudices, and shake them out of their complacent pride in the superiority of Greek masculinity.

But the play is more than a feminist melodrama. Before it is over, our sympathies have come full circle; the contempt with which we regard the Jason of the opening scenes turns to pity as we feel the measure of his loss and the ferocity of Medea's revenge. Medea's passion has carried her too far; the death of Creon and his daughter we might have accepted, but the murder of the children is too much. It was, of course, meant to be. Euripides' theme, like Homer's, is violence, but this is the unspeakable violence of the oppressed, which is greater than the violence of the oppressor and which, because it has been long pent up, cannot be controlled.

In this, as in the other plays, the gods have their place. In the *Agamemnon* the will of Zeus is manifested in every action and implied in every word; in the *Oedipus Tyrannus* the gods bide their time and watch Oedipus fulfill the truth of their prophecy, but in the *Medea*, the divine will, which is revealed at the end, is enigmatic and, far from bringing harmony, concludes the play with a terrifying discord. All through the *Medea* the human beings involved call on the gods; two especially are singled out for attention, Earth and Sun. It is by these two gods that Medea makes Aegeus swear to give her refuge in Athens, the chorus invokes them to prevent Medea's violence against her sons, and Jason wonders how Medea can look upon earth and sun after she has killed her own children. These emphatic appeals clearly raise the question of the attitude of the gods, and the answer to the question is a shock. We are not told what Earth does, but Sun sends the magic chariot on which Medea makes her escape. His reason, too, is stated; it is not any concern for justice, but the fact that Medea is his granddaughter. Euripides is here using the letter of the myth for his own purposes. This jarring detail emphasizes the significance of the whole. The play creates a world in which there is no relation whatsoever between the powers which rule the universe and the fundamental laws of human morality. It dramatizes disorder, not just the disorder of the family of Jason and Medea, but the disorder of the universe as a whole. It is the nightmare in which the dream of the fifth century was to end, the senseless fury and degradation of permanent violence. "Flow backward to your sources, sacred rivers," the chorus sings, "And let the world's great order be reversed."

THE TROJAN WOMEN

In *The Trojan Women*, produced in 415 B.C., the disorder is that of a defeated nation and of its conquerors. Here war is seen not as Homer saw it but through the eyes of the enslaved women who are its victims. The play has no real central character and no real plot; it presents the reality of defeat in war through the persons of a grandmother who has lost all her sons and now loses a daughter; of an unmarried girl who, though she is a priestess of Apollo, is taken as his concubine by the victorious king; of a married woman and mother who is handed over to the enemy whose father killed her husband; and lastly of a small child who is cruelly murdered in cold blood for political reasons. These separate individual fates are types of what happens to all that is left of Troy; the chorus of captive women will fare no better and sings in its lyric songs the dirge of a whole people.

As in the *Medea*, the gods, to whom mankind looks for justice, provide a discordant note. The prologue shows us Athene changing sides; because of a personal insult, she now joins Poseidon to punish the Greeks as they return home. The Greek atrocities which follow have nothing to do with the decision of the gods; that has already been made and for quite other reasons. We know that when the Greeks leave at the end of the play, they are going to their punishment—Agamemnon to his death in Argos, Odysseus to his wanderings—but whatever justice may be at work in these events is beyond our comprehension. The one thing that might demonstrate a justice at work in the world, the punishment of Helen, will clearly not take place; we are left in no doubt that Helen, the cause of all these deaths, will get off scot-free. Small wonder that to Hecuba, as she mourns over the corpse of her grandson, life seems senseless:

Fortune's ways—
here now, there now. She springs
away—back—and away, an idiot's
    dance.

COMEDY

By the fifth century both tragedy and comedy were regularly produced at the winter festivals of the god Dionysus in Athens. Comedy, like tragedy, employed a chorus, that is to say, a group of dancers (who also sang) and actors, who wore masks; its tone was burlesque and parodic, though there was often a serious theme emphasized by the crude clowning and the free play of wit. The only comic poet of the fifth century whose work has survived is Aris-

tophanes; in his thirteen extant comedies, produced over the years 425-388 B.C., the institutions and personalities of his time are caricatured and criticized in a brilliant combination of poetry and obscenity, of farce and wit, which has no parallel in European literature. It can be described only in terms of itself, by the adjective "Aristophanic."

LYSISTRATA

Lysistrata, which is outstanding among the Aristophanic comedies in its coherence of structure and underlying seriousness of theme, was first produced in 411 B.C. In 413 the news of the total destruction of the Athenian fleet in Sicily had reached Athens, and though heroic efforts to carry on the war were under way, the confidence in victory with which Athens had begun the war had gone forever. It is a recurring feature of Aristophanic comedy that the comic hero upsets the *status quo,* to produce a series of extraordinary results which are exploited to the full for their comic potential. In this play the Athenian women, who had no political rights, seize the Acropolis and leave the men without women. At the same time similar revolutions take place in all the Greek cities according to a coordinated plan. The men are eventually "starved" into submission and the Spartans come to Athens to end the war. We

Aristophanes does not miss a trick in his exploitation of the possibilities for ribald humor inherent in this situation, a female sex-strike against war; Myrrhine's teasing game with her husband Cinesias, for example, is rare fooling and the final appearance of the uncomfortably rigid Spartan ambassadors and their equally tense Athenian hosts is a visual and verbal climax of astonishing brilliance. But underneath all the fooling real issues are pursued, and they come to the surface with telling effect in the argument between Lysistrata and the magistrate who has been sent to suppress the revolt. Reversing the words of Hector to Andromache, which had become proverbial, Lysistrata claims that "War shall be the concern of Women!"—it is too important a matter to be left to men, for women are its real victims. And when asked what the women will do, she explains that they will treat politics just as they do wool in their household tasks: "when it's confused and snarled . . . draw out a thread here and a thread there . . . we'll unsnarl this war. . . ." There is no fooling here, and for Americans today the passage has an urgently contemporary note.

We do not know how the Athenians welcomed the play. All we know is that they were not impressed by its serious undertone; the war continued for seven more exhausting years, until Athens' last fleet was defeated, the city laid open to the enemy, the empire lost.

SOCRATES

In the last half of the fifth century the whole traditional basis of individual conduct was undermined, gradually at first by the critical approach of the Sophists and their pupils, and

then rapidly, as the war accelerated the process of moral disintegration. "In peace and prosperity," says Thucydides, "both states and individuals are actuated by higher motives . . . but war, which takes away the comfortable provision of daily life, is a hard master, and tends to assimilate men's characters to their conditions." The war brought to Athens the rule of the new politicians, who reckoned only in terms of power, who carried out the massacre of Melos, and many of whom, like Alcibiades and Critias, betrayed their city for their own ends. Community and individual were no longer one, and the individual, cast on his own resources for guidance, found only conflicting attitudes which he could not refer to any absolute standards. The mood of postwar Athens oscillated between a fanatic, unthinking reassertion of traditional values and a weary cynicism which wanted only to be left alone. The only thing common to the two extremes was a distrust of intelligence.

In the disillusioned gloom of the years of defeat the Athenians began to feel more and more exasperation with a voice they had been listening to for many years, the voice of Socrates, a stonemason who for most of his adult life had made it his business to discuss with his fellow citizens the great issues of which the Athenians were now so weary—the nature of justice, of truth, of piety. Unlike the Sophists, he did not lecture nor did he charge a fee; his method was dialectic, the search for truth by a process of questions and answers, and his dedication to his mission had kept him poor. But the initial results of his discussions were often infuriatingly like the results of sophistic teaching. By questions and answers he succeeded in exposing the illogicality of his opponent's position, but Socrates did not often provide a substitute for the erroneous belief he had destroyed. Yet it is clear that he did believe in absolute standards, and what is more, he believed they could be discovered by a process of logical inquiry and supported by logical proof. His ethics rested on an intellectual basis. The resentment against him, which came to a head in 399 B.C., is partly explained by the fact that he satisfied neither extreme of the postwar mood. He questioned the old standards in order to establish new, and he refused to let the Athenians live in peace, for he preached that it was every man's duty to think his way through to the truth. In this last respect he was the prophet of the new age; for him the city and the accepted code were no substitute for the task of self-examination which each individual must set himself and carry through to a conclusion. The characteristic statement of the old Athens was public, in the assembly or the theater; Socrates proclaimed the right and duty of each individual to work out his own salvation and made clear his distrust of public life: "he who will fight for the right . . . must have a private station and not a public one."

Socrates himself wrote nothing; we know what we do about him mainly from the writings of his pupil Plato, a philosophical and literary genius of the first rank. It is very difficult to distinguish between what Socrates actually said and what Plato put into his mouth, but there is general agreement that the *Apology*, which Plato wrote as a representation of what Socrates said at his trial, is the clearest picture we have of the historical Socrates. He is on trial for impiety and "corrupting the youth." He deals with these charges, but he also takes the opportunity to present a defense and explanation of the mission to which his life has been devoted.

The *Apology* is a defiant speech; Socrates rides roughshod over legal forms and seems to neglect no opportunity of outraging his hearers. But this defiance is not stupidity (as he hints himself, he could, if he had wished, have made a speech to please the court), nor is it a deliberate courting of martyrdom. It is the only course possible for him in the circumstances if he is not to betray his life's work, for Socrates knows as well as his accusers that what the Athenians really want is to silence him without having to take his life. What Socrates is making clear is that there is no such easy way out; he will have no part of any compromise that would restrict his freedom of speech or undermine his moral position. The speech is a sample of what the Athenians will have to put up with if they allow him to live; he will continue to be the gadfly which stings the sluggish horse. He will go on persuading them not to be concerned for their persons or their property, but first and chiefly to care about the improvement of the soul. He has spent his life denying the validity of worldly standards, and he will not accept them now.

He was declared guilty, and condemned to death. While in prison awaiting execution, he was approached by a wealthy friend, Crito, who had made arrangements for his escape from Athens. In the dialogue *Crito*, Plato reconstructs the discussion between the two men. Socrates refused to escape, and the arguments put into his mouth in this dialogue show that although he rejected the political life and the unwavering adherence to one political system which it demanded, he still felt himself bound by the laws of the city. Unlike Alcibiades, the typical representative of the sophistic spirit, who betrayed his country when it had found him guilty of a crime, Socrates refused to disobey the laws even when they demanded his own death.

The sentence was duly carried out. And in Plato's account of the execution we can see the calmness and kindness of a man who has led a useful life and who is secure in his faith that, contrary to appearances, "no evil can happen to a good man, either in life or after death."

THE DIFFUSION OF
GREEK CULTURE

The century that followed the death of Socrates saw the exhaustion of the Greek city-states in constant internecine warfare. Politically and economically bankrupt, they fell under the power of the semibarbarous kingdom of Macedon, in the north, whose king, Philip, combined a ferocious energy with a cynicism which enabled him to take full advantage of the corrupt governments of the city-states. Greek liberty ended at the battle of Chaeronea in 338 B.C., and Philip's son Alexander inherited a powerful army and the political control of all Greece. He led his Macedonian and Greek armies against Persia, and in a few brilliant campaigns became master of an empire which extended into Egypt in the south and to the borders of India in the east. He died at Babylon in 323 B.C., and his empire broke up into a number of independent kingdoms ruled by his generals; but the results of his fantastic achievements were more durable than might have been expected. Into the newly conquered territories came thousands of Greeks who wished to escape from the political futility and economic crisis of the homeland. Wherever they went they took with them their language, their culture, and their typical buildings, the gymnasium and the theater. At Alexandria in Egypt, for example, a Greek library was formed to preserve the texts of Greek literature for the scholars who edited them, a school of Greek poetry flourished, Greek mathematicians and geographers made new advances in science. The Middle East became, as far as the cities were concerned, a Greek-speaking area; and when, some two or three centuries later, the first accounts of Christ's life and teaching were written down, they were written in Greek, the language on which the cultural homogeneity of the whole area was based.

ROME

When Alexander died at Babylon in 323 B.C., the Italian city of Rome, situated on the Tiber in the western coastal plain, was engaged in a struggle for the control of central Italy. Less than a hundred years later (269 B.C.) Rome, in control of the whole Italian peninsula, was drawn into a hundred-year war against the Phoenician city of Carthage, on the West African coast, from which she emerged mistress of the western Mediterranean. At the end of the first century B.C., in spite of a series of civil wars fought with savage vindictiveness and on a continental scale, Rome was the capital of an empire which stretched from the Straits of Gibraltar to the frontiers of Palestine. This empire gave peace and orderly government to the Mediterranean area for the next two centuries, and for two centuries after that maintained a desperate but losing battle against the invading savage tribes moving in from the north and east. When it finally went down, it left behind it the ideal of the world-state, an ideal which was to be reconstituted as a reality by the medieval church, which ruled from the same center, Rome, and with a spiritual authority as great as the secular authority it replaced.

The achievements of the Romans, not only their conquests but also their success in consolidating the conquests and organizing the conquered, are best understood in the light of the Roman character. Unlike the Greek, the Roman was above all a practical man. He might have no aptitude for pure mathematics, but he could build an aqueduct to last two thousand years; he was not notable as a political theorist, but he organized a complicated yet stable federation which held Italy loyal to him in the presence of invading armies. He was conservative to the core; his strongest authority was *mos maiorum*, the custom of his predecessors; a monument of this conservatism, the great body of Roman law, is one of his greatest contributions to Western civilization. The quality he most admired was *gravitas*, seriousness of attitude and purpose, and his highest words of commendation were "manliness," "industry," "discipline." Pericles, in his funeral speech, praised the Athenian for his adaptability, versatility, and grace; this would have seemed strange praise to a Roman, whose idea of personal and civic virtue was different. "By her ancient custom and her men the Roman state stands," says Ennius the Roman poet, in a line which by its metrical heaviness emphasizes the stability implied in the key word "stands": *moribus antiquis res stat Romana virisque.*

LATIN LITERATURE—
LUCRETIUS AND CICERO

Greek history begins, not with a king, a battle, or the founding of a city, but with an epic poem; the literary achievement preceded the political by many centuries. The Romans, on the other hand, had conquered half the world before they began to write. The stimulus to the creation of Latin literature was the Greek literature which the Romans discovered when, in the second century B.C., they assumed political responsibility for Greece and the Near East. Latin literature began with a translation of the *Odyssey*, made by a Greek prisoner of war, and with the exception of satire, until Latin literature became Christian, the model was always Greek. The Latin writer (especially the poet) borrowed wholesale from his Greek original, not furtively, but openly and proudly, as a tribute to the master from whom he had learned. But this frank acknowledgment of indebtedness should not blind us to the fact that Latin literature is original, and sometimes profoundly so. Writing in the first century B.C., both Lucretius and Cicero, the one a poet and the other an orator and philosopher, followed Greek models in the works by which they are represented in this volume. Yet the results were not slavish imitations; each made what he borrowed peculiarly his own.

Lucretius' poem *On the Nature of Things* (*De rerum natura*) is a Latin presentation of the philosophical system of Epicurus, a Greek philosopher of the fourth century B.C. Epicurus had reacted to the hopelessness of his age, which saw the breakdown of the Greek city-states, by propounding a philosophy that described the universe as the result of blind combinations of atoms. With Epicurus the philosophy was not completely materialistic, for it allowed the existence of the gods, though it denied them any role in the government of the universe and asserted that they had no interest in human affairs. But in Lucretius' version, especially in his thoroughly materialistic account (in Book V) of the development of human civilization from primitive savagery, the gods play no part; far from creating man or his civilization, the gods are themselves created by humanity out of its dreams and ignorance.

The ethical precepts of Epicurus' philosophy are summed up in his famous admonition to pursue pleasure, which according to his definition, however, consisted in living a virtuous life. It is a philosophy which encourages a withdrawal from public life, and is in this respect a typical product of the political chaos of the fourth century. This is probably one of the reasons why it attracted Lucretius, for he too lived in an age of social conflict which every twenty years or so erupted in revolution and civil war. But it did not attract many Romans; their respect for action and their deep-rooted worship of duty were obstacles too great to be overcome even by Lucretius' great poetic power.

How great that power is can be seen in the conclusion of his third book, in which he draws the moral from his exposition of the atomic basis of phenomena, and proclaims that death is not to be feared. Death is merely not-being, a rearrangement of the atoms of which we are composed, the dead feel neither pleasure nor pain—so runs his argument, and if it were no more complicated than that it would be just a restatement, though admittedly a magnificent one, of an Epicurean commonplace. But as he develops the argument, we can detect beneath the authoritative calm of the teacher the cry of a man in an agony of doubt and fear. As we read Nature's speech to the coward who is afraid to die, we become increasingly aware that no one is more afraid of death than the poet himself. The vehemence and passion of these famous lines is the mark of a man trying to convince himself rather than his audience; the fears of the unenlightened, animal, part of the human being, which in the face of death will abandon everything except the will to live, are too vividly evoked to be stilled by Nature's argument. And the argument itself, that death is no more than the extinction of consciousness, is a frightening one, especially for an Epicurean, who narrows his ethical and intellectual concern to the restricted scope of his individual self, who "cultivates his garden," and who by his withdrawal from society rejects the corporate immortality of family, city, or race. Lucretius believes in the Epicurean system, but on this central point of the fear of death it brings him little comfort. The disturbance in the poet's own soul, expressed in the tension and violence of these great lines, has turned a philosophical sermon into great poetry.

Much more acceptable to the Roman temperament is the vision of a future life of happiness for those who have been outstanding in their service to the state which is the subject of Cicero's "Dream of Scipio." This is the final chapter of his great work *On the Republic* (*De republica*), the myth which concludes the philosophical discussion. The work as a whole is an imitation of Plato's *Republic*, which is also rounded off by a myth, the story told by Er, who returns from the dead and describes to the living the life of the souls, "the just going up the heavenly way to their reward, the unjust going down to the place of punishment." But Cicero's imitation is characteristically Roman. Instead of imagining, as Plato did, the ideal city, Cicero deals with the Roman republic, its birth, growth, and maturity, and his myth shows the same practical, social viewpoint that is the hallmark of Roman philosophy at its best. "But hold fast to this," says Scipio, Cicero's spokesman: "For all those who have guarded, aided, and increased the welfare of their fatherland there is a place reserved in heaven, where they shall dwell in happiness forever." Lucretius' desperate assertion that the individual must live for himself and accept the obliteration of his personality in death is counterpoised by a vision of an eternal heaven for those who devote themselves to the supreme duty, which, for the Roman, is the public duty.

CATULLUS

A contemporary of Lucretius and Cicero, the young Caius Valerius Catullus from Verona also imitated the Greek masters, but his models were the learned, sophisticated poets of Hellenistic Alexandria as well as the lyric poets of an earlier Greece—one of his poems, for example, is an astonishingly successful translation of Sappho's most passionate lyric (the second in our selection). The hundred or so poems of Catullus that have survived show a rich variety; his book contains long poems on Greek mythological themes, scurrilous personal attacks on contemporary politicians and private individuals, lighthearted verses designed to amuse his friends, a magnificent marriage hymn, and, above all, a series of poems (our selection represents them) which deal with his love affair, at first ecstatically happy, then despairing, with a Roman lady he calls Lesbia but who was probably Clodia, the enchanting but viciously corrupt sister of one of Rome's most cynical and violent aristocrats turned political gangster. These poems present all the phases of the liaison, from the unalloyed happiness of the first encounters through doubt and hesitation to despair and virulent accusation, ending in heartbroken resignation to the bitter fact. They express both the joy of passionate love requited and the torment of betrayal in language so direct and simple, so charged with ecstasy and fury, that they have been the despair of translators ever since.

LATIN LITERATURE—VIRGIL

When Cicero wrote "The Dream of Scipio" the republican form of government which was his larger subject still existed, but its days were numbered. The institutions of the city-state proved inadequate for world government. The civil conflict which had disrupted the republic for more than a hundred years ended finally in the establishment of a powerful executive. Although the Senate, which had been the controlling body of the republic, retained an impressive share of the power, the new arrangement developed inevitably toward autocracy, the rule of the executive, the emperor, as he was called once the system was stabilized. The first of the long line of Roman emperors who gave stable government to the Roman world during the first two centuries A.D. was Octavius, known generally by his title, Augustus. He had made his way cautiously through the intrigues and bloodshed that followed the murder of his uncle Julius Caesar in 44 B.C., until by 31 B.C., he controlled the western half of the empire. In that year he fought a decisive battle with the ruler of the eastern half of the empire, Mark Antony, who was supported by Cleopatra, queen of Egypt. Octavius' victory at Actium united the empire under one authority and ushered in an age of peace and reconstruction. It was in the opening years of the new age that Virgil wrote (and left unfinished at his early death) the great Roman epic, the *Aeneid*.

Like all the Latin poets, Virgil built on the solid foundations of his Greek predecessors. The story of Aeneas, the Trojan prince who came to Italy and whose descendants founded Rome, combines the themes of the *Odyssey* (the wanderer in search of home) and the *Iliad* (the hero in battle). Virgil borrows Homeric turns of phrase, similes, sentiments, whole incidents: his Aeneas, like Achilles, sacrifices prisoners to the shade of a friend and, like Odysseus, descends alive to the world of the dead. But unlike Achilles, Aeneas does not satisfy the great passion of his life, nor, like Odysseus, does he find a home in which to end his days in peace. The personal objectives of both of Homer's heroes are sacrificed by Aeneas for a greater objective. There is something greater than himself. His mission, imposed on him by the gods, is to found a city, from which, in the fullness of time, will spring the Roman state.

Homer presents us in the *Iliad* with the tragic pattern of the individual will, Achilles' wrath. But Aeneas is more than an individual. He is the prototype of the ideal Roman ruler; his qualities are the devotion to duty and the seriousness of purpose which were to give the Mediterranean world two centuries of ordered government. Aeneas' mission begins in disorder in the burning city of Troy, but he leaves it carrying his father on his shoulders and leading his little son by the hand. This famous picture emphasizes the fact that, unlike Achilles, he is securely set in a continuity of generations, the immortality of the family group, just as his mission to found a city, a home for the gods of Troy whose statues he carries with him, places him in a political and religious continuity. Achilles has no future. When he mentions his father and son, neither of whom he will see again, he emphasizes for us the loneliness

of his short career; the brilliance of his life is that of a meteor which burns itself out to darkness. Odysseus has a father, wife, and son, and his heroic efforts are directed toward re-establishing himself in his proper context, that home in which he will be no longer man in a world of magic and terror, but man in an organized and continuous community. But he fights for himself. Aeneas, on the other hand, suffers and fights, not for himself but for the future; his own life is unhappy and his death miserable. Yet he can console himself with the glory of his sons to come, the pageant of Roman achievement which he is shown by his father in the world below and which he carries on his shield. Aeneas' future is Virgil's present; the consolidation of the Roman peace under Augustus is the reward of Aeneas' unhappy life of effort and suffering.

Summarized like this, the *Aeneid* sounds like propaganda, which, in one sense of the word, it is. What saves it from the besetting fault of even the best propaganda—the partial concealment of the truth—is the fact that Virgil maintains an independence of the power which he is celebrating and sees his hero in the round. He knows that the Roman ideal of devotion to duty has another side, the suppression of many aspects of the personality; that the man who wins and uses power must sacrifice much of himself, must live a life which, compared with that of Achilles or Odysseus, is constricted. In Virgil's poem Aeneas betrays the great passion of his life, his love for Dido, queen of Carthage. He does it reluctantly, but nevertheless he leaves her, and the full realization of what he has lost comes to him only when he meets her ghost in the world below. He weeps (as he did not at Carthage) and he pleads, in stronger terms than he did then, the overriding power which forced him to depart: "It was not of my own will, Dido, I left your land." She leaves him without a word, her silence as impervious to pleas and tears as his at Carthage once, and he follows her weeping as she goes back to join her first love, her husband Sychaeus. He has sacrificed his love to something greater, but this does not insulate him from unhappiness. The limitations upon the dedicated man are emphasized by the contrasting figure of Dido, who follows her own impulse always, even in death. By her death, Virgil tells us expressly, she forestalls fate, breaks loose from the pattern in which Aeneas remains to the bitter end.

The angry reactions which this part of the poem has produced in many critics are the true measure of Virgil's success. Aeneas does act in such a way that he forfeits much of our sympathy, but this is surely exactly what Virgil intended. The Dido episode is not, as many critics have supposed, a flaw in the great design, a case of Virgil's sympathy outrunning his admiration for Aeneas; it is Virgil's emphatic statement of the sacrifice which the Roman ideal of duty demands. Aeneas' sacrifice is so great that few of us could make it ourselves, and none of us can contemplate it in another without a feeling of loss. It is an expression of the famous Virgilian sadness which informs every line of the *Aeneid* and which makes a poem that was in its historical context a command performance into the great epic which has dominated Western literature ever since.

OVID

Virgil had grown to manhood in the years of civil war, when no man's property, nor even his life, was safe. He knew all too well the horrors that would inevitably recur if Augustus' attempt to establish stable government should fail; like all his generation, he knew how precarious the newfound peace was and felt himself deeply engaged in the Augustan program. But a new generation of poets, who had not known the time of troubles, took all that had been achieved for granted, and turned to new themes. The most brilliant of them, Ovid, was a boy of eleven when Octavius defeated Anthony at Actium; the early years of his manhood, far from being dominated by fear of chaos come again, were marked by rapid literary and social success in the brilliant society of a capital intent on enjoying the peace and prosperity which had been restored with so much effort.

Ovid was a versifier of genius; "whatever I tried to say," he wrote, "came out in verse," and Pope adapted the line for his own case: "I lisped in numbers for the numbers came." Elegance, wit, and precision remained the hallmarks of Ovid's poetry throughout his long and productive career; though his themes are often frivolous, the technical perfection of the medium carries the dazzled reader along. His most influential work, the *Metamorphoses*, is a treasure house of Greek and Roman mythological stories brilliantly combined in a long narrative and retold with such wit, charm, and surpassing beauty that poets ever since, Shakespeare among them, have used it as a source. Ovid is represented here by selections from his earliest book, the *Amores*—unabashed chronicles of a Roman Don Juan. Ovid is working the same territory as Catullus, but with a world of difference. There is no passion here, no broken hearts; infidelity is taken for granted (but should be decently concealed). What saves the poems from banality is their unembarrassed enjoyment of the pleasures of life, their wit, and the perfection of their form (in this case admirably conveyed by the translation).

JESUS OF NAZARETH

In the last years of Augustus' life, in the Roman province of Judea, there was born to Joseph, a carpenter of Nazareth, and his wife, Mary, a son who was at once the final product of an old tradition and the starting point of a new. He was the last of the Hebrew prophets, but His message, unlike theirs, was to spread outside the boundaries of Palestine until it became the religion of the Roman Empire. His life on earth was short; it ended in the agony of crucifixion at about His thirty-third year. This event is a point of intersection of the three main lines of development of the ancient world—Hebrew, Greek, and Latin—for this Hebrew prophet was executed by a Roman governor, and His life and teachings were written down in the Greek language. These documents, which eventually, with some additions, constituted what we now know as the New Testament, circulated in the Greek-speaking half of the Roman Empire and later, in a Latin translation, in the West. They became the sacred texts of a church which, at first persecuted by and then triumphantly associated with Roman imperial power, outlasted the destruction of the empire and ruled over a spiritual kingdom which still exists.

The teaching of Christ was revolutionary not only in terms of Greek and Roman feeling but also in terms of the Hebrew religious tradition. The Hebrew idea of a personal God who is yet not anthropomorphic, who is omnipotent, omniscient, and infinitely just, was now broadened to include among His attributes an infinite mercy which tempered the justice. Greek and Roman religion was outward and visible, the formal practice of ritual acts in a social context; Christianity was inward and spiritual, the important relationship was that between the individual soul and God. All human beings were on an equal plane in the eyes of their Creator. This idea ran counter to the theory and practice of an institution basic to the economy of the ancient world, slavery. Christ was rejected by His own people, as prophets have always been, and His death on the cross and His resurrection provided His followers and the future converts with an unforgettable symbol of a new dispensation, the son of God in human form suffering to atone for the sins of humanity, the supreme expression of divine mercy. This conception is the basis of the teaching of Paul, the apostle to the gentiles, who in the middle years of the first century A.D. changed Christianity from a Jewish sect to a world-wide movement with flourishing churches all over Asia Minor and Greece, and even in Rome. The burden of his teaching was the frailty and corruption of this life and world, and the certainty of resurrection. "For this corruptible must put on incorruption, and this mortal must put on immortality." To those who had accepted this vision the secular materialism which was the dominant view in the new era of peace and progress guaranteed by the stabilization of Roman rule was no longer tenable.

LATIN LITERATURE—PETRONIUS

The pragmatic outlook which Christianity was to supplant is to be seen most clearly portrayed in the satiric masterpiece of the Roman aristocrat Petronius. The work which is attributed to him, the *Satyricon*, was probably written during the principate of Nero (A.D. 54-68), a period in which the material benefits and the spiritual weakness of the new order had already become apparent. The *Satyricon* itself has survived only in fragments; we know nothing certain about the scope of the work as a whole, but from the fragments it is clear that this book is the work of a satiric genius, perhaps the most original genius of Latin literature.

"Dinner with Trimalchio," one of the longer fragments, selections from which are included here, shows us a trades-man's world. The narrator, a student of literature, and his cronies may have an aristocratic disdain for the businessmen at whose tables they eat, but they know that Trimalchio and his kind have inherited the earth. Trimalchio began life as a foreign slave, but he is now a multimillionaire. The representative of culture, Agamemnon the teacher, drinks his wine and praises his fatuous remarks; he is content to be the court jester, the butt of Trimalchio's witticisms. Trimalchio knows no god but Mercury, the patron of business operations, but the gold bracelet, a percentage of his income which he has dedicated to Mercury, he wears on his own arm. He identifies himself with the god, and worships himself, the living embodiment of the power of money. The conversation at his table is a sardonic revelation of the temper of a whole civilization. Written in brilliantly humorous and colloquial style it exposes mercilessly a blindness to spiritual values of any kind, a distrust of the intellect, and a ferocious preoccupation with the art of cheating one's neighbor. The point is made more effective by the conscious evocation of the epic tradition throughout the work. The names alone of the teacher, Agamemnon, and his assistant in instruction, Menelaus; the wall paintings which show "the Iliad and the Odyssey and the gladiator's show given by Laenas"; Trimalchio's exhibition of monstrous ignorance of Homer (which nobody dares to correct); the Nestorian tone of Ganymede, who regrets the old days when men were men (he is

talking of the time when Safinius forced the bakers to lower
the price of bread)—one touch
after another reminds us that
these figures are the final product of a tradition that began
with Achilles and Odysseus.

The satire is witty, but it is
nonetheless profound. All of
them live for the moment, in
material enjoyment, but they
know that it cannot last. "Let us
remember the living" is their
watchword, but they cannot forget the dead. And as the banquet
goes on, the thought of death,
suppressed beneath the debased
Epicureanism of Trimalchio and
his associates, emerges slowly to
the surface of their consciousness and comes to dominate it
completely. The last arrival at
the banquet is Habinnas the
undertaker, and his coming co-
incides with the last stage of
Trimalchio's drunkenness, the
maudlin exhibition of his funeral clothes and the description
of his tomb. "I would that I
were dead," says the Sibyl in the
story Trimalchio tells early in
the evening; at its end he himself acts out his own funeral,
complete with ointment, robes,
wine, and trumpet players. The
fact of death, the one fact which
the practical materialism of
Trimalchio and his circle can
neither deny nor assimilate, as-
serts itself triumphantly as the
supreme fact in the emptiness
of Trimalchio's mind.

JUVENAL

There was one province of literature in which the Romans
claimed to owe nothing to the
Greeks: "Satire," said the Roman critic Quintilian, "is wholly
ours." The word itself originally
meant a mixture (of prose and
verse, of meters, of topics), but it
has come to mean what it does to
us mainly because it was the
name that Juvenal gave to his
poems. His subject is the whole
range of the vices and follies of
mankind, particularly those of
the huge imperial Rome in which
he lived, apparently in something near to poverty. Writing
under the emperors of the turn
of the first century A.D., when the
Augustan political compromise
had long since evolved into auto-
cratic rule, he was not so foolish
as to choose his examples of corruption among the powerful of
his own day; "I shall see," he
says, "how much I will be allowed
to say about those whose ashes lie
in tombs along the high roads."
But though his examples were
drawn from the Roman past,
their vices were still to be seen
on every hand, as they are still.
In his famous tenth satire, the
scope is broader: the folly of ambition, of praying for anything
at all but "a sound mind in a
sound body"—a theme which he
drives home with a series of vivid
pictures of the overthrow and
miserable end which come to all
the great ones of the earth,
couched in a pointed, bitter rhetoric which makes them impossible to forget.

ST. AUGUSTINE

When Augustine was born in
North Africa in A.D. 354, the era
of Roman peace was already
over. The invading barbarians
had pierced the empire's de-
fenses and were increasing their
pressure every year. The economic basis of the empire was
cracking under the strain of the
enormous taxation needed to
support the army; the land was

exhausted. The empire was Christian, but the Church was split, beset by heresies and organized heretical sects. The empire was about to go down to destruction, and there was every prospect that the Church would go down with it.

Augustine, one of the men responsible for the consolidation of the Church in the West, especially for the systematization of its doctrine and policy, was not converted to Christianity until he had reached middle life. "Late I loved you, Beauty so ancient and so new," he says in his *Confessions* (A.D.399), written long after his conversion. The lateness of his conversion and his regret for his wasted youth were among the sources of the energy which drove him to assume the intellectual leadership of the Western Church and to guarantee, by combating heresy on the one hand and laying new ideological foundations for Christianity on the other, the Church's survival through the dark centuries to come. Augustine had been brought up in the literary and philosophical tradition of the classical world, and it is partly because of his assimilation of classical literature and method to Christian training and teaching that the literature of the ancient world survived at all when Roman power collapsed in a welter of bloodshed and destruction which lasted for generations.

In his *Confessions* he set down, for the benefit of others, the story of his early life and his conversion to Christianity. This is, as far as we know, the first real ancient autobiography, and that fact itself is a significant expression of the Christian spirit, which proclaims the value of the individual soul and the importance of its relation with God. Throughout the *Confessions* Augustine talks directly to God, in humility, yet conscious that God is concerned for him personally. At the same time he comes to an understanding of his own feelings and development as a human being which marks his *Confessions* as one of the great literary documents of the Western world. His description of his childhood is the only detailed account of the childhood of a great man which antiquity has left us, and his accurate observation and keen perception are informed by the Hebrew and Christian idea of the sense of sin. "So young, and such a sinner"—from the beginning of his narrative to the end Augustine sees man not as the Greek at his most optimistic tended to see him, the center and potential master of the universe, but as a child, wandering in ignorance, capable of reclamation only through the divine mercy which waits eternally for him to turn to it.

In Augustine are combined the intellectual tradition of the ancient world at its best and the religious feeling which was the characteristic of the Middle Ages. The transition from the old world to the new can be seen in his pages; his analytical intellect pursues its Odyssey through strange and scattered islands—the mysticism of the Manichees, the skepticism of the Academic philosophers, the fatalism of the astrologers—until he finds his home in the Church, to which he was to render such great service. His account of his conversion in the garden at Milan records the true moment of transition from the ancient to the medieval world. The innumerable defeats and victories, the burning towns and ravaged farms, the bloodshed, dates, and statistics of the end of an era are all illuminated and ordered by this moment in the history of the human spirit. Here is the point of change itself.

LIVES, WRITINGS, AND CRITICISM
Biographical and critical works are listed only if they are available in English.

GREECE—GENERAL

Sir Alfred Zimmern, *The Greek Commonwealth* (1922) is a stimulating account of Greek geography, economy, and political practice. For a good one-volume history see J. B. Bury, *History of Greece*, revised by R. Meiggs (1951). See also H. D. F. Kitto, *The Greeks* (1951); C. M. Bowra, *The Greek Experience* (1957); M. I. Finley, *The Ancient Greeks* (1963); A. Andrewes, *The Greeks* (1967).

HOMER

LIFE AND WRITINGS. Nothing whatsoever is known about Homer's life. The traditional date for the composition of the poems is *ca.* 850 B.C., though the tendency of modern scholarship is to prefer a later date. On the "Homeric problem," see M. P. Nilsson, *Homer and Mycenae* (1933); G. S. Kirk, *The Songs of Homer* (1962); D. L. Page, *History and the Homeric Iliad* (1959); and H. L. Lorimer, *Homer and the Monuments* (1950).

CRITICISM. *Iliad*. J. P. Shephard, *The Pattern of the Iliad* (1922); C. M. Bowra, *Tradition and Design in the Iliad* (1930); C. H. Whitman, *Homer and the Heroic Tradition* (1958); G. Steiner and R. Fagles, *Homer, A Collection of Critical Essays* (1962). See also Richmond Lattimore's introduction to his translation, *The Iliad of Homer* (1951).

Odyssey. C. H. Taylor, Jr., ed., *Essays on the Odyssey* (1963); M. I. Finley, *The World of Odysseus* (1954).

GREEK LYRIC POETS

Except for Solon (who was a political reformer of note) information about their lives is sketchy and unreliable; in some cases even their century is a controversial matter. Except for Theognis, their works survive only in fragments preserved by later writers who quote them or battered papyri from Egypt.

ARCHILOCHUS. Born on the island of Paros, probably in the seventh century B.C., he served as a soldier and took part in the colonization of the island of Thasos. He was famous for his outspokenness and the savagery of his satire.

TYRTAEUS. Ancient traditions about his life are worthless; all we can say is that he seems to have been a Spartan and that his exhortations to warlike valor were probably connected with a war Sparta waged to extend her territory in Messenia, to the west.

MIMNERMUS. Lived in Colophon and Smyrna, both Greek colonies in Asia Minor. To later writers he was famous as the poet of love par excellence, but he seems also to have written (in works now lost) about the history of the two cities where he lived.

SAPPHO. Born about 630 B.C., a member of the aristocratic society of Mytilene on the island of Lesbos. She was married and had a daughter (mentioned in her poems). The ancient world possessed nine books of her poems; the few fragments that are left show how great is our loss.

ALCAEUS. A younger contemporary of Sappho and a member of the same aristocratic class, he took part in the civil strife which erupted on Lesbos and was exiled twice.

SOLON. In 594 B.C. he was appointed archon, chief magistrate of Athens, to institute political and economic reforms designed to prevent civil war and revolution. He steered a middle course between right and left, abolishing the debts of those who had sold themselves into slavery, but refused to please the extremists of either side.

ANACREON. Born ca. 520 B.C. on the island of Teos, he took part in the colonization of Abdera in Thrace, then became a sort of court poet to the dictatorial ruler of Samos, and finally moved to Athens.

XENOPHANES. Born in Colophon in Asia Minor, he left home when the Persians annexed the Greek cities of the coast (545 B.C.) and lived the rest of his life in the Greek cities of Sicily. His writings show a philosophical bent and contain sharp criticism of current attitudes to morals and religion.

THEOGNIS. An aristocrat of Megara, from which he was exiled as a result of a democratic revolution. His poem is addressed to a young man called Cyrnus, and contains advice, sometimes moral, sometimes cynical, with much lamentation for the loss of his lands and the end of the aristocratic world.

CRITICISM. C. M. Bowra, *Early Greek Elegists* (1938); *Greek Lyric Poetry*, 2d ed. (1961).

TRANSLATION. R. Lattimore, *Greek Lyrics*, 2d ed. (1960).

GREEK THEATER

For information about the theater—scenery, machinery, actors, audience, etc.—see A. W. Pickard-Cambridge, *The Theatre of Dionysus* (1946) and *The Dramatic Festivals of Athens*, 2d ed., revised by J. Gould and D. M. Lewis (1968); M. Bieber, *The History of the Greek and Roman Theater*, 2d ed. (1961); T. B. L. Webster, *Greek Theatre Production* (1956); and P. Arnott, *Greek Scenic Conventions* (1962). Critical works on the plays: H. D. F. Kitto, *Greek Tragedy, A Literary Study*, 3d ed. (1961); D. W. Lucas, *The Greek Tragic Poets*, 2d ed. (1959); T. G. Rosenmeyer, *The Masks of Tragedy* (1963); R. Lattimore, *The Poetry of Greek Tragedy* (1958).

AESCHYLUS

LIFE AND WRITINGS. Born in 524? B.C. He fought at Marathon against the Persians in 490 B.C. Among his plays are *The Persians* (472 B.C.); *The Seven against Thebes* (467 B.C.); the *Oresteia* (*Agamemnon, Choephoroe, Eumenides*, 458 B.C.). He died in Sicily in 456 B.C. His other surviving plays are *The Suppliants* and *Prometheus Bound*.

For a translation of the whole trilogy and an excellent introduction see Richmond Lattimore's *Oresteia of Aeschylus* (1953). Prose translations of the complete works are to be found in *The Plays of Aeschylus*, translated by Walter Headlam (1900). H. Weir Smith's prose version in the Loeb Classical Library is also noteworthy.

CRITICISM. H. Weir Smith, *Aeschylean Tragedy* (1924); Gilbert Murray, *Aeschylus, Creator of Tragedy* (1940); and E. T. Owen, *The Harmony of Aeschylus* (1952).

THUCYDIDES

LIFE AND WRITINGS. The only certain date in his biography is 424 B.C., the year in which he was exiled from Athens because of a failure as general in the north of Greece. He gives an account of his unsuccessful campaign in Book IV, Chapters 103-109, of his *History of the Peloponnesian War*, and mentions his exile in Book V, Chapter 26. He probably returned to Athens after the defeat in 404 B.C., but he did not live long enough to complete his history of the war; his book ends with the events of the year 411 B.C.

A translation by Benjamin Jowett of the complete work is included in *The Greek Historians*, edited by F. R. B. Godolphin, Vol. I (1942). There are also translations by R. Crawley (1876, reprinted 1934) and R. Warner (1954).

CRITICISM. J. H. Finley, Jr., *Thucydides* (1947): and F. E. Adcock, *Thucydides and his History* (1963).

SOPHOCLES

LIFE AND WRITINGS. Born in 495 B.C. He was victorious over Aeschylus in the dramatic contest in 468 B.C. In 440 B.C. he was appointed one of ten generals for the expedition against Samos. He died in 406 B.C. His plays are *Antigone* (441? B.C.); *Ajax; King Oedipus* (*Oedipus Tyrannus*); *Electra; Trachiniae; Philoctetes* (409 B.C.); *Oedipus at Colonus* (produced after his death, 401 B.C.).

The standard edition in English, by Sir Richard C. Jebb, consists of seven separate volumes (1884-1896), each containing a careful prose translation. More recent translations are to be found in *The Complete Greek Tragedies*, edited by D. Grene and R. Lattimore (1957–); H. D. F. Kitto, *Sophocles, Three Tragedies* (1962); T. H. Banks, *Three Theban Plays* (1956); B. M. W. Knox, *Oedipus the King* (1959).

CRITICISM. C. M. Bowra, *Sophoclean Tragedy* (1944); C. H. Whitman, *Sophocles, A Study in Heroic Humanism* (1951); S. M. Adams, *Sophocles the Playwright* (1957); A. J. A. Waldock, *Sophocles the Dramatist* (1951); B. M. W. Knox, *Oedipus at Thebes* (1957) and *The Heroic Temper* (1964); L. Berkowitz and T. Brunner, *Oedipus Tyrannus* (1970).

EURIPIDES

LIFE AND WRITINGS. Born in 480 B.C. His first dramatic victory was in 441 B.C. Among his plays are *Alcestis*, 438 B.C.; *Medea*, 431 B.C.; *Hippolytus*, 428 B.C.; *Trojan Women*, 415 B.C.; *Orestes*, 408 B.C. Some time after this he left Athens for Macedonia, where he died in 406 B.C. The *Bacchae* and *Iphigenia at Aulis* were produced at Athens after his death. Eighteen of his plays have been preserved. For translations see *The Complete Greek Tragedies* (1957–) and the versions by P. Vellacott in the Penguin Series. Also R. Warner, *Three Great Plays of Euripides* (1958).

CRITICISM. G. M. A. Grube, *The Drama of Euripides* (1941); D. J. Conacher, *Euripidean Drama* (1967); *Euripides, A Collection of Critical Essays*, edited by E. Segal (1968).

ARISTOPHANES

LIFE AND WRITINGS. Born around 450 B.C. Eleven of his comedies have survived; among the most famous are *The Clouds* (423 B.C.), *The Birds* (414 B.C.), and *The Frogs* (405 B.C.). He died around 385 B.C.

CRITICISM. G. Murray *Aristophanes, A Study* (1933); G. Norwood, *Greek Comedy* (1931) K. Lever, *The Art of Greek Comedy* (1956); and C. H. Whitman, *Aristophanes and the Comic Hero* (1964).

PLATO

LIFE. Born in Athens in 429 or 428 B.C. He was present at the trial of Socrates, his teacher, in 399 B.C. After this he traveled widely, eventually returning to Athens to found his philosophical school, the Academy. He made two visits to Sicily to act as philosophical and political tutor to the younger Dionysius, tyrant of Syracuse, but both of these interventions in practical affairs were unfortunate. He died in 347 B.C.

WRITINGS. The whole of his work is preserved; all of his writings except the last, *The Laws*, are dialogues in which Socrates is the chief speaker. A complete translation is Benjamin Jowett, *The Dialogues of Plato* (1925). The best translation of Plato's most famous work, *The Republic*, is by F. M. Cornford (1945). Translations by Percy Bysshe Shelley of the *Ion* and *Symposium* are to be found in *Five Dialogues of Plato*, Everyman's Library (1952).

CRITICISM. A. E. Taylor, *Plato, The Man and His Work* (1927); G. M. A. Grube, *Plato's Thought* (1935); R. S. Brumbaugh, *Plato for the Modern Age* (1962).

ARISTOTLE

LIFE. Born at Stagira (Macedonia) in 384 B.C. In 367 B.C. he went to Athens and became a pupil of Plato at the Academy. He left Athens in 347 B.C. (the year Plato died), spent some years in the Greek cities of Asia Minor, and in 342 B.C. went to Macedonia as tutor to the young Alexander, then thirteen years of age. In 335 B.C., when Alexander succeeded to the throne of Macedonia, Aristotle returned to Athens, where he founded a school, the Lyceum. He directed the school, lecturing and writing, until 323 BC., the year of Alexander's death at Babylon. Aristotle himself died at Chalcis, in Euboea, in the next year.

WRITINGS. His writings cover almost the whole field of human knowledge. Among the subjects he treated are logic, rhetoric, literary criticism, physics, metaphysics, politics, mathematics,

meteorology, zoology, and history. For the complete works see the Oxford translation, completed in 1931. For the *Poetics*, see Ingram Bywater, *Aristotle on the Art of Poetry* (1909); and S. H. Butcher, *Aristotle's Theory of Poetry and the Fine Arts* (1907).

CRITICISM. Werner Jaeger, *Aristotle*, (1936); *Aristotle's Poetics*, with an introductory essay by Francis Fergusson (1961); and H. House, *Aristotle's Poetics* (1961).

ROME—GENERAL

For a good one-volume history of Rome see M. Cary, *History of Rome* (1938); and R. H. Barrow, *The Romans* (1949).

LUCRETIUS

LIFE AND WRITINGS. Titus Lucretius Carus, born about 99 B.C. He died in 55 B.C., a suicide, according to rumor. His only work is the didactic poem *On the Nature of Things (De rerum natura)*, a philosophical poem in six books. The best edition (with prose translation) is by C. Bailey, 3 vol. (1946). For a verse translation of the whole poem see the version by W. E. Leonard, Everyman's Library (1947).

CRITICISM. E. E. Sikes, *Lucretius, Poet and Philosopher* (1936).

CICERO

LIFE AND WRITINGS. Marcus Tullius Cicero, born in 106 B.C. He studied at Athens, went into law, and soon became prominent in politics. In 70 B.C. he successfully pleaded the case of the Sicilians against Verres, a corrupt governor. In 63 B.C. he attained the highest republican office, the consulate, and during his term put down forcibly an insurrection led by Catiline. Later, a reaction against his policies caused him to retire from Rome; he returned in 55 B.C. When the civil war broke out in 49 B.C., he took sides with Pompey against Julius Caesar; after Pompey's defeat and death he was pardoned and returned to Rome. After Caesar's murder in 44 B.C. Cicero led the opposition against Caesar's lieutenant, Antony, and he was murdered in 43 B.C. at Antony's orders. He has left a great number of speeches, both forensic and political, which have served as models for Western oratory ever since; philosophical works, in which he made available to the Latin-speaking (and medieval) world the achievements of Greek philosophy; works on rhetoric; and a huge collection of private letters, which give a fascinating and uncensored picture of his life and times. Translations of almost all of his works are to be found in the Loeb Classical Library.

BIOGRAPHY AND CRITICISM. For a good biography see E. G. Sihler, *Cicero of Arpinum* (1914). See also J. L. Strachan-Davidson, *Cicero and the Fall of the Roman Republic* (1903).

CATULLUS

LIFE AND WRITINGS. Gaius Valerius Catullus was born at Verona in North Italy probably in 84 B.C. and died at the age of thirty. Moving in fashionable literary circles in Rome in the last decades of the republic, he fell in love with the woman called Lesbia in his poems whose real name was Clodia; she was probably the notorious sister of Clodius Pulcher, enemy of Cicero and agent of Caesar. This unhappy love is the theme of his most famous poems but he had a wide range of mood and subject; the one volume of his poems that has survived is probably a selection, put together after his death.

TRANSLATIONS. *The Poems of Catullus*, H. Gregory (1956).

CRITICISM. E. A. Havelock, *The Lyric Genius of Catullus*.

VIRGIL

LIFE AND WRITINGS. Publius Virgilius Maro, born in 79 B.C. in the north of Italy. Very little is known about his life. The earliest work which is certainly his is the *Bucolics*, a collection of poems in the pastoral genre which have had enormous influence. These were followed by the *Georgics*, a didactic poem on farming, in four books, which many critics consider his finest work. The *Aeneid*, the Roman epic, was left unfinished at his early death in 19 B.C. Recent translations are by Cecil Day Lewis, *The Georgics* (1940) and *The Aeneid of Virgil* (1952). John Dryden's classic versions of the *Georgics* and the *Aeneid* can be found in *The Complete Poems of John Dryden* (1949).

CRITICISM. W. F. J. Knight, *Roman Vergil* (1944); V. Pöschl, *The Art of Vergil* (1962); B. Otis, *Virgil, A Study in Civilized Poetry* (1963); M. C. J. Putnam, *The Poetry of the Aeneid* (1965); W. A. Camps, *An Introduction to Virgil's Aeneid* (1969).

OVID

LIFE AND WRITINGS. Publius Ovidius Naso, 43 B.C.–A.D. 17. Born at Sulmona in central Italy, he was destined by his father for a government career but became a poet instead. He is certainly the most professional and skillful of the Latin poets, and the most prolific. The *Amores* (from which our selections come) was his earliest publication; it was soon followed by the *Art of Love*, a handbook of seduction (originally in two books, for men— Book III, for women, was added by popular request). His most influential poem over the centuries has been the *Metamorphoses*, an epic poem in fifteen books which deals with stories of transformations and became for later ages the favorite handbook of Greek and

Roman mythology. In A.D. 8 Ovid was banished, by imperial decree, to the town of Tomi, in Romania, outside the frontiers of the empire, where he remained until his death. The reason for his banishment is not known: involvement in some scandal concerning Augustus' daughter Julia is a possibility but the love poetry may have been a contributory factor. Augustus was trying, by legislation, to revive the old Roman standards of strict morality and Ovid's *Amores* and *Art of Love* were not exactly helpful.

TRANSLATIONS. *Ovid's Amores*, Guy Lee (1968); *Metamorphoses*, R. Humphries (1955).

CRITICISM. H. Fraenkel, *Ovid: A Poet between Two Worlds* (1945); L. P. Wilkinson, *Ovid Recalled* (1955); B. Otis, *Ovid as an Epic Poet* (1966).

PETRONIUS

LIFE AND WRITINGS. It is not certain that Caius Petronius (Arbiter) was the author of the *Satyricon*, but he is the best candidate. A friend of Nero's, he committed suicide at the imperial order after becoming involved in the Pisonian conspiracy against the emperor in 65 A.D. A brilliant account of Petronius' character and death is given by Tacitus in the eighteenth and nineteenth chapters of Book XVI of the *Annals*.

For another recent translation with a critical introduction, see W. Arrowsmith, *The Satyricon of Petronius* (1959).

JUVENAL

Decimus Iunius Iuvenalis, of Aquinum. There are no reliable records of his life or dates: from internal evidence it seems clear that he was middle-aged when he published his first satires around A.D. 100; he was still writing in A.D. 127. His work consists of satires, which vary greatly in length.

CRITICISM. G. Highet, *Juvenal the Satirist* (1954).

ST. AUGUSTINE

LIFE AND WRITINGS. Aurelius Augustinus, born in 354 A.D. at Tagaste, in North Africa. He was baptized as a Christian in 387 A.D. and ordained bishop of Hippo, in North Africa, in 395 A.D. When he died there in 430 A.D., the city was besieged by Gothic invaders. Besides the *Confessions (Confessiones*, written in 397 A.D.) he wrote *The City of God* (*De civitate dei*, finished in 426 A.D.) and many polemical works against schismatics and heretics. Translations of *The City of God* may be found in Everyman's Library and also in the Loeb Classical Library, which also includes some of his letters. For a modern translation of the *Confessions* see F. J. Sheed, *The Confessions of St. Augustine* (1943), and for criticism and biography, P. Brown, *Augustine of Hippo* (1967).

The Old Testament*

[*The Creation—The Fall*]

1. In the beginning God created the heaven and the earth. And the earth was without form, and void; and darkness was upon the face of the deep. And the Spirit of God moved upon the face of the waters.

And God said, Let there be light: and there was light. And God saw the light, that it was good· and God divided the light from the darkness. And God called the light Day, and the darkness he called Night. And the evening and the morning were the first day.

And God said, Let there be a firmament in the midst of the waters,[1] and let it divide the waters from the waters. And God made the firmament, and divided the waters which were under the firmament from the waters which were above the firmament: and it was so. And God called the firmament Heaven. And the evening and the morning were the second day.

And God said, Let the waters under the heaven be gathered together unto one place, and let the dry land appear: and it was so. And God called the dry land Earth; and the gathering together of the waters called he Seas: and God saw that it was good. And God said, Let the earth bring forth grass, the herb yielding seed, and the fruit tree yielding fruit after his kind, whose seed is in itself, upon the earth: and it was so. And the earth brought forth grass, and herb yielding seed after his kind, and the tree yielding fruit, whose seed was in itself, after his kind: and God saw that it was good. And the evening and the morning were the third day.

And God said, Let there be lights in the firmament of the heaven to divide the day from the night; and let them be for signs, and for seasons, and for days, and years: and let them be for lights in the firmament of the heaven to give light upon the earth: and it was so. And God made two great lights; the greater light to rule the day, and the lesser light to rule the night: he made the stars also. And God set them in the firmament of the heaven to give light upon the earth, and to rule over the day and over the night, and to divide the light from the darkness: and God saw that it was good. And the evening and the morning were the fourth day. And God said, Let the waters bring forth abundantly the moving creature that hath life, and fowl[2] that may fly above the earth in the open firmament of heaven. And God created great whales, and every living creature that moveth,

---

* The text of these selections from the Holy Bible is that of the King James, or Authorized, Version.
† Genesis 1:1—3:24.

1. The firmament is the sky, which seen from below has the appearance of a ceiling; the waters above it are those which come down in the form of rain.
2. winged creatures of all kinds.

which the waters brought forth abundantly, after their kind, and every winged fowl after his kind: and God saw that it was good. And God blessed them, saying, Be fruitful, and multiply, and fill the waters in the seas, and let fowl multiply in the earth. And the evening and the morning were the fifth day.

And God said, Let the earth bring forth the living creature after his kind, cattle, and creeping thing, and beast of the earth after his kind: and it was so. And God made the beast of the earth after his kind, and cattle after their kind, and everything that creepeth upon the earth after his kind: and God saw that it was good.

And God said, Let us make man in our image, after our likeness: and let them have dominion over the fish of the sea, and over the fowl of the air, and over the cattle, and over all the earth, and over every creeping thing that creepeth upon the earth. So God created man in his own image, in the image of God created he him; male and female created he them. And God blessed them, and God said unto them, Be fruitful, and multiply, and replenish the earth, and subdue it: and have dominion over the fish of the sea, and over the fowl of the air, and over every living thing that moveth upon the earth.

And God said, Behold, I have given you every herb bearing seed, which is upon the face of all the earth, and every tree, in the which is the fruit of a tree yielding seed; to you it shall be for meat. And to every beast of the earth, and to every fowl of the air, and to every thing that creepeth upon the earth, wherein there is life, I have given every green herb for meat: and it was so. And God saw every thing that he had made, and, behold, it was very good. And the evening and the morning were the sixth day.

2. Thus the heavens and the earth were finished, and all the host of them. And on the seventh day God ended his work which he had made; and he rested on the seventh day from all his work which he had made. And God blessed the seventh day, and sanctified it: because that in it he had rested from all his work which God created and made.

These are the generations of the heavens and of the earth when they were created,[3] in the day that the Lord God made the earth and the heavens, and every plant of the field before it was in the earth, and every herb of the field before it grew: for the Lord God had not caused it to rain upon the earth, and there was not a man to till the ground. But there went up a mist from the earth, and watered the whole face of the ground. And the Lord God formed

---

3. This is the beginning of a different account of the Creation, which does not agree in all respects with the first.

man of the dust of the ground, and breathed into his nostrils the breath of life; and man became a living soul.

And the Lord God planted a garden eastward in Eden; and there he put the man whom he had formed. And out of the ground made the Lord God to grow every tree that is pleasant to the sight, and good for food; the tree of life also in the midst of the garden, and the tree of knowledge of good and evil. And a river went out of Eden to water the garden; and from thence it was parted, and became into four heads. The name of the first is Pison: that is it which compasseth the whole land of Havilah, where there is gold; and the gold of that land is good: there is bdellium and the onyx stone. And the name of the second river is Gihon: the same is it that compasseth the whole land of Ethiopia. And the name of the third river is Hiddekel: that is it which goeth toward the east of Assyria. And the fourth river is Euphrates. And the Lord God took the man, and put him into the garden of Eden to dress it and to keep it. And the Lord God commanded the man, saying, Of every tree of the garden thou mayest freely eat: but of the tree of the knowledge of good and evil, thou shalt not eat of it: for in the day that thou eatest thereof thou shalt surely die.

And the Lord God said, It is not good that the man should be alone; I will make him an help meet for him. And out of the ground the Lord God formed every beast of the field, and every fowl of the air; and brought them unto Adam to see what he would call them: and whatsoever Adam called every living creature, that was the name thereof. And Adam gave names to all cattle, and to the fowl of the air, and to every beast of the field; but for Adam there was not found an help meet for him. And the Lord God caused a deep sleep to fall upon Adam, and he slept: and he took one of his ribs, and closed up the flesh instead thereof; and the rib, which the Lord God had taken from man, made he a woman, and brought her unto the man. And Adam said, This is now bone of my bones, and flesh of my flesh: she shall be called Woman, because she was taken out of Man. Therefore shall a man leave his father and his mother, and shall cleave unto his wife: and they shall be one flesh. And they were both naked, the man and his wife, and were not ashamed.

3. Now the serpent was more subtil than any beast of the field which the Lord God had made. And he said unto the woman, Yea, hath God said, Ye shall not eat of every tree of the garden? And the woman said unto the serpent, We may eat of the fruit of the trees of the garden: but of the fruit of the tree which is in the midst of the garden, God hath said, Ye shall not eat of it, neither shall ye touch it, lest ye die. And the serpent said unto the woman, Ye shall not surely die: for God doth know that in the day ye eat

thereof, then your eyes shall be opened, and ye shall be as gods, knowing good and evil. And when the woman saw that the tree was good for food, and that it was pleasant to the eyes, and a tree to be desired to make one wise, she took the fruit thereof, and did eat, and gave also unto her husband with her; and he did eat. And the eyes of them both were opened, and they knew that they were naked; and they sewed fig leaves together, and made themselves aprons. And they heard the voice of the Lord God walking in the garden in the cool of the day: and Adam and his wife hid themselves from the presence of the Lord God amongst the trees of the garden. And the Lord God called unto Adam, and said unto him, Where art thou? And he said, I heard thy voice in the garden, and I was afraid, because I was naked; and I hid myself. And he said, Who told thee that thou wast naked? Hast thou eaten of the tree, whereof I commanded thee that thou shouldest not eat? And the man said, The woman whom thou gavest to be with me, she gave me of the tree, and I did eat. And the Lord God said unto the woman, What is this that thou hast done? And the woman said, The serpent beguiled me, and I did eat. And the Lord God said unto the serpent, Because thou hast done this, thou art cursed above all cattle, and above every beast of the field; upon thy belly shalt thou go, and dust shalt thou eat all the days of thy life: and I will put enmity between thee and the woman, and between thy seed and her seed; it shall bruise thy head, and thou shalt bruise his heel. Unto the woman he said, I will greatly multiply thy sorrow and thy conception; in sorrow thou shalt bring forth children; and thy desire shall be to thy husband, and he shall rule over thee. And unto Adam he said, Because thou hast hearkened unto the voice of thy wife, and hast eaten of the tree, of which I commanded thee, saying, Thou shalt not eat of it: cursed is the ground for thy sake; in sorrow shalt thou eat of it all the days of thy life; thorns also and thistles shall it bring forth to thee; and thou shalt eat the herb of the field; in the sweat of thy face shalt thou eat bread, till thou return unto the ground; for out of it wast thou taken: for dust thou art, and unto dust shalt thou return. And Adam called his wife's name Eve; because she was the mother of all living. Unto Adam also and to his wife did the Lord God make coats of skins, and clothed them.

And the Lord God said, Behold, the man is become as one of us, to know good and evil: and now, lest he put forth his hand, and take also of the tree of life, and eat, and live forever: therefore the Lord God sent him forth from the garden of Eden, to till the ground from whence he was taken. So he drove out the man; and he placed at the east of the garden of Eden Cherubims, and a flaming sword which turned every way, to keep the way of the tree of life.

[The First Murder]*

4. And Adam knew Eve his wife; and she conceived, and bare Cain, and said, I have gotten a man from the Lord. And she again bare his brother Abel. And Abel was a keeper of sheep, but Cain was a tiller of the ground. And in process of time it came to pass, that Cain brought of the fruit of the ground an offering unto the Lord. And Abel, he also brought of the firstlings of his flock and of the fat thereof. And the Lord had respect unto Abel and to his offering: But unto Cain and to his offering he had not respect. And Cain was very wroth,[1] and his countenance fell. And the Lord said unto Cain, Why art thou wroth? and why is thy countenance fallen? If thou doest well, shalt thou not be accepted? and if thou doest not well, sin lieth at the door. And unto thee shall be his desire, and thou shall rule over him.[2] And Cain talked with Abel his brother: and it came to pass, when they were in the field, that Cain rose up against Abel his brother, and slew him.

And the Lord said unto Cain, Where is Abel thy brother? And he said, I know not: Am I my brother's keeper? And he said, What hast thou done? the voice of thy brother's blood crieth unto me from the ground. And now art thou cursed from the earth, which hath opened her mouth to receive thy brother's blood from thy hand; When thou tillest the ground, it shall not henceforth yield unto thee her strength; a fugitive and a vagabond shalt thou be in the earth. And Cain said unto the Lord, My punishment is greater than I can bear. Behold, thou hast driven me out this day from the face of the earth; and from thy face shall I be hid; and I shall be a fugitive and a vagabond in the earth; and it shall come to pass, that every one that findeth me shall slay me. And the Lord said unto him, Therefore whosoever slayeth Cain, vengeance shall be taken on him sevenfold. And the Lord set a mark upon Cain, lest any finding him should kill him.

* From Genesis 4:1–15.
1. *wroth:* angry.
2. an obscure sentence. It seems to mean something like: "It (i.e., sin) shall be eager for you, but you must master it."

[The Flood]*

6. . . . And God saw that the wickedness of man was great in the earth, and that every imagination of the thoughts of his heart was only evil continually. And it repented the Lord that he had made man on the earth, and it grieved him at his heart. And the Lord said, I will destroy man whom I have created from the face of the earth; both man, and beast, and the creeeping thing, and the fowls of the air; for it repenteth me that I have made them. But Noah found grace in the eyes of the Lord.

These are the generations of Noah: Noah was a just man and perfect in his generations, and Noah walked with God. And Noah begat three sons, Shem, Ham, and Japheth.

* From Genesis 6:5–9:17.

The earth also was corrupt before God, and the earth was filled with violence. And God looked upon the earth, and, behold, it was corrupt; for all flesh had corrupted his way upon the earth. And God said unto Noah, The end of all flesh is come before me; for the earth is filled with violence through them; and, behold, I will destroy them with the earth. Make thee an ark of gopher[1] wood; rooms shalt thou make in the ark, and shalt pitch it within and without with pitch. And this is the fashion which thou shalt make it of: The length of the ark shall be three hundred cubits,[2] the breadth of it fifty cubits, and the height of it thirty cubits. A window[3] shalt thou make to the ark, and in a cubit shalt thou finish it above; and the door of the ark shalt thou set in the side thereof; with lower, second, and third stories shalt thou make it. And, behold, I, even I, do bring a flood of waters upon the earth, to destroy all flesh, wherein is the breath of life, from under heaven; and every thing that is in the earth shall die. But with thee will I establish my covenant; and thou shalt come into the ark, thou, and thy sons, and thy wife, and thy sons' wives with thee. And of every living thing of all flesh, two of every sort shalt thou bring into the ark, to keep them alive with thee; they shall be male and female. Of fowls after their kind, and of cattle after their kind, of every creeping thing of the earth after his kind, two of every sort shall come unto thee, to keep them alive. And take thou unto thee of all food that is eaten, and thou shalt gather it to thee; and it shall be for food for thee, and for them. Thus did Noah; according to all that God commanded him, so did he.

7. . . . And Noah was six hundred years old when the flood of waters was upon the earth. And Noah went in, and his sons, and his wife, and his sons' wives with him, into the ark, because of the waters of the flood. Of clean beasts, and of beasts that are not clean,[4] and of fowls, and of everything that creepeth upon the earth, There went in two and two unto Noah into the ark, the male and the female, as God had commanded Noah. And it came to pass after seven days, that the waters of the flood were upon the earth. In the six hundredth year of Noah's life, in the second month, the seventeenth day of the month, the same day were all the fountains of the great deep broken up, and the windows of heaven were opened. And the rain was upon the earth forty days and forty nights. In the selfsame day entered Noah, and Shem, and Ham, and Japheth, the sons of Noah, and Noah's wife, and the three wives of his sons with them, into the ark; They, and every beast after his kind, and all the cattle after their kind, and every creeping thing that creepeth upon the earth after his kind, and every fowl

---

1. *gopher:* cypress.
2. *cubit:* a Hebrew measure of length, about one and a half feet.
3. *window:* The text is obscure; it may refer to a skylight in the roof.
4. *not clean:* Certain animals were forbidden food to the Hebrews. For a list of them see Leviticus 11.

after his kind, every bird of every sort. And they went in unto Noah into the ark, two and two of all flesh, wherein is the breath of life. And they that went in, went in male and female of all flesh, as God had commanded him, and the Lord shut him in. And the flood was forty days upon the earth; and the waters increased, and bare up the ark, and it was lift up above the earth. And the waters prevailed, and were increased greatly upon the earth; and the ark went upon the face of the waters. And the waters prevailed exceedingly upon the earth; and all the high hills, that were under the whole heaven, were covered. Fifteen cubits upward did the waters prevail; and the mountains were covered. And all flesh died that moved upon the earth, both of fowl, and of cattle, and of beast, and of every creeping thing that creepeth upon the earth, and every man: All in whose nostrils was the breath of life, of all that was in the dry land, died. And every living substance was destroyed which was upon the face of the ground, both man, and cattle, and the creeping things, and the fowl of the heaven; and they were destroyed from the earth, and Noah only remained alive, and they that were with him in the ark. And the waters prevailed upon the earth an hundred and fifty days.

8. And God remembered Noah, and every living thing, and all the cattle that was with him in the ark: and God made a wind to pass over the earth, and the waters assuaged; The fountains also of the deep and the windows of heaven were stopped, and the rain from heaven was restrained; And the waters returned from off the earth continually: and after the end of the hundred and fifty days the waters were abated. And the ark rested in the seventh month, on the seventeenth day of the month, upon the mountains of Ararat.[5] And the waters decreased continually until the tenth month: in the tenth month, on the first day of the month, were the tops of the mountains seen.

And it came to pass at the end of forty days, that Noah opened the window of the ark which he had made: And he sent forth a raven, which went forth to and fro, until the waters were dried up from off the earth. Also he sent forth a dove from him, to see if the waters were abated from off the face of the ground; But the dove found no rest for the sole of her foot, and she returned unto him into the ark, for the waters were on the face of the whole earth: then he put forth his hand, and took her, and pulled her in unto him into the ark. And he stayed yet another seven days; and again he sent forth the dove out of the ark; And the dove came in to him in the evening; and, lo, in her mouth was an olive leaf plucked off: so Noah knew that the waters were abated from off the earth. And he stayed yet other seven days; and sent forth the dove; which returned not again unto him any more.

5. *Ararat:* a mountain in the eastern part of Asia Minor.

And it came to pass in the six hundredth and first year, in the first month, the first day of the month, the waters were dried up from off the earth: and Noah removed the covering of the ark, and looked, and, behold, the face of the ground was dry. And in the second month, on the seven and twentieth day of the month, was the earth dried.

And God spake unto Noah, saying, Go forth of the ark, thou, and thy wife, and thy sons, and thy sons' wives with thee. Bring forth with thee every living thing that is with thee, of all flesh, both of fowl, and of cattle, and of every creeping thing that creepeth upon the earth; that they may breed abundantly in the earth, and be fruitful, and multiply upon the earth. And Noah went forth, and his sons, and his wife, and his sons' wives with him: Every beast, every creeping thing, and every fowl, and whatsoever creepeth upon the earth, after their kinds, went forth out of the ark. And Noah builded an altar unto the Lord; and took of every clean beast, and of every clean fowl, and offered burnt offerings on the altar. And the Lord smelled a sweet savour; and the Lord said in his heart, I will not again curse the ground any more for man's sake; for the imagination of man's heart is evil from his youth; neither will I again smite any more every thing living, as I have done. While the earth remaineth, seedtime and harvest, and cold and heat, and summer and winter, and day and night shall not cease.

9. And God blessed Noah and his sons, and said unto them, Be fruitful, and multiply, and replenish the earth. And the fear of you and the dread of you shall be upon every beast of the earth, and upon every fowl of the air, upon all that moveth upon the earth, and upon all the fishes of the sea; into your hand are they delivered. Every moving thing that liveth shall be meat for you; even as the green herb have I given you all things. But flesh with the life thereof, which is the blood thereof, shall ye not eat.[6] And surely your blood of your lives will I require; at the hand of every beast will I require it, and at the hand of man; at the hand of every man's brother will I require the life of man. Whoso sheddeth man's blood, by man shall his blood be shed, for in the image of God made he man. And you, be ye fruitful, and multiply; bring forth abundantly in the earth, and multiply therein.

And God spake unto Noah, and to his sons with him, saying, And I, behold, I establish my covenant with you, and with your seed after you; And with every living creature that is with you, of the fowl, of the cattle, and of every beast of the earth with you; from all that go out of the ark, to every beast of the earth. And I will establish my covenant with you; neither shall all flesh be cut off any more by the waters of a flood; neither shall there any more be a

---

6. This sentence refers to the dietary laws: blood was drained from the slaugh- tered animal.

flood to destroy the earth. And God said, This is the token of the
covenant which I make between me and you and every living creature that is with you, for perpetual generations: I do set my bow in
the cloud, and it shall be for a token of a covenant between me and
the earth. And it shall come to pass, when I bring a cloud over the
earth, that the bow shall be seen in the cloud: And I will remember
my covenant, which is between me and you and every living creature of all flesh; and the waters shall no more become a flood to
destroy all flesh. And the bow shall be in the cloud; and I will look
upon it, that I may remember the everlasting covenant between
God and every living creature of all flesh that is upon the earth.
And God said unto Noah, This is the token of the covenant, which
I have established between me and all flesh that is upon the earth.

[The Origin of Languages]*

11. And the whole earth was of one language, and of one speech.
And it came to pass, as they[1] journeyed from the east, that they
found a plain in the land of Shinar;[2] and they dwelt there. And
they said one to another, Go to, let us make brick, and burn them
throughly. And they had brick for stone, and slime[3] had they for
mortar. And they said, Go to, let us build us a city and a tower,[4]
whose top may reach unto heaven; and let us make us a name, lest
we be scattered abroad upon the face of the whole earth. And the
Lord came down to see the city and the tower, which the children
of men builded. And the Lord said, Behold, the people is one, and
they have all one language; and this they begin to do: and now
nothing will be restrained from them, which they have imagined to
do. Go to, let us go down, and there confound their language, that
they may not understand one another's speech. So the Lord scattered them abroad from thence upon the face of all the earth: and
they left off to build the city. Therefore is the name of it called
Babel;[5] because the Lord did there confound the language of all the
earth: and from thence did the Lord scatter them abroad upon the
face of all the earth.

* From Genesis 11:1–9.
1. *they:* the human race.
2. *Shinar:* in Mesopotamia.
3. *slime:* bitumen.
4. *tower:* This story is based on the
Babylonian practice of building temples
in the form of terraced pyramids (zig-
gurats).
5. *Babel:* Babylon.

[The Story of Joseph]*

37. . . . Joseph, being seventeen years old, was feeding the flock
with his brethren; and the lad was with the sons of Bilhah, and
with the sons of Zilpah, his father's wives: and Joseph brought unto
his father[1] their evil report.[2] Now Israel loved Joseph more than
all his children, because he was the son of his old age: and he made
him a coat of many colours. And when his brethren saw that their

* From Genesis 37:2—46:7.

father loved him more than all his brethren, they hated him, and could not speak peaceably unto him.

And Joseph dreamed a dream, and he told it his brethren: and they hated him yet the more. And he said unto them, Hear, I pray you, this dream which I have dreamed: for, behold, we were binding sheaves in the field, and, lo, my sheaf arose, and also stood upright; and, behold, your sheaves stood round about, and made obeisance to[3] my sheaf. And his brethren said to him, Shalt thou indeed reign over us? or shalt thou indeed have dominion over us? And they hated him yet the more for his dreams, and for his words.

And he dreamed yet another dream, and told it his brethren, and said, Behold, I have dreamed a dream more; and, behold, the sun and the moon and the eleven stars made obeisance to me. And he told it to his father, and to his brethren: and his father rebuked him, and said unto him, What is this dream that thou hast dreamed? Shall I and thy mother and thy brethren indeed come to bow down ourselves to thee to the earth? And his brethren envied him; but his father observed the saying.

And his brethren went to feed their father's flock in Shechem. And Israel said unto Joseph, Do not thy brethren feed the flock in Shechem? come, and I will send thee unto them. And he said to him, Here am I. And he said to him, Go, I pray thee, see whether it be well with thy brethren, and well with the flocks; and bring me word again. So he sent him out of the vale of Hebron, and he came to Shechem.

And a certain man found him, and, behold, he was wandering in the field: and the man asked him, saying, What seekest thou? And he said, I seek my brethren: tell me, I pray thee, where they feed their flocks. And the man said, They are departed hence; for I heard them say, Let us go to Dothan. And Joseph went after his brethren, and found them in Dothan. And when they saw him afar off, even before he came near unto them, they conspired against him to slay him. And they said one to another, Behold, this dreamer cometh. Come now therefore, and let us slay him, and cast him into some pit, and we will say, Some evil beast hath devoured him: and we shall see what will become of his dreams. And Reuben heard it, and he delivered him out of their hands; and said, Let us not kill him. And Reuben said unto them, Shed no blood, but cast him into this pit that is in the wilderness, and lay no hand upon him; that he might rid him out of their hands, to deliver him to his father again.

And it came to pass, when Joseph was come unto his brethren, that they stripped Joseph out of his coat, his coat of many colours that was on him; and they took him, and cast him into a pit: and the pit was empty, there was no water in it. And they sat down to

---

1. Israel.
2. Joseph reported their misdeeds.
3. bowed down to.

eat bread: and they lifted up their eyes and looked, and, behold, a company of Ishmeelites came from Gilead with their camels bearing spicery and balm and myrrh, going to carry it down to Egypt. And Judah said unto his brethren, What profit is it if we slay our brother, and conceal his blood? Come, and let us sell him to the Ishmeelites, and let not our hand be upon him; for he is our brother and our flesh. And his brethren were content. Then there passed by Midianites merchantmen;[4] and they[5] drew and lifted up Joseph out of the pit, and sold Joseph to the Ishmeelites for twenty pieces of silver: and they[6] brought Joseph into Egypt.

And Reuben returned unto the pit; and, behold, Joseph was not in the pit; and he rent his clothes. And he returned unto his brethren, and said, The child is not; and I, whither shall I go? And they took Joseph's coat, and killed a kid of the goats, and dipped the coat in the blood; and they sent the coat of many colours, and they brought it to their father; and said, This have we found: know now whether it be thy son's coat or no. And he knew it, and said, It is my son's coat; an evil beast hath devoured him; Joseph is without doubt rent in pieces. And Jacob[7] rent his clothes, and put sackcloth upon his loins, and mourned for his son many days. And all his sons and all his daughters rose up to comfort him; but he refused to be comforted; and he said, For I will go down into the grave unto my son mourning. Thus his father wept for him. . . .

39. And Joseph was brought down to Egypt; and Potiphar, an officer of Pharaoh,[8] captain of the guard, an Egyptian, bought him of the hands of the Ishmeelites, which had brought him down thither. And the Lord was with Joseph, and he was a prosperous man; and he was in the house of his master the Egyptian. And his master saw that the Lord was with him, and that the Lord made all he did to prosper in his hand. And Joseph found grace in his sight, and he served him: and he made him overseer over his house, and all that he had he put into his hand. And it came to pass from the time that he had made him overseer in his house, and over all that he had, that the Lord blessed the Egyptian's house for Joseph's sake; and the blessing of the Lord was upon all that he had in the house, and in the field. And he left all that he had in Joseph's hand; and he knew not ought he had, save the bread which he did eat. And Joseph was a goodly person, and well favoured.[9]

And it came to pass after these things, that his master's wife cast her eyes upon Joseph; and she said, Lie with me. But he refused, and said unto his master's wife, Behold, my master wotteth not

4. The confusion in this passage may be due to the fact that the version we have is a composite of two different versions.

5. the brothers.

6. the Ishmeelites.

7. Israel.

8. the Egyptian king.

9. handsome.

what is with me in the house, and he hath committed all that he hath to my hand; there is none greater in this house than I; neither hath he kept back any thing from me but thee, because thou art his wife: how then can I do this great wickedness, and sin against God? And it came to pass, as she spake to Joseph day by day, that he hearkened not unto her, to lie by her, or to be with her. And it came to pass about this time, that Joseph went into the house to do his business; and there was none of the men of the house there within. And she caught him by his garment, saying, Lie with me: and he left his garment in her hand, and fled and got him out. And it came to pass, when she saw that he had left his garment in her hand, and was fled forth, that she called unto the men of her house, and spoke unto them, saying, See, he hath brought in an Hebrew unto us to mock us; he came in unto me to lie with me, and I cried with a loud voice: and it came to pass, when he heard that I lifted up my voice and cried, that he left his garment with me, and fled, and got him out. And she laid up his garment by her, until his lord came home. And she spake unto him according to these words, saying, The Hebrew servant, which thou hast brought unto us, came in unto me to mock me: and it came to pass, as I lifted up my voice and cried, that he left his garment with me, and fled out. And it came to pass, when his master heard the words of his wife, which she spake unto him, saying, After this manner did thy servant to me; that his wrath was kindled. And Joseph's master took him, and put him into the prison, a place where the king's prisoners were bound: and he was there in the prison.

But the Lord was with Joseph, and showed him mercy, and gave him favour in the sight of the keeper of the prison. And the keeper of the prison committed to Joseph's hand all the prisoners that were in the prison; and whatsoever they did there, he was the doer of it. The keeper of the prison looked not to any thing that was under his[10] hand; because the Lord was with him,[11] and that which he did, the Lord made it to prosper.

40. And it came to pass after these things that the butler of the king of Egypt and his baker had offended their lord the king of Egypt. And Pharaoh was wroth against two of his officers, against the chief of the butlers, and against the chief of the bakers. And he put them in ward in the house of the captain of the guard, into the prison, the place where Joseph was bound. And the captain of the guard charged Joseph with them, and he served them: and they continued a season in ward.

And they dreamed a dream both of them, each man his dream in one night, each man according to the interpretation of his dream, the butler and the baker of the king of Egypt, which were

10. Joseph's.　　　　11. Joseph.

bound in the prison. And Joseph came in unto them in the morning, and looked upon them, and, behold, they were sad. And he asked Pharaoh's officers that were with him in the ward of his lord's house, saying, Wherefore look ye so sadly to day? And they said unto him, We have dreamed a dream, and there is no interpreter of it. And Joseph said unto them, Do not interpretations belong to God? tell me them, I pray you. And the chief butler told his dream to Joseph, and said to him, In my dream, behold, a vine was before me; and in the vine were three branches: and it was as though it budded, and her blossoms shot forth; and the clusters thereof brought forth ripe grapes: and Pharaoh's cup was in my hand: and I took the grapes, and pressed them into Pharaoh's cup, and I gave the cup into Pharaoh's hand. And Joseph said unto him, This is the interpretation of it: the three branches are three days: yet within three days shall Pharaoh lift up thine head, and restore thee unto thy place: and thou shalt deliver Pharaoh's cup into his hand, after the former manner when thou wast his butler. But think on me when it shall be well with thee, and shew kindness, I pray thee, unto me, and make mention of me unto Pharaoh, and bring me out of this house: for indeed I was stolen away out of the land of the Hebrews: and here also have I done nothing that they should put me into the dungeon. When the chief baker saw that the interpretation was good, he said unto Joseph, I also was in my dream, and, behold, I had three white baskets on my head: and in the uppermost basket there was of all manner of bakemeats for Pharaoh; and the birds did eat them out of the basket upon my head. And Joseph answered and said, This is the interpretation thereof: the three baskets are three days: yet within three days shall Pharaoh lift up thy head from off thee, and shall hang thee on a tree; and the birds shall eat thy flesh from off thee.

And it came to pass the third day, which was Pharaoh's birthday, that he made a feast unto all his servants: and he lifted up the head of the chief butler and of the chief baker among his servants. And he restored the chief butler unto his butlership again; and he gave the cup into Pharaoh's hand. But he hanged the chief baker: as Joseph had interpreted to them. Yet did not the chief butler remember Joseph, but forgat him.

41. And it came to pass at the end of two full years, that Pharaoh dreamed: and, behold, he stood by the river. And, behold, there came up out of the river seven well favoured kine[12] and fat-fleshed; and they fed in a meadow. And, behold, seven other kine came up after them out of the river, ill favoured and leanfleshed; and stood by the other kine upon the brink of the river. And the

12. cattle.

ill favoured and leanfleshed kine did eat up the seven well favoured and fat kine. So Pharaoh awoke. And he slept and dreamed the second time: and, behold, seven ears of corn came up upon one stalk, rank[13] and good. And, behold, seven thin ears and blasted with the east wind sprung up after them. And the seven thin ears devoured the seven rank and full ears. And Pharaoh awoke, and, behold, it was a dream. And it came to pass in the morning that his spirit was troubled; and he sent and called for all the magicians of Egypt, and all the wise men thereof: and Pharaoh told them his dream; but there was none that could interpret them unto Pharaoh.

Then spake the chief butler unto Pharaoh, saying, I do remember my faults this day: Pharaoh was wroth with his servants, and put me in ward in the captain of the guard's house, both me and the chief baker: and we dreamed a dream in one night, I and he; we dreamed each man according to the interpretation of his dream. And there was there with us a young man, an Hebrew, servant to the captain of the guard; and we told him, and he interpreted to us our dreams; to each man according to his dream he did interpret. And it came to pass, as he interpreted to us, so it was; me he restored unto mine office, and him he hanged.

Then Pharaoh sent and called Joseph, and they brought him hastily out of the dungeon: and he shaved himself, and changed his raiment, and came in unto Pharaoh. And Pharaoh said unto Joseph, I have dreamed a dream, and there is none that can interpret it: and I have heard say of thee that thou canst understand a dream to interpret it. And Joseph answered Pharaoh, saying, It is not in me: God shall give Pharaoh an answer of peace. And Pharaoh said unto Joseph, In my dream, behold, I stood upon the bank of the river: and, behold, there came up out of the river seven kine, fatfleshed and well favoured; and they fed in a meadow: and, behold, seven other kine came up after them, poor and very ill favoured and leanfleshed, such as I never saw in all the land of Egypt for badness: and the lean and the ill favoured kine did eat up the first seven fat kine; and when they had eaten them up, it could not be known that they had eaten them; but they were still ill favoured, as at the beginning. So I awoke. And I saw in my dream, and, behold, seven ears came up in one stalk, full and good: and, behold, seven ears, withered, thin, and blasted with the east wind, sprung up after them: and the thin ears devoured the seven good ears: and I told this unto the magicians; but there was none that could declare it to me.

And Joseph said unto Pharaoh, The dream of Pharaoh is one: God hath shewed Pharaoh what he is about to do. The seven good kine are seven years; and the seven goods ears are seven years: the

13. fat.

dream is one. And the seven thin and ill favoured kine that came up after them are seven years; and the seven empty ears blasted with the east wind shall be seven years of famine. This is the thing which I have spoken unto Pharaoh: what God is about to do he sheweth unto Pharaoh. Behold, there come seven years of great plenty throughout all the land of Egypt: and there shall arise after them seven years of famine; and all the plenty shall be forgotten in the land of Egypt; and the famine shall consume the land; and the plenty shall not be known in the land by reason of that famine following; for it shall be very grievous. And for that the dream was doubled unto Pharaoh twice; it is because the thing is established by God, and God will shortly bring it to pass. Now therefore let Pharaoh look out a man discreet and wise, and set him over the land of Egypt. Let Pharaoh do this, and let him appoint officers over the land, and take up the fifth part of the land[14] of Egypt in the seven plenteous years. And let them gather all the food of those good years that come, and lay up corn under the hand of Pharaoh, and let them keep food in the cities. And that food shall be for store to the land against the seven years of famine, which shall be in the land of Egypt; that the land perish not through the famine.

And the thing was good in the eyes of Pharaoh, and in the eyes of all his servants. And Pharaoh said unto his servants, Can we find such a one as this is, a man in whom the Spirit of God is? And Pharaoh said unto Joseph, Forasmuch as God hath shewed thee all this, there is none so discreet and wise as thou art: thou shalt be over my house, and according unto thy word shall all my people be ruled: only in the throne will I be greater than thou. And Pharaoh said unto Joseph, See, I have set thee over all the land of Egypt. And Pharaoh took off his ring from his hand, and put it upon Joseph's hand, and arrayed him in vestures of fine linen, and put a gold chain about his neck; and he made him to ride in the second chariot which he had; and they cried before him, Bow the knee: and he made him ruler over all the land of Egypt. And Pharaoh said unto Joseph, I am Pharaoh, and without thee shall no man lift his hand or foot in all the land of Egypt. And Pharaoh called Joseph's name Zaphnath-paaneah; and he gave him to wife Asenath the daughter of Poti-pherah priest of On. And Joseph went out over all the land of Egypt.

And Joseph was thirty years old when he stood before Pharaoh king of Egypt. And Joseph went out from the presence of Pharaoh, and went throughout all the land of Egypt. And in the seven plenteous years the earth brought forth by handfuls. And he gathered up all the food of the seven years, which were in the land of Egypt, and laid up the food in the cities: the food of the field,

14. i.e., of the crop.

which was round about every city, laid he up in the same. And Joseph gathered corn as the sand of the sea, very much, until he left numbering; for it was without number. And unto Joseph were born two sons before the years of famine came, which Asenath the daughter of Poti-pherah priest of On bare unto him. And Joseph called the name of the first born Manasseh:[15] For God, said he, hath made me forget all my toil, and all my father's house. And the name of the second called he Ephraim:[16] For God hath caused me to be fruitful in the land of my affliction.

And the seven years of plenteousness, that was in the land of Egypt, were ended. And the seven years of dearth[17] began to come, according as Joseph had said: and the dearth was in all lands; but in all the land of Egypt there was bread. And when all the land of Egypt was famished, the people cried to Pharaoh for bread: and Pharaoh said unto all the Egyptians, Go unto Joseph; what he saith to you, do. And the famine was over all the face of the earth. And Joseph opened all the storehouses, and sold unto the Egyptians; and the famine waxed sore in the land of Egypt. And all countries came into Egypt to Joseph for to buy corn; because that the famine was so sore in all lands.

42. Now when Jacob saw that there was corn in Egypt, Jacob said unto his sons, Why do ye look one upon another? And he said, Behold, I have heard that there is corn in Egypt: get you down thither, and buy for us from thence; that we may live, and not die.

And Joseph's ten brethren went down to buy corn in Egypt. But Benjamin,[18] Joseph's brother, Jacob sent not with his brethren; for he said, Lest peradventure mischief befall him. And the sons of Israel came to buy corn among those that came: for the famine was in the land of Canaan. And Joseph was the governor over the land, and he it was that sold to all the people of the land: and Joseph's brethren came, and bowed down themselves before him with their faces to the earth. And Joseph saw his brethren, and he knew them, but made himself strange unto them, and spake roughly unto them; and he said unto them, Whence come ye? And they said, From the land of Canaan to buy food. And Joseph knew his brethren, but they knew not him. And Joseph remembered the dreams which he dreamed of them, and said unto them, Ye are spies; to see the nakedness of the land ye are come. And they said unto him, Nay, my lord, but to buy food are thy servants come. We are all one man's sons; we are true men, thy servants are no spies. And he said unto them, Nay, but to see the nakedness of the land ye are come. And

15. meaning "causing to forget."
16. meaning "fruitfulness."
17. scarcity.

18. more closely related than the other ten since he is the son of the same mother.

they said, Thy servants are twelve brethren, the sons of one man in the land of Canaan; and, behold, the youngest is this day with our father, and one is not. And Joseph said unto them, That is it that I spake unto you, saying, Ye are spies: Hereby ye shall be proved: By the life of Pharaoh ye shall not go forth hence, except your youngest brother come hither. Send one of you, and let him fetch your brother, and ye shall be kept in prison, that your words may be proved, whether there be any truth in you: or else by the life of Pharaoh surely ye are spies. And he put them all together into ward three days. And Joseph said unto them the third day, This do, and live; for I fear God: if ye be true men, let one of your brethren be bound in the house of your prison: go ye, carry corn for the famine of your houses: but bring your youngest brother unto me; so shall your words be verified, and ye shall not die. And they did so.

And they said one to another, We are verily guilty concerning our brother, in that we saw the anguish of his soul, when he besought us, and we would not hear; therefore is this distress come upon us. And Reuben answered them, saying, Spake I not unto you, saying, Do not sin against the child; and ye would not hear? therefore, behold, also his blood is required. And they knew not that Joseph understood them; for he spake unto them by an interpreter. And he turned himself about from them, and wept; and returned to them again, and communed with them, and took from them Simeon, and bound him before their eyes.

Then Joseph commanded to fill their sacks with corn, and to restore every man's money into his sack, and to give them provision for the way: and thus did he unto them. And they laded their asses with the corn, and departed thence. And as one of them opened his sack to give his ass provender in the inn, he espied his money; for, behold, it was in his sack's mouth. And he said unto his brethren, My money is restored; and, lo, it is even in my sack: and their heart failed them, and they were afraid, saying one to another, What is this that God hath done unto us?

And they came unto Jacob their father unto the land of Canaan, and told him all that befell unto them; saying, The man, who is lord of the land, spake roughly to us, and took us for spies of the country. And we said unto him, We are true men; we are no spies: we be twelve brethren, sons of our father; one is not, and the youngest is this day with our father in the land of Canaan. And the man, the lord of the country, said unto us, Hereby shall I know that ye are true men; leave one of your brethren here with me, and take food for the famine of your households, and be gone: and bring your youngest brother unto me: then shall I know that ye are no spies, but that ye are true men: so will I deliver you your brother, and ye shall traffick in the land.

And it came to pass as they emptied their sacks, that, behold, every man's bundle of money was in his sack: and when both they and their father saw the bundles of money, they were afraid. And Jacob their father said unto them, Me have ye bereaved of my children: Joseph is not, and Simeon is not; and ye will take Benjamin away: all these things are against me.

And Reuben spake unto his father, saying, Slay my two sons, if I bring him not to thee: deliver him into my hand, and I will bring him to thee again. And he said, My son shall not go down with you; for his brother is dead, and he is left alone: if mischief befall him by the way in the which ye go, then shall ye bring down my gray hairs with sorrow to the grave.

43. And the famine was sore in the land. And it came to pass, when they had eaten up the corn which they had brought out of Egypt,their father said unto them, Go again, buy us a little food. And Judah spake unto him, saying, The man did solemnly protest unto us, saying, Ye shall not see my face, except your brother be with you. If thou wilt send our brother with us, we will go down and buy thee food: but if thou wilt not send him, we will not go down: for the man said unto us, Ye shall not see my face, except your brother be with you. And Israel said, Wherefore dealt ye so ill with me, as to tell the man whether ye had yet a brother? And they said, The man asked us straitly[19] of our state, and of our kindred, saying, Is your father yet alive? have ye another brother? and we told him according to the tenor of these words: could we certainly know that he would say, Bring your brother down? And Judah said unto Israel his father, Send the lad with me, and we will arise and go; that we may live, and not die, both we, and thou, and also our little ones. I will be surety for him; of my hand shalt thou require him: if I bring him not unto thee, and set him before thee, then let me bear the blame for ever: for except we had lingered, surely now we had returned this second time. And their father Israel said unto them, If it must be so now, do this; take of the best fruits in the land in your vessels, and carry down the man a present, a little balm, and a little honey, spices, and myrrh, nuts, and almonds: and take double money in your hand; and the money that was brought again in the mouth of your sacks, carry it again in your hand; peradventure it was an oversight: take also your brother, and arise, go again unto the man: and God Almighty give you mercy before the man, that he may send away your other brother, and Benjamin.

19. strictly, precisely.

If I be bereaved of my children, I am bereaved.

And the men took that present, and they took double money in their hand, and Benjamin; and rose up, and went down to Egypt, and stood before Joseph. And when Joseph saw Benjamin with them, he said to the ruler of his house, Bring these men home, and slay,[20] and make ready; for these men shall dine with me at noon. And the man did as Joseph bade; and the man brought the men into Joseph's house. And the men were afraid, because they were brought into Joseph's house; and they said, Because of the money that was returned in our sacks at the first time are we brought in; that he may seek occasion against us, and fall upon us, and take us for bondmen,[21] and our asses. And they came near to the steward of Joseph's house, and they communed with him at the door of the house, and said, O sir, we came indeed down at the first time to buy food; and it came to pass, when we came to the inn, that we opened our sacks, and, behold, every man's money was in the mouth of his sack, our money in full weight: and we have brought it again in our hand. And other money have we brought down in our hands to buy food: we cannot tell who put our money in our sacks. And he said, Peace be to you, fear not: your God, and the God of your father, hath given you treasure in your sacks: I had your money. And he brought Simeon out unto them. And the man brought the men into Joseph's house, and gave them water, and they washed their feet; and he gave their asses provender. And they made ready the present against Joseph came at noon: for they heard that they should eat bread there.

And when Joseph came home, they brought him the present which was in their hand into the house, and bowed themselves to him to the earth. And he asked them of their welfare, and said, Is your father well, the old man of whom ye spoke? Is he yet alive? And they answered, Thy servant our father is in good health, he is yet alive. And they bowed down their heads, and made obeisance. And he lifted up his eyes, and saw his brother Benjamin, his mother's son, and said, Is this your younger brother, of whom ye spoke unto me? And he said, God be gracious unto thee, my son. And Joseph made haste; for his bowels did yearn upon his brother: and he sought where to weep; and he entered into his chamber, and wept there. And he washed his face, and went out, and refrained himself and said, Set on bread. And they set on for him by himself, and for them by themselves, and for the Egyptians, which did eat with him, by themselves: because the Egyptians might not eat bread with the Hebrews; for that is an abomination unto the Egyptians. And they sat before him, the firstborn according to his

20. kill an animal for meat. 21. slaves.

birthright, and the youngest according to his youth: and the men marvelled one at another. And he took and sent messes[22] unto them from before him: but Benjamin's mess was five times so much as any of theirs. And they drank, and were merry with him.

44. And he commanded the steward of his house, saying, Fill the men's sacks with food, as much as they can carry, and put every man's money in his sack's mouth. And put my cup, the silver cup, in the sack's mouth of the youngest, and his corn money. And he did according to the word that Joseph had spoken. As soon as the morning was light, the men were sent away, they and their asses. And when they were gone out of the city, and not yet far off, Joseph said unto his steward, Up, follow after the men; and when thou dost overtake them, say unto them, Wherefore have ye rewarded evil for good? Is not this it in which my lord drinketh, and whereby indeed he divineth?[23] ye have done evil in so doing.

And he overtook them, and he spake unto them these same words. And they said unto him, Wherefore saith my lord these words? God forbid that thy servants should do according to this thing: behold, the money, which we found in our sacks' mouths, we brought again unto thee out of the land of Canaan: how then should we steal out of thy lord's house silver or gold? With whomsoever of thy servants it be found, both let him die, and we also will be my lord's bondmen. And he said, Now also let it be according unto your words: he with whom it is found shall be my servant; and ye shall be blameless. Then they speedily took down every man his sack to the ground, and opened every man his sack. And he searched, and began at the eldest, and left at the youngest: and the cup was found in Benjamin's sack. Then they rent their clothes, and laded every man his ass, and returned to the city.

And Judah and his brethren came to Joseph's house; for he was yet there: and they fell before him on the ground. And Joseph said unto them, What deed is this that ye have done? wot ye not that such a man as I can certainly divine? And Judah said, What shall we say unto my lord? what shall we speak? or how shall we clear ourselves? God hath found out the iniquity of thy servants: behold, we are my lord's servants, both we, and he also with whom the cup is found. And he said, God forbid that I should do so: but the man in whose hand the cup is found, he shall be my servant; and as for you, get you up in peace unto your father.

Then Judah came near unto him, and said, Oh my lord, let thy servant, I pray thee, speak a word in my lord's ears, and let not thine anger burn against thy servant: for thou art even as Pharaoh.

22. portions.
23. Joseph's servant is to claim that this is the cup Joseph uses for clairvoy-ance; the diviner stared into a cup of water and foretold the future.

My lord asked his servants, saying, Have ye a father, or a brother? And we said unto my lord, We have a father, an old man, and a child of his old age, a little one; and his brother is dead, and he alone is left of his mother, and his father loveth him. And thou saidst unto thy servants, Bring him down unto me, that I may set mine eyes upon him. And we said unto my lord, The lad cannot leave his father: for if he should leave his father, his father would die. And thou saidst unto thy servants, Except your youngest brother come down with you, ye shall see my face no more. And it came to pass when we came up unto thy servant my father, we told him the words of my lord. And our father said, Go again, and buy us a little food. And we said, We cannot go down: if our youngest brother be with us, then will we go down: for we may not see the man's face, except our youngest brother be with us. And thy servant my father said unto us, Ye know that my wife bare me two sons; and the one went out from me, and I said, Surely he is torn in pieces; and I saw him not since: and if ye take this also from me, and mischief befall him, ye shall bring down my gray hairs with sorrow to the grave. Now therefore when I come to thy servant my father, and the lad be not with us; seeing that his life is bound up in the lad's life; it shall come to pass, when he seeth that the lad is not with us, that he will die: and thy servants[24] shall bring down the gray hairs of thy servant our father with sorrow to the grave. For thy servant[25] became surety for the lad unto my father, saying, If I bring him not unto thee, then I shall bear the blame to my father for ever. Now therefore, I pray thee, let thy servant[26] abide instead of the lad a bondman to my lord; and let the lad go up with his brethren. For how shall I go up to my father, and the lad be not with me? lest peradventure I see the evil that shall come on my father.

45. Then Joseph could not refrain himself before all them that stood by him; and he cried, Cause every man to go out from me. And there stood no man with him, while Joseph made himself known unto his brethren. And he wept aloud: and the Egyptians and the house of Pharaoh heard. And Joseph said unto his brethren, I am Joseph; doth my father yet live? And his brethren could not answer him; for they were troubled at his presence. And Joseph said unto his brethren, Come near to me, I pray you. And they came near. And he said, I am Joseph your brother, whom ye sold into Egypt. Now therefore be not grieved, nor angry with yourselves, that ye sold me hither: for God did send me before you to preserve life. For these two years hath the famine been in the land: and yet

24. we.   26. me.
25. I.

there are five years, in the which there shall neither be earing nor harvest. And God sent me before you to preserve you a posterity in the earth, and to save your lives by a great deliverance. So now it was not you that sent me hither, but God: and he hath made me a father to Pharaoh, and lord of all his house, and a ruler throughout all the land of Egypt. Haste ye, and go up to my father, and say unto him, Thus saith thy son Joseph, God hath made me lord of all Egypt: come down unto me, tarry not: and thou shalt dwell in the land of Goshen, and thou shalt be near unto me, thou, and thy children, and thy children's children, and thy flocks, and thy herds, and all thou hast: and there will I nourish thee; for yet there are five years of famine; lest thou, and thy household, and all that thou hast, come to poverty. And, behold, your eyes see, and the eyes of my brother Benjamin, that it is my mouth that speaketh unto you. And ye shall tell my father of all my glory in Egypt, and of all that ye have seen; and ye shall haste and bring down my father hither. And he fell upon his brother Benjamin's neck, and wept; and Benjamin wept upon his neck. Moreover he kissed all his brethren, and wept upon them: and after that his brethren talked with him.

And the fame thereof was heard in Pharaoh's house, saying, Joseph's brethren are come: and it pleased Pharaoh well, and his servants. And Pharaoh said unto Joseph, Say unto thy brethren, This do ye; lade[27] your beasts, and go, get you unto the land of Canaan; and take your father and your households, and come unto me: and I will give you the good of the land of Egypt, and ye shall eat the fat of the land. Now thou art commanded, this do ye; take you wagons out of the land of Egypt for your little ones, and for your wives, and bring your father, and come. Also regard not your stuff; for the good of all the land of Egypt is yours. And the children of Israel did so: and Joseph gave them wagons, according to the commandment of Pharaoh, and gave them provision for the way. To all of them he gave each man changes of raiment; but to Benjamin he gave three hundred pieces of silver, and five changes of raiment. And to his father he sent after this manner; ten asses laden with the good things of Egypt, and ten she-asses laden with corn and bread and meat for his father by the way. So he sent his brethren away, and they departed: and he said unto them, See that ye fall not out by the way.

And they went up out of Egypt, and came into the land of Canaan unto Jacob their father, and told him, saying, Joseph is yet alive, and he is governor over all the land of Egypt. And Jacob's heart fainted, for he believed them not. And they told him all the words of Joseph, which he had said unto them: and when he saw the wagons which Joseph had sent to carry him, the spirit of Jacob

27. load.

their father revived. And Israel said, It is enough; Joseph my son is yet alive: I will go and see him before I die.

46. And Israel took his journey with all that he had, and came to Beer-sheba, and offered sacrifices unto the God of his father Isaac. And God spake unto Israel in the visions of the night, and said, Jacob, Jacob. And he said, Here am I. And he said, I am God, the God of thy father: fear not to go down into Egypt; for I will there make of thee a great nation: I will go down with thee into Egypt; and I will also surely bring thee up again: and Joseph shall put his hand upon thine eyes. And Jacob rose up from Beer-sheba: and the sons of Israel carried Jacob their father, and their little ones, and their wives, in the wagons which Pharaoh had sent to carry him. And they took their cattle, and their goods, which they had gotten in the land of Canaan, and came into Egypt, Jacob, and all his seed with him: his sons, and his sons' sons with him, his daughters, and his sons' daughters, and all his seed brought he with him into Egypt.

The Book of Job*

1. There was a man in the land of Uz whose name was Job; and that man was perfect and upright, and one that feared God, and eschewed[1] evil. And there were born unto him seven sons and three daughters. His substance also was seven thousand sheep, and three thousand camels, and five hundred yoke of oxen, and five hundred she asses, and a very great household; so that this man was the greatest of all the men of the east. And his sons went and feasted in their houses, every one his day;[2] and sent and called for their three sisters to eat and to drink with them. And it was so, when the days of their feasting were gone about, that Job sent and sanctified them,[3] and rose up early in the morning, and offered burnt offerings according to the number of them all: for Job said, It may be that my sons have sinned, and cursed God in their hearts. Thus did Job continually.

Now there was a day when the sons of God came to present themselves before the Lord, and Satan[4] came also among them. And the Lord said unto Satan, Whence comest thou? Then Satan answered the Lord, and said, From going to and fro in the earth, and from walking up and down in it. And the Lord said unto Satan, Hast thou considered my servant Job, that there is none like him in the earth, a perfect and an upright man, one that feareth God, and echeweth evil? Then Satan answered the Lord, and said, Doth Job fear God for nought? Hast not thou made an hedge about him,

---

* Chapters 1–14, 29–31, 38–42.
1. avoided.
2. in rotation at each son's house.
3. by ritual purification.
4. His name means "the accuser," "the opposer."

and about his house, and about all that he hath on every side? thou hast blessed the work of his hands, and his substance is increased in the land. But put forth thine hand now, and touch all that he hath, and he will curse thee to thy face. And the Lord said unto Satan, Behold, all that he hath is in thy power; only upon himself put not forth thine hand. So Satan went forth from the presence of the Lord.

And there was a day when his sons and his daughters were eating and drinking wine in their eldest brother's house: and there came a messenger unto Job, and said, The oxen were plowing, and the asses feeding beside them: and the Sabeans fell upon them, and took them away; yea, they have slain the servants with the edge of the sword; and I only am escaped alone to tell thee. While he was yet speaking, there came also another, and said, The fire of God is fallen from heaven, and hath burned up the sheep, and the servants, and consumed them; and I only am escaped alone to tell thee. While he was yet speaking, there came also another, and said, The Chaldeans made out three bands,[5] and fell upon the camels, and have carried them away, yea, and slain the servants with the edge of the sword; and I only am escaped alone to tell thee. While he was yet speaking, there came also another, and said, Thy sons and thy daughters were eating and drinking wine in their eldest brother's house: and, behold, there came a great wind from the wilderness, and smote the four corners of the house, and it fell upon the young men, and they are dead; and I only am escaped alone to tell thee.

Then Job arose and rent[6] his mantle,[7] and shaved his head, and fell down upon the ground, and worshipped, and said, Naked came I out of my mother's womb, and naked shall I return thither: the Lord gave, and the Lord hath taken away; blessed be the name of the Lord. In all this Job sinned not, nor charged God foolishly.

2. Again there was a day when the sons of God came to present themselves before the Lord, and Satan came also among them to present himself before the Lord. And the Lord said unto Satan, From whence comest thou? And Satan answered the Lord, and said, From going to and fro in the earth, and from walking up and down in it. And the Lord said unto Satan, Hast thou considered my servant Job, that there is none like him in the earth, a perfect and an upright man, one that feareth God, and escheweth evil? and still he holdeth fast his integrity, although thou movedst me against him, to destroy him without cause. And Satan answered the Lord, and said, Skin for skin, yea, all that a man hath will he give for his life. But put forth thine hand now, and touch his bone

5. split up into three groups. 7. cloak.
6. tore.

and his flesh, and he will curse thee to thy face. And the Lord said unto Satan, Behold, he is in thine hand; but save his life.

So went Satan forth from the presence of the Lord, and smote Job with sore boils from the sole of his foot unto his crown. And he took him a potsherd to scrape himself withal;[8] and he sat down among the ashes.

Then said his wife unto him, Dost thou still retain thine integrity? curse God, and die. But he said unto her, Thou speakest as one of the foolish women speaketh. What? shall we receive good at the hand of God, and shall we not receive evil? In all this did not Job sin with his lips.

Now when Job's three friends heard of all this evil that was come upon him, they came every one from his own place; Eliphaz the Temanite, and Bildad the Shuhite, and Zophar the Naamathite: for they had made an appointment together to come to mourn with him and to comfort him. And when they lifted up their eyes afar off, and knew him not, they lifted up their voice, and wept; and they rent every one his mantle, and sprinkled dust upon their heads toward heaven. So they sat down with him upon the ground seven days and seven nights, and none spake a word unto him: for they saw that his grief was very great.

3. After this opened Job his mouth, and cursed his day. And Job spake, and said, Let the day perish wherein I was born, and the night in which it was said, There is a man child conceived. Let that day be darkness; let not God regard it from above, neither let the light shine upon it. Let darkness and the shadow of death stain it; let a cloud dwell upon it; let the blackness of the day terrify it. As for that night, let darkness seize upon it; let it not be joined unto the days of the year, let it not come into the number of the months. Lo, let that night be solitary, let no joyful voice come therein. Let them curse it that curse the day,[9] who are ready to raise up their mourning. Let the stars of the twilight thereof be dark; let it look for light, but have none; neither let it see the dawning of the day: because it shut not up the doors of my mother's womb, nor hid sorrow from mine eyes. Why died I not from the womb? Why did I not give up the ghost when I came out of the belly? Why did the knees prevent[10] me? or why the breasts that I should suck? For now should I have lain still and been quiet, I should have slept: then had I been at rest, with kings and counsellors of the earth, which built desolate places for themselves; or with princes that had gold, who filled their houses with silver: or as an hidden untimely birth

8. with.

9. sorcerers, magicians. A more literal translation of the next clause would read, "who are ready to rouse up levia-than." Leviathan was a dragon that was thought to produce darkness.

10. receive.

I had not been; as infants which never saw light. There the wicked cease from troubling; and there the weary be at rest. There the prisoners rest together; they hear not the voice of the oppressor. The small and great are there; and the servant is free from his master. Wherefore is light given to him that is in misery, and life unto the bitter in soul; which long for death, but it cometh not; and dig for it more than for hid treasures; which rejoice exceedingly, and are glad, when they can find the grave? Why is light given to a man whose way is hid, and whom God hath hedged in? For my sighing cometh before I eat, and my roarings are poured out like the waters. For the thing which I greatly feared is come upon me, and that which I was afraid of is come unto me. I was not in safety, neither had I rest, neither was I quiet;[11] yet trouble came.

4. Then Eliphaz the Temanite answered and said, If we assay to commune with thee, wilt thou be grieved? But who can withhold himself from speaking? Behold, thou hast instructed many, and thou hast strengthened the weak hands. Thy words have upholden him that was falling, and thou hast strengthened the feeble knees. But now it is come upon thee, and thou faintest; it toucheth thee, and thou art troubled. Is not this thy fear, thy confidence, thy hope, and the uprightness of thy ways?[12] Remember, I pray thee, who ever perished, being innocent? or where were the righteous cut off? Even as I have seen, they that plow iniquity, and sow wickedness, reap the same. By the blast of God they perish, and by the breath of his nostrils are they consumed. The roaring of the lion, and the voice of the fierce lion, and the teeth of the young lions, are broken. The old lion perisheth for lack of prey, and the stout lion's whelps are scattered abroad. Now a thing was secretly brought to me, and mine ear received a little[13] thereof. In thoughts from the visions of the night, when deep sleep falleth on men, fear came upon me, and trembling, which made all my bones to shake. Then a spirit passed before my face; the hair of my flesh stood up: It stood still, but I could not discern the form thereof: an image was before mine eyes, there was silence, and I heard a voice, saying, Shall mortal man be more just than God? Shall a man be more pure than his maker? Behold, he put no trust in his servants; and his angels he charged with folly: How much less[14] in them that dwell in houses of clay, whose foundation is in the dust, which are crushed before the moth? They are destroyed from morning to evening: they perish for ever without any regarding it. Doth not their excellency which is in them go away? They die, even without wisdom.

---

11. For *was, had,* and *was,* read, "am," "have," and "am."

12. A more literal translation of this sentence would read, "Is not thy fear of God thy confidence, and thy hope the uprightness of thy ways?"

13. a whisper.

14. how much less does he trust.

5. Call now, if there be any that will answer thee; and to which of the saints wilt thou turn? For wrath killeth the foolish man, and envy slayeth the silly one. I have seen the foolish taking root: but suddenly I cursed his habitation. His children are far from safety, and they are crushed in the gate, neither is there any to deliver them. Whose harvest the hungry eateth up, and taketh it even out of the thorns,[15] and the robber swalloweth up their substance. Although affliction cometh not forth of the dust, neither doth trouble spring out of the ground; yet man is born unto trouble, as the sparks fly upward. I would seek unto God, and unto God would I commit my cause: which doeth great things and unsearchable; marvellous things without number: who giveth rain upon the earth, and sendeth waters upon the fields: to set up on high those that be low; that those which mourn may be exalted to safety. He disappointeth the devices of the crafty, so that their hands cannot perform their enterprise. He taketh the wise in their own craftiness: and the counsel of the froward is carried headlong. They meet with darkness in the daytime, and grope in the noonday as in the night. But he saveth the poor from the sword, from their mouth, and from the hand of the mighty. So the poor hath hope, and iniquity stoppeth her mouth. Behold, happy is the man whom God correcteth: therefore despise not thou the chastening of the Almighty: for he maketh sore, and bindeth up: he woundeth, and his hands make whole. He shall deliver thee in six troubles: yea, in seven there shall no evil touch thee. In famine he shall redeem thee from death: and in war from the power of the sword. Thou shalt be hid from the scourge of the tongue: neither shalt thou be afraid of destruction when it cometh. At destruction and famine thou shalt laugh: neither shalt thou be afraid of the beasts of the earth. For thou shalt be in league with the stones of the field: and the beasts of the field shall be at peace with thee. And thou shalt know that thy tabernacle[16] shall be in peace; and thou shalt visit thy habitation, and shalt not sin. Thou shalt know also that thy seed shall be great, and thine offspring as the grass of the earth. Thou shalt come to thy grave in a full age, like as a shock of corn cometh in in his season. Lo this, we have searched it, so it is; hear it, and know thou it for thy good.

6. But Job answered and said, Oh that my grief were thoroughly weighed, and my calamity laid in the balances together! For now it would be heavier than the sand of the sea: therefore my words are swallowed up.[17] For the arrows of the Almighty are within me, the poison whereof drinketh up my spirit: the terrors of God do set

15. perhaps a hedge of thorn.
16. tent.
17. A more literal translation of this clause would read, "therefore have my words been rash." Job recognizes the exaggeration of his first outburst.

themselves in array against me. Doth the wild ass bray when he hath grass? or loweth the ox over his fodder?[18] Can that which is unsavoury be eaten without salt? or is there any taste in the white of an egg? The things that my soul refused to touch are as my sorrowful meat.[19] Oh that I might have my request; and that God would grant me the thing that I long for! Even that it would please God to destroy me; that he would let loose his hand, and cut me off! Then should I yet have comfort; yea, I would harden myself in sorrow: let him not spare; for I have not concealed[20] the words of the Holy One. What is my strength, that I should hope? and what is mine end, that I should prolong my life? Is my strength the strength of stones? or is my flesh of brass? Is not my help in me? and is wisdom driven quite from me?[21] To him that is afflicted pity should be shewed from his friend; but he forsaketh the fear of the Almighty. My brethren have dealt deceitfully as a brook, and as the stream of brooks they pass away; which are blackish by reason of the ice, and wherein the snow is hid: what time they wax warm, they vanish: when it is hot, they are consumed out of their place. The paths of their way are turned aside; they go to nothing, and perish. The troops of Tema looked, the companies of Sheba waited for them. They were confounded because they had hoped;[22] they came thither, and were ashamed. For now ye are nothing; ye see my casting down, and are afraid. Did I say, Bring unto me? or, Give a reward for me of your substance? or, Deliver me from the enemy's hand? or, Redeem me from the hand of the mighty? Teach me, and I will hold my tongue: and cause me to understand wherein I have erred. How forcible are right words! But what doth your arguing reprove? Do ye imagine to reprove words, and the speeches of one that is desperate, which are as wind? Yea, ye overwhelm the fatherless, and ye dig a pit for your friend. Now therefore be content, look upon me; for it is evident unto you if I lie. Return, I pray you, let it not be iniquity;[23] yea, return again, my righteousness is in it.[24] Is there iniquity in my tongue? Cannot my taste discern perverse things?

7. Is there not an appointed time to man upon earth? Are not his days also like the days of an hireling? As a servant earnestly desireth the shadow,[25] and as an hireling looketh for the reward of

18. Animals do not complain without reason; therefore when a rational man complains, he must have some justification for it.

19. more literally, "My soul refuseth to touch them, they are as loathsome meat to me." He is referring to the statements of his friends.

20. more literally, "denied."

21. more literally, "Is not my help within me gone, and is not wisdom driven quite away from me?"

22. The caravans reached the springs they had counted on and found them dry.

23. let there be no injustice.

24. my cause is righteous.

25. evening, the end of the working day.

his work: so am I made to possess months of vanity, and wearisome nights are appointed to me. When I lie down, I say, When shall I arise, and the night be gone? and I am full of tossings to and fro unto the dawning of the day. My flesh is clothed with worms and clods of dust; my skin is broken, and become loathsome. My days are swifter than a weaver's shuttle, and are spent without hope. O remember that my life is wind: mine eye shall no more see good. The eye of him that hath seen me shall see me no more: thine eyes are upon me, and I am not. As the cloud is consumed and vanisheth away: so he that goeth down to the grave shall come up no more. He shall return no more to his house, neither shall his place know him any more. Therefore I will not refrain my mouth; I will speak in the anguish of my spirit; I will complain in the bitterness of my soul. Am I a sea, or a whale, that thou settest a watch over me?[26] When I say, My bed shall comfort me, my couch shall ease my complaint; then thou scarest me with dreams, and terrifiest me through visions: so that my soul chooseth strangling, and death rather than my life. I loathe it; I would not live alway: let me alone; for my days are vanity. What is man, that thou shouldest magnify him? and that thou shouldest set thine heart upon him? and that thou shouldest visit him every morning, and try him every moment? How long wilt thou not depart from me, nor let me alone till I swallow down my spittle?[27] I have sinned; what shall I do unto thee, O thou preserver[28] of men? Why hast thou set me as a mark[29] against thee, so that I am a burden to myself? And why dost thou not pardon my transgression, and take away mine iniquity? For now shall I sleep in the dust; and thou shalt seek me in the morning, but I shall not be.

8. Then answered Bildad the Shuhite, and said, How long wilt thou speak these things? and how long shall the words of thy mouth be like a strong wind? Doth God pervert judgment? or doth the Almighty pervert justice? If thy children have sinned against him, and he have cast them away for their transgression; if thou wouldest seek unto God betimes,[30] and make thy supplication to the Almighty; if thou wert pure and upright; surely now he would awake for thee, and make the habitation of thy righteousness prosperous. Though thy beginning was small, yet thy latter end should greatly increase. For enquire, I pray thee, of the former age, and prepare thy self to the search of their fathers: (For we are but of yesterday, and know nothing, because our days upon earth are a shadow:)

---

26. Job, now addressing God directly, compares his situation with that of the sea monster whom a god fought against in the Babylonian myth. He reproves God for exerting His power against anything as small as himself.

27. even for a moment.
28. A more literal translation would read, "watcher."
29. target.
30. early.

shall not they teach thee, and tell thee, and utter words out of their heart? Can the rush[31] grow up without mire? Can the flag grow without water? Whilst it is yet in his greenness, and not cut down, it withereth before any other herb. So are the paths of all that forget God; and the hypocrite's hope shall perish: whose hope shall be cut off, and whose trust shall be a spider's web. He shall lean upon his house, but it shall not stand: he shall hold it fast, but it shall not endure. He is green before the sun, and his branch shooteth forth in his garden. His roots are wrapped about the heap, and seeth the place of stones. If he destroy him from his place, then it shall deny him, saying, I have not seen thee. Behold, this is the joy of his way, and out of the earth shall others grow. Behold, God will not cast away a perfect man, neither will he help the evil doers: till he fill thy mouth with laughing, and thy lips with rejoicing. They that hate thee shall be clothed with shame; and the dwelling place of the wicked shall come to nought.

9. Then Job answered and said, I know it is so of a truth: but how should man be just with God? If he will contend with him, he cannot answer him one of a thousand.[32] He is wise in heart, and mighty in strength: who hath hardened himself against him, and hath prospered? Which removeth the mountains, and they know not: which overturneth them in his anger. Which shaketh the earth out of her place, and the pillars thereof tremble. Which commandeth the sun, and it riseth not; and sealeth up the stars. Which alone spreadeth out the heavens, and treadeth upon the waves of the sea. Which maketh Arcturus, Orion, and Pleiades, and the chambers of the south. Which doeth great things past finding out; yea, and wonders without number. Lo, he goeth by me, and I see him not: he passeth on also, but I perceive him not. Behold, he taketh away, who can hinder him? Who will say unto him, What doest thou? If[33] God will not withdraw his anger, the proud helpers do stoop under him. How much less shall I answer him, and choose out my words to reason with him? Whom, though I were righteous, yet would I not answer, but I would make supplication to my judge. If I had called, and he had answered me; yet would I not believe that he had hearkened unto my voice. For he breaketh me with a tempest, and multiplieth my wounds without cause. He will not suffer me to take my breath, but filleth me with bitterness. If I speak of strength, lo, he is strong: and if of judgment, who shall set me a time to plead? If I justify myself, mine own mouth shall condemn me: if I say, I am perfect, it shall also prove me perverse. Though I were perfect, yet would I not know my soul: I would

31. the papyrus, which grows rapidly when the Nile is high, but withers at once when the waters go down.

32. one of a thousand questions.
33. In a more literal translation, *If* would be omitted.

despise my life.[34] This is one thing, therefore I said it, He destroyeth the perfect and the wicked. If the scourge slay suddenly, he will laugh at the trial of the innocent. The earth is given into the hand of the wicked: he covereth the faces of the judges thereof; if not,[35] where, and who is he? Now my days are swifter than a post:[36] they flee away, they see no good. They are passed away as the swift ships: as the eagle that hasteth to the prey. If I say, I will forget my complaint, I will leave off my heaviness, and comfort myself: I am afraid of all my sorrows, I know that thou wilt not hold me innocent. If I be wicked, why then labour I in vain? If I wash myself with snow water, and make my hands never so clean; yet shalt thou plunge me in the ditch, and mine own clothes abhor me.[37] For he is not a man, as I am, that I should answer him, and we should come together in judgment. Neither is there any daysman[38] betwixt us, that might lay his hand upon us both. Let him take his rod away from me, and let not his fear terrify me: then would I speak, and not fear him; but it is not so with me.

10. My soul is weary of my life; I will leave[39] my complaint upon[40] myself; I will speak in the bitterness of my soul. I will say unto God, Do not condemn me; shew me wherefore thou contendest with me. Is it good unto thee that thou shouldest oppress, that thou shouldest despise the work of thine hands, and shine upon the counsel of the wicked? Hast thou eyes of flesh? or seest thou as man seeth?[41] Are thy days as the days of man? Are thy years as man's days,[42] that thou enquirest after mine iniquity, and searchest after my sin? Thou knowest that I am not wicked; and there is none that can deliver out of thine hand. Thine hands have made me and fashioned me together round about; yet thou dost destroy me. Remember, I beseech thee, that thou hast made me as the clay; and wilt thou bring me into dust again? Hast thou not poured me out as milk and curdled me like cheese? Thou hast clothed me with skin and flesh, and hast fenced me with bones and sinews. Thou hast granted me life and favour, and thy visitation hath preserved my spirit. And these things hast thou hid in thine heart: I know that this is with thee.[43] If I sin, then thou markest me, and thou wilt not acquit me from mine iniquity. If I be wicked, woe unto me; and if I be righteous, yet will I not lift up my head. I am full of confusion; therefore see thou mine affliction; for it increaseth. Thou huntest me as a fierce lion: and again thou shewest thy-

34. In a more literal translation this sentence would read, "I am perfect, I regard not myself. I despise my life."
35. if not he.
36. courier.
37. shall abhor me.
38. arbitrator.
39. give free course to.
40. on behalf of.

41. Are you capable of mistakes, of seeing as a man sees?
42. Is your time, like man's, short, so that you have to judge hastily?
43. The meaning is, "My destruction (*this*) is your purpose." Job accuses God of planning his destruction while showing favor to him.

self marvellous upon me. Thou renewest thy witnesses[44] against me, and increasest thine indignation upon me; changes and war are against me. Wherefore then hast thou brought me forth out of the womb? Oh that I had given up the ghost, and no eye had seen me! I should have been as though I had not been; I should have been carried from the womb to the grave. Are not my days few? Cease then, and let me alone, that I may take comfort a little, before I go whence I shall not return, even to the land of darkness and the shadow of death: a land of darkness, as darkness itself; and of the shadow of death, without any order, and where the light is as darkness.

11. Then answered Zophar the Naamathite, and said, Should not the multitude of words be answered? And should a man full of talk be justified? Should thy lies make men hold their peace? And when thou mockest, shall no man make thee ashamed? For thou hast said, My doctrine is pure, and I am clean in thine eyes. But oh that God would speak, and open his lips against thee; and that he would shew thee the secrets of wisdom, that they are double to that which is![45] Know therefore that God exacteth of thee less than thine iniquity deserveth. Canst thou by searching find out God? Canst thou find out the Almighty unto perfection? It is as high as heaven; what canst thou do? Deeper than hell; what canst thou know? The measure thereof is longer than the earth, and broader than the sea. If he cut off, and shut up, or gather together,[46] then who can hinder him? For he knoweth vain men: he seeth wickedness also; will he not then consider it? For vain man would be wise, though man be born like a wild ass's colt. If thou prepare thine heart, and stretch out thine hands toward him; if iniquity be in thine hand, put it far away, and let not wickedness dwell in thy tabernacles. For then shalt thou lift up thy face without spot; yea, thou shalt be stedfast, and shalt not fear: because thou shalt forget thy misery, and remember it as waters that pass away: and thine age shall be clearer than the noonday; thou shalt shine forth, thou shalt be as the morning. And thou shalt be secure, because there is hope; yea, thou shalt dig[47] about thee, and thou shalt take thy rest in safety. Also thou shalt lie down, and none shall make thee afraid; yea, many shall make suit unto thee. But the eyes of the wicked shall fail, and they shall not escape, and their hope shall be as the giving up of the ghost.

12. And Job answered and said, No doubt but ye are the people, and wisdom shall die with you. But I have understanding as well as

---

44. his afflictions, which prove (to his friends) his guilt.

45. *double to that which is:* obscure in the original, usually taken to mean simply "manifold," "various."

46. for judgment.

47. search. The master inspects his property before retiring.

you; I am not inferior to you: yea, who knoweth not such things as these? I am as one mocked of his neighbour, who calleth upon God, and he answered him: the just upright man is laughed to scorn. He that is ready to slip with his feet is as a lamp despised in the thought of him that is at ease. The tabernacles of robbers prosper, and they that provoke God are secure; into whose hand God bringeth abundantly. But ask now the beasts, and they shall teach thee; and the fowls of the air, and they shall tell thee: or speak to the earth, and it shall teach thee: and the fishes of the sea shall declare unto thee. Who knoweth not in all these that the hand of the Lord hath wrought this? In whose hand is the soul of every living thing, and the breath of all mankind. Doth not the ear try words? and the mouth taste his meat? With the ancient is wisdom; and in length of days understanding. With him is wisdom and strength, he hath counsel and understanding. Behold, he breaketh down, and it cannot be built again: he shutteth up a man, and there can be no opening. Behold, he withholdeth the waters, and they dry up: also he sendeth them out, and they overturn the earth. With him is strength and wisdom: the deceived and the deceiver are his. He leadeth counsellors away spoiled, and maketh the judges fools. He looseth the bond of kings, and girdeth their loins with a girdle. He leadeth princes away spoiled, and overthroweth the mighty. He removeth away the speech of the trusty, and taketh away the understanding of the aged. He poureth contempt upon princes, and weakeneth the strength of the mighty. He discovereth deep things out of darkness, and bringeth out to light the shadow of death. He increaseth the nations, and destroyeth them: he enlargeth the nations, and straiteneth[48] them again. He taketh away the heart of the chief of the people of the earth, and causeth them to wander in a wilderness where there is no way. They grope in the dark without light, and he maketh them to stagger like a drunken man.

13. Lo, mine eye hath seen all this, mine ear hath heard and understood it. What ye know, the same do I know also: I am not inferior unto you. Surely I would speak to the Almighty, and I desire to reason with God. But ye are forgers of lies, ye are all physicians of no value. O that ye would altogether hold your peace! and it should be your wisdom. Hear now my reasoning, and hearken to the pleadings of my lips. Will ye speak wickedly for God? and talk deceitfully for him? Will ye accept[49] his person? Will ye contend for God? Is it good that he should search you out? or as one man mocketh another, do ye so mock him? He will surely reprove you, if ye do secretly accept persons.[50] Shall not his excellency make

48. contracts their boundaries.
49. respect.
50. This phrase seems to mean something like, "back the winning side for personal reasons."

you afraid? and his dread fall upon you? Your remembrances[51] are like unto ashes, your bodies to bodies of clay. Hold your peace, let me alone, that I may speak, and let come on me what will. Wherefore do I take my flesh in my teeth,[52] and put my life in mine hand? Though he slay me, yet will I trust in him: but I will maintain mine own ways before him. He also shall be my salvation: for an hypocrite shall not come before him. Hear diligently my speech, and my declaration with your ears. Behold now, I have ordered my cause; I know that I shall be justified. Who is he that will plead with me?[53] for now, if I hold my tongue, I shall give up the ghost.[54] Only do not two things unto me: then will I not hide myself from thee.[55] Withdraw thine hand far from me: and let not thy dread make me afraid. Then call thou, and I will answer: or let me speak, and answer thou me. How many are mine iniquities and sins? Make me to know my transgression and my sin. Wherefore hidest thou thy face, and holdest me for thine enemy? Wilt thou break a leaf driven to and fro? and wilt thou pursue the dry stubble? For thou writest bitter things against me, and makest me to possess[56] the iniquities of my youth. Thou puttest my feet also in the stocks, and lookest narrowly unto all my paths; thou settest a print upon[57] the heels of my feet. And he,[58] as a rotten thing, consumeth, as a garment that is moth eaten.

14. Man that is born of a woman is of few days, and full of trouble. He cometh forth like a flower, and is cut down: he fleeth also as a shadow, and continueth not. And dost thou open thine eyes upon such an one, and bringest me into judgment with thee? Who can bring a clean thing out of an unclean? not one. Seeing his days are determined, the number of his months are with thee, thou hast appointed his bounds that he cannot pass; turn from him, that he may rest, till he shall accomplish, as an hireling, his day. For there is hope of a tree, if it be cut down, that it will sprout again, and that the tender branch thereof will not cease. Though the root thereof wax old in the earth, and the stock thereof die in the ground; yet through the scent of water it will bud, and bring forth boughs like a plant. But man dieth, and wasteth away: yea, man giveth up the ghost, and where is he? As the waters fail from the sea, and the flood decayeth and drieth up: so man lieth down, and riseth not: till the heavens be no more, they shall not awake, nor be raised out of their sleep. O that thou wouldest hide me in the grave, that thou wouldest keep me secret, until thy wrath be past,

51. memorable sayings.
52. like a wild beast at bay, defending its life with its teeth.
53. accuse me.
54. In a more literal translation this would read, "If anyone does accuse me I shall hold my tongue and die."
55. He now addresses himself directly to God.
56. inherit.
57. drawest a line about.
58. the prisoner in the stocks, Job.

that thou wouldest appoint me a set time, and remember me! If a man die, shall he live again? All the days of my appointed time will I wait, till my change[59] come. Thou shalt call, and I will answer thee: thou wilt have a desire to[60] the work of thine hands. For now thou numberest my steps: dost thou not watch over my sin? My transgression is sealed up in a bag, and thou sewest up mine iniquity. And surely the mountain falling cometh to nought, and the rock is removed out of his place. The waters wear the stones: thou washest away the things which grow out of the dust of the earth; and thou destroyest the hope of man. Thou prevailest for ever against him, and he passeth. thou changest his countenance, and sendest him away. His sons come to honour, and he knoweth it not; and they are brought low, but he perceiveth it not of them. But his flesh upon him shall have pain, and his soul within him shall mourn.

29. Moreover Job continued his parable, and said, Oh that I were as in months past, as in the days when God preserved me; when his candle shined upon my head, and when by his light I walked through darkness; as I was in the days of my youth, when the secret of God was upon my tabernacle; when the Almighty was yet with me, when my children were about me; when I washed my steps with butter and the rock poured me out rivers of oil; when I went out to the gate[61] through the city, when I prepared my seat in the street! The young men saw me, and hid themselves: and the aged arose, and stood up. The princes refrained talking, and laid their hand on their mouth. The nobles held their peace, and their tongue cleaved to the roof of their mouth. When the ear heard me, then it blessed me; and when the eye saw me, it gave witness to me: because I delivered the poor that cried, and the fatherless, and him that had none to help him. The blessing of him that was ready to perish came upon me: and I caused the widow's heart to sing for joy. I put on righteousness, and it clothed me: my judgment was as a robe and a diadem. I was eyes to the blind, and feet was I to the lame. I was a father to the poor: and the cause which I knew not I searched out. And I brake the jaws of the wicked, and plucked the spoil out of his teeth. Then I said, I shall die in my nest, and I shall multiply my days as the sand. My root was spread out by the waters, and the dew lay all night upon my branch. My glory was fresh in me, and my bow was renewed in my hand. Unto me men gave ear, and waited, and kept silence at my counsel. After my words they spake not again; and my speech dropped upon them. And they waited for me as for the rain; and they opened their mouth wide

59. release.
60. for.

61. The town meeting place and law court was just inside the gate.

as for the latter rain. If I laughed on them, they believed it not;[62] and the light of my countenance they cast not down. I chose out their way, and sat chief, and dwelt as a king in the army, as one that comforteth the mourners.

30. But now they that are younger than I have me in derision, whose fathers I would have disdained to have set with the dogs of my flock. Yea, whereto might the strength of their hands profit me,[63] in whom old age was perished? For want and famine they were solitary; fleeing into the wilderness in former time desolate and waste. Who cut up mallows by the bushes, and juniper roots for their meat. They were driven forth from among men, (they cried after them as after a thief;) to dwell in the cliffs of the valleys, in caves of the earth, and in the rocks. Among the bushes they brayed; under the nettles they were gathered together. They were children of fools, yea, children of base men: they were viler than the earth. And now am I their song, yea, I am their byword. They abhor me, they flee far from me, and spare not to spit in my face. Because he hath loosed my cord, and afflicted me, they have also let loose the bridle before me. Upon my right hand rise the youth; they push away my feet, and they raise up against me the ways of their destruction. They mar my path, they set forward my calamity, they have no helper.[64] They came upon me as a wide breaking in of waters: in the desolation they rolled themselves upon me. Terrors are turned upon me: they pursue my soul as the wind: and my welfare passeth away as a cloud. And now my soul is poured out upon[65] me; the days of affliction have taken hold upon me. My bones are pierced in me in the night season: and my sinews take no rest. By the great force of my disease is my garment changed: it bindeth me about as the collar of my coat. He hath cast me into the mire, and I am become like dust and ashes. I cry unto thee, and thou dost not hear me: I stand up, and thou regardest me not. Thou art become cruel to me: with thy strong hand thou opposest thyself against me. Thou liftest me up to the wind; thou causest me to ride upon it, and dissolvest my substance. For I know that thou wilt bring me to death, and to the house appointed for all living. Howbeit he will not stretch out his hand to the grave, though they cry in his destruction.[66] Did not I weep for him that was in trouble? Was not my soul grieved for the poor? When I looked for good, then evil came unto me: and when I waited for light, there came darkness. My bowels boiled, and rested not: the days of afflic-

62. obscure in the original; perhaps, "I smiled on them and they were confident."

63. They were too old to work.

64. *they have no helper:* The text is uncertain at this point.

65. within.

66. This sentence is unintelligible in the original.

tion prevented me.[67] I went mourning without the sun: I stood up, and I cried in the congregation. I am a brother to dragons, and a companion to owls. My skin is black upon me, and my bones are burned with heat. My harp also is turned to mourning, and my organ[68] into the voice of them that weep.

31. I made a covenant with mine eyes; why then should I think upon a maid? For what portion of God is there from above? and what inheritance of the Almighty from on high? Is not destruction to the wicked? and a strange punishment to the workers of iniquity? Doth not he see my ways, and count all my steps? If I have walked with vanity, or if my foot hath hasted to deceit; let me be weighed in an even balance, that God may know mine integrity. If my step hath turned out of the way, and mine heart walked after mine eyes, and if any blot hath cleaved to mine hands; then let me sow, and let another eat; yea, let my offspring be rooted out. If mine heart have been deceived by a woman, or if I have laid wait at my neighbour's door; then let my wife grind unto another, and let others bow down upon her. For this is an heinous crime; yea, it is an iniquity to be punished by the judges. For it is a fire that consumeth to destruction, and would root out all mine increase.

If I did despise the cause of my manservant or of my maidservant, when they contended with me; what then shall I do when God riseth up? and when he visiteth, what shall I answer him? Did not he that made me in the womb make him? and did not one fashion us in the womb? If I have withheld the poor from their desire, or have caused the eyes of the widow to fail; or have eaten my morsel myself alone, and the fatherless hath not eaten thereof; (For from my youth he was brought up with me, as with a father, and I have guided her from my mother's womb;) if I have seen any perish for want of clothing, or any poor without covering; if his loins have not blessed me, and if he were not warmed with the fleece of my sheep; if I have lifted up my hand against the fatherless, when I saw my help in the gate:[69] then let mine arm fall from my shoulder blade, and mine arm be broken from the bone. For destruction from God was a terror to me, and by reason of his highness I could not endure. If I have made gold my hope, or have said to the fine gold, Thou art my confidence; if I rejoiced because my wealth was great, and because mine hand had gotten much; if I beheld the sun when it shined, or the moon walking in brightness; and my heart hath been secretly enticed, or my mouth hath kissed my hand:[70] this also were an iniquity to be punished by the

---

67. came upon me.
68. pipe.
69. The gate is the court; the clause means, "when I had influence in the court."

70. *my heart . . . my hand:* idolatrous acts of worship of the sun and moon.

judge: for I should have denied the God that is above.

If I rejoiced at the destruction of him that hated me, or lifted up myself when evil found him: neither have I suffered my mouth to sin by wishing a curse to his soul. If the men of my tabernacle said not, Oh that we had of his flesh! We cannot be satisfied.[71] The stranger did not lodge in the street: but I opened my doors to the traveller. If I covered my transgressions as Adam, by hiding mine iniquity in my bosom: did I fear a great multitude, or did the contempt of families terrify me, that I kept silence, and went not out of the door? Oh that one would hear me! Behold, my desire is, that the Almighty would answer me, and that mine adversary had written a book. Surely I would take it upon my shoulder, and bind it as a crown to me. I would declare unto him the number of my steps; as a prince would I go near unto him. If my land cry against me, or that the furrows likewise thereof complain; if I have eaten the fruits thereof without money, or have caused the owners thereof to lose their life: let thistles grow instead of wheat, and cockle instead of barley. The words of Job are ended.

. . .

38. Then the Lord answered Job out of the whirlwind, and said, Who is this that darkeneth counsel by words without knowledge? Gird up now thy loins like a man; for I will demand of thee, and answer thou me. Where wast thou when I laid the foundations of the earth? Declare, if thou hast understanding. Who hath laid the measures thereof, if thou knowest? or who hath stretched the line upon it? Whereupon are the foundations thereof fastened? or who laid the corner stone thereof; when the morning stars sang together, and all the sons of God shouted for joy? Or who shut up the sea with doors, when it brake forth, as if it had issued out of the womb? When I made the cloud the garment thereof, and thick darkness a swaddlingband for it, and brake up for it my decreed place,[72] and set bars and doors, and said, Hitherto shalt thou come, but no further: and here shall thy proud waves be stayed? Hast thou commanded the morning since thy days; and caused the dayspring[73] to know his place; that it might take hold of the ends of the earth, that the wicked might be shaken out of it? It is turned as clay to the seal;[74] and they[75] stand as a garment. And from the wicked their light is withholden, and the high arm shall be broken. Hast thou entered into the springs of the sea? or hast thou walked in the search of the depth? Have the gates of death been opened unto

71. Translated literally, the statement of the men of the tabernacle should probably read, "Who can find one that hath not been satisfied with his flesh?" i.e., with meat from his flocks.

72. the broken coastline.

73. dawn.

74. A more literal translation would read, "changed as clay under the seal."

75. all things. God is describing the moment of the creation of the universe.

thee? or hast thou seen the doors of the shadow of death? Hast thou perceived the breadth of the earth? Declare if thou knowest it all. Where is the way where light dwelleth? And as for darkness, where is the place thereof, that thou shouldest take it to the bound thereof, and that thou shouldest know the paths to the house thereof? Knowest thou it, because thou wast then born? or because the number of thy days is great? Hast thou entered into the treasures of the snow? or hast thou seen the treasures of the hail, which I have reserved against the time of trouble, against the day of battle and war? By what way is the light parted, which scattereth the east wind upon the earth?[76] Who hath divided a watercourse for the overflowing of waters, or a way for the lightning of thunder; to cause it to rain on the earth, where no man is; on the wilderness, wherein there is no man; to satisfy the desolate and waste ground; and to cause the bud of the tender herb to spring forth? Hath the rain a father? or who hath begotten the drops of dew? Out of whose womb came the ice? And the hoary frost of heaven, who hath gendered it? The waters are hid as with a stone, and the face of the deep is frozen. Canst thou bind the sweet influences of Pleiades, or loose the bands of Orion? Canst thou bring forth Mazzaroth[77] in his season? or canst thou guide Arcturus with his sons? Knowest thou the ordinances of heaven? Canst thou set the dominion thereof in the earth? Canst thou lift up thy voice to the clouds, that abundance of waters may cover thee? Canst thou send lightnings, that they may go, and say unto thee, Here we are? Who hath put wisdom in the inward parts? or who hath given understanding to the heart? Who can number the clouds in wisdom? or who can stay the bottles of heaven, when the dust groweth into hardness, and the clods cleave fast together? Wilt thou hunt the prey for the lion? or fill the appetite of the young lion, when they couch in their dens, and abide in the covert to lie in wait? Who provideth for the raven his food? when his young ones cry unto God, they[78] wander for lack of meat.

39. Knowest thou the time when the wild goats of the rock bring forth? or canst thou mark when the hinds do calve? Canst thou number the months that they fulfil? or knowest thou the time when they bring forth? They bow themselves, they bring forth their young ones, they cast out their sorrows. Their young ones are in good liking, they grow up with corn; they go forth, and return not unto them. Who hath sent out the wild ass free? or who hath loosed the bands of the wild ass? Whose house I have made the wilderness, and the barren land his dwellings. He scorneth the

76. more literally, "and the east wind scattered upon the earth."

77. meaning disputed; it may be a name for the signs of the zodiac, or for some particular constellation.

78. more literally, "and."

multitude of the city, neither regardeth he the crying of the driver. The range of the mountains is his pasture, and he searcheth after every green thing. Will the unicorn[79] be willing to serve thee, or abide by thy crib? Canst thou bind the unicorn with his band in the furrow? or will he harrow the valleys after thee? Wilt thou trust him, because his strength is great? or wilt thou leave thy labour to him? Wilt thou believe him, that he will bring home thy seed, and gather it into thy barn? Gavest thou the goodly wings unto the peacocks? or wings and feathers unto the ostrich? Which leaveth her eggs in the earth, and warmeth them in dust, and forgetteth that the foot may crush them, or that the wild beast may break them. She is hardened against her young ones, as though they were not her's: her labour is in vain without fear;[80] because God hath deprived her of wisdom, neither hath he imparted to her understanding. What time she lifteth up herself on high, she scorneth the horse and his rider. Hast thou given the horse strength? Hast thou clothed his neck with thunder? Canst thou make him afraid as a grasshopper? The glory of his nostrils is terrible. He paweth in the valley, and rejoiceth in his strength: he goeth on to meet the armed men. He mocketh at fear, and is not affrighted; neither turneth he back from the sword. The quiver rattleth against him, the glittering spear and the shield. He swalloweth the ground with fierceness and rage: neither believeth he that it is the sound of the trumpet. He saith among the trumpets, Ha, ha; and he smelleth the battle afar off, the thunder of the captains, and the shouting. Doth the hawk fly by thy wisdom, and stretch her wings toward the south? Doth the eagle mount up at thy command, and make her nest on high? She dwelleth and abideth on the rock, upon the crag of the rock, and the strong place. From thence she seeketh the prey, and her eyes behold afar off. Her young ones also suck up blood: and where the slain are, there is she.

40. Moreover the Lord answered Job, and said, Shall he that contendeth with the Almighty instruct him? He that reproveth God, let him answer it.

Then Job answered the Lord, and said, Behold, I am vile; what shall I answer thee? I will lay mine hand upon my mouth. Once have I spoken; but I will not answer: yea, twice; but I will proceed no further.

Then answered the Lord unto Job out of the whirlwind, and said, Gird up thy loins now like a man: I will demand of thee, and declare thou unto me. Wilt thou also disannul my judgment? Wilt thou condemn me, that thou mayest be righteous? Hast thou an

79. a mythical beast with one horn in the center of his forehead. The Hebrew is less imaginative; it says, "wild ox."

80. though her labor is in vain, she is without fear.

arm like God? or canst thou thunder with a voice like him? Deck thyself now with majesty and excellency; and array thyself with glory and beauty. Cast abroad the rage of thy wrath: and behold every one that is proud, and abase him. Look on every one that is proud, and bring him low; and tread down the wicked in their place. Hide them in the dust together; and bind their faces in secret. Then will I also confess unto thee that thine own right hand can save thee.

Behold now behemoth,[81] which I made with thee; he eateth grass as an ox. Lo now, his strength is in his loins, and his force is in the navel of his belly. He moveth his tail like a cedar: the sinews of his stone[82] are wrapped together. His bones are as strong pieces of brass; his bones are like bars of iron. He is the chief of the ways of God: he that made him can make his sword to approach unto him. Surely the mountains bring him forth food, where all the beasts of the field play. He lieth under the shady trees, in the covert of the reed, and fens. The shady trees cover him with their shadow; the willows of the brook compass him about. Behold, he drinketh up a river, and hasteth not: he trusteth that he can draw up Jordan into his mouth. He taketh it with his eyes:[83] his nose pierceth through snares.

41. Canst thou draw out leviathan[84] with an hook?[85] or his tongue with a cord which thou lettest down? Canst thou put an hook into his nose? or bore his jaw through with a thorn? Will he make many supplications unto thee? will he speak soft words unto thee? Will he make a covenant with thee? wilt thou take him for a servant for ever? Wilt thou play with him as with a bird? or wilt thou bind him for thy maidens? Shall the companions make a banquet of him? Shall they part him among the merchants? Canst thou fill his skin with barbed irons? or his head with fish spears? Lay thine hand upon him, remember the battle, do no more. Behold, the hope of him is in vain: shall not one be cast down even at the sight of him? None is so fierce that dare stir him up: who then is able to stand before me? Who hath prevented[86] me, that I should repay him? Whatsoever is under the whole heaven is mine. I will not conceal his parts, nor his power, nor his comely proportion. Who can discover the face of[87] his garment?[88] or who can come to him with his double bridle? Who can open the doors of his face? His teeth are terrible round about. His scales are his pride, shut up together as with a close seal. One is so near to another, that

---

81. generally identified with the hippopotamus.

82. A more literal translation would read, "thighs."

83. obscure in the original; probably, "None can attack him in the eyes."

84. here probably the crocodile.

85. The Greek historian Herodotus tells how the Egyptians captured the crocodile with a hook.

86. given anything to me first.

87. strip off.

88. his scales.

no air can come between them. They are joined one to another, they stick together, that they cannot be sundered. By his neesings[89] a light doth shine, and his eyes are like the eyelids of the morning. Out of his mouth go burning lamps, and sparks of fire leap out. Out of his nostrils goeth smoke, as out of a seething pot or caldron. His breath kindleth coals, and a flame goeth out of his mouth. In his neck remaineth strength, and sorrow is turned into joy before him. The flakes of his flesh are joined together: they are firm in themselves; they cannot be moved. His heart is as firm as a stone; yea, as hard as a piece of the nether millstone. When he raiseth up himself, the mighty are afraid: by reason of breakings they purify themselves.[90] The sword of him that layeth at him cannot hold: the spear, the dart, nor the habergeon. He esteemeth iron as straw, and brass as rotten wood. The arrow cannot make him flee: slingstones are turned with him into stubble. Darts are counted as stubble: he laugheth at the shaking of a spear. Sharp stones are under him: he spreadeth sharp pointed things upon the mire. He maketh the deep to boil like a pot: he maketh the sea like a pot of ointment. He maketh a path to shine after him; one would think the deep to be hoary.[91] Upon earth there is not his like, who is made without fear. He beholdeth all high things: he is a king over all the children of pride.

42. Then Job answered the Lord, and said, I know that thou canst do every thing, and that no thought can be withholden from thee. Who is he that hideth counsel without knowledge? Therefore have I uttered that I understood not; things too wonderful for me, which I knew not. Hear, I beseech thee, and I will speak: I will demand of thee, and declare thou unto me. I have heard of thee by the hearing of the ear: but now mine eye seeth thee. Wherefore I abhor myself, and repent in dust and ashes.

And it was so, that after the Lord had spoken these words unto Job, the Lord said to Eliphaz the Temanite, My wrath is kindled against thee, and against thy two friends: for ye have not spoken of me the thing that is right, as my servant Job hath. Therefore take unto you now seven bullocks and seven rams, and go to my servant Job, and offer up for yourselves a burnt offering; and my servant Job shall pray for you: for him will I accept: lest I deal with you after your folly, in that ye have not spoken of me the thing which is right, like my servant Job. So Eliphaz the Temanite and Bildad the Shuhite and Zophar the Naamathite went, and did according as the Lord commanded them: the Lord also accepted Job. And

89. his breath (compare, "sneeze"). The vapor exhaled by the crocodile appears luminous in the sunlight.

90. a corrupt text. The clause probably should read, "in consternation they are beside themselves."

91. white (with foam).

the Lord turned to the captivity[92] of Job, when he prayed for his friends: also the Lord gave Job twice as much as he had before. Then came there unto him all his brethren, and all his sisters, and all they that had been of his acquaintance before, and did eat bread with him in his house: and they bemoaned him, and comforted him over all the evil that the Lord had brought upon him: every man also gave him a piece of money, and every one an earring of gold. So the Lord blessed the latter end of Job more than his beginning: for he had fourteen thousand sheep, and six thousand camels, and a thousand yoke of oxen, and a thousand she asses. He had also seven sons and three daughters. And he called the name of the first, Jemima; and the name of the second, Kezia; and the name of the third, Kerenhappuch. And in all the land were no women found so fair as the daughters of Job: and their father gave them inheritance among their brethren. After this lived Job an hundred and forty years, and saw his sons, and his sons' sons, even four generations. So Job died, being old and full of days.

Ecclesiastes
*or, The Preacher**

1. . . . . Vanity of vanities, saith the Preacher, vanity of vanities; all is vanity.[1] What profit hath a man of all his labour which he taketh under the sun? One generation passeth away, and another generation cometh: but the earth abideth for ever. The sun also ariseth, and the sun goeth down and hasteth to his place where he arose. The wind goeth toward the south, and turneth about unto the north; it whirleth about continually, and the wind returneth again according to his circuits. All the rivers run into the sea; yet the sea is not full; unto the place from whence the rivers come, thither they return again. All things are full of labour; man cannot utter it; the eye is not satisfied with seeing, nor the ear filled with hearing. The thing that hath been, it is that which shall be; and that which is done is that which shall be done: and there is no new thing under the sun. Is there any thing whereof it may be said, See, this is new? it hath been already of old time, which was before us. There is no remembrance of former things; neither shall there be any remembrance of things that are to come with those that shall come after.

I the Preacher was king over Israel in Jerusalem. And I gave my heart to seek and search out by wisdom concerning all things that are done under heaven: this sore travail hath God given to the sons of man to be exercised therewith. I have seen all the works that are done under the sun; and, behold, all is vanity and vexation of spirit. That which is crooked cannot be made straight: and that which is wanting cannot be numbered. I communed with mine own heart,

---

* Selections (1:2–18; 2:1–24; 3; 9:2–   1. *vanity:* emptiness.
12; 11; 12:1–8).

saying, Lo, I am come to great estate, and have gotten more wisdom than all they that have been before me in Jerusalem: yea, my heart had great experience of wisdom and knowledge. And I gave my heart to know wisdom, and to know madness and folly: I perceived that this also is vexation of spirit. For in much wisdom is much grief: and he that increaseth knowledge increaseth sorrow.

2. I said in mine heart, Go to now, I will prove thee with mirth,[2] therefore enjoy pleasure: and, behold, this also is vanity. I said of laughter, It is mad: and of mirth, What doeth it? I sought in mine heart to give myself unto wine, yet acquainting mine heart with wisdom; and to lay hold on folly, till I might see what was that good for the sons of men, which they should do under the heaven all the days of their life. I made me great works; I builded me houses; I planted me vineyards: · I made me gardens and orchards, and I planted trees in them of all kinds of fruits: I made me pools of water, to water therewith the wood that bringeth forth trees; I got me servants[3] and maidens, and had servants born in my house; also I had great possessions of great and small cattle above all that were in Jerusalem before me: I gathered me also silver and gold, and the peculiar treasure of kings and of the provinces: I gat me men singers and women singers, and the delights of the sons of men, as musical instruments, and that of all sorts. So I was great, and increased more than all that were before me in Jerusalem: also my wisdom remained with me. And whatsoever mine eyes desired I kept not from them, I withheld not my heart from any joy; for my heart rejoiced in all my labour: and this was my portion of all my labour. Then I looked on all the works that my hands had wrought, and on the labour that I had laboured to do: and, behold, all was vanity and vexation of spirit, and there was no profit under the sun.

And I turned myself to behold wisdom, and madness, and folly: for what can the man do that cometh after the king? even that which hath been already done. Then I saw that wisdom excelleth folly, as far as light excelleth darkness. The wise man's eyes are in his head; but the fool walketh in darkness: and I myself perceived also that one event happeneth to them all. Then said I in my heart, As it happeneth to the fool, so it happeneth even to me; and why was I then more wise? Then I said in my heart, that this also is vanity. For there is no remembrance of the wise more than of the fool for ever; seeing that which now is in the days to come shall all be forgotten. And how dieth the wise man? as the fool. Therefore I hated life; because the work that is wrought under the sun is grievous unto me: for all is vanity and vexation of spirit.

---

2. *prove thee with mirth:* i.e., I will try pleasure.

3. *servants:* slaves.

Yea, I hated all my labour which I had taken under the sun: because I should leave it unto the man that shall be after me. And who knoweth whether he shall be a wise man or a fool? yet shall he have rule over all my labour wherein I have laboured, and wherein I have shewed myself wise under the sun. This is also vanity. Therefore I went about to cause my heart to despair of all the labour which I took under the sun. For there is a man whose labour is in wisdom, and in knowledge, and in equity; yet to a man that hath not laboured therein shall he leave it for his portion. This also is vanity and a great evil. For what hath man of all his labour, and of the vexation of his heart, wherein he hath laboured under the sun? For all his days are sorrows, and his travail grief; yea, his heart taketh not rest in the night. This is also vanity.

There is nothing better for a man, than that he should eat and drink, and that he should make his soul enjoy good in his labour. This also I saw, that it was from the hand of God.

3. To every thing there is a season, and a time to every purpose under the heaven: A time to be born, and a time to die; a time to plant, and a time to pluck up that which is planted; A time to kill, and a time to heal; a time to break down, and a time to build up; A time to weep, and a time to laugh; a time to mourn, and a time to dance; A time to cast away stones, and a time to gather stones together; a time to embrace, and a time to refrain from embracing; A time to get, and a time to lose; a time to keep, and a time to cast away; A time to rend, and a time to sew; a time to keep silence, and a time to speak; A time to love, and a time to hate; a time of war, and a time of peace. What profit hath he that worketh in that wherein he laboureth? I have seen the travail,[4] which God hath given to the sons of men to be exercised in it. He hath made every thing beautiful in his time; also he hath set the world in their heart, so that no man can find out the work that God maketh from the beginning to the end. I know that there is no good in them, but for a man to rejoice, and to do good in his life. And also that every man should eat and drink, and enjoy the good of all his labour, it is the gift of God. I know that, whatsoever God doeth, it shall be for ever: nothing can be put to it, nor any thing taken from it; and God doeth it, that men should fear before him. That which hath been is now; and that which is to be hath already been; and God requireth[5] that which is past.

And moreover I saw under the sun the place of judgment, that wickedness was there; and the place of righteousness, that iniquity was there. I said in mine heart, God shall judge the righteous and the wicked: for there is a time there for every purpose and for every work. I said in mine heart concerning the estate of the sons of men,

4. *travail:* labor.   5. *requireth:* calls back.

that God might manifest[6] them and that they might see that they themselves are beasts. For that which befalleth the sons of men befalleth beasts; even one thing befalleth them; as the one dieth, so dieth the other; yea, they have all one breath; so that a man hath no preeminence above a beast: for all is vanity. All go unto one place; all are of the dust, and all turn to dust again. Who knoweth the spirit of man that goeth upward, and the spirit of the beast that goeth downward to the earth?[7] Wherefore I perceive that there is nothing better, than that a man should rejoice in his own works; for that is his portion; for who shall bring him to see what shall be after him?

9. . . . All things come alike to all: there is one event to the righteous and to the wicked; to the good and to the clean, and to the unclean; to him that sacrificeth, and to him that sacrificeth not; as is the good, so is the sinner; and he that sweareth, as he that feareth[8] an oath. This is an evil among all things that are done under the sun, that there is one event unto all: yea, also the heart of the sons of men is full of evil, and madness is in their heart while they live, and after that they go to the dead.

For to him that is joined to all the living there is hope: for a living dog is better than a dead lion. For the living know that they shall die: but the dead know not any thing, neither have they any more a reward; for the memory of them is forgotten. Also their love, and their hatred, and their envy, is now perished; neither have they any more a portion for ever in any thing that is done under the sun.

Go thy way, eat thy bread with joy, and drink thy wine with a merry heart; for God now accepteth thy works. Let thy garments be always white; and let thy head lack no ointment. Live joyfully with the wife whom thou lovest all the days of the life of thy vanity, which he hath given thee under the sun, all the days of thy vanity; for that is thy portion in this life, and in thy labour which thou takest under the sun. Whatsoever thy hand findeth to do, do it with thy might; for there is no work, nor device, nor knowledge, nor wisdom, in the grave, whither thou goest.

I returned, and saw under the sun, that the race is not to the swift, nor the battle to the strong, neither yet bread to the wise, nor yet riches to men of understanding, nor yet favour to men of skill; but time and chance happeneth to them all. For man also knoweth not his time: as the fishes that are taken in an evil net, and as the birds that are caught in the snare; so are the sons of men snared in an evil time, when it falleth suddenly upon them.

6. *manifest:* make clear.
7. Who knows whether the spirit of man goes upward or whether . . . ?

8. *feareth:* dares not take the oath (that he is innocent).

11. Cast thy bread upon the waters: for thou shalt find it after many days. Give a portion to seven, and also to eight; for thou knowest not what evil shall be upon the earth. If the clouds be full of rain, they empty themselves upon the earth: and if the tree fall toward the south, or toward the north, in the place where the tree falleth, there shall it be. He that observeth the wind shall not sow; and he that regardeth the clouds shall not reap. As thou knowest not what is the way of the spirit, nor how the bones do grow in the womb of her that is with child: even so thou knowest not the works of God who maketh all. In the morning sow thy seed, and in the evening withhold not thine hand: for thou knowest not whether shall prosper, either this or that, or whether they both shall be alike good.

Truly the light is sweet, and a pleasant thing it is for the eyes to behold the sun: But if a man live many years, and rejoice in them all; yet let him remember the days of darkness; for they shall be many. All that cometh is vanity.

Rejoice, O young man, in thy youth; and let thy heart cheer thee in the days of thy youth, and walk in the ways of thine heart, and in the sight of thine eyes: but know thou, that for all these things God will bring thee into judgment. Therefore remove sorrow from thy heart, and put away evil from thy flesh, for childhood and youth are vanity.

12. Remember now thy Creator in the days of thy youth, while the evil days come not, nor the years draw nigh, when thou shalt say, I have no pleasure in them; While the sun, or the light, or the moon, or the stars, be not darkened, nor the clouds return after the rain: In the day when the keepers of the house shall tremble, and the strong men shall bow themselves, and the grinders[9] cease because they are few, and those that look out of the windows be darkened, And the doors shall be shut in the streets, when the sound of the grinding is low, and he shall rise up at the voice of the bird, and all the daughters of musick shall be brought low; Also when they shall be afraid of that which is high, and fears shall be in the way, and the almond tree shall flourish, and the grasshopper shall be a burden, and desire shall fail: because man goeth to his long home, and the mourners go about the streets: Or ever the silver cord be loosed, or the golden bowl be broken, or the pitcher be broken at the fountain, or the wheel broken at the cistern. Then shall the dust return to the earth as it was: and the spirit shall return unto God who gave it.

Vanity of vanities, saith the preacher; all is vanity.

---

9. *grinders:* the servants grinding the wheat at the mill.

Psalm 8

1. O Lord our Lord, how excellent is thy name in all the earth! who hast set thy glory above the heavens.

2. Out of the mouth of babes and sucklings hast thou ordained strength because of thine enemies, that thou mightest still the enemy and the avenger.

3. When I consider thy heavens, the work of thy fingers, the moon and the stars, which thou hast ordained;

4. What is man, that thou art mindful of him? and the son of man, that thou visitest him?

5. For thou hast made him a little lower than the angels, and hast crowned him with glory and honour.

6. Thou madest him to have dominion over the works of thy hands; thou hast put all things under his feet:

7. All sheep and oxen, yea, and the beasts of the field;

8. The fowl of the air, and the fish of the sea, and whatsoever passeth through the paths of the seas.

9. O Lord our Lord, how excellent is thy name in all the earth!

Psalm 19

1. The heavens declare the glory of God; and the firmament sheweth his handywork.

2. Day unto day uttereth speech, and night unto night sheweth knowledge.

3. There is no speech nor language, where their voice is not heard.

4. Their line is gone out through all the earth, and their words to the end of the world. In them hath he set a tabernacle for the sun,

5. Which is as a bridegroom coming out of his chamber, and rejoiceth as a strong man to run a race.

6. His going forth is from the end of the heaven, and his circuit unto the ends of it: and there is nothing hid from the heat thereof.

7. The law of the Lord is perfect, converting the soul: the testimony of the Lord is sure, making wise the simple.

8. The statutes of the Lord are right, rejoicing the heart: the commandment of the Lord is pure, enlightening the eyes.

9. The fear of the Lord is clean, enduring for ever: the judgments of the Lord are true and righteous altogether.

10. More to be desired are they than gold, yea, than much fine gold: sweeter also than honey and the honeycomb.

11. Moreover by them is thy servant warned: and in keeping of them there is great reward.

12. Who can understand his errors? cleanse thou me from secret faults.

13. Keep back thy servant also from presumptuous sins; let them not have dominion over me: then shall I be upright, and I shall be innocent from the great transgression.

14. Let the words of my mouth, and the meditation of my heart, be acceptable in thy sight, O Lord, my strength, and my redeemer.

Psalm 23

1. The Lord is my shepherd; I shall not want.

2. He maketh me to lie down in green pastures: he leadeth me beside the still waters.

3. He restoreth my soul: he leadeth me in the paths of righteousness for his name's sake.

4. Yea, though I walk through the valley of the shadow of death, I will fear no evil: for thou art with me; thy rod and thy staff they comfort me.

5. Thou preparest a table before me in the presence of mine enemies: thou anointest my head with oil; my cup runneth over.

6. Surely goodness and mercy shall follow me all the days of my life: and I will dwell in the house of the Lord for ever.

Psalm 104

1. Bless the Lord, O my soul. O Lord my God, thou art very great; thou art clothed with honour and majesty.

2. Who coverest thyself with light as with a garment: who stretchest out the heavens like a curtain:

3. Who layeth the beams of his chambers in the waters: who maketh the clouds his chariot: who walketh upon the wings of the wind:

4. Who maketh his angels spirits; his ministers a flaming fire:

5. Who laid the foundations of the earth, that it should not be removed for ever.

6. Thou coveredst it with the deep as with a garment: the waters stood above the mountains.

7. At thy rebuke they fled; at the voice of thy thunder they hasted away.

8. They go up by the mountains; they go down by the valleys unto the place which thou hast founded for them.

9. Thou hast set a bound that they may not pass over; that they turn not again to cover the earth.

10. He sendeth the springs into the valleys, which run among the hills.

11. They give drink to every beast of the field: the wild asses quench their thirst.

12. By them shall the fowls of the heaven have their habitation, which sing among the branches.

13. He watereth the hills from his chambers: the earth is satisfied with the fruit of thy works.

14. He causeth the grass to grow for the cattle, and herb for the service of man: that he may bring forth food out of the earth;

15. And wine that maketh glad the heart of man, and oil to make his face to shine, and bread which strengtheneth man's heart.

16. The trees of the Lord are full of sap; the cedars of Lebanon, which he hath planted;

17. Where the birds make their nests: as for the stork, the fir trees are her house.

18. The high hills are a refuge for the wild goats; and the rocks for the conies.

19. He appointed the moon for seasons: the sun knoweth his going down.

20. Thou makest darkness, and it is night: wherein all the beasts of the forest do creep forth.

21. The young lions roar after their prey, and seek their meat from God.

22. The sun ariseth, they gather themselves together, and lay them down in their dens.

23. Man goeth forth unto his work and to his labour until the evening.

24. O Lord, how manifold are thy works! in wisdom hast thou made them all: the earth is full of thy riches.

25. So is this great and wide sea, wherein are things creeping innumerable, both small and great beasts.

26. There go the ships: there is that leviathan, whom thou hast made to play therein.

27. These wait all upon thee; that thou mayest give them their meat in due season.

28. That thou givest them they gather: thou openest thine hand, they are filled with good.

29. Thou hidest thy face, they are troubled: thou takest away their breath, they die, and return to their dust.

30. Thou sendest forth thy spirit, they are created: and thou renewest the face of the earth.

31. The glory of the Lord shall endure for ever: the Lord shall rejoice in his works.

32. He looketh on the earth, and it trembleth: he toucheth the hills, and they smoke.

33. I will sing unto the Lord as long as I live: I will sing praise to my God while I have my being.

34. My meditation of him shall be sweet: I will be glad in the Lord.

35. Let the sinners be consumed out of the earth, and let the wicked be no more. Bless thou the Lord, O my soul. Praise ye the Lord.

Psalm 137

1. By the rivers of Babylon,[1] there we sat down, yea, we wept, when we remembered Zion.

2. We hanged our harps upon the willows in the midst thereof.

3. For there they that carried us away captive required of us a song; and they that wasted us required of us mirth, saying, Sing us one of the songs of Zion.

4. How shall we sing the Lord's song in a strange land?

5. If I forget thee, O Jerusalem, let my right hand forget her cunning.

6. If I do not remember thee, let my tongue cleave to the roof of my mouth; if I prefer not Jerusalem above my chief joy.

7. Remember, O Lord, the children of Edom[2] in the day of Jerusalem; who said, Rase it, rase it, even to the foundation thereof.

8. O daughter of Babylon, who art to be destroyed; happy shall he be, that rewardeth thee as thou hast served us.

9. Happy shall he be, that taketh and dasheth thy little ones against the stones.

1. on the river Euphrates. Jerusalem was captured and sacked by the Babylonians in 586 B.C. The Jews were taken away into captivity in Babylon.
2. The Edomites helped the Babylonians to capture Jerusalem.

Amos*

4. Hear this word, ye kine[1] of Bashan, that are in the mountain of Samaria, which oppress the poor, which crush the needy, which say to their masters, Bring, and let us drink. The Lord God hath sworn by his holiness, that, lo, the days shall come upon you, that he will take you away with hooks, and your posterity with fishhooks. And ye shall go out at the breaches,[2] every cow at that which is before her; and ye shall cast them into the palace, saith the Lord.

Come to Beth-el, and transgress; at Gilgal multiply transgression; and bring your sacrifices every morning, and your tithes after three years: And offer a sacrifice of thanksgiving with leaven, and proclaim and publish the free offerings: for this liketh you,[3] O ye children of Israel, saith the Lord God.

And I also have given you cleanness of teeth[4] in all your cities, and want of bread in all your places: yet have ye not returned unto me, saith the Lord. And also I have withholden the rain from you, when there were yet three months to the harvest: and I caused it to rain upon one city, and caused it not to rain upon another city: one piece was rained upon, and the piece whereupon it rained not with-

* Chapters 4, 5.
1. *kine:* cows.
2. *breaches:* made in the city walls by the conquerors.
3. *this liketh you:* this is what you like. The people of Israel observe the outward forms of religion, but do not repent.
4. *cleanness of teeth:* hunger.

ered. So two or three cities wandered unto one city, to drink water;
but they were not satisfied: yet have ye not returned unto me, saith
the Lord. I have smitten you with blasting and mildew: when your
gardens and your vineyards and your fig trees and your olive trees
increased, the palmerworm devoured them: yet have ye not
returned unto me, saith the Lord. I have sent among you the pestilence after the manner of Egypt:[5] your young men have I slain with
the sword, and have taken away your horses; and I have made the
stink of your camps to come up unto your nostrils: yet have ye not
returned unto me, saith the Lord. I have overthrown some of you,
as God overthrew Sodom and Gomorrah, and ye were as a firebrand
plucked out of the burning: yet have ye not returned unto me, saith
the Lord. Therefore thus will I do unto thee, O Israel: and because
I will do this unto thee, prepare to meet thy God, O Israel. For,
lo, he that formeth the mountains, and createth the wind, and
declareth unto man what is his thought, that maketh the morning
darkness, and treadeth upon the high places of the earth, The Lord,
The God of hosts, is his name.

5. Hear ye this word which I take up against you, even a lamentation, O house of Israel. The virgin of Israel is fallen; she shall no
more rise: she is forsaken upon her land; there is none to raise her
up. For thus saith the Lord God; The city that went out by a thousand shall leave an hundred, and that which went forth by an
hundred shall leave ten, to the house of Israel.

For thus saith the Lord unto the house of Israel, Seek ye me, and
ye shall live: but seek not Beth-el, nor enter into Gilgal, and pass
not to Beersheba: for Gilgal shall surely go to captivity, and Beth-el
shall come to nought. Seek the Lord, and ye shall live; lest he break
out like fire in the house of Joseph, and devour it, and there be
none to quench it in Beth-el. Ye who turn judgment to wormwood,
and leave off righteousness in the earth, Seek him that maketh the
seven stars[6] and Orion, and turneth the shadow of death into the
morning, and maketh the day dark with night: that calleth for the
waters of the sea, and poureth them out upon the face of the earth:
The Lord is his name: That strengtheneth the spoiled against the
strong, so that the spoiled shall come against the fortress. They hate
him that rebuketh in the gate,[7] and they abhor him that speaketh
uprightly. Forasmuch therefore as your treading is upon the poor,
and ye take from him burdens of wheat: ye have built houses of
hewn stone, but ye shall not dwell in them; ye have planted pleasant vineyards, but ye shall not drink wine of them. For I know your
manifold transgressions and your mighty sins: they afflict the
just, they take a bribe, and they turn aside the poor in the gate from

5. *Egypt:* a reference to the plagues the
Lord inflicted on the Egyptians, when
they held the Israelites enslaved (Exodus,
Chapters 7–10).

6. *seven stars:* the Pleiades.

7. *rebuketh in the gate:* brings the
wrongdoer to justice.

their right. Therefore the prudent shall keep silence in that time; for it is an evil time. Seek good, and not evil, that ye may live: and so the Lord, the God of hosts, shall be with you, as ye have spoken.[8] Hate the evil, and love the good, and establish judgment in the gate: it may be that the Lord God of hosts will be gracious unto the remnant of Joseph.

Therefore the Lord, the God of hosts, the Lord, saith thus; Wailing shall be in all streets; and they shall say in all the highways, Alas! alas! and they shall call the husbandman to mourning, and such as are skilful of lamentation.to wailing. And in all vineyards shall be wailing: for I will pass through thee, saith the Lord. Woe unto you that desire the day of the Lord! to what end is it for you? the day of the Lord is darkness, and not light. As if a man did flee from a lion, and a bear met him; or went into the house, and leaned his hand on the wall, and a serpent bit him. Shall not the day of the Lord be darkness, and not light? even very dark, and no brightness in it?

I hate, I despise your feast days, and I will not smell in your solemn assemblies. Though ye offer me burnt offerings and your meat offerings, I will not accept them: neither will I regard the peace offerings of your fat beasts. Take thou away from me the noise of thy songs; for I will not hear the melody of thy viols. But let judgment run down as waters, and righteousness as a mighty stream. Have ye offered unto me sacrifices and offerings in the wilderness forty years, O house of Israel? But ye have borne the tabernacle of your Moloch and Chiun[9] your images, the star of your god, which ye made to yourselves. Therefore will I cause you to go into captivity beyond Damascus, saith the Lord, whose name is The God of hosts.

8. *as ye have spoken:* as you have said He is.   9. *Moloch, Chiun:* pagan deities.

Jonah

1. Now the word of the Lord came unto Jonah the son of Amittai, saying, Arise, go to Nineveh,[1] that great city, and cry against it; for their wickedness is come up before me. But Jonah rose up to flee unto Tarshish[2] from the presence of the Lord, and went down to Joppa;[3] and he found a ship going to Tarshish: so he paid the fare thereof, and went down into it, to go with them unto Tarshish from the presence of the Lord. But the Lord sent out a great wind into the sea, and there was a mighty tempest in the sea, so that the

1. *Nineveh:* on the river Tigris, the capital city of the Assyrians.
2. *Tarshish:* probably Tartessus, in Spain. Jonah intends to go west (instead of east to Nineveh) and as far away as he can.
3. *Joppa:* seaport on the coast of Palestine.

ship was like to be broken. Then the mariners were afraid, and cried every man unto his god, and cast forth the wares that were in the ship into the sea, to lighten it of them. But Jonah was gone down into the sides of the ship; and he lay, and was fast asleep. So the shipmaster came to him, and said unto him, What meanest thou, O sleeper? arise, call upon thy God, if so be that God will think upon us, that we perish not. And they said every one to his fellow, Come, and let us cast lots, that we may know for whose cause this evil is upon us. So they cast lots, and the lot fell upon Jonah. Then said they unto him, Tell us, we pray thee, for whose cause this evil is upon us; What is thine occupation? and whence comest thou? what is thy country? and of what people art thou? And he said unto them, I am an Hebrew; and I fear the Lord, the God of heaven, which hath made the sea and the dry land. Then were the men exceedingly afraid, and said unto him, Why hast thou done this? For the men knew that he fled from the presence of the Lord, because he had told them. Then said they unto him, What shall we do unto thee, that the sea may be calm unto us? for the sea wrought, and was tempestuous. And he said unto them, Take me up, and cast me forth into the sea; so shall the sea be calm unto you: for I know that for my sake this great tempest is upon you. Nevertheless the men rowed hard to bring it to the land; but they could not: for the sea wrought, and was tempestuous against them. Wherefore they cried unto the Lord, and said, We beseech thee, O Lord, we beseech thee, let us not perish for this man's life, and lay not upon us innocent blood: for thou, O Lord, hast done as it pleased thee. So they took up Jonah, and cast him forth into the sea: and the sea ceased from her raging. Then the men feared the Lord exceedingly, and offered a sacrifice unto the Lord, and made vows.

Now the Lord had prepared a great fish to swallow up Jonah. And Jonah was in the belly of the fish three days and three nights.

2. Then Jonah prayed unto the Lord his God out of the fish's belly, And said, I cried by reason of mine affliction unto the Lord, and he heard me; out of the belly of hell cried I, and thou heardest my voice. For thou hadst cast me into the deep, in the midst of the seas; and the floods compassed me about; all thy billows and thy waves passed over me. Then I said, I am cast out of thy sight; yet I will look again toward thy holy temple. The waters compassed me about, even to the soul: the depth closed me round about, the weeds were wrapped about my head. I went down to the bottoms of the mountains; the earth with her bars was about me for ever: yet hast thou brought up my life from corruption, O Lord my God. When my soul fainted within me I remembered the Lord: and my

prayer came in unto thee, into thine holy temple. They that observe lying vanities forsake their own mercy.[4] But I will sacrifice unto thee with the voice of thanksgiving; I will pay that that I have vowed. Salvation is of the Lord. And the Lord spake unto the fish, and it vomited out Jonah upon the dry land.

3. And the word of the Lord came unto Jonah the second time, saying, Arise, go unto Nineveh, that great city, and preach unto it the preaching that I bid thee. So Jonah arose, and went unto Nineveh, according to the word of the Lord. Now Nineveh was an exceeding great city of three days' journey. And Jonah began to enter into the city a day's journey, and he cried, and said, Yet forty days, and Nineveh shall be overthrown.

So the people of Nineveh believed God, and proclaimed a fast, and put on sackcloth, from the greatest of them even to the least of them. For word came unto the king of Nineveh, and he arose from his throne, and he laid his robe from him, and covered him with sackcloth, and sat in ashes. And he caused it to be proclaimed and published through Nineveh by the decree of the king and his nobles, saying, Let neither man nor beast, herd nor flock, taste any thing: let them not feed, nor drink water: But let man and beast be covered with sackcloth, and cry mightily unto God: yea, let them turn every one from his evil way, and from the violence that is in their hands. Who can tell if God will turn and repent, and turn away from his fierce anger, that we perish not?

And God saw their works, that they turned from their evil way; and God repented of the evil, that he had said that he would do unto them; and he did it not.

4. But it displeased Jonah exceedingly, and he was very angry. And he prayed unto the Lord, and said, I pray thee, O Lord, was not this my saying, when I was yet in my country? Therefore I fled before unto Tarshish: for I knew that thou art a gracious God, and merciful, slow to anger, and of great kindness, and repentest thee of the evil.[5] Therefore now, O Lord, take, I beseech thee, my life from me; for it is better for me to die than to live. Then said the Lord, Doest thou well to be angry? So Jonah went out of the city, and sat on the east side of the city, and there made him a booth,[6] and sat under it in the shadow, till he might see what would become of the city. And the Lord God prepared a gourd,[7] and made it to come up over Jonah, that it might be a shadow over his head, to deliver him from his grief. So Jonah was exceeding glad of the gourd. But God prepared a worm when the morning rose the

---

4. The general sense is: "those that worship false gods forfeit their claim to mercy."

5. *a gracious God . . . evil:* Jonah is quoting Scripture (Exodus 34:6).

6. *booth:* a tent shelter.

7. *gourd:* some kind of climbing plant.

next day, and it smote the gourd that it withered. And it came to pass, when the sun did arise, that God prepared a vehement east wind; and the sun beat upon the head of Jonah, that he fainted, and wished in himself to die, and said, It is better for me to die than to live. And God said to Jonah, Doest thou well to be angry for the gourd? And he said, I do well to be angry, even unto death. Then said the Lord, Thou hast had pity on the gourd, for the which thou hast not laboured, neither madest it grow; which came up in a night, and perished in a night: And should not I spare Nineveh, that great city, wherein are more than sixscore thousand persons that cannot discern between their right hand and their left hand;[8] and also much cattle?

8. i.e., children.

[*The Song of the Suffering Servant*]*

52:13. Behold, my servant shall deal prudently, he shall be exalted and extolled, and be very high.

14. As many were astonied at thee; his visage was so marred more than any man, and his form more than the sons of men:

15. So shall he sprinkle many nations; the kings shall shut their mouths at him: for that which had not been told them shall they see; and that which they had not heard shall they consider.

53:1. Who hath believed our report? and to whom is the arm of the Lord revealed?

2. For he shall grow up before him as a tender plant, and as a root out of a dry ground: he hath no form nor comeliness; and when we shall see him, there is no beauty that we should desire him.

3. He is despised and rejected of men; a man of sorrows, and acquainted with grief: and we hid as it were our faces from him; he was despised, and we esteemed him not.

4. Surely he hath borne our griefs, and carried our sorrows: yet we did esteem him stricken, smitten of God, and afflicted.

5. But he was wounded for our transgressions, he was bruised for our iniquities: the chastisement of our peace was upon him; and with his stripes we are healed.

6. All we like sheep have gone astray; we have turned every one to his own way; and the Lord hath laid on him the iniquity of us all.

7. He was oppressed, and he was afflicted, yet he opened not his mouth: he is brought as a lamb to the slaughter, and as a sheep before her shearers is dumb, so he openeth not his mouth.

8. He was taken from prison and from judgment: and who shall declare his generation? for he was cut off out of the land of the living: for the transgression of my people was he stricken.

* Isaiah 52:13—53:12

9. And he made his grave with the wicked, and with the rich[1] in his death; because he had done no violence, neither was any deceit in his mouth.

10. Yet it pleased the Lord to bruise him; he hath put him to grief: when thou shalt make his soul an offering for sin, he shall see his seed, he shall prolong his days, and the pleasure of the Lord shall prosper in his hand.

11. He shall see the travail of his soul, and shall be satisfied: by his knowledge shall my righteous servant justify many; for he shall bear their iniquities.

12. Therefore will I divide him a portion with the great, and he shall divide the spoil with the strong; because he hath poured out his soul unto death: and he was numbered with the transgressors; and he bare the sin of many, and made intercession for the transgressors.

1. Some editors emend the Hebrew to give the meaning, "evildoers."

HOMER

The Iliad *

[The Quarrel of Achilles and Agamemnon]

Book I

Sing, goddess, the anger of Peleus' son Achilleus
and its devastation, which put pains thousandfold upon the
 Achaians,
hurled in their multitudes to the house of Hades strong souls
of heroes, but gave their bodies to be the delicate feasting
of dogs, of all birds, and the will of Zeus was accomplished   5
since that time when first there stood in division of conflict
Atreus' son the lord of men and brilliant Achilleus.

What god was it then set them together in bitter collision?
Zeus' son and Leto's, Apollo, who in anger at the king drove
the foul pestilence along the host, and the people perished,   10
since Atreus' son had dishonoured Chryses, priest of Apollo,
when he came beside the fast ships of the Achaians to ransom
back his daughter, carrying gifts beyond count and holding
in his hands wound on a staff of gold the ribbons of Apollo
who strikes from afar, and supplicated all the Achaians,   15

* Abridged. Traditionally supposed to have been composed *ca.* 850 B.C. From *The Iliad of Homer*, translated and with an introduction by Richmond Lattimore. University of Chicago Press. Copyright, 1951, by the University of Chicago.

1. *goddess:* the Muse. *Achilleus:* The translator has transliterated the original Greek names, rather than use the more familiar Latin forms. Thus we find "Achilleus" instead of "Achilles," "Achaians" instead of "Achaeans," and so on.

2. *Achaians:* the Greeks. Homer also calls them Danaans and Argives.

7. *Atreus' son:* Agamemnon, the commander of the Greek army.

11. *Chryses:* His daughter is called Chryseis, and the place where he lives, Chryse.

but above all Atreus' two sons, the marshals of the people:
'Sons of Atreus and you other strong-greaved Achaians,
to you may the gods grant who have their homes on Olympos
Priam's city to be plundered and a fair homecoming thereafter,
but may you give me back my own daughter and take the ransom,   20
giving honour to Zeus' son who strikes from afar, Apollo.'
    Then all the rest of the Achaians cried out in favour
that the priest be respected and the shining ransom be taken;
yet this pleased not the heart of Atreus' son Agamemnon,
but harshly he drove him away with a strong order upon him: 25
'Never let me find you again, old sir, near our hollow
ships, neither lingering now nor coming again hereafter,
for fear your staff and the god's ribbons help you no longer.
The girl I will not give back; sooner will old age come upon her
in my own house, in Argos, far from her own land, going   30
up and down by the loom and being in my bed as my companion.
So go now, do not make me angry; so you will be safer.'
    So he spoke, and the old man in terror obeyed him
and went silently away beside the murmuring sea beach.
Over and over the old man prayed as he walked in solitude   35
to King Apollo, whom Leto of the lovely hair bore: 'Hear me,
lord of the silver bow who set your power about Chryse
and Killa the sacrosanct, who are lord in strength over Tenedos,
Smintheus, if ever it pleased your heart that I built your temple,
if ever it pleased you that I burned all the rich thigh pieces   40
of bulls, of goats, then bring to pass this wish I pray for:
let your arrows make the Danaans pay for my tears shed.'
    So he spoke in prayer, and Phoibos Apollo heard him,
and strode down along the pinnacles of Olympos, angered
in his heart, carrying across his shoulders the bow and the hooded   45
quiver; and the shafts clashed on the shoulders of the god walking
angrily. He came as night comes down and knelt then
apart and opposite the ships and let go an arrow.
Terrible was the clash that rose from the bow of silver.
First he went after the mules and the circling hounds, then let go   50
a tearing arrow against the men themselves and struck them.
The corpse fires burned everywhere and did not stop burning.
    Nine days up and down the host ranged the god's arrows,
but on the tenth Achilleus called the people to assembly;

16. *Atreus' two sons:* Agamemnon
and his brother Menelaos.
    17. *strong-greaved:* The greave is a
piece of armor which fits over the leg
below the knee.
    19. *Priam's city:* Priam was king of
Troy.
    37–38. *Chryse and Killa:* cities near
Troy.
    38. *Tenedos:* an island off the Trojan
coast.

39. *Smintheus:* a cult name of Apollo,
probably a reference to his rôle as the
destroyer of field mice. The Greek
sminthos means "mouse."
    42. *Danaans:* Greeks.
    44. *Olympos:* the mountain in north-
ern Greece which was supposed to be
the home of the gods.

a thing put into his mind by the goddess of the white arms, Hera,
who had pity upon the Danaans when she saw them dying. 56
Now when they were all assembled in one place together,
Achilleus of the swift feet stood up among them and spoke forth:
'Son of Atreus, I believe now that straggling backwards
we must make our way home if we can even escape death, 60
if fighting now must crush the Achaians and the plague likewise.
No, come, let us ask some holy man, some prophet,
even an interpreter of dreams, since a dream also
comes from Zeus, who can tell why Phoibos Apollo is so angry,
if for the sake of some vow, some hecatomb he blames us, 65
if given the fragrant smoke of lambs, of he goats, somehow
he can be made willing to beat the bane aside from us.'

He spoke thus and sat down again, and among them stood up
Kalchas, Thestor's son, far the best of the bird interpreters, 69
who knew all things that were, the things to come and the things
    past,
who guided into the land of Ilion the ships of the Achaians
through that seercraft of his own that Phoibos Apollo gave him.
He in kind intention toward all stood forth and addressed them:
'You have bidden me, Achilleus beloved of Zeus, to explain to
you this anger of Apollo the lord who strikes from afar. Then 75
I will speak; yet make me a promise and swear before me
readily by word and work of your hands to defend me,
since I believe I shall make a man angry who holds great kingship
over the men of Argos, and all the Achaians obey him.
For a king when he is angry with a man beneath him is too strong,
and suppose even for the day itself he swallow down his anger, 81
he still keeps bitterness that remains until its fulfilment
deep in his chest. Speak forth then, tell me if you will protect me.'

Then in answer again spoke Achilleus of the swift feet:
'Speak, interpreting whatever you know, and fear nothing. 85
In the name of Apollo beloved of Zeus to whom you, Kalchas,
make your prayers when you interpret the gods' will to the Danaans,
no man so long as I am alive above earth and see daylight
shall lay the weight of his hands on you beside the hollow ships,
not one of all the Danaans, even if you mean Agamemnon, 90
who now claims to be far the greatest of all the Achaians.'

At this the blameless seer took courage again and spoke forth:
'No, it is not for the sake of some vow or hecatomb he blames us,
but for the sake of his priest whom Agamemnon dishonoured
and would not give him back his daughter nor accept the ransom.
Therefore the archer sent griefs against us and will send them 96

---

55. *Hera:* sister and wife of Zeus, the father of the gods; she was hostile to the Trojans.

65. *hecatomb:* Strictly, the word de-notes a sacrifice of a hundred animals, but it is often used to refer to smaller offerings.

71. *Ilion:* Troy.

still, nor sooner thrust back the shameful plague from the Danaans
until we give the glancing-eyed girl back to her father
without price, without ransom, and lead also a blessed hecatomb
to Chryse; thus we might propitiate and persuade him.'   100

He spoke thus and sat down again, and among them stood up
Atreus' son the hero wide-ruling Agamemnon
raging, the heart within filled black to the brim with anger
from beneath, but his two eyes showed like fire in their blazing.
First of all he eyed Kalchas bitterly and spoke to him: 105

'Seer of evil: never yet have you told me a good thing.
Always the evil things are dear to your heart to prophesy,
but nothing excellent have you said nor ever accomplished.
Now once more you make divination to the Danaans, argue
forth your reason why he who strikes from afar afflicts them,   110
because I for the sake of the girl Chryseis would not take
the shining ransom; and indeed I wish greatly to have her
in my own house; since I like her better than Klytaimnestra
my own wife, for in truth she is no way inferior,
neither in build nor stature nor wit, nor in accomplishment.   115
Still I am willing to give her back, if such is the best way.
I myself desire that my people be safe, not perish.
Find me then some prize that shall be my own, lest I only
among the Argives go without, since that were unfitting;
you are all witnesses to this thing, that my prize goes elsewhere.'   120

Then in answer again spoke brilliant swift-footed Achilleus:
'Son of Atreus, most lordly, greediest for gain of all men,
how shall the great-hearted Achaians give you a prize now?
There is no great store of things lying about I know of.
But what we took from the cities by storm has been distributed;   125
it is unbecoming for the people to call back things once given.
No, for the present give the girl back to the god; we Achaians
thrice and four times over will repay you, if ever Zeus gives
into our hands the strong-walled citadel of Troy to be plundered.

Then in answer again spoke powerful Agamemnon: 130
'Not that way, good fighter though you be, godlike Achilleus,
strive to cheat, for you will not deceive, you will not persuade me.
What do you want? To keep your own prize and have me sit here
lacking one? Are you ordering me to give this girl back?
Either the great-hearted Achaians shall give me a new prize   135
chosen according to my desire to atone for the girl lost,
or else if they will not give me one I myself shall take her,
your own prize, or that of Aias, or that of Odysseus,
going myself in person; and he whom I visit will be bitter.
Still, these are things we shall deliberate again hereafter.   140
Come, now, we must haul a black ship down to the bright sea,

---

138. *Aias*: Ajax, the bravest of the Greeks after Achilleus. *Odysseus*: the most
subtle and crafty of the Greeks.

and assemble rowers enough for it, and put on board it
the hecatomb, and the girl herself, Chryseis of the fair cheeks,
and let there be one responsible man in charge of her,
either Aias or Idomeneus or brilliant Odysseus,   145
or you yourself, son of Peleus, most terrifying of all men,
to reconcile by accomplishing sacrifice the archer.'
    Then looking darkly at him Achilleus of the swift feet spoke:
'O wrapped in shamelessness, with your mind forever on profit,
how shall any one of the Achaians readily obey you   150
either to go on a journey or to fight men strongly in battle?
I for my part did not come here for the sake of the Trojan
spearmen to fight against them, since to me they have done nothing.
Never yet have they driven away my cattle or my horses,
never in Phthia where the soil is rich and men grow great did they
spoil my harvest, since indeed there is much that lies between us, 156
the shadowy mountains and the echoing sea; but for your sake,
o great shamelessness, we followed, to do you favour,
you with the dog's eyes, to win your honour and Menelaos'
from the Trojans. You forget all this or else you care nothing.   160
And now my prize you threaten in person to strip from me,
for whom I laboured much, the gift of the sons of the Achaians.
Never, when the Achaians sack some well-founded citadel
of the Trojans, do I have a prize that is equal to your prize.
Always the greater part of the painful fighting is the work of 165
my hands; but when the time comes to distribute the booty
yours is far the greater reward, and I with some small thing
yet dear to me go back to my ships when I am weary with fighting.
Now I am returning to Phthia, since it is much better
to go home again with my curved ships, and I am minded no longer
to stay here dishonoured and pile up your wealth and your luxury.'
    Then answered him in turn the lord of men Agamemnon: 172
'Run away by all means if your heart drives you. I will not
entreat you to stay here for my sake. There are others with me
who will do me honour, and above all Zeus of the counsels.   175
To me you are the most hateful of all the kings whom the gods love.
Forever quarrelling is dear to your heart, and wars and battles;
and if you are very strong indeed, that is a god's gift.
Go home then with your own ships and your own companions,
be king over the Myrmidons. I care nothing about you.   180
I take no account of your anger. But here is my threat to you.
Even as Phoibos Apollo is taking away my Chryseis.
I shall convey her back in my own ship, with my own
followers; but I shall take the fair-cheeked Briseis,
your prize, I myself going to your shelter, that you may learn well 185

---

155. *Phthia:* Achilleus' home in northern Greece.

159. *and Menelaos':* The aim of the expedition was to recapture Helen, the wife of Menelaos, who had run off to Troy with Priam's son Paris.

180. *Myrmidons:* the name of Achilleus' people.

how much greater I am than you, and another man may shrink back
from likening himself to me and contending against me.'

So he spoke. And the anger came on Peleus' son, and within
his shaggy breast the heart was divided two ways, pondering
whether to draw from beside his thigh the sharp sword, driving   190
away all those who stood between and kill the son of Atreus,
or else to check the spleen within and keep down his anger.
Now as he weighed in mind and spirit these two courses
and was drawing from its scabbard the great sword, Athene descended
from the sky. For Hera the goddess of the white arms sent her,   195
who loved both men equally in her heart and cared for them.
The goddess standing behind Peleus' son caught him by the fair hair,
appearing to him only, for no man of the others saw her.
Achilleus in amazement turned about, and straightway
knew Pallas Athene and the terrible eyes shining.   200
He uttered winged words and addressed her: 'Why have you come now,
o child of Zeus of the aegis, once more? Is it that you may see
the outrageousness of the son of Atreus Agamemnon?
Yet will I tell you this thing, and I think it shall be accomplished.
By such acts of arrogance he may even lose his own life.'   205

Then in answer the goddess grey-eyed Athene spoke to him:
'I have come down to stay your anger—but will you obey me?—
from the sky; and the goddess of the white arms Hera sent me,
who loves both of you equally in her heart and cares for you.   209
Come then, do not take your sword in your hand, keep clear of
    fighting,
though indeed with words you may abuse him, and it will be that
    way.
And this also will I tell you and it will be a thing accomplished.
Some day three times over such shining gifts shall be given you
by reason of this outrage. Hold your hand then, and obey us.'

Then in answer again spoke Achilleus of the swift feet: 215
'Goddess, it is necessary that I obey the word of you two,
angry though I am in my heart. So it will be better.
If any man obeys the gods, they listen to him also.'

He spoke, and laid his heavy hand on the silver sword hilt
and thrust the great blade back into the scabbard nor disobeyed   220
the word of Athene. And she went back again to Olympos
to the house of Zeus of the aegis with the other divinities.

But Peleus' son once again in words of derision

---

194. *Athene:* a goddess, daughter
of Zeus, a patron of human ingenuity
and resourcefulness, whether exemplified
by handicrafts, such as spinning, or by
skill in human relations, such as her
favorite among the Greeks, Odysseus,
possessed. She supported the Greek
side in the war.

202. *aegis:* a terrible shield with
which Zeus (or any other god to whom
it was entrusted) stirred up storms or
threw panic into human beings.

spoke to Atreides, and did not yet let go of his anger:
'You wine sack, with a dog's eyes, with a deer's heart. Never   225
once have you taken courage in your heart to arm with your people
for battle, or go into ambuscade with the best of the Achaians.
No, for in such things you see death. Far better to your mind
is it, all along the widespread host of the Achaians
to take away the gifts of any man who speaks up against you.   230
King who feed on your people, since you rule nonentities;
otherwise, son of Atreus, this were your last outrage.
But I will tell you this and swear a great oath upon it:
in the name of this sceptre, which never again will bear leaf nor
branch, now that it has left behind the cut stump in the moun-
        tains,   235
nor shall it ever blossom again, since the bronze blade stripped
bark and leafage, and now at last the sons of the Achaians
carry it in their hands in state when they administer
the justice of Zeus. And this shall be a great oath before you:
some day longing for Achilleus will come to the sons of the
        Achaians,   240
all of them. Then stricken at heart though you be, you will be able
to do nothing, when in their numbers before man-slaughtering
        Hektor
they drop and die. And then you will eat out the heart within you
in sorrow, that you did no honour to the best of the Achaians.'

Thus spoke Peleus' son and dashed to the ground the sceptre   245
studded with golden nails, and sat down again. But Atreides
raged still on the other side, and between them Nestor
the fair-spoken rose up, the lucid speaker of Pylos,
from whose lips the streams of words ran sweeter than honey.
In his time two generations of mortal men had perished,   250
those who had grown up with him and they who had been born to
these in sacred Pylos, and he was king in the third age.
He in kind intention toward both stood forth and addressed them:
'Oh, for shame. Great sorrow comes on the land of Achaia.
Now might Priam and the sons of Priam in truth be happy,   255
and all the rest of the Trojans be visited in their hearts with glad-
        ness,
were they to hear all this wherein you two are quarrelling,
you, who surpass all Danaans in council, in fighting.
Yet be persuaded. Both of you are younger than I am.
Yes, and in my time I have dealt with better men than   260
you are, and never once did they disregard me. Never
yet have I seen nor shall see again such men as these were,
men like Peirithoös, and Dryas, shepherd of the people,
Kaineus and Exadios, godlike Polyphemos,

242. *Hektor:* son of Priam; the fore-most warrior of the Trojans.
246. *Atreides:* son of Atreus, i.e.,
Agamemnon.
248. *Pylos:* on the western shore of the Peloponnese.

or Theseus, Aigeus' son, in the likeness of the immortals.   265
These were the strongest generation of earth-born mortals,

the strongest, and they fought against the strongest, the beast men
living within the mountains, and terribly they destroyed them.
I was of the company of these men, coming from Pylos,
a long way from a distant land, since they had summoned me.   270
And I fought single-handed, yet against such men no one
of the mortals now alive upon earth could do battle. And also
these listened to the counsels I gave and heeded my bidding.
Do you also obey, since to be persuaded is better.
You, great man that you are, yet do not take the girl away   275
but let her be, a prize as the sons of the Achaians gave her
first. Nor, son of Peleus, think to match your strength with
the king, since never equal with the rest is the portion of honour
of the sceptred king to whom Zeus gives magnificence. Even
though you are the stronger man, and the mother who bore you was
         immortal,   280
yet is this man greater who is lord over more than you rule.
Son of Atreus, give up your anger; even I entreat you
to give over your bitterness against Achilleus, he who
stands as a great bulwark of battle over all the Achaians.'

     Then in answer again spoke powerful Agamemnon: 285
'Yes, old sir, all this you have said is fair and orderly.
Yet here is a man who wishes to be above all others,
who wishes to hold power over all, and to be lord of
all, and give them their orders, yet I think one will not obey him.
And if the everlasting gods have made him a spearman,   290
yet they have not given him the right to speak abusively.'

     Then looking at him darkly brilliant Achilleus answered him:
'So must I be called of no account and a coward
if I must carry out every order you may happen to give me.
Tell other men to do these things, but give me no more   295
commands, since I for my part have no intention to obey you.
And put away in your thoughts this other thing I tell you.
With my hands I will not fight for the girl's sake, neither
with you nor any other man, since you take her away who gave her.
But of all the other things that are mine beside my fast black   300
ship, you shall take nothing away against my pleasure.
Come, then, only try it, that these others may see also;
instantly your own black blood will stain my spearpoint.'

     So these two after battling in words of contention
stood up, and broke the assembly beside the ships of the Achaians.
Peleus' son went back to his balanced ships and his shelter   306
with Patroklos, Menoitios' son, and his own companions.
But the son of Atreus drew a fast ship down to the water

280. *mother:* Achilleus' mother was
Thetis, a sea nymph. She was married
to a mortal, Peleus (Achilleus' father),
but later left humankind and went to
live with her father, Nereus, in the
depths of the Aegean Sea.

and allotted into it twenty rowers and put on board it
the hecatomb for the god and Chryseis of the fair cheeks   310
leading her by the hand. And in charge went crafty Odysseus.
    These then putting out went over the ways of the water
while Atreus' son told his people to wash off their defilement.
And they washed it away and threw the washings into the salt sea.
Then they accomplished perfect hecatombs to Apollo,   315
of bulls and goats along the beach of the barren salt sea.
The savour of the burning swept in circles up to the bright sky.
    Thus these were busy about the army. But Agamemnon
did not give up his anger and the first threat he made to Achilleus,
but to Talthybios he gave his orders and Eurybates   320
who were heralds and hard-working henchmen to him: 'Go now
to the shelter of Peleus' son Achilleus, to bring back
Briseis of the fair cheeks leading her by the hand. And if he
will not give her, I must come in person to take her
with many men behind me, and it will be the worse for him.'   325
    He spoke and sent them forth with this strong order upon them.
They went against their will beside the beach of the barren
salt sea, and came to the shelters and the ships of the Myrmidons.
The man himself they found beside his shelter and his black ship
sitting. And Achilleus took no joy at all when he saw them.   330
These two terrified and in awe of the king stood waiting
quietly, and did not speak a word at all nor question him.
But he knew the whole matter in his own heart, and spoke first:
'Welcome, heralds, messengers of Zeus and of mortals.
Draw near. You are not to blame in my sight, but Agamemnon   335
who sent the two of you here for the sake of the girl Briseis.
Go then, illustrious Patroklos, and bring the girl forth
and give her to these to be taken away. Yet let them be witnesses
in the sight of the blessed gods, in the sight of mortal
men, and of this cruel king, if ever hereafter   340
there shall be need of me to beat back the shameful destruction
from the rest. For surely in ruinous heart he makes sacrifice
and has not wit enough to look behind and before him
that the Achaians fighting beside their ships shall not perish.'
    So he spoke, and Patroklos obeyed his beloved companion.   345
He led forth from the hut Briseis of the fair cheeks and gave her
to be taken away; and they walked back beside the ships of the
        Achaians,
and the woman all unwilling went with them still. But Achilleus
weeping went and sat in sorrow apart from his companions
beside the beach of the grey sea looking out on the infinite water. 350
Many times stretching forth his hands he called on his mother:
'Since, my mother, you bore me to be a man with a short life,

therefore Zeus of the loud thunder on Olympos should grant me
honour at least. But now he has given me not even a little.
Now the son of Atreus, powerful Agamemnon,   355
has dishonoured me, since he has taken away my prize and keeps it.'

So he spoke in tears and the lady his mother heard him
as she sat in the depths of the sea at the side of her aged father,
and lightly she emerged like a mist from the grey water.
She came and sat beside him as he wept, and stroked him   360
with her hand and called him by name and spoke to him: 'Why
        then,
child, do you lament? What sorrow has come to your heart now?
Tell me, do not hide it in your mind, and thus we shall both know.'

Sighing heavily Achilleus of the swift feet answered her:
'You know; since you know why must I tell you all this?   365
We went against Thebe, the sacred city of Eëtion,
and the city we sacked, and carried everything back to this place,
and the sons of the Achaians made a fair distribution
and for Atreus' son they chose out Chryseis of the fair cheeks.
Then Chryses, priest of him who strikes from afar, Apollo,   370
came beside the fast ships of the bronze-armoured Achaians to
        ransom
back his daughter, carrying gifts beyond count and holding
in his hands wound on a staff of gold the ribbons of Apollo
who strikes from afar, and supplicated all the Achaians,
but above all Atreus' two sons, the marshals of the people.   375
Then all the rest of the Achaians cried out in favour
that the priest be respected and the shining ransom be taken;
yet this pleased not the heart of Atreus' son Agamemnon,
but harshly he sent him away with a strong order upon him.
The old man went back again in anger, but Apollo   380
listened to his prayer, since he was very dear to him, and let go
the wicked arrow against the Argives. And now the people
were dying one after another while the god's shafts ranged
everywhere along the wide host of the Achaians, till the seer
knowing well the truth interpreted the designs of the archer.   385
It was I first of all urged then the god's appeasement;
and the anger took hold of Atreus' son, and in speed standing
he uttered his threat against me, and now it is a thing accomplished.
For the girl the glancing-eyed Achaians are taking to Chryse
in a fast ship, also carrying to the king presents. But even   390
now the heralds went away from my shelter leading
Briseus' daughter, whom the sons of the Achaians gave me.
You then, if you have power to, protect your own son, going

366. *Thebe:* a city in Trojan terri-   390. *the king:* Apollo.
tory.

to Olympos and supplicating Zeus, if ever before now
either by word you comforted Zeus' heart or by action.   395
Since it is many times in my father's halls I have heard you
making claims, when you said you only among the immortals
beat aside shameful destruction from Kronos' son the dark-misted,
that time when all the other Olympians sought to bind him,
Hera and Poseidon and Pallas Athene. Then you,   400
goddess, went and set him free from his shackles, summoning
in speed the creature of the hundred hands to tall Olympos,
that creature the gods name Briareus, but all men
Aigaios' son, but he is far greater in strength than his father.
He rejoicing in the glory of it sat down by Kronion,   405
and the rest of the blessed gods were frightened and gave up
    binding him.
Sit beside him and take his knees and remind him of these things
now, if perhaps he might be willing to help the Trojans,
and pin the Achaians back against the ships and the water,
dying, so that thus they may all have profit of their own king,   410
that Atreus' son wide-ruling Agamemnon may recognize
his madness, that he did no honour to the best of the Achaians.'
    Thetis answered him then letting the tears fall: 'Ah me,
my child. Your birth was bitterness. Why did I raise you?
If only you could sit by your ships untroubled, not weeping,   415
since indeed your lifetime is to be short, of no length.
Now it has befallen that your life must be brief and bitter
beyond all men's. To a bad destiny I bore you in my chambers.
But I will go to cloud-dark Olympos and ask this
thing of Zeus who delights in the thunder. Perhaps he will do it.   420
Do you therefore continuing to sit by your swift ships
be angry at the Achaians and stay away from all fighting.
For Zeus went to the blameless Aithiopians at the Ocean
yesterday to feast, and the rest of the gods went with him.
On the twelfth day he will be coming back to Olympos,   425
and then I will go for your sake to the house of Zeus, bronze-
    founded,
and take him by the knees and I think I can persuade him.'
    So speaking she went away from that place and left him
sorrowing in his heart for the sake of the fair-girdled woman
whom they were taking by force against his will. But Odysseus   430
meanwhile drew near to Chryse conveying the sacred hecatomb.

---

398. *Kronos' son:* Zeus. *dark-misted:*
Zeus is the god of the sky, who brings
rain and sunshine.
400. *Poseidon:* brother of Zeus; god
of the sea.
402. *Briareus:* a giant, son of
Poseidon.

405. *Kronion:* Zeus.
423. *Ocean:* the river which was believed to encircle the whole world. The
Aithiopians (Ethiopians) were thought
to live at the extreme edges of the
world.

These when they were inside the many-hollowed harbour
took down and gathered together the sails and stowed them in the
    black ship,
let down mast by the forestays, and settled it into the mast crutch
easily, and rowed her in with oars to the mooring.   435
They threw over the anchor stones and made fast the stern cables
and themselves stepped out on to the break of the sea beach,
and led forth the hecatomb to the archer Apollo,
and Chryseis herself stepped forth from the sea-going vessel.
Odysseus of the many designs guided her to the altar   440
and left her in her father's arms and spoke a word to him:
'Chryses, I was sent here by the lord of men Agamemnon
to lead back your daughter and accomplish a sacred hecatomb
to Apollo on behalf of the Danaans, that we may propitiate
the lord who has heaped unhappiness and tears on the Argives.'   445
    He spoke, and left her in his arms. And he received gladly
his beloved child. And the men arranged the sacred hecatomb
for the god in orderly fashion around the strong-founded altar.
Next they washed their hands and took up the scattering barley.
Standing among them with lifted arms Chryses prayed in a great
    voice: 450
'Hear me, lord of the silver bow, who set your power about
Chryse and Killa the sacrosanct, who are lord in strength over
Tenedos; if once before you listened to my prayers
and did me honour and smote strongly the host of the Achaians,
so one more time bring to pass the wish that I pray for.   455
Beat aside at last the shameful plague from the Danaans.'
    So he spoke in prayer, and Phoibos Apollo heard him.
And when all had made prayer and flung down the scattering barley
first they drew back the victims' heads and slaughtered them and
    skinned them,
and cut away the meat from the thighs and wrapped them in fat,   460
making a double fold, and laid shreds of flesh upon them.
The old man burned these on a cleft stick and poured the gleaming
wine over, while the young men with forks in their hands stood
    about him.
But when they had burned the thigh pieces and tasted the vitals,
they cut all the remainder into pieces and spitted them   465
and roasted all carefully and took off the pieces.
Then after they had finished the work and got the feast ready
they feasted, nor was any man's hunger denied a fair portion.
But when they had put away their desire for eating and drinking,
the young men filled the mixing bowls with pure wine, passing
a portion to all, when they had offered drink in the goblets.   471
All day long they propitiated the god with singing,

chanting a splendid hymn to Apollo, these young Achaians,
singing to the one who works from afar, who listened in gladness.
    Afterwards when the sun went down and darkness came on-
ward   475
they lay down and slept beside the ship's stern cables.
But when the young Dawn showed again with her rosy fingers,
they put forth to sea toward the wide camp of the Achaians.
And Apollo who works from afar sent them a favouring stern wind.
They set up the mast again and spread on it the white sails,   480
and the wind blew into the middle of the sail, and at the cutwater
a blue wave rose and sang strongly as the ship went onward.
She ran swiftly cutting across the swell her pathway.
But when they had come back to the wide camp of the Achaians
they hauled the black ship up on the mainland, high up   485
on the sand, and underneath her they fixed the long props.
Afterwards they scattered to their own ships and their shelters.
    But that other still sat in anger beside his swift ships,
Peleus' son divinely born, Achilleus of the swift feet.
Never now would he go to assemblies where men win glory,   490
never more into battle, but continued to waste his heart out
sitting there, though he longed always for the clamour and fighting.
    But when the twelfth dawn after this day appeared, the gods who
live forever came back to Olympos all in a body
and Zeus led them; nor did Thetis forget the entreaties   495
of her son, but she emerged from the sea's waves early
in the morning and went up to the tall sky and Olympos.
She found Kronos' broad-browed son apart from the others
sitting upon the highest peak of rugged Olympos.
She came and sat beside him with her left hand embracing   500
his knees, but took him underneath the chin with her right hand
and spoke in supplication to lord Zeus son of Kronos:
'Father Zeus, if ever before in word or action
I did you favour among the immortals, now grant what I ask for.
Now give honour to my son short-lived beyond all other   505
mortals. Since even now the lord of men Agamemnon
dishonours him, who has taken away his prize and keeps it.
Zeus of the counsels, lord of Olympos, now do him honour.
So long put strength into the Trojans, until the Achaians
give my son his rights, and his honour is increased among them.'   510
    She spoke thus. But Zeus who gathers the clouds made no answer
but sat in silence a long time. And Thetis, as she had taken
his knees, clung fast to them and urged once more her question:
'Bend your head and promise me to accomplish this thing,

500–501. *embracing his knees . . . chin:* the posture of the suppliant, who by this physical pressure emphasized his desperation and the urgency of the request. Zeus was above all other gods the protector of suppliants.

or else refuse it, you have nothing to fear, that I may know   515
by how much I am the most dishonoured of all gods.'
   Deeply disturbed Zeus who gathers the clouds answered her:
'This is a disastrous matter when you set me in conflict
with Hera, and she troubles me with recriminations.
Since even as things are, forever among the immortals   520
she is at me and speaks of how I help the Trojans in battle.
Even so, go back again now, go away, for fear she
see us. I will look to these things that they be accomplished.
See then, I will bend my head that you may believe me.
For this among the immortal gods is the mightiest witness   525
I can give, and nothing I do shall be vain nor revocable
nor a thing unfulfilled when I bend my head in assent to it.'
   He spoke, the son of Kronos, and nodded his head with the dark
     brows,
and the immortally anointed hair of the great god
swept from his divine head, and all Olympos was shaken.   530
   So these two who had made their plans separated, and Thetis
leapt down again from shining Olympos into the sea's depth,
but Zeus went back to his own house, and all the gods rose up
from their chairs to greet the coming of their father, not one had
     courage
to keep his place as the father advanced, but stood up to greet
     him.   535
Thus he took his place on the throne; yet Hera was not
ignorant, having seen how he had been plotting counsels
with Thetis the silver-footed, the daughter of the sea's ancient,
and at once she spoke revilingly to Zeus son of Kronos:
'Treacherous one, what god has been plotting counsels with you?   540
Always it is dear to your heart in my absence to think of
secret things and decide upon them. Never have you patience
frankly to speak forth to me the thing that you purpose.'
   Then to her the father of gods and men made answer:
'Hera, do not go on hoping that you will hear all my   545
thoughts, since these will be too hard for you, though you are my
     wife.
Any thought that it is right for you to listen to, no one
neither man nor any immortal shall hear it before you.
But anything that apart from the rest of the gods I wish to
plan, do not always question each detail nor probe me.'   550
   Then the goddess the ox-eyed lady Hera answered:
'Majesty, son of Kronos, what sort of thing have you spoken?
Truly too much in time past I have not questioned nor probed you,
but you are entirely free to think out whatever pleases you.

538. *the sea's ancient:* Nereus.

Now, though, I am terrible afraid you were won over   555
by Thetis the silver-footed, the daughter of the sea's ancient.
For early in the morning she sat beside you and took your
knees, and I think you bowed your head in assent to do honour
to Achilleus, and to destroy many beside the ships of the Achaians.'

Then in return Zeus who gathers the clouds made answer: 560
'Dear lady, I never escape you, you are always full of suspicion.
Yet thus you can accomplish nothing surely, but be more
distant from my heart than ever, and it will be the worse for you.
If what you say is true, then that is the way I wish it.
But go then, sit down in silence, and do as I tell you,   565
for fear all the gods, as many as are on Olympos, can do nothing
if I come close and lay my unconquerable hands upon you.'

He spoke, and the goddess the ox-eyed lady Hera was frightened
and went and sat down in silence wrenching her heart to obedience,
and all the Uranian gods in the house of Zeus were troubled.   570
Hephaistos the renowned smith rose up to speak among them,
to bring comfort to his beloved mother, Hera of the white arms:
'This will be a disastrous matter and not endurable
if you two are to quarrel thus for the sake of mortals
and bring brawling among the gods. There will be no pleasure   575
in the stately feast at all, since vile things will be uppermost.
And I entreat my mother, though she herself understands it,
to be ingratiating toward our father Zeus, that no longer
our father may scold her and break up the quiet of our feasting.
For if the Olympian who handles the lightning should be   580
minded to hurl us out of our places, he is far too strong for any.
Do you therefore approach him again with words made gentle,
and at once the Olympian will be gracious again to us.'

He spoke, and springing to his feet put a two-handled goblet
into his mother's hands and spoke again to her once more: 585
'Have patience, my mother, and endure it, though you be saddened,
for fear that, dear as you are, I see you before my own eyes
struck down, and then sorry though I be I shall not be able
to do anything. It is too hard to fight against the Olympian.
There was a time once before now I was minded to help you,   590
and he caught me by the foot and threw me from the magic
          threshold,
and all day long I dropped helpless, and about sunset
I landed in Lemnos, and there was not much life left in me.
After that fall it was the Sintian men who took care of me.'

He spoke, and the goddess of the white arms Hera smiled at
          him,   595

570. *Uranian:* The Greek word *uranos* means "sky," "heaven."

571. *Hephaistos:* the patron god of craftsmen, especially workers in metal.

593. *Lemnos:* an island in the Aegean Sea.

594. *Sintian men:* the ancient inhabitants of Lemnos.

and smiling she accepted the goblet out of her son's hand.
Thereafter beginning from the left he poured drinks for the other
gods, dipping up from the mixing bowl the sweet nectar.
But among the blessed immortals uncontrollable laughter
went up as they saw Hephaistos bustling about the palace.   600
    Thus thereafter the whole day long until the sun went under
they feasted, nor was anyone's hunger denied a fair portion,
nor denied the beautifully wrought lyre in the hands of Apollo
nor the antiphonal sweet sound of the Muses singing.
    Afterwards when the light of the flaming sun went under   605
they went away each one to sleep in his home where
for each one the far-renowned strong-handed Hephaistos
had built a house by means of his craftsmanship and cunning.
Zeus the Olympian and lord of the lightning went to
his own bed, where always he lay when sweet sleep came on him   610
Going up to the bed he slept and Hera of the gold throne beside him.

[The Greeks, in spite of Achilleus' withdrawal, continued to fight.
They did not suffer immoderately from Achilleus' absence; on the
contrary, they pressed the Trojans so hard that Hektor, the Trojan
leader, after rallying his men, returned to the city to urge the
Trojans to offer special prayers and sacrifices to the gods.]

[*The Meeting of Hector and Andromache*]

Book VI

    . . . Now as Hektor had come to the Skaian gates and the oak
        tree,
all the wives of the Trojans and their daughters came running about
        him
to ask after their sons, after their brothers and neighbours,
their husbands; and he told them to pray to the immortals,   240
all, in turn; but there were sorrows in store for many.
    Now he entered the wonderfully built palace of Priam.
This was fashioned with smooth-stone cloister walks, and within it
were embodied fifty sleeping chambers of smoothed stone
built so as to connect with each other; and within these slept   245
each beside his own wedded wife, the sons of Priam.
In the same inner court on the opposite side, to face these,
lay the twelve close smooth-stone sleeping chambers of his daughters
built so as to connect with each other; and within these slept,
each by his own modest wife, the lords of the daughters of Priam. 250

598. *nectar:* the drink of the gods.
237. *Skaian gates:* one of the entrances to Troy.

There there came to meet Hektor his bountiful mother
with Laodike, the loveliest looking of all her daughters.
She clung to his hand and called him by name and spoke to him:
    'Why then,
child, have you come here and left behind the bold battle?
Surely it is these accursed sons of the Achaians who wear you   255
out, as they fight close to the city, and the spirit stirred you
to return, and from the peak of the citadel lift your hands, praying
to Zeus. But stay while I bring you honey-sweet wine, to pour out
a libation to father Zeus and the other immortals
first, and afterwards if you will drink yourself, be strengthened.   260
In a tired man, wine will bring back his strength to its bigness,
in a man tired as you are tired, defending your neighbours.'
    Tall Hektor of the shining helm spoke to her answering:
'My honoured mother, lift not to me the kindly sweet wine,
for fear you stagger my strength and make me forget my courage;   265
and with hands unwashed I would take shame to pour the glittering
wine to Zeus; there is no means for a man to pray to the dark-misted
son of Kronos, with blood and muck all spattered upon him.
But go yourself to the temple of the spoiler Athene,
assembling the ladies of honour, and with things to be sacrificed,   270
and take a robe, which seems to you the largest and loveliest
in the great house, and that which is far your dearest possession.
Lay this along the knees of Athene the lovely haired. Also
promise to dedicate within the shrine twelve heifers,
yearlings, never broken, if only she will have pity   275
on the town of Troy, and the Trojan wives, and their innocent
    children,
if she will hold back from sacred Ilion the son of Tydeus,
that wild spear-fighter, the strong one who drives men to thoughts
    of terror.
So go yourself to the temple of the spoiler Athene,
while I go in search of Paris, to call him, if he will listen   280
to anything I tell him. How I wish at this moment the earth might
open beneath him. The Olympian let him live, a great sorrow
to the Trojans, and high-hearted Priam, and all of his children.
If only I could see him gone down to the house of the Death God,
then I could say my heart had forgotten its joyless affliction.'   285
    So he spoke, and she going into the great house called out
to her handmaidens, who assembled throughout the city the
    highborn
women; while she descended into the fragrant store-chamber.
There lay the elaborately wrought robes, the work of Sidonian

251. *mother:* Hekabe (Hecuba).
277. *son of Tydeus:* Diomedes, one
of the Greek champions, who has just
distinguished himself in the fighting.
289. *Sidonian:* Sidon was a Phoenician city on the coast of Palestine.

women, whom Alexandros himself, the godlike, had brought
    home   290
from the land of Sidon, crossing the wide sea, on that journey
when he brought back also gloriously descended Helen.
Hekabe lifted out one and took it as gift to Athene,
that which was the loveliest in design and the largest,
and shone like a star. It lay beneath the others. She went on   295
her way, and a throng of noble women hastened about her.
    When these had come to Athene's temple on the peak of the
    citadel,
Theano of the fair cheeks opened the door for them, daughter
of Kisseus, and wife of Antenor, breaker of horses,
she whom the Trojans had established to be Athene's priestess.   300
With a wailing cry all lifted up their hands to Athene,
and Theano of the fair cheeks taking up the robe laid it
along the knees of Athene the lovely haired, and praying
she supplicated the daughter of powerful Zeus: 'O lady,
Athene, our city's defender, shining among goddesses: 305
break the spear of Diomedes, and grant that the man be
hurled on his face in front of the Skaian gates; so may we
instantly dedicate within your shrine twelve heifers,
yearlings, never broken, if only you will have pity
on the town of Troy, and the Trojan wives, and their innocent
    children.'   310
    She spoke in prayer, but Pallas Athene turned her head from her.
    So they made their prayer to the daughter of Zeus the powerful.
But Hektor went away to the house of Alexandros,
a splendid place he had built himself, with the men who at that time
were the best men for craftsmanship in the generous Troad,   315
who had made him a sleeping room and a hall and a courtyard
near the houses of Hektor and Priam, on the peak of the citadel.
There entered Hektor beloved of Zeus, in his hand holding
the eleven-cubit-long spear, whose shaft was tipped with a shining
bronze spearhead, and a ring of gold was hooped to hold it.   320
He found the man in his chamber busy with his splendid armour,
the corselet and the shield, and turning in his hands the curved bow,
while Helen of Argos was sitting among her attendant women
directing the magnificent work done by her handmaidens.
    But Hektor saw him, and in words of shame he rebuked him: 325
'Strange man! It is not fair to keep in your heart this coldness.

---

290. *Alexandros:* another name for
Paris.
    319. *eleven-cubit-long:* The Greek
word translated as "cubit" means "the
length of the forearm."
    325. *rebuked him:* Paris, like Achil-
leus, was sulking at home. He had been

worsted in a duel with Menelaos, but
the goddess Aphrodite saved him from
the consequences of his defeat and
brought him to his house in Troy.
Paris was hated by his countrymen as
the cause of the war.

The people are dying around the city and around the steep wall
as they fight hard; and it is for you that this war with its clamour
has flared up about our city. You yourself would fight with another
whom you saw anywhere hanging back from the hateful en-
    counter.   330
Up then, to keep our town from burning at once in the hot fire.'
  Then in answer the godlike Alexandros spoke to him:
'Hektor, seeing you have scolded me rightly, not beyond measure,
therefore I will tell, and you in turn understand and listen.
It was not so much in coldness and bitter will toward the Trojans   335
that I sat in my room, but I wished to give myself over to sorrow.
But just now with soft words my wife was winning me over
and urging me into the fight, and that way seems to me also
the better one. Victory passes back and forth between men.
Come then, wait for me now while I put on my armour of battle,   340
or go, and I will follow, and I think I can overtake you.'
  He spoke, but Hektor of the shining helm gave him no answer,
but Helen spoke to him in words of endearment: 'Brother
by marriage to me, who am a nasty bitch evil-intriguing,
how I wish that on that day when my mother first bore me   345
the foul whirlwind of the storm had caught me away and swept me
to the mountain, or into the wash of the sea deep-thundering
where the waves would have swept me away before all these things
    had happened.
Yet since the gods had brought it about that these vile things must
    be,
I wish I had been the wife of a better man than this is,   350
one who knew modesty and all things of shame that men say.
But this man's heart is no steadfast thing, nor yet will it be so
ever hereafter; for that I think he shall take the consequence.
But come now, come in and rest on this chair, my brother,
since it is on your heart beyond all that the hard work has fallen 355
for the sake of dishonoured me and the blind act of Alexandros,
us two, on whom Zeus set a vile destiny, so that hereafter
we shall be made into things of song for the men of the future.'
  Then tall Hektor of the shining helm answered her: 'Do not,
    Helen,
make me sit with you, though you love me. You will not persuade
    me.   360
Already my heart within is hastening me to defend
the Trojans, who when I am away long greatly to have me.
Rather rouse this man, and let himself also be swift to action
so he may overtake me while I am still in the city.
For I am going first to my own house, so I can visit   365
my own people, my beloved wife and my son, who is little,

since I do not know if ever again I shall come back this way,
or whether the gods will strike me down at the hands of the
    Achaians.'
  So speaking Hektor of the shining helm departed
and in speed made his way to his own well-established dwelling,   370
but failed to find in the house Andromache of the white arms;
for she, with the child, and followed by one fair-robed attendant,
had taken her place on the tower in lamentation, and tearful.
When he saw no sign of his perfect wife within the house, Hektor
stopped in his way on the threshold and spoke among the hand-
    maidens: 375
'Come then, tell me truthfully as you may, handmaidens:
where has Andromache of the white arms gone? Is she
with any of the sisters of her lord or the wives of his brothers?
Or has she gone to the house of Athene, where all the other
lovely-haired women of Troy propitiate the grim goddess?'   380
  Then in turn the hard-working housekeeper gave him an answer:
Hektor, since you have urged me to tell you the truth, she is not
with any of the sisters of her lord or the wives of his brothers,
nor has she gone to the house of Athene, where all the other
lovely-haired women of Troy propitiate the grim goddess,   385
but she has gone to the great bastion of Ilion, because she heard that
the Trojans were losing, and great grew the strength of the Achaians.
Therefore she has gone in speed to the wall, like a woman
gone mad, and a nurse attending her carries the baby.'
  So the housekeeper spoke, and Hektor hastened from his home   390
backward by the way he had come through the well-laid streets. So
as he had come to the gates on his way through the great city,
the Skaian gates, whereby he would issue into the plain, there
at last his own generous wife came running to meet him,
Andromache, the daughter of high-hearted Eëtion;   395
Eëtion, who had dwelt underneath wooded Plakos,
in Thebe below Plakos, lord over the Kilikian people.
It was his daughter who was given to Hektor of the bronze helm.
She came to him there, and beside her went an attendant carrying
the boy in the fold of her bosom, a little child, only a baby,   400
Hektor's son, the admired, beautiful as a star shining,
whom Hektor called Skamandrios, but all of the others
Astyanax—lord of the city; since Hektor alone saved Ilion.
Hektor smiled in silence as he looked on his son, but she,
Andromache, stood close beside him, letting her tears fall,   405
and clung to his hand and called him by name and spoke to him:
    'Dearest,

---

402. *Skamandrios:* after the Trojan river Skamander.

403. *Astyanax:* The name does literally mean "lord of the city."

your own great strength will be your death, and you have no pity
on your little son, nor on me, ill-starred, who soon must be your
     widow;·
for presently the Achaians, gathering together,
will set upon you and kill you; and for me it would be far better   410
to sink into the earth when I have lost you, for there is no other
consolation for me after you have gone to your destiny—
only grief; since I have no father, no honoured mother.
It was brilliant Achilleus who slew my father, Eëtion,
when he stormed the strong-founded citadel of the Kilikians,   415
Thebe of the towering gates. He killed Eëtion
but did not strip his armour, for his heart respected the dead man,
but burned the body in all its elaborate war-gear
and piled a grave mound over it, and the nymphs of the mountains,
daughters of Zeus of the aegis, planted elm trees about it.   420
And they who were my seven brothers in the great house all went
upon a single day down into the house of the death god,
for swift-footed brilliant Achilleus slaughtered all of them
as they were tending their white sheep and their lumbering oxen;
and when he had led my mother, who was queen under wooded
     Plakos,   425
here, along with all his other possessions, Achilleus
released her again, accepting ransom beyond count, but Artemis
of the showering arrows struck her down in the halls of her father.
Hektor, thus you are father to me, and my honoured mother,
you are my brother, and you it is who are my young husband.   430
Please take pity upon me then, stay here on the rampart,
that you may not leave your child an orphan, your wife a widow,
but draw your people up by the fig tree, there where the city
is openest to attack, and where the wall may be mounted.
Three times their bravest came that way, and fought there to storm
     it   435
about the two Aiantes and renowned Idomeneus,
about the two Atreidai and the fighting son of Tydeus.
Either some man well skilled in prophetic arts had spoken,
or the very spirit within themselves had stirred them to the
     onslaught.'
    Then tall Hektor of the shining helm answered her: 'All these   440
things are in my mind also, lady; yet I would feel deep shame
before the Trojans, and the Trojan women with trailing garments,
if like a coward I were to shrink aside from the fighting;
and the spirit will not let me, since I have learned to be valiant
and to fight always among the foremost ranks of the Trojans,   445

427. *Artemis:* a virgin goddess, dispenser of natural and painless death to women.

436. *Aiantes:* There were two Greek warriors called Aias (Ajax). *Idomeneus:* a hero from Crete.
437. *Atreidai:* the sons of Atreus.

winning for my own self great glory, and for my father.
For I know this thing well in my heart, and my mind knows it:
there will come a day when sacred Ilion shall perish,
and Priam, and the people of Priam of the strong ash spear.
But it is not so much the pain to come of the Trojans   450
that troubles me, not even of Priam the king nor Hekabe,
not the thought of my brothers who in their numbers and valour
shall drop in the dust under the hands of men who hate them,
as troubles me the thought of you, when some bronze-armoured
Achaian leads you off, taking away your day of liberty,   455
in tears; and in Argos you must work at the loom of another,
and carry water from the spring Messeis or Hypereia,
all unwilling, but strong will be the necessity upon you;
and some day seeing you shedding tears a man will say of you:
"This is the wife of Hektor, who was ever the bravest fighter   460
of the Trojans, breakers of horses, in the days when they fought
    about Ilion."
So will one speak of you; and for you it will be yet a fresh grief,
to be widowed of such a man who could fight off the day of your
    slavery.
But may I be dead and the piled earth hide me under before I
hear you crying and know by this that they drag you captive.'   465
    So speaking glorious Hektor held out his arms to his baby,
who shrank back to his fair-girdled nurse's bosom
screaming, and frightened at the aspect of his own father,
terrified as he saw the bronze and the crest with its horse-hair,
nodding dreadfully, as he thought, from the peak of the helmet.   470
Then his beloved father laughed out, and his honoured mother,
and at once glorious Hektor lifted from his head the helmet
and laid it in all its shining upon the ground. Then taking
up his dear son he tossed him about in his arms, and kissed him,
and lifted his voice in prayer to Zeus and the other immortals: 475
'Zeus, and you other immortals, grant that this boy, who is my son,
may be as I am, pre-eminent among the Trojans,
great in strength, as am I, and rule strongly over Ilion;
and some day let them say of him: "He is better by far than his
    father",
as he comes in from the fighting; and let him kill his enemy   480
and bring home the blooded spoils, and delight the heart of his
    mother.'
    So speaking he set his child again in the arms of his beloved
wife, who took him back again to her fragrant bosom
smiling in her tears; and her husband saw, and took pity upon her,
and stroked her with his hand, and called her by name and spoke
    to her: 485

457. *Messeis or Hypereia:* one in central, the other in northern, Greece.

'Poor Andromache! Why does your heart sorrow so much for me?
No man is going to hurl me to Hades, unless it is fated,
but as for fate, I think that no man yet has escaped it
once it has taken its first form, neither brave man nor coward.
Go therefore back to our house, and take up your own work,   490
the loom and the distaff, and see to it that your handmaidens
ply their work also; but the men must see to the fighting,
all men who are the people of Ilion, but I beyond others.'
    So glorious Hektor spoke and again took up the helmet
with its crest of horse-hair, while his beloved wife went home-
        ward,   495
turning to look back on the way, letting the live tears fall.
And as she came in speed into the well-settled household
of Hektor the slayer of men, she found numbers of handmaidens
within, and her coming stirred all of them into lamentation.
So they mourned in his house over Hektor while he was living   500
still, for they thought he would never again come back from the
        fighting
alive, escaping the Achaian hands and their violence.
    But Paris in turn did not linger long in his high house,
but when he had put on his glorious armour with bronze elaborate
he ran in the confidence of his quick feet through the city.   505
As when some stalled horse who has been corn-fed at the manger
breaking free of his rope gallops over the plain in thunder
to his accustomed bathing place in a sweet-running river
and in the pride of his strength holds high his head, and the mane
        floats
over his shoulders; sure of his glorious strength, the quick knees   510
carry him to the loved places and the pasture of horses;
so from uttermost Pergamos came Paris, the son of
Priam, shining in all his armour of war as the sun shines,
laughing aloud, and his quick feet carried him; suddenly thereafter
he came on brilliant Hektor, his brother, where he yet lingered   515
before turning away from the place where he had talked with his
        lady.
It was Alexandros the godlike who first spoke to him:
'Brother, I fear that I have held back your haste, by being
slow on the way, not coming in time, as you commanded me.'
    Then tall Hektor of the shining helm spoke to him in answer: 520
'Strange man! There is no way that one, giving judgment in fairness,
could dishonour your work in battle, since you are a strong man.
But of your own accord you hang back, unwilling. And my heart
is grieved in its thought, when I hear shameful things spoken about
        you
by the Trojans, who undergo hard fighting for your sake.   525

    512. *Pergamos:* the citadel of Troy.

Let us go now; some day hereafter we will make all right
with the immortal gods in the sky, if Zeus ever grant it,
setting up to them in our houses the wine-bowl of liberty
after we have driven out of Troy the strong-greaved Achaians.'

[The Trojans rallied successfully and went over to the offensive.
They drove the Greeks back to the light fortifications they had built
around their beached ships. The Trojans lit their watchfires on the
plain, ready to deliver the attack in the morning.]

Book VIII
[*The Eve of Battle*]

. . . So with hearts made high these sat night-long by the out-
    works
of battle, and their watchfires blazed numerous about them.
As when in the sky the stars about the moon's shining   555
are seen in all their glory, when the air has fallen to stillness,
and all the high places of the hills are clear, and the shoulders out-
    jutting,
and the deep ravines, as endless bright air spills from the heavens
and all the stars are seen, to make glad the heart of the shepherd;
such in their numbers blazed the watchfires the Trojans were
    burning   560
between the waters of Xanthos and the ships, before Ilion.
A thousand fires were burning there in the plain, and beside each
one sat fifty men in the flare of the blazing firelight.
And standing each beside his chariot, champing white barley
and oats, the horses waited for the dawn to mount to her high
    place.   565

Book IX
[*The Embassy to Achilles*]

So the Trojans held their night watches. Meanwhile immortal
Panic, companion of cold Terror, gripped the Achaians
as all their best were stricken with grief that passes endurance.
As two winds rise to shake the sea where the fish swarm, Boreas
and Zephyros, north wind and west, that blow from Thraceward,   5
suddenly descending, and the darkened water is gathered
to crests, and far across the salt water scatters the seaweed;
so the heart in the breast of each Achaian was troubled.
And the son of Atreus, stricken at heart with the great sorrow,
went among his heralds the clear-spoken and told them   10
to summon calling by name each man into the assembly
but with no outcry, and he himself was at work with the foremost.

They took their seats in assembly, dispirited, and Agamemnon
stood up before them, shedding tears, like a spring dark-running
that down the face of a rock impassable drips its dim water.   15
So, groaning heavily, Agamemnon spoke to the Argives:
'Friends, who are leaders of the Argives and keep their counsel:
Zeus son of Kronos has caught me badly in bitter futility.
He is hard: who before this time promised me and consented
that I might sack strong-walled Ilion and sail homeward.   20
Now he has devised a vile deception and bids me go back
to Argos in dishonour having lost many of my people.
Such is the way it will be pleasing to Zeus, who is too strong,
who before now has broken the crests of many cities
and will break them again, since his power is beyond all others.   25
Come then, do as I say, let us all be won over; let us
run away with our ships to the beloved land of our fathers
since no longer now shall we capture Troy of the wide ways.'
  So he spoke, and all of them stayed stricken to silence.
For some time the sons of the Achaians said nothing in sorrow;   30
but at long last Diomedes of the great war cry addressed them:
'Son of Atreus: I will be first to fight with your folly,
as is my right, lord, in this assembly; then do not be angered.
I was the first of the Danaans whose valour you slighted
and said I was unwarlike and without courage. The young men   35
of the Argives know all these things, and the elders know it.
The son of devious-devising Kronos has given you
gifts in two ways: with the sceptre he gave you honour beyond all,
but he did not give you a heart, and of all power this is the greatest.
Sir, sir, can you really believe the sons of the Achaians   40
are so unwarlike and so weak of their hearts as you call them?
But if in truth your own heart is so set upon going,
go. The way is there, and next to the water are standing
your ships that came—so many of them!—with you from Mykenai,
and yet the rest of the flowing-haired Achaians will stay here   45
until we have sacked the city of Troy; let even these also
run away with their ships to the beloved land of their fathers,
still we two, Sthenelos and I, will fight till we witness
the end of Ilion; for it was with God that we made our way hither.'
  So he spoke, and all the sons of the Achaians shouted   50
acclaim for the word of Diomedes, breaker of horses.
And now Nestor the horseman stood forth among them and spoke
    to them:
'Son of Tydeus, beyond others you are strong in battle,
and in counsel also are noblest among all men of your own age.

34–35. *I was . . . courage:* This happened during Agamemnon's review of his
forces before the battle.

Not one man of all the Achaians will belittle your words nor   55
speak against them. Yet you have not made complete your argument,
since you are a young man still and could even be my own son
and my youngest born of all; yet still you argue in wisdom
with the Argive kings, since all you have spoken was spoken fairly.
But let me speak, since I can call myself older than you are,   60
and go through the whole matter, since there is none who can
    dishonour
the thing I say, not even powerful Agamemnon.
Out of all brotherhood, outlawed, homeless shall be that man
who longs for all the horror of fighting among his own people.
But now let us give way to the darkness of night, and let us   65
make ready our evening meal; and let the guards severally
take their stations by the ditch we have dug outside the ramparts.
This I would enjoin upon our young men; but thereafter
do you, son of Atreus, take command, since you are our kingliest.
Divide a feast among the princes; it befits you, it is not   70
unbecoming. Our shelters are filled with wine that the Achaian
ships carry day by day from Thrace across the wide water.
All hospitality is for you; you are lord over many.
When many assemble together follow him who advises
the best counsel, for in truth there is need for all the Achaians   75
of good close counsel, since now close to our ships the enemy
burn their numerous fires. What man could be cheered to see this?
Here is the night that will break our army, or else will preserve it.'

    So he spoke, and they listened hard to him, and obeyed him,
and the sentries went forth rapidly in their armour, gathering   80
about Nestor's son Thrasymedes, shepherd of the people,
and about Askalaphos and Ialmenos, sons both of Ares,
about Meriones and Aphareus and Deïpyros
and about the son of Kreion, Lykomedes the brilliant.
There were seven leaders of the sentinels, and with each one a
    hundred   85
fighting men followed gripping in their hands the long spears.
They took position in the space between the ditch and the rampart,
and there they kindled their fires and each made ready his supper.

    But the son of Atreus led the assembled lords of the Achaians
to his own shelter, and set before them the feast in abundance.   90
They put their hands to the good things that lay ready before them.
But when they had put away their desire for eating and drinking,
the aged man began to weave his counsel before them
first, Nestor, whose advice had shown best before this.
He in kind intention toward all stood forth and addressed them: 95

----

67. *ditch . . . ramparts:* The Greeks   Zeus' promise to Thetis is being ful-
are now besieged beside their ships;   filled.
                             82. *Ares:* god of war.

'Son of Atreus, most lordly and king of men, Agamemnon,
with you I will end, with you I will make my beginning, since you
are lord over many people, and Zeus has given into your hand
the sceptre and rights of judgment, to be king over the people.
It is yours therefore to speak a word, yours also to listen,   100
and grant the right to another also, when his spirit stirs him
to speak for our good. All shall be yours when you lead the way. Still
I will speak in the way it seems best to my mind, and no one
shall have in his mind any thought that is better than this one
that I have in my mind either now or long before now   105
ever since that day, illustrious, when you went from the shelter
of angered Achilleus, taking by force the girl Briseis
against the will of the rest of us, since I for my part
urged you strongly not to, but you, giving way to your proud heart's
anger, dishonoured a great man, one whom the immortals   110
honour, since you have taken his prize and keep it. But let us
even now think how we can make this good and persuade him
with words of supplication and with the gifts of friendship.'
    Then in turn the lord of men Agamemnon spoke to him:
'Aged sir, this was no lie when you spoke of my madness.   115
I was mad, I myself will not deny it. Worth many
fighters is that man whom Zeus in his heart loves, as now
he has honoured this man and beaten down the Achaian people.
But since I was mad, in the persuasion of my heart's evil,
I am willing to make all good, and give back gifts in abundance.   120
Before you all I will count off my gifts in their splendour:
seven unfired tripods; ten talents' weight of gold; twenty
shining cauldrons; and twelve horses, strong, race-competitors
who have won prizes in the speed of their feet. That man would not
        be
poor in possessions, to whom were given all these have won me,   125
nor be unpossessed of dearly honoured gold, were he given
all the prizes these single-foot horses have won for me.
I will give him seven women of Lesbos, the work of whose hands is
blameless, whom when he himself captured strong-founded Lesbos
I chose, and who in their beauty surpassed the races of women.   130
I will give him these, and with them shall go the one I took from
        him,
the daughter of Briseus. And to all this I will swear a great oath
that I never entered into her bed and never lay with her
as is natural for human people, between men and women.
All these gifts shall be his at once; but again, if hereafter   135

---

122. *unfired:* i.e., unused, brand new. *tripods:* A tripod was a three-footed kettle. *ten talents' weight of gold:* an enormous sum. The talent was the largest measure of weight.

128. *Lesbos:* a large island off the coast of what is now Turkey, famous in later times as the home of Sappho.

the gods grant that we storm and sack the great city of Priam,
let him go to his ship and load it deep as he pleases
with gold and bronze, when we Achaians divide the war spoils,
and let him choose for himself twenty of the Trojan women
who are the loveliest of all after Helen of Argos.   140
And if we come back to Achaian Argos, pride of the tilled land,
he may be my son-in-law; I will honour him with Orestes
my growing son, who is brought up there in abundant luxury.
Since, as I have three daughters there in my strong-built castle,
Chrysothemis and Laodike and Iphianassa,   145
let him lead away the one of these that he likes, with no bride-price,
to the house of Peleus, and with the girl I will grant him as dowry
many gifts, such as no man ever gave with his daughter.
I will grant to him seven citadels, strongly settled:
Kardamyle, and Enope, and Hire of the grasses,   150
Pherai the sacrosanct, and Antheia deep in the meadows,
with Aipeia the lovely and Pedasos of the vineyards.
All these lie near the sea, at the bottom of sandy Pylos,
and men live among them rich in cattle and rich in sheepflocks,
who will honour him as if he were a god with gifts given   155
and fulfil his prospering decrees underneath his sceptre.
All this I will bring to pass for him, if he changes from his anger.
Let him give way. For Hades gives not way, and is pitiless,
and therefore he among all the gods is most hateful to mortals.
And let him yield place to me, inasmuch as I am the kinglier   160
and inasmuch as I can call myself born the elder.'
   Thereupon the Gerenian horseman Nestor answered him:
'Son of Atreus, most lordly and king of men, Agamemnon,
none could scorn any longer these gifts you offer to Achilleus
the king. Come, let us choose and send some men, who in all
    speed   165
will go to the shelter of Achilleus, the son of Peleus;
or come, the men on whom my eye falls, let these take the duty.
First of all let Phoinix, beloved of Zeus, be their leader,
and after him take Aias the great, and brilliant Odysseus,
and of the heralds let Odios and Eurybates go with them.   170
Bring also water for their hands, and bid them keep words of good
    omen,
so we may pray to Zeus, son of Kronos, if he will have pity.'
   So he spoke, and the word he spoke was pleasing to all of them.
And the heralds brought water at once, and poured it over
their hands, and the young men filled the mixing-bowl with pure
    wine   175

---

168. *Phoinix:* He is especially suited for this embassy since he was tutor to the
young Achilleus.

and passed it to all, pouring first a libation in goblets.
Then when they had poured out wine, and drunk as much as their
    hearts wished,
they set out from the shelter of Atreus' son, Agamemnon.
And the Gerenian horseman Nestor gave them much instruction,
looking eagerly at each, and most of all at Odysseus,   180
to try hard, so that they might win over the blameless Peleion.
    So these two walked along the strand of the sea deep-thundering
with many prayers to the holder and shaker of the earth, that they
might readily persuade the great heart of Aiakides.
Now they came beside the shelters and ships of the Myrmidons   185
and they found Achilleus delighting his heart in a lyre, clear-
    sounding,
splendid and carefully wrought, with a bridge of silver upon it,
which he won out of the spoils when he ruined Eëtion's city.
With this he was pleasuring his heart, and singing of men's fame,
as Patroklos was sitting over against him, alone, in silence,   190
watching Aiakides and the time he would leave off singing.
Now these two came forward, as brilliant Odysseus led them,
and stood in his presence. Achilleus rose to his feet in amazement
holding the lyre as it was, leaving the place where he was sitting.
In the same way Patroklos, when he saw the men come, stood up.
And in greeting Achilleus the swift of foot spoke to them: 196
'Welcome. You are my friends who have come, and greatly I need
    you,
who even to this my anger are dearest of all the Achaians.'
    So brilliant Achilleus spoke, and guided them forward,
and caused them to sit down on couches with purple coverlets   200
and at once called over to Patroklos who was not far from him:
'Son of Menoitios, set up a mixing-bowl that is bigger,
and mix us stronger drink, and make ready a cup for each man,
since these who have come beneath my roof are the men that I love
    best.'
    So he spoke, and Patroklos obeyed his beloved companion,   205
and tossed down a great chopping-block into the firelight,
and laid upon it the back of a sheep, and one of a fat goat,
with the chine of a fatted pig edged thick with lard, and for him
Automedon held the meats, and brilliant Achilleus carved them,
and cut it well into pieces and spitted them, as meanwhile   210
Menoitios' son, a man like a god, made the fire blaze greatly.

---

176. *libation:* an offering to the gods
—before the wine was drunk, a little
was poured out on the ground.
181. *Peleion:* son of Peleus, i.e.,
Achilleus.
183. *holder and shaker:* Poseidon,
who was believed to be responsible for
earthquakes.
184. *Aiakides:* descendant of Aiakos
(father of Peleus), i.e., Achilleus.
209. *Automedon:* the charioteer of
Achilleus.

But when the fire had burned itself out, and the flames had died
    down,
he scattered the embers apart, and extended the spits across them
lifting them to the andirons, and sprinkled the meats with divine
    salt.
Then when he had roasted all, and spread the food on the platters,
Patroklos took the bread and set it out on a table   216
in fair baskets, while Achilleus served the meats. Thereafter
he himself sat over against the godlike Odysseus
against the further wall, and told his companion, Patroklos,
to sacrifice to the gods; and he threw the firstlings in the fire.   220
They put their hands to the good things that lay ready before
    them.
But when they had put aside their desire for eating and drinking,
Aias nodded to Phoinix, and brilliant Odysseus saw it,
and filled a cup with wine, and lifted it to Achilleus:
'Your health, Achilleus. You have no lack of your equal portion   225
either within the shelter of Atreus' son, Agamemnon,
nor here now in your own. We have good things in abundance
to feast on; here it is not the desirable feast we think of,
but a trouble all too great, beloved of Zeus, that we look on
and are afraid. There is doubt if we save our strong-benched ves-
    sels   230
or if they will be destroyed, unless you put on your war strength.
The Trojans in their pride, with their far-renowned companions,
have set up an encampment close by the ships and the rampart,
and lit many fires along their army, and think no longer
of being held, but rather to drive in upon the black ships.   235
And Zeus, son of Kronos, lightens upon their right hand, showing
    them
portents of good, while Hektor in the huge pride of his strength
    rages
irresistibly, reliant on Zeus, and gives way to no one
neither god nor man, but the strong fury has descended upon him.
He prays now that the divine Dawn will show most quickly,   240
since he threatens to shear the uttermost horns from the ship-sterns,
to light the ships themselves with ravening fire, and to cut down
the Achaians themselves as they stir from the smoke beside them.
All this I fear terribly in my heart, lest immortals
accomplish all these threats, and lest for us it be destiny   245
to die here in Troy, far away from horse-pasturing Argos.
Up, then! if you are minded, late though it be, to rescue
the afflicted sons of the Achaians from the Trojan onslaught.
It will be an affliction to you hereafter, there will be no remedy

found to heal the evil thing when it has been done. No, beforehand   250
take thought to beat the evil day aside from the Danaans.
Dear friend, surely thus your father Peleus advised you
that day when he sent you away to Agamemnon from Phthia:
"My child, for the matter of strength, Athene and Hera will give it
if it be their will, but be it yours to hold fast in your bosom   255
the anger of the proud heart, for consideration is better.
Keep from the bad complication of quarrel, and all the more for this
the Argives will honour you, both their younger men and their
elders."
So the old man advised, but you have forgotten. Yet even now
stop, and give way from the anger that hurts the heart. Agamemnon   260
offers you worthy recompense if you change from your anger.
Come then, if you will, listen to me, while I count off for you
all the gifts in his shelter that Agamemnon has promised:
Seven unfired tripods; ten talents' weight of gold; twenty
shining cauldrons; and twelve horses, strong, race-competitors   265
who have won prize in the speed of their feet. That man would not
be
poor in possessions, to whom were given all these have won him,
nor be unpossessed of dearly honoured gold, were he given
all the prizes Agamemnon's horses won in their speed for him.
He will give you seven women of Lesbos, the work of whose hands
is blameless, whom when you yourself captured strong-founded
Lesbos   271
he chose, and who in their beauty surpassed the races of women.
He will give you these, and with them shall go the one he took from
you,
the daughter of Briseus. And to all this he will swear a great oath
that he never entered into her bed and never lay with her   275
as is natural for human people, between men and women.
All these gifts shall be yours at once; but again, if hereafter
the gods grant that we storm and sack the great city of Priam,
you may go to your ship and load it deep as you please with
gold and bronze, when we Achaians divide the war spoils,   280
and you may choose for yourself twenty of the Trojan women,
who are the loveliest of all after Helen of Argos.
And if we come back to Achaian Argos, pride of the tilled land,
you could be his son-in-law; he would honour you with Orestes,
his growing son, who is brought up there in abundant luxury.   285
Since, as he has three daughters there in his strong-built castle,
Chrysothemis and Laodike and Iphianassa,
you may lead away the one of these that you like, with no bride-price,

to the house of Peleus; and with the girl he will grant you as dowry
many gifts, such as no man ever gave with his daughter.   290
He will grant you seven citadels, strongly settled:
Kardamyle and Enope and Hire of the grasses,
Pherai the sacrosanct, and Antheia deep in the meadows,
with Aipeia the lovely, and Pedasos of the vineyards.
All these lie near the sea, at the bottom of sandy Pylos,   295
and men live among them rich in cattle and rich in sheepflocks,
who will honour you as if you were a god with gifts given
and fulfil your prospering decrees underneath your sceptre.
All this he will bring to pass for you, if you change from your anger.
But if the son of Atreus is too much hated in your heart,   300
himself and his gifts, at least take pity on all the other
Achaians, who are afflicted along the host, and will honour you
as a god. You may win very great glory among them.
For now you might kill Hektor, since he would come very close to
        you
with the wicked fury upon him, since he thinks there is not his equal
among the rest of the Danaans the ships carried hither.'   306
      Then in answer to him spoke Achilleus of the swift feet:
'Son of Laertes and seed of Zeus, resourceful Odysseus:
without consideration for you I must make my answer,
the way I think, and the way it will be accomplished, that you may
        not   310
come one after another, and sit by me, and speak softly.
For as I detest the doorways of Death, I detest that man, who
hides one thing in the depths of his heart, and speaks forth another.
But I will speak to you the way it seems best to me: neither
do I think the son of Atreus, Agamemnon, will persuade me,   315
nor the rest of the Danaans, since there was no gratitude given
for fighting incessantly forever against your enemies.
Fate is the same for the man who holds back, the same if he fights
        hard.
We are all held in a single honour, the brave with the weaklings.
A man dies still if he has done nothing, as one who has done much.
Nothing is won for me, now that my heart has gone through its
        afflictions   321
in forever setting my life on the hazard of battle.
For as to her unwinged young ones the mother bird brings back
morsels, wherever she can find them, but as for herself it is suffering,
such was I, as I lay through all the many nights unsleeping,   325
such as I wore through the bloody days of the fighting,
striving with warriors for the sake of these men's women.
But I say that I have stormed from my ships twelve cities
of men, and by land eleven more through the generous Troad.

From all these we took forth treasures, goodly and numerous,   330
and we would bring them back, and give them to Agamemnon,
Atreus' son; while he, waiting back beside the swift ships,
would take them, and distribute them little by little, and keep many.
All the other prizes of honour he gave the great men and the princes
are held fast by them, but from me alone of all the Achaians   335
he has taken and keeps the bride of my heart. Let him lie beside her
and be happy. Yet why must the Argives fight with the Trojans?
And why was it the son of Atreus assembled and led here
these people? Was it not for the sake of lovely-haired Helen?
Are the sons of Atreus alone among mortal men the ones   340
who love their wives? Since any who is a good man, and careful,
loves her who is his own and cares for her, even as I now
loved this one from my heart, though it was my spear that won her.
Now that he has deceived me and taken from my hands my prize
        of honour,   344
let him try me no more. I know him well. He will not persuade
        me.
Let him take counsel with you, Odysseus, and the rest of the princes
how to fight the ravening fire away from his vessels.
Indeed, there has been much hard work done even without me;
he has built himself a wall and driven a ditch about it,
making it great and wide, and fixed the sharp stakes inside it.   350
Yet even so he cannot hold the strength of manslaughtering
Hektor; and yet when I was fighting among the Achaians
Hektor would not drive his attack beyond the wall's shelter
but would come forth only so far as the Skaian gates and the oak
        tree.
There once he endured me alone, and barely escaped my onslaught.
But, now I am unwilling to fight against brilliant Hektor,   356
tomorrow, when I have sacrificed to Zeus and to all gods,
and loaded well my ships, and rowed out on to the salt water,
you will see, if you have a mind to it and if it concerns you,
my ships in the dawn at sea on the Hellespont where the fish swarm
and my men manning them with good will to row. If the glorious   361
shaker of the earth should grant us a favouring passage
on the third day thereafter we might raise generous Phthia.
I have many possessions there that I left behind when I came here
on this desperate venture, and from here there is more gold, and red
        bronze,   365
and fair-girdled women, and grey iron I will take back;
all that was allotted to me. But my prize: he who gave it,
powerful Agamemnon, son of Atreus, has taken it back again
outrageously. Go back and proclaim to him all that I tell you,
openly, so other Achaians may turn against him in anger   370

if he hopes yet one more time to swindle some other Danaan,
wrapped as he is forever in shamelessness; yet he would not,
bold as a dog though he be, dare look in my face any longer.
I will join with him in no counsel, and in no action.
He cheated me and he did me hurt. Let him not beguile me   375
with words again. This is enough for him. Let him of his own will
be damned, since Zeus of the counsels has taken his wits away from
      him.
I hate his gifts. I hold him light as the strip of a splinter.
Not if he gave me ten times as much, and twenty times over
as he possesses now, not if more should come to him from else-
      where,   380
or gave all that is brought in to Orchomenos, all that is brought in
to Thebes of Egypt, where the greatest possessions lie up in the
      houses,
Thebes of the hundred gates, where through each of the gates two
      hundred
fighting men come forth to war with horses and chariots;
not if he gave me gifts as many as the sand or the dust is,   385
not even so would Agamemnon have his way with my spirit
until he had made good to me all this heartrending insolence.
Nor will I marry a daughter of Atreus' son, Agamemnon,
not if she challenged Aphrodite the golden for loveliness,
not if she matched the work of her hands with grey-eyed Athene;   390
not even so will I marry her; let him pick some other Achaian,
one who is to his liking and is kinglier than I am.
For if the gods will keep me alive, and I win homeward,
Peleus himself will presently arrange a wife for me.
There are many Achaian girls in the land of Hellas and Phthia,   395
daughters of great men who hold strong places in guard. And of
      these
any one that I please I might make my beloved lady.
And the great desire in my heart drives me rather in that place
to take a wedded wife in marriage, the bride of my fancy,
to enjoy with her the possessions won by aged Peleus. For not   400
worth the value of my life are all the possessions they fable
were won for Ilion, that strong-founded citadel, in the old days
when there was peace, before the coming of the sons of the Achaians;
not all that the stone doorsill of the Archer holds fast within it,
of Phoibos Apollo in Pytho of the rocks. Of possessions   405
cattle and fat sheep are things to be had for the lifting,
and tripods can be won, and the tawny high heads of horses,
but a man's life cannot come back again, it cannot be lifted

---

405. *Pytho:* at Delphi. The treasures consisted of offerings made to the god by grateful worshipers.

nor captured again by force, once it has crossed the teeth's barrier.
For my mother Thetis the goddess of the silver feet tells me   410
I carry two sorts of destiny toward the day of my death. Either,
if I stay here and fight beside the city of the Trojans,
my return home is gone, but my glory shall be everlasting;
but if I return home to the beloved land of my fathers,
the excellence of my glory is gone, but there will be a long life   415
left for me, and my end in death will not come to me quickly.
And this would be my counsel to others also, to sail back
home again, since no longer shall you find any term set
on the sheer city of Ilion, since Zeus of the wide brows has strongly
held his own hand over it, and its people are made bold.   420
    Do you go back therefore to the great men of the Achaians,
and take them this message, since such is the privilege of the princes:
that they think out in their minds some other scheme that is better,
which might rescue their ships, and the people of the Achaians
who man the hollow ships, since this plan will not work for them   425
which they thought of by reason of my anger. Let Phoinix
remain here with us and sleep here, so that tomorrow
he may come with us in our ships to the beloved land of our fathers,
if he will; but I will never use force to hold him.'
    So he spoke, and all of them stayed stricken to silence   430
in amazement at his words. He had spoken to them very strongly.
But at long last Phoinix the aged horseman spoke out
in a stormburst of tears, and fearing for the ships of the Achaians:
'If it is going home, glorious Achilleus, you ponder
in your heart, and are utterly unwilling to drive the obliterating   435
fire from the fast ships, since anger has descended on your spirit,
how then shall I, dear child, be left in this place behind you
all alone? Peleus the aged horseman sent me forth with you
on that day when he sent you from Phthia to Agamemnon
a mere child, who knew nothing yet of the joining of battle   440
nor of debate where men are made pre-eminent. Therefore
he sent me along with you to teach you of all these matters,
to make you a speaker of words and one who accomplished in action.
Therefore apart from you, dear child, I would not be willing
to be left behind, not were the god in person to promise   445
he would scale away my old age and make me a young man blos-
        soming
as I was that time when I first left Hellas, the land of fair women,
running from the hatred of Ormenos' son Amyntor,
my father; who hated me for the sake of a fair-haired mistress.
For he made love to her himself, and dishonoured his own wife,   450
my mother; who was forever taking my knees and entreating me

to lie with this mistress instead so that she would hate the old man.
I was persuaded and did it; and my father when he heard of it
    straightway
called down his curses, and invoked against me the dreaded furies
that I might never have any son born of my seed to dandle   455
on my knees; and the divinities, Zeus of the underworld
and Persephone the honoured goddess, accomplished his curses.
Then I took it into my mind to cut him down with the sharp bronze,
but some one of the immortals checked my anger, reminding me
of rumour among the people and men's maledictions repeated,   460
that I might not be called a parricide among the Achaians.
But now no more could the heart in my breast be ruled entirely
to range still among these halls when my father was angered.
Rather it was the many kinsmen and cousins about me
who held me closed in the house, with supplications repeated,   465
and slaughtered fat sheep in their numbers, and shambling horn-
    curved
cattle, and numerous swine with the fat abundant upon them
were singed and stretched out across the flame of Hephaistos,
and much wine was drunk that was stored in the jars of the old man.
Nine nights they slept nightlong in their places beside me,   470
and they kept up an interchange of watches, and the fire was never
put out; one below the gate of the strong-closed courtyard,
and one in the ante-chamber before the doors of the bedroom.
But when the tenth night had come to me in its darkness,
then I broke the close-compacted doors of the chamber   475
and got away, and overleapt the fence of the courtyard
lightly, unnoticed by the guarding men and the women servants.
Then I fled far away through the wide spaces of Hellas
and came as far as generous Phthia, mother of sheepflocks,
and to lord Peleus, who accepted me with a good will   480
and gave me his love, even as a father loves his own son
who is a single child brought up among many possessions.
He made me a rich man, and granted me many people,
and I lived, lord over the Dolopes, in remotest Phthia,
and, godlike Achilleus, I made you all that you are now,   485
and loved you out of my heart, for you would not go with another
out to any feast, nor taste any food in your own halls
until I had set you on my knees, and cut little pieces
from the meat, and given you all you wished, and held the wine for
    you.
And many times you soaked the shirt that was on my body   490

454. *furies:* avenging spirits, particularly concerned with crimes committed by kinsmen against kinsmen.

456. *Zeus of the underworld:* the god Hades.

457. *Persephone:* wife of Hades.

with wine you would spit up in the troublesomeness of your child-
    hood.
So I have suffered much through you, and have had much trouble,
thinking always how the gods would not bring to birth any children
of my own; so that it was you, godlike Achilleus, I made
my own child, so that some day you might keep hard affliction from
    me.   495
Then, Achilleus, beat down your great anger. It is not
yours to have a pitiless heart. The very immortals
can be moved; their virtue and honour and strength are greater than
    ours are,
and yet with sacrifices and offerings for endearment,
with libations and with savour men turn back even the immortals
in supplication, when any man does wrong and transgresses.   501
For there are also the spirits of Prayer, the daughters of great Zeus,
and they are lame of their feet, and wrinkled, and cast their eyes
    sidelong,
who toil on their way left far behind by the spirit of Ruin:
but she, Ruin, is strong and sound on her feet, and therefore   505
far outruns all Prayers, and wins into every country
to force men astray; and the Prayers follow as healers after her.
If a man venerates these daughters of Zeus as they draw near,
such a man they bring great advantage, and hear his entreaty;
but if a man shall deny them, and stubbornly with a harsh word   510
refuse, they go to Zeus, son of Kronos, in supplication
that Ruin may overtake this man, that he be hurt, and punished.
So, Achilleus: grant, you also, that Zeus' daughters be given
their honour, which, lordly though they be, curbs the will of others.
Since, were he not bringing gifts and naming still more hereafter,   515
Atreus' son; were he to remain still swollen with rancour,
even I would not bid you throw your anger aside, nor
defend the Argives, though they needed you sorely. But see now,
he offers you much straightway, and has promised you more here-
    after;
he has sent the best men to you to supplicate you, choosing them   520
out of the Achaian host, those who to yourself are the dearest
of all the Argives. Do not you make vain their argument
nor their footsteps, though before this one could not blame your
    anger.
Thus it was in the old days also, the deeds that we hear of   524
from the great men, when the swelling anger descended upon them.
The heroes would take gifts; they would listen, and be persuaded.
For I remember this action of old, it is not a new thing,
and how it went; you are all my friends, I will tell it among you.
    The Kouretes and the steadfast Aitolians were fighting

and slaughtering one another about the city of Kalydon, 530
the Aitolians in lovely Kalydon's defence, the Kouretes
furious to storm and sack it in war. For Artemis,
she of the golden chair, had driven this evil upon them,
angered that Oineus had not given the pride of the orchards
to her, first fruits; the rest of the gods were given due sacrifice, 535
but alone to this daughter of great Zeus he had given nothing.
He had forgotten, or had not thought, in his hard delusion,
and in wrath at his whole mighty line the Lady of Arrows
sent upon them the fierce wild boar with the shining teeth, who
after the way of his kind did much evil to the orchards of Oineus. 540
For he ripped up whole tall trees from the ground and scattered
    them headlong
roots and all, even to the very flowers of the orchard.
The son of Oineus killed this boar, Meleagros, assembling
together many hunting men out of numerous cities
with their hounds; since the boar might not have been killed by a
    few men, 545
so huge was he, and had put many men on the sad fire for burning.
But the goddess again made a great stir of anger and crying
battle, over the head of the boar and the bristling boar's hide,
between Kouretes and the high-hearted Aitolians. So long
as Meleagros lover of battle stayed in the fighting 550
it went the worse for the Kouretes, and they could not even
hold their ground outside the wall, though they were so many.
But when the anger came upon Meleagros, such anger
as wells in the hearts of others also, though their minds are careful,
he, in the wrath of his heart against his own mother, Althaia, 555
lay apart with his wedded bride, Kleopatra the lovely,
daughter of sweet-stepping Marpessa, child of Euenos,
and Idas, who was the strongest of all men upon earth
in his time; for he even took up the bow to face the King's onset,
Phoibos Apollo, for the sake of the sweet-stepping maiden; 560
a girl her father and honoured mother had named in their palace
Alkyone, sea-bird, as a by-name, since for her sake
her mother with the sorrow-laden cry of a sea-bird
wept because far-reaching Phoibos Apollo had taken her;
with this Kleopatra he lay mulling his heart-sore anger, 565
raging by reason of his mother's curses, which she called down

---

534. *Oineus:* king of Kalydon.
557. *Marpessa:* The story to which
Homer alludes runs as follows: Idas, the
famous archer, carried off and married
Marpessa, daughter of Euenos. Apollo
also had been her suitor, and he overtook Idas and carried off Marpessa.
Idas defied Apollo to combat, but Zeus
decided that the choice was up to

Marpessa, who preferred Idas. They
gave their daughter Kleopatra the nickname Alkyone (compare "halcyon"),
the name of a sea-bird that is supposed to mourn for its mate, to commemorate the time when Marpessa, carried off by Apollo, mourned for Idas.
564. *her:* Marpessa.

from the gods upon him, in deep grief for the death of her brother,
and many times beating with her hands on the earth abundant
she called on Hades and on honoured Persephone, lying
at length along the ground, and the tears were wet on her bosom, 570
to give death to her son; and Erinys, the mist-walking,
she of the heart without pity, heard her out of the dark places.
Presently there was thunder about the gates, and the sound rose
of towers under assault, and the Aitolian elders
supplicated him, sending their noblest priests of the immortals, 575
to come forth and defend them; they offered him a great gift:
wherever might lie the richest ground in lovely Kalydon,
there they told him to choose out a piece of land, an entirely
good one, of fifty acres, the half of it to be vineyard
and the half of it unworked ploughland of the plain to be fur-
    rowed. 580
And the aged horseman Oineus again and again entreated him,
and took his place at the threshold of the high-vaulted chamber
and shook against the bolted doors, pleading with his own son.
And again and again his honoured mother and his sisters
entreated him, but he only refused the more; then his own friends
who were the most honoured and dearest of all entreated him; 585
but even so they could not persuade the heart within him
until, as the chamber was under close assault, the Kouretes
were mounting along the towers and set fire to the great city.
And then at last his wife, the fair-girdled bride, supplicated 590
Meleagros, in tears, and rehearsed in their numbers before him
all the sorrows that come to men when their city is taken:
they kill the men, and the fire leaves the city in ashes,
and strangers lead the children away and the deep-girdled women.
And the heart, as he listened to all this evil, was stirred within
    him 595
and he rose, and went, and closed his body in shining armour.
So he gave way in his own heart, and drove back the day of evil
from the Aitolians; yet these no longer would make good
their many and gracious gifts; yet he drove back the evil from them.
    Listen, then; do not have such a thought in your mind; let not 600
the spirit within you turn you that way, dear friend. It would be
    worse
to defend the ships after they are burning. No, with gifts promised
go forth. The Achaians will honour you as they would an immortal.
But if without gifts you go into the fighting where men perish,
your honour will no longer be as great, though you drive back the
    battle.' 605

567. *her brother:* In the course of the battles Meleagros had killed one of his mother's brothers.

571. *Erinys:* the personified spirit of vengeance, a Fury (compare "furies," Book IX, l. 454).

Then in answer to him spoke Achilleus of the swift feet:
'Phoinix my father, aged, illustrious, such honour is a thing
I need not. I think I am honoured already in Zeus' ordinance
which will hold me here beside my curved ships as long as life's wind
stays in my breast, as long as my knees have their spring beneath
   me.   610
And put away in your thoughts this other thing I tell you.
Stop confusing my heart with lamentation and sorrow
for the favour of great Atreides. It does not become you
to love this man, for fear you turn hateful to me, who love you.
It should be your pride with me to hurt whoever shall hurt me. 615
Be king equally with me; take half of my honour.
These men will carry back the message; you stay here and sleep here
in a soft bed, and we shall decide tomorrow, as dawn shows,
whether to go back home again or else to remain here.'
  He spoke, and, saying nothing, nodded with his brows to Patroklos   620
to make up a neat bed for Phoinix, so the others might presently
think of going home from his shelter. The son of Telamon,
Aias the godlike, saw it, and now spoke his word among them:
'Son of Laertes and seed of Zeus, resourceful Odysseus:
let us go. I think that nothing will be accomplished 625
by argument on this errand; it is best to go back quickly
and tell this story, though it is not good, to the Danaans
who sit there waiting for us to come back, seeing that Achilleus
has made savage the proud-hearted spirit within his body.
He is hard, and does not remember that friends' affection 630
wherein we honoured him by the ships, far beyond all others.
Pitiless. And yet a man takes from his brother's slayer
the blood price, or the price for a child who was killed, and the guilty
one, when he has largely repaid, stays still in the country,
and the injured man's heart is curbed, and his pride, and his anger   635
when he has taken the price; but the gods put in your breast a
   spirit
not to be placated, bad, for the sake of one single
girl. Yet now we offer you seven, surpassingly lovely,
and much beside these. Now make gracious the spirit within you.
Respect your own house; see, we are under the same roof with
   you,   640
from the multitude of the Danaans, we who desire beyond all
others to have your honour and love, out of all the Achaians.'
  Then in answer to him spoke Achilleus of the swift feet:
'Son of Telamon, seed of Zeus, Aias, lord of the people:
all that you have said seems spoken after my own mind. 645

Yet still the heart in me swells up in anger, when I remember
the disgrace that he wrought upon me before the Argives,
the son of Atreus, as if I were some dishonoured vagabond.
Do you then go back to him, and take him this message:
that I shall not think again of the bloody fighting   650
until such time as the son of wise Priam, Hektor the brilliant,
comes all the way to the ships of the Myrmidons, and their shelters,
slaughtering the Argives, and shall darken with fire our vessels.
But around my own shelter, I think, and beside my black ship
Hektor will be held, though he be very hungry for battle.'   655
    He spoke, and they taking each a two-handled cup poured out
a libation, then went back to their ships, and Odysseus led them.
Now Patroklos gave the maids and his followers orders
to make up without delay a neat bed for Phoinix.
And these obeyed him and made up the bed as he had commanded,
laying fleeces on it, and a blanket, and a sheet of fine linen.   661
There the old man lay down and waited for the divine Dawn.
But Achilleus slept in the inward corner of the strong-built shelter,
and a woman lay beside him, one he had taken from Lesbos,
Phorbas' daughter, Diomede of the fair colouring.   665
In the other corner Patroklos went to bed; with him also
was a girl, Iphis the fair-girdled, whom brilliant Achilleus
gave him, when he took sheer Skyros, Enyeus' citadel.
    Now when these had come back to the shelters of Agamemnon,
the sons of the Achaians greeted them with their gold cups   670
uplifted, one after another, standing, and asked them questions.
And the first to question them was the lord of men, Agamemnon:
'Tell me, honoured Odysseus, great glory of the Achaians:
is he willing to fight the ravening fire away from our vessels,
or did he refuse, and does the anger still hold his proud heart?'   675
    Then long-suffering great Odysseus spoke to him in answer:
'Son of Atreus, most lordly, king of men, Agamemnon.
That man will not quench his anger, but still more than ever
is filled with rage. He refuses you and refuses your presents.
He tells you yourself to take counsel among the Argives   680
how to save your ships, and the people of the Achaians.
And he himself has threatened that tomorrow as dawn shows
he will drag down his strong-benched, oarswept ships to the
        water.
He said it would be his counsel to others also, to sail back
home again, since no longer will you find any term set   685
on the sheer city of Ilion, since Zeus of the wide brows has strongly
held his own hand over it, and its people are made bold.
So he spoke. There are these to attest it who went there with me
also, Aias, and the two heralds, both men of good counsel.

But aged Phoinix stayed there for the night, as Achilleus urged
him,   690
so he might go home in the ships to the beloved land of his fathers
if Phoinix will; but he will never use force to persuade him.'
    So he spoke, and all of them stayed stricken to silence
in amazement at his words. He had spoken to them very strongly.
For a long time the sons of the Achaians said nothing, in sorrow,   695
but at long last Diomedes of the great war cry spoke to them:
'Son of Atreus, most lordly and king of men, Agamemnon,
I wish you had not supplicated the blameless son of Peleus
with innumerable gifts offered. He is a proud man without this,
and now you have driven him far deeper into his pride. Rather   700
we shall pay him no more attention, whether he comes in with us
or stays away. He will fight again, whenever the time comes
that the heart in his body urges him to, and the god drives him.
Come then, do as I say, and let us all be won over.
Go to sleep, now that the inward heart is made happy   705
with food and drink, for these are the strength and courage within
    us.
But when the lovely dawn shows forth with rose fingers, Atreides,
rapidly form before our ships both people and horses
stirring them on, and yourself be ready to fight in the foremost.'
    So he spoke, and all the kings gave him their approval,   710
acclaiming the word of Diomedes, breaker of horses.
Then they poured a libation, and each man went to his shelter,
where they went to their beds and took the blessing of slumber.

[After Achilleus' refusal, the situation of the Greeks worsened
rapidly. Agamemnon, Diomedes, and Odysseus were all wounded.
The Trojans breached the stockade and fought beside the ships.
Patroklos tried to bring Achilleus to the aid of the Greeks, but the
most he could obtain was permission for himself to fight, clad in
Achilleus' armor, at the head of the Myrmidons. He turned the tide
of battle and drove the Trojans back to their walls, only to fall himself through the direct intervention of Apollo. Hektor stripped
Achilleus' armor from the body. A fierce fight for the body itself
ended in partial success for the Greeks; they took Patroklos' body
but had to retreat to their camp, with the Trojans at their heels.]

Book XVIII

[*The Arming of Achilles*]

So these fought on in the likeness of blazing fire. Meanwhile,
Antilochos came, a swift-footed messenger, to Achilleus,

2. *Antilochos:* a son of Nestor.

and found him sitting in front of the steep-horned ships, thinking
over in his heart of things which had now been accomplished.
Disturbed, Achilleus spoke to the spirit in his own great heart: 5
'Ah me, how is it that once again the flowing-haired Achaians
are driven out of the plain on their ships in fear and confusion?
May the gods not accomplish vile sorrows upon the heart in me
in the way my mother once made it clear to me, when she told me
how while I yet lived the bravest of all the Myrmidons   10
must leave the light of the sun beneath the hands of the Trojans.
Surely, then, the strong son of Menoitios has perished.
Unhappy! and yet I told him, once he had beaten the fierce fire
off, to come back to the ships, not fight in strength against Hektor.'
   Now as he was pondering this in his heart and his spirit,   15
meanwhile the son of stately Nestor was drawing near him
and wept warm tears, and gave Achilleus his sorrowful message:
'Ah me, son of valiant Peleus; you must hear from me
the ghastly message of a thing I wish never had happened.
Patroklos has fallen, and now they are fighting over his body   20
which is naked. Hektor of the shining helm has taken his armour.'
   He spoke, and the black cloud of sorrow closed on Achilleus.
In both hands he caught up the grimy dust, and poured it
over his head and face, and fouled his handsome countenance,
and the black ashes were scattered over his immortal tunic.   25
And he himself, mightily in his might, in the dust lay
at length, and took and tore at his hair with his hands, and defiled it.
And the handmaidens Achilleus and Patroklos had taken
captive, stricken at heart cried out aloud, and came running
out of doors about valiant Achilleus, and all of them   30
beat their breasts with their hands, and the limbs went slack in each
      of them.
On the other side Antilochos mourned with him, letting the tears
      fall,
and held the hands of Achilleus as he grieved in his proud heart,
fearing Achilleus might cut his throat with the iron. He cried out
terribly, aloud, and the lady his mother heard him   35
as she sat in the depths of the sea at the side of her aged father,
and she cried shrill in turn, and the goddesses gathered about her,
all who along the depth of the sea were daughters of Nereus.
For Glauke was there, Kymodoke and Thaleia,
Nesaie and Speio and Thoë, and ox-eyed Halia;   40
Kymothoë was there, Aktaia and Limnoreia,
Melite and Iaira, Amphithoë and Agauë,
Doto and Proto, Dynamene and Pherousa,
Dexamene and Amphinome and Kallianeira;
Doris and Panope and glorious Galateia,   45

12. *son of Menoitios:* Patroklos.

Nemertes and Apseudes and Kallianassa;
Klymene was there, Ianeira and Ianassa,
Maira and Oreithyia and lovely-haired Amatheia,
and the rest who along the depth of the sea were daughters of
    Nereus.
The silvery cave was filled with these, and together all of them   50
beat their breasts, and among them Thetis led out the threnody:
'Hear me, Nereids, my sisters; so you may all know
well all the sorrows that are in my heart, when you hear of them
    from me.
Ah me, my sorrow, the bitterness in this best of child-bearing,
since I gave birth to a son who was without fault and powerful,   55
conspicuous among heroes; and he shot up like a young tree,
and I nurtured him, like a tree grown in the pride of the orchard.
I sent him away with the curved ships into the land of Ilion
to fight with the Trojans; but I shall never again receive him
won home again to his country and into the house of Peleus.   60
Yet while I see him live and he looks on the sunlight, he has
sorrows, and though I go to him I can do nothing to help him.
Yet I shall go, to look on my dear son, and to listen
to the sorrow that has come to him as he stays back from the
    fighting.'
    So she spoke, and left the cave, and the others together   65
went with her in tears, and about them the wave of the water
was broken. Now these, when they came to the generous Troad,
followed each other out on the sea-shore, where close together
the ships of the Myrmidons were hauled up about swift Achilleus.
There as he sighed heavily the lady his mother stood by him   70
and cried out shrill and aloud, and took her son's head in her arms,
    then
sorrowing for him she spoke to him in winged words: 'Why then,
child, do you lament? What sorrow has come to your heart now?
Speak out, do not hide it. These things are brought to accomplish-
    ment
through Zeus: in the way that you lifted your hands and prayed
    for,   75
that all the sons of the Achaians be pinned on their grounded vessels
by reason of your loss, and suffer things that are shameful.'
    Then sighing heavily Achilleus of the swift feet answered her:
'My mother, all these things the Olympian brought to accomplish-
    ment.
But what pleasure is this to me, since my dear companion has per-
    ished,   80
Patroklos, whom I loved beyond all other companions,
as well as my own life. I have lost him, and Hektor, who killed him,

51. *threnody:* song of mourning.   79. *the Olympian:* Zeus.

has stripped away that gigantic armour, a wonder to look on
and splendid, which the gods gave Peleus, a glorious present,
on that day they drove you to the marriage bed of a mortal.   85
I wish you had gone on living then with the other goddesses
of the sea, and that Peleus had married some mortal woman.
As it is, there must be on your heart a numberless sorrow
for your son's death, since you can never again receive him
won home again to his country; since the spirit within does not
  drive me   90
to go on living and be among men, except on condition
that Hektor first be beaten down under my spear, lose his life
and pay the price for stripping Patroklos, the son of Menoitios.'
  Then in turn Thetis spoke to him, letting the tears fall:
'Then I must lose you soon, my child, by what you are saying,   95
since it is decreed your death must come soon after Hektor's.'
  Then deeply disturbed Achilleus of the swift feet answered her:
'I must die soon, then; since I was not to stand by my companion
when he was killed. And now, far away from the land of his fathers,
he has perished, and lacked my fighting strength to defend him.   100
Now, since I am not going back to the beloved land of my fathers,
since I was no light of safety to Patroklos, nor to my other
companions, who in their numbers went down before glorious Hektor,
but sit here beside my ships, a useless weight on the good land,
I, who am such as no other of the bronze-armoured Achaians   105
in battle, though there are others also better in council—
why, I wish that strife would vanish away from among gods and
  mortals,
and gall, which makes a man grow angry for all his great mind,
that gall of anger that swarms like smoke inside of a man's heart
and becomes a thing sweeter to him by far than the dripping of
  honey.   110
So it was here that the lord of men Agamemnon angered me.
Still, we will let all this be a thing of the past, and for all our
sorrow beat down by force the anger deeply within us.
Now I shall go, to overtake that killer of a dear life,
Hektor; then I will accept my own death, at whatever   115
time Zeus wishes to bring it about, and the other immortals.
For not even the strength of Herakles fled away from destruction,
although he was dearest of all to lord Zeus, son of Kronos,
but his fate beat him under, and the wearisome anger of Hera.
So I likewise, if such is the fate which has been wrought for me,   120
shall lie still, when I am dead. Now I must win excellent glory,

117. *Herakles:* son of Zeus; pursued
by the jealousy of Hera, he was forced
to undertake twelve great labors and
finally died in agony from the effects
of a poisoned garment.

and drive some one of the women of Troy, or some deep-girdled
Dardanian woman, lifting up to her soft cheeks both hands
to wipe away the close bursts of tears in her lamentation,
and learn that I stayed too long out of the fighting. Do not   125
hold me back from the fight, though you love me. You will not
    persuade me.'
   In turn the goddess Thetis of the silver feet answered him:
'Yes, it is true, my child, this is no cowardly action,
to beat aside sudden death from your afflicted companions.
Yet, see now, your splendid armour, glaring and brazen,   130
is held among the Trojans, and Hektor of the shining helmet
wears it on his own shoulders, and glories in it. Yet I think
he will not glory for long, since his death stands very close to him.
Therefore do not yet go into the grind of the war god,
not before with your own eyes you see me come back to you.   135
For I am coming to you at dawn and as the sun rises
bringing splendid armour to you from the lord Hephaistos.'
   So she spoke, and turned, and went away from her son,
and turning now to her sisters of the sea she spoke to them:
'Do you now go back into the wide fold of the water   140
to visit the ancient of the sea and the house of our father,
and tell him everything. I am going to tall Olympos
and to Hephaistos, the glorious smith, if he might be willing
to give me for my son renowned and radiant armour.'
   She spoke, and they plunged back beneath the wave of the water,
while she the goddess Thetis of the silver feet went onward   146
to Olympos, to bring back to her son the glorious armour.
   So her feet carried her to Olympos; meanwhile the Achaians
with inhuman clamour before the attack of manslaughtering Hektor
fled until they were making for their own ships and the Hellespont;
nor could the strong-greaved Achaians have dragged the body   151
of Patroklos, henchman of Achilleus, from under the missiles,
for once again the men and the horses came over upon him,
and Hektor, Priam's son, who fought like a flame in his fury.
Three times from behind glorious Hektor caught him   155
by the feet, trying to drag him, and called aloud on the Trojans.
Three times the two Aiantes with their battle-fury upon them
beat him from the corpse, but he, steady in the confidence of his
   great strength,
kept making, now a rush into the crowd, or again at another time
stood fast, with his great cry, but gave not a bit of ground backward.   160
And as herdsmen who dwell in the fields are not able to frighten
a tawny lion in his great hunger away from a carcass,

123. *Dardanian:* Trojan.

so the two Aiantes, marshals of men, were not able
to scare Hektor, Priam's son, away from the body.
And now he would have dragged it away and won glory forever 165
had not swift wind-footed Iris come running from Olympos
with a message for Peleus' son to arm. She came secretly
from Zeus and the other gods, since it was Hera who sent her.
She came and stood close to him and addressed him in winged
    words:
'Rise up, son of Peleus, most terrifying of all men. 170
Defend Patroklos, for whose sake the terrible fighting
stands now in front of the ships. They are destroying each other;
the Achaians fight in defence over the fallen body
while the others, the Trojans, are rushing to drag the corpse off
to windy Ilion, and beyond all glorious Hektor 175
rages to haul it away, since the anger within him is urgent
to cut the head from the soft neck and set it on sharp stakes.
Up, then, lie here no longer; let shame come into your heart, lest
Patroklos become sport for the dogs of Troy to worry,
your shame, if the body goes from here with defilement upon it.' 180
    Then in turn Achilleus of the swift feet answered her:
'Divine Iris, what god sent you to me with a message?'
    Then in turn swift wind-footed Iris spoke to him:
'Hera sent me, the honoured wife of Zeus; but the son of
Kronos, who sits on high, does not know this, nor any other 185
immortal, of all those who dwell by the snows of Olympos.'
    Then in answer to her spoke Achilleus of the swift feet:
'How shall I go into the fighting? They have my armour.
And my beloved mother told me I must not be armoured,
not before with my own eyes I see her come back to me. 190
She promised she would bring magnificent arms from Hephaistos.
Nor do I know of another whose glorious armour I could wear
unless it were the great shield of Telamonian Aias.
But he himself wears it, I think, and goes in the foremost
of the spear-fight over the body of fallen Patroklos.' 195
    Then in turn swift wind-footed Iris spoke to him:
'Yes, we also know well how they hold your glorious armour.
But go to the ditch, and show yourself as you are to the Trojans,
if perhaps the Trojans might be frightened, and give way
from their attack, and the fighting sons of the Achaians get wind 200
again after hard work. There is little breathing space in the fighting.'
    So speaking Iris of the swift feet went away from him;
but Achilleus, the beloved of Zeus, rose up, and Athene
swept about his powerful shoulders the fluttering aegis;

---

166. *Iris:* messenger of the gods, particularly of Hera.

193. *Telamonian:* The more famous of the two heroes called Aias (Ajax) was the son of Telamon.

and she, the divine among goddesses, about his head circled   205
a golden cloud, and kindled from it a flame far-shining.
As when a flare goes up into the high air from a city
from an island far away, with enemies fighting about it
who all day long are in the hateful division of Ares
fighting from their own city, but as the sun goes down signal   210
fires blaze out one after another, so that the glare goes
pulsing high for men of the neighbouring islands to see it,
in case they might come over in ships to beat off the enemy;
so from the head of Achilleus the blaze shot into the bright air.
He went from the wall and stood by the ditch, nor mixed with the
       other   215
Achaians, since he followed the close command of his mother.
There he stood, and shouted, and from her place Pallas Athene
gave cry, and drove an endless terror upon the Trojans.
As loud as comes the voice that is screamed out by a trumpet
by murderous attackers who beleaguer a city,   220
so then high and clear went up the voice of Aiakides.
But the Trojans, when they heard the brazen voice of Aiakides,
the heart was shaken in all, and the very floating-maned horses
turned their chariots about, since their hearts saw the coming afflic-
       tions.
The charioteers were dumbfounded as they saw the unwearied dan-
       gerous   225
fire that played above the head of great-hearted Peleion
blazing, and kindled by the goddess grey-eyed Athene.
Three times across the ditch brilliant Achilleus gave his great cry,
and three times the Trojans and their renowned companions were
       routed.
There at that time twelve of the best men among them perished   230
upon their own chariots and spears. Meanwhile the Achaians
gladly pulled Patroklos out from under the missiles
and set him upon a litter, and his own companions about him
stood mourning, and along with them swift-footed Achilleus
went, letting fall warm tears as he saw his steadfast companion   235
lying there on a carried litter and torn with the sharp bronze,
the man he had sent off before with horses and chariot
into the fighting; who never again came home to be welcomed.
      Now the lady Hera of the ox eyes drove the unwilling
weariless sun god to sink in the depth of the Ocean,   240
and the sun went down, and the brilliant Achaians gave over
their strong fighting, and the doubtful collision of battle.
      The Trojans on the other side moved from the strong encounter

---

209. *Ares:* the god of war.   221. *Aiakides:* Achilleus, grandson
of Aiakos.

in their turn, and unyoked their running horses from under the
 chariots,
and gathered into assembly before taking thought for their supper.
They stood on their feet in assembly, nor did any man have the patience   246
to sit down, but the terror was on them all, seeing that Achilleus
had appeared, after he had stayed so long from the difficult fighting.
First to speak among them was the careful Poulydamas,
Panthöos' son, who alone of them looked before and behind him. 250
He was companion to Hektor, and born on the same night with him,
but he was better in words, the other with the spear far better.
He in kind intention toward all stood forth and addressed them:
'Now take careful thought, dear friends; for I myself urge you
to go back into the city and not wait for the divine dawn 255
in the plain beside the ships. We are too far from the wall now.
While this man was still angry with great Agamemnon,
for all that time the Achaians were easier men to fight with.
For I also used then to be one who was glad to sleep out
near their ships, and I hoped to capture the oarswept vessels. 260
But now I terribly dread the swift-footed son of Peleus.
So violent is the valour in him, he will not be willing
to stay here in the plain, where now Achaians and Trojans
from either side sunder between them the wrath of the war god.
With him, the fight will be for the sake of our city and women. 265
Let us go into the town; believe me; thus it will happen.
For this present, immortal night has stopped the swift-footed
son of Peleus, but if he catches us still in this place
tomorrow, and drives upon us in arms, a man will be well
aware of him, be glad to get back into sacred Ilion, 270
the man who escapes; there will be many Trojans the vultures
and dogs will feed on. But let such a word be out of my hearing!
If all of us will do as I say, though it hurts us to do it,
this night we will hold our strength in the market place, and the
 great walls
and the gateways, and the long, smooth-planed, close-joined gate
 timbers   275
that close to fit them shall defend our city. Then, early
in the morning, under dawn, we shall arm ourselves in our war gear
and take stations along the walls. The worse for him, if he endeavours
to come away from the ships and fight us here for our city.
Back he must go to his ships again, when he wears out the strong
 necks   280

  250. *before and behind him:* He was a prophet; he knew the past and foresaw
the future.

of his horses, driving them at a gallop everywhere by the city.
His valour will not give him leave to burst in upon us
nor sack our town. Sooner the circling dogs will feed on him.'
   Then looking darkly at him Hektor of the shining helm spoke:
'Poulydamas, these things that you argue please me no longer   285
when you tell us to go back again and be cooped in our city.
Have you not all had your glut of being fenced in our outworks?
There was a time when mortal men would speak of the city
of Priam as a place with much gold and much bronze. But now
the lovely treasures that lay away in our houses have vanished,   290
and many possessions have been sold and gone into Phrygia
and into Maionia the lovely, when great Zeus was angry.
But now, when the son of devious-devising Kronos has given
me the winning of glory by the ships, to pin the Achaians
on the sea, why, fool, no longer show these thoughts to our people.
Not one of the Trojans will obey you. I shall not allow it.   296
Come, then, do as I say and let us all be persuaded.
Now, take your supper by positions along the encampment,
and do not forget your watch, and let every man be wakeful.
And if any Trojan is strongly concerned about his possessions,   300
let him gather them and give them to the people, to use them in
      common.
It is better for one of us to enjoy them than for the Achaians.
In the morning, under dawn, we shall arm ourselves in our war gear
and waken the bitter god of war by the hollow vessels.
If it is true that brilliant Achilleus is risen beside their   305
ships, then the worse for him if he tries it, since I for my part
will not run from him out of the sorrowful battle, but rather
stand fast, to see if he wins the great glory, or if I can win it.
The war god is impartial. Before now he has killed the killer.'
   So spoke Hektor, and the Trojans thundered to hear him;   310
fools, since Pallas Athene had taken away the wits from them.
They gave their applause to Hektor in his counsel of evil,
but none to Poulydamas, who had spoken good sense before them.
They took their supper along the encampment. Meanwhile the
      Achaians
mourned all night in lamentation over Patroklos.   315
Peleus' son led the thronging chant of their lamentation,
and laid his manslaughtering hands over the chest of his dear friend
with outbursts of incessant grief. As some great bearded lion
when some man, a deer hunter, has stolen his cubs away from him
out of the close wood; the lion comes back too late, and is an-
      guished,   320
and turns into many valleys quartering after the man's trail
on the chance of finding him, and taken with bitter anger;

so he, groaning heavily, spoke out to the Myrmidons:
'Ah me. It was an empty word I cast forth on that day
when in his halls I tried to comfort the hero Menoitios.   325
I told him I would bring back his son in glory to Opous
with Ilion sacked, and bringing his share of war spoils allotted.
But Zeus does not bring to accomplishment all thoughts in men's
        minds.
Thus it is destiny for us both to stain the same soil
here in Troy; since I shall never come home, and my father,   330
Peleus the aged rider, will not welcome me in his great house,
nor Thetis my mother, but in this place the earth will receive me.
But seeing that it is I, Patroklos, who follow you underground,
I will not bury you till I bring to this place the armour
and the head of Hektor, since he was your great-hearted murderer.
Before your burning pyre I shall behead twelve glorious   336
children of the Trojans, for my anger over your slaying.
Until then, you shall lie where you are in front of my curved ships
and beside you women of Troy and deep-girdled Dardanian women
shall sorrow for you night and day and shed tears for you, those
        whom   340
you and I worked hard to capture by force and the long spear
in days when we were storming the rich cities of mortals.'
        So speaking brilliant Achilleus gave orders to his companions
to set a great cauldron across the fire, so that with all speed
they could wash away the clotted blood from Patroklos.   345
They set up over the blaze of the fire a bath-water cauldron
and poured water into it and put logs underneath and kindled them.
The fire worked on the swell of the cauldron, and the water heated.
But when the water had come to a boil in the shining bronze, then
they washed the body and anointed it softly with olive oil   350
and stopped the gashes in his body with stored-up unguents
and laid him on a bed, and shrouded him in a thin sheet
from head to foot, and covered that over with a white mantle.
        Then all night long, gathered about Achilleus of the swift feet,
the Myrmidons mourned for Patroklos and lamented over him.   355
But Zeus spoke to Hera, who was his wife and his sister:
'So you have acted, then, lady Hera of the ox eyes.
You have roused up Achilleus of the swift feet. It must be then
that the flowing-haired Achaians are born of your own generation.'
        Then the goddess the ox-eyed lady Hera answered him: 360
'Majesty, son of Kronos, what sort of thing have you spoken?
Even one who is mortal will try to accomplish his purpose
for another, though he be a man and knows not such wisdom as
        we do.
As for me then, who claim I am highest of all the goddesses,

both ways, since I am eldest born and am called your consort,   365
yours, and you in turn are lord over all the immortals,
how could I not weave sorrows for the men of Troy, when I hate
    them?'
    Now as these two were saying things like this to each other,
Thetis of the silver feet came to the house of Hephaistos,
imperishable, starry, and shining among the immortals,   370
built in bronze for himself by the god of the dragging footsteps.
She found him sweating as he turned here and there to his bellows
busily, since he was working on twenty tripods
which were to stand against the wall of his strong-founded dwelling.
And he had set golden wheels underneath the base of each one   375
so that of their own motion they could wheel into the immortal
gathering, and return to his house: a wonder to look at.
These were so far finished, but the elaborate ear handles
were not yet on. He was forging these, and beating the chains out.
As he was at work on this in his craftsmanship and his cunning   380
meanwhile the goddess Thetis the silver-footed drew near him.
Charis of the shining veil saw her as she came forward,
she, the lovely goddess the renowned strong-armed one had married.
She came, and caught her hand and called her by name and spoke
    to her:
'Why is it, Thetis of the light robes, you have come to our house
    now?   385
We honour you and love you; but you have not come much before
    this.
But come in with me, so I may put entertainment before you.'
    She spoke, and, shining among divinities, led the way forward
and made Thetis sit down in a chair that was wrought elaborately
and splendid with silver nails, and under it was a footstool.   390
She called to Hephaistos the renowned smith and spoke a word to
    him:
'Hephaistos, come this way; here is Thetis, who has need of you.'
    Hearing her the renowned smith of the strong arms answered her:
'Then there is a goddess we honour and respect in our house.
She saved me when I suffered much at the time of my great fall   395
through the will of my own brazen-faced mother, who wanted
to hide me, for being lame. Then my soul would have taken much
    suffering
had not Eurynome and Thetis caught me and held me,
Eurynome, daughter of Ocean, whose stream bends back in a circle.

371. *dragging footsteps:* Hephaistos
was lame.
382. *Charis:* Her name means
"grace," "beauty."

399. *in a circle:* since the river
Ocean was supposed to surround the
earth.

With them I worked nine years as a smith, and wrought many
    intricate   400
things; pins that bend back, curved clasps, cups, necklaces, working
there in the hollow of the cave, and the stream of Ocean around us
went on forever with its foam and its murmur. No other
among the gods or among mortal men knew about us
except Eurynome and Thetis. They knew, since they saved me.   405
Now she has come into our house; so I must by all means
do everything to give recompense to lovely-haired Thetis
for my life. Therefore set out before her fair entertainment
while I am putting away my bellows and all my instruments.'
    He spoke, and took the huge blower off from the block of the anvil
limping; and yet his shrunken legs moved lightly beneath him.   411
He set the bellows away from the fire, and gathered and put away
all the tools with which he worked in a silver strongbox.
Then with a sponge he wiped clean his forehead, and both hands,
and his massive neck and hairy chest, and put on a tunic,   415
and took up a heavy stick in his hand, and went to the doorway
limping. And in support of their master moved his attendants.
These are golden, and in appearance like living young women.
There is intelligence in their hearts, and there is speech in them
and strength, and from the immortal gods they have learned how
    to do things.   420
These stirred nimbly in support of their master, and moving
near to where Thetis sat in her shining chair, Hephaistos
caught her by the hand and called her by name and spoke a word to
    her:
'Why is it, Thetis of the light robes, you have come to our house
    now?
We honour you and love you; but you have not come much before
    this.   425
Speak forth what is in your mind. My heart is urgent to do it
if I can, and if it is a thing that can be accomplished.'
    Then in turn Thetis answered him, letting the tears fall:
'Hephaistos, is there among all the goddesses on Olympos
one who in her heart has endured so many grim sorrows   430
as the griefs Zeus, son of Kronos, has given me beyond others?
Of all the other sisters of the sea he gave me to a mortal,
to Peleus, Aiakos' son, and I had to endure mortal marriage
though much against my will. And now he, broken by mournful
old age, lies away in his halls. Yet I have other troubles.   435
For since he has given me a son to bear and to raise up
conspicuous among heroes, and he shot up like a young tree,
I nurtured him, like a tree grown in the pride of the orchard.
I sent him away in the curved ships to the land of Ilion

to fight with the Trojans; but I shall never again receive him   440
won home again to his country and into the house of Peleus.
Yet while I see him live and he looks on the sunlight, he has
sorrows, and though I go to him I can do nothing to help him.
And the girl the sons of the Achaians chose out for his honour
powerful Agamemnon took her away again out of his hands.   445
For her his heart has been wasting in sorrow; but meanwhile the
          Trojans
pinned the Achaians against their grounded ships, and would not
let them win outside, and the elders of the Argives entreated
my son, and named the many glorious gifts they would give him.
But at that time he refused himself to fight the death from them;   450
nevertheless he put his own armour upon Patroklos
and sent him into the fighting, and gave many men to go with him.
All day they fought about the Skaian Gates, and on that day
they would have stormed the city, if only Phoibos Apollo
had not killed the fighting son of Menoitios there in the first
          ranks   455
after he had wrought much damage, and given the glory to Hektor.
Therefore now I come to your knees; so might you be willing
to give me for my short-lived son a shield and a helmet
and two beautiful greaves fitted with clasps for the ankles
and a corslet. What he had was lost with his steadfast companion
when the Trojans killed him. Now my son lies on the ground, heart
          sorrowing.'   461
    Hearing her the renowned smith of the strong arms answered her:
'Do not fear. Let not these things be a thought in your mind.
And I wish that I could hide him away from death and its sorrow
at that time when his hard fate comes upon him, as surely   465
as there shall be fine armour for him, such as another
man out of many men shall wonder at, when he looks on it.'
    So he spoke, and left her there, and went to his bellows.
He turned these toward the fire and gave them their orders for
          working.
And the bellows, all twenty of them, blew on the crucibles,   470
from all directions blasting forth wind to blow the flames high
now as he hurried to be at this place and now at another,
wherever Hephaistos might wish them to blow, and the work went
          forward.
He cast on the fire bronze which is weariless, and tin with it
and valuable gold, and silver, and thereafter set forth   475
upon its standard the great anvil, and gripped in one hand
the ponderous hammer, while in the other he grasped the pincers.
    First of all he forged a shield that was huge and heavy,
elaborating it about, and threw around it a shining

triple rim that glittered, and the shield strap was cast of silver.   480
There were five folds composing the shield itself, and upon it
he elaborated many things in his skill and craftsmanship.

He made the earth upon it, and the sky, and the sea's water,
and the tireless sun, and the moon waxing into her fullness,
and on it all the constellations that festoon the heavens,   485
the Pleiades and the Hyades and the strength of Orion
and the Bear, whom men give also the name of the Wagon,
who turns about in a fixed place and looks at Orion
and she alone is never plunged in the wash of the Ocean.

On it he wrought in all their beauty two cities of mortal   490
men. And there were marriages in one, and festivals.
They were leading the brides along the city from their maiden
   chambers
under the flaring of torches, and the loud bride song was arising.
The young men followed the circles of the dance, and among them
the flutes and lyres kept up their clamour as in the meantime   495
the women standing each at the door of her court admired them.
The people were assembled in the market place, where a quarrel
had arisen, and two men were disputing over the blood price
for a man who had been killed. One man promised full restitution
in a public statement, but the other refused and would accept
   nothing.   500
Both then made for an arbitrator, to have a decision;
and people were speaking up on either side, to help both men.
But the heralds kept the people in hand, as meanwhile the elders
were in session on benches of polished stone in the sacred circle
and held in their hands the staves of the heralds who lift their
   voices.   505
The two men rushed before these, and took turns speaking their
   cases,
and between them lay on the ground two talents of gold, to be given
to that judge who in this case spoke the straightest opinion.

But around the other city were lying two forces of armed men
shining in their war gear. For one side counsel was divided   510
whether to storm and sack, or share between both sides the property
and all the possessions the lovely citadel held hard within it.
But the city's people were not giving way, and armed for an ambush.
Their beloved wives and their little children stood on the rampart
to hold it, and with them the men with age upon them, but meanwhile   515
the others went out. And Ares led them, and Pallas Athene.

---

487. *Bear:* the Big Dipper. It is a female bear (Ursa Major), hence "she" in
l. 489.

These were gold, both, and golden raiment upon them, and they
were
beautiful and huge in their armour, being divinities,
and conspicuous from afar, but the people around them were smaller.
These, when they were come to the place that was set for their
ambush,   520
in a river, where there was a watering place for all animals,
there they sat down in place shrouding themselves in the bright
bronze.
But apart from these were sitting two men to watch for the rest of
them
and waiting until they could see the sheep and the shambling cattle,
who appeared presently, and two herdsmen went along with them
playing happily on pipes, and took no thought of the treachery.   526
Those others saw them, and made a rush, and quickly thereafter
cut off on both sides the herds of cattle and the beautiful
flocks of shining sheep, and killed the shepherds upon them.
But the other army, as soon as they heard the uproar arising   530
from the cattle, as they sat in their councils, suddenly mounted
behind their light-foot horses, and went after, and soon overtook
them.
These stood their ground and fought a battle by the banks of the
river,
and they were making casts at each other with their spears bronze-
headed;
and Hate was there with Confusion among them, and Death the
destructive;   535
she was holding a live man with a new wound, and another
one unhurt, and dragged a dead man by the feet through the carnage.
The clothing upon her shoulders showed strong red with the men's
blood.
All closed together like living men and fought with each other
and dragged away from each other the corpses of those who had
fallen.   540
    He made upon it a soft field, the pride of the tilled land,
wide and triple-ploughed, with many ploughmen upon it
who wheeled their teams at the turn and drove them in either
direction.
And as these making their turn would reach the end-strip of the
field,
a man would come up to them at this point and hand them a
flagon   545
of honey-sweet wine, and they would turn again to the furrows
in their haste to come again to the end-strip of the deep field.

The earth darkened behind them and looked like earth that has
    been ploughed
though it was gold. Such was the wonder of the shield's forging.
    He made on it the precinct of a king, where the labourers   550
were reaping, with the sharp reaping hooks in their hands. Of the
    cut swathes
some fell along the lines of reaping, one after another,
while the sheaf-binders caught up others and tied them with bind-
    ropes.
There were three sheaf-binders who stood by, and behind them
were children picking up the cut swathes, and filled their arms with
    them   555
and carried and gave them always; and by them the king in silence
and holding his staff stood near the line of the reapers, happily.
And apart and under a tree the heralds made a feast ready
and trimmed a great ox they had slaughtered. Meanwhile the women
scattered, for the workmen to eat, abundant white barley.   560
    He made on it a great vineyard heavy with clusters,
lovely and in gold, but the grapes upon it were darkened
and the vines themselves stood out through poles of silver. About
    them
he made a field-ditch of dark metal, and drove all around this
a fence of tin; and there was only one path to the vineyard,   565
and along it ran the grape-bearers for the vineyard's stripping.
Young girls and young men, in all their light-hearted innocence,
carried the kind, sweet fruit away in their woven baskets,
and in their midst a youth with a singing lyre played charmingly
upon it for them, and sang the beautiful song for Linos   570
in a light voice, and they followed him, and with singing and
    whistling
and light dance-steps of their feet kept time to the music.
    He made upon it a herd of horn-straight oxen. The cattle
were wrought of gold and of tin, and thronged in speed and with
    lowing
out of the dung of the farmyard to a pasturing place by a sounding
river, and beside the moving field of a reed bed.   576
The herdsmen were of gold who went along with the cattle,
four of them, and nine dogs shifting their feet followed them.
But among the foremost of the cattle two formidable lions
had caught hold of a bellowing bull, and he with loud lowings   580
was dragged away, as the dogs and the young men went in pursuit
    of him.
But the two lions, breaking open the hide of the great ox,

---

570. *song for Linos:* an ancient folk song commemorating Linos, the favorite
of Apollo.

gulped the black blood and the inward guts, as meanwhile the
    herdsmen
were in the act of setting and urging the quick dogs on them.
But they, before they could get their teeth in, turned back from
    the lions,   585
but would come and take their stand very close, and bayed, and kept
    clear.
    And the renowned smith of the strong arms made on it a meadow
large and in a lovely valley for the glimmering sheepflocks,
with dwelling places upon it, and covered shelters, and sheepfolds.
    And the renowned smith of the strong arms made elaborate on
    it   590
a dancing floor, like that which once in the wide spaces of Knosos
Daidalos built for Ariadne of the lovely tresses.
And there were young men on it and young girls, sought for their
    beauty
with gifts of oxen, dancing, and holding hands at the wrist. These
wore, the maidens long light robes, but the men wore tunics   595
of finespun work and shining softly, touched with olive oil.
And the girls wore fair garlands on their heads, while the young men
carried golden knives that hung from sword-belts of silver.
At whiles on their understanding feet they would run very lightly,
as when a potter crouching makes trial of his wheel, holding   600
it close in his hands, to see if it will run smooth. At another
time they would form rows, and run, rows crossing each other.
And around the lovely chorus of dancers stood a great multitude
happily watching, while among the dancers two acrobats
led the measures of song and dance revolving among them.   605
    He made on it the great strength of the Ocean River
which ran around the uttermost rim of the shield's strong structure.
    Then after he had wrought this shield, which was huge and heavy,
he wrought for him a corselet brighter than fire in its shining,
and wrought him a helmet, massive and fitting close to his
    temples,   610
lovely and intricate work, and laid a gold top-ridge along it,
and out of pliable tin wrought him leg-armour. Thereafter
when the renowned smith of the strong arms had finished the
    armour
he lifted it and laid it before the mother of Achilleus.
And she like a hawk came sweeping down from the snows of
    Olympos   615
and carried with her the shining armour, the gift of Hephaistos.

591. *Knosos:* in Crete.
592. *Daidalos:* the "fabulous artif-
icer" who built the labyrinth and, with
his son Icarus, escaped from Crete on
wings. *Ariadne:* daughter of Minos
king of Crete.

Book XIX

[Achilles Returns to the Battle]

Now Dawn the yellow-robed arose from the river of Ocean
to carry her light to men and to immortals. And Thetis
came to the ships and carried with her the gifts of Hephaistos.
She found her beloved son lying in the arms of Patroklos
crying shrill, and his companions in their numbers about him   5
mourned. She, shining among divinities, stood there beside them.
She clung to her son's hand and called him by name and spoke to
   him:
'My child, now, though we grieve for him, we must let this man lie
dead, in the way he first was killed through the gods' designing.
Accept rather from me the glorious arms of Hephaistos,   10
so splendid, and such as no man has ever worn on his shoulders.'
   The goddess spoke so, and set down the armour on the ground
before Achilleus, and all its elaboration clashed loudly.
Trembling took hold of all the Myrmidons. None had the courage
to look straight at it. They were afraid of it. Only Achilleus   15
looked, and as he looked the anger came harder upon him
and his eyes glittered terribly under his lids, like sunflare.
He was glad, holding in his hands the shining gifts of Hephaistos.
But when he had satisfied his heart with looking at the intricate
armour, he spoke to his mother and addressed her in winged
   words: 20
'My mother, the god has given me these weapons; they are such
as are the work of immortals. No mortal man could have made them.
Therefore now I shall arm myself in them. Yet I am sadly
afraid, during this time, for the warlike son of Menoitios
that flies might get into the wounds beaten by bronze in his body   25
and breed worms in them, and these make foul the body, seeing
that the life is killed in him, and that all his flesh may be rotted.'
   In turn the goddess Thetis the silver-footed answered him:
'My child, no longer let these things be a care in your mind.
I shall endeavour to drive from him the swarming and fierce
   things,   30
those flies, which feed upon the bodies of men who have perished;
and although he lie here till a year has gone to fulfilment,
still his body shall be as it was, or firmer than ever.
Go then and summon into assembly the fighting Achaians,
and unsay your anger against Agamemnon, shepherd of the people,
and arm at once for the fighting, and put your war strength upon
   you.'   36
   She spoke so, and drove the strength of great courage into him;
and meanwhile through the nostrils of Patroklos she distilled

ambrosia and red nectar, so that his flesh might not spoil.
But he, brilliant Achilleus, walked along by the sea-shore   40
crying his terrible cry, and stirred up the fighting Achaians.
And even those who before had stayed where the ships were assembled,
they who were helmsmen of the ships and handled the steering oar,
they who were stewards among the ships and dispensers of rations,
even these came then to assembly, since now Achilleus   45
had appeared, after staying so long from the sorrowful battle.
And there were two who came limping among them, henchmen of Ares
both, Tydeus' son the staunch in battle, and brilliant Odysseus,
leaning on spears, since they had the pain of their wounds yet upon them,
and came and took their seats in the front rank of those assembled.
And last of them came in the lord of men Agamemnon   51
with a wound on him, seeing that Koön, the son of Antenor,
had stabbed him with the bronze edge of the spear in the strong encounter.
But now, when all the Achaians were in one body together,
Achilleus of the swift feet stood up before them and spoke to them: 55
'Son of Atreus, was this after all the better way for
both, for you and me, that we, for all our hearts' sorrow,
quarrelled together for the sake of a girl in soul-perishing hatred?
I wish Artemis had killed her beside the ships with an arrow
on that day when I destroyed Lyrnessos and took her.   60
For thus not all these too many Achaians would have bitten
the dust, by enemy hands, when I was away in my anger.
This way was better for the Trojans and Hektor; yet I think
the Achaians will too long remember this quarrel between us.
Still, we will let all this be a thing of the past, though it hurts us,   65
and beat down by constraint the anger that rises inside us.
Now I am making an end of my anger. It does not become me
unrelentingly to rage on. Come, then! The more quickly
drive on the flowing-haired Achaians into the fighting,
so that I may go up against the Trojans, and find out   70
if they still wish to sleep out beside the ships. I think rather
they will be glad to rest where they are, whoever among them
gets away with his life from the fury of our spears' onset.'
   He spoke, and the strong-greaved Achaians were pleasured to hear him
and how the great-hearted son of Peleus unsaid his anger.   75
Now among them spoke forth the lord of men Agamemnon
    39. *ambrosia:* the food of the gods.

from the place where he was sitting, and did not stand up among
      them:
'Fighting men and friends, o Danaans, henchmen of Ares:
it is well to listen to the speaker, it is not becoming
to break in on him. This will be hard for him, though he be able. 80
How among the great murmur of people shall anyone listen
or speak either? A man, though he speak very clearly, is baffled.
I shall address the son of Peleus; yet all you other
Argives listen also, and give my word careful attention.
This is the word the Achaians have spoken often against me 85
and found fault with me in it, yet I am not responsible
but Zeus is, and Destiny, and Erinys the mist-walking
who in assembly caught my heart in the savage delusion
on that day I myself stripped from him the prize of Achilleus.
Yet what could I do? It is the god who accomplishes all things. 90
Delusion is the elder daughter of Zeus, the accursed
who deludes all; her feet are delicate and they step not
on the firm earth, but she walks the air above men's heads
and leads them astray. She has entangled others before me.
Yes, for once Zeus even was deluded, though men say 95
he is the highest one of gods and mortals. Yet Hera
who is female deluded even Zeus in her craftiness
on that day when in strong wall-circled Thebe Alkmene
was at her time to bring forth the strength of Herakles. Therefore
Zeus spoke forth and made a vow before all the immortals: 100
"Hear me, all you gods and all you goddesses: hear me
while I speak forth what the heart within my breast urges.
This day Eileithyia of women's child-pains shall bring forth
a man to the light who, among the men sprung of the generation
of my blood, shall be lord over all those dwelling about him." 105
Then in guileful intention the lady Hera said to him:
"You will be a liar, not put fulfilment on what you have spoken.
Come, then, lord of Olympos, and swear before me a strong oath
that he shall be lord over all those dwelling about him
who this day shall fall between the feet of a woman, 110
that man who is born of the blood of your generation." So Hera
spoke. And Zeus was entirely unaware of her falsehood,
but swore a great oath, and therein lay all his deception.
But Hera in a flash of speed left the horn of Olympos
and rapidly came to Argos of Achaia, where she knew 115
was the mighty wife of Sthenelos, descended of Perseus.
And she was carrying a son, and this was the seventh month for her,

87. *Erinys:* an avenger, a Fury. Here
mentioned without reference to the
Furies' proper function, simply as a
power of darkness.
      99. *Herakles:* son of Zeus (see note
to Book XVIII, l. 117).

103. *Eileithyia:* the goddess who presided over human birth.
      110. *fall between the feet of a
woman:* be born.
      116. *Perseus:* a son of Zeus.

but she brought him sooner into the light, and made him premature,
and stayed the childbirth of Alkmene, and held back the birth pangs.
She went herself and spoke the message to Zeus, son of Kronos: 120
"Father Zeus of the shining bolt, I will tell you a message
for your heart. A great man is born, who will be lord over the
    Argives,
Eurystheus, son of Sthenelos, of the seed of Perseus,
your generation. It is not unfit that he should rule over
the Argives." She spoke, and the sharp sorrow struck at his deep
    heart. 125
He caught by the shining hair of her head the goddess Delusion
in the anger of his heart, and swore a strong oath, that never
after this might Delusion, who deludes all, come back
to Olympos and the starry sky. So speaking, he whirled her
about in his hand and slung her out of the starry heaven, 130
and presently she came to men's establishments. But Zeus
would forever grieve over her each time that he saw his dear son
doing some shameful work of the tasks that Eurystheus set him.
So I in my time, when tall Hektor of the shining helm
was forever destroying the Argives against the sterns of their ves-
    sels, 135
could not forget Delusion, the way I was first deluded.
But since I was deluded and Zeus took my wits away from me,
I am willing to make all good and give back gifts in abundance.
Rise up, then, to the fighting and rouse the rest of the people.
Here am I, to give you all those gifts, as many 140
as brilliant Odysseus yesterday went to your shelter and promised.
Or if you will, hold back, though you lean hard into the battle,
while my followers take the gifts from my ship and bring them
to you, so you may see what I give to comfort your spirit.'

    Then in answer to him spoke Achilleus of the swift feet: 145
'Son of Atreus, most lordly and king of men, Agamemnon,
the gifts are yours to give if you wish, and as it is proper,
or to keep with yourself. But now let us remember our joy in
    warcraft,
immediately, for it is not fitting to stay here and waste time
nor delay, since there is still a big work to be done. 150
So can a man see once more Achilleus among the front fighters
with the bronze spear wrecking the Trojan battalions. Therefore
let each of you remember this and fight his antagonist.'

    Then in answer to him spoke resourceful Odysseus:
'Not that way, good fighter that you are, godlike Achilleus. 155
Do not drive the sons of the Achaians on Ilion when they are
    hungry,

123. *Eurystheus:* He became king of Argos, and taskmaster of Herakles, who performed twelve great labors for him.

124. *your generation:* descended from Zeus through Perseus.

to fight against the Trojans, since not short will be the time
of battle, once the massed formations of men have encountered
together, with the god inspiring fury in both sides.
Rather tell the men of Achaia here by their swift ships,   160
to take food and wine, since these make fighting fury and warcraft.
For a man will not have strength to fight his way forward all day
long until the sun goes down if he is starved for food. Even
though in his heart he be very passionate for the battle,
yet without his knowing it his limbs will go heavy, and hunger   165
and thirst will catch up with him and cumber his knees as he moves
      on.
But when a man has been well filled with wine and with eating
and then does battle all day long against the enemy,
why, then the heart inside him is full of cheer, nor do his limbs
get weary, until all are ready to give over the fighting.   170
Come then, tell your men to scatter and bid them get ready
a meal; and as for the gifts, let the lord of men Agamemnon
bring them to the middle of our assembly so all the Achaians
can see them before their eyes, so your own heart may be pleasured.
And let him stand up before the Argives and swear an oath to you
that he never entered into her bed and never lay with her   176
as is natural for people, my lord, between men and women.
And by this let the spirit in your own heart be made gracious.
After that in his own shelter let him appease you
with a generous meal, so you will lack nothing of what is due you.
And you, son of Atreus, after this be more righteous to another 181
man. For there is no fault when even one who is a king
appeases a man, when the king was the first one to be angry.'
    Then in turn the lord of men Agamemnon answered him:
'Hearing what you have said, son of Laertes, I am pleased with
      you.   185
Fairly have you gone through everything and explained it.
And all this I am willing to swear to, and my heart urges me,
and I will not be foresworn before the gods. Let Achilleus
stay here the while, though he lean very hard toward the work of
      the war god,
and remain the rest of you all here assembled, until the gifts come
back from my shelter and while we cut our oaths of fidelity.   191
And for you yourself, Odysseus, I give you this errand, this order,
that you choose out excellent young men of all the Achaians
and bring the gifts back here from my ship, all that you promised
yesterday to Achilleus, and bring the women back also.   195
And in the wide host of the Achaians let Talthybios make ready

176. *her:* Briseis.
191. *cut our oaths:* "cut" refers to
the killing of the animals sacrificed to
seal the oath.
196. *Talthybios:* Agamemnon's herald.

a boar for me, and dedicate it to Zeus and Helios.'
    Then in answer to him spoke Achilleus of the swift feet:
'Son of Atreus, most lordly and king of men, Agamemnon,
at some other time rather you should busy yourself about these
     things,   200
when there is some stopping point in the fighting, at some time
when there is not so much fury inside of my heart. But now
as things are they lie there torn whom the son of Priam
Hektor has beaten down, since Zeus was giving him glory,
and then you urge a man to eating. No, but I would now   205
drive forward the sons of the Achaians into the fighting
starving and unfed, and afterwards when the sun sets
make ready a great dinner, when we have paid off our defilement.
But before this, for me at least, neither drink nor food shall
go down my very throat, since my companion has perished   210
and lies inside my shelter torn about with the cutting
bronze, and turned against the forecourt while my companions
mourn about him. Food and drink mean nothing to my heart
but blood does, and slaughter, and the groaning of men in the hard
     work.'
    Then in answer to him spoke resourceful Odysseus: 215
'Son of Peleus, Achilleus, far greatest of the Achaians,
you are stronger than I am and greater by not a little
with the spear, yet I in turn might overpass you in wisdom
by far, since I was born before you and have learned more things.
Therefore let your heart endure to listen to my words.   220
When there is battle men have suddenly their fill of it
when the bronze scatters on the ground the straw in most numbers
and the harvest is most thin, when Zeus has poised his balance,
Zeus, who is administrator to men in their fighting.
There is no way the Achaians can mourn a dead man by denying   225
the belly. Too many fall day by day, one upon another,
and how could anyone find breathing space from his labour?
No, but we must harden our hearts and bury the man who
dies, when we have wept over him on the day, and all those
who are left about from the hateful work of war must remember   230
food and drink, so that afterwards all the more strongly
we may fight on forever relentless against our enemies
with the weariless bronze put on about our bodies. Let one not
wait longing for any other summons to stir on the people.
This summons now shall be an evil on anyone left behind   235
by the ships of the Argives. Therefore let us drive on together
and wake the bitter war god on the Trojans, breakers of horses.'
    He spoke, and went away with the sons of glorious Nestor,

197. *Helios:* the sun.

with Meges, the son of Phyleus, and Meriones, and Thoas,
and Lykomedes, the son of Kreion, and Melanippos. These went
on their way to the shelter of Atreus' son Agamemnon.   241
No sooner was the order given than the thing had been done.
They brought back seven tripods from the shelter, those Agamemnon
had promised, and twenty shining cauldrons, twelve horses. They
     brought back
immediately the seven women the work of whose hands was   245
blameless, and the eighth of them was Briseis of the fair cheeks.
Odysseus weighed out ten full talents of gold and led them
back, and the young men of the Achaians carried the other gifts.
They brought these into the midst of assembly, and Agamemnon
stood up, and Talthybios in voice like an immortal   250
stood beside the shepherd of the people with the boar in his hands.
Atreus' son laid hands upon his work-knife, and drew it
from where it hung ever beside the great sheath of his war sword,
and cut first hairs away from the boar, and lifting his hands up
to Zeus, prayed, while all the Argives stayed fast at their places 255
in silence and in order of station, and listened to their king.
He spoke before them in prayer gazing into the wide sky:
'Let Zeus first be my witness, highest of the gods and greatest,
and Earth, and Helios the Sun, and Furies, who underground
avenge dead men, when any man has sworn to a falsehood,   260
that I have never laid a hand on the girl Briseis
on pretext to go to bed with her, or for any other
reason, but she remained, not singled out, in my shelter.
If any of this is falsely sworn, may the gods give me many   264
griefs, all that they inflict on those who swear falsely before them.'
     So he spoke, and with pitiless bronze he cut the boar's throat.
Talthybios whirled the body about, and threw it in the great reach
of the grey sea, to feed the fishes. Meanwhile Achilleus
stood up among the battle-fond Achaians, and spoke to them:
'Father Zeus, great are the delusions with which you visit men. 270
Without you, the son of Atreus could never have stirred so
the heart inside my breast, nor taken the girl away from me
against my will, and be in helplessness. No, but Zeus somehow
wished that death should befall great numbers of the Achaians.
Go now and take your dinner, so we may draw on the battle.'   275
     So he spoke, and suddenly broke up the assembly.
Now these scattered away each man to his own ship. Meanwhile
the great-hearted Myrmidons disposed of the presents.
They went on their way carrying them to the ship of godlike
     Achilleus,   279
and stowed the gifts in the shelters, and let the women be settled,
while proud henchmen drove the horses into Achilleus' horse-herd.

And now, in the likeness of golden Aphrodite, Briseis
when she saw Patroklos lying torn with sharp bronze, folding
him in her arms cried shrilly above him and with her hands tore
at her breasts and her soft throat and her beautiful forehead.   285
The woman like the immortals mourning for him spoke to him:
'Patroklos, far most pleasing to my heart in its sorrows,
I left you here alive when I went away from the shelter,
but now I come back, lord of the people, to find you have fallen.
So evil in my life takes over from evil forever.   290
The husband on whom my father and honoured mother bestowed
      me
I saw before my city lying torn with the sharp bronze,
and my three brothers, whom a single mother bore with me
and who were close to me, all went on one day to destruction.
And yet you would not let me, when swift Achilleus had cut down
my husband, and sacked the city of godlike Mynes, you would not
let me sorrow, but said you would make me godlike Achilleus'
wedded lawful wife, that you would take me back in the ships
to Phthia, and formalize my marriage among the Myrmidons.
Therefore I weep your death without ceasing. You were kind
      always.'   300
      So she spoke, lamenting, and the women sorrowed around her
grieving openly for Patroklos, but for her own sorrows
each. But the lords of Achaia were gathered about Achilleus
beseeching him to eat, but he with a groan denied them:
'I beg of you, if any dear companion will listen   305
to me, stop urging me to satisfy the heart in me
with food and drink, since this strong sorrow has come upon me.
I will hold out till the sun goes down and endure, though it be hard.'
      So he spoke, and caused the rest of the kings to scatter;
but the two sons of Atreus stayed with him, and brilliant Odys-
      seus,   310
and Nestor, and Idomeneus, and the aged charioteer, Phoinix,
comforting him close in his sorrow, yet his heart would not
be comforted, till he went into the jaws of the bleeding battle.
Remembering Patroklos he sighed much for him, and spoke aloud:
'There was a time, ill fated, o dearest of all my companions,   315
when you yourself would set the desirable dinner before me
quickly and expertly, at the time the Achaians were urgent
to carry sorrowful war on the Trojans, breakers of horses.
But now you lie here torn before me, and my heart goes starved
for meat and drink, though they are here beside me, by reason   320
of longing for you. There is nothing worse than this I could suffer,
not even if I were to hear of the death of my father
who now, I think, in Phthia somewhere lets fall a soft tear

for bereavement of such a son, for me, who now in a strange land
make war upon the Trojans for the sake of accursed Helen;   325
or the death of my dear son, who is raised for my sake in Skyros
now, if godlike Neoptolemos is still one of the living.
Before now the spirit inside my breast was hopeful
that I alone should die far away from horse-pasturing Argos
here in Troy; I hoped you would win back again to Phthia   330
so that in a fast black ship you could take my son back
from Skyros to Phthia, and show him all my possessions,
my property, my serving men, my great high-roofed house.
For by this time I think that Peleus must altogether
have perished, or still keeps a little scant life in sorrow   335
for the hatefulness of old age and because he waits ever from me
the evil message, for the day he hears I have been killed.'
    So he spoke, mourning, and the elders lamented around him
remembering each those he had left behind in his own halls.
The son of Kronos took pity on them as he watched them mourn-
        ing   340
and immediately spoke in winged words to Athene:
'My child, have you utterly abandoned the man of your choice?
Is there no longer deep concern in your heart for Achilleus?
Now he has sat down before the steep horned ships and is mourning
for his own beloved companion, while all the others   345
have gone to take their dinner, but he is fasting and unfed.
Go then to him and distil nectar inside his chest, and delicate
ambrosia, so the weakness of hunger will not come upon him.'
    Speaking so, he stirred Athene, who was eager before this,
and she in the likeness of a wide-winged, thin-crying   350
hawk plummeted from the sky through the bright air. Now the
        Achaians
were arming at once along the encampment. She dropped the
        delicate
ambrosia and the nectar inside the breast of Achilleus
softly, so no sad weakness of hunger would come on his knees,
and she herself went back to the close house of her powerful   355
father, while they were scattering out away from the fast ships.
As when in their thickness the snowflakes of Zeus come fluttering
cold beneath the blast of the north wind born in the bright sky,
so now in their thickness the pride of the helms bright shining
were carried out from the ships, and shields massive in the middle
and the corselets strongly hollowed and the ash spears were worn
        forth.   361
The shining swept to the sky and all earth was laughing about them
under the glitter of bronze and beneath their feet stirred the thunder
of men, within whose midst brilliant Achilleus helmed him.
A clash went from the grinding of his teeth, and his eyes glowed   365

as if they were the stare of a fire, and the heart inside him
was entered with sorrow beyond endurance. Raging at the Trojans
he put on the gifts of the god, that Hephaistos wrought him with
    much toil.
  First he placed along his legs the fair greaves linked with
silver fastenings to hold the greaves at the ankles.   370
Afterward he girt on about his chest the corselet,
and across his shoulders slung the sword with the nails of silver,
a bronze sword, and caught up the great shield, huge and heavy
next, and from it the light glimmered far, as from the moon.
And as when from across water a light shines to mariners   375
from a blazing fire, when the fire is burning high in the mountains
in a desolate steading, as the mariners are carried unwilling
by storm winds over the fish-swarming sea, far away from their loved
    ones;
so the light from the fair elaborate shield of Achilleus
shot into the high air. And lifting the helm he set it   380
massive upon his head, and the helmet crested with horse-hair
shone like a star, the golden fringes were shaken about it
which Hephaistos had driven close along the horn of the helmet.
And brilliant Achilleus tried himself in his armour, to see
if it fitted close, and how his glorious limbs ran within it,   385
and the armour became as wings and upheld the shepherd of the
    people.
Next he pulled out from its standing place the spear of his father,
huge, heavy, thick, which no one else of all the Achaians
could handle, but Achilleus alone knew how to wield it,
the Pelian ash spear which Cheiron had brought to his father   390
from high on Pelion, to be death for fighters in battle.
Automedon and Alkimos, in charge of the horses,
yoked them, and put the fair breast straps about them, and forced
    the bits home
between their jaws, and pulled the reins back against the compacted
chariot seat, and one, Automedon, took up the shining   395
whip caught close in his hand and vaulted up to the chariot,
while behind him Achilleus helmed for battle took his stance
shining in all his armour like the sun when he crosses above us,
and cried in a terrible voice on the horses of his father:
'Xanthos, Balios, Bay and Dapple, famed sons of Podarge,   400
take care to bring in another way your charioteer back
to the company of the Danaans, when we give over fighting,
not leave him to lie fallen there, as you did to Patroklos.'
  Then from beneath the yoke the gleam-footed horse answered
    him,
Xanthos, and as he spoke bowed his head, so that all the mane   405
fell away from the pad and swept the ground by the cross-yoke;

the goddess of the white arms, Hera, had put a voice in him:
'We shall still keep you safe for this time, o hard Achilleus.
And yet the day of your death is near, but it is not we
who are to blame, but a great god and powerful Destiny.   410
For it was not because we were slow, because we were careless,
that the Trojans have taken the armour from the shoulders of
    Patroklos,
but it was that high god, the child of lovely-haired Leto,
who killed him among the champions and gave the glory to Hektor.
But for us, we two could run with the blast of the west wind   415
who they say is the lightest of all things; yet still for you
there is destiny to be killed in force by a god and a mortal.'
    When he had spoken so the Furies stopped the voice in him,
but deeply disturbed, Achilleus of the swift feet answered him:
'Xanthos, why do you prophesy my death? This is not for you.   420
I myself know well it is destined for me to die here
far from my beloved father and mother. But for all that
I will not stop till the Trojans have had enough of my fighting.'
    He spoke, and shouting held on in the foremost his single-foot
    horses.

[Achilleus' return to the fighting brought terror to the Trojans,
and turned the battle into a rout in which Achilleus killed every
Trojan that crossed his path. As he pursued Agenor, Apollo tricked
him by rescuing his intended victim (he spirited him away in a
mist) and assumed Agenor's shape to lead Achilleus away from the
walls of Troy. The Trojans took refuge in the city, all except Hektor.]

[The Death of Hector]

Book XXII

    So along the city the Trojans, who had run like fawns, dried
the sweat off from their bodies and drank and slaked their thirst,
    leaning
along the magnificent battlements. Meanwhile the Achaians
sloping their shields across their shoulders came close to the rampart.
But his deadly fate held Hektor shackled, so that he stood fast   5
in front of Ilion and the Skaian gates. Now Phoibos
Apollo spoke aloud to Peleion: 'Why, son of Peleus,
do you keep after me in the speed of your feet, being mortal
while I am an immortal god? Even yet you have not
seen that I am a god, but strain after me in your fury.   10

---

413. *child of . . . Leto:* Apollo.
417. *god . . . mortal:* Achilleus will eventually fall by the hand of Paris as a result of the intervention of Apollo.

418. *Furies:* One of the functions of these goddesses was to ensure that all the creatures of the universe observed their proper limits.

Now hard fighting with the Trojans whom you stampeded means
     nothing
to you. They are crowded in the city, but you bent away here.
You will never kill me. I am not one who is fated.'
   Deeply vexed Achilleus of the swift feet spoke to him:
'You have balked me, striker from afar, most malignant of all
     gods,   15
when you turned me here away from the rampart, else many Trojans
would have caught the soil in their teeth before they got back into
     Ilion.
Now you have robbed me of great glory, and rescued these people
lightly, since you have no retribution to fear hereafter.
Else I would punish you, if only the strength were in me.'   20
   He spoke, and stalked away against the city, with high thoughts
in mind, and in tearing speed, like a racehorse with his chariot
who runs lightly as he pulls the chariot over the flat land.
Such was the action of Achilleus in feet and quick knees.
   The aged Priam was the first of all whose eyes saw him   25
as he swept across the flat land in full shining, like that star
which comes on in the autumn and whose conspicuous brightness
far outshines the stars that are numbered in the night's darkening,
the star they give the name of Orion's Dog, which is brightest
among the stars, and yet is wrought as a sign of evil   30
and brings on the great fever for unfortunate mortals.
Such was the flare of the bronze that girt his chest in his running.
The old man groaned aloud and with both hands high uplifted
beat his head, and groaned amain, and spoke supplicating
his beloved son, who there still in front of the gateway   35
stood fast in determined fury to fight with Achilleus.
The old man stretching his hands out called pitifully to him:
'Hektor, beloved child, do not wait the attack of this man
alone, away from the others. You might encounter your destiny
beaten down by Peleion, since he is far stronger than you are.   40
A hard man: I wish he were as beloved of the immortal
as loved by me. Soon he would lie dead, and the dogs and the
     vultures
would eat him, and bitter sorrow so be taken from my heart.
He has made me desolate of my sons, who were brave and many.
He killed them, or sold them away among the far-lying islands.   45
Even now there are two sons, Lykaon and Polydoros,
whom I cannot see among the Trojans pent up in the city,
sons Laothoë a princess among women bore to me.
But if these are alive somewhere in the army, then I can

---

46. *Lykaon:* he had already been   youngest son, already killed by
killed by Achilleus. *Polydoros:* Priam's   Achilleus.

set them free for bronze and gold; it is there inside, since   50
Altes the aged and renowned gave much with his daughter.
But if they are dead already and gone down to the house of Hades,
it is sorrow to our hearts, who bore them, myself and their mother,
but to the rest of the people a sorrow that will be fleeting
beside their sorrow for you, if you go down before Achilleus.   55
Come then inside the wall, my child, so that you can rescue
the Trojans and the women of Troy, neither win the high glory
for Peleus' son, and yourself be robbed of your very life. Oh, take
pity on me, the unfortunate still alive, still sentient
but ill-starred, whom the father, Kronos' son, on the threshold of
    old age   60
will blast with hard fate, after I have looked upon evils
and seen my sons destroyed and my daughters dragged away captive
and the chambers of marriage wrecked and the innocent children
    taken
and dashed to the ground in the hatefulness of war, and the wives
of my sons dragged off by the accursed hands of the Achaians.   65
And myself last of all, my dogs in front of my doorway
will rip me raw, after some man with stroke of the sharp bronze
spear, or with spearcast, has torn the life out of my body;
those dogs I raised in my halls to be at my table, to guard my
gates, who will lap my blood in the savagery of their anger   70
and then lie down in my courts. For a young man all is decorous
when he is cut down in battle and torn with the sharp bronze, and
    lies there
dead, and though dead still all that shows about him is beautiful;
but when an old man is dead and down, and the dogs mutilate
the grey head and the grey beard and the parts that are secret,   75
this, for all sad mortality, is the sight most pitiful.'
    So the old man spoke, and in his hands seizing the grey hairs
tore them from his head, but could not move the spirit in Hektor.
And side by side with him his mother in tears was mourning
and laid the fold of her bosom bare and with one hand held out   80
a breast, and wept her tears for him and called to him in winged
    words:
'Hektor, my child, look upon these and obey, and take pity
on me, if ever I gave you the breast to quiet your sorrow.
Remember all these things, dear child, and from inside the wall
beat off this grim man. Do not go out as champion against him,   85
o hard one; for if he kills you I can no longer
mourn you on the death-bed, sweet branch, o child of my bearing,
nor can your generous wife mourn you, but a big way from us
beside the ships of the Argives the running dogs will feed on you.'

51. *Altes:* father of Laothoë.

So these two in tears and with much supplication called out   90
to their dear son, but could not move the spirit in Hektor,
but he awaited Achilleus as he came on, gigantic.
But as a snake waits for a man by his hole, in the mountains,
glutted with evil poisons, and the fell venom has got inside him,
and coiled about the hole he stares malignant, so Hektor   95
would not give ground but kept unquenched the fury within him
and sloped his shining shield against the jut of the bastion.
Deeply troubled he spoke to his own great-hearted spirit:
'Ah me! If I go now inside the wall and the gateway,
Poulydamas will be first to put a reproach upon me,   100
since he tried to make me lead the Trojans inside the city
on that accursed night when brilliant Achilleus rose up,
and I would not obey him, but that would have been far better.
Now, since by my own recklessness I have ruined my people,
I feel shame before the Trojans and the Trojan women with
trailing   105
robes, that someone who is less of a man than I will say of me:
"Hektor believed in his own strength and ruined his people."
Thus they will speak; and as for me, it would be much better
at that time, to go against Achilleus, and slay him, and come back,
or else be killed by him in glory in front of the city.   110
Or if again I set down my shield massive in the middle
and my ponderous helm, and lean my spear up against the rampart
and go out as I am to meet Achilleus the blameless
and promise to give back Helen, and with her all her possessions,
all those things that once in the hollow ships Alexandros   115
brought back to Troy, and these were the beginning of the quarrel;
to give these to Atreus' sons to take away, and for the Achaians
also to divide up all that is hidden within the city,
and take an oath thereafter for the Trojans in conclave
not to hide anything away, but distribute all of it,   120
as much as the lovely citadel keeps guarded within it;
yet still, why does the heart within me debate on these things?
I might go up to him, and he take no pity upon me
nor respect my position, but kill me naked so, as if I were
a woman, once I stripped my armour from me. There is no   125
way any more from a tree or a rock to talk to him gently
whispering like a young man and a young girl, in the way
a young man and a young maiden whisper together.
Better to bring on the fight with him as soon as it may be.
We shall see to which one the Olympian grants the glory.'   130
So he pondered, waiting, but Achilleus was closing upon him
in the likeness of the lord of battles, the helm-shining warrior,
and shaking from above his shoulder the dangerous Pelian

ash spear, while the bronze that closed about him was shining
like the flare of blazing fire or the sun in its rising.   135
And the shivers took hold of Hektor when he saw him, and he
        could no longer
stand his ground there, but left the gates behind, and fled, fright-
        ened,
and Peleus' son went after him in the confidence of his quick feet.
As when a hawk in the mountains who moves lightest of things flying
makes his effortless swoop for a trembling dove, but she slips away
from beneath and flies and he shrill screaming close after her   141
plunges for her again and again, heart furious to take her;
so Achilleus went straight for him in fury, but Hektor
fled away under the Trojan wall and moved his knees rapidly.
They raced along by the watching point and the windy fig tree   145
always away from under the wall and along the wagon-way
and came to the two sweet-running well springs. There there are
        double
springs of water that jet up, the springs of whirling Skamandros.
One of these runs hot water and the steam on all sides
of it rises as if from a fire that was burning inside it.   150
But the other in the summer-time runs water that is like hail
or chill snow or ice that forms from water. Beside these
in this place, and close to them, are the washing-hollows
of stone, and magnificent, where the wives of the Trojans and their
        lovely
daughters washed the clothes to shining, in the old days   155
when there was peace, before the coming of the sons of the
        Achaians.
They ran beside these, one escaping, the other after him.
It was a great man who fled, but far better he who pursued him
rapidly, since here was no festal beast, no ox-hide
they strove for, for these are prizes that are given men for their
        running.   160
No, they ran for the life of Hektor, breaker of horses.
As when about the turnposts racing single-foot horses
run at full speed, when a great prize is laid up for their winning,
a tripod or a woman, in games for a man's funeral,
so these two swept whirling about the city of Priam   165
in the speed of their feet, while all the gods were looking upon
        them.
First to speak among them was the father of gods and mortals:
'Ah me, this is a man beloved whom now my eyes watch
being chased around the wall; my heart is mourning for Hektor
who has burned in my honour many thigh pieces of oxen   170
on the peaks of Ida with all her folds, or again on the uttermost

part of the citadel, but now the brilliant Achilleus
drives him in speed of his feet around the city of Priam.
Come then, you immortals, take thought and take counsel, whether
to rescue this man or whether to make him, for all his valour,   175
go down under the hands of Achilleus, the son of Peleus.'
   Then in answer the goddess grey-eyed Athene spoke to him:
'Father of the shining bolt, dark misted, what is this you said?
Do you wish to bring back a man who is mortal, one long since
doomed by his destiny, from ill-sounding death and release
      him?   180
Do it, then; but not all the rest of us gods shall approve you.'
   Then Zeus the gatherer of the clouds spoke to her in answer:
'Tritogeneia, dear daughter, do not lose heart; for I say this
not in outright anger, and my meaning toward you is kindly.
Act as your purpose would have you do, and hold back no
      longer.'   185
   So he spoke, and stirred on Athene, who was eager before this,
and she went in a flash of speed down the pinnacles of Olympos.
   But swift Achilleus kept unremittingly after Hektor,
chasing him, as a dog in the mountains who has flushed from his
      covert
a deer's fawn follows him through the folding ways and the
      valleys,   190
and though the fawn crouched down under a bush and be hidden
he keeps running and noses him out until he comes on him;
so Hektor could not lose himself from swift-footed Peleion.
If ever he made a dash right on for the gates of Dardanos
to get quickly under the strong-built bastions, endeavouring   195
that they from above with missiles thrown might somehow defend
      him,
each time Achilleus would get in front and force him to turn back
into the plain, and himself kept his flying course next the city.
As in a dream a man is not able to follow one who runs
from him, nor can the runner escape, nor the other pursue him,   200
so he could not run him down in his speed, nor the other get clear.
How then could Hektor have escaped the death spirits, had not
Apollo, for this last and uttermost time, stood by him
close, and driven strength into him, and made his knees light?
But brilliant Achilleus kept shaking his head at his own people   205
and would not let them throw their bitter projectiles at Hektor
for fear the thrower might win the glory, and himself come second.
But when for the fourth time they had come around to the well
      springs
then the Father balanced his golden scales, and in them

183. *Tritogeneia:* a title of Athene; its origin and meaning are unknown.

he set two fateful portions of death, which lays men prostrate, 210
one for Achilleus, and one for Hektor, breaker of horses,
and balanced it by the middle; and Hektor's death-day was heavier
and dragged downward toward death, and Phoibos Apollo forsook
    him.
But the goddess grey-eyed Athene came now to Peleion
and stood close beside him and addressed him in winged words:
    'Beloved   215
of Zeus, shining Achilleus, I am hopeful now that you and I
will take back great glory to the ships of the Achaians, after
we have killed Hektor, for all his slakeless fury for battle.
Now there is no way for him to get clear away from us,
not though Apollo who strikes from afar should be willing to
    undergo   220
much, and wallow before our father Zeus of the aegis.
Stand you here then and get your wind again, while I go
to this man and persuade him to stand up to you in combat.'
    So spoke Athene, and he was glad at heart, and obeyed her,
and stopped, and stood leaning on his bronze-barbed ash spear.
    Meanwhile   225
Athene left him there, and caught up with brilliant Hektor,
and likened herself in form and weariless voice to Deïphobos.
She came now and stood close to him and addressed him in winged
    words:
'Dear brother, indeed swift-footed Achilleus is using you roughly
and chasing you on swift feet around the city of Priam.   230
Come on, then; let us stand fast against him and beat him back
    from us.'
    Then tall Hektor of the shining helm answered her: 'Deïphobos,
before now you were dearest to me by far of my brothers,
of all those who were sons of Priam and Hekabe, and now
I am minded all the more within my heart to honour you,   235
you who dared for my sake, when your eyes saw me, to come forth
from the fortifications, while the others stand fast inside them.'
    Then in turn the goddess grey-eyed Athene answered him:
'My brother, it is true our father and the lady our mother, taking
my knees in turn, and my companions about me, entreated   240
that I stay within, such was the terror upon all of them.
But the heart within me was worn away by hard sorrow for you.
But now let us go straight on and fight hard, let there be no sparing
of our spears, so that we can find out whether Achilleus
will kill us both and carry our bloody war spoils back   245
to the hollow ships, or will himself go down under your spear.'
    So Athene spoke and led him on by beguilement.

227. *Deïphobos:* one of Hecktor's brothers.

Now as the two in their advance were come close together,
first of the two to speak was tall helm-glittering Hektor:
'Son of Peleus, I will no longer run from you, as before this   250
I fled three times around the great city of Priam, and dared not
stand to your onfall. But now my spirit in turn has driven me
to stand and face you. I must take you now, or I must be taken.
Come then, shall we swear before the gods? For these are the highest
who shall be witnesses and watch over our agreements.   255
Brutal as you are I will not defile you, if Zeus grants
to me that I can wear you out, and take the life from you.
But after I have stripped your glorious armour, Achilleus,
I will give your corpse back to the Achaians. Do you do likewise.'
    Then looking darkly at him swift-footed Achilleus answered: 260
'Hektor, argue me no arguments. I cannot forgive you.
As there are no trustworthy oaths between men and lions,
nor wolves and lambs have spirit that can be brought to agreement
but forever these hold feelings of hate for each other,
so there can be no love between you and me, nor shall there be   265
oaths between us, but one or the other must fall before then
to glut with his blood Ares the god who fights under the shield's
        guard.
Remember every valour of yours, for now the need comes
hardest upon you to be a spearman and a bold warrior.
There shall be no more escape for you, but Pallas Athene   270
will kill you soon by my spear. You will pay in a lump for all those
sorrows of my companions you killed in your spear's fury.'
    So he spoke, and balanced the spear far shadowed, and threw it;
but glorious Hektor kept his eyes on him, and avoided it,
for he dropped, watchful, to his knee, and the bronze spear flew
        over his shoulder   275
and stuck in the ground, but Pallas Athene snatched it, and gave it
back to Achilleus, unseen by Hektor shepherd of the people.
But now Hektor spoke out to the blameless son of Peleus:
'You missed; and it was not, o Achilleus like the immortals,
from Zeus that you knew my destiny; but you thought so; or
        rather   280
you are someone clever in speech and spoke to swindle me,
to make me afraid of you and forget my valour and war strength.
You will not stick your spear in my back as I run away from you
but drive it into my chest as I storm straight in against you;
if the god gives you that; and now look out for my brazen   285
spear. I wish it might be taken full length in your body.
And indeed the war would be a lighter thing for the Trojans
if you were dead, seeing that you are their greatest affliction.'
    So he spoke, and balanced the spear far shadowed, and threw it,

and struck the middle of Peleïdes' shield, nor missed it,   290
but the spear was driven far back from the shield, and Hektor was
    angered
because his swift weapon had been loosed from his hand in a vain
    cast.
He stood discouraged, and had no other ash spear; but lifting
his voice he called aloud on Deïphobos of the pale shield,
and asked him for a long spear, but Deïphobos was not near
    him.   295
And Hektor knew the truth inside his heart, and spoke aloud:
'No use. Here at last the gods have summoned me deathward.
I thought Deïphobos the hero was here close beside me,
but he is behind the wall and it was Athene cheating me,
and now evil death is close to me, and no longer far away,   300
and there is no way out. So it must long since have been pleasing
to Zeus, and Zeus' son who strikes from afar, this way; though
    before this
they defended me gladly. But now my death is upon me.
Let me at least not die without a struggle, inglorious,
but do some big thing first, that men to come shall know of it.'   305
    So he spoke, and pulling out the sharp sword that was slung
at the hollow of his side, huge and heavy, and gathering
himself together, he made his swoop, like a high-flown eagle
who launches himself out of the murk of the clouds on the flat land
to catch away a tender lamb or a shivering hare; so   310
Hektor made his swoop, swinging his sharp sword, and Achilleus
charged, the heart within him loaded with savage fury.
In front of his chest the beautiful elaborate great shield
covered him, and with the glittering helm with four horns
he nodded; the lovely golden fringes were shaken about it   315
which Hephaistos had driven close along the horn of the helmet.
And as a star moves among stars in the night's darkening,
Hesper, who is the fairest star who stands in the sky, such
was the shining from the pointed spear Achilleus was shaking
in his right hand with evil intention toward brilliant Hektor.   320
He was eyeing Hektor's splendid body, to see where it might best
give way, but all the rest of the skin was held in the armour,
brazen and splendid, he stripped when he cut down the strength of
    Patroklos;
yet showed where the collar-bones hold the neck from the shoulders,
the throat, where death of the soul comes most swiftly; in this
    place   325
brilliant Achilleus drove the spear as he came on in fury,

318. *Hesper:* the evening star.

and clean through the soft part of the neck the spearpoint was
    driven.
Yet the ash spear heavy with bronze did not sever the windpipe,
so that Hektor could still make exchange of words spoken.
But he dropped in the dust, and brilliant Achilles vaunted above
    him: 330
'Hektor, surely you thought as you killed Patroklos you would be
safe, and since I was far away you thought nothing of me,
o fool, for an avenger was left, far greater than he was,
behind him and away by the hollow ships. And it was I;
and I have broken your strength; on you the dogs and the
    vultures   335
shall feed and foully rip you; the Achaians will bury Patroklos.'
    In his weakness Hektor of the shining helm spoke to him:
'I entreat you, by your life, by your knees, by your parents,
do not let the dogs feed on me by the ships of the Achaians,
but take yourself the bronze and gold that are there in abun-
    dance,   340
those gifts that my father and the lady my mother will give you,
and give my body to be taken home again, so that the Trojans
and the wives of the Trojans may give me in death my rite of
    burning.'
    But looking darkly at him swift-footed Achilleus answered:
'No more entreating of me, you dog, by knees or parents.   345
I wish only that my spirit and fury would drive me
to hack your meat away and eat it raw for the things that
you have done to me. So there is no one who can hold the dogs off
from your head, not if they bring here and set before me ten times
and twenty times the ransom, and promise more in addition,   350
not if Priam son of Dardanos should offer to weigh out
your bulk in gold; not even so shall the lady your mother
who herself bore you lay you on the death-bed and mourn you:
no, but the dogs and the birds will have you all for their feasting.'
    Then, dying, Hektor of the shining helmet spoke to him: 355
'I know you well as I look upon you, I know that I could not
persuade you, since indeed in your breast is a heart of iron.
Be careful now; for I might be made into the gods' curse
upon you, on that day when Paris and Phoibos Apollo
destroy you in the Skaian gates, for all your valour.'   360
    He spoke, and as he spoke the end of death closed in upon him,
and the soul fluttering free of the limbs went down into Death's
    house
mourning her destiny, leaving youth and manhood behind her.
Now though he was a dead man brilliant Achilleus spoke to him:

'Die: and I will take my own death at whatever time   365
Zeus and the rest of the immortals choose to accomplish it.'

He spoke, and pulled the brazen spear from the body, and laid it
on one side, and stripped away from the shoulders the bloody
armour. And the other sons of the Achaians came running about
       him,
and gazed upon the stature and on the imposing beauty   370
of Hektor; and none stood beside him who did not stab him;
and thus they would speak one to another, each looking at his
       neighbour:
'See now, Hektor is much softer to handle than he was
when he set the ships ablaze with the burning firebrand.'
  So as they stood beside him they would speak, and stab him.   375
But now, when he had despoiled the body, swift-footed brilliant
Achilleus stood among the Achaians and addressed them in winged
       words:
'Friends, who are leaders of the Argives and keep their counsel:
since the gods have granted me the killing of this man
who has done us much damage, such as not all the others
       together   380
have done, come, let us go in armour about the city
to see if we can find out what purpose is in the Trojans,
whether they will abandon their high city, now that this man
has fallen, or are minded to stay, though Hektor lives no longer.
Yet still, why does the heart within me debate on these things?   385
There is a dead man who lies by the ships, unwept, unburied:
Patroklos: and I will not forget him, never so long as
I remain among the living and my knees have their spring beneath
       me.
And though the dead forget the dead in the house of Hades,
even there I shall still remember my beloved companion.   390
But now, you young men of the Achaians, let us go back, singing
a victory song, to our hollow ships; and take this with us.
We have won ourselves enormous fame; we have killed the great
       Hektor
whom the Trojans glorified as if he were a god in their city.'

He spoke, and now thought of shameful treatment for glorious
       Hektor.   395
In both of his feet at the back he made holes by the tendons
in the space between ankle and heel, and drew thongs of ox-hide
       through them,
and fastened them to the chariot so as to let the head drag,
and mounted the chariot, and lifted the glorious armour inside it,
then whipped the horses to a run, and they winged their way
       unreluctant.   400

A cloud of dust rose where Hektor was dragged, his dark hair was
   falling   [tumbled
about him, and all that head that was once so handsome was
in the dust; since by this time Zeus had given him over
to his enemies, to be defiled in the land of his fathers.
   So all his head was dragged in the dust; and now his mother   405
tore out her hair, and threw the shining veil far from her
and raised a great wail as she looked upon her son; and his father
beloved groaned pitifully, and all his people about him
were taken with wailing and lamentation all through the city.
It was most like what would have happened, if all lowering   410
Ilion had been burning top to bottom in fire.
His people could scarcely keep the old man in his impatience
from storming out of the Dardanian gates; he implored them all,
and wallowed in the muck before them calling on each man
and naming him by his name: 'Give way, dear friends,   415
and let me alone though you care for me, leave me to go out
from the city and make my way to the ships of the Achaians.
I must be suppliant to this man, who is harsh and violent,
and he might have respect for my age and take pity upon it
since I am old, and his father also is old, as I am,   420
Peleus, who begot and reared him to be an affliction
on the Trojans. He has given us most sorrow, beyond all others,
such is the number of my flowering sons he has cut down.
But for all of these I mourn not so much, in spite of my sorrow,
as for one, Hektor, and the sharp grief for him will carry me
   downward   425
into Death's house. I wish he had died in my arms, for that way
we two, I myself and his mother who bore him unhappy,
might so have glutted ourselves with weeping for him and
   mourning.'
   So he spoke, in tears, and beside him mourned the citizens.
But for the women of Troy Hekabe led out the thronging   430
chant of sorrow: 'Child, I am wretched. What shall my life be
in my sorrows, now you are dead, who by day and in the night
were my glory in the town, and to all of the Trojans
and the women of Troy a blessing throughout their city. They
   adored you
as if you were a god, since in truth you were their high honour   435
while you lived. Now death and fate have closed in upon you.'
   So she spoke in tears but the wife of Hektor had not yet
heard: for no sure messenger had come to her and told her
how her husband had held his ground there outside the gates;
but she was weaving a web in the inner room of the high
   house,   440

a red folding robe, and inworking elaborate figures.
She called out through the house to her lovely-haired handmaidens
to set a great cauldron over the fire, so that there would be
hot water for Hektor's bath as he came back out of the fighting;
poor innocent, nor knew how, far from waters for bathing,   445
Pallas Athene had cut him down at the hands of Achilleus.
She heard from the great bastion the noise of mourning and sorrow.
Her limbs spun, and the shuttle dropped from her hand to the
    ground. Then
she called aloud to her lovely-haired handmaidens: 'Come here.
Two of you come with me, so I can see what has happened.   450
I heard the voice of Hektor's honoured mother; within me
my own heart rising beats in my mouth, my limbs under me
are frozen. Surely some evil is near for the children of Priam.
May what I say come never close to my ear; yet dreadfully
I fear that great Achilleus might have cut off bold Hektor   455
alone, away from the city, and be driving him into the flat land,
might put an end to that bitter pride of courage, that always
was on him, since he would never stay back where the men were in
    numbers
but break far out in front, and give way in his fury to no man.'
    So she spoke, and ran out of the house like a raving woman   460
with pulsing heart, and her two handmaidens went along with her.
But when she came to the bastion and where the men were gathered
she stopped, staring, on the wall; and she saw him
being dragged in front of the city, and the running horses
dragged him at random toward the hollow ships of the
    Achaians.   465
The darkness of night misted over the eyes of Andromache.
She fell backward, and gasped the life breath from her, and far off
threw from her head the shining gear that ordered her headdress,
the diadem and the cap, and the holding-band woven together,
and the circlet, which Aphrodite the golden once had given her   470
on that day when Hektor of the shining helmet led her forth
from the house of Eëtion, and gave numberless gifts to win her.
And about her stood thronging her husband's sisters and the wives
    of his brothers
and these, in her despair for death, held her up among them.
But she, when she breathed again and the life was gathered back
    into her,   475
lifted her voice among the women of Troy in mourning:
'Hektor, I grieve for you. You and I were born to a single
destiny, you in Troy in the house of Priam, and I
in Thebe, underneath the timbered mountain of Plakos
in the house of Eëtion, who cared for me when I was little,   480

ill-fated he, I ill-starred. I wish he had never begotten me.
Now you go down to the house of Death in the secret places
of the earth, and left me here behind in the sorrow of mourning,
a widow in your house, and the boy is only a baby
who was born to you and me, the unfortunate. You cannot help
    him,   485
Hektor, any more, since you are dead. Nor can he help you.
Though he escape the attack of the Achaians with all its sorrows,
yet all his days for your sake there will be hard work for him
and sorrows, for others will take his lands away from him. The day
of bereavement leaves a child with no agemates to befriend
    him.   490
He bows his head before every man, his cheeks are bewept, he
goes, needy, a boy among his father's companions,
and tugs at this man by the mantle, that man by the tunic,
and they pity him, and one gives him a tiny drink from a goblet,
enough to moisten his lips, not enough to moisten his palate. 495
But one whose parents are living beats him out of the banquet
hitting him with his fists and in words also abuses him:
"Get out, you! Your father is not dining among us."
And the boy goes away in tears to his widowed mother,
Astyanax, who in days before on the knees of his father   500
would eat only the marrow or the flesh of sheep that was fattest.
And when sleep would come upon him and he was done with his
    playing,
he would go to sleep in a bed, in the arms of his nurse, in a soft
bed, with his heart given all its fill of luxury.
Now, with his dear father gone, he has much to suffer: 505
he, whom the Trojans have called Astyanax, lord of the city,
since it was you alone who defended the gates and the long
    walls.
But now, beside the curving ships, far away from your parents,
the writhing worms will feed, when the dogs have had enough of
    you,
on your naked corpse, though in your house there is clothing
    laid up   510
that is fine-textured and pleasant, wrought by the hands of women.
But all of these I will burn up in the fire's blazing,
no use to you, since you will never be laid away in them;
but in your honour, from the men of Troy and the Trojan women.'
    So she spoke, in tears; and the women joined in her mourn-
    ing.   515

[Achilleus buried Patroklos, and the Greeks celebrated the dead
hero's fame with athletic games, for which Achilleus gave the prizes.]

Book XXIV

[Achilles and Priam]

And the games broke up, and the people scattered to go away, each man
to his fast-running ship, and the rest of them took thought of their dinner
and of sweet sleep and its enjoyment; only Achilleus
wept still as he remembered his beloved companion, nor did sleep
who subdues all come over him, but he tossed from one side to the other   5
in longing for Patroklos, for his manhood and his great strength
and all the action he had seen to the end with him, and the hardships
he had suffered; the wars of men; hard crossing of the big waters.
Remembering all these things he let fall the swelling tears, lying
sometimes along his side, sometimes on his back, and now again   10
prone on his face; then he would stand upright, and pace turning
in distraction along the beach of the sea, nor did dawn rising
escape him as she brightened across the sea and the beaches.
Then, when he had yoked running horses under the chariot
he would fasten Hektor behind the chariot, so as to drag him,   15
and draw him three times around the tomb of Menoitios' fallen
son, then rest again in his shelter, and throw down the dead man
and leave him to lie sprawled on his face in the dust. But Apollo
had pity on him, though he was only a dead man, and guarded
the body from all ugliness, and hid all of it under the golden   20
aegis, so that it might not be torn when Achilleus dragged it.
   So Achilleus in his standing fury outraged great Hektor.
The blessed gods as they looked upon him were filled with compassion
and kept urging clear-sighted Argeïphontes to steal the body.
There this was pleasing to all the others, but never to Hera   25
nor Poseidon, nor the girl of the grey eyes, who kept still
their hatred for sacred Ilion as in the beginning,
and for Priam and his people, because of the delusion of Paris
who insulted the goddesses when they came to him in his courtyard
and favoured her who supplied the lust that led to disaster.   30
But now, as it was the twelfth dawn after the death of Hektor,
Phoibos Apollo spoke his word out among the immortals:
'You are hard, you gods, and destructive. Now did not Hektor

---

24. *Argeïphontes:* a title of Hermes (its meaning is disputed). Hermes was the messenger of Zeus, and was also renowned for his trickery and thieving.

26. *girl of the grey eyes:* Athene.

28. *delusion of Paris:* He was appointed judge in a contest of beauty between Aphrodite, Hera, and Athene. All three goddesses offered bribes, but Aphrodite's promise to give him Helen proved the most attractive.

burn thigh pieces of oxen and unblemished goats in your honour?
Now you cannot bring yourselves to save him, though he is only   35
a corpse, for his wife to look upon, his child and his mother
and Priam his father, and his people, who presently thereafter
would burn his body in the fire and give him his rites of burial.
No, you gods; your desire is to help this cursed Achilleus
within whose breast there are no feelings of justice, nor can   40
his mind be bent, but his purposes are fierce, like a lion
who when he has given way to his own great strength and his
     haughty
spirit, goes among the flocks of men, to devour them.
So Achilleus has destroyed pity, and there is not in him
any shame; which does much harm to men but profits them
     also.   45
For a man must some day lose one who was even closer
than this; a brother from the same womb, or a son. And yet
he weeps for him, and sorrows for him, and then it is over,
for the Destinies put in mortal men the heart of endurance.
But this man, now he has torn the heart of life from great
     Hektor,   50
ties him to his horses and drags him around his beloved companion's
tomb; and nothing is gained thereby for his good, or his honour.
Great as he is, let him take care not to make us angry;
for see, he does dishonour to the dumb earth in his fury.'
     Then bitterly Hera of the white arms answered him, saying: 55
'What you have said could be true, lord of the silver bow, only
if you give Hektor such pride of place as you give to Achilleus.
But Hektor was mortal, and suckled at the breast of a woman,
while Achilleus is the child of a goddess, one whom I myself
nourished and brought up and gave her as bride to her husband   60
Peleus, one dear to the hearts of the immortals, for you all
went, you gods, to the wedding; and you too feasted among them
and held your lyre, o friend of the evil, faithless forever.'
     In turn Zeus who gathers the clouds spoke to her in answer:
'Hera, be not utterly angry with the gods, for there shall not   65
be the same pride of place given both. Yet Hektor also
was loved by the gods, best of all the mortals in Ilion.
I loved him too. He never failed of gifts to my liking.
Never yet has my altar gone without fair sacrifice,
the smoke and the savour of it, since that is our portion of
     honour.   70
The stealing of him we will dismiss, for it is not possible
to take bold Hektor secretly from Achilleus, since always
his mother is near him night and day; but it would be better
if one of the gods would summon Thetis here to my presence
so that I can say a close word to her, and see that Achilleus   75

is given gifts by Priam and gives back the body of Hektor.'
He spoke, and Iris storm-footed sprang away with the message,
and at a point between Samos and Imbros of the high cliffs
plunged in the dark water, and the sea crashed moaning about her.
She plummeted to sea floor like a lead weight which, mounted   80
along the horn of an ox who ranges the fields, goes downward
and takes death with it to the raw-ravening fish. She found Thetis
inside the hollow of her cave, and gathered about her
sat the rest of the sea goddesses, and she in their midst
was mourning the death of her blameless son, who so soon was destined   85
to die in Troy of the rich soil, far from the land of his fathers.
Iris the swift-foot came close beside her and spoke to her:
'Rise, Thetis. Zeus whose purposes are infinite calls you.'
    In turn Thetis the goddess, the silver-footed, answered her:
'What does he, the great god, want with me? I feel shamefast   90
to mingle with the immortals, and my heart is confused with sorrows.
But I will go. No word shall be in vain, if he says it.'
    So she spoke, and shining among the divinities took up
her black veil, and there is no darker garment. She went
on her way, and in front of her rapid wind-footed Iris   95
guided her, and the wave of the water opened about them.
They stepped out on the dry land and swept to the sky. There they found
the son of Kronos of the wide brows, and gathered about him
sat all the rest of the gods, the blessed, who live forever.
She sat down beside Zeus father, and Athene made a place for her.   100
Hera put into her hand a beautiful golden goblet
and spoke to her to comfort her, and Thetis accepting drank from it.
The father of gods and men began the discourse among them:
'You have come to Olympos, divine Thetis, for all your sorrow,
with an unforgotten grief in your heart. I myself know this.   105
But even so I will tell you why I summoned you hither.
For nine days there has risen a quarrel among the immortals
over the body of Hektor, and Achilleus, stormer of cities.
They keep urging clear-sighted Argeïphontes to steal the body,
but I still put upon Achilleus the honour that he has, guarding   110
your reverence and your love for me into time afterwards. Go then
in all speed to the encampment and give to your son this message:
tell him that the gods frown upon him, that beyond all other

---

78. *Samos and Imbros:* two islands
in the north Aegean.

81. *horn of an ox:* a lure for big
fish, a "plug."

immortals I myself am angered that in his heart's madness
he holds Hektor beside the curved ships and did not give him   115
back. Perhaps in fear of me he will give back Hektor.
Then I will send Iris to Priam of the great heart, with an order
to ransom his dear son, going down to the ships of the Achaians
and bringing gifts to Achilleus which might soften his anger.'
   He spoke and the goddess silver-foot Thetis did not disobey
     him   120
but descended in a flash of speed from the peaks of Olympos
and made her way to the shelter of her son, and there found him
in close lamentation, and his beloved companions about him
were busy at their work and made ready the morning meal, and
     there
stood a great fleecy sheep being sacrificed in the shelter.   125
His honoured mother came close to him and sat down beside him,
and stroked him with her hand and called him by name and spoke
     to him:
'My child, how long will you go on eating your heart out in sorrow
and lamentation, and remember neither your food nor going
to bed? It is a good thing even to lie with a woman   130
in love. For you will not be with me long, but already
death and powerful destiny stand closely above you.
But listen hard to me, for I come from Zeus with a message.
He says that the gods frown upon you, that beyond all other
immortals he himself is angered that in your heart's madness   135
you hold Hektor beside the curved ships and did not redeem him.
Come, then, give him up and accept ransom for the body.'
   Then in turn Achilleus of the swift feet answered her:
'So be it. He can bring the ransom and take off the body,
if the Olympian himself so urgently bids it.'   140
   So, where the ships were drawn together, the son and his mother
conversed at long length in winged words. But the son of Kronos
stirred Iris to go down to sacred Ilion, saying:
'Go forth, Iris the swift, leaving your place on Olympos,
and go to Priam of the great heart within Ilion, tell him   145
to ransom his dear son, going down to the ships of the Achaians
and bringing gifts to Achilleus which might soften his anger:
alone, let no other man of the Trojans go with him, but only
let one elder herald attend him, one who can manage
the mules and the easily running wagon, so he can carry   150
the dead man, whom great Achilleus slew, back to the city.
Let death not be a thought in his heart, let him have no fear;
such an escort shall I send to guide him, Argeïphontes
who shall lead him until he brings him to Achilleus. And after
he has brought him inside the shelter of Achilleus, neither   155

will the man himself kill him, but will hold back all the others,
for he is no witless man nor unwatchful, nor is he wicked,
but will in all kindness spare one who comes to him as a suppliant.'
    He spoke, and storm-footed Iris swept away with the message
and came to the house of Priam. There she found outcry and
        mourning.   160
The sons sitting around their father inside the courtyard
made their clothes sodden with their tears, and among them the old
        man
sat veiled, beaten into his mantle. Dung lay thick
on the head and neck of the aged man, for he had been rolling
in it, he had gathered and smeared it on with his hands. And his
        daughters   165
all up and down the house and the wives of his sons were mourning
as they remembered all those men in their numbers and valour
who lay dead, their lives perished at the hands of the Argives.
The messenger of Zeus stood beside Priam and spoke to him
in a small voice, and yet the shivers took hold of his body: 170
'Take heart, Priam, son of Dardanos, do not be frightened.
I come to you not eyeing you with evil intention
but with the purpose of good toward you. I am a messenger
of Zeus, who far away cares much for you and is pitiful.
The Olympian orders you to ransom Hektor the brilliant,   175
to bring gifts to Achilleus which may soften his anger:
alone, let no other man of the Trojans go with you, but only
let one elder herald attend you, one who can manage
the mules and the easily running wagon, so he can carry
the dead man, whom great Achilleus slew, back to the city.   180
Let death not be a thought in your heart, you need have no fear,
such an escort shall go with you to guide you, Argeïphontes
who will lead you till he brings you to Achilleus. And after
he has brought you inside the shelter of Achilleus, neither
will the man himself kill you but will hold back all the others;   185
for he is no witless man nor unwatchful, nor is he wicked
but will in all kindness spare one who comes to him as a suppliant.'
    So Iris the swift-footed spoke and went away from him.
Thereupon he ordered his sons to make ready the easily rolling
mule wagon, and to fasten upon it the carrying basket.   190
He himself went into the storeroom, which was fragrant
and of cedar, and high-ceilinged, with many bright treasures inside
        it.
He called out to Hekabe his wife, and said to her:
'Dear wife, a messenger came to me from Zeus on Olympos,
that I must go to the ships of the Achaians and ransom my dear
        son,   195

bringing gifts to Achilleus which may soften his anger.
Come then, tell me. What does it seem best to your own mind
for me to do? My heart, my strength are terribly urgent
that I go there to the ships within the wide army of the Achaians.'
  So he spoke, and his wife cried out aloud, and answered him: 200
'Ah me, where has that wisdom gone for which you were famous
in time before, among outlanders and those you rule over?
How can you wish to go alone to the ships of the Achaians
before the eyes of a man who has slaughtered in such numbers
such brave sons of yours? The heart in you is iron. For if 205
he has within his grasp and lays eyes upon you, that man
who is savage and not to be trusted will not take pity upon you
nor have respect for your rights. Let us sit apart in our palace
now, and weep for Hektor, and the way at the first strong Destiny
spun with his life line when he was born, when I gave birth to
    him, 210
that the dogs with their shifting feet should feed on him, far from
    his parents,
gone down before a stronger man; I wish I could set teeth
in the middle of his liver and eat it. That would be vengeance
for what he did to my son; for he slew him when he was no coward
but standing before the men of Troy and the deep-girdled
    women 215
of Troy, with no thought in his mind of flight or withdrawal.'
  In turn the aged Priam, the godlike, answered her saying:
'Do not hold me back when I would be going, neither yourself be
a bird of bad omen in my palace. You will not persuade me.
If it had been some other who ordered me, one of the mortals, 220
one of those who are soothsayers, or priests, or diviners,
I might have called it a lie and we might rather have rejected it.
But now, for I myself heard the god and looked straight upon her,
I am going, and this word shall not be in vain. If it is my destiny
to die there by the ships of the bronze-armoured Achaians, 225
then I wish that. Achilleus can slay me at once, with my own son
caught in my arms, once I have my fill of mourning above him.'
  He spoke, and lifted back the fair covering of his clothes-chest
and from inside took out twelve robes surpassingly lovely
and twelve mantles to be worn single, as many blankets, 230
as many great white cloaks, also the same number of tunics.
He weighed and carried out ten full talents of gold, and brought
    forth
two shining tripods, and four cauldrons, and brought out a goblet
of surpassing loveliness that the men of Thrace had given him
when he went to them with a message, but now the old man spared
    not 235

even this in his halls, so much was it his heart's desire
to ransom back his beloved son. But he drove off the Trojans
all from his cloister walks, scolding them with words of revilement:
'Get out, you failures, you disgraces. Have you not also
mourning of your own at home that you come to me with your sorrows?   240
Is it not enough that Zeus, son of Kronos, has given me sorrow
in losing the best of my sons? You also shall be aware of this
since you will be all the easier for the Achaians to slaughter
now he is dead. But, for myself, before my eyes look
upon this city as it is destroyed and its people are slaughtered,   245
my wish is to go sooner down to the house of the death god.'
    He spoke, and went after the men with a stick, and they fled out-
side
before the fury of the old man. He was scolding his children
and cursing Helenos, and Paris, Agathon the brilliant,
Pammon and Antiphonos, Polites of the great war cry,   250
Deïphobos and Hippothoös and proud Dios. There were nine
sons to whom now the old man gave orders and spoke to them
roughly:
'Make haste, wicked children, my disgraces. I wish all of you
had been killed beside the running ships in the place of Hektor.
Ah me, for my evil destiny. I have had the noblest   255
of sons in Troy, but I say not one of them is left to me,
Mestor like a god and Troilos whose delight was in horses,
and Hektor, who was a god among men, for he did not seem like
one who was child of a mortal man, but of a god. All these
Ares has killed, and all that are left me are the disgraces,   260
the liars and the dancers, champions of the chorus, the plunderers
of their own people in their land of lambs and kids. Well then,
will you not get my wagon ready and be quick about it,
and put all these things on it, so we can get on with our journey?'
    So he spoke, and they in terror at the old man's scolding   265
hauled out the easily running wagon for mules, a fine thing
new-fabricated, and fastened the carrying basket upon it.
They took away from its peg the mule yoke made of boxwood
with its massive knob, well fitted with guiding rings, and brought
forth
the yoke lashing (together with the yoke itself) of nine cubits   270
and snugged it well into place upon the smooth-polished wagon-
pole
at the foot of the beam, then slipped the ring over the peg, and
lashed it
with three turns on either side to the knob, and afterwards
fastened it all in order and secured it under a hooked guard.

Then they carried out and piled into the smooth-polished mule
    wagon   275
all the unnumbered spoils to be given for the head of Hektor,
then yoked the powerful-footed mules who pulled in the harness
and whom the Mysians gave once as glorious presents to Priam;
but for Priam they led under the yoke those horses the old man
himself had kept, and cared for them at his polished manger.   280
    Now in the high house the yoking was done for the herald
and Priam, men both with close counsels in their minds. And now
    came
Hekabe with sorrowful heart and stood close beside them
carrying in her right hand the kind, sweet wine in a golden
goblet, so that before they went they might pour a drink-offering. 285
She stood in front of the horses, called Priam by name and spoke to
    him:
'Here, pour a libation to Zeus father, and pray you may come back
home again from those who hate you, since it seems the spirit
within you drives you upon the ships, though I would not have it.
Make your prayer then to the dark-misted, the son of Kronos   290
on Ida, who looks out on all the Troad, and ask him
for a bird of omen, a rapid messenger, which to his own mind
is dearest of all birds and his strength is the biggest, one seen
on the right, so that once your eyes have rested upon him
you can trust in him and go to the ships of the fast-mounted
    Danaans.   295
But if Zeus of the wide brows will not grant you his own messenger,
then I, for one, would never urge you on nor advise you
to go to the Argive ships, for all your passion to do it.'
    Then in answer to her again spoke Priam the godlike:
'My lady, I will not disregard this wherein you urge me.   300
It is well to lift hands to Zeus and ask if he will have mercy.'
    The old man spoke, and told the housekeeper who attended them
to pour unstained water over his hands. She standing beside them
and serving them held the washing-bowl in her hands, and a pitcher.
He washed his hands and took the cup from his wife. He stood
    up   305
in the middle of the enclosure, and prayed, and poured the wine out
looking up into the sky, and gave utterance and spoke, saying·
'Father Zeus, watching over us from Ida, most high, most honoured:
grant that I come to Achilleus for love and pity; but send me
a bird of omen, a rapid messenger which to your own mind   310
is dearest of all birds and his strength is biggest, one seen
on the right, so that once my eyes have rested upon him
I may trust in him and go to the ships of the fast-mounted Dan-
    aans.'

So he spoke in prayer, and Zeus of the counsels heard him.
Straightway he sent down the most lordly of birds, an eagle,   315
the dark one, the marauder, called as well the black eagle.
And as big as is the build of the door to a towering chamber
in the house of a rich man, strongly fitted with bars, of such size
was the spread of his wings on either side. He swept through the
    city
appearing on the right hand, and the people looking upon him   320
were uplifted and the hearts made glad in the breasts of all of them.
   Now in urgent haste the old man mounted into his chariot
and drove out through the forecourt and the thundering close. Be-
    fore him
the mules hauled the wagon on its four wheels, Idaios
the sober-minded driving them, and behind him the horses   325
came on as the old man laid the lash upon them and urged them
rapidly through the town, and all his kinsmen were following
much lamenting, as if he went to his death. When the two men
had gone down through the city, and out, and come to the flat land,
the rest of them turned back to go to Ilion, the sons   330
and the sons-in-law. And Zeus of the wide brows failed not to notice
the two as they showed in the plain. He saw the old man and took
    pity
upon him, and spoke directly to his beloved son, Hermes:
'Hermes, for to you beyond all other gods it is dearest
to be man's companion, and you listen to whom you will, go
    now   335
on your way, and so guide Priam inside the hollow ships
of the Achaians, that no man shall see him, none be aware of him,
of the other Danaans, till he has come to the son of Peleus.'
   He spoke, nor disobeyed him the courier, Argeïphontes.
Immediately he bound upon his feet the fair sandals   340
golden and immortal, that carried him over the water
as over the dry land of the main abreast of the wind's blast.
He caught up the staff, with which he mazes the eyes of those
    mortals
whose eyes he would maze, or wakes again the sleepers. Holding
this in his hands, strong Argeïphontes winged his way onward   345
until he came suddenly to Troy and the Hellespont, and there
walked on, and there took the likeness of a young man, a noble,
with beard new grown, which is the most graceful time of young
    manhood.
   Now when the two had driven past the great tomb of Ilos
they stayed their mules and horses to water them in the river,   350
for by this time darkness had descended on the land; and the herald
made out Hermes, who was coming toward them at a short distance.

He lifted his voice and spoke aloud to Priam: 'Take thought,
son of Dardanos. Here is work for a mind that is careful.
I see a man; I think he will presently tear us to pieces..   355
Come then, let us run away with our horses, or if not, then
clasp his knees and entreat him to have mercy upon us.'
   So he spoke, and the old man's mind was confused, he was badly
frightened, and the hairs stood up all over his gnarled body
and he stood staring, but the kindly god himself coming closer   360
took the old man's hand, and spoke to him and asked him a question:
'Where, my father, are you thus guiding your mules and horses
through the immortal night while other mortals are sleeping?
Have you no fear of the Achaians whose wind is fury,
who hate you, who are your enemies, and are near? For if one   365
of these were to see you, how you are conveying so many
treasures through the swift black night, what then could you think
of?
You are not young yourself, and he who attends you is aged
for beating off any man who might pick a quarrel with you.
But I will do you no harm myself, I will even keep off   370
another who would. You seem to me like a beloved father.'
   In answer to him again spoke aged Priam the godlike:
'Yes, in truth, dear child, all this is much as you tell me;
yet still there is some god who has held his hand above me,
who sent such a wayfarer as you to meet me, an omen   375
of good, for such you are by your form, your admired beauty
and the wisdom in your mind. Your parents are fortunate in you.'
   Then in turn answered him the courier Argeïphontes:
'Yes, old sir, all this that you said is fair and orderly.
But come, tell me this thing and recite it to me accurately.   380
Can it be you convey these treasures in all their numbers and
beauty
to outland men, so that they can be still kept safe for you?
Or are all of you by now abandoning sacred Ilion
in fear, such a one was he who died, the best man among you,
your son; who was never wanting when you fought against the
Achaians.'   385
   In answer to him again spoke aged Priam the godlike:
'But who are you, o best of men, and who are your parents?
Since you spoke of my ill-starred son's death, and with honour.'
   Then in turn answered him the courier Argeïphontes:
'You try me out, aged sir. You ask me of glorious Hektor   390
whom many a time my eyes have seen in the fighting where men
win
glory, as also on that time when he drove back the Argives

on their ships and kept killing them with the stroke of the sharp
    bronze,
and we stood by and wondered at him; for then Achilleus
would not let us fight by reason of his anger at Agamemnon.   395
For I am Achilleus' henchman, and the same strong-wrought vessel
brought us here; and I am a Myrmidon, and my father
is Polyktor; a man of substance, but aged, as you are.
He has six sons beside, and I am the seventh, and I shook
lots with the others, and it was my lot to come on this venture.   400
But now I have come to the plain away from the ships, for at day-
    break
the glancing-eyed Achaians will do battle around the city.
They chafe from sitting here too long, nor have the Achaians'
kings the strength to hold them back as they break for the fighting.'
    In answer to him again spoke aged Priam the godlike: 405
'If then you are henchman to Peleïd Achilleus,
come, tell me the entire truth, and whether my son lies
still beside the ships, or whether by now he has been hewn
limb from limb and thrown before the dogs by Achilleus.'
    Then in turn answered him the courier Argeïphontes: 410
'Aged sir, neither have any dogs eaten him, nor have
the birds, but he lies yet beside the ship of Achilleus
at the shelters, and as he was; now here is the twelfth dawn
he has lain there, nor does his flesh decay, nor do worms feed
on him, they who devour men who have fallen in battle.   415
It is true, Achilleus drags him at random around his beloved
companion's tomb, as dawn on dawn appears, yet he cannot
mutilate him; you yourself can see when you go there
how fresh with dew he lies, and the blood is all washed from him,
nor is there any corruption, and all the wounds have been closed
    up   420
where he was struck, since many drove the bronze in his body.
So it is that the blessed immortals care for your son, though
he is nothing but a dead man; because in their hearts they loved
    him.'
    He spoke, and the old man was made joyful and answered him,
    saying:
'My child, surely it is good to give the immortals   425
their due gifts; because my own son, if ever I had one,
never forgot in his halls the gods who live on Olympos.
Therefore they remembered him even in death's stage. Come, then,
accept at my hands this beautiful drinking-cup, and give me
protection for my body, and with the gods' grace be my escort   430
until I make my way to the shelter of the son of Peleus.'

In turn answered him the courier Argeïphontes:
'You try me out, aged sir, for I am young, but you will not
persuade me, telling me to accept your gifts when Achilleus
does not know. I fear him at heart and have too much reverence   435
to rob him. Such a thing might be to my sorrow hereafter.
But I would be your escort and take good care of you, even
till I came to glorious Argos in a fast ship or following
on foot, and none would fight you because he despised your escort.'
   The kind god spoke, and sprang up behind the horses and
        into   440
the chariot, and rapidly caught in his hands the lash and the guide
        reins,
and breathed great strength into the mules and horses. Now after
they had got to the fortifications about the ships, and the ditch,
        there
were sentries, who had just begun to make ready their dinner,
but about these the courier Argeïphontes drifted   445
sleep, on all, and quickly opened the gate, and shoved back
the door-bars, and brought in Priam and the glorious gifts on the
        wagon.
But when they had got to the shelter of Peleus' son: a towering
shelter the Myrmidons had built for their king, hewing
the timbers of pine, and they made a roof of thatch above it   450
shaggy with grass that they had gathered out of the meadows;
and around it made a great courtyard for their king, with hedgepoles
set close together; the gate was secured by a single door-piece
of pine, and three Achaians could ram it home in its socket
and three could pull back and open the huge door-bar; three other
Achaians, that is, but Achilleus all by himself could close it.   456
At this time Hermes, the kind god, opened the gate for the old man
and brought in the glorious gifts for Peleus' son, the swift-footed,
and dismounted to the ground from behind the horses, and spoke
        forth:
'Aged sir, I who came to you am a god immortal,   460
Hermes. My father sent me down to guide and go with you.
But now I am going back again, and I will not go in
before the eyes of Achilleus, for it would make others angry
for an immortal god so to face mortal men with favour.
But go you in yourself and clasp the knees of Peleion   465
and entreat him in the name of his father, the name of his mother
of the lovely hair, and his child, and so move the spirit within him.'
   So Hermes spoke, and went away to the height of Olympos,
but Priam vaulted down to the ground from behind the horses

and left Idaios where he was, for he stayed behind, holding   470
in hand the horses and mules. The old man made straight for the
   dwelling
where Achilleus the beloved of Zeus was sitting. He found him
inside, and his companions were sitting apart, as two only,
Automedon the hero and Alkimos, scion of Ares,
were busy beside him. He had just now got through with his
   dinner,   475
with eating and drinking, and the table still stood by. Tall Priam
came in unseen by the other men and stood close beside him
and caught the knees of Achilleus in his arms, and kissed the hands
that were dangerous and manslaughtering and had killed so many
of his sons. As when dense disaster closes on one who has murdered   480
a man in his own land, and he comes to the country of others,
to a man of substance, and wonder seizes on those who behold him,
so Achilleus wondered as he looked on Priam, a godlike
man, and the rest of them wondered also, and looked at each other.
But now Priam spoke to him in the words of a suppliant: 485
'Achilleus like the gods, remember your father, one who
is of years like mine, and on the door-sill of sorrowful old age.
And they who dwell nearby encompass him and afflict him,
nor is there any to defend him against the wrath, the destruction.
Yet surely he, when he hears of you and that you are still living,   490
is gladdened within his heart and all his days he is hopeful
that he will see his beloved son come home from the Troad.
But for me, my destiny was evil. I have had the noblest
of sons in Troy, but I say not one of them is left to me.
Fifty were my sons, when the sons of the Achaians came here.   495
Nineteen were born to me from the womb of a single mother,
and other women bore the rest in my palace; and of these
violent Ares broke the strength in the knees of most of them,
but one was left me who guarded my city and people, that one
you killed a few days since as he fought in defence of his country,   500
Hektor; for whose sake I come now to the ships of the Achaians
to win him back from you, and I bring you gifts beyond number.
Honour then the gods, Achilleus, and take pity upon me
remembering your father, yet I am still more pitiful;
I have gone through what no other mortal on earth has gone
   through;   505
I put my lips to the hands of the man who has killed my children.
  So he spoke, and stirred in the other a passion of grieving
for his own father. He took the old man's hand and pushed him

gently away, and the two remembered, as Priam sat huddled
at the feet of Achilleus and wept close for manslaughtering
    Hektor   510
and Achilleus wept now for his own father, now again
for Patroklos. The sound of their mourning moved in the house.
    Then
when great Achilleus had taken full satisfaction in sorrow
and the passion for it had gone from his mind and body, thereafter
he rose from his chair, and took the old man by the hand, and set
    him   515
on his feet again, in pity for the grey head and the grey beard,
and spoke to him and addressed him in winged words: 'Ah, un-
    lucky,
surely you have had much evil to endure in your spirit.
How could you dare to come alone to the ships of the Achaians
and before my eyes, when I am one who have killed in such num-
    bers   520
such brave sons of yours? The heart in you is iron. Come, then,
and sit down upon this chair, and you and I will even let
our sorrows lie still in the heart for all our grieving. There is not
any advantage to be won from grim lamentation.
Such is the way the gods spun life for unfortunate mortals,   525
that we live in unhappiness, but the gods themselves have no sor-
    rows.
There are two urns that stand on the door-sill of Zeus. They are
    unlike
for the gifts they bestow: an urn of evils, an urn of blessings.
If Zeus who delights in thunder mingles these and bestows them
on man, he shifts, and moves now in evil, again in good for-
    tune,   530
But when Zeus bestows from the urn of sorrows, he makes a failure
of man, and the evil hunger drives him over the shining
earth, and he wanders respected neither of gods nor mortals.
Such were the shining gifts given by the gods to Peleus
from his birth, who outshone all men beside for his riches   535
and pride of possession, and was lord over the Myrmidons. Thereto
the gods bestowed an immortal wife on him, who was mortal.
But even on him the god piled evil also. There was not
any generation of strong sons born to him in his great house
but a single all-untimely child he had, and I give him   540
no care as he grows old, since far from the land of my fathers
I sit here in Troy, and bring nothing but sorrow to you and your
    children.
And you, old sir, we are told you prospered once; for as much
as Lesbos, Makar's hold, confines to the north above it

and Phrygia from the north confines, and enormous Hellespont, 545
of these, old sir, you were lord once in your wealth and your children.
But now the Uranian gods brought us, an affliction upon you,
forever there is fighting about your city, and men killed.
But bear up, nor mourn endlessly in your heart, for there is not
anything to be gained from grief for your son; you will never 550
bring him back; sooner you must go through yet another sorrow.'
    In answer to him again spoke aged Priam the godlike:
'Do not, beloved of Zeus, make me sit on a chair while Hektor
lies yet forlorn among the shelters; rather with all speed
give him back, so my eyes may behold him, and accept the ran-
        som 555
we bring you, which is great. You may have joy of it, and go back
to the land of your own fathers, since once you have permitted me
to go on living myself and continue to look on the sunlight.'
    Then looking darkly at him spoke swift-footed Achilleus:
'No longer stir me up, old sir. I myself am minded 560
to give Hektor back to you. A messenger came to me from Zeus,
my mother, she who bore me, the daughter of the sea's ancient.
I know you, Priam, in my heart, and it does not escape me
that some god led you to the running ships of the Achaians.
For no mortal would dare come to our encampment, not even 565
one strong in youth. He could not get by the pickets, he could not
lightly unbar the bolt that secures our gateway. Therefore
you must not further make my spirit move in my sorrows,
for fear, old sir, I might not let you alone in my shelter,
suppliant as you are; and be guilty before the god's orders.' 570
    He spoke, and the old man was frightened and did as he told him.
The son of Peleus bounded to the door of the house like a lion,
nor went alone, but the two henchmen followed attending,
the hero Automedon and Alkimos, those whom Achilleus
honoured beyond all companions after Patroklos dead. These
        two 575
now set free from under the yoke the mules and the horses,
and led inside the herald, the old king's crier, and gave him
a chair to sit in, then from the smooth-polished mule wagon
lifted out the innumerable spoils for the head of Hektor,
but left inside it two great cloaks and a finespun tunic 580
to shroud the corpse in when they carried him home. Then Achilleus
called out to his serving-maids to wash the body and anoint it
all over; but take it first aside, since otherwise Priam
might see his son and in the heart's sorrow not hold in his anger
at the sight, and the deep heart in Achilleus be shaken to an-
        ger; 585

that he might not kill Priam and be guilty before the god's orders.
Then when the serving-maids had washed the corpse and anointed
    it
with olive oil, they threw a fair great cloak and a tunic
about him, and Achilleus himself lifted him and laid him
on a litter, and his friends helped him lift it to the smooth-
    polished   590
mule wagon. He groaned then, and called by name on his beloved
    companion:
'Be not angry with me, Patroklos, if you discover,
though you be in the house of Hades, that I gave back great Hektor
to his loved father, for the ransom he gave me was not unworthy.
I will give you your share of the spoils, as much as is fitting.'   595
    So spoke great Achilleus and went back into the shelter
and sat down on the elaborate couch from which he had risen,
against the inward wall, and now spoke his word to Priam:
'Your son is given back to you, aged sir, as you asked it.
He lies on a bier. When dawn shows you yourself shall see him   600
as you take him away. Now you and I must remember our supper.
For even Niobe, she of the lovely tresses, remembered
to eat, whose twelve children were destroyed in her palace,
six daughters, and six sons in the pride of their youth, whom Apollo
killed with arrows from his silver bow, being angered   605
with Niobe, and shaft-showering Artemis killed the daughters;
because Niobe likened herself to Leto of the fair colouring
and said Leto had borne only two, she herself had borne many;
but the two, though they were only two, destroyed all those others.
Nine days long they lay in their blood, nor was there anyone   610
to bury them, for the son of Kronos made stones out of
the people; but on the tenth day the Uranian gods buried them.
But she remembered to eat when she was worn out with weeping.
And now somewhere among the rocks, in the lonely mountains,
in Sipylos, where they say is the resting place of the goddesses   615
who are nymphs, and dance beside the waters of Acheloios,
there, stone still, she broods on the sorrows that the gods gave her.
Come then, we also, aged magnificent sir, must remember
to eat, and afterwards you may take your beloved son back
to Ilion, and mourn for him; and he will be much lamented.'   620
    So spoke fleet Achilleus and sprang to his feet and slaughtered
a gleaming sheep, and his friends skinned it and butchered it fairly,
and cut up the meat expertly into small pieces, and spitted them,
and roasted all carefully and took off the pieces.
Automedon took the bread and set it out on the table   625

---

607. *Leto:* mother of Apollo and
Artemis.

617. *stone still:* She was changed
into a rock.

in fair baskets, while Achilleus served the meats. And thereon
they put their hands to the good things that lay ready before them.
But when they had put aside their desire for eating and drinking,
Priam, son of Dardanos, gazed upon Achilleus, wondering
at his size and beauty, for he seemed like an outright vision   630
of gods. Achilleus in turn gazed on Dardanian Priam
and wondered, as he saw his brave looks and listened to him talking.
But when they had taken their fill of gazing one on the other,
first of the two to speak was the aged man, Priam the godlike:
'Give me, beloved of Zeus, a place to sleep presently, so that   635
we may even go to bed and take the pleasure of sweet sleep.
For my eyes have not closed underneath my lids since that time
when my son lost his life beneath your hands, but always
I have been grieving and brooding over my numberless sorrows
and wallowed in the muck about my courtyard's enclosure.   640
Now I have tasted food again and have let the gleaming
wine go down my throat. Before, I had tasted nothing.'
    He spoke, and Achilleus ordered his serving-maids and com-
        panions
to make a bed in the porch's shelter and to lay upon it
fine underbedding of purple, and spread blankets above it   645
and fleecy robes to be an over-all covering. The maid-servants
went forth from the main house, and in their hands held torches,
and set to work, and presently had two beds made. Achilleus
of the swift feet now looked at Priam and said, sarcastic:
'Sleep outside, aged sir and good friend, for fear some Achaian   650
might come in here on a matter of counsel, since they keep coming
and sitting by me and making plans; as they are supposed to.
But if one of these come through the fleeting black night should
        notice you,
he would go straight and tell Agamemnon, shepherd of the people,
and there would be delay in the ransoming of the body.   655
But come, tell me this and count off for me exactly
how many days you intend for the burial of great Hektor.
Tell me, so I myself shall stay still and hold back the people.'
    In answer to him again spoke aged Priam the godlike:
'If you are willing that we accomplish a complete funeral   660
for great Hektor, this, Achilleus, is what you could do and give
me pleasure. For you know surely how we are penned in our city,
and wood is far to bring in from the hills, and the Trojans are
        frightened
badly. Nine days we would keep him in our palace and mourn him,
and bury him on the tenth day, and the people feast by him,   665
and on the eleventh day we would make the grave-barrow for him.
and on the twelfth day fight again; if so we must do.'

Then in turn swift-footed brilliant Achilleus answered him:
'Then all this, aged Priam, shall be done as you ask it.
I will hold off our attack for as much time as you bid me.'   670
    So he spoke, and took the aged king by the right hand
at the wrist, so that his heart might have no fear. Then these two,
Priam and the herald who were both men of close counsel,
slept in the place outside the house, in the porch's shelter;
but Achilleus slept in the inward corner of the strong-built shel-
    ter,   675
and at his side lay Briseis of the fair colouring.
    Now the rest of the gods and men who were lords of chariots
slept nightlong, with the easy bondage of slumber upon them,
only sleep had not caught Hermes the kind god, who pondered
now in his heart the problem of how to escort King Priam   680
from the ships and not be seen by the devoted gate-wardens.
He stood above his head and spoke a word to him, saying:
'Aged sir, you can have no thought of evil from the way
you sleep still among your enemies now Achilleus has left you
unharmed. You have ransomed now your dear son and given much
    for him.   685
But the sons you left behind would give three times as much ransom
for you, who are alive, were Atreus' son Agamemnon
to recognize you, and all the other Achaians learn of you.'
    He spoke, and the old man was afraid, and wakened his herald,
and lightly Hermes harnessed for them the mules and the
    horses   690
and himself drove them through the encampment. And no man
    knew of them.
    But when they came to the crossing-place of the fair-running
    river,
of whirling Xanthos, a stream whose father was Zeus the immortal,
there Hermes left them and went away to the height of Olympos,
and dawn, she of the yellow robe, scattered over all earth,   695
and they drove their horses on to the city with lamentation
and clamour, while the mules drew the body. Nor was any other
aware of them at the first, no man, no fair-girdled woman,
only Kassandra, a girl like Aphrodite the golden,
who had gone up to the height of the Pergamos. She saw   700
her dear father standing in the chariot, his herald and crier
with him. She saw Hektor drawn by the mules on a litter.
She cried out then in sorrow and spoke to the entire city:
'Come, men of Troy and Trojan women; look upon Hektor
if ever before you were joyful when you saw him come back liv-
    ing   705
from battle; for he was a great joy to his city, and all his people.'

She spoke, and there was no man left there in all the city
nor woman, but all were held in sorrow passing endurance.
They met Priam beside the gates as he brought the dead in.
First among them were Hektor's wife and his honoured mother   710
who tore their hair, and ran up beside the smooth-rolling wagon,
and touched his head. And the multitude, wailing, stood there about
    them.
And now and there in front of the gates they would have lamented
all day till the sun went down and let fall their tears for Hektor,
except that the old man spoke from the chariot to his people: 715
'Give me way to get through with my mules; then afterwards
you may sate yourselves with mourning, when I have him inside the
    palace.'
So he spoke, and they stood apart and made way for the wagon.
And when they had brought him inside the renowned house, they
    laid him
then on a carved bed, and seated beside him the singers   720
who were to lead the melody in the dirge, and the singers
chanted the song of sorrow, and the women were mourning beside
    them.
Andromache of the white arms led the lamentation
of the women, and held in her arms the head of manslaughtering
    Hektor:
'My husband, you were lost young from life, and have left me   725
a widow in your house, and the boy is only a baby
who was born to you and me, the unhappy. I think he will never
come of age, for before then head to heel this city
will be sacked, for you, its defender, are gone, you who guarded
the city, and the grave wives, and the innocent children,   730
wives who before long must go away in the hollow ships,
and among them I shall also go, and you, my child, follow
where I go, and there do much hard work that is unworthy
of you, drudgery for a hard master; or else some Achaian
will take you by hand and hurl you from the tower into hor-
    rible   735
death, in anger because Hektor once killed his brother,
or his father, or his son; there were so many Achaians
whose teeth bit the vast earth, beaten down by the hands of Hektor.
Your father was no merciful man in the horror of battle.
Therefore your people are grieving for you all through their
    city,   740
Hektor, and you left for your parents mourning and sorrow
beyond words, but for me passing all others is left the bitterness

---

735. *hurl . . . tower:* After the fall of Troy Astyanax was, in fact, hurled from
the walls.

and the pain, for you did not die in bed, and stretch your arms to
    me,
nor tell me some last intimate word that I could remember
always, all the nights and days of my weeping for you.'   745
    So she spoke in tears, and the women were mourning about her.
Now Hekabe led out the thronging chant of their sorrow:
'Hektor, of all my sons the dearest by far to my spirit;
while you still lived for me you were dear to the gods, and even
in the stage of death they cared about you still. There were
    others   750
of my sons whom at times swift-footed Achilleus captured,
and he would sell them as slaves far across the unresting salt water
into Samos, and Imbros, and Lemnos in the gloom of the mists.
    You,
when he had taken your life with the thin edge of the bronze sword,
he dragged again and again around his beloved companion's   755
tomb, Patroklos', whom you killed, but even so did not
bring him back to life. Now you lie in the palace, handsome
and fresh with dew, in the likeness of one whom he of the silver
bow, Apollo, has attacked and killed with his gentle arrows.'
    So she spoke, in tears, and wakened the endless mourning.   760
Third and last Helen led the song of sorrow among them:
'Hektor, of all my lord's brothers dearest by far to my spirit:
my husband is Alexandros, like an immortal, who brought me
here to Troy; and I should have died before I came with him;
and here now is the twentieth year upon me since I came   765
from the place where I was, forsaking the land of my fathers. In this
    time
I have never heard a harsh saying from you, nor an insult.
No, but when another, one of my lord's brothers or sisters, a fair-
    robed
wife of some brother, would say a harsh word to me in the palace,
or my lord's mother—but his father was gentle always, a father   770
indeed—then you would speak and put them off and restrain them
by your own gentleness of heart and your gentle words. Therefore
I mourn for you in sorrow of heart and mourn myself also
and my ill luck. There was no other in all the wide Troad
who was kind to me, and my friend; all others shrank when they
    saw me.'   775
    So she spoke in tears, and the vast populace grieved with her.
Now Priam the aged king spoke forth his word to his people:
'Now, men of Troy, bring timber into the city, and let not
your hearts fear a close ambush of the Argives. Achilleus
promised me, as he sent me on my way from the black ships,   780
that none should do us injury until the twelfth dawn comes.'

He spoke, and they harnessed to the wagons their mules and
    their oxen
and presently were gathered in front of the city. Nine days
they spent bringing in an endless supply of timber. But when
the tenth dawn had shone forth with her light upon mortals,   785
they carried out bold Hektor, weeping, and set the body
aloft a towering pyre for burning. And set fire to it.
    But when the young dawn showed again with her rosy fingers,
the people gathered around the pyre of illustrious Hektor.
But when all were gathered to one place and assembled together, 790
first with gleaming wine they put out the pyre that was burning,
all where the fury of the fire still was in force, and thereafter
the brothers and companions of Hektor gathered the white bones
up, mourning, as the tears swelled and ran down their cheeks. Then
they laid what they had gathered up in a golden casket   795
and wrapped this about with soft robes of purple, and presently
put it away in the hollow of the grave, and over it
piled huge stones laid close together. Lightly and quickly
they piled up the grave-barrow, and on all sides were set watchmen
for fear the strong-greaved Achaians might too soon set upon them.
They piled up the grave-barrow and went away, and thereafter   801
assembled in a fair gathering and held a glorious
feast within the house of Priam, king under God's hand.
    Such was their burial of Hektor, breaker of horses.

The Odyssey*

[Ten years after the fall of Troy, Odysseus, king of Ithaca, on
the west coast of Greece, has still not returned home to his wife
Penelope and his son Telemakhos. He is stranded on the far-off
island of the nymph Kalypso, where he was cast up, sole survivor of
his fleet, seven years before, after many adventures in unknown
seas. But in the tenth year the gods contrive his homecoming.
Kalypso releases him, and on a raft he makes his way toward his
home, only to be cast up, naked and battered, on the shore of
Phaiakia, home of rich merchant princes. He meets the king's
daughter and under her protection is introduced to the royal court,
where he is welcomed by the king Alkinoos and the queen Arete. He

* An extract: three books of the
twenty-four. From *The Odyssey*, translated by Robert Fitzgerald. Copyright ©
1961 by Robert Fitzgerald. Reprinted
by permission of the author and Doubleday & Company, Inc.

has learned caution in his adventures and does not reveal his name.
But at a feast in the great hall, when the minstrel sings of the war
at Troy and mentions Odysseus and the wooden horse, he betrays
himself by giving way to his emotions and weeping. The king
Alkinoos presses him for his name and story, and Odysseus proceeds to tell, at great length, the full tale of his adventures since he
left Troy with his fleet.]

Book IX

Now this was the reply Odysseus made:
"Alkínoös, king and admiration of men,
how beautiful this is, to hear a minstrel
gifted as yours: a god he might be, singing!
There is no boon in life more sweet, I say,   5
than when a summer joy holds all the realm,
and banqueters sit listening to a harper
in a great hall, by rows of tables heaped
with bread and roast meat, while a steward goes
to dip up wine and brim your cups again.   10
Here is the flower of life, it seems to me!
But now you wish to know my cause for sorrow—
and thereby give me cause for more.
                            What shall I say first? What
shall I keep until the end?
The gods have tried me in a thousand ways.   15
But first my name: let that be known to you,
and if I pull away from pitiless death,
friendship will bind us, though my land lies far.

I am Laërtês' son, Odysseus.
                            Men hold me
formidable for guile in peace and war: 20
this fame has gone abroad to the sky's rim.
My home is on the peaked sea-mark of Ithaka
under Mount Neion's wind-blown robe of leaves,
in sight of other islands—Doulíkhion,
Samê, wooded Zakynthos—Ithaka   25
being most lofty in that coastal sea,
and northwest, while the rest lie east and south.
A rocky isle, but good for a boy's training;
I shall not see on earth a place more dear,
though I have been detained long by Kalypso,   30

30. *Kalypso:* At the end of the wanderings which Odysseus is about to describe, he was cast up, sole survivor of
the wreckage of his ship, on the island
of Ogygia, where the nymph Kalypso
(whose name is connected with the
Greek word which means to "cover or
hide") kept him for seven years.

loveliest among goddesses, who held me
in her smooth caves, to be her heart's delight,
as Kirkê of Aiaia, the enchantress,
desired me, and detained me in her hall.
But in my heart I never gave consent.   35
Where shall a man find sweetness to surpass
his own home and his parents? In far lands
he shall not, though he find a house of gold.

What of my sailing, then, from Troy?
                     What of those years
of rough adventure, weathered under Zeus?   40
The wind that carried west from Ilion
brought me to Ísmaros, on the far shore,
a strongpoint on the coast of the Kikonês.
I stormed that place and killed the men who fought.
Plunder we took, and we enslaved the women,   45
to make division, equal shares to all—
but on the spot I told them: 'Back, and quickly!
Out to sea again!' My men were mutinous,
fools, on stores of wine. Sheep after sheep
they butchered by the surf, and shambling cattle,   50
feasting,—while fugitives went inland, running
to call to arms the main force of Kikonês.
This was an army, trained to fight on horseback
or, where the ground required, on foot. They came
with dawn over that terrain like the leaves   55
and blades of spring. So doom appeared to us,
dark word of Zeus for us, our evil days.
My men stood up and made a fight of it—
backed on the ships, with lances kept in play,
from bright morning through the blaze of noon   60
holding our beach, although so far outnumbered;
but when the sun passed toward unyoking time,
then the Akhaians, one by one, gave way.
Six benches were left empty in every ship
that evening when we pulled away from death.   65
And this new grief we bore with us to sea:
our precious lives we had, but not our friends.
No ship made sail next day until some shipmate
had raised a cry, three times, for each poor ghost
unfleshed by the Kikonês on that field.   70

---

43. *Kikonês:* allies of the Trojans,   this fact to excuse the piratical raid; he
but Odysseus does not even mention.   did not think any excuse was needed.

Now Zeus the lord of cloud roused in the north
a storm against the ships, and driving veils
of squall moved down like night on land and sea.
The bows went plunging at the gust; sails
cracked and lashed out strips in the big wind.   75
We saw death in that fury, dropped the yards,
unshipped the oars, and pulled for the nearest lee:
then two long days and nights we lay offshore
worn out and sick at heart, tasting our grief,
until a third Dawn came with ringlets shining.   80
Then we put up our masts, hauled sail, and rested,
letting the steersmen and the breeze take over.

I might have made it safely home, that time,
but as I came round Malea the current
took me out to sea, and from the north   85
a fresh gale drove me on, past Kythera.
Nine days I drifted on the teeming sea
before dangerous high winds. Upon the tenth
we came to the coastline of the Lotos Eaters,
who live upon that flower. We landed there   90
to take on water. All ships' companies
mustered alongside for the mid-day meal.
Then I sent out two picked men and a runner
to learn what race of men that land sustained.
They fell in, soon enough, with Lotos Eaters,   95
who showed no will to do us harm, only
offering the sweet Lotos to our friends—
but those who ate this honeyed plant, the Lotos,
never cared to report, nor to return:
they longed to stay forever, browsing on   100
that native bloom, forgetful of their homeland.
I drove them, all three wailing, to the ships,
tied them down under their rowing benches,
and called the rest: 'All hands aboard;
come, clear the beach and no one taste   105
the Lotos, or you lose your hope of home.'
Filing in to their places by the rowlocks
my oarsmen dipped their long oars in the surf,
and we moved out again on our sea faring.

84. *Malea:* the southeastern tip of the Peloponnese. *Kythera:* a large island off the headland.

89. *Lotos Eaters:* It is generally thought that this story contains some memory of early Greek contact with North Africa; the north wind Odysseus describes would have taken him to the area of Cyrenaica, modern Libya. Modern identifications of the lotos range from dates to hashish.

In the next land we found were Kyklopês,   110
giants, louts, without a law to bless them.
In ignorance leaving the fruitage of the earth in mystery
to the immortal gods, they neither plow
nor sow by hand, nor till the ground, though grain—
wild wheat and barley—grows untended, and   115
wine-grapes, in clusters, ripen in heaven's rain.
Kyklopês have no muster and no meeting,
no consultation or old tribal ways,
but each one dwells in his own mountain cave
dealing out rough justice to wife and child,   120
indifferent to what the others do.
                                        Well, then:
across the wide bay from the mainland
there lies a desert island, not far out,
but still not close inshore. Wild goats in hundreds
breed there; and no human being comes   125
upon the isle to startle them—no hunter
of all who ever tracked with hounds through forests
or had rough going over mountain trails.
The isle, unplanted and untilled, a wilderness,
pastures goats alone. And this is why: 130
good ships like ours with checkpaint at the bows
are far beyond the Kyklopês. No shipwright
toils among them, shaping and building up
symmetrical trim hulls to cross the sea
and visit all the seaboard towns, as men do   135
who go and come in commerce over water.
This isle—seagoing folk would have annexed it
and built their homesteads on it: all good land,
fertile for every crop in season: lush
well-watered meads along the shore, vines in profusion, 140
prairie, clear for the plow, where grain would grow
chin high by harvest time, and rich sub-soil.
The island cove is landlocked, so you need
no hawsers out astern, bow-stones or mooring:
run in and ride there till the day your crews   145
chafe to be under sail, and a fair wind blows.
You'll find good water flowing from a cavern
through dusky poplars into the upper bay.
Here we made harbor. Some god guided us
that night, for we could barely see our bows   150

110. *next land:* According to ancient tradition the Kyklopes lived· in Sicily.
131. *cheekpaint:* On a Greek ship an emblem (often shown as a huge eye on vase-paintings) was painted on the bows.
144. *bow-stones:* a primitive anchor made of a stone attached to a rope.

in the dense fog around us, and no moonlight
filtered through the overcast. No look-out,
nobody saw the island dead ahead,
nor even the great landward rolling billow
that took us in: we found ourselves in shallows,   155
keels grazing shore: so furled our sails
and disembarked where the low ripples broke.
There on the beach we lay, and slept till morning.

When Dawn spread out her finger tips of rose
we turned out marvelling, to tour the isle,   160
while Zeus's shy nymph daughters flushed wild goats
down from the heights—a breakfast for my men.
We ran to fetch our hunting bows and long-shanked
lances from the ships, and in three companies
we took our shots. Heaven gave us game a-plenty: 165
for every one of twelve ships in my squadron
nine goats fell to be shared; my lot was ten.
So there all day, until the sun went down,
we made our feast on meat galore, and wine—
wine from the ship, for our supply held out,   170
so many jars were filled at Ísmaros
from stores of the Kikonês that we plundered.
We gazed, too, at Kyklopês Land, so near,
we saw their smoke, heard bleating from their flocks.
But after sundown, in the gathering dusk,   175
we slept again above the wash of ripples.

When the young Dawn with finger tips of rose
came in the east, I called my men together
and made a speech to them:
                        'Old shipmates, friends,
the rest of you stand by; I'll make the crossing   180
in my own ship, with my own company,
and find out what the mainland natives are—
for they may be wild savages, and lawless,
or hospitable and god fearing men.'

At this I went aboard, and gave the word   185
to cast off by the stern. My oarsmen followed,
filing in to their benches by the rowlocks,
and all in line dipped oars in the grey sea.

As we rowed on, and nearer to the mainland,
at one end of the bay, we saw a cavern   190

yawning above the water, screened with laurel,
and many rams and goats about the place
inside a sheepfold—made from slabs of stone
earthfast between tall trunks of pine and rugged
towering oak trees.

          A prodigious man   195
slept in this cave alone, and took his flocks
to graze afield—remote from all companions,
knowing none but savage ways, a brute
so huge, he seemed no man at all of those
who eat good wheaten bread; but he seemed rather   200
a shaggy mountain reared in solitude.
We beached there, and I told the crew
to stand by and keep watch over the ship;
as for myself I took my twelve best fighters
and went ahead. I had a goatskin full   205
of that sweet liquor that Euanthês' son,
Maron, had given me. He kept Apollo's
holy grove at Ísmaros; for kindness
we showed him there, and showed his wife and child,
he gave me seven shining golden talents   210
perfectly formed, a solid silver winebowl,
and then this liquor—twelve two-handled jars
of brandy, pure and fiery. Not a slave
in Maron's household knew this drink; only
he, his wife and the storeroom mistress knew;   215
and they would put one cupful—ruby-colored,
honey-smooth—in twenty more of water,
but still the sweet scent hovered like a fume
over the winebowl. No man turned away
when cups of this came round.   220
          A wineskin full
I brought along, and victuals in a bag.
for in my bones I knew some towering brute
would be upon us soon—all outward power,
a wild man, ignorant of civility.

We climbed, then, briskly to the cave. But Kyklops   225
had gone afield, to pasture his fat sheep,
so we looked round at everything inside:
a drying rack that sagged with cheeses, pens
crowded with lambs and kids, each in its class:
firstlings apart from middlings, and the 'dewdrops,'   230

---

210. *talents:* ingots of gold; the talent was a standard weight.

or newborn lambkins, penned apart from both.
And vessels full of whey were brimming there—
bowls of earthenware and pails for milking.
My men came pressing round me, pleading:
                                    'Why not   235
take these cheeses, get them stowed, come back,
throw open all the pens, and make a run for it?
We'll drive the kids and lambs aboard. We say
put out again on good salt water!'
                            Ah,
how sound that was! Yet I refused, I wished   240
to see the caveman, what he had to offer—
no pretty sight, it turned out, for my friends.
We lit a fire, burnt an offering,
and took some cheese to eat; then sat in silence
around the embers, waiting. When he came   245
he had a load of dry boughs on his shoulder
to stoke his fire at suppertime. He dumped it
with a great crash into that hollow cave,
and we all scattered fast to the far wall.
Then over the broad cavern floor he ushered   250
the ewes he meant to milk. He left his rams
and he-goats in the yard outside, and swung
high overhead a slab of solid rock
to close the cave. Two dozen four-wheeled wagons,
with heaving wagon teams, could not have stirred 255
the tonnage of that rock from where he wedged it
over the doorsill. Next he took his seat
and milked his bleating ewes. A practiced job
he made of it, giving each ewe her suckling:
thickened his milk, then, into curds and whey,   260
sieved out the curds to drip in withy baskets,
and poured the whey to stand in bowls
cooling until he drank it for his supper.
When all these chores were done, he poked the fire,
heaping on brushwood. In the glare he saw us.   265

'Strangers,' he said, 'who are you? And where from?
What brings you here by sea ways—a fair traffic?
Or are you wandering rogues, who cast your lives
like dice, and ravage other folk by sea?'

We felt a pressure on our hearts, in dread   270
of that deep rumble and that mighty man.

But all the same I spoke up in reply:
'We are from Troy, Akhaians, blown off course
by shifting gales on the Great South Sea;
homeward bound, but taking routes and ways   275
uncommon; so the will of Zeus would have it.
We served under Agamémnon, son of Atreus—
the whole world knows what city
he laid waste, what armies he destroyed.
It was our luck to come here; here we stand,   280
beholden for your help, or any gifts
you give—as custom is to honor strangers.
We would entreat you, great Sir, have a care
for the gods' courtesy; Zeus will avenge
the unoffending guest.'
               He answered this   285
from his brute chest, unmoved:
                       'You are a ninny,
or else you come from the other end of nowhere,
telling me, mind the gods! We Kyklopês
care not a whistle for your thundering Zeus
or all the gods in bliss; we have more force by far.   290
I would not let you go for fear of Zeus—
you or your friends—unless I had a whim to.
Tell me, where was it, now, you left your ship—
around the point, or down the shore, I wonder?'

He thought he'd find out, but I saw through this,   295
and answered with a ready lie:
                   'My ship?
Poseidon Lord, who sets the earth a-tremble,
broke it up on the rocks at your land's end.
A wind from seaward served him, drove us there.
We are survivors, these good men and I.'   300

Neither reply nor pity came from him,
but in one stride he clutched at my companions
and caught two in his hands like squirming puppies
to beat their brains out, spattering the floor.
Then he dismembered them and made his meal,   305
gaping and crunching like a mountain lion—
everything: innards, flesh, and marrow bones.
We cried aloud, lifting our hands to Zeus,
powerless, looking on at this, appalled;

281. *gifts:* it is the mark of civilized men in the *Odyssey* that they welcome the stranger and send him on his way with gifts.

but Kyklops went on filling up his belly   310
with manflesh and great gulps of whey,
then lay down like a mast among his sheep.
My heart beat high now at the chance of action,
and drawing the sharp sword from my hip I went
along his flank to stab him where the midriff   315
holds the liver. I had touched the spot
when sudden fear stayed me: if I killed him
we perished there as well, for we could never
move his ponderous doorway slab aside.
So we were left to groan and wait for morning.   320

When the young Dawn with finger tips of rose
lit up the world, the Kyklops built a fire
and milked his handsome ewes, all in due order,
putting the sucklings to the mothers. Then,
his chores being all dispatched, he caught   325
another brace of men to make his breakfast,
and whisked away his great door slab
to let his sheep go through—but he, behind,
reset the stone as one would cap a quiver.
There was a din of whistling as the Kyklops   330
rounded his flock to higher ground, then stillness.
And now I pondered how to hurt him worst,
if but Athena granted what I prayed for.

Here are the means I thought would serve my turn:
a club, or staff, lay there along the fold—   335
an olive tree, felled green and left to season
for Kyklops' hand. And it was like a mast
a lugger of twenty oars, broad in the beam—
a deep-sea-going craft—might carry:
so long, so big around, it seemed. Now I   340
chopped out a six foot section of this pole
and set it down before my men, who scraped it;
and when they had it smooth, I hewed again
to make a stake with pointed end. I held this
in the fire's heart and turned it, toughening it,   345
then hid it, well back in the cavern, under
one of the dung piles in profusion there.
Now came the time to toss for it: who ventured
along with me? whose hand could bear to thrust
and grind that spike in Kyklops' eye, when mild   350

---

333. *Athena:* the goddess who shows   Odysseus   particular   marks   of   favor
throughout.

sleep had mastered him? As luck would have it,
the men I would have chosen, won the toss—
four strong men, and I made five as captain.

At evening came the shepherd with his flock,
his woolly flock. The rams as well, this time,   355
entered the cave: by some sheep-herding whim—
or a god's bidding—none were left outside.
He hefted his great boulder into place
and sat him down to milk the bleating ewes
in proper order, put the lambs to suck,   360
and swiftly ran through all his evening chores.
Then he caught two more men and feasted on them.
My moment was at hand, and I went forward
holding an ivy bowl of my dark drink,
looking up, saying:
                'Kyklops, try some wine.   365
Here's liquor to wash down your scraps of men.
Taste it, and see the kind of drink we carried
under our planks. I meant it for an offering
if you would help us home. But you are mad,
unbearable, a bloody monster! After this,   370
will any other traveller come to see you?'

He seized and drained the bowl, and it went down
so fiery and smooth he called for more:
'Give me another, thank you kindly. Tell me,
how are you called? I'll make a gift will please you.   375
Even Kyklopês know the wine-grapes grow
out of grassland and loam in heaven's rain,
but here's a bit of nectar and ambrosia!'

Three bowls I brought him and he poured them down.
I saw the fuddle and flush come over him,   380
then I sang out in cordial tones:
                     'Kyklops,
you ask my honorable name? Remember
the gift you promised me, and I shall tell you.
My name is Nohbdy: mother, father, and friends,
everyone calls me Nohbdy.'

                    And he said: 385
'Nohbdy's my meat, then, after I eat his friends.

378. *nectar* and *ambrosia*: the drink and food of the gods.

Others come first. There's a noble gift, now.'

Even as he spoke, he reeled and tumbled backward,
his great head lolling to one side; and sleep
took him like any creature. Drunk, hiccuping,   390
he dribbled streams of liquor and bits of men.

Now, by the gods, I drove my big hand spike
deep in the embers, charring it again,
and cheered my men along with battle talk
to keep their courage up: no quitting now.   395
The pike of olive, green though it had been,
reddened and glowed as if about to catch.
I drew it from the coals and my four fellows
gave me a hand, lugging it near the Kyklops
as more than natural force nerved them; straight   400
forward they sprinted, lifted it, and rammed it
deep in his crater eye, and I leaned on it
turning it as a shipwright turns a drill
in planking, having men below to swing
the two-handled strap that spins it in the groove.   405
So with our brand we bored that great eye socket
while blood ran out around the red hot bar.
Eyelid and lash were seared; the pierced ball
hissed broiling, and the roots popped.

                In a smithy
one sees a white-hot axehead or an adze   410
plunged and wrung in a cold tub, screeching steam—
the way they make soft iron hale and hard—:
just so that eyeball hissed around the spike.
The Kyklops bellowed and the rock roared round him,
and we fell back in fear. Clawing his face   415
he tugged the bloody spike out of his eye,
threw it away, and his wild hands went groping;
then he set up a howl for Kyklopês
who lived in caves on windy peaks nearby.
Some heard him; and they came by divers ways   420
to clump around outside and call:
                       'What ails you,
Polyphêmos? Why do you cry so sore
in the starry night? You will not let us sleep.
Sure no man's driving off your flock? No man
has tricked you, ruined you?'

Out of the cave   425
the mammoth Polyphêmos roared in answer:
'Nohbdy, Nohbdy's tricked me, Nohbdy's ruined me!'

To this rough shout they made a sage reply;
'Ah well, if nobody has played you foul
there in your lonely bed, we are no use in pain   430
given by great Zeus. Let it be your father,
Poseidon Lord, to whom you pray.'
                                        So saying
they trailed away. And I was filled with laughter
to see how like a charm the name deceived them.
Now Kyklops, wheezing as the pain came on him,   435
fumbled to wrench away the great doorstone
and squatted in the breach with arms thrown wide
for any silly beast or man who bolted—
hoping somehow I might be such a fool.
But I kept thinking how to win the game: 440
death sat there huge; how could we slip away?
I drew on all my wits, and ran through tactics,
reasoning as a man will for dear life,
until a trick came—and it pleased me well.
The Kyklops' rams were handsome, fat, with heavy   445
fleeces, a dark violet.

                        Three abreast
I tied them silently together, twining
cords of willow from the ogre's bed;
then slung a man under each middle one
to ride there safely, shielded left and right.   450
So three sheep could convey each man. I took
the woolliest ram, the choicest of the flock,
and hung myself under his kinky belly,
pulled up tight, with fingers twisted deep
in sheepskin ringlets for an iron grip.   455
So, breathing hard, we waited until morning.

When Dawn spread out her finger tips of rose
the rams began to stir, moving for pasture,
and peals of bleating echoed round the pens
where dams with udders full called for a milking.   460
Blinded, and sick with pain from his head wound,
the master stroked each ram, then let it pass,
but my men riding on the pectoral fleece
the giant's blind hands blundering never found.
Last of them all my ram, the leader, came,   465

weighted by wool and me with my meditations.
The Kyklops patted him, and then he said:
'Sweet cousin ram, why lag behind the rest
in the night cave? You never linger so,
but graze before them all, and go afar   470
to crop sweet grass, and take your stately way
leading along the streams, until at evening
you run to be the first one in the fold.
Why, now, so far behind? Can you be grieving
over your Master's eye? That carrion rogue   475
and his accurst companions burnt it out
when he had conquered all my wits with wine.
Nohbdy will not get out alive, I swear.
Oh, had you brain and voice to tell
where he may be now, dodging all my fury!   480
Bashed by this hand and bashed on this rock wall
his brains would strew the floor, and I should have
rest from the outrage Nohbdy worked upon me.'
He sent us into the open, then. Close by,
I dropped and rolled clear of the ram's belly,   485
going this way and that to untie the men.
With many glances back, we rounded up
his fat, stiff-legged sheep to take aboard,
and drove them down to where the good ship lay.
We saw, as we came near, our fellows' faces   490
shining; then we saw them turn to grief
tallying those who had not fled from death.
I hushed them, jerking head and eyebrows up,
and in a low voice told them: 'Load this herd;
move fast, and put the ship's head toward the breakers.'   495
They all pitched in at loading, then embarked
and struck their oars into the sea. Far out,
as far off shore as shouted words would carry,
I sent a few back to the adversary:
'O Kyklops! Would you feast on my companions?   500
Puny, am I, in a Caveman's hands?
How do you like the beating that we gave you,
you damned cannibal? Eater of guests
under your roof! Zeus and the gods have paid you!'

The blind thing in his doubled fury broke   505
a hilltop in his hands and heaved it after us.
Ahead of our black prow it struck and sank
whelmed in a spuming geyser, a giant wave
that washed the ship stern foremost back to shore.

I got the longest boathook out and stood   510
fending us off, with furious nods to all
to put their backs into a racing stroke—
row, row, or perish. So the long oars bent
kicking the foam sternward, making head
until we drew away, and twice as far.   515
Now when I cupped my hands I heard the crew
in low voices protesting:
                          'Godsake, Captain!
Why bait the beast again? Let him alone!'
'That tidal wave he made on the first throw
all but beached us.'

                    'All but stove us in!'   520

'Give him our bearing with your trumpeting,
he'll get the range and lob a boulder.'

                              'Aye
He'll smash our timbers and our heads together!'

I would not heed them in my glorying spirit,
but let my anger flare and yelled:
                              'Kyklops,   525
if ever mortal man inquire
how you were put to shame and blinded, tell him
Odysseus, raider of cities, took your eye:
Laërtês' son, whose home's on Ithaka!'

At this he gave a mighty sob and rumbled: 530
'Now comes the weird upon me, spoken of old.
A wizard, grand and wondrous, lived here—Télemos,
a son of Eurymos; great length of days
he had in wizardry among the Kyklopês,
and these things he foretold for time to come: 535
my great eye lost, and at Odysseus' hands.
Always I had in mind some giant, armed
in giant force, would come against me here.
But this, but you—small, pitiful and twiggy—
you put me down with wine, you blinded me.   540
Come back, Odysseus, and I'll treat you well,
praying the god of earthquake to befriend you—
his son I am, for he by his avowal
fathered me, and, if he will, he may

542. *god of earthquake*: Poseidon, the sea-god, the earth-shaker.

heal me of this black wound—he and no other   545
of all the happy gods or mortal men.'

Few words I shouted in reply to him:
'If I could take your life I would and take
your time away, and hurl you down to hell!
The god of earthquake could not heal you there!'   550

At this he stretched his hands out in his darkness
toward the sky of stars, and prayed Poseidon:
'O hear me, lord, blue girdler of the islands,
if I am thine indeed, and thou art father:
grant that Odysseus, raider of cities, never   555
see his home: Laërtês' son, I mean,
who kept his hall on Ithaka. Should destiny
intend that he shall see his roof again
among his family in his father land,
far be that day, and dark the years between.   560
Let him lose all companions, and return
under strange sail to bitter days at home.'

In these words he prayed, and the god heard him.
Now he laid hands upon a bigger stone
and wheeled around, titanic for the cast,   565
to let it fly in the black-prowed vessel's track.
But it fell short, just aft the steering oar,
and whelming seas rose giant above the stone
to bear us onward toward the island.
                                            There
as we ran in we saw the squadron waiting,   570
the trim ships drawn up side by side, and all
our troubled friends who waited, looking seaward.
We beached her, grinding keel in the soft sand,
and waded in, ourselves, on the sandy beach.
Then we unloaded all the Kyklops' flock   575
to make division, share and share alike,
only my fighters voted that my ram,
the prize of all, should go to me. I slew him
by the sea side and burnt his long thighbones
to Zeus beyond the stormcloud, Kronos' son,   580
who rules the world. But Zeus disdained my offering;
destruction for my ships he had in store
and death for those who sailed them, my companions.
Now all day long until the sun went down
we made our feast on mutton and sweet wine,   585

till after sunset in the gathering dark
we went to sleep above the wash of ripples.

When the young Dawn with finger tips of rose
touched the world, I roused the men, gave orders
to man the ships, cast off the mooring lines;   590
and filing in to sit beside the rowlocks
oarsmen in line dipped oars in the grey sea.
So we moved out, sad in the vast offing,
having our precious lives, but not our friends.

Book X

We made our landfall on Aiolia Island,
domain of Aiolos Hippotadês,
the wind king, dear to the gods who never die—
an isle adrift upon the sea, ringed round
with brazen ramparts on a sheer cliffside.   5
Twelve children had old Aiolos at home—
six daughters and six lusty sons—and he
gave girls to boys to be their gentle brides;
now those lords, in their parents' company,
sup every day in hall—a royal feast   10
with fumes of sacrifice and winds that pipe
'round hollow courts; and all the night they sleep
on beds of filigree beside their ladies.
Here we put in, lodged in the town and palace,
while Aiolos played host to me. He kept me   15
one full month to hear the tale of Troy,
the ships and the return of the Akhaians,
all which I told him point by point in order.
When in return I asked his leave to sail
and asked provisioning, he stinted nothing,   20
adding a bull's hide sewn from neck to tail
into a mighty bag, bottling storm winds;
for Zeus had long ago made Aiolos
warden of winds, to rouse or calm at will.
He wedged this bag under my afterdeck,   25
lashing the neck with shining silver wire
so not a breath got through; only the west wind
he lofted for me in a quartering breeze

1. *Aiolia:* a moving island, the home
of the king of the winds (whose name
in Greek means "shifting, changeable").
It has been located by modern geographers in the Lipari Islands of the Sicilian
coast. The great ancient geographer Era-
tosthenes was not so confident. He once
said that we would know exactly where
Odysseus wandered after we had traced
the leatherworker who made the bag in
which the winds were contained.

to take my squadron spanking home.
                                No luck:
the fair wind failed us when our prudence failed.   30

Nine days and nights we sailed without event,
till on the tenth we raised our land. We neared it,
and saw men building fires along the shore;
but now, being weary to the bone, I fell
into deep slumber; I had worked the sheet   35
nine days alone, and given it to no one,
wishing to spill no wind on the homeward run.
But while I slept, the crew began to parley:
silver and gold, they guessed, were in that bag
bestowed on me by Aiolos' great heart;   40
and one would glance at his benchmate and say:
'It never fails. He's welcome everywhere:
hail to the captain when he goes ashore!
He brought along so many presents, plunder
out of Troy, that's it. How about ourselves—   45
his shipmates all the way? Nigh home we are
with empty hands. And who has gifts from Aiolos?
He has. I say we ought to crack that bag,
there's gold and silver, plenty, in that bag!'

Temptation had its way with my companions,   50
and they untied the bag.
                         Then every wind
roared into hurricane; the ships went pitching
west with many cries; our land was lost.
Roused up, despairing in that gloom, I thought:
"Should I go overside for a quick finish   55
or clench my teeth and stay among the living?'
Down in the bilge I lay, pulling my sea cloak
over my head, while the rough gale blew the ships
and rueful crews clear back to Aiolia.

We put ashore for water; then all hands   60
gathered alongside for a mid-day meal.
When we had taken bread and drink, I picked
one soldier, and one herald, to go with me
and called again on Aiolos. I found him
at meat with his young princes and his lady,   65
but there beside the pillars, in his portico,
we sat down silent at the open door.
The sight amazed them, and they all exclaimed:

'Why back again, Odysseus?'
                'What sea fiend
rose in your path?'
                    'Did we not launch you well   70
for home, or for whatever land you chose?'

Out of my melancholy I replied:
'Mischief aboard and nodding at the tiller—
a damned drowse—did for me. Make good my loss,
dear friends! You have the power!'
                   Gently I pleaded,   75
but they turned cold and still. Said Father Aiolos:
'Take yourself out of this island, creeping thing—
no law, no wisdom, lays it on me now
to help a man the blessed gods detest—
out! Your voyage here was cursed by heaven!'   80

He drove me from the place, groan as I would,
and comfortless we went again to sea,
days of it, till the men flagged at the oars—
no breeze, no help in sight, by our own folly—
six indistinguishable nights and days   85
before we raised the Laistrygonian height
and far stronghold of Lamos. In that land
the daybreak follows dusk, and so the shepherd
homing calls to the cowherd setting out;
and he who never slept could earn two wages,   90
tending oxen, pasturing silvery flocks,
where the low night path of the sun is near
the sun's path by day. Here, then, we found
a curious bay with mountain walls of stone
to left and right, and reaching far inland,—   95
a narrow entrance opening from the sea
where cliffs converged as though to touch and close.
All of my squadron sheltered here, inside
the cavern of this bay.
                Black prow by prow
those hulls were made fast in a limpid calm   100
without a ripple, stillness all around them.
My own black ship I chose to moor alone
on the sea side, using a rock for bollard;
and climbed a rocky point to get my bearings.
No farms, no cultivated land appeared,   105

    95. *sun's path by day:* generally   the short summer nights of the far north,
thought to be a confused reference to

but puffs of smoke rose in the wilderness;
so I sent out two picked men and a herald
to learn what race of men this land sustained.

My party found a track—a wagon road
for bringing wood down from the heights to town; 110
and near the settlement they met a daughter
of Antiphatês the Laistrygon—a stalwart
young girl taking her pail to Artakía,
the fountain where these people go for water.
My fellows hailed her, put their questions to her: 115
who might the king be? ruling over whom?
She waved her hand, showing her father's lodge,
so they approached it. In its gloom they saw
a woman like a mountain crag, the queen—
and loathed the sight of her. But she, for greeting, 120
called from the meeting ground her lord and master,
Antiphatês, who came to drink their blood.
He seized one man and tore him on the spot,
making a meal of him; the other two
leaped out of doors and ran to join the ships. 125
Behind, he raised the whole tribe howling, countless
Laistrygonês—and more than men they seemed,
gigantic when they gathered on the sky line
to shoot great boulders down from slings; and hell's own
crashing rose, and crying from the ships, 130
as planks and men were smashed to bits—poor gobbets
the wildmen speared like fish and bore away.
But long before it ended in the anchorage—
havoc and slaughter—I had drawn my sword
and cut my own ship's cable. 'Men,' I shouted, 135
'man the oars and pull till your hearts break
if you would put this butchery behind!'
The oarsmen rent the sea in mortal fear
and my ship spurted out of range, far out
from that deep canyon where the rest were lost. 140
So we fared onward, and death fell behind,
and we took breath to grieve for our companions.

Our next landfall was on Aiaia, island
of Kirkê, dire beauty and divine,
sister of baleful Aiêtês, like him 145
fathered by Hêlios the light of mortals
on Persê, child of the Ocean stream.
                                    We came

washed in our silent ship upon her shore,
and found a cove, a haven for the ship—
some god, invisible, conned us in. We landed,   150
to lie down in that place two days and nights,
worn out and sick at heart, tasting our grief.
But when Dawn set another day a-shining
I took my spear and broadsword, and I climbed
a rocky point above the ship, for sight   155
or sound of human labor. Gazing out
from that high place over a land of thicket,
oaks and wide watercourses, I could see
a smoke wisp from the woodland hall of Kirke.
So I took counsel with myself: should I   160
go inland scouting out that reddish smoke?
No: better not, I thought, but first return
to waterside and ship, and give the men
breakfast before I sent them to explore.
Now as I went down quite alone, and came   165
a bowshot from the ship, some god's compassion
set a big buck in motion to cross my path—
a stag with noble antlers, pacing down
from pasture in the woods to the riverside,
as long thirst and the power of sun constrained him.   170
He started from the bush and wheeled: I hit him
square in the spine midway along his back
and the bronze point broke through it. In the dust
he fell and whinnied as life bled away.
I set one foot against him, pulling hard   175
to wrench my weapon from the wound, then left it,
butt-end on the ground. I plucked some withies
and twined a double strand into a rope—
enough to tie the hocks of my huge trophy;
then pickaback I lugged him to the ship,   180
leaning on my long spearshaft; I could not
haul that mighty carcass on one shoulder.
Beside the ship I let him drop, and spoke
gently and low to each man standing near:
'Come, friends, though hard beset, we'll not go down   185
into the House of Death before our time.
As long as food and drink remain aboard
let us rely on it, not die of hunger.'

At this those faces, cloaked in desolation
upon the waste sea beach, were bared;   190
their eyes turned toward me and the mighty trophy,

lighting, foreseeing pleasure, one by one.
So hands were washed to take what heaven sent us.
And all that day until the sun went down
we had our fill of venison and wine,   195
till after sunset in the gathering dusk
we slept at last above the line of breakers.
When the young Dawn with finger tips of rose
made heaven bright, I called them round and said:
'Shipmates, companions in disastrous time,   200
O my dear friends, where Dawn lies, and the West,
and where the great Sun, light of men, may go
under the earth by night, and where he rises—
of these things we know nothing. Do we know
any least thing to serve us now? I wonder.   205
All that I saw when I went up the rock
was one more island in the boundless main,
a low landscape, covered with woods and scrub,
and puffs of smoke ascending in mid-forest.'

They were all silent, but their hearts contracted,   210
remembering Antiphatês the Laistrygon
and that prodigious cannibal, the Kyklops.
They cried out, and the salt tears wet their eyes.
But seeing our time for action lost in weeping,
I mustered those Akhaians under arms,   215
counting them off in two platoons, myself
and my godlike Eurýlokhos commanding.
We shook lots in a soldier's dogskin cap
and his came bounding out—valiant Eurýlokhos!—
So off he went, with twenty-two companions   220
weeping, as mine wept, too, who stayed behind.

In the wild wood they found an open glade,
around a smooth stone house—the hall of Kirkê—
and wolves and mountain lions lay there, mild
in her soft spell, fed on her drug of evil.   225
None would attack—oh, it was strange, I tell you—
but switching their long tails they faced our men
like hounds, who look up when their master comes
with tidbits for them—as he will—from table.
Humbly those wolves and lions with mighty paws   230
fawned on our men—who met their yellow eyes

---

201. *where Dawn lies, etc.*: in view of
the immediately preceding lines, this
can hardly be taken literally. It is possibly a sailor's metaphorical way of
saying, "we don't know where we are."

and feared them.
                    In the entrance way they stayed
to listen there: inside her quiet house
they heard the goddess Kirkê.

                    Low she sang
in her beguiling voice, while on her loom   235
she wove ambrosial fabric sheer and bright,
by that craft known to the goddesses of heaven.
No one would speak, until Politês—most
faithful and likable of my officers, said:
'Dear friends, no need for stealth: here's a young weaver   240
singing a pretty song to set the air
a-tingle on these lawns and paven courts.
Goddess she is, or lady. Shall we greet her?'

So reassured, they all cried out together,
and she came swiftly to the shining doors   245
to call them in. All but Eurýlokhos—
who feared a snare—the innocents went after her.
On thrones she seated them, and lounging chairs,
while she prepared a meal of cheese and barley
and amber honey mixed with Pramnian wine,   250
adding her own vile pinch, to make them lose
desire or thought of our dear father land.
Scarce had they drunk when she flew after them
with her long stick and shut them in a pigsty—
bodies, voices, heads, and bristles, all   255
swinish now, though minds were still unchanged.
So, squealing, in they went. And Kirkê tossed them
acorns, mast, and cornel berries—fodder
for hogs who rut and slumber on the earth.

Down to the ship Eurýlokhos came running   260
to cry alarm, foul magic doomed his men!
But working with dry lips to speak a word
he could not, being so shaken; blinding tears
welled in his eyes; foreboding filled his heart.
When we were frantic questioning him, at last   265
we heard the tale: our friends were gone. Said he:
'We went up through the oak scrub where you sent us,
Odysseus, glory of commanders,
until we found a palace in a glade,
a marble house on open ground, and someone   270
singing before her loom a chill, sweet song—
goddess or girl, we could not tell. They hailed her,

and then she stepped through shining doors and said,
"Come, come in!" Like sheep they followed her,
but I saw cruel deceit, and stayed behind.   275
Then all our fellows vanished. Not a sound,
and nothing stirred, although I watched for hours.'

When I heard this I slung my silver-hilted
broadsword on, and shouldered my long bow,
and said, 'Come, take me back the way you came.'   280
But he put both his hands around my knees
in desperate woe, and said in supplication:
'Not back there, O my lord! Oh, leave me here!
You, even you, cannot return, I know it,
I know you cannot bring away our shipmates;   285
better make sail with these men, quickly too,
and save ourselves from horror while we may.'

But I replied:
            'By heaven, Eurýlokhos,
rest here then; take food and wine;
stay in the black hull's shelter. Let me go,   290
as I see nothing for it but to go.'

I turned and left him, left the shore and ship,
and went up through the woodland hushed and shady
to find the subtle witch in her long hall.
But Hermês met me, with his golden wand,   295
barring the way—a boy whose lip was downy
in the first bloom of manhood, so he seemed.
He took my hand and spoke as though he knew me:
    'Why take the inland path alone,
    poor seafarer, by hill and dale   300
    upon this island all unknown?
    Your friends are locked in Kirkê's pale;
    all are become like swine to see;
    and if you go to set them free
    you go to stay, and never more make sail   305
    for your old home upon Thaki.
    But I can tell you what to do
    to come unchanged from Kirkê's power
    and disenthrall your fighting crew:

298ff. The four rhymed stanzas which
follow are a translator's license; in the
original there is no change of meter and,
of course, no rhyme.
306. *Thaki:* Ithaka.

take with you to her bower   310
as amulet, this plant I know—
it will defeat her horrid show,
so pure and potent is the flower;
no mortal herb was ever so.

Your cup with numbing drops of night   315
and evil, stilled of all remorse,
she will infuse to charm your sight;
but this great herb with holy force
will keep your mind and senses clear:
when she turns cruel, coming near   320
with her long stick to whip you out of doors,
then let your cutting blade appear,

Let instant death upon it shine,
and she will cower and yield her bed—
a pleasure you must not decline,   325
so may her lust and fear bestead
you and your friends, and break her spell;
but make her swear by heaven and hell
no witches' tricks, or else, your harness shed,
you'll be unmanned by her as well.'   330

He bent down glittering for the magic plant
and pulled it up, black root and milky flower—
a *molü* in the language of the gods—
fatigue and pain for mortals to uproot;
but gods do this, and everything, with ease.   335

Then toward Olympos through the island trees
Hermês departed, and I sought out Kirkê,
my heart high with excitement, beating hard.
Before her mansion in the porch I stood
to call her, all being still. Quick as a cat   340
she opened her bright doors and sighed a welcome;
then I strode after her with heavy heart
down the long hall, and took the chair she gave me,
silver-studded, intricately carved,
made with a low footrest. The lady Kirkê   345
mixed me a golden cup of honeyed wine,
adding in mischief her unholy drug.
I drank, and the drink failed. But she came forward
aiming a stroke with her long stick, and whispered:

'Down in the sty and snore among the rest!'   350

Without a word, I drew my sharpened sword
and in one bound held it against her throat.
She cried out, then slid under to take my knees,
catching her breath to say, in her distress:
'What champion, of what country, can you be?   355
Where are your kinsmen and your city?
Are you not sluggish with my wine? Ah, wonder!
Never a mortal man that drank this cup
but when it passed his lips he had succumbed.
Hale must your heart be and your tempered will.   360
Odysseus then you are, O great contender,
of whom the glittering god with golden wand
spoke to me ever, and foretold
the black swift ship would carry you from Troy.
Put up your weapon in the sheath. We two   365
shall mingle and make love upon our bed.
So mutual trust may come of play and love.'

To this I said:
                  'Kirkê, am I a boy,
that you should make me soft and doting now?
Here in this house you turned my men to swine;   370
now it is I myself you hold, enticing
into your chamber, to your dangerous bed,
to take my manhood when you have me stripped.
I mount no bed of love with you upon it.
Or swear me first a great oath, if I do,   375
you'll work no more enchantment to my harm.'
She swore at once, outright, as I demanded,
and after she had sworn, and bound herself,
I entered Kirkê's flawless bed of love.

Presently in the hall her maids were busy,   380
the nymphs who waited upon Kirkê: four,
whose cradles were in fountains, under boughs,
or in the glassy seaward-gliding streams.
One came with richly colored rugs to throw
on seat and chairback, over linen covers;   385
a second pulled the tables out, all silver,
and loaded them with baskets all of gold;
a third mixed wine as tawny-mild as honey
in a bright bowl, and set out golden cups.

362. *god with the golden wand:* Hermes.

The fourth came bearing water, and lit a blaze   390
under a cauldron. By and by it bubbled,
and when the dazzling brazen vessel seethed
she filled a bathtub to my waist, and bathed me,
pouring a soothing blend on head and shoulders,
warming the soreness of my joints away.   395
When she had done, and smoothed me with sweet oil,
she put a tunic and a cloak around me
and took me to a silver-studded chair
with footrest, all elaborately carven.
Now came a maid to tip a golden jug   400
of water into a silver finger bowl,
and draw a polished table to my side.
The larder mistress brought her tray of loaves
with many savory slices, and she gave
the best, to tempt me. But no pleasure came;   405
I huddled with my mind elsewhere, oppressed.

Kirkê regarded me, as there I sat
disconsolate, and never touched a crust.
Then she stood over me and chided me:
'Why sit at table mute, Odysseus?   410
Are you mistrustful of my bread and drink?
Can it be treachery that you fear again,
after the gods' great oath I swore for you?'
I turned to her at once, and said:
                             'Kirkê'
where is the captain who could bear to touch   415
this banquet, in my place? A decent man
would see his company before him first.
Put heart in me to eat and drink—you may,
by freeing my companions. I must see them.'

But Kirkê had already turned away.   420
Her long staff in her hand, she left the hall
and opened up the sty. I saw her enter,
driving those men turned swine to stand before me.
She stroked them, each in turn, with some new chrism;
and then, behold! their bristles fell away,   425
the coarse pelt grown upon them by her drug
melted away, and they were men again,
younger, more handsome, taller than before.
Their eyes upon me, each one took my hands,
and wild regret and longing pierced them through,   430
so the room rang with sobs, and even Kirkê

pitied that transformation. Exquisite
the goddess looked as she stood near me, saying:
'Son of Laërtês and the gods of old,
Odysseus, master mariner and soldier,   435
go to the sea beach and sea-breasting ship;
drag it ashore, full length upon the land;
stow gear and stores in rock-holes under cover;
return; be quick; bring all your dear companions.'

Now, being a man, I could not help consenting.   440
So I went down to the sea beach and the ship,
where I found all my other men on board,
weeping, in despair along the benches.
Sometimes in farmyards when the cows return
well fed from pasture to the barn, one sees   445
the pens give way before the calves in tumult,
breaking through to cluster about their mothers,
bumping together, bawling. Just that way
my crew poured round me when they saw me come—
their faces wet with tears as if they saw   450
their homeland, and the crags of Ithaka,
even the very town where they were born.
And weeping still they all cried out in greeting:
'Prince, what joy this is, your safe return!
Now Ithaka seems here, and we in Ithaka!   455
But tell us now, what death befell our friends?'

And, speaking gently, I replied:
'First we must get the ship high on the shingle,
and stow our gear and stores in clefts of rock
for cover. Then come follow me, to see   460
your shipmates in the magic house of Kirkê
eating and drinking, endlessly regaled.'

They turned back, as commanded, to this work;
only one lagged, and tried to hold the others;
Eurýlokhos it was, who blurted out: 465
'Where now, poor remnants? is it devil's work
you long for? Will you go to Kirkê's hall?
Swine, wolves, and lions she will make us all,
beasts of her courtyard, bound by her enchantment.
Remember those the Kyklops held, remember   470
shipmates who made that visit with Odysseus!
The daring man! They died for his foolishness!'

When I heard this I had a mind to draw
the blade that swung against my side and chop him,
bowling his head upon the ground—kinsman   475
or no kinsman, close to me though he was.
But others came between, saying, to stop me,
'Prince, we can leave him, if you say the word;
let him stay here on guard. As for ourselves,
show us the way to Kirkê's magic hall.'   480

So all turned inland, leaving shore and ship,
and Eurýlokhos—he, too, came on behind,
fearing the rough edge of my tongue. Meanwhile
at Kirkê's hands the rest were gently bathed,
anointed with sweet oil, and dressed afresh   485
in tunics and new cloaks with fleecy linings.
We found them all at supper when we came.
But greeting their old friends once more, the crew
could not hold back their tears; and now again
the rooms rang with sobs. Then Kirkê, loveliest   490
of all immortals, came to counsel me:
'Son of Laërtês and the gods of old.
Odysseus, master mariner and soldier,
enough of weeping fits. I know—I, too—
what you endured upon the inhuman sea,   495
what odds you met on land from hostile men.
Remain with me, and share my meat and wine;
restore behind your ribs those gallant hearts
that served you in the old days, when you sailed
from stony Ithaka. Now parched and spent,   500
your cruel wandering is all you think of,
never of joy, after so many blows.'

As we were men we could not help consenting.
So day by day we lingered, feasting long
on roasts and wine, until a year grew fat.   505
But when the passing months and wheeling seasons
brought the long summery days, the pause of summer,
my shipmates one day summoned me and said:
'Captain, shake off this trance, and think of home—
if home indeed awaits us,
                                if we shall ever see   510
your own well-timbered hall on Ithaka.'

They made me feel a pang, and I agreed.

475. *kinsman*: Eurýlokhos was related to Odysseus by marriage.

That day, and all day long, from dawn to sundown,
we feasted on roast meat and ruddy wine,
and after sunset when the dusk came on   515
my men slept in the shadowy hall, but I
went through the dark to Kirkê's flawless bed
and took the goddess' knees in supplication,
urging, as she bent to hear:
              'O Kirkê,
now you must keep your promise; it is time.   520
Help me make sail for home. Day after day
my longing quickens, and my company
give me no peace, but wear my heart away
pleading when you are not at hand to hear.'

The loveliest of goddesses replied: 525
'Son of Laërtês and the gods of old,
Odysseus, master mariner and soldier,
you shall not stay here longer against your will;
but home you may not go
unless you take a strange way round and come   530
to the cold homes of Death and pale Perséphonê.
You shall hear prophecy from the rapt shade
of blind Teirêsias of Thebes, forever
charged with reason even among the dead;
to him alone, of all the flitting ghosts,   535
Perséphonê has given a mind undarkened.'

At this I felt a weight like stone within me,
and, moaning, pressed my length against the bed,
with no desire to see the daylight more.
But when I had wept and tossed and had my fill   540
of this despair, at last I answered her:
'Kirkê, who pilots me upon this journey?
No man has ever sailed to the land of Death.'

That loveliest of goddesses replied:
'Son of Laërtês and the gods of old,   545
Odysseus, master of land ways and sea ways,
feel no dismay because you lack a pilot;
only set up your mast and haul your canvas
to the fresh blowing North; sit down and steer,
and hold that wind, even to the bourne of Ocean,   550
Perséphonê's deserted strand and grove,

531. *Perséphonê*: queen of the underworld.

dusky with poplars and the drooping willow.
Run through the tide-rip, bring your ship to shore,
land there, and find the crumbling homes of Death.
Here, toward the Sorrowing Water, run the streams   555
of Wailing, out of Styx, and quenchless Burning—
torrents that join in thunder at the Rock.
Here then, great soldier, setting foot obey me:
dig a well shaft a forearm square; pour out
libations round it to the unnumbered dead: 560
sweet milk and honey, then sweet wine, and last
clear water, scattering handfulls of white barley.
Pray now, with all your heart, to the faint dead;
swear you will sacrifice your finest heifer,
at home in Ithaka, and burn for them   565
her tenderest parts in sacrifice; and vow
to the lord Teirêsias, apart from all,
a black lamb, handsomest of all your flock—
thus to appease the nations of the dead.
Then slash a black ewe's throat, and a black ram,   570
facing the gloom of Erebos; but turn
your head away toward Ocean. You shall see, now
souls of the buried dead in shadowy hosts,
and now you must call out to your companions
to flay those sheep the bronze knife has cut down,   575
for offerings, burnt flesh to those below,
to sovereign Death and pale Perséphonê.
Meanwhile draw sword from hip, crouch down, ward off
the surging phantoms from the bloody pit
until you know the presence of Teirêsias.   580
He will come soon, great captain; be it he
who gives you course and distance for your sailing
homeward across the cold fish-breeding sea.'

As the goddess ended, Dawn came stitched in gold.
Now Kirkê dressed me in my shirt and cloak,   585
put on a gown of subtle tissue, silvery,
then wound a golden belt about her waist
and veiled her head in linen,
while I went through the hall to rouse my crew.
I bent above each one, and gently said: 590
'Wake from your sleep; no more sweet slumber. Come,
we sail: the Lady Kirkê so ordains it.'

555-556. *Sorrowing Water ... Burning*: translations of the Greek names for the rivers of the underworld: Acheron, Cocytus, and Pyriphlegethon.

577. *Erebos*: the darkest region of the underworld, usually imagined as below the underworld itself but here to the west.

They were soon up, and ready at that word;
but I was not to take my men unharmed
from this place, even from this. Among them all   595
the youngest was Elpênor—
no mainstay in a fight nor very clever—
and this one, having climbed on Kirkê's roof
to taste the cool night, fell asleep with wine.
Waked by our morning voices, and the tramp   600
of men below, he started up, but missed
his footing on the long steep backward ladder
and fell that height headlong. The blow smashed
the nape cord, and his ghost fled to the dark.
But I was outside, walking with the rest,   605
saying:
        'Homeward you think we must be sailing
to our own land; no, elsewhere is the voyage
Kirkê has laid upon me. We must go
to the cold homes of Death and pale Perséphonê   610
to hear Teirêsias tell of time to come.'

They felt so stricken, upon hearing this,
they sat down wailing loud, and tore their hair.
But nothing came of giving way to grief.
Down to the shore and ship at last we went,
bowed with anguish, cheeks all wet with tears,   615
to find that Kirkê had been there before us
and tied nearby a black ewe and a ram:
she had gone by like air.
For who could see the passage of a goddess
unless she wished his mortal eyes aware?   620

Book XI

We bore down on the ship at the sea's edge
and launched her on the salt immortal sea,
stepping our mast and spar in the black ship;
embarked the ram and ewe and went aboard
in tears, with bitter and sore dread upon us.   5
But now a breeze came up for us astern—
a canvas-bellying landbreeze, hale shipmate
sent by the singing nymph with sun-bright hair;
so we made fast the braces, took our thwarts,
and let the wind and steersman work the ship   10

598. *roof*: a flat roof. and the coolest place to sleep.

with full sail spread all day above our coursing,
till the sun dipped, and all the ways grew dark
upon the fathomless unresting sea.
                                    By night
our ship ran onward toward the Ocean's bourne,
the realm and region of the Men of Winter,   15
hidden in mist and cloud. Never the flaming
eye of Hêlios lights on those men
at morning, when he climbs the sky of stars,
nor in descending earthward out of heaven;
ruinous night being rove over those wretches.   20
We made the land, put ram and ewe ashore,
and took our way along the Ocean stream
to find the place foretold for us by Kirkê.
There Perimêdês and Eurýlokhos
pinioned the sacred beasts. With my drawn blade   25
I spaded up the votive pit, and poured
libations round it to the unnumbered dead:
sweet milk and honey, then sweet wine, and last
clear water; and I scattered barley down.
Then I addressed the blurred and breathless dead,   30
vowing to slaughter my best heifer for them
before she calved, at home in Ithaka,
and burn the choice bits on the altar fire;
as for Teirêsias, I swore to sacrifice
a black lamb, handsomest of all our flock.   35
Thus to assuage the nations of the dead
I pledged these rites, then slashed the lamb and ewe,
letting their black blood stream into the wellpit.
Now the souls gathered, stirring out of Erebos,
brides and young men, and men grown old in pain,   40
and tender girls whose hearts were new to grief;
many were there, too, torn by brazen lanceheads,
battle-slain, bearing still their bloody gear.
From every side they came and sought the pit
with rustling cries; and I grew sick with fear.   45
But presently I gave command to my officers
to flay those sheep the bronze cut down, and make
burnt offerings of flesh to the gods below—
to sovereign Death, to pale Perséphonê.
Meanwhile I crouched with my drawn sword to keep   50
the surging phantoms from the bloody pit
till I should know the presence of Teirêsias.

15. *Men of Winter:* Although Homer
usually places Hades below the earth,
here he puts it across a great expanse
of sea, apparently in the far north.

One shade came first—Elpênor, of our company,
who lay unburied still on the wide earth
as we had left him—dead in Kirkê's hall,   55
untouched, unmourned, when other cares compelled us.
Now when I saw him there I wept for pity
and called out to him:
                              'How is this, Elpênor,
how could you journey to the western gloom
swifter afoot than I in the black lugger?'   60

He sighed, and answered:
                              'Son of great Laërtês,
Odysseus, master mariner and soldier,
bad luck shadowed me, and no kindly power;
ignoble death I drank with so much wine.
I slept on Kirkê's roof, then could not see   65
the long steep backward ladder, coming down,
and fell that height. My neck bone, buckled under,
snapped, and my spirit found this well of dark.
Now hear the grace I pray for, in the name
of those back in the world, not here—your wife   70
and father, he who gave you bread in childhood,
and your own child, your only son, Telémakhos,
long ago left at home.
                              When you make sail
and put these lodgings of dim Death behind,
you will moor ship, I know, upon Aiaia Island;   75
there, O my lord, remember me, I pray,
do not abandon me unwept, unburied,
to tempt the gods' wrath, while you sail for home;
but fire my corpse, and all the gear I had,
and build a cairn for me above the breakers—   80
an unknown sailor's mark for men to come.
Heap up the mound there and implant upon it
the oar I pulled in life with my companions.'

He ceased, and I replied:
                              'Unhappy spirit,
I promise you the barrow and the burial.'   85

So we conversed, and grimly, at a distance,
with my long sword between, guarding the blood,
while the faint image of the lad spoke on.
Now came the soul of Antikleía, dead,
my mother, daughter of Autólykos,   90
dead now, though living still when I took ship

for holy Troy. Seeing this ghost I grieved,
but held her off, through pang on pang of tears,
till I should know the presence of Teirêsias.
Soon from the dark that prince of Thebes came forward   95
bearing a golden staff; and he addressed me:
'Son of Laërtês and the gods of old,
Odysseus, master of land ways and sea ways,
why leave the blazing sun, O man of woe,
to see the cold dead and the joyless region?   100
Stand clear, put up your sword;
let me but taste of blood, I shall speak true.'

At this I stepped aside, and in the scabbard
let my long sword ring home to the pommel silver,
as he bent down to the sombre blood. Then spoke   105
the prince of those with gift of speech:
                                        'Great captain,
a fair wind and the honey lights of home
are all you seek. But anguish lies ahead;
the god who thunders on the land prepares it,
not to be shaken from your track, implacable,   110
in rancor for the son whose eye you blinded.
One narrow strait may take you through his blows:
denial of yourself, restraint of shipmates.
When you make landfall on Thrinakia first
and quit the violet sea, dark on the land   115
you'll find the grazing herds of Hêlios
by whom all things are seen, all speech is known.
Avoid those kine, hold fast to your intent,
and hard seafaring brings you all to Ithaka.
But if you raid the beeves, I see destruction   120
for ship and crew. Though you survive alone,
bereft of all companions, lost for years,
under strange sail shall you come home, to find
your own house filled with trouble: insolent men
eating your livestock as they court your lady.   125
Aye, you shall make those men atone in blood!

114ff.: Tiresias here predicts the future of Odysseus. Like many Greek prophecies, it contains alternatives. The second (l. 120ff.) is what happens. In Book XII (not in our selection) Odysseus and his crew land on Thrinakia (Sicily), and while Odysseus goes off to explore, his crew kill and eat the cattle of the Sun-god Helios. As a result the ship is wrecked when they put to sea again. Odysseus is the only survivor and is cast up on the island of Kalypso, where he is detained for seven years before he makes his way to the land of the Phaeakians, at whose court he is telling this story. From there he reaches Ithaka and after great trials kills the suitors who besiege his wife and waste his wealth. The journey inland to find a people who have never seen the sea (and so mistake an oar for a winnowing-fan—l. 136) does not take place within the Odyssey itself.

But after you have dealt out death—in open
combat or by stealth—to all the suitors,
go overland on foot, and take an oar,
until one day you come where men have lived   130
with meat unsalted, never known the sea,
nor seen seagoing ships, with crimson bows
and oars that fledge light hulls for dipping flight.
The spot will soon be plain to you, and I
can tell you how: some passerby will say,   135
"What winnowing fan is that upon your shoulder?"
Halt, and implant your smooth oar in the turf
and make fair sacrifice to Lord Poseidon:
a ram, a bull, a great buck boar; turn back,
and carry out pure hekatombs at home   140
to all wide heaven's lords, the undying gods,
to each in order. Then a seaborne death
soft as this hand of mist will come upon you
when you are wearied out with rich old age,
your country folk in blessed peace around you.   145
And all this shall be just as I foretell.'

When he had done, I said at once,
                                 'Teirêsias,
my life runs on then as the gods have spun it.
But come, now, tell me this; make this thing clear:
I see my mother's ghost among the dead   150
sitting in silence near the blood. Not once
has she glanced this way toward her son, nor spoken.
Tell me, my lord,
may she in some way come to know my presence?'

To this he answered:
                      'I shall make it clear   155
in a few words and simply. Any dead man
whom you allow to enter where the blood is
will speak to you, and speak the truth; but those
deprived will grow remote again and fade.'
When he had prophesied, Teirêsias' shade   160
retired lordly to the halls of Death;
but I stood fast until my mother stirred,
moving to sip the black blood; then she knew me
and called out sorrowfully to me:
                                  'Child,
how could you cross alive into this gloom   165

140. *hekatombs*: sacrifices of a hundred head of cattle.

at the world's end?—No sight for living eyes;
great currents run between, desolate waters,
the Ocean first, where no man goes a journey
without ship's timber under him.

                        Say, now,
is it from Troy, still wandering, after years,   170
that you come here with ship and company?
Have you not gone at all to Ithaka?
Have you not seen your lady in your hall?'

She put these questions, and I answered her:
'Mother, I came here, driven to the land of death   175
in want of prophecy from Teirêsias' shade;
nor have I yet coasted Akhaia's hills
nor touched my own land, but have had hard roving
since first I joined Lord Agamémnon's host
by sea for Ilion, the wild horse country,   180
to fight the men of Troy.
But come now, tell me this, and tell me clearly,
what was the bane that pinned you down in Death?
Some ravaging long illness, or mild arrows
a-flying down one day from Artemis?   185
Tell me of Father, tell me of the son
I left behind me; have they still my place,
my honors, or have other men assumed them?
Do they not say that I shall come no more?
And tell me of my wife: how runs her thought,   190
still with her child, still keeping our domains,
or bride again to the best of the Akhaians?'

To this my noble mother quickly answered:
'Still with her child indeed she is, poor heart,
still in your palace hall. Forlorn her nights   195
and days go by, her life used up in weeping.
But no man takes your honored place. Telémakhos
has care of all your garden plots and fields,
and holds the public honor of a magistrate,
feasting and being feasted. But your father   200
is country bound and comes to town no more.
He owns no bedding, rugs, or fleecy mantles,
but lies down, winter nights, among the slaves,
rolled in old cloaks for cover, near the embers
Or when the heat comes at the end of summer,   205
the fallen leaves, all round his vineyard plot,

184-185. *arrows . . . from Artemis:* death for women.
a formula for mysterious but painless

heaped into windrows, make his lowly bed.
He lies now even so, with aching heart,
and longs for your return, while age comes on him.
So I, too, pined away, so doom befell me,   210
not that the keen-eyed huntress with her shafts
had marked me down and shot to kill me; not
that illness overtook me—no true illness
wasting the body to undo the spirit;
only my loneliness for you, Odysseus,   215
for your kind heart and counsel, gentle Odysseus,
took my own life away.'

                I bit my lip,
rising perplexed, with longing to embrace her,
and tried three times, putting my arms around her,
but she went sifting through my hands, impalpable   220
as shadows are, and wavering like a dream.
Now this embittered all the pain I bore,
and I cried in the darkness:
                'O my mother,
will you not stay, be still, here in my arms,
may we not, in this place of Death, as well,   225
hold one another, touch with love, and taste
salt tears' relief, the twinge of welling tears?
Or is this all hallucination, sent
against me by the iron queen, Perséphonê,
to make me groan again?'

                My noble mother   230
answered quickly:
                'O my child—alas,
most sorely tried of men—great Zeus's daughter,
Perséphonê, knits no illusion for you.
All mortals meet this judgment when they die.
No flesh and bone are here, none bound by sinew,   235
since the bright-hearted pyre consumed them down—
the white bones long exanimate—to ash;
dreamlike the soul flies, insubstantial.
You must crave sunlight soon.
                Note all things strange
seen here, to tell your lady in after days.'   240

So went our talk; then other shadows came,
ladies in company, sent by Perséphonê—
consorts or daughters of illustrious men—

211. *huntress:* Artemis.

crowding about the black blood.
                    I took thought
how best to separate and question them,   245
and saw no help for it, but drew once more
the long bright edge of broadsword from my hip,
that none should sip the blood in company
but one by one, in order; so it fell
that each declared her lineage and name.   250

Here was great loveliness of ghosts! I saw
before them all, that princess of great ladies,
Tyro, Salmoneus' daughter, as she told me,
and queen to Krêtheus, a son of Aiolos.
She had gone daft for the river Enipeus,   255
most graceful of all running streams, and ranged
all day by Enipeus' limpid side,
whose form the foaming girdler of the islands,
the god who makes earth tremble, took and so
lay down with her where he went flooding seaward,   260
their bower a purple billow, arching round
to hide them in a sea-vale, god and lady.
Now when his pleasure was complete, the god
spoke to her softly, holding fast her hand:
'Dear mortal, go in joy! At the turn of seasons,   265
winter to summer, you shall bear me sons;
no lovemaking of gods can be in vain.
Nurse our sweet children tenderly, and rear them.
Home with you now, and hold your tongue, and tell
no one your lover's name—though I am yours,   270
Poseidon, lord of surf that makes earth tremble.'

He plunged away into the deep sea swell,
and she grew big with Pelias and Neleus,
powerful vassals, in their time, of Zeus.
Pelias lived on broad Iolkos seaboard   275
rich in flocks, and Neleus at Pylos.
As for the sons borne by that queen of women
to Krêtheus, their names were Aison, Pherês,
and Amytháon, expert charioteer.
Next after her I saw Antiopê,   280

---

251. *loveliness of ghosts:* There follows a "catalogue of women," a list of
famous and beautiful women of former
times.
    253. *Tyro:* a queen of Thessaly;
among her famous descendants were
Nestor and Jason.
    255. *Enipeus:* a river of Thessaly.

Tyro had fallen in love with the river-
god; Poseidon, the "god who makes
earth tremble," assumed his shape.
    273. *Neleus:* father of Nestor of
Pylos.
    278. *Aison:* father of Jason, the Argo-
naut.

daughter of Ásopos. She too could boast
a god for lover, having lain with Zeus
and borne two sons to him: Amphion and
Zêthos, who founded Thebes, the upper city,
and built the ancient citadel. They sheltered   285
no life upon that plain, for all their power,
without a fortress wall.

               And next I saw
Amphitrion's true wife, Alkmênê, mother,
as all men know, of lionish Heraklês,
conceived when she lay close in Zeus's arms;   290
and Megarê, high-hearted Kreon's daughter,
wife of Amphitrion's unwearying son.

I saw the mother of Oidipous, Epikastê,
whose great unwitting deed it was
to marry her own son. He took that prize   295
from a slain father; presently the gods
brought all to light that made the famous story.
But by their fearsome wills he kept his throne
in dearest Thebes, all through his evil days,
while she descended to the place of Death,   300
god of the locked and iron door. Steep down
from a high rafter, throttled in her noose,
she swung, carried away by pain, and left him
endless agony from a mother's Furies.

And I saw Khloris, that most lovely lady,   305
whom for her beauty in the olden time
Neleus wooed with countless gifts, and married.
She was the youngest daughter of Amphion,
son of Iasos. In those days he held
power at Orkhómenos, over the Minyai.   310
At Pylos then as queen she bore her children—
Nestor, Khromios, Periklýmenos,
and Pêro, too, who turned the heads of men
with her magnificence. A host of princes
from nearby lands came courting her; but Neleus   315
would hear of no one, not unless the suitor
could drive the steers of giant Iphiklos
from Phylakê—longhorns, broad in the brow,
so fierce that one man only, a diviner,
offered to round them up. But bitter fate   320
saw him bound hand and foot by savage herdsmen.

---

281. *Ásopos:* a river in Boeotia, the territory of Thebes.
293. *Epikastê:* usually known as Jocasta.

309. *he:* Amphion (not the same Amphion who founded Thebes, l. 284).
319. *a diviner:* named Melampus.

Then days and months grew full and waned, the year
went wheeling round, the seasons came again,
before at last the power of Iphiklos,
relenting, freed the prisoner, who foretold   325
all things to him. So Zeus's will was done.

And I saw Lêda, wife of Tyndareus,
upon whom Tyndareus had sired twins
indomitable: Kastor, tamer of horses,
and Polydeukês, best in the boxing ring.   330
Those two live still, though life-creating earth
embraces them: even in the underworld
honored as gods by Zeus, each day in turn
one comes alive, the other dies again.

Then after Lêda to my vision came   335
the wife of Aloeus, Iphimedeia,
proud that she once had held the flowing sea
and borne him sons, thunderers for a day,
the world-renowned Otos and Ephialtês.
Never were men on such a scale   340
bred on the plowlands and the grainlands, never
so magnificent any, after Orion.
At nine years old they towered nine fathoms tall,
nine cubits in the shoulders, and they promised
furor upon Olympos, heaven broken by battle cries,   345
the day they met the gods in arms.
                With Ossa's
mountain peak they meant to crown Olympos
and over Ossa Pelion's forest pile
for footholds up the sky. As giants grown
they might have done it, but the bright son of Zeus   350
by Lêto of the smooth braid shot them down
while they were boys unbearded; no dark curls
clustered yet from temples to the chin.
Then I saw Phaidra, Prokris; and Ariadnê,

---

327. *Lêda:* she bore Helen to Zeus; to
her husband Tyndareus, she bore the
two sons, Kastor and Polydeuces, and
Clytemnestra, who was to be the wife
of Agamemnon.

333. *each day in turn:* they shared,
as it were, one immortality between
them.

337. *flowing sea:* Poseidon.

342. *Orion:* the hunter who was, according to later legend, transformed into
the constellation which still bears his
name; in Homer he is in the underworld
after his death (see l. 643*ff.*).

346-347. *Ossa's mountain peak:* Ossa
and Pelion are mountains near Olympus
in Thessaly.

350. *son of Zeus:* Apollo, son of Zeus
and Lêto.

354. *Phaidra:* the Cretan wife of
Theseus of Athens, who fell in love with
her stepson Hippolytus. *Prokris:* the unfaithful wife of Cephalus, king of Athens. *Ariadnê:* sister of Phaidra; she
helped Theseus slay the Minotaur on
Crete and escaped with him, only to die
on the island of Dia.

daughter of Minos, the grim king. Theseus took her   355
aboard with him from Krete for the terraced land
of ancient Athens; but he had no joy of her.
Artemis killed her on the Isle of Dia
at a word from Dionysos.

                Maira, then,
and Klymênê, and that detested queen,   360
Eriphylê, who betrayed her lord for gold . . .
but how name all the women I beheld there,
daughters and wives of kings? The starry night
wanes long before I close.

                Here, or aboard ship,
amid the crew, the hour for sleep has come.   365
Our sailing is the gods' affair and yours."

Then he fell silent. Down the shadowy hall
the enchanted banqueters were still. Only
the queen with ivory pale arms, Arêtê, spoke,
saying to all the silent men:

                "Phaiákians,   370
how does he stand, now, in your eyes, this captain,
the look and bulk of him, the inward poise?
He is my guest, but each one shares that honor.
Be in no haste to send him on his way
or scant your bounty in his need. Remember   375
how rich, by heaven's will, your possessions are."

Then Ekhenêos, the old soldier, eldest
of all Phaiákians, added his word:
"Friends, here was nothing but our own thought spoken,
the mark hit square. Our duties to her majesty.   380
For what is to be said and done,
we wait upon Alkínoös' command."

At this the king's voice rang:

355. *Minos*: king of Crete, father of Phaidra and Ariadnê.

359. *at a word from Dionysus*: we have no other account of this version of the episode which explains why Dionysus wanted Ariadne killed; the prevalent version of the story in later times is that Dionysus carried Ariadne off to be his bride. *Maira*: a nymph of Artemis who broke her vow of chastity and was killed by the goddess.

360. *Klymênê*: some story must have been attached to this name, but we do not know what it was.

361. *Eriphylê*: bribed with a golden necklace by Polynices, son of Oedipus, she persuaded her husband Amphiaraus to take part in the attack on Thebes, where he was killed.

367. Odysseus breaks off the story of his wanderings, and we are transported back to the scene of the banqueting hall of the Phaiákians.

371. *how does he stand, now*: before Odysseus revealed his identity and told his story, some of the Phaiákians had treated him with a certain lack of respect.

375. *scant your bounty*: Arêtê is appealing to the Phaiákian chiefs to give Odysseus parting gifts.

"I so command—
as sure as it is I who, while I live,
rule the sea rovers of Phaiákia. Our friend   385
longs to put out for home, but let him be
content to rest here one more day, until
I see all gifts bestowed. And every man
will take thought for his launching and his voyage,
I most of all, for I am master here."   390

Odysseus, the great tactician, answered:
"Alkínoös, king and admiration of men,
even a year's delay, if you should urge it,
in loading gifts and furnishing for sea—
I too could wish it; better far that I   395
return with some largesse of wealth about me—
I shall be thought more worthy of love and courtesy
by every man who greets me home in Ithaka."
The king said:
            "As to that, one word, Odysseus:
from all we see, we take you for no swindler—   400
though the dark earth be patient of so many,
scattered everywhere, baiting their traps with lies
of old times and of places no one knows.
You speak with art, but your intent is honest.
The Argive troubles, and your own troubles,   405
you told as a poet would, a man who knows the world.
But now come tell me this: among the dead
did you meet any of your peers, companions
who sailed with you and met their doom at Troy?
Here's a long night—an endless night—before us,   410
and no time yet for sleep, not in this hall.
Recall the past deeds and the strange adventures.
I could stay up until the sacred Dawn
as long as you might wish to tell your story."

Odysseus the great tactician answered: 415
"Alkínoös, king and admiration of men,
there is a time for story telling; there is
also a time for sleep. But even so,
if, indeed, listening be still your pleasure,
I must not grudge my part. Other and sadder   420
tales there are to tell, of my companions,
of some who came through all the Trojan spears,
clangor and groan of war,
only to find a brutal death at home—

396. *wealth about me:* he lost at sea all the loot he took at Troy and Ismaros.

and a bad wife behind it.

After Perséphonê,

icy and pale, dispersed the shades of women,
the soul of Agamémnon, son of Atreus,
came before me, sombre in the gloom,
and others gathered round, all who were with him
when death and doom struck in Aegísthos' hall.
Sipping the black blood, the tall shade perceived me,
and cried out sharply, breaking into tears;
then tried to stretch his hands toward me, but could not,
being bereft of all the reach and power
he once felt in the great torque of his arms.
Gazing at him, and stirred, I wept for pity,
and spoke across to him:

'O son of Atreus,

illustrious Lord Marshal, Agamémnon,
what was the doom that brought you low in death?
Were you at sea, aboard ship, and Poseidon
blew up a wicked squall to send you under,
or were you cattle-raiding on the mainland
or in a fight for some strongpoint, or women,
when the foe hit you to your mortal hurt?'

But he replied at once:

'Son of Laërtês,

Odysseus, master of land ways and sea ways,
neither did I go down with some good ship
in any gale Poseidon blew, nor die
upon the mainland, hurt by foes in battle.
It was Aigísthos who designed my death,
he and my heartless wife, and killed me, after
feeding me, like an ox felled at the trough.
That was my miserable end—and with me
my fellows butchered, like so many swine
killed for some troop, or feast, or wedding banquet
in a great landholder's household. In your day
you have seen men, and hundreds, die in war,
in the bloody press, or downed in single combat,
but these were murders you would catch your breath at:
think of us fallen, all our throats cut, winebowl
brimming, tables laden on every side,
while blood ran smoking over the whole floor.
In my extremity I heard Kassandra,

---

430. *Aegísthos*: cousin of Agamémnon, who remained at home while Agamémnon went to Troy, seduced his wife Clytemnestra, and helped her murder her husband when he returned.

463. *Kassandra*: She was part of Agamemnon's share of the booty at Troy.

Priam's daughter, piteously crying
as the traitress Klytaimnéstra made to kill her   465
along with me. I heaved up from the ground
and got my hands around the blade, but she
eluded me, that whore. Nor would she close
my two eyes as my soul swam to the underworld
or shut my lips. There is no being more fell,   470
more bestial than a wife in such an action,
and what an action that one planned!
The murder of her husband and her lord.
Great god, I thought my children and my slaves
at least would give me welcome. But that woman,   475
plotting a thing so low, defiled herself
and all her sex, all women yet to come,
even those few who may be virtuous.'
He paused then, and I answered:
                              'Foul and dreadful.
That was the way that Zeus who views the wide world   480
vented his hatred on the sons of Atreus—
intrigues of women, even from the start.
                              Myriads
died by Helen's fault, and Klytaimnéstra
plotted against you half the world away.'

And he at once said:
                              'Let it be a warning   485
even to you. Indulge a woman never,
and never tell her all you know. Some things
a man may tell, some he should cover up.
Not that I see a risk for you, Odysseus,
of death at your wife's hands. She is too wise,   490
too clear-eyed, sees alternatives too well,
Penélopê, Ikários' daughter—
that young bride whom we left behind—think of it!—
when we sailed off to war. The baby boy
still cradled at her breast—now he must be   495
a grown man, and a lucky one. By heaven,
you'll see him yet, and he'll embrace his father
with old fashioned respect, and rightly.
                              My own
lady never let me glut my eyes
on my own son, but bled me to death first.   500
One thing I will advise, on second thought;

468-469. *close my two eyes: i.e.,*   500. *own son:* Crestes.
give me a proper burial.

stow it away and ponder it.

Land your ship

in secret on your island; give no warning.
The day of faithful wives is gone forever.

But tell me, have you any word at all   505
about my son's life? Gone to Orkhómenos
or sandy Pylos, can he be? Or waiting
with Meneláos in the plain of Sparta?
Death on earth has not yet taken Orestés.'

But I could only answer:

'Son of Atreus,   510

why do you ask these questions of me? Neither
news of home have I, nor news of him,
alive or dead. And empty words are evil.'

So we exchanged our speech, in bitterness,
weighed down by grief, and tears welled in our eyes,   515
when there appeared the spirit of Akhilleus,
son of Peleus; then Patróklos' shade,
and then Antílokhos, and then Aias,
first among all the Danaans in strength
and bodily beauty, next to prince Akhilleus.   520
Now that great runner, grandson of Aíakhos,
recognized me and called across to me:
'Son of Laërtês and the gods of old,
Odysseus, master mariner and soldier,
old knife, what next? What greater feat remains   525
for you to put your mind on, after this?
How did you find your way down to the dark
where these dimwitted dead are camped forever,
the after images of used-up men?'

I answered:

'Akhilleus, Peleus' son, strongest of all   530
among the Akhaians, I had need of foresight
such as Teirêsias alone could give
to help me, homeward bound for the crags of Ithaka.
I have not yet coasted Akhaia, not yet
touched my land; my life is all adversity.   535
But was there ever a man more blest by fortune
than you, Akhilleus? Can there ever be?
We ranked you with immortals in your lifetime,
we Argives did, and here your power is royal

---

518. *Antílokhos*: son of Nestor.   521. *grandson of Aíakhos*: Akhilleus.

among the dead men's shades. Think, then, Akhilleus: 540
you need not be so pained by death.'

                  To this
he answered swiftly:

               'Let me hear no smooth talk
of death from you, Odysseus, light of councils.
Better, I say, to break sod as a farm hand
for some poor country man, on iron rations,   545
than lord it over all the exhausted dead.
Tell me, what news of the prince my son: did he
come after me to make a name in battle
or could it be he did not? Do you know
if rank and honor still belong to Peleus   550
in the towns of the Myrmidons? Or now, may be,
Hellas and Phthia spurn him, seeing old age
fetters him, hand and foot. I cannot help him
under the sun's rays, cannot be that man
I was on Troy's wide seaboard, in those days   555
when I made bastion for the Argives
and put an army's best men in the dust.
Were I but whole again, could I go now
to my father's house, one hour would do to make
my passion and my hands no man could hold   560
hateful to any who shoulder him aside.'

Now when he paused I answered:

                'Of all that—
of Peleus' life, that is—I know nothing;
but happily I can tell you the whole story
of Neoptólemos, as you require.   565
In my own ship I brought him out from Skyros
to join the Akhaians under arms.

                And I can tell you,
in every council before Troy thereafter
your son spoke first and always to the point;
no one but Nestor and I could out-debate him.   570
And when we formed against the Trojan line
he never hung back in the mass, but ranged
far forward of his troops—no man could touch him
for gallantry. Aye, scores went down before him

---

547. *my son:* Neoptolemos (the name
means "new war").
566. *brought him out from Skyros:*
The Greeks were told by a prophet that

Troy would fall only to the son of Achilles, who was living on the rocky island
of Skyros.

in hard fights man to man. I shall not tell   575
all about each, or name them all—the long
roster of enemies he put out of action,
taking the shock of charges on the Argives.
But what a champion his lance ran through
in Eurýpulos the son of Télephos! Keteians   580
in throngs around that captain also died—
all because Priam's gifts had won his mother
to send the lad to battle; and I thought
Memnon alone in splendor ever outshone him.

But one fact more: while our picked Argive crew   585
still rode that hollow horse Epeios built,
and when the whole thing lay with me, to open
the trapdoor of the ambuscade or not,
at that point our Danaan lords and soldiers
wiped their eyes, and their knees began to quake,   590
all but Neoptólemos. I never saw
his tanned cheek change color or his hand
brush one tear away. Rather he prayed me,
hand on hilt, to sortie, and he gripped
his tough spear, bent on havoc for the Trojans.   595
And when we had pierced and sacked Priam's tall city
he loaded his choice plunder and embarked
with no scar on him; not a spear had grazed him
nor the sword's edge in close work—common wounds
one gets in war. Arês in his mad fits   600
knows no favorites.'

        But I said no more,
for he had gone off striding the field of asphodel,
the ghost of our great runner, Akhilleus Aiákidês,
glorying in what I told him of his son.

Now other souls of mournful dead stood by,   605
each with his troubled questioning, but one
remained alone, apart: the son of Télamon,
Aías, it was—the great shade burning still
because I had won favor on the beachhead
in rivalry over Akhilleus' arms.   610
The Lady Thetis, mother of Akhilleus,

580. *Eurýpulos*: He came to the aid of the Trojans with a fresh army.

610. *Akhilleus' arms*: After Akhilleus was killed by the Trojan Paris, his mother Thetis offered them as a prize to the Greek who had done most harm to the Trojans. They were awarded to Odysseus. Ajax, after an attempt to kill Odysseus and the two kings, Menelaus and Agamemnon, committed suicide.

laid out for us the dead man's battle gear,
and Trojan children, with Athena,
named the Dannan fittest to own them. Would
god I had not borne the palm that day! 615
For earth took Aías then to hold forever,
the handsomest and, in all feats of war,
noblest of the Danaans after Akhilleus.
Gently therefore I called across to him:
'Aías, dear son of royal Télamon, 620
you would not then forget, even in death,
your fury with me over those accurst
calamitous arms?—and so they were, a bane
sent by the gods upon the Argive host.
For when you died by your own hand we lost 625
a tower, formidable in war. All we Akhaians
mourn you forever, as we do Akhilleus;
and no one bears the blame but Zeus.
He fixed that doom for you because he frowned
on the whole expedition of our spearmen. 630
My lord, come nearer, listen to our story!
Conquer your indignation and your pride.'

But he gave no reply, and turned away,
following other ghosts toward Erebos.
Who knows if in that darkness he might still 635
have spoken, and I answered?
                                              But my heart
longed, after this, to see the dead elsewhere.
And now there came before my eyes Minos,
the son of Zeus, enthroned, holding a golden staff,
dealing out justice among ghostly pleaders 640
arrayed about the broad doorways of Death.

And then I glimpsed Orion, the huge hunter,
gripping his club, studded with bronze, unbreakable,
with wild beasts he had overpowered in life
on lonely mountainsides, now brought to bay 645
on fields of asphodel.
                              And I saw Títyos,
the son of Gaia, lying
abandoned over nine square rods of plain.
Vultures, hunched above him, left and right,
rifling his belly, stabbed into the liver, 650
and he could never push them off.

This hulk
had once committed rape of Zeus's mistress,
Léto, in her glory, when she crossed
the open grass of Panopeus toward Pytho.

Then I saw Tántalos put to the torture: 655
in a cool pond he stood, lapped round by water
clear to the chin, and being athirst he burned
to slake his dry weasand with drink, though drink
he would not ever again. For when the old man
put his lips down to the sheet of water   660
it vanished round his feet, gulped underground,
and black mud baked there in a wind from hell.
Boughs, too, drooped low above him, big with fruit,
pear trees, pomegranates, brilliant apples,
luscious figs, and olives ripe and dark;   665
but if he stretched his hand for one, the wind
under the dark sky tossed the bough beyond him.

Then Sísyphos in torment I beheld
being roustabout to a tremendous boulder.
Leaning with both arms braced and legs driving,   670
he heaved it toward a height, and almost over,
but then a Power spun him round and sent
the cruel boulder bounding again to the plain.
Whereon the man bent down again to toil,
dripping sweat, and the dust rose overhead.   675
Next I saw manifest the power of Heraklês—
a phantom, this, for he himself has gone
feasting amid the gods, reclining soft
with Hêbê of the ravishing pale ankles,
daughter of Zeus and Hêra, shod in gold.   680
But, in my vision, all the dead around him
cried like affrighted birds; like Night itself
he loomed with naked bow and nocked arrow
and glances terrible as continual archery.
My hackles rose at the gold swordbelt he wore   685
sweeping across him: gorgeous intaglio
of savage bears, boars, lions with wildfire eyes,
swordfights, battle, slaughter, and sudden death—
the smith who had that belt in him, I hope
he never made, and never will make, another.   690

655. *Tántalos*: king of Lydia. He was
the confidant of the gods and ate at
their table, but he betrayed their secrets.

668. *Sísyphos*: king of Corinth, the
archetype of the liar and trickster. We
do not know what misdeed he is being
punished for in this passage.

The eyes of the vast figure rested on me,
and of a sudden he said in kindly tones:
'Son of Laërtês and the gods of old,
Odysseus, master mariner and soldier,
under a cloud, you too? Destined to grinding   695
labors like my own in the sunny world?
Son of Kroníon Zeus or not, how many
days I sweated out, being bound in servitude
to a man far worse than I, a rough master!
He made me hunt this place one time   700
to get the watchdog of the dead: no more
perilous task, he thought, could be; but I
brought back that beast, up from the underworld
Hermês and grey-eyed Athena showed the way.'

And Heraklês, down the vistas of the dead,   705
faded from sight; but I stood fast, awaiting
other great souls who perished in times past.
I should have met, then, god-begotten Theseus
and Peirithoös, whom both I longed to see,
but first came shades in thousands, rustling   710
in a pandemonium of whispers, blown together,
and the horror took me that Perséphonê
had brought from darker hell some saurian death's head.
I whirled then, made for the ship, shouted to crewmen
to get aboard and cast off the stern hawsers,   715
an order soon obeyed. They took their thwarts,
and the ship went leaping toward the stream of Ocean
first under oars, then with a following wind.

699. *rough master*: Heraklês, son of
Zeus, was made subject to the orders of
Eurýstheus of Argos who ordered him
to perform the twelve famous labors.
One of them was to bring back from
Hades the dog which guarded the gate.

708. *Theseus*: After his adventures in
Krete, he went with his friend Peirithoös
to Hades to kidnap Perséphonê; the
venture failed, and the two heroes, imprisoned in Hades, were rescued by
Heraklês.

Greek Lyric Poetry[*]

ARCHILOCHUS OF PAROS
(seventh century B.C.)

1

I don't like the towering captain with the spraddly length of leg,
one who swaggers in his lovelocks and cleanshaves beneath the chin.
Give me a man short and squarely set upon his legs, a man

*These selections are reprinted from *Greek
Lyrics* by Richmond Lattimore. Translations by Richmond Lattimore. University
of Chicago Press • Copyright, 1960, by
the University of Chicago.

full of heart, not to be shaken from the place he plants his feet.

2

Heart, my heart, so battered with misfortune far beyond your
    strength,
up, and face the men who hate us. Bare your chest to the assault
of the enemy, and fight them off. Stand fast among the beamlike
    spears.
Give no ground; and if you beat them, do not brag in open show,
nor, if they beat you, run home and lie down on your bed and cry.
Keep some measure in the joy you take in luck, and the degree
you give way to sorrow. All our life is up-and-down like this.

3

To the gods all things are easy. Many times from circumstance
of disaster they set upright those who have been sprawled at length
on the ground, but often again when men stand planted on firm
    feet,
these same gods will knock them on their backs, and then the evils
    come,
so that a man wanders homeless, destitute, at his wit's end.

TYRTAEUS OF SPARTA

(seventh century B.C.?)

I would not say anything for a man nor take account of him
    for any speed of his feet or wrestling skill he might have,
not if he had the size of a Cyclops and strength to go with it,
    not if he could outrun Bóreas, the North Wind of Thrace,
not if he were more handsome and gracefully formed than
    Tithónos,   5
    or had more riches than Midas had, or Kínyras too,
not if he were more of a king than Tantalid Pelops,
    or had the power of speech and persuasion Adrastos had,
not if he had all splendors except for a fighting spirit.
    For no man ever proves himself a good man in war   10
unless he can endure to face the blood and the slaughter,
    go close against the enemy and fight with his hands.
Here is courage, mankind's finest possession, here is
    the noblest prize that a young man can endeavor to win,
and it is a good thing his city and all the people share with him   15

---

5. *Tithónos:* a handsome Trojan prince.
The goddess Eos (Dawn) fell in love with
him and persuaded Zeus to make him immortal.

6. *Midas:* king of Phrygia, whose touch
turned everything to gold. *Kínyras:* a
king of Cyprus, famous for his wealth.

7. *Pelops:* son of Tantalus, king of Lydia. Pelops came to Greece, became king,
and left his name there forever (Pelo-
ponnese=island of Pelops).

8. *Adrastos:* king of Argos.

when a man plants his feet and stands in the foremost spears
relentlessly, all thought of foul flight completely forgotten,
   and has well trained his heart to be steadfast and to endure,
and with words encourages the man who is stationed beside him.
   Here is a man who proves himself to be valiant in war.   20
With a sudden rush he turns to flight the rugged battalions
   of the enemy, and sustains the beating waves of assault.
And he who so falls among the champions and loses his sweet life,
   so blessing with honor his city, his father, and all his people,
with wounds in his chest, where the spear that he was facing has
     transfixed   25
   that massive guard of his shield, and gone through his breastplate
     as well,
why, such a man is lamented alike by the young and the elders,
   and all his city goes into mourning and grieves for his loss.
His tomb is pointed to with pride, and so are his children,
   and his children's children, and afterward all the race that
     is his.   30
His shining glory is never forgotten, his name is remembered,
   and he becomes an immortal, though he lies under the ground,
when one who was a brave man has been killed by the furious War
     God
   standing his ground and fighting hard for his children and land.
But if he escapes the doom of death, the destroyer of bodies,   35
   and wins his battle, and bright renown for the work of his spear,
all men give place to him alike, the youth and the elders,
   and much joy comes his way before he goes down to the dead.
Aging, he has reputation among his citizens. No one
   tries to interfere with his honors or all he deserves;   40
all men withdraw before his presence, and yield their seats to him,
   the youth, and the men his age, and even those older than he.
Thus a man should endeavor to reach this high place of courage
   with all his heart, and, so trying, never be backward in war.

MIMNERMUS OF COLOPHON

(late seventh century B.C.?)

What, then, is life if love the golden is gone? What is pleasure?
   Better to die when the thought of these is lost from my heart:
the flattery of surrender, the secret embrace in the darkness.
   These alone are such charming flowers of youth as befall
women and men. But once old age with its sorrows advances   5
   upon us, it makes a man feeble and ugly alike,
heart worn thin with the hovering expectation of evil,
   lost all joy that comes out of the sight of the sun.
Hateful to boys a man goes then, unfavored of women.
   Such is the thing of sorrow God has made of old age.   10

SAPPHO OF LESBOS
(born ca. 630 B.C.)

1

Throned in splendor, deathless, O Aphrodite,
child of Zeus, charm-fashioner, I entreat you
not with griefs and bitternesses to break my
      spirit, O goddess;

standing by me rather, if once before now   5
far away you heard, when I called upon you,
left your father's dwelling place and descended,
      yoking the golden

chariot to sparrows, who fairly drew you
down in speed aslant the black world, the bright air   10
trembling at the heart to the pulse of countless
      fluttering wingbeats.

Swiftly then they came, and you, blessed lady,
smiling on me out of immortal beauty,
asked me what affliction was on me, why I   15
      called thus upon you,

what beyond all else I would have befall my
tortured heart: "Whom then would you have Persuasion
force to serve desire in your heart? Who is it,
      Sappho, that hurt you?   20

Though she now escape you, she soon will follow;
though she take not gifts from you, she will give them:
though she love not, yet she will surely love you
      even unwilling."

In such guise come even again and set me
free from doubt and sorrow; accomplish all those   25
things my heart desires to be done; appear and
      stand at my shoulder.

1. a prayer to the goddess of love, Aphrodite. The translator has skillfully reproduced the metrical form of the Greek, the "Sapphic" stanza.
9. *sparrows:* Aphrodite's sacred birds.

2

Like the very gods in my sight is he who
sits where he can look in your eyes, who listens

close to you, to hear the soft voice, its sweetness
    murmur in love and

laughter, all for him. But it breaks my spirit;   5
underneath my breast all the heart is shaken.
Let me only glance where you are, the voice dies,
    I can say nothing,

but my lips are stricken to silence, underneath my skin the tenuous flame suffuses;   10
nothing shows in front of my eyes, my ears are
    muted in thunder.

And the sweat breaks running upon me, fever
shakes my body, paler I turn than grass is;
I can feel that I have been changed, I feel that   15
    death has come near me.

3

Some there are who say that the fairest thing seen
on the black earth is an array of horsemen;
some, men marching; some would say ships; but I say
    she whom one loves best

is the loveliest. Light were the work to make this   5
plain to all, since she, who surpassed in beauty
all mortality, Helen, once forsaking
    her lordly husband,

fled away to Troy-land across the water.
Not the thought of child nor beloved parents   10
was remembered, after the Queen of Cyprus
    won her at first sight.

Since young brides have hearts that can be persuaded
easily, light things, palpitant to passion
as am I, remembering Anaktória   15
    who has gone from me

and whose lovely walk and the shining pallor
of her face I would rather see before my
eyes than Lydia's chariots in all their glory
    armored for battle.   20

11. *Queen of Cyprus:* Aphrodite.

ALCAEUS OF LESBOS

(born ca. 620 B.C.)

The great hall is aglare with bronze armament and the whole inside
    made fit for war

with helms glittering and hung high, crested over with white horse-
    manes that nod and wave
and make splendid the heads of men who wear them. Here are shin-
    ing greaves made out of bronze,
hung on hooks, and they cover all the house's side. They are strong
    to stop arrows and spears.
Here are war-jackets quilted close of new linen, with hollow shields
    stacked on the floor,   5
with broad swords of the Chalkis make, many tunics and many
    belts heaped close beside.
These shall not lie neglected, now we have stood to our task and
    have this work to do.

SOLON OF ATHENS*

(early sixth century B.C.)

My purpose was to bring my scattered people back
together. Where did I fall short of my design?
I call to witness at the judgment seat of time
one who is noblest, mother of Olympian
divinities, and greatest of them all, Black Earth.   5
I took away the mortgage stones stuck in her breast,
and she, who went a slave before, is now set free.
Into this sacred land, our Athens, I brought back
a throng of those who had been sold, some by due law,
though others wrongly; some by hardship pressed to escape   10
the debts they owed; and some of these no longer spoke
Attic, since they had drifted wide around the world,
while those in the country had the shame of slavery
upon them, and they served their masters' moods in fear.
These I set free; and I did this by strength of hand,   15
welding right law with violence to a single whole.
So have I done, and carried through all that I pledged.
I have made laws, for the good man and the bad alike,
and shaped a rule to suit each case, and set it down.
Had someone else not like myself taken the reins,   20
some ill-advised or greedy person, he would not
have held the people in. Had I agreed to do
what pleased their adversaries at that time, or what
they themselves planned to do against their enemies,
our city would have been widowed of her men. Therefore,   25
I put myself on guard at every side, and turned
among them like a wolf inside a pack of dogs.

---

* Chief Athenian magistrate, 594–593   12. *Attic:* the dialect of Athens and its
B.C.   territory.

ANACREON OF TEOS
(born ca. 570 B.C.)

1

The love god with his golden curls
puts a bright ball into my hand,
shows a girl in her fancy shoes,
    and suggests that I take her.

Not that girl—she's the other kind,   5
one from Lesbos. Disdainfully,
nose turned up at my silver hair,
    she makes eyes at the ladies.

2

I have gone gray at the temples,
yes, my head is white, there's nothing
of the grace of youth that's left me,
and my teeth are like an old man's.
Life is lovely. But the lifetime   5
that remains for me is little.
For this cause I mourn. The terrors
of the Dark Pit never leave me.
For the house of Death is deep down
underneath; the downward journey   10
to be feared, for once I go there
I know well there's no returning.

XENOPHANES OF COLOPHON
(second half of sixth century B.C.)

Now, supposing a man were to win the prize for the foot race
    at Olympia, there where the precinct of Zeus stands beside
the river, at Pisa: or if he wins the five-contests, or the wrestling,
    or if he endures the pain of boxing and wins, or that new
and terrible game they call the pankrátion, contest of all holds: 5
    why, such a man will obtain honor, in the citizens' sight,
and be given a front seat and be on display at all civic occasions,
    and he would be given his meals all at the public expense,
and be given a gift from the city to take and store for safekeeping.
    If he won with the chariot, too, all this would be granted
        to him,   10

and yet he would not deserve it, as I do. Better than brute strength
of men, or horses either, is the wisdom that is mine.
But custom is careless in all these matters, and there is no justice
in putting strength on a level above wisdom which is sound.
For if among the people there is one who is a good boxer, 15
or one who excels in wrestling or in the five-contests,
or else for speed of his feet, and this is prized beyond other
feats of strength that men display in athletic games,
the city will not, on account of this man, have better government.
Small is the pleasure the city derives from one of its men 20
if he happens to come first in the games by the banks of Pisa.
This does not make rich the treasure house of the state.

THEOGNIS OF MEGARA

(sixth century B.C.)

1

Kyrnos, this city is still the same city, but its people are different.
Those who before knew nothing of lawsuits, nothing of laws,
who went about in goatskins flapping over their shoulders,
who lived on the ranges, far out from the town, like wild deer,
these are now the Great Men, son of Pólypas. Our former nobles 5
are Rabble now. Who could endure it when things are so?
They swindle each other, they mock at one another, and meanwhile
understand nothing at all of what good and bad men think.
Never make one of these citizens your friend, son of Pólypas,
however much you may need to use them: not from the heart: 10
pretend to all that you are their friend: talk as if you were one:
but never communicate to any one of these men
anything important. You must know that their purposes are
unpleasant,
and there is no trusting them in any matter at all,
but treachery, and deception, and catch-as-catch-can is their nature.
Such are the desperate men who have no future assured. 15

1. *Kyrnos:* son of Pólypas (1. 5), the   addressed.
young man to whom Theognis' lines are

2

I heard the voice of that bird, son of Pólypas, whose piercing outcry
and whose arrival announces to men the season when fields
are plowed, and the voice of her broke the heart that darkens within
me,
since other men possess my flourishing acres now,
and not for me are the mules dragging the plow through the grain-
land, 5
since I have given my heart to the restless seafarer's life.

AESCHYLUS
(524?–456 B.C.)
Agamemnon*

[The myth on which this play is based is the story of a family
which suffered through many generations from a series of acts of
vengeance to which there was no foreseeable end as long as private
vengeance was a recognized system of justice. Pelops, son of
Tantalus, had two sons, Atreus and Thyestes, who quarreled when
Thyestes seduced Atreus' wife. Atreus revenged himself by killing
the children of Thyestes and serving their flesh to their father at a
feast. One son of Thyestes, Aegisthus, escaped the slaughter, and
lived to avenge his father. The sons of Atreus, Agamemnon and
Menelaus, were kings of Argos and Sparta respectively. Menelaus'
wife was Helen, whose abduction caused the Trojan War. Agamemnon, leader of the Greek army, sacrificed his daughter Iphigenia to ensure the departure of the fleet when it lay wind-bound
at the port of Aulis. His wife, Clytemnestra, committed adultery
with Aegisthus while Agamemnon was away at Troy, and when her
husband returned, with Aegisthus' aid, she murdered him. He was
avenged seven years later by his son Orestes, who killed Aegisthus
and Clytemnestra. (This action is the subject of the second play
of the Aeschylean trilogy, the *Choephoroe.*) The *Agamemnon*
begins with the moment when the news of the fall of Troy reaches
Argos. The play was first produced in the open-air theater of
Dionysus at Athens.]

Characters

WATCHMAN	HERALD
CHORUS OF OLD MEN	AGAMEMNON
OF THE CITY	CASSANDRA
CLYTEMNESTRA	AEGISTHUS

SCENE—*A space in front of the palace of Agamemnon in Argos.
Night. A* WATCHMAN *on the roof of the palace.*

WATCHMAN. The gods it is I ask to release me from this watch
A year's length now, spending my nights like a dog,
Watching on my elbow on the roof of the sons of Atreus
So that I have come to know the assembly of the nightly stars

---

* First produced in the spring of 458
B.C. Our text is a translation by Louis
MacNeice, published as *The Agamemnon
of Aeschylus*, Harcourt, Brace and Company, New York, 1936.

2. *like a dog:* explained by the following words, "Watching on my elbow"; head on arms like a reclining
dog.
3. *sons of Atreus:* Agamemnon and
Menelaus.

Those which bring storm and those which bring summer to
    men,   5
The shining Masters riveted in the sky—
I know the decline and rising of those stars.
And now I am waiting for the sign of the beacon,
The flame of fire that will carry the report from Troy,
News of her taking. Which task has been assigned me   10
By a woman of sanguine heart but a man's mind.
Yet when I take my restless rest in the soaking dew,
My night not visited with dreams—
For fear stands by me in the place of sleep
That I cannot firmly close my eyes in sleep—   15
Whenever I think to sing or hum to myself
As an antidote to sleep, then every time I groan
And fall to weeping for the fortunes of this house
Where not as before are things well ordered now.
But now may a good chance fall, escape from pain,   20
The good news visible in the midnight fire.
    [*Pause. A light appears, gradually increasing, the light of
      the beacon.*]
Ha! I salute you, torch of the night whose light
Is like the day, an earnest of many dances
In the city of Argos, celebration of Peace.
I call to Agamemnon's wife; quickly to rise   25
Out of her bed and in the house to raise
Clamour of joy in answer to this torch
For the city of Troy is taken—
Such is the evident message of the beckoning flame.
And I myself will dance my solo first   30
For I shall count my master's fortune mine
Now that this beacon has thrown me a lucky throw.
And may it be when he comes, the master of this house,
That I grasp his hand in my hand.
As to the rest, I am silent. A great ox, as they say,   35
Stands on my tongue. The house itself, if it took voice,
Could tell the case most clearly. But I will only speak
To those who know. For the others I remember nothing.
    [*Enter* CHORUS OF OLD MEN. *During the following chorus
      the day begins to dawn.*]
CHORUS. The tenth year it is since Priam's high
    Adversary, Menelaus the king   40
    And Agamemnon, the double-throned and sceptred

---

8. *beacon:* Clytemnestra had arranged to be informed of the fall of
Troy by a chain of signal fires stretching from Troy across the islands of
the Aegean Sea to Argos.
11. *woman . . . mind:* Clytemnestra.

27. *Clamour of joy:* the triumphant
cry with which the women of a city
greeted the news of victory.
40. *Adversary. Menelaus:* Priam's
son Paris carried off Menelaus' wife
Helen.

Yoke of the sons of Atreus
Ruling in fee from God,
From this land gathered an Argive army
On a mission of war a thousand ships,   45
Their hearts howling in boundless bloodlust
In eagles' fashion who in lonely
Grief for nestlings above their homes hang
Turning in cycles
Beating the air with the oars of their wings,   50
    Now to no purpose
    Their love and task of attention.

But above there is One,
Maybe Pan, maybe Zeus or Apollo,
Who hears the harsh cries of the birds   55
Guests in his kingdom,
Wherefore, though late, in requital
He sends the Avenger.
Thus Zeus our master
Guardian of guest and of host   60
Sent against Paris the sons of Atreus
For a woman of many men
Many the dog-tired wrestlings
Limbs and knees in the dust pressed—
    For both the Greeks and Trojans   65
    An overture of breaking spears.

Things are where they are, will finish
In the manner fated and neither
Fire beneath nor oil above can soothe
The stubborn anger of the unburnt offering.   70
As for us, our bodies are bankrupt,
The expedition left us behind
And we wait supporting on sticks
Our strength—the strength of a child;
For the marrow that leaps in a boy's body   75
Is no better than that of the old

54. *Pan:* a god particularly associated with the forest and all forms of wild life.

56. *guests in his kingdom:* since they live in the sky, his domain.

58. *Avenger:* a Fury. The Furies avenged those who could not avenge themselves. So, later in the trilogy, they come to demand retribution for the murder of Clytemnestra, who has left no avenger behind her.

60. *Guardian of guest and of host:* Zeus himself punished violations of the code of hospitality. In this case he punishes the abduction of Helen by Paris, who was a guest in the house of Menelaus.

73 ff. *And we wait . . . :* The general sense of the passage is that only two classes of the male population are left in Argos, those who are too young to fight and those who, like the chorus, are too old. The emphasis on the age and weakness of the members of the chorus prepares the audience for their complete failure of nerve at the moment of Agamemnon's murder.

For the War God is not in his body;
While the man who is very old
And his leaf withering away
Goes on the three-foot way   80
No better than a boy, and wanders
A dream in the middle of the day.

But you, daughter of Tyndareus,
Queen Clytemnestra,
What is the news, what is the truth, what have you learnt,   85
On the strength of whose word have you thus
Sent orders for sacrifice round?
All the gods, the gods of the town,
Of the worlds of Below and Above,
By the door, in the square,   90
Have their altars ablaze with your gifts,
From here, from there, all sides, all corners,
Sky-high leap the flame-jets fed
By gentle and undeceiving
Persuasion of sacred unguent,   95
Oil from the royal stores.
Of these things tell
That which you can, that which you may,
Be healer of this our trouble
Which at times torments with evil   100
Though at times by propitiations
A shining hope repels
The insatiable thought upon grief
Which is eating away our hearts.

Of the omen which powerfully speeded   105
That voyage of strong men, by God's grace even I
Can tell, my age can still
Be galvanized to breathe the strength of song,
To tell how the kings of all the youth of Greece
Two-throned but one in mind   110
Were launched with pike and punitive hand
Against the Trojan shore by angry birds.
Kings of the birds to our kings came,
One with a white rump, the other black,
Appearing near the palace on the spear-arm side   115
Where all could see them,

80. *three-foot:* two feet and a stick.
82. **Enter Clytemnestra.**
104. Clytemnestra leaves the stage without giving them an answer.
105. *omen:* The chorus proceeds to describe the omen which accompanied the departure of the army for Troy ten years before. Two eagles seized and tore a pregnant hare; this was interpreted by the prophet Calchas as meaning that the two kings would destroy the city of Troy, thus killing not only the living Trojans but the Trojan generations yet unborn.
113. *Kings of the birds:* eagles.
115. *spear-arm side:* the right.

Tearing a pregnant hare with the unborn young
Foiled of their courses.
    Cry, cry upon Death; but may the good prevail

But the diligent prophet of the army seeing the sons   120
Of Atreus twin in temper knew
That the hare-killing birds were the two
Generals, explained it thus—
"In time this expedition sacks the town
Of Troy before whose towers   125
By Fate's force the public
Wealth will be wasted.
Only let not some spite from the gods benight the bulky
    battalions,
The bridle of Troy, nor strike them untimely;
For the goddess feels pity, is angry   130
With the winged dogs of her father
Who killed the cowering hare with her unborn young;
Artemis hates the eagles' feast."
    Cry, cry upon Death; but may the good prevail.

"But though you are so kind, goddess,   135
To the little cubs of lions
And to all the sucking young of roving beasts
In whom your heart delights,
Fulfil us the signs of these things,
The signs which are good but open to blame,   140
And I call on Apollo the Healer
That his sister raise not against the Greeks
Unremitting gales to baulk their ships,
Hurrying on another kind of sacrifice, with no feasting,
Barbarous building of hates and disloyalties   145
Grown on the family. For anger grimly returns
Cunningly haunting the house, avenging the death of a child,
    never forgetting its due."

---

120. *prophet:* Calchas.

130. *goddess:* Artemis, a virgin goddess, patron of hunting and the protectress of wild life. She is angry that the eagles have destroyed a pregnant animal. The prophet fears that she may turn her wrath against the kings whom the eagles represent.

135. *goddess:* Calchas addresses a prayer to Artemis.

143. *Unremitting gales:* He foresees the future. Artemis will send unfavorable winds to prevent the sailing of the Greek expedition from Aulis, the port of embarkation. She will demand the sacrifice of Agamemnon's daughter Iphigenia as the price of the fleet's release.

144. *with no feasting:* At an ordinary sacrifice the celebrants gave the gods their due portion and then feasted on the animal's flesh. The word "sacrifice" comes to have the connotation of "feast." There will be no feast at this sacrifice, since the victim will be a human being. The ominous phrase reminds us of a feast of human flesh which has already taken place, Thyestes' feasting on his children.

147. *avenging the death of a child:* This prophecy is fulfilled in this play, by the murder of Agamemnon.

So cried the prophet—evil and good together,
Fate that the birds foretold to the king's house.
In tune with this   150
   Cry, cry upon Death; but may the good prevail.

Zeus, whoever He is, if this
Be a name acceptable,
By this name I will call him.
There is no one comparable   155
When I reckon all of the case
Excepting Zeus, if ever I am to jettison
The barren care which clogs my heart.
Not He who formerly was great
With brawling pride and mad for broils   160
Will even be said to have been.
And He who was next has met
His match and is seen no more,
But Zeus is the name to cry in your triumph-song
And win the prize for wisdom.   165

Who setting us on the road
Made this a valid law—
   "That men must learn by suffering."
Drop by drop in sleep upon the heart
Falls the laborious memory of pain,   170
Against one's will comes wisdom;
The grace of the gods is forced on us
   Throned inviolably.

So at that time the elder
Chief of the Greek ships   175
Would not blame any prophet
Nor face the flail of fortune;
For unable to sail, the people
Of Greece were heavy with famine,
Waiting in Aulis where the tides   180
   Flow back, opposite Chalcis.

---

159. *He who formerly was great:*
Uranus, father of Cronos, grandfather
of Zeus, the first lord of heaven. This
whole passage refers to a primitive
legend which told how Uranus was
violently supplanted by his son Cronos,
who was in his turn overthrown by his
son Zeus. This legend is made to bear
new meaning by Aeschylus, for he suggests that it is not a meaningless series
of acts of violence, but a progression to
the rule of Zeus, who stands for order

and justice. Thus the law of human life
which Zeus proclaims and administers,
that wisdom comes through suffering,
has its counterpart in the history of the
establishment of the divine rule.
162. *He who was next:* Cronos.
174–175. *elder chief:* Agamemnon.
180–181. *Aulis . . . Chalcis:* the unruly water of the narrows between Aulis
on the mainland and Chalcis on the
island of Euboea.

But the winds that blew from the Strymon,
Bringing delay, hunger, evil harbourage,
Crazing men, rotting ships and cables,
By drawing out the time   185
Were shredding into nothing the flower of Argos,
When the prophet screamed a new
Cure for that bitter tempest
And heavier still for the chiefs,
Pleading the anger of Artemis so that the sons of Atreus   190
Beat the ground with their sceptres and shed tears.

Then the elder king found voice and answered:
"Heavy is my fate, not obeying,
And heavy it is if I kill my child, the delight of my house,
And with a virgin's blood upon the altar   195
Make foul her father's hands.
Either alternative is evil.
How can I betray the fleet
And fail the allied army?
It is right they should passionately cry for the winds to be
        lulled   200
By the blood of a girl. So be it. May it be well."

But when he had put on the halter of Necessity
Breathing in his heart a veering wind of evil
Unsanctioned, unholy, from that moment forward
He changed his counsel, would stop at nothing.   205
For the heart of man is hardened by infatuation,
A faulty adviser, the first link of sorrow.
Whatever the cause, he brought himself to slay
His daughter, an offering to promote the voyage
To a war for a runaway wife.   210

Her prayers and her cries of father,
Her life of a maiden,
Counted for nothing with those militarists;
But her father, having duly prayed, told the attendants
To lift her, like a goat, above the altar   215
With her robes falling about her,
To lift her boldly, her spirit fainting,
And hold back with a gag upon her lovely mouth
By the dumb force of a bridle
The cry which would curse the house.   220
Then dropping on the ground her saffron dress,

182. *Strymon:* a river in Thrace;   190. *anger of Artemis:* The prophet
the winds blew from the north.   announces Artemis' demand for the sac-
                                       rifice of Iphigenia.

Glancing at each of her appointed
Sacrificers a shaft of pity,
Plain as in a picture she wished
To speak to them by name, for often   225
At her father's table where men feasted
She had sung in celebration for her father
With a pure voice, affectionately, virginally,
The hymn for happiness at the third libation.
The sequel to this I saw not and tell not   230
But the crafts of Calchas gained their object.
To learn by suffering is the equation of Justice; the Future
Is known when it comes, let it go till then.
To know in advance is to sorrow in advance.
The facts will appear with the shining of the dawn.   235
   [*Enter* CLYTEMNESTRA.]
But may good, at the least, follow after
As the queen here wishes, who stands
Nearest the throne, the only
  Defence of the land of Argos.
LEADER OF THE CHORUS. I have come, Clytemnestra, reverencing
  your authority.   240
For it is right to honour our master's wife
When the man's own throne is empty.
But you, if you have heard good news for certain, or if
You sacrifice on the strength of flattering hopes,
I would gladly hear. Though I cannot cavil at silence.   245
CLYTEMNESTRA. Bearing good news, as the proverb says, may Dawn
  Spring from her mother Night.
You will hear something now that was beyond your hopes.
The men of Argos have taken Priam's city.
LEAD. What! I cannot believe it. It escapes me.   250
CLYT. Troy in the hands of the Greeks. Do I speak plain?
LEAD. Joy creeps over me, calling out my tears.
CLYT. Yes. Your eyes proclaim your loyalty.
LEAD. But what are your grounds? Have you a proof of it?
CLYT. There is proof indeed—unless God has cheated us.   255
LEAD. Perhaps you believe the inveigling shapes of dreams?
CLYT. I would not be credited with a dozing brain!
LEAD. Or are you puffed up by Rumour, the wingless flyer?
CLYT. You mock my common sense as if I were a child.
LEAD. But at what time was the city given to sack?   260
CLYT. In this very night that gave birth to this day.
LEAD. What messenger could come so fast?

229. *at the third libation:* At the
banquet three libations (offerings of
wine) were poured, the third and last
to Zeus the Savior. The last libation
was accompanied by a hymn of praise.

CLYT. Hephaestus, launching a fine flame from Ida,
   Beacon forwarding beacon, despatch-riders of fire,
   Ida relayed to Hermes' cliff in Lemnos   265
   And the great glow from the island was taken over third
   By the height of Athos that belongs to Zeus,
   And towering then to straddle over the sea
   The might of the running torch joyfully tossed
   The gold gleam forward like another sun,   270
   Herald of light to the heights of Mount Macistus,
   And he without delay, nor carelessly by sleep
   Encumbered, did not shirk his intermediary role,
   His farflung ray reached the Euripus' tides
   And told Messapion's watchers, who in turn   275
   Sent on the message further
   Setting a stack of dried-up heather on fire.
   And the strapping flame, not yet enfeebled, leapt
   Over the plain of Asopus like a blazing moon
   And woke on the crags of Cithaeron   280
   Another relay in the chain of fire.
   The light that was sent from far was not declined
   By the look-out men, who raised a fiercer yet,
   A light which jumped the water of Gorgopis
   And to Mount Aegiplanctus duly come   285
   Urged the reveille of the punctual fire.
   So then they kindle it squanderingly and launch
   A beard of flame big enough to pass
   The headland that looks down upon the Saronic gulf,

263. *Hephaestus:* i.e., fire. Hephaestus was the god of fire and of the crafts dependent upon fire.

263 ff. *Ida:* the mountain range near Troy. The names which follow in this speech designate the places where beacon fires flashed the message of Troy's fall to Argos. The chain extends from Ida to Hermes' cliff on the island of Lemnos (off the coast of Asia Minor), to Mount Athos (which is situated on a rocky peninsula in north Greece), to Mount Macistus on the island of Euboea (off the coast of central Greece), to Messapion, a mountain of the mainland, to Cithaeron, a mountain near Thebes, across Lake Gorgopis to Mount Aegiplanctus on the Isthmus of Corinth, across the sea (the Saronic Gulf) to Mount Arachnaeus in Argive territory. This fire is the one seen by the watchman at the beginning of the play. The speech has often been criticized as discursive, but it has great poetic importance. The image of the light which will dispel the darkness, first introduced by the watchman, is one of the dominant images of the trilogy, and is here developed by Clytemnestra with magnificent ambiguous effect. For the watchman the light means the safe return of Agamemnon and the restoration of order in the house; for Clytemnestra it means the return of Agamemnon to his death at her hands. Each swift jump of the racing light is one step nearer home and death for Agamemnon. The light the watchman longs for brings only greater darkness, but eventually it brings darkness for Clytemnestra too. The final emergence of the true light comes in the glare of the torchlight procession which ends the last play of the trilogy, a procession which symbolizes perfect reconciliation on both the human and the divine levels, and the working out of the will of Zeus in the substitution of justice for vengeance. The conception of the beacons as a chain of descendants (compare, "Issue and image of the fire on Ida," l. 293), is also important; the fire at Argos which announces Agamemnon's imminent death is a direct descendant of the fire on Ida which announces the sack of Troy and Agamemnon's sacrilegious conduct there. The metaphor thus reminds us of the sequence of crimes from generation to generation which is the history of the house of Pelops.

Blazing and bounding till it reached at length   290
The Arachnaean steep, our neighbouring heights;
And leaps in the latter end on the roof of the sons of Atreus
Issue and image of the fire on Ida.
Such was the assignment of my torch-racers,
The task of each fulfilled by his successor,   295
And victor is he who ran both first and last.
Such is the proof I offer you, the sign
My husband sent me out of Troy.

LEAD. To the gods, queen, I shall give thanks presently.
But I would like to hear this story further,   300
To wonder at it in detail from your lips.

CLYT. The Greeks hold Troy upon this day.
The cries in the town I fancy do not mingle.
Pour oil and vinegar into the same jar,
You would say they stand apart unlovingly;   305
Of those who are captured and those who have conquered
Distinct are the sounds of their diverse fortunes,
For *these* having flung themselves about the bodies
Of husbands and brothers, or sons upon the bodies
Of aged fathers from a throat no longer   310
Free, lament the fate of their most loved.
But *those* a night's marauding after battle
Sets hungry to what breakfast the town offers
Not billeted duly in any barracks order
But as each man has drawn his lot of luck.   315
So in the captive homes of Troy already
They take their lodging, free of the frosts
And dews of the open. Like happy men
They will sleep all night without sentry.
But if they respect duly the city's gods,   320
Those of the captured land and the sanctuaries of the gods,
They need not, having conquered, fear reconquest.
But let no lust fall first upon the troops
To plunder what is not right, subdued by gain,
For they must still, in order to come home safe,   325
Get round the second lap of the doubled course.
So if they return without offence to the gods
The grievance of the slain may learn at last
A friendly talk—unless some fresh wrong falls.
Such are the thoughts you hear from me, a woman.   330
But may the good prevail for all to see.
We have much good. I only ask to enjoy it.

LEAD. Woman, you speak with sense like a prudent man.
I, who have heard your valid proofs, prepare

---

296. *he who ran both first and last:*
The chain of beacons is compared to
a relay race in which the runners carry
torches: the last runner (who runs the
final lap) comes in first to win.

323. *But let no lust fall:* The audience was familiar with the traditional
account, according to which Agamemnon and his army failed signally to
respect the gods and temples of Troy.

To give the glory to God.   335
Fair recompense is brought us for our troubles.
    [CLYTEMNESTRA *goes back into the palace.*]
CHOR. O Zeus our king and Night our friend
  Donor of glories,
  Night who cast on the towers of Troy
  A close-clinging net so that neither the grown   340
  Nor any of the children can pass
  The enslaving and huge
  Trap of all-taking destruction.
  Great Zeus, guardian of host and guest,
  I honour who has done his work and taken   345
  A leisured aim at Paris so that neither
  Too short nor yet over the stars
    He might shoot to no purpose.

From Zeus is the blow they can tell of,
This at least can be established,   350
They have fared according to his ruling. For some
Deny that the gods deign to consider those among men
Who trample on the grace of inviolate things;
It is the impious man says this,
For Ruin is revealed the child   355
Of not to be attempted actions
When men are puffed up unduly
And their houses are stuffed with riches.
Measure is the best. Let danger be distant,
This should suffice a man   360
With a proper part of wisdom.
  For a man has no protection
  Against the drunkenness of riches
  Once he has spurned from his sight
  The high altar of Justice.   365

Sombre Persuasion compels him,
Intolerable child of calculating Doom;
All cure is vain, there is no glozing it over
But the mischief shines forth with a deadly light
And like bad coinage   370
By rubbings and frictions
He stands discoloured and black
Under the test—like a boy
Who chases a winged bird.

337. *Night:* Troy fell to a night attack.

353. *Who trample . . . things:* The language throughout this passage is significantly general. The chorus refers to Paris, but everything it says is equally applicable to Agamemnon, who sacrificed his daughter for his ambitions.

359. *Measure:* the mean, moderation.

373–374. *like a boy . . . bird:* a proverbial expression describing a person of insane ambitions.

He has branded his city for ever. 375
His prayers are heard by no god.
Who makes such things his practice
The gods destroy him.
  This way came Paris
    To the house of the sons of Atreus 380
    And outraged the table of friendship
    Stealing the wife of his host.

Leaving to her countrymen clanging of
Shields and spears and
Launching of warships 385
And bringing instead of a dowry destruction to Troy
Lightly she was gone through the gates daring
Things undared. Many the groans
Of the palace spokesmen on this theme—
"O the house, the house, and its princes, 390
O the bed and the imprint of her limbs;
One can see him crouching in silence
Dishonoured and unreviling."
Through desire for her who is overseas, a ghost
Will seem to rule the household. 395
  And now her husband hates
    The grace of shapely statues;
    In the emptiness of their eyes
    All their appeal is departed.

But appearing in dreams persuasive 400
  Images come bringing a joy that is vain,
Vain for when in fancy he looks to touch her—
Slipping through his hands the vision
Rapidly is gone
Following on wings the walks of sleep. 405
Such are his griefs in his house on his hearth,
Such as these and worse than these,
But everywhere through the land of Greece which men have left
Are mourning women with enduring hearts
To be seen in all houses; many 410
Are the thoughts which stab their hearts;
  For those they sent to war
    They know, but in place of men
    That which comes home to them
    Is merely an urn and ashes. 415

But the money-changer War, changer of bodies,

406. *his:* Menelaus'.

Holding his balance in the battle
Home from Troy refined by fire
Sends back to friends the dust
That is heavy with tears, stowing   420
A man's worth of ashes
In an easily handled jar.
And they wail speaking well of the men how that one
Was expert in battle, and one fell well in the carnage—
But for another man's wife.   425
Muffled and muttered words;
And resentful grief creeps up against the sons
Of Atreus and their cause.
> But others there by the wall
> Entombed in Trojan ground   430
> Lie, handsome of limb,
> Holding and hidden in enemy soil.

Heavy is the murmur of an angry people
Performing the purpose of a public curse;
There is something cowled in the night   435
That I anxiously wait to hear.
For the gods are not blind to the
Murderers of many and the black
Furies in time
When a man prospers in sin   440
By erosion of life reduce him to darkness,
Who, once among the lost, can no more
Be helped. Over-great glory
Is a sore burden. The high peak
Is blasted by the eyes of Zeus.   445
> I prefer an unenvied fortune,
> Not to be a sacker of cities
> Nor to find myself living at another's
> Ruling, myself a captive.

AN OLD MAN. From the good news' beacon a swift   450
Rumour is gone through the town.
Who knows if it be true
Or some deceit of the gods?
ANOTHER OLD MAN. Who is so childish or broken in wit
To kindle his heart at a new-fangled message of flame   455
And then be downcast
At a change of report?
ANOTHER OLD MAN. It fits the temper of a woman.
To give her assent to a story before it is proved.
ANOTHER OLD MAN. The over-credulous passion of women
expands   460
In swift conflagration but swiftly declining is gone

417. *balance:* scales.

The news that a woman announced.

LEAD. Soon we shall know about the illuminant torches,
The beacons and the fiery relays,
Whether they were true or whether like dreams   465
That pleasant light came here and hoaxed our wits.
Look: I see, coming from the beach, a herald
Shadowed with olive shoots; the dust upon him,
Mud's thirsty sister and colleague, is my witness
That he will not give dumb news nor news by lighting   470
A flame of fire with the smoke of mountain timber;
In words he will either corroborate our joy—
But the opposite version I reject with horror.
To the good appeared so far may good be added.

ANOTHER SPEAKER. Whoever makes other prayers for this our
    city,   475
May he reap himself the fruits of his wicked heart.

[*Enter the* HERALD, *who kisses the ground before speaking.*]

HERALD. Earth of my fathers, O the earth of Argos,
In the light of the tenth year I reach you thus
After many shattered hopes achieving one,
For never did I dare to think that here in Argive land   480
I should win a grave in the dearest soil of home;
But now hail, land, and hail, light of the sun.
And Zeus high above the country and the Pythian king—
May he no longer shoot his arrows at us
(Implacable long enough beside Scamander)   485
But now be saviour to us and be healer,
King Apollo. And all the Assembly's gods
I call upon, and him my patron, Hermes,
The dear herald whom all heralds adore,
And the Heroes who sped our voyage, again with favour   490
Take back the army that has escaped the spear.
O cherished dwelling, palace of royalty,
O august thrones and gods facing the sun,
If ever before, now with your bright eyes
Gladly receive your king after much time,   495
Who comes bringing light to you in the night time,
And to all these as well—King Agamemnon.
Give him a good welcome as he deserves,
Who with the axe of judgment-awarding God
Has smashed Troy and levelled the Trojan land;   500
The altars are destroyed, the seats of the gods,
And the seed of all the land is perished from it.
Having cast this halter round the neck of Troy

468. *Shadowed with olive shoots:*
wearing a wreath of olive.
483. *Pythian king:* Apollo.
484. *arrows:* Compare the opening
scenes of the *Iliad*, Book 1.
488. *Hermes:* As the messenger of
Zeus, he was the patron deity of heralds.

The King, the elder son of Atreus, a blessed man,
Comes, the most worthy to have honour of all   505
Men that are now. Paris nor his guilty city
Can boast that the crime was greater than the atonement.
Convicted in a suit for rape and robbery
He has lost his stolen goods and with consummate ruin
Mowed down the whole country and his father's house.   510
The sons of Priam have paid their account with interest.

LEAD. Hail and be glad, herald of the Greek army.
HER. Yes. Glad indeed! So glad that at the gods' demand
    I should no longer hesitate to die.
LEAD. Were you so harrowed by desire for home?   515
HER. Yes. The tears come to my eyes for joy.
LEAD. Sweet then is the fever which afflicts you.
HER. What do you mean? Let me learn your drift.
LEAD. Longing for those whose love came back in echo.
HER. Meaning the land was homesick for the army?   520
LEAD. Yes. I would often groan from a darkened heart.
HER. This sullen hatred—how did it fasten on you?
LEAD. I cannot say. Silence is my stock prescription.
HER. What? In your masters' absence were there some you feared?
LEAD. Yes. In your phrase, death would now be a gratification. 525
HER. Yes, for success is ours. These things have taken time.
    Some of them we could say have fallen well,
    While some we blame. Yet who except the gods
    Is free from pain the whole duration of life?
    If I were to tell of our labours, our hard lodging,   530
    The sleeping on crowded decks, the scanty blankets,
    Tossing and groaning, rations that never reached us—
    And the land too gave matter for more disgust,
    For our beds lay under the enemy's walls.
    Continuous drizzle from the sky, dews from the marshes,   535
    Rotting our clothes, filling our hair with lice.
    And if one were to tell of the bird-destroying winter
    Intolerable from the snows of Ida
    Or of the heat when the sea slackens at noon
    Waveless and dozing in a depressed calm—   540
    But why make these complaints? The weariness is over;
    Over indeed for some who never again
    Need even trouble to rise.
    Why make a computation of the lost?
    Why need the living sorrow for the spites of fortune?   545
    I wish to say a long goodbye to disasters.

---

523. *Silence:* Throughout this dialogue the chorus has been nerving itself to warn the herald that there is danger for Agamemnon at home; at this point its nerve fails, and it abandons the attempt.

For us, the remnant of the troops of Argos,
The advantage remains, the pain can not outweigh it;
So we can make our boast to this sun's light,
Flying on words above the land and sea: 550
"Having taken Troy the Argive expedition
Has nailed up throughout Greece in every temple
These spoils, these ancient trophies."
Those who hear such things must praise the city
And the generals. And the grace of God be honoured   555
Which brought these things about. You have the whole story.

LEAD. I confess myself convinced by your report.
    Old men are always young enough to learn.
        [*Enter* CLYTEMNESTRA *from the palace*.]
    This news belongs by right first to the house
    And Clytemnestra—though I am enriched also.   560

CLYT. Long before this I shouted at joy's command
    At the coming of the first night-messenger of fire
    Announcing the taking and capsizing of Troy.
    And people reproached me saying, "Do mere beacons
    Persuade you to think that Troy is already down?   565
    Indeed a woman's heart is easily exalted."
    Such comments made me seem to be wandering but yet
    I began my sacrifices and in the women's fashion
    Throughout the town they raised triumphant cries
    And in the gods' enclosures   570
    Lulling the fragrant, incense-eating flame.
    And now what need is there for you to tell me more?
    From the King himself I shall learn the whole story.
    But how the best to welcome my honoured lord
    I shall take pains when he comes back—For what   575
    Is a kinder light for a woman to see than this,
    To open the gates to her man come back from war
    When God has saved him? Tell this to my husband,
    To come with all speed, the city's darling;
    May he returning find a wife as loyal   580
    As when he left her, watchdog of the house,
    Good to *him* but fierce to the ill-intentioned,
    And in all other things as ever, having destroyed
    No seal or pledge at all in the length of time.
    I know no pleasure with another man, no scandal,   585
    More than I know how to dye metal red.
    Such is my boast, bearing a load of truth,
    A boast that need not disgrace a noble wife.   [*Exit*.]

LEAD. Thus has she spoken; if you take her meaning,
    Only a specious tale to shrewd interpreters.   590

569. *triumpha*. *-ies:* the women's victory cry mentioned by the watchman.

But do you, herald, tell me; I ask after Menelaus
Whether he will, returning safe preserved,
Come back with you, our land's loved master.

HER. I am not able to speak the lovely falsehood
To profit you, my friends, for any stretch of time.   595

LEAD. But if only the true tidings could be also good!
It is hard to hide a division of good and true.

HER. The prince is vanished out of the Greek fleet,
Himself and ship. I speak no lie.

LEAD. Did he put forth first in the sight of all from Troy,   600
Or a storm that troubled all sweep him apart?

HER. You have hit the target like a master archer,
Told succinctly a long tale of sorrow.

LEAD. Did the rumours current among the remaining ships
Represent him as alive or dead?   605

HER. No one knows so as to tell for sure
Except the sun who nurses the breeds of earth.

LEAD. Tell me how the storm came on the host of ships
Through the divine anger, and how it ended.

HER. Day of good news should not be fouled by tongue   610
That tells ill news. To each god his season.
When, despair in his face, a messenger brings to a town
The hated news of a fallen army—
One general wound to the city and many men
Outcast, outcursed, from many homes   615
By the double whip which War is fond of,
Doom with a bloody spear in either hand,
One carrying such a pack of grief could well
Recite this hymn of the Furies at your asking.
But when our cause is saved and a messenger of good   620
Comes to a city glad with festivity,
How am I to mix good news with bad, recounting
The storm that meant God's anger on the Greeks?
For they swore together, those inveterate enemies,
Fire and sea, and proved their alliance, destroying   625
The unhappy troops of Argos.
In night arose ill-waved evil,
Ships on each other the blasts from Thrace
Crashed colliding, which butting with horns in the violence
Of big wind and rattle of rain were gone   630

591. *Menelaus:* The relevance of this question and the following speeches lies in the fact that Menelaus' absence makes Agamemnon's murder easier (his presence might have made it impossible), and in the fact that Menelaus is bringing Helen home; the choral ode which follows shows how much the chorus is obsessed with Helen's guilt—so much that it fails to recognize the true responsibility for the war and the imminence of disaster.

625. *Fire:* lightning.

To nothing, whirled all ways by a wicked shepherd.
But when there came up the shining light of the sun
We saw the Aegean sea flowering with corpses
Of Greek men and their ships' wreckage.
But for us, our ship was not damaged,   635
Whether someone snatched it away or begged it off,
Some god, not a man, handling the tiller;
And Saving Fortune was willing to sit upon our ship
So that neither at anchor we took the tilt of waves
Nor ran to splinters on the crag-bound coast.   640
But then having thus escaped death on the sea,
In the white day, not trusting our fortune,
We pastured this new trouble upon our thoughts,
The fleet being battered, the sailors weary,
And now if any of *them* still draw breath,   645
They are thinking no doubt of us as being lost
And we are thinking of them as being lost.
May the best happen. As for Menelaus
The first guess and most likely is a disaster.
But still—if any ray of sun detects him   650
Alive, with living eyes, by the plan of Zeus
Not yet resolved to annul the race completely,
There is some hope then that he will return home.
So much you have heard. Know that it is the truth.   [*Exit.*]
CHOR. Who was it named her thus   655
    In all ways appositely
    Unless it was Someone whom we do not see,
    Fore-knowing fate
    And plying an accurate tongue?
    Helen, bride of spears and conflict's   660
    Focus, who as was befitting
    Proved a hell to ships and men,
    Hell to her country, sailing
    Away from delicately-sumptuous curtains,
    Away on the wind of a giant Zephyr,   665
    And shielded hunters mustered many
    On the vanished track of the oars,
    Oars beached on the leafy
    Banks of a Trojan river
    For the sake of a bloody war.   670

    But on Troy was thrust a marring marriage
    By the Wrath that working to an end exacts
    In time a price from guests

656. *appositely:* Helen's name contains a Greek root (*hele-*) which means "to destroy."

Who dishonoured their host
And dishonoured Zeus of the Hearth,   675
From those noisy celebrants
Of the wedding hymn which fell
To the brothers of Paris
To sing upon that day.
But learning this, unlearning that,   680
Priam's ancestral city now
Continually mourns, reviling
Paris the fatal bridegroom.
The city has had much sorrow,
Much desolation in life,   685
From the pitiful loss of her people.

So in his house a man might rear
A lion's cub caught from the dam
In need of suckling,
In the prelude of its life   690
Mild, gentle with children,
For old men a playmate,
Often held in the arms
Like a new-born child,
Wheedling the hand,   695
Fawning at belly's bidding.

But matured by time he showed
The temper of his stock and payed
Thanks for his fostering
With disaster of slaughter of sheep   700
Making an unbidden banquet
And now the house is a shambles,
Irremediable grief to its people,
Calamitous carnage;
For the pet they had fostered was sent   705
By God as a priest of Ruin.

So I would say there came
To the city of Troy
A notion of windless calm,
Delicate adornment of riches,   710
Soft shooting of the eyes and flower
Of desire that stings the fancy.
But swerving aside she achieved
A bitter end to her marriage,
Ill guest and ill companion,   715

675. *Zeus of the Hearth:* Zeus in his capacity as protector of host and guest.

Hurled upon Priam's sons, convoyed
By Zeus, patron of guest and host,
Dark angel dowered with tears.

Long current among men an old saying
Runs that a man's prosperity   720
When grown to greatness
Comes to birth, does not die childless—
His good luck breeds for his house
Distress that shall not be appeased.
I only, apart from the others,   725
Hold that the unrighteous action
Breeds true to its kind,
Leaves its own children behind it.
But the lot of a righteous house
Is a fair offspring always.   730

Ancient self-glory is accustomed
To bear to light in the evil sort of men
A new self-glory and madness,
Which sometime or sometime finds
The appointed hour for its birth,   735
And born therewith is the Spirit, intractable, unholy, irresistible,
The reckless lust that brings black Doom upon the house,
A child that is like its parents.

But Honest Dealing is clear
Shining in smoky homes,   740
Honours the god-fearing life.
Mansions gilded by filth of hands she leaves,
Turns her eyes elsewhere, visits the innocent house,
Not respecting the power
Of wealth mis-stamped with approval,   745
But guides all to the goal.

[*Enter* AGAMEMNON *and* CASSANDRA *on chariots.*]

CHOR. Come then my King, stormer of Troy,
Offspring of Atreus,
How shall I hail you, how give you honour
Neither overshooting nor falling short   750
Of the measure of homage?
There are many who honour appearance too much

719–724. *Long current . . . appeased:*
These lines state the traditional Greek
view that immoderate good fortune (or
excellence of any kind beyond the average) is itself the cause of disaster. In
the lines which follow, the chorus rejects this view and states that only an
act of evil produces evil consequences.
It later admits by implication (ll. 739
ff.) that those who are less prosperous
are less likely to commit such an act.
740. *smoky homes:* i.e., poor homes.
752. *There are many . . . :* The
chorus is trying to warn Agamemnon,

Passing the bounds that are right.
To condole with the unfortunate man
Each one is ready but the bite of the grief   755
  Never goes through to the heart.
And they join in rejoicing, affecting to share it,
Forcing their face to a smile.
But he who is shrewd to shepherd his sheep
Will fail not to notice the eyes of a man   760
Which seem to be loyal but lie,
  Fawning with watery friendship.
Even you, in my thought, when you marshalled the troops
For Helen's sake, I will not hide it,
Made a harsh and ugly picture,   765
Holding badly the tiller of reason,
Paying with the death of men
  Ransom for a willing whore.
But now, not unfriendly, not superficially,
I offer my service, well-doers' welcome.   770
In time you will learn by inquiry
Who has done rightly, who transgressed
  In the work of watching the city.

AGAMEMNON. First to Argos and the country's gods
My fitting salutations, who have aided me   775
To return and in the justice which I exacted
From Priam's city. Hearing the unspoken case
The gods unanimously had cast their vote
Into the bloody urn for the massacre of Troy;
But to the opposite urn   780
Hope came, dangled her hand, but did no more.
Smoke marks even now the city's capture.
Whirlwinds of doom are alive, the dying ashes
Spread on the air the fat savour of wealth.
For these things we must pay some memorable return   785
To Heaven, having exacted enormous vengeance
For wife-rape; for a woman
The Argive monster ground a city to powder,
Sprung from a wooden horse, shield-wielding folk,
Launching a leap at the setting of the Pleiads,   790
Jumping the ramparts, a ravening lion,
Lapped its fill of the kingly blood.
To the gods I have drawn out this overture

and goes much further than it did in its
dialogue with the herald.
779. *bloody urn:* The Greeks voted
with pebbles, which were put into
different urns and then counted.

789. *wooden horse:* The stratagem
with which the Greeks captured the
city.
790. *at the setting of the Pleiads:*
late in the fall.

But as for your concerns, I bear them in my mind
And say the same, you have me in agreement.   795
To few of men does it belong by nature
To congratulate their friends unenviously,
For a sullen poison fastens on the heart,
Doubling the pain of a man with this disease;
He feels the weight of his own griefs and when   800
He sees another's prosperity he groans.
I speak with knowledge, being well acquainted
With the mirror of comradeship—ghost of a shadow
Were those who seemed to be so loyal to me.
Only Odysseus, who sailed against his will,   805
Proved, when yoked with me, a ready tracehorse;
I speak of him not knowing if he is alive.
But for what concerns the city and the gods
Appointing public debates in full assembly
We shall consult. That which is well already   810
We shall take steps to ensure it remain well.
But where there is need of medical remedies,
By applying benevolent cautery or surgery
We shall try to deflect the dangers of disease.
But now, entering the halls where stands my hearth,   815
First I shall make salutation to the gods
Who sent me a far journey and have brought me back.
And may my victory not leave my side.

> [*Enter* CLYTEMNESTRA, *followed by women slaves carrying*
> *purple tapestries.*]

CLYT. Men of the city, you the aged of Argos,
I shall feel no shame to describe to you my love   820
Towards my husband. Shyness in all of us
Wears thin with time. Here are the facts first hand.
I will tell you of my own unbearable life
I led so long as this man was at Troy.
For first that the woman separate from her man   825
Should sit alone at home is extreme cruelty,
Hearing so many malignant rumours—First
Comes one, and another comes after, bad news to worse,
Clamour of grief to the house. If Agamemnon
Had had so many wounds as those reported   830
Which poured home through the pipes of hearsay, then—

---

805. *Odysseus:* Feigning madness in
order to escape going to Troy, he was
tricked into demonstrating his sanity.
The remark shows that the truth is
far from Agamemnon's mind; he has no
thought that his danger comes from a
woman

820–821. *love towards my husband*
The Greek is ambiguous, and may mean
also "love for men."
821. *Shyness·* The word also means
"modesty," "virtue." Almost every
statement in this speech has a double
meaning.

Then he would be gashed fuller than a net has holes!
And if only he had died . . . as often as rumour told us,
He would be like the giant in the legend,
Three-bodied. Dying once for every body, 835
He should have by now three blankets of earth above him—
All that above him; I care not how deep the mattress under!
Such are the malignant rumours thanks to which
They have often seized me against my will and undone
The loop of a rope from my neck. 840
And this is why our son is not standing here,
The guarantee of your pledges and mine,
As he should be, Orestes. Do not wonder;
He is being brought up by a friendly ally and host,
Strophius the Phocian, who warned me in advance 845
Of dubious troubles, both your risks at Troy
And the anarchy of shouting mobs that might
Overturn policy, for it is born in men
To kick the man who is down.
This is not a disingenuous excuse. 850
For me the outrushing wells of weeping are dried up,
There is no drop left in them.
My eyes are sore from sitting late at nights
Weeping for you and for the baffled beacons,
Never lit up. And, when I slept, in dreams 855
I have been waked by the thin whizz of a buzzing
Gnat, seeing more horrors fasten on you
Than could take place in the mere time of my dream.
Having endured all this, now, with unsorrowed heart
I would hail this man as the watchdog of the farm, 860
Forestay that saves the ship, pillar that props
The lofty roof, appearance of an only son
To a father or of land to sailors past their hope,
The loveliest day to see after the storm,
Gush of well-water for the thirsty traveller. 865
Such are the metaphors I think befit him,
But envy be absent. Many misfortunes already
We have endured. But now, dear head, come down
Out of that car, not placing upon the ground
Your foot, O King, the foot that trampled Troy. 870
Why are you waiting, slaves, to whom the task is assigned
To spread the pavement of his path with tapestries?

---

834. *giant:* Geryon, a fabulous giant
with three heads and six arms.
845. *Phocian:* Phocis is in central
Greece. Orestes grew up there in exile
and later returned to avenge his father.

872. *tapestries:* To walk on these
tapestries, wall hangings dyed with the
expensive purple (crimson), would be
an act of extravagant pride. Pride is
the keynote of Agamemnon's character,

At once, at once let his way be strewn with purple
That Justice lead him toward his unexpected home.
The rest a mind, not overcome by sleep   875
Will arrange rightly, with God's help, as destined.

AGAM. Daughter of Leda, guardian of my house,
You have spoken in proportion to my absence.
You have drawn your speech out long. Duly to praise me,
That is a duty to be performed by others.   880
And further—do not by women's methods make me
Effeminate nor in barbarian fashion
Gape ground-grovelling acclamations at me
Nor strewing my path with cloths make it invidious.
It is the gods should be honoured in this way.   885
But being mortal to tread embroidered beauty
For me is no way without fear.
I tell you to honour me as a man, not god.
Footcloths are very well—Embroidered stuffs
Are stuff for gossip. And not to think unwisely   890
Is the greatest gift of God. Call happy only him
Who has ended his life in sweet prosperity.
I have spoken. This thing I could not do with confidence.

CLYT. Tell me now, according to your judgment.

AGAM. I tell you you shall not override my judgment.   895

CLYT. Supposing you had feared something . . .
Could you have vowed to God to do this thing?

AGAM. Yes. If an expert had prescribed that vow.

CLYT. And how would Priam have acted in your place?

AGAM. He would have trod the cloths, I think, for certain.   900

CLYT. Then do not flinch before the blame of men.

AGAM. The voice of the multitude is very strong.

CLYT. But the man none envy is not enviable.

AGAM. It is not a woman's part to love disputing.

CLYT. But it is a conqueror's part to yield upon occasion.   905

AGAM. You think such victory worth fighting for?

CLYT. Give way. Consent to let me have the mastery.

AGAM. Well, if such is your wish, let someone quickly loose
My vassal sandals, underlings of my feet,
And stepping on these sea-purples may no god   910
Shoot me from far with the envy of his eye.

---

and it suits Clytemnestra's sense of
fitness that he should go into his death
in godlike state, treading a way "strewn
with purple," the color of blood.

877. *Daughter of Leda:* Clytemnestra and Helen are both daughters of
Leda.

882. *barbarian:* foreign, especially
Asiatic. Aeschylus is thinking of the
pomp and servility of the contemporary
Persian court.

898. *expert:* a priest, or prophet;
Calchas for instance.

910. *sea-purples:* The dye was made
from shellfish.

Great shame it is to ruin my house and spoil
The wealth of costly weavings with my feet.
But of this matter enough. This stranger woman here
Take in with kindness. The man who is a gentle master   915
God looks on from far off complacently.
For no one of his will bears the slave's yoke.
This woman, of many riches being the chosen
Flower, gift of the soldiers, has come with me.
But since I have been prevailed on by your words   920
I will go to my palace home, treading on purples.

> [*He dismounts from the chariot and begins to walk up the
> tapestried path. During the following speech he enters the
> palace.*]

CLYT. There is the sea and who shall drain it dry? It breeds
Its wealth in silver of plenty of purple gushing
And ever-renewed, the dyeings of our garments.
The house has its store of these by God's grace, King.   925
This house is ignorant of poverty
And I would have vowed a pavement of many garments
Had the palace oracle enjoined that vow
Thereby to contrive a ransom for his life.
For while there is root, foliage comes to the house   930
Spreading a tent of shade against the Dog Star.
So now that you have reached your hearth and home
You prove a miracle—advent of warmth in winter;
And further this—even in the time of heat
When God is fermenting wine from the bitter grape,   935
Even then it is cool in the house if only
Its master walk at home, a grown man, ripe.
O Zeus the Ripener, ripen these my prayers;
Your part it is to make the ripe fruit fall.

> [*She enters the palace.*]

CHOR. Why, why at the doors   940
Of my fore-seeing heart
Does this terror keep beating its wings?
And my song play the prophet
Unbidden, unhired—
Which I cannot spit out   945
Like the enigmas of dreams
Nor plausible confidence
Sit on the throne of my mind?

---

914. *stranger woman:* Cassandra, daughter of Priam, Agamemnon's share of the human booty of the sack of Troy. She was loved by Apollo and by him given the gift of prophecy; but when she refused her love to the god he added to his gift the proviso that her prophecies, though true, should never be believed until it was too late.

It is long time since
The cables let down from the stern 950
Were chafed by the sand when the seafaring army started for
    Troy.

And I learn with my eyes
And witness myself their return;
But the hymn without lyre goes up,
The dirge of the Avenging Fiend, 955
In the depths of my self-taught heart
Which has lost its dear
Possession of the strength of hope.
But my guts and my heart
Are not idle which seethe with the waves 960
Of trouble nearing its hour.
But I pray that these thoughts
May fall out not as I think
    And not be fulfilled in the end.

Truly when health grows much 965
It respects not limit; for disease,
Its neighbour in the next door room,
Presses upon it.
A man's life, crowding sail,
Strikes on the blind reef: 970
But if caution in advance
Jettison part of the cargo
With the derrick of due proportion,
The whole house does not sink,
Though crammed with a weight of woe 975
The hull does not go under.
The abundant bounty of God
And his gifts from the year's furrows
Drive the famine back.

But when upon the ground there has fallen once 980
The black blood of a man's death,
Who shall summon it back by incantations?
Even Asclepius who had the art
To fetch the dead to life, even to him
Zeus put a provident end. 985
But, if of the heaven-sent fates

971–979. *But if caution . . . back:* These lines refer to a traditional Greek belief that the fortunate man could avert the envy of heaven by deliberately getting rid of some precious possession.

983. *Asclepius:* the great physician, who was so skillful that he finally succeeded in restoring a dead man to life. Zeus struck him with a thunderbolt for going too far.

One did not check the other,
Cancel the other's advantage,
My heart would outrun my tongue
In pouring out these fears.   990
But now it mutters in the dark,
Embittered, no way of hoping
To unravel a scheme in time
   From a burning mind.
    [CLYTEMNESTRA *appears in the door of the palace.*]
CLYT. Go in too, you; I speak to you, Cassandra,   995
   Since God in his clemency has put you in this house
   To share our holy water, standing with many slaves
   Beside the altar that protects the house,
   Step down from the car there, do not be overproud.
   Heracles himself they say was once   1000
   Sold, and endured to eat the bread of slavery.
   But should such a chance inexorably fall,
   There is much advantage in masters who have long been rich.
   Those who have reaped a crop they never expected
   Are in all things hard on their slaves and overstep the line.   1005
   From us you will have the treatment of tradition.
LEAD. You, it is you she has addressed, and clearly.
   Caught as you are in these predestined toils
   Obey her if you can. But should you disobey . . .
CLYT. If she has more than the gibberish of the swallow,   1010
   An unintelligible barbaric speech,
   I hope to read her mind, persuade her reason.
LEAD. As things now stand for you, she says the best.
   Obey her; leave that car and follow her.
CLYT. I have no leisure to waste out here, outside the door.   1015
   Before the hearth in the middle of my house
   The victims stand already, wait the knife.
   You, if you will obey me, waste no time.
   But if you cannot understand my language—
    [To CHORUS LEADER]
   You make it plain to her with the brute and voiceless hand.   1020
LEAD. The stranger seems to need a clear interpreter.
   She bears herself like a wild beast newly captured.
CLYT. The fact is she is mad, she listens to evil thoughts,
   Who has come here leaving a city newly captured
   Without experience how to bear the bridle   1025

---

997. *holy water:* used in the sacrifice
in honor of Agamemnon's return which
is about to take place inside the house.
   1000. *Heracles:* The Greek hero,
famous for his twelve labors which
rid the earth of monsters, was at one

time forced to be slave to Omphale, an
Eastern queen.
   1010. *gibberish of the swallow:* The
comparison of foreign speech to the
twittering of the swallow was a Greek
commonplace.

So as not to waste her strength in foam and blood.
I will not spend more words to be ignored.
　　[*She re-enters the palace.*]
CHOR. But I, for I pity her, will not be angry.
　Obey, unhappy woman. Leave this car.
　Yield to your fate. Put on the untried yoke.　　　1030
CASSANDRA. Apollo! Apollo!
CHOR. Why do you cry like this upon Apollo?
　He is not the kind of god that calls for dirges.
CASS. Apollo! Apollo!
CHOR. Once more her funereal cries invoke the god　　1035
　Who has no place at the scene of lamentation.
CASS. Apollo! Apollo!
　God of the Ways! My destroyer!
　Destroyed again—and this time utterly!
CHOR. She seems about to predict her own misfortunes.　　1040
　The gift of the god endures, even in a slave's mind.
CASS. Apollo! Apollo!
　God of the Ways! My destroyer!
　Where? To what house, Where, where have you brought me?
CHOR. To the house of the sons of Atreus. If you do not know
　　it,　　　1045
　I will tell you so. You will not find it false.
CASS. No, no, but to a god-hated, but to an accomplice
　In much kin-killing, murdering nooses,
　Man-shambles, a floor asperged with blood.
CHOR. The stranger seems like a hound with a keen scent,　　1050
　Is picking up a trail that leads to murder.
CASS. Clues! I have clues! Look! They are these.
　These wailing, these children, butchery of children;
　Roasted flesh, a father sitting to dinner.
CHOR. Of your prophetic fame we have heard before　　1055
　But in this matter prophets are not required.
CASS. What is she doing? What is she planning?
　What is this new great sorrow?
　Great crime . . . within here . . . planning
　Unendurable to his folk, impossible　　1060
　Ever to be cured. For help
　　Stands far distant.

1038. *God of the Ways:* A statue of Apollo was often placed outside the house overlooking the street. (Perhaps there was one on stage in this scene.) *destroyer:* The Greek word is *apollon,* a pun on the god's name.
　1044. *brought:* another pun on the god's name; the word translated "brought" echoes, in the Greek, the word translated "God of the ways."
　1049. *asperged with blood:* She sees Agamemnon murdered in his bath.
　1054. *a father sitting to dinner:* Thyestes at his feast.
　1057. *she:* Clytemnestra.
　1061–1062. *help stands far distant:* a reference to Menelaus (distant in space) and Orestes (distant in time).

CHOR. This reference I cannot catch. But the children
   I recognized; that refrain is hackneyed.
CASS. Damned, damned, bringing this work to completion—   1065
   Your husband who shared your bed
   To bathe him, to cleanse him, and then—
   How shall I tell of the end?
   Soon, very soon, it will fall.
      The end comes hand over hand   1070
      Grasping in greed.
CHOR. Not yet do I understand. After her former riddles
   Now I am baffled by these dim pronouncements.
CASS. Ah God, the vision! God, God, the vision!
   A net, is it? Net of Hell!   1075
   But herself is the net; shared bed; shares murder.
   O let the pack ever-hungering after the family
   Howl for the unholy ritual, howl for the victim.
CHOR. What black Spirit is this you call upon the house—
   To raise aloft her cries? Your speech does not lighten me.   1080
   Into my heart runs back the blood
   Yellow as when for men by the spear fallen
   The blood ebbs out with the rays of the setting life
      And death strides quickly.
CASS. Quick! Be on your guard! The bull—   1085
   Keep him clear of the cow.
   Caught with a trick, the black horn's point,
   She strikes. He falls; lies in the water.
   Murder; a trick in a bath. I tell what I see.
CHOR. I would not claim to be expert in oracles   1090
   But these, as I deduce, portend disaster.
   Do men ever get a good answer from oracles?
   No. It is only through disaster
   That their garrulous craft brings home
   The meaning of the prophet's panic.   1095
CASS. And for me also, for me, chance ill-destined!
   My own now I lament, pour into the cup my own.
   Where is this you have brought me in my misery?
   Unless to die as well. What else is meant?
CHOR. You are mad, mad, carried away by the god,   1100
   Raising the dirge, the tuneless
   Tune, for yourself. Like the tawny

1077. *pack ever-hungering*: the Furies.

1102–1103. *tawny unsatisfied singer*: the nightingale. Philomela was raped by Tereus, the husband of her sister Procne. The two sisters avenged themselves by killing Tereus' son Itys, and serving up his flesh to Tereus to eat. Philomela was changed into a nightingale, mourning for Itys (the name is an imitation of the sound of the nightingale's song).

Unsatisfied singer from her luckless heart
Lamenting "Itys, Itys," the nightingale
Lamenting a life luxuriant with grief.   1105
CASS. Oh the lot of the songful nightingale!
    The gods enclosed her in a winged body,
    Gave her a sweet and tearless passing.
    But for me remains the two-edged cutting blade.
CHOR. From whence these rushing and God-inflicted   1110
    Profitless pains?
    Why shape with your sinister crying
    The piercing hymn—fear-piercing?
    How can you know the evil-worded landmarks
        On the prophetic path?   1115
CASS. Oh the wedding, the wedding of Paris—death to his people!
    O river Scamander, water drunk by my fathers!
    When I was young, alas, upon your beaches
    I was brought up and cared for.
    But now it is the River of Wailing and the banks of Hell   1120
        That shall hear my prophecy soon.
CHOR. What is this clear speech, too clear?
    A child can understand it.
    I am bitten with fangs that draw blood
    By the misery of your cries,   1125
    Cries harrowing the heart.
CASS. O trouble on trouble of a city lost, lost utterly!
    My father's sacrifices before the towers,
    Much killing of cattle and sheep,
    No cure—availed not at all   1130
    To prevent the coming of what came to Troy,
    And I, my brain on fire, shall soon enter the trap.
CHOR. This speech accords with the former.
    What god, malicious, over-heavy, persistently pressing,
    Drives you to chant of these lamentable   1135
    Griefs with death their burden?
    But I cannot see the end.
        [CASSANDRA *now steps down from the car.*]
CASS. The oracle now no longer from behind veils
    Will be peeping forth like a newly-wedded bride;
    But I can feel it like a fresh wind swoop   1140
    And rush in the face of the dawn and, wave-like, wash
    Against the sun a vastly greater grief
    Than this one. I shall speak no more conundrums.
    And bear me witness, pacing me, that I
    Am trailing on the scent of ancient wrongs.   1145
    For this house here a choir never deserts,

Chanting together ill. For they mean ill,
And to puff up their arrogance they have drunk
Men's blood, this band of revellers that haunts the house,
Hard to be rid of, fiends that attend the family.   1150
Established in its rooms they hymn their hymn
Of that original sin, abhor in turn
The adultery that proved a brother's ruin.
A miss? Or do my arrows hit the mark?
Or am I a quack prophet who knocks at doors, a babbler?   1155
Give me your oath, confess I have the facts,
The ancient history of this house's crimes.

LEAD. And how could an oath's assurance, however finely assured,
Turn out a remedy? I wonder, though, that you
Being brought up overseas, of another tongue,   1160
Should hit on the whole tale as if you had been standing by.

CASS. Apollo the prophet set me to prophesy.

LEAD. Was he, although a god, struck by desire?

CASS. Till now I was ashamed to tell the story.

LEAD. Yes. Good fortune keeps us all fastidious.   1165

CASS. He wrestled hard upon me, panting love.

LEAD. And did you come, as they do, to child-getting?

CASS. No. I agreed to him. And I cheated him.

LEAD. Were you already possessed by the mystic art?

CASS. Already I was telling the townsmen all their future
            suffering.   1170

LEAD. Then how did you escape the doom of Apollo's anger?

CASS. I did not escape. No one ever believed me.

LEAD. Yet to us your words seem worthy of belief.

CASS. Oh misery, misery!
Again comes on me the terrible labour of true   1175
Prophecy, dizzying prelude; distracts . . .
Do you see these who sit before the house,
Children, like the shapes of dreams?
Children who seem to have been killed by their kinsfolk,
Filling their hands with meat, flesh of themselves,   1180
Guts and entrails, handfuls of lament—
Clear what they hold—the same their father tasted.
For this I declare someone is plotting vengeance—
A lion? Lion but coward, that lurks in bed,
Good watchdog truly against the lord's return—   1185
My lord, for I must bear the yoke of serfdom.
Leader of the ships, overturner of Troy,
He does not know what plots the accursed hound

1153. *adultery:* Thyestes seduced
the wife of Atreus. This was the beginning of strife between the brothers.

1184. *Lion but coward:* Aegisthus.
1188. *hound:* Clytemnestra.

With the licking tongue and the pricked-up ear will plan
In the manner of a lurking doom, in an evil hour.   1190
A daring criminal! Female murders male.
What monster could provide her with a title?
An amphisbaena or hag of the sea who dwells
In rocks to ruin sailors—
A raving mother of death who breathes against her folk   1195
War to the finish. Listen to her shout of triumph,
Who shirks no horrors, like men in a rout of battle.
And yet she poses as glad at their return.
If you distrust my words, what does it matter?
That which will come will come. You too will soon stand
        here   1200
And admit with pity that I spoke too truly.
LEAD. Thyestes' dinner of his children's meat
    I understood and shuddered, and fear grips me
    To hear the truth, not framed in parables.
    But hearing the rest I am thrown out of my course.   1205
CASS. It is Agamemnon's death I tell you you shall witness.
LEAD. Stop! Provoke no evil. Quiet your mouth!
CASS. The god who gives me words is here no healer.
LEAD. Not if this shall be so. But may some chance avert it.
CASS. You are praying. But others are busy with murder.   1210
LEAD. What man is he promotes this terrible thing?
CASS. Indeed you have missed my drift by a wide margin!
LEAD. But I do not understand the assassin's method.
CASS. And yet too well I know the speech of Greece!
LEAD. So does Delphi but the replies are hard.   1215
CASS. Ah what a fire it is! It comes upon me.

    Apollo, Wolf-Destroyer, pity, pity . . .
    It is the two-foot lioness who beds
    Beside a wolf, the noble lion away,
    It is she will kill me. Brewing a poisoned cup   1220
    She will mix my punishment too in the angry draught
    And boasts, sharpening the dagger for her husband,
    To pay back murder, for my bringing here.
    Why then do I wear these mockeries of myself,
    The wand and the prophet's garland round my neck?   1225
    My hour is coming—but you shall perish first.
    Destruction! Scattered thus you give me my revenge;
    Go and enrich some other woman with ruin.

1193. *amphisbaena:* a fabulous serpent with a head at either end; the
word means literally "going in both
directions."
1208. *healer:* one of Apollo's titles.

1212. *missed my drift:* in speaking
of a man instead of a woman.
1215. *Delphi:* The replies of the Delphic oracle were celebrated for their
obscurity and ambiguity.

See: Apollo himself is stripping me
Of my prophetic gear, who has looked on   1230
When in this dress I have been a laughing-stock
To friends and foes alike, and to no purpose;
They called me crazy, like a fortune-teller,
A poor starved beggar-woman—and I bore it.
And now the prophet undoing his prophetess   1235
Has brought me to this final darkness.
Instead of my father's altar the executioner's block
Waits me the victim, red with my hot blood.
But the gods will not ignore me as I die.
One will come after to avenge my death,   1240
A matricide, a murdered father's champion.
Exile and tramp and outlaw he will come back
To gable the family house of fatal crime;
His father's outstretched corpse shall lead him home.
Why need I then lament so pitifully?   1245
For now that I have seen the town of Troy
Treated as she was treated, while her captors
Come to their reckoning thus by the gods' verdict,
I will go in and have the courage to die.
Look, these gates are the gates of Death. I greet them.   1250
And I pray that I may meet a deft and mortal stroke
So that without a struggle I may close
My eyes and my blood ebb in easy death.
LEAD. Oh woman very unhappy and very wise,
    Your speech was long. But if in sober truth   1255
    You know your fate, why like an ox that the gods
    Drive, do you walk so bravely to the altar?
CASS. There is no escape, strangers. No; not by postponement.
LEAD. But the last moment has the privilege of hope.
CASS. The day is here. Little should I gain by flight.   1260
LEAD. This patience of yours comes from a brave soul.
CASS. A happy man is never paid that compliment.
LEAD. But to die with credit graces a mortal man.
CASS. Oh my father! You and your noble sons!
    [*She approaches the door, then suddenly recoils.*]
LEAD. What is it? What is the fear that drives you back?   1265
CASS. Faugh.
LEAD. Why faugh? Or is this some hallucination?
CASS. These walls breathe out a death that drips with blood.
LEAD. Not so. It is only the smell of the sacrifice.
CASS. It is like a breath out of a charnel-house.   1270
LEAD. You think our palace burns odd incense then!

1240 ff., *one will come after* . . . : These lines refer to Orestes.

CASS. But I will go to lament among the dead
My lot and Agamemnon's. Enough of life!
Strangers,
I am not afraid like a bird afraid of a bush   1275
But witness you my words after my death
When a woman dies in return for me a woman
And a man falls for a man with a wicked wife.
I ask this service, being about to die.
LEAD. Alas, I pity you for the death you have foretold.   1280
CASS. One more speech I have; I do not wish to raise
The dirge for my own self. But to the sun I pray
In face of his last light that my avengers
May make my murderers pay for this my death,
Death of a woman slave, an easy victim.   1285
    [*She enters the palace.*]

LEAD. Ah the fortunes of men! When they go well
A shadow sketch would match them, and in ill-fortune
The dab of a wet sponge destroys the drawing.
It is not myself but the life of man I pity.
CHOR. Prosperity in all men cries   1290
For more prosperity. Even the owner
Of the finger-pointed-at palace never shuts
His door against her, saying "Come no more."
So to our king the blessed gods had granted
To take the town of Priam, and heaven-favoured   1295
He reaches home. But now if for former bloodshed
    He must pay blood
And dying for the dead shall cause
    Other deaths in atonement
What man could boast he was born   1300
    Secure, who heard this story?
AGAM. [*Within*] Oh! I am struck a mortal blow—within!
LEAD. Silence! Listen. Who calls out, wounded with a mortal stroke?
AGAM. Again—the second blow—I am struck again.
LEAD. You heard the king cry out. I think the deed is done.   1305
    Let us see if we can concert some sound proposal.
2ND OLD MAN. Well, I will tell you my opinion—
    Raise an alarm, summon the folk to the palace.
3RD OLD MAN. I say burst in with all speed possible,
    Convict them of the deed while still the sword is wet.   1310
4TH OLD MAN. And I am partner to some such suggestion.
    I am for taking some course. No time to dawdle.
5TH OLD MAN. The case is plain. This is but the beginning.
    They are going to set up dictatorship in the state.

6TH OLD MAN. We are wasting time. The assassins tread to
    earth   1315
  The decencies of delay and gives their hands no sleep.
7TH OLD MAN. I do not know what plan I could hit on to pro-
    pose.
  The man who acts is in the position to plan.
8TH OLD MAN. So I think, too, for I am at a loss
  To raise the dead man up again with words.   1320
9TH OLD MAN. Then to stretch out our life shall we yield thus
  To the rule of these profaners of the house?
10TH OLD MAN. It is not to be endured. To die is better.
  Death is more comfortable than tyranny.
11TH OLD MAN. And are we on the evidence of groans   1325
  Going to give oracle that the prince is dead?
12TH OLD MAN. We must know the facts for sure and *then* be
    angry.
  Guesswork is not the same as certain knowledge.
LEAD. Then all of you back me and approve this plan—
  To ascertain how it is with Agamemnon   1330
    [*The doors of the palace open, revealing the bodies of*
    AGAMEMNON *and* CASSANDRA. CLYTEMNESTRA *stands above*
    them.]
CLYT. Much having been said before to fit the moment,
  To say the opposite now will not outface me.
  How else could one serving hate upon the hated,
  Thought to be friends, hang high the nets of doom
  To preclude all leaping out?   1335
  For me I have long been training for this match,
  I tried a fall and won—a victory overdue.
  I stand here where I struck, above my victims;
  So I contrived it—this I will not deny—
  That he could neither fly nor ward off death;   1340
  Inextricable like a net for fishes
  I cast about him a vicious wealth of raiment
  And struck him twice and with two groans he loosed
  His limbs beneath him, and upon him fallen
  I deal him the third blow to the God beneath the earth,   1345
  To the safe keeper of the dead a votive gift,
  And with that he spits his life out where he lies
  And smartly spouting blood he sprays me with
  The sombre drizzle of bloody dew and I
  Rejoice no less than in God's gift of rain   1350
  The crops are glad when the ear of corn gives birth.

1345. *third blow to the God beneath the earth:* like the third libation to Zeus above.

These things being so, you, elders of Argos,
Rejoice if rejoice you will. Mine is the glory.
And if I could pay this corpse his due libation
I should be right to pour it and more than right;   1355
With so many horrors this man mixed and filled
The bowl—and, coming home, has drained the draught himself.

LEAD. Your speech astonishes us. This brazen boast
Above the man who was your king and husband!

CLYT. You challenge me as a woman without foresight   1360
But I with unflinching heart to you who know
Speak. And you, whether you will praise or blame,
It makes no matter. Here lies Agamemnon,
My husband, dead, the work of this right hand,
An honest workman. There you have the facts.   1365

CHOR. Woman, what poisoned
Herb of the earth have you tasted
Or potion of the flowing sea
To undertake this killing and the people's curses?
You threw down, you cut off—The people will cast you out,   1370
Black abomination to the town.

CLYT. Now your verdict—in my case—is exile
And to have the people's hatred, the public curses,
Though then in no way you opposed this man
Who carelessly, as if it were a head of sheep   1375
Out of the abundance of his fleecy flocks,
Sacrificed his own daughter, to me the dearest
Fruit of travail, charm for the Thracian winds.
He was the one to have banished from this land,
Pay off the pollution. But when you hear what I   1380
Have done, you judge severely. But I warn you—
Threaten me on the understanding that I am ready
For two alternatives—Win by force the right
To rule me, but, if God brings about the contrary,
Late in time you will have to learn self-discipline.   1385

CHOR. You are high in the thoughts,
You speak extravagant things,
After the soiling murder your crazy heart
Fancies your forehead with a smear of blood.
Unhonoured, unfriended, you must   1390
Pay for a blow with a blow.

CLYT. Listen then to this—the sanction of my oaths:
By the Justice totting up my child's atonement,
By the Avenging Doom and Fiend to whom I killed this man,
For me hope walks not in the rooms of fear   1395
So long as my fire is lit upon my hearth

By Aegisthus, loyal to me as he was before.
The man who outraged me lies here,
The darling of each courtesan at Troy,
And here with him is the prisoner clairvoyant,   1400
The fortune-teller that he took to bed,
Who shares his bed as once his bench on shipboard,
A loyal mistress. Both have their deserts.
He lies so; and she who like a swan
Sang her last dying lament   1405
Lies his lover, and the sight contributes
An appetiser to my own bed's pleasure.

CHOR. Ah would some quick death come not overpainful,
Not overlong on the sickbed,
Establishing in us the ever-   1410
Lasting unending sleep now that our guardian
Has fallen, the kindest of men,
Who suffering much for a woman
By a woman has lost his life.

    O Helen, insane, being one   1415
    One to have destroyed so many
    And many souls under Troy,
    Now is your work complete, blossomed not for oblivion,
    Unfading stain of blood. Here now, if in any home,
    Is Discord, here is a man's deep-rooted ruin.   1420

CLYT. Do not pray for the portion of death
Weighed down by these things, do not turn
Your anger on Helen as destroyer of men,
One woman destroyer of many
Lives of Greek men,   1425
    A hurt that cannot be healed.

CHOR. O Evil Spirit, falling on the family,
On the two sons of Atreus and using
Two sisters in heart as your tools,
A power that bites to the heart—   1430
See on the body
Perched like a raven he gloats
Harshly croaking his hymn.

CLYT. Ah, now you have amended your lips' opinion,
Calling upon this family's three times gorged   1435
Genius—demon who breeds
Blood-hankering lust in the belly:
Before the old sore heals, new pus collects.

CHOR. It is a great spirit—great—
You tell of, harsh in anger,   1440
A ghastly tale, alas,

Of unsatisfied disaster
Brought by Zeus, by Zeus,
Cause and worker of all.
For without Zeus what comes to pass among us?   1445
Which of these things is outside Providence?
> O my king, my king,
> How shall I pay you in tears,
> Speak my affection in words?
> You lie in that spider's web,   1450
> In a desecrating death breathe out your life,
> Lie ignominiously
> Defeated by a crooked death
> And the two-edged cleaver's stroke.

CLYT. You say this is *my* work—mine?   1455
Do not cozen yourself that I am Agamemnon's wife.
Masquerading as the wife
Of the corpse there the old sharp-witted Genius
Of Atreus who gave the cruel banquet
Has paid with a grown man's life   1460
The due for children dead.

CHOR. That you are not guilty of
This murder who will attest?
No, but you may have been abetted
By some ancestral Spirit of Revenge.   1465
Wading a millrace of the family's blood
The black Manslayer forces a forward path
To make the requital at last
For the eaten children, the blood-clot cold with time.
> O my king, my king,   1470
> How shall I pay you in tears,
> Speak my affection in words?
> You lie in that spider's web,
> In a desecrating death breathe out your life,
> Lie ignominiously   1475
> Defeated by a crooked death
> And the two-edged cleaver's stroke.

CLYT. Did he not, too, contrive a crooked
Horror for the house? My child by him,
Shoot that I raised, much-wept-for Iphigeneia,   1480
He treated her like this;
So suffering like this he need not make
Any great brag in Hell having paid with death
Dealt by the sword for work of his own beginning.

CHOR. I am at a loss for thought, I lack   1485
All nimble counsel as to where

To turn when the house is falling.
I fear the house-collapsing crashing
Blizzard of blood—of which these drops are earnest.
Now is Destiny sharpening her justice   1490
On other whetstones for a new infliction.
    O earth, earth, if only you had received me
    Before I saw this man lie here as if in bed
      In a bath lined with silver.
    Who will bury him? Who will keen him?   1495
    Will you, having killed your own husband,
    Dare now to lament him
    And after great wickedness make
      Unamending amends to his ghost?
    And who above this godlike hero's grave   1500
    Pouring praises and tears
      Will grieve with a genuine heart?
CLYT. It is not your business to attend to that.
    By my hand he fell low, lies low and dead,
    And I shall bury him low down in the earth,   1505
    And his household need not weep him
    For Iphigeneia his daughter
    Tenderly, as is right,
    Will meet her father at the rapid ferry of sorrows,
    Put her arms round him and kiss him!   1510
CHOR. Reproach answers reproach,
    It is hard to decide,
    The catcher is caught, the killer pays for his kill.
    But the law abides while Zeus abides enthroned
    That the wrongdoer suffers. That is established.   1515
    Who could expel from the house the seed of the Curse?
    The race is soldered in sockets of Doom and Vengeance.
CLYT. In this you say what is right and the will of God.
    But for my part I am ready to make a contract
    With the Evil Genius of the House of Atreus   1520
    To accept what has been till now, hard though it is,
    But that for the future he shall leave this house
    And wear away some other stock with deaths
    Imposed among themselves. Of my possessions
    A small part will suffice if only I   1525
    Can rid these walls of the mad exchange of murder.
      [*Enter* AEGISTHUS, *followed by soldiers.*]
AEGISTHUS. O welcome light of a justice-dealing day!
    From now on I will say that the gods, avenging men,
    Look down from above on the crimes of earth,
    Seeing as I do in woven robes of the Furies   1530
    This man lying here—a sight to warm my heart—

1495. *keen:* mourn for.

Paying for the crooked violence of his father.
For his father Atreus, when he ruled the country,
Because his power was challenged, hounded out
From state and home his own brother Thyestes.   1535
My father—let me be plain—was this Thyestes,
Who later came back home a suppliant,
There, miserable, found so much asylum
As not to die on the spot, stain the ancestral floor.
But to show his hospitality godless Atreus   1540
Gave him an eager if not a loving welcome,
Pretending a day of feasting and rich meats
Served my father with his children's flesh.
The hands and feet, fingers and toes, he hid
At the bottom of the dish. My father sitting apart   1545
Took unknowing the unrecognizable portion
And ate of a dish that has proved, as you see, expensive.
But when he knew he had eaten worse than poison
He fell back groaning, vomiting their flesh,
And invoking a hopeless doom on the sons of Pelops   1550
Kicked over the table to confirm his curse—
So may the whole race perish!
Result of this—you see this man lie here.
I stitched this murder together; it was my title.
Me the third son he left, an unweaned infant,   1555
To share the bitterness of my father's exile.
But I grew up and Justice brought me back,
I grappled this man while still beyond his door,
Having pieced together the programme of his ruin.
So now would even death be beautiful to me   1560
Having seen Agamemnon in the nets of Justice.
LEAD. Aegisthus. I cannot respect brutality in distress.
You claim that you deliberately killed this prince
And that you alone planned this pitiful murder.
Be sure that in your turn your head shall not escape   1565
The people's volleyed curses mixed with stones.
AEG. Do you speak so who sit at the lower oar
While those on the upper bench control the ship?
Old as you are, you will find it is a heavy load
To go to school when old to learn the lesson of tact.   1570
For old age, too, gaol and hunger are fine
Instructors in wisdom, second-sighted doctors.
You have eyes. Cannot you see?
Do not kick against the pricks. The blow will hurt you.
LEAD. You woman waiting in the house for those who return from
      battle   1575
While you seduce their wives! Was it you devised

1550. *Pelops:* the founder of the line.

The death of a master of armies?

AEG. And these words, too, prepare the way for tears.
Contrast your voice with the voice of Orpheus: he
Led all things after him bewitched with joy, but you   1580
Having stung me with your silly yelps shall be
Led off yourself, to prove more mild when mastered.

LEAD. Indeed! So you are now to be king of Argos,
You who, when you had plotted the king's death,
Did not even dare to do that thing yourself!   1585

AEG. No. For the trick of it was clearly woman's work.
I was suspect, an enemy of old.
But now I shall try with Agamemnon's wealth
To rule the people. Any who is disobedient
I will harness in a heavy yoke, no tracehorse work for him   1590
Like barley-fed colt, but hateful hunger lodging
Beside him in the dark will see his temper soften.

LEAD. Why with your cowardly soul did you yourself
Not strike this man but left that work to a woman
Whose presence pollutes our country and its gods?   1595
But Orestes—does he somewhere see the light
That he may come back here by favour of fortune
And kill this pair and prove the final victor?

AEG. [Summoning his guards] Well, if such is your design in deeds
and words, you will quickly learn—
Here my friends, here my guards, there is work for you at
hand.   1600

LEAD. Come then, hands on hilts, be each and all of us prepared.
[The old men and the guards threaten each other.]

AEG. Very well! I too am ready to meet death with sword in hand.

LEAD. We are glad you speak of dying. We accept your words for
luck.

CLYT. No, my dearest, do not so. Add no more to the train of wrong.
To reap these many present wrongs is harvest enough of
misery.   1605
Enough of misery. Start no more. Our hands are red.
But do you, and you old men, go home and yield to fate in time,
In time before you suffer. We have acted as we had to act.
If only our afflictions now could prove enough, we should agree—
We who have been so hardly mauled in the heavy claws of the
evil god.   1610
So stands my word, a woman's, if any man thinks fit to hear.

AEG. But to think that these should thus pluck the blooms of an
idle tongue
And should throw out words like these, giving the evil god his
chance,

1590. *tracehorse:* an extra horse, outside the yoke, which does less work than
the others.

And should miss the path of prudence and insult their master so!
LEAD. It is not the Argive way to fawn upon a cowardly man.   1615
AEG. Perhaps. But I in later days will take further steps with you.
LEAD. Not if the god who rules the family guides Orestes to his home.
AEG. Yes. I know that men in exile feed themselves on barren hopes.
LEAD. Go on, grow fat defiling justice . . . while you have your hour.
AEG. Do not think you will not pay me a price for your   1620
    stupidity.
LEAD. Boast on in your self-assurance, like a cock beside his hen.
CLYT. Pay no heed, Aegisthus, to these futile barkings. You and I,
Masters of this house, from now shall order all things well.

    [*They enter the palace.*]

Prometheus Bound*

The scene is a lonely rock in the far North. FORCE *and* VIOLENCE,
the henchmen of Zeus, have brought PROMETHEUS *to his place of
punishment, and* HÆPHESTUS *is now ordered to chain and nail him
to the rock.*

FORCE. Far have we come to this far spot of earth,
    this narrow Scythian land, a desert all untrodden.
    God of the forge and fire, yours the task
    the Father laid upon you.
    To this high-piercing, head-long rock   5
    in adamantine chairs that none can break
    bind him—him here, who dared all things.
    Your flaming flower he stole to give to men,
    fire, the master craftsman, through whose power
    all things are wrought, and for such error now   10
    he must repay the gods; be taught to yield
    to Zeus' lordship and to cease
    from his man-loving way.
HEPHESTUS. Force, Violence, what Zeus enjoined on you
    has here an end. Your task is done.   15
    But as for me, I am not bold to bind
    a god, a kinsman, to this stormy crag.
    Yet I must needs be bold.
    His load is heavy who dares disobey the Father's word.
    O high-souled child of Justice, the wise counselor,   20

* Reprinted from *Three Greek Plays*, translated with introductions by Edith Hamilton, by permission of W. W. Norton & Company, Inc. Copyright 1937 by W. W. Norton & Company, Inc.

2. *Scythian:* Scythia for the Greeks was a vast and ill-defined area, stretching from the Balkans into southern Russia.

19. *Father's:* Hephestus is the son of Zeus.

20. *Justice:* Prometheus is the son of the goddess Themis, whose name suggests, in Greek, age-old and customary right.

against my will as against yours I nail you fast
in brazen fetters never to be loosed
to this rock peak, where no man ever comes,
where never voice or face of mortal you will see.
The shining splendor of the sun shall wither you.   25
Welcome to you will be the night
when with her mantle star-inwrought
she hides the light of day.
And welcome then in turn the sun
to melt the frost the dawn has left behind.   30
Forever shall the intolerable present grind you down,
and he who will release you is not born.
Such fruit you reap for your man-loving way.
A god yourself, you did not dread God's anger,
but gave to mortals honor not their due,   35
and therefore you must guard this joyless rock—
no rest, no sleep, no moment's respite.
Groans shall your speech be, lamentation
your only words—all uselessly.
Zeus has no mind to pity. He is harsh,   40
like upstarts always.

FORCE. Well then, why this delay and foolish talk?
A god whom gods hate is abominable.

HEPHESTUS. The tie of blood has a strange power,
and old acquaintance too.   45

FORCE. And so say I—but don't you think
that disobedience to the Father's words
might have still stranger power?

HEPHESTUS. You're rough, as always. Pity is not in you.

FORCE. Much good is pity here. Why all this pother   50
that helps him not a whit?

HEPHESTUS. O skill of hand now hateful to me.

FORCE. Why blame your skill? These troubles here
were never caused by it. That's simple truth.

HEPHESTUS. Yet would it were another's and not mine.   55

FORCE. Trouble is everywhere except in heaven.
No one is free but Zeus.

HEPHESTUS. I know—I've not a word to say.

FORCE. Come then. Make haste. On with his fetters.
What if the Father sees you lingering?   60

HEPHESTUS. The chains are ready here if he should look.

FORCE. Seize his hands and master him.

27. *star-inwrought:* "Shelley's adjective is the perfect translation. Anything
else would be less exact and less like
Aeschylus." [Translator's note.]

32. *is not born:* Hephestus means, of
course, that there is no chance of release for Prometheus, but the words
have another meaning, of which he is
not aware. Prometheus will eventually
be released by Heracles, who will be
born many generations later, of the line
of Io.

Now to your hammer. Pin him to the rocks.
HEPHESTUS. All done, and quick work too.
FORCE. Still harder. Tighter. Never loose your hold.   65
    For he is good at finding a way out where there is none.
HEPHESTUS. This arm at least he will not ever free.
FORCE. Buckle the other fast, and let him learn
    with all his cunning he's a fool to Zeus.
HEPHESTUS. No one but he, poor wretch, can blame my work.   70
FORCE. Drive stoutly now your wedge straight through his breast,
    the stubborn jaw of steel that cannot break.
HEPHESTUS. Alas, Prometheus, I grieve for your pain.
FORCE. You shirk your task and grieve for those Zeus hates?
    Take care; you may need pity for yourself.   75
HEPHESTUS. You see a sight eyes should not look upon.
FORCE. I see one who has got what he deserves.
    But come. The girdle now around his waist.
HEPHESTUS. What must be shall be done. No need to urge me.
FORCE. I will and louder too. Down with you now.   80
    Make fast his legs in rings. Use all your strength.
HEPHESTUS. Done and small trouble.
FORCE. Now for his feet. Drive the nails through the flesh.
    The judge is stern who passes on our work.
HEPHESTUS. Your tongue and face match well.   85
FORCE. Why, you poor weakling. Are you one to cast
    a savage temper in another's face?
HEPHESTUS. Oh, let us go. Chains hold him, hand and foot.
FORCE. Run riot now, you there upon the rocks.
    Go steal from gods to give their goods to men—   90
    to men whose life is but a little day.
    What will they do to lift these woes from you?
    Forethought your name means, falsely named.
    Forethought you lack and need now for yourself
    if you would slip through fetters wrought like these.   95
        [*Exeunt* FORCE, VIOLENCE, HEPHESTUS.]
PROMETHEUS. O air of heaven and swift-winged winds,
    O running river waters,
    O never numbered laughter of sea waves,
    Earth, mother of all, Eye of the sun, all seeing,
    on you I call.   100
    Behold what I, a god, endure from gods.
    See in what tortures I must struggle
    through countless years of time.
    This shame, these bonds, are put upon me
    by the new ruler of the gods.   105
    Sorrow enough in what is here and what is still to come.
    It wrings groans from me.
    When shall the end be, the appointed end?

And yet why ask?
All, all I knew before,   110
all that should be.
Nothing, no pang of pain
that I did not foresee.
Bear without struggle what must be.
Necessity is strong and ends our strife.   115
But silence is intolerable here.
So too is speech.
I am fast bound, I must endure.
I gave to mortals gifts.
I hunted out the secret source of fire.   120
I filled a reed therewith,
fire, the teacher of all arts to men,
the great way through.
These are the crimes that I must pay for,
pinned to a rock beneath the open sky.   125
But what is here? What comes?
What sound, what fragrance, brushed me with faint wings,
of deities or mortals or of both?
Has someone found a way to this far peak
to view my agony? What else?   130
Look at me then, in chains, a god who failed,
the enemy of Zeus, whom all gods hate,
all that go in and out of Zeus' hall.
The reason is that I loved men too well.
Oh, birds are moving near me. The air murmurs   135
with swift and sweeping wings.
Whatever comes to me is terrible.

> [*Enter* CHORUS. *They are sea nymphs. It is clear from what*
> *follows that a winged car brings them on to the stage.*]

LEADER OF CHORUS. Oh, be not terrified, for friends are here,
each eager to be first,
on swift wings flying to your rock.   140
I prayed my father long
before he let me come.
The rushing winds have sped me on.
A noise of ringing brass went through the sea-caves,
and for all a maiden's fears it drove me forth,   145
so swift, I did not put my sandals on,
but in my winged car I came to you.

PROMETHEUS. To see this sight—
Daughters of fertile Tethys,

---

121. *reed:* the dried hollow stalk of
the fennel plant which would keep the
spark alive inside and conceal it as in
a tube.

128. *of deities . . . :* "This line of

Keats is the exact translation." [Trans-
lator's note.]

141. *my father:* They are the daughters of Ocean.

149. *Tethys:* wife of Ocean.

children of Ocean who forever flows   150
unresting round earth's shores,
behold me, and my bonds
that bind me fast upon the rocky height
of this cleft mountain side,
keeping my watch of pain.   155

A SEA NYMPH. I look upon you and a mist of tears,
of grief and terror, rises as I see
your body withering upon the rocks,
in shameful fetters.
For a new helmsman steers Olympus.   160
By new laws Zeus is ruling without law.
He has put down the mighty ones of old.

PROMETHEUS. Oh, had I been sent deep, deep into earth,
to that black boundless place where go the dead,
though cruel chains should hold me fast forever,   165
I should be hid from sight of gods and men.
But now I am a plaything for the winds.
My enemies exult—and I endure.

ANOTHER NYMPH. What god so hard of heart to look on these things
      gladly?
Who, but Zeus only, would not suffer with you?   170
He is malignant always and his mind
unbending. All the sons of heaven
he drives beneath his yoke.
Nor will he make an end
until his heart is sated or until   175
someone, somehow, shall seize his sovereignty—
if that could be.

PROMETHEUS. And yet—and yet—all tortured though I am,
      fast fettered here,
he shall have need of me, the lord of heaven,   180
to show to him the strange design
by which he shall be stripped of throne and scepter.
But he will never win me over
with honeyed spell of soft, persuading words,
nor will I ever cower beneath his threats   185
to tell him what he seeks.
First he must free me from this savage prison
and pay for all my pain.

ANOTHER. Oh, you are bold. In bitter agony

181. *strange design:* It was fated that the sea-nymph Thetis would bear a son stronger than his father. Zeus did not know this, and his union with Thetis would give birth to a son who would overthrow him as he had overthrown his father Kronos. Knowledge of this secret is the one advantage Prometheus has in his struggle with the power of Zeus. He merely hints at it here; later he becomes more explicit, but of course he never mentions the name of Thetis; Zeus is listening, as we find out at the end of the play. The prophecy about Thetis was eventually fulfilled: she was married to Peleus and her son was Achilles.

you will not yield.   190
These are such words as only free men speak.
Piercing terror stings my heart.
I fear because of what has come to you.
Where are you fated to put in to shore
and find a haven from this troubled sea?   195
Prayers cannot move,
persuasions cannot turn,
the heart of Kronos' son.

PROMETHEUS. I know that he is savage.
He keeps his righteousness at home.   200
But yet some time he shall be mild of mood,
when he is broken.
He will smooth his stubborn temper,
and run to meet me.
Then peace will come and love between us two.   205

LEADER. Reveal the whole to us. Tell us your tale.
What guilt does Zeus impute
to torture you in shame and bitterness?
Teach us, if you may speak.

PROMETHEUS. To speak is pain, but silence too is pain,   210
and everywhere is wretchedness.
When first the gods began to quarrel
and faction rose among them,
some wishing to throw Kronos out of heaven,
that Zeus, Zeus, mark you, should be lord,   215
others opposed, pressing the opposite,
that Zeus should never rule the gods,
then I, giving wise counsel to the Titans,
children of Earth and Heaven, could not prevail.
My way out was a shrewd one, they despised it,   220
and in their arrogant minds they thought to conquer
with ease, by their own strength.
But Justice, she who is my mother, told me—
Earth she is sometimes called,
whose form is one, whose name is many—   225
she told me, and not once alone,
the future, how it should be brought to pass,
that neither violence nor strength of arm
but only subtle craft could win.
I made all clear to them.   230
They scorned to look my way.
The best then left me was to stand with Zeus
in all good will, my mother with me,

---

218. *Titans:* the older generation of
gods, the brothers of Kronos.
223. *Justice:* Themis, see l. 20.

230. *them:* the Titans, of whom
Prometheus was one.

and, through my counsel, the black underworld
covered, and hides within its secret depths   235
Kronos the aged and his host.
Such good the ruler of the gods had from me,
and with such evil he has paid me back.
There is a sickness that infects all tyrants,
they cannot trust their friends.   240
But you have asked a question I would answer:
What is my crime that I am tortured for?
Zeus had no sooner seized his father's throne
than he was giving to each god a post
and ordering his kingdom,   245
but mortals in their misery
he took no thought for.
His wish was they should perish
and he would then beget another race.
And there were none to cross his will save I.   250
I dared it, I saved men.
Therefore I am bowed down in torment,
grievous to suffer, pitiful to see.
I pitied mortals,
I never thought to meet with this.   255
Ruthlessly punished here I am
an infamy to Zeus.
LEADER. Iron of heart or wrought from rock is he
    who does not suffer in your misery.
    Oh, that these eyes had never looked upon it.   260
    I see it and my heart is wrung.
PROMETHEUS. A friend must feel I am a thing to pity.
LEADER. Did you perhaps go even further still?
PROMETHEUS. I made men cease to live with death in sight.
LEADER. What potion did you find to cure this sickness?   265
PROMETHEUS. Blind hopes I caused to dwell in them.
ANOTHER SEA NYMPH. Great good to men that gift.
PROMETHEUS. To it I added the good gift of fire.
ANOTHER. And now the creatures of a day
    have flaming fire?   270
PROMETHEUS. Yes, and learn many crafts therefrom.
LEADER. For deeds like these Zeus holds you guilty,
    and tortures you with never ease from pain?
    Is no end to your anguish set before you?
PROMETHEUS. None other except when it pleases him.   275
LEADER. It pleases him? What hope there? You must see
    you missed your mark. I tell you this with pain
    to give you pain.
    But let that pass. Seek your deliverance.
PROMETHEUS. Your feet are free.   280

Chains bind mine fast.
Advice is easy for the fortunate.
All that has come I knew full well.
Of my own will I shot the arrow that fell short,
of my own will.   285
Nothing do I deny.
I helped men and found trouble for myself.
I knew—and yet not all.
I did not think to waste away
hung high in air upon a lonely rock.   290
But now, I pray you, no more pity
for what I suffer here. Come, leave your ear,
and learn the fate that steals upon me,
all, to the very end.
Hear me, oh, hear me. Share my pain. Remember,   295
trouble may wander far and wide
but it is always near.

LEADER. You cry to willing ears, Prometheus.
Lightly I leave my swift speeding car
and the pure ways of air where go the birds.   300
I stand upon this stony ground.
I ask to hear your troubles to the end.
        [*Enter* OCEAN *riding on a four-footed bird. The* CHORUS *draw
        back, and he does not see them.*]

OCEAN. Well, here at last, an end to a long journey.
I've made my way to you, Prometheus.
This bird of mine is swift of wing   305
but I can guide him by my will,
without a bridle.
Now you must know, I'm grieved at your misfortunes.
Of course I must be, I'm your kinsman.
And that apart, there's no one I think more of.   310
And you'll find out the truth of what I'm saying.
It isn't in me to talk flattery.
Come: tell me just what must be done to help you,
and never say that you've a firmer friend
than you will find in me.   315

PROMETHEUS. Oho! What's here? You? Come to see my troubles?
How did you dare to leave your ocean river,
vour rock caves hollowed by the sea,
and stand upon the iron mother earth?
Was it to see what has befallen me,   320
because you grieve with me?
Then see this sight: here is the friend of Zeus,
who helped to make him master.
This twisted body is his handiwork.

OCEAN. I see, Prometheus. I do wish   325

You'd take some good advice.
I know you're very clever,
but real self-knowledge—that you haven't got.
New fashions have come in with this new ruler.
Why can't you change your own to suit?   330
Don't talk like that—so rude and irritating.
Zeus isn't so far off but he might hear,
and what would happen then would make these troubles
seem child's play.
You're miserable. Then do control your temper   335
and find some remedy.
Of course you think you know all that I'm saying.
You certainly should know the harm
that blustering has brought you.
But you're not humbled yet. You won't give in.   340
You're looking for more trouble.
Just learn one thing from me:
Don't kick against the pricks.
You see he's savage—why not? He's a tyrant.
He doesn't have to hand in his accounts.   345
Well, now I'm going straight to try
if I can free you from this wretched business.
Do you keep still. No more of this rash talking.
Haven't you yet learned with all your wisdom
the mischief that a foolish tongue can make?   350
PROMETHEUS. Wisdom? The praise for that is yours alone,
who shared and dared with me and yet were able
to shun all blame.
But—let be now. Give not a thought more to me.
You never would persuade him.   355
He is not easy to win over.
Be cautious. Keep a sharp look out,
or on your way back you may come to harm.
OCEAN. You counsel others better than yourself,
to judge by what I hear and what I see.   360
But I won't let you turn me off.
I really want to serve you.
And I am proud, yes, proud to say
I know that Zeus will let you go
just as a favor done to me.   365
PROMETHEUS. I thank you for the good will you would show me.
But spare your pains. Your trouble would be wasted.

345. *accounts:* In democratic Athens
the magistrates gave an account of their
stewardship to the people at the end of
their year of office.
352. *who shared and dared:* These
words seem to imply that Ocean took the
side of Prometheus and Zeus in the fight
against the Titans and even helped in
the theft of fire (though this is contradicted by l. 250). We have no other
source for this part of the story.

The effort, if indeed you wish to make it,
could never help me.
Now you are out of harm's way. Stay there.   370
Because I am unfortunate myself
I would not wish that others too should be.
Not so. Even here the lot of Atlas, of my brother,
weighs on me. In the western country
he stands, and on his shoulders is the pillar   375
that holds apart the earth and sky,
a load not easy to be borne.
Pity too filled my heart when once I saw
swift Typhon overpowered.
Child of the Earth was he, who lived   380
in caves in the Cilician land,
a flaming monster with a hundred heads,
who rose up against all the gods.
Death whistled from his fearful jaws.
His eyes flashed glaring fire.   385
I thought he would have wrecked God's sovereignty.
But to him came the sleepless bolt of Zeus,
down from the sky, thunder with breath of flame,
and all his high boasts were struck dumb.
Into his very heart the fire burned.   390
His strength was turned to ashes.
And now he lies a useless thing,
a sprawling body, near the narrow sea-way
by Aetna, underneath the mountain's roots.
High on the peak the god of fire sits,   395
welding the molten iron in his forge,
whence sometimes there will burst
rivers red hot, consuming with fierce jaws
the level fields of Sicily,
lovely with fruits.   400
And that is Typhon's anger boiling up,
his darts of flame none may abide,
of fire-breathing spray,
scorched to a cinder though he is
by Zeus' bolt.   405
But you are no man's fool; you have no need
to learn from me. Keep yourself safe,
as you well know the way.
And I will drain my cup to the last drop,
until Zeus shall abate his insolence of rage.   410

373. *Atlas*: one of the defeated Titans
whose punishment was to bear the weight
of the sky on his shoulders.
379. *Typhon*: another Titan; Cilicia
is in Asia Minor. His punishment is to
be imprisoned under the weight of Aetna,
the Sicilian volcano.
395. *god of fire*: Hephaestus. Ll. 396ff.
refer to one of the frequent eruptions of
Aetna (two are attested for the fifth
century B.C.).

OCEAN. And yet you know the saying,
  when anger reaches fever heat
  wise words are a physician.
PROMETHEUS. Not when the heart is full to bursting.
  Wait for the crisis; then the balm will soothe.   415
OCEAN. But if one were discreet as well as daring—?
  You don't see danger then? Advise me.
PROMETHEUS. I see your trouble wasted,
  and you good-natured to the point of folly.
OCEAN. That's a complaint I don't mind catching.   420
  Let be: I'll choose to seem a fool
  if I can be a loyal friend.
PROMETHEUS. But he will lay to me all that you do.
OCEAN. There you have said what needs must send me home.
PROMETHEUS. Just so. All your lamenting over me   425
  will not have got you then an enemy.
OCEAN. Meaning—the new possessor of the throne?
PROMETHEUS. Be on your guard. See that you do not vex him.
OCEAN. Your case, Prometheus, may well teach me—
PROMETHEUS. Off with you. Go—and keep your present mind.   430
OCEAN. You urge one who is eager to be gone.
  For my four-footed bird is restless
  to skim with wings the level ways of air.
  He'll be well pleased to rest in his home stable.
  [*Exit* OCEAN. *The* CHORUS *now come forward.*]
CHORUS. I mourn for you, Prometheus.   435
  Desolation is upon you.
  My face is wet with weeping.
  Tears fall as waters which run continually.
  The floods overflow me.
  Terrible are the deeds of Zeus.   440
  He rules by laws that are his own.
  High is his spear above the others,
  turned against the gods of old.
  All the land now groans aloud,
  mourning for the honor of the heroes of your race.   445
  Stately were they, honored ever in the days of long ago.
  Holy Asia is hard by.
  Those that dwell there suffer in your trouble, great and sore.
  In the Colchian land maidens live,
  fearless in fight.   450
  Scythia has a battle throng,
  the farthest place of earth is theirs,
  where marsh grass grows around Maeotis lake.
  Arabia's flower is a warrior host;

---

449. *Colchian land:* on the Black Sea   453. *Maeotis lake:* the sea of Azov.
coast of Asia Minor.

high on a cliff their fortress stands,   455
Caucasus towers near;
men fierce as the fire, like the roar of the fire
they shout when the sharp spears clash.
All suffer with you in your trouble, great and sore.
Another Titan too, Earth mourns,   460
bound in shame and iron bonds.
I saw him, Atlas the god.
He bears on his back forever
the cruel strength of the crushing world
and the vault of the sky.   465
He groans beneath them.
The foaming sea-surge roars in answer,
the deep laments,
the black place of death far down in earth is moved exceedingly,
and the pure-flowing river waters grieve for him in his piteous
        pain.   470

PROMETHEUS. Neither in insolence nor yet in stubbornness
have I kept silence.
It is thought that eats my heart,
seeing myself thus outraged.
Who else but I, but I myself,   475
gave these new gods their honors?
Enough of that. I speak to you who know.
Hear rather all that mortals suffered.
Once they were fools. I gave them power to think.
Through me they won their minds.   480
I have no blame for them. All I would tell you
is my good will and my good gifts to them.
Seeing they did not see, nor hearing hear.
Like dreams they led a random life.
They had no houses built to face the sun,   485
of bricks or well-wrought wood,
but like the tiny ant who has her home
in sunless crannies deep down in the earth,
they lived in caverns.
The signs that speak of winter's coming,   490
of flower-faced spring, of summer's heat
with mellowing fruits,
were all unknown to them.
From me they learned the stars that tell the seasons,
their risings and their settings hard to mark.   495
And number, that most excellent device,
I taught to them, and letters joined in words.
I gave to them the mother of all arts,
hard working memory.
I, too, first brought beneath the yoke   500

great beasts to serve the plow,
to toil in mortals' stead.
Up to the chariot I led the horse that loves the rein.
the glory of the rich man in his pride.
None else but I first found   505
the seaman's car, sail-winged, sea-driven.
Such ways to help I showed them, I who have
no wisdom now to help myself.

LEADER. You suffer shame as a physician must
who cannot heal himself.   510
You who cured others now are all astray,
distraught of mind and faint of heart,
and find no medicine to soothe your sickness.

PROMETHEUS. Listen, and you shall find more cause for wonder.
Best of all gifts I gave them was the gift of healing.   515
For if one fell into a malady
there was no drug to cure, no draught, or soothing ointment.
For want of these men wasted to a shadow
until I showed them how to use
the kindly herbs that keep from us disease.   520
The ways of divination I marked out for them,
and they are many; how to know
the waking vision from the idle dream;
to read the sounds hard to discern;
the signs met on the road; the flight of birds,   525
eagles and vultures,
those that bring good or ill luck in their kind,
their way of life, their loves and hates
and council meetings.
And of those inward parts that tell the future,   530
the smoothness and the color and fair shape
that please the gods.
And how to wrap the flesh in fat
and the long thigh bone, for the altar fire
in honor to the gods.   535
So did I lead them on to knowledge
of the dark and riddling art.
The fire omens, too, were dim to them
until I made them see.
Deep within the earth are hidden   540
precious things for men,
brass and iron, gold and silver.

530. *inward parts, . . . future:* methods of foretelling the future from signs found in the entrails of the animals killed for sacrifice.
533-535 *flesh . . . altar fire:* These are the parts of the animal burned on the altar as the gods' portion. It is noteworthy that this earliest account of human progress from savagery to civilization includes religion among the great discoveries.

Would any say he brought these forth to light
until I showed the way?
No one, except to make an idle boast. 545
All arts, all goods, have come to men from me.
LEADER. Do not care now for mortals
but take thought for yourself, O evil-fated. •
I have good hope that still loosed from your bonds
you shall be strong as Zeus. 550
PROMETHEUS. Not thus—not yet—is fate's appointed end,
fate that brings all to pass.
I must be bowed by age-long pain and grief.
So only will my bonds be loosed.
All skill, all cunning, is as foolishness 555
before necessity.
A SEA NYMPH. Who is the helmsman of necessity?
PROMETHEUS. Fate, threefold, Retribution, unforgetting.
ANOTHER. And Zeus is not so strong?
PROMETHEUS. He cannot shun what is foredoomed. 560
ANOTHER. And is he not foredoomed to rule forever?
PROMETHEUS. No word of that. Ask me no further.
ANOTHER. Some solemn secret hides behind your silence.
PROMETHEUS. Think of another theme. It is not yet
the time to speak of this. 565
It must be wrapped in darkness, so alone
I shall some time be saved
from shame and grief and bondage.
CHORUS. Zeus orders all things.
May he never set his might against purpose of mine, 570
like a wrestler in the match.
May I ever be found where feast the holy gods,
and the oxen are slain,
where ceaselessly flows the pathway
of Ocean, my father. 575
May the words of my lips forever
be free from sin.
May this abide with me and not depart
like melting snow.
Long life is sweet when there is hope 580
and hope is confident.
And it is sweet when glad thoughts make the heart grow strong,
and there is joy.
But you, crushed by a thousand griefs,
I look upon you and I shudder. 585
You did not tremble before Zeus.
You gave your worship where you would, to men,
a gift too great for mortals,

a thankless favor.
What help for you there? What defense in those   590
whose life is but from morning unto evening?
Have you not seen?
Their little strength is feebleness,
fast bound in darkness,
like a dream.   595
The will of man shall never break
the harmony of God.
This I have learned beholding your destruction.
Once I spoke different words to you
from those now on my lips.   600
A song flew to me.
I stood beside your bridal bed,
I sang the wedding hymn,
glad in your marriage.
And with fair gifts persuading her,   605
you led to share your couch
Hesione, child of the sea.

     [*Enter* 10.]

10. What land—what creatures here?
This, that I see—
A form storm-beaten,   610
bound to the rock.
Did you do wrong?
Is this your punishment?
You perish here.
Where am I?   615
Speak to a wretched wanderer.
Oh! Oh! he stings again—
the gadfly—oh, miserable!
But you must know he's not a gadfly.
He's Argus, son of Earth, the herdsman,   620
He has a thousand eyes.
I see him. Off! Keep him away!
No, he comes on.
His eyes can see all ways at once.
He's dead but no grave holds him.   625
He comes straight up from hell.
He is the huntsman,

s.d. *Io:* daughter of Inachus, king of Argos. Zeus fell in love with her, but Hera, the wife of Zeus, changed her into a cow. The actor in the play wore a horned mask to represent this shape.

619. *gadfly:* Hera set Argus, a monstrous herdsman with a hundred eyes, to guard Io from Zeus. Zeus sent Hermes to kill Argus, but Hera replaced him with a gadfly which stung Io to distraction. In her delirium she confuses Argus with the gadfly. The realistic basis of this part of the story is the fact that in the hot Greek summer cattle are in fact sometimes driven wild by stinging flies.

and I his wretched quarry.
He drives me all along the long sea strand.
I may not stop for food or drink.   630
He has a shepherd's pipe,
a reed with beeswax joined.
Its sound is like the locust's shrilling,
a drowsy note—that will not let me sleep.
Oh, misery. Oh, misery.   635
Where is it leading me,
my wandering—far wandering.
What ever did I do,
how ever did I sin,
that you have yoked me to calamity,   640
O son of Kronos,
that you madden a wretched woman
driven mad by the gadfly of fear.
Oh, burn me in fire or hide me in earth
or fling me as food to the beasts of the sea.   645
Master, grant me my prayer.
Enough—I have been tried enough—
my wandering—long wandering.
Yet I have found no place
to leave my misery.   650
—I am a girl who speak to you,
but horns are on my head.

PROMETHEUS. Like one caught in an eddy, whirling round and round,
     the gadfly drives you.
     I know you, girl. You are Inachus' daughter.   655
     You made the god's heart hot with love,
     and Hera hates you. She it is
     who drives you on this flight that never stops.

10. How is it that you speak my father's name?
     Who are you? Tell me for my misery.   660
     Who are you, sufferer, that speak the truth
     to one who suffers?
     You know the sickness God has put upon me,
     that stings and maddens me and drives me on
     and wastes my life away.   665
     I am a beast, a starving beast,
     that frenzied runs with clumsy leaps and bounds,
     oh, shame,
     mastered by Hera's malice.
     Who among the wretched   670
     suffer as I do?
     Give me a sign, you there.

Tell to me clearly
the pain still before me.
Is help to be found? 675
A medicine to cure me?
Speak, if you know.

PROMETHEUS. I will and in plain words,
as friend should talk to friend.
—You see Prometheus, who gave mortals fire. 680

IO. You, he who succored the whole race of men?
You, that Prometheus, the daring, the enduring?
Why do you suffer here?

PROMETHEUS. Just now I told the tale—

IO. But will you not still give to me a boon? 685

PROMETHEUS. Ask what you will. I know all you would learn.

IO. Then tell me who has bound you to this rock.

PROMETHEUS. Zeus was the mind that planned.
The hand that did the deed the god of fire.

IO. What was the wrong that you are punished for? 690

PROMETHEUS. No more. Enough of me.

IO. But you will tell the term set to my wandering?
My misery is great. When shall it end?

PROMETHEUS. Here not to know is best.

IO. I ask you not to hide what I must suffer. 695

PROMETHEUS. I do so in no grudging spirit.

IO. Why then delay to tell me all?

PROMETHEUS. Not through ill will. I would not terrify you.

IO. Spare me not more than I would spare myself.

PROMETHEUS. If you constrain me I must speak. Hear then— 700

LEADER. Not yet. Yield to my pleasure too.
For I would hear from her own lips
what is the deadly fate, the sickness
that is upon her. Let her say—then teach her
the trials still to come. 705

PROMETHEUS. If you would please these maidens, Io—
they are your father's sisters,
and when the heart is sorrowful, to speak
to those who will let fall a tear
is time well spent. 710

IO. I do not know how to distrust you.
You shall hear all. And yet—
I am ashamed to speak,
to tell of that god-driven storm

707. *father's sisters*: Inachus, her father, was the river of Argos and, since
the rivers are sons of Ocean, a brother
of the daughters of Ocean who compose
the chorus.

that struck me, changed me, ruined me.   715
How shall I tell you who it was?
How ever to my maiden chamber
visions came by night,
persuading me with gentle words:
"Oh happy, happy girl,   720
Why are you all too long a maid
when you might marry with the highest?
The arrow of desire has pierced Zeus.
For you he is on fire.
With you it is his will to capture love.   725
Would you, child, fly from Zeus' bed?
Go forth to Lerna, to the meadows deep in grass.
There is a sheep-fold there,
an ox-stall, too, that holds your father's oxen—
so shall Zeus find release from his desire."   730
Always, each night, such dreams possessed me.
I was unhappy and at last I dared
to tell my father of these visions.
He sent to Pytho and far Dodona
man after man to ask the oracle   735
what he must say or do to please the gods.
But all brought answers back of shifting meaning,
hard to discern, like golden coins unmarked.
At last a clear word came. It fell upon him
like lightning from the sky. It told him   740
to thrust me from his house and from his country,
to wander to the farthest bounds of earth
like some poor dumb beast set apart
for sacrifice, whom no man will restrain.
And if my father would not, Zeus would send   745
his thunder-bolt with eyes of flame to end
his race, all, everyone.
He could not but obey such words
from the dark oracle. He drove me out.
He shut his doors to me—against his will   750
as against mine. Zeus had him bridled.
He drove him as he would.
Straightway I was distorted, mind and body.
A beast—with horns—look at me—
stung by a fly, who madly leaps and bounds.   755
And so I ran and found myself beside
the waters, sweet to drink, of Kerchneia

727. *Lerna*: a marshy district near Argos.
734. *Pytho*: the oracle of Apollo at Delphi. *Dodona*: an oracle of Zeus in northwest Greece.

and Lerna's well-spring.
Beside me went the herdsman Argus,
the violent of heart, the earth-born,   760
watching my footsteps with his hundred eyes.
But death came to him, swift and unforeseen.
Plagued by a gadfly then, the scourge of God,
I am driven on from land to land.
So for what has been. But what still remains   765
of anguish for me, tell me.
Do not in pity soothe me with false tales.
Words strung together by a lie
are like a foul disease.

LEADER. Oh, shame. Oh, tale of shame.   770
Never, oh never, would I have believed that my ears
would hear words such as these, of strange meaning.
Evil to see and evil to hear,
misery, defilement, and terror.
They pierce my heart with a two-edged sword.   775
A fate like that—
I shudder to look upon Io.

PROMETHEUS. You are too ready with your tears and fears.
Wait for the end.

LEADER. Speak. Tell us, for when one lies sick,   780
to face with clear eyes all the pain to come
is sweet.

PROMETHEUS. What first you asked was granted easily,
to hear from her own lips her trials.
But for the rest, learn now the sufferings   785
she still must suffer, this young creature,
at Hera's hands. Child of Inachus,
keep in your heart my words, so you shall know
where the road ends. First to the sunrise,
over furrows never plowed, where wandering Scythians   790
live in huts of wattles made, raised high
on wheels smooth-rolling. Bows they have,
and they shoot far. Turn from them.
Keep to the shore washed by the moaning sea.

789. *where the road ends*: the long prophecy that follows details the wanderings of Io all the way to Egypt where she is to regain human shape and bear a son to Zeus. Many of the places and people she is to visit are clearly mythical. The general direction of her wandering is to be north and east round the Black Sea, then south, and then west to the sources of the Nile, from which she is to make her way up to the Egyptian delta. The description of movement through far-off lands helps to liberate the spectator's imagination from the immobility of the stage situation, but it has a more important function too. Prometheus is to be released by Heracles, a descendant of Io. The wandering of Io to Egypt, where she will bear a son to Zeus and so found the line which will in the fullness of time produce a hero to liberate Prometheus, gives us a sense of the vastness of time and space which must be covered before Prometheus' deliverance can come.

Off to the left live the Chalybians,   795
workers of iron. There be on your guard.
A rough people they, who like not strangers.
Here rolls a river called the Insolent,
true to its name. You cannot find a ford
until you reach the Caucasus itself,   800
highest of mountains. From beneath its brow
the mighty river rushes. You must cross
the summit, neighbor to the stars.
Then by the southward road, until you reach
the warring Amazons, men-haters, who one day   805
will found a city by the Thermodon,
where Salmydessus thrusts
a fierce jaw out into the sea that sailors hate,
stepmother of ships.
And they will bring you on your way right gladly   810
to the Cimmerian isthmus, by a shallow lake,
Maeotis, at the narrows.
Here you must cross with courage.
And men shall tell forever of your passing.
The strait shall be named for you, Bosporus,   815
Ford of the Cow. There leave the plains of Europe,
and enter Asia, the great Continent.
—Now does he seem to you, this ruler of the gods,
evil, to all, in all things?
A god desired a mortal—drove her forth   820
to wander thus.
A bitter lover you have found, O girl,
for all that I have told you is not yet
the prelude even.
IO. Oh, wretched, wretched.   825
PROMETHEUS. You cry aloud for this? What then
  when you have learned the rest?
LEADER. You will not tell her of more trouble?
PROMETHEUS. A storm-swept sea of grief and ruin.
IO. What gain to me is life? Oh, now to fling myself   830
  down from this rock peak to the earth below,
  and find release there from my trouble.
  Better to die once than to suffer
  through all the days of life.
PROMETHEUS. Hardly would you endure my trial,   835
  whose fate it is not ever to find death
  that ends all pain. For me there is no end
  until Zeus falls from power.
IO. Zeus fall from power?
PROMETHEUS. You would rejoice, I think, to see that happen?   840

io. How could I not, who suffer at his hands?

PROMETHEUS. Know then that it shall surely be.

io. But who will strip the tyrant of his scepter?

PROMETHEUS. He will himself and hs own empty mind.

io. How? Tell me, if it is not wrong to ask.   845

PROMETHEUS. He will make a marriage that will vex him.

io. Goddess or mortal, if it may be spoken?

PROMETHEUS. It may not be. Seek not to know.

io. His wife shall drive him from his throne?

PROMETHEUS. Her child shall be more than his father's match. 850

io. And is there no way of escape for him?

PROMETHEUS. No way indeed, unless my bonds are loosed.

io. But who can loose them against Zeus' will?

PROMETHEUS. A son of yours—so fate decrees.

io. What words are these? A child of mine shall free you?   855

PROMETHEUS. Ten generations first must pass and then three more.

io. Your prophecy grows dim through generations.

PROMETHEUS. So let it be. Seek not to know your trials.

io. Do not hold out a boon and then withdraw it.

PROMETHEUS. One boon of two I will bestow upon you.   860

io. And they are? Speak. Give me the choice.

PROMETHEUS. I give it you: the hardships still before you,
    or his name who shall free me. Choose.

LEADER. Of these give one to her, but give to me
    a grace as well—I am not quite unworthy.   865
    Tell her where she must wander, and to me
    tell who shall free you. It is my heart's desire.

PROMETHEUS. And to your eagerness I yield.
    Hear, Io, first, of your far-driven journey.
    And bear in mind my words, inscribe them   870
    upon the tablets of your heart.
    When you have crossed the stream that bounds
    the continents, turn to the East where flame
    the footsteps of the sun, and pass
    along the sounding sea to Cisthene.   875
    Here on the plain live Phorcys' children, three,
    all maidens, very old, and shaped like swans,
    who have one eye and one tooth to the three.
    No ray of sun looks ever on that country,
    nor ever moon by night. Here too their sisters dwell. 880
    And they are three, the Gorgons, winged,
    with hair of snakes, hateful to mortals.
    Whom no man shall behold and draw again
    the breath of life. They garrison that place.
    And yet another evil sight, the hounds of Zeus   885
    who never bark, griffins with beaks like birds.

The one-eyed Arimaspi too, the riders,
who live beside a stream that flows with gold,
a way of wealth. From all these turn aside.
Far off there is a land where black men live, 890
close to the sources of the sun, whence springs
a sun-scorched river. When you reach it,
go with all care along the banks up to
the great descent, where from the mountains
the holy Nile pours forth its waters 895
pleasant to drink from. It will be your guide
to the Nile land, the Delta. A long exile
is fated for you and your children here.
If what I speak seems dark and hard to know,
ask me again and learn all clearly. 900
For I have time to spare and more
than I could wish.

LEADER. If in your story of her fatal journey
there is yet somewhat left to tell her,
speak now. If not, give then to us 905
the grace we asked. You will remember.

PROMETHEUS. The whole term of her roaming has been told.
But I will show she has not heard in vain,
and tell her what she suffered coming hither,
in proof my words are true. 910
A moving multitude of sorrows were there,
too many to recount, but at the end
you came to where the levels of Molossa
surround the lofty ridge of Dodona,
seat of God's oracle. 915
A wonder past belief is there, oak trees that speak.
They spoke, not darkly but in shining words,
calling you Zeus' glorious spouse.
The frenzy seized you then. You fled
along the sea-road washed by the great inlet, 920
named for God's mother. Up and down you wandered,
storm-tossed. And in the time to come that sea
shall have its name from you, Ionian,
that men shall not forget your journey.
This is my proof to you my mind can see 925
farther than meets the eye.
From here the tale I tell is for you all,
and of the future, leaving now the past.

---

914. *Dodona:* in northwest Greece; the oak trees were supposed to convey the voice and will of Zeus.
921. *God's mother:* Rhea, the mother of Zeus. By the gulf or inlet of Rhea.
Aeschylus apparently means the Adriatic Sea.
923. *Ionian:* the sea between western Greece and Sicily.

There is a city, Canobus, at the land's end,
where the Nile empties, on new river soil. 930
There Zeus at last shall make you sane again,
stroking you with a hand you will not fear.
And from this touch alone you will conceive
and bear a son, a swarthy man,
whose harvest shall be reaped on many fields, 935
all that are washed by the wide-watered Nile.
In the fifth generation from him, fifty sisters
will fly from marriage with their near of kin,
who, hawks in close pursuit of doves, a-quiver
with passionate desire, shall find that death 940
waits for the hunters on the wedding night.
God will refuse to them the virgin bodies.
Argos will be the maidens' refuge, to their suitors
a slaughter dealt by women's hands,
bold in the watches of the night. 945
The wife shall kill her husband,
dipping her two-edged sword in blood.
O Cyprian goddess, thus may you come to my foes.
One girl, bound by love's spell, will change
her purpose, and she will not kill 950
the man she lay beside, but choose the name
of coward rather than be stained with blood.
In Argos she will bear a kingly child—
a story overlong if all were told.
Know this, that from that seed will spring 955
one glorious with the bow, bold-hearted,
and he shall set me free.
This is the oracle my mother told me,
Justice, who is of old, Earth's daughter.
But how and where would be too long a tale, 960
nor would you profit.

. 10. Oh, misery. Oh, misery.
    A frenzy tears me.
    Madness strikes my mind.
    I burn. A frantic sting— 965

934. *a son*: born from the touch of Zeus's hand stroking Io, he was called Epaphus (which means "touch of the hand"). The story referred to in the lines which follow was familiar to the audience and was in fact the subject of another play of Aeschylus, the *Suppliant Maidens*. The descendants of Epaphus in the fourth generation were Aegyptus, who had fifty sons, and Danaus, who had fifty daughters. The sons of Aegyptus demanded the daughters of Danaus in marriage but were refused. When they threatened force, the daughters and their father fled to Argos, the home of their ancestor Io and claimed protection. It was granted, but the sons of Aegyptus, who had followed them, defeated the Argives and married the girls. They agreed among themselves that each one on her marriage night would murder her husband. All of them did, except one, Hypermnestra, and from this daughter's line, Heracles was eventually born.

948. *Cyprian goddess:* Aphrodite, the goddess of love.

an arrow never forged with fire.
My heart is beating at its walls in terror.
My eyes are whirling wheels.
Away. Away. A raging wind of fury
sweeps through me.   970
My tongue has lost its power.
My words are like a turbid stream,
wild waves that dash against a surging sea,
the black sea of madness.   [*Exit* 10.]

CHORUS. Wise, wise was he,   975
who first weighed this in thought
and gave it utterance:
Marriage within one's own degree is best,
not with one whom wealth has spoiled,
nor yet with one made arrogant by birth.   980
Such as these he must not seek
who lives upon the labor of his hands.
Fate, dread deity,
may you never, oh, never behold me
sharing the bed of Zeus.   985
May none of the dwellers in heaven
draw near to me ever.
Terrors take hold of me
seeing her maidenhood
turning from love of man,   990
torn by Hera's hate,
driven in misery.
For me, I would not shun marriage nor fear it,
so it were with my equal.
But the love of the greater gods,   995
from whose eyes none can hide,
may that never be mine.
To war with a god-lover is not war,
it is despair.
For what could I do,   1000
or where could I fly
from the cunning of Zeus?

PROMETHEUS. In very truth shall Zeus, for all his stubborn pride,
be humbled, such a marriage he will make
to cast him down from throne and power.   1005
And he shall be no more remembered.
The curse his father put on him
shall be fulfilled.
The curse that he cursed him with as he fell
from his age-long throne.   1010

The way from such trouble no one of the gods
can show him save I.
These things I know and how they shall come to pass.
So let him sit enthroned in confidence,
trust to his crashing thunder high in air,   1015
shake in his hands his fire-breathing dart.
Surely these shall be no defense,
but he will fall, in shame unbearable.
Even now he makes ready against himself
one who shall wrestle with him and prevail,   1020
a wonder of wonders, who will find
a flame that is swifter than lightning,
a crash to silence the thunder,
who will break into pieces the sea-god's spear,
the bane of the ocean that shakes the earth.   1025
Before this evil Zeus shall be bowed down.
He will learn how far apart are a king and a slave.
LEADER. These words of menace on your tongue
speak surely only your desire.
PROMETHEUS. They speak that which shall surely be—   1030
and also my desire.
LEADER. And we must look to see Zeus mastered?
PROMETHEUS. Yes, and beneath a yoke more cruel than this I bear.
LEADER. You have no fear to utter words like these?
PROMETHEUS. I am immortal—and I have no fear.   1035
ANOTHER SEA NYMPH. But agony still worse he might inflict—
PROMETHEUS. So let him do. All that must come I know.
ANOTHER. The wise bow to the inescapable.
PROMETHEUS. Be wise then. Worship power.
 Cringe before each who wields it.   1040
To me Zeus counts as less than nothing.
Let him work his will, show forth his power
for his brief day, his little moment
of lording it in heaven.
—But see. There comes a courier from Zeus,   1045
a lackey in his new lord's livery.
Some curious news is surely on his lips.
  [*Enter* HERMES.]
HERMES. You trickster there, you biter bitten,
sinner against the gods, man-lover, thief of fire,
my message is to you.   1050
The great father gives you here his orders:
Reveal this marriage that you boast of,
by which he shall be hurled from power.

1024. *sea-god*: Poseidon, the brother of Zeus.

And, mark you, not in riddles, each fact clearly,
—Don't make me take a double journey, Prometheus. 1055
    You can see Zeus isn't going to be made kinder
    by this sort of thing.
PROMETHEUS. Big words and insolent. They well become you,
  O lackey of the gods.
  Young—young—your thrones just won, 1060
you think you live in citadels grief cannot reach.
Two dynasties I have seen fall from heaven,
  and I shall see the third fall fastest,
  most shamefully of all.
Is it your thought to see me tremble 1065
and crouch before your upstart gods?
Not so—not such a one am I.
Make your way back. You will not learn from me.
HERMES. Ah, so? Still stubborn? Yet this willfulness
  has anchored you fast in these troubled waters. 1070
PROMETHEUS. And yet I would not change my lot
  with yours, O lackey.
HERMES. Better no doubt to be slave to a rock
  than be the Father's trusted herald. 1074
PROMETHEUS. I must be insolent when I must speak to insolence.
HERMES. You are proud, it seems, of what has come to you.
PROMETHEUS. I proud? May such pride be
  the portion of my foes—I count you of them.
HERMES. You blame me also for your sufferings?
PROMETHEUS. In one word, all gods are my enemies. 1080
  They had good from me. They return me evil.
HERMES. I heard you were quite mad.
PROMETHEUS. Yes, I am mad, if to abhor such foes is madness.
HERMES. You would be insufferable, Prometheus, if you were not
  so wretched.
PROMETHEUS. Alas! 1085
HERMES. Alas? That is a word Zeus does not understand.
PROMETHEUS. Time shall teach it him, gray time,
  that teaches all things.
HERMES. It has not taught you wisdom yet.
PROMETHEUS. No, or I had not wrangled with a slave. 1090
HERMES. It seems that you will tell the Father nothing.
PROMETHEUS. Paying the debt of kindness that I owe him?
HERMES. You mock at me as though I were a child.
PROMETHEUS. A child you are or what else has less sense
  if you expect to learn from me. 1095
  There is no torture and no trick of skill,
there is no force, which can compel my speech,
until Zeus wills to loose these deadly bonds.

So let him hurl his blazing bolt,
and with the white wings of the snow, 1100
with thunder and with earthquake,
confound the reeling world.
None of all this will bend my will
to tell him at whose hands he needs must fall.
HERMES. I urge you, pause and think if this will help you. 1105
PROMETHEUS. I thought long since of all. I planned for all.
HERMES. Submit, you fool. Submit. In agony learn wisdom.
PROMETHEUS. Go and persuade the sea wave not to break.
You will persuade me no more easily.
I am no frightened woman, terrified 1110
at Zeus' purpose. Do you think to see me
ape women's ways, stretch out my hands
to him I hate, and pray him for release?
A world apart am I from prayer for pity.
HERMES. Then all I say is said in vain. 1115
Nothing will move you, no entreaty
soften your heart.
Like a young colt new-bridled,
you have the bit between your teeth,
and rear and fight against the rein. 1120
But all this vehemence is feeble bombast.
A fool, bankrupt of all but obstinacy,
is the poorest thing on earth.
Oh, if you will not hear me, yet consider
the storm that threatens you from which 1125
you cannot fly, a great third wave of evil.
Thunder and flame of lightning will rend
this jagged peak. You shall be buried deep,
held by a splintered rock.
After long length of time you will return 1130
to see the light, but Zeus' winged hound,
an eagle red with blood,
shall come a guest unbidden to your banquet.
All day long he will tear to rags your body,
great rents within the flesh, 1135
feasting in fury on the blackened liver.
Look for no ending to this agony
until a god will freely suffer for you,
will take on him your pain, and in your stead
descend to where the sun is turned to darkness, 1140
the black depths of death.

1138. *freely suffer*: Hermes of course thinks of this as an impossible set of circumstances. But the centaur Chiron, accidentally wounded by one of Hera- cles' arrows and unable to find release from his pain because he was immortal, accepted death as a substitute for Pro- metheus.

Take thought: this is no empty boast
but utter truth. Zeus does not lie.
Each word shall be fulfilled.
Pause and consider. Never think   1145
self-will is better than wise counsel.
LEADER. To us the words he speaks are not amiss.
He bids you let your self-will go and seek
good counsel. Yield.
For to the wise a failure is disgrace.   1150
PROMETHEUS. These tidings that the fellow shouts at me
were known to me long since.
A foe to suffer at the hands of foes
is nothing shameful.
Then let the twisting flame of forked fire   1155
be hurled upon me. Let the very air
be rent by thunder-crash.
Savage winds convulse the sky,
hurricanes shake the earth from its foundations,
the waves of the sea rise up and drown the stars,   1160
and let me be swept down to hell,
caught in the cruel whirlpool of Necessity.
He cannot kill me.
HERMES. Why, these are ravings you may hear from madmen.
His case is clear. Frenzy can go no further.   1165
You maids who pity him, depart, be swift.
The thunder peals and it is merciless.
Would you too be struck down?
LEADER. Speak other words, another counsel,
if you would win me to obey.   1170
Now, in this place, to urge
that I should be a coward is intolerable.
I choose with him to suffer what must be.
Not to stand by a friend—there is no evil
I count more hateful.   1175
I spit it from my mouth.
HERMES. Remember well I warned you,
when you are swept away in utter ruin.
Blame then yourselves, not fate, nor ever say
that Zeus delivered you   1180
to a hurt you had not thought to see.
With open eyes,
not suddenly, not secretly,
into the net of utter ruin
whence there is no escape,   1185
you fall by your own folly.   [*Exit* HERMES.]

PROMETHEUS. An end to words. Deeds now.
The world is shaken.
The deep and secret way of thunder
is rent apart.   1190
Fiery wreaths of lightning flash.
Whirlwinds toss the swirling dust.
The blasts of all the winds are battling in the air,
and sky and sea are one.
On me the tempest falls.   1195
It does not make me tremble.
O holy Mother Earth, O air and sun,
behold me. I am wronged.

1198. *I am wronged*: We know that the play had a sequel, *Prometheus Unbound;* the title of a third Prometheus play is mentioned, and it is possible (though disputed) that the *Prometheus Bound* is part of a trilogy. Of the second play only fragments remain, but they are interesting. The chorus of the play consisted of Titans, the older generation of gods overthrown by Zeus, the brothers of Prometheus. They have been released from captivity by Zeus. Prometheus is tortured by the eagle mentioned by Hermes in his final threats but will not surrender and reveal the secret of the fatal marriage. Heracles arrives, and in a long scene which resembles the Io episode in our play, Prometheus tells Heracles where his wanderings will take him. Heracles shoots the eagle which has been feeding on Prometheus' liver, and this seems to be the occasion of Prometheus' reconciliation wih Zeus. We have the line which he speaks: "this dearest son of the father my enemy."

THUCYDIDES

History of the Peloponnesian War*

*[Athenian Democracy—The Athenians from the
Enemy's Point of View]†*

[This is an extract from a speech made by the representatives of Corinth, a city bitterly hostile to Athens, at a congress of Spartan allies meeting at Sparta in 432 B.C. to discuss the question of peace or war with Athens. The Spartans were hesitant, and in this speech the Corinthian ambassadors urge them to take a firm stand.]

You have never considered what manner of men are these Athenians with whom you will have to fight, and how utterly unlike yourselves. They are revolutionary, equally quick in the conception and in the execution of every new plan; while you are conservative —careful only to keep what you have, originating nothing, and not acting even when action is most necessary. They are bold beyond their strength; they run risks which prudence would condemn; and in the midst of misfortune they are full of hope. Whereas it is your

* Translated by Benjamin Jowett.   † From Book I, Chapter 70.

nature, though strong, to act feebly; when your plans are most prudent, to distrust them; and when calamities come upon you, to think that you will never be delivered from them. They are impetuous, and you are dilatory; they are always abroad, and you are always at home. For they hope to gain something by leaving their homes; but you are afraid that any new enterprise may imperil what you have already. When conquerors, they pursue their victory to the utmost; when defeated, they fall back the least. Their bodies they devote to their country as though they belonged to other men; their true self is their mind, which is most truly their own when employed in her service. When they do not carry out an intention which they have formed, they seem to have sustained a personal bereavement; when an enterprise succeeds, they have gained a mere instalment of what is to come; but if they fail, they at once conceive new hopes and so fill up the void. With them alone to hope is to have, for they lose not a moment in the execution of an idea. This is the life-long task, full of danger and toil, which they are always imposing upon themselves. None enjoy their good things less, because they are always seeking for more. To do their duty is their only holiday, and they deem the quiet of inaction to be as disagreeable as the most tiresome business. If a man should say of them, in a word, that they were born neither to have peace themselves nor to allow peace to other men, he would simply speak the truth.

[Athenian Democracy—The Athenians, a Self-Portrait]*

During the same winter,[1] in accordance with an old national custom, the funeral of those who first fell in this war was celebrated by the Athenians at the public charge. The ceremony is as follows: Three days before the celebration they erect a tent in which the bones of the dead are laid out, and every one brings to his own dead any offering which he pleases. At the time of the funeral the bones are placed in chests of cypress wood, which are conveyed on hearses; there is one chest for each tribe.[2] They also carry a single empty litter decked with a pall for all whose bodies are missing, and cannot be recovered after the battle. The procession is accompanied by any one who chooses, whether citizen or stranger, and the female relatives of the deceased are present at the place of interment and make lamentation. The public sepulchre is situated in the most beautiful spot outside the walls; there they always bury those who fall in war; only after the battle of Marathon[3] the dead, in recognition of their pre-eminent valor, were interred on the field. When the remains

---

* From Book II, Chapters 34–46.
1. 431–430 B.C.
2. The Athenian citizen body was organized in ten tribes.

3. on the coast of Attica. In this battle (490 B.C.) the Athenians, alone except for a small contingent from the neighboring city of Plataea, defeated a Persian expeditionary force.

have been laid in the earth, some man of known ability and high reputation, chosen by the city, delivers a suitable oration over them; after which the people depart. Such is the manner of interment; and the ceremony was repeated from time to time throughout the war. Over those who were the first buried Pericles[4] was chosen to speak. At the fitting moment he advanced from the sepulchre to a lofty stage, which had been erected in order that he might be heard as far as possible by the multitude, and spoke as follows:

"Most of those who have spoken here before me have commended the lawgiver who added this oration to our other funeral customs; it seemed to them a worthy thing that such an honor should be given at their burial to the dead who have fallen on the field of battle. But I should have preferred that, when men's deeds have been brave, they should be honored in deed only, and with such an honor as this public funeral, which you are now witnessing. Then the reputation of many would not have been imperilled on the eloquence or want of eloquence of one, and their virtues believed or not as he spoke well or ill. For it is difficult to say neither too little nor too much; and even moderation is apt not to give the impression of truthfulness. The friend of the dead who knows the facts is likely to think that the words of the speaker fall short of his knowledge and of his wishes; another who is not so well informed, when he hears of anything which surpasses his own powers, will be envious and will suspect exaggeration. Mankind are tolerant of the praises of others so long as each hearer thinks that he can do as well or nearly as well himself, but, when the speaker rises above him, jealousy is aroused and he begins to be incredulous. However, since our ancestors have set the seal of their approval upon the practice, I must obey, and to the utmost of my power shall endeavor to satisfy the wishes and beliefs of all who hear me.

"I will speak first of our ancestors, for it is right and becoming that now, when we are lamenting the dead, a tribute should be paid to their memory. There has never been a time when they did not inhabit this land,[5] which by their valor they have handed down from generation to generation, and we have received from them a free state. But if they were worthy of praise, still more were our fathers, who added to their inheritance, and after many a struggle transmitted to us their sons this great empire.[6] And we ourselves

4. the statesman who guided the policies of the Athenian democracy during its greatest years. He died in the next year, 430 B.C.
5. The Athenians boasted uninterrupted descent from the first inhabitants of the land.
6. After the defeat of the Persian invaders in 479 B.C. the Athenians organized a league of the Greek cities on the islands and the Asiatic mainland for defense against any renewed Persian attack; as the years went by this league was transformed from a league dominated by the Athenians into an empire which they ruled.

assembled here to-day, who are still most of us in the vigor of life, have chiefly done the work of improvement, and have richly endowed our city with all things, so that she is sufficient for herself both in peace and war. Of the military exploits by which our various possessions were acquired, or of the energy with which we or our fathers drove back the tide of war, Hellenic or Barbarian,[7] I will not speak; for the tale would be long and is familiar to you. But before I praise the dead, I should like to point out by what principles of action we rose to power, and under what institutions and through what manner of life our empire became great. For I conceive that such thoughts are not unsuited to the occasion,[8] and that this numerous assembly of citizens and strangers may profitably listen to them.

"Our form of government does not enter into rivalry with the institutions of others. We do not copy our neighbors, but are an example to them. It is true that we are called a democracy, for the administration is in the hands of the many and not of the few.[9] But while the law secures equal justice to all alike in their private disputes, the claim of excellence is also recognized; and when a citizen is in any way distinguished, he is preferred to the public service, not as a matter of privilege, but as the reward of merit. Neither is poverty a bar, but a man may benefit his country whatever be the obscurity of his condition. There is no exclusiveness in our public life, and in our private intercourse we are not suspicious of one another, nor angry with our neighbor if he does what he likes; we do not put on sour looks at him which, though harmless, are not pleasant. While we are thus unconstrained in our private intercourse, a spirit of reverence pervades our public acts; we are prevented from doing wrong by respect for authority and for the laws, having an especial regard to those which are ordained for the protection of the injured as well as to those unwritten laws which bring upon the transgressor of them the reprobation of the general sentiment.

"And we have not forgotten to provide for our weary spirits many relaxations from toil; we have regular games and sacrifices throughout the year; at home the style of our life is refined; and the delight which we daily feel in all these things helps to banish melancholy.

7. *Hellenic or Barbarian:* Greek or Persian.
8. Thucydides tells his readers (Book I, Chapter 22) how he composed this and other speeches: "As to the speeches . . . it was hard for me, and for others who reported them to me, to recollect the exact words. I have therefore put into the mouth of each speaker the sentiments proper to the occasion, expressed as I thought he would be likely to express them, while at the same time I endeavoured, as nearly as I could, to give the general purport of what was actually said."
9. The word "democracy" is composed of the two Greek words *demos* and *kratos,* which mean "people" and "power" respectively.

Because of the greatness of our city the fruits of the whole earth flow in upon us; so that we enjoy the goods of other countries as freely as of our own.

"Then, again, our military training is in many respects superior to that of our adversaries. Our city is thrown open to the world, and we never expel a foreigner or prevent him from seeing or learning anything of which the secret if revealed to an enemy might profit him.[10] We rely not upon management or trickery, but upon our own hearts and hands. And in the matter of education, whereas they from early youth are always undergoing laborious exercises which are to make them brave, we live at ease, and yet are equally ready to face the perils which they face. And here is the proof. The Lacedaemonians[11] come into Attica not by themselves, but with their whole confederacy following; we go alone into a neighbor's country; and although our opponents are fighting for their homes and we on a foreign soil, we have seldom any difficulty in overcoming them. Our enemies have never yet felt our united strength; the care of a navy divides our attention, and on land we are obliged to send our own citizens everywhere. But they, if they meet and defeat a part of our army, are as proud as if they had routed us all, and when defeated they pretend to have been vanquished by us all.

"If then we prefer to meet danger with a light heart but without laborious training, and with a courage which is gained by habit and not enforced by law, are we not greatly the gainers? Since we do not anticipate the pain, although, when the hour comes, we can be as brave as those who never allow themselves to rest; and thus too our city is equally admirable in peace and in war. For we are lovers of the beautiful, yet simple in our tastes, and we cultivate the mind without loss of manliness. Wealth we employ, not for talk and ostentation, but when there is a real use for it. To avow poverty with us is no disgrace: the true disgrace is in doing nothing to avoid it. An Athenian citizen does not neglect the state because he takes care of his own household; and even those of us who are engaged in business have a very fair idea of politics. We alone regard a man who takes no interest in public affairs, not as a harmless, but as a useless character; and if few of us are originators, we are all sound judges of a policy. The great impediment to action is, in our opinion, not discussion, but the want of that knowledge which is gained by discussion preparatory to action. For we have a peculiar power of thinking before we act and of acting too, whereas other men are courageous from ignorance but hesitate upon reflection. And they are surely to be esteemed the bravest spirits who, having the clearest

10. in contrast to Sparta, where foreigners were admitted only on state business and then kept under surveillance. The next sentence contrasts the Athenian system of education with the Spartan.

11. Spartans.

sense both of the pains and pleasures of life, do not on that account shrink from danger. In doing good, again, we are unlike others; we make our friends by conferring, not by receiving favors. Now he who confers a favor is the firmer friend, because he would fain by kindness keep alive the memory of an obligation; but the recipient is colder in his feelings, because he knows that in requiting another's generosity he will not be winning gratitude, but only paying a debt. We alone do good to our neighbors not upon a calculation of interest, but in the confidence of freedom and in a frank and fearless spirit. To sum up: I say that Athens is the school of Hellas, and that the individual Athenian in his own person seems to have the power of adapting himself to the most varied forms of action with the utmost versatility and grace. This is no passing and idle word, but truth and fact; and the assertion is verified by the position to which these qualities have raised the state. For in the hour of trial Athens alone among her contemporaries is superior to the report of her. No enemy who comes against her is indignant at the reverses which he sustains at the hands of such a city; no subject complains that his masters are unworthy of him. And we shall assuredly not be without witnesses; there are mighty monuments of our power which will make us the wonder of this and of succeeding ages;[12] we shall not need the praises of Homer or of any other panegyrist whose poetry may please for the moment, although his representation of the facts will not bear the light of day. For we have compelled every land and every sea to open a path for our valor, and have everywhere planted eternal memorials of our friendship and of our enmity. Such is the city for whose sake these men nobly fought and died; they could not bear the thought that she might be taken from them; and every one of us who survive should gladly toil on her behalf.

"I have dwelt upon the greatness of Athens because I want to show you that we are contending for a higher prize than those who enjoy none of these privileges, and to establish by manifest proof the merit of these men whom I am now commemorating. Their loftiest praise has been already spoken. For in magnifying the city I have magnified them, and men like them whose virtues made her glorious. And of how few Hellenes can it be said as of them, that their deeds when weighed in the balance have been found equal to their fame! Methinks that a death such as theirs has been given the true measure of a man's worth; it may be the first revelation of his virtues, but is at any rate their final seal. For even those who come short in other ways may justly plead the valor with which they have fought for their country; they have blotted out the evil with the

12. The ruins of the fifth-century buildings on the Acropolis of Athens are still the wonder of the world.

good, and have benefited the state more by their public services than they have injured her by their private actions. None of these men were enervated by wealth or hesitated to resign the pleasures of life; none of them put off the evil day in the hope, natural to poverty, that a man, though poor, may one day become rich. But, deeming that the punishment of their enemies was sweeter than any of these things, and that they could fall in no nobler cause, they determined at the hazard of their lives to be honorably avenged, and to leave the rest. They resigned to hope their unknown chance of happiness; but in the face of death they resolved to rely upon themselves alone. And when the moment came they were minded to resist and suffer, rather than to fly and save their lives; they ran away from the word of dishonor, but on the battle-field their feet stood fast, and in an instant, at the height of their fortune, they passed away from the scene, not of their fear, but of their glory.

"Such was the end of these men; they were worthy of Athens, and the living need not desire to have a more heroic spirit, although they may pray for a less fatal issue. The value of such a spirit is not to be expressed in words. Any one can discourse to you for ever about the advantages of a brave defence which you know already. But instead of listening to him I would have you day by day fix your eyes upon the greatness of Athens, until you become filled with the love of her; and when you are impressed by the spectacle of her glory, reflect that this empire has been acquired by men who knew their duty and had the courage to do it, who in the hour of conflict had the fear of dishonor always present to them, and who, if ever they failed in an enterprise, would not allow their virtues to be lost to their country, but freely gave their lives to her as the fairest offering which they could present at her feast. The sacrifice which they collectively made was individually repaid to them; for they received again each one for himself a praise which grows not old, and the noblest of all sepulchres—I speak not of that in which their remains are laid, but of that in which their glory survives, and is proclaimed always and on every fitting occasion both in word and deed. For the whole earth is the sepulchre of famous men; not only are they commemorated by columns and inscriptions in their own country, but in foreign lands there dwells also an unwritten memorial of them, graven not on stone but in the hearts of men. Make them your examples, and, esteeming courage to be freedom and freedom to be happiness, do not weigh too nicely the perils of war. The unfortunate who has no hope of a change for the better has less reason to throw away his life than the prosperous who, if he survive, is always liable to a change for the worse, and to whom any accidental fall makes the most serious difference. To a man of spirit, cowardice and disaster coming together are far more bitter than death, striking him unperceived at a time when he is full of courage and animated by the general hope.

"Wherefore I do not now commiserate the parents of the dead who stand here; I would rather comfort them. You know that your life has been passed amid manifold vicissitudes; and that they may be deemed fortunate who have gained most honor, whether an honorable death like theirs, or an honorable sorrow like yours, and whose days have been so ordered that the term of their happiness is likewise the term of their life. I know how hard it is to make you feel this, when the good fortune of others will too often remind you of the gladness which once lightened your hearts. And sorrow is felt at the want of those blessings, not which a man never knew, but which were a part of his life before they were taken from him. Some of you are of an age at which they may hope to have other children, and they ought to bear their sorrow better; not only will the children who may hereafter be born make them forget their own lost ones, but the city will be doubly a gainer. She will not be left desolate, and she will be safer. For a man's counsel cannot have equal weight or worth, when he alone has no children to risk in the general danger. To those of you who have passed their prime, I say: 'Congratulate yourselves that you have been happy during the greater part of your days; remember that your life of sorrow will not last long, and be comforted by the glory of those who are gone. For the love of honor alone is ever young, and not riches, as some say, but honor is the delight of men when they are old and useless.'

"To you who are the sons and brothers of the departed, I see that the struggle to emulate them will be an arduous one. For all men praise the dead, and, however pre-eminent your virtue may be, hardly will you be thought, I do not say to equal, but even to approach them. The living have their rivals and detractors, but when a man is out of the way, the honor and good-will which he receives is unalloyed. And, if I am to speak of womanly virtues to those of you who will henceforth be widows, let me sum them up in one short admonition: To a woman not to show more weakness than is natural to her sex is a great glory, and not to be talked about for good or for evil among men.

"I have paid the required tribute, in obedience to the law, making use of such fitting words as I had. The tribute of deeds has been paid in part; for the dead have been honorably interred, and it remains only that their children should be maintained at the public charge until they are grown up; this is the solid prize with which, as with a garland, Athens crowns her sons living and dead, after a struggle like theirs. For where the rewards of virtue are greatest, there the noblest citizens are enlisted in the service of the state. And now, when you have duly lamented, every one of his own dead, you may depart."

SOPHOCLES
(495?–406 B.C.)
Oedipus Tyrannus*

Characters

OEDIPUS, RULER OF THEBES	MESSENGER 2
JOCASTA, WIFE OF OEDIPUS	A SHEPHERD
CREON, BROTHER OF JOCASTA	AN ATTENDANT
TEIRESIAS, A BLIND PROPHET	ANTIGONE ⎱ DAUGHTERS OF OEDIPUS
A PRIEST	ISMENE ⎰ AND JOCASTA
MESSENGER 1	CHORUS OF THEBAN ELDERS

SCENE.—*In front of the doors of the palace of Oedipus at Thebes. A crowd of citizens sits at an altar in supplication. Among them is an old man, the* PRIEST *of Zeus.*
[*Enter, through the doors,* OEDIPUS.]

OEDIPUS: What is it, children, sons of the ancient house of Cadmus?[1] Why do you sit as suppliants crowned with laurel branches? What is the meaning of the incense which fills the city? The pleas to end pain? The cries of sorrow? I chose not to hear it from my messengers, but came myself—I came, Oedipus, Oedipus, whose name is known to all. You, old one—age gives you the right to speak for all of them—you tell me why they sit before my altar. Has something frightened you? What brings you here? Some need? Some want? I'll help you all I can. I would be cruel did I not greet you with compassion when you are gathered here before me.

PRIEST: My Lord and King, we represent the young and old; some are priests and some the best of Theban youth. And I—I am a priest of Zeus. There are many more who carry laurel boughs[2] like these—in the market-places, at the twin altars of Pallas,[3] by the sacred ashes of Ismenus' oracle.[4] You see yourself how torn our city is, how she craves relief from the waves of death which now crash over her. Death is everywhere—in the harvests of the land, in the flocks that roam the pastures, in the unborn children

---

* Translated by Luci Berkowitz and Theodore F. Brunner. Copyright © 1970 by W. W. Norton & Company, Inc. The date of the play's first production is unknown but is usually taken to be 430 B.C. or a few years later.

1. *Cadmus:* founder of Thebes and its first king.

2. *laurel boughs:* the suppliant carried a branch, which he laid on the altar and left there until his request was granted. At the end of this scene, Oedipus tells the suppliants to take their branches away.

3. *Pallas:* Athena.

4. *Ismenus' oracle:* in a temple of Apollo near the river Ismenus, where burnt offerings were made and prophecies given.

of our mothers' wombs. A fiery plague is ravaging the city, festering, spreading its pestilence, wasting the house of Cadmus, filling the house of Hades with screams of pain and of fear. This is the reason why we come to you, these children and I. No, we do not think you a god. But we deem you a mortal set apart to face life's common issues and the trials which the gods dispense to men. It was you who once before came to Thebes and freed us from the spell that hypnotized our lives.[5] You did this, and yet you knew no more than we—less even. You had no help from us. God aided you. Yes, you restored our life. And now a second time, great Oedipus, we turn to you for help. Find some relief for us, whether with god or man to guide your way. You helped us then. Yes. And we believe that you will help us now. O Lord, revive our city; restore her life. Think of your fame, your own repute. The people know you saved us from our past despair. Let no one say you raised us up to let us fall. Save us and keep us safe. You found good omens once to aid you and brought us fortune then. Find them again. If you will rule this land as king and lord, rule over men and not a wall encircling emptiness. No city wall, no ship can justify its claim to strength if it is stripped of men who give it life.

OEDIPUS: O my children, I know well the pain you suffer and understand what brings you here. You suffer—and yet not one among you suffers more than I. Each of you grieves for himself alone, while my heart must bear the strain of sorrow for all—myself and you and all our city's people. No, I am not blind to it. I have wept and in my weeping set my thoughts on countless paths, searching for an answer. I have sent my own wife's brother Creon, son of Menoeceus, to Apollo's Pythian shrine[6] to learn what I might say or do to ease our city's suffering. I am concerned that he is not yet here—he left many days ago. But this promise: whenever he returns, whatever news he brings, whatever course the god reveals—*that* is the course that I shall take.

PRIEST: Well spoken. Look! They are giving signs that Creon is returning.

OEDIPUS: O God! If only he brings news as welcome as his smiling face.

PRIEST: I think he does. His head is crowned with laurel leaves.

OEDIPUS: We shall know soon enough. There. My Lord Creon, what word do you bring from the god?

[*Enter* CREON.]

CREON: Good news. I tell you this: if all goes well, our troubles will be past.

OEDIPUS: But what was the oracle? Right now I'm swaying between hope and fear.

---

5. *spell:* the Sphinx, a winged female monster which terrorized the city of Thebes until her riddle was finally answered by Oedipus. The riddle was: "What is it that walks on four feet and two feet and three feet and has only one voice; when it walks on most feet, it is weakest?" Oedipus' answer was Man. (He has four feet as a child crawling on all fours, and three feet in old age when he walks with the aid of a stick.)

6. *Pythian shrine:* the oracle of Apollo at Delphi.

CREON: If you want to hear it in the presence of these people, I shall tell you. If not, let's go inside.

OEDIPUS: Say it before all of us. I sorrow more for them than for myself.

CREON: Then I shall tell you exactly what the god Apollo answered. These are his words: Pollution. A hidden sore is festering in our land. We are to stop its growth before it is too late.

OEDIPUS: Pollution? How are we to save ourselves?

CREON: Blood for blood. To save ourselves we are to banish a man or pay for blood with blood. It is a murder which has led to this despair.

OEDIPUS: Murder? Whose? Did the god say whose . . . ?

CREON: My Lord, before you came to rule our city, we had a king. His name was Laius . . .

OEDIPUS: I know, although I never saw him.

CREON: He was murdered. And the god's command is clear: we must find the assassin and destroy him.

OEDIPUS: But where? Where is he to be found? How can we find the traces of a crime committed long ago?

CREON: He lives among us. If we seek, we will find; what we do not seek cannot be found.

OEDIPUS: Where was it that Laius met his death? At home? The country? In some foreign land?

CREON: One day he left and told us he would go to Delphi. That was the last we saw of him.

OEDIPUS: And there was no one who could tell what happened? No one who traveled with him? Did no one see? Is there no evidence?

CREON: All perished. All—except one who ran in panic from the scene and could not tell us anything for certain, except . . .

OEDIPUS: Except? What? What was it? One clue might lead to many. We have to grasp the smallest shred of hope.

CREON: He said that robbers—many of them—fell upon Laius and his men and murdered them.

OEDIPUS: Robbers? Who committed *murder*? Why? Unless they were paid assassins?

CREON: We considered that. But the king was dead and we were plagued with trouble. No one came forth as an avenger.

OEDIPUS: Trouble? What could have kept you from investigating the death of your king?

CREON: The Sphinx. The Sphinx was confounding us with her riddles, forcing us to abandon our search for the unknown and to tend to what was then before us.

OEDIPUS: Then I—I shall begin again. I shall not cease until I bring the truth to light. Apollo has shown, and you have shown, the duty which we owe the dead. You have my gratitude. You will find me a firm ally, and together we shall exact vengeance for our land and for the god. I shall not rest till I dispel this defilement—not just for another man's sake, but for my own as well. For whoever the assassin—he might turn his hand against me too. Yes, I shall be serving Laius and myself. Now go, my chil-

dren. Leave the steps of my altar. Go. Take away your laurel
branches. Go to the people of Cadmus. Summon them.[7] Tell
them that I, their king, will leave nothing untried. And with the
help of God, we shall find success—or ruin.

[*Exit* OEDIPUS.]

PRIEST: Come, children. We have learned what we came to learn.
Come, Apollo, come yourself, who sent these oracles!
Come as our savior! Come! Deliver us from this plague!

CHORUS:

O prophecy of Zeus,[8] sweet is the sound of your words
as they come to our glorious city of Thebes
from Apollo's glittering shrine.
Yet I quake and I dread and I tremble at those words.
Io, Delian Lord![9]

What will you bring to pass? Disaster unknown,
or familiar to us, as the ever recurring seasons?
Tell me, O oracle,
heavenly daughter of blessèd hope.

Foremost I call on you, daughter of Zeus,
Athena, goddess supreme;
and on Artemis,[10] shielding the world,
shielding this land from her circular shrine
graced with renown.
And on you I call, Phoebus,[11] Lord of the unerring bow.

Come to my aid, you averters of doom!
Come to my aid if ever you came!
Come to my aid as once you did, when you quenched
the fires of doom that fell on our soil!
Hear me, and come to my aid!

Boundless the pain, boundless the grief I bear;
sickness pervades this land,
affliction without reprieve.
Barren the soil, barren of fruit;
children are born no longer to light;
all of us flutter in agony
winging our way into darkness and death.

Countless the number of dead in the land;
corpses of children cover the plain,
children dying before they have lived,
no one to pity them,
reeking, and spreading diseases and death.

Moaning and wailing our wives,

7. **Summon them:** The people of Thebes
are represented by the chorus, which
comes into the orchestra at the end of
the scene.
8. *Zeus:* Apollo was his son, and spoke
for him.
9. *Delian:* Apollo was born on the sacred island of Delos.
10. *Artemis:* sister of Apollo.
11. *Phoebus:* Apollo.

moaning and wailing our mothers
stream to the altars this way and that,
scream to the air with helpless cries.
Hear us, golden daughter of Zeus,
hear us! Send us release!

Ares[12] now rages in our midst
brandishing in his hands
the firebrands of disease,
raving, consuming, rousing the screams of death.
Hear us, O goddess!
Help us, and still his rage!
Turn back his assault!
Help us! Banish him from our land!
Drive him into the angry sea,
to the wave-swept border of Thrace!

We who escape him tonight
will be struck down at dawn.
Help us, O father Zeus,
Lord of the thunderbolt,
crush him! Destroy him!
Burn him with fires of lightning!

Help us, Apollo, Lycean[13] Lord!
Stand at our side with your golden bow!
Artemis, help us!
Come from the Lycian[14] hills!
Come with your torches aflame!
Dionysus,[15] protector, come to our aid,
come with your revelers' band!
Burn with your torch the god
hated among the gods!

[*Enter* OEDIPUS.]

OEDIPUS: I have heard your prayers and answer with relief and
help, if you will heed my words and tend the sickness with the
cure it cries for. My words are uttered as a stranger to the act, a
stranger to its tale. I cannot trace its path alone, without a sign.
As a citizen newer to Thebes than you, I make this proclamation: If one among you knows who murdered Laius, the son of
Labdacus, let him tell us now. If he fears for his life, let him confess and know a milder penalty. He will be banished from this
land. Nothing more. Or if you know the assassin to be an alien,
do not protect him with your silence. You will be rewarded. But
if in fear you protect yourself or any other man and keep your
silence, then hear what I say now: Whoever he is, this assassin

---

12. *Ares:* god of war and destruction.
He was thought to be at home among the
savages of Thrace, to the northeast of
Greece proper.

13. *Lycean:* an epithet of Apollo, sug-
gestive of his connection with light (like
Phoebus = shining) and also of his role

as protector of the flocks against wolves.

14. *Lycian:* from Lycia, in southern
Turkey. The connection of this region with
Artemis is not clear.

15. *Dionysus:* son of Zeus, god of the
forest and the vine.

must be denied entrance to your homes. Any man where I rule is forbidden to receive him or speak to him or share with him his prayers and sacrifice or offer him the holy rites of purification. I command you to drive this hideous curse out of your homes; I command you to obey the will of Pythian Apollo. I will serve the god and the dead. On the assassin or assassins, I call down the most vile damnation—for this vicious act, may the brand of shame be theirs to wear forever. And if I knowingly harbor their guilt within my own walls, I shall not exempt myself from the curse that I have called upon them. It is for me, for God, and for this city that staggers toward ruin that you must fulfill these injunctions. Even if Heaven gave you no sign, you had the sacred duty to insure that this act did not go unexamined, unavenged! It was the assassination of a noble man—your king! Now that I hold the powers that he once held, his bed, his wife—had fate been unopposed, his children would have bound us closer yet—and now on him has this disaster fallen. I will avenge him as I would avenge my own father. I will leave nothing untried to expose the murderer of Laius, the son of Labdacus, heir to the house of Cadmus and Agenor.[16] On those who deny me obedience, I utter this curse: May the gods visit them with barrenness in their harvests, barrenness in their women, barrenness in their fate. Worse still—may they be haunted and tormented and never know the peace that comes with death. But for you, my people, in sympathy with me—I pray that Justice and all the gods attend you forever.

CHORUS: You have made me swear an oath, my Lord, and under oath I speak. I did not kill the king and cannot name the man who did. The question was Apollo's. He could name the man you seek.

OEDIPUS: I know. And yet no mortal can compel a god to speak.

CHORUS: The next-best thing, it seems to me . . .

OEDIPUS: Tell me. Tell me all your thoughts. We must consider everything.

CHORUS: There is one man, second only to Apollo, who can see the truth, who can clearly help us in our search—Teiresias.[17]

OEDIPUS: I thought of this. On Creon's advice, I sent for him. Twice. He should be here.

CHORUS: There were some rumors once, but no one hears them now.

OEDIPUS: What rumors? I want to look at every tale that is told.

CHORUS: They said that travelers murdered Laius.

OEDIPUS: I have heard that too. And yet there's no one to be found who saw the murderer in the act.

CHORUS: He will come forth himself, once he has heard your curse, if he knows what it means to be afraid.

OEDIPUS: Why? Why should a man now fear words if then he did not fear to kill?

---

16. *Agenor:* king of Phoenicia, father of Cadmus.

17. *Teiresias:* the blind prophet of Thebes (the same one whose ghost Odysseus goes to consult in Hades, p. 242).

CHORUS: But there is one man who can point him out—the man in whom the truth resides, the god-inspired prophet. And there—they are bringing him now.

[*Enter* TEIRESIAS, *guided by a servant.*]

OEDIPUS: Teiresias, all things are known to you—the secrets of heaven and earth, the sacred and profane. Though you are blind, you surely see the plague that rakes our city. My Lord Teiresias, we turn to you as our only hope. My messengers may have told you—we have sent to Apollo and he has answered us. We must find Laius' murderers and deal with them. Or drive them out. Then—only then will we find release from our suffering. I ask you not to spare your gifts of prophecy. Look to the voices of prophetic birds or the answers written in the flames. Spare nothing. Save all of us—yourself, your city, your king, and all that is touched by this deathly pollution. We turn to you. My Lord, it is man's most noble role to help his fellow man the best his talents will allow.

TEIRESIAS: O God! How horrible wisdom is! How horrible when it does not help the wise! How could I have forgotten? I should not have come.

OEDIPUS: Why? What's wrong?

TEIRESIAS: Let me go. It will be better if you bear your own distress and I bear mine. It will be better this way.

OEDIPUS: This city gave you life and yet you refuse her an answer! You speak as if you were her enemy.

TEIRESIAS: No! No! It is because I see the danger in your words. And mine would add still more.

OEDIPUS: For God's sake, if you know, don't turn away from us! We are pleading. We are begging you.

TEIRESIAS: Because you are blind! No! I shall not reveal my secrets. I shall not reveal yours.

OEDIPUS: What? You know, and yet you refuse to speak? Would you betray us and watch our city fall helplessly to her death?

TEIRESIAS: I will not cause you further grief. I will not grieve myself. Stop asking me to tell; I will tell you nothing.

OEDIPUS: You will not tell? You monster! You could stir the stones of earth to a burning rage! You will never tell? What will it take?

TEIRESIAS: Know yourself, Oedipus. You denounce me, but you do not yet know yourself.

OEDIPUS: Yes! You disgrace your city. And then you expect us to control our rage!

TEIRESIAS: It does not matter if I speak; the future has already been determined.

OEDIPUS: And if it has, then it is for you to tell me, *prophet*!

TEIRESIAS: I shall say no more. Rage, if you wish.

OEDIPUS: I *am* enraged. And now I will tell you what I think. I think this was *your* doing. *You* plotted the crime, *you* saw it carried out. It was *your* doing. All but the actual killing. And had you not been blind, you would have done *that*, too!

TEIRESIAS: Do you believe what you have said? Then accept your own decree! From this day on, deny yourself the right to speak to anyone. You, Oedipus, are the desecrator, the polluter of this land!

OEDIPUS: You traitor! Do you think that you can get away with this?

TEIRESIAS: The truth is my protection.

OEDIPUS: Who taught you this? It did not come from prophecy!

TEIRESIAS: *You* taught me. *You* drove me, *you* forced me to say it against my will.

OEDIPUS: Say it again. I want to make sure that I understand you.

TEIRESIAS: Understand me? Or are you trying to provoke me?

OEDIPUS: No, I want to be sure, I want to know. Say it again.

TEIRESIAS: I say that you, Oedipus Tyrannus, are the murderer you seek.

OEDIPUS: So! A second time! Now twice you will regret what you have said!

TEIRESIAS: Shall I tell you more? Shall I fan your flames of anger?

OEDIPUS: Yes. Tell me more. Tell me more—whatever suits you. It will be in vain.

TEIRESIAS: I say you live in shame with the woman you love, blind to your own calamity.

OEDIPUS: Do you think you can speak like this forever?

TEIRESIAS: I do, if there is any strength in truth.

OEDIPUS: There is—for everyone but you. You—you cripple! Your ears are deaf, your eyes are blind, your mind—your *mind* is crippled!

TEIRESIAS: You fool! You slander me when one day you will hear the same . . .

OEDIPUS: You live in night, Teiresias, in night that never turns to day. And so, you cannot hurt me—or any man who sees the light.

TEIRESIAS: No—it is not I who will cause your fall. That is Apollo's office—and he will discharge it.

OEDIPUS: Was this *your* trick—or Creon's?

TEIRESIAS: No, not Creon's. No, Oedipus. You are destroying yourself!

OEDIPUS: Ah, wealth and sovereignty and skill surpassing skill in life's contentions, why must envy always attend them? This city *gave* me power; I did not ask for it. And Creon, my friend, my trusted friend, would plot to overthrow me—with this charlatan, this impostor, who auctions off his magic wares! His eyes see profit clearly, but they are blind in prophecy. Tell me, Teiresias, what makes you a prophet? Where were you when the monster was here weaving her spells and taunts? What words of relief did Thebes hear from you? Her riddle would stagger the simple mind; it demanded the mind of a seer. Yet, put to the test, all your birds and god-craft proved useless; you had no answer. Then *I* came—ignorant Oedipus—I came and smothered her, using only my wit. There were no birds to tell me what to do. I am the man you would overthrow so you can stand near Creon's throne. You will regret—you and your conspirator—you will regret your attempt to purify this land. If you were not an old man, I would make you suffer the pain which you deserve for your audacity.

CHORUS: Both of you, my Lord, have spoken in bitter rage. No more—not when we must direct our every thought to obey the god's command

TEIRESIAS: Though you are king, the right to speak does not belong to you alone. It is *my* right as well and I shall claim it. I am not your servant and Creon is not my patron. I serve only Loxian[18] Apollo. And I tell you this, since you mock my blindness. You have eyes, Oedipus, and do not see your own destruction. You have eyes and do not see what lives with you. Do you know whose son you are? I say that you have sinned and do not know it; you have sinned against your own—the living and the dead. A double scourge, your mother's and your father's curse, will drive you from this land. Then darkness will shroud those eyes that now can see the light. Cithæron,[19]—the whole earth will resound with your mournful cries when you discover the meaning of the wedding-song that brought you to this place you falsely thought a haven. More sorrow still awaits you—more than you can know—to show you what you are and what your children are. Damn Creon, if you will; damn the words I say. No man on earth will ever know the doom that waits for you.

OEDIPUS: How much of this am I to bear? Leave! Now! Leave my house!

TEIRESIAS: I would not be here had you not sent for me.

OEDIPUS: I never would have sent for you had I known the madness I would hear.

TEIRESIAS: To you, I am mad; but not to your parents . . .

OEDIPUS: Wait! My parents? Who are my parents?

TEIRESIAS: This day shall bring you birth *and* death.

OEDIPUS: Why must you persist with riddles?

TEIRESIAS: Are you not the best of men when it comes to riddles?

OEDIPUS: You mock the very skill that proves me great.

TEIRESIAS: A great misfortune—which will destroy you.

OEDIPUS: I don't care. If I have saved this land, I do not care.

TEIRESIAS: Then I shall go. [*To his servant.*] Come, take me home.

OEDIPUS: Yes, go home. You won't be missed.

TEIRESIAS: I will go when I've said all that I came to say. I am not afraid of you. You cannot hurt me. And I tell you this: The man you seek—the man whose death or banishment you ordered, the man who murdered Laius—that man is here, passing as an alien, living in our midst. Soon it will be known to all of you—he is a native Theban. And he will find no joy in that discovery. His eyes now see, but soon they will be blind: rich now, but soon a beggar. Holding a scepter now, but soon a cane, he will grope for the earth beneath him—in a foreign land. Both brother and father to the children that he loves. Both son and husband to the woman who bore him. Both heir and spoiler of his father's bed

---

18. *Loxian:* an epithet of Apollo which means "crooked, ambiguous."

19. *Cithaeron:* the mountain range near Thebes.

and the one who took his life. Go, think of this. And if you find
the words I speak are lies, *then* say that I am blind.

[*Exeunt* OEDIPUS, TEIRESIAS.]

CHORUS:
Who is he? Who is the man?
Who is the man whom the voice of the Delphian shrine
denounced as the killer, the murderer,
the man who committed the terrible crime?
Where is he? Where is he now?
Let him run, let him flee!
Let him rush with the speed of the wind on his flight!
For with fire and lightning the god will attack,
and relentlessly fate will pursue him and haunt him
and drive him to doom.

Do you hear? Do you hear the command of the god?
From Parnassus[20] he orders the hunt.
In vain will the murderer hide,
in vain will he run,
in vain will he lurk in the forests and caves
like an animal roaming the desolate hills.
Let him flee to the edge of the world:
On his heels he will find
the command of the god!

Confusion and fear
have been spread by the prophet's words.
For I cannot affirm, yet I cannot refute
what he spoke. And I'm lost, I am lost—
What am I to believe?
Now foreboding is gripping my heart.
Was there ever a strife between Laius and Polybus'[21] house?
Can I test? Can I prove?
Can I ever believe that the name of my king
has been soiled by a murder unknown?

It is Zeus and Apollo who know,
who can see the affairs of men.
But the seer and I,
we are mortal, and blind.
Who is right? Who can judge?
We are mortal, our wisdom assigned in degrees.
Does the seer know? Do I?
No, I will not believe in the prophet's charge
till the charge has been proved to my mind.
For I saw how the king
in the test with the Sphinx
proved his wisdom and worth
when he saved this city from doom.

---

20. *Parnassus:* mountain above Delphi.
21. *Polybus:* king of Corinth and, so far as anyone yet knows, the father of Oedipus.

No! I can *never* condemn the king!

[*Enter* CREON.]

CREON: My fellow-citizens, anger has impelled me to come because I have heard the accusation which Oedipus has brought against me—and I will not tolerate it. If he thinks that I—in the midst of this torment—*I* have thought to harm him in any way, I will not spend the rest of my life branded by his charge. Doesn't he see the implications of such slander? To you, to my friends, to my city—I would be a traitor!

CHORUS: He spoke in anger—without thinking.

CREON: Yes—and who was it who said that the prophet lied on my advice?

CHORUS: It was said, but I don't know how it was meant.

CREON: And was this a charge leveled by one whose eyes were clear? Whose head was clear?

CHORUS: I don't know. I do not judge my master's actions. But here he comes.

[*Enter* OEDIPUS.]

OEDIPUS: Why have you come, Creon? Do you have the audacity to show your face in my presence? Assassin! And now you would steal my throne! What drove you to this plot? Did you see cowardice in me? Stupidity? Did you imagine that I would not see your treachery? Did you expect that I wouldn't act to stop you? You fool! Your plot was mad! You go after a throne without money, without friends! How do you think thrones are won?

CREON: You listen to me! And when you have heard me out, when you have heard the truth, *then* judge for yourself.

OEDIPUS: Ah yes, your oratory! I can learn nothing from that. This is what I have learned—you are my enemy!

CREON: Just let me say . . .

OEDIPUS: Say one thing—say that you are not a traitor.

CREON: If you think that senseless stubbornness is a precious gift, you are a fool.

OEDIPUS: If you think that you can threaten the house of Cadmus —your own house—and not pay for it, you are mad.

CREON: I grant you that. But tell me: just what is this terrible thing you say I have done to you?

OEDIPUS: Did you or did you not tell me to send for that—that— prophet?

CREON: I did. And I would again.

OEDIPUS: Then, how long since Laius . . . ?

CREON: What? I do not follow . . .

OEDIPUS: . . . Disappeared?

CREON: A long time ago.

OEDIPUS: Your Teiresias—was he—was he a prophet then?

CREON: Yes—and just as honored and just as wise.

OEDIPUS: Did he ever mention me—then?

CREON: Not in my presence.

OEDIPUS: But didn't you investigate the murder?

CREON: Of course we did—

OEDIPUS: And why didn't the prophet say anything *then*?

CREON: I do not know. It's not for me to try to understand.

OEDIPUS: You know this much which you will try to tell me . . .

CREON: What is it? I will tell you if I can.

OEDIPUS: Just this: Had he not acted under your instructions, he would not have named *me* killer of Laius.

CREON: If this is what he said, you ought to know. You heard him. But now I claim the right to question you, as you have me.

OEDIPUS: Ask what you wish. I am not the murderer.

CREON: Then answer me. Did you marry my sister?

OEDIPUS: Of course I did.

CREON: And do you rule on equal terms with her?

OEDIPUS: She has all that she wants from me.

CREON: And am I not the third and equal partner?

OEDIPUS: You are—and that is where you have proved yourself a traitor.

CREON: Not true. Consider rationally, as I have done. First ask yourself—would any man prefer a life of fear to one in which the self-same rank, the self-same rights are guaranteed untroubled peace? I have no wish to be a king when I can act as one without a throne. And any man would feel the same, if he were wise. I share with you a king's prerogatives, yet you alone must face the danger lurking around the throne. If *I* were king, I would have to act in many ways against my pleasure. What added benefit could kingship hold when I have rank and rule without the threat of pain? I am not deluded—no, I would not look for honors beyond the ones which profit me. I have the favor of every man; each greets me first when he would hope to have *your* favor. Why should I exchange this for a throne? Only a fool would. No, I am not a traitor nor would I aid an act of treason. You want proof? Go to Delphi; ask if I have brought you the truth. Then, if you find me guilty of conspiracy with the prophet, command my death. I will face that. But do not condemn me without proof. You are wrong to judge the guilty innocent, the innocent guilty —without proof. Casting off a true friend is like casting off your greatest prize—your life. You will know in time that this is true. Time alone reveals the just; a single day condemns the guilty.

CHORUS: He is right, my Lord. Respect his words. A man who plans in haste will gamble the result.

OEDIPUS: This is a plot conceived in rashness. It must be met with quick response. I cannot sit and wait until the plot succeeds.

CREON: What will you do then? Do you intend to banish me?

OEDIPUS: No. No, not banish you. I want to see you *dead*—to make you an example for all aspiring to my throne.

CREON: Then you won't do as I suggest? You won't believe me?

OEDIPUS: You have not shown that you deserve belief.

CREON: No, because I see that you are mad.

OEDIPUS: In my own eyes, I am sane.

CREON: You should be sane in mine as well.

OEDIPUS: No. You are a traitor!

CREON: And what if you are wrong?

OEDIPUS: Still—*I* will rule.

CREON: Not when you rule treacherously.

OEDIPUS: O Thebes! My city! Listen to him!

CREON: My city too!

CHORUS: My Lords, no more. Here comes Jocasta. Perhaps the queen can end this bitter clash.

[*Enter* JOCASTA.]

JOCASTA: Why do you behave like senseless fools and quarrel without reason? Are you not ashamed to add trouble of your own when your city is sick and dying? Go, Creon. Go and leave us alone. Forget those petty grievances which you exaggerate. How important can they be?

CREON: This important, sister: Oedipus, your husband, in his insanity, has threatened me with banishment or death.

OEDIPUS: Yes, for I have realized his plot—a plot against my person.

CREON: May the gods haunt me forever, if that is true—if I am guilty of that charge.

JOCASTA: In the name of God, believe him, Oedipus! Believe him for the sake of his oath, for my own sake, and for theirs!

CHORUS: Listen to her, my Lord. I beg you to consider and comply.

OEDIPUS: What would you have me do?

CHORUS: Respect the oath that Creon gave you. Respect his past integrity.

OEDIPUS: Do you know what you are asking?

CHORUS: Yes, I know.

OEDIPUS: Then, tell me what you mean.

CHORUS: I mean that you are wrong to charge a friend who has invoked a curse upon his head. You are wrong to slander without proof and be the cause for his dishonor.

OEDIPUS: Then you must know that when you ask for this, you ask for banishment or doom—for *me*.

CHORUS:
O God, no!
O Helios, [22] no!
May Heaven and Earth exact my doom
if that is what I thought!
When our city is torn by sickness
and my heart is torn with pain—
do not compound the troubles
that beset us!

OEDIPUS: Then, let him go, although it surely means my death—or banishment with dishonor. *Your* words—not his—have touched my heart. But Creon—wherever he may be—I will hate him.

CREON: You are hard when you should yield, cruel when you should pity. Such natures deserve the pain they bear.

OEDIPUS: Just go—and leave me in peace.

22. *Helios:* the sun. He is appealed to as a witness to oaths since, in his daily passage over the earth, he sees everything that happens.

CREON: I will go—my guilt pronounced by you alone. Behold my
judge and jury—Oedipus Tyrannus!
[*Exit* CREON.]

CHORUS: My queen, persuade your husband to rest awhile.

JOCASTA: I will—when I have learned the truth.

CHORUS: Blind suspicion has consumed the king. And Creon's passions flared beneath the sting of unjust accusations.

JOCASTA: Are *both* at fault?

CHORUS: Yes, both of them.

JOCASTA: But what is the reason for their rage?

CHORUS: Don't ask again. Our city is weary enough from suffering.
Enough. Let the matter rest where it now stands.

OEDIPUS: Do you see what you have done? Do you see where you
have come—with your good intentions, your noble efforts to dull
the sharpness of my anger?

CHORUS:
My Lord, I have said before
and now I say again:
I would be mad,
a reckless fool
to turn away my king,
who saved us from a sea of troubles
and set us on a fairer course,
and who will lead us once again
to peace, a haven from our pain.

JOCASTA: In the name of Heaven, my Lord, tell me the reason for
your bitterness.

OEDIPUS: I will—because you mean more to me than anyone. The
reason is Creon and his plot against my throne.

JOCASTA: But can you *prove* a plot?

OEDIPUS: He says that I—Oedipus—bear the guilt of Laius' death.

JOCASTA: How does he justify this charge?

OEDIPUS: He does not stain his own lips by saying it. No. He uses
that false prophet to speak for him.

JOCASTA: Then, you can exonerate yourself because no mortal has
the power of divination. And I can prove it. An oracle came to
Laius once from the Pythian priests—I'll not say from Apollo
himself—that he would die at the hands of his own child, his
child and mine. Yet the story which *we* heard was that robbers
murdered Laius in a place where three roads meet. As for the child
—when he was three days old, Laius drove pins into his ankles
and handed him to someone to cast upon a deserted mountain
path—to die. And so, Apollo's prophecy was unfulfilled—the
child did not kill his father. And Laius' fears were unfulfilled—he
did not die by the hand of his child. Yet, these had been the
prophecies. You need not give them any credence. For the god
will reveal what he wants.

OEDIPUS: Jocasta—my heart is troubled at your words. Suddenly, my
thoughts are wandering, disturbed . . .

JOCASTA: What is it? What makes you so frightened?

OEDIPUS: Your statement—that Laius was murdered in a place where three roads meet. Isn't that what you said?

JOCASTA: Yes. That was the story then; that is the story now.

OEDIPUS: Where is this place where three roads meet?

JOCASTA: In the land called Phocis where the roads from Delphi and from Daulia converge.

OEDIPUS: How long a time has passed since then?

JOCASTA: We heard it shortly before you came.

OEDIPUS: O God, what have you planned for me?

JOCASTA: What is it, Oedipus? What frightens you?

OEDIPUS: Do not ask me. Do not ask. Just tell me—what was Laius like? How old was he?

JOCASTA: He was tall and his hair was lightly cast with silver tones, the contour of his body much like yours.

OEDIPUS: O God! Am I cursed and cannot see it?

JOCASTA: What is it, Oedipus? You frighten me.

OEDIPUS: It cannot be—that the prophet sees! Tell me one more thing.

JOCASTA: You frighten me, my Lord, but I will try to tell you what I know.

OEDIPUS: Who traveled with the king? Was he alone? Was there a guide? An escort? A few? Many?

JOCASTA: There were five—one of them a herald—and a carriage in which Laius rode.

OEDIPUS: O God! O God! I see it all now! Jocasta, who told you this?

JOCASTA: A servant—the only one who returned alive.

OEDIPUS: Is he here now? In our house?

JOCASTA: No. When he came back and saw you ruling where once his master was, he pleaded with me—begged me—to send him to the fields to tend the flocks, far from the city. And so I did. He was a good servant and I would have granted him more than that, if he had asked.

OEDIPUS: Could we arrange to have him here—now?

JOCASTA: Yes, but what do you want with him?

OEDIPUS: I am afraid, Jocasta. I have said too much and now I have to see him.

JOCASTA: Then he shall be brought. But I, too, must know the cause of your distress. I have the right to know.

OEDIPUS: Yes, you have that right. And I must tell you—now. You, more than anyone, will have to know what I am going through. My father was Polybus of Corinth, my mother a Dorian—Merope. I was held in high regard in Corinth until—until something strange occurred—something uncanny and strange, although I might have given it too much concern. There was a man dining with us one day who had had far too much wine and shouted at me—half-drunk and shouting that I was not rightly called my father's son. I could barely endure the rest of that day and on the next I went to my parents and questioned them. They were enraged at the remark. I felt relieved at their response. But still, this—this thing—kept gnawing at my heart. And it was spread about in vulgar whispers. And then, without my parents' knowledge, I went to Delphi, but Apollo did not say what I had gone to hear. Instead, he answered questions I had not asked and told of horror and misery beyond belief—how I would know my mother's bed and bring to the world a race of children too terrible for men to see and cause the death of my own father. I trembled at those words and fled from Corinth—as far as I could—to where no star could ever guide me back, where I could never see that infamous prophecy fulfilled. And as I traveled, I came to that place where you say the king was murdered. This is the truth, Jocasta—I was in that place where the three roads meet. There was a herald leading a carriage drawn by horses and a man riding in the carriage—just as you described. The man in front, and the old one, ordered me out of the path. I refused. The driver pushed. In anger, I struck him. The old man saw it, reached for his lash and waited till I had passed. Then he struck me on the head. But he paid—oh yes, he paid. He lost his balance and fell from the carriage and as he lay there helpless—on his back—I killed him. I killed them all. But if this stranger had any tie with Laius—O God—who could be more hated in the eyes of Heaven and Earth? *I* am the one whom strangers and citizens are forbidden to receive! *I* am the one to whom all are forbidden to speak! *I* am the one who must be driven out! *I* am the one for whom my curse was meant! I have touched his bed with the very hands that killed him! O God! The sin! The horror! *I* am to be banished, never to see my people, never to walk in my fatherland. Or else I must take my mother for a bride and kill my father Polybus, who gave me life and cared for me. What cruel god has sent this torture? Hear me, you gods, you holy gods—I will never see that day! I will die before I ever see the stain of this abominable act!

CHORUS: Your words frighten us, my Lord. But you must have hope until you hear the story from the man who saw.

OEDIPUS: Yes—hope. My only hope is waiting for this shepherd.

JOCASTA: Why? What do you hope to find with him?

OEDIPUS: This—if his story agrees with what you say, then I am safe.

JOCASTA: What did I say that makes you sure of this?

OEDIPUS: You said he told of *robbers*—that *robbers* killed the king. If he still says *robbers*, then I am not the guilty one—because no man can talk of many when he means a single one. But if he names a *single* traveler, there will be no doubt—the guilt is mine.

JOCASTA: You can be sure that this was what he said—and he cannot deny it. The whole city heard him—not I alone. But even if he alters what he said before, he cannot prove that Laius met his death as it was prophesied. For Apollo said that he would die at the hand of a child—of mine. And as it happens, the child is dead. So prophecy is worthless. I wouldn't dignify it with a moment's thought.

OEDIPUS: You are right. But still—send someone for the shepherd. Now.

JOCASTA: I shall—immediately. I shall do what you ask. But now —let us go inside.

[*Exeunt* OEDIPUS, JOCASTA.]

CHORUS:

I pray, may destiny permit
that honestly I live my life
in word and deed.
That I obey the laws
the heavens have begotten
and prescribed.
Those laws created by Olympus,[23]
laws pure, immortal,
forever lasting, essence of the god
who lives in them.
On arrogance and pride
a tyrant feeds.
The goad of insolence,
of senseless overbearing, blind conceit,
of seeking things unseasonable,
unreasonable,
will prick a man to climb to heights
where he must lose his footing
and tumble to his doom.
Ambition must be used
to benefit the state;
else it is wrong, and God
must strike it from this earth.
Forever, God, I pray,
may you stand at my side!

A man who goes through life
with insolence in word and deed,
who lacks respect for law and right,
and scorns the shrines and temples of the gods,
may he find evil fate and doom
as his reward for wantonness,
for seeking ill-begotten gains
and reaching after sacred things
with sacrilegious hands.
No! Surely no such man
escapes the wrath, the vengeance of the god!
For if he did, if he could find reward
in actions which are wrong,

23. *Olympus:* the highest mountain on the Greek peninsula, considered by the Greeks to be the home of the gods.

why should I trouble to acclaim,
to honor you, God, in my song?

No longer shall my feet
take me to Delphi's sacred shrine;
no longer shall they Abae or Olympia's altars[24] seek
unless the oracles are shown to tell the truth
to mortals without fail!
Where are you, Zeus, all-powerful, all-ruling?
You must be told,
you must know in your all-pervading power:
Apollo's oracles now fall into dishonor,
and what the god has spoken about Laius
finds disregard.
Could God be dead?

[*Enter* JOCASTA.]

JOCASTA: My Lords, I want to lay these laurel wreaths and incense offerings at the shrines of Thebes—for Oedipus is torturing himself, tearing his heart with grief. His vision to weigh the present against the past is blurred by fear and terror. He devours every word of dread, drinks in every thought of pain, destruction, death. And I no longer have the power to ease his suffering. Now I turn to you, Apollo, since you are nearest, with prayer and suppliant offerings. Find some way to free us, end our agony! O God of Light, release us! You see the fear that grips us—like sailors who watch their captain paralyzed by some unknown terror on the seas.

[*Enter* MESSENGER 1.]

MESSENGER 1: Strangers, would you direct me to the house of Oedipus? Or if you know where I might find the king himself, please tell me.

CHORUS: This is his house, stranger. He is inside. But this is the queen—his wife, and mother of his children.

MESSENGER 1: Then, blessings on the house of Oedipus—his house, his children, and his wife.

JOCASTA: Blessings on you as well, stranger. Your words are kind. But why have you come? What is it?

MESSENGER 1: Good news, my lady—for your husband and your house.

JOCASTA: What news? Where do you come from?

MESSENGER 1: From Corinth, my lady. My news will surely bring you joy—but sorrow, too.

JOCASTA: What? How can that be?

MESSENGER 1: Your husband now is ruler of the Isthmus![25]

JOCASTA: Do you mean that Polybus of Corinth has been deposed?

MESSENGER 1: Deposed by death, my lady. He has passed away.

JOCASTA: What! Polybus dead?

---

24. *Abae, Olympia:* Abae was a city in central Greece and Olympia a site in the western Peloponnese, where there were important oracles of Apollo and Zeus, respectively.

25. *Isthmus:* Corinth owed its importance to its situation on the narrow neck of land separating the Gulf of Corinth and the westward route from the Saronic gulf to the south.

MESSENGER 1.: I swear on my life that this is true.

JOCASTA: [*to a servant*]: Go! Quickly! Tell your master. [*To the heavens.*] You prophecies—you divinely-uttered prophecies! Where do you stand now? The man that Oedipus feared, the man he dared not face lest he should be his killer—that man is dead! Time claimed his life—not Oedipus!

[*Enter* OEDIPUS.]

OEDIPUS: Why, Jocasta? Why have you sent for me again?

JOCASTA: I want you to listen to this man. Listen to him and judge for yourself the worth of those holy prophecies.

OEDIPUS: Who is he? What news could he have for me?

JOCASTA: He comes from Corinth with the news that—that Polybus—is dead.

OEDIPUS: What! Tell me.

MESSENGER 1: If you must know this first, then I shall tell you—plainly. Polybus has died.

OEDIPUS: How? An act of treason? Sickness? How?

MESSENGER 1: My Lord, only a slight shift in the scales is required to bring the agèd to their rest.

OEDIPUS: Then it was sickness. Poor old man.

MESSENGER 1: Sickness—yes. And the weight of years.

OEDIPUS: Oh, Jocasta! Why? Why should we even look to oracles, the prophetic words delivered at their shrines or the birds that scream above us? They led me to believe that I would kill my father. But he is dead and in his grave, while I stand here—never having touched a weapon. Unless he died of longing for his son. If that is so, then I *was* the instrument of his death. And those oracles! Where are they now? Polybus has taken them to his grave. What worth have they now?

JOCASTA: Have I not been saying this all along?

OEDIPUS: Yes, you have. But I was misled by fear.

JOCASTA: Now you will no longer have to think of it.

OEDIPUS: But—my mother's bed. I still have *that* to fear.

JOCASTA: No. No, mortals have no need to fear when chance reigns supreme. The knowledge of the future is denied to us. It is better to live as you will, live as you can. You need not fear a union with your mother. Men often, in their dreams, approach their mothers' beds, lie with them, possess them. But the man who sees that this is meaningless can live without the threat of fear.

OEDIPUS: You would be right, Jocasta, if my mother were not alive. But she *is* alive. And no matter what you say, I have reason to fear.

JOCASTA: At least your father's death has brought some comfort.

OEDIPUS: Yes—some comfort. But my fear is of *her*—as long as she lives.

MESSENGER 1: Who is *she*? The woman you fear?

OEDIPUS: Queen Merope, old man, the wife of Polybus.

MESSENGER 1: But why does *she* instill fear in you?

OEDIPUS: There was an oracle—a dreadful oracle sent by the gods.

MESSENGER 1: Can you tell me—a stranger—what it is?

OEDIPUS: Yes, it is all right to tell. Once Loxian Apollo said that I would take my mother for my bride and murder my father with my own hands. This is the reason that I left Corinth long ago. Fortunately. And yet, I have often longed to see my parents.

MESSENGER 1: Is this the fear that drove you away from Corinth?

OEDIPUS: Yes. I did not want to kill my father.

MESSENGER 1: But I can free you from this fear, my Lord. My purpose for coming was a good one.

OEDIPUS: And I shall see that you receive a fitting reward.

MESSENGER 1: Yes—that's why I came. To fare well myself by your returning home.

OEDIPUS: Home? To Corinth? To my parents? Never.

MESSENGER 1: My son, you do not realize what you are doing.

OEDIPUS: What do you mean, old man? For God's sake, tell me what you mean.

MESSENGER 1: I mean—the reasons why you dread returning home.

OEDIPUS: I dread Apollo's prophecy—and its fulfillment.

MESSENGER 1: You mean the curse—the stain they say lies with your parents?

OEDIPUS: Yes, old man. That is the fear that lives with me.

MESSENGER 1: Then you must realize that this fear is groundless.

OEDIPUS: How can that be—if I am their son?

MESSENGER 1: Because Polybus was no relative of yours.

OEDIPUS: What are you saying! Polybus was *not* my father?

MESSENGER 1: No more than I.

OEDIPUS: No more than you? But you are nothing to me.

MESSENGER 1: He was not your father any more than I.

OEDIPUS: Then why did he call me his son?

MESSENGER 1: You were a gift to him—from me.

OEDIPUS: A gift? From you? And yet he loved me as his son?

MESSENGER 1: Yes, my Lord. He had been childless.

OEDIPUS: And when you gave me to him—had you bought me? Or found me?

MESSENGER 1: I found you—in the hills of Cithaeron.

OEDIPUS: What were you doing there?

MESSENGER 1: Tending sheep along the mountain side.

OEDIPUS: Then you were a—hired shepherd?

MESSENGER 1: Yes, my son—a hired shepherd who saved you at that time.

OEDIPUS: Saved me? Was I in pain when you found me? Was I in trouble?

MESSENGER 1: Yes, your ankles are the proof of that.

OEDIPUS: Ah, you mean this old trouble. What has that to do with it?

MESSENGER 1: When I found, your ankles were pierced with rivets. And I freed you.

OEDIPUS: Yes, I have had this horrible stigma since infancy.

MESSENGER 1: And so it was the swelling in your ankles that caused your name: Oedipus—"Clubfoot."

OEDIPUS: Oh! Who did this to me? My father? Or my mother?

MESSENGER 1: I don't know. You will have to ask the man who handed you to me.

OEDIPUS: You mean—*you* did not find me? It was someone else?

MESSENGER 1: Another shepherd.

OEDIPUS: Who? Do you remember who he was?

MESSENGER 1: I think—he was of the house of Laius.

OEDIPUS: The king who ruled this city?

MESSENGER 1: Yes. He was a shepherd in the service of the king.

OEDIPUS: Is he still alive? Can I see him?

MESSENGER 1: [*addressing the* CHORUS]: You—you people here—could answer that.

OEDIPUS: Do any of you know this shepherd? Have you seen him in the fields? Here in Thebes? Tell me now! Now is the time to unravel this mystery—once and for all.

CHORUS: I think it is the shepherd you asked to see before. But the queen will know.

OEDIPUS: Jocasta, is that the man he means? Is it the shepherd we have sent for? Is *he* the one?

JOCASTA: Why? What difference does it make? Don't think about it. Pay no attention to what he said. It makes no difference.

OEDIPUS: No difference? When I must have every clue to untangle the line of mystery surrounding my birth?

JOCASTA: In the name of God, if you care at all for your own life, you must not go on with this. I cannot bear it any longer.

OEDIPUS: Do not worry, Jocasta. Even if I am a slave—a third-generation slave, it is no stain on your nobility.

JOCASTA: Oedipus! I beg you—don't do this!

OEDIPUS: I can't grant you that. I cannot leave the truth unknown.

JOCASTA: It is for *your* sake that I beg you to stop. For your own good.

OEDIPUS: My own good has brought me pain too long.

JOCASTA: God help you! May you never know what you are!

OEDIPUS: Go, someone, and bring the shepherd to me. Leave the queen to exult in her noble birth.

JOCASTA: God help you! This is all that I can say to you—now or ever.

[*Exit* JOCASTA.]

CHORUS: Why has the queen left like this—grief-stricken and tortured with pain? My Lord, I fear—I fear that from her silence some horror will burst forth.

OEDIPUS: Let it explode! I will still want to uncover the secret of my birth—no matter how horrible. She—she is a woman with a woman's pride—and she feels shame for my humble birth. But I am the child of Fortune—beneficent Fortune—and I shall not be shamed! She is my mother. My sisters are the months and they have seen me rise and fall. This is my family. I will never deny my birth—and I will learn its secret!

[*Exit* OEDIPUS.]

CHORUS:
Ah Cithaeron,
if in my judgment I am right,
if I interpret what I hear correctly,
then—by Olympus' boundless majesty!—

364 · *Sophocles*

tomorrow's full moon will not pass
before, Cithaeron, you will find
that Oedipus will honor you
as mother and as nurse!
That we will praise you in our song,
benevolent and friendly to our king.
Apollo, our Lord, may you find joy in this!

Who bore you, Oedipus? A nymph?
Did Pan[26] beget you in the hills?
Were you begotten by Apollo?
Perhaps so, for he likes the mountain glens.
Could Hermes[27] be your father?
Or Dionysus? Could it be
that he received you as a gift
high in the mountains from a nymph
with whom he lay?

[*Enter* OEDIPUS.]

OEDIPUS: My Lords, I have never met him, but could that be the
shepherd we have been waiting for? He seems to be of the same
age as the stranger from Corinth. And I can see now—those are
my servants who are bringing him here. But, perhaps you know
—if you have seen him before. Is he the shepherd?

[*Enter* SHEPHERD.]

CHORUS: Yes. I recognize him. He was a shepherd in the service of
Laius—as loyal as any man could be.

OEDIPUS: Corinthian, I ask you—is this the man you mean?

MESSENGER 1: Yes, my Lord. This is the man.

OEDIPUS: And you, old man, look at me and answer what I ask.
Were you in the service of Laius?

SHEPHERD: I was. But not bought. I was reared in his house.

OEDIPUS: What occupation? What way of life?

SHEPHERD: Tending flocks—for most of my life.

OEDIPUS: And where did you tend those flocks?

SHEPHERD: Sometimes Cithaeron, sometimes the neighboring
places.

OEDIPUS: Have you ever seen this man before?

SHEPHERD: What man do you mean? Doing what?

OEDIPUS: This man. Have you ever met him before?

SHEPHERD: Not that I recall, my Lord.

MESSENGER 1: No wonder, my Lord. But I shall help him to recall.
I am sure that he'll remember the time we spent on Cithaeron—
he with his two flocks and I with one. Six months—spring to
autumn—every year—for three years. In the winter I would drive
my flocks to my fold in Corinth, and he to the fold of Laius.
Isn't that right, sir?

SHEPHERD: That is what happened. But it was a long time ago.

MESSENGER 1: Then tell me this. Do you remember a child you
gave me to bring up as my own?

26. *Pan:* a woodland god; patron of shepherds and flocks.

27. *Hermes:* son of Zeus and Maia; god of flocks and shepherds.

SHEPHERD: What are you saying? Why are you asking me this?

MESSENGER 1: This, my friend, this—is that child.

SHEPHERD: Damn you! Will you keep your mouth shut!

OEDIPUS: Save your reproaches, old man. It is you who deserve them—your words deserve them.

SHEPHERD: But master—how have I offended?

OEDIPUS: By refusing to answer his question about the child.

SHEPHERD: He doesn't know what he's saying. He's crazy.

OEDIPUS: If you don't answer of your own accord, we'll make you talk.

SHEPHERD: No! My Lord, please! Don't hurt an old man.

OEDIPUS [*to the* CHORUS]: One of you—twist his hands behind his back!

SHEPHERD: Why? Why? What do you want to know?

OEDIPUS: Did you or did you not give him that child?

SHEPHERD: I did. I gave it to him—and I wish that I had died that day.

OEDIPUS: You tell the truth, or you'll have your wish now.

SHEPHERD: If I tell, it will be worse.

OEDIPUS: Still he puts it off!

SHEPHERD: I said that I gave him the child!

OEDIPUS: Where did you get it? Your house? Someone else's? Where?

SHEPHERD: Not mine. Someone else's.

OEDIPUS: Whose? One of the citizens'? Whose house?

SHEPHERD: O God, master! Don't ask me any more.

OEDIPUS: This is the last time that I ask you.

SHEPHERD: It was a child—of the house of Laius.

OEDIPUS: A slave? Or of his own line?

SHEPHERD: Ah master, do I *have* to speak?

OEDIPUS: You have to. And I *have* to hear.

SHEPHERD: They said—it was his child. But the queen could tell you best.

OEDIPUS: Why? Did *she* give you the child?

SHEPHERD: Yes, my Lord.

OEDIPUS: Why?

SHEPHERD: To—kill!

OEDIPUS: Her own child!

SHEPHERD: Yes. Because she was terrified of some dreadful prophecy.

OEDIPUS: What prophecy?

SHEPHERD: The child would kill his father.

OEDIPUS: Then why did you give him to this man?

SHEPHERD: I felt sorry for him, master. And I thought that he would take him to his own home. But he saved him from his suffering—for worse suffering yet. My Lord, if you are the man he says you are—O God—you were born to suffering!

OEDIPUS: O God! O no! I see it now! All clear! O Light! I will never look on you again! Sin! Sin in my birth! Sin in my marriage! Sin in blood!

[*Exit* OEDIPUS.]

CHORUS:

O generations of men, you are nothing!
You are nothing!
And I count you as not having lived at all!
Was there ever a man,
was there ever a man on this earth
who could say he was happy,
who knew happiness, true happiness,
not an image, a dream,
an illusion, a vision, which would disappear?
Your example, Oedipus,
your example, your fate, your disaster,
show that none of us mortals
ever knew, ever felt what happiness truly is.

Here is Oedipus,
fortune and fame and bliss
leading him by the hand,
prodding him on to heights
mortals had never attained.
Zeus, it was he who removed
the scourge of the riddling maid,
of the sharp-clawed, murderous Sphinx!
He restored me to life from the brink
of disaster, of doom and of death.
It was he who was honored and hailed,
who was crowned and acclaimed as our king.

Here is Oedipus:
Anyone on this earth
struck by a harder blow,
stung by a fate more perverse?
Wretched Oedipus!
Father and son alike,
pleasures you took from where
once you were given life.
Furrows your father ploughed
bore you in silence. How, how, oh how could it be?

Time found you out,
all-seeing, irrepressible time.
Time sits in judgment on
the union that never could be;
judges you, father and son,
begot and begetter alike.
Would that I never had
laid eyes on Laius' child!
Now I wail and I weep,
and my lips are drenched in lament.
It was you, who offered me life;
it is you, who now bring me death.

[*Enter* MESSENGER 2.]

MESSENGER 2: O you most honored citizens of Thebes, you will mourn for the things you will hear, you will mourn for the things you will see, you will ache from the burden of sorrow—if you are true sons of the house of Labdacus, if you care, if you feel. The waters of Ister and Phasis[28] can never cleanse this house of the horrors hidden within it and soon to be revealed—horrors willfully done! Worst of the sorrows we know are those that are willfully done!

CHORUS: We have mourned enough for sorrows we have known. What more is there that you can add?

MESSENGER 2: One more and only one—Jocasta, the queen, is dead.

CHORUS: O God—no! How?

MESSENGER 2: By her own hand. But the most dreadful pain you have not seen. You have not seen the worst. I have seen it and I shall tell you what I can of her terrible suffering. She ran in frenzied despair through the palace halls and rushed straight to her bridal bed—her fingers clutching and tearing at her hair. Then, inside the bedroom, she flung the doors closed and cried out to Laius, long since dead. She cried out to him, remembering the son that she had borne long ago, the son who killed his father, the son who left her to bear a dread curse—the children of her own son! She wept pitifully for that bridal bed which she had twice defiled—husband born of husband, child born of child. I didn't see what happened then. I didn't see her die. At that moment the king rushed in and shrieked in horror. All eyes turned to him as he paced in frantic passion and confusion. He sprang at each of us and begged to have a sword. He begged to know where he could find the wife that was no wife to him, the woman who had been mother to him and to his children. Some power beyond the scope of man held him in its sway and guided him to her. It was none of us. Then—as if someone had beckoned to him and bade him follow—he screamed in terror and threw himself against the doors that she had locked. His body's weight and force shattered the bolts and thrust them from their sockets and he rushed into the room. There we saw the queen hanging from a noose of twisted cords. And when the king saw her, he cried out and moaned in deep, sorrowful misery. Then he untied the rope that hung about her neck and laid her body on the ground. But what happened then was even worse. Her gold brooches, her pins—he tore them from her gown and plunged them into his eyes again and again and again and screamed, "No longer shall you see the suffering you have known and caused! You saw what was forbidden to be seen, yet failed to recognize those whom you longed to see! Now you shall see only darkness!" And as he cried out in such desperate misery, he struck his eyes over and over—until a

---

28. *Ister and Phasis:* the Danube and a river flowing into the Black Sea, both large.

shower of blood and tears splattered down his beard, like a torrent of crimson rain and hail. And now suffering is mingled with pain for man and wife for the sins that both have done. Not one alone. Once—long ago—this house was happy—and rightly so. But now—today—sorrow, destruction, death, shame—all torments that have a name—all, all are theirs to endure.

CHORUS: But the king—does he have any relief from his suffering now?

MESSENGER 2: He calls for someone to unlock the gates and reveal to Thebes his father's killer, his mother's—I can't say it. I cannot say this unholy word. He cries out that he will banish himself from the land to free this house of the curse that he has uttered. But he is weak, drained. There is no one to guide his way. The pain is more than he can bear. You will see for yourselves. The palace gates are opening. You will see a sight so hideous that even his most bitter enemy would pity him.

[*Enter* OEDIPUS.]

CHORUS:
Ah!
Dread horror for men to see!
Most dreadful of all that I have seen!
Ah!
Wretched one,
what madness has possessed you?
What demon has descended upon you
and bound you to this dire fate?
Ah!
Wretched one,
I cannot bear to look at you.
I want to ask you more
and learn still more
and understand—
but I shudder at the sight of you!

OEDIPUS: Ah! Ah! Where has this misery brought me? Is this my own voice I hear—carried on the wings of the air? O Fate! What have you done to me?

CHORUS: Terrible! Too terrible to hear! Too terrible to see!

OEDIPUS: O cloud of darkness! Cruel! Driven by the winds of fate! Assaulting me! With no defense to hold you back! O God! The pain! The pain! My flesh aches from its wounds! My soul aches from the memory of its horrors!

CHORUS: Body and soul—each suffers and mourns.

OEDIPUS: Ah! You still remain with me—a constant friend. You still remain to care for me—a blind man now. Now there is darkness and I cannot see your face. But I can hear your voice and I know that you are near.

CHORUS: O my Lord, how could you have done this? How could you blind yourself? What demon drove you?

OEDIPUS: Apollo! It was Apollo! *He* brought this pain, this suffering to me. But it was my own hand that struck the blow. Not his. O God! Why should I have sight when all that I would see is ugliness?

CHORUS: It is as you say.

OEDIPUS: What is there for me to see and love? What sight would give me joy? What sound? Take me away! Take me out of this land! I am cursed! Doomed! I am the man most hated by the gods!

CHORUS: You have suffered equally for your fortune and for your disaster. I wish that you had never come to Thebes.

OEDIPUS: Damn the man who set me free! Who loosed the fetters from my feet and let me live! I will never forgive him. If he had let me die, I would never have become the cause—the grief . . .

CHORUS: I wish that it had been this way.

OEDIPUS: If it had been, I would not have come to this—killer of my father, bridegroom of the woman who gave me birth, despised by the gods, child of shame, father and brother to my children. Is there any horror worse than these—any horror that has not fallen upon Oedipus?

CHORUS: My Lord, I cannot condone what you have done. You would have been better dead than alive and blind.

OEDIPUS: I did what I had to. You know I did. No more advice. Could these eyes have looked upon my father in the house of Hades? Could these eyes have faced my mother in her agony? I sinned against them both—a sin no suicide could purge. Could I have joy at the sight of my children—born as they were born? With these eyes? Never! Could I look upon the city of Thebes? The turrets that grace her walls? The sacred statues of her gods? Never! Damned! I—the noblest of the sons of Thebes—I have damned myself. It was I who commanded that Thebes must cast out the one who is guilty, unholy, cursed by the heavenly gods. *I* was the curse of Thebes! Could these eyes look upon the people? Never! And if I could raise a wall to channel the fountain of my hearing, I would spare nothing to build a prison for this defiled body where sight and sound would never penetrate. Then only would I have peace—where grief could not reach my mind. O Cithaeron! Why did you receive me? Why did you not let me die then? Why did you let me live to show the world how I was born? O Polybus! O Corinth! My home that was no home! You raised me, thinking I was fair and never knowing the evil that festered beneath. Now—now see the evil from which I was born, the evil I have become. O God! The three roads! The hidden glen! The thickets! The pathway where three roads meet! The blood you drank from my hands—do you not know—it was the blood of my father! Do you remember? Do you remember what I did then and what I did for Thebes? Wedding-rites! You gave me birth and gave my children birth! Born of the same womb that bore my children! Father! Brother! Child! Incestuous sin! Bride! Wife! Mother! All of one union! All the most heinous sins that man can know! The most horrible shame—I can no longer speak of it. For the love of God, hide me somewhere. Hide me away from this land! Kill me! Cast me into the sea where you will never have to look at me again! I beg you—touch me—in

my misery. Touch me. Do not be afraid. My sins are mine alone
to bear and touch no other man.

[*Enter* CREON.]

CHORUS: My Lord, Creon is here to act or counsel in what you ask.
In your stead—he is now our sole protector.

OEDIPUS: What can I say to him? How can I ask for his trust? I
have wronged him. I know that now.

CREON: I have not come to mock you, Oedipus, nor to reproach
you for the past. But you—if you have no respect for men, at
least respect the lord of the sun whose fires give life to men. Hide
your naked guilt from his sight. No earth or sacred rain or light
can endure its presence. [*To a servant.*] Take him inside. It is
impious for any but his own family to see and hear his suffering.

OEDIPUS: I ask you in the name of God to grant one favor. You
have been kinder to me than I deserved. But one favor. I ask it
for you—not for myself?

CREON: What do you ask of me?

OEDIPUS: Cast me out of this land. Cast me out to where no man
can see me. Cast me out now.

CREON: I would have done so, you can be sure. But I must wait and
do the will of the god.

OEDIPUS: He has signified his will—with clarity. Destroy the parricide! Destroy the unholy one! Destroy Oedipus!

CREON: That was the god's command, I know. But now—with
what has happened—I think it better to wait and learn what we
must do.

OEDIPUS: You mean that you would ask for guidance for a man
so sorrowful as I?

CREON: Surely, you are ready to put your trust in the god—now.

OEDIPUS: Yes, I am ready now. But I ask this of you. Inside—she is
lying inside—give her whatever funeral rites you wish. You will
do the right thing for her. She is your sister. But for me—do not
condemn this city—my father's city—to suffer any longer from
my presence as long as I live. Let me go and live upon Cithaeron
—O Cithaeron, your name is ever linked with mine! Where my
parents chose a grave for me. Where they would have had me
die. Where I shall die in answer to their wish. And yet, I know,
neither sickness nor anything else will ever bring me death. For I
would not have been saved from death that once. No—I was
saved for a more dreadful fate. Let it be. Creon, do not worry
about my sons. They are boys and will have all they need, no
matter where they go. But my daughters—poor creatures! They
never ate a single meal without their father. We shared everything together. Creon, take care of them. Creon, let me touch
them one last time. And let me weep—one last time. Please, my
Lord, please, allow it—you're generous, you're kind. If I could
only touch them and feel that they are with me—as I used to—
when I could see them. [*Enter* ANTIGONE *and* ISMENE.] What is
that crying? Is it my daughters? Has Creon taken pity on me?
Has he sent my daughters to me? Are they here?

CREON: Yes, Oedipus, they are here. I had them brought to you. I know how much you love them, how much you have always loved them.

OEDIPUS: Bless you for this, Creon. Heaven bless you and grant you greater kindness than it has granted me. Ah, children, where are you? Come—come, touch my hands, the hands of your father, the hands of your brother, the hands that blinded these eyes which once were bright—these eyes—your father's eyes which neither saw nor knew what he had done when he became your father. I weep for you, my children. I cannot see you now. But when I think of the bitterness that waits for you in life, what you will have to suffer—the festivals, the holidays—the sadness you will know when you should share in gaiety! And when you are old enough to marry—who will there be, who will be the man strong enough to bear the slander that will haunt you—because you are *my* children? What disgrace will you not know? Your father killed his father. And lay with the woman that bore him and his children. These are the taunts that will follow you. And what man will marry you? No man, my children. You will spend your lives unwed—without children of your own—barren and wasted. Ah, Creon, you are the only father left to them. We—their parents—are lost. We gave them life. And we are lost to them. Take care of them. See that they do not wander poor and lonely. Do not let them suffer for what I have done. Pity them. They are so young. So lost. They have no one but you. Take my hand and promise me. And oh, my children, if you were older, I could make you understand. But now, make this your prayer—to find some place where you can live and have a better life than what your father knew.

CREON: Enough, my Lord. Go inside now.
OEDIPUS: Yes. I do not want to, but I will go.
CREON: All things have their time and their place.
OEDIPUS: I shall go—on this condition.
CREON: What condition? I am listening.
OEDIPUS: That you will send me away.
CREON: That is the god's decision, not mine.
OEDIPUS: The gods will not care where I go.
CREON: Then you shall have your wish.
OEDIPUS: Then—you consent?
CREON: It has nothing to do with my consent.
OEDIPUS: Let me go away from here.
CREON: Go then—but leave the children.
OEDIPUS: No! Do not take them away from me!
CREON: Do not presume that you are still in power. Your power has not survived with you.
CHORUS:
There goes Oedipus—
he was the man who was able
to answer the riddle proposed by the Sphinx.
Mighty Oedipus—
he was an object of envy
to all for his fortune and fame.

There goes Oedipus—
now he is drowning in waves of dread and despair.
Look at Oedipus—
proof that none of us mortals
can truly be thought of as happy
until he is granted deliverance from life,
until he is dead
and must suffer no more.

Antigone*

SCENE:—*Courtyard of the royal palace at Thebes. Daybreak.*

[*Enter* ANTIGONE *and* ISMENE.]

ANTIGONE. Dear sister! Dear Ismene! How many evils
Our father, Oedipus, bequeathed to us!
And is there one of them—do you know of one
That Zeus has not showered down upon our heads?
I have seen pain, dishonor, shame, and ruin,   5
I have seen them all, in what we have endured.
And now comes this new edict by the King
Proclaimed throughout the city. Have you heard?
Do you not know, even yet, our friends are threatened?
They are to meet the fate of enemies.   10
ISMENE. Our friends, Antigone? No, I have heard
Nothing about them either good or bad.
I have no news except that we two sisters
Lost our two brothers when they killed each other.
I know the Argive army fled last night,   15
But what that means, or whether it makes my life
Harder or easier, I cannot tell.
ANTIGONE. This I was sure of. So I brought you here
Beyond the palace gates to talk alone.   19
ISMENE. What is the matter? I know you are deeply troubled.
ANTIGONE. Yes, for our brothers' fate. Creon has given
An honored burial to one, to the other
Only unburied shame. Eteocles
Is laid in the earth with all the rites observed
That give him his due honor with the dead.   25
But the decree concerning Polyneices
Published through Thebes is that his wretched body
Shall lie unmourned, unwept, unsepulchered.
Sweet will he seem to the vultures when they find him,

* From *Three Theban Plays*, translated by T. H. Banks. Copyright © 1956 by Theodore Howard Banks. Reprinted by permission of Oxford University Press, Inc. First produced in 441 B.C.

A welcome feast that they are eager for.   30
This is the edict the good Creon uttered
For your observance and for mine—yes, mine.
He is coming here himself to make it plain
To those who have not heard. Nor does he think it
Of little consequence, because whoever   35
Does not obey is doomed to death by stoning.
Now you can show you are worthy of your birth,
Or bring disgrace upon a noble house.

ISMENE. What can I do, Antigone? As things are,
    What can I do that would be of any help?   40
ANTIGONE. You can decide if you will share my task.
ISMENE. What do you mean? What are you planning to do?
ANTIGONE. I intend to give him burial. Will you help?
ISMENE. To give him burial! Against the law?
ANTIGONE. He is our brother. I will do my duty.   45
    Yours too, perhaps. I never will be false.
ISMENE. Creon forbids it! You are too rash, too headstrong.
ANTIGONE. He has no right to keep me from my own.
ISMENE. Antigone! Think! Think how our father perished
    In scorn and hatred when his sins, that he   50
    Himself discovered, drove him to strike blind
    His eyes by his own hand. Think how his mother,
    His wife—both names were hers—ended her life
    Shamefully hanging in a twisted noose.
    Think of that dreadful day when our two brothers,   55
    Our wretched brothers, fought and fell together,
    Each slayer and each slain. And now we too,
    Left all alone, think how in turn we perish,
    If, in defiance of the law, we brave
    The power of the commandment of a king.   60
    O think Antigone! We who are women
    Should not contend with men; we who are weak
    Are ruled by the stronger, so that we must obey
    In this and in matters that are yet more bitter.
    And so I pray the dead to pardon me   65
    If I obey our rulers, since I must.
    To be too bold in what we do is madness.
ANTIGONE. I will not urge you. And I would not thank you
    For any help that you might care to give me.
    Do what you please, but I will bury him,   70
    And if I die for that, I shall be happy.
    Loved, I shall rest beside the one I loved.
    My crime is innocence, for I owe the dead
    Longer allegiance than I owe the living.
    With the dead I lie forever. Live, if you choose,   75
    Dishonoring the laws the gods have hallowed.

ISMENE. No, I dishonor nothing. But to challenge
    Authority—I have not strength enough.
ANTIGONE. Then make that your excuse. I will go heap
    The earth above the brother that I love.   80
ISMENE. O Sister, Sister! How I fear for you!
ANTIGONE. No, not for me. Set your own life in order.
ISMENE. Well then, at least, tell no one of your plan.
    Keep it close hidden, as I too will keep it.
ANTIGONE. Oh! Publish it! Proclaim it to the world!   85
    Then I will hate you less than for your silence.
ISMENE. Your heart is hot for deeds that chill the blood.
ANTIGONE. I know that I give pleasure where I should.
ISMENE. Yes, if you can, but you will try in vain.
ANTIGONE. When my strength fails, then I shall try no longer. 90
ISMENE. A hopeless task should never be attempted.
ANTIGONE. Your words have won their just reward: my hatred
    And the long-lasting hatred of the dead.
    But leave me and the folly that is mine
    To undergo the worst that can befall me.   95
    I shall not suffer an ignoble death.
ISMENE. Go then, Antigone, if you must go.
    And yet remember, though your act is foolish,
    That those who love you do so with all their hearts.
    [*Exeunt* ANTIGONE *and* ISMENE. *Enter* CHORUS.]

CHORUS.
    Sunbeam, eye of the golden day, on Thebes the seven-gated,   100
        On Dircé's streams you have dawned at last, O fairest of light.
        Dawned on our foes, who had come enflamed by the quarrel
            of Polyneices,
        Shone on their glittering arms, made swifter their headlong
            flight.
           From Argos they came with their white shields flashing,
           Their helmets, crested with horsehair, agleam: 105
           An army that flew like a snow-white eagle
           Across our borders with shrilling scream.

    Above our roofs it soared, at our gates with greedy jaws it was
        gaping;
        But before their spears tasted our blood, and before our
        circle of towers
    Felt the flame of their torches, they turned to flight. The foes
        of the Theban dragon   110

101*ff*. The chorus of old men cele-
brates the victory won over the Argive
forces and Polyneices. Dircé is a river
of the Theban plain.

110. *Theban dragon*: According to
legend, the Thebans sprang from the
dragon's teeth sown by Cadmus.

Found the surge and clamor of battle too fierce for their
    feebler powers.
For Zeus, who abhors a proud tongue's boasting,
    Seeing their river of armor flow
Clashing and golden, struck with his lightning
To silence the shout of our foremost foe.   115

He crashed to the earth with his torch, who had scaled the top
    of our ramparts.
Raging in frenzy against us, breathing tempestuous hate,
Raging and threatening in vain. And mighty Ares, our ally,
    Dealing havoc around him, apportioned to other foemen their
    fate.
    For at seven portals, their seven leaders,   120
      Down to the earth their bronze arms threw
    In tribute to Zeus, the lord of the battle;
      Save the fated brothers, the wretched two,
      Who went to their common doom together,
        Each wielding a spear that the other slew.   125

Now glorious Victory smiles upon jubilant Thebes rich in
    chariots.
    Let us give free rein to our joy, forgetting our late-felt war;
Let us visit in night-long chorus the temples of all the immortals,
    With Bacchus, who shakes the land in the dances, going
    before.
      But behold! The son of Menoeceus approaches,   130
      Creon, the new-crowned King of the land,
    Made King by new fortunes the gods have allotted.
      What step has he pondered? What has he planned
    To lay before us, his council of elders,
      Who have gathered together at his command?   135

    [*Enter* CREON.]
CREON. Elders of Thebes, our city has been tossed
  By a tempestuous ocean, but the gods
  Have steadied it once more and made it safe.
  You, out of all the citizens, I have summoned,
  Because I knew that you once reverenced   140
  The sovereignty of Laius, and that later,
  When Oedipus was King and when he perished,
  Your steadfast loyalty upheld his children.
  And now his sons have fallen, each one stained
  By his brother's blood, killed by his brother's hand,   145

---

116. *He crashed* . . .: Capaneus, the
most violent of the Seven against Thebes.
    118. *Ares:* god of war and a patron
deity of Thebes.

So that the sovereignty devolves on me,
Since I by birth am nearest to the dead.
Certainly no man can be fully known,
Known in his soul, his will, his intellect,
Until he is tested and has proved himself   150
In statesmanship. Because a city's ruler,
Instead of following the wisest counsel,
May through some fear keep silent. Such a man
I think contemptible. And one whose friend
Has stronger claims upon him than his country,   155
Him I consider worthless. As for me,
I swear by Zeus, forever all-beholding,
That I would not keep silence, if I saw
Ruin instead of safety drawing near us;
Nor would I think an enemy of the state   160
Could be my friend. For I remember this:
Our country bears us all securely onward,
And only while it sails a steady course
Is friendship possible. Such are the laws
By which I guard the greatness of the city.   165
And kindred to them is the proclamation
That I have made to all the citizens
Concerning the two sons of Oedipus:
Eteocles, who has fallen in our defence,
Bravest of warriors, shall be entombed   170
With every honor, every offering given
That may accompany the noble dead
Down to their rest. But as for Polyneices,
He came from exile eager to consume
The city of his fathers with his fire   175
And all the temples of his father's gods,
Eager to drink deep of his kindred's blood,
Eager to drag us off to slavery.
To this man, therefore, nothing shall be given.
None shall lament him, none shall do him honor.   180
He shall be left without a grave, his corpse
Devoured by birds and dogs, a loathsome sight.
Such is my will. For never shall the wicked
Be given more approval than the just,
If I have power to stop it. But whoever   185
Feels in his heart affection for his city
Shall be rewarded both in life and death.
CHORUS. Creon, son of Menoeceus, it has pleased you
So to pass judgment on our friend and foe.
And you may give commands to all of us,   190
The living and the dead. Your will is law.
CREON. Then see that this command is carried out.

CHORUS. Sir, lay that burden on some younger man.
CREON. Sentries have been assigned to guard the body.
CHORUS. Then what additional duty would you give us?   195
CREON. Never to countenance the disobedient.
CHORUS. Who is so stupid as to long for death?
CREON. Death is indeed the punishment. Yet men
    Have often been destroyed by hope of gain.

    [*Enter* GUARD.]
GUARD. My Lord, I cannot say that I have hurried,   200
    Or that my running has made me lose my breath.
    I often stopped to think, and turned to go back.
    I stood there talking to myself: 'You fool,'
    I said, 'Why do you go to certain death?'
    And then: 'You idiot, are you still delaying?   205
    If someone else tells Creon, you will suffer.'
    I changed my mind this way, getting here slowly,
    Making a short road long. But still, at last,
    I did decide to come. And though my story
    Is nothing much to tell, yet I will tell it.   210
    One thing I know. I must endure my fate,
    But nothing more than that can happen to me.
CREON. What is the matter? What is troubling you?
GUARD. Please let me tell you first about myself.
    I did not do it. I did not see who did.   215
    It is not right for me to be punished for it.
CREON. You take good care not to expose yourself.
    Your news must certainly be something strange.
GUARD. Yes, it is strange—dreadful. I cannot speak.
CREON. Oh, tell it, will you? Tell it and go away!   220
GUARD. Well, it is this. Someone has buried the body,
    Just now, and gone—has sprinkled it with dust
    And given it other honors it should have.
CREON. What are you saying? Who has dared to do it?
GUARD. I cannot tell. Nothing was to be seen: 225
    No mark of pickaxe, no spot where a spade
    Had turned the earth. The ground was hard and dry,
    Unbroken—not a trace of any wheels—
    No sign to show who did it. When the sentry
    On the first watch discovered it and told us,   230
    We were struck dumb with fright. For he was hidden
    Not by a tomb but a light coat of dust,
    As if a pious hand had scattered it.
    There were no tracks of any animal,
    A dog or wild beast that had come to tear him.   235
    We all began to quarrel, and since no one
    Was there to stop us, nearly came to blows.

Everyone was accused, and everyone
Denied his guilt. We could discover nothing.
We were quite willing to handle red-hot iron,   240
To walk through fire, to swear by all the gods
That we were innocent of the deed itself,
And innocent of taking any part
In planning it or doing it. At last
One of us spoke. We trembled and hung our heads,   245
For he was right; we could not argue with him,
Yet his advice was bound to cause us trouble.
He told us all this had to be reported,
Not kept a secret. We all agreed to that.
We drew lots for it, and I had no luck.   250
I won the prize and was condemned to come.
So here I stand, unwilling, because I know
The bringer of bad news is never welcome.

CHORUS. Sir, as he spoke, I have been wondering.
Can this be, possibly, the work of gods?   255

CREON. Be silent! Before you madden me! You are old.
Would you be senseless also? What you say
Is unendurable. You say the gods
Cared for this corpse. Then was it for reward,
Mighty to match his mighty services,   260
That the gods covered him? He who came to burn
Their pillared temples and their votive offerings,
Ravage their land, and trample down the state.
Or is it your opinion that the gods
Honor the wicked? Inconceivable!   265
However, from the first, some citizens
Who found it difficult to endure this edict,
Muttered against me, shaking their heads in secret,
Instead of bowing down beneath the yoke,
Obedient and contented with my rule.   270
These are the men who are responsible,
For I am certain they have bribed the guards
To bury him. Nothing is worse than money.
Money lays waste to cities, banishes
Men from their homes, indoctrinates the heart,   275
Perverting honesty to works of shame,
Showing men how to practice villainy,
Subduing them to every godless deed.
But all those men who got their pay for this
Need have no doubt their turn to pay will come.   280
[To *the* GUARD] Now, you. As I still honor Zeus the King,
I tell you, and I swear it solemnly,
Either you find the man who did this thing,

The very man, and bring him here to me,
Or you will not just die. Before you die,   285
You will be tortured until you have explained
This outrage; so that later when you steal
You will know better where to look for money
And not expect to find it everywhere.
Ill-gotten wealth brings ruin and not safety.   290
GUARD. Sir, may I speak? Or shall I merely go?
CREON. You can say nothing that is not offensive.
GUARD. Do I offend your hearing or your heart?
CREON. Is it your business to define the spot?
GUARD. The criminal hurts your heart, and I your ears.   295
CREON. Still talking? Why, you must have been born talking!
GUARD. Perhaps. But I am not the guilty man.
CREON. You are. And what is more you sold yourself.
GUARD. You have judged me, sir, and have misjudged me, too.
CREON. Be clever about judging if you care to.   300
But you will say that treachery leads to sorrow
Unless you find the man and show him to me.
        [*Exit* CREON.]

GUARD. Finding him is the best thing that could happen.
Fate will decide. But however that may be,
You never are going to see me here again.   305
I have escaped! I could not have hoped for that.
I owe the gods my thanks for guarding me.
        [*Exit* GUARD.]

CHORUS.
Many the marvelous things; but none that can be
More of a marvel than man! This being that braves   309
With the south wind of winter the whitened streaks of the sea,
Threading his way through the troughs of engulfing waves.
And the earth most ancient, the eldest of all the gods,
Earth, undecaying, unwearied, he wears away with his toil;
Forward and back with his plowshare, year after year, he plods,
With his horses turning the soil.   315

Man in devising excels. The birds of the air,
That light-minded race, he entangles fast in his toils.
Wild creatures he catches, casting about them his snare,
And the salt-sea brood he nets in his woven coils.
The tireless bull he has tamed, and the beast whose lair   320
Is hidden deep in the wilds, who roams in the wooded hills.
He has fitted a yoke that the neck of the shaggy-maned horse will
        bear;
He is master of all through his skills.

He has taught himself speech, and wind-like thought, and the lore
    Of ruling a town. He has fled the arrows of rain,   325
The searching arrows of frost he need fear no more,
    That under a starry sky are endured with pain.
Provision for all he has made—unprovided for naught,
    Save death itself, that in days to come will take shape.
From obscure and deep-seated disease he has subtly wrought   330
    A way of escape.

Resourceful and skilled, with an inconceivable art,
    He follows his course to a good or an evil end.
When he holds the canons of justice high in his heart
    And has sworn to the gods the laws of the land to defend,   335
Proud stands his city; without a city is he
    Who with ugliness, rashness, or evil dishonors the day.
Let me shun his thoughts. Let him share no hearthstone with me,
    Who acts in this way!

CHORUS. Look there! Look there! What portent can this be?   340
    Antigone! I know her, it is she!
    Daughter of Oedipus a prisoner brought?
    You defied Creon? You in folly caught?

      [*Enter* GUARD *with* ANTIGONE.]
GUARD. She did it. Here she is. We caught this girl   345
    As she was burying him. Where is the King?
CHORUS. Leaving the palace there, just as we need him.

      [*Enter* CREON.]
CREON. Why do you need my presence? What has happened?
GUARD. My Lord, no one should take a solemn oath
    Not to do something, for his second thoughts
    Make him a liar. I vowed not to hurry back.   350
    I had been battered by your storm of threats.
    But when a joy comes that exceeds our hopes,
    No other happiness can equal it.
    So I have broken my vow. I have returned,
    Bringing this girl along. She was discovered   355
    Busy with all the rites of burial.
    There was no casting lots, no, not this time!
    Such luck as this was mine and no one else's.
    Now sir, take her yourself, examine her,
    Convict her, do what you like. But as for me,   360
    I have the right to a complete acquittal.
CREON. This is the girl you caught? How? Where was she?
GUARD. Burying the dead man, just as I have told you.

CREON. Do you mean that? Or have you lost your mind?
GUARD. Your order was that he should not be buried.   365
   I saw her bury him. Is that all clear?
CREON. How was she seen? You caught her in the act?
GUARD. This was what happened. When we had gotten back, ˙
   With your threats following us, we swept away
   The dust that covered him. We left him bare,   370
   A rotting corpse. And then we sat to windward,
   Up on the hillside, to avoid the stench.
   All of us were alert, and kept awake
   Threatening each other. No one could get careless.
   So the time passed, until the blazing sun   375
   Stood at the zenith, and the heat was burning.
   Then suddenly the wind came in a blast,
   Lifting a cloud of dust up from the earth,
   Troubling the sky and choking the whole plain,
   Stripping off all the foliage of the woods,   380
   Filling the breadth of heaven. We closed our eyes
   And bore the affliction that the gods had sent us.
   When it had finally stopped, we saw this girl.
   She wailed aloud with a sharp, bitter cry,
   The cry a bird gives seeing its empty nest   385
   Robbed of its brood. And she too, when she saw
   The naked body, was loud in her lament
   And cursed the men who had uncovered him.
   Quickly she sprinkled him with dust, and then
   Lifting a pitcher, poured out three libations   390
   To do him honor. When we ran and caught her,
   She was unterrified. When we accused her
   Both of her earlier and her present act,
   She made no effort to deny the charges.
   I am part glad, part sorry. It is good   395
   To find that you yourself have gotten clear,
   But to bring trouble on your friends is hard.
   However, nothing counts except my safety.
CREON. [*To* ANTIGONE] You there. You, looking at the ground. Tell
   me.
   Do you admit this or deny it? Which?   400
ANTIGONE. Yes, I admit it. I do not deny it.
CREON. [*To* GUARD] Go. You are free. The charge is dropped.
     [*Exit* GUARD.]
                              Now you,
   Answer this question. Make your answer brief.
   You knew there was a law forbidding this?
ANTIGONE. Of course I knew it. Why not? It was public.   405
CREON. And you have dared to disobey the law?

ANTIGONE. Yes. For this law was not proclaimed by Zeus,
Or by the gods who rule the world below.
I do not think your edicts have such power
That they can override the laws of heaven,   410
Unwritten and unfailing, laws whose life
Belongs not to today or yesterday
But to time everlasting; and no man
Knows the first moment that they had their being.
If I transgressed these laws because I feared   415
The arrogance of man, how to the gods
Could I make satisfaction? Well I know,
Being a mortal, that I have to die,
Even without your proclamations. Yet
If I must die before my time is come,   420
That is a blessing. Because to one who lives,
As I live, in the midst of sorrows, death
Is of necessity desirable.
For me, to face death is a trifling pain
That does not trouble me. But to have left   425
The body of my brother, my own brother,
Lying unburied would be bitter grief.
And if these acts of mine seem foolish to you,
Perhaps a fool accuses me of folly.
CHORUS. The violent daughter of a violent father,   430
She cannot bend before a storm of evils.
CREON. [*To* ANTIGONE] Stubborn? Self-willed? People like that, I tell
    you,
Are the first to come to grief. The hardest iron,
Baked in the fire, most quickly flies to pieces.
An unruly horse is taught obedience   435
By a touch of the curb. How can you be so proud?
You, a mere slave? [*To* CHORUS] She was well schooled already
In insolence, when she defied the law.
And now look at her! Boasting, insolent,
Exulting in what she did. And if she triumphs
And goes unpunished, I am no man—she is.   440
If she were more than niece, if she were closer
Than anyone who worships at my altar,
She would not even then escape her doom,
A dreadful death. Nor would her sister. Yes,
Her sister had a share in burying him.   445
[*To* ATTENDANT] Go bring her here. I have just seen her, raving,
Beside herself. Even before they act,
Traitors who plot their treason in the dark
Betray themselves like that. Detestable!

[*To* ANTIGONE] But hateful also is an evil-doer   450
    Who, caught red-handed, glorifies the crime.

ANTIGONE. Now you have caught me, will you do more than kill me?

CREON. No, only that. With that I am satisfied.

ANTIGONE. Then why do you delay? You have said nothing
    I do not hate. I pray you never will.   455
    And you hate what I say. Yet how could I
    Have won more splendid honor than by giving
    Due burial to my brother? All men here
    Would grant me their approval, if their lips
    Were not sealed up in fear. But you, a king,   460
    Blessed by good fortune in much else besides,
    Can speak and act with perfect liberty.

CREON. All of these Thebans disagree with you.

ANTIGONE. No. They agree, but they control their tongues.

CREON. You feel no shame in acting without their help?   465

ANTIGONE. I feel no shame in honoring a brother.

CREON. Another brother died who fought against him.

ANTIGONE. Two brothers. The two sons of the same parents.

CREON. Honor to one is outrage to the other.

ANTIGONE. Eteocles will not feel himself dishonored.   470

CREON. What! When his rites are offered to a traitor?

ANTIGONE. It was his brother, not his slave, who died.

CREON. One who attacked the land that he defended.

ANTIGONE. The gods still wish those rites to be performed.

CREON. Are the just pleased with the unjust as their equals?   475

ANTIGONE. That may be virtuous in the world below.

CREON. No. Even there a foe is never a friend.

ANTIGONE. I am not made for hatred but for love.

CREON. Then go down to the dead. If you must love,
    Love them. While I yet live, no woman rules me.   480

CHORUS. Look there. Ismene, weeping as sisters weep.
    The shadow of a cloud of grief lies deep
    On her face, darkly flushed; and in her pain
    Her tears are falling like a flood of rain.

[*Enter* ISMENE *and* ATTENDANTS.]

CREON. You viper! Lying hidden in my house,   485
    Sucking my blood in secret, while I reared,
    Unknowingly, two subverters of my throne.
    Do you confess that you have taken part
    In this man's burial, or deny it? Speak.

ISMENE. If she will recognize my right to say so,   490
    I shared the action and I share the blame.

ANTIGONE. No. That would not be just. I never let you

Take any part in what you disapproved of.
ISMENE. In your calamity, I am not ashamed
  To stand beside you, beaten by this tempest.   495
ANTIGONE. The dead are witnesses of what I did,
  To love in words alone is not enough.
ISMENE. Do not reject me, Sister! Let me die
  Beside you, and do honor to the dead.
ANTIGONE. No. You will neither share my death nor claim   500
  What I have done. My death will be sufficient.
ISMENE. What happiness can I have when you are gone?
ANTIGONE. Ask Creon that. He is the one you value.
ISMENE. Do you gain anything by taunting me?
ANTIGONE. Ah, no! By taunting you, I hurt myself.   505
ISMENE. How can I help you? Tell me what I can do.
ANTIGONE. Protect yourself. I do not grudge your safety.
ISMENE. Antigone! Shall I not share your fate?
ANTIGONE. We both have made our choices: life, and death.
ISMENE. At least I tried to stop you. I protested.   510
ANTIGONE. Some have approved your way; and others, mine.
ISMENE. Yet now I share your guilt. I too am ruined.
ANTIGONE. Take courage. Live your life. But I long since
  Gave myself up to death to help the dead.
CREON. One of them has just lost her senses now.   515
  The other has been foolish all her life.
ISMENE. We cannot always use our reason clearly.
  Suffering confuses us and clouds our minds.
CREON. It clouds your mind. You join in her wrong-doing.
ISMENE. How is life possible without my sister?   520
CREON. Your sister? You have no sister. She is dead.
ISMENE. Then you will kill the wife your son has chosen?
CREON. Yes. There are other fields that he can plow.
ISMENE. He will not find such an enduring love.
CREON. A wicked woman for my son? No, never!   525
ANTIGONE. O Haemon, Haemon! How your father wrongs you!
CREON. You and your marriage! Let me hear no more!
CHORUS. You are unyielding? You will take her from him?
CREON. Death will act for me. Death will stop the marriage.
CHORUS. It seems, then, you have sentenced her to death.   530
CREON. Yes. And my sentence you yourselves accepted.
  Take them inside. From now on, they are women,
  And have no liberty. For even the bold
  Seek an escape when they see death approaching.
    [*Exeunt* ANTIGONE, ISMENE, *and* ATTENDANTS.]
CHORUS.
    Blessèd the life that has no evil known,   535
  For the gods, striking, strike down a whole race—

Doomed parent and doomed child both overthrown.
As when the fierce breath of the winds of Thrace
   Across the darkness of the sea has blown
A rushing surge; black sand from deep below   540
   Comes boiling up; wind-beaten headlands moan,
Fronting the full shock of the billow's blow.

The race of Oedipus, from days of old,
To long dead sorrows add new sorrows' weight.
   Some god has sent them sufferings manifold.   545
None may release another, for their fate
   Through generations loosens not its hold.
Now is their last root cut, their last light fled,
   Because of frenzy's curse, words overbold,
And dust, the gods' due, on the bloodstained dead.   550

O Zeus, what human sin restricts thy might?
Thou art unsnared by all-ensnaring sleep
   Or tireless months. Unaging thou dost keep
Thy court in splendor of Olympian light.
   And as this law was true when time began,   555
Tomorrow and forever it shall be:
   Naught beyond measure in the life of man
      From fate goes free.

For hope, wide-ranging, that brings good to some,
To many is a false lure of desire   560
   Light-minded, giddy; and until the fire
Scorches their feet, they know not what will come.
   Wise is the famous adage: that to one
Whom the gods madden, evil, soon or late,
   Seems good; then can he but a moment shun   565
      The stroke of fate.

But Haemon comes, of your two sons the last.
Is his heart heavy for the sentence passed
   Upon Antigone, his promised bride,
And for his hope of marriage now denied?   570

   [*Enter* HAEMON.]
CREON. We soon shall know better than seers could tell us.
   My son, Antigone is condemned to death.
   Nothing can change my sentence. Have you learned
   Her fate and come here in a storm of anger,
   Or do you love me and support my acts?   575
HAEMON. Father, I am your son. Your greater knowledge

Will trace the pathway that I mean to follow.
My marriage cannot be of more importance
Than to be guided always by your wisdom.

CREON. Yes, Haemon, this should be the law you live by! 580
In all things to obey your father's will.
Men pray for children round them in their homes
Only to see them dutiful and quick
With hatred to requite their father's foe,
With honor to repay their father's friend. 585
But what is there to say of one whose children
Prove to be valueless? That he has fathered
Grief for himself and laughter for his foes.
Then, Haemon, do not, at the lure of pleasure,
Unseat your reason for a woman's sake. 590
This comfort soon grows cold in your embrace:
A wicked wife to share your bed and home.
Is there a deeper wound than to find worthless
The one you love? Turn from this girl with loathing.
As from an enemy, and let her go 595
To get a husband in the world below.
For I have found her openly rebellious,
Her only out of all the city. Therefore,
I will not break the oath that I have sworn.
I will have her killed. Vainly she will invoke 600
The bond of kindred blood the gods make sacred.
If I permit disloyalty to breed
In my own house, I nurture it in strangers.
He who is righteous with his kin is righteous
In the state also. Therefore, I cannot pardon 605
One who does violence to the laws or thinks
To dictate to his rulers; for whoever
May be the man appointed by the city,
That man must be obeyed in everything,
Little or great, just or unjust. And surely 610
He who was thus obedient would be found
As good a ruler as he was a subject;
And in a storm of spears he would stand fast
With loyal courage at his comrade's side.
But disobedience is the worst of evils. 615
For it is this that ruins cities; this
Makes our homes desolate; armies of allies
Through this break up in rout. But most men find
Their happiness and safety in obedience.
Therefore we must support the law, and never 620
Be beaten by a woman. It is better
To fall by a man's hand, if we must fall,

Than to be known as weaker than a girl.
CHORUS. We may in our old age have lost our judgment,
  And yet to us you seem to have spoken wisely.   625
HAEMON. The gods have given men the gift of reason,
  Greatest of all things that we call our own.
  I have no skill, nor do I wish to have it,
  To show where you have spoken wrongly. Yet
  Some other's thought, beside your own, might prove   630
  To be of value. Therefore it is my duty,
  My natural duty as your son, to notice,
  On your behalf, all that men say, or do,
  Or find to blame. For your frown frightens them,
  So that the citizen dares not say a word   635
  That would offend you. I can hear, however,
  Murmurs in darkness and laments for her.
  They say: "No woman ever less deserved
  Her doom, no woman ever was to die
  So shamefully for deeds so glorious.   640
  For when her brother fell in bloody battle,
  She would not let his body lie unburied
  To be devoured by carrion dogs or birds.
  Does such a woman not deserve reward,
  Reward of golden honor?" This I hear,   645
  A rumor spread in secrecy and darkness.
  Father, I prize nothing in life so highly
  As your well-being. How can children have
  A nobler honor than their father's fame
  Or father than his son's? Then do not think   650
  Your mood must never alter; do not feel
  Your word, and yours alone, must be correct.
  For if a man believes that he is right
  And only he, that no one equals him
  In what he says or thinks, he will be found   655
  Empty when searched and tested. Because a man
  Even if he be wise, feels no disgrace
  In learning many things, in taking care
  Not to be over-rigid. You have seen
  Trees on the margin of a stream in winter: 660
  Those yielding to the flood save every twig,
  And those resisting perish root and branch.
  So, too, the mariner who never slackens
  His taut sheet overturns his craft and spends
  Keel uppermost the last part of his voyage.   665
  Let your resentment die. Let yourself change.
  For I believe—if I, a younger man,
  May have a sound opinion—it is best

That men by nature should be wise in all things.
But most men find they cannot reach that goal; 670
And when this happens, it is also good
To learn to listen to wise counselors.

CHORUS. Sir, when his words are timely, you should heed them.
And Haemon, you should profit by his words.
Each one of you has spoken reasonably. 675

CREON. Are men as old as I am to be taught
How to behave by men as young as he?

HAEMON: Not to do wrong. If I am young, ignore
My youth. Consider only what I do.

CREON. Have you done well in honoring the rebellious? 680

HAEMON. Those who do wrong should not command respect.

CREON. Then that disease has not infected her?

HAEMON. All of our city with one voice denies it.

CREON. Does Thebes give orders for the way I rule?

HAEMON. How young you are! How young in saying that! 685

CREON. Am I to govern by another's judgment?

HAEMON. A city that is one man's is no city.

CREON. A city is the king's. That much is sure.

HAEMON. You would rule well in a deserted country.

CREON. This boy defends a woman, it appears. 690

HAEMON. If you are one. I am concerned for you.

CREON. To quarrel with your father does not shame you?

HAEMON. Not when I see you failing to do justice.

CREON. Am I unjust when I respect my crown?

HAEMON. Respect it! When you trample down religion? 695

CREON. Infamous! Giving first place to a woman!

HAEMON. But never to anything that would disgrace me.

CREON. Each word you utter is a plea for her.

HAEMON. For you, too, and for me, and for the gods.

CREON. You shall not marry her this side of death. 700

HAEMON. Then if she dies, she does not die alone.

CREON. What! Has it come to this? You threaten me?

HAEMON. No. But I tell you your decree is useless.

CREON. You will repent this. You! Teaching me wisdom!

HAEMON. I will not call you mad. You are my father. 705

CREON. You woman's slave! Your talk will not persuade me.

HEAMON. Then what you want is to make all the speeches.

CREON. So. Now by all the gods in heaven above us,
One thing is certain: you are going to pay
For taunting and insulting me. [*To* ATTENDANTS] Bring out 710
That hated object. Let her die this moment,
Here, at her bridegroom's feet, before his eyes.

HAEMON. No, you are wrong. Not at my feet. And never

Will you set eyes upon my face again.   714
  Rage, rave, with anyone who can bear to listen.   [*Exit* HAEMON.]
CHORUS. Sir, he is gone; his anger gives him speed.
  Young men are bitter in their agony.
CREON. Let him imagine more than man can do,
  Or let him do more. Never shall he save
  These two girls; they are going to their doom.   720
CHORUS. Do you intend to put them both to death?
CREON. That was well said. No, not the innocent.
CHORUS. And the other? In what way is she to die?
CREON. Along a desolate pathway I will lead her,
  And shut her, living, in a rocky vault   725
  With no more food than will appease the gods,
  So that the city may not be defiled.
  Hades, who is the only god she worships,
  May hear her prayers, and rescue her from death.
  Otherwise she will learn at last, though late,   730
  That to revere the dead is useless toil.   [*Exit* CREON.]
CHORUS.
  None may withstand you, O love unconquered,
    Seizing the wealth of man as your prey,
  In the cheek of a maiden keeping your vigil,
    Till night has faded again to day.   735
  You roam the wilds to men's farthest dwellings,
    You haunt the boundless face of the sea.
  No god may escape you, no short-lived mortal
    From the madness that love inflicts may flee.

  You twist our minds until ruin follows.   740
    The just to unrighteous ways you turn.
  You have goaded kinsman to strive with kinsman
    Till the fires of bitter hatred burn.
  In the eyes of a bride you shine triumphant;
    Beside the eternal laws your throne   745
  Eternal stands, for great Aphrodite,
    Resistless, works her will on her own.

  But now I too am moved. I cannot keep
    Within the bounds of loyalty. I weep
  When I behold Antigone, the bride,   750
    Near the room where all at last abide.

726-727. *With no more food . . . de-*
filed: This passage is obscure; the penalty proposed by Creon seems to be imprisonment in a tomb with a certain
ration of food. Since Antigone would die
of starvation but not actually by anyone's hand, Creon seems to think that
the city will not be "defiled," *i.e.* incur
blood-guilt.

[*Enter* ANTIGONE, *guarded.*]

ANTIGONE.

See me, my countrymen! See with what pain
I tread the path I shall not tread again,
Looking my last upon the light of day
  That shines for me no more.   755
Hades, who gives his sleep to all, me, living, leads away
  To Acheron's dark shore.
Not mine the hymeneal chant, not mine the bridal song,
  For I, a bride, to Acheron belong.

CHORUS.

Glorious, therefore, and with praise you tread   760
The pathway to the deep gulf of the dead.
You have not felt the force of fate's decrees,
Struck down by violence, wasted by disease;
But of your own free will you choose to go,
Alone of mortals, to the world below.   765

ANTIGONE.

I know how sad a death she suffered, she
Who was our guest here, Phrygian Niobe.
Stone spread upon her, close as ivy grows,
  And locked her in its chains.
Now on her wasted form, men say, fall ceaselessly the snows, 770
  Fall ceaselessly the rains;
While from her grieving eyes drop tears, tears that her bosom
  steep.
And like hers, my fate lulls me now to sleep.

CHORUS.

She was a goddess of the gods' great race;
Mortals are we and mortal lineage trace.   775
But for a woman the renown is great
In life and death to share a godlike fate.

ANTIGONE.

By our fathers' gods, I am mocked! I am mocked! Ah! why,
  You men of wealth, do you taunt me before I die? 780
O sacred grove of the city! O waters that flow
  From the spring of Dircé! Be witness; to you I cry.
What manner of woman I am you know
And by what laws, unloved, unlamented, I go
  To my rocky prison, to my unnatural tomb. 785
   Alas, how ill-bestead!

767. *Niobe:* a Phrygian princess married to Amphion, king of Thebes. She boasted that she had borne more children than Leto, mother of Apollo and Artemis; these two killed her children. She returned to Phrygia where she was turned into a rock on Mount Sipylus; the melting of the snow on the mountain caused 'tears' to flow down the rock formation which resembled a woman's face.

No fellowship have I; no others can share my doom,
Neither mortals nor corpses, neither the quick nor the dead.

CHORUS.

You have rushed forward with audacious feet
And dashed yourself against the law's high seat. 790
That was a grievous fall, my child, and yet
In this ordeal you pay your father's debt.

ANTIGONE.

You have touched on the heaviest grief that my heart can hold:
Grief for my father, sorrow that never grows old
For our famous house and its doom that the fates have spun. 795
My mother's bed! Ah! How can its horrors be told?
My mother who yielded her love to one
Who was at once my father and her son.
Born of such parents, with them henceforth I abide,
Wretched, accursed, unwed. 800
And you, Polyneices, you found an ill-fated bride,
And I, the living, am ruined by you, the dead.

CHORUS.

A pious action may of praise be sure,
But he who rules a land cannot endure
An act of disobedience to his rule. 805
Your own self-will you have not learned to school.

ANTIGONE.

Unwept, unfriended, without marriage song,
Forth on my road I miserable am led;
I may not linger. Not for long
Shall I, most wretched, see the holy sun. 810
My fate no friend bewails, not one;
For me no tear is shed.

[*Enter* CREON.]

CREON. Do you not know that singing and lamentation
Would rise incessantly as death approached,
If they could be of service? Lead her away! 815
Obey my orders. Shut her in her grave
And leave her there, alone. Then she can take
Her choice of living in that home, or dying.
I am not stained by the guilt of this girl's blood,
But she shall see the light of day no longer. 820

ANTIGONE. O tomb! O cavern! Everlasting prison!
O bridal-chamber! To you I make my way
To join my kindred, all those who have died
And have been greeted by Persephone.

824. *Persephone:* the queen of the underworld.

The last and far most miserable of all,   825
I seek them now, before I have lived my life.
Yet high are the hopes I cherish that my coming
Will be most welcome to my father; welcome,
Mother, to you; and welcome to you, Brother.
For when you died I ministered to you all,   830
With my own hands washed you and dressed your bodies,
And poured libations at your graves. And now,
Because I have given to you, too, Polyneices,
Such honors as I could, I am brought to this.
And yet all wise men will approve my act.   835
Not for my children, had I been a mother,
Not for a husband, for his moldering body,
Would I have set myself against the city
As I have done. And the law sanctions me.
Losing a husband, I might find another.   840
I could have other children. But my parents
Are hidden from me in the underworld,
So that no brother's life can bud and bloom
Ever again. And therefore, Polyneices,
I paid you special honor. And for this   845
Creon has held me guilty of evil-doing,
And leads me captive for my too great boldness.
No bridal bed is mine, no bridal song,
No share in the joys of marriage, and no share
In nursing children and in tending them.   850
But thus afflicted, destitute of friends,
Living, I go down to the vaults of death.
What is the law of heaven that I have broken?
Why should I any longer look to the gods,
Ill-fated as I am? Whose aid should I invoke,   855
When I for piety am called impious?
If this pleases the gods, then I shall learn
That sin brought death upon me. But if the sin
Lies in my judges, I could wish for them
No harsher fate than they have decreed for me.   860

CHORUS. Still the storm rages; still the same gusts blow,
   Troubling her spirit with their savage breath.
CREON. Yes. And her guards will pay for being slow.
ANTIGONE. Ah! With those words I have drawn close to death.
CREON. You cannot hope that you will now be freed   865
   From the fulfillment of the doom decreed.
ANTIGONE.
   O Thebes, O land of my fathers, O city!
   O gods who begot and guarded my house from of old!
      They seize me, they snatch me away!

Now, now! They show no pity. 870
They give no second's delay.
You elders, you leaders of Thebes, behold me, behold!
The last of the house of your kings, the last
See what I suffer. See the doom
That is come upon me, and see from whom, 875
Because to the laws of heaven I held fast.

[*Exeunt* ANTIGONE *and* GUARDS.]

CHORUS.

This likewise Danaë endured:
The light of heaven she changed for a home brass-bound,
In a tomb-like chamber close immured.
And yet, O my child, her race was with honor crowned, 880
And she guarded the seed of Zeus gold-showered.
But naught from the terrible power of fate is free.
Neither war, nor city walls high-towered,
Nor wealth, nor black ships beaten by the sea.

He too bowed down beneath his doom, 885
The son of Dryas, swift-angered Edonian king,
Shut fast in a rocky prison's gloom.
How he roused the god with his mad tongue's mocking sting,
As his frenzy faded, he came to know;
For he sought to make the god-filled maenads mute, 890
To quench the Bacchic torches' glow,
And angered the Muses, lovers of the flute.

By the double sea and the dark rocks steely blue
The beach of Bosporus lies and the savage shore
Of Thracian Salmydessus. There the bride 895
Of Phineus, whose fierce heart no mercy knew,
Dealt his two sons a blow that for vengeance cried;
Ares beheld her hand, all stained with gore,
Grasping the pointed shuttle that pierced through
Their eyes that saw no more. 900

877. *Danaë:* daughter of Acrisius, king of Argos. It was prophesied that he would be killed by his daughter's son; so he shut her up in a bronze tower. But Zeus came to her in the form of a golden rainshower and she bore a son, Perseus, who did in the end kill his grandfather.

886. *son of Dryas:* Lycurgus, the Thracian (Edonian) king. He opposed the introduction of Dionysiac religion into his kingdom and was imprisoned by the god.

893ff. *By the double sea . . . :* The whole story is difficult to follow and its application to the case of Antigone obscure. Cleopatra, the daughter of the Athenian princess Orithyia, whom Boreas, the North Wind, carried off to his home in Thrace (*cf. l.* 902ff.), was married to Phineus, the Thracian king, and bore him two sons. He tired of her, abandoned her, and married Eidothea, "the bride of Phineus" (ll. 895-896). Eidothea put out the eyes of the two sons of Cleopatra. Ares, the god of war, associated with Thrace, watched the savage act.

In misery pining, their lot they lamented aloud,
    So is of a mother whose fortune in marriage was ill.
From the ancient line of Erechtheus her blood she traced;
    Nurtured in caves far-distant and nursed in cloud,
Daughter of Boreas, daughter of gods, she raced   905
    Swift as a steed on the slope of the soaring hill.
And yet, O child, O child, she also bowed
    To the long-lived fates' harsh will.

[*Enter* TIRESIAS *and* BOY.]

TIRESIAS. Elders of Thebes, we have come to you with one
    Finding for both the pathway that we followed,   910
    For in this fashion must the blind be guided.
CREON. What tidings, old Tiresias, are you bringing?
TIRESIAS. I will inform you, I the seer. Give heed.
CREON. To ignore your counsel has not been my custom.
TIRESIAS. Therefore you kept Thebes on a steady course.   915
CREON. I can bear witness to the help you gave.
TIRESIAS. Mark this. You stand upon the brink of ruin.
CREON. What terrible words are those? What do you mean?
TIRESIAS. My meaning is made manifest by my art
    And my art's omens. As I took my station   920
    Upon my ancient seat of augury,
    Where round me birds of every sort come flocking,
    I could no longer understand their language.
    It was drowned out in a strange, savage clamor,
    Shrill, evil, frenzied, inarticulate.   925
    The whirr of wings told me their murderous talons
    Tore at each other. Filled with dread, I then
    Made trial of burnt sacrifice. The altar
    Was fully kindled, but no clear, bright flame
    Leaped from the offering; only fatty moisture   930
    Oozed from the flesh and trickled on the embers,
    Smoking and sputtering. The bladder burst,
    And scattered in the air. The folds of fat
    Wrapping the thigh-bones melted and left them bare.
    Such was the failure of the sacrifice,   935
    That did not yield the sign that I was seeking.
    I learned these things from this boy's observation;
    He is my guide as I am guide to others.
    Your edict brings this suffering to the city,
    For every hearth of ours has been defiled   940
    And every altar. There the birds and dogs
    Have brought their carrion, torn from the corpse
    Of ill-starred Polyneices. Hence, the gods
    Refuse our prayers, refuse our sacrifice,
    Refuse the flame of our burnt-offerings.   945

No birds cry clearly and auspiciously,
For they are glutted with a slain man's blood.
Therefore, my son, consider what has happened.
All men are liable to grievous error;
But he who, having erred, does not remain   950
Inflexible, but rather makes amends
For ill, is not unwise or unrewarded.
Stubborn self-will incurs the charge of folly.
Give to the fallen the honors he deserves
And do not stab him. Are you being brave   955
When you inflict new death upon the dead?
Your good I think of; for your good I speak,
And a wise counselor is sweet to hear
When the advice he offers proves of value.
CREON. Old man, all of you shoot your arrows at me   960
Like archers at a target. You have used
Even the art of prophecy in your plotting.
Long have the tribe of prophets traded in me,
Like a ship's cargo. Drive whatever bargain
May please you, buy, sell, heap up for yourself   965
Silver of Sardis, gold of India. Yet
I tell you this: that man shall not be buried,
Not though the eagles of Zeus himself should bear
The carrion morsels to their master's throne.
Not even from the dread of such pollution   970
Will I permit his burial, since I know
There is no mortal can defile the gods.
But even the wisest men disastrously
May fall, Tiresias, when for money's sake
They utter shameful words with specious wisdom.   975
TIRESIAS. Ah! Do men understand, or even consider—
CREON. Consider what? Doubtless some platitude!
TIRESIAS. How precious beyond any wealth is prudence.
CREON. How full of evil is the lack of prudence.
TIRESIAS. Yet you are sick, sick with that same disease. 980
CREON. I will not in reply revile a prophet.
TIRESIAS. You do. You say my prophecy is false.
CREON. Well, all the race of seers are mercenary.
TIRESIAS. And love of base wealth marks the breed of tyrants.
CREON. Are you aware that you address your King?   985
TIRESIAS. I made you King by helping you save Thebes.
CREON. Wise in your art and vicious in your acts.
TIRESIAS. Do not enrage me. I should keep my secret.
CREON. Reveal it. Speak. But do not look for profit.
TIRESIAS. You too will find no profit in my words.   990
CREON. How can you earn your pay? I will not change.
TIRESIAS. Then know this. Yes, be very sure of it.

Only a few more times will you behold
The swift course of the chariot of the sun
Before you give as payment for the dead   995
Your own dead flesh and blood. For you have thrust
A living soul to darkness, in a tomb
Imprisoned without pity. And a corpse,
Belonging to the gods below you keep
Unpurified, unburied, unrevered.   1000
The dead are no concern either of yours
Or of the gods above, yet you offend them.
So the avengers, the destroyers, Furies
Of Hades and the gods, lurking in ambush,
Wait to inflict your sins upon your head.   1005
Do you still think my tongue is lined with silver?
A time will come, and will not linger coming,
That will awaken in your house the wailing
Of men and women. Hatred shakes the cities,
Hatred of you. Their sons are mangled corpses,   1010
Hallowed with funeral rites by dogs or beasts
Or birds who bear the all-polluting stench
To every city having hearth or altar.
You goaded me, and therefore like an archer
I shoot my angry arrows at your heart,   1015
Sure arrows; you shall not escape their sting.
Boy, lead me home. Let him expend his rage
On younger men, and let him learn to speak
With a more temperate tongue, and school his heart
To feelings finer than his present mood.   1020
     [*Exeunt* TIRESIAS *and* BOY.]
CHORUS. Sir, he is gone, with fearful prophecies.
    And from the time that these dark hairs have whitened,
    I have known this: never has he foretold
    Anything that proved false concerning Thebes.
CREON. I also know it well, and it dismays me.   1025
    To yield is bitter. But to resist, and bring
    A curse upon my pride is no less bitter.
CHORUS. Son of Menoeceus, listen. You must listen.
CREON. What should I do? Tell me, I will obey.
CHORUS. Go. Free the girl. Release her from the cavern,   1030
    And build a tomb for the man you would not bury.
CREON. So that is your advice—that I should yield?
CHORUS. Sir, you should not delay. The gods are swift
    In cutting short man's folly with their curse.
CREON. How hard it is to change! Yet I obey.   1035
    I will give up what I had set my heart on.

1009. *Hatred shakes the cities:* Creon   champions, not only Polynices.
had exposed the corpses of all seven

No one can stand against the blows of fate.
CHORUS. Go. Go yourself. These things are not for others.
CREON. I will go this moment. Guards there! All of you!
    Take up your axes. Quick! Quick! Over there.   1040
    I imprisoned her myself, and I myself
    Will set her free. And yet my mind misgives me.
    Never to break the ancient law is best.   [*Exit* CREON.]
CHORUS.
        Thou art known by many a name.
        O Bacchus! To thee we call.   1045
        Cadmean Semele's glory and pride,
    Begotten of Zeus, whose terrible lightnings flame,
            Whose thunders appall.
    Bacchus, thou dost for us all in thy love provide.
        Over Icaria thou dost reign,   1050
        And where the worshippers journey slow
        To the rites of Eleusis, where mountains shield
    The multitudes crossing Demeter's welcoming plain.
    Thou makest this mother-city of maenads thine own,
        A city beside the rippling flow   1055
    Of the gentle river, beside the murderous field
        Where the teeth of the dragon were sown.

        In the torches' wind-blown flare
        Thou art seen, in their flicker and smoke.
    Where the two-fold peaks of Parnassus gleam,   1060
    Corycian nymphs, as they move through the ruddy glare,
            Thee, Bacchus, invoke.
    They move in their dance beside the Castalian stream.
        O Bacchus, guardian divine!
        Down from the slopes of Nysa's hills   1065
        Where a mantle of ivy covers the ground,
    From headlands rich with the purple grape and the vine,
    Thou comest to us, thou comest. O be not long!
        Thy triumph the echoing city fills.
    The streets are loud with thy praises; the highways resound,   1070
        Resound with immortal song.

1044*ff*. *Thou art known* . . . : a hymn to the god Dionysus (Bacchus), whose mother was a Theban princess, Semele. When she was pregnant by her lover Zeus, she asked the god to appear to her in his own shape; he did, and she was blasted with the fire of his lightning.

1050. *Icaria:* the place where Dionysus was welcomed to Attica.

1052. *Eleusis:* on the coast near Athens, the site of the great mystery religion which had as its cult-deities Demeter and her daughter Persephone.

1060. *Parnassus:* the great mountain above Delphi, where Dionysus was worshipped as well as Apollo.

1061. *Corycian nymphs:* named from the Corycian cave on the heights above Delphi.

1063. *Castalian stream:* the spring at Delphi.

1065. *Nysa:* on the island of Euboea, opposite the Boeotian (Theban) coast.

Thou honorest highly our Theban city,
   Thou, and thy mother by lightning slain.
Our people sicken. O Bacchus have pity!
   Across the strait with its moaning wave,   1075
Down from Parnassus, come thou again!
   Come with thy healing feet, and save!

O thou who leadest the stars in chorus,
   Jubilant stars with their breath of fire,
Offspring of Zeus, appear before us!   1080
   Lord of the tumult of night, appear!
With the frenzied dance of thy maenad choir,
   Bacchus, thou giver of good, draw near!

    [*Enter* MESSENGER.]
MESSENGER. You of the house of Cadmus and Amphíon,
   No man's estate can ever be established   1085
   Firmly enough to warrant praise or blame.
   Fortune, from day to day, exalts the lucky
   And humbles the unlucky. No one knows
   Whether his present lot can long endure.
   For Creon once was blest, as I count blessings;   1090
   He had saved this land of Cadmus from its foes;
   He was the sovereign and ruled alone,
   The noble father of a royal house.
   And now, all has been lost. Because a man
   Who has forfeited his joy is not alive,   1095
   He is a living corpse. Heap, if you will,
   Your house with riches; live in regal pomp.
   Yet if your life is unhappy, all these things
   Are worth not even the shadow of a vapor
   Put in the balance against joy alone.   1100
CHORUS. What new disaster has the King's house suffered?
MESSENGER. Death. And the guilt of death lies on the living.
CHORUS. The guilt of death! Who has been killed? Who killed him?
MESSENGER. Haemon is killed, and by no stranger's hand.
CHORUS. He killed himself? Or did his father kill him?   1105
MESSENGER. He killed himself, enraged by his murderous father.
CHORUS. Tiresias! Now your prophecy is fulfilled.
MESSENGER. Consider, therefore, what remains to do.
CHORUS. There is the Queen, wretched Eurydice.
   Perhaps mere chance has brought her from the palace;   1110
   Perhaps she has learned the news about her son.
    [*Enter* EURYDICE.]
EURYDICE. Thebans, I heard you talking here together
   When I was on my way to greet the goddess,

Pallas Athene, and to pray to her.
Just as I loosed the fastening of the door,   1115
The words that told of my calamity
Struck heavily upon my ear. In terror
I fell back fainting in my women's arms.
But now, repeat your story. I shall hear it
As one who is not ignorant of grief.   1120
MESSENGER. My Lady, I will bear witness to what I saw,
And will omit no syllable of the truth.
Why should I comfort you with words that later
Would prove deceitful? Truth is always best.
Across the plain I guided my Lord Creon   1125
To where unpitied Polyneices lay,
A corpse mangled by dogs. Then we besought
Hecate, goddess of the roads, and Pluto
To moderate their wrath, and to show mercy.
We washed the dead with ceremonial water.   1130
Gathering the scattered fragments that remained,
With fresh-cut boughs we burned them. We heaped up
A mound of native earth above his ashes.
Then we approached the cavern of Death's bride,
The rock-floored marriage-chamber. While as yet   1135
We were far distant, someone heard the sound
Of loud lament in that unhallowed place,
And came to tell our master. As the King
Drew near, there floated through the air a voice,
Faint, indistinct, that uttered a bitter cry.   1140
The King burst out in anguish: 'Can it be
That I, in my misery, have become a prophet?
Will this be the saddest road I ever trod?
My son's voice greets me. Quickly, slaves! Go quickly!
When you have reached the sepulcher, get through   1145
The opening where the stones are wrenched away,
Get to the mouth of the burial chamber. Look,
See if I know his voice—Haemon's, my son's—
Or if I am deluded by the gods.'
We followed our despairing master's bidding   1150
And in the farthest recess of the tomb
We found Antigone, hanging, with her veil
Noosed round her neck. And with her we found Haemon,
His arms flung round her waist, grieving aloud
For his bride lost in death, his ruined marriage,   1155
His father's deeds. But when his father saw him,
Creon cried piteously and going in,
Called to him brokenly: "My son, my son,

1128. *Hecate . . . and Pluto:* divinities of the underworld.

What have you done? What are you thinking of?
What dreadful thing has driven you out of your mind?　　1160
Son, come away. I beg you. I beseech you."
But Haemon glared at him with furious eyes
Instead of answering, spat in his face,
And drew his sword. His father turned to fly
So that he missed his aim. Immediately,　　1165
In bitter self-reproach, the wretched boy
Leaned hard against his sword, and drove it deep
Into his side. Then while his life yet lingered,
With failing strength he drew Antigone close;
And as he lay there gasping heavily,　　1170
Over her white cheek his blood ebbed away.
The dead lie clasped together. He is wedded,
Not in this world but in the house of Death.
He has borne witness that of all the evils　　1174
Afflicting man, the worst is lack of wisdom.　　[*Exit* EURYDICE.]
CHORUS. What does that mean? Who can interpret it?
　The Queen has gone without a single word.
MESSENGER. It startles me. And yet I hope it means
　That hearing these dreadful things about her son,
　She will not let herself show grief in public　　1180
　But will lament in private with her women.
　Schooled in discretion, she will do no wrong.
CHORUS. How can we tell? Surely too great a silence
　Is no less ominous than too loud lament.
MESSENGER. Then I will enter. Perhaps she is concealing　　1185
　Some secret purpose in her passionate heart.
　I will find out, for you are right in saying
　Too great a silence may be ominous.
　　　　[*Exit* MESSENGER. *Enter* CREON *with* ATTENDANTS, *carrying*
　　　　the body of HAEMON *on a bier.*]
CHORUS. Thebans, look there! The King himself draws near,
　Bearing a load whose tale is all too clear.　　1190
　This is a work—if we dare speak our thought—
　That not another's but his own hands wrought.
CREON.
　　O, how may my sin be told?
The stubborn, death-fraught sin of a darkened brain!
　　Behold us here, behold　　1195
Father and son, the slayer and the slain!
　　Pain, only pain
Has come of my design.
　　Fate struck too soon; too soon your spirit fled.
My son, my young son, you are lying dead　　1200
Not for your folly, but for mine, for mine.
CHORUS. Sir, you have come to learn the right too late.

CREON.

    My lesson has been bitter and complete.

  Some god has struck me down with crushing weight,

  Filling my heart with cruelty and hate,   1205

    Trampling my happiness beneath his feet.

        Grief, bitter grief, is man's fate.

[*Enter* MESSENGER.]

MESSENGER. [*Indicating* HAEMON] Your load is heavy, Sir, but there
  is more.

  That is the burden you are bearing now.

  Soon you must bear new woe within your house.   1210

CREON. And what worse misery can follow this?

MESSENGER. Your wife is dead, a mother like her son.

  Poor woman, by her own hand she has died.

CREON.

    By her own hand she died.

  Death, spare me! Can you never have your fill?   1215

    Never be satisfied?

  Herald of evil, messenger of ill,

    Your harsh words kill,

  They smite me now anew.

    My wife is dead—You tell me my wife is dead.   1220

    Death after death is heaped upon my head.

  Speak to me, boy. Is what you tell me true?

MESSENGER. It is no longer hidden. Sir, look there.

    [*The body of* EURYDICE *is disclosed through the palace doors.*]

CREON.

    Another horror that makes blind mine eyes!

  What further agony has fate in store?   1225

  My dead son's body in my arms I bore,

    And now beside him his dead mother lies.

    I can endure no more.

MESSENGER. There at the altar with a keen-edged knife

  She stabbed herself; and as her eyes were darkened,   1230

  She wailed the death of Megareus, her son,

  Who earlier had met a noble fate;

  She wailed for Haemon; then, with her last breath,

  You, as the slayer of your sons, she cursed.

CREON.

    I am shaken with terror, with terror past belief.   1235

  Is there none here to end my anguish? None?

    No sword to pierce me? Broken with my grief,

  So steeped in agony that we are one.

MESSENGER. Sir, as she died, she burdened you with guilt,

  Charging you with the death of both your sons.   1240

1231. *Megareus:* killed during the siege of the city.

CREON. And by what act of violence did she die?
MESSENGER. Hearing the shrill lament for Haemon's fate,
  Deep in her heart she drove the bright blade home.
CREON. [*To* HAEMON]
    I am your slayer, I alone.
  I am guilty, only I.   1245
    I, and none other, must atone.
  Lead me away. The truth I own.
    Nothing is left, except to die.
CHORUS. If anything can be good, those words are good.
  For when calamity has come upon us,   1250
  The thing that is the briefest is the best.
CREON.
    Draw near me, death! O longed for death, draw near!
  Most welcome destiny, make no delay.
    To tell me my last hour, my last breath, is here.
  I have no wish to see another day.   1255
CHORUS. Such things are yet to come. We are concerned
  With doing what must needs be done today.
  The future rests in other hands than ours.
CREON. That is my whole desire. That is my prayer.
CHORUS. No. Do not pray. Men must accept their doom.   1260
CREON.
    My life's work there before me lies.
  My folly slew my wife, my son.
    I know not where to turn mine eyes.
  All my misdeeds before me rise.   1264
    Lead me away, brought low, undone.   [*Exit* CREON.]

CHORUS.
    The crown of happiness is to be wise.
  Honor the gods, and the gods' edicts prize.
  They strike down boastful men and men grown bold.
  Wisdom we learn at last, when we are old.   1269

THUCYDIDES

History of the Peloponnesian War*

The Melian Dialogue†

[The war between Athens and Sparta which began in 431 B.C.
came to a temporary stop in 421. The uneasy truce which ensued
was only a breathing space in which both sides prepared for the

* Translated by Benjamin Jowett.   † From Book V, Chapters 84-116.

renewal of the war and the decisive struggle. The spirit of Athenian democracy had changed during the hard years of the war; Pericles was dead and his place had been taken by younger and less scrupulous politicians. Thucydides describes the Athenian attack on the small island of Melos, in 416 B.C., an incident which, in Thucydides' hands, is made to reveal the depths of cynicism of the new Athenian policies.]

. . . The Athenians next made an expedition against the island of Melos[1] with thirty ships of their own, six Chian, and two Lesbian,[2] twelve hundred hoplites[3] and three hundred archers besides twenty mounted archers of their own, and about fifteen hundred hoplites furnished by their allies in the islands. The Melians are colonists of the Lacedaemonians who would not submit to Athens like the other islanders. At first they were neutral and took no part. But when the Athenians tried to coerce them by ravaging their lands they were driven into open hostilities. The generals, Cleomedes the son of Lycomedes and Tisias the son of Tisimachus, encamped with the Athenian forces on the island. But before they did the country any harm they sent envoys to negotiate with the Melians. Instead of bringing these envoys before the people, the Melians desired them to explain their errand to the magistrates and to the chief men.[4] They spoke as follows:—

"Since we are not allowed to speak to the people, lest, forsooth, they should be deceived by seductive and unanswerable arguments which they would hear set forth in a single uninterrupted oration (for we are perfectly aware that this is what you mean in bringing us before a select few), you who are sitting here may as well make assurance yet surer. Let us have no set speeches at all, but do you reply to each several statement of which you disapprove, and criticise it at once. Say first of all how you like this mode of proceeding."

The Melian representatives answered:—"The quiet interchange of explanations is a reasonable thing, and we do not object to that. But your warlike movements, which are present not only to our fears but to our eyes, seem to belie your words. We see that, although you may reason with us, you mean to be our judges; and that at the end of the discussion, if the justice of our cause prevail and we therefore refuse to yield, we may expect war; if we are convinced by you, slavery."

ATHENIANS. Nay, but if you are only going to argue from fancies about the future, or if you meet us with any other purpose than

---

1. a barren, unimportant island in the Aegean Sea, off the east coast of the Peloponnese.

2. Chios and Lesbos are two large islands off the coast of Asia Minor,

which were at this time subject to Athens.

3. heavy infantry.

4. Melos was governed by an oligarchy.

that of looking your circumstances in the face and saving your city, we have done; but if this is your intention we will proceed.

MELIANS. It is an excusable and natural thing that men in our position should have much to say and should indulge in many fancies. But we admit that this conference has met to consider the question of our preservation; and therefore let the argument proceed in the manner which you propose.

ATH. Well, then, we Athenians will use no fine words; we will not go out of our way to prove at length that we have a right to rule, because we overthrew the Persians;[5] or that we attack you now because we are suffering any injury at your hands. We should not convince you if we did; nor must you expect to convince us by arguing that, although a colony of the Lacedaemonians, you have taken no part in their expeditions, or that you have never done us any wrong. But you and we should say what we really think, and aim only at what is possible, for we both alike know that into the discussion of human affairs the question of justice only enters where the pressure of necessity is equal, and that the powerful exact what they can, and the weak grant what they must.

MEL. Well, then, since you set aside justice and invite us to speak of expediency, in our judgment it is certainly expedient that you should respect a principle which is for the common good; and that to every man when in peril a reasonable claim should be accounted a claim of right, and any plea which he is disposed to urge, even if failing of the point a little, should help his cause. Your interest in this principle is quite as great as ours, inasmuch as you, if you fall, will incur the heaviest vengeance, and will be the most terrible example to mankind.

ATH. The fall of our empire, if it should fall, is not an event to which we look forward with dismay; for ruling states such as Lacedaemon are not cruel to their vanquished enemies.[6] And we are fighting not so much against the Lacedaemonians as against our own subjects who may some day rise up and overcome their former masters. But this is a danger which you may leave to us. And we will now endeavor to show that we have come in the interests of our empire, and that in what we are about to say we are only seeking the preservation of your city. For we want to make you ours with the least trouble to ourselves, and it is for the interests of us both that you should not be destroyed.

MEL. It may be your interest to be our masters, but how can it be ours to be your slaves?

---

5. during the Persian invasion of 480–479 B.C. and during the subsequent offensives against the Persians, which were led by Athens as the most important power in the Delian League.

6. This cynical prophecy turned out to be correct, for after their victory in 404 B.C. the Spartans treated Athens with comparative mildness.

ATH. To you the gain will be that by submission you will avert the worst; and we shall be all the richer for your preservation.

MEL. But must we be your enemies? Will you not receive us as friends if we are neutral and remain at peace with you?

ATH. No, your enmity is not half so mischievous to us as your friendship; for the one is in the eyes of our subjects an argument of our power, the other of our weakness.

MEL. But are your subjects really unable to distinguish between states in which you have no concern, and those which are chiefly your own colonies, and in some cases have revolted and been subdued by you?

ATH. Why, they do not doubt that both of them have a good deal to say for themselves on the score of justice, but they think that states like yours are left free because they are able to defend themselves, and that we do not attack them because we dare not. So that your subjection will give us an increase of security, as well as an extension of empire. For we are masters of the sea, and you who are islanders, and insignificant islanders too, must not be allowed to escape us.

MEL. But do you not recognize another danger? For once more, since you drive us from the plea of justice and press upon us your doctrine of expediency, we must show you what is for our interest, and, if it be for yours also, may hope to convince you:—Will you not be making enemies of all who are now neutrals? When they see how you are treating us they will expect you some day to turn against them; and if so, are you not strengthening the enemies whom you already have, and bringing upon you others who, if they could help, would never dream of being your enemies at all?

ATH. We do not consider our really dangerous enemies to be any of the peoples inhabiting the mainland who, secure in their freedom, may defer indefinitely any measures of precaution which they take against us, but islanders who, like you, happen to be under no control, and all who may be already irritated by the necessity of submission to our empire—these are our real enemies, for they are the most reckless and most likely to bring themselves as well as us into a danger which they cannot but foresee.

MEL. Surely then, if you and your subjects will brave all this risk, you to preserve your empire and they to be quit of it, how base and cowardly it would be in us, who retain our freedom, not to do and suffer anything rather than be your slaves.

ATH. Not so, if you calmly reflect: for you are not fighting against equals to whom you cannot yield without disgrace, but you are taking counsel whether or no you shall resist an overwhelming force. The question is not one of honor but of prudence.

MEL. But we know that the fortune of war is sometimes impartial, and not always on the side of numbers. If we yield now all is over; but if we fight there is yet a hope that we may stand upright.

ATH. Hope is a good comforter in the hour of danger, and when men have something else to depend upon, although hurtful, she is not ruinous. But when her spendthrift nature has induced them to stake their all, they see her as she is in the moment of their fall, and not till then. While the knowledge of her might enable them to be ware of her, she never fails. You are weak and a single turn of the scale might be your ruin. Do not you be thus deluded; avoid the error of which so many are guilty, who, although they might still be saved if they would take the natural means, when visible grounds of confidence forsake them, have recourse to the invisible, to prophecies and oracles and the like, which ruin men by the hopes which they inspire in them.

MEL. We know only too well how hard the struggle must be against your power, and against fortune, if she does not mean to be impartial. Nevertheless we do not despair of fortune; for we hope to stand as high as you in the favor of heaven, because we are righteous, and you against whom we contend are unrighteous; and we are satisfied that our deficiency in power will be compensated by the aid of our allies the Lacedaemonians; they cannot refuse to help us, if only because we are their kinsmen, and for the sake of their own honor. And therefore our confidence is not so utterly blind as you suppose.

ATH. As for the Gods, we expect to have quite as much of their favor as you: for we are not doing or claiming anything which goes beyond common opinion about divine or men's desires about human things. For of the Gods we believe, and of men we know, that by a law of their nature wherever they can rule they will. This law was not made by us, and we are not the first who have acted upon it; we did but inherit it, and shall bequeath it to all time, and we know that you and all mankind, if you were as strong as we are, would do as we do. So much for the Gods; we have told you why we expect to stand as high in their good opinion as you. And then as to the Lacedaemonians—when you imagine that out of very shame they will assist you, we admire the simplicity of your idea, but we do not envy you the folly of it. The Lacedaemonians are exceedingly virtuous among themselves, and according to their national standard of morality. But in respect of their dealings with others, although many things might be said, a word is enough to describe them—of all men whom we know they are the most notorious for identifying what is pleasant with what is honorable, and what is expedient with what is just. But how inconsistent is such a character with your present blind hope of deliverance!

MEL. That is the very reason why we trust them; they will look to their interest, and therefore will not be willing to betray the Melians, who are their own colonists, lest they should be distrusted by their friends in Hellas[7] and play into the hands of their enemies.

ATH. But do you not see that the path of expediency is safe, whereas justice and honor involve danger in practice, and such dangers the Lacedaemonians seldom care to face?

MEL. On the other hand, we think that whatever perils there may be, they will be ready to face them for our sakes, and will consider danger less dangerous where we are concerned. For if they need our aid we are close at hand, and they can better trust our loyal feeling because we are their kinsmen.

ATH. Yes, but what encourages men who are invited to join in a conflict is clearly not the good-will of those who summon them to their side, but a decided superiority in real power. To this no men look more keenly than the Lacedaemonians; so little confidence have they in their own resources that they only attack their neighbors when they have numerous allies, and therefore they are not likely to find their way by themselves to an island, when we are masters of the sea.

MEL. But they may send their allies: the Cretan sea[8] is a large place; and the masters of the sea will have more difficulty in overtaking vessels which want to escape than the pursued in escaping. If the attempt should fail they may invade Attica itself, and find their way to allies of yours whom Brasidas[9] did not reach; and then you will have to fight, not for the conquest of a land in which you have no concern, but nearer home, for the preservation of your confederacy and of your own territory.

ATH. Help may come from Lacedaemon to you as it has come to others, and should you ever have actual experience of it, then you will know that never once have the Athenians retired from a siege through fear of a foe elsewhere. You told us that the safety of your city would be your first care, but we remark that, in this long discussion, not a word has been uttered by you which would give a reasonable man expectation of deliverance. Your strongest grounds are hopes deferred, and what power you have is not to be compared with that which is already arrayed against you. Unless after we have withdrawn you mean to come, as even now you may, to a wiser conclusion, you are showing a great want of sense. For surely you cannot dream of flying to that false sense of honor which has been the ruin of so many when danger and dishonor were staring them in the face. Many men with their eyes still open to the conse-

7. Greece.
8. Melos lies some seventy miles north of Crete.
9. a Spartan commander who had stirred up a great deal of trouble among the Athenian subjects in the north of Greece earlier in the war.

quences have found the word honor too much for them, and have suffered a mere name to lure them on, until it has drawn upon them real and irretrievable calamities; through their own folly they have incurred a worse dishonor than fortune would have inflicted upon them. If you are wise you will not run this risk; you ought to see that there can be no disgrace in yielding to a great city which invites you to become her ally on reasonable terms, keeping your own land, and merely paying tribute; and that you will certainly gain no honor if, having to choose between two alternatives, safety and war, you obstinately prefer the worse. To maintain our rights against equals, to be politic with superiors, and to be moderate towards inferiors is the path of safety. Reflect once more when we have withdrawn, and say to yourselves over and over again that you are deliberating about your one and only country, which may be saved or may be destroyed by a single decision.

The Athenians left the conference: the Melians, after consulting among themselves, resolved to persevere in their refusal, and made answer as follows:—"Men of Athens, our resolution is unchanged; and we will not in a moment surrender that liberty which our city, founded seven hundred years ago, still enjoys; we will trust to the good-fortune which by the favor of the Gods has hitherto preserved us, and for human help to the Lacedaemonians, and endeavor to save ourselves. We are ready however to be your friends, and the enemies neither of you nor of the Lacedaemonians, and we ask you to leave our country when you have made such a peace as may appear to be in the interest of both parties."

Such was the answer of the Melians; the Athenians, as they quitted the conference, spoke as follows:—"Well, we must say, judging from the decision at which you have arrived, that you are the only men who deem the future to be more certain than the present, and regard things unseen as already realized in your fond anticipation, and that the more you cast yourselves upon the Lacedaemonians and fortune, and hope, and trust them, the more complete will be your ruin."

The Athenian envoys returned to the army; and the generals, when they found that the Melians would not yield, immediately commenced hostilities. They surrounded the town of Melos with a wall, dividing the work among the several contingents. They then left troops of their own and of the allies to keep guard both by land and by sea, and retired with the greater part of their army; the remainder carried on the blockade.

. . . The Melians took that part of the Athenian wall which looked towards the agora[10] by a night assault, killed a few men, and brought in as much corn and other necessaries as they could; they

10. market place.

then retreated and remained inactive. After this the Athenians set a better watch. So the summer ended.

In the following winter . . . the Melians took another part of the Athenian wall; for the fortifications were insufficiently guarded. Whereupon the Athenians sent fresh troops, under the command of Philocrates the son of Demeas. The place was now closely invested, and there was treachery among the citizens themselves. So the Melians were induced to surrender at discretion. The Athenians thereupon put to death all who were of military age, and made slaves of the women and children. They then colonized the island, sending thither five hundred settlers of their own.

EURIPIDES
(480–406 B.C.)
Medea *

Characters

MEDEA, *princess of Colchis and wife of Jason*
JASON, *son of Aeson, king of Iolcos*
TWO CHILDREN *of Medea and Jason*
KREON, *king of Corinth*
AIGEUS, *king of Athens*
NURSE *to Medea*
TUTOR *to Medea's children*
MESSENGER
CHORUS OF CORINTHIAN WOMEN

SCENE—*In front of Medea's house in Corinth. Enter from the house Medea's* NURSE.

NURSE. How I wish the Argo never had reached the land
Of Colchis, skimming through the blue Symplegades,
Nor ever had fallen in the glades of Pelion
The smitten fir-tree to furnish oars for the hands
Of heroes who in Pelias's name attempted   5
The Golden Fleece! For then my mistress Medea
Would not have sailed for the towers of the land of Iolcos,
Her heart on fire with passionate love for Jason;
Nor would she have persuaded the daughters of Pelias

---

* Produced in 431 B.C. Our text is a translation by Rex Warner, from *The Medea of Euripides*, John Lane The Bodley Head, Ltd., London, 1944.

1. *Argo:* the ship in which Jason and his companions sailed on the quest for the Golden Fleece.

2. *Symplegades:* clashing rocks, which crushed ships endeavoring to pass between them. They were supposed to be located at the Hellespont, the passage between the Mediterranean and the Black Sea.

3. *Pelion:* a mountain in the north of Greece near Iolcos, the place from which Jason sailed.

5. *Pelias:* He seized the kingdom of Iolcos, expelling Aeson, Jason's father. When Jason came to claim his rights, Pelias sent him to get the Golden Fleece.

To kill their father, and now be living here   10
In Corinth with her husband and children. She gave
Pleasure to the people of her land of exile,
And she herself helped Jason in every way.
This is indeed the greatest salvation of all,—
For the wife not to stand apart from the husband.   15
But now there's hatred everywhere. Love is diseased.
For, deserting his own children and my mistress,
Jason has taken a royal wife to his bed,
The daughter of the ruler of this land, Kreon.
And poor Medea is slighted, and cries aloud on the   20
Vows they made to each other, the right hands clasped
In eternal promise. She calls upon the gods to witness
What sort of return Jason has made to her love.
She lies without food and gives herself up to suffering,
Wasting away every moment of the day in tears.   25
So it has gone since she knew herself slighted by him.
Not stirring an eye, not moving her face from the ground,
No more than either a rock or surging sea water
She listens when she is given friendly advice.
Except that sometimes she twists back her white neck and   30
Moans to herself, calling out on her father's name,
And her land, and her home betrayed when she came away with
A man who now is determined to dishonour her.
Poor creature, she has discovered by her sufferings
What it means to one not to have lost one's own country.   35
She has turned from the children and does not like to see them.
I am afraid she may think of some dreadful thing,
For her heart is violent. She will never put up with
The treatment she is getting. I know and fear her
Lest she may sharpen a sword and thrust to the heart,   40
Stealing into the palace where the bed is made,
Or even kill the king and the new-wedded groom,
And thus bring a greater misfortune on herself.
She's a strange woman. I know it won't be easy
To make an enemy of her and come off best.   45
But here the children come. They have finished playing.
They have no thought at all of their mother's trouble.

10. *kill . . . father:* After Jason returned to Iolcos with the Fleece and Medea, Pelias' daughters were persuaded by Medea, who had a reputation as a sorceress, to cut Pelias up and boil the pieces, in order to restore him to youth. The experiment was, of course, unsuccessful, but the son of Pelias expelled Jason and Medea from the kingdom, and they took refuge in Corinth.

11. *Corinth:* on the isthmus between the Peloponnese and Attica. In Euripides' time it was a wealthy trading city, a commercial rival of Athens.

19. *Kreon:* Creon.

32. *home betrayed:* Medea, daughter of the king of Colchis, fell in love with Jason and helped him to take the Golden Fleece away from her own country.

Indeed it is not usual for the young to grieve.

[*Enter from the right the slave who is the* TUTOR *to Medea's two small children. The* CHILDREN *follow him.*]

TUTOR. You old retainer of my mistress's household,
Why are you standing here all alone in front of the   50
Gates and moaning to yourself over your misfortune?
Medea could not wish you to leave her alone.
NURSE. Old man, and guardian of the children of Jason,
If one is a good servant, it's a terrible thing
When one's master's luck is out; it goes to one's heart.   55
So I myself have got into such a state of grief
That a longing stole over me to come outside here
And tell the earth and air of my mistress's sorrows.
TUTOR. Has the poor lady not yet given up her crying?
NURSE. Given up? She's at the start, not half-way through her
tears.   60
TUTOR. Poor fool,—if I may call my mistress such a name,—
How ignorant she is of trouble more to come.
NURSE. What do you mean, old man? You needn't fear to speak.
TUTOR. Nothing. I take back the words which I used just now.
NURSE. Don't, by your beard, hide this from me, your fellow-
servant.   65
If need be, I'll keep quiet about what you tell me.
TUTOR. I heard a person saying, while I myself seemed
Not to be paying attention, when I was at the place
Where the old draught-players sit, by the holy fountain,
That Kreon, ruler of the land, intends to drive   70
These children and their mother in exile from Corinth.
But whether what he said is really true or not
I do not know. I pray that it may not be true.
NURSE. And will Jason put up with it that his children
Should suffer so, though he's no friend to their mother?   75
TUTOR. Old ties give place to new ones. As for Jason, he
No longer has a feeling for this house of ours.
NURSE. It's black indeed for us, when we add new to old
Sorrows before even the present sky has cleared.
TUTOR. But you be silent, and keep all this to yourself.   80
It is not the right time to tell our mistress of it.
NURSE. Do you hear, children, what a father he is to you?
I wish he were dead,—but no, he is still my master.
Yet certainly he has proved unkind to his dear ones.
TUTOR. What's strange in that? Have you only just discovered   85
That everyone loves himself more than his neighbour?
Some have good reason, others get something out of it.

69. *draught-players:* checker-players.

So Jason neglects his children for the new bride.
NURSE. Go indoors, children. That will be the best thing.
And you, keep them to themselves as much as possible.   90
Don't bring them near their mother in her angry mood.
For I've seen her already blazing her eyes at them
As though she meant some mischief and I am sure that
She'll not stop raging until she has struck at someone.
May it be an enemy and not a friend she hurts!   95
    [MEDEA *is heard inside the house.*]
MEDEA. Ah, wretch! Ah, lost in my sufferings,
I wish, I wish I might die.
NURSE. What did I say, dear children? Your mother
Frets her heart and frets it to anger.
Run away quickly into the house,   100
And keep well out of her sight.
Don't go anywhere near, but be careful
Of the wildness and bitter nature
Of that proud mind.
Go now! Run quickly indoors.   105
It is clear that she soon will put lightning
In that cloud of her cries that is rising
With a passion increasing. Oh, what will she do,
Proud-hearted and not to be checked on her course,
A soul bitten into with wrong?   110
    [*The* TUTOR *takes the children into the house.*]
MEDEA. Ah I have suffered
What should be wept for bitterly. I hate you,
Children of a hateful mother. I curse you
And your father. Let the whole house crash.
NURSE. Ah, I pity you, you poor creature.   115
How can your children share in their father's
Wickedness? Why do you hate them? Oh children,
How much I fear that something may happen!
Great people's tempers are terrible, always
Having their own way, seldom checked,   120
Dangerous they shift from mood to mood.
How much better to have been accustomed
To live on equal terms with one's neighbours.
I would like to be safe and grow old in a
Humble way. What is moderate sounds best,   125
Also in practice is best for everyone.
Greatness brings no profit to people.
God indeed, when in anger, brings
Greater ruin to great men's houses.

[*Enter, on the right, a* CHORUS OF CORINTHIAN WOMEN. *They have come to enquire about* MEDEA *and to attempt to console her.*]

CHORUS. I heard the voice, I heard the cry 130
 Of Colchis' wretched daughter.
 Tell me, mother, is she not yet
 At rest? Within the double gates
 Of the court I heard her cry. I am sorry
 For the sorrow of this home. O, say, what has happened? 135

NURSE. There is no home. It's over and done with.
 Her husband holds fast to his royal wedding,
 While she, my mistress, cries out her eyes
 There in her room, and takes no warmth from
 Any word of any friend. 140

MEDEA. Oh, I wish
 That lightning from heaven would split my head open.
 Oh, what use have I now for life?
 I would find my release in death
 And leave hateful existence behind me. 145

CHOR. O God and Earth and Heaven!
 Did you hear what a cry was that
 Which the sad wife sings?
 Poor foolish one, why should you long
 For that appalling rest? 150
 The final end of death comes fast.
 No need to pray for that.
 Suppose your man gives honour
 To another woman's bed.
 It often happens. Don't be hurt. 155
 God will be your friend in this.
 You must not waste away
 Grieving too much for him who shared your bed.

MEDEA. Great Themis, lady Artemis, behold
 The things I suffer, though I made him promise, 160
 My hateful husband. I pray that I may see him,
 Him and his bride and all their palace shattered
 For the wrong they dare to do me without cause.
 Oh, my father! Oh, my country! In what dishonour
 I left you, killing my own brother for it. 165

NURSE. Do you hear what she says, and how she cries
 On Themis, the goddess of Promises, and on Zeus,
 Whom we believe to be the Keeper of Oaths?

159. *Themis:* justice. *Artemis:* the protector of women in pain and distress. 165. *my own brother:* Medea killed him to delay the pursuit when she escaped with Jason.

Of this I am sure, that no small thing
Will appease my mistress's anger.   170
CHOR. Will she come into our presence?
    Will she listen when we are speaking
    To the words we say?
    I wish she might relax her rage
    And temper of her heart.   175
    My willingness to help will never
    Be wanting to my friends.
    But go inside and bring her
    Out of the house to us,
    And speak kindly to her: hurry,   180
    Before she wrongs her own.
    This passion of hers moves to something great.
NURSE. I will, but I doubt if I'll manage
    To win my mistress over.
    But still I'll attempt it to please you.   185
    Such a look she will flash on her servants
    If any comes near with a message,
    Like a lioness guarding her cubs.
    It is right, I think, to consider
    Both stupid and lacking in foresight   190
    Those poets of old who wrote songs
    For revels and dinners and banquets,
    Pleasant sounds for men living at ease;
    But none of them all has discovered
    How to put an end with their singing   195
    Or musical instruments grief,
    Bitter grief, from which death and disaster
    Cheat the hopes of a house. Yet how good
    If music could cure men of this! But why raise
    To no purpose the voice at a banquet? For *there* is   200
    Already abundance of pleasure for men
    With a joy of its own.
        [*The* NURSE *goes into the house.*]
CHOR. I heard a shriek that is laden with sorrow.
    Shrilling out her hard grief she cries out
    Upon him who betrayed both her bed and her marriage.   205
    Wronged, she calls on the gods,
    On the justice of Zeus, the oath sworn,
    Which brought her away
    To the opposite shore of the Greeks
    Through the gloomy salt straits to the gateway   210
    Of the salty unlimited sea.
        [MEDEA, *attended by servants, comes out of the house.*]

MEDEA. Women of Corinth, I have come outside to you
  Lest you should be indignant with me; for I know
  That many people are overproud, some when alone,
  And others when in company. And those who live   215
  Quietly, as I do, get a bad reputation.
  For a just judgement is not evident in the eyes
  When a man at first sight hates another, before
  Learning his character, being in no way injured;
  And a foreigner especially must adapt himself.   220
  I'd not approve of even a fellow-countryman
  Who by pride and want of manners offends his neighbours.
  But on me this thing has fallen so unexpectedly,
  It has broken my heart. I am finished. I let go
  All my life's joy. My friends, I only want to die.   225
  It was everything to me to think well of one man,
  And he, my own husband, has turned out wholly vile.
  Of all things which are living and can form a judgement
  We women are the most unfortunate creatures.
  Firstly, with an excess of wealth it is required   230
  For us to buy a husband and take for our bodies
  A master; for not to take one is even worse.
  And now the question is serious whether we take
  A good or bad one; for there is no easy escape
  For a woman, nor can she say no to her marriage.   235
  She arrives among new modes of behaviour and manners,
  And needs prophetic power, unless she has learnt at home,
  How best to manage him who shares the bed with her.
  And if we work out all this well and carefully,
  And the husband lives with us and lightly bears his yoke,   240
  Then life is enviable. If not, I'd rather die.
  A man, when he's tired of the company in his home,
  Goes out of the house and puts an end to his boredom
  And turns to a friend or companion of his own age.
  But we are forced to keep our eyes on one alone.   245
  What they say of us is that we have a peaceful time
  Living at home, while they do the fighting in war.
  How wrong they are! I would very much rather stand
  Three times in the front of battle than bear one child.
  Yet what applies to me does not apply to you.   250
  You have a country. Your family home is here.
  You enjoy life and the company of your friends.

220. *a foreigner . . . himself:* Foreign residents were encouraged to come to Athens, but were rarely admitted to the rights of full citizenship, which was a jealously guarded privilege.

229. *women:* Athenian rights and institutions were made for men; the women had few privileges and almost no legal rights. The following two lines refer to the dowry which had to be provided for the bride.

But I am deserted, a refugee, thought nothing of
By my husband,—something he won in a foreign land.
I have no mother or brother, nor any relation   255
With whom I can take refuge in this sea of woe.
This much then is the service I would beg from you:
If I can find the means or devise any scheme
To pay my husband back for what he has done to me,—
Him and his father-in-law and the girl who married him,—   260
Just to keep silent. For in other ways a woman
Is full of fear, defenceless, dreads the sight of cold
Steel; but, when once she is wronged in the matter of love,
No other soul can hold so many thoughts of blood.

CHOR. This I will promise. You are in the right, Medea,   265
   In paying your husband back. I am not surprised at you
   For being sad.
           But look! I see our king Kreon
   Approaching. He will tell us of some new plan.
    [*Enter, from the right,* KREON, *with attendants.*]

KREON. You, with that angry look, so set against your husband,
   Medea, I order you to leave my territories   270
   An exile, and take along with you your two children,
   And not to waste time doing it. It is my decree,
   And I will see it done. I will not return home
   Until you are cast from the boundaries of my land.

MEDEA. Oh, this is the end for me. I am utterly lost.   275
   Now I am in the full force of the storm of hate
   And have no harbour from ruin to reach easily.
   Yet still, in spite of it all, I'll ask the question:
   What is your reason, Kreon, for banishing me?

KREON. I am afraid of you,—why should I dissemble it?—   280
   Afraid that you may injure my daughter mortally.
   Many things accumulate to support my feeling.
   You are a clever woman, versed in evil arts,
   And are angry at having lost your husband's love.
   I hear that you are threatening, so they tell me,   285
   To do something against my daughter and Jason
   And me, too. I shall take my precautions first.
   I tell you, I prefer to earn your hatred now
   Than to be soft-hearted and afterwards regret it.

MEDEA. This is not the first time, Kreon. Often previously   290
   Through being considered clever I have suffered much.
   A person of sense ought never to have his children
   Brought up to be more clever than the average.
   For, apart from cleverness bringing them no profit,
   It will make them objects of envy and ill-will.   295

If you put new ideas before the eyes of fools
They'll think you foolish and worthless into the bargain;
And if you are thought superior to those who have
Some reputation for learning, you will become hated.
I have some knowledge myself of how this happens;   300
For being clever, I find that some will envy me,
Others object to me. Yet all my cleverness
Is not so much.
           Well, then, are you frightened, Kreon,
That I should harm you? There is no need. It is not
My way to transgress the authority of a king.   305
How have you injured me? You gave your daughter away
To the man you wanted. O, certainly I hate
My husband, but you, I think, have acted wisely;
Nor do I grudge it you that your affairs go well.
May the marriage be a lucky one! Only let me   310
Live in this land. For even though I have been wronged,
I will not raise my voice, but submit to my betters.
KREON. What you say sounds gentle enough. Still in my heart
  I greatly dread that you are plotting some evil,
  And therefore I trust you even less than before.   315
  A sharp-tempered woman, or for that matter a man,
  Is easier to deal with than the clever type
  Who holds her tongue. No. You must go. No need for more
  Speeches. The thing is fixed. By no manner of means
  Shall you, an enemy of mine, stay in my country.   320
MEDEA. I beg you. By your knees, by your new-wedded girl.
KREON. Your words are wasted. You will never persuade me.
MEDEA. Will you drive me out, and give no heed to my prayers?
KREON. I will, for I love my family more than you.
MEDEA. O my country! How bitterly now I remember you!   325
KREON. I love my country too,—next after my children.
MEDEA. O what an evil to men is passionate love!
KREON. That would depend on the luck that goes along with it.
MEDEA. O God, do not forget who is the cause of this!
KREON. Go. It is no use. Spare me the pain of forcing you.   330
MEDEA. I'm spared no pain. I lack no pain to be spared me.
KREON. Then you'll be removed by force by one of my men.
MEDEA. No, Kreon, not that! But do listen, I beg you.
KREON. Woman, you seem to want to create a disturbance.
MEDEA. I *will* go into exile. *This* is not what I beg for.   335
KREON. Why then this violence and clinging to my hand?
MEDEA. Allow me to remain here just for this one day,
  So I may consider where to live in my exile,
  And look for support for my children, since their father

Chooses to make no kind of provision for them.   340
Have pity on them! You have children of your own.
It is natural for you to look kindly on them.
For myself I do not mind if I go into exile.
It is the children being in trouble that I mind.

KREON. There is nothing tyrannical about my nature,   345
And by showing mercy I have often been the loser.
Even now I know that I am making a mistake.
All the same you shall have your will. But this I tell you,
That if the light of heaven tomorrow shall see you,
You and your children in the confines of my land,   350
You die. This word I have spoken is firmly fixed.
But now, if you must stay, stay for this day alone.
For in it you can do none of the things I fear.

[*Exit* KREON *with his attendants.*]

CHOR. Oh, unfortunate one! Oh, cruel!
Where will you turn? Who will help you?   355
What house or what land to preserve you
From ill can you find?
Medea, a god has thrown suffering
Upon you in waves of despair.

MEDEA. Things have gone badly every way. No doubt of that   360
But not these things this far, and don't imagine so.
There are still trials to come for the new-wedded pair,
And for their relations pain that will mean something
Do you think that I would ever have fawned on that man
Unless I had some end to gain or profit in it?   365
I would not even have spoken or touched him with my hands.
But he has got to such a pitch of foolishness
That, though he could have made nothing of all my plans
By exiling me, he has given me this one day
To stay here, and in this I will make dead bodies   370
Of three of my enemies,—father, the girl and my husband.
I have many ways of death which I might suit to them,
And do not know, friends, which one to take in hand;
Whether to set fire underneath their bridal mansion,
Or sharpen a sword and thrust it to the heart,   375
Stealing into the palace where the bed is made.
There is just one obstacle to this. If I am caught
Breaking into the house and scheming against it,
I shall die, and give my enemies cause for laughter.
It is best to go by the straight road, the one in which   380
I am most skilled, and make away with them by poison.
So be it then.

And now suppose them dead. What town will receive me?
What friend will offer me a refuge in his land,
Or the guarantee of his house and save my own life? 385
There is none. So I must wait a little time yet,
And if some sure defence should then appear for me,
In craft and silence I will set about this murder.
But if my fate should drive me on without help,
Even though death is certain, I will take the sword 390
Myself and kill, and steadfastly advance to crime.
It shall not be,—I swear it by her, my mistress,
Whom most I honour and have chosen as partner,
Hecate, who dwells in the recesses of my hearth,—
That any man shall be glad to have injured me. 395
Bitter I will make their marriage for them and mournful,
Bitter the alliance and the driving me out of the land.
Ah, come, Medea, in your plotting and scheming
Leave nothing untried of all those things which you know.
Go forward to the dreadful act. The test has come 400
For resolution. You see how you are treated. Never
Shall you be mocked by Jason's Corinthian wedding,
Whose father was noble, whose grandfather Helios.
You have the skill. What is more, you were born a woman,
And women, though most helpless in doing good deeds, 405
Are of every evil the cleverest of contrivers.

CHOR. Flow backward to your sources, sacred rivers,
And let the world's great order be reversed.
It is the thoughts of *men* that are deceitful,
Their pledges that are loose. 410
Story shall now turn my condition to a fair one,
Women are paid their due.
No more shall evil-sounding fame be theirs.

Cease now, you muses of the ancient singers,
To tell the tale of my unfaithfulness; 415
For not on us did Phoebus, lord of music,
Bestow the lyre's divine
Power, for otherwise I should have sung an answer
To the other sex. Long time
Has much to tell of us, and much of them. 420

You sailed away from your father's home,
With a heart on fire you passed

---

394. *Hecate:* the patron of witch-
craft, sometimes identified with
Artemis. Medea has a statue and
shrine of Hecate in the house.

403. *Helios:* the sun, father of
Medea's father, Aeëtes.
416. *Phoebus:* Apollo.

The double rocks of the sea.
And now in a foreign country
You have lost your rest in a widowed bed,   425
And are driven forth, a refugee
In dishonour from the land.

Good faith has gone, and no more remains
In great Greece a sense of shame.
It has flown away to the sky.   430
No father's house for a haven
Is at hand for you now, and another queen
Of your bed has dispossessed you and
Is mistress of your home.

       [*Enter* JASON, *with attendants.*]

JASON. This is not the first occasion that I have noticed   435
How hopeless it is to deal with a stubborn temper.
For, with reasonable submission to our ruler's will,
You might have lived in this land and kept your home.
As it is you are going to be exiled for your loose speaking.
Not that I mind myself. You are free to continue   440
Telling everyone that Jason is a worthless man.
But as to your talk about the king, consider
Yourself most lucky that exile is your punishment.
I, for my part, have always tried to calm down
The anger of the king, and wished you to remain.   445
But you will not give up your folly, continually
Speaking ill of him, and so you are going to be banished.
All the same, and in spite of your conduct, I'll not desert
My friends, but have come to make some provision for you,
So that you and the children may not be penniless   450
Or in need of anything in exile. Certainly
Exile brings many troubles with it. And even
If you hate me, I cannot think badly of you.

MEDEA. O coward in every way,—that is what I call you,
With bitterest reproach for your lack of manliness,   455
You have come, you, my worst enemy, have come to me!
It is not an example of over-confidence
Or of boldness thus to look your friends in the face,
Friends you have injured,—no, it is the worst of all
Human diseases, shamelessness. But you did well   460
To come, for I can speak ill of you and lighten
My heart, and you will suffer while you are listening.
And first I will begin from what happened first.
I saved your life, and every Greek knows I saved it,
Who was a ship-mate of yours aboard the Argo,   465

When you were sent to control the bulls that breathed fire
And yoke them, and when you would sow that deadly field.
Also that snake, who encircled with his many folds
The Golden Fleece and guarded it and never slept,
I killed, and so gave you the safety of the light.   470
And I myself betrayed my father and my home,
And came with you to Pelias' land of Iolcos.
And then, showing more willingness to help than wisdom,
I killed him, Pelias, with a most dreadful death
At his own daughters' hands, and took away your fear.   475
This is how I behaved to you, you wretched man,
And you forsook me, took another bride to bed
Though you had children; for, if that had not been,
You would have had an excuse for another wedding.
Faith in your word has gone. Indeed I cannot tell   480
Whether you think the gods whose names you swore by then
Have ceased to rule and that new standards are set up,
Since you must know you have broken your word to me.
O my right hand, and the knees which you often clasped
In supplication, how senselessly I am treated   485
By this bad man, and how my hopes have missed their mark!
Come, I will share my thoughts as though you were a friend,—
You! Can I think that you would ever treat me well?
But I will do it, and these questions will make you
Appear the baser. Where am I to go? To my father's?   490
Him I betrayed and his land when I came with you.
To Pelias' wretched daughters? What a fine welcome
They would prepare for me who murdered their father!
For this is my position,—hated by my friends
At home, I have, in kindness to you, made enemies   495
Of others whom there was no need to have injured.
And how happy among Greek women you have made me
On your side for all this! A distinguished husband
I have,—for breaking promises. When in misery
I am cast out of the land and go into exile,   500
Quite without friends and all alone with my children,
That will be a fine shame for the new-wedded groom,
For his children to wander as beggars and she who saved him.
O God, you have given to mortals a sure method
Of telling the gold that is pure from the counterfeit;   505
Why is there no mark engraved upon men's bodies,

466. *bulls . . . fire:* This and the following lines refer to ordeals through which Jason had to pass to win the Fleece, and in which Medea helped him. He had to yoke a team of fire-breathing bulls, then sow a field which immediately sprouted armed warriors, then deal with the snake which guarded the Fleece.

By which we could know the true ones from the false ones?
CHOR. It is a strange form of anger, difficult to cure
    When two friends turn upon each other in hatred.
JASON. As for me, it seems I must be no bad speaker.   510
    But, like a man who has a good grip of the tiller,
    Reef up his sail, and so run away from under
    This mouthing tempest, woman, of your bitter tongue.
    Since you insist on building up your kindness to me,
    My view is that Cypris was alone responsible   515
    Of men and gods for the preserving of my life.
    You are clever enough,—but really I need not enter
    Into the story of how it was love's inescapable
    Power that compelled you to keep my person safe.
    On this I will not go into too much detail.   520
    In so far as you helped me, you did well enough.
    But on this question of saving me, I can prove
    You have certainly got from me more than you gave.
    Firstly, instead of living among barbarians,
    You inhabit a Greek land and understand our ways,   525
    How to live by law instead of the sweet will of force.
    And all the Greeks considered you a clever woman.
    You were honoured for it; while, if you were living at
    The ends of the earth, nobody would have heard of you.
    For my part, rather than stores of gold in my house   530
    Or power to sing even sweeter songs than Orpheus,
    I'd choose the fate that made me a distinguished man.
    There is my reply to your story of my labours.
    Remember it was you who started the argument.
    Next for your attack on my wedding with the princess: 535
    Here I will prove that, first, it was a clever move,
    Secondly, a wise one, and, finally, that I made it
    In your best interests and the children's. Please keep calm.
    When I arrived here from the land of Iolcos,
    Involved, as I was, in every kind of difficulty,   540
    What luckier chance could I have come across than this,
    An exile to marry the daughter of the king?
    It was not,—the point that seems to upset you—that I
    Grew tired of your bed and felt the need of a new bride;
    Nor with any wish to outdo your number of children.   545
    We have enough already. I am quite content.
    But,—this was the main reason—that we might live well,
    And not be short of anything. I know that all
    A man's friends leave him stone-cold if he becomes poor.
    Also that I might bring my children up worthily   550

515. *Cypris:* Aphrodite, goddess of love.

Of my position, and, by producing more of them
To be brothers of yours, we would draw the families
Together and all be happy. You need no children.
And it pays me to do good to those I have now
By having others. Do you think this a bad plan? 555
You wouldn't if the love question hadn't upset you.
But you women have got into such a state of mind
That, if your life at night is good, you think you have
Everything; but, if in that quarter things go wrong,
You will consider your best and truest interests 560
Most hateful. It would have been better far for men
To have got their children in some other way, and women
Not to have existed. Then life would have been good.

CHOR. Jason, though you have made this speech of yours look well,
Still I think, even though others do not agree, 565
You have betrayed your wife and are acting badly.

MEDEA. Surely in many ways I hold different views
From others, for I think that the plausible speaker
Who is a villain deserves the greatest punishment.
Confident in his tongue's power to adorn evil, 570
He stops at nothing. Yet he is not really wise.
As in your case. There is no need to put on the airs
Of a clever speaker, for one word will lay you flat.
If you were not a coward, you would not have married
Behind my back, but discussed it with me first. 575

JASON. And you, no doubt, would have furthered the proposal,
If I had told you of it, you who even now
Are incapable of controlling your bitter temper.

MEDEA. It was not that. No, you thought it was not respectable
As you got on in years to have a foreign wife. 580

JASON. Make sure of this: it was not because of a woman
I made the royal alliance in which I now live,
But, as I said before, I wished to preserve you
And breed a royal progeny to be brothers
To the children I have now, a sure defence to us. 585

MEDEA. Let me have no happy fortune that brings pain with it,
Or prosperity which is upsetting to the mind!

JASON. Change your ideas of what you want, and show more
   sense.
Do not consider painful what is good for you,
Nor, when you are lucky, think yourself unfortunate. 590

MEDEA. You can insult me. You have somewhere to turn to.
But I shall go from this land into exile, friendless.

JASON. It was what you chose yourself. Don't blame others for it.

MEDEA. And how did I choose it? Did I betray my husband?

JASON. You called down wicked curses on the king's family.   595
MEDEA. A curse, that is what I am become to your house too.
JASON. I do not propose to go into all the rest of it;
    But, if you wish for the children or for yourself
    In exile to have some of my money to help you,
    Say so, for I am prepared to give with open hand,   600
    Or to provide you with introductions to my friends
    Who will treat you well. You are a fool if you do not
    Accept this. Cease your anger and you will profit.
MEDEA. I shall never accept the favours of friends of yours,
    Nor take a thing from you, so you need not offer it.   605
    There is no benefit in the gifts of a bad man.
JASON. Then, in any case, I call the gods to witness that
    I wish to help you and the children in every way,
    But you refuse what is good for you. Obstinately
    You push away your friends. You are sure to suffer for it.   610
MEDEA. Go! No doubt you hanker for your virginal bride,
    And are guilty of lingering too long out of her house.
    Enjoy your wedding. But perhaps,—with the help of God—
    You will make the kind of marriage that you will regret.
        [JASON *goes out with his attendants.*]
CHOR. When love is in excess   615
    It brings a man no honour
    Nor any worthiness.
    But if in moderation Cypris comes,
    There is no other power at all so gracious.
    O goddess, never on me let loose the unerring   620
    Shaft of your bow in the poison of desire.

    Let my heart be wise.
    It is the gods' best gift.
    On me let mighty Cypris
    Inflict no wordy wars or restless anger   625
    To urge my passion to a different love.
    But with discernment may she guide women's weddings,
    Honouring most what is peaceful in the bed.

    O country and home,
    Never, never may I be without you,   630
    Living the hopeless life,
    Hard to pass through and painful,
    Most pitiable of all.
    Let death first lay me low and death
    Free me from this daylight.   635
    There is no sorrow above
    The loss of a native land.

I have seen it myself,
Do not tell of a secondhand story.
Neither city nor friend   640
Pitied you when you suffered
The worst of sufferings.
O let him die ungraced whose heart
Will not reward his friends,
Who cannot open an honest mind   645
No friend will he be of mine.

[*Enter* AIGEUS, *king of Athens, an old friend of* MEDEA.]

AIGEUS. Medea, greeting! This is the best introduction
Of which men know for conversation between friends.
MEDEA. Greeting to you too, Aigeus, son of King Pandion,
Where have you come from to visit this country's soil?   650
AIGEUS. I have just left the ancient oracle of Phoebus.
MEDEA. And why did you go to earth's prophetic centre?
AIGEUS. I went to inquire how children might be born to me.
MEDEA. Is it so? Your life still up to this point childless?
AIGEUS. Yes. By the fate of some power we have no children.   655
MEDEA. Have you a wife, or is there none to share your bed?
AIGEUS. There is. Yes, I am joined to my wife in marriage.
MEDEA. And what did Phoebus say to you about children?
AIGEUS. Words too wise for a mere man to guess their meaning.
MEDEA. Is it proper for me to be told the God's reply?   660
AIGEUS. It is. For sure what is needed is cleverness.
MEDEA. Then what was his message? Tell me, if I may hear.
AIGEUS. I am not to loosen the hanging foot of the wine-skin . . .
MEDEA. Until you have done something, or reached some country?
AIGEUS. Until I return again to my hearth and house.   665
MEDEA. And for what purpose have you journeyed to this land?
AIGEUS. There is a man called Pittheus, king of Troezen.
MEDEA. A son of Pelops, they say, a most righteous man.
AIGEUS. With him I wish to discuss the reply of the god.
MEDEA. Yes. He is wise and experienced in such matters.   670
AIGEUS. And to me also the dearest of all my spear-friends.
MEDEA. Well, I hope you have good luck, and achieve your will.
AIGEUS. But why this downcast eye of yours, and this pale cheek?
MEDEA. O Aigeus, my husband has been the worst of all to me.
AIGEUS. What do you mean? Say clearly what has caused this
    grief.   675
MEDEA. Jason wrongs me, though I have never injured him.

---

647. *Aigeus:* Aegeus.
663. *not to loosen . . . wine-skin:*
This cryptic phrase probably means
"not to have intercourse."

667. *Pittheus:* Aigeus' father-in-law.
Troezen: in the Peloponnese. Corinth
was on the way from Delphi to Troezen.
671. *spear-friends:* allies in war,
companions in fighting.

AIGEUS. What has he done? Tell me about it in clearer words.

MEDEA. He has taken a wife to his house, supplanting me.

AIGEUS. Surely he would not dare to do a thing like that.

MEDEA. Be sure he has. Once dear, I now am slighted by him.   680

AIGEUS. Did he fall in love? Or is he tired of your love?

MEDEA. He was greatly in love, this traitor to his friends.

AIGEUS. Then let him go, if, as you say, he is so bad.

MEDEA. A passionate love,—for an alliance with the king.

AIGEUS. And who gave him his wife? Tell me the rest of it.   685

MEDEA. It was Kreon, he who rules this land of Corinth.

AIGEUS. Indeed, Medea, your grief was understandable.

MEDEA. I am ruined. And there is more to come: I am banished.

AIGEUS. Banished? By whom? Here you tell me of a new wrong.

MEDEA. Kreon drives me an exile from the land of Corinth.   690

AIGEUS. Does Jason consent? I cannot approve of this.

MEDEA. He pretends not to, but he will put up with it.
    Ah, Aigeus, I beg and beseech you, by your beard
    And by your knees I am making myself your suppliant,
    Have pity on me, have pity on your poor friend,   695
    And do not let me go into exile desolate,
    But receive me in your land and at your very hearth.
    So may your love, with God's help, lead to the bearing
    Of children, and so may you yourself die happy.
    You do not know what a chance you have come on here.   700
    I will end your childlessness, and I will make you able
    To beget children. The drugs I know can do this.

AIGEUS. For many reasons, woman, I am anxious to do
    This favour for you. First, for the sake of the gods,
    And then for the birth of children which you promise,   705
    For in that respect I am entirely at my wits' end.
    But this is my position: if you reach my land,
    I, being in my rights, will try to befriend you.
    But this much I must warn you of beforehand:
    I shall not agree to take you out of this country;   710
    But if you by yourself can reach my house, then you
    Shall stay there safely. To none will I give you up.
    But from this land you must make your escape yourself,
    For I do not wish to incur blame from my friends.

MEDEA. It shall be so. But, if I might have a pledge from you   715
    For this, then I would have from you all I desire.

AIGEUS. Do you not trust me? What is it rankles with you?

MEDEA. I trust you, yes. But the house of Pelias hates me,
    And so does Kreon. If you are bound by this oath,
    When they try to drag me from your land, you will not   720
    Abandon me; but if our pact is only words,

With no oath to the gods, you will be lightly armed,
Unable to resist their summons. I am weak,
While they have wealth to help them and a royal house.
AIGEUS. You show much foresight for such negotiations.   725
Well, if you will have it so, I will not refuse.
For, both on my side this will be the safest way
To have some excuse to put forward to your enemies,
And for you it is more certain. You may name the gods.
MEDEA. Swear by the plain of Earth, and Helios, father   730
Of my father, and name together all the gods. . . .
AIGEUS. That I will act or not act in what way? Speak.
MEDEA. That you yourself will never cast me from your land,
Nor, if any of my enemies should demand me,
Will you, in your life, willingly hand me over.   735
AIGEUS. I swear by the Earth, by the holy light of Helios,
By all the gods, I will abide by this you say.
MEDEA. Enough. And, if you fail, what shall happen to you?
AIGEUS. What comes to those who have no regard for heaven.
MEDEA. Go on your way. Farewell. For I am satisfied,   740
And I will reach your city as soon as I can,
Having done the deed I have to do and gained my end.
        [AIGEUS *goes out.*]
CHOR. May Hermes, god of travellers,
Escort you, Aigeus, to your home!
And may you have the things you wish   745
So eagerly; for you
Appear to me to be a generous man.
MEDEA. God, and God's daughter, justice, and light of Helios!
Now, friends, has come the time of my triumph over
My enemies, and now my foot is on the road.   750
Now I am confident they will pay the penalty.
For this man, Aigeus, has been like a harbour to me
In all my plans just where I was most distressed.
To him I can fasten the cable of my safety
When I have reached the town and fortress of Pallas.   755
And now I shall tell to you the whole of my plan.
Listen to these words that are not spoken idly.
I shall send one of my servants to find Jason
And request him to come once more into my sight.
And when he comes, the words I'll say will be soft ones.   760
I'll say that I agree with him, that I approve
The royal wedding he has made, betraying me.
I'll say it was profitable, an excellent idea.
But I shall beg that my children may remain here:

755. *town . . . Pallas:* Athens, city of Pallas Athene.

Not that I would leave in a country that hates me 765
Children of mine to feel their enemies' insults,
But that by a trick I may kill the king's daughter.
For I will send the children with gifts in their hands
To carry to the bride, so as not to be banished,—
A finely woven dress and a golden diadem. 770
And if she takes them and wears them upon her skin
She and all who touch the girl will die in agony;
Such poison will I lay upon the gifts I send.
But there, however, I must leave that account paid.
I weep to think of what a deed I have to do 775
Next after that; for I shall kill my own children.
My children, there is none who can give them safety.
And when I have ruined the whole of Jason's house,
I shall leave the land and flee from the murder of my
Dear children, and I shall have done a dreadful deed. 780
For it is not bearable to be mocked by enemies.
So it must happen. What profit have I in life?
I have no land, no home, no refuge from my pain.
My mistake was made the time I left behind me
My father's house, and trusted the words of a Greek, 785
Who, with heaven's help, will pay me the price for that.
For those children he had from me he will never
See alive again, nor will he on his new bride
Beget another child, for she is to be forced
To die a most terrible death by these my poisons. 790
Let no one think me a weak one, feeble-spirited,
A stay-at-home, but rather just the opposite,
One who can hurt my enemies and help my friends;
For the lives of such persons are most remembered.
CHOR. Since you have shared the knowledge of your plan with us, 795
I both wish to help you and support the normal
Ways of mankind, and tell you not to do this thing.
MEDEA. I can do no other thing. It is understandable
For you to speak thus. You have not suffered as I have.
CHOR. But can you have the heart to kill your flesh and blood? 800
MEDEA. Yes, for this is the best way to wound my husband.
CHOR. And you too. Of women you will be most unhappy.
MEDEA. So it must be. No compromise is possible.
　　　[*She turns to the* NURSE.]
Go, you, at once, and tell Jason to come to me.
You I employ on all affairs of greatest trust. 805
Say nothing of these decisions which I have made,
If you love your mistress, if you were born a woman.
CHOR. From of old the children of Erechtheus are

808. *Erechtheus:* an early king of Athens, a son of Hephaestus.

Splendid, the sons of blessed gods. They dwell
In Athens' holy and unconquered land,   810
Where famous Wisdom feeds them and they pass gaily
Always through that most brilliant air where once, they say,
That golden Harmony gave birth to the nine
Pure Muses of Pieria.

And beside the sweet flow of Cephisos' stream,   815
Where Cypris sailed, they say, to draw the water,
And mild soft breezes breathed along her path,
And on her hair were flung the sweet-smelling garlands
Of flowers of roses by the Lovers, the companions
Of Wisdom, her escort, the helpers of men   820
In every kind of excellence.

How then can these holy rivers
Or this holy land love you,
Or the city find you a home,
You, who will kill your children,   825
You, not pure with the rest?
O think of the blow at your children
And think of the blood that you shed.
O, over and over I beg you,
By your knees I beg you do not   830
Be the murderess of your babes!

O where will you find the courage
Or the skill of hand and heart,
When you set yourself to attempt
A deed so dreadful to do?   835
How, when you look upon them,
Can you tearlessly hold the decision
For murder? You will not be able,
When your children fall down and implore you,
You will not be able to dip   840
Steadfast your hand in their blood.

[*Enter* JASON *with attendants.*]

JASON. I have come at your request. Indeed, although you are
　　Bitter against me, this you shall have: I will listen
　　To what new thing you want, woman, to get from me.

---

810. *unconquered:* It was the
Athenians' boast that their descent
from the original settlers was uninterrupted by any invasion. There is a
topical reference here, for the play was
produced in 431 B.C., in a time of imminent war.
　809–814. *They dwell . . . Pieria:*
The sentence means that the fortunate
balance ("Harmony") of the elements

and the genius of the people produced
the cultivation of the arts ("the nine
pure Muses"). Pieria was a fountain
in Boeotia where the Muses were supposed to live.
　815. *Cephisos:* an Athenian river.
Cypris, mentioned in the next line, is
the goddess of love and therefore of
the principle of fertility.

MEDEA. Jason, I beg you to be forgiving towards me   845
    For what I said. It is natural for you to bear with
    My temper, since we have had much love together.
    I have talked with myself about this and I have
    Reproached myself. 'Fool' I said, 'why am I so mad?
    Why am I set against those who have planned wisely?   850
    Why make myself an enemy of the authorities
    And of my husband, who does the best thing for me
    By marrying royalty and having children who
    Will be as brothers to my own? What is wrong with me?
    Let me give up anger, for the gods are kind to me.   855
    Have I not children, and do I not know that we
    In exile from our country must be short of friends?'
    When I considered this I saw that I had shown
    Great lack of sense, and that my anger was foolish.
    Now I agree with you. I think that you are wise   860
    In having this other wife as well as me, and I
    Was mad. I should have helped you in these plans of yours,
    Have joined in the wedding, stood by the marriage bed,
    Have taken pleasure in attendance on your bride.
    But we women are what we are,—perhaps a little   865
    Worthless; and you men must not be like us in this,
    Nor be foolish in return when we are foolish.
    Now I give in, and admit that then I was wrong.
    I have come to a better understanding now.
        [*She turns towards the house.*]
    Children, come here, my children, come outdoors to us!   870
    Welcome your father with me, and say goodbye to him,
    And with your mother, who just now was his enemy,
    Join again in making friends with him who loves us.
        [*Enter the* CHILDREN, *attended by the* TUTOR.]
    We have made peace, and all our anger is over.
    Take hold of his right hand,—O God, I am thinking   875
    Of something which may happen in the secret future.
    O children, will you just so, after a long life,
    Hold out your loving arms at the grave? O children,
    How ready to cry I am, how full of foreboding!
    I am ending at last this quarrel with your father,   880
    And, look, my soft eyes have suddenly filled with tears.
CHOR. And the pale tears have started also in my eyes.
    O may the trouble not grow worse than now it is!
JASON. I approve of what you say. And I cannot blame you
    Even for what you said before. It is natural   885
    For a woman to be wild with her husband when he
    Goes in for secret love. But now your mind has turned

To better reasoning. In the end you have come to
The right decision, like the clever woman you are.
And of you, children, your father is taking care. 890
He has made, with God's help, ample provision for you.
For I think that a time will come when you will be
The leading people in Corinth with your brothers.
You must grow up. As to the future, your father
And those of the gods who love him will deal with that. 895
I want to see you, when you have become young men,
Healthy and strong, better men than my enemies.
Medea, why are your eyes all wet with pale tears?
Why is your cheek so white and turned away from me?
Are not these words of mine pleasing for you to hear? 900

MEDEA. It is nothing. I was thinking about these children.

JASON. You must be cheerful. I shall look after them well.

MEDEA. I will be. It is not that I distrust your words,
But a woman is a frail thing, prone to crying.

JASON. But why then should you grieve so much for these
children? 905

MEDEA. I am their mother. When you prayed that they might
live
I felt unhappy to think that these things will be.
But come, I have said something of the things I meant
To say to you, and now I will tell you the rest.
Since it is the king's will to banish me from here,— 910
And for me too I know that this is the best thing,
Not to be in your way by living here or in
The king's way, since they think me ill-disposed to them,—
I then am going into exile from this land;
But do you, so that you may have the care of them, 915
Beg Kreon that the children may not be banished.

JASON. I doubt if I'll succeed, but still I'll attempt it.

MEDEA. Then you must tell your wife to beg from her father
That the children may be reprieved from banishment.

JASON. I will, and with her I shall certainly succeed. 920

MEDEA. If she is like the rest of us women, you will.
And I too will take a hand with you in this business,
For I will send her some gifts which are far fairer,
I am sure of it, than those which now are in fashion,
A finely-woven dress and a golden diadem, 925
And the children shall present them. Quick, let one of you
Servants bring here to me that beautiful dress.

[*One of her attendants goes into the house.*]

She will be happy not in one way, but in a hundred,
Having so fine a man as you to share her bed,

And with this beautiful dress which Helios of old,   930
My father's father, bestowed on his descendants.
    [*Enter attendant carrying the poisoned dress and diadem.*]
There, children, take these wedding presents in your hands.
Take them to the royal princess, the happy bride,
And give them to her. She will not think little of them.

JASON. No, don't be foolish, and empty your hands of these.   935
Do you think the palace is short of dresses to wear?
Do you think there is no gold there? Keep them, don't give them
Away. If my wife considers me of any value,
She will think more of me than money, I am sure of it.

MEDEA. No, let me have my way. They say the gods themselves   940
Are moved by gifts, and gold does more with men than words.
Hers is the luck, her fortune that which god blesses;
She is young and a princess; but for my children's reprieve
I would give my very life, and not gold only.
Go children, go together to that rich palace,   945
Be suppliants to the new wife of your father,
My lady, beg her not to let you be banished.
And give her the dress,—for this is of great importance,
That she should take the gift into her hand from yours.
Go, quick as you can. And bring your mother good news   950
By your success of those things which she longs to gain.
    [JASON *goes out with his attendants, followed by the* TUTOR
    and the CHILDREN *carrying the poisoned gifts.*]

CHOR. Now there is no hope left for the children's lives.
Now there is none. They are walking already to murder.
The bride, poor bride, will accept the curse of the gold,
Will accept the bright diadem.   955
Around her yellow hair she will set that dress
Of death with her own hands.
The grace and the perfume and glow of the golden robe
Will charm her to put them upon her and wear the wreath,
And now her wedding will be with the dead below,   960
Into such a trap she will fall,
Poor thing, into such a fate of death and never
Escape from under that curse.

You too, O wretched bridegroom, making your match with kings,
You do not see that you bring   965
Destruction on your children and on her,
Your wife, a fearful death.
Poor soul, what a fall is yours!

In your grief too I weep, mother of little children,
You who will murder your own,   970

In vengeance for the loss of married love
Which Jason has betrayed
As he lives with another wife.
    [*Enter the* TUTOR *with the* CHILDREN.]
TUTOR. Mistress, I tell you that these children are reprieved,
    And the royal bride has been pleased to take in her hands   975
    Your gifts. In that quarter the children are secure.
    But come,
    Why do you stand confused when you are fortunate?
    Why have you turned round with your cheek away from me?
    Are not these words of mine pleasing for you to hear?   980
MEDEA. Oh! I am lost!
TUTOR. That word is not in harmony with my tidings.
MEDEA. I am lost, I am lost!
TUTOR.   Am I in ignorance telling you
    Of some disaster, and not the good news I thought?
MEDEA. You have told what you have told. I do not blame you.   985
TUTOR. Why then this downcast eye, and this weeping of tears?
MEDEA. Oh, I am forced to weep, old man. The gods and I,
    I in a kind of madness have contrived all this.
TUTOR. Courage! You too will be brought home by your children.
MEDEA. Ah, before that happens I shall bring others home.   990
TUTOR. Others before you have been parted from their children.
    Mortals must bear in resignation their ill luck.
MEDEA. That is what I shall do. But go inside the house,
    And do for the children your usual daily work.
       [*The* TUTOR *goes into the house.* MEDEA *turns to her*
       CHILDREN.]
O children, O my children, you have a city,   995
You have a home, and you can leave me behind you,
And without your mother you may live there for ever.
But I am going in exile to another land
Before I have seen you happy and taken pleasure in you,
Before I have dressed your brides and made your marriage beds
And held up the torch at the ceremony of wedding.   1001
Oh, what a wretch I am in this my self-willed thought!
What was the purpose, children, for which I reared you?
For all my travail and wearing myself away?
They were sterile, those pains I had in the bearing of you.   1005
O surely once the hopes in you I had, poor me,
Were high ones: you would look after me in old age,
And when I died would deck me well with your own hands;
A thing which all would have done. O but now it is gone,
That lovely thought. For, once I am left without you,   1010
Sad will be the life I'll lead and sorrowful for me.

And you will never see your mother again with
Your dear eyes, gone to another mode of living.
Why, children, do you look upon me with your eyes?
Why do you smile so sweetly that last smile of all?   1015
Oh, Oh, what can I do? My spirit has gone from me,
Friends, when I saw that bright look in the children's eyes.
I cannot bear to do it. I renounce my plans
I had before. I'll take my children away from
This land. Why should I hurt their father with the pain   1020
They feel, and suffer twice as much of pain myself?
No, no, I will not do it. I renounce my plans.
Ah, what is wrong with me? Do I want to let go
My enemies unhurt and be laughed at for it?
I must face this thing. Oh, but what a weak woman   1025
Even to admit to my mind these soft arguments.
Children, go into the house. And he whom law forbids
To stand in attendance at my sacrifices,
Let him see to it. I shall not mar my handiwork.
Oh! Oh!   1030
Do not, O my heart, you must not do these things!
Poor heart, let them go, have pity upon the children.
If they live with you in Athens they will cheer you.
No! By Hell's avenging furies it shall not be,—
This shall never be, that I should suffer my children   1035
To be the prey of my enemies' insolence.
Every way is it fixed. The bride will not escape.
No, the diadem is now upon her head, and she,
The royal princess, is dying in the dress, I know it.
But,—for it is the most dreadful of roads for me   1040
To tread, and them I shall send on a more dreadful still—
I wish to speak to the children.

    [*She calls the* CHILDREN *to her.*]

                         Come, children, give
Me your hands, give your mother your hands to kiss them.
O the dear hands, and O how dear are these lips to me,   1045
And the generous eyes and the bearing of my children!
I wish you happiness, but not here in this world.
What is here your father took. O how good to hold you!
How delicate the skin, how sweet the breath of children!
Go, go! I am no longer able, no longer   1050
To look upon you. I am overcome by sorrow.

    [*The* CHILDREN *go into the house.*]

I know indeed what evil I intend to do,
But stronger than all my afterthoughts is my fury,
Fury that brings upon mortals the greatest evils.

[*She goes out to the right, towards the royal palace.*]

CHOR. Often before   1055
  I have gone through more subtle reasons,
  And have come upon questionings greater
  Than a woman should strive to search out.
  But we too have a goddess to help us
  And accompany us into wisdom.   1060
  Not all of us. Still you will find
  Among many women a few,
  And our sex is not without learning.
  This I say, that those who have never
  Had children, who know nothing of it,   1065
  In happiness have the advantage
  Over those who are parents.
  The childless, who never discover
  Whether children turn out as a good thing
  Or as something to cause pain, are spared   1070
  Many troubles in lacking this knowledge.
  And those who have in their homes
  The sweet presence of children, I see that their lives
  Are all wasted away by their worries.
  First they must think how to bring them up well and   1075
  How to leave them something to live on.
  And then after this whether all their toil
  Is for those who will turn out good or bad,
  Is still an unanswered question.
  And of one more trouble, the last of all,   1080
  That is common to mortals I tell.
  For suppose you have found them enough for their living,
  Suppose that the children have grown into youth
  And have turned out good, still, if God so wills it,
  Death will away with your children's bodies,   1085
  And carry them off into Hades.
  What is our profit, then, that for the sake of
  Children the gods should pile upon mortals
  After all else
  This most terrible grief of all?   1090
      [*Enter* MEDEA, *from the spectators' right.*]
MEDEA. Friends, I can tell you that for long I have waited
  For the event. I stare towards the place from where
  The news will come. And now, see one of Jason's servants
  Is on his way here, and that laboured breath of his
  Shows he has tidings for us, and evil tidings.   1095
      [*Enter, also from the right, the* MESSENGER.]
MESSENGER. Medea, you who have done such a dreadful thing,

So outrageous, run for your life, take what you can,
A ship to bear you hence or chariot on land.

MEDEA. And what is the reason deserves such flight as this?

MESS. She is dead, only just now, the royal princess,   1100
And Kreon dead too, her father, by your poisons.

MEDEA. The finest words you have spoken. Now and hereafter
I shall count you among my benefactors and friends.

MESS. What! Are you right in the mind? Are you not mad,
Woman? The house of the king is outraged by you.   1105
Do you enjoy it? Not afraid of such doings?

MEDEA. To what you say I on my side have something too
To say in answer. Do not be in a hurry, friend,
But speak. How did they die? You will delight me twice
As much again if you say they died in agony.   1110

MESS. When those two children, born of you, had entered in,
Their father with them, and passed into the bride's house,
We were pleased, we slaves who were distressed by your wrongs.
All through the house we were talking of but one thing,
How you and your husband had made up your quarrel.   1115
Some kissed the children's hands and some their yellow hair,
And I myself was so full of my joy that I
Followed the children into the women's quarters.
Our mistress, whom we honour now instead of you,
Before she noticed that your two children were there,   1120
Was keeping her eye fixed eagerly on Jason.
Afterwards however she covered up her eyes,
Her cheek paled and she turned herself away from him,
So disgusted was she at the children's coming there.
But your husband tried to end the girl's bad temper,   1125
And said 'You must not look unkindly on your friends.
Cease to be angry. Turn your head to me again.
Have as your friends the same ones as your husband has.
And take these gifts, and beg your father to reprieve
These children from their exile. Do it for my sake.'   1130
She, when she saw the dress, could not restrain herself.
She agreed with all her husband said, and before
He and the children had gone far from the palace,
She took the gorgeous robe and dressed herself in it,
And put the golden crown around her curly locks,   1135
And arranged the set of the hair in a shining mirror,
And smiled at the lifeless image of herself in it.
Then she rose from her chair and walked about the room,
With her gleaming feet stepping most soft and delicate,
All overjoyed with the present. Often and often   1140
She would stretch her foot out straight and look along it.

But after that it was a fearful thing to see.
The colour of her face changed, and she staggered back,
She ran, and her legs trembled, and she only just
Managed to reach a chair without falling flat down.   1145
An aged woman servant who, I take it, thought
This was some seizure of Pan or another god,
Cried out 'God bless us,' but that was before she saw
The white foam breaking through her lips and her rolling
The pupils of her eyes and her face all bloodless.   1150
Then she raised a different cry from that 'God bless us,'
A huge shriek, and the women ran, one to the king,
One to the newly wedded husband to tell him
What had happened to his bride; and with frequent sound
The whole of the palace rang as they went running.   1155
One walking quickly round the course of a race-track
Would now have turned the bend and be close to the goal,
When she, poor girl, opened her shut and speechless eye,
And with a terrible groan she came to herself.
For a two-fold pain was moving up against her.   1160
The wreath of gold that was resting around her head
Let forth a fearful stream of all-devouring fire,
And the finely-woven dress your children gave to her,
Was fastening on the unhappy girl's fine flesh.
She leapt up from the chair, and all on fire she ran,   1165
Shaking her hair now this way and now that, trying
To hurl the diadem away; but fixedly
The gold preserved its grip, and, when she shook her hair,
Then more and twice as fiercely the fire blazed out.
Till, beaten by her fate, she fell down to the ground,   1170
Hard to be recognised except by a parent.
Neither the setting of her eyes was plain to see,
Nor the shapeliness of her face. From the top of
Her head there oozed out blood and fire mixed together.
Like the drops on pine-bark, so the flesh from her bones   1175
Dropped away, torn by the hidden fang of the poison.
It was a fearful sight; and terror held us all
From touching the corpse. We had learned from what had
    happened.
But her wretched father, knowing nothing of the event,
Came suddenly to the house, and fell upon the corpse,   1180
And at once cried out and folded his arms about her,
And kissed her and spoke to her, saying 'O my poor child,

1147. *Pan:* As the god of wild nature he was supposed to be the source of the sudden, apparently causeless terror which solitude in wild surroundings may produce, and thence of all kinds of sudden madness. (Compare our word "panic".)

What heavenly power has so shamefully destroyed you?
And who has set me here like an ancient sepulchre,
Deprived of you? O let me die with you, my child!'   1185
And when he had made an end of his wailing and crying,
Then the old man wished to raise himself to his feet;
But, as the ivy clings to the twigs of the laurel,
So he stuck to the fine dress, and he struggled fearfully.
For he was trying to lift himself to his knee,   1190
And she was pulling him down, and when he tugged hard
He would be ripping his aged flesh from his bones.
At last his life was quenched and the unhappy man
Gave up the ghost, no longer could hold up his head.
There they lie close, the daughter and the old father,   1195
Dead bodies, an event he prayed for in his tears.
As for your interests, I will say nothing of them,
For you will find your own escape from punishment.
Our human life I think and have thought a shadow,
And I do not fear to say that those who are held   1200
Wise amongst men and who search the reasons of things
Are those who bring the most sorrow on themselves.
For of mortals there is no one who is happy.
If wealth flows in upon one, one may be perhaps
Luckier than one's neighbour, but still not happy.   1205
    [*Exit.*]
CHOR. Heaven, it seems, on this day has fastened many
    Evils on Jason, and Jason has deserved them.
    Poor girl, the daughter of Kreon, how I pity you
    And your misfortunes, you who have gone quite away
    To the house of Hades because of marrying Jason.   1210
MEDEA. Women, my task is fixed: as quickly as I may
    To kill my children, and start away from this land,
    And not, by wasting time, to suffer my children
    To be slain by another hand less kindly to them.
    Force every way will have it they must die, and since 1215
    This must be so, then I, their mother, shall kill them.
    O arm yourself in steel, my heart! Do not hang back
    From doing this fearful and necessary wrong.
    O come, my hand, poor wretched hand, and take the sword,
    Take it, step forward to this bitter starting point,   1220
    And do not be a coward, do not think of them,
    How sweet they are, and how you are their mother. Just for
    This one short day be forgetful of your children,
    Afterwards weep; for even though you will kill them,
    They were very dear,—O, I am an unhappy woman!   1225
    [*With a cry she rushes into the house.*]

CHOR. O Earth, and the far shining
    Ray of the sun, look down, look down upon
    This poor lost woman, look, before she raises
    The hand of murder against her flesh and blood.
    Yours was the golden birth from which   1230
    She sprang, and now I fear divine
    Blood may be shed by men.
    O heavenly light, hold back her hand,
    Check her, and drive from out the house
    The bloody Fury raised by fiends of Hell.   1235

    Vain waste, your care of children;
    Was it in vain you bore the babes you loved,
    After you passed the inhospitable strait
    Between the dark blue rocks, Symplegades?
    O wretched one, how has it come,   1240
    This heavy anger on your heart,
    This cruel bloody mind?
    For God from mortals asks a stern
    Price for the stain of kindred blood
    In like disaster falling on their homes.   1245
       [A *cry from one of the* CHILDREN *is heard.*]
CHOR. Do you hear the cry, do you hear the children's cry?
    O you hard heart, O woman fated for evil!
ONE OF THE CHILDREN. [*From within*] What can I do and how
    escape my mother's hands?
ANOTHER CHILD. [*From within*] O my dear brother, I cannot tell.
    We are lost.
CHOR. Shall I enter the house? O surely I should   1250
    Defend the children from murder.
A CHILD. [*From within*] O help us, in God's name, for now we need
    your help.
    Now, now we are close to it. We are trapped by the sword.
CHOR. O your heart must have been made of rock or steel,
    You who can kill   1255
    With your own hand the fruit of your own womb.
    Of one alone I have heard, one woman alone
    Of those of old who laid her hands on her children,
    Ino, sent mad by heaven when the wife of Zeus
    Drove her out from her home and made her wander;   1260
    And because of the wicked shedding of blood
    Of her own children she threw
    Herself, poor wretch, into the sea and stepped away
    Over the sea-cliff to die with her two children.
    What horror more can be? O women's love,   1265

So full of trouble,
How many evils have you caused already!
[*Enter* JASON, *with attendants.*]

JASON. You women, standing close in front of this dwelling,
Is she, Medea, she who did this dreadful deed,
Still in the house, or has she run away in flight?   1270
For she will have to hide herself beneath the earth,
Or raise herself on wings into the height of air,
If she wishes to escape the royal vengeance.
Does she imagine that, having killed our rulers,
She will herself escape uninjured from this house?   1275
But I am thinking not so much of her as for
The children,—her the king's friends will make to suffer
For what she did. So I have come to save the lives
Of my boys, in case the royal house should harm them
While taking vengeance for their mother's wicked deed.   1280

CHOR. O Jason, if you but knew how deeply you are
Involved in sorrow, you would not have spoken so.

JASON. What is it? That she is planning to kill me also?

CHOR. Your children are dead, and by their own mother's hand.

JASON. What! This is it? O woman, you have destroyed me.   1285

CHOR. You must make up your mind your children are no more.

JASON. Where did she kill them? Was it here or in the house?

CHOR. Open the gates and there you will see them murdered.

JASON. Quick as you can unlock the doors, men, and undo
The fastenings and let me see this double evil,   1290
My children dead and her,—O her I will repay.

[*His attendants rush to the door.* MEDEA *appears above the
house in a chariot drawn by dragons. She has the dead bodies
of the children with her.*]

MEDEA. Why do you batter these gates and try to unbar them,
Seeking the corpses and for me who did the deed?
You may cease your trouble, and, if you have need of me,
Speak, if you wish. You will never touch me with your hand,   1295
Such a chariot has Helios, my father's father,
Given me to defend me from my enemies.

JASON. You hateful thing, you woman most utterly loathed
By the gods and me and by all the race of mankind,
You who have had the heart to raise a sword against   1300
Your children, you, their mother, and left me childless,—
You have done this, and do you still look at the sun
And at the earth, after these most fearful doings?
I wish you dead. Now I see it plain, though at that time
I did not, when I took you from your foreign home   1305
And brought you to a Greek house, you, an evil thing,

A traitress to your father and your native land.
The gods hurled the avenging curse of yours on me.
For your own brother you slew at your own hearthside,
And then came aboard that beautiful ship, the Argo.   1310
And that was your beginning. When you were married
To me, your husband, and had borne children to me,
For the sake of pleasure in the bed you killed them.
There is no Greek woman who would have dared such deeds,
Out of all those whom I passed over and chose you   1315
To marry instead, a bitter destructive match,
A monster not a woman, having a nature
Wilder than that of Scylla in the Tuscan sea.
Ah! no, not if I had ten thousand words of shame
Could I sting you. You are naturally so brazen.   1320
Go, worker in evil, stained with your children's blood.
For me remains to cry aloud upon my fate,
Who will get no pleasure from my newly-wedded love,
And the boys whom I begot and brought up, never
Shall I speak to them alive. Oh, my life is over!   1325

MEDEA. Long would be the answer which I might have made to
These words of yours, if Zeus the father did not know
How I have treated you and what you did to me.
No, it was not to be that you should scorn my love,
And pleasantly live your life through, laughing at me;   1330
Nor would the princess, nor he who offered the match,
Kreon, drive me away without paying for it.
So now you may call me a monster, if you wish,
O Scylla housed in the caves of the Tuscan sea
I too, as I had to, have taken hold of your heart.   1335

JASON. You feel the pain yourself. You share in my sorrow.

MEDEA. Yes, and my grief is gain when you cannot mock it.

JASON. O children, what a wicked mother she was to you!

MEDEA. They died from a disease they caught from their father.

JASON. I tell you it was not my hand that destroyed them.   1340

MEDEA. But it was your insolence, and your virgin wedding.

JASON. And just for the sake of that you chose to kill them.

MEDEA. Is love so small a pain, do you think, for a woman?

JASON. For a wise one, certainly. But you are wholly evil.

MEDEA. The children are dead. I say this to make you suffer.   1345

JASON. The children, I think, will bring down curses on you.

MEDEA. The gods know who was the author of this sorrow.

JASON. Yes, the gods know indeed, they know your loathsome heart.

MEDEA. Hate me. But I tire of your barking bitterness.

1318. *Scylla:* a monster located in the straits between Italy and Sicily, who snatched sailors off passing ships and devoured them.

JASON. And I of yours. It is easier to leave you.   1350
MEDEA. How then? What shall I do? I long to leave you too.
JASON. Give me the bodies to bury and to mourn them.
MEDEA. No, that I will not. I will bury them myself,
    Bearing them to Hera's temple on the promontory;
    So that no enemy may evilly treat them   1355
    By tearing up their grave. In this land of Corinth
    I shall establish a holy feast and sacrifice
    Each year for ever to atone for the blood guilt.
    And I myself go to the land of Erechtheus
    To dwell in Aigeus' house, the son of Pandion.   1360
    While you, as is right, will die without distinction,
    Struck on the head by a piece of the Argo's timber,
    And you will have seen the bitter end of my love.
JASON. May a Fury for the children's sake destroy you,
    And justice, requitor of blood.   1365
MEDEA. What heavenly power lends an ear
    To a breaker of oaths, a deceiver?
JASON. O, I hate you, murderess of children.
MEDEA. Go to your palace. Bury your bride.
JASON. I go, with two children to mourn for.   1370
MEDEA. Not yet do you feel it. Wait for the future.
JASON. Oh, children I loved!
MEDEA.   I loved them, you did not.
JASON. You loved them, and killed them.
MEDEA.   To make you feel
    pain.   1375
JASON. Oh, wretch that I am, how I long
    To kiss the dear lips of my children!
MEDEA. Now you would speak to them, now you would kiss them.
    Then you rejected them.
JASON.   Let me, I beg you,   1380
    Touch my boys' delicate flesh.
MEDEA. I will not. Your words are all wasted.
JASON. O God, do you hear it, this persecution,
    These my sufferings from this hateful
    Woman, this monster, murderess of children?   1385
    Still what I can do that I will do:
    I will lament and cry upon heaven,
    Calling the gods to bear me witness
    How you have killed my boys and prevent me from
    Touching their bodies or giving them burial.   1390
    I wish I had never begot them to see them

1357. *feast and sacrifice:* Some such ceremony was still performed at Corinth in
Euripides' time.

Afterwards slaughtered by you.

CHOR. Zeus in Olympus is the overseer
 Of many doings. Many things the gods
 Achieve beyond our judgment. What we thought 1395
 Is not confirmed and what we thought not god
 Contrives. And so it happens in this story.

The Trojan Women*

*The scene is a space of waste ground except for a few huts to
right and left, where the women selected for the Greek leaders are
housed. Far in the background, Troy, the wall in ruins, is slowly
burning, as yet more smoke than flame. In front a woman with white
hair lies on the ground. It is just before dawn. A tall dim figure is
seen, back of the woman.*

POSEIDON. I am the sea god. I have come
 up from the salt sea depths of the Aegean,
 from where the sea nymphs' footsteps fall,
 weaving the lovely measures of the dance.
 For since that day I built the towers of stone 5
 around this town of Troy, Apollo with me,
 —and straight we raised them, true by line and plummet—
 good will for them has never left my heart,
 my Trojans and their city.
 City? Smoke only—all is gone, 10
 perished beneath Greek spears.
 A horse was fashioned, big with arms.
 Parnassus was the workman's home,
 in Phocia, and his name Epeius.
 The skill he had Athena gave him. 15
 He sent it through the walls—it carried death.
 The wooden horse, so men will call it always,
 which held and hid those spears.
 A desert now where groves were. Blood drips down
 from the gods' shrines. Beside his hearth 20
 Priam lies dead upon the altar steps
 of Zeus, the hearth's protector.
 While to the Greek ships pass the Trojan treasure,
 gold, gold in masses, armor, clothing,

* Reprinted from *Three Greek Plays*, translated with introductions by Edith Hamilton, by permission of W. W. Norton & Company, Inc. Copyright 1937 by W. W. Norton & Company, Inc. First produced in 415 B.C.

stripped from the dead.   25
The Greeks who long since brought war to the town,
—ten times the seed was sown before Troy fell—
wait now for a fair wind for home,
the joyful sight of wife and child again.
Myself defeated by the Argive goddess   30
Hera and by Athena, both in league together—
I too must take my leave of glorious Troy,
forsake my altars. When a town is turned
into a desert, things divine fall sick.
Not one to do them honor.   35
Scamander's stream is loud with lamentation,
so many captive women weeping.
Their masters drew lots for them. Some will go
to Arcady and some to Thessaly.
Some to the lords of Athens, Theseus' sons.   40
Huts here hold others spared the lot, but chosen
for the great captains.
With them, like them a captive of the spear,
the Spartan woman, Helen.
But if a man would look on misery,   45
it is here to see—Hecuba lies there
before the gates. She weeps.
Many tears for many griefs.
And one still hidden from her.
But now upon Achilles' grave her daughter   50
was killed—Polyxena. So patiently she died.
Gone is her husband, gone her sons, all dead.
One daughter whom the Lord Apollo loved,
yet spared her wild virginity, Cassandra,
Agamemnon, in the dark, will force upon his bed.   55
No thought for what was holy and was God's.
O city happy once, farewell.
O shining towers, crumbling now
beneath Athena's hand, the child of God,
or you would still stand firm on deep foundations.   60

    [*As he turns to go the goddess* PALLAS ATHENA *enters.*]

ATHENA. Am I allowed to speak to one who is
    my father's nearest kinsman,
    a god among gods honored, powerful?

---

30. *Argive goddess:* Hera, the wife of
Zeus, was the principal deity worshipped
at Argos.
    39. *Arcady:* Arcadia, the central area
of the Peloponnese. *Thessaly :* the north-

eastern part of Greece.
    51. *Polyxena:* She was sacrificed by
the Greeks to appease the ghost of
Achilles.

If I put enmity aside, will he?

POSEIDON. He will, most high Athena. We are kin,   65
old comrades too, and these have magic power.

ATHENA. Thanks for your gentleness. What I would say
touches us both, great king.

POSEIDON. A message from the gods? A word from Zeus?
Some spirit, surely?   70

ATHENA. No, but for Troy's sake, where we stand, I seek
your power to join my own with it.

POSEIDON. What! Now—at last? Has that long hatred left you?
Pity—when all is ashes—burned to ashes?

ATHENA. The point first, please. Will you make common cause   75
with me? What I wish done will you wish, too?

POSEIDON. Gladly. But what you wish I first must know.
You come to me for Troy's sake or for Greece?

ATHENA. I wish to make my Trojan foes rejoice,
and give the Greeks a bitter home-coming.   80

POSEIDON. The way you change! Here—there—then back again.
Now hate, now love—no limit ever.

ATHENA. You know how I was outraged and my temple.

POSEIDON. Oh that—when Ajax dragged Cassandra out?   84

ATHENA. And not one Greek to punish him—not one to blame him.

POSEIDON. Even though your power ruined Troy for them.

ATHENA. Therefore with you I mean to hurt them.

POSEIDON. Ready for all you wish. But—hurt them? How?

ATHENA. Give them affliction for their coming home.

POSEIDON. Held here, you mean? Or out on the salt sea?   90

ATHENA. Whenever the ships sail.
Zeus shall send rain, unending rain, and sleet,
and darkness blown from heaven.
He will give me—he has promised—his thunderbolt,
to strike the ships with fire. They shall burn.   95
Your part, to make your sea-roads roar—
wild waves and whirlwinds,
while dead men choke the winding bay.
So Greeks shall learn to reverence my house
and dread all gods.   100

POSEIDON. These things shall be. No need of many words
to grant a favor. I will stir the sea,
the wide Aegean. Shores and reefs and cliffs
will hold dead men, bodies of many dead.

66. *these:* kinship and comradeship.
84. *Ajax:* not the great Ajax, son of Telamon, but the lesser Ajax, son of Oileus. He dragged Cassandra away from the temple of Athena where she had taken refuge during the sack of the city.

Off to Olympus with you now, and get   105
those fiery arrows from the hand of Zeus.
Then when a fair wind sends the Greeks to sea,
watch the ships sail.
    [*Exit* ATHENA.]
Oh, fools the men who lay a city waste,
giving to desolation temples, tombs,   110
the sanctuaries of the dead—so soon
to die themselves.   [*Exit* POSEIDON.]
    [*The two gods have been talking before daylight, but now
    the day begins to dawn and the woman lying on the ground
    in front moves. She is* HECUBA, *the aged queen of Troy.*]

HECUBA. Up from the ground—O weary head, O breaking neck.
This is no longer Troy. And we are not
the lords of Troy.   115
Endure. The ways of fate are the ways of the wind.
Drift with the stream—drift with fate.
No use to turn the prow to breast the waves.
Let the boat go as it chances.
Sorrow, my sorrow.   120
What sorrow is there that is not mine,
grief to weep for.
Country lost and children and husband.
Glory of all my house brought low.
All was nothing—nothing, always.   125
Keep silent? Speak?
Weep then? Why? For what?
    [*She begins to get up.*]
Oh, this aching body—this bed—
it is very hard. My back pressed to it—
Oh, my side, my brow, my temples.   130
Up! Quick, quick. I must move.
Oh, I'll rock myself this way, that way,
to the sound of weeping, the song of tears,
dropping down forever.
The song no feet will dance to ever,   135
for the wretched, the ruined.

O ships, O prows, swift oars,
out from the fair Greek bays and harbors,
over the dark shining sea,
you found your way to our holy city,   140
and the fearful music of war was heard,
the war song sung to flute and pipe,
as you cast on the shore your cables,

ropes the Nile dwellers twisted and coiled,
and you swung, oh, my grief, in Troy's waters.   145

What did you come for? A woman?
A thing of loathing, of shame,
to husband, to brother, to home.
She slew Priam, the king,
father of fifty sons,   150
she wrecked me upon
the reef of destruction.
Who am I that I wait
here at a Greek king's door?
A slave that men drive on,   155
an old gray woman that has no home.
Shaven head brought low in dishonor.
O wives of the bronze-armored men who fought,
and maidens, sorrowing maidens,
plighted to shame,   160
see—only smoke left where was Troy.
Let us weep for her.
As a mother bird cries to her feathered brood,
so will I cry.
Once another song I sang   165
when I leaned on Priam's scepter,
and the beat of dancing feet
marked the music's measure.
Up to the gods
the song of Troy rose at my signal.   170

[*The door of one of the huts opens and a woman steals
out, then another, and another.*]

FIRST WOMAN. Your cry, O Hecuba—oh, such a cry—
   What does it mean? There in the tent
   we heard you call so piteously,
   and through our hearts flashed fear.
   In the tent we were weeping, too,   175
   for we are slaves.

HECUBA. Look, child, there where the Greek ships lie—

ANOTHER WOMAN. They are moving. The men hold oars.

ANOTHER. O God, what will they do? Carry me off
   over the sea in a ship far from home?   180

HECUBA. You ask and I know nothing,
   but I think ruin is here.

153. This is the way Professor [Gilbert] Murray translates the line and the one following. The translation is so simple and beautiful, I cannot bear to give it up for a poorer one of my own [Translator's note].

ANOTHER WOMAN. Oh, we are wretched. We shall hear the summons.
Women of Troy, go forth from your home,
for the Greeks set sail.   185
HECUBA. But not Cassandra, oh, not her.
She is mad—she has been driven mad. Leave her within.
Not shamed before the Greeks—not that grief too.
I have enough.
    O Troy, unhappy Troy, you are gone   190
and we, the unhappy, leave you,
we who are living and we who are dead.
        [*More women now come out from a second hut.*]
A WOMAN. Out of the Greek king's tent
trembling I come, O Queen,
to hear my fate from you.   195
Not a death—They would not think of death
for a poor woman.
ANOTHER. The sailors—they are standing on the prow.
Already they are running out the oars.
ANOTHER. [*She comes out of a third hut and several follow her.*]
It is so early—but a terror woke me.   200
    My heart beats so.
ANOTHER. Has a herald come from the Greek camp?
Whose slave shall I be? I—bear that?
HECUBA. Wait for the lot drawing. It is near.
ANOTHER. Argos shall it be, or Phthia?   205
    or an island of the sea?
    A Greek soldier lead me there,
far, far from Troy?
HECUBA. And I a slave—to whom—where—how?
You old gray woman, patient to endure,   210
you bee without a sting,
only an image of what was alive
    or the ghost of one dead.
I watch a master's door?
    I nurse his children?   215
    Once I was queen in Troy.
ONE WOMAN TO ANOTHER. Poor thing. What are your tears
to the shame before you?
THE OTHER. The shuttle will still pass through my hands,
but the loom will not be in Troy.   220
ANOTHER. My dead sons. I would look at them once more.
Never again.
ANOTHER. Worse to come.
    A Greek's bed—and I—

205. *Phthia:* in Northern Greece, the home of Achilles.

ANOTHER. A night like that? Oh, never— 225
oh, no—not that for me.

ANOTHER. I see myself a water carrier,
dipping my pitcher in the great Pirenian spring.

ANOTHER. The land of Theseus, Athens, it is known
to be a happy place. I wish I could go there. 230

ANOTHER. But not to the Eurotas, hateful river,
where Helen lived. Not there, to be a slave
to Menelaus who sacked Troy.

ANOTHER. Oh, look. A man from the Greek army—
a herald. Something strange has happened, 235
he comes so fast. To tell us—what?
What will he say? Only Greek slaves are here,
waiting for orders.

[*Enter* TALTHYBIUS *with soldiers.*]

TALTHYBIUS. You know me, Hecuba. I have often come
with messages to Troy from the Greek camp. 240
Talthybius—these many years you've known me.
I bring you news.

HECUBA. It has come, women of Troy. Once we only feared it.

TALTHYBIUS. The lots are drawn, if that is what you feared.

HECUBA. Who—where? Thessaly? Phthia? Thebes? 245

TALTHYBIUS. A different man takes each. You're not to go together.

HECUBA. Then which takes which? Has any one good fortune?

TALTHYBIUS. I know, but ask about each one, not all at once.

HECUBA. My daughter, who—who drew her? Tell me—
Cassandra. She has had so much to bear. 250

TALTHYBIUS. King Agamemnon chose her out from all.

HECUBA. Oh! but—of course—to serve his Spartan wife?

TALTHYBIUS. No, no—but for the king's own bed at night.

HECUBA. Oh, never. She is God's, a virgin, always.
That was God's gift to her for all her life. 255

TALTHYBIUS. He loved her for that same strange purity.

HECUBA. Throw away, daughter, the keys of the temple.
Take off the wreath and the sacred stole.

TALTHYBIUS. Well, now—a king's bed is not so bad.

HECUBA. My other child you took from me just now? 260

TALTHYBIUS. [*Speaking with constraint*] Polyxena, you mean? Or
someone else?

HECUBA. Her. Who drew her?

TALTHYBIUS. They told her off to watch Achilles' tomb.

HECUBA. To watch a tomb? My daughter?

---

228. *Pirenian spring:* at Corinth.
231. *Eurotas:* the river of Sparta.
241. *Talthybius:* the herald of Agamemnon.

256. This line, too, is Professor Murray's, retained here for the reason given
above [Translator's note].

That a Greek custom? 265
What strange ritual is that, my friend?

TALTHYBIUS. [*Speaking fast and trying to put her off*]
Just think of her as happy—all well with her.

HECUBA. Those words—Why do you speak like that?
She is alive?

TALTHYBIUS. [*Determined not to tell her*]
What happened was—well, she is free from trouble. 270

HECUBA. [*Wearily giving the riddle up*]
Then Hector's wife—my Hector, wise in war—
Where does she go, poor thing—Andromache?

TALTHYBIUS. Achilles' son took her. He chose her out.

HECUBA. And I, old gray head, whose slave am I,
creeping along with my crutch? 275

TALTHYBIUS. Slave of the king of Ithaca, Odysseus.

HECUBA. Beat, beat my shorn head! Tear, tear my cheek!
His slave—vile lying man. I have come to this—
There is nothing good he does not hurt—a lawless beast.
He twists and turns, this way and that, and back again. 280
A double tongue, as false in hate as false in love.
Pity me, women of Troy,
I have gone. I am lost—oh, wretched.
An evil fate fell on me,
a lot the hardest of all. 285

A WOMAN. You know what lies before you, Queen, but I—
What man among the Greeks owns me?

TALTHYBIUS. [*To the soldiers*] Off with you. Bring Cassandra here.
Be quick,
you fellows. We must give her to the chief,
into his very hand. And then these here 290
to all the other generals. But what's that—
that flash of light inside there?
[*Light shines through the crevices of one of the huts.*]
Set fire to the huts—is that their plan,
these Trojan women? Burn themselves to death
rather than sail to Greece. Choosing to die instead. 295
How savagely these days the yoke bears down
on necks so lately free.
Open there, open the door. [*Aside*] As well for them perhaps,
but for the Greeks—they'd put the blame on me.

HECUBA. No, no, there is nothing burning. It is my daughter, 300
Cassandra. She is mad.
[CASSANDRA *enters from the hut dressed like a priestess, a
wreath in her hair, a torch in her hand. She does not seem to*

see anyone.]

CASSANDRA. Lift it high—in my hand—light to bring.
I praise him. I bear a flame.
With my torch I touch to fire
this holy place.   305
Hymen, O Hymen.
Blessed the bridegroom,
blessed am I
to lie with a king in a king's bed in Argos.
Hymen, O Hymen.   310
Mother, you weep
tears for my father dead,
mourning for the beloved
country lost.
I for my bridal here   315
lift up the fire's flame
to the dawn, to the splendor,
to you, O Hymen.
Queen of night,
give your starlight   320
to a virgin bed,
as of old you did.
Fly, dancing feet.
Up with the dance.
Oh, joy, oh, joy!   325
Dance for my father dead,
most blest to die.
Oh, holy dance!
Apollo—you?
Lead on then.   330
There in the laurel grove
I served your altar.
Dance, Mother, come.
Keep step with me.
Dear feet with my feet   335
tracing the measure
this way and that.
Sing to the Marriage god,
oh, joyful song.
Sing for the bride, too,   340
joyously all.

302ff. In these lines Cassandra performs a mock bridal hymn for her "marriage" to Agamemnon. Torches were carried at a wedding, and the guests greeted
the bride and groom with the cry "Hymen, O Hymen" which Cassandra repeats throughout her song.

Maidens of Troy,
dressed in your best,
honor my marriage.
Honor too him   345
whose bed fate drives me to share.

A WOMAN. Hold her fast, Queen, poor frenzied girl.
She might rush straight to the Greek camp.

HECUBA. O fire, fire, when men make marriages
you light the torch, but this flame flashing here   360
is for grief only. Child, such great hopes once I had.
I never thought that to your bridal bed
Greek spears would drive you.
Give me your torch. You do not hold it straight,
you move so wildly. Your sufferings, my child,   355
have never taught you wisdom.
You never change. Here! Someone take the torch
into the hut. This marriage needs no songs,
but only tears.

CASSANDRA. O Mother, crown my triumph with a wreath.   360
Be glad, for I am married to a king.
Send me to him, and if I shrink away,
drive me with violence. If Apollo lives,
my marriage shall be bloodier than Helen's.
Agamemnon, the great, the glorious lord of Greece—   365
I shall kill him, Mother, lay his house as low
as he laid ours, make him pay for all
he made my father suffer, brothers, and—
But no. I must not speak of that—that axe
which on my neck—on others' too—   370
nor of that murder of a mother.
All, all because he married me and so
pulled his own house down.
But I will show you. This town now, yes, Mother,
is happier than the Greeks. I know that I am mad,   375
but Mother, dearest, now, for this one time
I do not rave.
One woman they came hunting, and one love,
Helen, and men by tens of thousands died.
Their king, so wise, to get what most he hated   380
destroyed what most he loved,
his joy at home, his daughter, killing her
for a brother's sake, to get him back a woman

---

363. *If Apollo lives: i.e.*, if Apollo is
a god and his prophecies true.

382. *his daughter:* Iphigenia.

who had fled because she wished—not forced to go.
And when they came to the banks of the Scamander   385
those thousands died. And why?
No man had moved their landmarks
or laid siege to their high-walled towns.
But those whom war took never saw their children.
No wife with gentle hands shrouded them for their grave.   390
They lie in a strange land. And in their homes
are sorrows, too, the very same.
Lonely women who died, old men who waited
for sons that never came—no son left to them
to make the offering at their graves.   395
That was the glorious victory they won.
But we—we Trojans died to save our people,
no glory greater. All those the spear slew,
friends bore them home and wrapped them in their shroud
with dutiful hands. The earth of their own land   400
covered them. The rest, through the long days they fought,
had wife and child at hand, not like the Greeks,
whose joys were far away.
And Hector's pain—your Hector. Mother, hear me.
This is the truth: he died, the best, a hero.   405
Because the Greeks came, he died thus.
Had they stayed home, we never would have known him.
This truth stands firm: the wise will fly from war.
But if war comes, to die well is to win
the victor's crown.   410
The only shame is not to die like that.
So, Mother, do not pity Troy,
or me upon my bridal bed.

TALTHYBIUS. [*Has been held awestruck through all this, but can
        bear no more*]
Now if Apollo had not made you mad
I would have paid you for those evil words,   415
bad omens, and my general sailing soon.
        [*Grumbles to himself*]
The great, who seem so wise, have no more sense
than those who rank as nothing.
Our king, the first in Greece, bows down
before this mad girl, loves her, chooses her   420
out of them all. Well, I am a poor man,
but I'd not go to bed with her.
        [*Turns to* CASSANDRA]
Now you—you know your mind is not quite right.

So all you said against Greece and for Troy,
I never heard—the wind blew it away.   425
Come with me to the ship now.
[Aside] A grand match for our general, she is.
        [To HECUBA, gently]
And you, do follow quietly when Odysseus' men come.
His wife's a good, wise woman, so they say.

CASSANDRA. [Seeming to see TALTHYBIUS for the first time and looking
        him over haughtily] A strange sort of slave, surely.   430
Heralds such men are called,
hated by all, for they are tyrants' tools.
You say my mother goes to serve Odysseus?
        [She turns away and speaks to herself.]
But where then is Apollo's word, made clear
to me, that death will find her here?   435
And—no, that shame I will not speak of.
Odysseus! wretched—but he does not know.
    Soon all these sorrows, mine and Troy's, will seem
compared to his like golden hours.
Ten years behind him here, ten years before him.   440
Then only, all alone, will he come home,
and there find untold trouble has come first.
But his cares—why let fly one word at him?
Come, let us hasten to my marriage.
We two shall rest, the bridegroom and the bride,   445
within the house of death.
O Greek king, with your dreams of grandeur yet to come,
vile as you are, so shall your end be,
in darkness—all light gone.
And me—a cleft in the hills,   450
washed by winter rains,
his tomb near by.
There—dead—cast out—naked—
and wild beasts seeking food—
It is I there—I myself—Apollo's servant.   455
O flowers of the God I love, mysterious wreaths,
away. I have forgotten temple festival,
I have forgotten joy.
Off. I tear them from my neck.
Swift winds will carry them   460
up to you, O God of truth.
My flesh still clean, I give them back to you.

436. *that shame:* the legend was that
Hecuba, after blinding King Polymestor
of Thrace in revenge for his murder of

her last remaining son, was changed into
a dog and drowned in the sea off the
coast.

Where is the ship? How do I go on board?
Spread the sail—the wind comes swift.
Those who bring vengeance—three are they,   465
And one of them goes with you on the sea.
Mother, my Mother, do not weep. Farewell,
dear City. Brothers, in Troy's earth laid, my father,
a little time and I am with you.
You dead, I shall come to you a victor.   470
Those ruined by my hand who ruined us.
      [*She goes out with* TALTHYBIUS *and the soldiers.* HECUBA,
      motionless for a moment, falls.]
A WOMAN. The Queen! See—see—she is falling.
Oh, help! She cannot speak.
Miserable slaves, will you leave her on the ground,
old as she is. Up—lift her up.   475
HECUBA. Let me be. Kindness not wanted is unkindness.
I cannot stand. Too much is on me.
Anguish here and long since and to come—
O God—Do I call to you? You did not help.
But there is something that cries out for God   480
when trouble comes.
Oh, I will think of good days gone,
days to make a song of,
crowning my sorrow by remembering.
We were kings and a king I married.   485
Sons I bore him, many sons.
That means little—but fine, brave lads.
They were the best in all Troy.
No woman, Trojan, Greek, or stranger,
had sons like mine to be proud of.   490
I saw them fall beneath Greek spears.
My hair I shore at the grave of the dead.
Their father—I did not learn from others
that I must weep for him—these eyes beheld him.
I, my own self, saw him fall murdered   495
upon the altar, when his town was lost.
My daughters, maidens reared to marry kings,
are torn from me. For the Greeks I reared them.
All gone—no hope that I shall look upon
their faces any more, or they on mine.   500
And now the end—no more can lie beyond—
an old gray slave woman I go to Greece.

---

465. *three are they:* Euripides is following a legend that there were three
Erinyes, the avenging spirits; Cassandra
claims that she has become one of them.

The tasks they know for my age hardest, mine.
The door to shut and open, bowing low
—I who bore Hector—meal to grind; upon   505
the ground lay this old body down that once
slept in a royal bed; torn rags around me,
torn flesh beneath.
And all this misery and all to come
because a man desired a woman.   510
Daughter, who knew God's mystery and joy,
what strange chance lost you your virginity?
And you, Polyxena—where are you gone?
No son, no daughter, left to help my need,
and I had many, many—   515
Why lift me up? What hope is there to hold to?
　　This slave that once went delicately in Troy,
take her and cast her on her bed of clay,
rocks for her pillow, there to fall and die,
wasted with tears. Count no one happy,   520
however fortunate, before he dies.
CHORUS. Sing me, O Muse, a song for Troy,
　a strange song sung to tears,
　a music for the grave.
　O lips, sound forth a melody   525
　　for Troy.

A four-wheeled cart brought the horse to the gates,
brought ruin to me,
　captured, enslaved me.
Gold was the rein and the bridle,   530
deadly the arms within,
and they clashed loud to heaven as the threshold was
　　passed.

High on Troy's rock the people cried,
"Rest at last, trouble ended.
Bring the carven image in.   535
Bear it to Athena,
fit gift for the child of God."

Who of the young but hurried forth?
Who of the old would stay at home?
With song and rejoicing they brought death in,   540
treachery and destruction.
All that were in Troy,

hastening to the gate,
drew that smooth-planed horse of wood
carven from a mountain pine,   545
where the Greeks were hiding,
where was Troy's destruction,
gave it to the goddess,
gift for her, the virgin,
driver of the steeds that never die.   550

With ropes of twisted flax,
as a ship's dark hull is drawn to land,
they brought it to her temple of stone,
to her floor that soon would run with blood,
    to Pallas Athena.   555

    On their toil and their joy
the dark of evening fell,
but the lutes of Egypt still rang out
    to the songs of Troy.
And girls with feet light as air   560
dancing, sang happy songs.
The houses blazed with light
through the dark splendor,
    and sleep was not.

A GIRL. I was among the dancers.   565
I was singing to the maiden of Zeus,
the goddess of the hills.
A shout rang out in the town,
a cry of blood through the houses,
and a frightened child caught his mother's skirt   570
and hid himself in her cloak.
Then War came forth from his hiding place—
Athena, the virgin, devised it.
Around the altars they slaughtered us.
Within on their beds lay headless men,   575
young men cut down in their prime.
This was the triumph-crown of Greece.
We shall bear children for her to rear,
grief and shame to our country.
    [A *chariot approaches, loaded with spoils. In it sits a woman
    and a child.*]
A WOMAN. Look, Hecuba, it is Andromache.   580

567. *goddess of the hills:* Artemis.

See, in the Greek car yonder.
Her breast heaves with her sobs and yet
the baby sleeps there, dear Astyanax,
 the son of Hector.

ANOTHER. Most sorrowful of women, where do you go?   585
Beside you the bronze armor that was Hector's,
the spoil of the Greek spear, stripped from the dead.
Will Achilles' son use it to deck his temples?

ANDROMACHE. I go where my Greek masters take me.

HECUBA. Oh, our sorrow—our sorrow.   590

ANDROMACHE. Why should you weep? This sorrow is mine.

HECUBA. O God—

ANDROMACHE. What has come to me is mine.

HECUBA. My children—

ANDROMACHE. Once we lived, not now.   595

HECUBA. Gone—gone—happiness—Troy—

ANDROMACHE. And you bear it.

HECUBA. Sons, noble sons, all lost.

ANDROMACHE. Oh, sorrow is here.

HECUBA. For me—for me.   600

ANDROMACHE. For the city, in its shroud of smoke.
Come to me, O my husband.

HECUBA. What you cry to lies in the grave.
My son, wretched woman, mine.

ANDROMACHE. Defend me—me, your wife.   605

HECUBA. My son, my eldest son,
whom I bore to Priam,
whom the Greeks used shamefully,
come to me, lead me to death.

ANDROMACHE. Death—oh, how deep a desire.   610

HECUBA. Such is our pain—

ANDROMACHE. For a city that has fallen, fallen.

HECUBA. For anguish heaped upon anguish.

ANDROMACHE. For the anger of God against Paris,
your son, who fled from death,   615
who laid Troy's towers low

---

615. *fled from:* escaped from. This refers not to the immediate present (for Paris was killed in the sack of the city) but to the story of his birth. Hecuba, before she bore him, dreamed she had brought forth a firebrand which burned down the city. The prophets advised her that the child would be the ruin of Troy and should be killed at birth. Instead Hecuba sent the child out to be exposed on the mountain. There Paris survived and grew to be a handsome shepherd. Later, when his identity was discovered, Hecuba and Priam took him back into the family. These events were the subject of a play of Euripides, which was produced in the same year as *The Trojan Women.*

to win an evil love.
Dead men—bodies—blood—
vultures hovering—
Oh, Athena the goddess is there, be sure,   620
and the slave's yoke is laid upon Troy.
HECUBA. O country, desolate, empty.
ANDROMACHE. My tears fall for you.
HECUBA. Look and see the end—
ANDROMACHE. Of the house where I bore my children.   625
HECUBA. O children, your mother has lost her city,
and you—you have left her alone.
Only grief is mine and mourning.
Tears and more tears, falling, falling.
The dead—they have forgotten their pain.   630
They weep no more.
A WOMAN. [*Aside to another*] Tears are sweet in bitter grief,
and sorrow's song is lamentation.
ANDROMACHE. Mother of him whose spear of old brought death
to Greeks unnumbered, you see what is here.   635
HECUBA. I see God's hand that casts the mighty down
and sets on high the lowly.
ANDROMACHE. Driven like cattle captured in a raid,
my child and I—the free changed to a slave.
Oh, changed indeed.   640
HECUBA. It is fearful to be helpless. Men just now
have taken Cassandra—forced her from me.
ANDROMACHE. And still more for you—more than that—
HECUBA. Number my sorrows, will you? Measure them?
One comes—the next one rivals it.   645
ANDROMACHE. Polyxena lies dead upon Achilles' tomb,
a gift to a corpse, to a lifeless thing.
HECUBA. My sorrow! That is what Talthybius meant—
I could not read his riddle. Oh, too plain.
ANDROMACHE. I saw her there and left the chariot   650
and covered her dead body with my cloak,
and beat my breast.
HECUBA. Murdered—my child. Oh, wickedly!
Again I cry to you. Oh, cruelly slain!
ANDROMACHE. She has died her death, and happier by far   655
dying than I alive.
HECUBA. Life cannot be what death is, child.
Death is empty—life has hope.
ANDROMACHE. Mother, O Mother, hear a truer word.
Now let me bring joy to your heart.   660

I say to die is only not to be,
and rather death than life with bitter grief.
They have no pain, they do not feel their wrongs.
But the happy who has come to wretchedness,
his soul is a lost wanderer,   665
the old joys that were once, left far behind.
She is dead, your daughter—to her the same
as if she never had been born.
She does not know the wickedness that killed her.
While I—I aimed my shaft at good repute.   670
I gained full measure—then missed happiness.
For all that is called virtuous in a woman
I strove for and I won in Hector's house.
Always, because we women, whether right or wrong,
are spoken ill of   675
unless we stay within our homes, my longing
I set aside and kept the house.
Light talk, glib women's words,
could never gain an entrance there.
My own thoughts were enough for me,   680
best of all teachers to me in my home.
Silence, a tranquil eye, I brought my husband,
knew well in what I should rule him,
and when give him obedience.
And this report of me came to the Greeks   685
for my destruction. When they captured me
Achilles' son would have me.
I shall be a slave to those who murdered—
O Hector, my beloved—shall I thrust him aside,
open my heart to the man that comes to me,   690
and be a traitor to the dead?
And yet to shrink in loathing from him
and make my masters hate me—
One night, men say, one night in a man's bed
will make a woman tame—   695
Oh, shame! A woman throw her husband off
and in a new bed love another—
Why, a young colt will not run in the yoke
with any but her mate—not a dumb beast
that has no reason, of a lower nature.   700
O Hector, my beloved, you were all to me,
wise, noble, mighty, in wealth, in manhood, both.
No man had touched me when you took me,
took me from out my father's home

and yoked a girl fast to you.   705
And you are dead, and I, with other plunder,
am sent by sea to Greece. A slave's yoke there.
Your dead Polyxena you weep for,
what does she know of pain like mine?
The living must have hope. Not I, not any more.   710
I will not lie to my own heart. No good will ever come.
But oh, to think it would be sweet.

A WOMAN. We stand at the same point of pain. You mourn your
        ruin,
    and in your words I hear my own calamity.

HECUBA. Those ships—I never have set foot on one,   715
    but I have heard of them, seen pictures of them.
    I know that when a storm comes which they think
    they can ride out, the sailors do their best,
    one by the sail, another at the helm,
    and others bailing.   720
    But if great ocean's raging overwhelms them,
    they yield to fate.
    They give themselves up to the racing waves.
    So in my many sorrows I am dumb.
    I yield, I cannot speak.   725
    The great wave from God has conquered me.
    But, O dear child, let Hector be,
    and let be what has come to him.
    Your tears will never call him back.
    Give honor now to him who is your master.   730
    Your sweet ways—use them to allure him.
    So doing you will give cheer to your friends.
    Perhaps this child, my own child's son,
    you may rear to manhood and great aid for Troy,
    and if ever you should have more children,   735
    they might build her again. Troy once more be a city!
    Oh—one thought leads another on.
    But why again that servant of the Greeks?
    I see him coming. Some new plan is here.

        [*Enter* TALTHYBIUS *with soldiers. He is troubled and advances
        hesitatingly.*]

TALTHYBIUS. Wife of the noblest man that was in Troy,   740
    O wife of Hector, do not hate me.
    Against my will I come to tell you.
    The people and the kings have all resolved—

ANDROMACHE. What is it? Evil follows words like those.

TALTHYBIUS. This child they order—Oh, how can I say it—   745

ANDROMACHE. Not that he does not go with me to the same master—
TALTHYBIUS. No man in Greece shall ever be his master.
ANDROMACHE. But—leave him here—all that is left of Troy?
TALTHYBIUS. I don't know how to tell you. What is bad,
    words can't make better—   750
ANDROMACHE. I feel you kind. But you have not good news.
TALTHYBIUS. Your child must die. There, now you know
    the whole, bad as it is.
ANDROMACHE. Oh, I have heard an evil worse
    than a slave in her master's bed.   755
TALTHYBIUS. It was Odysseus had his way. He spoke
    to all the Greeks.
ANDROMACHE. O God. There is no measure to my pain.
TALTHYBIUS. He said a hero's son must not grow up—
ANDROMACHE. God, on his own sons may that counsel fall.   760
TALTHYBIUS. —but from the towering wall of Troy be thrown.
    Now, now—let it be done—that's wiser.
    Don't cling so to him. Bear your pain
    the way a brave woman suffers.
    You have no strength—don't look to any help.   765
    There's no help for you anywhere. Think—think.
    The city gone—your husband too. And you
    a captive and alone, one woman—how
    can you do battle with us? For your own good
    I would not have you try, and draw   770
    hatred down on you and be shamed.
    Oh, hush—never a curse upon the Greeks.
    If you say words that make the army angry
    the child will have no burial, and without pity—
    Silence now. Bear your fate as best you can.   775
    So then you need not leave him dead without a grave,
    and you will find the Greeks more kind.
ANDROMACHE. Go die, my best beloved, my own, my treasure,
    in cruel hands, leaving your mother comfortless.
    Your father was too noble. That is why   780
    they kill you. He could save others,
    he could not save you for his nobleness.
    My bed, my bridal—all for misery—
    when long ago I came to Hector's halls
    to bear my son—oh, not for Greeks to slay,   785
    but for a ruler over teeming Asia.
    Weeping, my little one? There, there.
    You cannot know what waits for you.
    Why hold me with your hands so fast, cling so fast to me?

You little bird, flying to hide beneath my wings.   790
And Hector will not come—he will not come,
up from the tomb, great spear in hand, to save you.
Not one of all his kin, of all the Trojan might.
How will it be? Falling down—down—oh, horrible.
And his neck—his breath—all broken.   795
And none to pity. You little thing,
curled in my arms, you dearest to your mother,
how sweet the fragrance of you.
All nothing then—this breast from where
your baby mouth drew milk, my travail too,   800
my cares, when I grew wasted watching you.
Kiss me—Never again. Come, closer, closer.
Your mother who bore you—put your arms around my neck.
Now kiss me, lips to lips.
O Greeks, you have found out ways to torture   805
that are not Greek.
A little child, all innocent of wrong—
you wish to kill him.
O Helen, evil growth, that was sown by Tyndareus,
you are no child of Zeus, as people say.   810
Many the fathers you were born of,
Madness, Hatred, Red Death, whatever poison
the earth brings forth—no child of Zeus,
but Greece's curse and all the world's.
God curse you, with those beautiful eyes   815
that brought to shame and ruin
Troy's far-famed plains.
Quick! take him—seize him—cast him down—
if so you will. Feast on his flesh.
God has destroyed me, and I cannot—   820
I cannot save my child from death.
Oh hide my head for shame and fling me
into the ship.
        [*She falls, then struggles to her knees.*]
My fair bridal—I am coming—
Oh, I have lost my child, my own.   825

A WOMAN. O wretched Troy, tens of thousands lost
    for a woman's sake, a hateful marriage bed.
TALTHYBIUS. [*Drawing the child away*]
    Come, boy, let go. Unclasp those loving hands,
    poor mother.

809. *Tyndareus:* Helen's earthly fa-   and she was considered Zeus's child.
ther; but Zeus loved her mother, Leda,

Come now, up, up, to the very height,   830
where the towers of your fathers crown the wall,
and where it is decreed that you must die.
    [*To the soldiers*]
Take him away.
A herald who must bring such orders
should be a man who feels no pity,   835
and no shame either—not like me.

HECUBA. Child, son of my poor son, whose toil was all in vain,
we are robbed, your mother and I, oh, cruelly—
robbed of your life. How bear it?
What can I do for you, poor piteous child?   840
Beat my head, my breast—all I can give you.
Troy lost, now you—all lost.
The cup is full. Why wait? For what?
Hasten on—swiftly on to death.
    [*The soldiers, who have waited while* HECUBA *speaks, go out
    with the child and* TALTHYBIUS. *One of them takes* ANDRO-
    MACHE *to the chariot and drives off with her.*]

CHORUS. The waves make a ring around Salamis.   845
The bees are loud in the island.
King Telamon built him a dwelling.
It fronted the holy hills,
where first the gray gleaming olive
Athena showed to men,   850
the glory of shining Athens,
her crown from the sky.
He joined himself to the bowman,
the son of Alcmena, for valorous deeds.
Troy, Troy he laid waste, my city,   855
long ago when he went forth from Greece.
When he led forth from Greece the bravest
in his wrath for the steeds withheld,
and by fair-flowing Simois stayed his oar
that had brought him over the sea.   860
Cables there made the ship fast.
In his hand was the bow that never missed.
It brought the king to his death.
Walls of stone that Phœbus had built
he wrecked with the red breath of fire.   865

845ff. The chorus sings of the first fall of Troy, in the previous generation. "When Troy was destroyed the first time, the reason was that the Trojan king had promised two immortal horses to Hercules (the son of Alcmena) but did not give them to him. Hercules in revenge ruined the city. The son of this king was Ganymede, cup-bearer to Zeus" [Translator's note].

He wasted the plain of Troy.
Twice her walls have fallen. Twice
a blood-stained spear struck her down,
    laid her in ruin.

In vain, O you who move   870
with delicate feet where the wine-cups are gold,
son of that old dead king,
who fill with wine the cup Zeus holds,
service most fair—
she who gave you birth is afire.   875
The shores of the sea are wailing for her.
As a bird cries over her young,
women weep for husbands, for children,
for the old, too, who gave them birth.
Your dewy baths are gone,   880
and the race-course where you ran.
Yet your young face keeps the beauty of peace
in joy, by the throne of Zeus.
While Priam's land
lies ruined by Greek spearsmen.   885

Love, O Love,
once you came to the halls of Troy,
and your song rose up to the dwellers in heaven.
How did you then exalt Troy high,
binding her fast to the gods, by a union—   890
No—I will not speak blame of Zeus.
But the light of white-winged Dawn, dear to men,
is deadly over the land this day,
shining on fallen towers.
And yet Dawn keeps in her bridal bower   895
her children's father, a son of Troy.
Her chariot bore him away to the sky.
It was gold, and four stars drew it.
Hope was high then for our town.
But the magic that brought her the love of the gods   900
has gone from Troy.
        [As the song ends MENELAUS enters with a bodyguard of
        soldiers.]
MENELAUS. How bright the sunlight is today—
    this day, when I shall get into my power

---

896. *a son of Troy:* Tithonus, a Trojan prince, was carried off by the Dawn
goddess to be her husband.

Helen, my wife. For I am Menelaus,
the man of many wrongs.   905
I came to Troy and brought with me my army,
not for that woman's sake, as people say,
but for the man who from my house,
and he a guest there, stole away my wife.
Ah, well, with God's help he has paid the price,   910
he and his country, fallen beneath Greek spears.
I am come to get her—wretch—I cannot speak her name
who was my wife once.
In a hut here, where they house the captives,
she is numbered with the other Trojan women.   915
The men who fought and toiled to win her back,
have given her to me—to kill, or else,
if it pleases me, to take her back to Argos.
And it has seemed to me her death in Troy
is not the way. I will take her overseas,   920
with swift oars speeding on the ship,
and there in Greece give her to those to kill
whose dearest died because of her.
[*To his men*] Attention! Forward to the huts.   925
Seize her and drag her out by that long blood-drenched hair—
    [*Stops suddenly and controls himself*]
And when fair winds come, home with her to Greece.
    [*Soldiers begin to force the door of one of the huts.*]
HECUBA. [*Comes slowly forward*] O thou who dost uphold the world,
    whose throne is high above the world,
    thou, past our seeking hard to find, who art thou?
    God, or Necessity of what must be,   930
    or Reason of our reason?
    Whate'er thou art, I pray to thee,
    seeing the silent road by which
    all mortal things are led by thee to justice.
MENELAUS. What have we here? A queer prayer that.   935
HECUBA. [*She comes still nearer to him and he recognizes her.*]
    Kill her, Menelaus? You will? Oh, blessings on you!
    But—shun her, do not look at her.
    Desire for her will seize you, conquer you.
    For through men's eyes she gets them in her power.
    She ruins them and ruins cities too.   940
    Fire comes from her to burn homes,
    magic for death. I know her—so do you,
    and all these who have suffered.
        [HELEN *enters from the hut. The soldiers do not touch her.*

She is very gentle and undisturbed.]
HELEN. [*With sweet, injured dignity. Not angry at all*]
  Menelaus, these things might well make a woman fear.
  Your men with violence have driven me from my room,   945
  have laid their hands upon me.
  Of course I know—almost I know—you hate me,
  but yet I ask you, what is your decision,
  yours and the Greeks? Am I to live or not?
MENELAUS. Nothing more clear. Unanimous, in fact.   950
  Not one who did not vote you should be given me,
  whom you have wronged, to kill you.
HELEN. Am I allowed to speak against the charge?
  To show you if I die that I shall die
  most wronged and innocent?   955
MENELAUS. I have come to kill you, not to argue with you.
HECUBA. Oh, hear her. She must never die unheard.
  Then, Menelaus, let me answer her.
  The evil that she did in Troy, you do not know.
  But I will tell the story. She will die.   960
  She never can escape.
MENELAUS. That means delay. Still—if she wants to speak,
  she can. I grant her this because of what you say,
  not for her sake. She can be sure of that.
HELEN. And perhaps, no matter if you think I speak   965
  the truth or not, you will not talk to me,
  since you believe I am your enemy.
  Still, I will try to answer what I think
  you would say if you spoke your mind,
  and my wrongs shall be heard as well as yours.   970
  First: who began these evils? She, the day
  when she gave birth to Paris. Who next was guilty?
  The old king who decreed the child should live,
  and ruined Troy and me—Paris, the hateful,
  the firebrand.   975
  What happened then? Listen and learn.
  This Paris—he was made the judge for three,
  all yoked together in a quarrel—goddesses.
  Athena promised he should lead the Trojans
  to victory and lay all Greece in ruins.   980
  And Hera said if he thought her the fairest
  she would make him lord of Europe and of Asia.

977. *judge for three:* the judgment
of Paris. He was appointed to award the
golden apple inscribed "To the most
beautiful"; the contestants were the goddesses Athena, Hera, and Aphrodite, who
all offered him bribes, but Aphrodite's
was the most alluring.

But Aphrodite—well, she praised my beauty—
astonishing, she said—and promised him
that she would give me to him if he judged   985
that she was loveliest. Then, see what happened.
She won, and so my bridal brought all Greece
great good. No strangers rule you,
no foreign spears, no tyrant.
Oh, it was well for Greece, but not for me,   990
sold for my beauty and reproached besides
when I deserved a crown.
But—to the point. Is that what you are thinking?
Why did I go—steal from your house in secret?
That man, Paris, or any name you like to call him,   995
his mother's curse—oh, when he came to me
a mighty goddess walked beside him.
And you, poor fool, you spread your sails for Crete,
left Sparta—left him in your house.
Ah well—Not you, but my own self I ask,   1000
what was there in my heart that I went with him,
a strange man, and forgot my home and country?
Not I, but Aphrodite. Punish her,
be mightier than Zeus who rules
the other gods, but is her slave.   1005
She is my absolution—
One thing with seeming justice you might say.
When Paris died and went down to the grave,
and when no god cared who was in my bed,
I should have left his house—gone to the Greeks.   1010
Just what I tried to do—oh, many times.
I have witnesses—the men who kept the gates,
the watchmen on the walls. Not once, but often
they found me swinging from a parapet,
a rope around this body, stealthily   1015
feeling my way down.
The Trojans then no longer wanted me,
but the man who next took me—and by force—
would never let me go.
My husband, must I die, and at your hands?   1020
You think that right? Is that your justice?
I was forced—by violence. I lived a life
that had no joy, no triumph. In bitterness
I lived a slave.
Do you wish to set yourself above the gods?   1025

1018. *the man who next took me:* Deiphobus, a younger brother of Paris.

Oh, stupid, senseless wish!

A WOMAN. O Queen, defend your children and your country.
Her soft persuasive words are deadly.
She speaks so fair and is so vile.
A fearful thing.   1030

HECUBA. Her goddesses will fight on my side while
I show her for the liar that she is.
Not Hera, not virgin Athena, do I think
would ever stoop to folly great enough
to sell their cities. Hera sell her Argos,   1035
Athena Athens, to be the Trojan's slave!
playing like silly children there on Ida,
and each one in her insolence demanding
the prize for beauty. Beauty—why was Hera
so hot for it? That she might get herself   1040
a better mate than Zeus?
Athena—who so fled from marriage that she begged
one gift from Zeus, virginity.
But she would have the prize, you say. And why?
To help her hunt some god to marry her?   1045
Never make gods out fools to whitewash your own evil.
No one with sense will listen to you.
And Aphrodite, did you say—who would not laugh?
—must take my son to Menelaus' house?
Why? Could she not stay quietly in heaven   1050
and send you on—and all your town—to Troy?
My son was beautiful exceedingly.
You saw him—your own desire was enough.
No need of any goddess.
Men's follies—they are Aphrodite.   1055
She rose up from the sea-foam; where the froth
and foam of life are, there she is.
It was my son. You saw him in his Eastern dress
all bright with gold, and you were mad with love.
Such little things had filled your mind in Argos,   1060
busied with this and that.
Once free of Sparta and in Troy where gold,
you thought, flowed like a river, you would spend
and spend, until your spendthrift hand
had drowned the town.   1065
Your luxuries, your insolent excesses,
Menelaus' halls had grown too small for them.

1037. *Ida:* Trojan mountain where   have taken place.
the judgment of Paris was supposed to

Enough of that. By force you say he took you?
You cried out? Where? No one in Sparta heard you.
Young Castor was there and his brother too,   1070
not yet among the stars.
And when you came to Troy and on your track the Greeks,
and death and agony in battle,
if they would tell you, "Greece has won today,"
you would praise this man here, Menelaus,   1075
to vex my son, who feared him as a rival.
Then Troy had victories, and Menelaus
was nothing to you.
Looking to the successful side—oh yes,
you always followed there.   1080
There was no right or wrong side in your eyes.
And now you talk of ropes—letting your body down
in secret from the wall, longing to go.
Who found you so?
Was there a noose around your neck?   1085
A sharp knife in your hand? Such ways
as any honest woman would have found,
who loved the husband she had lost?
Often and often I would tell you, Go,
my daughter. My sons will find them other wives.   1090
I will help you. I will send you past the lines
to the Greek ships. Oh, end this war
between our foes and us. But this was bitter to you.
In Paris' house you had your insolent way.
You liked to see the Eastern men fall at your feet.   1095
These were great things to you.
Look at the dress you wear, your ornaments.
Is that the way to meet your husband?
You should not dare to breathe the same air with him.
Oh, men should spit upon you.   1100
Humbly, in rags, trembling and shivering,
with shaven head—so you should come,
with shame at last, instead of shamelessness,
for all the wickedness you did.
King, one word more and I am done.   1105
Give Greece a crown, be worthy of yourself.
Kill her. So shall the law stand for all women,
that she who plays false to her husband's bed,
shall die.

A WOMAN. O son of an ancient house, O King, now show   1110

1070. *brother:* Polydeuces (Pollux)   after their deaths they became the con-
and Castor were Helen's brothers;   stellation Gemini ("the twins").

that you are worthy of your fathers.
The Greeks called you a woman, shamed you
with that reproach. Be strong. Be noble. Punish her.

MENELAUS. [*Impatiently*] I see it all as you do. We agree.   1115
She left my house because she wanted to—
went to a stranger's bed. Her talk of Aphrodite—
big words, no more. [*Turns to* HELEN] Go. Death is near.
Men there are waiting for you. In their hands are stones.
Die—a small price for the Greeks' long suffering.
You shall not any more dishonor me.   1120

HELEN. [*Kneeling and clinging to him*] No! No! Upon my knees—
see, I am praying to you.
It was the gods, not me. Oh, do not kill me.
Forgive.

HECUBA. The men she murdered. Think of those
who fought beside you—of their children too.   1125
Never betray them. Hear that prayer.

MENELAUS. [*Roughly*] Enough, old woman. She is nothing to me.
Men, take her to the ships and keep her safe
until she sails.   1129

HECUBA. But not with you! She must not set foot on your ship.

MENELAUS. [*Bitterly*] And why? Her weight too heavy for it?

HECUBA. A lover once, a lover always.

MENELAUS. [*Pauses a moment to think*] Not so when what he loved
has gone.
But it shall be as you would have it.
Not on the same ship with me. The advice is good.   1135
And when she gets to Argos she shall die
a death hard as her heart.
So in the end she will become a teacher,
teach women chastity—no easy thing,
but yet her utter ruin will strike terror   1140
into their silly hearts,
even women worse than she.   [*Exit* MENELAUS.]

CHORUS. And so your temple in Ilium,
your altar of frankincense,
are given to the Greek,   1145
the flame from the honey, the corn and the oil,
the smoke from the myrrh floating upward,
the holy citadel.
And Ida, the mountain where the ivy grows,
and rivers from the snows rush through the glens,   1150
and the boundary wall of the world
where the first sunlight falls,

1143. the chorus addresses Zeus.

the blessed home of the dawn.

The sacrifice is gone, and the glad call
of dancers, and the prayers at evening to the gods   1155
that last the whole night long.
Gone too the golden images,
and the twelve Moons, to Trojans holy.
Do you care, do you care, do you heed these things,
O God, from your throne in high heaven?   1160
My city is perishing,
ending in fire and onrushing flame.

A WOMAN. O dear one, O my husband,
you are dead, and you wander
unburied, uncared for, while over-seas   1165
the ships shall carry me,
swift-winged ships darting onward,
on to the land the riders love,
Argos, where the towers of stone
built by giants reach the sky.   1170

ANOTHER. Children, our children.
At the gate they are crying, crying,
calling to us with tears,
Mother, I am all alone.
They are driving me away   1175
to a black ship, and I cannot see you.

ANOTHER. Where, oh where? To holy Salamis,
with swift oars dipping?
Or to the crest of Corinth,
the city of two seas,   1180
Where the gates King Pelops built
for his dwelling stand?

ANOTHER. Oh, if only, far out to sea,
the crashing thunder of God
would fall down, down on Menelaus' ship,   1185
crashing down upon her oars,
the Aegean's wild-fire light.
He it was drove me from Troy.
He is driving me in tears
over to Greece to slavery.   1190

ANOTHER. And Helen, too, with her mirrors of gold,
looking and wondering at herself,
as pleased as a girl.
May she never come to the land of her fathers,
never see the hearth of her home,   1195

1194. *May she never come:* Helen, of   spared by Menelaus. They are shown
course, did reach home safely and was   living affectionately together many years

her city, the temple with brazen doors
of goddess Athena.
Oh, evil marriage that brought
shame to Greece, the great,
and to the waters of Simois   1200
sorrow and suffering.

> [TALTHYBIUS *approaches with a few soldiers. He is carrying
> the dead child.*]

ANOTHER WOMAN. Before new sufferings are grown old
come other new.
Look, unhappy wives of Troy,
the dead Astyanax.   1205
They threw him from the tower as one might pitch a ball.
Oh, bitter killing.
And now they have him there.

TALTHYBIUS. [*He gives the body into* HECUBA's *arms.*]
One ship is waiting, Hecuba, to take aboard
the last of all the spoil Achilles' son was given,   1210
and bear it with the measured beat of oars
to Thessaly's high headlands.
The chief himself has sailed because of news
he heard, his father's father
driven from his land by his own son.   1215
So, more for haste even than before,
he went and with him went Andromache.
She drew tears from me there upon the ship
mourning her country, speaking to Hector's grave,
begging a burial for her child, your Hector's son,   1220
who thrown down from the tower lost his life.
And this bronze-fronted shield, the dread of many a Greek,
which Hector used in battle,
that it should never, so she prayed,
hang in strange halls, her grief before her eyes,   1225
nor in that bridal chamber where she must be a wife,
Andromache, this dead boy's mother.
She begged that he might lie upon it in his grave,
instead of cedar wood or vault of stone.
And in your arms she told me I must lay him,   1230
for you to cover the body, if you still
have anything, a cloak left—
And to put flowers on him if you could,
since she has gone. Her master's haste
kept her from burying her child.   1235

later in the fourth book of Homer's
Odyssey.
1214. *father's father:* Peleus, father of
Achilles.

1215. *own son:* Acastus, son of Pelias,
monarch of the neighboring kingdom of
Iolcos.

So now, whenever you have laid him out,
we'll heap the earth above him, then
up with the sails!
Do all as quickly as you can. One trouble
I saved you. When we passed Scamander's stream   1240
I let the water run on him and washed his wounds.
I am off to dig his grave now, break up the hard earth.
Working together, you and I,
will hurry to the goal, oars swift for home.   1244

HECUBA. Set the shield down—the great round shield of Hector.
I wish I need not look at it.

      [TALTHYBIUS *goes out with the soldiers.*]

You Greeks, your spears are sharp but not your wits.
You feared a child. You murdered him.
Strange murder. You were frightened, then? You thought
he might build up our ruined Troy? And yet   1250
when Hector fought and thousands at his side,
we fell beneath you. Now, when all is lost,
the city captured and the Trojans dead,
a little child like this made you afraid.
The fear that comes when reason goes away—   1255
Myself, I do not wish to share it.

      [*She dismisses the Greeks and their ways.*]

Beloved, what a death has come to you.
If you had fallen fighting for the city,
if you had known strong youth and love
and godlike power, if we could think   1260
you had known happiness—if there is
happiness anywhere—
But now—you saw and knew, but with your soul
you did not know, and what was in your house
you could not use.   1265
Poor little one. How savagely our ancient walls,
Apollo's towers, have torn away the curls
your mother's fingers wound and where she pressed
her kisses—here where the broken bone grins white—
Oh no—I cannot—   1270
Dear hands, the same dear shape your father's had,
how loosely now you fall. And dear proud lips
forever closed. False words you spoke to me
when you would jump into my bed, call me sweet names
and tell me, Grandmother, when you are dead,   1275
I'll cut off a great lock of hair and lead my soldiers all
to ride out past your tomb.
Not you, but I, old, homeless, childless,

must lay you in your grave, so young,
so miserably dead.   1280
Dear God. How you would run to greet me.
And I would nurse you in my arms, and oh,
so sweet to watch you sleep. All gone.
What could a poet carve upon your tomb?
"A child lies here whom the Greeks feared and slew."   1285
Ah, Greece should boast of that.
Child, they have taken all that was your father's,
but one thing, for your burying, you shall have,
the bronze-barred shield.
It kept safe Hector's mighty arm, but now   1290
it has lost its master.
The grip of his own hand has marked it—dear to me then—
His sweat has stained the rim. Often and often
in battle it rolled down from brows and beard
while Hector held the shield close.   1295
Come, bring such covering for the pitiful dead body
as we still have. God has not left us much
to make a show with. Everything I have
I give you, child.
O men, secure when once good fortune comes—   1300
fools, fools. Fortune's ways—
here now, there now. She springs
away—back—and away, an idiot's dance.
No one is ever always fortunate.
          [*The women have come in with coverings and garlands.*]
A WOMAN. Here, for your hands, they bring you clothing for the
          dead,   1305
     got from the spoils of Troy.
HECUBA. [*Shrouding the body and putting garlands beside it*]
     Oh, not because you conquered when the horses raced,
     or with the bow outdid your comrades,
     your father's mother lays these wreaths beside you,
     and of all that was yours, gives you this covering.   1310
     A woman whom God hates has robbed you,
     taken your life, when she had taken your treasure
     and ruined all your house.
A WOMAN. Oh, my heart! As if you touched it—touched it.
     Oh, this was once our prince, great in the city.   1315
HECUBA. So on your wedding day I would have dressed you,
     the highest princess of the East your bride.
     Now on your body I must lay the raiment,
     all that is left of the splendor that was Troy's.
     And the dear shield of Hector, glorious in battle,   1320

mother of ten thousand triumphs won,
it too shall have its wreath of honor,
undying it will lie beside the dead.
More honorable by far than all the armor
Odysseus won, the wicked and the wise.   1325

A WOMAN. You, O child, our bitter sorrow,
earth will now receive.
Mourn, O Mother.

HECUBA. Mourn, indeed.

A WOMAN. Weeping for all the dead.   1330

HECUBA. Bitter tears.

A WOMAN. Your sorrows that can never be forgotten.

[*The funeral rite is now begun,* HECUBA *symbolically healing
the wounds.*]

HECUBA. I heal your wounds; with linen I bind them.
Ah, in words only, not in truth—
a poor physician.   1335
But soon among the dead your father
will care for you.

WOMAN. Beat, beat your head.
Lift your hands and let them fall,
moving in measure.   1340

HECUBA. O Women. Dearest—

A WOMAN. Oh, speak to us. Your cry—what does it mean?

HECUBA. Only this the gods would have,
pain for me and pain for Troy,
those they hated bitterly.   1345
Vain, vain, the bulls we slew.
And yet—had God not bowed us down,
not laid us low in dust,
none would have sung of us or told our wrongs
in stories men will listen to forever.   1350
Go: lay our dead in his poor grave,
with these last gifts of death given to him.
I think those that are gone care little
how they are buried. It is we, the living,
our vanity.   1355

[*Women lift the shield with the body on it and carry it out.*]

A WOMAN. Poor mother—her high hopes were stayed on you
and they are broken.
They called you happy at your birth,
a good man's son.
Your death was miserable exceedingly.   1360

ANOTHER. Oh, see, see—
On the crested height of Troy

fiery hands. They are flinging torches.
Can it be
some new evil?   1365
Something still unknown?
TALTHYBIUS. [*Stops as he enters and speaks off stage*]
Captains, attention. You have been given charge
to burn this city. Do not let your torches sleep.
Hurry the fire on.
When once the town is level with the ground   1370
then off for home and glad goodbye to Troy.
And you, you Women—I will arrange for you
as well, one speech for everything—
whenever a loud trumpet-call is sounded,
go to the Greek ships, to embark.   1375
Old woman, I am sorriest for you,
follow. Odysseus' men are here to get you.
He drew you—you must leave here as his slave.
HECUBA. The end then. Well—the height of sorrow, I stand there.
Troy is burning—I am going.   1380
But—hurry, old feet, if you can,
a little nearer—here, where I can see
my poor town, say goodbye to her.
You were so proud a city, in all the East
the proudest. Soon your name the whole world knew,   1385
will be taken from you. They are burning you
and leading us away, their slaves.
O God—What makes me say that word?
The gods—I prayed, they never listened.
Quick, into the fire—Troy, I will die with you.   1390
Death then—oh, beautiful.
TALTHYBIUS. Out of your head, poor thing, with all you've suffered.
Lead her away—Hold her, don't be too gentle.
She must be taken to Odysseus.
Give her into his hands. She is his—   1395
[*Shakes his head*] his prize. [*It grows darker.*]
A WOMAN. Ancient of days, our country's Lord,
Father, who made us,
You see your children's sufferings.
Have we deserved them?   1400
ANOTHER. He sees—but Troy has perished, the great city.
No city now, never again.
ANOTHER. Oh, terrible!
The fire lights the whole town up.
The inside rooms are burning.   1405
The citadel—it is all flame now.

ANOTHER. Troy is vanishing.
  War first ruined her.
  And what was left is rushing up in smoke,
  the glorious houses fallen.   1410
  First the spear and then the fire.
HECUBA. [*She stands up and seems to be calling to someone far
    away.*] Children, hear, your mother is calling.
A WOMAN. [*Gently*] They are dead, those you are speaking to.
HECUBA. My knees are stiff, but I must kneel.
  Now, strike the ground with both my hands—   1415
A WOMAN. I too, I kneel upon the ground.
  I call to mine down there.
  Husband, poor husband.
HECUBA. They are driving us like cattle—taking us away.
A WOMAN. Pain, all pain.   1420
ANOTHER. To a slave's house, from my country.
HECUBA. Priam, Priam, you are dead,
  and not a friend to bury you.
  The evil that has found me—
  do you know?   1425
A WOMAN. No. Death has darkened his eyes.
  He was good and the wicked killed him.
HECUBA. O dwellings of gods and O dear city,
  the spear came first and now
  only the red flame lives there.   1430
A WOMAN. Fall and be forgotten. Earth is kind.
ANOTHER. The dust is rising, spreading out like a great wing of
    smoke.
  I cannot see my house.
ANOTHER. The name has vanished from the land,
  and we are gone, one here, one there.   1435
  And Troy is gone forever.
    [*A great crash is heard.*]
HECUBA. Did you hear? Did you know—
A WOMAN. The fall of Troy—
ANOTHER. Earthquake and flood and the city's end—
HECUBA. Trembling body—old weak limbs,   1440
  you must carry me on to the new day of slavery.
    [*A trumpet sounds.*]
A WOMAN. Farewell, dear city.
  Farewell, my country, where once my children lived.
  On to the ships—
  There below, the Greek ships wait.   1445
    [*The trumpet sounds again and the women pass out.*]

ARISTOPHANES

(448?–380? B.C.)

Lysistrata*

Characters in the Play†

LYSISTRATA ⎫
CALONICE ⎬ *Athenian women*
MYRRHINE ⎭
LAMPITO, *a Spartan woman*
LEADER *of the Chorus of Old Men*
CHORUS *of Old Men*
LEADER *of the Chorus of Old Women*
CHORUS *of Old Women*
ATHENIAN MAGISTRATE
THREE ATHENIAN WOMEN
CINESIAS, *an Athenian, husband of Myrrhine*
SPARTAN HERALD
SPARTAN AMBASSADORS
ATHENIAN AMBASSADORS
TWO ATHENIAN CITIZENS
CHORUS *of Athenians*
CHORUS *of Spartans*

SCENE: *In Athens, beneath the Acropolis. In the center of the stage is the Propylaea, or gate-way to the Acropolis; to one side is a small grotto, sacred to Pan. The Orchestra represents a slope leading up to the gate-way.*

It is early in the morning. LYSISTRATA *is pacing impatiently up and down.*

LYSISTRATA. If they'd been summoned to worship the God of Wine, or Pan, or to visit the Queen of Love, why, you couldn't have pushed your way through the streets for all the timbrels.[1] But now there's not a single woman here—except my neighbour;

---

* From *Greek Literature in Translation* by W. J. Oates and C. T. Murphy. Translation by Charles T. Murphy. Longmans, Green & Co., Inc., 1944. Used by permission of David McKay Company, Inc.

† As is usual in ancient comedy, the leading characters have significant names. *Lysistrata* is "She who disbands the armies"; *Myrrhine's* name is chosen to suggest *myrton*, a Greek word meaning *pudenda muliebria; Lampito* is a celebrated Spartan name; *Cinesias*, although a real name in Athens, is chosen to suggest a Greek verb *kinein, to move*, then *to make love, to have intercourse,* and the name of his deme, *Paionidai,* suggests the verb *paiein,* which has about the same significance.

1. *timbrels:* These instruments were

here she comes.

[*Enter* CALONICE.]

Good day to you, Calonice.

CALONICE. And to you, Lysistrata. [*Noticing* LYSISTRATA'S *impatient air*] But what ails you? Don't scowl, my dear; it's not becoming to you to knit your brows like that.

LYSISTRATA. [*Sadly*] Ah, Calonice, my heart aches; I'm so annoyed at us women. For among men we have a reputation for sly trickery—

CALONICE. And rightly too, on my word!

LYSISTRATA. —but when they were told to meet here to consider a matter of no small importance, they lie abed and don't come.

CALONICE. Oh, they'll come all right, my dear. It's not easy for a woman to get out, you know. One is working on her husband, another is getting up the maid, another has to put the baby to bed, or wash and feed it.

LYSISTRATA. But after all, there are other matters more important than all that.

CALONICE. My dear Lysistrata, just what is this matter you've summoned us women to consider? What's up? Something big?

LYSISTRATA. Very big.

CALONICE. [*Interested*] Is it stout, too?

LYSISTRATA. [*Smiling*] Yes indeed—both big and stout.

CALONICE. What? And the women still haven't come?

LYSISTRATA. It's not what you suppose; they'd have come soon enough for *that*. But I've worked up something, and for many a sleepless night I've turned it this way and that.

CALONICE. [*In mock disappointment*] Oh, I guess it's pretty fine and slender, if you've turned it this way and that.

LYSISTRATA. So fine that the safety of the whole of Greece lies in us women.

CALONICE. In us women? It depends on a very slender reed then.

LYSISTRATA. Our country's fortunes are in our hands; and whether the Spartans shall perish—

CALONICE. Good! Let them perish, by all means.

LYSISTRATA. —and the Boeotians shall be completely annihilated.

CALONICE. Not completely! Please spare the eels.[2]

LYSISTRATA. As for Athens, I won't use any such unpleasant words. But you understand what I mean. But if the women will meet here—the Spartans, the Boeotians, and we Athenians—then all together we will save Greece.

CALONICE. But what could women do that's clever or distinguished? We just sit around all dolled up in silk robes, looking pretty in

used in most orgiastic cults, especially in the worship of Dionysus, the "God of Wine."

2. Eels were a favorite Athenian delicacy from the Boeotian lakes; eels were then very rare in Athens because of the war.

our sheer gowns and evening slippers.

LYSISTRATA. These are just the things I hope will save us: these silk robes, perfumes, evening slippers, rouge, and our chiffon blouses.

CALONICE. How so?

LYSISTRATA. So never a man alive will lift a spear against the foe—

CALONICE. I'll get a silk gown at once.

LYSISTRATA. —or take up his shield—

CALONICE. I'll put on my sheerest gown!

LYSISTRATA. —or sword.

CALONICE. I'll buy a pair of evening slippers.

LYSISTRATA. Well then, shouldn't the women have come?

CALONICE. Come? Why, they should have *flown* here.

LYSISTRATA. Well, my dear, just watch: they'll act in true Athenian fashion—everything too late! And now there's not a woman here from the shore or from Salamis.[3]

CALONICE. They're coming. I'm sure; at daybreak they were laying —to their oars to cross the straits.

LYSISTRATA. And those I expected would be the first to come—the women of Acharnae[4]—they haven't arrived.

CALONICE. Yet the wife of Theagenes[5] means to come: she consulted Hecate about it. [*Seeing a group of women approaching*] But look! Here come a few. And there are some more over here. Hurrah! Where do they come from?

LYSISTRATA. From Anagyra.[6]

CALONICE. Yes indeed! We've raised up quite a stink from Anagyra anyway.

[*Enter* MYRRHINE *in haste, followed by several other women.*]

MYRRHINE. [*Breathlessly*] Have we come in time, Lysistrata? What do you say? Why so quiet?

LYSISTRATA. I can't say much for you, Myrrhine, coming at this hour on such important business.

MYRRHINE. Why, I had trouble finding my girdle in the dark. But if it's so important, we're here now; tell us.

LYSISTRATA. No. Let's wait a little for the women from Boeotia and the Peloponnesus.

MYRRHINE. That's a much better suggestion. Look! Here comes Lampito now.

[*Enter* LAMPITO *with two other women.*]

LYSISTRATA. Greetings, my dear Spartan friend. How pretty you

3. just across the bay from Piraeus, the port of Athens.

4. a large village a few miles northwest of Athens.

5. was a very superstitious Athenian (perhaps he was sitting in the audience) who never went out without consulting the shrine of Hecate at his doorstep.

6. a district south of Athens. It was also the name of a bad-smelling shrub and the phrase "to stir up the anagyra" was proverbially used to describe people who brought trouble on themselves by interfering.

look, my dear. What a smooth complexion and well-developed figure! You could throttle an ox.

LAMPITO. Faith, yes, I think I could. I take exercises and kick my heels against my bum. [*She demonstrates with a few steps of the Spartan "bottom-kicking" dance.*]

LYSISTRATA. And what splendid breasts you have.

LAMPITO. La! You handle me like a prize steer.

LYSISTRATA. And who is this young lady with you?

LAMPITO. Faith, she's an Ambassadress from Boeotia.

LYSISTRATA. Oh yes, a Boeotian, and blooming like a garden too.

CALONICE. [*Lifting up her skirt*] My word! How neatly her garden's weeded!

LYSISTRATA. And who is the other girl?

LAMPITO. Oh, she's a Corinthian swell.

MYRRHINE. [*After a rapid examination*] Yes indeed. She swells very nicely [*Pointing*] here and here.

LAMPITO. Who has gathered together this company of women?

LYSISTRATA. I have.

LAMPITO. Speak up, then. What do you want?

MYRRHINE. Yes, my dear, tell us what this important matter is.

LYSISTRATA. Very well, I'll tell you. But before I speak, let me ask you a little question.

MYRRHINE. Anything you like.

LYSISTRATA. [*Earnestly*] Tell me: don't you yearn for the fathers of your children, who are away at the wars? I know you all have husbands abroad.

CALONICE. Why, yes; mercy me! my husband's been away for five months in Thrace keeping guard on—Eucrates.[7]

MYRRHINE. And mine for seven whole months in Pylus.[8]

LAMPITO. And mine, as soon as ever he returns from the fray, readjusts his shield and flies out of the house again.

LYSISTRATA. And as for lovers, there's not even a ghost of one left. Since the Milesians revolted from us,[9] I've not even seen an eight-inch dingus to be a leather consolation for us widows. Are you willing, if I can find a way, to help me end the war?

MYRRHINE. Goodness, yes! I'd do it, even if I had to pawn my dress and—get drunk on the spot!

CALONICE. And I, even if I had to let myself be split in two like a flounder.

LAMPITO. I'd climb up Mt. Taygetus[10] if I could catch a glimpse of peace.

7. *Eucrates:* We have no details on this campaign in Thrace.

8. *Pylus:* a point on the west coast of the Peloponnese held by an Athenian garrison.

9. The city of Miletus, an Athenian ally ever since the Persian war, had de-serted the Athenian cause in the previous year. The objects Lysistrata speaks of were supposed to be manufactured there.

10. The mountain which towers over Sparta.

LYSISTRATA. I'll tell you, then, in plain and simple words. My friends, if we are going to force our men to make peace, we must do without—

MYRRHINE. Without what? Tell us.

LYSISTRATA. Will you do it?

MYRRHINE. We'll do it, if it kills us.

LYSISTRATA. Well, then we must do without sex altogether. [*General consternation*] Why do you turn away? Where go you? Why turn so pale? Why those tears? Will you do it or not? What means this hesitation?

MYRRHINE. I won't do it! Let the war go on.

CALONICE. Nor I! Let the war go on.

LYSISTRATA. So, my little flounder? Didn't you say just now you'd split yourself in half?

CALONICE. Anything else you like. I'm willing, even if I have to walk through fire. Anything rather than sex. There's nothing like it, my dear.

LYSISTRATA. [*To* MYRRHINE] What about you?

MYRRHINE. [*Sullenly*] I'm willing to walk through fire, too.

LYSISTRATA. Oh vile and cursed breed! No wonder they make tragedies about us: we're naught but "love-affairs and bassinets."[11] But you, my dear Spartan friend, if you alone are with me, our enterprise might yet succeed. Will you vote with me?

LAMPITO. 'Tis cruel hard, by my faith, for a woman to sleep alone without her nooky; but for all that, we certainly do need peace.

LYSISTRATA. O my dearest friend! You're the only real woman here.

CALONICE. [*Wavering*] Well, if we do refrain from—[*Shuddering*] what you say (God forbid!), would that bring peace?

LYSISTRATA. My goodness, yes! If we sit at home all rouged and powdered, dressed in our sheerest gowns, and neatly depilated, our men will get excited and want to take us; but if you don't come to them and keep away, they'll soon make a truce.

LAMPITO. Aye; Menelaus caught sight of Helen's naked breast and dropped his sword, they say.

CALONICE. What if the men give us up?

LYSISTRATA. "Flay a skinned dog,"[12] as Pherecrates says.

CALONICE. Rubbish! These make-shifts are no good. But suppose they grab us and drag us into the bedroom?

LYSISTRATA. Hold on to the door.

CALONICE. And if they beat us?

LYSISTRATA. Give in with a bad grace. There's no pleasure in it for them when they have to use violence. And you must torment

---

11. In the *Tyro* of Sophocles, which had recently been produced, the heroine, who had borne twin sons to the god Poseidon, left them exposed in a bas- sinet.

12. a proverb for useless activity Pherecrates: a fifth-century comic poet

them in every possible way. They'll give up soon enough; a man gets no joy if he doesn't get along with his wife.

MYRRHINE. If this is your opinion, we agree.

LAMPITO. As for our own men, we can persuade them to make a just and fair peace; but what about the Athenian rabble? Who will persuade them not to start any more monkey-shines?

LYSISTRATA. Don't worry. We guarantee to convince them.

LAMPITO. Not while their ships are rigged so well and they have that mighty treasure in the temple of Athene.

LYSISTRATA. We've taken good care for that too: we shall seize the Acropolis today. The older women have orders to do this, and while we are making our arrangements, they are to pretend to make a sacrifice and occupy the Acropolis.

LAMPITO. All will be well then. That's a very fine idea.

LYSISTRATA. Let's ratify this, Lampito, with the most solemn oath.

LAMPITO. Tell us what oath we shall swear.

LYSISTRATA. Well said. Where's our Policewoman? [*To a Scythian slave*] What are you gaping at? Set a shield upside-down here in front of me, and give me the sacred meats.

CALONICE. Lysistrata, what sort of an oath are we to take?

LYSISTRATA. What oath? I'm going to slaughter a sheep over the shield, as they do in Aeschylus.[13]

CALONICE. Don't, Lysistrata! No oaths about peace over a shield.

LYSISTRATA. What shall the oath be, then?

CALONICE. How about getting a white horse somewhere and cutting out its entrails for the sacrifice?

LYSISTRATA. White horse indeed!

CALONICE. Well then, how shall we swear?

MYRRHINE. I'll tell you: let's place a large black bowl upside-down and then slaughter—a flask of Thasian wine.[14] And then let's swear—not to pour in a single drop of water.

LAMPITO. Lord! How I like that oath!

LYSISTRATA. Someone bring out a bowl and a flask.

[*A slave brings the utensils for the sacrifice.*]

CALONICE. Look, my friends! What a big jar! Here's a cup that 'twould give me joy to handle. [*She picks up the bowl.*]

LYSISTRATA. Set it down and put your hands on our victim. [*As CALONICE places her hands on the flask*] O Lady of Persuasion and dear Loving Cup, graciously vouchsafe to receive this sacrifice from us women. [*She pours the wine into the bowl.*]

CALONICE. The blood has a good colour and spurts out nicely.

13. In Aeschylus' *Seven against Thebes*, the enemy champions are described as swearing loyalty to each other and slaughtering a bull so that the blood flowed into the hollow of a shield.

14. strong wine from the island of Thasos in the northern Aegean. In Athens the wife was in charge of the household supplies and it is a frequent Aristophanic joke to present her as addicted to the bottle.

LAMPITO. Faith, it has a pleasant smell, too.

MYRRHINE. Oh, let me be the first to swear, ladies![15]

CALONICE. No, by our Lady! Not unless you're allotted the first turn.

LYSISTRATA. Place all your hands on the cup, and one of you repeat on behalf of all what I say. Then all will swear and ratify the oath. *I will suffer no man, be he husband or lover,*

CALONICE. *I will suffer no man, be he husband or lover,*

LYSISTRATA. *To approach me all hot and horny.* [*As* CALONICE *hesitates*] Say it!

CALONICE. [*Slowly and painfully*] *To approach me all hot and horny.* O Lysistrata, I feel so weak in the knees!

LYSISTRATA. *I will remain at home unmated,*

CALONICE. *I will remain at home unmated,*

LYSISTRATA. *Wearing my sheerest gown and carefully adorned,*

CALONICE. *Wearing my sheerest gown and carefully adorned,*

LYSISTRATA. *That my husband may burn with desire for me.*

CALONICE. *That my husband may burn with desire for me.*

LYSISTRATA. *And if he takes me by force against my will,*

CALONICE. *And if he takes me by force against my will,*

LYSISTRATA. *I shall do it badly and keep from moving.*

CALONICE. *I shall do it badly and keep from moving.*

LYSISTRATA. *I will not stretch my slippers toward the ceiling,*

CALONICE. *I will not stretch my slippers toward the ceiling,*

LYSISTRATA. *Nor will I take the posture of the lioness on the knife-handle.*

CALONICE. *Nor will I take the posture of the lioness on the knife-handle.*

LYSISTRATA. *If I keep this oath, may I be permitted to drink from this cup,*

CALONICE. *If I keep this oath, may I be permitted to drink from this cup,*

LYSISTRATA. *But if I break it, may the cup be filled with water.*

CALONICE. *But if I break it, may the cup be filled with water.*

LYSISTRATA. Do you all swear to this?

ALL. I do, so help me!

LYSISTRATA. Come then, I'll just consummate this offering. [*She takes a long drink from the cup.*]

CALONICE. [*Snatching the cup away*] Shares, my dear! Let's drink to our continued friendship.
[*A shout is heard from off-stage.*]

LAMPITO. What's that shouting?

LYSISTRATA. That's what I was telling you: the women have just seized the Acropolis. Now, Lampito, go home and arrange matters in Sparta; and leave these two ladies here as hostages. We'll enter the Acropolis to join our friends and help them

15. *first to swear:* and so the first to drink.

lock the gates.

CALONICE. Don't you suppose the men will come to attack us?

LYSISTRATA. Don't worry about them. Neither threats nor fire will suffice to open the gates, except on the terms we've stated.

CALONICE. I should say not! Else we'd belie our reputation as unmanageable pests.

[LAMPITO *leaves the stage. The other women retire and enter the Acropolis through the Propylaea.*]

[*Enter the* CHORUS OF OLD MEN, *carrying fire-pots and a load of heavy sticks.*]

LEADER OF MEN. Onward, Draces, step by step, though your shoulder's aching.

Cursèd logs of olive-wood, what a load you're making!

FIRST SEMI-CHORUS OF OLD MEN. [*Singing*]

Aye, many surprises await a man who lives to a ripe old age;

For who could suppose, Strymodorus my lad, that the women we've nourished (alas!),

Who sat at home to vex our days,

Would seize the holy image here

And occupy this sacred shrine,

With bolts and bars, with fell design,

To lock the Propylaea?

LEADER OF MEN. Come with speed, Philourgus, come! to the temple hast'ning.

There we'll heap these logs about in a circle round them,

And whoever has conspired, raising this rebellion,

Shall be roasted, scorched, and burnt, all without exception,

Doomed by one unanimous vote—but first the wife of Lycon.[16]

SECOND SEMI-CHORUS. [*Singing*]

No, no! by Demeter, while I'm alive, no woman shall mock at me.

Not even the Spartan Cleomenes,[17] our citadel first to seize,

Got off unscathed; for all his pride

And haughty Spartan arrogance,

He left his arms and sneaked away,

Stripped to his shirt, unkempt, unshav'd,

With six years' filth still on him.

LEADER OF MEN. I besieged that hero bold, sleeping at my station,

16. The ancient commentaries tell us that she was called Rhodia and was not too careful about her reputation.

17. *Cleomenes:* In 508 B.C., the Athenians expelled the tyrant Hippias and were about to install a democratic regime under the leadership of Cleisthenes when the oligarchic party appealed to Sparta for help. The Spartan king Cleomenes invaded Attica, seized the city, and began a purge of the democrats. A popular uprising, however, forced him into the Acropolis, where he was besieged; after two days he was allowed to withdraw with his troops and Cleisthenes began the reforms which established the democracy.

Marshalled at these holy gates sixteen deep against him.
Shall I not these cursèd pests punish for their daring,
Burning these Euripides-and-God-detested women?[18]
Aye! or else may Marathon overturn my trophy.[19]

FIRST SEMI-CHORUS. [*Singing*]

> There remains of my road
> Just this brow of the hill;
> There I speed on my way.
Drag the logs up the hill, though we've got no ass to help.
> (God! my shoulder's bruised and sore!)
> Onward still must we go
> Blow the fire! Don't let it go out
> Now we're near the end of our road.

ALL. [*Blowing on the fire-pots*]
Whew! Whew! Drat the smoke!

SECOND SEMI-CHORUS. [*Singing*]

> Lord, what smoke rushing forth
> From the pot, like a dog
> Running mad, bites my eyes!
This must be Lemnos-fire.[20] What a sharp and stinging smoke!
> Rushing onward to the shrine
> Aid the gods. Once for all
> Show your mettle, Laches my boy!
> To the rescue hastening all!

ALL. [*Blowing on the fire-pots*] Whew! Whew! Drat the smoke!

> [*The chorus has now reached the edge of the Orchestra nearest the stage, in front of the Propylaea. They begin laying their logs and fire-pots on the ground.*]

LEADER OF MEN. Thank heaven, this fire is still alive. Now let's first put down these logs here and place our torches in the pots to catch; then let's make a rush for the gates with a battering-ram. If the women don't unbar the gate at our summons, we'll have to smoke them out.

Let me put down my load. Ouch! That hurts! [*To the audience*] Would any of the generals in Samos[21] like to lend a hand with this log? [*Throwing down a log*] Well, *that* won't break my back any more, at any rate. [*Turning to his fire-pot*] Your job, my little pot, is to keep those coals alive and furnish me shortly with a red-hot torch.

18. Euripides is always presented in Aristophanic comedy as a misogynist and hence hated by women in return. There does not seem to be any foundation for Aristophanes' view, though Euripides' realistic (if sympathetic) presentation of women may possibly have enraged Athenian society ladies.

19. If the chorus really fought at Marathon, they are very old men. The trophy was on a high mound which covered the Athenian dead and is still in place.

20. *Lemnos:* a volcanic island in the Aegean.

21. at this time, the headquarters of the Athenian fleet.

O mistress Victory, be my ally and grant me to rout these audacious women in the Acropolis.

[*While the men are busy with their logs and fires, the* CHORUS OF OLD WOMEN *enters, carrying pitchers of water.*]

LEADER OF WOMEN. What's this I see? Smoke and flames? Is that a fire ablazing?

Let's rush upon them. Hurry up! They'll find us women ready.

FIRST SEMI-CHORUS OF OLD WOMEN. [*Singing*]

With wingèd foot onward I fly,
Ere the flames consume Neodice;
Lest Critylla be overwhelmed
By a lawless, accurst herd of old men.
I shudder with fear. Am I too late to aid them?
At break of the day filled we our jars with water
Fresh from the spring, pushing our way straight through the
crowds. Oh, what a din!
Mid crockery crashing, jostled by slave-girls,
Sped we to save them, aiding our neighbours,
Bearing this water to put out the flames.

SECOND SEMI-CHORUS OF OLD WOMEN. [*Singing*]

Such news I've heard: doddering fools
Come with logs, like furnace-attendants,
Loaded down with three hundred pounds,
Breathing many a vain, blustering threat,
That all these abhorred sluts will be burnt to charcoal.
O goddess, I pray never may they be kindled;
Grant them to save Greece and our men; madness and war help
them to end.
With this as our purpose, golden-plumed Maiden,
Guardian of Athens, seized we thy precinct.
Be my ally, Warrior-maiden,
'Gainst these old men, bearing water with me.

[*The women have now reached their position in the* Orchestra, *and their* LEADER *advances toward the* LEADER OF THE MEN.]

LEADER OF WOMEN. Hold on there! What's this, you utter scoundrels? No decent, God-fearing citizens would act like this.

LEADER OF MEN. Oho! Here's something unexpected: a swarm of women have come out to attack us.

LEADER OF WOMEN. What, do we frighten you? Surely you don't think we're too many for you. And yet there are ten thousand times more of us whom you haven't even seen.

LEADER OF MEN. What say, Phaedria?[22] Shall we let these women

22. a man's name; the remark is addressed to another member of the male chorus.

wag their tongues? Shan't we take our sticks and break them over their backs?

LEADER OF WOMEN. Let's set our pitchers on the ground; then if anyone lays a hand on us, they won't get in our way.

LEADER OF MEN. By God! If someone gave them two or three smacks on the jaw, like Bupalus,[23] they wouldn't talk so much!

LEADER OF WOMEN. Go on, hit me, somebody! Here's my jaw! But no other bitch will bite a piece out of you before me.

LEADER OF MEN. Silence! or I'll knock out your—senility!

LEADER OF WOMEN. Just lay one finger on Stratyllis, I dare you!

LEADER OF MEN. Suppose I dust you off with this fist? What will you do?

LEADER OF WOMEN. I'll tear the living guts out of you with my teeth.

LEADER OF MEN. No poet is more clever than Euripides: "There is no beast so shameless as a woman."

LEADER OF WOMEN. Let's pick up our jars of water, Rhodippe.

LEADER OF MEN. Why have you come here with water, you detestable slut?

LEADER OF WOMEN. And why have you come with fire, you funeral vault? To cremate yourself?

LEADER OF MEN. To light a fire and singe your friends.

LEADER OF WOMEN. And I've brought water to put out your fire.

LEADER OF MEN. What? You'll put out my fire?

LEADER OF WOMEN. Just try and see!

LEADER OF MEN. I wonder: shall I scorch you with this torch of mine?

LEADER OF WOMEN. If you've got any soap, I'll give you a bath.

LEADER OF MEN. Give *me* a bath, you stinking hag?

LEADER OF WOMEN. Yes—a bridal bath!

LEADER OF MEN. Just listen to her! What crust!

LEADER OF WOMEN. Well, I'm a free citizen.

LEADER OF MEN. I'll put an end to your bawling. [*The men pick up their torches.*]

LEADER OF WOMEN. You'll never do jury-duty[24] again. [*The women pick up their pitchers.*]

LEADER OF MEN. Singe her hair for her!

LEADER OF WOMEN. Do your duty, water! [*The women empty their pitchers on the men.*]

LEADER OF MEN. Ow! Ow! For heaven's sake!

LEADER OF WOMEN. Is it too hot?

LEADER OF MEN. What do you mean "hot"? Stop! What are you doing?

23. a sixth-century sculptor, the target of the poet Hipponax's satirical attacks.

24. paid attendance at the courts, the usual source of income for older Athenians.

LEADER OF WOMEN. I'm watering you, so you'll be fresh and green.

LEADER OF MEN. But I'm all withered up with shaking.

LEADER OF WOMEN. Well, you've got a fire; why don't you dry yourself?

[*Enter an Athenian* MAGISTRATE, *accompanied by four Scythian policemen.*[25]]

MAGISTRATE. Have these wanton women flared up again with their timbrels and their continual worship of Sabazius?[26] Is this another Adonis-dirge[27] upon the roof-tops—which we heard not long ago in the Assembly? That confounded Demostratus was urging us to sail to Sicily, and the whirling women shouted, "Woe for Adonis!" And then Demostratus said we'd best enroll the infantry from Zacynthus, and a tipsy woman on the roof shrieked, "Beat your breasts for Adonis!" And that vile and filthy lunatic forced his measure through. Such license do our women take.

LEADER OF MEN. What if you heard of the insolence of these women here? Besides their other violent acts, they threw water all over us, and we have to shake out our clothes just as if we'd leaked in them.

MAGISTRATE. And rightly, too, by God! For we ourselves lead the women astray and teach them to play the wanton; from these roots such notions blossom forth. A man goes into the jeweler's shop and says, "About that necklace you made for my wife, goldsmith: last night, while she was dancing, the fastening-bolt slipped out of the hole. I have to sail over to Salamis today; if you're free, do come around tonight and fit in a new bolt for her." Another goes to the shoe-maker, a strapping young fellow with manly parts, and says, "See here, cobbler, the sandal-strap chafes my wife's little—toe; it's so tender. Come around during the siesta and stretch it a little, so she'll be more comfortable." Now we see the results of such treatment: here I'm a special Councillor and need money to procure oars for the galleys; and I'm locked out of the Treasury by these women.

But this is no time to stand around. Bring up crow-bars there! I'll put an end to their insolence. [*To one of the policemen*] What

---

25. the regular police of Athens. They carried bows and arrows.

26. The cult of the oriental deity Sabazius had been recently introduced in Athens. It was considered somewhat disorderly and immoral by religious conservatives.

27. the lament of the women for Adonis (Tammuz), another oriental cult. When the great expedition to Sicily set

sail, the women were mourning the death of Adonis—a bad omen which proved all too true. Demostratus was one of the supporters of the expedition (the most prominent was Alcibiades) and he proposed to enroll heavy armed infantry from the island of Zacynthus, on the way to Sicily.

are you gaping at, you wretch? What are you staring at? Got an eye out for a tavern, eh? Set your crow-bars here to the gates and force them open. [*Retiring to safe distance*] I'll help from over here.

> [*The gates are thrown open and* LYSISTRATA *comes out followed by several other women.*]

LYSISTRATA. Don't force the gates; I'm coming out of my own accord. We don't need crow-bars here; what we need is good sound common-sense.

MAGISTRATE. Is that so, you strumpet? Where's my policeman? Officer, arrest her and tie her arms behind her back.

LYSISTRATA. By Artemis, if he lays a finger on me, he'll pay for it, even if he is a public servant.

> [*The policeman retires in terror.*]

MAGISTRATE. You there, are you afraid? Seize her round the waist —and you, too. Tie her up, both of you!

FIRST WOMAN. [*As the second policeman approaches* LYSISTRATA] By Pandrosus,[28] if you but touch her with your hand, I'll kick the stuffings out of you.

> [*The second policeman retires in terror.*]

MAGISTRATE. Just listen to that: "kick the stuffings out." Where's another policeman? Tie *her* up first, for her chatter.

SECOND WOMAN. By the Goddess of the Light, if you lay the tip of your finger on her, you'll soon need a doctor.

> [*The third policeman retires in terror.*]

MAGISTRATE. What's this? Where's my policeman? Seize *her* too. I'll soon stop your sallies.

THIRD WOMAN. By the Goddess of Tauros,[29] if you go near her, I'll tear out your hair until it shrieks with pain.

> [*The fourth policeman retires in terror.*]

MAGISTRATE. Oh, damn it all! I've run out of policemen. But women must never defeat us. Officers, let's charge them all together. Close up your ranks!

> [*The policemen rally for a mass attack.*]

LYSISTRATA. By heaven, you'll soon find out that we have four companies of warrior-women, all fully equipped within!

MAGISTRATE. [*Advancing*] Twist their arms off, men!

LYSISTRATA. [*Shouting*] To the rescue, my valiant women!
O sellers-of-barley-green-stuffs-and-eggs,
O sellers-of-garlic, ye keepers-of-taverns, and vendors-of-bread,
Grapple! Smite! Smash!
Won't you heap filth on them? Give them a tongue-lashing!
> [*The women beat off the policemen.*]

28. a mythical Athenian princess.   29. Artemis.

Halt! Withdraw! No looting on the field.

MAGISTRATE. Damn it! My police-force has put up a very poor show.

LYSISTRATA. What did you expect? Did you think you were attacking slaves? Didn't you know that women are filled with passion?

MAGISTRATE. Aye, passion enough—for a good strong drink!

LEADER OF MEN. O chief and leader of this land, why spend your words in vain?

Don't argue with these shameless beasts. You know not how we've fared:

A soapless bath they've given us; our clothes are soundly soaked.

LEADER OF WOMEN. Poor fool! You never should attack or strike a peaceful girl.

But if you do, your eyes must swell. For I am quite content

To sit unmoved, like modest maids, in peace and cause no pain;

But let a man stir up my hive, he'll find me like a wasp.

CHORUS OF MEN. [*Singing*]

O God, whatever shall we do with creatures like Womankind?

This can't be endured by any man alive. Question them!

Let us try to find out what this means.

To what end have they seized on this shrine,

This steep and rugged, high and holy,

Undefiled Acropolis?

LEADER OF MEN. Come, put your questions; don't give in, and probe her every statement.

For base and shameful it would be to leave this plot untested.

MAGISTRATE. Well then, first of all I wish to ask her this: for what purpose have you barred us from the Acropolis?

LYSISTRATA. To keep the treasure safe, so you won't make war on account of it.

MAGISTRATE. What? Do we make war on account of the treasure?

LYSISTRATA. Yes, and you cause all our other troubles for it, too. Peisander[30] and those greedy office-seekers keep things stirred up so they can find occasions to steal. Now let them do what they like: they'll never again make off with any of this money.

MAGISTRATE. What will you do?

LYSISTRATA. What a question! We'll administer it ourselves.

MAGISTRATE. *You* will administer the treasure?

LYSISTRATA. What's so strange in that? Don't we administer the household money for you?

MAGISTRATE. That's different.

LYSISTRATA. How is it different?

MAGISTRATE. We've got to make war with this money.

LYSISTRATA. But that's the very first thing: you mustn't make war.

30. a leader of the war party.

MAGISTRATE. How else can we be saved?

LYSISTRATA. We'll save you.

MAGISTRATE. *You?*

LYSISTRATA. Yes, we!

MAGISTRATE. God forbid!

LYSISTRATA. We'll save you, whether you want it or not.

MAGISTRATE. Oh! This is terrible!

LYSISTRATA. You don't like it, but we're going to do it none the less.

MAGISTRATE. Good God! it's illegal!

LYSISTRATA. We *will* save you, my little man!

MAGISTRATE. Suppose I don't want you to?

LYSISTRATA. That's all the more reason.

MAGISTRATE. What business have you with war and peace?

LYSISTRATA. I'll explain.

MAGISTRATE. [*Shaking his fist*] Speak up, or you'll smart for it.

LYSISTRATA. Just listen, and try to keep your hands still.

MAGISTRATE. I can't. I'm so mad I can't stop them.

FIRST WOMAN. Then you'll be the one to smart for it.

MAGISTRATE. Croak to yourself, old hag! [*To* LYSISTRATA] Now then, speak up.

LYSISTRATA. Very well. Formerly we endured the war for a good long time with our usual restraint, no matter what you men did. You wouldn't let us say "boo," although nothing you did suited us. But we watched you well, and though we stayed at home we'd often hear of some terribly stupid measure you'd proposed. Then, though grieving at heart, we'd smile sweetly and say, "What was passed in the Assembly today about writing on the treaty-stone?"[31] "What's that to you?" my husband would say. "Hold your tongue!" And I held my tongue.

FIRST WOMAN. But I wouldn't have—not I!

MAGISTRATE. You'd have been soundly smacked, if you hadn't kept still.

LYSISTRATA. So I kept still at home. Then we'd hear of some plan still worse than the first; we'd say, "Husband, how could you pass such a stupid proposal?" He'd scowl at me and say, "If you don't mind your spinning, your head will be sore for weeks. *War shall be the concern of Men.*"[32]

MAGISTRATE. And he was right, upon my word!

LYSISTRATA. Why right, you confounded fool, when your proposals were so stupid and we weren't allowed to make suggestions?

"There's not a *man* left in the country," says one. "No, not one," says another. Therefore all we women have decided in council to make a common effort to save Greece. How long should

31. The text of a treaty was inscribed on a stone which was set up in a public place.

32. *War shall be the concern of Men:* Hector to Andromache, *Iliad* VI, 492.

we have waited? Now, if you're willing to listen to our excellent
proposals and keep silence for us in your turn, we still may save you.

MAGISTRATE. We men keep silence for you? That's terrible; I won't
endure it!

LYSISTRATA. Silence!

MAGISTRATE. Silence for *you*, you wench, when you're wearing a
snood? I'd rather die!

LYSISTRATA. Well, if that's all that bothers you—here! take my snood
and tie it round your head. [*During the following words the
women dress up the* MAGISTRATE *in women's garments.*] And
now keep quiet! Here, take this spinning-basket, too, and card
your wool with robes tucked up, munching on beans. *War shall
be the concern of Women!*

LEADER OF WOMEN. Arise and leave your pitchers, girls; no time
is this to falter.

We too must aid our loyal friends; our turn has come for action.

CHORUS OF WOMEN. [*Singing*]
I'll never tire of aiding them with song and dance; never may
Faintness keep my legs from moving to and fro endlessly.
For I yearn to do all for my friends;
They have charm, they have wit, they have grace,
With courage, brains, and best of virtues—
Patriotic sapience.

LEADER OF WOMEN. Come, child of manliest ancient dames, offspring of stinging nettles,

Advance with rage unsoftened; for fair breezes speed you onward.

LYSISTRATA. If only sweet Eros and the Cyprian Queen of Love
shed charm over our breasts and limbs and inspire our men with
amorous longing and priapic spasms, I think we may soon be
called Peacemakers among the Greeks.

MAGISTRATE. What will you do?

LYSISTRATA. First of all, we'll stop those fellows who run madly about
the Marketplace in arms.

FIRST WOMAN. Indeed we shall, by the Queen of Paphos.[33]

LYSISTRATA. For now they roam about the market, amid the pots and
greenstuffs, armed to the teeth like Corybantes.[34]

MAGISTRATE. That's what manly fellows ought to do!

LYSISTRATA. But it's so silly: a chap with a Gorgon-emblazoned
shield buying pickled herring.

FIRST WOMAN. Why, just the other day I saw one of those long-haired
dandies who command our cavalry ride up on horseback and
pour into his bronze helmet the egg-broth he'd bought from an

---

33. Aphrodite.   34. the armed priests of the goddess
                                  Cybele.

old dame. And there was a Thracian slinger too, shaking his lance like Tereus[35]; he'd scared the life out of the poor fig-peddler and was gulping down all her ripest fruit.

MAGISTRATE. How can you stop all the confusion in the various states and bring them together?

LYSISTRATA. Very easily.

MAGISTRATE. Tell me how.

LYSISTRATA. Just like a ball of wool, when it's confused and snarled: we take it thus, and draw out a thread here and a thread there with our spindles; thus we'll unsnarl this war, if no one prevents us, and draw together the various states with embassies here and embassies there.

MAGISTRATE. Do you suppose you can stop this dreadful business with balls of wool and spindles, you nit-wits?

LYSISTRATA. Why, if *you* had any wits, you'd manage all affairs of state like our wool-working.

MAGISTRATE. How so?

LYSISTRATA. First you ought to treat the city as we do when we wash the dirt out of a fleece: stretch it out and pluck and thrash out of the city all those prickly scoundrels; aye, and card out those who conspire and stick together to gain office, pulling off their heads. Then card the wool, all of it, into one fair basket of good-will, mingling in the aliens residing here, any loyal foreigners, and anyone who's in debt to the Treasury; and consider that all our colonies lie scattered round about like remnants; from all of these collect the wool and gather it together here, wind up a great ball, and then weave a good stout cloak for the democracy.

MAGISTRATE. Dreadful! Talking about thrashing and winding balls of wool, when you haven't the slightest share in the war!

LYSISTRATA. Why, you dirty scoundrel, we bear more than twice as much as you. First, we bear children and send off our sons as soldiers.

MAGISTRATE. Hush! Let bygones be bygones!

LYSISTRATA. Then, when we ought to be happy and enjoy our youth, we sleep alone because of your expeditions abroad. But never mind us married women: I grieve most for the maids who grow old at home unwed.

MAGISTRATE. Don't men grow old, too?

LYSISTRATA. For heaven's sake! That's not the same thing. When a man comes home, no matter how grey he is, he soon finds a girl to marry. But woman's bloom is short and fleeting; if she doesn't grasp her chance, no man is willing to marry her and she sits at home a prey to every fortune-teller.

MAGISTRATE. [*Coarsely*] But if a man can still get it up—

35. a mythical king of Thrace. Thracian mercenaries had served in the Athenian ranks during the war.

LYSISTRATA. See here, you: what's the matter? Aren't you dead yet? There's plenty of room for you. Buy yourself a shroud and I'll bake you a honey-cake.[36] [*Handing him a copper coin for his passage across the Styx*] Here's your fare! Now get yourself a wreath.

[*During the following dialogue the women dress up the* MAGISTRATE *as a corpse.*]

FIRST WOMAN. Here, take these fillets.

SECOND WOMAN. Here, take this wreath.

LYSISTRATA. What do you want? What's lacking? Get moving; off to the ferry! Charon is calling you; don't keep him from sailing.

MAGISTRATE. Am I to endure these insults? By God! I'm going straight to the magistrates to show them how I've been treated.

LYSISTRATA. Are you grumbling that you haven't been properly laid out? Well, the day after tomorrow we'll send around all the usual offerings early in the morning.

[*The* MAGISTRATE *goes out still wearing his funeral decorations.* LYSISTRATA *and the women retire into the Acropolis.*]

LEADER OF MEN. Wake, ye sons of freedom, wake! 'Tis no time for sleeping. Up and at them, like a man! Let us strip for action.

[*The* CHORUS OF MEN *remove their outer cloaks.*]

CHORUS OF MEN. [*Singing*]
Surely there is something here greater than meets the eye;
For without a doubt I smell Hippias'[37] tyranny.
Dreadful fear assails me lest certain bands of Spartan men,
Meeting here with Cleisthenes,[38] have inspired through treachery
All these god-detested women secretly to seize
Athens' treasure in the temple, and to stop that pay
    Whence I live at my ease.

LEADER OF MEN. Now isn't it terrible for them to advise the state and chatter about shields, being mere women?

And they think to reconcile us with the Spartans—men who hold nothing sacred any more than hungry wolves. Surely this is a web of deceit, my friends, to conceal an attempt at tyranny. But they'll never lord it over me; I'll be on my guard and from now on,
    "The blade I bear   A myrtle spray shall wear."
I'll occupy the market under arms and stand next to Aristogeiton.[39]
    Thus I'll stand beside him. [*He strikes the pose of the famous*

---

36. The dead were provided with a honey cake to throw to Cerberus, the three-headed dog which guarded the entry to the underworld. The copper coin was to pay the fare required by Charon, the ferryman over the river Styx.

37. the last tyrant of Athens, driven out in 510 B.C.

38. not the great reformer who set up the democracy, but a contemporary of Aristophanes, notorious for his effeminacy (and therefore suspect as a fellow-conspirator of the women).

39. one of the two heroes of the democracy who assassinated Hipparchus, the brother of the tyrant Hippias. A drinking song which was frequently heard at Athenian banquets ran: "In a branch of myrtle, I'll hide my sword, like Harmodius and Aristogeiton, who killed the tyrant, and made Athens free."

statue of the tyrannicides, with one arm raised.] And here's my chance to take this accurst old hag and—[*Striking the* LEADER OF WOMEN] smack her on the jaw!

LEADER OF WOMEN. You'll go home in such a state your Ma won't recognize you!
Ladies all, upon the ground let us place these garments.
[*The* CHORUS OF WOMEN *remove their outer garments.*]
CHORUS OF WOMEN. [*Singing*]
Citizens of Athens, hear useful words for the state.
Rightly; for it nurtured me in my youth royally.
As a child of seven years carried I the sacred box;[40]
Then I was a Miller-maid, grinding at Athene's shrine;
Next I wore the saffron robe and played Brauronia's Bear;
And I walked as Basket-bearer, wearing chains of figs,
    As a sweet maiden fair.
LEADER OF WOMEN. Therefore, am I not bound to give good advice to the city?
Don't take it ill that I was born a woman, if I contribute something better than our present troubles. I pay my share; for I contribute MEN. But you miserable old fools contribute nothing, and after squandering our ancestral treasure, the fruit of the Persian Wars, you make no contribution in return. And now, all on account of you, we're facing ruin.
What, muttering, are you? If you annoy me, I'll take this hard, rough slipper and—[*Striking the* LEADER OF MEN] smack you on the jaw!

CHORUS OF MEN. [*Singing*]
This is outright insolence! Things go from bad to worse.
If you're men with any guts, prepare to meet the foe.
Let us strip our tunics off! We need the smell of male
Vigour. And we cannot fight all swaddled up in clothes.
    [*They strip off their tunics.*]
Come then, my comrades, on to the battle, ye who once to
        Leipsydrion[41] came;
Then ye were MEN. Now call back your youthful vigour.
    With light, wingèd footstep advance,
    Shaking old age from your frame.
LEADER OF MEN. If any of us give these wenches the slightest hold,

40. This and the next four lines describe the religious duties of a well-born Athenian girl. The sacred box contained religious objects connected with the worship of Athena in the Erechtheum. The miller-maids ground flour for sacred cakes. At Brauron in Attica, young girls who represented themselves as bears (the saffron robe was a substitute for a more primitive bearskin) worshipped Artemis. In the Panathenaic procession certain selected girls carried baskets on their heads.
41. the base of the aristocratic family of the Almaeonidae (the family of Pericles) in their first attempt to overthrow Hippias.

they'll stop at nothing: such is their cunning.

They will even build ships and sail against us, like Artemisia.[42] Or if they turn to mounting, I count our Knights as done for: a woman's such a tricky jockey when she gets astraddle, with a good firm seat for trotting. Just look at those Amazons that Micon[43] painted, fighting on horseback against men!

But we must throw them all in the pillory—[*Seizing and choking the* LEADER OF WOMEN] grabbing hold of yonder neck!

CHORUS OF WOMEN. [*Singing*]

'Ware my anger! Like a boar 'twill rush upon you men.

Soon you'll bawl aloud for help, you'll be so soundly trimmed!

Come, my friends, let's strip with speed, and lay aside these robes;

Catch the scent of women's rage. Attack with tooth and nail!

[*They strip off their tunics.*]

Now then, come near me, you miserable man! you'll never eat garlic or black beans again.

And if you utter a single hard word, in rage I will "nurse" you as once

The beetle[44] requited her foe.

LEADER OF WOMEN. For you don't worry me; no, not so long as my Lampito lives and our Theban friend, the noble Ismenia.

You can't do anything, not even if you pass a dozen—decrees! You miserable fool, all our neighbours hate you. Why, just the other day when I was holding a festival for Hecate, I invited as playmate from our neighbours the Boeotians a charming, well-bred Copaic—eel. But they refused to send me one on account of your decrees.

And you'll never stop passing decrees until I grab your foot and—[*Tripping up the* LEADER OF MEN] toss you down and break your neck!

[*Here an interval of five days is supposed to elapse.* LYSISTRATA *comes out from the Acropolis*]

LEADER OF WOMEN. [*Dramatically*] Empress[45] of this great emprise and undertaking,

Why come you forth, I pray, with frowning brow?

LYSISTRATA. Ah, these cursèd women! Their deeds and female notions make me pace up and down in utter despair.

LEADER OF WOMEN. Ah, what sayest thou?

LYSISTRATA. The truth, alas! the truth.

42. queen of Halicarnassus in Asia Minor. She played a prominent part in Xerxes' invasion of Greece and her ships fought at Salamis.

43. a painter who had lately decorated several public buildings with frescos. The battles of the Greeks and Amazons were favorite subjects of sculptors and painters all through the fifth century.

44. In a fable of Aesop the beetle revenges itself on the eagle by breaking its eggs.

45. The tone of the following passage is mock-tragic.

LEADER OF WOMEN. What dreadful tale hast thou to tell thy friends?

LYSISTRATA. 'Tis shame to speak, and not to speak is hard.

LEADER OF WOMEN. Hide not from me whatever woes we suffer.

LYSISTRATA. Well then, to put it briefly, we want—laying!

LEADER OF WOMEN. O Zeus, Zeus!

LYSISTRATA. Why call on Zeus? That's the way things are. I can no longer keep them away from the men, and they're all deserting. I caught one wriggling through a hole near the grotto of Pan, another sliding down a rope, another deserting her post; and yesterday I found one getting on a sparrow's back to fly off to Orsilochus,[46] and had to pull her back by the hair. They're digging up all sorts of excuses to get home. Look, here comes one of them now. [A *woman comes hastily out of the Acropolis.*] Here you! Where are you off to in such a hurry?

FIRST WOMAN. I want to go home. My very best wool is being devoured by moths.

LYSISTRATA. Moths? Nonsense! Go back inside.

FIRST WOMAN. I'll come right back; I swear it. I just want to lay it out on the bed.

LYSISTRATA. Well, you won't lay it out, and you won't go home, either.

FIRST WOMAN. Shall I let my wool be ruined?

LYSISTRATA. If necessary, yes. [*Another woman comes out.*]

SECOND WOMAN. Oh dear! Oh dear! My precious flax! I left it at home all unpeeled.

LYSISTRATA. Here's another one, going home for her "flax." Come back here!

SECOND WOMAN. But I just want to work it up a little and then I'll be right back.

LYSISTRATA. No indeed! If you start this, all the other women will want to do the same. [A *third woman comes out.*]

THIRD WOMAN. O Eilithyia, gooddess of travail, stop my labour till I come to a lawful spot![47]

LYSISTRATA. What's this nonsense?

THIRD WOMAN. I'm going to have a baby—right now!

LYSISTRATA. But you weren't even even pregnant yesterday.

THIRD WOMAN. Well, I am today. O Lysistrata, do send me home to see a midwife, right away.

LYSISTRATA. What are you talking about? [*Putting her hand on her stomach*] What's this hard lump here?

THIRD WOMAN. A little boy.

LYSISTRATA. My goodness, what have you got there? It seems hollow; I'll just find out. [*Pulling aside her robe*] Why, you silly goose,

---

46. the sparrow, Aphrodite's bird, pulled her chariot. *Orsilochus* ran a house of ill-fame.

47. *lawful spot:* The Acropolis was holy ground, and would be polluted by either birth or death.

you've got Athene's sacred helmet there. And you said you were having a baby!

THIRD WOMAN. Well, I *am* having one, I swear!

LYSISTRATA. Then what's this helmet for?

THIRD WOMAN. If the baby starts coming while I'm still in the Acropolis, I'll creep into this like a pigeon and give birth to it there.

LYSISTRATA. Stuff and nonsense! It's plain enough what you're up to. You just wait here for the christening of this—helmet.

THIRD WOMAN. But I can't sleep in the Acropolis since I saw the sacred snake.[48]

FIRST WOMAN. And I'm dying for lack of sleep: the hooting of the owls[49] keeps me awake.

LYSISTRATA. Enough of these shams, you wretched creatures. You want your husbands, I suppose. Well, don't you think they want us? I'm sure they're spending miserable nights. Hold out, my friends, and endure for just a little while. There's an oracle that we shall conquer, if we don't split up. [*Producing a roll of paper*] Here it is.

FIRST WOMAN. Tell us what it says.

LYSISTRATA. Listen.

"When in the length of time the Swallows shall gather together,
Fleeing the Hoopoe's amorous flight and the Cockatoo shunning,
Then shall your woes be ended and Zeus who thunders in heaven
Set what's below on top—"

FIRST WOMAN. What? Are we going to be on top?

LYSISTRATA. "But if the Swallows rebel and flutter away from the temple,
Never a bird in the world shall seem more wanton and worthless."

FIRST WOMAN. That's clear enough, upon my word!

LYSISTRATA. By all that's holy, let's not give up the struggle now. Let's go back inside. It would be a shame, my dear friends, to disobey the oracle.

[*The women all retire to the Acropolis again.*]

CHORUS OF MEN. [*Singing*]
I have a tale to tell,
Which I know full well.
It was told me
In the nursery.

Once there was a likely lad,

---

48. A snake was kept in the Erechtheum.

49. the sacred bird of Athene.

Melanion they name him;
The thought of marriage made him mad,
    For which I cannot blame him.[50]

So off he went to mountains fair;
    (No women to upbraid him!)
A mighty hunter of the hare,
    He had a dog to aid him.

He never came back home to see
    Detested women's faces.
He showed a shrewd mentality.
    With him I'd fain change places!

ONE OF THE MEN. [*To one of the women*] Come here, old dame,
  give me a kiss.
WOMAN. You'll ne'er eat garlic, if you dare!
MAN. I want to kick you—just like this!
WOMAN. Oh, there's a leg with bushy hair!
MAN. Myronides and Phormio[51]
    Were hairy—and they thrashed the foe.

CHORUS OF WOMEN. [*Singing*]
    I have another tale,
    With which to assail
      Your contention
      'Bout Melanion.

Once upon a time a man
    Named Timon[52] left our city,
To live in some deserted land.
    (We thought him rather witty.)

He dwelt alone amidst the thorn;
    In solitude he brooded.
From some grim Fury he was born:
    Such hatred he exuded.

He cursed you men, as scoundrels through
    And through, till life he ended.
He couldn't stand the sight of YOU!
    But women he befriended.

---

50. The chorus of men here recasts a well-known myth for its own purposes. In the myth it was Atalanta who avoided marriage, challenging her suitors to a foot race which she always won; Melanion threw a golden apple in front of her; when she stopped to pick it up, she lost the race to him.

51. successful Athenian generals.

52. the famous misanthrope, the subject of Shakespeare's play. There is no evidence that he "befriended" women his hatred seems to have been directed at the whole human race.

WOMAN. [*To one of the men*] I'll smash your face in, if you like.

MAN. Oh no, please don't! You frighten me.

WOMAN. I'll lift my foot—and thus I'll strike.

MAN. Aha! Look there! What's that I see?

WOMAN. Whate'er you see, you cannot say
   That I'm not neatly trimmed today.

   [LYSISTRATA *appears on the wall of the Acropolis.*]

LYSISTRATA. Hello! Hello! Girls, come here quick!

   [*Several women appear beside her.*]

WOMAN. What is it? Why are you calling?

LYSISTRATA. I see a man coming: he's in a dreadful state. He's mad
   with passion. O Queen of Cyprus, Cythera, and Paphos, just keep
   on this way!

WOMAN. Where is the fellow?

LYSISTRATA. There, beside the shrine of Demeter.

WOMAN. Oh yes, so he is. Who is he?

LYSISTRATA. Let's see. Do any of you know him?

MYRRHINE. Yes indeed. That's my husband, Cinesias.

LYSISTRATA. It's up to you, now: roast him, rack him, fool him,
   love him—and leave him! Do everything, except what our oath
   forbids.

MYRRHINE. Don't worry; I'll do it.

LYSISTRATA. I'll stay here to tease him and warm him up a bit. Off
   with you.

   [*The other women retire from the wall. Enter* CINESIAS *followed by a slave carrying a baby.* CINESIAS *is obviously in
   great pain and distress.*]

CINESIAS. [*Groaning*] Oh-h! Oh-h-h! This is killing me! O God,
   what tortures I'm suffering!

LYSISTRATA. [*From the wall*] Who's that within our lines?

CINESIAS. Me.

LYSISTRATA. A *man*?

CINESIAS. [*Pointing*] A *man*, indeed!

LYSISTRATA. Well, go away!

CINESIAS. Who are you to send me away?

LYSISTRATA. The captain of the guard.

CINESIAS. Oh, for heaven's sake, call out Myrrhine for me.

LYSISTRATA. Call Myrrhine? Nonsense! Who are you?

CINESIAS. Her husband, Cinesias of Paionidai.

LYSISTRATA. [*Appearing much impressed*] Oh, greetings, friend.
   Your name is not without honour here among us. Your wife is
   always talking about you, and whenever she takes an egg or an
   apple, she says, "Here's to my dear Cinesias!"

CINESIAS. [*Quivering with excitement*] Oh, ye gods in heaven!

LYSISTRATA. Indeed she does! And whenever our conversations turn
   to men, your wife immediately says, "All others are mere rubbish

compared with Cinesias."

CINESIAS. [*Groaning*] Oh! Do call her for me.

LYSISTRATA. Why should I? What will you give me?

CINESIAS. Whatever you want. All I have is yours—and you see what I've got.

LYSISTRATA. Well then, I'll go down and call her. [*She descends.*]

CINESIAS. And hurry up! I've had no joy of life ever since she left home. When I go in the house, I feel awful: everything seems so empty and I can't enjoy my dinner. I'm in such a state all the time!

MYRRHINE. [*From behind the wall*] I *do* love him so. But he won't let me love him. No, no! Don't ask me to see him!

CINESIAS. O my darling, O Myrrhine honey, why do you do this to me? [MYRRHINE *appears on the wall.*] Come down here!

MYRRHINE. No, I won't come down.

CINESIAS. Won't you come, Myrrhine, when I call you?

MYRRHINE. No; you don't want me.

CINESIAS. *Don't want you?* I'm in agony!

MYRRHINE. I'm going now.

CINESIAS. Please don't! At least, listen to your baby. [*To the baby*] Here you, call your mamma! [*Pinching the baby*]

BABY. Ma-ma! Ma-ma! Ma-ma!

CINESIAS. [*To* MYRRHINE] What's the matter with you? Have you no pity for your child, who hasn't been washed or fed for five whole days?

MYRRHINE. Oh, poor child; your father pays no attention to you.

CINESIAS. Come down then, you heartless wretch, for the baby's sake.

MYRRHINE. Oh, what it is to be a mother! I've got to come down, I suppose. [*She leaves the wall and shortly reappears at the gate.*]

CINESIAS. [*To himself*] She seems much younger, and she has such a sweet look about her. Oh, the way she teases me! And her pretty, provoking ways make me burn with longing

MYRRHINE. [*Coming out of the gate and taking the baby*]. O my sweet little angel. Naughty papa! Here, let Mummy kiss you, Mamma's little sweetheart! [*She fondles the baby lovingly.*]

CINESIAS. [*In despair*] You heartless creature, why do you do this? Why follow these other women and make both of us suffer so? [*He tries to embrace her.*]

MYRRHINE. Don't touch me!

CINESIAS. You're letting all our things at home go to wrack and ruin.

MYRRHINE. I don't care.

CINESIAS. You don't care that your wool is being plucked to pieces by the chickens?

MYRRHINE. Not in the least.

CINESIAS. And you haven't celebrated the rites of Aphrodite for ever so long. Won't you come home?

MYRRHINE. Not on your life, unless you men make a truce and stop the war.

CINESIAS. Well then, if that pleases you, we'll do it.

MYRRHINE. Well then, if that pleases *you*, I'll come home—afterwards! Right now I'm on oath not to.

CINESIAS. Then just lie down here with me for a moment.

MYRRHINE. No—[*In a teasing voice*] and yet, I won't say I don't love you.

CINESIAS. You love me? Oh, do lie down here, Myrrhine dear!

MYRRHINE. What, you silly fool! in front of the baby?

CINESIAS. [*Hastily thrusting the baby at the slave*] Of course not. Here—home! Take him Manes! [*The slave goes off with the baby.*] See, the baby's out of the way. Now won't you lie down?

MYRRHINE. But where, my dear?

CINESIAS. Where? The grotto of Pan's a lovely spot.

MYRRHINE. How could I purify myself before returning to the shrine?

CINESIAS. Easily: just wash here in the Clepsydra.[53]

MYRRHINE. And then, shall I go back on my oath?

CINESIAS. On my head be it! Don't worry about the oath.

MYRRHINE. All right, then. Just let me bring out a bed.

CINESIAS. No, don't. The ground's all right.

MYRRHINE. Heavens, no! Bad as you are, I won't let you lie on the bare ground. [*She goes into the Acropolis.*]

CINESIAS. Why, she really loves me; it's plain to see.

MYRRHINE. [*Returning with a bed*] There! Now hurry up and lie down. I'll just slip off this dress. But—let's see: oh yes, I must fetch a mattress.

CINESIAS. Nonsense! No mattress for me.

MYRRHINE. Yes indeed! It's not nice on the bare springs.

CINESIAS. Give me a kiss.

MYRRHINE. [*Giving him a hasty kiss*] There! [*She goes.*]

CINESIAS. [*In mingled distress and delight*] Oh-h! Hurry back!

MYRRHINE. [*Returning with a mattress*] Here's the mattress; lie down on it. I'm taking my things off now—but—let's see: you have no pillow.

CINESIAS. I don't *want* a pillow!

MYRRHINE. But I do. [*She goes.*]

CINESIAS. Cheated again, just like Heracles and his dinner![54]

MYRRHINE. [*Returning with a pillow*] Here, lift your head. [*To her-*

---

53. a spring on the Acropolis.
54. The point of this proverb seems to be that the hero is such a glutton that his hosts are never quick enough with their entertainment.

self, wondering how else to tease him] Is that all?

CINESIAS. Surely that's all! Do come here, precious!

MYRRHINE. I'm taking off my girdle. But remember: don't go back on your promise about the truce.

CINESIAS. Hope to die, if I do.

MYRRHINE. You don't have a blanket.

CINESIAS. [*Shouting in exasperation*] I *don't want one!* I WANT TO—

MYRRHINE. Sh-h! There, there, I'll be back in a minute. [*She goes.*]

CINESIAS. She'll be the death of me with these bed-clothes.

MYRRHINE. [*Returning with a blanket*] Here, get up.

CINESIAS. I've got *this* up!

MYRRHINE. Would you like some perfume?

CINESIAS. Good heavens, no! I won't have it!

MYRRHINE. Yes, you shall, whether you want it or not. [*She goes.*]

CINESIAS. O lord! Confound all perfumes anyway!

MYRRHINE. [*Returning with a flask*] Stretch out your hand and put some on.

CINESIAS. [*Suspiciously*] By God, I don't much like this perfume. It smells of shilly-shallying, and has no scent of the marriage-bed.

MYRRHINE. Oh dear! This is Rhodian perfume I've brought.

CINESIAS. It's quite all right dear. Never mind.

MYRRHINE. Don't be silly! [*She goes out with the flask.*]

CINESIAS. Damm the man who first concocted perfumes!

MYRRHINE. [*Returning with another flask*] Here, try this flask.

CINESIAS. I've got another one all ready for you. Come, you wretch, lie down and stop bringing me things.

MYRRHINE. All right; I'm taking off my shoes. But, my dear, see that you vote for peace.

CINESIAS. [*Absently*] I'll consider it. [MYRRHINE *runs away to the Acropolis.*] I'm ruined! The wretch has skinned me and run away! [*Chanting, in tragic style*] Alas! Alas! Deceived, deserted by this fairest of women, whom shall I—lay? Ah, my poor little child, how shall I nurture thee? Where's Cynalopex?[55] I needs must hire a nurse!

LEADER OF MEN. [*Chanting*] Ah, wretched man, in dreadful wise beguiled, bewrayed, thy soul is sore distressed. I pity thee, alas! alas! What soul, what loins, what liver could stand this strain? How firm and unyielding he stands, with naught to aid him of a morning.

CINESIAS. O lord! O Zeus! What tortures I endure!

LEADER OF MEN. This is the way she's treated you, that vile and cursèd wanton.

LEADER OF WOMEN. Nay, not vile and cursèd, but sweet and dear.

LEADER OF MEN. Sweet, you say? Nay, hateful, hateful!

55. a local brothel-keeper.

CINESIAS. Hateful indeed! O Zeus, Zeus!
  Seize her and snatch her away,
  Like a handful of dust, in a mighty,
  Fiery tempest! Whirl her aloft, then let her drop
  Down to the earth, with a crash, as she falls—
  On the point of this waiting
  Thingummybob! [*He goes out.*]
    [*Enter a Spartan* HERALD, *in an obvious state of excitement,
    which he is doing his best to conceal.*]
HERALD. Where can I find the Senate or the Prytanes?[56] I've got an
  important message.
    [*The Athenian* MAGISTRATE *enters.*]
MAGISTRATE. Say there, are you a man or Priapus?[57]
HERALD. [*In annoyance*] I'm a herald, you lout! I've come from Sparta
  about the truce.
MAGISTRATE. Is that a spear you've got under your cloak?
HERALD. No, of course not!
MAGISTRATE. Why do you twist and turn so? Why hold your cloak in
  front of you? Did you rupture yourself on the trip?
HERALD. By gum, the fellow's an old fool.
MAGISTRATE. [*Pointing*] Why, you dirty rascal, you're all excited.
HERALD. Not at all. Stop this tom-foolery.
MAGISTRATE. Well, what's that I see?
HERALD. A Spartan message-staff.[58]
MAGISTRATE. Oh, certainly! That's just the kind of message-staff I've
  got. But tell me the honest truth: How are things going in Sparta?
HERALD. All the land of Sparta is up in arms—and our allies are up,
  too. We need Pellene.[59]
MAGISTRATE. What brought this trouble on you? A sudden Panic?
HERALD. No, Lampito started it and then all the other women in
  Sparta with one accord chased their husbands out of their beds.
MAGISTRATE. How do you feel?
HERALD. Terrible. We walk around the city bent over like men light-
  ing matches in a wind. For our women won't let us touch them
  until we all agree and make peace throughout Greece.
MAGISTRATE. This is a general conspiracy of the women; I see it now.
  Well, hurry back and tell the Spartans to send ambassadors here
  with full powers to arrange a truce. And I'll go tell the Council to
  choose ambassadors from here; I've got a little something here that

56. *Prytanes:* the permanent committee of the Council (Senate).
  57. a god whose grossly phallic statue was set to guard orchards and gardens.
  58. an encoding device. The papyrus
was wrapped round the staff on a spiral

and the message could be read only
when the papyrus was wound round an
exactly similar staff.
  59. a city held by the Athenians and
claimed by the Spartans; also the name
of a famous Athenian prostitute.

will soon persuade them!

HERALD. I'll fly there; for you've made an excellent suggestion.

[*The* HERALD *and the* MAGISTRATE *depart on opposite sides of the stage.*]

LEADER OF MEN. No beast or fire is harder than womankind to tame.
Nor is the spotted leopard so devoid of shame.

LEADER OF WOMEN. Knowing this, you dare provoke us to attack?
I'd be your steady friend, if you'd but take us back.

LEADER OF MEN. I'll never cease my hatred keen of womankind.

LEADER OF WOMEN. Just as you will. But now just let me help you find
That cloak you threw aside. You look so silly there
Without your clothes. Here, put it on and don't go bare.

LEADER OF MEN. That's very kind, and shows you're not entirely bad.
But I threw off my things when I was good and mad.

LEADER OF WOMEN. At last you seem a man, and won't be mocked, my lad.
If you'd been nice to me, I'd take this little gnat
That's in your eye and pluck it out for you, like that.

LEADER OF MEN. So that's what's bothered me and bit my eye so long!
Please dig it out for me. I own that I've been wrong.

LEADER OF WOMEN. I'll do so, though you've been a most ill-natured brat.
Ye gods! See here! A huge and monstrous little gnat!

LEADER OF MEN. Oh, how that helps! For it was digging wells in me.
And now it's out, my tears can roll down hard and free.

LEADER OF WOMEN. Here, let me wipe them off, although you're such a knave
And kiss me.

LEADER OF MEN. No!

LEADER OF WOMEN. Whate'er you say, a kiss I'll have. [*She kisses him.*]

LEADER OF MEN. Oh, confound these women! They've a coaxing way about them.
He was wise and never spoke a truer word, who said,
"We can't live with women, but we cannot live without them."
Now I'll make a truce with you. We'll fight no more: instead,
I will not injure you if you do me no wrong.
And now let's join our ranks and then begin a song.

COMBINED CHORUS. [*Singing*]
Athenians, we're not prepared,
To say a single ugly word

About our fellow-citizens.
Quite the contrary: we desire but to say and to do
Naught but good. Quite enough are the ills now on hand.

Men and women, be advised:
   If anyone requires
Money—minae two or three—
   We've got what he desires.

My purse is yours, on easy terms:
   When Peace shall reappear,
Whate'er you've borrowed will be due.
   So speak up without fear.

You needn't pay me back, you see,
If you can get a cent from me!

We're about to entertain
   Some foreign gentlemen;
We've soup and tender, fresh-killed pork.
   Come round to dine at ten.

Come early; wash and dress with care,
   And bring the children, too.
Then step right in, no "by your leave."
   We'll be expecting you.

Walk in as if you owned the place.
You'll find the door—shut in your face!

[*Enter a group of Spartan Ambassadors; they are in the same
desperate condition as the Herald in the previous scene.*]

LEADER OF CHORUS. Here come the envoys from Sparta, sprouting
   long beards and looking for all the world as if they were carrying
   pig-pens in front of them.
      Greetings, gentlemen of Sparta. Tell me, in what state have you
   come?
SPARTAN. Why waste words? You can plainly see what state
   we're come in!
LEADER OF CHORUS. Wow! You're in a pretty high-strung condition,
   and it seems to be getting worse.
SPARTAN. It's indescribable. Won't someone please arrange a peace
   for us—in any way you like.
LEADER OF CHORUS. Here come our own, native ambassadors, crouch-

ing like wrestlers and holding their clothes in front of them; this seems an athletic kind of malady.

[*Enter several Athenian Ambassadors.*]

ATHENIAN. Can anyone tell us where Lysistrata is? You see our condition.

LEADER OF CHORUS. Here's another case of the same complaint. Tell me, are the attacks worse in the morning?

ATHENIAN. No, we're always afflicted this way. If someone doesn't soon arrange this truce, you'd better not let me get my hands on— Cleisthenes!

LEADER OF CHORUS. If you're smart, you'll arrange your cloaks so none of the fellows who smashed the Hermae[60] can see you.

SPARTAN. Right you are; a very good suggestion.

ATHENIAN. Greetings, Spartan. We've suffered dreadful things.

SPARTAN. My dear fellow, we'd have suffered still worse if one of those fellows had seen us in this condition.

ATHENIAN. Well, gentlemen, we must get down to business. What's your errand here?

SPARTAN. We're ambassadors about peace.

ATHENIAN. Excellent; so are we. Only Lysistrata can arrange things for us; shall we summon her?

SPARTAN. Aye, and Lysistratus too, if you like.

LEADER OF CHORUS. No need to summon her, it seems. She's coming out of her own accord.

[*Enter* LYSISTRATA *accompanied by a statue of a nude female figure, which represents Reconciliation.*]

Hail, noblest of women; now must thou be
A judge shrewd and subtle, mild and severe,
Be sweet yet majestic: all manners employ.
The leaders of Hellas, caught by thy love-charms
Have come to thy judgment, their charges submitting.

LYSISTRATA. This is no difficult task, if one catch them still in amorous passion, before they've resorted to each other. But I'll soon find out. Where's Reconciliation? Go, first bring the Spartans here, and don't seize them rudely and violently, as our tactless husbands used to do, but as befits a woman, like an old, familiar friend; if they won't give you their hands, take them however you can. Then go fetch these Athenians here, taking hold of whatever they offer you. Now then, men of Sparta, stand here beside me, and you Athenians on the other side, and listen to my words.

60. small statues of the god Hermes equipped with *phalloi*, which stood at the door of most Athenian houses. Just before the great expedition left for Sicily, rioters (probably oligarchic conspirators opposed to the expedition) smashed many of these statues.

I am a woman, it is true, but I have a mind; I'm not badly off in native wit, and by listening to my father and my elders, I've had a decent schooling.

Now I intend to give you a scolding which you both deserve. With one common font you worship at the same altars, just like brothers, at Olympia, at Thermopylae, at Delphi—how many more might I name, if time permitted;—and the Barbarians stand by waiting with their armies; yet you are destroying the men and towns of Greece.

ATHENIAN. Oh, this tension is killing me!

LYSISTRATA. And now, men of Sparta,—to turn to you—don't you remember how the Spartan Pericleidas came here once as a suppliant, and sitting at our altar, all pale with fear in his crimson cloak, begged us for an army?[61] For all Messene had attacked you and the god sent an earthquake too? Then Cimon went forth with four thousand hoplites and saved all Lacedaemon. Such was the aid you received from Athens, and now you lay waste the country which once treated you so well.

ATHENIAN. [*Hotly*] They're in the wrong, Lysistrata, upon my word, they are!

SPARTAN. [*Absently, looking at the statue of Reconciliation*] We're in the wrong. What hips! How lovely they are!

LYSISTRATA. Don't think I'm going to let you Athenians off. Don't you remember how the Spartans came in arms when you were wearing the rough, sheepskin cloak of slaves and slew the host of Thessalians, the comrades and allies of Hippias?[62] Fighting with you on that day, alone of all the Greeks, they set you free and instead of a sheepskin gave your folk a handsome robe to wear.

SPARTAN. [*Looking at* LYSISTRATA] I've never seen a more distinguished woman.

ATHENIAN. [*Looking at Reconciliation*] I've never seen a more voluptuous body!

LYSISTRATA. Why then, with these many noble deeds to think of, do you fight each other? Why don't you stop this villainy? Why not make peace? Tell me, what prevents it?

SPARTAN. [*Waving vaguely at Reconciliation*] We're willing, if you're willing to give up your position on yonder flank.

LYSISTRATA. What position, my good man?

SPARTAN. Pylus; we've been panting for it for ever so long.

ATHENIAN. No, by God! You shan't have it!

LYSISTRATA. Let them have it, my friend.

61. After a disastrous earthquake the Spartans were in great danger as a result of a rebellion of their serfs, the Helots. The Athenians under Cimon sent a large force of soldiers to help them (464 B.C.).

62. Hippias the tyrant had allowed exiled democrats to return to Attica but they had to stay outside the city and wear sheepskins so that they could readily be identified. With the help of Spartan soldiers the exiles and the people of Attica finally defeated the Thessalian troops of Hippias.

ATHENIAN. Then, what shall we have to rouse things up?

LYSISTRATA. Ask for another place in exchange.

ATHENIAN. Well, let's see: first of all [*Pointing to various parts of Reconciliation's anatomy*] give us Echinus[63] here, this Maliac Inlet in back there, and these two Megarian legs.

SPARTAN. No, by heavens! You can't have *everything*, you crazy fool!

LYSISTRATA. Let it go. Don't fight over a pair of legs.

ATHENIAN. [*Taking off his cloak*] I think I'll strip and do a little planting now.

SPARTAN. [*Following suit*] And I'll just do a little fertilizing, by gosh!

LYSISTRATA. Wait until the truce is concluded. Now if you've decided on this course, hold a conference and discuss the matter with your allies.

ATHENIAN. Allies? Don't be ridiculous! They're in the same state we are. Won't all our allies want the same thing we do—to jump in bed with their women?

SPARTAN. Ours will, I know.

ATHENIAN. Especially the Carystians,[64] by God!

LYSISTRATA. Very well. Now purify yourselves, that your wives may feast and entertain you in the Acropolis; we've provisions by the basketful. Exchange your oaths and pledges there, and then each of you may take his wife and go home.

ATHENIAN. Let's go at once.

SPARTAN. Come on, where you will.

ATHENIAN. For God's sake, let's hurry!

[*They all go into the Acropolis.*]

CHORUS. [*Singing.*]

Whate'er I have of coverlets
　　And robes of varied hue
And golden trinkets,—without stint
　　I offer them to you.

Take what you will and bear it home,
　　Your children to delight,
Or if your girl's a Basket-maid;
　　Just choose whate'er's in sight.

There's naught within so well secured
　　You cannot break the seal
And bear it off; just help yourselves;
　　No hesitation feel.

---

63. Like Pylus (on the "flank" of the Peloponnese), these names are all double-barrelled references to territories in dispute in the war and salient portions of the anatomy of Reconciliation.

64. The people of Carystus on the island of Euboea were supposed to be of pre-Hellenic stock and therefore primitive and savage.

But you'll see nothing, though you try,
Unless you've sharper eyes than I!

If anyone needs bread to feed
   A growing family,
I've lots of wheat and full-grown loaves;
   So just apply to me.

Let every poor man who desires
   Come round and bring a sack
To fetch the grain; my slave is there
   To load it on his back.

But don't come near my door, I say.
Beware the dog, and stay away!

[*An* ATHENIAN *enters carrying a torch; he knocks at the gate.*]

ATHENIAN. Open the door! [*To the* CHORUS, *which is clustered around the gate*] Make way, won't you! What are you hanging around for? Want me to singe you with this torch? [*To himself*] No; it's a stale trick, I won't do it! [*To the audience*] Still, if I've got to do it to please *you*, I suppose I'll have to take the trouble.

[*A* SECOND ATHENIAN *comes out of the gate.*]

SECOND ATHENIAN. And I'll help you.

FIRST ATHENIAN. [*Waving his torch at the* CHORUS] Get out! Go bawl your heads off! Move on there, so the Spartans can leave in peace when the banquet's over.

[*They brandish their torches until the* CHORUS *leaves the Orchestra.*]

SECOND ATHENIAN. I've never seen such a pleasant banquet: the Spartans are charming fellows, indeed they are! And we Athenians are very witty in our cups.

FIRST ATHENIAN. Naturally: for when we're sober we're never at our best. If the Athenians would listen to me, we'd always get a little tipsy on our embassies. As things are now, we go to Sparta when we're sober and look around to stir up trouble. And then we don't hear what they say—and as for what they *don't* say, we have all sorts of suspicions. And then we bring back varying reports about the mission. But this time everything is pleasant; even if a man should sing the Telamon-song when he ought to sing "Cleitagoras,"[65] we'd praise him and swear it was excellent.

[*The two* CHORUSES *return, as a* CHORUS OF ATHENIANS *and a* CHORUS OF SPARTANS.]

65. At an Athenian banquet each guest in turn, when the time came to sing, was supposed to cap the singer before him by choosing an appropriate drinking song.

Here they come back again. Go to the devil, you scoundrels!
SECOND ATHENIAN. Get out, I say! They're coming out from the feast.

[*Enter the Spartan and Athenian envoys, followed by* LYSIS-TRATA *and all the women.*]

SPARTAN. [*To one of his fellow-envoys*] My good fellow, take up your pipes; I want to do a fancy two-step and sing a jolly song for the Athenians.

ATHENIAN. Yes, do take your pipes, by all means. I'd love to see you dance.

SPARTAN. [*Singing and dancing with the* CHORUS OF SPARTANS]

These youths inspire
To song and dance, O Memory;
Stir up my Muse, to tell how we
And Athens' men, in our galleys clashing
At Artemisium,[66] 'gainst foemen dashing
    In godlike ire,
Conquered the Persian and set Greece free.

    Leonidas
Led on his valiant warriors
Whetting their teeth like angry boars.
Abundant foam on their lips was flow'ring,
A stream of sweat from their limbs was show'ring.
    The Persian was
Numberless as the sand on the shores.

O Huntress[67] who slayest the beasts in the glade,
O Virgin divine, hither come to our truce,
Unite us in bonds which all time will not loose.
Grant us to find in this treaty, we pray,
An unfailing source of true friendship today,
And all of our days, helping us to refrain
From weaseling tricks which bring war in their train.
    Then hither, come hither! O huntress maid.

LYSISTRATA. Come then, since all is fairly done, men of Sparta, lead away your wives, and you, Athenians, take yours. Let every man stand beside his wife, and every wife beside her man, and then, to celebrate our fortune, let's dance. And in the future, let's take care to avoid these misunderstandings.

CHORUS OF ATHENIANS. [*Singing and dancing*]
    Lead on the dances, your graces revealing.
    Call Artemis hither, call Artemis' twin,

---

66. the indecisive naval battle which took place off the coast while Leonidas held the pass at Thermopylae.
67. Artemis.

Leader of dances, Apollo the Healing,
Kindly God—hither! let's summon him in!

Nysian Bacchus call,
Who with his Maenads, his eyes flashing fire,
Dances, and last of all
Zeus of the thunderbolt flaming, the Sire.
And Hera in majesty,
Queen of prosperity.

Come, ye Powers who dwell above
Unforgetting, our witnesses be
Of Peace with bonds of harmonious love—
The Peace which Cypris has wrought for me.
Alleluia! Io Paean!
Leap in joy—hurrah! hurrah!
'Tis victory—hurrah! hurrah!
Euoi! Euoi! Euai! Euai!

LYSISTRATA. [*To the Spartans*] Come now, sing a new song to cap ours.
CHORUS OF SPARTANS. [*Singing and dancing*]
Leaving Taygetus fair and renown'd,
Muse of Laconia,[68] hither come:
Amyclae's god[69] in hymns resound,
Athene of the Brazen Home,[70]
And Castor and Pollux, Tyndareus' sons,
Who sport where Eurotas[71] murmuring runs.

On with the dance! Heia! Ho!
All leaping along,
Mantles a-swinging as we go!
Of Sparta our song.
There the holy chorus ever gladdens,
There the beat of stamping feet,
As our winsome fillies, lovely maidens,
Dance, beside Eurotas' banks a-skipping,—
Nimbly go to and fro
Hast'ning, leaping feet in measures tripping,
Like the Bacchae's revels, hair a-streaming.
Leda's child, divine and mild,
Leads the holy dance, her fair face beaming.
On with the dance! as your hand
Presses the hair
Streaming away unconfined.

68. the Spartan region.
69. *Amyclae:* part of Sparta.
70. the bronze-plated temple of Athena in Sparta.
71. the river of Sparta.

> Leap in the air
> Light as the deer; footsteps resound
> Aiding our dance, beating the ground.
> Praise Athene, Maid divine, unrivalled in her might,
> Dweller in the Brazen Home, unconquered in the fight.
> [*All go out singing and dancing.*]

PLATO
(429?–347 B.C.)
The Apology of Socrates*

How you, O Athenians, have been affected by my accusers, I cannot tell; but I know that they almost made me forget who I was—so persuasively did they speak; and yet they have hardly uttered a word of truth. But of the many falsehoods told by them, there was one which quite amazed me;—I mean when they said that you should be upon your guard and not allow yourselves to be deceived by the force of my eloquence. To say this, when they were certain to be detected as soon as I opened my lips and proved myself to be anything but a great speaker, did indeed appear to me most shameless—unless by the force of eloquence they mean the force of truth; for if such is their meaning, I admit that I am eloquent. But in how different a way from theirs! Well, as I was saying, they have scarcely spoken the truth at all; but from me you shall hear the whole truth: not, however, delivered after their manner in a set oration duly ornamented with words and phrases. No, by heaven! but I shall use the words and arguments which occur to me at the moment; for I am confident in the justice of my cause: at my time of life I ought not to be appearing before you, O men of Athens, in the character of a juvenile orator—let no one expect it of me. And I must beg of you to grant me a favour:—If I defend myself in my accustomed manner, and you hear me using the words which I have been in the habit of using in the agora,[1] at the tables of the money-changers, or anywhere else, I would ask you not to be surprised, and not to interrupt me on this account. For I am more than seventy years of age, and appearing now for the first time in a court of law, I am quite a stranger to the language of the place; and therefore I would have you regard me as if I were really a stranger, whom you would excuse if he spoke in his native tongue, and after the fashion of his country:—Am I making an unfair request of you? Never mind the manner, which may or may not be

---

* Translated by Benjamin Jowett.   1. the market place.
"Apology" means "defense."

good; but think only of the truth of my words, and give heed to that: let the speaker speak truly and the judge decide justly.

And first, I have to reply to the older charges[2] and to my first accusers, and then I will go on to the later ones. For of old I have had many accusers, who have accused me falsely to you during many years; and I am more afraid of them than of Anytus and his associates, who are dangerous, too, in their own way. But far more dangerous are the others, who began when you were children, and took possession of your minds with their falsehoods, telling of one Socrates, a wise man, who speculated about the heaven above, and searched into the earth beneath, and made the worse appear the better cause.[3] The disseminators of this tale are the accusers whom I dread; for their hearers are apt to fancy that such enquirers do not believe in the existence of the gods. And they are many, and their charges against me are of ancient date, and they were made by them in the days when you were more impressible than you are now—in childhood, or it may have been in youth—and the cause when heard went by default, for there was none to answer. And hardest of all, I do not know and cannot tell the names of my accusers; unless in the chance case of a Comic poet.[4] All who from envy and malice have persuaded you—some of them having first convinced themselves—all this class of men are most difficult to deal with; for I cannot have them up here, and cross-examine them, and therefore I must simply fight with shadows in my own defence, and argue when there is no one who answers. I will ask you then to assume with me, as I was saying, that my opponents are of two kinds; one recent, the other ancient: and I hope that you will see the propriety[5] of my answering the latter first, for these accusations you heard long before the others, and much oftener.

Well, then, I must make my defence, and endeavor to clear away in a short time, a slander which has lasted a long time. May I succeed, if to succeed be for my good and yours, or likely to avail me in my cause! The task is not an easy one; I quite understand the

2. Socrates had been the object of much criticism and satire for many years before the trial. He here disregards legal forms and announces that he will deal first with the prejudices that lie behind the formal charge that has been brought against him.

3. He was accused by some of his enemies of being a materialist philosopher who speculated about the physical nature of the universe, and by others of being one of the Sophists, professional teachers of rhetoric and other subjects, many of whom taught methods which were more effective than honest. (See footnotes 7 and 29, on Protagoras and Anaxagoras.)

4. He is referring to the poet Aristophanes, whose play *The Clouds* (produced in 423 B.C.) is a broad satire on Socrates and his associates, and a good example of the prejudice Socrates is dealing with, for it presents him propounding fantastic theories about matter and religion, and teaching students how to avoid payment of debts.

5. He says this with his tongue in his cheek, for he is actually paying no attention to legal propriety. This becomes clearer below, where he goes so far as to paraphrase the actual terms of the indictment and put into the mouths of his accusers the prejudice he claims is the basis of their action.

nature of it. And so leaving the event with God, in obedience to the law I will now make my defence.

I will begin at the beginning, and ask what is the accusation which has given rise to the slander of me, and in fact has encouraged Meletus to prefer this charge against me. Well, what do the slanderers say? They shall be my prosecutors, and I will sum up their words in an affidavit: 'Socrates is an evil-doer, and a curious person, who searches into things under the earth and in heaven, and he makes the worse appear the better cause; and he teaches the aforesaid doctrines to others.' Such is the nature of the accusation: it is just what you have yourselves seen in the comedy of Aristophanes, who has introduced a man whom he calls Socrates, going about and saying that he walks in air,[6] and talking a deal of nonsense concerning matters of which I do not pretend to know either much or little—not that I mean to speak disparagingly of any one who is a student of natural philosophy. I should be very sorry if Meletus could bring so grave a charge against me. But the simple truth is, O Athenians, that I have nothing to do with physical speculations. Very many of those here present are witnesses to the truth of this, and to them I appeal. Speak then, you who have heard me, and tell your neighbours whether any of you have ever known me hold forth in few words or in many upon such matters. . . . You hear their answer. And from what they say of this part of the charge you will be able to judge of the truth of the rest.

As little foundation is there for the report that I am a teacher, and take money;[7] this accusation has no more truth in it than the other. Although, if a man were really able to instruct mankind, to receive money for giving instruction would, in my opinion, be an honour to him. There is Gorgias[8] of Leontium, and Prodicus[9] of Ceos, and Hippias[10] of Elis, who go the round of the cities, and are able to persuade the young men to leave their own citizens by whom they might be taught for nothing, and come to them whom they not only pay, but are thankful if they may be allowed to pay them. There is at this time a Parian[11] philosopher residing in

---

6. In the comedy of Aristophanes Socrates first appears suspended in a basket, and when asked what he is doing replies, "I walk in air and contemplate the sun." He explains that only by suspending his intelligence can he investigate celestial matters.

7. Unlike Socrates, who beggared himself in the quest for truth, the professional teachers made great fortunes. The wealth of Protagoras, the first of the Sophists who demanded fees, was proverbial.

8. from Leontium in Sicily; he was famous as the originator of an antithetical, ornate prose style which had great influence.

9. from Ceos, an island in the Aegean; he taught rhetoric and was well-known for his pioneering grammatical studies.

10. from Elis, in the Peloponnese; he claimed to be able to teach any and all subjects, including handicrafts.

11. from Paros, a small island in the Aegean.

Athens, of whom I have heard; and I came to hear of him in this way:—I came across a man who has spent a world of money on the Sophists, Callias, the son of Hipponicus, and knowing that he had sons, I asked him: 'Callias,' I said, 'if your two sons were foals or calves, there would be no difficulty in finding some one to put over them; we should hire a trainer of horses, or a farmer probably, who would improve and perfect them in their own proper virtue and excellence; but as they are human beings, whom are you thinking of placing over them? Is there any one who understands human and political virtue? You must have thought about the matter, for you have sons; is there any one?' 'There is,' he said. 'Who is he?' said I; 'and of what country? and what does he charge?' 'Evenus the Parian,' he replied; 'he is the man, and his charge is five minae.'[12] Happy is Evenus, I said to myself; if he really has this wisdom, and teaches at such a moderate charge. Had I the same, I should have been very proud and conceited; but the truth is that I have no knowledge of the kind.

I dare say, Athenians, that some one among you will reply, 'Yes, Socrates, but what is the origin of these accusations which are brought against you; there must have been something strange which you have been doing? All these rumours and this talk about you would never have arisen if you had been like other men: tell us, then, what is the cause of them, for we should be sorry to judge hastily of you.' Now I regard this as a fair challenge, and I will endeavour to explain to you the reason why I am called wise and have such an evil fame. Please to attend then. And although some of you may think that I am joking, I declare that I will tell you the entire truth. Men of Athens, this reputation of mine has come of a certain sort of wisdom which I possess. If you ask me what kind of wisdom, I reply, wisdom such as may perhaps be attained by man, for to that extent I am inclined to believe that I am wise; whereas the persons of whom I was speaking have a superhuman wisdom, which I may fail to describe, because I have it not myself; and he who says that I have, speaks falsely, and is taking away my character. And here, O men of Athens, I must beg you not to interrupt me, even if I seem to say something extravagant. For the word which I will speak is not mine. I will refer you to a witness who is worthy of credit; that witness shall be the God of Delphi[13]—he will tell you about my wisdom, if I have any, and of what sort it is. You must have known Chaerephon;[14] he was early a friend of mine, and also a friend of yours, for he shared in the recent exile of the people,[15] and returned with you. Well, Chaerephon, as you

---

12. a relatively moderate sum; Protagoras is said to have charged a hundred minae for a course of instruction.
13. the oracle of Apollo at Delphi.

14. one of Socrates' closest associates; he appears in Aristophanes' comedy.
15. Chaerephon was an enthusiastic

know, was very impetuous in all his doings, and he went to Delphi
and boldly asked the oracle to tell him whether—as I was saying,
I must beg you not to interrupt—he asked the oracle to tell him
whether any one was wiser than I was, and the Pythian prophetess
answered, that there was no man wiser. Chaerephon is dead himself;
but his brother, who is in court, will confirm the truth of what I
am saying.

Why do I mention this? Because I am going to explain to you
why I have such an evil name. When I heard the answer, I said to
myself, What can the god mean? and what is the interpretation of
his riddle? for I know that I have no wisdom, small or great. What
then can he mean when he says that I am the wisest of men? And
yet he is a god, and cannot lie; that would be against his nature.
After long consideration, I thought of a method of trying the question. I reflected that if I could only find a man wiser than myself,
then I might go to the god with a refutation in my hand. I should
say to him, 'Here is a man who is wiser than I am; but you said
that I was the wisest.' Accordingly I went to one who had the
reputation of wisdom, and observed him—his name I need not
mention; he was a politician whom I selected for examination—and
the result was as follows: When I began to talk with him, I could
not help thinking that he was not really wise, although he was
thought wise by many, and still wiser by himself; and thereupon I
tried to explain to him that he thought himself wise, but was not
really wise; and the consequence was that he hated me, and his
enmity was shared by several who were present and heard me. So
I left him, saying to myself, as I went away: Well, although I do
not suppose that either of us knows anything really beautiful and
good, I am better off than he is,—for he knows nothing, and thinks
that he knows; I neither know nor think that I know. In this latter
particular, then, I seem to have slightly the advantage of him. Then
I went to another who had still higher pretensions to wisdom, and
my conclusion was exactly the same. Whereupon I made another
enemy of him, and of many others besides him.

Then I went to one man after another, being not unconscious
of the enmity which I provoked, and I lamented and feared this:
But necessity was laid upon me,—the word of God, I thought,
ought to be considered first. And I said to myself, Go I must to all
who appear to know, and find out the meaning of the oracle. And
I swear to you, Athenians, by the dog I swear![16]—for I must tell
you the truth—the result of my mission was just this: I found that

enough partisan of the democratic
regime to have to go into exile in 404
B.C. when the Thirty Tyrants carried
on an oligarchic reign of terror. The
phrase "the recent exile of the people"
refers to the exile into which all known
champions of democracy were forced
until the democracy was restored.
16. a euphemistic oath (compare,
"by George")

the men most in repute were all but the most foolish; and that others less esteemed were really wiser and better. I will tell you the tale of my wanderings and of the 'Herculean' labours, as I may call them, which I endured only to find at last the oracle irrefutable. After the politicians, I went to the poets; tragic, dithyrambic,[17] and all sorts. And there, I said to myself, you will be instantly detected; now you will find out that you are more ignorant than they are. Accordingly, I took them some of the most elaborate passages in their own writings, and asked what was the meaning of them—thinking that they would teach me something. Will you believe me? I am almost ashamed to confess the truth, but I must say that there is hardly a person present who would not have talked better about their poetry than they did themselves. Then I knew that not by wisdom do poets write poetry, but by a sort of genius and inspiration; they are like diviners or soothsayers who also say many fine things, but do not understand the meaning of them.[18] The poets appeared to me to be much in the same case; and I further observed that upon the strength of their poetry they believed themselves to be the wisest of men in other things in which they were not wise. So I departed, conceiving myself to be superior to them for the same reason that I was superior to the politicians.

At last I went to the artisans, for I was conscious that I knew nothing at all, as I may say, and I was sure that they knew many fine things; and here I was not mistaken, for they did know many things of which I was ignorant, and in this they certainly were wiser than I was. But I observed that even the good artisans fell into the same error as the poets;—because they were good workmen they thought that they also knew all sorts of high matters, and this defect in them overshadowed their wisdom; and therefore I asked myself on behalf of the oracle, whether I would like to be as I was, neither having their knowledge nor their ignorance, or like them in both; and I made answer to myself and to the oracle that I was better off as I was.

This inquisition has led to my having many enemies of the worst and most dangerous kind, and has given occasion also to many calumnies. And I am called wise, for my hearers always imagine that I myself possess the wisdom which I find wanting in others: but the truth is, O men of Athens, that God only is wise; and by his answer he intends to show that the wisdom of men is worth little or nothing; he is not speaking of Socrates, he is only using my name by way of illustration, as if he said, He, O men, is the wisest, who, like Socrates, knows that his wisdom is in truth worth

17. The dithyramb was a short performance by a chorus, produced, like tragedy, at state expense and at a public festival.

18. For a fuller exposition of this famous theory of poetic inspiration see Plato's *Ion*.

nothing. And so I go about the world, obedient to the god, and search and make enquiry into the wisdom of any one, whether citizen or stranger, who appears to be wise; and if he is not wise, then in vindication of the oracle I show him that he is not wise; and my occupation quite absorbs me, and I have no time to give either to any public matter of interest or to any concern of my own, but I am in utter poverty by reason of my devotion to the god.

There is another thing:—young men of the richer classes, who have not much to do, come about me of their own accord; they like to hear the pretenders examined, and they often imitate me, and proceed to examine others; there are plenty of persons, as they quickly discover, who think that they know something, but really know little or nothing; and then those who are examined by them instead of being angry with themselves are angry with me: This confounded Socrates, they say; this villainous misleader of youth! —and then if somebody asks them, Why, what evil does he practice or teach? they do not know, and cannot tell; but in order that they may not appear to be at a loss, they repeat the ready-made charges which are used against all philosophers about teaching things up in the clouds and under the earth, and having no gods, and making the worse appear the better cause; for they do not like to confess that their pretence of knowledge has been detected—which is the truth; and as they are numerous and ambitious and energetic, and are drawn up in battle array and have persuasive tongues, they have filled your ears with their loud and inveterate calumnies. And this is the reason why my three accusers, Meletus and Anytus and Lycon, have set upon me; Meletus, who has a quarrel with me on behalf of the poets; Anytus, on behalf of the craftsmen and politicians; Lycon,[19] on behalf of the rhetoricians: and as I said at the beginning, I cannot expect to get rid of such a mass of calumny all in a moment. And this, O men of Athens, is the truth and the whole truth; I have concealed nothing, I have dissembled nothing. And yet, I know that my plainness of speech makes them hate me, and what is their hatred but a proof that I am speaking the truth?— Hence has arisen the prejudice against me; and this is the reason of it, as you will find out either in this or in any future enquiry.

I have said enough in my defence against the first class of my accusers; I turn to the second class. They are headed by Meletus, that good man and true lover of his country, as he calls himself. Against these, too, I must try to make a defence:—Let their affidavit be read: it contains something of this kind: It says that Socrates is a doer of evil, who corrupts the youth; and who does not believe in the gods of the state, but has other new divinities[20] of his own.

19. the three accusers. Anytus was a prominent politician; the connection of Meletus with poetry and of Lycon with rhetoric is known only from this passage.

20. The precise meaning of the

Such is the charge; and now let us examine the particular counts. He says that I am a doer of evil, and corrupt the youth; but I say, O men of Athens, that Meletus is a doer of evil, in that he pretends to be in earnest when he is only in jest, and is so eager to bring men to trial from a pretended zeal and interest about matters in which he really never had the smallest interest. And the truth of this I will endeavour to prove to you.

Come hither, Meletus, and let me ask a question[21] of you. You think a great deal about the improvement of youth?

Yes, I do.

Tell the judges, then, who is their improver; for you must know, as you have taken the pains to discover their corrupter, and are citing and accusing me before them. Speak, then, and tell the judges who their improver is.—Observe, Meletus, that you are silent, and have nothing to say. But is not this rather disgraceful, and a very considerable proof of what I was saying, that you have no interest in the matter? Speak up, friend, and tell us who their improver is.

The laws.

But that, my good sir, is not my meaning. I want to know who the person is, who, in the first place, knows the laws.

The judges,[22] Socrates, who are present in court.

What, do you mean to say, Meletus, that they are able to instruct and improve youth?

Certainly they are.

What, all of them, or some only and not others?

All of them.

By the goddess Herè,[23] that is good news! There are plenty of improvers, then. And what do you say of the audience,—do they improve them?

Yes, they do.

And the senators?[24]

charge is not clear. As this translation indicates, the Greek words may mean "new divinities," with a reference to Socrates' famous inner voice, which from time to time warned him against action on which he had decided. Or the words may mean "practicing strange rites," though this charge is difficult to understand. In any case, the importance of the phrase is that it implies religious belief of some sort and can later be used against Meletus when he loses his head and accuses Socrates of atheism.

21. Socrates avails himself of his right to interrogate the accuser. He is, of course, a master in this type of examination, for he has spent his life in the practice of puncturing inflated pretensions and exposing logical contradictions in the arguments of his adversaries. He is here fulfilling his

earlier promise to defend himself in the manner to which he has been accustomed and use the words which he has been in the habit of using in the agora (p. 297).

22. the jury. There was no judge in the Athenian law court. The Athenian jury was large; in this trial it probably consisted of five hundred citizens. In the following questions Socrates forces Meletus to extend the capacity to improve the youth to successively greater numbers, until it appears that the entire citizen body is a good influence and Socrates the only bad one. Meletus is caught in the trap of his own demagogic appeal.

23. Hera.

24. the members of the standing council of the assembly, five hundred in number.

Yes, the senators improve them.

But perhaps the members of the assembly[25] corrupt them?—or do they too improve them?

They improve them.

Then every Athenian improves and elevates them; all with the exception of myself; and I alone am their corrupter? Is that what you affirm?

That is what I stoutly affirm.

I am very unfortunate if you are right. But suppose I ask you a question: How about horses?[26] Does one man do them harm and all the world good? Is not the exact opposite the truth? One man is able to do them good, or at least not many;—the trainer of horses, that is to say, does them good, and others who have to do with them rather injure them? Is not that true, Meletus, of horses, or any other animals? Most assuredly it is; whether you and Anytus say yes or no. Happy indeed would be the condition of youth if they had one corrupter only, and all the rest of the world were their improvers. But you, Meletus, have sufficiently shown that you never had a thought about the young: your carelessness is seen in your not caring about the very things which you bring against me.

And now, Meletus, I will ask you another question—by Zeus I will: Which is better, to live among bad citizens, or among good ones? Answer, friend, I say; the question is one which may be easily answered. Do not the good do their neighbours good, and the bad do them evil?

Certainly.

And is there any one who would rather be injured than benefited by those who live with him? Answer, my good friend, the law requires you to answer—does any one like to be injured?

Certainly not.

And when you accuse me of corrupting and deteriorating the youth, do you allege that I corrupt them intentionally or unintentionally?

Intentionally, I say.

But you have just admitted that the good do their neighbours good, and evil do them evil. Now, is that a truth which your superior wisdom has recognized thus early in life, and am I, at my age, in such darkness and ignorance as not to know that if a man with whom I have to live is corrupted by me, I am very likely to be harmed by him; and yet I corrupt him, and intentionally, too—so you say, although neither I nor any other human being is ever likely to be convinced by you. But either I do not corrupt them, or I

25. the sovereign body in the Athenian constitution, theoretically an assembly of the whole citizen body.

26. This simple analogy is typical of the Socratic method; he is still defending himself in his accustomed manner.

corrupt them unintentionally; and on either view of the case you lie. If my offence is unintentional, the law has no cognizance of unintentional offences: you ought to have taken me privately, and warned and admonished me; for if I had been better advised, I should have left off doing what I only did unintentionally—no doubt I should; but you would have nothing to say to me and refused to teach me. And now you bring me up in this court, which is not a place of instruction, but of punishment.

It will be very clear to you, Athenians, as I was saying, that Meletus has no care at all, great or small, about the matter. But still I should like to know, Meletus, in what I am affirmed to corrupt the young. I suppose you mean, as I infer from your indictment, that I teach them not to acknowledge the gods which the state acknowledges, but some other new divinities or spiritual agencies in their stead. These are the lessons by which I corrupt the youth, as you say.

Yes, that I say emphatically.

Then, by the gods, Meletus, of whom we are speaking, tell me and the court, in somewhat plainer terms, what you mean! for I do not as yet understand whether you affirm that I teach other men to acknowledge some gods, and therefore that I do believe in gods, and am not an entire atheist—this you do not lay to my charge,—but only you say that they are not the same gods which the city recognizes—the charge is that they are different gods. Or, do you mean that I am an atheist simply, and a teacher of atheism?

I mean the latter—that you are a complete atheist.[27]

What an extraordinary statement! Why do you think so, Meletus? Do you mean that I do not believe in the godhead of the sun or moon, like other men?

I assure you, judges, that he does not: for he says that the sun is stone, and the moon earth.[28]

Friend Meletus, you think that you are accusing Anaxagoras: and you have but a bad opinion of the judges, if you fancy them illiterate to such a degree as not to know that these doctrines are found in the books of Anaxagoras[29] the Clazomenian, which are full of them. And so, forsooth, the youth are said to be taught them by Socrates, when there are not unfrequently exhibitions of them at the theatre[30] (price of admission one drachma at the most); and

27. Meletus jumps at the most damaging charge, and falls into the trap.

28. Meletus falls back on the old prejudices which Socrates claims are the real indictment against him.

29. a fifth-century philosopher from Clazomenae in Asia Minor. He was an intimate friend of Pericles, but this did not save him from indictment for impiety. He was condemned, and forced to leave Athens. He is famous for his doctrine that matter was set in motion and ordered by Intelligence (Nous), which, however, did not create it. He also declared that the sun was a mass of red-hot metal larger than the Peloponnese, and that there were hills and ravines on the moon.

30. I.e., the doctrines of Anaxagoras are reflected in the works of the tragic

they might pay their money, and laugh at Socrates if he pretends to father these extraordinary views. And so, Meletus, you really think that I do not believe in any god?

I swear by Zeus that you believe absolutely in none at all.

Nobody will believe you, Meletus, and I am pretty sure that you do not believe yourself. I cannot help thinking, men of Athens, that Meletus is reckless and impudent, and that he has written this indictment in a spirit of mere wantonness and youthful bravado. Has he not compounded a riddle, thinking to try me? He said to himself:—I shall see whether the wise Socrates will discover my facetious contradiction, or whether I shall be able to deceive him and the rest of them. For he certainly does appear to me to contradict himself in the indictment as much as if he said that Socrates is guilty of not believing in the gods, and yet of believing in them—but this is not like a person who is in earnest.

I should like you, O men of Athens, to join me in examining what I conceive to be his inconsistency; and do you, Meletus, answer. And I must remind the audience of my request that they would not make a disturbance[31] if I speak in my accustomed manner:

Did ever man, Meletus, believe in the existence of human things, and not of human beings? . . . I wish, men of Athens, that he would answer, and not be always trying to get up an interruption. Did ever any man believe in horsemanship, and not in horses? or in flute-playing, and not in flute-players? No, my friend; I will answer to you and to the court, as you refuse to answer for yourself. There is no man who ever did. But now please to answer the next question: Can a man believe in spiritual and divine agencies, and not in spirits or demigods?

He cannot.

How lucky I am to have extracted that answer, by the assistance of the court! But then you swear in the indictment that I teach and believe in divine or spiritual agencies (new or old, no matter for that); at any rate, I believe in spiritual agencies,—so you say and swear in the affidavit; and yet if I believe in divine beings, how can I help believing in spirits or demigods;—must I not? To be sure I must; and therefore I may assume that your silence gives consent. Now what are spirits or demigods? are they not either gods or the sons of gods?

Certainly they are.

But this is what I call the facetious riddle invented by you: the

poets; or the words may mean simply that Anaxagoras' book was on sale at the theater.

31. The disturbance is presumably due to the frustration of the enemies of Socrates, who see him assuming complete control of the proceedings and turning them into a street-corner argument of the type in which he is invincible.

demigods or spirits are gods, and you say first that I do not believe in gods, and then again that I do believe in gods; that is, if I believe in demigods. For if the demigods are the illegitimate sons of gods, whether by the nymphs or by any other mothers, of whom they are said to be the sons—what human being will ever believe that there are no gods if they are the sons of gods? You might as well affirm the existence of mules, and deny that of horses and asses. Such nonsense, Meletus, could only have been intended by you to make trial of me. You have put this into the indictment because you had nothing real of which to accuse me. But no one who has a particle of understanding will ever be convinced by you that the same men can believe in divine and superhuman things, and yet not believe that there are gods and demigods and heroes.

I have said enough in answer to the charge of Meletus: any elaborate defence is unnecessary; but I know only too well how many are the enmities which I have incurred, and this is what will be my destruction if I am destroyed;—not Meletus, nor yet Anytus, but the envy and detraction of the world, which has been the death of many good men, and will probably be the death of many more; there is no danger of my being the last of them.

Some one will say: And are you not ashamed, Socrates, of a course of life which is likely to bring you to an untimely end? To him I may fairly answer: There you are mistaken: a man who is good for anything ought not to calculate the chance of living or dying; he ought only to consider whether in doing anything he is doing right or wrong—acting the part of a good man or of a bad. Whereas, upon your view, the heroes who fell at Troy were not good for much, and the son of Thetis[32] above all, who altogether despised danger in comparison with disgrace; and when he was so eager to slay Hector, his goddess mother said to him, that if he avenged his companion Patroclus, and slew Hector, he would die himself—'Fate,' she said, in these or the like words, 'waits for you next after Hector;' he, receiving this warning, utterly despised danger and death, and instead of fearing them, feared rather to live in dishonour, and not to avenge his friend. 'Let me die forthwith,' he replies, 'and be avenged of my enemy, rather than abide here by the beaked ships, a laughing-stock and a burden of the earth.' Had Achilles any thought of death and danger? For wherever a man's place is, whether the place which he has chosen or that in which he has been placed by a commander, there he ought to remain in hour of danger; he should not think of death or of anything but of disgrace. And this, O men of Athens, is a true saying.

Strange, indeed, would be my conduct, O men of Athens, if I who, when I was ordered by the generals whom you chose to com-

32. Achilles. See the *Iliad*, Book XVIII, ll. 94 ff.

mand me at Potidaea and Amphipolis and Delium,[33] remained
where they placed me, like any other man, facing death—if now,
when, as I conceive and imagine, God orders me to fulfil the
philosopher's mission of searching into myself and other men, I
were to desert my post through fear of death, or any other fear; that
would indeed be strange, and I might justly be arraigned in court
for denying the existence of the gods, if I disobeyed the oracle
because I was afraid of death, fancying that I was wise when I was
not wise. For the fear of death is indeed the pretence of wisdom,
and not real wisdom, being a pretence of knowing the unknown;
and no one knows whether death, which men in their fear appre-
hend to be the greatest evil, may not be the greatest good. Is not
this ignorance of a disgraceful sort, the ignorance which is the
conceit that man knows what he does not know? And in this respect only I believe myself to differ from men in general, and may
perhaps claim to be wiser than they are:—that whereas I know but
little of the world below,[34] I do not suppose that I know: but I do
know that injustice and disobedience to a better, whether God or
man, is evil and dishonourable, and I will never fear or avoid a
possible good rather than a certain evil. And therefore if you let
me go now, and are not convinced by Anytus, who said that since
I had been prosecuted I must be put to death (or if not that I ought
never to have been prosecuted at all); and that if I escape now, your
sons will all be utterly ruined by listening to my words—if you say
to me, Socrates, this time we will not mind Anytus, and you shall
be let off, but upon one condition, that you are not to enquire and
speculate in this way any more, and that if you are caught doing so
again you shall die:—if this was the condition on which you let me
go, I should reply: Men of Athens, I honour and love you; but I
shall obey God rather than you, and while I have life and strength
I shall never cease from the practice and teaching of philosophy,
exhorting any one whom I meet and saying to him after my manner:
You, my friend,—a citizen of the great and mighty and wise city of
Athens,—are you not ashamed of heaping up the greatest amount
of money and honour and reputation, and caring so little about
wisdom and truth and the greatest improvement of the soul, which
you never regard or heed at all? And if the person with whom I
am arguing, says: Yes, but I do care; then I do not leave him or let
him go at once; but I proceed to interrogate and examine and cross-
examine him, and if I think that he has no virtue in him, but only

33. three of the battles in the Peloponnesian War in which Socrates had
fought as an infantryman. The battle
at Potidaea (in northern Greece) occurred in 432 B.C. (For a fuller account
of Socrates' conduct there see Plato's
Symposium.) The date of the battle at
Amphipolis (in northern Greece) is uncertain. The battle at Delium (in central
Greece) took place in 424 B.C.

34. the next world. The dead were
supposed to carry on a sort of existence below the earth.

says that he has, I reproach him with undervaluing the greater, and overvaluing the less. And I shall repeat the same words to every one whom I meet, young and old, citizen and alien, but especially to the citizens, inasmuch as they are my brethren. For know that this is the command of God; and I believe that no greater good has ever happened in the state than my service to the God. For I do nothing but go about persuading you all, old and young alike, not to take thought for your persons or your properties, but first and chiefly to care about the greatest improvement of the soul. I tell you that virtue is not given by money, but that from virtue comes money and every other good of man, public as well as private. This is my teaching, and if this is the doctrine which corrupts the youth, I am a mischievous person. But if any one says that this is not my teaching, he is speaking an untruth. Wherefore, O men of Athens, I say to you, do as Anytus bids or not as Anytus bids, and either acquit me or not; but whichever you do, understand that I shall never alter my ways, not even if I have to die many times.

Men of Athens, do not interrupt,[35] but hear me; there was an understanding between us that you should hear me to the end: I have something more to say, at which you may be inclined to cry out; but I believe that to hear me will be good for you, and therefore I beg that you will not cry out. I would have you know, that if you kill such an one as I am, you will injure yourselves more than you will injure me. Nothing will injure me, not Meletus nor yet Anytus—they cannot, for a bad man is not permitted to injure a better than himself. I do not deny that Anytus may, perhaps, kill him, or drive him into exile, or deprive him of civil rights; and he may imagine, and others may imagine, that he is inflicting a great injury upon him: but there I do not agree. For the evil of doing as he is doing—the evil of unjustly taking away the life of another—is greater far.

And now, Athenians, I am not going to argue for my own sake, as you may think, but for yours, that you may not sin against the God by condemning me, who am his gift to you. For if you kill me you will not easily find a successor to me, who, if I may use such a ludicrous figure of speech, am a sort of gadfly, given to the state by God; and the state is a great and noble steed who is tardy in his motions owing to his very size, and requires to be stirred into life. I am that gadfly which God has attached to the state, and all day long and in all places am always fastening upon you, arousing and persuading and reproaching you. You will not easily find another like me, and therefore I would advise you to spare me. I dare say that you may feel out of temper (like a person who is suddenly

---

35. The disturbance this time is presumably more general, for Socrates is defying the court and the people.

awakened from sleep), and you think that you might easily strike me dead as Anytus advises, and then you would sleep on for the remainder of your lives, unless God in his care of you sent you another gadfly. When I say that I am given to you by God, the proof of my mission is this:—if I had been like other men, I should not have neglected all my own concerns or patiently seen the neglect of them during all these years, and have been doing yours, coming to you individually like a father or elder brother, exhorting you to regard virtue; such conduct, I say, would be unlike human nature. If I had gained anything, or if my exhortations had been paid, there would have been some sense in my doing so; but now, as you will perceive, not even the impudence of my accusers dares to say that I have ever exacted or sought pay of any one; of that they have no witness. And I have a sufficient witness to the truth of what I say— my poverty.

Some one may wonder why I go about in private giving advice and busying myself with the concerns of others, but do not venture to come forward in public and advise the state. I will tell you why. You have heard me speak at sundry times and in divers places of an oracle or sign which comes to me, and is the divinity which Meletus ridicules in the indictment. This sign, which is a kind of voice, first began to come to me when I was a child; it always forbids but never commands me to do anything which I am going to do. This is what deters me from being a politician. And rightly, as I think. For I am certain, O men of Athens, that if I had engaged in politics, I should have perished long ago, and done no good either to you or to myself. And do not be offended at my telling you the truth: for the truth is, that no man who goes to war with you or any other multitude, honestly striving against the many lawless and unrighteous deeds which are done in a state, will save his life; he who will fight for the right, if he would live even for a brief space, must have a private station and not a public one.

I can give you convincing evidence of what I say, not words only, but what you value far more—actions. Let me relate to you a passage of my own life which will prove to you that I should never have yielded to injustice from any fear of death, and that 'as I should have refused to yield' I must have died at once. I will tell you a tale of the courts, not very interesting perhaps, but nevertheless true. The only office of state which I ever held, O men of Athens, was that of senator:[36] the tribe Antiochis,[37] which is my tribe, had the

36. The Council of the Five Hundred consisted of fifty members of each of the ten tribes into which the population was divided. Each tribal delegation acted as a standing committee of the whole body for a part of the year. The members of this standing committee were called Prytanes. In acting as a member of the council Socrates was not "engaging in politics" but simply fulfilling his duty as a citizen when called upon.

37. Socrates' tribe, like the other nine, was named after a mythical hero, in this case Antiochus.

presidency at the trial of the generals who had not taken up the bodies of the slain after the battle of Arginusae;[38] and you proposed to try them in a body, contrary to law, as you all thought afterwards; but at the time I was the only one of the Prytanes who was opposed to the illegality, and I gave my vote against you; and when the orators threatened to impeach and arrest me, and you called and shouted, I made up my mind that I would run the risk, having law and justice with me, rather than take part in your injustice because I feared imprisonment and death. This happened in the days of the democracy.[39] But when the oligarchy of the Thirty[40] was in power, they sent for me and four others into the rotunda,[41] and bade us bring Leon the Salaminian from Salamis,[42] as they wanted to put him to death. This was a specimen of the sort of commands which they were always giving with the view of implicating as many as possible in their crimes; and then I showed, not in word only but in deed, that, if I may be allowed to use such an expression, I cared not a straw for death, and that my great and only care was lest I should do an unrighteous or unholy thing. For the strong arm of that oppressive power did not frighten me into doing wrong; and when we came out of the rotunda the other four went to Salamis and fetched Leon, but I went quietly home. For which I might have lost my life, had not the power of the Thirty shortly afterwards come to an end. And many will witness to my words.

Now do you really imagine that I could have survived all these years, if I had led a public life, supposing that like a good man I had always maintained the right and had made justice, as I ought, the first thing? No indeed, men of Athens, neither I nor any other man. But I have been always the same in all my actions, public as well as private, and never have I yielded any base compliance to those who are slanderously termed my disciples, or to any other. Not that I have any regular disciples. But if any one likes to come and hear me while I am pursuing my mission, whether he be young or old, he is not excluded. Nor do I converse only with those who pay; but any one, whether he be rich or poor, may ask and answer me and listen

---

38. an Athenian naval victory over Sparta, in 406 B.C. The Athenian commanders failed to pick up the bodies of a large number of Athenians whose ships had been destroyed. Whether they were prevented from doing so by the wind or simply neglected this duty in the excitement of victory is not known; in any case, the Athenian population suspected the worst and put all ten generals on trial, not in a court of law but before the assembly. The generals were tried not individually, but in a group, and condemned to death. The six who had returned to Athens were executed, among them a son of Pericles.

39. Socrates gives two instances of his political actions, one under the democracy and one under the Thirty Tyrants. In both cases, he was in opposition to the government.

40. In 404 B.C., with Spartan backing, the Thirty Tyrants (as they were known to their enemies) ruled for eight months over a defeated Athens. Prominent among them was Critias, who had been one of the rich young men who listened eagerly to Socrates.

41. the circular building in which the Prytanes held their meetings.

42. Athenian territory, an island off Piraeus, the port of Athens.

to my words; and whether he turns out to be a bad man or a good one, neither result can be justly imputed to me; for I never taught or professed to teach him anything. And if any one says that he has ever learned or heard anything from me in private which all the world has not heard, let me tell you that he is lying.

But I shall be asked, Why do people delight in continually conversing with you? I have told you already, Athenians, the whole truth about this matter: they like to hear the cross-examination of the pretenders to wisdom; there is amusement in it. Now this duty of cross-examining other men has been imposed upon me by God; and has been signified to me by oracles, visions, and in every way in which the will of divine power was ever intimated to any one. This is true, O Athenians; or, if not true, would be soon refuted. If I am or have been corrupting the youth, those of them who are now grown up and become sensible that I gave them bad advice in the days of their youth should come forward as accusers, and take their revenge; or if they do not like to come themselves, some of their relatives, fathers, brothers, or other kinsmen, should say what evil their families have suffered at my hands. Now is their time. Many of them I see in the court. There is Crito,[43] who is of the same age and of the same deme[44] with myself, and there is Critobulus his son, whom I also see. Then again there is Lysanias of Sphettus, who is the father of Aeschines—he is present; and also there is Antiphon of Cephisus, who is the father of Epigenes; and there are the brothers of several who have associated with me. There is Nicostratus the son of Theosdotides, and the brother of Theodotus (now Theodotus himself is dead, and therefore he, at any rate, will not seek to stop him); and there is Paralus the son of Demodocus, who had a brother Theages; and Adeimantus the son of Ariston, whose brother Plato[45] is present; and Acantodorus, who is the brother of Apollodorus, whom I also see. I might mention a great many others, some of whom Meletus should have produced as witnesses in the course of his speech; and let him still produce them, if he has forgotten—I will make way for him. And let him say, if he has any testimony of the sort which he can produce. Nay, Athenians, the very opposite is the truth. For all these are ready to witness on behalf of the corrupter, of the injurer of their kindred, as Meletus and Anytus call me; not the corrupted youth only—there might have been a motive for that—but their uncorrupted elder relatives. Why should they too support me with their testimony? Why, indeed, except for the sake of truth and justice, and because they know that I am speaking the truth, and that Meletus is a liar.

Well, Athenians, this and the like of this is all the defence which

43. a friend of Socrates who later tried to persuade him to escape from prison.

44. precinct; the local unit of Athenian administration.

45. the writer of the *Apology*.

I have to offer. Yet a word more. Perhaps there may be some one who is offended at me, when he calls to mind how he himself on a similar, or even a less serious occasion, prayed and entreated the judges with many tears, and how he produced his children in court, which was a moving spectacle, together with a host of relations and friends;[46] whereas I, who am probably in danger of my life, will do none of these things. The contrast may occur to his mind, and he may be set against me, and vote in anger because he is displeased at me on this account. Now if there be such a person among you,— mind, I do not say that there is,—to him I may fairly reply: My friend, I am a man, and like other men, a creature of flesh and blood, and not 'of wood or stone,' as Homer says;[47] and I have a family, yes, and sons, O Athenians, three in number, one almost a man, and two others who are still young; and yet I will not bring any of them hither in order to petition you for an acquittal. And why not? Not from any self-assertion or want of respect for you. Whether I am or am not afraid of death is another question, of which I will not now speak. But, having regard to public opinion, I feel that such conduct would be discreditable to myself, and to you, and to the whole state. One who has reached my years, and who has a name for wisdom, ought not to demean himself. Whether this opinion of me be deserved or not, at any rate the world has decided that Socrates is in some way superior to other men. And if those among you who are said to be superior in wisdom and courage, and any other virtue, demean themselves in this way, how shameful is their conduct! I have seen men of reputation, when they have been condemned, behaving in the strangest manner: they seemed to fancy that they were going to suffer something dreadful if they died, and that they could be immortal if you only allowed them to live; and I think that such are a dishonour to the state, and that any stranger coming in would have said of them that the most eminent men of Athens, to whom the Athenians themselves give honour and command, are no better than women. And I say that these things ought not to be done by those of us who have a reputation; and if they are done, you ought not to permit them; you ought rather to show that you are far more disposed to condemn the man who gets up a doleful scene and makes the city ridiculous, than him who holds his peace.

But, setting aside the question of public opinion, there seems to be something wrong in asking a favour of a judge, and thus procuring an acquittal, instead of informing and convincing him. For his

46. The accepted ending of the speech for the defense was an unrestrained appeal to the pity of the jury. Socrates' refusal to make it is another shock for the prejudices of the audience.

47. In the Odyssey, Book XIX, ll. 162–163, Penelope says to her husband Odysseus (who is disguised as a beggar), "Tell me of your family and where you come from. For you did not spring from an oak or a rock, as the old saying goes."

duty is, not to make a present of justice, but to give judgment; and he has sworn that he will judge according to the laws, and not according to his own good pleasure; and we ought not to encourage you, nor should you allow yourself to be encouraged, in this habit of perjury—there can be no piety in that. Do not then require me to do what I consider dishonourable and impious and wrong, especially now, when I am being tried for impiety on the indictment of Meletus. For if, O men of Athens, by force of persuasion and entreaty I could overpower your oaths, then I should be teaching you to believe that there are no gods, and in defending should simply convict myself of the charge of not believing in them. But that is not so—far otherwise. For I do believe that there are gods, and in a sense higher than that in which any of my accusers believe in them. And to you and to God I commit my cause, to be determined by you as is best for you and me.[48]

There are many reasons why I am not grieved, O men of Athens, at the vote of condemnation. I expected it, and am only surprised that the votes are so nearly equal; for I had thought that the majority against me would have been far larger; but now, had thirty votes gone over to the other side, I should have been acquitted. And I may say, I think, that I have escaped Meletus. I may say more; for without the assistance of Anytus and Lycon, any one may see that he would not have had a fifth part of the votes,[49] as the law requires, in which case he would have incurred a fine of a thousand drachmae.

And so he proposes death as the penalty. And what shall I propose on my part, O men of Athens? Clearly that which is my due. And what is my due? What return shall be made to the man who has never had the wit to be idle during his whole life; but has been careless of what the many care for—wealth, and family interests, and military offices, and speaking in the assembly, and magistracies, and plots, and parties. Reflecting that I was really too honest a man to be a politician and live, I did not go where I could do no good to you or to myself; but where I could do the greatest good privately to every one of you, thither I went, and sought to persuade every man among you that he must look to himself, and seek virtue and wisdom before he looks to his private interests, and look to the state before he looks to the interests of the state; and that this

48. The jury reaches a verdict of guilty. It appears from what Socrates says later that the jury was split, 280 for this verdict and 220 against it. The penalty is to be settled by the jury's choice between the penalty proposed by the prosecution and that offered by the defense. Meletus demands death. Socrates must propose the lightest sentence he thinks he can get away with, but one heavy enough to satisfy the majority of the jury who voted him guilty. The prosecution probably expects him to propose exile from Athens, but Socrates surprises them.

49. Socrates jokingly divides the votes against him into three parts, one for each of his three accusers, and points out that Meletus' votes fall below the minimum necessary to justify the trial.

should be the order which he observes in all his actions. What shall be done to such an one? Doubtless some good thing, O men of Athens, if he has his reward; and ·the good should be of a kind suitable to him. What would be a reward suitable to a poor man who is your benefactor, and who desires leisure that he may instruct you? There can be no reward so fitting as maintenance in the Prytaneum,[50] O men of Athens, a reward which he deserves far more than the citizen who has won the prize at Olympia in the horse or chariot race, whether the chariots were drawn by two horses or by many. For I am in want, and he has enough; and he only gives you the appearance of happiness, and I give you the reality. And if I am to estimate the penalty fairly, I should say that maintenance in the Prytaneum is the just return.

Perhaps you think that I am braving you in what I am saying now, as in what I said before about the tears and prayers. But this is not so. I speak rather because I am convinced that I never intentionally wronged any one, although I cannot convince you—the time has been too short; if there were a law at Athens, as there is in other cities, that a capital cause should not be decided in one day,[51] then I believe that I should have convinced you. But I cannot in a moment refute great slander; and, as I am convinced that I never wronged another, I will assuredly not wrong myself. I will not say of myself that I deserve any evil, or propose any penalty. Why should I? Because I am afraid of the penalty of death which Meletus proposes? When I do not know whether death is a good or an evil, why should I propose a penalty which would certainly be an evil? Shall I say imprisonment? And why should I live in prison, and be the slave of the magistrates of the year—of the Eleven?[52] Or shall the penalty be a fine, and imprisonment until the fine is paid? There is the same objection. I should have to lie in prison, for money I have none, and cannot pay. And if I say exile (and this may possibly be the penalty which you will affix), I must indeed be blinded by the love of life, if I am so irrational as to expect that when you, who are my own citizens, cannot endure my discourses and words, and have found them so grievous and odious that you will have no more of them, others are likely to endure me. No indeed, men of Athens, that is not very likely. And what a life should I lead, at my age, wandering from city to city, ever changing my place of exile, and always being driven out! For I am quite sure that wherever I go, there, as here, the young men will flock to me; and if I drive them away, their elders will drive me out at their request; and if I

---

50. the place in which the Prytanes, as representatives of the city, entertained distinguished visitors and winners at the athletic contests at Olympia.

51. There was such a law in Sparta.
52. a committee which had charge of prisons and of public executions.

let them come, their fathers and friends will drive me out for their sakes.

Some one will say: Yes, Socrates, but cannot you hold your tongue, and then you may go into a foreign city, and no one will interfere with you? Now I have great difficulty in making you understand my answer to this. For if I tell you that to do as you say would be a disobedience to the God, and therefore that I cannot hold my tongue, you will not believe that I am serious; and if I say again that daily to discourse about virtue, and of those other things about which you hear me examining myself and others, is the greatest good of man, and that the unexamined life is not worth living, you are still less likely to believe me. Yet I say what is true, although a thing of which it is hard for me to persuade you. Also, I have never been accustomed to think that I deserve to suffer any harm. Had I money I might have estimated the offence at what I was able to pay, and not have been much the worse. But I have none, and therefore I must ask you to proportion the fine to my means. Well, perhaps I could afford a mina,[53] and therefore I propose that penalty: Plato, Crito, Critobulus, and Appollodorus, my friends here, bid me say thirty minae, and they will be the sureties. Let thirty minae be the penalty; for which sum they will be ample security to you.[54]

Not much time will be gained, O Athenians, in return for the evil name which you will get from the detractors of the city, who will say that you killed Socrates, a wise man; for they will call me wise, even although I am not wise, when they want to reproach you. If you had waited a little while, your desire would have been fulfilled in the course of nature. For I am far advanced in years, as you may perceive, and not far from death. I am speaking now not to all of you, but only to those who have condemned me to death. And I have another thing to say to them: You think that I was convicted because I had no words of the sort which would have procured my acquittal—I mean, if I had thought fit to leave nothing undone or unsaid. Not so; the deficiency which led to my conviction was not of words—certainly not. But I had not the boldness or impudence or inclination to address you as you would have liked me to do, weeping and wailing and lamenting, and saying and doing many things which you have been accustomed to hear from others, and

53. It is almost impossible to express the value of ancient money in modern terms. A mina was a considerable sum; in Aristotle's time (fourth century B.C.) one mina was recognized as a fair ransom for a prisoner of war.

54. The jury decides for death (according to a much later source, the vote this time was 300 to 200). The decision is not surprising in view of Socrates' intransigence. Socrates now makes a final statement to the court.

which, as I maintain, are unworthy of me. I thought at the time that I ought not to do anything common or mean when in danger: nor do I now repent of the style of my defence; I would rather die having spoken after my manner, than speak in your manner and live. For neither in war nor yet at law ought I or any man to use every way of escaping death. Often in battle there can be no doubt that if a man will throw away his arms, and fall on his knees before his pursuers, he may escape death; and in other dangers there are other ways of escaping death, if a man is willing to say and do anything. The difficulty, my friends, is not to avoid death, but to avoid unrighteousness; for that runs faster than death. I am old and move slowly, and the slower runner has overtaken me, and my accusers are keen and quick, and the faster runner, who is unrighteousness, has overtaken them. And now I depart hence condemned by you to suffer the penalty of death,—they too go their ways condemned by the truth to suffer the penalty of villainy and wrong; and I must abide by my award—let them abide by theirs. I suppose that these things may be regarded as fated,—and I think that they are well.

And now, O men who have condemned me, I would fain prophesy to you; for I am about to die, and in the hour of death men are gifted with prophetic power.[55] And I prophesy to you who are my murderers, that immediately after my departure punishment far heavier than you have inflicted on me will surely await you. Me you have killed because you wanted to escape the accuser, and not to give an account of your lives. But that will not be as you suppose: far otherwise. For I say that there will be more accusers of you than there are now;[56] accusers whom hitherto I have restrained: and as they are younger they will be more inconsiderate with you, and you will be more offended at them. If you think that by killing men you can prevent some one from censuring your evil lives, you are mistaken; that is not a way of escape which is either possible or honourable; the easiest and the noblest way is not to be disabling others, but to be improving yourselves. This is the prophecy which I utter before my departure to the judges who have condemned me.

Friends, who would have acquitted me, I would like also to talk with you about the thing which has come to pass, while the magistrates are busy, and before I go to the place at which I must die. Stay then a little, for we may as well talk with one another while there is time. You are my friends, and I should like to show you

---

55. as the dying Hector foretells the death of Achilles; see the *Iliad*, Book XXII, ll. 355–360.

56. Socrates' prophecy was fulfilled, for all of the many different philo-sophical schools of the early fourth century claimed descent from Socrates and developed one or another aspect of his teachings.

the meaning of this event which has happened to me. O my judges —for you I may truly call judges—I should like to tell you of a wonderful circumstance. Hitherto the divine faculty of which the internal oracle is the source has constantly been in the habit of opposing me even about trifles, if I was going to make a slip or error in any matter; and now as you see there has come upon me that which may be thought, and is generally believed to be, the last and worst evil. But the oracle made no sign of opposition, either when I was leaving my house in the morning, or when I was on my way to the court, or while I was speaking, at anything which I was going to say; and yet I have often been stopped in the middle of a speech, but now in nothing I either said or did touching the matter in hand has the oracle opposed me. What do I take to be the explanation of this silence? I will tell you. It is an intimation that what has happened to me is a good, and that those of us who think that death is an evil are in error. For the customary sign would surely have opposed me had I been going to evil and not to good.

Let us reflect in another way, and we shall see that there is great reason to hope that death is a good; for one of two things—either death is a state of nothingness and utter unconsciousness, or, as men say, there is a change and migration of the soul from this world to another. Now if you suppose that there is no consciousness, but a sleep like the sleep of him who is undisturbed even by dreams, death will be an unspeakable gain. For if a person were to select the night in which his sleep was undisturbed even by dreams, and were to compare with this the other days and nights of his life, and then were to tell us how many days and nights he had passed in the course of his life better and more pleasantly than this one, I think that any man, I will not say a private man, but even the great king will not find many such days or nights, when compared with the others. Now if death be of such a nature, I say that to die is gain; for eternity is then only a single night. But if death is the journey to another place, and there, as men say, all the dead abide, what good, O my friends and judges, can be greater than this? If indeed when the pilgrim arrives in the world below, he is delivered from the professors of justice in this world, and finds the true judges who are said to give judgment there, Minos and Rhadamanthus and Aeacus and Triptolemus,[57] and other sons of God who were righteous in their own life, that pilgrimage will be worth making. What would not a man give if he might converse with Orpheus and

---

57. Minos appears as a judge of the dead in Homer's *Odyssey*, Book XI; Rhadamanthus and Aeacus, like Minos, were models of just judges in life and after death; Triptolemus, the mythical inventor of agriculture, is associated with judgment in the next world only in this passage. The first three are sons of Zeus.

Musaeus[58] and Hesiod[59] and Homer? Nay, if this be true, let me die again and again. I myself, too, shall have a wonderful interest in there meeting and conversing with Palamedes, and Ajax[60] the son of Telamon, and any other ancient hero who has suffered death through an unjust judgment; and there will be no small pleasure, as I think, in comparing my own sufferings with theirs. Above all, I shall then be able to continue my search into true and false knowledge; as in this world, so also in the next and I shall find out who is wise, and who pretends to be wise, and is not. What would not a man give, O judges, to be able to examine the leader of the great Trojan expedition; or Odysseus or Sisyphus,[61] or numberless others, men and women too! What infinite delight would there be in conversing with them and asking them questions! In another world they do not put a man to death for asking questions: assuredly not. For besides being happier than we are, they will be immortal, if what is said is true.

Wherefore, O judges, be of good cheer about death, and know of a certainty, that no evil can happen to a good man, either in life or after death. He and his are not neglected by the gods; nor has my own approaching end happened by mere chance. But I see clearly that the time had arrived when it was better for me to die and be released from trouble; wherefore the oracle gave no sign. For which reason, also, I am not angry with my condemners, or with my accusers; they have done me no harm, although they did not mean to do me any good; and for this I may gently blame them.

Still I have a favour to ask of them. When my sons are grown up, I would ask you, O my friends, to punish them; and I would have you trouble them, as I have troubled you, if they seem to care about riches, or anything more than about virtue; or if they pretend to be something when they are really nothing,—then reprove them, as I have reproved you, for not caring about that for which they ought to care, and thinking that they are something when they are really nothing. And if you do this, both I and my sons will have received justice at your hands.

The hour of departure has arrived, and we go our ways—I to die, and you to live. Which is better God only knows.

---

58. legendary poets and religious teachers.

59. early Greek poet (eighth century B.C.?) who wrote *The Works and Days*, a didactic poem containing precepts for the farmer.

60. both victims of unjust trials. Palamedes, one of the Greek chieftains at Troy, was unjustly executed for treason on the false evidence of his enemy Odysseus, and Ajax committed suicide after the arms of the dead Achilles were adjudged to his enemy Odysseus as the bravest warrior on the Greek side.

61. Odysseus was the most cunning of the Greek chieftains at Troy, the hero of Homer's *Odyssey;* Sisyphus, was famous for his unscrupulousness and cunning. Each is presumably an example of the man who "pretends to be wise, and is not."

Crito*

Persons of the Dialogue

SOCRATES   CRITO

SCENE—*The prison of Socrates.*

SOCRATES. Why have you come at this hour, Crito?[1] It must be quite early?

CRITO. Yes, certainly.

SOC. What is the exact time?

CR. The dawn is breaking.

SOC. I wonder that the keeper of the prison would let you in.

CR. He knows me, because I often come, Socrates; moreover, I have done him a kindness.

SOC. And are you only just arrived?

CR. No, I came some time ago.

SOC. Then why did you sit and say nothing, instead of at once awakening me?

CR. I should not have liked myself, Socrates, to be in such great trouble and unrest as you are—indeed I should not: I have been watching with amazement your peaceful slumbers; and for that reason I did not awake you, because I wished to minimize the pain. I have always thought you to be of a happy disposition; but never did I see anything like the easy, tranquil manner in which you bear this calamity.

SOC. Why, Crito, when a man has reached my age[2] he ought not to be repining at the approach of death.

CR. And yet other old men find themselves in similar misfortunes, and age does not prevent them from repining.

SOC. That is true. But you have not told me why you come at this early hour.

CR. I come to bring you a message which is sad and painful; not, as I believe, to yourself, but to all of us who are your friends, and saddest of all to me.

SOC. What? Has the ship come from Delos,[3] on the arrival of which I am to die?

CR. No, the ship has not actually arrived, but she will probably be here to-day, as persons who have come from Sunium tell me that they left her there; and therefore to-morrow, Socrates, will be the last day of your life.

SOC. Very well, Crito; if such is the will of God, I am willing; but my belief is that there will be a delay of a day.

* Translated by Benjamin Jowett.

1. an Athenian of ample means, the same age as Socrates, who offered to stand surety for him at his trial.

2. Socrates was seventy years old.

3. Socrates' execution had been delayed by an annual religious ceremony. A ship had been dispatched to the island of Delos (a center of the worship of Apollo) and until it returned no public execution could take place.

CR. Why do you think so?

SOC. I will tell you. I am to die on the day after the arrival of the ship.

CR. Yes; that is what the authorities say.

SOC. But I do not think that the ship will be here until to-morrow; this I infer from a vision which I had last night, or rather only just now, when you fortunately allowed me to sleep.

CR. And what was the nature of the vision?

SOC. There appeared to me the likeness of a woman, fair and comely, clothed in bright raiment, who called to me and said: O Socrates, The third day hence to fertile Phthia shalt thou go.[4]

CR. What a singular dream, Socrates!

SOC. There can be no doubt about the meaning, Crito, I think.

CR. Yes; the meaning is only too clear. But, oh! my beloved Socrates, let me entreat you once more to take my advice and escape. For if you die I shall not only lose a friend who can never be replaced, but there is another evil: people who do not know you and me will believe that I might have saved you if I had been willing to give money,[5] but that I did not care. Now, can there be a worse disgrace than this—that I should be thought to value money more than the life of a friend? For the many will not be persuaded that I wanted you to escape, and that you refused.

SOC. But why, my dear Crito, should we care about the opinion of the many? Good men, and they are the only persons who are worth considering, will think of these things truly as they occurred.

CR. But you see, Socrates, that the opinion of the many must be regarded, for what is now happening shows that they can do the greatest evil to any one who has lost their good opinion.

SOC. I only wish it were so, Crito; and that the many could do the greatest evil; for then they would also be able to do the greatest good—and what a fine thing this would be! But in reality they can do neither; for they cannot make a man either wise or foolish; and whatever they do is the result of chance.

CR. Well, I will not dispute with you; but please tell me, Socrates, whether you are not acting out of regard to me and your other friends: are you not afraid that if you escape from prison we may get into trouble with the informers[6] for having stolen you away, and lose either the whole or a great part of our property; or that even a worse evil may happen to us? Now, if you fear on our account, be at ease; for in order to save you, we ought surely to run this, or even a greater risk; be persuaded, then, and do as I say.

---

4. Socrates adapts the words of Achilles, who, threatening to leave Troy, declares that "on the third day thereafter we might raise generous Phthia." (*Iliad*, Book IX, l. 363.)

5. to bribe the jailers and "fix" the politicians, as he explains below.

6. private citizens who made a living by detecting and prosecuting breaches of the laws.

soc. Yes, Crito, that is one fear which you mention, but by no means the only one.

cr. Fear not—there are persons who are willing to get you out of prison at no great cost; and as for the informers, they are far from being exorbitant in their demands—a little money will satisfy them. My means, which are certainly ample, are at your service, and if you have a scruple about spending all mine, here are strangers[7] who will give you the use of theirs; and one of them, Simmias the Theban, has brought a large sum of money for this very purpose; and Cebes and many others are prepared to spend their money in helping you to escape. I say, therefore, do not hesitate on our account, and do not say, as you did in the court,[8] that you will have a difficulty in knowing what to do with yourself anywhere else. For men will love you in other places to which you may go, and not in Athens only; there are friends of mine in Thessaly,[9] if you like to go to them, who will value and protect you, and no Thessalian will give you any trouble. Nor can I think that you are at all justified, Socrates, in betraying your own life when you might be saved; in acting thus you are playing into the hands of your enemies, who are hurrying on your destruction. And further I should say that you are deserting your own children; for you might bring them up and educate them; instead of which you go away and leave them, and they will have to take their chance; and if they do not meet with the usual fate of orphans, there will be small thanks to you. No man should bring children into the world who is unwilling to persevere to the end in their nurture and education. But you appear to be choosing the easier part, not the better and manlier, which would have been more becoming in one who professes to care for virtue in all his actions, like yourself. And indeed, I am ashamed not only of you, but of us who are your friends, when I reflect that the whole business will be attributed entirely to our want of courage. The trial need never have come on,[10] or might have been managed differently; and this last act, or crowning folly, will seem to have occurred through our negligence and cowardice, who might have saved you, if we had been good for anything; and you might have saved yourself, for there was no difficulty at all. See now, Socrates, how sad and discreditable are the consequences, both to us and you. Make up your mind then, or rather have your mind already made up, for the time of deliberation is over, and there is only one thing to be done, which must be done this very night, and if we delay at all will be no longer practicable or possible; I beseech you therefore, Socrates, be persuaded by me, and do as I say.

7. foreigners. Simmias and Cebes both came from Thebes.
8. See pp. 534–35
9. in the north; an uncivilized part of Greece.
10. Crito probably means that Socrates could have left Athens as soon as proceedings were started.

soc. Dear Crito, your zeal is invaluable, if a right one; but if wrong, the greater the zeal the greater the danger; and therefore we ought to consider whether I shall or shall not do as you say. For I am and always have been one of those natures who must be guided by reason, whatever the reason may be which upon reflection appears to me to be the best; and now that this chance has befallen me, I cannot repudiate my own words: the principles which I have hitherto honoured and revered I still honour, and unless we can at once find other and better principles, I am certain not to agree with you; no, not even if the power of the multitude could inflict many more imprisonments, confiscations, deaths, frightening us like children with hobgoblin terrors. What will be the fairest way of considering the question? Shall I return to your old argument about the opinions of men?—we are saying that some of them are to be regarded, and others not. Now were we right in maintaining this before I was condemned? And has the argument which was once good now proved to be talk for the sake of talking—mere childish nonsense? That is what I want to consider with your help, Crito:—whether, under my present circumstances, the argument appears to be in any way different or not; and is to be allowed by me or disallowed. That argument, which, as I believe, is maintained by many persons of authority, was to the effect, as I was saying, that the opinions of some men are to be regarded, and of other men not to be regarded. Now you, Crito, are not going to die to-morrow—at least, there is no human probability of this—and therefore you are disinterested and not liable to be deceived by the circumstances in which you are placed. Tell me then, whether I am right in saying that some opinions, and the opinions of some men only, are to be valued, and that other opinions, and the opinions of other men, are not to be valued. I ask you whether I was right in maintaining this?

cr. Certainly.

soc. The good are to be regarded, and not the bad?

cr. Yes.

soc. And the opinions of the wise are good, and the opinions of the unwise are evil?

cr. Certainly.

soc. And what was said about another matter? Is the pupil who devotes himself to the practice of gymnastics supposed to attend to the praise and blame and opinion of every man, or of one man only—his physician or trainer, whoever he may be?

cr. Of one man only.

soc. And he ought to fear the censure and welcome the praise of that one only, and not of the many?

cr. Clearly so.

soc. And he ought to act and train, and eat and drink in the

way which seems good to his single master who has understanding, rather than according to the opinion of all other men put together?

CR. True.

SOC. And if he disobeys and disregards the opinion and approval of the one, and regards the opinion of the many who have no understanding, will he not suffer evil?

CR. Certainly he will.

SOC. And what will the evil be, whither tending and what affecting, in the disobedient person?

CR. Clearly, affecting the body; that is what is destroyed by the evil.

SOC. Very good; and is not this true, Crito, of other things which we need not separately enumerate? In questions of just and unjust, fair and foul, good and evil, which are the subjects of our present consultation, ought we to follow the opinion of the many and to fear them; or the opinion of the one man who has understanding? ought we not to fear and reverence him more than all the rest of the world: and if we desert him shall we not destroy and injure that principle in us which may be assumed to be improved by justice and deteriorated by injustice;—there is such a principle?

CR. Certainly there is, Socrates.

SOC. Take a parallel instance:—if, acting under the advice of those who have no understanding, we destroy that which is improved by health and is deteriorated by disease, would life be worth having? And that which has been destroyed is—the body?

CR. Yes.

SOC. Could we live, having an evil and corrupted body?

CR. Certainly not.

SOC. And will life be worth having, if that higher part of man be destroyed, which is improved by justice and depraved by injustice? Do we suppose that principle, whatever it may be in man, which has to do with justice and injustice, to be inferior to the body?

CR. Certainly not.

SOC. More honourable than the body?

CR. Far more.

SOC. Then, my friend, we must not regard what the many say of us: but what he, the one man who has understanding of just and unjust, will say, and what the truth will say. And therefore you begin in error when you advise that we should regard the opinion of the many about just and unjust, good and evil, honourable and dishonourable,—'Well,' some one will say, 'but the many can kill us.'

CR. Yes, Socrates; that will clearly be the answer.

SOC. And it is true: but still I find with surprise that the old argument is unshaken as ever. And I should like to know whether I may say the same of another proposition—that not life, but a good life, is to be chiefly valued?

CR. Yes, that also remains unshaken.

SOC. And a good life is equivalent to a just and honourable one—that holds also?

CR. Yes, it does.

SOC. From these premises I proceed to argue the question whether I ought or ought not to try and escape without the consent of the Athenians: and if I am clearly right in escaping, then I will make the attempt; but if not, I will abstain. The other considerations which you mention, of money and loss of character and the duty of educating one's children, are, I fear, only the doctrines of the multitude, who would be as ready to restore people to life, if they were able, as they are to put them to death—and with as little reason. But now, since the argument has thus far prevailed, the only question which remains to be considered is, whether we shall do rightly either in escaping or in suffering others to aid in our escape and paying them in money and thanks, or whether in reality we shall not do rightly; and if the latter, then death or any other calamity which may ensue on my remaining here must not be allowed to enter into the calculation.

CR. I think that you are right, Socrates; how then shall we proceed?

SOC. Let us consider the matter together, and do you either refute me if you can, and I will be convinced; or else cease, my dear friend, from repeating to me that I ought to escape against the wishes of the Athenians: for I highly value your attempts to persuade me to do so, but I may not be persuaded against my own better judgment. And now please to consider my first position, and try how you can best answer me.

CR. I will.

SOC. Are we to say that we are never intentionally to do wrong, or that in one way we ought and in another we ought not to do wrong, or is doing wrong always evil and dishonourable, as I was just now saying, and as has been already acknowledged by us? Are all our former admissions which were made within a few days to be thrown away? And have we, at our age, been earnestly discoursing with one another all our life long only to discover that we are no better than children? Or, in spite of the opinion of the many, and in spite of consequences whether better or worse, shall we insist on the truth of what was then said, that injustice is always an evil and dishonour to him who acts unjustly? Shall we say so or not?

CR. Yes.

SOC. Then we must do no wrong?

CR. Certainly not.

soc. Nor when injured injure in return, as the many imagine; for we must injure no one at all?

cr. Clearly not.

soc. Again, Crito, may we do evil?

cr. Surely not, Socrates.

soc. And what of doing evil in return for evil, which is the morality of the many—is that just or not?

cr. Not just.

soc. For doing evil to another is the same as injuring him?

cr. Very true.

soc. Then we ought not to retaliate or render evil for evil to any one, whatever evil we may have suffered from him. But I would have you consider, Crito, whether you really mean what you are saying. For this opinion has never been held, and never will be held, by any considerable number of persons; and those who are agreed and those who are not agreed upon this point have no common ground, and can only despise one another when they see how widely they differ. Tell me, then, whether you agree with and assent to my first principle, that neither injury nor retaliation nor warding off evil by evil is ever right. And shall that be the premiss of our argument? Or do you decline and dissent from this? For so I have ever thought, and continue to think; but, if you are of another opinion, let me hear what you have to say. If, however, you remain of the same mind as formerly, I will proceed to the next step.

cr. You may proceed, for I have not changed my mind.

soc. Then I will go on to the next point, which may be put in the form of a question:—Ought a man to do what he admits to be right, or ought he to betray the right?

cr. He ought to do what he thinks right.

soc. But if this is true, what is the application? In leaving the prison against the will of the Athenians, do I wrong any? or rather do I not wrong those whom I ought least to wrong? Do I not desert the principles which were acknowledged by us to be just—what do you say?

cr. I cannot tell, Socrates; for I do not know.

soc. Then consider the matter in this way:—Imagine that I am about to play truant (you may call the proceeding by any name which you like), and the laws and the government come and interrogate me: 'Tell us, Socrates,' they say, 'what are you about? are you not going by an act of yours to overturn us—the laws, and the whole state, as far as in you lies? Do you imagine that a state can subsist and not be overthrown, in which the decisions of law have no power, but are set aside and trampled upon by individuals?' What will be our answer, Crito, to these and the like words? Any one, and especially a rhetorician, will have a good deal to say on behalf of the law which requires a sentence to be carried out. He will argue that this law should not be set aside; and shall we reply, 'Yes; but the state has injured us and given an unjust sentence.' Suppose I say that?

CR. Very good, Socrates.

SOC. 'And was that our agreement with you?' the law would answer; 'or were you to abide by the sentence of the state?' And if I were to express my astonishment at their words, the law would probably add: 'Answer, Socrates, instead of opening your eyes—you are in the habit of asking and answering questions. Tell us,—What complaint have you to make against us which justifies you in attempting to destroy us and the state? In the first place did we not bring you into existence? Your father married your mother by our aid and begat you. Say whether you have any objection to urge against those of us who regulate marriage?' None, I should reply. 'Or against those of us who after birth regulate the nurture and education of children, in which you also were trained? Were not the laws, which have the charge of education, right in commanding your father to train you in music[11] and gymnastic?' Right, I should reply. 'Well then, since you were brought into the world and nurtured and educated by us, can you deny in the first place that you are our child and slave, as your fathers were before you? And if this is true you are not on equal terms with us; nor can you think that you have a right to do to us what we are doing to you. Would you have any right to strike or revile or do any other evil to your father or your master, if you had one, because you have been struck or reviled by him, or received some other evil at his hands?—you would not say this? And because we think right to destroy you, do you think that you have any right to destroy us in return, and your country as far as in you lies? Will you, O professor of true virtue, pretend that you are justified in this? Has a philosopher like you failed to discover that our country is more to be valued and higher and holier far than mother or father or any ancestor, and more to be regarded in the eyes of the gods and of men of understanding? also to be soothed, and gently and reverently entreated when angry, even more than a father, and either to be persuaded, or if not persuaded, to be obeyed? And when we are punished by her, whether with imprisonment or stripes, the punishment is to be endured in silence; and if she leads us to wounds or death in battle, thither we follow as is right; neither may any one yield or retreat or leave his rank, but whether in battle or in a court of law, or in any other place, he must do what his city and his country order him; or he must change their view of what is just: and if he may do no violence to his father or mother, much less may he do violence to his

11. The Greek term includes literature as well as music.

country.' What answer shall we make to this, Crito? Do the laws speak truly, or do they not?

CR. I think that they do.

SOC. Then the laws will say, 'Consider, Socrates, if we are speaking truly that in your present attempt you are going to do us an injury. For, having brought you into the world, and nurtured and educated you, and given you and every other citizen a share in every good which we had to give, we further proclaim to any Athenian by the liberty which we allow him, that if he does not like us when he has become of age and has seen the ways of the city, and made our acquaintance, he may go where he pleases and take his goods with him. None of us laws will forbid him or interfere with him. Any one who does not like us and the city, and who wants to emigrate to a colony or to any other city, may go where he likes, retaining his property. But he who has experience of the manner in which we order justice and administer the state, and still remains, has entered into an implied contract that he will do as we command him. And he who disobeys us is, as we maintain, thrice wrong; first, because in disobeying us he is disobeying his parents; secondly, because we are the authors of his education; thirdly, because he has made an agreement with us that he will duly obey our commands; and he neither obeys them nor convinces us that our commands are unjust; and we do not rudely impose them, but give him the alternative of obeying or convincing us;—that is what we offer, and he does neither.

'These are the sort of accusations to which, as we were saying, you, Socrates, will be exposed if you accomplish your intentions; you, above all other Athenians.' Suppose now I ask, why I rather than anybody else? they will justly retort upon me that I above all other men have acknowledged the agreement. 'There is clear proof,' they will say, 'Socrates, that we and the city were not displeasing to you. Of all Athenians you have been the most constant resident in the city, which, as you never leave, you may be supposed to love. For you never went out of the city either to see the games, except once when you went to the Isthmus,[12] or to any other place unless when you were on military service; nor did you travel as other men do. Nor had you any curiosity to know other states or their laws: your affections did not go beyond us and our state; we were your special favourites, and you acquiesced in our government of you; and here in this city you begat your children, which is a proof of your satisfaction. Moreover, you might in the course of the trial, if you had liked, have fixed the penalty at banishment; the state which refuses to let you go now would have let you go then. But you pretended that you preferred death to exile, and that you were not

12. Nothing is known of this journey.

unwilling to die. And now you have forgotten these fine sentiments, and pay no respect to us the laws, of whom you are the destroyer; and are doing what only a miserable slave would do, running away and turning your back upon the compacts and agreements which you made as a citizen. And first of all answer this very question: Are we right in saying that you agreed to be governed according to us in deed, and not in word only? Is that true or not?' How shall we answer, Crito? Must we not assent?

CR. We cannot help it, Socrates.

SOC. Then will they not say: 'You, Socrates, are breaking the covenants and agreements which you made with us at your leisure, not in any haste or under any compulsion or deception, but after you have had seventy years to think of them, during which time you were at liberty to leave the city, if we were not to your mind, or if our covenants appeared to you to be unfair. You had your choice, and might have gone either to Lacedaemon or Crete, both which states are often praised by you for their good government, or to some other Hellenic or foreign state. Whereas you, above all other Athenians, seemed to be so fond of the state, or, in other words, of us her laws (and who would care about a state which has no laws?), that you never stirred out of her; the halt, the blind, the maimed were not more stationary in her than you were. And now you run away and forsake your agreements. Not so, Socrates, if you will take our advice; do not make yourself ridiculous by escaping out of the city.

'For just consider, if you transgress and err in this sort of way, what good will you do either to yourself or to your friends? That your friends will be driven into exile and deprived of citizenship, or will lose their property, is tolerably certain; and you yourself, if you fly to one of the neighboring cities, as, for example, Thebes or Megara, both of which are well governed, will come to them as an enemy, Socrates, and their government will be against you, and all patriotic citizens will cast an evil eye upon you as a subverter of the laws, and you will confirm in the minds of the judges the justice of their own condemnation of you. For he who is a corrupter of the laws is more than likely to be a corrupter of the young and foolish portion of mankind. Will you then flee from well-ordered cities and virtuous men? and is existence worth having on these terms? Or will you go to them without shame, and talk to them, Socrates? And what will you say to them? What you say here about virtue and justice and institutions and laws being the best things among men? Would that be decent of you? Surely not. But if you go away from well-governed states to Crito's friends in Thessaly, where there is great disorder and licence, they will be charmed to hear the tale of your escape from prison, set off with ludicrous particulars of the manner in which you were wrapped in a goatskin or some other disguise, and metamorphosed as the manner is of runaways; but will there be no one to remind you that in your old age you were not ashamed to violate the most sacred laws from a miserable desire of a little more life? Perhaps not, if you keep them in a good temper; but if they are out of temper you will hear many degrading things; you will live, but how?—as the flatterer of all men, and the servant of all men; and doing what?—eating and drinking in Thessaly, having gone abroad in order that you may get a dinner. And where will be your fine sentiments about justice and virtue? Say that you wish to live for the sake of your children —you want to bring them up and educate them—will you take them into Thessaly and deprive them of Athenian citizenship? Is this the benefit which you will confer upon them? Or are you under the impression that they will be better cared for and educated here if you are still alive, although absent from them; for your friends will take care of them? Do you fancy that if you are an inhabitant of Thessaly they will take care of them, and if you are an inhabitant of the other world that they will not take care of them? Nay; but if they who call themselves friends are good for anything, they will—to be sure they will.

'Listen, then, Socrates, to us who have brought you up. Think not of life and children first, and of justice afterwards, but of justice first, that you may be justified before the princes of the world below.[13] For neither will you nor any that belong to you be happier or holier or juster in this life, or happier in another, if you do as Crito bids. Now you depart in innocence, a sufferer and not a doer of evil; a victim, not of the laws but of men. But if you go forth, returning evil for evil, and injury for injury, breaking the covenants and agreements which you have made with us, and wronging those whom you ought least of all to wrong, that is to say, yourself, your friends, your country, and us, we shall be angry with you while you live, and our brethren, the laws of the world below, will receive you as an enemy; for they will know that you have done your best to destroy us. Listen, then, to us and not to Crito.'

This, dear Crito, is the voice which I seem to hear murmuring in my ears, like the sound of the flute in the ears of the mystic;[14] that voice, I say, is humming in my ears, and prevents me from hearing any other. And I know that anything more which you may say will be vain. Yet speak, if you have anything to say.

CR. I have nothing to say, Socrates.

SOC. Leave me then, Crito, to fulfil the will of God, and to follow whither he leads.

---

13. the judges of the dead.
14. like the worshipers at the mysteries, who seem to hear the flutes still playing, after they have stopped.

Phaedo*

[The Death of Socrates]

[The narrator, Phaedo, who was present at the execution of Socrates, gives his friend Echecrates an account of Socrates' last hours. Many of his friends were with him on that day, among them Crito and two Theban philosophers, Simmias and Cebes. These two engaged him in an argument about the immortality of the soul, which Socrates succeeded in proving to their satisfaction. He concluded with an account of the next world, describing the place of reward for the virtuous and of punishment for the wicked. The opening words of the following selection are his conclusion of the argument.]

A man of sense ought not to say, nor will I be very confident, that the description which I have given of the soul and her mansions is exactly true. But I do say that, inasmuch as the soul is shown to be immortal, he may venture to think, not improperly or unworthily, that something of the kind is true. The venture is a glorious one, and he ought to comfort himself with words like these, which is the reason why I lengthen out the tale. Wherefore, I say, let a man be of good cheer about his soul, who having cast away the pleasures and ornaments of the body as alien to him and working harm rather than good, has sought after the pleasures of knowledge; and has arrayed the soul, not in some foreign attire, but in her own proper jewels, temperance, and justice, and courage, and nobility, and truth—in these adorned she is ready to go on her journey to the world below, when her hour comes. You, Simmias and Cebes, and all other men, will depart at some time or other. Me already, as a tragic poet would say, the voice of fate calls. Soon I must drink the poison;[1] and I think that I had better repair to the bath first, in order that the women may not have the trouble of washing my body after I am dead.

When he had done speaking, Crito said: And have you any commands for us, Socrates—anything to say about your children, or any other matter in which we can serve you?

Nothing particular, Crito, he replied: only, as I have always told you, take care of yourselves; that is a service which you may be ever rendering to me and mine and to all of us, whether you promise to do so or not. But if you have no thought for yourselves, and care not to walk according to the rule which I have prescribed for you,

---

* Translated by Benjamin Jowett.
1. hemlock. This was the regular method of execution at Athens. The action of the poison is described below.

not now for the first time, however much you may profess or promise at the moment, it will be of no avail.

We will do our best, said Crito: And in what way shall we bury you?

In any way that you like; but you must get hold of me, and take care that I do not run away from you. Then he turned to us, and added with a smile:—I cannot make Crito believe that I am the same Socrates who have been talking and conducting the argument; he fancies that I am the other Socrates whom he will soon see, a dead body—and he asks, How shall he bury me? And though I have spoken many words in the endeavour to show that when I have drunk the poison I shall leave you and go to the joys of the blessed, —these words of mine, with which I was comforting you and myself, have had, as I perceive, no effect upon Crito. And therefore I want you to be surety for me to him now, as at the trial he was surety to the judges for me: but let the promise be of another sort; for he was surety for me to the judges that I would remain, and you must be my surety to him that I shall not remain, but go away and depart; and then he will suffer less at my death, and not be grieved when he sees my body being burned or buried. I would not have him sorrow at my hard lot, or say at the burial, Thus we lay out Socrates, or, Thus we follow him to the grave or bury him; for false words are not only evil in themselves, but they inflict the soul with evil. Be of good cheer then, my dear Crito, and say that you are burying my body only, and do with that whatever is usual, and what you think best.

When he had spoken these words, he arose and went into a chamber to bathe; Crito followed him and told us to wait. So we remained behind, talking and thinking of the subject of discourse, and also of the greatness of our sorrow; he was like a father of whom we were being bereaved, and we were about to pass the rest of our lives as orphans. When he had taken the bath his children were brought to him (he had two young sons and an elder one); and the women of his family also came, and he talked to them and gave them a few directions in the presence of Crito; then he dismissed them and returned to us.

Now the hour of sunset was near, for a good deal of time had passed while he was within. When he came out, he sat down with us again after his bath, but not much was said. Soon the jailer, who was the servant of the Eleven, entered and stood by him, saying:— To you, Socrates, whom I know to be the noblest and gentlest and best of all who ever came to this place, I will not impute the angry feeling of other men, who rage and swear at me, when, in obedience to the authorities, I bid them drink the poison—indeed, I am sure that you will not be angry with me; for others, as you are aware, and not I, are to blame. And so fare you well, and try to bear lightly what must needs be—you know my errand. Then bursting into tears he turned away and went out.

Socrates looked at him and said: I return your good wishes, and will do as you bid. Then turning to us, he said, How charming the man is: since I have been in prison he has always been coming to see me, and at times he would talk to me, and was as good to me as could be, and now see how generously he sorrows on my account. We must do as he says, Crito; and therefore let the cup be brought, if the poison is prepared: if not, let the attendant prepare some.

Yet, said Crito, the sun is still upon the hill-tops, and I know that many a one has taken the draught late, and after the announcement has been made to him, he has eaten and drunk, and enjoyed the society of his beloved: do not hurry—there is time enough.

Socrates said: Yes, Crito, and they of whom you speak are right in so acting, for they think that they will be gainers by the delay; but I am right in not following their example, for I do not think that I should gain anything by drinking the poison a little later; I should only be ridiculous in my own eyes for sparing and saving a life which is already forfeit. Please then to do as I say, and not to refuse me.

Crito made a sign to the servant, who was standing by; and he went out, and having been absent for some time, returned with the jailer carrying the cup of poison. Socrates said: You, my good friend, who are experienced in these matters, shall give me directions how I am to proceed. The man answered: You have only to walk about until your legs are heavy, and then to lie down, and the poison will act. At the same time he handed the cup to Socrates, who in the easiest and gentlest manner, without the least fear or change of colour or feature, looking at the man with all his eyes, Echecrates, as his manner was,[2] took the cup and said: What do you say about making a libation[3] out of this cup to any god? May I, or not? The man answered: We only prepare, Socrates, just so much as we deem enough. I understand, he said: but I may and must ask the gods to prosper my journey from this to the other world—even so—and so be it according to my prayer. Then raising the cup to his lips, quite readily and cheerfully he drank off the poison. And hitherto most of us had been able to control our sorrow; but now when we saw him drinking, and saw too that he had finished the draught, we could no longer forbear, and in spite of myself my own tears were flowing fast; so that I covered my face and wept, not for him, but at the thought of my own calamity in having to part from such a friend.

2. Socrates was famous for his projecting eyes and his intent stare.

3. He asks if he may pour a little of it out in honor of the gods, as if it were wine.

Nor was I the first; for Crito, when he found himself unable to restrain his tears, had got up, and I followed; and at that moment, Apollodorus, who had been weeping all the time, broke out in a loud and passionate cry which made cowards of us all. Socrates alone retained his calmness: What is this strange outcry? he said. I sent away the women mainly in order that they might not misbehave in this way, for I have been told that a man should die in peace. Be quiet then, and have patience. When we heard his words we were ashamed, and refrained our tears; and he walked about until, as he said, his legs began to fail, and then he lay on his back, according to directions, and the man who gave him the poison now and then looked at his feet and legs; and after a while he pressed his foot hard, and asked him if he could feel; and he said, No; and then his leg, and so upwards and upwards, and showed us that he was cold and stiff. And he felt them himself, and said: When the poison reaches the heart, that will be the end. He was beginning to grow cold about the groin, when he uncovered his face, for he had covered himself up, and said—they were his last words—he said: Crito, I owe a cock to Asclepius;[4] will you remember to pay the debt? The debt shall be paid, said Crito; is there anything else? There was no answer to this question; but in a minute or two a movement was heard, and the attendants uncovered him; his eyes were set, and Crito closed his eyes and mouth.

Such was the end, Echecrates, of our friend; concerning whom I may truly say, that of all men of his time whom I have known, he was the wisest and justest and best.

4. *a cock to Asclepius:* a sacrifice to the god of healing, perhaps as a thank offering for the painlessness of his death.

ARISTOTLE
(384–322 B.C.)
Poetics*

. . . Tragedy, then, is an imitation of an action that is serious, complete, and of a certain magnitude; in language embellished with each kind of artistic ornament, the several kinds being found in separate parts of the play; in the form of action, not of narrative; through pity and fear effecting the proper purgation[1] of these emo-

* Selected passages. Our text is the translation by S. H. Butcher, published by the Oxford University Press.

1. The Greek word is *katharsis*. This is probably the most disputed passage in European literary criticism. There are two main schools of interpretation; they differ in their understanding of the metaphor implied in the word *katharsis*.

Some critics take the word to mean "purification," implying a metaphor from the religious process of purification from guilt; the passions are "purified" by the tragic performance since the excitement of these passions by the performance weakens them and reduces them to just proportions in the individual. (This theory was supported by

tions. By 'language embellished,' I mean language into which rhythm, 'harmony,' and song enter. By 'the several kinds in separate parts,' I mean, that some parts are rendered through the medium of verse alone, others again with the aid of song.

Now as tragic imitation implies persons acting, it necessarily follows, in the first place, that Scenic equipment will be a part of Tragedy. Next, Song and Diction, for these are the means of imitation. By 'Diction' I mean the mere metrical arrangement of the words: as for 'Song,' it is a term whose full sense is well understood.

Again, Tragedy is the imitation of an action; and an action implies personal agents, who necessarily possess certain qualities both of character and thought. It is these that determine the qualities of actions themselves; these—thought and character—are the two natural causes from which actions spring: on these causes, again, all success or failure depends. Hence, the Plot is the imitation of the action—for by plot I here mean the arrangement of the incidents. By Character I mean that in virtue of which we ascribe certain qualities to the agents. By Thought, that whereby a statement is proved, or a general truth expressed. Every Tragedy, therefore, must have six parts, which parts determine its quality—namely, Plot, Character, Diction, Thought, Scenery, Song. Two of the parts constitute the means of imitation, one the manner, and three the objects of imitation. And these complete the list. These elements have been employed, we may say, by almost all poets; in fact, every play contains Scenic accessories as well as Character, Plot, Diction, Song, and Thought.

But most important of all is the structure of the incidents. For Tragedy is an imitation, not of men, but of an action and of life— of happiness and misery; and happiness and misery consist in action, the end of human life being a mode of action, not a quality. Now the characters of men determine their qualities, but it is by their actions that they are happy or the reverse. Dramatic action, therefore, is not with a view to the representation of character: character comes in as subsidiary to the action. Hence the incidents and the plot are the end of a tragedy; and the end[2] is the chief thing of all. Again, without action there cannot be a tragedy; there may be without character. . . .

These principles being established, let us now discuss the proper structure of the Plot, since this is the first, and also the most important part of Tragedy.

the German critic Lessing.) Others take the metaphor to be medical, reading the word as "purging" and interpreting the phrase to mean that the tragic performance excites the emotions only to allay them, thus ridding the spectator of the disquieting emotions from which he suffers in everyday life; tragedy thus has a therapeutic effect.

2. purpose.

Now, according to our definition, Tragedy is an imitation of an action, that is complete, and whole, and of a certain magnitude; for there may be a whole that is wanting in magnitude. A whole is that which has beginning, middle, and end. A beginning is that which does not itself follow anything by causal necessity, but after which something naturally is or comes to be. An end, on the contrary, is that which itself naturally follows some other thing, either by necessity, or in the regular course of events, but has nothing following it. A middle is that which follows something as some other thing follows it. A well constructed plot, therefore, must neither begin nor end at haphazard, but conform to the type here described. . . .

Unity of plot does not, as some persons think, consist in the unity of the hero. For infinitely various are the incidents in one man's life, which cannot be reduced to unity; and so, too, there are many actions of one man out of which we cannot make one action. Hence the error, as it appears, of all poets who have composed a Heracleid, a Theseid, or other poems of the kind. They imagine that as Heracles was one man, the story of Heracles ought also to be a unity. . . .

It is, moreover, evident from what has been said, that it is not the function of the poet to relate what has happened, but what may happen—what is possible according to the law of probability or necessity. The poet and the historian differ not by writing in verse or in prose. The work of Herodotus[3] might be put into verse, and it would still be a species of history, with metre no less than without it. The true difference is that one relates what has happened, the other what may happen. Poetry, therefore, is a more philosophical and a higher thing than history: for poetry tends to express the universal, history the particular. The universal tells us how a person of given character will on occasion speak or act, according to the law of probability or necessity; and it is this universality at which Poetry aims in giving expressive names to the characters. The particular is—for example—what Alcibiades did or suffered. . . .

Of all plots and actions the episodic are the worst. I call a plot episodic in which the episodes or acts succeed one another without probable or necessary sequence. Bad poets compose such pieces by their own fault, good poets, to please the players; for, as they write for competing rivals, they draw out the plot beyond its capacity, and are often forced to break the natural continuity. . . .

Plots are either simple or complicated; for such too, in their very nature, are the actions of which the plots are an imitation. An action which is one and continuous in the sense above defined,

3. the fifth-century historian of the Persian wars.

I call Simple, when the turning point is reached without Reversal of Fortune or Recognition:[4] Complicated, when it is reached with Reversal of Fortune, or Recognition, or both. These last should arise from the internal structure of the plot, so that what follows should be the necessary or probable result of the preceding action. It makes all the difference whether one event is the consequence of another, or merely subsequent to it.

A reversal of fortune is, as we have said, a change by which a train of action produces the opposite of the effect intended; and that, according to our rule of probability or necessity. Thus in the *Oedipus*, the messenger,[5] hoping to cheer Oedipus, and to free him from his alarms about his mother, reveals his[6] origin, and so produces the opposite effect. . . .

A Recognition, as the name indicates, is a change from ignorance to knowledge, producing love or hate between the persons destined by the poet for good or bad fortune. The best form of recognition is coincident with a reversal of fortune, as in the *Oedipus*. . . .

As the sequel to what has already been said, we must proceed to consider what the poet should aim at, and what he should avoid, in constructing his plots; and by what means Tragedy may best fulfil its function.

A perfect tragedy should, as we have seen, be arranged not on the simple but on the complex plan. It should, moreover, imitate actions which excite pity and fear, this being the distinctive mark of tragic imitation. It follows plainly, in the first place, that the change of fortune presented must not be the spectacle of a perfectly good man brought from prosperity to adversity: for this moves neither pity nor fear; it simply shocks us. Nor, again, that of a bad man passing from adversity to prosperity: for nothing can be more alien to the spirit of Tragedy; it possesses no single tragic quality; it neither satisfies the moral sense, nor calls forth pity or fear. Nor, again, should the downfall of the utter villain be exhibited. A plot of this kind would, doubtless, satisfy the moral sense, but it would inspire neither pity nor fear; for pity is aroused by unmerited misfortune, fear by the misfortune of a man like ourselves. Such an event, therefore, will be neither pitiful nor terrible. There remains, then, the character between these two extremes—that of a man who is not eminently good and just, yet whose misfortune is brought about not by vice or depravity, but by some error or frailty. He must be one who is highly renowned and prosperous—a personage like Oedipus, Thyestes, or other illustrious men of such families.

---

4. defined in the following paragraph. 6. Oedipus'.
5. Messenger 1.

A well constructed plot should, therefore, be single, rather than double as some maintain. The change of fortune should be not from bad to good, but, reversely, from good to bad. It should come about as the result not of vice, but of some great error or frailty, in a character either such as we have described, or better rather than worse. The practice of the stage bears out our view. At first the poets recounted any legends that came in their way. Now, tragedies are founded on the story of a few houses—on the fortunes of Alcmaeon, Oedipus, Orestes, Meleager, Thyestes, Telephus, and those others who have done or suffered something terrible. A tragedy, then, to be perfect according to the rules of art should be of this construction. Hence they are in error who censure Euripides just because he follows this principle in his plays, many of which end unhappily. It is, as we have said, the right ending. The best proof is that on the stage and in dramatic competition, such plays, if they are well represented, are most tragic in their effect; and Euripides, faulty as he is in the general management of his subject, yet is felt to be the most tragic of poets. . . .

As in the structure of the plot, so too in the portraiture of character, the poet should always aim either at the necessary or the probable. Thus a person of a given character should speak or act in a given way, by the rule either of necessity or of probability; just as this event should follow that by necessary or probable sequence. It is therefore evident that the unravelling of the plot, no less than the complication, must be brought about by the plot itself, and not by Machinery[7]—as in the *Medea*, or in the Return of the Greeks[8] in the *Iliad*. Machinery should be employed only for events external to the drama—either such as are previous to it and outside the sphere of human knowledge, or subsequent to it and which need to be foretold and announced; for to the gods we ascribe the power of seeing all things. Within the action there must be nothing irrational. If the irrational cannot be excluded, it should be outside the scope of the tragedy. Such is the irrational element in the *Oedipus* of Sophocles. . . .

The Chorus too should be regarded as one of the actors; it should be an integral part of the whole, and share in the action, in the manner not of Euripides but of Sophocles. As for the later poets, their choral songs pertain as little to the subject of the piece as to that of any other tragedy. They are, therefore, sung as mere inter-

7. literally the machine which was employed in the theater to show the gods flying in space. It has come to mean any implausible way of solving the complications of the plot. Medea escapes from Corinth "on the machine" in her magic chariot.

8. Aristotle refers to an incident in the second book of the *Iliad*; an attempt of the Greek rank and file to return home and abandon the siege is arrested by the intervention of Athene. (If it were a drama she would appear "on the machine.")

ludes—a practice first begun by Agathon. Yet what difference is there between introducing such choral interludes, and transferring a speech, or even a whole act, from one play to another? . . .

LUCRETIUS
(99?–55 B.C.)
On the Nature of Things (De rerum natura)

[Against the Fear of Death]*

What has this bugbear death to frighten man,
If souls can die, as well as bodies can?
For, as before our birth we felt no pain,
When Punic arms infested land and main,
When heav'n and earth were in confusion hurl'd,   5
For the debated empire of the world,
Which aw'd with dreadful expectation lay,
Sure to be slaves, uncertain who should sway:
So, when our mortal frame shall be disjoin'd,
The lifeless lump uncoupled from the mind,   10
From sense of grief and pain we shall be free;
We shall not feel, because we shall not *be*.
Tho' earth in seas, and seas in heav'n were lost,
We should not move, we only should be toss'd.
Nay, ev'n suppose when we have suffer'd fate,   15
The soul could feel in her divided state,
What's that to us? for we are only we
While souls and bodies in one frame agree.
Nay, tho' our atoms should revolve by chance,
And matter leap into the former dance;   20
Tho' time our life and motion could restore,
And make our bodies what they were before,
What gain to us would all this bustle bring?
The new-made man would be another thing.
When once an interrupting pause is made,   25
That individual being is decay'd.
We, who are dead and gone, shall bear no part
In all the pleasures, nor shall feel the smart
Which to that other mortal shall accrue,
Whom of our matter time shall mold anew.   30
For backward if you look on that long space

---

* From Book III. Translated by John Dryden.

4. *Punic . . . main:* the Second Punic War (218–201 B.C.). In this decisive struggle for the domination of the western Mediterranean, the Carthaginian (Punic) general Hannibal invaded Italy and came close to taking Rome. Lucretius is writing some hundred and fifty years after these events.

Of ages past, and view the changing face
Of matter, toss'd and variously combin'd
In sundry shapes, 't is easy for the mind
From thence t' infer, that seeds of things have **been**   35
In the same order as they now are seen:
Which yet our dark remembrance cannot trace,
Because a pause of life, a gaping space,
Has come betwixt, where memory lies dead,
And all the wand'ring motions from the sense are fled.   40
For whosoe'er shall in misfortunes live,
Must *be*, when those misfortunes shall arrive;
And since the man who *is* not, feels not woe,
(For death exempts him, and wards off the blow,
Which we, the living, only feel and bear,)   45
What is there left for us in death to fear?
When once that pause of life has come between,
'T is just the same as we had never been.
   And therefore if a man bemoan his lot,
That after death his mold'ring limbs shall rot,   50
Or flames, or jaws of beasts devour his mass,
Know, he's an unsincere, unthinking ass.
A secret sting remains within his mind;
The fool is to his own cast offals kind.
He boasts no sense can after death remain, ⎫   55
Yet makes himself a part of life again, ⎬
As if some other He could feel the pain. ⎭
If, while he live, this thought molest his head,
What wolf or vulture shall devour me dead?
He wastes his days in idle grief, nor can   60
Distinguish 'twixt the body and the man;
But thinks himself can still himself survive;
And, what when dead he feels not, feels alive.
Then he repines that he was born to die,
Nor knows in death there is no other He,   65
No living He remains his grief to vent,
And o'er his senseless carcass to lament.
If after death 't is painful to be torn
By birds, and beasts, then why not so to burn;
Or, drench'd in floods of honey, to be soak'd;   70
Imbalm'd, to be at once preserv'd and chok'd;
Or on an airy mountain's top to lie,
Expos'd to cold and heav'n's inclemency;
Or crowded in a tomb to be oppress'd

---

35. *seeds of things:* atoms.
51. *flames:* Cremation was the normal method of disposition of dead bodies.
70. *honey:* used in an expensive type of embalming.

With monumental marble on thy breast?   75
   But to be snatch'd from all thy houshold joys,
From thy chaste wife, and thy dear prattling boys,
Whose little arms about thy legs are cast,
And climbing for a kiss prevent their mother's haste,
Inspiring secret pleasure thro' thy breast—   80
All these shall be no more: thy friends oppress'd
Thy care and courage now no more shall free;
"Ah! wretch!" thou cry'st, "ah! miserable me!
One woful day sweeps children, friends, and wife,
And all the brittle blessings of my life!"   85
Add one thing more, and all thou say'st is true;
Thy want and wish of them is vanish'd too:
Which, well consider'd, were a quick relief
To all thy vain imaginary grief.
For thou shalt sleep, and never wake again,   90
And, quitting life, shalt quit thy living pain.
But we, thy friends, shall all those sorrows find,
Which in forgetful death thou leav'st behind;
No time shall dry our tears, nor drive thee from our mind.
The worst that can befall thee, measur'd right,   95
Is a sound slumber, and a long good-night.
   Yet thus the fools, that would be thought the wits,
Disturb their mirth with melancholy fits:
When healths go round, and kindly brimmers flow,
Till the fresh garlands on their foreheads glow,   100
They whine, and cry: "Let us make haste to live.
Short are the joys that human life can give."
Eternal preachers, that corrupt the draught,
And pall the god, that never thinks, with thought;
Idiots with all that thought, to whom the worst   105
Of death is want of drink, and endless thirst,
Or any fond desire as vain as these.
For ev'n in sleep, the body, wrapp'd in ease,
Supinely lies, as in the peaceful grave;
And, wanting nothing, nothing can it crave.   110
Were that sound sleep eternal, it were death;
Yet the first atoms then, the seeds of breath,
Are moving near to sense; we do but shake
And rouse that sense, and straight we are awake.
Then death to us, and death's anxiety,   115
Is less than nothing, if a less could be.

---

79. *prevent:* anticipate.
99. *brimmers:* full cups (of wine).
104. *the god, that never thinks:* Bacchus.
113. *moving near to sense:* The only difference between sleep and death is that in sleep the atoms of which we are composed are still in ordered motion and combination, while in death they are scattered; in neither state are we conscious.

For then our atoms, which in order lay,
Are scatter'd from their heap, and puff'd away,
And never can return into their place,
When once the pause of life has left an empty space.   120
    And last, suppose great Nature's voice should call
To thee, or me, or any of us all:
"What dost thou mean, ungrateful wretch, thou vain,
Thou mortal thing, thus idly to complain,
And sigh and sob that thou shalt be no more?   125
For if thy life were pleasant heretofore,
If all the bounteous blessings, I could give, ⎫
Thou hast enjoy'd; if thou hast known to live, ⎬
And pleasure not leak'd thro' thee like a sieve; ⎭
Why dost thou not give thanks as at a plenteous feast,   130
Cramm'd to the throat with life, and rise and take thy rest?
But if my blessings thou hast thrown away,
If indigested joys pass'd thro', and would not stay,
Why dost thou wish for more to squander still?
If life be grown a load, a real ill,   135
And I would all thy cares and labors end,
Lay down thy burden, fool, and know thy friend.

To please thee, I have emptied all my store; ⎫
I can invent and can supply no more, ⎬
But run the round again, the round I ran before. ⎭   140
Suppose thou art not broken yet with years,
Yet still the selfsame scene of things appears,
And would be ever, couldst thou ever live;
For life is still but life, there's nothing new to give."
What can we plead against so just a bill?   145
We stand convicted, and our cause goes ill.
    But if a wretch, a man oppress'd by fate,
Should beg of Nature to prolong his date,
She speaks aloud to him with more disdain:
"Be still, thou martyr fool, thou covetous of pain."   150
But if an old decrepit sot lament;
"What, thou," she cries, "who hast outliv'd content!
Dost thou complain, who hast enjoy'd my store?
But this is still th' effect of wishing more.
Unsatisfied with all that Nature brings;   155
Loathing the present, liking absent things;
From hence it comes, thy vain desires, at strife
Within themselves, have tantaliz'd thy life;
And ghastly death appear'd before thy sight,
Ere thou hadst gorg'd thy soul and senses with delight.   160
Now leave those joys, unsuiting to thy age,
To a fresh comer, and resign the stage."

Is Nature to be blam'd if thus she chide?
No, sure; for 't is her business to provide,
Against this ever-changing frame's decay,
New things to come, and old to pass away.   165
One being, worn, another being makes;
Chang'd, but not lost; for Nature gives and takes:
New matter must be found for things to come,
And these must waste like those, and follow Nature's doom.   170
All things, like thee, have time to rise and rot;
And from each other's ruin are begot:
For life is not confin'd to him or thee;
'T is given to all for use, to none for property.

Consider former ages past and gone,   175
Whose circles ended long ere thine begun,
Then tell me, fool, what part in them thou hast.
Thus may'st thou judge the future by the past.
What horror see'st thou in that quiet state?
What bugbear dreams to fright thee after fate?   180
No ghost, no goblins, that still passage keep;
But all is there serene, in that eternal sleep.

For all the dismal tales that poets tell
Are verified on earth, and not in hell.
No Tantalus looks up with fearful eye,   185
Or dreads th' impending rock to crush him from on high;
But fear of chance on earth disturbs our easy hours,
Or vain imagin'd wrath of vain imagin'd pow'rs.
No Tityus torn by vultures lies in hell;   ⎫
Nor could the lobes of his rank liver swell   ⎬   190
To that prodigious mass for their eternal meal: ⎭
Not tho' his monstrous bulk had cover'd o'er   ⎫
Nine spreading acres, or nine thousand more;   ⎬
Not tho' the globe of earth had been the giant's floor: ⎭
Nor in eternal torments could he lie,   195
Nor could his corpse sufficient food supply.
But he 's the Tityus, who by love oppress'd,   ⎫
Or tyrant passion preying on his breast,   ⎬
And ever-anxious thoughts, is robb'd of rest.   ⎭
The Sisyphus is he, whom noise and strife   200

184. *on earth, and not in hell:* in the following lines Lucretius interprets the fabled punishments of great evildoers in hell as allegories of the woes of this life.

185. *Tantalus:* He was confined beneath an overhanging rock which every minute seemed about to fall.

189. *Tityus:* a giant who was punished for his attempted rape of Artemis by a pair of vultures' tearing perpetually at his liver. His body was supposed to cover nine acres.

200. *Sisyphus:* condemned to roll a huge rock to the top of a hill; every time he reached the summit the rock rolled back down again.

Seduce from all the soft retreats of life,
To vex the government, disturb the laws:
Drunk with the fumes of popular applause,
He courts the giddy crowd to make him great,
And sweats and toils in vain, to mount the sovereign seat.   205
For still to aim at pow'r, and still to fail,
Ever to strive, and never to prevail,
What is it, but, in reason's true account,
To heave the stone against the rising mount?
Which urg'd, and labor'd, and forc'd up with pain,   210
Recoils, and rolls impetuous down, and smokes along the plain.
Then still to treat thy ever-craving mind
With ev'ry blessing, and of ev'ry kind,
Yet never fill thy rav'ning appetite;
Tho' years and seasons vary thy delight,   215
Yet nothing to be seen of all the store,
But still the wolf within thee barks for more;
This is the fable's moral, which they tell
Of fifty foolish virgins damn'd in hell
To leaky vessels, which the liquor spill;   220
To vessels of their sex, which none could ever fill.
As for the Dog, the Furies, and their snakes,
The gloomy caverns, and the burning lakes,
And all the vain infernal trumpery,
They neither are, nor were, nor e'er can be.   225
But here on earth the guilty have in view
The mighty pains to mighty mischiefs due;
Racks, prisons, poisons, the Tarpeian rock,
Stripes, hangmen, pitch, and suffocating smoke;
And last, and most, if these were cast behind,   230
Th' avenging horror of a conscious mind,
Whose deadly fear anticipates the blow,
And sees no end of punishment and woe;
But looks for more, at the last gasp of breath:
This makes a hell on earth, and life a death.   235
     Meantime, when thoughts of death disturb thy head;
Consider, Ancus, great and good, is dead;
Ancus, thy better far, was born to die;
And thou, dost thou bewail mortality?
So many monarchs with their mighty state,   240

211. *smokes:* races.
219. *fifty foolish virgins:* the fifty daughters of Danaus, who murdered their husbands. They were condemned to carry water in a sieve.

222. *Dog:* Cerberus, the dog which guarded the gates of hell.
228. *Tarpeian rock:* a cliff at Rome from which traitors were hurled.
237. *Ancus:* the fourth of the legendary kings of Rome.

Who rul'd the world, were overrul'd by fate.
That haughty king, who lorded o'er the main,
And whose stupendous bridge did the wild waves restrain,
(In vain they foam'd, in vain they threaten'd wreck,
While his proud legions march'd upon their back,)   245
Him death, a greater monarch, overcame;
Nor spar'd his guards the more, for their immortal name.
The Roman chief, the Carthaginian dread, ⎫
Scipio, the thunderbolt of war, is dead, ⎬
And, like a common slave, by fate in triumph led. ⎭   250
The founders of invented arts are lost;
And wits, who made eternity their boast.
Where now is Homer, who possess'd the throne?
Th' immortal work remains, the mortal author's gone.
Democritus, perceiving age invade,   255
His body weaken'd, and his mind decay'd,
Obey'd the summons with a cheerful face;
Made haste to welcome death, and met him half the race.
That stroke ev'n Epicurus could not bar, ⎫
Tho' he in wit surpass'd mankind, as far ⎬   260
As does the midday sun the midnight star. ⎭
And thou, dost thou disdain to yield thy breath,
Whose very life is little more than death?
More than one half by lazy sleep possess'd; ⎫
And when awake, thy soul but nods at best, ⎬   265
Day-dreams and sickly thoughts revolving in thy breast. ⎭
Eternal troubles haunt thy anxious mind,
Whose cause and cure thou never hop'st to find;
But still uncertain, with thyself at strife,
Thou wander'st in the labyrinth of life.   270

O, if the foolish race of man, who find
A weight of cares still pressing on their mind,
Could find as well the cause of this unrest,
And all this burden lodg'd within the breast;
Sure they would change their course, nor live as now,   275
Uncertain what to wish or what to vow.

---

243. *stupendous bridge:* The reference is to the bridge over the Hellespont built by Xerxes, king of Persia,
for his invasion of Greece in 480 B.C.
249. *Scipio:* the Roman general who
defeated Hannibal at Zama in 202 B.C.
255. *Democritus:* a Greek philosopher; one of the pioneers of the
atomic theory on which the doctrines
of Epicurus (and Lucretius) were
based. According to tradition he starved
himself to death when he was over
ninety years old.

259. *Epicurus:* Greek philosopher
(342–270 B.C.) whose philosophy is
presented in Lucretius' poem. Basing
himself on the atomic theories of his
predecessors, he put forward a materialistic scheme of the universe and stated
that the gods, if they exist, have no
concern for human life. He recommended the pursuit of happiness, which
he defined as the peace of mind which
comes from the cultivation of virtue.
273. *Could . . . unrest:* through the
study of the Epicurean system. See ll.
294 ff.

Uneasy both in country and in town,
They search a place to lay their burden down.
One, restless in his palace, walks abroad,
And vainly thinks to leave behind the load;   280
But straight returns, for he's as restless there,
And finds there's no relief in open air.
Another to his villa would retire,
And spurs as hard as if it were on fire;
No sooner enter'd at his country door,   285
But he begins to stretch, and yawn, and snore;
Or seeks the city which he left before.
Thus every man o'erworks his weary will,
To shun himself, and to shake off his ill;
The shaking fit returns, and hangs upon him still.   290
No prospect of repose, nor hope of ease;
The wretch is ignorant of his disease;
Which known would all his fruitless trouble spare,
For he would know the world not worth his care;
Then would he search more deeply for the cause;   295
And study nature well, and nature's laws:
For in this moment lies not the debate,
But on our future, fix'd, eternal state;
That never-changing state, which all must keep,
Whom death has doom'd to everlasting sleep.   300
    Why are we then so fond of mortal life,
Beset with dangers, and maintain'd with strife?
A life which all our care can never save;
One fate attends us, and one common grave.
Besides, we tread but a perpetual round;   305
We ne'er strike out, but beat the former ground,
And the same mawkish joys in the same track are found.
For still we think an absent blessing best,
Which cloys, and is no blessing when possess'd;
A new arising wish expels it from the breast.   310
The fev'rish thirst of life increases still;
We call for more and more, and never have our fill,
Yet know not what to-morrow we shall try,
What dregs of life in the last draught may lie:
Nor, by the longest life we can attain,   315
One moment from the length of death we gain;
For all behind belongs to his eternal reign.
When once the Fates have cut the mortal thread,
The man as much to all intents is dead,
Who dies to-day, and will as long be so,   320
As he who died a thousand years ago.

CICERO

(106–43 B.C.)

On the Republic (De republica)*

The Dream of Scipio

On landing in Africa [1]—I had gone there, as you both know, as a military tribune[2] in the Fourth Legion for the consul Manius Manilius[3]—there was nothing that I wanted so much as to meet King Masinissa,[4] who for the best of reasons[5] was a great friend of our family. When I came to his house the old man burst into tears as he embraced me and then lifting his eyes to heaven cried: "Thanks give I to thee, O Sun supreme, and to you, ye other dwellers in the skies, that before I take my leave of this life I see in my kingdom and under my own roof P. Cornelius Scipio whose very name refreshes me; for never from my heart has faded the memory of that great and unconquerable hero!"[6] Then, we spent the whole day in conversing together—I asking him about his kingdom and he questioning me in turn about our country.

And later, after we had dined amidst regal state we prolonged our talk until far into the night. The old man would talk about nothing except of Africanus and remembered not only all that he had done but all as well that he had said. Then, when we had parted to take our rest a sleep much deeper than was usual fell upon me, for I was weary from my journey and had stayed awake until very late. And then—(I suppose it was a result of what we had been talking about; for it happens often that the things that we have been thinking and speaking of bring about something in our sleep. So Ennius[7] relates in his dream about Homer, of whom in hours of wakefulness he used so often to think and speak)—Africanus stood there before me, in figure familiar to me from his bust[8] rather than from life. I shuddered with dread as I recognized

* Written from 54 B.C. on; published before 51 B.C. Our selection is the principal surviving fragment of this work. This translation by H. A. Rice is here first published.

1. The speaker is Publius Cornelius Scipio Africanus the Younger, the Roman general who led the legions to victory in the Third Punic War (149–146 B.C.), which resulted in the final subjugation of Rome's rival in the West, Carthage. He is supposed to be speaking at a conversation which took place twenty years later; he tells the story of what happened to him in the first year of the war which made his name, when he was an undistinguished junior officer.

2. officer on the staff of a legion.

3. The consuls were the two chief magistrates at home, and commanders of the armies in the field. Scipio was later to replace Manius Manilius as commander.

4. king of Numidia; he became a trusted ally of the Romans in the Second Punic War (218–201 B.C.). He was a close friend of the first Scipio Africanus, who had adopted as his grandson the Scipio who tells this story.

5. among others because the elder Scipio had enlarged his dominions.

6. the elder Scipio.

7. Roman epic poet (239–169 B.C.) who began his epic of Roman history with an account of Homer's appearance to him in a dream.

8. The Roman aristocrat displayed

him but he said, "Be calm, Scipio, and have no fear, but fail not to remember the things that I shall tell.

"Do you see that city[9] which by me was forced to kneel before the Roman people and is now renewing battle as of old and will not rest in peace?" And from a place high up above, studded with stars and blazing with light, he pointed to Carthage far below. "To the siege of that city you are now marching, a soldier almost in the ranks. Two years from now you will destroy it as consul in command, and will win thereby a surname which hitherto you have held as a legacy from me.[10] And then, after you have blotted out Carthage, celebrated your triumph and become censor[11] and gone as legate[12] to Egypt, Syria, Asia and Greece, you will be chosen, while absent,[13] consul for the second time, complete a mighty war and destroy Numantia.[14] But just when you have been driven in triumph up to the Capitol, you will find the state in turmoil through the schemings of a grandson of mine.[15]

"It is here, Africanus, that you must needs show to our country the lustre of your genius, your capacity and your wisdom. But at that hour, I foresee, the path of your destiny divides. For when the years of your life have completed seven times eight circlings of the sun and those two numbers, each for a different reason, held to be perfect,[16] have fulfilled the sum allotted for you in the revolving ordained by fate, then the whole state will turn to you alone and to the name you bear. To you will turn the eyes of the senate, of all good citizens, allies and Latins, and you will be the man on whom alone the salvation of the state will depend. In a word, it will be your duty to bring back order in the state as dictator[17]— if only you escape the impious hands of your own kinsmen."[18] A cry burst from Laelius at this and deep groans from the others,[19] but Scipio, gently smiling, continued, "Hush, I beg of you! Do not rouse me from my sleep. Listen a while and hear the rest."

the busts of his ancestors in his house.

9. Carthage.

10. Hitherto he has been called Africanus in virtue of his adoption by the elder Scipio; after the capture of Carthage he will deserve the name by his own deeds.

11. the magistrate in charge of the senatorial rolls, who passed judgment on the senators' moral and financial fitness to continue in office.

12. ambassador.

13. He would be elected to the office without campaigning for it.

14. in Spain; it was destroyed in 133 B.C.

15. the agrarian reformer Tiberius Gracchus, son of Africanus' daughter Cornelia. His land law (enacted in 133 B.C.) restricted the holdings of the wealthy families and provided for the resettlement of small landholders. His

law marked the beginning of the century of internal struggle which was to end in the establishment of authoritarian power at Rome. Scipio is here made to speak of him from a conservative standpoint, which is in character, and was Cicero's own standpoint too.

16. Both these numbers were regarded as especially important in various mystical and philosophical systems. Scipio is fifty-six years old at the imagined time of the dialogue.

17. a temporary constitutional office; in times of crisis the Senate appointed a dictator for a specific term.

18. Scipio died in 129 B.C. while trying to bring about a compromise between the two parties; there was a rumor that his death was the work of the partisans of Gracchus.

19. the audience to whom Scipio is talking.

"But hold fast to this, Africanus, that you may be more eager to defend the state: For all those who have guarded, aided, and increased the welfare of their fatherland there is a place reserved in heaven, where they shall dwell in happiness forever. For to that all-ruling God whose power is over all that is there is nothing that is done on earth more acceptable than those meetings for conference of men joined together by the bond of law which are called states. Those who guide and preserve these have come from this heaven and to it they return."

At this, though I was filled with fear more at the thought of treachery from my own kin than by dread of death, I asked whether he and my father Paulus[20] and the others whom we deem to be dead were really living. "In all truth," said he, "they live, for they have made their escape from the fetters of the body as though out of a prison: it is that life of yours—you call it life—that is really death. Do you not see yonder your father Paulus coming to greet you?" When I saw him, I wept a flood of tears, but he embracing and kissing me bade me not to weep.

As soon as I could overcome my weeping and was able to speak I cried, "Tell me, best and most saintly of fathers, since here is life, as I hear Africanus say, why should I linger longer on earth? Why should I not make haste to join you here?" "That may not be," he replied, "for until that God, whose dominion is all that you can see, shall free you from the prison-house of the body, there can be for you no entrance here. For to men life has been given for this purpose, that they shall be care-takers of that sphere called the earth, which you see in the centre of this abode of the divine, and to them a soul has been given out of those never-dying fires which you call planets and stars, which, perfect in their form as spheres, are informed by souls divine and, in their orbits ordained, complete their courses with a motion marvellous in its swiftness. Therefore you, O Publius, and all good men must keep that soul in the guardianship of the body and must not seek to set forth from the life of men save at the bidding of him by whom it was entrusted to you, lest you be found to have fled from the trust imposed upon man by God.

"Rather do you, O Scipio, do as your grandfather here and as I who begat you have done: cherish righteousness and that loyalty, so greatly due to parents and kinsmen but most of all to one's fatherland. That is the life that is the road to the sky overhead and to this gathering of those whose life on earth has been lived. There are they who, lightened of the body's burden, now dwell in that place which you see yonder (it was a circle of light shining out with a radiant glory among the other fires) which you of earth call by a term learned from the Greeks, the Milky Way."

20. Scipio's father won a decisive victory at Pydna, in Greece, in 168 B.C.

To me, as I surveyed from that point all that I could see, wondrous and glorious was the sight. There were those stars that we never see from the earth, all larger than we have ever imagined, of these the smallest was one farthest from heaven[21] and nearest to the earth, shining with a reflected light. Much larger than the earth were these starry spheres: to me the earth seemed so small in comparison that I felt ashamed of our empire which includes but a single point on its surface.

As I gazed more and more intently upon the earth, Africanus said, "Tell me, how long will your mind devote itself to the earth below? Do you not see into what lofty heights you have come? Before you are the nine circles or rather spheres which bind together all that is. Of these the outermost is that of the heavens, enclosing all the rest—the God supreme guarding and embracing all the other spheres; within it are included the stars in their courses, revolving without ceasing. Beneath it are the seven other spheres whirling in their course opposite to that of the heaven. Of these one is that which among men is called Saturn. Next comes that radiance so helpful and healthful to mankind that men call Jupiter. Beneath this, red and fearful to mankind, is the star that you call Mars. Next below, almost midway between heaven and earth, is the sun, the leader, chief and ruler of the other lights, the soul of the universe and its controlling power, of such greatness of size that he fills all things and floods them with his light. In his train as companions are the orbits of Venus and Mercury, and in the lowest of the spheres the moon revolves, lighted by the rays of the sun. But below this there is nothing that is not impermanent and doomed to die save only the souls bestowed by nature's gift on the race of men, while above all things are imperishable. For that central sphere the earth, which is the ninth, is motionless and of all things the lowest, and toward it all bodies tend because of their weight."

As I gazed with awe at these marvellous things I said as soon as I could recover from my amazement, "But what is that wondrous sound, so loud and sweet, that fills my ears?"

"That," said he, "is that harmony of the spheres, produced by the sweep of their onward motion, with the intervals between them unequal but composed, by the blending of notes high with low in exact proportion, to produce various harmonies. For not in silence can such mighty motions speed on their way, and it is nature's will that the lowest spheres sound forth in heaviest tones and those above in highest. So that this uppermost sphere of the heavens bearing the stars, since it revolves at greater speed, moves apace with notes of highest pitch, while that one of the moon, the lowest, gives out the lowest tones; for the earth, ninth of the spheres, re-

21. the moon.

mains without motion in its fixed place in the centre of the universe. But the other eight spheres, two of which move at the same rate,[22] send out seven different sounds,—that number which is the key of almost everything. It is this harmony that inspired men have reproduced both on strings and in songs and thus have won a return to this place, as have those others who during their life on earth have devoted outstanding gifts to the pursuit of things divine. To this music our human ears, though filled with it, have become deaf—for there is no duller sense in man than that of hearing. So it is that where the Nile falls headlong from those lofty mountains at the place called the Cataracts, the race of men that lives nearby has, because of the loudness of the sound, lost its power of hearing. So this sound so glorious, made by the revolving at the highest speed of the whole universe, cannot be heard by human ears, just as you cannot look directly at the sun, since your sight is blinded by its radiance."

Though I marvelled at these things, I yet kept turning my eyes again and again back to the earth.

Then Africanus continued: "You are still, I see, fixing your eyes upon the abode and the home of men. If it seems a small thing, as it is, to you, keep rather your eyes upon these things of the heavens, scorning those of mankind. For what glory can you gain from what men say, what fame worth striving for? The earth, as you can see, is inhabited in but scattered parts and these small, while between those spots, as it were, where men dwell, stretch vast desert places. Those who inhabit the earth are from each other so widely apart that no word can spread from one group to another, for some live in parts slantwise,[23] others crosswise,[24] and some even opposite[25] to you; from these surely there is no glory that you can hope to have.

"You can see besides, that the earth is girdled and encircled by zones of a sort, of which the two that are farthest apart, supported by the opposite poles of the sky, are both held fast in bonds of ice, while that middle and widest one is scorched by the blazing heat of the sun. Two of the zones are fit for habitation; of these the southern, where men dwell whose footprints press against yours, has no concern for you; while if you consider this northern one inhabited by you, see how small a part of it belongs to you. For that whole stretch of earth which you hold, narrow from north to south and wider from east to west, is in fact only a small island surrounded by that sea which you call the Atlantic, the Great Sea, or the Ocean. See how small it is, in spite of its lordly name. Do you suppose that your name or that of anyone of our people has ever passed from

22. Mercury and Venus.
23. in the opposite (southern) temperate zone of the same hemisphere.

24. in the same (northern) temperate zone of the opposite hemisphere.
25. in the opposite temperate zone of the opposite hemisphere.

those lands that are cultivated and known to us and scaled the Caucasus which you see there, or crossed beyond the Ganges? Who among those who dwell in those remote lands of the rising or the setting sun, or of the farthest north or south will ever hear your name? With these left out you see, surely, within what narrow limits the fame for which you long can spread. And how long will even those who now speak about you continue to do so?

"Why, even if generations yet to be should want to pass on to those yet unborn the praises of anyone of us received from their fathers, still, because of the floods and conflagrations that are bound at certain intervals to happen on the earth, we could not count upon a long-lasting fame among men, much less an endless one. Yet how much does it concern you to be spoken of by those who come after you when you have never been mentioned by those who have lived before you?

"Indeed they were not fewer than the men of now and surely were better; especially since not one of those by whom our names can now be heard will, after a year has passed, have any memory of it. For men generally reckon a year by the circling of only one of the stars, that is, the sun: but when all the stars have come back to the point where they started and have, at long intervals, restored the same arrangement of the whole heavens, then comes about that which can truly be called a completed year.[26] How many generations of men are included in such a year I would not venture to say. For as the sun seemed to men to fail of its light and to be eclipsed at the hour when the soul of Romulus[27] made its way to these shining heights, so when the sun shall again be eclipsed at the same point and the same hour, then, since all the planets and stars will have returned to their starting point you can be assured that such a year has been completed. But you may be sure that one twentieth[28] of such a year has not yet passed.

"If, therefore, you despair of a return to this place where all belongs to great and noble men, of what worth, I ask you, is that fame of yours among men? It can hardly extend to the smallest part of a single year. So if you will but fix your gaze on things on high and on this eternal home and dwelling-place, you will cease to listen to the talking of the common herd, nor will you longer put your trust in the rewards that men can bestow for what you have done; let rather the charm of virtue itself lead you on to the only true glory; whatever men may say of you leave to them; they will say it anyway, and all that they have to say will be confined within those narrow limits which you see: all that they say about any man has not been

---

26. reckoned by ancient authorities at from twelve thousand to fifteen thousand years.

27. the traditional founder of the city of Rome; the legendary date of his death is 716 B.C.

28. from the death of Romulus to the supposed time of Scipio's dream is 567 years.

for long, for it dies with them and is blotted out by the forgetfulness of those who come after them." As he said this, "If it is true, Africanus," said I, "that for those who have well served their country there lies open a path to heaven here, then, though from my boyhood I have tried to follow in the footsteps of my father and of you and to be worthy of your fame, now indeed with such a reward before my eyes I shall strive with even greater zeal." "Strive on," said he, "and be assured that you are not, though your body is, born but to die; for that form which your body shows is not your true self: the spirit within each man is the man himself—not the bodily form to which one can point. Know then that you are divine, for that is divine which throbs with life, feels, remembers, foresees, which rules, controls, and makes to move the body over which it has been placed in charge; as over this universe rules that supreme God; so this mortal body is made to move by a deathless soul within.

"For that which is ever in motion is eternal, but that which sets in motion something else but is itself moved by a force outside it, must needs, when the cause of its motion ends, cease to live. Only that therefore which gives itself motion ceases not to move, since it never abandons itself: more than that, it is for all other things that move, the first cause and beginning of their motion. Of a first cause there is of course no beginning, for it is from this first cause that all things begin, while it can never take its beginning from anything else; for it would not be a first cause if it found its beginning outside itself. Moreover because it never had a beginning it will never have an end. For if a first cause were destroyed it could never be born again from anything else, nor could it create another thing from itself, since only from a first cause must everything begin to be. So it follows that motion must begin from that which is self-moving: this can neither be born nor die: otherwise all heaven above would fall and all nature cease to be since they are endowed with no power from which they can receive a beginning of motion.

"Since then that which is self-moving is everlasting, who would dare deny that this is the essential nature given to living spirits? For everything that is set in motion by an outside force is without a spirit within it, but that which is animated by spirit is moved by its own power within, for this is the essential property and power of spirit,—which, since it is the only thing among all things that moves itself, cannot have had a beginning nor can it ever have an end. Devote this, then, to the highest tasks! Of these surely the noblest are those on behalf of one's fatherland: a spirit dedicated and devoted to these will swiftly wing its way to this, its own abode and home. And more swiftly will it speed here if, while still prisoned in the body, it soars above it and fixing its gaze on things beyond, it rids itself as much as is in its power from the body. The souls of those, however, who have surrendered to the pleasures of the body as slaves to them and who at the bidding of desires of the body have transgressed the laws of gods and men, when they have left their bodies, flit about the earth below, and do not return to this place until after they have, through many ages, suffered retribution." He left me then, and I awoke from my sleep.

CATULLUS*

(84?–54? B.C.)

1

Come, Lesbia, let us live and love,
nor give a damn what sour old men say.
The sun that sets may rise again
but when our light has sunk into the earth,
it is gone forever.   5
      Give me a thousand kisses,
then a hundred, another thousand,
another hundred
      and in one breath
still kiss another thousand,   10
another hundred.
      O then with lips and bodies joined
many deep thousands;
      confuse
their number,   15
      so that poor fools and cuckolds (envious
even now) shall never
learn our wealth and curse us
with their
evil eyes.   20

2

There are many who think of Quintia in terms of beauty,
but to me she is merely tall and golden white, erect,
and I admit each of these separate distinctions in her favour,
yet I object, deny,
that the word "beauty" describes her person;   5
for she has no charm, not even a grain of salt in her whole body
to give you appetite—
now Lesbia has beauty, she is everything
that's handsome, glorious,
and she has captured all that Venus has to offer   10
in ways of love.

* A selection (fifteen poems out of 116). Translated and copyrighted © by Horace Gregory 1956: reprinted by permission of Grove Press, Inc.

The numbers of the poems in the original text are: 5, 86, 87, 107, 109, 83, 70, 72, 60, 85, 75, 8, 58, 11, 76.]

3

No woman, if she is honest, can say that she's
been blessed with greater love, my Lesbia,
than I have given you;
nor has any man held to a contract made
with more fidelity   5
than I have shown, my dear,
in loving you.

4

When at last after long despair, our hopes ring true again
and long-starved desire eats, O then the mind leaps in the sunlight
     —Lesbia
so it was with me when you returned. Here was a treasure
more valuable than gold; you, whom I love beyond hope, giving
     yourself
to me again. That hour, a year of holidays, radiant,   5
where is the man more fortunate than I,
where can he find anything in life more glorious
than the sight of all his wealth restored?

5

My life, my love, you say our love will last forever;
O gods remember
her pledge, convert the words of her avowal into a prophecy.
Now let her blood speak, let sincerity govern each syllable fallen
from her lips, so that the long years of our lives shall be   5
a contract of true love inviolate
against time itself, a symbol of eternity.

6

Lesbia speaks evil of me with her husband near and he (damned
     idiot) loves to hear her.
Chuckling, the fool is happy, seeing nothing, understanding
     nothing.
If she forgetting me fell silent, her heart would be his alone, con-
     tent and peaceful;
but she raves, spitting hatred upon me, all of which carries this
     meaning:
I am never out of her mind, and what is more, she rises in fury
     against me   5
with words that make her burn, her blood passionate for me.

7

My woman says that she would rather wear the wedding-veil for me
than anyone: even if Jupiter himself came storming after her;
that's what she says, but when a woman talks to a hungry,
ravenous lover, her words should be written upon the wind
and engraved in rapid waters.   5

8

There was a time, O Lesbia, when you said Catullus was the only
     man on earth who could understand you,
who could twine his arms round you, even Jove himself less wel-
     come.

And when I thought of you, my dear, you were not the mere flesh
  and
the means by which a lover finds momentary rapture.
My love was half paternal, as a father greets his son or   5
smiles at his daughter's husband.

Although I know you well (too well), my love now turns to fire
and you are small and shallow.
Is this a miracle? Your wounds in love's own battle
have made me your companion, perhaps, a greater lover,   10
but O, my dear, I'll never be
the modest boy who saw you as a lady, delicate and sweet,
a paragon of virtue.

9

Were you born of a lioness in the Libyan Mountains,
or that half-woman monster, Scylla,
screaming in the lowest chambers of her womb,
sent forth already merciless and hard,
one who could never hear the cries of a man, even in his mortal
  agony,   5
O heart made bitter and cruel beyond all measure.

2. *Scylla:* a sea monster who snatched them. She was woman above the waist
sailors from their ships and devoured and a pack of ravenous hounds below.

10

I hate and love.
   And if you ask me why,
I have no answer, but I discern,
can feel, my senses rooted in eternal torture.

11

You are the cause of this destruction, Lesbia,
that has fallen upon my mind;
this mind that has ruined itself
by fatal constancy.
And now it cannot rise from its own misery   5
to wish that you become
best of women, nor can it fail
to love you even though all is lost and you destroy
all hope.

12

Poor damned Catullus, here's no time for nonsense,
open your eyes, O idiot, innocent boy, look at what has happened:
once there were sunlit days when you followed after
where ever a girl would go, she loved with greater
love than any woman knew.   5
Then you took your pleasure
and the girl was not unwilling. Those were the bright days, gone;
now she's no longer yielding; you must be, poor idiot,
more like a man! not running after
her your mind all tears; stand firm, insensitive.   10
Say with a smile, voice steady, "Good-bye, my girl," Catullus

strong and manly no longer follows you, nor comes when you are
calling
him at night and you shall need him.
You whore! Where's your man to cling to, who will praise your
beauty,
where's the man that you love and who will call you his,   15
and when you fall to kissing, whose lips will you devour?
But always, your Catullus will be as firm as rock is.

13

Caelius, my Lesbia, that one, that only Lesbia,
Lesbia whom Catullus loved more than himself and all things
he ever owned or treasured.
Now her body's given up in alley-ways,
on highroads to these fine Roman gentlemen,   5
fathered centuries ago by the noble Remus.

6. *Remus:* brother of Romulus, founder of Rome.

14

Furius, Aurelius, bound to Catullus
though he marches piercing farthest India
where echoing waves of the Eastern Oceans
          break upon the shores:

Under Caspian seas, to mild Arabia,   5
east of Parthia, dark with savage bowmen,
or where the Nile, sevenfold and uprising,
          stains its leveled sands,—

Even though he marches over Alps to gaze on
great Caesar's monuments: the Gallic Rhine and   10
Britons who live beyond torn seas, remotest
          men of distant lands—

Friends who defy with me all things, whatever
gods may send us, go now, friends, deliver
these words to my lady, nor sweet—flattering,   15
          nor kind nor gentle:

Live well and sleep with adulterous lovers,
three hundred men between your thighs, embracing
all love turned false, again, again, and breaking
          their strength, now sterile.   20

She will not find my love (once hers) returning;
she it was who caused love, this lonely flower,
tossed aside, to fall by the plough dividing
          blossoming meadows.

10. *Caesar's monuments:* Julius Caesar   in 55 B.C. made an expedition to Britain.
began the conquest of Gaul in 58 B.C. and

15

If man can find rich consolation, remembering his good deeds and
          all he has done,
if he remembers his loyalty to others, nor abuses his religion by
          heartless betrayal

of friends to the anger of powerful gods,
then, my Catullus, the long years before you shall not sink in darkness with all hope gone,
wandering, dismayed, through the ruins of love.   5
All the devotion that man gives to man, you have given, Catullus,
your heart and your brain flowed into a love that was desolate,
    wasted, nor can it return.
But why, why do you crucify love and yourself through the years?
Take what the gods have to offer and standing serene, rise forth as a
    rock against darkening skies;
and yet you do nothing but grieve, sunken deep in your sorrow,
    Catullus,   10
for it is hard, hard to throw aside years lived in poisonous love that
    has tainted your brain
and must end.
If this seems impossible now, you must rise
to salvation. O gods of pity and mercy, descend and witness my
    sorrow, if ever
you have looked upon man in his hour of death, see me now in
    despair.   15
Tear this loathsome disease from my brain. Look, a subtle corruption has entered my bones,
no longer shall happiness flow through my veins like a river.
            No longer I pray
that she love me again, that her body be chaste, mine forever.
Cleanse my soul of this sickness of love, give me power to rise, resurrected, to thrust love aside,   20
I have given my heart to the gods, O hear me, omnipotent heaven,
and ease me of love and its pain.

VIRGIL

(70–19 B.C.)

The Aeneid*

Book I

I tell about war and the hero who first from Troy's frontier,
Displaced by destiny, came to the Lavinian shores,
To Italy—a man much travailed on sea and land

* Abridged. Left unfinished when the poet died in 19 B.C. Our text is from *The Aeneid of Virgil,* translated by C. Day Lewis, copyright 1952 by C. Day Lewis, reprinted by permission of Oxford University Press, Inc.
1. *the hero:* Aeneas, one of the Trojan champions in the fight for Troy, son of Aphrodite (Venus) and Anchises, a member of the royal house of Troy. Aeneas survived the fall of the city and set off in search of another home. After years of wandering he settled in Italy, and from his line sprang, in the fullness of time, the founders of Rome.
2. *Lavinian shores:* the west coast of Italy in the vicinity of Rome, named after the nearby city of Lavinium. Lavinia is the name of the Italian princess whom Aeneas is eventually to marry.

By the powers above, because of the brooding anger of Juno,
Suffering much in war until he could found a city   5
And march his gods into Latium, whence rose the Latin race,
The royal line of Alba and the high walls of Rome.
Where lay the cause of it all? How was her godhead injured?
What grievance made the queen of heaven so harry a man
Renowned for piety, through such toils, such a cycle of calamity?   10
Can a divine being be so persevering in anger?
There was a town of old—men from Tyre colonised it—
Over against Italy and Tiber mouth, but afar off,
Carthage, rich in resources, fiercely efficient in warfare.
This town, they say, was Juno's favourite dwelling, preferred   15
To all lands, even Samos: here were her arms, her chariot:
And even from the long-ago time she cherished the aim that this
Should be, if fate allowed, the metropolis of all nations.
Nevertheless, she had heard a future race was forming
Of Trojan blood, which one day would topple that Tyrian strong-
    hold—   20
A people arrogant in war, born to be everywhere rulers
And root up her Libyan empire—so the Destiny-Spinners planned.
Juno, afraid of this, and remembering well the old war
Wherein she had championed the Greeks whom she loved against
    the Trojans—
Besides, she has other reasons for rage, bitter affronts   25
Unblotted as yet from her heart: deep in her mind rankle
The judgment of Paris, the insult of having her beauty scorned,
Her hate for Troy's origin, Ganymede taken and made a favourite—
Furious at these things too, she tossed all over the sea
The Trojans, the few that the Greeks and relentless Achilles had
    left,   30
And rode them off from their goal, Latium. Many years
They were wandering round the seven seas, moved on by destiny.
So massive a task it was to found the Roman race.

[*Aeneas at Carthage*]

[The story opens with a storm, provoked by Juno's agency, which
scatters Aeneas' fleet off Sicily and separates him from his com-

4. *Juno:* the Latin equivalent of
Hera, the ruler of the gods,
Zeus (Jupiter, the "Juppiter" of this
translation). As in the *Iliad*, she is
a bitter enemy of the Trojans.
6. *Latium:* the coastal plain on which
Rome is situated.
7. *Alba:* The city of Alba Longa was
to be founded by Aeneas' son Ascanius,
and from it were to come Romulus and
Remus, the builders of Rome.
14. *Carthage:* founded in North
Africa by the Phoenicians who came
from Tyre and Sidon in Palestine. It
was their chief colony in the western
Mediterranean. In the third and second
centuries B.C. Carthage fought a series
of bitter wars against Rome for the
domination of the area.
16. *Samos:* Greek island in the
Aegean, famous as a center for the
worship of Hera (Juno).
22. *Libyan:* African. *Destiny-Spinners:* the Fates.
27. *judgment of Paris:* Paris, son to
King Priam of Troy, was chosen to
judge which was the most beautiful goddess—Hera, Aphrodite, or Athene. All
three attempted to bribe him, but
Aphrodite's promise, the love of Helen,
prevailed, and he awarded her the prize.
28. *Ganymede:* a beautiful Trojan
boy taken up into heaven by Juppiter.

panions. He lands on the African coast near Carthage. Setting out
with his friend Achates to explore the country, he meets his mother,
Venus, who tells him that the rest of his ships are safe and directs
him to the city just founded by Dido, the queen of Carthage. Venus
surrounds Aeneas and Achates with a mist so that they can see
without being seen.]

Meanwhile the two pressed on apace, where the track pointed.
And now they were climbing a hill whose massive bulk looms over
The city and commands a prospect of soaring towers.   420
Aeneas marvels at great buildings, where once were shanties,
Marvels at city gates and the din of the paved streets.
The Tyrians are busy at work there, some extending the walls,
Manhandling blocks of stone and building the citadel,
Others choosing a site for a house and trenching foundations: 425
Laws are being made, magistrates and a parliament elected:
Here they dig out a harbour basin; here they are laying
Foundations deep for a theatre, and hewing from stone immense
Columns to grace one day a tall proscenium.
So in the youth of summer throughout the flowering land   430
The bees pursue their labours under the sun: they lead
A young brood from the hive, or press the flowing honey
And fill the cells to bursting with a delicious nectar;
Relieve incoming bees of their burden, or closing ranks
Shoo the drones, that work-shy gang, away from the bee-folds. 435
The work goes on like wild-fire, the honey smells of thyme.
"Ah, fortunate you are, whose town is already building!"
Aeneas said, and gazed up at the city's heights.
Then, in his cloak of darkness he went—a miraculous thing—
Into their midst and joined the crowds, but none perceived
him.   440
There was a grove, most genial its shade, at the city centre,
Just where the Carthaginians, after their rough passage,
First dug and found the sign which royal Juno had promised—
The skull of a spirited horse; it was a sign that henceforth
Their nation would thrive in wealth and war throughout the
ages.   445
Dido was building here, in Juno's honour, a huge
Temple, made rich by offerings and the indwelling presence of Juno:
Bronze was its threshold, approached by a flight of steps; the door-
posts
Were braced with bronze, and the door with its grinding hinges
was bronze.
This grove had seen Dido's fear allayed by a chance of renewal   450
For the first time; and here Aeneas first dared to hope for

---

418. *The two:* Aeneas and his companion, Achates.
423. *Tyrians:* Phoenicians, Carthaginians.

444. *skull of a . . . horse:* a sign
that they were to be a warlike race and
inhabit a rich land (one that could
support horses).

Salvation and believe that at last his luck was turning.
For, while he awaited the queen and his eyes roved over the detail
Of that immense façade, amazed by the town's good fortune,
Admiring the skill of the rival craftsmen, the scope of their
    work,   455
He noticed a series of frescoes depicting the Trojan war,
Whose fame had already gone round the world; the sons of Atreus
Were there, and Priam, Achilles too, hostile to both.
Aeneas stood; wept:—

               Oh, Achates, is there anywhere,
Any place left on earth unhaunted by our sorrows?   460
Look!—Priam. Here too we find virtue somehow rewarded,
Tears in the nature of things, hearts touched by human transience.
Then cast off fear; the fame of our deeds will ensure your welfare.
    He spoke, and fed his soul on those insubstantial figures,
Heavily sighing, the large tears rivering down his cheeks.   465
Pictured there, he beheld scenes of the fight round Troy—
Here the Greeks fled with the Trojan warriors hard behind them,
Here fled the Trojans before the chariot of plumed Achilles.
He recognised through his tears, not far away, the snow-white
Tents of Rhesus taken by surprise, while all slept deep,   470
And wrecked with terrible slaughter by Diomed, man of blood,
And Diomed driving away to his camp the fiery horses
Before they could graze the meadows of Troy or drink the Xanthus.
Another scene was of Troilus in flight, his weapons gone
(Unhappy the lad, unequal the fight with Achilles): his horses 475
Are bolting; heels over head he hangs backwards out of the chariot,
Yet gripping the reins; his neck and his hair are being dragged along
Over the ground, and his trailing spearpoint scribbles in the dust.
Meanwhile to the shrine of their goddess, their foe's friend, the
    Trojan women
Are walking to make intercession: their hair is unbound, they
    carry   480
The goddess' ritual robe, they mourn and beat their breasts:
But the goddess keeps her eyes on the ground and regards them not.
Thrice round the walls of Troy Achilles has dragged Hector
And now is demanding a ransom of gold for the lifeless body.
At this point Aeneas uttered a deep groan   485
To see the spoils, the chariot, the actual body of
His friend, and Priam's defenceless hands stretched out to Achilles.
He noticed himself, too, in the forefront of the battle,
Noticed the Aethiopian brigade and the arms of black Memnon;

470. *Rhesus:* king of Thrace, who
came to the help of Troy just before
the end of the war. An oracle proclaimed that if his horses ate Trojan
grass and drank the water of the river
Xanthus, Troy would not fall. Odysseus
and Diomed went into the Trojan lines
at night, killed the king, and stole the
horses.
    474. *Troilus:* a son of Priam.
    479–482. *Meanwhile . . . not:* Com-
pare this scene with the *Iliad*, Book VI,
ll. 297–311.
    489. *Memnon:* king of the Aethio-
pians, who fought on the Trojan side.

Picked out Penthesilea leading the crescent shields of   490
The Amazons and storming through the mêlée like a fire,
Her bare breast thrusting out over the golden girdle,
A warrior queen, a girl who braved heroes in combat.
    Now while Aeneas viewed with wonder all these scenes,
And stood at gaze, rooted in a deep trance of attention,   495
There came in royal state to the temple, a crowd of courtiers
Attending her, queen Dido, most beautiful to see.
As, by the banks of Eurotas or over the Cynthian slopes
Diana foots the dance, and a thousand Oreads following
Weave a constellation around that arrowy one,   500
Who in grace of movement excels all goddesses,
And happiness runs through the still heart of Latona—
So Dido was, even so she went her radiant way
Through the crowds, eager to forward the work and growth of her
    realm.
Now, at the holy doors, under the temple porch,   505
Hedged by the spears of her guard, she throned herself on high;
Gave laws and ordinances, appointed the various tasks
In equitable proportions or else by drawing lots.
Just then, all of a sudden, Aeneas saw approaching
Amid the multitude Antheus, Sergestus, valiant   510
Cloanthus and other Trojans, whom the black hurricane
Had sundered at sea and driven afar to different beaches.
He and Achates together were thrilled through, were dumbfounded
With anxious joy: they eagerly yearned to join hands with their
    friends,
But the mystery of the whole affair disquieted them.   515
So they keep dark, and peering out from their womb of cloud,
Speculate what befell these friends, where their ships are beached,
Why they are here: for spokesmen from each of the ships were
    coming
To sue the queen's favour, and shouting aloud as they neared the
    temple.
    When they had entered and Dido had granted to them an
    audience,   520
The eldest, Ilioneus, began in collected tones:—
    O queen, who, under God, have founded a new city
And curbed the arrogance of proud clans with your justice,
We hapless Trojans, wanderers over a world of seas,
Implore you, stop your people from wickedly burning our ships.   525
God-fearing men we are. Incline your heart to spare us.

---

490. *Penthesilea:* queen of the Amazons, killed by Achilles.
    498. *Eurotas:* a river near Sparta
where Artemis (Diana) was worshiped.
Cynthian: Cynthus is a mountain on
the island of Delos, Diana's birthplace.
    499. *Oreads:* mountain nymphs.

502. *Latona:* mother of Diana.
    510–511. *Antheus . . . Cloanthus:*
Aeneas' captains from whom he had
been parted by the storm.
    516. *womb of cloud:* Aeneas' mother,
Venus, has enfolded Aeneas and Achates
in a cloud, so that they are invisible.

We are not come as pirates to waste your Libyan homes
With the sword, and carry down their plunder to the beaches.
We've no mind for marauding; the conquered lack such effrontery.
There is a place—the Greeks call it Hesperia—   530
An antique land, well warded, possessed of a rich soil:
Oenotrians colonised it; whose heirs, so rumour says now,
Have named it, after their first founder, Italy.
That was our bourne. . . .
But rainy Orion rose, and the sea got up of a sudden: 535
We drove on chartless shoals, the winds wantonly pitched us
Far apart on the deep amid toppling waves and unchannelled
Reefs. A handful of us have drifted to your shores.
What manner of men are these? What land is this that allows them
Such barbarous ways? They bar us even from the sanctuary   540
Of the sands: they threaten, and forbid us to touch the hem of
    their country.
If humankind and mortal arms mean nothing to you,
Think of the gods—they do not forget good deeds and bad.
Aeneas was our king: never was a man more just,
More duteous of heart, more adept in warlike arts, than he.   545
If destiny has preserved him, if still he breathes the air
Of day, and is not sleeping in death's unwelcome shade,
We need not fear; and you should have no cause to regret
That you were prompt to aid us. In Sicily, too, we have towns
And resources, and noble Acestes who comes of Trojan stock.   550
We pray you, let us lay up the vessels the storm shattered,
And shape new oars and timbers for them out of your forests;
So that, if we are meant to get back our friends and our king
And make for Italy, to Italy we may go;
But if that hope is lost—if the Libyan sea has drowned you,   555
Lord Aeneas, and there's no future in Iulus—
We may at least sail back to our last port of call, to Sicily,
Where homes are ready for us, and make Acestes our king.
    Ilioneus stopped speaking. A shout of assent rose from
The Trojans all. . . .   560
Then Dido, with her eyes downcast, addressed them briefly:—
    Trojans, put fear away from your hearts and forget your troubles!
Mine's a hard task, with a young country: that's why I have to
Do such things, to guard my frontiers everywhere.
Who has not heard of Troy and the men of Aeneas—their
    manly   565
Virtues, and all that famous conflagration of war?
We Carthaginians are not so insensitive of heart,
Nor is our city quite so out of the way or benighted.

---

530. *Hesperia:* Italy, literally, "the western country."
532. *Oenotrians:* the original in-

habitants of Italy.
533. *first founder:* Italus.
556. *Iulus:* Ascanius, Aeneas son.

Whether your choice is great Hesperia, land of Saturn,
Or you decide upon Sicily and king Acestes,   570
I will give you an escort there and what provision you need.
Or would you like to share my kingdom, on equal terms?
This city I am building—it's yours: draw up your ships, then;
There shall be no preference, I say, between you and us.

    Oh, if only your king, Aeneas himself, could come here,   575
Fetched by the same storm. Well, I will send couriers abroad
With orders to comb the furthest corners of Libya, in case
He is wandering somewhere, in woods or towns, a castaway.

    Arrested by Dido's words, Aeneas and brave Achates
For some time now had been on fire to slough off their cloak   580
Of darkness. Achates first spoke urgently to Aeneas:—

    Tell me, goddess-born, what idea forms in your mind now.
All is saved, you can see, our fleet and our friends restored to us.
One only is missing, and him we saw drowned in the welter
Before our eyes: all else bears out what your mother told us.   585

    These words were hardly spoken, when in a flash the cloud-cloak
They wore was shredded and purged away into pure air.
Aeneas was standing there in an aura of brilliant light,
Godlike of face and figure: for Venus herself had breathed
Beauty upon his head and the roseate sheen of youth on   590
His manhood and a gallant light into his eyes;
As an artist's hand adds grace to the ivory he works on,
As silver or marble when they're plated with yellow gold.
So then Aeneas addressed the queen, and startling them all
At once began:—

             I am here, before you, the one you look for,   595
Trojan Aeneas, saved from the Libyan sea.
O lady, you alone have pitied the tragic ordeal
Of Troy, and now you offer to share your home and city
With us, the remnant of Troy—men utterly spent by
Every disaster on land and sea, deprived of everything.   600
Dido, we have not the means to repay your goodness, nor have
Any of our kin, wherever they are, scattered over the world.
If angels there be who look after the good, if indeed just dealing
And minds informed with the right mean anything to heaven,
May God reward you as you deserve! What happy age,   605
What great parentage was it gave life to the like of you?
So long as rivers run to the sea, and shadows wheel round
The hollows of the hills, and star-flocks browse in the sky,
Your name, your fame, your glory shall perish not from the land
Wherever I am summoned to go.

---

569. *Saturn:* An old legend connected Italy with Saturn (Cronos), the
father of Juppiter (Zeus). The "age of
Saturn" was the Golden Age.

570. *Acestes:* a Sicilian king; his
mother was a Trojan, and he had
offered Aeneas a home in his dominions.

584. *him we saw drowned:* One ship,
captained by Orontes, was sunk in the
storm in sight of Aeneas.

He spoke: he stretched out   610
His right hand to Ilioneus, his friend, and his left to Serestus,
Then to others, brave Gyas and brave Cloanthus.
    Sidonian Dido, amazed first by the man's appearance
Then by the magnitude of his downfall, thus addressed him:—
    O goddess-born, what doom is pursuing you through so many   615
Hazards? What violent fate casts you on this harsh coast?
Are *you* the famed Aeneas, whom gentle Venus bore
To Trojan Anchises by the waters of Simois?
Indeed I well recollect Teucer coming to Sidon,
An exile from his homeland, and seeking a new kingdom   620
With the help of Belus: at that time Belus, my father, was sacking
Rich Cyprus and holding the island down in subjection to him.
Now from that time I have known about the fall of Troy,
And known your name, Aeneas, and the kings who led the Greeks.
Even their enemy held the Trojans in high esteem   625
And claimed blood kinship with the ancient line of Troy.
So, gentlemen, do not hesitate to come under my roof.
I too have gone through much; like you, have been roughly handled
By fortune; but now at last it has willed me to settle here.
Being acquainted with grief, I am learning to help the unlucky.
    She spoke: she led Aeneas into the royal palace,   631
And ordered a thanksgiving service to be held in the gods' temple.
Besides, she sent to his companions on the shore
Twenty bulls, a hundred head of bristle-backed swine,
A hundred fatted lambs together with their ewes,   635
And the good cheer of the Wine-god.
Within, the palace was being arrayed in all the glitter
Of regal luxury, and a banquet being made ready:
Richly embroidered the hangings of princely purple; a service
Of solid silver on the tables; and golden vessels chased   640
With the legends of family history—a long lineage of glory
Traced through many heroes right from its earliest source. . . .

[At the banquet which Dido gives for Aeneas, he relates, at her
request, the story of the fall of Troy (Book II) and of his wanderings in search of a new home (Book III). Dido, already falling in
love with him before the banquet (through the intervention of
Venus and Juno, who both promote the affair, each for different
reasons), now feels the full force of her passion for Aeneas.]

[Aeneas Abandons Dido]

Book IV

But now for some while the queen had been growing more grievously love-sick,

---

619. *Teucer:* a Greek warrior who
fought at Troy and afterward was
exiled from his home. He founded a
city on the island of Cyprus.

Feeding the wound with her life-blood, the fire biting within her.
Much did she muse on the hero's nobility, and much
On his family's fame. His look, his words had gone to her heart
And lodged there: she could get no peace from love's disquiet.   5
    The morrow's morn had chased from heaven the dewy darkness,
Was carrying the sun's torch far and wide over earth,
When, almost beside herself, she spoke to her sister, her confi-
        dante:—
Anna, sister, why do these nerve-racking dreams haunt me?
This man, this stranger I've welcomed into my house—what of
        him?   10
How gallantly he looks, how powerful in chest and shoulders!
I really do think, and have reason to think, that he is heaven-born.
Mean souls convict themselves by cowardice. Oh, imagine
The fates that have harried him, the fight to a finish he told of!
Were it not that my purpose is fixed irrevocably   15
Never to tie myself in wedlock again to anyone,
Since that first love of mine proved false and let death cheat me;
Had I not taken a loathing for the idea of marriage,
For him, for this one man, I could perhaps have weakened.
Anna, I will confess it, since poor Sychaeus, my husband,   20
Was killed and our home broken up by my brother's murderous act,
This man is the only one who has stirred my senses and sapped
My will. I feel once more the scars of the old flame.
But no, I would rather the earth should open and swallow me
Or the Father of heaven strike me with lightning down to the
        shades—   25
The pale shades and deep night of the Underworld—before
I violate or deny pure widowhood's claim upon me.
He who first wedded me took with him, when he died,
My right to love: let him keep it, there, in the tomb, for ever.
    So Dido spoke, and the rising tears flooded her bosom.   30
Anna replied:—
            You are dearer to me than the light of day.
Must you go on wasting your youth in mourning and solitude,
Never to know the blessings of love, the delight of children?
Do you think that ashes, or ghosts underground, can mind about
        such things?
I know that in Libya, yes, and in Tyre before it, no wooers   35
Could touch your atrophied heart: Iarbas was rejected
And other lords of Africa, the breeding-ground of the great.
Very well: but when love comes, and pleases, why fight against it?
Besides, you should think of the nations whose land you have
        settled in—

---

17. *first love of mine:* Her first husband, Sychaeus, was murdered by Pygmalion, king of Tyre, Dido's brother.
Her husband's ghost warned her in a
dream to leave Tyre and seek a new
home.
    36. *Iarbas:* the most prominent of
Dido's African suitors.

Threatening encirclement are the Gaetuli, indomitable   40
In war, the Numidians (no bridle for them), the unfriendly Syrtes;
On your other frontier, a waterless desert and the far-raging
Barcaei: I need not mention the prospect of Tyrian aggression,
Your brother's menacing attitude.
I hold it was providential indeed, and Juno willed it,   45
That hither the Trojan fleet should have made their way. Oh, sister,
Married to such a man, what a city you'll see, what a kingdom
Established here! With the Trojans as our comrades in arms,
What heights of glory will not we Carthaginians soar to!
Only solicit the gods' favour, perform the due rites,   50
And plying our guest with attentions, spin a web to delay him,
While out at sea the winter runs wild and Orion is stormy,
While his ships are in bad repair, while the weather is unacquies-
   cent.

   These words blew to a blaze the spark of love in the queen's heart,
Set hope to her wavering will and melted her modesty's rigour.   55
So first they went to the shrines, beseeching at every altar
For grace: as religion requires, they sacrificed chosen sheep to
Ceres, giver of increase, to Phoebus, and to the Wine-god;
To Juno, chief of all, for the marriage-bond is her business.
Dido herself, most beautiful, chalice in hand, would pour   60
Libations between the horns of a milk-white heifer, and slowly
Would pace by the dripping altars, with the gods looking on,
And daily renew her sacrifice, poring over the victims'
Opened bodies to see what their pulsing entrails signified.
Ah, little the soothsayers know! What value have vows or
   shrines   65
For a woman wild with passion, the while love's flame eats into
Her gentle flesh and love's wound works silently in her breast?
So burns the ill-starred Dido, wandering at large through the town
In a rage of desire, like a doe pierced by an arrow—a doe which
Some hunting shepherd has hit with a long shot while unwary   70
She stepped through the Cretan woods, and all unknowing has left
   his
Winged weapon within her: the doe runs fleetly around the Dictaean
Woods and clearings, the deathly shaft stuck deep in her flank.

---

40. *Gaetuli:* a savage African people living southwest of Carthage.

41. *Numidian:* the most powerful of the local tribes. *Syrtes:* on the coast to the west.

43. *Barcaei:* to the east.

44. *Your brother's:* The reference is to Pygmalion of Tyre, from whom Dido fled to found Carthage.

58. *Ceres:* goddess of the crops. Ceres, the Wine-god, and Phoebus Apollo are selected as deities especially connected with the founding of cities;

one of Apollo's titles is "Founder," and Ceres and Dionysus (Bacchus) control the essential crops which will enable the colonists to live. Dido prays to these gods at the moment when she is about to abandon her responsibilities as founder of a city; a similar irony is present in her prayer to Juno, whose "business" is the marriage-bond, at the moment when she is about to break her long fidelity to the memory of Sychaeus.

72. *Dictaean:* Dicte is a mountain in Crete.

Now she conducts Aeneas on a tour of her city, and shows him
The vast resources of Carthage, the home there ready and wait-
    ing;   75
Begins to speak, then breaks off, leaving a sentence unfinished.
Now, as the day draws out, she wants to renew that first feast,
In fond distraction begs to hear once again the Trojan
Story, and hangs on his words as once again he tells it.
Then, when the company's broken up, when the moon is dim-
    ming   80
Her beams in turn and the dipping stars invite to sleep,
Alone she frets in the lonely house, lies down on her bed,
Then leaves it again: he's not there, not there, but she hears him
    and sees him.
Or charmed by his likeness to his father, she keeps Ascanius
Long in her lap to assuage the passion she must not utter.   85
Work on the half-built towers is closed down meanwhile; the men
Of Carthage have laid off drilling, or building the wharves and vital
Defences of their town; the unfinished works are idle—
Great frowning walls, head-in-air cranes, all at a standstill.

[Juno proposes to Venus that Dido and Aeneas be married,
which would guarantee the unity of Carthage and Troy and peace
between Juno and Venus. Her aim is of course to ensure that the
imperial destiny reserved for Rome be transferred to Carthage.
Venus, confident of the future, which has been explained to her by
Juppiter, consents to the scheme. Dido organizes a hunt, which is
broken up by a storm, and Dido and Aeneas take shelter in a cave,
where their love is consummated. There is no formal marriage, but
Dido henceforth feels justified in assuming the dignity and rights
of a wife. Their love is rumored abroad, and when the African
prince Iarbas hears of it, he appeals to Juppiter for satisfaction.]

    Thus did Iarbas pray, with his hands on the altar; and Jove
Omnipotent, hearing him, bent down his gaze upon Dido's   220
City and on those lovers lost to their higher fame.
Then he addressed Mercury, entrusting to him this errand:—
    Go quick, my son, whistle up the Zephyrs and wing your way
Down to the Trojan leader, who is dallying now in Carthage
Without one thought for the city which fate has assigned to be
    his.   225
Carry my dictate along the hastening winds and tell him,
Not for such ways did his matchless mother guarantee him
To us, nor for such ends rescue him twice from the Greeks;
Rather, that he should rule an Italy fertile in leadership

---

222. *Mercury:* the Latin equivalent of the Greek Hermes, the divine messenger.

228. *rescue him:* during the sack of Troy (Book II).

And loud with war, should hand on a line which sprang from the
   noble   230
Teucer and bring the whole world under a system of law.
If the glory of such great exploits no longer fires his heart
And for his own renown he will make no effort at all,
Does he grudge his son, Ascanius, the glory of Rome to be?
What aim, what hope does he cherish, delaying there in a hos-
   tile   235
Land, with no thought for posterity or his Italian kingdom?
Let him sail. That is the gist. Give him that message from me.
   Jove spake. Mercury now got ready to obey
His father's command. So first he bound on his feet the sandals,
The golden sandals whose wings waft him aloft over sea   240
And land alike with the hurrying breath of the breezes. Then
He took up his magic wand (with this he summons wan ghosts
From Orcus and consigns others to dreary Tartarus,
Gives sleep or takes it away, seals up the eyes of dead men).
Now, with that trusty wand, he drove the winds and threshed
   through   245
The cloud-wrack; descried as he flew the peak and precipitous
   flanks of
Atlas, that dour mountain which props the sky with his summit—
Atlas, his pine-bristled head for ever wrapped in a bandeau
Of glooming cloud, for ever beaten by wind and rain;
Snow lies deep on his shoulders, and watercourses plunge down   250
That ancient's chin, while his shaggy beard is stiff with ice.
Here first did Mercury pause, hovering on beautifully-balanced
Wings; then stooped, dived bodily down to the sea below,
Like a bird which along the shore and around the promontories
Goes fishing, flying low, wave-hopping over the water.   255
Even so did Mercury skim between earth and sky
Towards the Libyan coast, cutting his path through the winds,
On his way from that mountain giant, Atlas, his mother's sire.
As soon as his winged feet had carried him to the shacks there,
He noticed Aeneas superintending the work on towers   260
And new buildings: he wore a sword studded with yellow
Jaspers, and a fine cloak of glowing Tyrian purple
Hung from his shoulders—the wealthy Dido had fashioned it,
Interweaving the fabric with threads of gold, as a present for him.
Mercury went for him at once:—
                           So now you are laying   265
Foundations for lofty Carthage, building a beautiful city
To please a woman, lost to the interests of your own realm?
The king of the gods, who directs heaven and earth with his deity,

---

231. *Teucer:* the first of the Trojan kings; to be distinguished from the Teucer of Book I, l. 619.

243. *Orcus:* the abode of the dead.

Tartarus: the place of punishment of the wicked in the lower world.

247. *Atlas:* mountain range in western North Africa.

Sends me to you from bright Olympus: the king of the gods
Gave me this message to carry express through the air:—What do
    you   270
Aim at or hope for, idling and fiddling here in Libya?
If you're indifferent to your own high destiny
And for your own renown you will make no effort at all,
Think of your young hopeful, Ascanius, growing to manhood,
The inheritance which you owe him—an Italian kingdom, the soil
    of   275
Rome.
        Such were the words which Mercury delivered;
And breaking off abruptly, was manifest no more,
But vanished into thin air, far beyond human ken.
   Dazed indeed by that vision was Aeneas, and dumbfounded:
His hair stood on end with terror, the voice stuck in his throat.   280
Awed by this admonition from the great throne above,
He desired to fly the country, dear though it was to him.
But oh, what was he to do? What words could he find to get round
The temperamental queen? How broach the matter to her?
His mind was in feverish conflict, tossed from one side to the
    other,   285
Twisting and turning all ways to find a way past his dilemma.
So vacillating, at last he felt this the better decision:—
Sending for Mnestheus, Sergestus and brave Serestus, he bade them
Secretly get the ships ready, muster their friends on the beach,
Be prepared to fight: the cause of so drastic a change of plan   290
They must keep dark: in the meanwhile, assuming that generous
    Dido
Knew nothing and could not imagine the end of so great a love,
Aeneas would try for a way to approach her, the kindest moment
For speaking, the best way to deal with this delicate matter. His
    comrades
Obeyed the command and did as he told them with cheerful
    alacrity.   295
   But who can ever hoodwink a woman in love? The queen,
Apprehensive even when things went well, now sensed his de-
    ception,
Got wind of what was going to happen. That mischievous Rumour,
Whispering the fleet was preparing to sail, put her in a frenzy.
Distraught, she witlessly wandered about the city, raving   300
Like some Bacchante driven wild, when the emblems of sanctity
Stir, by the shouts of "Hail, Bacchus!" and drawn to Cithaeron
At night by the din of revellers, at the triennial orgies.
Finding Aeneas at last, she cried, before he could speak:—

301. *Bacchante:* a female devotee of
the god Dionysus (Bacchus), in an
ecstatic trance at the Dionysian festival,
which was held every three years.
302. *Cithaeron:* mountain near
Thebes, sacred to Dionysus.

Unfaithful man, did you think you could do such a dreadful
     thing   305
And keep it dark? yes, skulk from my land without one word?
Our love, the vows you made me—do these not give you pause,
Nor even the thought of Dido meeting a painful death?
Now, in the dead of winter, to be getting your ships ready
And hurrying to set sail when northerly gales are blowing,   310
You heartless one! Suppose the fields were not foreign, the home
     was
Not strange that you are bound for, suppose Troy stood as of old,
Would you be sailing for Troy, now, in this stormy weather?
Am I your reason for going? By these tears, by the hand you gave
     me—
They are all I have left, to-day, in my misery—I implore you,   315
And by our union of hearts, by our marriage hardly begun,
If I have ever helped you at all, if anything
About me please you, be sad for our broken home, forgo
Your purpose, I beg you, unless it's too late for prayers of mine!
Because of you, the Libyan tribes and the Nomad chieftains   320
Hate me, the Tyrians are hostile: because of you I have lost
My old reputation for faithfulness—the one thing that could have
     made me
Immortal. Oh, I am dying! To what, my guest, are you leaving me?
"Guest"—that is all I may call you now, who have called you hus-
     band.
Why do I linger here? Shall I wait till my brother, Pygmalion,   325
Destroys this place, or Iarbas leads me away captive?
If even I might have conceived a child by you before
You went away, a little Aeneas to play in the palace
And, in spite of all this, to remind me of you by his looks, oh then
I should not feel so utterly finished and desolate.   330
     She had spoken. Aeneas, mindful of Jove's words, kept his eyes
Unyielding, and with a great effort repressed his feeling for her.
In the end he managed to answer:—
                              Dido, I'll never pretend
You have not been good to me, deserving of everything
You can claim. I shall not regret my memories of Elissa   335
As long as I breathe, as long as I remember my own self.
For my conduct—this, briefly: I did not look to make off from here
In secret—do not suppose it; nor did I offer you marriage
At any time or consent to be bound by a marriage contract.
If fate allowed me to be my own master, and gave me   340
Free will to choose my way of life, to solve my problems,

---

314. *hand you gave me;* the hand-
clasp with which he pledged his love
and which Dido takes as an earnest of
marriage.
335. *Elissa:* another name for Dido.

Old Troy would be my first choice: I would restore it, and honour
My people's relics—the high halls of Priam perpetuated,
Troy given back to its conquered sons, a renaissant city,
Had been my task. But now Apollo and the Lycian   345
Oracle have told me that Italy is our bourne.
There lies my heart, my homeland. You, a Phoenician, are held by
These Carthaginian towers, by the charm of your Libyan city:
So can you grudge us Trojans our vision of settling down
In Italy? We too may seek a kingdom abroad.   350
Often as night envelops the earth in dewy darkness,
Often as star-rise, the troubled ghost of my father, Anchises,
Comes to me in my dreams, warns me and frightens me.
I am disturbed no less by the wrong I am doing Ascanius,
Defrauding him of his destined realm in Hesperia.   355
What's more, just now the courier of heaven, sent by Juppiter—
I swear it on your life and mine—conveyed to me, swiftly flying,
His orders: I saw the god, as clear as day, with my own eyes,
Entering the city, and these ears drank in the words he uttered.
No more reproaches, then—they only torture us both.   360
God's will, not mine, says "Italy".
    All the while he was speaking she gazed at him askance,
Her glances flickering over him, eyes exploring the whole man
In deadly silence. Now, furiously, she burst out:—
    Faithless and false! No goddess mothered you, no Dardanus   365
Your ancestor! I believe harsh Caucasus begat you
On a flint-hearted rock and Hyrcanian tigers suckled you.
Why should I hide my feelings? What worse can there be to keep
    them for?
Not one sigh from him when I wept! Not a softer glance!
Did he yield an inch, or a tear, in pity for her who loves him?   370
I don't know what to say first. It has come to this,—not Juno,
Not Jove himself can view my plight with the eye of justice.
Nowhere is it safe to be trustful. I took him, a castaway,
A pauper, and shared my kingdom with him—I must have been
    mad—
Rescued his lost fleet, rescued his friends from death.   375
Oh, I'm on fire and drifting! And now Apollo's prophecies,
Lycian oracles, couriers of heaven sent by Juppiter
With stern commands—all these order you to betray me.
Oh, of course this is just the sort of transaction that troubles the
    calm of

345. *Lycian:* There was an oracle of
Apollo at Patara, in Lycia.
    352. *Anchises:* Aeneas had rescued
him from the burning city of Troy, but
the old man died in Sicily, just before
Aeneas went to Carthage.
    365. *Dardanus:* an ancestor of the
Trojans.

366. *Caucasus:* a mountain range
near the Caspian Sea. It has connota-
tions of outlandishness and of cruelty.
(It was the place of punishment of
Prometheus.)
    367. *Hyrcanian:* from the same gen-
eral area as the Caucasus.

The gods. I'll not keep you, nor probe the dishonesty of your words.   380
Chase your Italy, then! Go, sail to your realm overseas!
I only hope that, if the just spirits have any power,
Marooned on some mid-sea rock you may drink the full cup of agony
And often cry out for Dido. I'll dog you, from far, with the death-fires;
And when cold death has parted my soul from my body, my spectre   385
Will be wherever you are. You shall pay for the evil you've done me.
The tale of your punishment will come to me down in the shades.
  With these words Dido suddenly ended, and sick at heart
Turned from him, tore herself away from his eyes, ran indoors,
While he hung back in dread of a still worse scene, although   390
He had much to say. Her maids bore up the fainting queen
Into her marble chamber and laid her down on the bed.
  But the god-fearing Aeneas, much as he longed to soothe
Her anguish with consolation, with words that would end her troubles,
Heavily sighing, his heart melting from love of her,   395
Nevertheless obeyed the gods and went off to his fleet.
Whereupon the Trojans redoubled their efforts, all along
The beach dragging down the tall ships, launching the well-tarred bottoms,
Fetching green wood to make oars and baulks of unfashioned timber
From the forest, so eager they were to be gone.   400
You could see them on the move, hurrying out of the city.
It looked like an army of ants when, provident for winter,
They're looting a great big corn-heap and storing it up in their own house;
Over a field the black file goes, as they carry the loot
On a narrow track through the grass; some are strenuously pushing   405
The enormous grains of corn with their shoulders, while others marshal
The traffic and keep it moving: their whole road seethes with activity.
Ah, Dido, what did you feel when you saw these things going forward?
What moans you gave when, looking forth from your high roof-top,
You beheld the whole length of the beach aswarm with men, and the sea's face   410
Alive with the sound and fury of preparations for sailing!

379–380. *calm of the gods:* Dido is referring to the Epicurean idea that the gods are unaffected by human events.

Excess of love, to what lengths you drive our human hearts!
Once again she was driven to try what tears and entreaties
Could do, and let love beggar her pride—she would leave no appeal
Untried, lest, for want of it, she should all needlessly die.   415

　Anna, you see the bustle down there on the beach; from all sides
They have assembled; their canvas is stretched to the winds already,
And the elated mariners have garlanded their ships.
If I was able to anticipate this deep anguish,
I shall be able to bear it. But do this one thing, Anna,   420
For your poor sister. You were the only confidante
Of that faithless man: he told you even his secret thoughts:
You alone know the most tactful way, the best time to approach
　him.
Go, sister, and make this appeal to my disdainful enemy:—
Say that *I* never conspired with the Greeks at Aulis to ruin   425
The Trojan people, nor sent squadrons of ships against Troy;
I never desecrated the ashes of dead Anchises,
So why must Aeneas be deaf and obdurate to my pleading?
Why off so fast? Will he grant a last wish to her who unhappily
Loves him, and wait for a favouring wind, an easier voyage?   430
Not for our marriage that was do I plead now—he has forsworn it,
Nor that he go without his dear Latium and give up his kingdom.
I ask a mere nothing—just time to give rein to despair and thus
　calm it,
To learn from ill luck how to grieve for what I have lost, and to
　bear it.
This last favour I beg—oh, pity your sister!—and if he   435
Grants it, I will repay him; my death shall be his interest.

　　Such were her prayers, and such the tearful entreaties her
　agonised
Sister conveyed to Aeneas again and again. But unmoved by
Tearful entreaties he was, adamant against all pleadings:
Fate blocked them, heaven stopped his ears lest he turn com-
　plaisant.
　　　　　　　　　　　　　　　　　　　　　　　　　　　　440
As when some stalwart oak-tree, some veteran of the Alps,
Is assailed by a wintry wind whose veering gusts tear at it,
Trying to root it up; wildly whistle the branches,
The leaves come flocking down from aloft as the bole is battered;
But the tree stands firm on its crag, for high as its head is car-
　ried   445
Into the sky, so deep do its roots go down towards Hades:
Even thus was the hero belaboured for long with every kind of
Pleading, and his great heart thrilled through and through with the
　pain of it;
Resolute, though, was his mind; unavailingly rolled her tears.

　　But hapless Dido, frightened out of her wits by her destiny,   450
Prayed for death: she would gaze no more on the dome of daylight.

And now, strengthening her resolve to act and to leave this world,
She saw, as she laid gifts on the incense-burning altars—
Horrible to relate—the holy water turn black
And the wine she poured changing uncannily to blood.   455
She told no one, not even her sister, of this phenomenon.
Again, she had dedicated a chantry of marble within
The palace to her first husband; held it in highest reverence;
Hung it with snow-white fleeces and with festoons of greenery:
Well, from this shrine, when night covered the earth, she
    seemed   460
To be hearing words—the voice of that husband calling upon her.
There was something dirge-like, too, in the tones of the owl on the
    roof-top
Whose lonely, repeated cries were drawn out to a long keening.
Besides, she recalled with horror presages, dread forewarnings
Of the prophets of old. Aeneas himself pursued her remorse-
    lessly   465
In dreams, driving her mad; or else she dreamed of unending
Solitude and desertion, of walking alone and eternally
Down a long road, through an empty land, in search of her Tyrians.
Just so does the raving Pentheus see covens of Furies and has the
Delusion of seeing two suns in the sky and a double Thebes: 470
Just so on the stage does Orestes, the son of Agamemnon,
Move wildly about while his mother pursues him with torches and
    black snakes,
And at the door the avenging Furies cut off his retreat.
    So when, overmastered by grief, she conceived a criminal mad-
    ness
And doomed herself to death, she worked out the time and
    method   475
In secret; then, putting on an expression of calm hopefulness
To hide her resolve, she approached her sorrowing sister with these
    words:—
    I have found out a way, Anna—oh, wish me joy of it—
To get him back or else get free of my love for him.
Near Ocean's furthest bound and the sunset is Aethiopia,   480
The very last place on earth, where giant Atlas pivots
The wheeling sky, embossed with fiery stars, on his shoulders.

469. *Pentheus:* king of Thebes. He persecuted the worshipers of the new god Dionysus, and imprisoned the god himself. He was later mocked by the god, who inspired him with the Dionysiac spirit (and perhaps with wine) so that he saw double. In this state he was led off to his death on Cithaeron. These events are dramatized in Euripides' play *The Bacchanals (Bacchae)*. The refer-ence to the Eumenides (Furies) in this passage is obscure.
471. *Orestes:* another reference to Greek tragedy. In the *Choephoroe*, the Aeschylean play which follows immediately on the *Agamemnon*, Orestes kills his mother Clytemnestra, and is pursued by the Furies. In other tragic contexts he is represented as pursued by the ghost of his mother.

I have been in touch with a priestess from there, a Massylian, who
    once,
As warden of the Hesperides' sacred close, was used to
Feed the dragon which guarded their orchard of golden apples,   485
Sprinkling its food with moist honey and sedative poppy-seeds.
Now this enchantress claims that her spells can liberate
One's heart, or can inject love-pangs, just as she wishes;
Can stop the flow of rivers, send the stars flying backwards,
Conjure ghosts in the night: she can make the earth cry out   490
Under one's feet, and elm trees come trooping down from the moun-
    tains.
Dear sister, I solemnly call to witness the gods and you whom
I love, that I do not willingly resort to her magic arts.
You must build up a funeral pyre high in the inner courtyard,
And keep it dark: lay on it the arms which that godless man   495
Has left on the pegs in our bedroom, all relics of him, and the
    marriage-bed
That was the ruin of me. To blot out all that reminds me
Of that vile man is my pleasure and what the enchantress directs.
    So Dido spoke, and fell silent, her face going deadly white.
Yet Anna never suspected that Dido was planning her own
    death   500
Through these queer rites, nor imagined how frantic a madness
    possessed her,
Nor feared any worse would happen than when Sychaeus had died.
So she made the arrangements required of her.
    When in the innermost court of the palace the pyre had been
    built up
To a great height with pinewood and logs of ilex, the queen   505
Festooned the place with garlands and wreathed it with funereal
Foliage: then she laid on it the clothes, the sword which Aeneas
Had left, and an effigy of him; she well knew what was to happen.
Altars are set up all round. Her hair unloosed, the enchantress
Loudly invokes three hundred deities—Erebus, Chaos,   510
Hecate, three in one, and three-faced Diana, the virgin.
She had sprinkled water which came, she pretended, from Lake
    Avernus:
Herbs she had gathered, cut by moonlight with a bronze knife—
Poisonous herbs all rank with juices of black venom;

483. *Massylian:* from an African tribe.

484. *Hesperides:* the daughters of Hesperus, in the west, who lived in a garden which contained golden apples, guarded by a serpent.

510. *Erebus:* the lowest depth of the underworld. *Chaos:* a Greek personification of the disorder which preceded the creation of the universe.

511. *Hecate:* title of Diana as goddess of sorcery. *Three-faced Diana:* She is Hecate, the moon, and Diana the virgin huntress.

512. *Avernus:* a lake in southern Italy which was supposed to be the entrance to the lower world.

She has found a love charm, a gland torn from the forehead of a
    new-born   515
Foal before its mother could get it.
Dido, the sacramental grain in her purified hands,
One foot unsandalled, her dress uncinctured, stood by the altars
Calling upon the gods and the stars that know fate's secrets,
Death at her heart, and prayed to whatever power it is   520
Holds unrequited lovers in its fair, faithful keeping.
    Was night. All over the earth, creatures were plucking the flower
Of soothing sleep, the woods and the wild seas fallen quiet—
A time when constellations have reached their mid-career,
When the countryside is all still, the beasts and the brilliant
    birds   525
That haunt the lakes' wide waters or the tangled undergrowth
Of the champain, stilled in sleep under the quiet night—
Cares are lulled and hearts can forget for a while their travails.
Not so the Phoenician queen: death at her heart, she could not
Ever relax in sleep, let the night in to her eyes   530
Or mind: her agonies mounted, her love reared up again
And savaged her, till she writhed in a boiling sea of passion.
So thus she began, her thoughts whirling round in a vicious circle:—
    What shall I do? Shall I, who've been jilted, return to my former
Suitors? go down on my knees for marriage to one of the
    Nomads   535
Although, time and again, I once rejected their offers?
Well then, am I to follow the Trojan's fleet and bow to
Their lightest word? I helped them once. Will that help me now?
Dare I think they remember with gratitude my old kindness?
But even if I wished it, who would suffer me, welcome me   540
Aboard those arrogant ships? They hate me. Ah, duped and
    ruined!—
Surely by now I should know the ill faith of Laomedon's people?
So then? Shall I sail, by myself, with those exulting mariners,
Or sail against them with all my Tyrian folk about me—
My people, whom once I could hardly persuade to depart from
    Sidon—   545
Bidding them man their ships and driving them out to sea again?
Better die—I deserve it—end my pain with the sword.
Sister, you started it all: overborne by my tears, you laid up
These evils to drive me mad, put me at the mercy of a foe.
Oh, that I could have been some child of nature and lived   550
An innocent life, untouched by marriage and all its troubles!
I have broken the faith I vowed to the memory of Sichaeus.

---

542. *Laomedon's people:* Laomedon was a king of Troy who twice broke his promise, once to Heracles and once to Apollo and Poseidon.

Such were the reproaches she could not refrain from uttering.
High on the poop of his ship, resolute now for departure,
Aeneas slept; preparations for sailing were fully completed.   555
To him in a dream there appeared the shape of the god, returning
Just as he'd looked before, as if giving the same admonitions—
Mercury's very image, the voice, the complexion, the yellow
Hair and the handsome youthful body identical:—
      Goddess-born, can you go on sleeping at such a crisis?   560
Are you out of your mind, not to see what dangers are brewing up
Around you, and not to hear the favouring breath of the West wind?
Being set upon death, her heart is aswirl with conflicting passions,
Aye, she is brooding now some trick, some desperate deed.
Why are you not going, all speed, while the going is good?   565
If dawn finds you still here, delaying by these shores,
You'll have the whole sea swarming with hostile ships, there will be
Firebrands coming against you, you'll see this beach ablaze.
Up and away, then! No more lingering! Woman was ever
A veering, weathercock creature.
                        He spoke, and vanished in the darkness.   570
Then, startled by the shock of the apparition, Aeneas
Snatched himself out of sleep and urgently stirred up his comrades:—
      Jump to it, men! To your watch! Go to the rowing benches!
Smartly! Hoist the sails! A god from heaven above
Spurs me to the cut cables, make off and lose not a moment: 575
This was his second warning. O blessed god, we follow you,
God indeed, and once more we obey the command joyfully!
Be with us! Look kindly upon us! Grant us good sailing weather!
    Thus did Aeneas cry, and flashing his sword from its scabbard,
With the drawn blade he severed the moorings. The same sense
      of   580
Urgency fired his comrades all; they cut and ran for it.
The shore lay empty. The ships covered the open sea.
The oarsmen swept the blue and sent the foam flying with hard
      strokes.
    And now was Aurora, leaving the saffron bed of Tithonus,
Beginning to shower upon earth the light of another day.   585
The queen, looking forth from her roof-top, as soon as she saw the
      sky
Grow pale and the Trojan fleet running before the wind,
Aware that the beach and the roadstead were empty, the sailors
      gone,
Struck herself three times, four times, upon her lovely breast,
Tore at her yellow hair, and exclaimed:—
                        In god's name! shall that foreigner   590
Scuttle away and make a laughing-stock of my country?

Will not my people stand to arms for a mass pursuit?
Will some not rush the warships out of the docks? Move, then!
Bring firebrands apace, issue the weapons, pull on the oars!
What am I saying? Where am I? What madness veers my
    mind?   595
Poor Dido, the wrong you have done—is it only now coming home
    to you?
You should have thought of that when you gave him your sceptre.
              So this is
The word of honour of one who, men say, totes round his home-
    gods
Everywhere, and bore on his back a doddering father!
Why could I not have seized him, torn up his body and littered 600
The sea with it? finished his friends with the sword, finished his
    own
Ascanius and served him up for his father to banquet on?
The outcome of battle had been uncertain?—Let it have been so:
Since I was to die, whom had I to fear? I should have stormed
Their bulwarks with fire, set alight their gangways, gutted the whole
    lot—   605
Folk, father and child—then flung myself on the conflagration.
O sun, with your beams surveying all that is done on earth!
Juno, the mediator and witness of my tragedy!
Hecate, whose name is howled by night at the city crossroads!
Avenging Furies, and you, the patrons of dying Elissa!—   610
Hear me! Incline your godheads to note this wickedness
So worthy of your wrath! And hear my prayer! If he,
That damned soul, must make port and get to land, if thus
Jove destines it, if that bourne is fixed for him irrevocably,
May he be harried in war by adventurous tribes, and exiled   615
From his own land; may Ascanius be torn from his arms; may he
    have to
Sue for aid, and see his own friends squalidly dying.
Yes, and when he's accepted the terms of a harsh peace,
Let him never enjoy his realm or the allotted span,

---

598. *home-gods:* Aeneas carries with
him on his journeys the images of the
gods of Troy, rescued from the flames
on the night of Troy's fall.
599. *on his back:* Dido recalls
Aeneas' story of the sack of Troy which
he told her at the banquet (Book II);
he left the city leading his son by the
hand and carrying his old father on his
shoulders.
615 ff. *May he be harried . . . :*
This prophecy of Dido's, expressed in
the form of a wish, is destined to come

true. Aeneas meets resistance in Italy;
at one point in the war he has to leave
Ascanius behind and go to beg aid from
an Italian king, Evander. The final
peace is made on condition that the
name of his people be changed from
"Trojans" to "Latins"; and he is
eventually drowned in an Italian river.
Aeneas' reward for all his struggles is
to come not during his life, but in the
glory of the generations which succeed
him.

But fall before his time and lie on the sands, unburied.   **620**
That is my last prayer. I pour it out, with my lifeblood.
Let you, my Tyrians, sharpen your hatred upon his children
And all their seed for ever: send this as a present to
My ghost. Between my people and his, no love, no alliance!
Rise up from my dead bones, avenger! Rise up, one   **625**
To hound the Trojan settlers with fire and steel remorselessly,
Now, some day, whenever the strength for it shall be granted!
Shore to shore, sea to sea, weapon to weapon opposed—
I call down a feud between them and us to the last generation!
    These things she said; then tried to think of every expedient,   **630**
Seeking the quickest way out of the life she hated.
Briefly now she addressed Barce, the nurse of Sychaeus,
Her own being dust and ashes, interred in her native land:—
    Dear nurse, please will you get my sister, Anna. She must
Hasten to purify herself with living water, and fetch   **635**
The cattle, tell her—the atonement offerings, as directed;
Then let her come. And do you go and put on the holy headband.
These rites to Jove of the Underworld, duly made ready and
    started,
I mean to go through with now, and put an end to my troubles,
Committing to the flames the funeral pyre of that Trojan.   **640**
    She spoke. The nurse hurried off with senile officiousness.
But Dido, trembling, distraught by the terrible thing she was doing,
Her bloodshot eyes all restless, with hectic blotches upon
Her quivering cheeks, yet pale with the shade of advancing death,
Ran to the innermost court of the palace, climbed the lofty   **645**
Pyre, frantic at heart, and drew Aeneas' sword—
Her present to him, procured once for a far different purpose.
Then, after eyeing the clothes he had left behind, and the memoried
Bed, pausing to weep and brood on him for a little,
She lay down on the bed and spoke her very last words:—   **650**
    O relics of him, things dear to me while fate, while heaven al-
    lowed it,
Receive this life of mine, release me from my troubles!
I have lived, I have run to the finish the course which fortune gave
    me:
And now, a queenly shade, I shall pass to the world below.
I built a famous city, saw my own place established,   **655**
Avenged a husband, exacted a price for a brother's enmity.
Happy I would have been, ah, beyond words happy,
If only the Trojan ships had never come to my shore!

<hr>

625. *avenger:* Dido foresees the har-
rying of Italy by the Carthaginian general Hannibal, who in the third century
B.C. invaded Italy, defeating the Romans
in battle after battle, but failed to capture Rome.

These words; then, burying her face in the bed:—
                            Shall I die unavenged?
At least, let me die. Thus, thus! I go to the dark, go gladly.   660
May he look long, from out there on the deep, at my flaming pyre,
The heartless! And may my death-fires signal bad luck for his
    voyage!
    She had spoken; and with these words, her attendants saw her
        falling
Upon the sword, they could see the blood spouting up over
The blade, and her hands spattered. Their screams rang to the
    roofs of   665
The palace; then rumour ran amok through the shocked city.
All was weeping and wailing, the streets were filled with a keening
Of women, the air resounded with terrible lamentations.
It was as if Carthage or ancient Tyre should be falling,
With enemy troops breaking into the town and a conflagration   670
Furiously sweeping over the abodes of men and of gods.
Anna heard it: half dead from extreme fear, she ran through
The crowd, tearing her cheeks with her nails, beating her breast
With her fists, and called aloud by name on the dying woman:—
    So this was your purpose, Dido? You were making a dupe of
        me?   675
That pyre, those lighted altars—for me, they were leading to this?
How shall I chide you for leaving me? Were you too proud to let
    your
Sister die with you? You should have called me to share your end:
One hour, one pang of the sword could have carried us both away.
Did I build this pyre with my own hands, invoking our family
    gods,   680
So that you might lie on it, and I, the cause of your troubles, not
    be there?
You have destroyed more than your self—me, and the lords
And commons and city of Sidon. Quick! Water for her wounds!
Let me bathe them, and if any last breath is fluttering from her
    mouth,
Catch it in mine!
                    So saying, she had scaled the towering pyre,   685
Taken the dying woman into her lap, was caressing her,
Sobbing, trying to staunch the dark blood with her own dress.
Dido made an effort to raise her heavy eyes,
Then gave it up: the sword-blade grated against her breast bone.
Three times she struggled to rise, to lift herself on an elbow,   690
Three times rolled back on the bed. Her wandering gaze went up

---

660. *Thus, thus:* The repetition represents the two strokes of the sword.
669–671. *as if Carthage . . . gods:* In these lines is prefigured the capture and total destruction of Carthage by the army of Scipio Africanus the Younger in 146 B.C.

To the sky, looking for light: she gave a moan when she saw it.
  Then did almighty Juno take pity on her long-drawn-out
Sufferings and hard going, sent Iris down from Olympus
To part the agonised soul from the body that still clung to it.   695
Since she was dying neither a natural death nor from others'
Violence, but desperate and untimely, driven to it
By a crazed impulse, not yet had Proserpine clipped from her
    head
The golden tress, or consigned her soul to the Underworld.
So now, all dewy, her pinions the colour of yellow crocus,   700
Her wake a thousand rainbow hues refracting the sunlight,
Iris flew down, and over Dido hovering, said:—
  As I was bidden, I take this sacred thing, the Death-god's
Due: and you I release from your body.
                                    She snipped the tress.
Then all warmth went at once, the life was lost in air.   705

  [After his hurried departure from Carthage, Aeneas goes to Sicily,
to the kingdom of his friend Acestes. There he organizes funeral
games in honor of his father, Anchises (who had died in Sicily on
their first visit there), and leaves behind those of his following who
are unwilling to go on to the uncertainty of a settlement in Italy.
Arrived in Italy, he consults the Sibyl, who guides him down to the
world of the dead. There he is to see his father and the vision of
the future of his race, which is to be his only reward.]

[Aeneas in the Underworld]

Book VI

  . . . You gods who rule the kingdom of souls! You soundless
    shades!
Chaos, and Phlegethon! O mute wide leagues of Nightland!—   265
Grant me to tell what I have heard! With your assent
May I reveal what lies deep in the gloom of the Underworld!
  Dimly through the shadows and dark solitudes they wended,
Through the void domiciles of Dis, the bodiless regions:
Just as, through fitful moonbeams, under the moon's thin light,   270
A path lies in a forest, when Jove has palled the sky
With gloom, and the night's blackness has bled the world of colour.
See! At the very porch and entrance way to Orcus
Grief and ever-haunting Anxiety make their bed:
Here dwell pallid Diseases, here morose Old Age,   275
With Fear, ill-prompting Hunger, and squalid Indigence,
Shapes horrible to look at, Death and Agony;
Sleep, too, which is the cousin of Death; and Guilty Joys,

694. *Iris:* a messenger of the gods, particularly of Juno; also identified with the rainbow.

265. *Phlegethon:* an underworld river of fire.
269. *Dis:* Pluto, the ruler of the underworld.

And there, against the threshold, War, the bringer of Death:
Here are the iron cells of the Furies, and lunatic Strife   280
Whose viperine hair is caught up with a headband soaked in
    blood. . . .
    From here is the road that leads to the dismal waters of
    Acheron.   295
Here a whirlpool boils with mud and immense swirlings
Of water, spouting up all the slimy sand of Cocytus.
A dreadful ferryman looks after the river crossing,
Charon; appallingly filthy he is, with a bush of unkempt
White beard upon his chin, with eyes like jets of fire;   300
And a dirty cloak draggles down, knotted about his shoulders.
He poles the boat, he looks after the sails, he is all the crew
Of that rust-coloured wherry which takes the dead across—
An ancient now, but a god's old age is green and sappy.
This way came fast and streaming up to the bank the whole
    throng: 305
Matrons and men were there, and there were great-heart heroes
Finished with earthly life, boys and unmarried maidens,
Young men laid on the pyre before their parents' eyes;
Multitudinous as the leaves that fall in a forest
At the first frost of autumn, or the birds that out of the deep-
    sea   310
Fly to land in migrant flocks, when the cold of the year
Has sent them overseas in search of a warmer climate.
So they all stood, each begging to be ferried across first,
Their hands stretched out in longing for the shore beyond the river.
But the surly ferryman embarks now this, now that group,   315
While others he keeps away at a distance from the shingle.
Aeneas, being astonished and moved by the great stir, said:—
    Tell me, O Sibyl, what means this rendezvous at the river?
What purpose have these souls? By what distinction are some
Turned back, while other souls sweep over the wan water?   320
    To which the long-lived Sibyl uttered this brief reply:—
    O son of Anchises' loins and true-born offspring of heaven,
What you see is the mere of Cocytus, the Stygian marsh
By whose mystery even the gods, having sworn, are afraid to be for-
    sworn.
All this crowd you see are the helpless ones, the unburied: 325
That ferryman is Charon: the ones he conveys have had burial.
None may be taken across from bank to awesome bank of
That harsh-voiced river until his bones are laid to rest.

295. *Acheron:* a river of the underworld.

297. *Cocytus:* the river of lamentation.

323. *Stygian:* The Styx is another
infernal river.

Otherwise, he must haunt this place for a hundred years
Before he's allowed to revisit the longed-for stream at last.   330
  The son of Anchises paused and stood stock still, in deep
Meditation; pierced to the heart by pity for their hard fortune.
He saw there, sorrowing because deprived of death's fulfilment,
Leucaspis and Orontes, the commodore of the Lycian
Squadron, who had gone down, their ship being lost with all
      hands   335
In a squall, sailing with him the stormy seas from Troy. . . .
  At once were voices heard, a sound of mewling and wailing,
Ghosts of infants sobbing there at the threshold, infants
From whom a dark day stole their share of delicious life,
Snatched them away from the breast, gave them sour death to
      drink.
Next to them were those condemned to death on a false charge.   430
Yet every place is duly allotted and judgment is given.
Minos, as president, summons a jury of the dead: he hears
Every charge, examines the record of each; he shakes the urn.
Next again are located the sorrowful ones who killed
Themselves, throwing their lives away, not driven by guilt   435
But because they loathed living: how they would like to be
In the world above now, enduring poverty and hard trials!
God's law forbids: that unlovely fen with its glooming water
Corrals them there, the nine rings of Styx corral them in.
Not far from here can be seen, extending in all directions,   440
The vale of mourning—such is the name it bears: a region
Where those consumed by the wasting torments of merciless love
Haunt the sequestered alleys and myrtle groves that give them
Cover; death itself cannot cure them of love's disease.
Here Aeneas descried Phaedra and Procris, sad   445
Eriphyle displaying the wounds her heartless son once dealt her,
Evadne and Pasiphae; with them goes Laodamia;
Here too is Caeneus, once a young man, but next a woman

432. *Minos:* judge of the dead.

445 ff. *Here Aeneas descried* . . . .
A catalogue of unhappy lovers follows.

445. *Phaedra:* wife of Theseus, king of Athens, who fell in love with Hippolytus, her husband's son by another woman; the result was her death by suicide and Hippolytus' death through his father's curse. *Procris:* killed by her husband in an accident which was brought about by her own jealousy.

446. *Eriphyle:* betrayed her husband for gold and was killed by her own son.

447. *Evadne:* threw herself on the pyre of her husband, who was killed by Zeus for impiety. *Pasiphae:* wife of Minos of Crete, she conceived a mon-
strous love for a bull. *Laodamia:* begged to be allowed to talk with her dead husband; the request was granted by the gods and when his time came to return, she went back with him to the land of the dead.

448. *Caeneus:* Virgil's words in the original are ambiguous (perhaps to reflect the ambiguity of the sex of Caeneus). The usual explanation of the passage is that Caenis (a woman) was changed by Poseidon into a man (Caeneus), but returned to her original sex after death. Since the name occurs here in a catalogue of women, this seems the most likely explanation.

And now changed back by fate to his original sex.
Amongst them, with her death-wound still bleeding, through the
    deep wood   450
Was straying Phoenician Dido. Now when the Trojan leader
Found himself near her and knew that the form he glimpsed
    through the shadows
Was hers—as early in the month one sees, or imagines he sees,
Through a wrack of cloud the new moon rising and glimmering—
He shed some tears, and addressed her in tender, loving
    tones:—   455
    Poor, unhappy Dido, so the message was true that came to me
Saying you'd put an end to your life with the sword and were dead?
Oh god! was it death I brought you, then? I swear by the stars,
By the powers above, by whatever is sacred in the Underworld,
It was not of my own will, Dido, I left your land.   460
Heaven's commands, which now force me to traverse the shades,
This sour and derelict region, this pit of darkness, drove me
Imperiously from your side. I did not, could not imagine
My going would ever bring such terrible agony on you.
Don't move away! Oh, let me see you a little longer!   465
To fly from me, when this is the last word fate allows us!
    Thus did Aeneas speak, trying to soften the wild-eyed,
Passionate-hearted ghost, and brought the tears to his own eyes.
She would not turn to him; she kept her gaze on the ground,
And her countenance remained as stubborn to his appeal   470
As if it were carved from recalcitrant flint or a crag of marble.
At last she flung away, hating him still, and vanished
Into the shadowy wood where her first husband, Sychaeus,
Understands her unhappiness and gives her an equal love.
None the less did Aeneas, hard hit by her piteous fate,   475
Weep after her from afar, as she went, with tears of compassion. . . .

[Aeneas returns to the upper air and begins his settlement in Italy.
He is offered the hand of the princess Lavinia by her father Latinus,
but this provokes a war against the Trojans, led by Turnus of
Laurentum, in the course of which Aeneas is wounded and stops by
a stream to rest. At this point his mother, Venus, comes to him with
the armor made for him by Vulcan (Hephaestus), her husband; on
the shield is carved a representation of the future glories of Rome.]

[*The Shield of Aeneas*]

Book VIII

    . . . Venus, divinely shining among the dark clouds, descended
Bringing her presents: when she had seen from afar Aeneas
On the other side of a cool stream in a secluded dell,   610
She offered herself to his view quite unexpectedly, saying:—

Look! Here are the presents my consort promised. All his science
Has gone to their making. Now you need not shrink from challenging
Haughty Laurentines and hot-headed Turnus to battle, my son.

With these words, the Cytherean went into her son's em-
brace: 615
The radiant arms she had propped up against an oak, before him.
Aeneas, overjoyed by her gifts and the glory of them,
Eyed each piece, couldn't have enough of gazing: in wonder
He took them up with his hands, in his arms, examining each—
The formidable helmet with plumes like fountains of fire,   620
The sword that would deal out doom, the breastplate of hard
bronze,
Massive and ruddy-coloured, like to some louring cloud
When it catches fire from the rays of the sun and glows afar;
Then the burnished greaves of gold-alloy inlaid with high-carat
Gold, and the spear, and the shield's miraculous workmanship.   625
Upon this shield the Fire-god, with knowledge of things to come,
Being versed in the prophets, had wrought events from Italian
history
And Roman triumphs; upon it appeared the whole line that would
spring from
Ascanius' stock, and the wars they would fight in, one by one.
He had depicted the mother wolf as she lay full length in   630
The green-swarded cave of Mars, with the twin boy babies fondling
And suckling at her udders, fearlessly nuzzling their dam;
She, her graceful neck bent sideways and back, is caressing
Each child in turn with her tongue, licking them into shape.
Nearby he had pictured the Sabine women so unceremoniously   635
Snatched from among the crowds around the arena at Rome
During the Great Games; then the war that immediately came,
Between Romulus' people and the hard-living Sabines of old Tatius.
Next, these same two kings, their quarrel laid aside,
Are standing at Jove's altar, armed, with bowls in their hands, 640
Ratifying a treaty by the sacrifice of a sow.
Near this was the scene where chariots, driven apart, had torn
Mettus to pieces (but you should have kept to your word, Al-
ban!)—

614. *Laurentines . . . Turnus:* Turnus of Laurentum is the leader of the
Italian resistance to Aeneas.
615. *the Cytherean:* Venus; Cythera
is one of her cult centers.
626. *Fire-god:* Vulcan.
630. *mother wolf:* The twins who
were to build Rome, Romulus and
Remus sons of Mars, were cast out into
the woods and there suckled by a she-
wolf.
635. *Sabine women:* The newly

founded city consisted almost entirely
of men; the Romans decided to steal
the wives of their neighbors, the Sabines.
They invited them to an athletic festival,
and at a given signal, every Roman
carried off a Sabine bride. The war
which followed ended in the amalgama-
tion of the Roman and Sabine peoples.
638. *Tatius:* the Sabine king.
643. *Mettus:* of Alba. He broke an
agreement made during the early wars
of Rome and was punished by being

Tullus is dragging away the remains of that false-tongued man
Through a wood, and the brambles there are drenched with a
    bloody dew.   645
Again, you could see Porsenna telling the Romans to take back
The banished Tarquin, and laying strenuous siege to Rome,
While the sons of Aeneas took up the sword for freedom's sake:
He was pictured there to the life, pouring out threats and wild with
Chagrin, seeing that Cocles dared to break down the bridge   650
And Cloelia had slipped her fetters and was swimming across the
    river.
At the top of the shield, Manlius, warden of the Tarpeian
Fortress, stood before the temple, guarding the Capitol—
The palace, just built by Romulus, being shown with a rough
    thatched roof.
Here too a silvery goose went fluttering through a golden   655
Colonnade, honking out an alarum, that the Gauls are on us:
Under the cover of a dark night, lucky for them, the Gauls
Creep closer through the brushwood, some have already scaled
The citadel's heights: their clothing and hair were done in gold;
The stripes on their cloaks are gleaming; about their fair-skinned
    throats   660
Are necklaces fastened; each of them brandishes two Alpine
Spears in his hand, and carries a tall, narrow shield for protection.
Vulcan had also embossed the dancing Salii and naked
Luperci, their head-dresses bound with wool, and the shields that
    fell from
Heaven: a solemn procession of virtuous ladies was moving   665
In cushioned carriages through the city. Elsewhere the deep gates
Of hell were represented, the domicile of the damned
And the torments they suffer—Catiline hangs from the edge of a
    terrible

torn apart by two chariots moving in opposite directions.

644. *Tullus:* the Roman king who punished Mettus.

646. *Porsenna:* the Etruscan king who attempted to restore the last of the Roman kings, Tarquin, to the throne from which he had been expelled.

650. *Cocles:* Horatius Cocles, who with two companions defended the bridge across the Tiber to give the Romans time to destroy it.

651. *Cloelia:* a Roman hostage held by Porsenna, who escaped by swimming the Tiber.

652. *Manlius:* consul in 392 B.C.; he was in charge of the citadel ("Tarpeian fortress") at a time when the Gauls from the north held all the rest of the city. They made a night attack on the citadel, but Manlius, awakened by the

cackling of the sacred geese, beat it off, and saved Rome.

654. *Romulus:* In Virgil's time there was still preserved at Rome a rustic building which was supposed to have been the dwelling place of Romulus.

663. *Salii:* the twelve priests of Mars, the war-god, who danced in his honor carrying shields which had fallen from heaven.

664. *Luperci:* priests of Lupercus, a Roman god corresponding to the Greek Pan.

668. *Catiline:* leader of a conspiracy to overthrow the republic which was halted mainly through the efforts of Cicero, consul in 63 B.C. Catiline is the type of discord, representing the civil war which almost destroyed the Roman state, and to which Augustus later put an end.

Precipice, shrinking away from the faces of Furies above him:
But the righteous are set apart, with Cato as their law-giver.   670
Among these subjects extended a wide and swelling sea;
It was done in gold, yet it looked like the blue sea foaming with
    white-caps:
Dolphins, picked out in silver, were cart-wheeling all around,
Lashing the face of the deep with their tails and cleaving the water.
Centrally were displayed two fleets of bronze, engaged in   675
The battle of Actium; all about Cape Leucas you saw
Brisk movement of naval formations; the sea was a blaze of gold.
On one side Augustus Caesar, high up on the poop, is leading
The Italians into battle, the Senate and People with him,
His home-gods and the great gods: two flames shoot up from his
    helmet   680
In jubilant light, and his father's star dawns over its crest.
Elsewhere in the scene is Agrippa—the gods and the winds fight
    for him—
Prominent, leading his column: the naval crown with its miniature
Ships' beaks, a proud decoration of war, shines on his head.
On the other side, with barbaric wealth and motley equipment,   685
Is Anthony, fresh from his triumphs in the East, by the shores of
    the Indian
Ocean; Egypt, the powers of the Orient and uttermost Bactra
Sail with him; also—a shameful thing—his Egyptian wife.
The fleets are converging at full speed, the sea is all churned and
    foaming
As the oarsmen take their long strokes and the trident bows drive
    on.   690
They manœuvre for sea-room: you'd think the Cyclades isles were
    unmoored
And afloat, or mountains were charging at mountains, to see those
    massive
Galleys on one side attacking the turreted ships of the other.
Volleys of flaming material and iron missiles fly thick
And fast; a strange new slaughter reddens the plains of Nep-
    tune.   695

670. *Cato:* the noblest of the republicans who had fought Julius Caesar; he stood for honesty and the seriousness which the Romans most admired. He committed suicide in 47 B.C. after Caesar's victory in Africa. Before taking his life he read through Plato's *Phaedo,* a dialogue concerned with the immortality of the soul, which ends with an account of the death of Socrates.

676. *Actium:* on the west coast of Greece. The naval battle fought here in 31 B.C. was the decisive engagement of the civil war. Augustus, the master of the western half of the empire, defeated Anthony, who held the eastern half and was supported by Cleopatra, queen of Egypt. *Cape Leucas:* a promontory near Actium; there was a temple of Apollo on it (see l. 704).

682. *Agrippa:* Augustus' admiral at Actium.

687. *Bactra:* on the borders of India.

691. *Cyclades:* the islands of the southern Aegean Sea.

In the midst, Cleopatra rallies her fleet with Egyptian timbrel,
For she cannot yet see the two serpents of death behind her.
Barking Anubis, a whole progeny of grotesque
Deities are embattled against Neptune and Minerva
And Venus. Mars is raging in the thick of the fight, his figure   700
Wrought from iron, and ominous Furies look on from above;
Here Discord strides exulting in her torn mantle, and she is
Followed by Bellona wielding a bloodstained scourge.
Viewing this, Apollo of Actium draws his bow
From aloft: it creates a panic; all the Egyptians, all   705
The Indians, Arabians and Sabaeans now turn tail.
You could see the queen Cleopatra praying a fair wind, making
All sail, in the very act of paying the sheets out and running.
The Fire-god had rendered her, pale with the shadow of her own
    death,
Amid the carnage, borne on by the waves and the westerly gale;   710
And, over against her, the Nile, sorrowing in all its length,
Throws wide the folds of its watery garment, inviting the con-
    quered
To sail for refuge into that blue, protective bosom.
But Caesar has entered the walls of Rome in triumphal procession,
Three times a victor; he dedicates now a thanks-offering im-
    mortal   715
To Italy's gods—three hundred great shrines all over the city.
The streets resound with cheering, rejoicing and merrymaking:
In all the temples women are chanting, altars are lit up;
At the foot of the altars lie the bodies of sacrificed bullocks.
Caesar, enthroned in the marble-white temple of dazzling
    Apollo,   720
Inspects the gifts from the nations and hangs them up on the
    splendid
Portals: subjected tribes pass by in a long procession—
A diversity of tongues, of national dress and equipment.
Here Vulcan had represented the Nomads, the flowing robes of
Africans, here the Leleges, Carians, Gelonian bowmen;   725
Some carry a picture of Euphrates, its waters pacified;
There go the Morini, furthest of men, the branching Rhine,
The Scythians untamed, the Araxes fretting about its bridge.
     Such were the scenes that Aeneas admired on the shield of
          Vulcan

698. *Anubis:* an Egyptian god, represented with the face of a dog.
    703. *Bellona:* a Roman goddess of
war.
    725. *Leleges, Carians:* peoples of
Asia Minor. *Gelonian:* from Scythia (in
the Balkans).
    726. *Euphrates:* an Eastern river.
    727. *Morini:* a Belgian people.
    728. *Araxes:* a turbulent river in
Armenia. Augustus built a new bridge
over it.

His mother gave him. Elated by its portrayal of things   730
Beyond his ken, he shouldered his people's glorious future.

[In the course of the desperate battles which follow, the young
Pallas, entrusted to Aeneas' care by his father, is killed by the
Italian champion Turnus, who takes and wears the belt of Pallas
as the spoil of victory. The fortunes of the war later change in favor
of the Trojans, and Aeneas kills the Etruscan King Mezentius,
Turnus' ally. Eventually, as the Italians prepare to accept the
generous peace terms offered by Aeneas, Turnus forestalls them by
accepting Aeneas' challenge to single combat to decide the issue.
But this solution is frustrated by the intervention of Juno, who
foresees Aeneas' victory. She prompts Turnus' sister, the river
nymph Juturna, to intervene in an attempt to save Turnus' life.
Juturna stirs up the Italians who are watching the champions prepare for the duel; the truce is broken, and in the subsequent fighting Aeneas is wounded by an arrow. Healed by Venus, he returns to
the fight, and the Italians are driven back. Turnus finally faces his
adversary. His sword breaks on the armor forged by Vulcan, and he
runs from Aeneas; he is saved by Juturna, who, assuming the shape
of his charioteer, hands him a fresh sword. At this point Juppiter
intervenes to stop the vain attempts of Juno and Juturna to save
Turnus.]

[*The Death of Turnus*]

Book XII

  . . . Meantime the king of all-powerful Olympus addresses Juno
As she looks down at the combat out of a golden cloud:—
    My wife, how shall it end now? What more is there you can
      do?
For you know, and admit the knowledge, that Aeneas is called of
    heaven
As a national hero, and fate is exalting him to the stars.   795
What are you planning? Why do you linger here in the chill
    clouds?
Was it right that Aeneas, the heaven-born, should be hurt by the
    hand of a mortal?
Or that Juturna should give back the missing sword to her brother—
Ah yes, without you she was powerless—and strengthen the loser's
    hand?
Then yield to my persuasions, give up the long feud now at last!   800
No more of the hidden rancour that so consumes you, the sullen
Recriminations your sweet lips have troubled me with so often!
This is the end, I say. You had power to harry the Trojans
All over lands and seas, to kindle accursed war,

Bring tragic disgrace on a king's home and drape a betrothal in
    mourning.   805
I forbid you to carry the feud any further.
                        So Juppiter spoke.
Juno, the daughter of Saturn, with lowered eyes, replied:—
    It is because your wishes, great consort, were known to me,
That I have reluctantly given up Turnus and quit the earth.
Otherwise I'd not be sitting apart here and putting up with   810
Every humiliation: no, armed with flame, I'd be there
In action, dragging the Trojans into a fatal fight.
I admit I encouraged Juturna to go and help her unfortunate
Brother, approved of her acting more boldly still to preserve him;
But not that she should use her bow and shoot at the Trojans: 815
This I swear by the source of the inexorable river,
Styx—the one dreadful and binding oath for us heaven-dwellers.
And now I do truly yield; I give up the fight—I am sick of it.
One thing, and no ruling of fate forbids you to grant it, I do
Entreat, for Latium's sake and the dignity of your own kin: 820
When they make peace through a prosperous—aye, let it be so—
    a prosperous
Marriage, and when they are making agreements and laws to unite
    them,
Do not command the indigenous Latins to change their ancient
Name, to become Trojans and to be called the Teucrians: 825
Allow them to keep the old language and their traditional dress:
Let it be Latium for ever, and the kings be Alban kings;
Let the line be Roman, the qualities making it great be Italian.
Troy's gone; may it be gone in name as well as reality.
    The creator of man and of all things replied to her with a smile:—
    Jove's sister you are indeed and the second child of Saturn,   830
So powerful the tides of wrath sweeping within your breast!
But come, there was no need for this violent emotion; calm yourself.
Willingly I grant what you ask: you have won me over.
The Italians shall keep their native tongue and their old traditions;
Their name shall not be altered. The Trojans will but sink down
    in   835
The mass and be made one with them. I'll add the rites and usage
Of Trojan worship to theirs. All will be Latins, speaking
One tongue. From this blend of Italian and Trojan blood shall arise

805. *betrothal in mourning:* a reference not only to the Italian losses but
also to the suicide of Amata, wife of
King Latinus, who hanged herself when
the Trojans assaulted the city just before the duel between Aeneas and Turnus
began.
    822. *Marriage:* the marriage between
Aeneas and Lavinia, daughter of Latinus.
    824. *Teucrians:* Trojans, from the
name of Teucer, the first Trojan king.
    826. *Alban:* the city of Alba Longa
was founded by Ascanius.
    830. *Jove's sister:* Jove (Juppiter)
and Juno were brother and sister as well
as husband and wife.

A people surpassing all men, nay even the gods, in godliness.
No other nation on earth will pay such reverence to Juno.   840
   The goddess bowed and agreed, glad now to change her whole
    policy,
Passed forthwith from the sky, leaving her place in the clouds.
   This being accomplished, the Father brooded awhile on another
Question—how to detach from her brother's side Juturna.
Two demon fiends there are, called by the name of Furies,   845
Whom darkest Night brought forth at one and the same birth with
Hellish Megaera, breeding all three alike with the twining
Coils of serpents and giving them wings like the wind. These
   creatures
Attend on Juppiter's throne, at the house of heaven's stern Ruler,
Ready to stab fear into the hearts of anguished mortals   850
Whenever the king of the gods is dealing out pestilences
And hideous death, or affrighting guilty cities with war.
Juppiter now sent one of these demons hurrying down from
Heaven, to confront Juturna with a forbidding omen.
Off she flew, and swiftly was borne to earth in a whirlwind.   855
Just as an arrow flies through the clouds from a bowstring—a shaft
Whose tip some Parthian or Cretan archer has doped with a deadly
Poison, and then shot it; fatal the wound it will give—
Whirring and unsuspected it flies through the mirk of the clouds:
So sped the spawn of Night upon her way to the earth.   860
When she could see the Trojan lines and Turnus' army,
She suddenly dwindled and changed into the shape of that small owl
Which often at night, when no one's about, perches on tombs
Or gables, and hoots for hours disquietingly through the darkness.
Thus transformed, the Fury flittered about the face of   865
Turnus, screeching, and kept on bumping his shield with her wings.
The thing was so uncanny that he went numb with fear
And his hair stood on end, and the voice died in his throat.
But Juturna recognised from afar the creaking wings of
The demon. It broke her spirit: she rent her dishevelled hair,   870
Scratched at her cheeks and beat her breast in grief for her
   brother:—
   Oh, Turnus, what can your sister do for you now? What worse
Remains for this much-tried heart? I have used all my powers
To save you. But how can I face a manifestation so dreadful?
No, no, I give up the fight now. I tremble—oh, spare me your
   terrors,   875
You sinister bird: I know the beat of your wings, I know that

---

857. *Parthian:* Parthia was the most dangerous neighbor of the Roman Empire in the east. Parthian mounted archers were famous.

They sound the tocsin of death, and Jove's high purpose has given
These high-handed orders. So thus he requites me who took my
    virginity?
Why did he make me immortal? disfranchise me from the common
Law of death? But for that, I could end my terrible anguish   880
This very moment, and go through the shades with my poor brother.
I immortal! What joy can I have from immortal life,
Bereft of my brother? Alas, that nowhere may earth yawn deep
And let me go down to the ghosts below, for I am a deity!
    So saying, the goddess veiled her face in her grey-green mantle,
And heavily sighing, vanished into the depths of the river.   886
    Aeneas moved up on his enemy, hefting and flashing his spear
Which was huge as a tree, and shouted out with extreme ferocity:—
Turnus, you'll get no more reprieves. Are you still recoiling?
It's cold steel now, hand to hand, not fleetness of foot, that will
    tell.   890
Try all the transformations of Proteus! Summon up
Your powers, whether of courage or magic! Take wings, if you like,
And shoot straight up to the stars, or go to ground in the deep earth!
    Turnus, shaking his head, replied:—
                               It's the gods and Juppiter's
Enmity frighten me, not your sneers or your bloodthirsty speeches.
    Without a word more he looked round and his eyes alit on a huge
    stone—   896
A huge old stone which for years had been lying there on the plain
As a boundary mark between fields, to prevent disputes about owner-
    ship.
Hardly could twelve strong men, of such physique as the earth
Produces nowadays, pick up and carry it on their shoulders.   900
Well, Turnus pounced on it, lifted it, and taking a run to give it
More impetus, hurled this stone from his full height at Aeneas.
But as he moved, as he ran, as he raised his hands, as he threw
That boulder, for him it was just as if somebody else were doing
    it.
Ice-bound were his veins, and his legs felt like water.   905
So too the stone he hurled, flying through empty air,
Failed to make the distance, fell short of its objective.
But, as it is in a nightmare, when sleep's narcotic hand
Is leaden upon our eyes, we seem to be desperately trying
To run and run, but we cannot—for all our efforts, we sink
    down   910
Nerveless; our usual strength is just not there, and our tongue
Won't work at all—we can't utter a word or produce one sound:

    879. he: Juppiter.
    891. *Proteus:* the old man of the
sea, who lived on the Egyptian island
of Pharos. For an account of his
power to change his shape, see Homer's
Odyssey, Book IV.

So with Turnus, each move he bravely attempted to make,
The unearthly demon brought it to nothing. Now did his feelings
Veer this way and that in distraction: he gazed at the city, the
    Rutuli;   915
Faltered with fear; trembled at the weapon menacing him.
He could see no way to escape and no way to get at Aeneas;
His chariot, his sister who drove it, were nowhere to be seen.
So Turnus faltered: the other brandished his fateful spear,
And watching out for an opening, hurled it with all his might   920
From a distance. The noise it made was louder than that of any
Great stone projected by siege artillery, louder than
A meteorite's explosion. The spear flew on its sinister
Mission of death like a black tornado, and piercing the edge of
The seven-fold shield, laid open the corselet of Turnus, low
    down.   925
Right through his thigh it ripped, with a hideous sound. The impact
Brought giant Turnus down on bent knee to the earth.
The Italians sprang to their feet, crying out: the hills all round
Bayed back their howl of dismay, far and wide the deep woods
    echoed it.
Turnus, brought low, stretched out a pleading hand, looked up
    at   930
His foe in appeal:—
               I know, I've deserved it. I'll not beg life.
Yours was the luck. Make the most of it. But if the thought of a
    father's
Unhappiness can move you—a father such as you had
In Anchises—I ask you, show compassion for aged Daunus
And give me back to him; or if that is the way it must be,   935
Give back my dead body. You have won. The Italians have seen me
Beaten, these hands outstretched. Lavinia is yours to wed.
Don't carry hatred further.
                 Aeneas stood over him, poised
On the edge of the stroke; but his eyes were restless, he did not
    strike.
And now what Turnus had said was taking effect, was making
    him   940
More and more indecisive, when on his enemy's shoulder
He noticed the fatal baldric, the belt with its glittering studs—
How well he knew it!—which Turnus had stripped from young
    Pallas after
He'd killed him, and put on himself—a symbol of triumph and
    doom.

---

915. *Rutuli:* the Italian troops watching the combat between **Turnus and**
Aeneas.

Aeneas fastened his eyes on this relic, this sad reminder   945
Of all the pain Pallas' death had caused. Rage shook him. He looked
Frightening. He said:—
                    Do you hope to get off now, wearing the spoils
You took from my Pallas? It's he, it's Pallas who strikes this blow—
The victim shedding his murderer's blood in retribution!
    So saying, Aeneas angrily plunged his sword full into   950
Turnus' breast. The body went limp and cold. With a deep sigh
The unconsenting spirit fled to the shades below.

PUBLIUS OVIDIUS NASO (OVID)

(43 B.C.–A.D. 17)

Amores*

1

Another collection of verse by the man from Sulmona,
that embarrassingly personal poet Naso.

Another of Cupid's commissions. Hands off, moralists!
Love's tender strains will shock you.

I write for the girl who responds to her sweetheart,   5
and the boy in love for the first time.

I want every young man wounded like me by Cupid's bow
to recognize the symptoms of his fever

and ask himself in amazement "How does this poet know
about me and my personal problems?"   10

Once, rashly, I sang of war in heaven and giants
with a hundred arms. My diction soared to the occasion—

the cruel vengeance of Mother Earth, and the piling
of Pelion upon Ossa upon Olympus.

But while I was busy with Jupiter standing on a storm-cloud,   15
thunderbolt at the ready to defend his heaven,

Corinna slammed her door. I dropped the thunderbolt
and even forgot the Almighty.

Forgive me, Lord. Your weapons couldn't help me.
That locked door had a far more effective bolt.   20

I returned to couplets and compliments, my own weapons,
and broke down its resistance with soft words.

---

* Our selection is from the translation by Guy Lee. Copyright © 1968 by Guy Lee. The original numbering of the selections is as follows: Book II.1, I.4, III.14, I.9, II.10, II.7, III.8, II.9b.
    1. *Sulmona:* Ovid's birthplace, in central Italy.

11 ff. a well-known epic theme, the war of the giants, sons of Earth, against the Olympian gods. The giants piled mountains on each other to reach the heavens (ll. 13–14).

The magic of verse can pull the blood-red moon out of orbit,
turn back the journeying sun's white steeds,

make rivers flow upstream,   25
split hooded snakes,

fling doors wide open, sliding
the strongest bolts from their staples.

What good are epic heroes to me—the two Atridae,
Achilles fleet of foot,   30

Ulysses wasting twenty years in war and wanderings,
Hector dragged in the dust by Greek horses?

But sing the prasies of a lovely girl
and she'll pay for the song in person.

A fair reward. Those famous names are out—   35
their gratitude means nothing to me.

My poems are written at Cupid's dictation
to catch the eye of Beauty.

23. Thessalian witches were popularly supposed to bring down the moon by their incantations.

29. *Atridae:* Agamemnon and Menelaus.
31. *Ulysses:* Latin form of the name of Odysseus.

2

Your husband? Going to the same dinner as us?
I hope it chokes him.

So I'm only to gaze at you, darling? Play gooseberry
while another man enjoys your touch?

You'll lie there snuggling up to him? He'll put his arm   5
round your neck whenever he wants?

No wonder Centaurs fought over Hippodamia
when the wedding wine began to flow.

I don't live in the forest nor am I part horse
but I find it hard to keep my hands off you.   10

However here's my plan. Listen carefully.
Don't throw my words of wisdom to the winds.

Arrive before him—not that I see what good
arriving first will do but arrive first all the same.

When he takes his place on the couch and you go to join him   15
looking angelic, secretly touch my foot.

Watch me for nods and looks that talk
and unobserved return my signals

7. *Centaurs:* half horse, half man. At the wedding feast they got drunk and tried to carry off all the women.

15. *couch:* The Romans dined reclining on couches which usually (as here) had room for three.

in the language of eyebrows and fingers
with annotations in wine.   20

Whenever you think of our love-making
stroke that rosy cheek with your thumb.

If you're cross with me, darling,
press the lobe of your ear

but turn your ring round if you're pleased   25
with anything I say or do.

When you feel like cursing your fool of a husband
touch the table as if you were praying.

If he mixes you a drink, beware—tell him to drink it himself,
then quietly ask the waiter for what you want.   30

I'll intercept the glass as you hand it back
and drink from the side you drank from.

Refuse all food he has tasted first—
it has touched his lips.

Don't lean your gentle head against his shoulder   35
and don't let him embrace you

or slide a hand inside your dress
or touch your breasts. Above all don't kiss him.

If you do I'll cause a public scandal,
grab you and claim possession.   40

I'm bound to see all this. It's what I shan't see
that worries me—the goings on under your cloak.

Don't press your thigh or your leg against his
or touch his coarse feet with your toes.

I know all the tricks. That's why I'm worried.   45
I hate to think of him doing what I've done.

We've often made love under your cloak, sweetheart,
in a glorious race against time.

You won't do that, I know. Still,
to avoid all doubt don't wear one.   50

Encourage him to drink but mind—no kisses.
Keep filling his glass when he's not looking.

If the wine's too much for him and he drops off
we can take our cue from what's going on around us.

When you get up to leave and we all follow   55
move to the middle of the crowd.

You'll find me there—or I'll find you
so touch me anywhere you can.

But what's the good? I'm only temporizing.
Tonight decrees our separation.   60

Tonight he'll lock you in and leave me
desolated at your door.

Then he'll kiss you, then go further,
forcing his right to our secret joy.

But you *can* show him you're acting under duress.   65
Be mean with your love—give grudgingly—in silence.

He won't enjoy it if my prayers are answered.
And if they're not, at least assure me you won't.

But whatever happens tonight tell me tomorrow
you didn't sleep with him—and stick to that story.   70

3

Your loveliness, I don't deny, needs lovers,
but spare me facts and figures—please.

My moral code does not require you to be chaste,
but it does demand concealment.

Any woman who pleads Not Guilty is innocent;   5
only confession gives her a bad name.

What madness to parade your nightlife in the daylight
and publicize your private affairs!

Even prostitutes insist on privacy
and lock the door before obliging a client.   10

Will *you* expose your naked guilt to scandalmongers
and give full details of your own misconduct?

Have *some* decency, please—or at least pretend to have,
so I can think you're faithful even if you aren't.

Carry on as before, but don't admit it,   15
and don't be ashamed of decorum in public.

There's a proper place for impropriety—
enjoy it there, shedding your inhibitions.

But don't forget them when you leave.
Confine your faults to bed.   20

It's no disgrace to undress there,
press thigh to thigh,

kiss as you please, and figure out
love's total variety,

moaning and whispering sweet words,   25
shaking the bedstead in abandon.

But when you dress put on your moral make-up too
and wear the negative look of virtue.

Take whoever you please—provided you take me in.
Don't enlighten me. Let me keep my illusions.   30

Need I see those notes coming and going?
That double hollow in the bed?

Your hair in sleepless disarray?
Those love-bites on your neck?

You'll soon be committing adultery before my very eyes.   35
Destroy your good name if you must, but spare my feelings.

These endless confessions bring me out in a cold sweat—
honestly, they're killing me.

My love becomes frustrated hate for what I can't help loving.
I'd gladly die—if only you'd die with me.   40

I'll ask no questions, I promise, and ferret out no secrets
if you'll do me the simple favour of deceit.

But if ever I catch you in the act,
if ever I'm forced to see the worst,

then flatly deny I saw what I did,   45
and your words shall stand in for my eyes.

It's so easy for you to beat a willing loser.
Only remember to say Not Guilty.

Two words can clear you—speak them and win.
Your case may be weak but your judge is weaker.   50

4

Yes, Atticus, take it from me—
lovers are all soldiers, in Cupid's private army.

Military age equals amatory age—
fighting and making love don't suit the old.

Commanders expect gallantry of their men—   5
and so do pretty girls.

Lovers too keep watch, bivouac, mount guard—
at their mistress' door instead of H.Q.

They have their forced marches,
tramping miles for love,   10

crossing rivers, climbing mountains,
trudging through the snow.

Ordered abroad they brave the storm
and steer by winter stars.

Hardened to freezing nights,   15
to showers of hail and sleet,

they go out on patrol,
observe their rivals' movements,

lay siege to rebel mistresses
and batter down front doors.   20

Tacticians recommend the night attack,
use of the spearhead, catching the foe asleep.

These tactics wiped out Rhesus and his Thracians,
capturing the famous horses.

Lovers use them too—to exploit a sleeping husband,   25
thrusting hard while the enemy snores,

eluding guards and night patrols,
moving under cover.

If war's a gamble, love's a lottery. Both have ups and downs.
In both apparent heroes can collapse.   30

So think again if you think of love as a soft option—
it calls for enterprise and courage.

Achilles loved Briseis, sulked when he lost her—
Trojans, now's your chance to hammer the Greeks!

Andromache strapped Hector's helmet on   35
and sent him into battle with a kiss.

Great Agamemnon fell in love at first sight—
with Cassandra's wind-swept hair.

Even Mars was caught. Trapped in the blacksmith's net
he caused an epic scandal in the sky.   40

And what about me? I was soft—born in a dressing-gown.
A reading-couch in the shade had sapped my morale.

But a pretty girl soon put me on my feet—
Fall in she ordered, *follow me*.

And look at me now—alive and alert, the night-fighter.   45
Yes, if you want an active life try love.

23. *Rhesus:* king of Thrace. He arrived
at Troy to save the city from the Greeks
but was killed (and his horses captured)
in a night raid made by Odysseus and
Diomedes.

39. *Mars:* Roman equivalent of Ares,
who was caught in bed with Aphrodite
by her husband Hephaestus, the smith
god, who had made a golden net to trap
the lovers.

5

Graecinus, I blame *you*. Yours that memorable remark
"No one can love two girls at once."

I trusted you and dropped my guard. The result
is too embarrassing—a double love-life.

They're both beautiful, both sophisticated.   5
It's hard to say which has more to offer.

Certainly one is more attractive—but which one?
I love each more than either,

torn by a schizophrenic passion,
a catamaran in contrary winds.   10

Great Aphrodite, one girl's hell enough on earth—
why double-damn me?

Why add leaves to trees, stars to the Milky Way,
water to the deep blue sea?

Still, two loves are better than none at all.   15
God send my enemies a moral life,

single sleep and limbs relaxed
in mid-mattress.

But give *me* ruthless love—to interrupt my slumbers
with company in bed.   20

Let woman be my undoing—one, if one's enough—
otherwise two.

I can take it. I may be thin and under weight
but I've muscle and stamina.

Pleasure's a food that builds me up.   25
I've never disappointed a girl.

Many's the night I've spent in love
and been fighting fit the morning after.

To die in love's duel—what final bliss!
It's the death I should choose.   30

Let soldiers impale their hearts on a pike
and pay down blood for glory.

Let seafaring merchants make their millions
till they and their lies are shipwrecked at last.

But when *I* die let me faint in the to and fro of love   35
and fade out at its climax.

I can just imagine the mourners' comment:
"Death was the consummation of his life."

6

So that's my role—the professional defendant?
I'm sick of standing trial—though I always win.

At the theatre I've only to glance at the back rows
and your jealous eye pin-points a rival.

A pretty girl need only look at me   5
and you're sure the look is a signal.

I compliment another woman—you grab my hair.
I criticize her—and you think I've something to hide.

If I'm looking well I don't love you.
If pale, I'm pining for someone else.   10

I wish to God I had been unfaithful—
the guilty can take their punishment.

As it is you accuse me blindly, believing anything.
It's your own fault your anger cuts no ice.

Remember the donkey, putting his long ears back—   15
the more he's beaten the slower he goes.

So that's the latest count against me—
I'm carrying on with your maid Cypassis?

Good God, if I wanted variety
is it likely I'd pick on a drudge like her?   20

What man of breeding would sleep with a slave
or embrace a body scarred by the lash?

Besides, she's your coiffeuse—her skill
makes her a favourite of yours.

I'd be mad to ask a maid so devoted to you.   25
She'd only turn me down and tell.

By Venus and Cupid's bow,
I'm innocent—I swear it!

7

Does anyone these days respect the artist
or value elegiac verse?

Time was when imagination meant more than money
but today *poor* and *boor* mean the same thing.

"I adore your poetry" she says,   5
and allows it in where I can't follow.

After the compliments the door curtly closes
and I, her poet, moon about humiliated,

displaced by a new-rich upstart, a bloody soldier
who butchered his way to wealth and a knighthood.   10

Him in your lovely arms! You in his clutches!
Light of my life, how could you?

That head wore a helmet, remember—
that obliging flank a sword.

His left hand, flashing the new equestrian ring,   15
once gripped a shield. His right has killed.

How can you hold hands with a killer?
Have you no sensibility?

2. *elegiac:* This word refers only to the
form employed by Ovid and other Latin
poets for love poetry—couplets with a
second line shorter than the first.
  10. *knighthood:* The soldier had been
raised to the so-called "equestrian" class
which gave him certain social and political
privileges and the right to wear the ring
mentioned in line 15.

Look at his scars, marks of a brutal trade—
that body earned him all he has.   20

I expect he even brags about his killings.
How can you touch him after that, gold-digger,

and allow me, the priest of Phoebus and the Muses,
to serenade your locked door in vain?

No man of taste should waste his time on art—   25
he'd better enlist and rough it under canvas.

Don't turn out couplets, turn out on parade.
Homer, join up if you want a date!

Jove Almighty realized gold's omnipotence
when he cashed himself to seduce a girl.   30

Before the transaction father looked grim, daughter prudish,
her turret steely, the doorposts coppered.

But when the crafty lecher arrived in cash
she opened her lap and gave as golden as she got.

Long ago, when Saturn ruled in the kingdom of heaven,   35
Earth sank all her capital in darkness—

stowed bronze and silver, gold and heavy iron in hell.
Ingots were not yet known:

she had better things to offer—crops without cultivation,
fruit on the bough, honey in the hollow oak.   40

No one tore the ground with ploughshares
or parcelled out the land

or swept the sea with dipping oars—
the shore was the world's end.

Clever human nature, victim of your inventions,   45
disastrously creative,

Why cordon cities with towered walls?
Why arm for war?

Why take to the sea—as if happiness were far away?
Why not annex the sky too?   50

We have, in a modest way—by deifying Bacchus
and Hercules and Romulus and now Caesar.

We dig for gold instead of food.
Our soldiers earn blood-money.

29 ff. a cynical reference to the story
of Acrisius, his daughter Danae, and her
seduction by Zeus in the form of a shower
of gold. See note on page 393.

35. *Saturn:* predecessor of Jupiter
(Zeus) as king of the gods. In his days
mankind was supposed to have lived in
rural peace, before the discovery of
metals.

51. *Bacchus:* Dionysus—here thought
of as a deified man.

52. *Romulus:* the founder of Rome,
was supposed to have been raised to the
heavens at his death, and Julius Caesar,
murdered in 44 B.C., was officially declared a god by his nephew Octavian,
now the all-powerful ruler of Rome.

The Senate's barred to the poor. Capital is king,   55
creates the solemn judge and the censorious knight.

Let them own the world—knights controlling Campus and Forum,
Senate dictating peace and war,

but hands off love! Sweethearts shouldn't be up for auction.
Leave the poor man his little corner.   60

As it is, if my girl were chaste as a Sabine prude
she'd crawl for anyone with money.

So I am locked out. When I'm around she's scared of her husband.
He'd vanish quick enough if I could pay.

O for a god in heaven to right a lover's wrongs   65
and turn those fat pickings to a pile of dust!

---

61. *Sabine:* one of the early Roman tribes, a synonym for puritan virtue.

8

Offered a sexless heaven I'd say *No thank you*—
women are such sweet hell.

Of course one gets bored, and passion cools, but always
desire begins to spiral again.

Like a horse bolting, with helpless rider   5
tugging at the reins,

or a gust catching a yacht about to tie up
and driving her out to sea,

Cupid's erratic air-stream hits me,
announcing love's target practice.   10

Then shoot, boy! I can't resist you.
Your aim strikes home in my heart.

Love's missiles lodge there automatically now—
they hardly know your quiver.

I pity the man whose idea of bliss   15
is eight hours' sleep.

Poor fool—what's sleep but death warmed up?
Resting in peace comes later.

Lead me astray, beguiling female voices.
Feed me on hope,   20

cooing today, cursing tomorrow,
locking me out and letting me in.

The fortunes of love. Cupid, Mars takes after you—
like stepson, like stepfather.

You're unpredictable, far more flighty than your wings,   25
giving delight, denying delight, evading question.

But maybe you and your lovely mother will hear this prayer:
be king of my heart for ever,

let women, those floating voters, crowd into the kingdom
and both sexes join there in your worship.   30

The New Testament*

[*The Birth and Youth of Jesus*]†

2. And it came to pass in those days, that there went out a
decree from Cæsar Augustus, that all the world[1] should be taxed.
(And this taxing was first made when Cyrenius was governor of
Syria.) And all went to be taxed, every one into his own city. And
Joseph also went up from Galilee, out of the city of Nazareth, into
Judæa, unto the city of David, which is called Bethlehem; (because
he was of the house and lineage of David:) to be taxed with Mary
his espoused wife, being great with child. And so it was, that, while
they were there, the days were accomplished that she should be
delivered. And she brought forth her firstborn son, and wrapped
him in swaddling clothes, and laid him in a manger; because there
was no room for them in the inn. And there were in the same
country shepherds abiding in the field, keeping watch over their
flock by night. And, lo, the angel of the Lord came upon them, and
the glory of the Lord shone round about them: and they were sore
afraid. And the angel said unto them, Fear not: for, behold, I bring
you good tidings of great joy, which shall be to all people. For unto
you is born this day in the city of David a Saviour, which is Christ[2]
the Lord. And this shall be a sign unto you; ye shall find the babe
wrapped in swaddling clothes, lying in a manger. And suddenly
there was with the angel a multitude of the heavenly host praising
God, and saying, Glory to God in the highest, and on earth peace,
good will toward men. And it came to pass, as the angels were
gone away from them into heaven, the shepherds said one to another, Let us now go even unto Bethlehem, and see this thing which
is come to pass, which the Lord hath made known unto us. And
they came with haste, and found Mary, and Joseph, and the babe
lying in a manger. And when they had seen it, they made known

---

* The text of these selections from
the Holy Bible is that of the King
James, or Authorized, Version.
† Luke 2:1–52.

1. the Roman Empire.
2. A Greek word meaning "anointed,"
used of kings, priests, and the De-
liverer promised by the Prophets.

abroad the saying which was told them concerning this child. And all they that heard it wondered at those things which were told them by the shepherds. But Mary kept all these things, and pondered them in her heart. And the shepherds returned, glorifying and praising God for all the things that they had heard and seen, as it was told unto them. And when eight days were accomplished for the circumcising of the child, his name was called JESUS,[3] which was so named of the angel[4] before he was conceived in the womb. And when the days of her purification[5] according to the law of Moses were accomplished, they brought him to Jerusalem, to present him to the Lord; (as it is written in the law of the Lord, Every male that openeth the womb[6] shall be called holy to the Lord;) and to offer a sacrifice according to that which is said in the law of the Lord, A pair of turtledoves, or two young pigeons. And, behold, there was a man in Jerusalem, whose name was Simeon; and the same man was just and devout, waiting for the consolation of Israel: and the Holy Ghost was upon him. And it was revealed unto him by the Holy Ghost, that he should not see death, before he had seen the Lord's Christ. And he came by the Spirit into the temple: and when the parents brought in the child Jesus, to do for him after the custom of the law, then took he him up in his arms, and blessed God, and said, Lord, now lettest thou thy servant depart in peace, according to thy word: for mine eyes have seen thy salvation, which thou hast prepared before the face of all people; a light to lighten the Gentiles,[7] and the glory of thy people Israel. And Joseph and his mother marvelled at those things which were spoken of him. And Simeon blessed them, and said unto Mary his mother, Behold this child is set for the fall and rising again[8] of many in Israel; and for a sign which shall be spoken against; (yea, a sword shall pierce through thy own soul also,) that the thoughts of many hearts may be revealed. And there was one Anna, a prophetess, the daughter of Phanuel, of the tribe of Aser: she was of a great age, and had lived with an husband seven years from her virginity; and she was a widow of about fourscore and four years, which departed not from the temple, but served God with fastings and prayers night and day. And she coming in that instant gave thanks likewise unto the Lord, and spoke of him to all them that looked for redemption in Jerusalem. And when they had performed all things according to the law of the Lord, they returned into Galilee, to their own city Nazareth. And the child grew, and waxed strong in spirit, filled with wisdom: and the grace of God was upon

3. a form of the name Joshua, which means "he shall save."

4. in the Annunciation to Mary. (Luke 1:31.)

5. For the law here referred to, see Leviticus 12.

6. first-born son. The first-born son was regarded as belonging to God. See Exodus 13:2.

7. non-Jews.

8. The Greek word is the one always used of the resurrection of the dead.

him. Now his parents went to Jerusalem every year at the feast of the passover. And when he was twelve years old, they went up to Jerusalem after the custom of the feast. And when they had fulfilled the days, as they returned, the child Jesus tarried behind in Jerusalem; and Joseph and his mother knew not of it. But they, supposing him to have been in the company, went a day's journey; and they sought him among their kinsfolk and acquaintance. And when they found him not, they turned back again to Jerusalem, seeking him. And it came to pass that after three days they found him in the temple, sitting in the midst of the doctors,[9] both hearing them, and asking them questions. And all that heard him were astonished at his understanding and answers. And when they saw him, they were amazed: and his mother said unto him, Son, why hast thou thus dealt with us? behold, thy father and I have sought thee sorrowing. And he said unto them, How is it that ye sought me? wist ye not that I must be about my Father's business? And they understood not the saying which he spoke unto them. And he went down with them, and came to Nazareth, and was subject unto them: but his mother kept all these sayings in her heart. And Jesus increased in wisdom and stature, and in favour with God and man.

9. teachers, rabbis.

[*The Teaching of Jesus*]

[THE SERMON ON THE MOUNT]*

5. And seeing the multitudes, he went up into a mountain: and when he was set, his disciples came unto him: and he opened his mouth, and taught them, saying, Blessed are the poor in spirit: for their's is the kingdom of heaven. Blessed are they that mourn: for they shall be comforted. Blessed are the meek: for they shall inherit the earth. Blessed are they which do hunger and thirst after righteousness: for they shall be filled. Blessed are the merciful: for they shall obtain mercy. Blessed are the pure in heart: for they shall see God. Blessed are the peacemakers: for they shall be called the children of God. Blessed are they which are persecuted for righteousness' sake: for their's is the kingdom of heaven. Blessed are ye, when men shall revile you, and persecute you, and shall say all manner of evil against you falsely, for my sake. Rejoice, and be exceeding glad: for great is your reward in heaven: for so persecuted they the prophets which were before you.

Ye are the salt of the earth: but if the salt have lost his savour, wherewith shall it be salted?[1] it is thenceforth good for nothing, but to be cast out, and to be trodden under foot of men. Ye are the light of the world. A city that is set on a hill cannot be hid.

* Matthew 5:1—7:29.   1. how can it regain its savor?

Neither do men light a candle, and put it under a bushel,[2] but on a candlestick; and it giveth light unto all that are in the house. Let your light so shine before men, that they may see your good works, and glorify your Father which is in heaven.

Think not that I am come to destroy the law, or the prophets: I am not come to destroy, but to fulfil. For verily I say unto you, Till heaven and earth pass, one jot or one tittle shall in no wise pass from the law, till all be fulfilled. Whosoever therefore shall break one of these least commandments, and shall teach men so, he shall be called the least in the kingdom of heaven: but whosoever shall do and teach them, the same shall be called great in the kingdom of heaven. For I say unto you, That except your righteousness shall exceed the righteousness of the scribes[3] and Pharisees,[4] ye shall in no case enter into the kingdom of heaven.

Ye have heard that it was said by them of old time, Thou shalt not kill; and whosoever shall kill shall be in danger of the judgment: but I say unto you, That whosoever is angry with his brother without a cause shall be in danger of the judgment: and whosoever shall say to his brother, Raca,[5] shall be in danger of the council: but whosoever shall say, Thou fool, shall be in danger of hell fire.[6] Therefore if thou bring thy gift to the altar, and there rememberest that thy brother hath ought against thee; leave there thy gift before the altar, and go thy way; first be reconciled to thy brother, and then come and offer thy gift. Agree with thine adversary quickly, whiles thou art in the way with him; lest at any time the adversary deliver thee to the judge, and the judge deliver thee to the officer, and thou be cast into prison. Verily I say unto thee, Thou shalt by no means come out thence, till thou hast paid the uttermost farthing.

Ye have heard that it was said by them of old time, Thou shalt not commit adultery: but I say unto you, That whosoever looketh on a woman to lust after her hath committed adultery with her already in his heart. And if thy right eye offend thee, pluck it out, and cast it from thee: for it is profitable for thee that one of thy members should perish, and not that thy whole body should be cast into hell. And if thy right hand offend thee, cut it off, and cast it from thee: for it is profitable for thee that one of thy members should perish, and not that thy whole body should be cast into

2. a household vessel with the capacity of a bushel.

3. the official interpreters of the Sacred Scriptures.

4. a sect which insisted on strict observance of the Mosaic law.

5. The word means "empty."

6. The reference is to Jewish legal institutions. The penalties which might be inflicted for murder (see the opening sentence of this paragraph) were death by the sword (a sentence of a local court, "the judgment"), death by stoning (the sentence of a higher court, "the council"), and lastly the burning of the criminal's body in the place where refuse was thrown, Gehenna, which is hence used as a name for hell. Jesus compares the different degrees of punishment (administered by God) for the new sins which he here lists to the degrees of punishment recognized by Jewish law.

hell. It hath been said, Whosoever shall put away his wife, let him give her a writing of divorcement: but I say unto you, That whosoever shall put away his wife, saving for the cause of fornication, causeth her to commit adultery: and whosoever shall marry her that is divorced committeth adultery.

Again, ye have heard that it hath been said by them of old time, Thou shalt not forswear thyself, but shalt perform unto the Lord thine oaths: but I say unto you, Swear not at all; neither by heaven; for it is God's throne: nor by the earth; for it is his footstool: neither by Jerusalem; for it is the city of the great King. Neither shalt thou swear by thy head, because thou canst not make one hair white or black. But let your communication be, Yea, yea; Nay, nay: for whatsoever is more than these cometh of evil.

Ye have heard that it hath been said, An eye for an eye, and a tooth for a tooth: but I say unto you, That ye resist not evil: but whosoever shall smite thee on thy right cheek, turn to him the other also. And if any man will sue thee at the law, and take away thy coat, let him have thy cloak also. And whosoever shall compel thee to go a mile, go with him twain. Give to him that asketh thee, and from him that would borrow of thee turn not thou away.

Ye have heard that it hath been said, Thou shalt love thy neighbour, and hate thine enemy. But I say unto you, Love your enemies, bless them that curse you, do good to them that hate you, and pray for them which despitefully use you, and persecute you; that ye may be the children of your Father which is in heaven: for he maketh his sun to rise on the evil and on the good, and sendeth rain on the just and on the unjust. For if ye love them which love you, what reward have ye? do not even the publicans[7] the same? And if ye salute your brethren only, what do ye more than others? do not even the publicans so? Be ye therefore perfect, even as your Father which is in heaven is perfect.

6. Take heed that ye do not your alms[8] before men, to be seen of them: otherwise ye have no reward of your Father which is in heaven. Therefore when thou doest thine alms, do not sound a trumpet before thee, as the hypocrites do in the synagogues and in the streets, that they may have glory of men. Verily I say unto you, They have their reward. But when thou doest alms, let not thy left hand know what thy right hand doeth: that thine alms may be in secret: and thy Father which seeth in secret himself shall reward thee openly.

And when thou prayest, thou shalt not be as the hypocrites are: for they love to pray standing in the synagogues and in the corners

---

7. the men who collected the taxes for the Roman tax-farming corpora- tions; they were, naturally, universally despised and hated.

8. charitable actions.

of the streets, that they may be seen of men. Verily I say unto you, They have their reward. But thou, when thou prayest, enter into thy closet, and when thou hast shut thy door, pray to thy Father which is in secret; and thy Father which seeth in secret shall reward thee openly. But when ye pray, use not vain repetitions, as the heathen do; for they think that they shall be heard for their much speaking. Be not ye therefore like unto them: for your Father knoweth what things ye have need of, before ye ask him. After this manner therefore pray ye: Our Father which art in heaven, Hallowed be thy name. Thy kingdom come. Thy will be done in earth, as it is in heaven. Give us this day our daily bread. And forgive us our debts, as we forgive our debtors. And lead us not into temptation, but deliver us from evil: For thine is the kingdom, and the power, and the glory, for ever. Amen. For if ye forgive men their trespasses, your heavenly Father will also forgive you: but if ye forgive not men their trespasses, neither will your Father forgive your trespasses.

Moreover when ye fast, be not, as the hypocrites, of a sad countenance: for they disfigure their faces, that they may appear unto men to fast. Verily I say unto you, They have their reward. But thou, when thou fastest, anoint thine head, and wash thy face; that thou appear not unto men to fast, but unto thy Father which is in secret: and thy Father, which seeth in secret shall reward thee openly.

Lay not up for yourselves treasures upon earth, where moth and rust doth corrupt, and where thieves break through and steal: but lay up for yourselves treasures in heaven, where neither moth nor rust doth corrupt, and where thieves do not break through nor steal: for where your treasure is, there will your heart be also. The light of the body is the eye: if therefore thine eye be single,[9] thy whole body shall be full of light. But if thine eye be evil, thy whole body shall be full of darkness. If therefore the light that is in thee be darkness, how great is that darkness!

No man can serve two masters: for either he will hate the one, and love the other; or else he will hold to the one, and despise the other. Ye cannot serve God and Mammon. Therefore I say unto you, Take no thought for your life, what ye shall eat, or what ye shall drink; nor yet for your body, what ye shall put on. Is not the life more than meat, and the body than raiment? Behold the fowls of the air: for they sow not, neither do they reap, nor gather into barns; yet your heavenly Father feedeth them. Are ye not much better than they? Which of you by taking thought can add one cubit unto his stature? And why take ye thought for raiment? Consider the lilies of the field, how they grow; they toil not, neither do they spin: and yet I say unto you that even Solomon in all his

9. clear.

glory was not arrayed like one of these. Wherefore, if God so clothe
the grass of the field, which to-day is, and to-morrow is cast into the
oven, shall he not much more clothe you, O ye of little faith? Therefore take no thought, saying, What shall we eat? or, What shall we
drink? or, Wherewithal shall we be clothed? (For after all these
things do the Gentiles[10] seek:) for your heavenly Father knoweth
that ye have need of all these things. But seek ye first the kingdom
of God, and his righteousness; and all these things shall be added
unto you. Take therefore no thought for the morrow: for the morrow shall take thought for the things of itself. Sufficient unto the
day is the evil thereof.

7. Judge not, that ye be not judged. For with what judgment ye
judged, ye shall be judged: and with what measure ye mete, it shall
be measured to you again. And why beholdest thou the mote that
is in thy brother's eye, but considerest not the beam that is in thine
own eye? Or how wilt thou say to thy brother, Let me pull out the
mote out of thine eye; and, behold, a beam is in thine own eye?
Thou hypocrite, first cast out the beam out of thine own eye; and
then shalt thou see clearly to cast out the mote out of thy brother's
eye.

Give not that which is holy unto the dogs, neither cast ye your
pearls before swine, lest they trample them under their feet, and
turn again and rend you.

Ask, and it shall be given you; seek, and ye shall find; knock, and
it shall be opened unto you: for every one that asketh receiveth; and
he that seeketh findeth; and to him that knocketh it shall be opened.
Or what man is there of you, whom if his son ask bread, will he give
him a stone? Or if he ask a fish, will he give him a serpent? If ye
then, being evil, know how to give good gifts unto your children,
how much more shall your Father which is in heaven give good
things to them that ask him? Therefore all things whatsoever ye
would that men should do to you, do ye even so to them: for this
is the law and the prophets.

Enter ye in at the strait[11] gate: for wide is the gate, and broad
is the way, that leadeth to destruction, and many there be which
go in thereat: because strait is the gate, and narrow is the way, which
leadeth unto life, and few there be that find it.

Beware of false prophets, which come to you in sheep's clothing,
but inwardly they are ravening wolves. Ye shall know them by their
fruits. Do men gather grapes of thorns, or figs of thistles? Even so
every good tree bringeth forth good fruit; but a corrupt tree bringeth
forth evil fruit. A good tree cannot bring forth evil fruit, neither
can a corrupt tree bring forth good fruit. Every tree that bringeth

10. non-Jews.   11. narrow.

not forth good fruit is hewn down, and cast into the fire. Wherefore by their fruits ye shall know them.

Not every one that saith unto me, Lord, Lord, shall enter into the kingdom of heaven; but he that doeth the will of my Father which is in heaven. Many will say to me in that day, Lord, Lord, have we not prophesied in thy name? and in thy name have cast out devils? and in thy name done many wonderful works? And then will I profess unto them, I never knew you: depart from me, ye that work iniquity.

Therefore whosoever heareth these sayings of mine, and doeth them, I will liken him unto a wise man, which built his house upon a rock: and the rain descended, and the floods came and the winds blew, and beat upon that house; and it fell not: for it was founded upon a rock. And every one that heareth these sayings of mine, and doeth them not, shall be likened unto a foolish man, which built his house upon the sand: and the rain descended, and the floods came, and the winds blew, and beat upon that house; and it fell: and great was the fall of it. And it came to pass, when Jesus had ended these sayings, the people were astonished at his doctrine: for he taught them as one having authority, and not as the scribes.

[PARABLES OF JESUS]*

15. Then drew near unto him all the publicans and sinners for to hear him. And the Pharisees and scribes murmured, saying, This man receiveth sinners, and eateth with them.

And he spoke this parable unto them, saying, What man of you, having a hundred sheep, if he lose one of them, doth not leave the ninety and nine in the wilderness, and go after that which is lost, until he find it? And when he hath found it, he layeth it on his shoulders, rejoicing. And when he cometh home, he calleth together his friends and neighbours, saying unto them, Rejoice with me; for I have found my sheep which was lost. I say unto you that likewise joy shall be in heaven over one sinner that repenteth, more than over ninety and nine just persons, which need no repentance.

Either what woman having ten pieces of silver, if she lose one piece, doth not light a candle, and sweep the house, and seek diligently till she find it? And when she hath found it, she calleth her friends and her neighbours together, saying, Rejoice with me; for I have found the piece which I had lost. Likewise, I say unto you, there is joy in the presence of the angels of God over one sinner that repenteth.

And he said, A certain man had two sons: and the younger of them said to his father, Father, give me the portion of goods that falleth to me. And he divided unto them his living. And not many

* Luke 15:1–32.

days after the younger son gathered all together, and took his journey into a far country, and there wasted his substance with riotous living. And when he had spent all, there arose a mighty famine in that land; and he began to be in want. And he went and joined himself to a citizen of that country; and he sent him into his fields to feed swine. And he would fain have filled his belly with the husks that the swine did eat: and no man gave unto him. And when he came to himself, he said, How many hired servants of my father's have bread enough and to spare, and I perish with hunger! I will arise and go to my father, and will say unto him, Father, I have sinned against heaven, and before thee, and am no more worthy to be called thy son: make me as one of thy hired servants. And he arose, and came to his father. But when he was yet a great way off, his father saw him, and had compassion, and ran, and fell on his neck, and kissed him. And the son said unto him, Father, I have sinned against heaven, and in thy sight, and am no more worthy to be called thy son. But the father said to his servants, Bring forth the best robe, and put it on him; and put a ring on his hand, and shoes on his feet: and bring hither the fatted calf, and kill it; and let us eat, and be merry: for this my son was dead, and is alive again; he was lost, and is found. And they began to be merry. Now his elder son was in the field: and as he came and drew nigh to the house, he heard musick and dancing. And he called one of the servants, and asked what these things meant. And he said unto him, Thy brother is come; and thy father hath killed the fatted calf, because he hath received him safe and sound. And he was angry, and would not go in: therefore came his father out, and intreated him. And he answering said to his father, Lo, these many years do I serve thee, neither transgressed I at any time thy commandment: and yet thou never gavest me a kid, that I might make merry with my friends: but as soon as this thy son was come, which hath devoured thy living with harlots, thou hast killed for him the fatted calf. And he said unto him, Son, thou art ever with me, and all that I have is thine. It was meet that we should make merry, and be glad: for this thy brother was dead, and is alive again; and was lost, and is found.

[The Betrayal of Jesus]*

26. . . . Then one of the twelve, called Judas Iscariot, went unto the chief priests, and said unto them, What will ye give me, and I will deliver him unto you? And they covenanted with him for thirty pieces of silver. And from that time he sought opportunity to betray him.

* Matthew 26:14–75.

Now the first day of the feast of unleavened bread[1] the disciples came to Jesus, saying unto him, Where wilt thou that we prepare for thee to eat the passover? And he said, Go into the city to such a man, and say unto him, The Master saith, My time is at hand; I will keep the passover at thy house with my disciples. And the disciples did as Jesus had appointed them; and they made ready the passover. Now when the even was come, he sat down with the twelve. And as they did eat, he said, Verily I say unto you, that one of you shall betray me. And they were exceeding sorrowful, and began every one of them to say unto him, Lord, is it I? And he answered and said, He that dippeth his hand with me in the dish, the same shall betray me. The Son of man goeth as it is written of him: but woe unto that man by whom the Son of man is betrayed! it had been good for that man if he had not been born. Then Judas, which betrayed him, answered and said, Master, is it I? He said unto him, Thou hast said.

And as they were eating, Jesus took bread, and blessed it, and brake it, and gave it to the disciples, and said, Take, eat; this is my body. And he took the cup, and gave thanks, and gave it to them, saying, Drink ye all of it; for this is my blood of the new testament,[2] which is shed for many for the remission of sins. But I say unto you, I will not drink henceforth of this fruit of the vine, until that day when I drink it new with you in my Father's kingdom. And when they had sung an hymn, they went out into the mount of Olives. Then saith Jesus unto them, All ye shall be offended[3] because of me this night: for it is written,[4] I will smite the shepherd, and the sheep of the flock shall be scattered abroad. But after I am risen again, I will go before you into Galilee. Peter answered and said unto him, Though all men shall be offended because of thee, yet will I never be offended. Jesus said unto him, Verily i say unto thee, That this night, before the cock crow, thou shalt deny me thrice. Peter said unto him, Though I should die with thee, yet will I not deny thee. Likewise also said all the disciples.

Then cometh Jesus with them unto a place called Gethsemane, and saith unto the disciples, Sit ye here, while I go and pray yonder. And he took with him Peter and the two sons of Zebedee,[5] and began to be sorrowful and very heavy. Then saith he unto them, My soul is exceeding sorrowful, even unto death: tarry ye here, and watch[6] with me. And he went a little farther, and fell on his face,

---

1. held in remembrance of the delivery of the Jews from captivity in Egypt. See Exodus 12.
2. i.e., of the new covenant, or agreement. Jesus compares himself to the lamb that was killed at the Passover as a sign of the covenant between God and the Jews.
3. The Greek means literally, "you will be made to stumble."
4. See Zechariah 13:7.
5. James and John.
6. stay awake.

and prayed, saying, O my Father, if it be possible, let this cup pass from me: nevertheless, not as I will, but as thou wilt. And he cometh unto the disciples, and findeth them asleep, and saith unto Peter, What, could ye not watch with me one hour? Watch and pray, that ye enter not into temptation: the spirit indeed is willing, but the flesh is weak. He went away again the second time, and prayed, saying, O my Father, if this cup may not pass away from me, except I drink it, thy will be done. And he came and found them asleep again: for their eyes were heavy. And he left them, and went away again, and prayed the third time, saying the same words. Then cometh he to his disciples, and saith unto them, Sleep on now, and take your rest: behold, the hour is at hand, and the Son of man is betrayed into the hands of sinners. Rise, let us be going: behold, he is at hand that doth betray me.

And while he yet spake, lo, Judas, one of the twelve, came, and with him a great multitude with swords and staves,[7] from the chief priests and elders of the people. Now he that betrayed him gave them a sign, saying, Whomsoever I shall kiss, that same is he: hold him fast. And forthwith he came to Jesus and said, Hail, master; and kissed him. And Jesus said unto him, Friend, wherefore art thou come? Then came they and laid hands on Jesus, and took him. And behold, one of them[8] which were with Jesus stretched out his hand, and drew his sword, and struck a servant of the high priest's, and smote off his ear. Then said Jesus unto him, Put up again thy sword into his place: for all they that take the sword shall perish with the sword. Thinkest thou that I cannot now pray to my Father, and he shall presently give me more than twelve legions[9] of angels? But how then shall the scriptures be fulfilled, that thus it must be? In that same hour said Jesus to the multitudes, Are ye come out as against a thief with swords and staves for to take me? I sat daily with you teaching in the temple, and ye laid no hold on me. But all this was done that the scriptures of the prophets might be fulfilled. Then all the disciples forsook him, and fled.

And they that had laid hold on Jesus led him away to Caiaphas the high priest, where the scribes and the elders were assembled. But Peter followed him afar off unto the high priest's palace, and went in, and sat with the servants, to see the end. Now the chief priests, and elders, and all the council, sought false witness[10] against Jesus, to put him to death; but found none: yea, though many false witnesses came, yet found they none. At the last came two false witnesses, and said, This fellow said, I am able to destroy the temple of God, and to build it in three days. And the high priest arose, and said unto him, Answerest thou nothing? What is it which these

---

7. clubs, sticks.
8. This was Peter.
9. The legion was a Roman military

formation; its full complement was six thousand men.
10. evidence.

witness against thee? But Jesus held his peace. And the high priest answered and said unto him, I adjure thee by the living God, that thou tell us whether thou be the Christ, the Son of God. Jesus saith unto him, Thou hast said:[11] nevertheless I say unto you, Hereafter shall ye see the Son of man sitting on the right hand of power, and coming in the clouds of heaven. Then the high priest rent[12] his clothes, saying, He hath spoken blasphemy; what further need have we of witnesses? behold, now ye have heard his blasphemy. What think ye? They answered and said, He is guilty of death.[13] Then did they spit in his face, and buffeted [14] him; and others smote him with the palms of their hands, saying, Prophesy unto us, thou Christ, Who is he that smote thee?

Now Peter sat without in the palace: and a damsel came unto him, saying, Thou also wast with Jesus of Galilee. But he denied before them all, saying, I know not what thou sayest. And when he was gone out into the porch, another maid saw him and said unto them that were there, This fellow was also with Jesus of Nazareth. And again he denied with an oath, I do not know the man. And after a while came unto him they that stood by, and said to Peter, Surely thou also art one of them; for thy speech bewrayeth[15] thee. Then began he to curse and to swear, saying, I know not the man. And immediately the cock crew. And Peter remembered the word of Jesus, which said unto him, Before the cock crow thou shalt deny me thrice. And he went out, and wept bitterly.

11. an affirmative phrase.
12. tore.
13. liable to the death penalty.

14. beat.
15. betrays. Peter's speech revealed his Galilean origin.

[*The Trial and Crucifixion of Jesus*]*

27. When the morning was come, all the chief priests and elders of the people took counsel against Jesus to put him to death: and when they had bound him, they led him away, and delivered him to Pontius Pilate the governor.[1]

Then Judas, which had betrayed him, when he saw that he was condemned, repented himself, and brought again the thirty pieces of silver to the chief priests and elders, saying, I have sinned in that I have betrayed the innocent blood. And they said, What is that to us? see thou to that. And he cast down the pieces of silver in the temple, and departed, and went and hanged himself. And the chief priests took the silver pieces, and said, It is not lawful for to put them into the treasury, because it is the price of blood. And they

* Matthew 27:1–66.
1. His official title was procurator of the province of Judea. The Roman policy was to allow the Jews as much independence as possible (especially in religious matters), but only the Roman authorities could impose a death sentence.

took counsel, and bought with them the potter's field,[2] to bury strangers in. Wherefore that field was called, The field of blood, unto this day. Then was fulfilled that which was spoken by Jeremy[3] the prophet, saying, And they took the thirty pieces of silver, the price of him that was valued, whom they of the children of Israel did value; and gave them for the potter's field, as the Lord appointed me. And Jesus stood before the governor: and the governor asked him, saying, Art thou the King of the Jews? And Jesus said unto him, Thou sayest.

And when he was accused of[4] the chief priests and elders, he answered nothing. Then said Pilate unto him, Hearest thou not how many things they witness against thee? And he answered him to never a word; insomuch that the governor marvelled greatly. Now at that feast the governor was wont to release unto the people a prisoner, whom they would. And they had then a notable prisoner, called Barabbas.[5] Therefore when they were gathered together, Pilate said unto them, Whom will ye that I release unto you? Barabbas, or Jesus which is called Christ? For he knew that for envy they had delivered him.[6]

When he was set down on the judgment seat, his wife sent unto him, saying, Have thou nothing to do with that just man: for I have suffered many things this day in a dream because of him. But the chief priests and elders persuaded the multitude that they should ask Barabbas, and destroy Jesus. The governor answered and said unto them, Whether of the twain will ye that I release unto you? They said, Barabbas. Pilate saith unto them, What shall I do then with Jesus which is called Christ? They all say unto him, Let him be crucified.[7] And the governor said, Why, what evil hath he done? But they cried out the more, saying, Let him be crucified.

When Pilate saw that he could prevail nothing, but that rather a tumult was made, he took water, and washed his hands before the multitude, saying, I am innocent of the blood of this just person: see ye to it. Then answered all the people, and said, His blood be on us, and on our children.

Then released he Barabbas unto them: and when he had scourged[8] Jesus, he delivered him to be crucified. Then the soldiers of the governor took Jesus into the common hall, and gathered unto him the whole band of soldiers. And they stripped him, and put on him a scarlet robe.

And when they had platted a crown of thorns, they put it upon

2. a field which had been dug for potter's clay, and was consequently not worth very much as land.

3. Jeremiah. The prophecy here quoted is a version of Zechariah 11:13.

4. by

5. under sentence of death for sedition and murder.

6. i.e., to the Roman authorities.

7. the regular Roman punishment for sedition.

8. whipped, a routine part of the punishment.

his head, and a reed[9] in his right hand: and they bowed the knee before him, and mocked him, saying, Hail, King of the Jews! And they spit upon him, and took the reed, and smote him on the head. And after that they had mocked him, they took the robe off from him, and put his own raiment on him, and led him away to crucify him. And as they came out, they found a man of Cyrene,[10] Simon by name: him they compelled to bear his cross. And when they were come unto a place called Golgotha, that is to say, a place of a skull,

They gave him vinegar to drink mingled with gall:[11] and when he had tasted thereof, he would not drink. And they crucified him, and parted his garments, casting lots: that it might be fulfilled which was spoken by the prophet, They parted my garments among them, and upon my vesture did they cast lots.[12] And sitting down they watched him there; and set up over his head his accusation written, THIS IS JESUS THE KING OF THE JEWS. Then were there two thieves crucified with him, one on the right hand, and another on the left.

And they that passed by reviled him, wagging their heads, and saying, Thou that destroyest the temple, and buildest it in three days, save thyself. If thou be the Son of God, come down from the cross. Likewise also the chief priests mocking him, with the scribes and elders, said, He saved others; himself he cannot save. If he be the King of Israel, let him now come down from the cross, and we will believe him. He trusted in God; let him deliver him now, if he will have him: for he said, I am the Son of God. The thieves also, which were crucified with him, cast the same in his teeth. Now from the sixth hour there was darkness over all the land unto the ninth hour. And about the ninth hour Jesus cried with a loud voice, saying, Eli, Eli, lama sabachthani? that is to say, My God, my God, why hast thou forsaken me?[13] Some of them that stood there, when they heard that, said, This man calleth for Elias. And straightway one of them ran, and took a sponge, and filled it with vinegar,[14] and put it on a reed, and gave him to drink. The rest said, Let be, let us see whether Elias[15] will come to save him.

Jesus, when he had cried again with a loud voice, yielded up the ghost. And, behold, the veil of the temple[16] was rent in twain from the top to the bottom; and the earth did quake, and the rocks rent; and the graves were opened; and many bodies of the saints which slept arose, and came out of the graves after his resurrection, and

---

9. to represent the king's scepter.
10. on the coast of North Africa.
11. The Greek word translated "vinegar" describes a sour wine which was the regular drink of the Roman soldiery. The addition of bitter gall is further mockery.
12. *that it might . . . cast lots:* It is generally agreed that this is a late addition to the text.

13. the opening words of Psalm 22. The actual words of Jesus, "Eli, Eli, lama sabachthani?" are Aramaic, the spoken Hebrew of the period.
14. See footnote 11.
15. the prophet Elijah.
16. the curtain which screened off the holy of holies.

went into the holy city, and appeared unto many. Now when the centurion,[17] and they that were with him, watching Jesus, saw the earthquake, and those things that were done, they feared greatly, saying, Truly this was the Son of God. And many women were there beholding afar off, which followed Jesus from Galilee, ministering unto him: among which was Mary Magdalene, and Mary the mother of James and Joses, and the mother of Zebedee's children. When the even was come, there came a rich man of Arimathæa, named Joseph, who also himself was Jesus' disciple. He went to Pilate, and begged the body of Jesus. Then Pilate commanded the body to be delivered. And when Joseph had taken the body, he wrapped it in clean linen cloth, and laid it in his own new tomb, which he had hewn out in the rock: and he rolled a great stone to the door of the sepulchre, and departed. And there was Mary Magdalene, and the other Mary, sitting over against the sepulchre.

Now the next day, that followed the day of the preparation, the chief priests and Pharisees came together unto Pilate, saying, Sir, we remember that that deceiver said, while he was yet alive, After three days I will rise again. Command therefore that the sepulchre be made sure[18] until the third day, lest his disciples come by night, and steal him away, and say unto the people, He is risen from the dead: so the last error shall be worse than the first. Pilate said unto them, Ye have a watch:[19] go your way, make it as sure as ye can. So they went, and made the sepulchre sure, sealing the stone, and setting a watch.

17. the Roman officer in charge of the execution.

18. guarded.

19. police force.

[The Resurrection]*

28. In the end of the sabbath, as it began to dawn toward the first day of the week, came Mary Magdalene and the other Mary to see the sepulchre. And, behold, there was a great earthquake: for the angel of the Lord descended from heaven, and came and rolled back the stone from the door, and sat upon it. His countenance was like lightning, and his raiment white as snow: and for fear of him the keepers did shake, and became as dead men. And the angel answered and said unto the women, Fear not ye: for I know that ye seek Jesus, which was crucified. He is not here: for he is risen, as he said. Come, see the place where the Lord lay. And go quickly, and tell his disciples that he is risen from the dead; and, behold, he goeth before you into Galilee; there shall ye see him: lo, I have told you. And they departed quickly from the sepulchre with fear and great joy; and did run to bring his disciples word.

And as they went to tell his disciples, behold, Jesus met them, saying, All hail! And they came and held him by the feet, and worshipped him. Then said Jesus unto them, Be not afraid: go tell my brethren that they go into Galilee, and there shall they see me.

* Matthew 28:1–20.

Now when they were going, behold, some of the watch came into the city, and shewed unto the chief priests all the things that were done. And when they were assembled with the elders, and had taken counsel, they gave large money unto the soldiers, saying, Say ye, His disciples came by night, and stole him away while we slept. And if this come to the governor's ears, we will persuade him, and secure you. So they took the money, and did as they were taught: and this saying is commonly reported among the Jews until this day.

Then the eleven disciples went away into Galilee, into a mountain where Jesus had appointed them. And when they saw him, they worshipped him: but some doubted. And Jesus came and spake unto them, saying, All power is given unto me in heaven and in earth.

Go ye therefore, and teach all nations, baptizing them in the name of the Father, and of the Son, and of the Holy Ghost: teaching them to observe all things whatsoever I have commanded you: and, lo, I am with you alway, even unto the end of the world. Amen.

PETRONIUS
(died A.D. 65)
Dinner with Trimalchio*

[The narrator, Encolpius, is a penniless vagabond who is a student of rhetoric under a master named Agamemnon. His close associates are Ascyltus, a fellow student, and Giton, a handsome boy who has no particular occupation. After some disreputable and very tiring adventures they are invited, as pupils of Agamemnon, to a banquet. The scene of the story is an unidentified city in southern Italy, the time probably about A.D. 50.]

The next day but one finally arrived. But we were so knocked about that we wanted to run rather than rest. We were mournfully discussing how to avoid the approaching storm,[1] when one of Agamemnon's slaves broke in on our frantic debate.

"Here," said he, "don't you know who's your host today? It's Trimalchio[2]—he's terribly elegant. . . . He has a clock[3] in the dining-room and a trumpeter[4] all dressed up to tell him how much longer he's got to live."

This made us forget all our troubles. We dressed carefully and

---

*From the work known as the *Satyricon*, probably written during the principate of Nero (A.D. 54–68). Our selection is one of the best-known incidents in the work. The translation is by J. P. Sullivan (copyright © J. P. Sullivan 1965, 1969) and is reprinted by permission of Penguin Books Ltd.

1. a repetition of the unsavory incidents they have just experienced.
2. *Trimalchio:* the name suggests "triply blessed" or "triply powerful."
3. at this period a rare and expensive article.
4. to sound off every hour on the hour.

told Giton, who was very kindly acting as our servant, to attend us at the baths.[5]

We did not take our clothes off but began wandering around, or rather exchanging jokes while circulating among the little groups. Suddenly we saw a bald old man in a reddish shirt, playing ball with some long-haired boys. It was not so much the boys that made us watch, although they alone were worth the trouble, but the old gentleman himself. He was taking his exercise in slippers and throwing a green ball around. But he didn't pick it up if it touched the ground; instead there was a slave holding a bagful, and he supplied them to the players. We noticed other novelties. Two eunuchs stood around at different points: one of them carried a silver chamber pot, the other counted the balls, not those flying from hand to hand according to the rules, but those that fell to the ground. We were still admiring these elegant arrangements when Menelaus[6] hurried up to us.

"This is the man you'll be dining with," he said. "In fact, you are now watching the beginning of the dinner."

No sooner had Menelaus spoken than Trimalchio snapped his fingers. At the signal the eunuch brought up the chamber pot for him, while he went on playing. With the weight off his bladder, he demanded water for his hands, splashed a few drops on his fingers and wiped them on a boy's head.

It would take too long to pick out isolated incidents. Anyway, we entered the baths where we began sweating at once and we went immediately into the cold water. Trimalchio had been smothered in perfume and was already being rubbed down, not with linen towels, but with bath-robes of the finest wool. As this was going on, three masseurs sat drinking Falernian[7] in front of him. Through quarreling they spilled most of it and Trimalchio said they were drinking his health.[8] Wrapped in thick scarlet felt he was put into a litter. Four couriers with lots of medals went in front, as well as a go-cart in which his favourite boy was riding—a wizened, bleary-eyed youngster, uglier than his master. As he was carried off, a musician with a tiny set of pipes took his place by Trimalchio's head and whispered a tune in his ear the whole way.

We followed on, choking with amazement by now, and arrived at the door with Agamemnon at our side. On the doorpost a notice was fastened which read:

ANY SLAVE LEAVING THE HOUSE WITHOUT HIS MASTER'S
PERMISSION WILL RECEIVE ONE HUNDRED LASHES

5. a public institution. They were magnificent buildings, containing not only baths of many types and temperatures, but places for conversation and games and even libraries.

6. appropriately enough, Agamemnon's assistant in instruction.

7. *Falernian:* a famous wine from Campania south of Rome.

8. *drinking his health:* He claims they are pouring a libation.

Just at the entrance stood the hall-porter, dressed in a green uniform with a belt of cherry red. He was shelling peas into a silver basin. Over the doorway hung—of all things—a golden cage from which a spotted magpie greeted visitors.

As I was gaping at all this, I almost fell over backwards and broke a leg. There on the left as one entered, not far from the porter's cubbyhole, was a huge dog with a chain round its neck. It was painted on the wall and over it, in big capitals, was written:

BEWARE OF THE DOG

My colleagues laughed at me, but when I got my breath back I went to examine the whole wall. There was a mural of a slave market, price tags and all. Then Thimalchio himself, holding a wand of Mercury[9] and being led into Rome by Minerva.[10] After this a picture of how he learned accounting and, finally how he became a steward. The painstaking artist had drawn it all in great detail with descriptions underneath. Just where the colonnade ended Mercury hauled him up by the chin and rushed him to a high platform. . . .

I began asking the porter what were the pictures they had in the middle.

"The Iliad, the Odyssey, and the gladiatorial show given by Laenas," he told me.

Time did not allow us to look at many things there . . . by now we had reached the dining-room. . . .

Finally we took our places. Boys from Alexandria poured iced water over our hands. Others followed them and attended to our feet, removing any hangnails with great skill. But they were not quiet even during this troublesome operation: they sang away at their work. I wanted to find out if the whole staff were singers, so I asked for a drink. In a flash a boy was there, singing in a shrill voice while he attended to me—and anyone else who was asked to bring something did the same. It was more like a musical comedy than a respectable dinner party.

Some extremely elegant hors d'oeuvre were served at this point—by now everyone had taken his place with the exception of Trimalchio, for whom, strangely enough, the place at the top was reserved. The dishes for the first course included an ass of Corinthian bronze with two panniers, white olives on one side and black on the other. Over the ass were two pieces of plate, with Trimalchio's name and the weight of the silver inscribed on the rims. There were some small iron frames shaped like bridges supporting dormice sprinkled with

9. *Mercury* (Hermes): as a trickster, the patron god of thieves and businessmen. 10. *Minerva* (Athena): patron goddess of arts and skills.

honey and poppy seed. There were steaming hot sausages too, on a silver gridiron with damsons and pomegranate seeds underneath.

We were in the middle of these elegant dishes when Trimalchio himself was carried in to the sound of music and set down on a pile of tightly stuffed cushions. The sight of him drew an astonished laugh from the guests. His cropped head stuck out from a scarlet coat; his neck was well muffled up and he had put round it a napkin with a broad purple stripe and tassels dangling here and there. On the little finger of his left hand he wore a heavy gilt ring and a smaller one on the last joint of the next finger. This I thought was solid gold, but actually it was studded with little iron stars. And to show off even more of his jewellery, he had his right arm bare and set off by a gold armlet and an ivory circlet fastened with a gleaming metal plate.

After picking his teeth with a silver toothpick, he began: "My friends, I wasn't keen to come into the dining room yet. But if I stayed away any more, I would have kept you back, so I've deprived myself of all my little pleasures for you. However, you'll allow me to finish my game."

A boy was at his heels with a board of terebinth wood[11] with glass squares, and I noticed the very last word in luxury—instead of white and black pieces he had gold and silver coins. While he was swearing away like a trooper over his game and we were still on the hors d'oeuvre, a tray was brought in with a basket on it. There sat a wooden hen, its wings spread round it the way hens are when they are broody. Two slaves hurried up and as the orchestra played a tune they began searching through the straw and dug out peahens' eggs, which they distributed to the guests.

Trimalchio turned to look at this little scene and said: "My friends, I gave orders for that bird to sit on some peahens' eggs. I hope to goodness they are not starting to hatch. However, let's try them and see if they are still soft."

We took up our spoons (weighing at least half a pound each) and cracked the eggs, which were made of rich pastry. To tell the truth, I nearly threw away my share, as the chicken seemed already formed. But I heard a guest who was an old hand say: "There should be something good here." So I searched the shell with my fingers and found the plumpest little figpecker, all covered with yolk and seasoned with pepper.

At this point Trimalchio became tired of his game and demanded that all the previous dishes be brought to him. He gave permission in a loud voice for any of us to have another glass of mead if we wanted it. Suddenly there was a crash from the orchestra and a troop of waiters—still singing—snatched away the hors d'oeuvre. However in the confusion one of the side-dishes happened to fall

11. *terebinth:* a very hard wood which takes a high polish and is very expensive (like everything Trimalchio has).

and a slave picked it up from the floor. Trimalchio noticed this, had the boy's ears boxed and told him to throw it down again. A cleaner came in with a broom and began to sweep up the silver plate along with the rest of the rubbish. Two long-haired Ethiopians followed him, carrying small skin bottles like those they use for scattering sand in the circus, and they poured wine over our hands—no one ever offered us water.

Our host was complimented on these elegant arrangements. "You've got to fight fair," he replied. "That is why I gave orders for each guest to have his own table. At the same time these smelly slaves won't crowd so."

Carefully sealed wine bottles were immediately brought, their necks labelled:

FALERNIAN

CONSUL OPIMIUS

ONE HUNDRED YEARS OLD[12]

While we were examining the labels, Trimalchio clapped his hands and said with a sigh:

"Wine has a longer life than us poor folks. So let's wet our whistles. Wine is life. I'm giving you real Opimian. I didn't put out such good stuff yesterday, though the company was much better class."

Naturally we drank and missed no opportunity of admiring his elegant hospitality. In the middle of this a slave brought in a silver skeleton, put together in such a way that its joints and backbone could be pulled out and twisted in all directions. After he had flung it about on the table once or twice, its flexible joints falling into various postures, Trimalchio recited:

> "Man's life alas! is but a span,
> So let us live it while we can,
> We'll be like this when dead."

After our applause the next course was brought in. Actually it was not as grand as we expected, but it was so novel that everyone stared. It was a deep circular tray with the twelve signs of the Zodiac arranged round the edge. . . .

After this course Trimalchio got up and went to the toilet. Free of his domineering presence, we began to strike up a general conversation. Dama[13] started off by calling for bigger glasses.

"The day's nothin'," he said, "It's night 'fore y'can turn around. So the best thing's get out of bed and go straight to dinner. Lovely

---

12. The wine was labeled with the name of the man who was consul in the year it was bottled. Opimius was consul in 121 B.C. Since it was in this year that the custom of dating the wine by the consul's name began, Trimalchio's wine was the oldest possible. If genuine, it would have been undrinkable.

13. *Dama:* one of Trimalchio's friends. Like those of Seleucus and Phileros who join the conversation later, his name is Greek.

cold weather we've had too. M'bath hardly thawed me out. Still, a hot drink's as good as an overcoat. I've been throwin' it back neat, and I'm pretty tight—the wine's gone to m'head."

This started Seleucus off.

"Me now," he said, "I don't have a bath every day. It's like gettin' rubbed with fuller's[14] earth, havin' a bath. The water bites into you, and as the days go by, your heart turns to water. But when I've knocked back a hot glass of wine and honey, kiss-my-arse I say to the cold weather. Mind you, I couldn't have a bath—I was at a funeral today. Poor old Chrysanthus has just given up the ghost —nice man he was! It was only the other day he stopped me in the street. I still seem to hear his voice. Dear, dear! We're just so many walking bags of wind. We're worse than flies—at least flies have got some strength in them, but we're no more than empty bubbles.

"And what would he have been like if he hadn't been on a diet? For five days he didn't take a drop of water or a crumb of bread into his mouth. But he's gone to join the majority. The doctors finished him—well, hard luck, more like. After all, a doctor is just to put your mind at rest. Still, he got a good sendoff—he had a bier and all beautifully draped. His mourners—several of his slaves were left their freedom—did him proud, even though his window was a bit mean with her tears. Suppose now he hadn't been so good to her! But women as a sex are real vultures. It's no good doing them a favour, you might as well throw it down a well. An old passion is just an ulcer."

He was being a bore and Phileros said loudly:

"Let's think of the living. He's got what he deserved. He lived an honest life and he died an honest death. What has he got to complain about? He started out in life with just a penny and he was ready to pick up less than that from a muck-heap, if he had to use his teeth. He went up in the world. He got bigger and bigger till he got where you see, like a honeycomb. I honestly think he left a solid hundred thousand and he had the lot in hard cash. But I'll be honest about it—seeing I'm a bit of a cynic—he had a foul mouth and too much lip. He wasn't a man, he was just murder.

"Now his brother was a fine man, a real friend to his friends, always ready with a helping hand or a decent meal.

"Chrysanthus had bad luck at first, but the first vintage set him on his feet. He fixed his own price when he sold the wine. And what properly kept his head above water was a legacy he came in for, when he pocketed more than was left to him. And the block-head, when he had a quarrel with his brother, cut him out of his will in favour of some sod we've never heard of. You're leaving a lot behind when you leave your own flesh and blood. But he took advice from his slaves and they really fixed him. It's never right to believe all you're told, especially for a business man. But it's true he

---

14. *fuller:* a cleaner (of woollen cloaks). They used very strong solvents.

enjoyed himself while he lived. You got it, you keep it. He was certainly Fortune's favourite—lead turned to gold in his hand. Mind you, it's easy when everything runs smoothly.

"And how old do you think he was? Seventy or more! But he was hard as nails and carried his age well. His hair was black as a raven's wing. I knew the man for ages and ages and he was still an old lecher. I honestly don't think he left the dog alone. What's more, he liked little boys—he could turn his hand to anything. Well, I don't blame him—after all, he couldn't take anything else with him."

This was Phileros, then Ganymedes said:

"You're all talking about things that don't concern heaven or earth. Meanwhile, no one gives a damn the way we're hit by the corn situation. Honest to God, I couldn't get hold of a mouthful of bread today. And look how there's still no rain. It's been absolute starvation for a whole year now. To hell with the food officers! They're in with the bakers—'You be nice to me and I'll be nice to you.' So the little man suffers, while those grinders of the poor never stop celebrating. Oh, if only we still had the sort of men I found here when I first arrived from Asia. Like lions they were. That was the life! Come one, come all! If white flour was inferior to the very finest, they'd thrash those bogeymen till they thought God Almighty was after them.

"I remember Safinius—he used to live by the old arch then; I was a boy at the time. He wasn't a man, he was all pepper. He used to scorch the ground wherever he went. But he was dead straight—don't let him down and he wouldn't let you down. You'd be ready to play *morra*[15] with him in the dark. But on the city council, how he used to wade into some of them—no beating about the bush, straight from the shoulder! And when he was in court, his voice got louder and louder like a trumpet. He never sweated or spat—I think there was a touch of the old acid about him. And very affable he was when you met him, calling everyone by name just like one of us. Naturally at the time corn was dirt cheap. You could buy a penny loaf that two of you couldn't get through. Today—I've seen bigger bull's-eyes.

"Ah me! It's getting worse every day. This place is going down like a calf's tail. But why do we have a third-rate food officer who wouldn't lose a penny to save our lives? He sits at home laughing and rakes in more money a day than anyone else's whole fortune. I happen to know he's just made a thousand in gold. But if we had any balls at all, he wouldn't be feeling so pleased with himself. People today are lions at home and foxes outside.

"Take me, I've already sold the rags off my back for food and if this shortage continues, I'll be selling my bit of a house. What's

15. *morra:* a game (still played in southern Italy) which requires the players to match the number of fingers held out by the opponent.

going to happen to this place if neither god nor man will help us? As I hope to go home tonight, I'm sure all this is heaven's doing.

"Nobody believes in heaven, see, nobody fasts, nobody gives a damn for the Almighty. No, people only bow their heads to count their money. In the old days high-class ladies used to climb up the hill barefoot, their hair loose and their hearts pure, and ask God for rain. And he'd send it down in bucketfuls right away—it was then or never—and everyone went home like drowned rats. Since we've given up religion the gods nowadays keep their feet well wrapped up. The fields just lie . . ."

"Please, please," broke in Echion the rag merchant, "be a bit more cheerful. 'First it's one thing, then another,' as the yokel said when he lost his spotted pig. What we haven't got today, we'll have tomorrow. That's the way life goes. Believe me, you couldn't name a better country, if it had the people. As things are, I admit, it's having a hard time, but it isn't the only place. We mustn't be soft. The sky don't get no nearer wherever you are. If you were somewhere else, you'd be talking about the pigs walking round ready roasted back here.

"And another thing, we'll be having a holiday with a three-day show that's the best ever—and not just a hack troupe of gladiators but freedmen for the most part. My old friend Titus has a big heart and a hot head. Maybe this, maybe that, but something at all events. I'm a close friend of his and he does nothing by halves. He'll give us cold steel, no quarter and the slaughterhouse right in the middle where all the stands can see it. And he's got the wherewithal—he was left thirty million when his poor father died. Even if he spent four hundred thousand, his pocket won't feel it and he'll go down in history. He's got some big brutes already, and a woman who fights in a chariot and Glyco's steward,[16] who was caught having fun with his mistress. You'll see quite a quarrel in the crowd between jealous husbands and romantic lovers. But that half-pint Glyco threw his steward to the lions, which is just giving himself away. How is it the servant's fault when he's forced into it? It's that old pisspot who really deserves to be tossed by a bull. But if you can't beat the ass you beat the saddle. But how did Glyco imagine the poisonous daughter of Hermogenes[17] would ever turn out well? The old man could cut the claws off a flying kite, and a snake don't hatch old rope. Glyco—well, Glyco's got his. He's branded for as long as he lives and only the grave will get rid of it. But everyone pays for their mistakes.

"But I can almost smell the dinner[18] Mammaea is going to give us—two denarii apiece for me and the family. If he really does it,

16. *steward:* a household slave. His master was permitted by law to punish him by forcing him to fight wild beasts in the arena.

17. *Hermogenes:* presumably the father of Glyco's wife.

18. *dinner:* a public banquet, given by Mammaea as part of his electoral campaign. His rival Norbanus has been giving gladiatorial shows.

he'll make off with all Norbanus's votes, I tell you he'll win at a
canter. After all, what good has Nobanus done us? He put on some
half-pint gladiators, so done in already that they'd have dropped if
you blew at them. I've seen animal-killers[19] fight better. As for the
horsemen killed, he got them off a lamp[20]—they ran round like
cocks in a backyard. One was just a carthorse, the other couldn't
stand up, and the reserve was just one corpse instead of another—
he was practically hamstrung. One boy did have a bit of spirit—he
was in Thracian armour,[21] and even he didn't show any initiative.
In fact, they were all flogged afterwards, there were so many shouts
of 'Give 'em what for!' from the crowd. Pure yellow, that's all.

"'Well, I've put on a show for you,' he says. 'And I'm clapping
you,' says I. 'Reckon it up—I'm giving more than I got. So we're
quits.'

"Hey, Agamemnon! I suppose you're saying 'What is that bore
going on and on about?' It's because a good talker like you don't
talk. You're a cut above us, and so you laugh at what us poor
people say. We all know you're off your head with all that reading.
But never mind! Some day I'll get you to come down to my place
in the country and have a look at our little cottage. We'll find something to eat—a chicken, some eggs. It'll be nice, even though the
unreliable weather this year has made off with everything. Anyway,
we'll find enough to fill our bellies.

"And my kid is growing up to be a pupil of yours. He can divide
by four already. If God spares him, you'll have him ready to do anything for you. In his spare time, he won't take his head out of his
exercise book. He's clever and there's good stuff in him, even if he
is crazy about birds. Only yesterday I killed his three goldfinches
and told him a weasel ate them. But he's found some other silly
hobbies, and he's having a fine time painting. Still, he's already well
ahead with his Greek, and he's starting to take to his Latin, though
his tutor is too pleased with himself and unreliable—he just comes
and goes. He knows his stuff but doesn't want to work. There is
another one as well, not so clever but he is conscientious—he
teaches the boy more than he knows himself. In fact, he makes a
habit of coming around on holidays, and whatever you give him,
he's happy.

"Anyway, I've just bought the boy some law books, as I want him
to pick up some legal training for home use. There's a living in that
sort of thing. He's done enough dabbling in poetry and such like. If
he objects, I've decided he'll learn a trade—barber, auctioneer, or
at least a barrister—something he can't lose till he dies. Well, yesterday I gave it to him straight: 'Believe me, my lad, any studying
you do will be for your own good. You see Phileros the solicitor—if

19. *animal-killers:* professional fighters
of wild animals, considered inferior to
gladiators.
20. *lamp:* as small as the horsemen
depicted on a lamp.
21. *Thracian armour:* light armor, such
as that worn by soldiers from Thrace, a
savage country northeast of Greece.

he hadn't studied, he'd be starving today. It's not so long since he was humping round loads on his back. Now he can even look Norbanus in the face. An education is an investment, and a proper profession never goes dead on you.' "

This was the sort of conversation flying round when Trimalchio came in, dabbed his forehead and washed his hands in perfume. There was a short pause, then he said:

"Excuse me, dear people, my inside has not been answering the call for several days now. The doctors are puzzled. But some pomegranate rind and resin in vinegar has done me good. But I hope now it will be back on its good behaviour. Otherwise my stomach rumbles like a bull. So if any of you wants to go out, there's no need for him to be embarrassed. None of us was born solid. I think there's nothing so tormenting as holding yourself in. This is the one thing even God Almighty can't object to. Yes, laugh, Fortunata,[22] but you generally keep me up all night with this sort of thing.

"Anyway, I don't object to people doing what suits them even in the middle of dinner—and the doctors forbid you to hold yourself in. Even if it's a longer business, everything is there just outside—water, bowls, and all the other little comforts. Believe me, if the wind goes to your brain it starts flooding your whole body too. I've known a lot of people die from this because they wouldn't be honest with themselves."

We thanked him for being so generous and considerate and promptly proceeded to bury our amusement in our glasses. Up to this point we'd not realized we were only in mid-stream, as you might say.

The orchestra played, the tables were cleared, and then three white pigs were brought into the dining-room, all decked out in muzzles and bells. The first, the master of ceremonies announced, was two years old, the second three, and the third six. I was under the impression that some acrobats were on their way in and the pigs were going to do some tricks, the way they do in street shows. But Trimalchio dispelled this impression by asking:

"Which of these would you like for the next course? Any clodhopper can do you a barnyard cock or a stew and trifles like that, but my cooks are used to boiling whole calves."

He immediately sent for the chef and without waiting for us to choose he told him to kill the oldest pig.

He then said to the man in a loud voice:

"Which division are you from?"

When he replied he was from number forty, Trimalchio asked:

"Were you bought or were you born here?"

"Neither," said the chef, "I was left to you in Pansa's will."

"Well, then," said Trimalchio, "see you serve it up carefully—otherwise I'll have you thrown into the messenger's division."

22. *Fortunata:* Trimalchio's wife.

So the chef, duly reminded of his master's magnificence, went back to his kitchen, the next course leading the way.

Trimalchio looked round at us with a gentle smile: "If you don't like the wine, I'll have it changed. It is up to you to do it justice. I don't buy it, thank heaven. In fact, whatever wine really tickles your palate this evening, it comes from an estate of mine which as yet I haven't seen. It's said to join my estates at Tarracina and Tarentum. What I'd like to do now is add Sicily to my little bit of land, so that when I want to go to Africa, I could sail there without leaving my own property.

"But tell me, Agamemnon, what was your debate about today? Even though I don't go in for the law, still I've picked up enough education for home consumption. And don't you think I turn my nose up at studying, because I have two libraries, one Greek, one Latin. So tell us, just as a favour, what was the topic of your debate?"

Agamemnon was just beginning, "A poor man and a rich man were enemies . . ." when Trimalchio said: "What's a poor man?" "Oh, witty!" said Agamemnon, and then told us about some fictitious case or other. Like lightning Trimalchio said: "If this happened, it's not a fictitious case—if it didn't happen, then it's nothing at all."

We greeted this witticism and several more like it with the greatest enthusiasm.

"Tell me, my dear Agamemnon," continued Trimalchio, "do you remember the twelve labours of Hercules and the story of Ulysses —how the Cyclops tore out his thumb with a pair of pincers.[23] I used to read about them in Homer, when I was a boy. In fact, I actually saw the Sibyl at Cumae with my own eyes dangling in a bottle, and when the children asked her in Greek: 'What do you want, Sybil?' she used to answer: 'I want to die.' "

[Presents for the guests are distributed with a slave announcing the nature of each gift and making in each case an atrocious pun on the name of the guest.]

We laughed for ages. There were hundreds of things like this but they've slipped my mind now.

Ascyltus, with his usual lack of restraint, found everything extremely funny, lifting up his hands and laughing till the tears came. Eventually one of Trimalchio's freedman[24] friends flared up at him—the one sitting above me, in fact.

"You with the sheep's eyes," he said, "what's so funny? Isn't our host elegant enough for you? You're better off, I suppose, and used

23. *pincers:* Trimalchio refers to Odysseus' adventures in the cave of the Cyclops (*Odyssey*, Book IX). In spite of what he goes on to say, he has obviously not read Homer.

24. *freedman:* a former slave who had bought his freedom.

to a bigger dinner. Holy guardian here preserve me! If I was sitting by him, I'd make him bleat! A fine pippin he is to be laughing at other people! Some fly-by-night from god knows where—not worth his own piss. In fact, if I pissed round him, he wouldn't know where to turn.

"By god, it takes a lot to make me boil, but if you're too soft, worms like this only come to the top. Look at him laughing! What's he got to laugh at? Did his father pay cash for him? You're a Roman knight,[25] are you? Well, my father was a king.

" '*Why are you only a freedman?*' did you say? Because I went into service voluntarily. I wanted to be a Roman citizen, not a subject with taxes to pay. And today, I hope no one can laugh at the way I live. I'm a man among men, and I walk with my head up. I don't owe anybody a penny—there's never been a court-order out for me. No one's said '*Pay up!*' to me in the street.

"I've bought a bit of land and some tiny pieces of plate. I've twenty bellies to feed, as well as a dog. I bought my old woman's freedom so nobody could wipe his dirty hands on *her* hair. Four thousand I paid for myself. I was elected to the Augustan College[26] and it cost me nothing. I hope when I die I won't have to blush in my coffin.

"But you now, you're such a busybody you don't look behind you. You see a louse on somebody else, but not the fleas on your own back. You're the only one who finds us funny. Look at the professor now—he's an older man than you and we get along with him. But you're still wet from your mother's milk and not up to your ABC yet. Just a crackpot—you're like a piece of wash-leather in soak, softer but no better! You're grander than us—well, have two dinners and two suppers! I'd rather have my good name than any amount of money. When all's said and done, who's ever asked me for money twice? For forty years I slaved but nobody ever knew if I was a slave or a free man. I came to this colony when I was a lad with long hair—the town-hall hadn't been built then. But I worked hard to please my master—there was a real gentleman, with more in his little finger-nail than there is in your whole body. And I had people in the house who tried to trip me up one way or another, but still—thanks be to his guardian spirit!—I kept my head above water. That's real success: being born free is as easy as all get-out. Now what are you gawping at, like a goat in a vetch field?"

At this remark, Giton, who was waiting on me, could not suppress his laughter and let out a filthy guffaw, which did not pass unnoticed by Ascyltus's opponent. He turned his abuse on the boy.

"So!" he said, "you're amused too, are you, you curly-headed

25. *knight:* a Roman class including all who had property above a certain amount.
26. The state religion was the worship of Augustus, the emperor. The office of priest might be sold or conferred.

onion? A merry Saturnalia[27] to you! Is it December, I'd like to know? When did *you* pay your liberation tax?[28] Look, he doesn't know what to do, the gallow's bird, the crow's meat.

"God's curse on you, and your master too, for not keeping you under control! As sure as I get my bellyful, it's only because of Trimalchio that I don't take it out of you here and now. He's a freedman like myself. We're doing all right, but those good-for-nothings, well—. It's easy to see, like master, like man. I can hardly hold myself back, and I'm not naturally hot-headed—but once I start, I don't give a penny for my own mother.

"All right! I'll see you when we get outside, you rat, you excrescence. I'll knock your master in the dirt before I'm an inch taller or shorter. And I won't let you off either, by heaven, even if you scream down God Almighty. Your cheap curls and your no-good master won't be much use to you then—I'll see to that. I'll get my teeth into you, all right. Either I'm much mistaken about myself or you won't be laughing at us behind your golden beard. Athena's curse on you and the man who first made you such a forward brat.

"I didn't learn no geometry or criticism and such silly rubbish, but I can read the letters on a notice board and I can do my percentages in metal, weights, and money. In fact, if you like, we'll have a bet. Come on, here's my cash. Now you'll see how your father wasted his money, even though you do know how to make a speech.

"Try this:

> Something we all have.
> Long I come, broad I come. What am I?

"I'll give you it: something we all have that runs and doesn't move from its place; something we all have that grows and gets smaller.[29]

"You're running round in circles, you've had enough, like the mouse in the pisspot. So either keep quiet or keep out of the way of your betters, they don't even know you're alive—unless you think I care about your box-wood rings that you swiped from your girl friend! Lord make me lucky! Let's go into town and borrow some money. You'll soon see they trust this iron one.

"Pah! a drownded fox makes a nice sight, I must say. As I hope to make my pile and die so famous that people swear by my dead body, I'll hound you to death. And he's a nice thing too—the one who taught you all these tricks—a muttonhead, not a master. We

---

27. *Saturnalia:* a December festival in honor of an ancient Italian deity at which the normal order of everyday life was reversed and the slaves and children made fun of their masters.

28. *liberation tax:* The freed slave had to pay 5 per cent of his value to the treasury.

29. There is no agreement about the correct answer to these riddles. Suggested answers are, to the first, the foot; the second, the eye; the third, the hair.

learned different. Our teacher used to say: 'Are your things in order? Go straight home. No looking around. And be polite to your elders.' Nowadays it's all an absolute muck-heap. They turn out nobody worth a penny. I'm like you see me and I thank God for the way I was learnt." . . .

In the middle of all this, a lictor[30] knocked at the double doors and a drunken guest entered wearing white, followed by a large crowd of people. I was terrified by this lordly apparition and thought it was the chief magistrate arriving. So I tried to rise and get my bare feet on the floor. Agamemnon laughed at this panic and said:

"Get hold of yourself, you silly fool. This is Habinnas—Augustan College and monumental mason."

Relieved by this information I resumed my position and watched Habinnas' entry with huge admiration. Being already drunk, he had his hands on his wife's shoulders; loaded with several garlands, oil pouring down his forehead and into his eyes, he settled himself into the place of honour and immediately demanded some wine and hot water. Trimalchio, delighted by these high spirits, demanded a larger cup for himself and asked how he had enjoyed it all.

"The only thing we missed," replied Habinnas, "was yourself— the apple of my eye was here. Still, it was damn good. Scissa was giving a ninth-day dinner[31] in honour of a poor slave of hers she'd freed on his death-bed. And I think she'll have a pretty penny to pay in liberation tax because they reckon he was worth fifty thousand. Still, it was pleasant enough, even if we did have to pour half our drinks over his wretched bones."

"Well," said Trimalchio, "what did you have for dinner?"

"I'll tell you if I can—I've such a good memory that I often forget my own name. For the first course we had a pig crowned with sausages and served with blood-puddings and very nicely done giblets, and of course beetroot and pure wholemeal bread—which I prefer to white myself: it's very strengthening and I don't regret it when I do my business. The next course was cold tart and a concoction of first-class Spanish wine poured over hot honey. I didn't eat anything at all of the actual tart, but I dived right into the honey. Scattered round were chickpeas, lupines, a choice of nuts and an apple apiece —though I took two. And look, I've got them tied up in a napkin, because if I don't take something in the way of a present to my youngster, I'll have a row on my hands.

"Oh, yes, my good lady reminds me. We had a hunk of bearmeat set before us, which Scintilla was foolish enough to try, and she practically spewed up her guts; but I ate more than a pound of it, as it tasted like real wild-boar. And I say if bears can eat us poor people, it's all the more reason why us poor people should eat bears.

---

30. *lictor:* a magistrate's attendant.
31. *ninth-day dinner:* on the last day of the mourning period.

"To finish up with, we had some cheese basted with new wine, snails all round, chitterlings, plates of liver, eggs in pastry hoods, turnips, mustard, and some filthy concoction—good riddance to that. There were pickled cumin seeds too, passed round in a bowl and some people were that bad-mannered they took three handfuls. You see, we sent the ham away.

"But tell me something, Gaius, now I ask—why isn't Fortunata at the table?"

"You know her," replied Trimalchio, "unless she's put the silver away and shared out the left-overs among the slaves, she won't put a drop of water to her mouth."

"All the same," retorted Habinnas, "unless she sits down, I'm shagging off."

And he was starting to get up, when at a given signal all the servants shouted *"Fortunata"* four or five times. So in she came with her skirt tucked up under a yellow sash to show her cerise petticoat underneath, as well as her twisted anklets and gold-embroidered slippers. Wiping her hands on a handkerchief which she carried round her neck, she took her place on the couch where Habbinas' wife was reclining. She kissed her. "Is it really you?" she said, clapping her hands together.

It soon got to the point where Fortunata took the bracelets from her great fat arms and showed them to the admiring Scintilla. In the end she even undid her anklets and her gold hair net, which she said was pure gold. Trimalchio noticed this and had it all brought to him and commented:

"A woman's chains, you see. This is the way us poor fools get robbed. She must have six and a half pounds on her. Still, I've got a bracelet myself, made up from one-tenth per cent to Mercury[32]— and it weighs not an ounce less than ten pounds."

Finally, for fear he looked like a liar, he even had some scales brought in and had them passed round to test the weight.

Scintilla was no better. From round her neck she took a little gold locket, which she called her "lucky box." From it she extracted two earrings and in her turn gave them to Fortunata to look at.

"A present from my good husband," she said, "and no one has a finer set."

"Hey!" said Habinnas, "you cleaned me out to buy you a glass bean. Honestly, if I had a daughter, I'd cut her little ears off. If there weren't any women, everything would be dirt cheap. As it is, we've got to drink cold water and piss it out hot."

Meanwhile, the women giggled tipsily between themselves and kissed each other drunkenly, one crying up her merits as a housewife, the other crying about her husband's demerits and boy friends.

---

32. *Mercury:* Trimalchio sets aside a percentage of his profits to offer to his patron deity.

While they had their heads together like this, Habinnas rose stealth-ily and taking Fortunata's feet, flung them up over the couch.

"Oh, oh!" she shrieked, as her underskirt wandered up over her knees. So she settled herself in Scintilla's lap and hid her disgusting red face in her handkerchief.

Then came an interval, after which Trimalchio called for dessert. . . .

Fortunata was now wanting to dance, and Scintilla was doing more clapping than talking, when Trimalchio said:

"Philargyrus—even though you are such a terrible fan of the Greens[33]—you have my permission to join us. And tell your dear Menophila to sit down as well."

Need I say more? We were almost thrown out of our places, so completely did the household fill the dining-room. I even noticed that the chef was actually given a place above me, and he was reek-ing of pickles and sauce. And he wasn't satisfied with just having a place, but he had to start straight off on an imitation of the trage-dian Ephesus, and then challenge his master to bet against the Greens winning at the next races.

Trimalchio became expansive after this argument.

"My dear people," he said, "slaves are human beings too. They drink the same milk as anybody else, even though luck's been agin 'em. Still, if nothing happens to me, they'll have their taste of free-dom soon. In fact, I'm setting them all free in my will. I'm giving Philargyrus a farm, what's more, and the woman he lives with. As for Cario, I'm leaving him a block of flats, his five per cent manu-mission tax, and a bed with all the trimmings. I'm making Fortunata my heir, and I want all my friends to look after her.

"The reason I'm telling everyone all this is so my household will love me now as much as if I was dead."

Everyone began thanking his lordship for his kindness, when he became very serious and had a copy of his will brought in. Amid the sobs of his household he read out the whole thing from beginning to end.

Then looking at Habinnas, he said:

"What have you to say, my dear old friend? Are you building my monument the way I told you? I particularly want you to keep a place at the foot of my statue and put a picture of my pup there, as well as paintings of wreaths, scent-bottles, and all the contests of Petraites,[34] and thanks to you I'll be able to live on after I'm dead. And another thing! See that it's a hundred feet facing the road and two hundred back into the field. I want all the various sorts of fruit round my ashes and lots and lots of vines. After all, it's a big mis-take to have nice houses just for when you're alive and not worry

---

33. *Greens:* one of the teams in the chariot races.
34. *Petraites:* a popular gladiator.

about the one we have to live in for much longer. And that's why I
want this written up before anything else:

THIS MONUMENT DOES NOT GO TO THE HEIR

"But I'll make sure in my will that I don't get done down once
I'm dead. I'll put one of my freedmen in charge of my tomb to look
after it and not let people run up and shit on my monument. I'd
like you to put some ships there too, sailing under full canvas, and
me sitting on a high platform in my robes of office, wearing five
gold rings and pouring out a bagful of money for the people. You
know I gave them all a dinner and two denarii apiece. Let's have in
a banqueting hall as well, if you think it's a good idea, and show
the whole town having a good time. Put up a statue of Fortunata
on my right, holding a dove, and have her leading her little dog tied
to her belt—and this dear little chap as well, and great big wine jars
sealed up so the wine won't spill. And perhaps you could carve me
a broken wine jar and boy crying over it. A clock in the middle, so
that anybody who looks at the time, like it or not, has got to read
my name. As for the inscription now, take a good look and see if
this seems suitable enough:

> HERE SLEEPS
> GAIUS POMPEIUS TRIMALCHIO
> MAECENATIANUS
> ELECTED TO THE AUGUSTAN COLLEGE IN HIS ABSENCE
> HE COULD HAVE BEEN ON EVERY BOARD IN ROME
> BUT HE REFUSED
> GOD-FEARING BRAVE AND TRUE
> A SELF-MADE MAN
> HE LEFT AN ESTATE OF 30,000,000
> AND HE NEVER HEARD A PHILOSOPHER
> FAREWELL
> AND YOU FARE WELL, TRIMALCHIO."

[After a visit to the baths, where Encolpius and his friends make
an unsuccessful attempt to escape, the dinner is resumed.]

After this dish Trimalchio looked at the servants and said:
"Why haven't you had dinner yet? Off you go and let some
others come on duty."

Up came another squad and as the first set called out: "Good
night, Gaius!" the new arrivals shouted: "Good evening, Gaius!"

This led to the first incident that damped the general high spirits. Not a bad-looking boy entered with the newcomers and Trimalchio jumped at him and began kissing him at some length. Fortunata, asserting her just and legal rights, began hurling insults at Trimalchio, calling him a low scum and a disgrace, who couldn't con-

trol his beastly desires. "You dirty dog!" she finally added.

Trimalchio took offence at this abuse and flung his glass into Fortunata's face. She screamed as though she'd lost an eye and put her trembling hands across her face. Scintilla was terrified too and hugged the quaking woman to her breast. An obliging slave pressed a little jug of cold water to her cheek, while Fortunata rested her head on it and began weeping. Trimalchio just said:

"Well, well, forgotten her chorus days, has she? She doesn't remember, but she was bought and sold, and I took her away from it all and made her as good as the next. Yet she puffs herself up like a frog and doesn't even spit for luck. Just a great hunk, not a woman. But those as are born over a shop don't dream of a house. May I never have a day's good luck again, if I don't teach that Cassandra in clogs some manners!

"There was I, not worth twopence, and I could have had ten million. And you know I'm not lying about it. Agatho, who ran a perfume shop for the lady next door, he took me on one side and said: 'You don't want to let your family die out, you know!' But me, trying to do the right thing and not wanting to look changeable, I cut my own throat.

"All right! I'll make you want to dig me up with your bare nails. Just so you'll know on the spot what you've done for yourself—Habinnas! I don't want you to put her statue on my tomb, so at least when I'm dead I won't have any more squabbles. And another thing! just to show I can get my own back—when I'm dead I don't want her to kiss me."

After this thunderbolt, Habinnas began asking him to calm down: "None of us are without faults," he said, "we're not gods, we're human!" Scintilla said the same, calling him Gaius, and she began asking him, in the name of his guardian spirit, to give in.

Trimalchio held back his tears no longer. "I ask you, Habinnas," he said, "as you hope to enjoy your bit of savings—if I did anything wrong, spit in my face. I kissed this very careful little fellow, not for his pretty face, but because he's careful with money—he says his ten times table, he reads a book at sight, he's got himself some Thracian kit out of his daily allowance, and he's bought himself an easy chair and two cups out of his own pocket. Doesn't he deserve to be the apple of my eye? But Fortunata won't have it.

"Is that the way you feel, high heels? I'll give you a piece of advice: don't let your good luck turn your head, you kite, and don't make me show my teeth, my little darling—otherwise you'll feel my temper. You know me: once I've decided on something, it's fixed with a twelve-inch nail.

"But to come back to earth—I want you to enjoy yourselves, my dear people. After all, I was once like you are, but being the right sort, I got where I am. It's the old headpiece that makes a man, the rest is all rubbish. 'Buy right—sell right!'—that's me! Different people will give you a different line. I'm just on top of the world, I'm that lucky.

"But you, you snoring thing, are you still moaning? I'll give you something to moan about in a minute.

"However, as I'd started to say, it was my shrewd way with money that got me to my present position. I came from Asia as big as this candlestick. In fact, every day I used to measure myself against it, and to get some whiskers round my beak quicker, I used to oil my lips from the lamp. Still, for fourteen years I was the old boy's fancy. And there's nothing wrong if the boss wants it. But I did all right by the old girl too. You know what I mean—I don't say anything because I'm not the boasting sort.

"Well, as heaven will have it, I became boss in the house, and the old boy, you see, couldn't think of anything but me. That's about it— he made me co-heir with the Emperor[35] and I got a senator's fortune. But nobody gets enough, never. I wanted to go into business. Not to make a long story of it, I built five ships, I loaded them with wine —it was absolute gold at the time—and I sent them to Rome. You'd have thought I ordered it—every single ship was wrecked. That's fact, not fable! In one single day Neptune[36] swallowed up thirty million. Do you think I gave up? This loss honestly wasn't more than a flea-bite to me—it was as if nothing had happened. I built more boats, bigger and better and luckier, so nobody could say I wasn't a man of courage. You know, the greater the ship, the greater the confidence. I loaded them again—with wine, bacon, beans, perfumes and slaves. At this point Fortunata did the decent thing, because she sold off all her gold trinkets, all her clothes, and put ten thousand in gold pieces in my hand. This was the yeast my fortune needed to rise. What heaven wants, soon happens. In one voyage I carved out a round ten million. I immediately bought back all my old master's estates. I built a house, I invested in slaves, and I bought up the horse trade. Whatever I touched grew like a honeycomb. Once I had more than the whole country, then down tools! I retired from business and began advancing loans through freedmen.

"Actually I was tired of trading on my own account, but it was an astrologer who convinced me. He happened to come to our colony, a sort of Greek, Serapa by name, and he could have told heaven itself what to do. He even told me things I'd forgotten. He went through everything for me from A to Z. He knew me inside out—the only thing he didn't tell me was what I ate for dinner the day before. You'd have thought he'd never left my side.

"Wasn't there that thing, Habinnas?—I think you were there: 'You got your lady wife out of those *certain circumstances*. You are

35. *co-heir with the Emperor:* an honor which Trimalchio shared with many others, for it was customary (as a prudent measure, to avoid confiscation on some pretext or other) to include a bequest to the emperor in one's will.

36. *Neptune* (Poseidon): the sea god.

not lucky in your friends. Nobody thanks you enough for your trouble. You have large estates. You are nursing a viper in your bosom.'

"And he said—though I shouldn't tell you—I have thirty years, four months, two days to live. What's more, I shall soon receive a legacy. My horoscope tells me this. If I'm allowed to join my estates to Apulia,[37] I'll have lived enough.

"Meantime, under the protection of Mercury, I built this house. As you know, it was still a shack, now it's a shrine. It has four dining-rooms, twenty bedrooms, two marble colonnades, a row of box-rooms up above, a bedroom where I sleep myself, a nest for this viper, and a really good lodge for the porter. The guest apartment takes a hundred guests. In fact, when Scaurus[38] came here, he didn't want to stay anywhere else, even though he's got his father's guest house down by the sea. And there are a lot of other things I'll show you in a second.

"Believe me: have a penny, and you're worth a penny. You got something, you'll be thought something. Like your old friend—first a frog, now a king.

"Meantime, Stichus, bring out the shroud and the things I want to be buried in. Bring some cosmetic cream too, and a sample from that jar of wine I want my bones washed in."

Stichus did not delay over it, but brought his white shroud and his formal dress into the dining-room . . . Trimalchio told us to examine them and see if they were made of good wool. Then he said with a smile:

"Now you, Stichus, see no mice or moths get at those—otherwise I'll burn you alive. I want to be buried in style, so the whole town will pray for my rest."

He opened a bottle of nard[39] on the spot, rubbed some on all of us and said:

"I hope this'll be as nice when I'm dead as when I'm alive." The wine he had poured into a big decanter and he said:

"I want you to think you've been invited to my wake."

The thing was becoming absolutely sickening, when Trimalchio, showing the effects of his disgusting drunkenness, had a fresh entertainment brought into the dining-room, some cornet players. Propped up on a lot of cushions, he stretched out along the edge of the couch and said: "Pretend I'm dead and say something nice."

The cornet players struck up a dead march. One man in particular, the slave of his undertaker (who was the most respectable person present) blew so loudly that he roused the neighbourhood. As a result, the fire brigade, thinking Trimalchio's house was on fire, sud-

37. *Apulia:* the southeastern extremity of Italy.
38. *Scaurus:* unknown. The name is aristocratic but our translator suggests Trim-

alchio may be referring to a well-known manufacturer of fish sauce from Pompeii.
39. *nard:* a perfumed ointment.

denly broke down the front door and began kicking up their own
sort of din with their water and axes.

Seizing this perfect chance, we gave Agamemnon the slip and
escaped as rapidly as if there really were a fire.

JUVENAL

(A.D.55?–127?)

The Vanity of Human Wishes (Satire X) *

In every land as far as man can go,
from Spain to the Aurora or the poles,
few know, and even fewer choose what's true.
What do we fear with reason, or desire?
Is a step made without regret? The gods   5
ruin whole households for a foolish prayer.
Devoured by peace, we seek devouring war,
the orator is drowned by his torrential speech,
the gladiator's murdered by his skill
at murder. Wealth is worse; how many pile   10
fortune on fortune—like the Atlantic whale,
they bulk above the lesser fish and die.
For this in the dark years and at the word
of Nero, Seneca's high gardens fell;
Longinus died; a cohort of praetorians   15
besieged the Laterani. No soldiers purge
a garret. If you take a walk at night,
carrying a little silver, be prepared
to think each shadow hides a knife or spear.
You'll fear each wavering of the moonlit reed,   20
while beggars whistle in the robber's face.

Almost the first and last prayer made in all
the temples is for wealth: "Let my estate
stand first in Rome!" But who drinks arsenic
from earthenware? Fear death each time you lift   25

---

* Translated by Robert Lowell copyright © 1961. Reprinted by permission of
Farrar, Straus & Giroux, Inc.
  2. *Aurora:* the dawn—i.e., the East.
  14. *Nero:* emperor A.D. 54–68. In A.D.
65 he accused Plautius Lateranus, a senator, and Lucius Annaeus Seneca, the
philosopher who had been his tutor and
advisor, of conspiring against him;
Lateranus was exiled, Seneca committed

suicide. Seneca's wealth was enormous
and his gardens famous.
  15. *Longinus:* Cassius Longinus, a lawyer
who had been consul, was exiled earlier.
The only charge against him, we are told
by the historian Tacitus, was that he surpassed Nero in inherited wealth. *praetorians:* imperial guards.
  16. *Laterani:* Lateranus' family seat.

the jewelled goblet, or when vintage wine
purples the golden bowl.

                 Which wise man shall
I praise, Democritus or Heraclitus,
he who smiled or he who wept each time
he left his house? But the dry smile comes easy,   30
I marvel any finds sufficient tears.
Democritus could laugh till he was sick,
and yet in those days in his little town,
there were no fasces, litters, canopies,
no tribune bawling from the tribunal.   35
What if he'd seen the praetor riding high
in his triumphal car across the Circus,
dragging his palm-embroidered robes of Zeus,
a gold-stitched toga, and a cloud of dust?
What if he'd seen him in his cardboard crown,   40
a millstone that no mortal neck could bear—
there elbowed by a sweating German slave,
crowding the praetor to deflate his pride?
And now the eagle on its ivory staff,
the hornblowers, the herd of toadies mixed   45
with citizens of Rome, in snow-white robes,
his dearest friends, the lackeys in his pay.
Democritus could laugh at everything;
his neighbors' self-importance made him smile,
he even found amusement in their tears,   50
and by his courage and good humor proved
that honesty and wisdom can survive
the smothering air of a provincial town.
When Superstition shouted for his head,
he laughed, and left her hanging in her noose.   55

Why do we hunger so for vicious things?
Our wishes bend the statues of the gods.

How many men are killed by Power, by Power
and Power's companion, Envy! Your long list

28. **Democritus:** of Abdera. A Greek
philosopher (fifth century B.C.) who, with
Leucippus, first put forward an atomic
theory. He was known to later ages as
"the laughing philosopher," though there
is little in the remaining fragments of his
work to justify that title. *Heraclitus* of
Ephesus (sixth to fifth century B.C.).
Known as "the obscure" because of the
paradoxical nature of his pronouncements,
he was taken by later antiquity as the
type of the pessimist.
34. *fasces:* a bundle of rods with an
axe inserted, the symbol of Roman authority.
36. *praetor:* a high Roman official, responsible for the public games, which
included gladiatorial fights. He opened the
games with a procession reminiscent of
the triumphal procession of a victorious

general under the long-dead republican
regime—riding a chariot, dressed in a
triumphal robe, a crown held over his
head by a slave who "deflates his pride,"
probably by whispering to him (as a
slave once whispered to the victorious
general), "Remember, you are only a
man."

59 ff. refer to the fall of Sejanus, influential commander of the praetorian
guard under Augustus' successor Tiberius
(A.D. 19–37). By A.D. 31 Sejanus' power
was so great that Tiberius decided to
overthrow him; from his pleasure palace
on Capri he sent a "long wordy epistle"
to the Senate accusing him of treason.
Sejanus was executed, his body dragged
through the streets on a hook, his statues
smashed or melted down.

of honors breaks your neck. Statues follow   60
the rope and crash, the axe cuts down the two-
wheeled chariot's wheels and snaps the horse's legs.
Fierce hiss the fires, the bellows roar, the head,
all-popular and adored by all once, burns—
Sejanus crackles, and his crude bronze face,   65
the second in the world, melts down to jars,
frying pans, basins, platters, chamber pots.
Hang out your streamers, lead the great chalked bull
to the high altar at the Capitol—
men lead Sejanus on a hook, and all   70
rejoice. "What flannel lips he has! No man,
I tell you, ever loved this man!" "But tell us,
what was his crime, friend? Who were the informers?
What witness swore away his life?" "No witness!
A wordy long epistle came from Capri."   75
"Tiberius spoke, enough, I'll hear no more."
But what about the Roman mob? Their rule
is always follow fortune and despise
the fallen. One thing's certain, if the gods
had spared Sejanus, if some accident   80
had choked Tiberius in his green old age,
the mob would hail Sejanus Caesar now.

Now that we have no suffrage left to sell,
we have no troubles; we who once conferred
legions, fasces, empires, everything,   85
are simply subjects; restlessly we ask
for two things: bread and circuses. But listen—
"I hear that many more are going to die."
"No doubt about it, they have built a fire."
"My closest friend, Brutidius, looked white   90
just now at Mars's altar, Caesar stirs,
I fear fresh heads will fall for negligence."
"Quick, Caesar's enemy is still exposed;
let's run; there's time to trample on the corpse."
"I'll bring my slaves for witnesses; no paid   95
accuser shall drag me haltered into court."
Thus, thus, the secret murmurs of the crowd—
would you be cheered and flattered like Sejanus?
Be rich as Croesus, give the ivory chair
to one, and armies to another? Would you be   100
Tiberius' right hand, while he sits and suns
himself at Capri, fed by eastern fags?
Surely you'd like to have his lances, cohorts,
blue-blooded knights and army corps of slaves.

68–69. refer to celebrations and sacrifices. The sacrificial bull had to be white; it if had dark patches on the skin, they were chalked over.

82. *Caesar:* i.e., emperor.

83. *suffrage:* vote. A cynical comment on the loss of republican freedom. It is true that in the last years of the republic electoral corruption was rampant.

99. *Croesus:* king of Lydia, a name still proverbial for enormous wealth. *ivory chair:* reserved for high magistrates.

Why not, friend? Even if you never wished   105
to murder, you would like to have the power.
But would you want to glitter and rise this high,
if ruin's counterweight must crush your life?
Who would prefer Sejanus' rod of office
to being mayor of Gabii, or Fidenae,   110
some rural aedile smashing crooked weights,
wearing a threadbare cloak at Ulubrae?
Let's say then that Sejanus was insane;
wanting authority and wealth, he added
story on story to his towering house—   115
so much the higher for the blinding crash!
What ruined Crassus, Pompey, he who scourged
Gaul and the torn Republic with his lash?
What brought them down? High places and the art
of climbing, wishes answered by the gods,   120
who send few kings to Pluto without wounds,
still fewer cherished by their people's love.
                              Each schoolboy
who cultivates Minerva with a penny fee,
and one poor slave to lug his satchel, prays through
the summer holidays for eloquence,   125
to be Demosthenes or Cicero.
Yet eloquence destroyed both orators,
this, this condemned and drowned them in its flood.
Eloquence lopped off Cicero's right hand,
and cut his throat, but no cheap shyster ever   130
dirtied the Roman rostrum with his blood.
"My consulate, how fortunate the state":
if this were all you wrote, you might have scorned
the swords and vengeance of Antonius.
Yes, all in all, I like such pompous verse   135
more than your force, immortal fifth Philippic!
Dark too the murder of the patriot Greek,
who stunned the men of Athens with his words,

110. *Gabii, Fidenae:* middle-sized country towns.

111. *aedile:* the lowest rank of magistrate.

112. *Ulubrae:* a small (and unhealthy) country town.

117. *Crassus:* a millionaire politician of the last years of the republic; killed in battle in the East 53 B.C. *Pompey:* rival of Julius Caesar, murdered in Egypt in 48 B.C.

117–118. *he who scourged . . . :* Julius Caesar, who added Gaul (France) to the Roman empire, put an end to the republic and was murdered in Rome in 44 B.C.

121. *Pluto:* god of the underworld.

123. *Minerva* (Athena): goddess of arts and learning.

126. *Demosthenes, Cicero:* The greatest of the Athenian orators (384–322 B.C.), Demosthenes, committed suicide to avoid execution. Cicero was murdered by soldiers sent by Mark Antony, whom he had denounced in a series of magnificent speeches known as Philippics (because they were comparable to the speeches Demosthenes made against Philip of Macedon, father of Alexander). The soldiers cut off Cicero's head and right hand. Antony nailed them to the *rostra*, the speakers' platform in the Forum.

132. *"My consulate . . .":* a quotation from Cicero's poem on his own consulate: his poetry was as bad as his prose was superb. Lowell's translation reproduces the inept vowel repetitions of the Latin.

137. *patriot Greek:* Demosthenes.

and held the hushed assembly in his palm.
Under unfriendly gods and an ill star,   140
your blacksmith father raised and sent you forth,
red-eyed and sooty from the glowering forge,
from anvil, pincers, hammer and the coals
to study rhetoric, Demosthenes!

War souvenirs and trophies nailed to trees,   145
a cheek strap dangling from a clobbered helmet,
a breastplate, or a trireme's figurehead,
or captives weeping on the victor's arch:
these are considered more than human prizes.
For these Greek, Roman, and barbarian   150
commanders march; for these they pledge their lives
and freedom—such their thirst for fame, and such
their scorn of virtue, for who wants a life
of virtue without praise? Whole nations die
to serve the glory of the few; all lust   155
for honors and inscriptions on their tombs—
those tombs a twisting fig tree can uproot,
for tombs too have their downfall and their doom.

Throw Hannibal on the scales, how many pounds
does the great captain come to? This is he   160
who found the plains of Africa too small,
rich Carthage with her mercenary grip
stretched from Gibraltar to the steaming Nile
and back to Ethiopia, her stud
for slaves and elephants. He set his hand   165
firmly on Spain, then scaled the Pyrenees;
when snows, the Alps, and Nature blocked his road,
he derricked rocks, and split the mountainsides
with vinegar. Now Italy is his;
the march goes on. "Think nothing done," he says,   170
"until my Punic soldiers hack through Rome,
and plant my standard over the Suburva's
whorehouses." What a face for painters! Look,
the one-eyed leader prods his elephant!
And what's the end? O glory! Like the others,   175
he is defeated, then the worried flight,
the great, world-famous client cools his heels

141. Demosthenes' father owned a weapons factory.

147. *trireme:* warship.

159. *Hannibal:* Carthaginian general (247–183 B.C.). Starting from his base in Spain he crossed the Alps (cutting through a mountain side at one point by heating it and then pouring vinegar on it to split the rock—or so we are told) and invaded Italy in 218 B.C. He defeated the Romans in every battle (the most important at Cannae, in 216 B.C.) but lost the war. Forced to return to Africa, he was defeated by the Romans on his home ground: he fled for refuge to the Greek kingdoms of the East where he lived as an exile and finally, to avoid being handed over to the Romans, committed suicide.

172. *Suburva:* a slum district of Rome.

174. *one-eyed leader:* Hannibal lost an eye in one of his first battles.

in royal anterooms, and waits on some
small despot, sleeping off a drunken meal.
What is the last day of this mighty spirit   180
whose valor turned the known world on its head?
Not swords, or pikes, or legions—no, not these,
his crown for Cannae and those seas of blood
is poison in a ring. March, madman, cross
the Alps, the Tiber—be a purple patch   185
for schoolboys, and a theme for declamation!

One world was much too small for Alexander,
racing to gain the limits of the globe,
as if he were a circling charioteer;
early however he reached his final city,   190
Babylon, fortified with frail dry brick.
A grave was all he wanted. Death alone
shows us what tedious things our bodies are.
Fleets climbed the slopes of Athos (such the lies
of Greek historians) yes, and paved the sea;   195
wheels rumbled down a boulevard of decks,
breakfasting Persians drank whole rivers dry—
that's how the perjured laureates puffed their songs.
But tell us how the King of Kings returned
from Salamis? Xerxes, whose amusement was   200
whipping the winds, and bragging how he'd drag
Neptune in chains, and branded to his throne—
a lovely master for the gods to serve!
Tell us of his return. A single ship,
scything for sea-room through the Persian dead.   205
That was his sentence for his dreams of glory.
"Give us long life, O God, and years to live,"
in sickness or in health, this is our prayer;
but age's ills are strong and never fail.
Look at the face, deformed and paralyzed,   210
unlike itself, its skin a hide, gone cheeks,
a thousand wrinkles like a mother ape.
But youth's unique: each boy is handsomer
than the next one, or cleverer, or stronger;
all old men look alike, their voices shake   215
worse than their fingers, every head is hairless,
each snivels like a child; they mess their bread,
their gums are toothless—how heavily they weigh

---

186. *theme for declamation:* Roman
school exercises stressed rhetoric. Students
were assigned historical and mythical subjects on which to compose speeches.

187. *Alexander:* died at Babylon in 323
B.C. at the age of thirty-three.

194 ff. These lines refer to the invasion
of Greece by Xerxes, king of Persia, in
480 B.C. According to the Greek historian
Herodotus, a canal was cut through the
peninsula behind Mt. Athos and a bridge
of boats was constructed across the

Hellespont; in spite of Juvenal's skepticism, we have no reason to doubt the
truth of this account. Xerxes' fleet was
defeated at Salamis, an island off the
coast of Attica, and Xerxes returned to
Persia (but surely not unaccompanied, as
Juvenal suggests).

201. *whipping the winds:* According to
Herodotus, when a storm damaged the
bridge of boats, Xerxes had the sea (Neptune) whipped and branded.

upon their wives, their children, and themselves!
Even the fortune-hunter turns them down,   220
now food and even wine are one more torture,
a long oblivion falls on intercourse,
the shy nerve, pumping, drops like a wet leaf,
though tickled through the night, it cannot rise.
What do you hope from your white pubic hairs?   225
Sex hounds you, when its power is gone. Or take
the loss of other senses—the best voice
strikes on the coughing ear like lead, the harp
of the best harpist screams like a ground knife.
What good are bosoms jingling with gold coins,   230
the best seat in the Colosseum, when you
can hardly tell a trumpet from a drum?
The boy announcing visitors or meals
half kills himself with baying in your ear.

Now only fevers warm the thinning blood,   235
diseases of all kinds lock hands and dance,
even their names escape you—let me list
the many lechers Oppia will love,
slow-coming Maura drain a day, how many
schoolboys Hamillus will crouch on, the partners   240
Hirrus will swindle, the sick men Themiston will kill
this autumn—I could more easily count
the villas bought up by the barber whose
razor once grated on my stiff young beard . . .
One man has a sagging shoulder, one a hernia,   245
another has a softening hipbone, and another
has cataracts; another's spoonfed: listen,
they yawn like baby swallows for their swill!
But the worst evil is the loss of mind;
we do not know our slaves, the friend we dined with,   250
then even our own children are forgotten.
"Who are they? Parasites!" The will's rewritten:
All goes to Phiale, so lulling are
the acrobatics of that quick, moist mouth
that used to sell her body in the streets.   255

Let's say you keep your mind, you'll live to see
your wife and sons laid out, the ashes of
brothers and sisters shut in marble urns.
These the rewards of living long: repeated
groaning that fills an empty house, yourself   260
in black, a ghost, disaster on disaster!
Nestor, if one believes the lines from Homer,
lived longer than a crow—how fortunate,
outwitting death and tasting the new wine

220. *fortune-hunter:* parasites who attached themselves to childless old men and hoped by flattery to win their inheritance. This was apparently a common type in Roman high society.
238. *Oppia:* This and the following names are fictitious.
241. *Themiston:* a doctor.

a hundred autumns! Was this all? Fate's grace,   265
and his long thread of years were all too much
for Nestor. He saw the beard of his son, Antilochus,
flame on the pyre, asked: "Why have I lived? What crime
have I committed?" Peleus felt the same
for his Achilles, and Laertes for   270
Odysseus. What of Priam? Would that he had died
the day when Paris launched his robber galley;
he would have met his city's shades, with Troy
still standing, Hector and all his sons on hand
to bear him on their shoulders, with Cassandra,   275
unravished, free to wail the song of mourning.
What good was his long life? He saw his house
fallen, all Asia burning—swords, then fire!
Then dropping his tiara, and putting on
armor, the poor old doddering soldier rushed   280
before the altar of his gods, and fell
like some old ox discarded by the plow,
craning his thin neck for the master's knife.
But Priam's death was human; Hecuba
survived him to die barking like a dog.   285

I pass by Mithridates; why repeat
Solon's old saws to Croesus—take our own men,
take Marius. Age brought him prison, exile,
weeks on his belly in Minturnae's marsh,
then back to Rome, his seventh consulship,   290
a few brief apoplectic days of blood.
Did Nature ever raise a Roman higher?
Did Rome? if he had died with all the pomp
of war, his army marshalled out to cheer him,
one foot descending on a Teuton's back?   295
How provident was the Campanian fever
for Pompey; but the tears of many cities,
all praying for his life, prevailed. He lived,
his stars preserved him, and a eunuch's slave
cut off his head. Was Lentulus so tortured?   300

275. *Cassandra:* a prophetess whose destiny it was not to be believed.

284–285. *Hecuba:* According to later legend (not in Homer), after great sufferings and the loss of all her children, she was changed into a dog.

286. *Mithridates:* king of Pontus in Asia Minor. He fought the Romans successfully for many years but ended in defeat and died by violence.

287. *Solon:* told Croesus of Lydia to call no man happy until he was dead.

288. *Marius:* Caius Marius (157–86 B.C.) was elected consul seven times. He saved Rome by defeating the Teutons who were about to invade Italy but later fled from Rome during a civil war (hiding in the marshes at Minturnae on the way). He returned to Rome for his seventh consulship, which he signalized by a massacre of his political opponents just before he died.

297. *Pompey* (see note to l. 117). He almost died of a fever in 50 B.C. but recovered—only to lose a civil war against Julius Caesar and be murdered by the Egyptians to whom he had fled for refuge.

300 ff. *Lentulus . . . Cethegus, Catiline:* leaders of an attempt to overthrow the republic in 63 B.C. It was thwarted by the consul Cicero (hence his self-congratulatory poem quoted above). Lentulus and Cethegus were strangled in prison at Rome; Catiline was cut down on the field of battle.

Was Cethegus? Or even Catiline,
whose corpse lay undishonored on the field?

The nervous mother passing Venus' altar
prays for good-looking sons and lovelier daughters.
"Why not?" she says. "Latona bore Diana!"   305
Why not? And yet Lucretia's fate forbids
us to desire her face. Virginia
would swap her figure for Rutila's hump.
A handsome son has shy and trembling parents.
Luck seldom goes with beauty. But suppose   310
a simple household teaches him the fathers'
virtues and Sabine manners, say that nature
moreover makes him kind, intelligent,
with warm blood rising to his cheeks—
what better gifts can nature give the boy,   315
all-giving nature, gentler than his teachers?
And yet the boy will never be a man.
Some prodigal seducer will seduce
the parents—money never fails its giver.
No overweight tyrant castrates the deformed.   320
Trust Nero, Nero had an eye for beauty:
he never picked a spastic or a lout.

Let's say your son survives, and reaches twenty.
He'll look for softer and more practiced hands
than Nero's. He will fly to women. Would   325
you have him an adulterer like Mars,
almost as handsome, but no luckier,
his bronze foot kicking in the cripple's net?
Risk the worst punishments the laws allow
an injured husband? Often the revenge   330
outdoes the law: the cuckold chops the lover's
balls off, or jams a mullet up his arse.
Then let him choose a widow; soon he'll have
her money, all her unloved body has
to give. What can Catulla, what can Chloris   335
deny his swelling prick—sad sacks in heat,
their conscience washing out between their legs.
But beauty never hurts the good! Go ask
Bellerophon, go ask Hippolytus.

305. *Latona, Diana:* goddesses corresponding to the Greek Leto and Artemis.

306. *Lucretia:* in Roman legend, the chaste wife of a Roman noble. She was raped by the king's son Tarquinius and committed suicide. This incident led to the overthrow of the monarchy and the establishment of the republic.

307. *Virginia:* daughter of Virginius, was killed by her father to save her from dishonor at the hands of a powerful official, Appius Claudius.

308. *Rutila:* a fictitious name.

312. *Sabine:* See Ovid's *Amores*, p. 623, ll. 61–62.

326. *Mars:* Ares—another reference to the Homeric story about Ares caught in a trap by the lame Hephaestus.

339 ff. *Bellerophon:* Tempted by Sthenoboea, the wife of his host, he refused her advances, whereupon she told her husband that he had tried to rape her. The same thing happened to Hippolytus but this time the temptress was Phaedra, the second wife of his father, Theseus. Hippolytus paid with his life; Bellerophon was sent to his death but escaped.

Chastity couldn't save their lives from Phaedra,   340
or Sthenoboea, faithful wives, then scorned
lovers screwed on to murder by their shame.
Now tell me what advice you have to give
the fellow Caesar's consort wants to marry—
the best man, the most beautiful, an old   345
patrician house could raise, soon caught, soon shoved
from life to death by Messalina's eyes.
She's long been seated, and her bridal veil
rustles, the lovers' bed of full-blown roses
rustles quite openly inside the garden;   350
by ancient rule, a dowry of a million
brass sesterces must now be counted—clerks,
lawyers, the thin-lipped priest, attend on tiptoe
"What, did you want a hole-in-corner marriage?
The lady has a right to her religion.   355
What will you do? Speak up! Say no, you'll die
before the lamps are lit. Say yes, you'll live
until the city hears, and someone squeals
in Claudius's ear—he'll be the last in Rome
to know of his disgrace. Meanwhile obey   360
your love, if one or two days' life mean much—
whatever's best or costs the smallest effort,
to bring your fair white body to the sword."

There's nothing then to pray for? If you pray,
pray for the gods and Jupiter to help.   365
What's best, what serves us, only He can know.
We're dearer to the gods than to ourselves.
Hurried by impulse and diseased desire,
we ask for wives, and children by our wives—
what wives, what children, heaven only knows.   370
Still, if you ask for something, if you must
buy holy sausages and dedicate
the tripe of bulls at every altar, pray for
a healthy body and a healthy soul,
a soul that is not terrified by death,   375
that thinks long life the least of nature's gifts,
courage that takes whatever comes—this hero
like Hercules, all pain and labor, loathes
the lecherous gut of Sardanapalus.
Success is worshipped as a god; it's we   380
who set up shrines and temples in her name.
I give you simply what you have already.

343 ff. These lines refer to the scandal which led to the death of Messalina, the young wife of the emperor Claudius (A.D. 41–54). She was so confident that Claudius was hopelessly infatuated and blind to her infidelities that, not content with clandestine lovers, she decided to marry one of them at a private but magnificent ceremony. This was too much even for Claudius, who arrested and executed the whole lot of them, Messalina included. The unfortunate bridegroom who is offered the choice in lines 354 ff. was Caius Silius.

379. *Sardanapalus:* king of Nineveh, proverbial for luxury and gluttony.

ST. AUGUSTINE
(354–430 A.D.)
Confessions (Confessiones)*

[Childhood]

Book I

. . . I know not whence I came into this dying life (shall I call it?) or living death. Then immediately did the comforts of Thy compassion take me up, as I heard (for I remember it not) from the parents of my flesh, out of whose substance Thou didst sometime fashion me. Thus there received me the comforts of woman's milk. For neither my mother nor my nurses stored their own breasts for me; but Thou didst bestow the food of my infancy through them, according to Thine ordinance, whereby Thou distributest Thy riches through the hidden springs of all things. Thou also gavest me to desire no more than Thou gavest; and to my nurses willingly to give me what Thou gavest them. For they, with an heaven-taught affection, willingly gave me, what they abounded with from Thee. For this my good from them, was good for them. Nor, indeed, from them was it, but through them; for from Thee, O God, are all good things, and *from my God is all my health.* This I since learned, Thou, through these Thy gifts, within me and without, proclaiming Thyself unto me. For then I knew but to suck; to repose in what pleased, and cry at what offended my flesh; nothing more.

Afterwards I began to smile; first in sleep, then waking: for so it was told me of myself, and I believed it; for we see the like in other infants, though of myself I remember it not. Thus, little by little, I became conscious where I was; and to have a wish to express my wishes to those who could content them, and I could not; for the wishes were within me, and they without; nor could they by any sense of theirs enter within my spirit. So I flung about at random limbs and voice, making the few signs I could, and such as I could, like, though in truth very little like, what I wished. And when I was not obeyed, (my wishes being hurtful or unintelligible,) then I was indignant with my elders for not submitting to me, with those owing me no service, for not serving me; and avenged myself on them by tears. Such have I learnt infants to be from observing them; and, that I was myself such, they, all unconscious, have shewn me better than my nurses who knew it.

---

* Abridged. Written in A.D. 397.

. . . I came to boyhood, or rather it came to me, displacing infancy. Nor did that depart,—(for whither went it?)—and yet it was no more. For I was no longer a speechless infant, but a speaking boy. This I remember; and have since observed how I learned to speak. It was not that my elders taught me words (as, soon after, other learning) in any set method; but I, longing by cries and broken accents and various motions of my limbs to express my thoughts, that so I might have my will, and yet unable to express all I willed, or to whom I willed, did myself, by the understanding which Thou, my God, gavest me, practise the sounds in my memory. When they named any thing, and as they spoke turned towards it, I saw and remembered that they called what they would point out, by the name they uttered. And that they meant this thing and no other, was plain from the motion of their body, the natural language, as it were, of all nations, expressed by the countenance, glances of the eye, gestures of the limbs, and tones of the voice, indicating the affections of the mind, as it pursues, possesses, rejects, or shuns. And thus by constantly hearing words, as they occurred in various sentences, I realized gradually for what they stood; and having broken in my mouth to these signs, I thereby gave utterance to my will. Thus I exchanged with those about me these current signs of our wills, and so launched deeper into the stormy intercourse of human life, yet depending on parental authority and the beck of elders.

O God my God, what miseries and mockeries did I now experience, when obedience to my teachers was proposed to me, as proper in a boy, in order that in this world I might prosper, and excel in tongue-science,[1] which should serve to the praise of men, and to deceitful riches. Next I was put to school to get learning, in which I (poor wretch) knew not what use there was; and yet, if idle in learning, I was beaten. For this was judged right by our forefathers; and many, passing the same course before us, framed for us weary paths, through which we were fain to pass; multiplying toil and grief upon the sons of Adam. But, Lord, we found that men called upon Thee, and we learnt from them to think of Thee (according to our powers) as of some great One, who, though hidden from our senses, couldst hear and help us. For so I began, as a boy, to pray to Thee, my aid and refuge; and broke the fetters of my tongue to call on Thee, praying Thee, though small, yet with no small earnestness, that I might not be beaten at school. And when Thou heardest me not, (*not thereby giving me over to folly*,[2]) my

---

1. the study of rhetoric, which was the passport to eminence in public life.

2. Augustine recognizes the necessity of this rigorous training; that he never forgot its harshness is clear from his remark in the *City of God*, Book XXI, Section 14: "If a choice were given him between suffering death and living his early years over again, who would not shudder and choose death?"

elders, yea, my very parents, who yet wished me no ill, mocked my stripes, my then great and grievous ill.

Is there, Lord, any of soul so great, and cleaving to Thee with so intense affection, (for a sort of stupidity will in a way do it); but is there any one, who, from cleaving devoutly to Thee, is endued with so great a spirit, that he can think as lightly of the racks and hooks and other torments,[3] (against which, throughout all lands, men call on Thee with extreme dread,) mocking at those by whom they are feared most bitterly, as our parents mocked the torments which we suffered in boyhood from our masters? For we feared not our torments less; nor prayed we less to Thee to escape them. And yet we sinned, in writing or reading or studying less than was exacted of us. For we wanted not, O Lord, memory or capacity, whereof Thy will gave enough for our age; but our sole delight was play; and for this we were punished by those who yet themselves were doing the like. But elder folks' idleness is called "business"; that of boys, being really the same, is punished by those elders; and none commiserates either boys or men. For will any of sound discretion approve of my being beaten as a boy, because, by playing at ball, I made less progress in studies which I was to learn, only that, as a man, I might play more unbeseemingly? And what else did he, who beat me? who, if worsted in some trifling discussion with his fellow-teachers, was more embittered and jealous than I, when beaten at ball by a play-fellow? . . .

In boyhood itself, however, (so much less dreaded for me than youth,) I loved not study, and hated to be forced to it. Yet I was forced; and this was well done towards me, but I did not well; for, unless forced, I had not learnt. But no one doeth well against his will, even though what he doth, be well. Yet neither did they well who forced me, but what was well came to me from Thee, my God. For they were regardless how I should employ what they forced me to learn, except to satiate the insatiate desires of a wealthy beggary, and a shameful glory. But Thou, *by whom the very hairs of our head are numbered*, didst use for my good the error of all who urged me to learn; and my own, who would not learn, Thou didst use for my punishment—a fit penalty for one, so small a boy and so great a sinner. So by those who did not well, Thou didst well for me; and by my own sin Thou didst justly punish me. For Thou hast commanded, and so it is, that every inordinate affection should be its own punishment.

But why did I so much hate the Greek,[4] which I studied as a

3. *racks and hooks and other torments:* the instruments of public execution.

4. important not only for gaining knowledge of Greek literature but also because it was the official language of the Eastern half of the Roman Empire. Augustine never really mastered Greek, though his remark elsewhere that he had acquired so little Greek that it amounted to practically none, is overmodest.

boy? I do not yet fully know. For the Latin I loved; not what my first masters, but what the so-called grammarians[5] taught me. For those first lessons, reading, writing, and arithmetic, I thought as great a burden and penalty as any Greek. And yet whence was this too, but from the sin and vanity of this life, because *I was flesh, and a breath that passeth away and cometh not again?* For those first lessons were better certainly, because more certain; by them I obtained, and still retain, the power of reading what I find written, and myself writing what I will; whereas in the others, I was forced to learn the wanderings of one Aeneas,[6] forgetful of my own, and to weep for dead Dido, because she killed herself for love; the while, with dry eyes, I endured my miserable self dying among these things, far from Thee, O God my life.

For what more miserable than a miserable being who commiserates not himself; weeping the death of Dido[7] for love to Aeneas, but weeping not his own death for want of love to Thee, O God. Thou light of my heart, Thou bread of my inmost soul, Thou Power who givest vigour to my mind, who quickenest my thoughts, I loved Thee not. I committed fornication[8] against Thee, and all around me thus fornicating there echoed "Well done! well done!" *for the friendship of this world is fornication against Thee*; and "Well done! well done!" echoes on till one is ashamed not to be thus a man. And all this I wept not, I who wept for Dido slain, and "seeking by the sword a stroke and wound extreme,"[9] myself seeking the while a worse extreme, the extremest and lowest of Thy creatures, having forsaken Thee, earth passing into the earth. And if forbid to read all this, I was grieved that I might not read what grieved me. Madness like this is thought a higher and a richer learning, than that by which I learned to read and write.

But now, my God, cry Thou aloud in my soul; and let Thy truth tell me, "Not so, not so. Far better was that first study." For, lo, I would readily forget the wanderings of Aeneas and all the rest, rather than how to read and write. But over the entrance of the Grammar School is a curtain[10] drawn! true; yet is this not so much an emblem of anything recondite, as a cloak of error. Let not those, whom I no longer fear, cry out against me, while I confess to Thee, my God, whatever my soul will, and acquiesce in the condemnation of my evil ways, that I may love Thy good ways. Let not either buyers or sellers of grammar-learning cry out against me. For if I

5. the teachers in the grammar school (see below), who taught the students how to read the poets, historians, and orators, and exercised them in textual and literary criticism.
6. the third book of Virgil's *Aeneid*.

7. See Book IV of the *Aeneid*.
8. metaphorically in this instance.
9. See the *Aeneid*, Book VI, l. 457.
10. School was often held in a building open on one side and curtained off from the street.

question them whether it be true, that Aeneas came on a time to Carthage, as the Poet tells, the less learned will reply that they know not, the more learned that he never did.[11] But should I ask with what letters the name "Aeneas" is written, every one who has learnt this will answer me aright, as to the signs which men have conventionally settled. If, again, I should ask, which might be forgotten with least detriment to the concerns of life, reading and writing or these poetic fictions? who does not foresee, what all must answer who have not wholly forgotten themselves? I sinned, then, when as a boy I preferred those empty to those more profitable studies, or rather loved the one and hated the other. "One and one, two;" "two and two, four;" this was to me a hateful sing-song: the wooden horse lined with armed men, and the burning of Troy, and "Creusa's shade and sad similitude,"[12] were the choice spectacle of my vanity. . . .

Bear with me, my God, while I say something of my wit, Thy gift, and on what dotages I wasted it. For a task was set me, troublesome enough to my soul, upon terms of praise or shame, and fear of blows, to speak the words of Juno,[13] as she raged and mourned that she could not

This Trojan prince from Latium turn.

Which words I had heard that Juno never uttered; but we were forced to go astray in the footsteps of these poetic fictions, and to say in prose the sort of thing which he expressed in verse. And his speaking was most applauded, in whom the passions of rage and grief were most pre-eminent, and clothed in the most fitting language, maintaining the dignity of the character. What is it to me, O my true life, my God, that my declamation was applauded above so many of my own age and class? Is not all this smoke and wind? And was there nothing else whereon to exercise my wit and tongue? Thy praises, Lord, Thy praises might have stayed the yet tender shoot of my heart by the prop of Thy Scriptures; so had it not trailed away amid these empty trifles, a defiled prey for the fowls of the air. For in more ways than one do men sacrifice to the rebellious angels. . . .

---

11. Augustine's point is that the historical truth of the poet's story may be doubted, but the spelling of Aeneas' name is certain.

12. *Aeneid*, Book II, l. 772.

13. Augustine was assigned the task of delivering a prose paraphrase of Juno's angry speech in the *Aeneid*, Book I. (She complains that her enemies, the Trojans under Aeneas, are on their way to their destined goal in Italy in spite of her resolution to prevent them.) Rhetorical exercises such as this were common in the schools, since they served the double purpose of teaching literature and rhetorical composition at the same time.

[The Pear Tree]

Book II

I will now call to mind my past foulness, and the carnal corruptions of my soul: not because I love them, but that I may love Thee, O my God. For love of Thy love I do it; reviewing my most wicked ways in the very bitterness of my remembrance, that Thou mayest grow sweet unto me; (Thou sweetness never failing, Thou blissful and assured sweetness;) and gathering me again out of that my dissipation, wherein I was torn piecemeal, while turned from Thee, the One Good, I lost myself among a multiplicity of things. For I even burnt in my youth heretofore, to be satiated in things below; and I dared to grow wild again, with these various and shadowy loves: *my beauty consumed away*, and I stank in Thine eyes; pleasing myself, and desirous to please in the eyes of men.

And what was it that I delighted in, but to love, and be beloved? but I kept not the measure of love, of mind to mind, friendship's bright boundary; but out of the muddy concupiscence of the flesh, and the bubblings of youth, mists fumed up which beclouded and overcast my heart, that I could not discern the clear brightness of love, from the fog of lustfulness. Both did confusedly boil in me, and hurried my unstayed youth over the precipice of unholy desires, and sunk me in a gulf of flagitiousnesses. Thy wrath had gathered over me, and I knew it not. I was grown deaf by the clanking of the chain of my mortality, the punishment of the pride of my soul, and I strayed further from Thee, and Thou lettest me alone, and I was tossed about, and wasted, and dissipated, and I boiled over in my fornications, and Thou heldest Thy peace, O Thou my tardy joy! Thou then heldest Thy peace, and I wandered further and further from Thee, into more and more fruitless seed-plots of sorrows, with a proud dejectedness, and a restless weariness. . . .

Where was I, and how far was I exiled from the delights of Thy house in that sixteenth year of the age of my flesh, when the madness of lust (to which human shamelessness giveth free license, though unlicensed by Thy laws) took the rule over me, and I resigned myself wholly to it? My friends meanwhile took no care by marriage to save my fall; their only care was that I should learn to speak excellently, and be a persuasive orator. . . .

Theft is punished by Thy law, O Lord, and the law written in the hearts of men, which iniquity itself effaces not. For what thief will abide a thief? not even a rich thief, one stealing through want. Yet I lusted to thieve, and did it, compelled by no poverty except want of righteousness and indeed contempt for it, and an over-abundance of wickedness. For I stole that, of which I had enough, and much better. Nor cared I to enjoy what I stole, but joyed in the theft and sin itself. A pear tree there was near our vineyard, laden with fruit, tempting neither for colour nor taste. To shake and rob this, some wild young fellows of us went, late one night, (having according to our pestilent custom prolonged our sports in the streets till then,) and took huge loads, not for our eating, but to fling to the very hogs, having only tasted them. And this, but to do, what we liked only, because it was misliked. Behold my heart, O God, behold my heart, which Thou hadst pity upon in the bottom of the bottomless pit. Now, behold let my heart tell Thee, what it sought there, that I should be gratuitously evil, having no temptation to ill, but the ill itself. It was foul, and I loved it; I loved to perish, I loved mine own fault, not that for which I was faulty, but my fault itself. Foul soul, falling from Thy firmament to utter destruction; not seeking aught through the shame but the shame itself! . . .

[*Student at Carthage*]

Book III

To Carthage[1] I came, where there sang all around me in my ears a cauldron of unholy loves. I loved not yet, yet I loved to love, and out of a deep-seated want, I hated myself for wanting not. I sought what I might love, in love with loving, and safety I hated, and a way without snares. For within me was a famine of that inward food, Thyself, my God; yet, through that famine I was not hungered; but was without all longing for incorruptible sustenance, not because filled therewith, but the more empty, the more I loathed it. For this cause my soul was sickly and full of sores, it miserably cast itself forth, desiring to be scraped by the touch of objects of sense. Yet if these had not a soul, they would not be objects of love. To love them, and to be beloved, was sweet to me; but more, when I obtained to enjoy the person I loved. I defiled, therefore, the spring of friendship with the filth of concupiscence, and I beclouded its brightness with the hell of lustfulness; and thus foul and unseemly, I would fain, through exceeding vanity, be fine and courtly. I fell headlong then into the love, wherein I longed to be ensnared. My God, my Mercy, with how much gall didst thou out of thy great goodness besprinkle for me that sweetness? For I was both beloved, and secretly arrived at the bond of enjoying; and was with joy fettered with sorrow-bringing bonds, that I might be scourged with the iron burning rods of jealousy, and suspicions, and fears, and angers, and quarrels.

Stage-plays also carried me away, full of images of my miseries,

1. the capital city of the province, where Augustine went to study rhetoric.

and of fuel to my fire. Why is it, that man desires to be made sad, beholding doleful and tragical things, which yet himself would by no means suffer? yet he desires as a spectator to feel sorrow at them, and this very sorrow is his pleasure. What is this but a miserable madness? for a man is the more affected with these actions, the less free he is from such affections. Howsoever, when he suffers in his own person, it is usually called misery: when he compassionates others, then it is mercy. But what sort of compassion is this for feigned and scenical passions? for the auditor is not called on to relieve, but only to grieve: and he applauds the actor of these fictions the more, the more he grieves. And if the calamities of those persons (whether of old times, or mere fiction) be so acted, that the spectator is not moved to tears, he goes away disgusted and criticising; but if he be moved to passion, he stays intent, and weeps for joy. . . .

Those studies[2] also, which were accounted commendable, had a view to excelling in the courts of litigation; the more bepraised, the craftier. Such is men's blindness, glorying even in their blindness. And now I was chief[3] in the rhetoric school, whereat I joyed proudly, and I swelled with arrogancy, though (Lord, Thou knowest) far quieter and altogether removed from the subvertings of those "Subverters"[4] (for this ill-omened and devilish name, was the very badge of gallantry) among whom I lived, with a shameless shame that I was not even as they. With them I lived, and was sometimes delighted with their friendship, whose doings I ever did abhor, i.e. their "subvertings," wherewith they wantonly persecuted the modesty of strangers, which they disturbed by a gratuitous jeering, feeding thereon their malicious mirth. Nothing can be liker the very actions of devils than these. What then could they be more truly called than "subverters?" themselves subverted and altogether perverted first, the deceiving spirits secretly deriding and seducing them, wherein themselves delight to jeer at, and deceive others.

Among such as these, in that unsettled age of mine, learned I books of eloquence, wherein I desired to be eminent, out of a damnable and vain glorious end, a joy in human vanity. In the ordinary course of study, I fell upon a certain book of Cicero, whose speech[5] almost all admire, not so his heart. This book of his contains an exhortation to philosophy, and is called "Hortensius."[6] But this book altered my affections, and turned my prayers to Thyself, O Lord; and made me have other purposes and desires. Every

---

2. rhetorical studies.
3. the best student.
4. a group of students who prided themselves on their wild actions and indiscipline.

5. style.
6. Only fragments of this dialogue remain. In it Cicero replies to an opponent of philosophy with an impassioned defense of the intellectual life.

vain hope at once became worthless to me; and I longed with an incredibly burning desire for an immortality of wisdom, and began now to arise, that I might return to Thee. For not to sharpen my tongue, (which thing I seemed to be purchasing with my mother's allowances, in that my nineteenth year, my father being dead two years before,) not to sharpen my tongue did I employ that book; nor did it infuse into me its style, but its matter. . . .

I resolved then to bend my mind to the holy Scriptures, that I might see what they were. But behold, I see a thing not understood by the proud, nor laid open to children, lowly in access, in its recesses lofty, and veiled with mysteries; and I was not such as could enter into it, or stoop my neck to follow its steps. For not as I now speak, did I feel when I turned to those Scriptures; but they seemed to me unworthy to be compared to the stateliness of Cicero, for my swelling pride shrunk from their lowliness, nor could my sharp wit pierce the interior thereof. Yet were they such as would grow up in a little one. But I disdained to be a little one; and, swoln with pride, took myself to be a great one.

[At Carthage, Augustine was converted to the doctrines of the Manichees, a sect of which he remained a member for the next nine years. The founder of this religion was the Babylonian Mani (or Manes), who was crucified in the third century A.D. His doctrines consisted of an amalgam of various beliefs (some borrowed from Christianity), out of which his followers constructed a complicated and somewhat contradictory system. Its most important feature was the stress laid on Evil as an independent power, engaged in a struggle with the power of Good. This conception had the effect of relieving the individual of any feeling of responsibility for his evil actions—they were manifestations of an outside power working in him. The members of the sect were divided into two classes, the Elect and the Hearers; the Elect were forbidden to eat meat. The Manichees were exceedingly powerful in the fourth century, and they remained a serious obstacle to the progress of Christianity for many years afterward.]

[Death of a Friend]

Book IV

For this space of nine years then (from my nineteenth year, to my eight and twentieth) we lived seduced and seducing, deceived and deceiving, in divers lusts; openly, by sciences which they call liberal;[1] secretly, with a false named religion; here proud, there superstitious, every where vain! Here, hunting after the emptiness

---

1. the rhetorical and literary studies which Augustine pursued.

of popular praise, down even to theatrical applauses,[2] and poetic prizes, and strifes for grassy garlands,[3] and the follies of shows, and the intemperance of desires. There, desiring to be cleansed from these defilements, by carrying food to those who were called "elect" and "holy," out of which, in the workhouse of their stomachs, they should forge for us Angels and Gods, by whom we might be cleansed.[4] These things did I follow, and practise with my friends, deceived by me, and with me. . . .

In those years I taught rhetoric, and, overcome by cupidity, made sale of loquacity to overcome by. Yet I preferred (Lord, Thou knowest) honest scholars, (as they are accounted,) and these I, without artifice, taught artifices, not to be practised against the life of the guiltless, though sometimes for the life of the guilty. And Thou, O God, from afar perceivedst me stumbling in that slippery course, and amid much smoke sending out some sparks of faithfulness, which I shewed in that my guidance of *such as loved vanity,* and *sought after lying,* myself their companion. In those years I had one,—not in that which is called lawful marriage, but whom I had found out in a wayward passion, void of understanding; yet but one, remaining faithful even to her; in whom I in my own case experienced, what difference there is betwixt the self-restraint of the marriage-covenant, for the sake of issue, and the bargain of a lustful love, where children are born against their parents' will, although, once born,[5] they constrain love. . . .

In those years when I first began to teach rhetoric in my native town, I had made one my friend, but too dear to me, from a community of pursuits, of mine own age, and, as myself, in the first opening flower of youth. He had grown up of a child with me, and we had been both school-fellows, and play-fellows. But he was not yet my friend as afterwards, nor even then, as true friendship is; for true it cannot be, unless in such as Thou cementest together, cleaving unto Thee, by that *love which is shed abroad in our hearts by the Holy Ghost, which is given unto us.* Yet was it but too sweet, ripened by the warmth of kindred studies: for, from the true faith (which he as a youth had not soundly and thoroughly imbibed,) I had warped him also to those superstitious and pernicious fables, for which my mother[6] bewailed me. With me he now erred in mind, nor could my soul be without him. But behold Thou wert close on the steps of Thy fugitives, at once *God of vengeance,* and Fountain of mercies, turning us to Thyself by wonderful means;

2. at rhetorical contests held in the theater.

3. the prize for the winner of the contest.

4. Certain vegetables were supposed to contain elements of Light, which were liberated when the vegetables were eaten by the Elect.

5. The liaison referred to in this passage resulted in the birth of a son, Adeodatus, who later accompanied Augustine to Italy.

6. Augustine's mother, Monica, was a Christian, and lamented her son's Manichaean beliefs.

Thou tookest that man out of this life, when he had scarce filled up one whole year of my friendship, sweet to me above all sweetness of that my life.

Who can recount all Thy praises, which he hath felt in his one self? What diddest Thou then, my God, and how unsearchable is the *abyss of Thy judgments?* For long, sore sick of a fever, he lay senseless in a death-sweat; and his recovery being despaired of, he was baptized,[7] unknowing; myself meanwhile little regarding, and presuming that his soul would retain rather what it had received of me, not what was wrought on his unconscious body. But it proved far otherwise: for he was refreshed, and restored. Forthwith, as soon as I could speak with him, (and I could, so soon as he was able, for I never left him, and we hung but too much upon each other,) I essayed to jest with him, as though he would jest with me at that baptism which he had received, when utterly absent in mind and feeling, but had now understood that he had received. But he so shrunk from me, as from an enemy; and with a wonderful and sudden freedom bade me, as I would continue his friend, forbear such language to him. I, all astonished and amazed, suppressed all my emotions till he should grow well, and his health were strong enough for me to deal with him, as I would. But he was taken away from my phrensy, that with Thee he might be preserved for my comfort; a few days after, in my absence, he was attacked again by the fever, and so departed.

At this grief my heart was utterly darkened; and whatever I beheld was death. My native country was a torment to me, and my father's house a strange unhappiness; and whatever I had shared with him, wanting him, became a distracting torture. Mine eyes sought him every where, but he was not granted them; and I hated all places, for that they had not him; nor could they now tell me, "he is coming," as when he was alive and absent. I became a great riddle to myself, and I asked my soul, *why she was so sad, and why she disquieted me sorely:* but she knew not what to answer me. And if I said, *Trust in God,* she very rightly obeyed me not; because that most dear friend, whom she had lost, was, being man, both truer and better, than that phantasm she was bid to trust in. Only tears were sweet to me, for they succeeded my friend, in the dearest of my affections. . . .

[Professor at Milan]

Book V

. . . Thou didst deal with me, that I should be persuaded to go to Rome, and to teach there rather, what I was teaching at Carthage. And how I was persuaded to this, I will not neglect to

7. as a Christian; the Manichees did not use this rite.

confess to Thee: because herein also the deepest recesses of Thy
wisdom and Thy most present mercy to us, must be considered and
confessed. I did not wish therefore to go to Rome, because higher
gains and higher dignities were warranted me by my friends who
persuaded me to this, (though even these things had at that time
an influence over my mind,) but my chief and almost only reason was, that I heard that young men studied there more peacefully, and were kept quiet under a restraint of more regular discipline; so that they did not, at their pleasures, petulantly rush into
the school of one, whose pupils they were not, nor were even admitted without his permission. Whereas at Carthage, there reigns
among the scholars a most disgraceful and unruly licence. They
burst in audaciously, and with gestures almost frantic, disturb all
order which any one hath established for the good of his scholars.
Divers outrages they commit, with a wonderful stolidity, punishable
by law, did not custom uphold them; that custom shewing them to
be the more miserable, in that they now do as lawful, what by Thy
eternal law shall never be lawful; and they think they do it unpunished, whereas they are punished with the very blindness whereby
they do it, and suffer incomparably worse than what they do. The
manners then which, when a student, I would not make my own, I
was fain, as a teacher, to endure in others: and so I was well pleased
to go where, all that knew it, assured me that the like was not done.
But Thou, *my refuge and my portion in the land of the living,* that
I might change my earthly dwelling for the salvation of my soul,
at Carthage didst goad me, that I might thereby be torn from it;
and at Rome didst proffer me allurements, whereby I might be
drawn thither, by men in love with a dying life, the one doing frantic, the other promising vain, things; and, to correct my steps, didst
secretly use their and my own perverseness. For both they who
disturbed my quiet, were blinded with a disgraceful phrenzy, and
they who invited me elsewhere, savoured of earth. And I, who here
detested real misery, was there seeking unreal happiness.

But why I went hence, and went thither, Thou knewest, O God,
yet shewedst it neither to me, nor to my mother, who grievously
bewailed my journey, and followed me as far as the sea. But I deceived her, holding me by force, that either she might keep me
back, or go with me, and I feigned that I had a friend whom I
could not leave, till he had a fair wind to sail. And I lied to my
mother, and such a mother, and escaped: for this also hast Thou
mercifully forgiven me, preserving me, thus full of execrable defilements, from the waters of the sea, for the water of Thy Grace;
whereby when I was cleansed, the streams of my mother's eyes
should be dried, with which for me she daily watered the ground

under her face. And yet refusing to return without me, I scarcely persuaded her to stay that night in a place hard by our ship, where was an Oratory[1] in memory of the blessed Cyprian.[2] That night I privily departed, but she was not behind in weeping and prayer And what, O Lord, was she with so many tears asking of Thee, but that Thou wouldest not suffer me to sail? But Thou, in the depth of Thy counsels and hearing the main point of her desire, regardest not what she then asked, that Thou mightest make me what she ever asked. The wind blew and swelled our sails, and withdrew the shore from our sight; and she on the morrow was there, frantic with sorrow, and with complaints and groans filled Thine ears, who didst then disregard them; whilst through my desires, Thou wert hurrying me to end all desire, and the earthly part of her affection to me was chastened by the allotted scourge of sorrows. For she loved my being with her, as mothers do, but much more than many; and she knew not how great joy Thou wert about to work for her out of my absence. She knew not; therefore did she weep and wail, and by this agony there appeared in her the inheritance of Eve, with sorrow seeking, what in sorrow she had brought forth. And yet, after accusing my treachery and hardheartedness, she betook herself again to intercede to Thee for me, went to her wonted place, and I to Rome. . . .

But now despairing to make proficiency in that false doctrine,[3] even those things (with which if I should find no better, I had resolved to rest contented) I now held more laxly and carelessly. For there half arose a thought in me, that those philosophers, whom they call Academics,[4] were wiser than the rest, for that they held, men ought to doubt every thing, and laid down that no truth can be comprehended by man: for so, not then understanding even their meaning, I also was clearly convinced that they thought, as they are commonly reported.[5] Yet did I freely and openly discourage that host[6] of mine from that over-confidence which I perceived him to have in those fables, which the books of Manichaeus are full of. Yet I lived in more familiar friendship with them, than with others who were not of this heresy. Nor did I maintain it with my ancient eagerness; still my intimacy with that sect (Rome secretly harbouring many of them) made me slower to seek any other way: especially since I despaired of finding the truth, from which they had

1. chapel.
2. bishop of Carthage, beheaded during a persecution of the Christians in 258 A.D.
3. the doctrine of the Manichees.
4. members of a Greek philosophical school which questioned the validity of all belief. Augustine probably became acquainted with their position through Cicero's work on the subject.
5. Augustine then thought the Academic position more simple than it was; it is still a matter of controversy how far they carried their skeptical attitude.
6. The man in whose house Augustine was living was a member of the Manichaean community in Rome.

turned me aside, in Thy Church, O Lord of heaven and earth, Creator of all things visible and invisible. . . .

I began then diligently to practise that for which I came to Rome, to teach rhetoric; and first, to gather some to my house, to whom, and through whom, I had begun to be known; when lo, I found other offences committed in Rome, to which I was not exposed in Africa. True, those "subvertings" by profligate young men, were not here practised, as was told me: but on a sudden, said they, to avoid paying their master's stipend, a number of youths plot together, and remove to another;—breakers of faith, who for love of money hold justice cheap. . . .

When therefore they of Milan[7] had sent to Rome to the prefect of the city, to furnish them with a rhetoric reader for their city, and send him at the public expense, I made application (through those very persons, intoxicated with Manichaean vanities, to be freed I was to go, neither of us however knowing it) that Symmachus, then prefect of the city, would try me by setting me some subject,[8] and so send me. To Milan I came, to Ambrose[9] the Bishop, known to the whole world as among the best of men, Thy devout servant; whose eloquent discourse did then plentifully dispense unto Thy people the flour of Thy wheat, the gladness of Thy oil, and the sober inebriation of Thy wine. To him was I unknowing led by Thee, that by him I might knowingly be led to Thee. That man of God received me as a father, and shewed me an Episcopal kindness[10] on my coming. Thenceforth I began to love him, at first indeed not as a teacher of the truth, (which I utterly despaired of in Thy Church,) but as a person kind towards myself. And I listened diligently to him preaching to the people, not with that intent I ought, but, as it were, trying his eloquence, whether it answered the fame thereof, or flowed fuller or lower than was reported; and I hung on his words attentively; but of the matter I was as a careless and scornful looker-on; and I was delighted with the sweetness of his discourse, more recondite, yet in manner, less winning and harmonious, than that of Faustus. Of the matter, however, there was no comparison; for the one was wandering amid Manichaean delusions, the other teaching salvation most

---

7. a city in the north of Italy, which because it was nearer to the frontiers was growing in importance and was soon to replace Rome as the capital, in practice, of the Western Empire.
8. on which to deliver an exhibition speech.
9. the leading personality among the Christians of the West. Not many years after this he defied the power of the emperor Theodosius, and forced him to beg for God's pardon in the church at Milan for having put the inhabitants of Thessalonica to the sword.
10. In the First Epistle to Timothy, Paul lists the qualifications of a bishop; he must, among other things, be "given to hospitality, apt to teach." (I Timothy 3:2.)

soundly. But *salvation is far from sinners*, such as I then stood before him; and yet was I drawing nearer by little and little, and unconsciously.

For though I took no pains to learn what he spake, but only to hear how he spake; (for that empty care alone was left me, despairing of a way open for man, to Thee,) yet together with the words which I would choose, came also into my mind the things which I would refuse; for I could not separate them. And while I opened my heart to admit "how eloquently he spake," there also entered "how truly he spake;" but this by degrees. For first, these things also had now begun to appear to me capable of defence; and the Catholic faith, for which I had thought nothing could be said against the Manichees' objections, I now thought might be maintained without shamelessness; especially after I had heard one or two places of the Old Testament resolved, and ofttimes *"in a figure,"*[11] which when I understood literally, I was slain spiritually. Very many places then of those books having been explained, I now blamed my despair, in believing, that no answer could be given to such as hated and scoffed at the Law and the Prophets. Yet did I not therefore then see, that the Catholic way was to be held, because it also could find learned maintainers, who could at large and with some shew of reason answer objections; nor that what I held was therefore to be condemned, because both sides could be maintained. For the Catholic cause seemed to me in such sort not vanquished, as still not as yet to be victorious.

Hereupon I earnestly bent my mind, to see if in any way I could by any certain proof convict the Manichees of falsehood. Could I once have conceived a spiritual substance,[12] all their strong holds had been beaten down, and cast utterly out of my mind; but I could not. Notwithstanding, concerning the frame of this world, and the whole of nature, which the senses of the flesh can reach to, as I more and more considered and compared things, I judged the tenets of most of the philosophers to have been much more probable. So then after the manner of the Academics (as they are supposed) doubting of every thing, and wavering between all, I settled so far, that the Manichees were to be abandoned; judging that, even while doubting, I might not continue in that sect, to which I already preferred some of the philosophers; to which philosophers notwithstanding, for that they were without the saving Name of Christ, I utterly refused to commit the cure of my sick soul. I determined

11. Ambrose was famous for his allegorical explanations of difficult passages in the Scriptures.

12. One of the Manichaean criticisms of Christian doctrine which Augustine so far found impossible to answer was their objection to the concept of an infinite god who took on a corporeal nature.

therefore so long to be a Catechumen[13] in the Catholic Church, to which I had been commended by my parents, till something certain should dawn upon me, whither I might steer my course.

[*Worldly Ambitions*]

Book VI

. . . My mother had now come to me, resolute through piety, following me over sea and land, in all perils confiding in Thee. For in perils of the sea, she comforted the very mariners, (by whom passengers unacquainted with the deep, use rather to be comforted when troubled,) assuring them of a safe arrival, because Thou hadst by a vision assured her thereof. She found me in grievous peril, through despair of ever finding truth. But when I had discovered to her, that I was now no longer a Manichee, though not yet a Catholic Christian, she was not overjoyed, as at something unexpected; although she was now assured concerning that part of my misery, for which she bewailed me as one dead. . . .

Nor did I yet groan in my prayers, that Thou wouldest help me; but my spirit was wholly intent on learning, and restless to dispute. And Ambrose himself, as the world counts happy, I esteemed a happy man, whom personages so great held in such honour; only his celibacy seemed to me a painful course. But what hope he bore within him, what struggles he had against the temptations which beset his very excellencies, or what comfort in adversities, and what sweet joys Thy Bread had for the hidden mouth of his spirit, when chewing the cud thereof, I neither could conjecture, nor had experienced. Nor did he know the tides of my feelings, or the abyss of my danger. For I could not ask of him, what I would as I would, being shut out both from his ear and speech by multitudes of busy people, whose weaknesses he served. With whom when he was not taken up, (which was but a little time,) he was either refreshing his body with the sustenance absolutely necessary, or his mind with reading. But when he was reading, his eye glided over the pages, and his heart searched out the sense, but his voice and tongue were at rest. Oft-times when we had come, (for no man was forbidden to enter, nor was it his wont that any who came should be announced to him,) we saw him thus reading to himself, and never otherwise; and having long sat silent, (for who durst intrude on one so intent?) we were fain to depart, conjecturing, that in the small interval, which he obtained, free from the din of others' business, for the recruiting of his mind, he was loath to be taken off; and perchance he dreaded lest if the author he read should deliver any thing obscurely, some attentive or perplexed hearer should desire him to expound it, or to discuss some of the

13. one who is preparing himself for baptism.

harder questions; so that his time being thus spent, he could not turn over so many volumes as he desired; although the preserving of his voice (which a very little speaking would weaken) might be the truer reason for his reading to himself. But with what intent soever he did it, certainly in such a man it was good. . . .

I panted after honours, gains, marriage; and Thou deridest me. In these desires I underwent most bitter crosses, Thou being the more gracious, the less Thou sufferedst aught to grow sweet to me, which was not Thou. Behold my heart, O Lord, who wouldest I should remember all this, and confess to Thee. Let my soul cleave unto Thee, now that Thou hast freed it from that fast-holding bird-lime of death. How wretched was it! and Thou didst irritate the feeling of its wound, that forsaking all else, it might be converted unto Thee, who art above all, and without whom all things would be nothing; be converted, and be healed. How miserable was I then, and how didst Thou deal with me, to make me feel my misery on that day, when I was preparing to recite a panegyric of the Emperor,[1] wherein I was to utter many a lie, and lying, was to be applauded by those who knew I lied, and my heart was panting with these anxieties, and boiling with the feverishness of consuming thoughts. For, passing through one of the streets of Milan, I observed a poor beggar, then, I suppose, with a full belly, joking and joyous: and I sighed and spoke to the friends around me, of the many sorrows of our phrenzies; for that by all such efforts of ours, as those wherein I then toiled, dragging along, under the goading of desire, the burthen of my own wretchedness, and, by dragging, augmenting it, we yet looked to arrive only at that very joyousness, whither that beggar-man had arrived before us, who should never perchance attain it. For what he had obtained by means of a few begged pence, the same was I plotting for by many a toilsome turning and winding; the joy of a temporary felicity. For he verily had not the true joy; but yet I with those my ambitious designs was seeking one much less true. And certainly he was joyous, I anxious; he void of care, I full of fears. But should any ask me, had I rather be merry or fearful? I would answer, merry. Again, if he asked had I rather be such as he was, or what I then was? I should choose to be myself, though worn with cares and fears; but out of wrong judgement; for, was it the truth? For I ought not to prefer myself to him, because more learned than he, seeing I had no joy therein, but sought to please men by it; and that not to instruct, but simply to please. Wherefore also Thou didst break my bones with the staff of thy correction. . . .

Continual effort was made to have me married. I wooed, I was promised, chiefly through my mother's pains, that so once married,

1. probably the young Valentinian, whose court was at Milan.

the health-giving baptism might cleanse me,[2] towards which she rejoiced that I was being daily fitted, and observed that her prayers, and Thy promises, were being fulfilled in my faith. At which time verily, both at my request and her own longing, with strong cries of heart she daily begged of Thee, that Thou wouldest by a vision discover unto her something concerning my future marriage; Thou never wouldest. She saw indeed certain vain and phantastic things, such as the energy of the human spirit, busied thereon, brought together; and these she told me of, not with that confidence she was wont, when Thou shewedst her any thing, but slighting them. For she could, she said, through a certain feeling, which in words she could not express, discern betwixt Thy revelations and the dreams of her own soul. Yet the matter was pressed on, and a maiden asked in marriage, two years under the fit age;[3] and, as pleasing, was waited for.

And many of us friends conferring about, and detesting the turbulent turmoils of human life, had debated and now almost resolved on living apart from business and the bustle of men; and this was to be thus obtained; we were to bring whatever we might severally procure, and make one household of all; so that through the truth of our friendship nothing should belong especially to any; but the whole thus derived from all, should as a whole belong to each, and all to all. We thought there might be some ten persons in this society; some of whom were very rich, especially Romanianus our townsman, from childhood a very familiar friend of mine, whom the grievous perplexities of his affairs had brought up to court; who was the most earnest for this project; and therein was his voice of great weight, because his ample estate far exceeded any of the rest. We had settled also, that two annual officers, as it were, should provide all things necessary, the rest being undisturbed. But when we began to consider whether the wives, which some of us already had, others hoped to have, would allow this, all that plan, which was being so well moulded, fell to pieces in our hands, was utterly dashed and cast aside. Thence we betook us to sighs, and groans, and our steps to follow the *broad and beaten ways* of the world; for many thoughts were in our heart, *but Thy counsel standeth for ever.* Out of which counsel Thou didst deride ours, and preparedst Thine own; purposing to *give us meat in due season, and to open Thy hand, and to fill our souls with blessing.*

Meanwhile my sins were being multiplied, and my concubine being torn from my side as a hindrance to my marriage, my heart which clave unto her was torn and wounded and bleeding. And she returned to Afric, vowing unto Thee never to know any other man,

2. He could not be baptized while living in sin with his mistress.

3. The legal age was twelve years.

leaving with me my son by her. But unhappy I, who could not imitate a very woman, impatient of delay, inasmuch as not till after two years was I to obtain her I sought, not being so much a lover of marriage, as a slave to lust, procured another, though no wife, that so by the servitude of an enduring custom, the disease of my soul might be kept up and carried on in its vigor or even augmented, into the dominion of marriage. Nor was that my wound cured, which had been made by the cutting away of the former, but after inflammation and most acute pain, it mortified, and my pains became less acute, but more desperate. . . .

[Book VII is an account of the intellectual difficulties which still stood in the way of his full conversion to the Church, and of the solution of those difficulties to which he finally came. Augustine tells how he rejected astrology and accepted the concept of free will, but was still puzzled by the problem of evil. He finally realized that evil is not an independent entity, existing in opposition to God (as the Manichees taught), but something negative, the absence of good, "not a substance but a perversity of the will turned away to lower things from the highest substance." The resolution of his intellectual difficulties did not bring him the Christian virtue of humility; this he learned through the writings of the Apostle Paul.

The opening chapters of Book VIII tell how, influenced by the examples of other conversions, he began to desire to become not simply a member of the Church, but one dedicated to the service of God, which meant that he would have to live a life of chastity. This was for him the most difficult break with secular life: "I had now found the pearl of great price," he says, "and I ought to have sold all I had and bought it. But still I hesitated."]

[Conversion]

Book VIII

. . . Thus soul-sick was I, and tormented, accusing myself much more severely than my wont, rolling and turning me in my chain, till that were wholly broken, whereby I now was but just, but still was, held. And Thou, O Lord, pressedst upon me in my inward parts by a severe mercy, redoubling the lashes of fear and shame, lest I should again give way, and not bursting that same slight remaining tie, it should recover strength, and bind me the faster. For I said within myself, "Be it done now, be it done now." And as I spake, I all but enacted it. I all but did it, and did it not: yet sunk not back to my former state, but kept my stand hard by, and took breath. And I essayed again, and wanted somewhat less of it, and somewhat less, and all but touched and laid hold of it; and yet came not at it, nor touched, nor laid hold of it: hesitating to die to death and to live to life: and the worse whereto I was inured, prevailed more with me than the better, whereto I was unused: and the very moment wherein I was to become other than I was, the nearer it approached me, the greater horror did it strike into me; yet did it not strike me back, nor turned me away, but held me in suspense.

The very toys of toys, and vanities of vanities, my ancient mistresses, still held me; they plucked my fleshly garment, and whispered softly, "Dost thou cast us off? and from that moment shall we no more be with thee for ever? and from that moment shall not this or that be lawful for thee for ever?" And what was it which they suggested in that I said, "this or that," what did they suggest, O my God? Let Thy mercy turn it away from the soul of Thy servant. What defilements did they suggest! what shame! And now I much less than half heard them, and not openly shewing themselves and contradicting me, but muttering as it were behind my back, and privily plucking me, as I was departing, but to look back on them. Yet they did retard me, so that I hesitated to burst and shake myself free from them, and to spring over whither I was called; a violent habit saying to me, "Thinkest thou, thou canst live without them?"

But now it spake very faintly. For on that side whither I had set my face, and whither I trembled to go, there appeared unto me the chaste dignity of Continency, serene, yet not relaxedly gay, honestly alluring me to come, and doubt not; and stretching forth to receive and embrace me, her holy hands full of multitudes of good examples. There were so many young men and maidens here, a multitude of youth and every age, grave widows and aged virgins; and Continence herself in all, not barren, but a *fruitful mother of children* of joys, by Thee her Husband, O Lord. And she smiled on me with a persuasive mockery, as would she say, "Canst not thou what these youths, what these maidens can? or can they either in themselves, and not rather in the Lord their God? The Lord their God gave me unto them. Why standest thou in thyself, and so standest not? Cast thyself upon Him, fear not He will not withdraw Himself that thou shouldest fall; cast thyself fearlessly upon Him, He will receive, and will heal thee." And I blushed exceedingly, for that I yet heard the muttering of those toys, and hung in suspense. And she again seemed to say, "Stop thine ears against *those* thy unclean *members on the earth, that they may be mortified. They tell thee of delights, but not as doth the law of the Lord thy God.* This controversy in my heart was self against self only. But Alypius[1] sitting

---

1. a student of Augustine's at Carthage; he had joined the Manichees with him, followed him to Rome and Milan, and now shared the desires and

close by my side, in silence waited the issue of my unwonted emotion.

But when a deep consideration had from the secret bottom of my soul drawn together and heaped up all my misery in the sight of my heart; there arose a mighty storm, bringing a mighty shower of tears. Which that I might pour forth wholly, in its natural expressions, I rose from Alypius: solitude was suggested to me as fitter for the business of weeping; so I retired so far that even his presence could not be a burthen to me. Thus was it then with me, and he perceived something of it; for something I suppose I had spoken, wherein the tones of my voice appeared choked with weeping, and so had risen up. He then remained where we were sitting, most extremely astonished. I cast myself down I know not how, under a certain fig-tree, giving full vent to my tears; and the floods of mine eyes gushed out, an *acceptable sacrifice to Thee*. And, not indeed in these words, yet to this purpose, spake I much unto Thee: *And Thou, O Lord, how long? how long, Lord, wilt Thou be angry, for ever? Remember not our former iniquities*, for I felt that I was held by them. I sent up these sorrowful words; How long? how long? to-morrow, and to-morrow? Why not now? why is there not this hour an end to my uncleanness?

So was I speaking, and weeping in the most bitter contrition of my heart, when, lo! I heard from a neighbouring house a voice, as of boy or girl, I know not, chanting, and oft repeating, "Take up and read; Take up and read." Instantly, my countenance altered, I began to think most intently, whether children were wont in any kind of play to sing such words: nor could I remember ever to have heard the like. So checking the torrent of my tears, I arose; interpreting it to be no other than a command from God, to open the book, and read the first chapter I should find. For I had heard of Antony,[2] that coming in during the reading of the Gospel, he received the admonition, as if what was being read, was spoken to him; *Go, sell all that thou hast, and give to the poor, and thou shalt have treasure in heaven, and come and follow me.*[3] And by such oracle he was forthwith converted unto Thee. Eagerly then I returned to the place where Alypius was sitting; for there had I laid the volume of the Apostle,[4] when I arose thence. I seized, opened, and in silence read that section, on which my eyes first fell: *Not in rioting and drunkenness, not in chambering and wantonness, not in strife and envying: but put ye on the Lord Jesus Christ, and make not provision for the flesh*,[5] in concupiscence. No further would I

doubts which he felt. Alypius finally became a bishop in North Africa.

2. the Egyptian saint whose abstinence and self-control are still proverbial; he was one of the founders of the system of monastic life.

3. Luke 18:22.
4. Paul.
5. Romans 13:13–14.

read; nor needed I: for instantly at the end of this sentence, by a light as it were of serenity infused into my heart, all the darkness of doubt vanished away.

Then putting my finger between, or some other mark, I shut the volume, and with a calmed countenance made it known to Alypius. And what was wrought in him, which I knew not, he thus shewed me. He asked to see what I had read: I shewed him; and he looked even further than I had read, and I knew not what followed. This followed, *him that is weak in the faith, receive*; which he applied to himself, and disclosed to me. And by this admonition was he strengthened; and by a good resolution and purpose, and most corresponding to his character, wherein he did always very far differ from me, for the better, without any turbulent delay he joined me. Thence we go into my mother; we tell her; she rejoiceth: we relate in order how it took place; she leaps for joy, and triumpheth, and blesseth Thee, *Who art able to do above that which we ask or think*; for she perceived that Thou hadst given her more for me, than she was wont to beg by her pitiful and most sorrowful groanings. For Thou convertedst me unto Thyself, so that I sought neither wife, nor any hope of this world, standing in that rule of faith, where Thou hadst shewed me unto her in a vision,[6] so many years before. And Thou didst *convert her mourning into joy*, much more plentiful than she had desired, and in a much more precious and purer way than she erst required, by having grandchildren of my body.

[Death of His Mother]

Book IX

. . . And I resolved in Thy sight, not tumultuously to tear, but gently to withdraw, the service of my tongue from the marts of lip-labour: that the young, no students in Thy law, nor in Thy peace, but in lying dotages and law-skirmishes, should no longer buy at my mouth arms for their madness. And very seasonably, it now wanted but very few days unto the Vacation of the Vintage,[1] and I resolved to endure them, then in a regular way to take my leave, and having been purchased by Thee, no more to return for sale. Our purpose then was known to Thee; but to men, other than our own friends, was it not known. For we had agreed among ourselves not to let it out abroad to any: although to us, now ascending from the *valley of tears*, and singing that *song of degrees*, Thou hadst given *sharp arrows*, and *destroying coals* against the *subtile tongue*, which as though advising for us, would thwart, and would out of love devour us, as it doth its meat. . . .

6. At Carthage, when Augustine was still a Manichee, Monica had dreamed that she was standing on a wooden rule weeping for her son, and then saw that he was standing on the same rule as herself.

1. This holiday lasted from the end of August to the middle of October.

Moreover, it had at first troubled me, that in this very summer my lungs began to give way, amid too great literary labour,[2] and to breathe deeply with difficulty, and by the pain in my chest to shew that they were injured, and to refuse any full or lengthened speaking; this had troubled me, for it almost constrained me of necessity, to lay down that burthen of teaching, or, if I could be cured and recover, at least to intermit it. But when the full wish for leisure, that I might see *how that Thou art the Lord*, arose, and was fixed, in me; my God, Thou knowest, I began even to rejoice that I had this secondary, and that no feigned, excuse, which might something moderate the offence taken by those, who for their sons' sake, wished me never to have the freedom of Thy sons. Full then of such joy, I endured till that interval of time were run; it may have been some twenty days, yet they were endured manfully; endured, for the covetousness which aforetime bore a part of this heavy business, had left me, and I remained alone, and had been overwhelmed, had not patience taken its place. Perchance, some of Thy servants, my brethren, may say, that I sinned in this, that with a heart fully set on Thy service, I suffered myself to sit even one hour in the chair of lies. Nor would I be contentious. But hast not Thou, O most merciful Lord, pardoned and remitted this sin also, with my other most horrible and deadly sins, in the holy water? . . .

Now was the day come, wherein I was in deed to be freed of my Rhetoric Professorship, whereof in thought I was already freed. And it was done. Thou didst rescue my tongue, whence Thou hadst before rescued my heart. And I blessed Thee, rejoicing; retiring with all mine to the villa.[3] What I there did in writing, which was now enlisted in Thy service, though still, in this breathing-time as it were, panting from the school of pride, my books may witness,[4] as well what I debated with others, as what with myself alone, before Thee: what with Nebridius, who was absent, my Epistles[5] bear witness. . . .

The vintage-vacation ended, I gave notice to the Milanese to provide their scholars with another master to sell words to them; for that I had both made choice to serve Thee, and through my difficulty of breathing and pain in my chest, was not equal to the Professorship. And by letters I signified to Thy Prelate, the holy man Ambrose, my former errors and present desires, begging his advice what of Thy Scriptures I had best read, to become readier

2. since he not only lectured but also read aloud, as is suggested by his comments on Ambrose's silent reading (Book VI).
3. at Cassiciacum, in the country, placed at his disposal by a friend.

4. While at Cassiciacum, Augustine wrote a book attacking the Academic philosophers, a book on the happy life, and another entitled *De ordine*, a treatise on divine providence.
5. His letters to Nebridius are still extant.

and fitter for receiving so great grace. He recommended Isaiah the Prophet: I believe, because he above the rest is a more clear fore-shewer of the Gospel and of the calling of the Gentiles. But I, rot understanding the first lesson in him, and imagining the whole to be like it, laid it by, to be resumed when better practised in our Lord's own words.

Thence, when the time was come, wherein I was to give in my name,[6] we left the country and returned to Milan. It pleased Alypius also to be with me born again in Thee, being already clothed with the humility befitting Thy Sacraments; and a most valiant tamer of the body, so as, with unwonted venture, to wear the frozen ground of Italy with his bare feet. We joined with us the boy Adeodatus, born after the flesh, of my sin. Excellently hadst Thou made him. He was not quite fifteen, and in wit sur-passed many grave and learned men. I confess unto Thee Thy gifts, O Lord my God, Creator of all, and abundantly able to re-form our deformities: for I had no part in that boy, but the sin. For that we brought him up in Thy discipline, it was Thou, none else, had inspired us with it. I confess unto Thee Thy gifts. There is a book of ours entitled The Master; it is a dialogue between him and me. Thou knowest, that all there ascribed to the person con-versing with me, were his ideas, in his sixteenth year. Much be-sides, and yet more admirable, I found in him. That talent struck awe into me. And who but Thou could be the workmaster of such wonders? Soon didst Thou take his life from the earth: and I now remember him without anxiety, fearing nothing for his childhood or youth, or his whole self. Him we joined with us, our contem-porary in grace, to be brought up in Thy discipline; and we were baptized, and anxiety for our past life vanished from us. Nor was I sated in those days with the wondrous sweetness of considering the depth of Thy counsels concerning the salvation of mankind. How did I weep, in Thy Hymns and Canticles, touched to the quick by the voices of Thy sweet-attuned Church! The voices flowed into mine ears, and the Truth distilled into my heart, whence the affec-tions of my devotion overflowed, and tears ran down, and happy was I therein.

Not long had the Church of Milan begun to use this kind of consolation and exhortation, the brethren zealously joining with harmony of voice and hearts. For it was a year, or not much more, that Justina, mother to the Emperor Valentinian, a child, per-secuted Thy servant Ambrose, in favour of her heresy, to which she was seduced by the Arians.[7] The devout people kept watch in

---

6. as a candidate for baptism.

7. members of a heretical sect who followed the doctrine of Arius (A.D. 250?–336) that the Son had not existed from all eternity and was therefore inferior to the Father. At the Council of Nicaea (A.D. 325) Arius and his followers were declared heretical, but the Arian heresy

the Church, ready to die with their Bishop Thy servant. There my mother Thy handmaid, bearing a chief part of those anxieties and watchings, lived for prayer. We, yet unwarmed by the heat of Thy Spirit, still were stirred up by the sight of the amazed and disquieted city. Then it was first instituted that after the manner of the Eastern Churches,[8] Hymns and Psalms should be sung, lest the people should wax faint through the tediousness of sorrow: and from that day to this the custom is retained, divers, yea, almost all Thy congregations, throughout other parts of the world, following herein.

Then didst Thou by a vision discover to Thy forenamed Bishop, where the bodies of Gervasius and Protasius the martyrs lay hid, (whom Thou hadst in Thy secret treasury stored uncorrupted so many years,) whence Thou mightest seasonably produce them to repress the fury of a woman, but an Empress. For when they were discovered and dug up, and with due honour translated to the Ambrosian Basilica,[9] not only they who were vexed with unclean spirits (the devils confessing themselves) were cured, but a certain man, who had for many years been blind, a citizen, and well known to the city, asking and hearing the reason of the people's confused joy, sprang forth, desiring his guide to lead him thither. Led thither, he begged to be allowed to touch with his handkerchief the bier of Thy *saints, whose death is precious in Thy sight.* Which when he had done, and put to his eyes, they were forthwith opened. Thence did the fame spread, thence Thy praises glowed, shone; thence the mind of that enemy,[10] though not turned to the soundness of believing, was yet turned back from her fury of persecuting. Thanks to Thee, O my God. Whence and whither hast Thou thus led my remembrance, that I should confess these things also unto Thee? which great though they be, I had passed by in forgetfulness. And yet then, when *the odour of Thy ointments was so fragrant,* did we not *run after Thee.* Therefore did I more weep among the singing of Thy Hymns, formerly sighing after Thee, and at length breathing in Thee, as far as the breath may enter into this our house of grass.

Thou *that makest men to dwell of one mind in one house,* didst join with us Euodius also, a young man of our own city. Who being an officer of Court,[11] was before us converted to Thee and baptized: and quitting his secular warfare, girded himself to Thine. We were together, about to dwell together in our devout purpose. We sought where we might serve Thee most usefully, and were together re-

remained as a serious problem for the Church for many years. Justina demanded that Ambrose allow the Arians to hold public services inside the walls of Milan.

8. the Greek-speaking churches of the Eastern half of the empire. They split off from the Catholic Church in the ninth century.

9. church.

10. Justina.

11. an administrative officer.

turning to Africa: whitherward being as far as Ostia,[12] my mother departed this life. Much I omit, as hastening much. Receive my confessions and thanksgivings, O my God, for innumerable things whereof I am silent. But I will not omit whatsoever my soul would bring forth concerning that Thy handmaid, who brought me forth, both in the flesh, that I might be born to this temporal light, and in heart, that I might be born to Light eternal. Not her gifts, but Thine in her, would I speak of; for neither did she make nor educate herself. Thou createdst her; nor did her father and mother know what a one should come from them. And the sceptre of Thy Christ, the discipline of Thine only Son, in a Christian house, a good member of Thy Church, educated her in Thy fear. Yet for her good discipline, was she wont to commend not so much her mother's diligence, as that of a certain decrepit maid-servant, who had carried her father when a child, as little ones used to be carried at the backs of elder girls. For which reason, and for her great age, and excellent conversation, was she, in that Christian family, well respected by its heads. Whence also the charge of her master's daughters was entrusted to her, to which she gave diligent heed, restraining them earnestly, when necessary, with a holy severity, and teaching them with a grave discretion. For, except at those hours wherein they were most temperately fed at their parents' table, she would not suffer them, though parched with thirst, to drink even water; preventing an evil custom, and adding this wholesome advice; "Ye drink water now, because you have not wine in your power; but when you come to be married, and be made mistresses of cellars and cupboards, you will scorn water, but the custom of drinking will abide." By this method of instruction, and the authority she had, she refrained the greediness of childhood, and moulded their very thirst to such an excellent moderation, that what they should not, that they would not.

And yet (as Thy handmaid told me her son) there had crept upon her a love of wine. For when (as the manner was) she, as though a sober maiden, was bidden by her parents to draw wine out of the hogshead, holding the vessel under the opening, before she poured the wine into the flagon, she sipped a little with the tip of her lips; for more her instinctive feelings refused. For this she did, not out of any desire of drink, but out of the exuberance of youth, whereby it boils over in mirthful freaks, which in youthful spirits are wont to be kept under by the gravity of their elders. And thus by adding to that little, daily littles, (*for whoso despiseth little things, shall fall by little and little,*) she had fallen into such a habit, as greedily to drink off her little cup brimfull almost of wine. Where

12. a port on the southwest coast of Italy; it was the port of Rome and the point of departure for Africa.

was then that discreet old woman, and that her earnest counter-
manding? Would aught avail against a secret disease, if Thy healing hand, O Lord, watched not over us? Father, mother, and
governors absent, Thou present, who createdst, who callest, who
also by those set over us, workest something towards the salvation
of our souls, what didst Thou then, O my God? how didst Thou
cure her? how heal her? didst Thou not out of another soul bring
forth a hard and a sharp taunt, like a lancet out of Thy secret
store, and with one touch remove all that foul stuff? For a maid-
servant with whom she used to go to the cellar, falling to words (as
it happens) with her little mistress, when alone with her, taunted
her with this fault, with most bitter insult, calling her wine-bibber.
With which taunt she, stung to the quick, saw the foulness of her
fault, and instantly condemned and forsook it. As flattering friends
pervert, so reproachful enemies mostly correct. Yet not what by
them Thou doest, but what themselves purposed, dost Thou repay
them. For she in her anger sought to vex her young mistress, not to
amend her; and did it in private, either for that the time and place
of the quarrel so found them; or lest herself also should have anger,
for discovering it thus late. But Thou, Lord, Governor of all in
heaven and earth, who turnest to Thy purposes the deepest currents, and the ruled turbulence of the tide of times, didst by the
very unhealthiness of one soul, heal another; lest any, when he observes this, should ascribe it to his own power, even when another,
whom he wished to be reformed, is reformed through words of his.

Brought up thus modestly and soberly, and made subject rather
by Thee to her parents, than by her parents to Thee, so soon as
she was of marriageable age, being bestowed upon a husband, she
served him as her lord; and did her diligence to win him unto Thee,
preaching Thee unto him by her conversation; by which Thou
ornamentedst her, making her reverently amiable, and admirable
unto her husband. And she so endured the wronging of her bed,
as never to have any quarrel with her husband thereon. For she
looked for Thy mercy upon him, that believing in Thee, he might
be made chaste. But besides this, he was fervid, as in his affections,
so in anger: but she had learnt, not to resist an angry husband,
not in deed only, but not even in word. Only when he was
smoothed and tranquil, and in a temper to receive it, she would
give an account of her actions, if haply he had overhastily taken
offence. In a word, while many matrons, who had milder husbands,
yet bore even in their faces marks of shame, would in familiar talk
blame their husbands' lives, she would blame their tongues, giving
them, as in jest, earnest advice; "That from the time they heard
the marriage writings read to them, they should account them as
indentures, whereby they were made servants; and so, remember-

ing their condition, ought not to set themselves up against their lords." And when they, knowing what a choleric husband she endured, marvelled, that it had never been heard, nor by any token perceived, that Patricius had beaten his wife, or that there had been any domestic difference between them, even for one day, and confidentially asking the reason, she taught them her practice above mentioned. Those wives who observed it found the good, and returned thanks; those who observed it not, found no relief, and suffered.

Her mother-in-law also, at first by whisperings of evil servants incensed against her, she so overcame by observance and persevering endurance and meekness, that she[13] of her own accord discovered to her son the meddling tongues, whereby the domestic peace betwixt her and her daughter-in-law had been disturbed, asking him to correct them. Then, when in compliance with his mother, and for the well-ordering of the family, and the harmony of its members, he had with stripes corrected those discovered, at her will who had discovered them, she promised the like reward to any who, to please her, should speak ill of her daughter-in-law to her: and none now venturing, they lived together with a remarkable sweetness of mutual kindness.

This great gift also Thou bestowedst, O my God, my mercy, upon that good handmaid of Thine, in whose womb Thou createdst me, that between any disagreeing and discordant parties where she was able, she shewed herself such a peacemaker, that hearing on both sides most bitter things, such as swelling and indigested choler uses to break out into, when the crudities of enmities are breathed out in sour discourses to a present friend against an absent enemy, she never would disclose aught of the one unto the other, but what might tend to their reconcilement. A small good this might appear to me, did I not to my grief know numberless persons, who through some horrible and wide-spreading contagion of sin, not only disclose to persons mutually angered things said in anger, but add withal things never spoken, whereas to humane humanity, it ought to seem a light thing, not to foment or increase ill will by ill words, unless one study withal by good words to quench it. Such was she, Thyself, her most inward Instructor, teaching her in the school of the heart.

Finally, her own husband, towards the very end of his earthly life, did she gain unto Thee; nor had she to complain of that in him as a believer, which before he was a believer she had borne from him. She was also the servant of thy servants; whosoever of them knew her, did in her much praise and honour and love Thee; for that through the witness of the fruits of a holy conversation

13. the mother-in-law.

they perceived Thy presence in her heart. For she had been *the wife of one man*, had *requited her parents*, had *governed her house* piously, *was well reported of for good works, had brought up children*,[14] so often *travailing in birth of them*, as she saw them swerving from Thee. Lastly, of all of us Thy servants, O Lord, (whom on occasion of Thy own gift Thou sufferest to speak,) us, who before her sleeping in Thee lived united[15] together, having received the grace of Thy baptism, did she so take care of, as though she had been mother of us all; so served us, as though she had been child to us all.

The day now approaching whereon she was to depart this life, (which day Thou well knewest, we knew not,) it came to pass, Thyself, as I believe, by Thy secret ways so ordering it, that she and I stood alone, leaning in a certain window, which looked into the garden of the house where we now lay, at Ostia; where removed from the din of men, we were recovering from the fatigues of a long journey, for the voyage. We were discoursing then together, alone, very sweetly; and *forgetting those things which are behind, and reaching forth unto those things which are before*, we were enquiring between ourselves in the presence of the Truth, which Thou art, of what sort the eternal life of the saints was to be, *which eye hath not seen, nor ear heard, nor hath it entered into the heart of man*. But yet we gasped with the mouth of our heart, after those heavenly streams of Thy fountain, *the fountain of life*, which is *with Thee*; that being bedewed thence according to our capacity, we might in some sort meditate upon so high a mystery.

And when our discourse was brought to that point, that the very highest delight of the earthly senses, in the very purest material light, was, in respect of the sweetness of that life, not only not worthy of comparison, but not even of mention; we raising up ourselves with a more glowing affection towards the Being itself[16] did by degrees pass through all things bodily, even the very heaven, whence sun and moon, and stars shine upon the earth; yea, we were soaring higher yet, by inward musing, and discourse, and admiring of Thy works; and we came to our own souls, and went beyond them, that we might arrive at that region of never-failing plenty, where *Thou feedest Israel* for ever with the food of truth, and where life is the *Wisdom by whom all* these *things are made*, and what have been, and what shall be, and she is not made, but is, as she hath been, and so shall she be ever; yea rather, to "have been," and "hereafter to be," are not in her, but only "to be,"

14. Augustine is quoting Paul's description of the duties of a widow. (I Timothy 5.)

15. Augustine and his fellow converts.

16. reality, the divine principle. This ecstasy of Augustine and Monica is throughout described in philosophical terms.

seeing she is eternal. For to "have been," and to "be hereafter," are not eternal. And while we were discoursing and panting after her, we slightly touched on her with the whole effort of our heart; and we sighed, and there we leave bound *the first fruits of the Spirit*; and returned to vocal expressions of our mouth, where the word spoken has beginning and end. And what is like unto Thy Word, our Lord, who *endureth in Himself* without becoming old, and *maketh all things new?*

We were saying then: If to any the tumult of the flesh were hushed, hushed the images of earth, and waters, and air, hushed also the poles of heaven, yea the very soul be hushed to herself, and by not thinking on self surmount self, hushed all dreams and imaginary revelations, every tongue and every sign, and whatsoever exists only in transition, since if any could hear, all these say, *We made not ourselves, but He made us that abideth for ever*—If then having uttered this, they too should be hushed, having roused only our ears to Him who made them, and He alone speak, not by them, but by Himself, that we may hear His Word, not through any tongue of flesh, nor Angel's voice, nor sound of thunder, nor in the dark riddle of a similitude, but, might hear Whom in these things we love, might hear His Very Self without these, (as we two now strained ourselves, and in swift thought touched on that Eternal Wisdom, which abideth over all;)—could this be continued on, and other visions of kind far unlike be withdrawn, and this one ravish, and absorb, and wrap up its beholder amid these inward joys, so that life might be for ever like that one moment of understanding which now we sighed after; were not this, *Enter into thy Master's joy?*[17] And when shall that be? When *we shall all rise again*, though we *shall not all be changed?*

Such things was I speaking, and even if not in this very manner, and these same words, yet, Lord, Thou knowest, that in that day when we were speaking of these things, and this world with all its delights became, as we spake, contemptible to us, my mother said, "Son, for mine own part I have no further delight in any thing in this life. What I do here any longer, and to what end I am here, I know not, now that my hopes in this world are accomplished. One thing there was, for which I desired to linger for a while in this life, that I might see thee a Catholic Christian before I died. My God hath done this for me more abundantly, that I should now see thee, despising earthly happiness, become His servant: what do I here?"

What answer I made her unto these things, I remember not. For scarce five days after, or not much more, she fell sick of a fever; and in that sickness one day she fell into a swoon, and was

17. Matthew 25:21.

for a while withdrawn from these visible things. We hastened round her; but she was soon brought back to her senses; and looking on me and my brother standing by her, said to us enquiringly, "Where was I?" And then looking fixedly on us, with grief amazed; "Here," saith she, "shall you bury your mother." I held my peace and refrained weeping; but my brother spake something, wishing for her, as the happier lot, that she might die, not in a strange place, but in her own land. Whereat, she with anxious look, checking him with her eyes, for that he still *savoured such things*, and then looking upon me; "Behold," saith she, "what he saith:" and soon after to us both, "Lay," she saith, "this body any where; let not the care for that any way disquiet you: this only I request, that you would remember me at the Lord's altar, wherever you be." And having delivered this sentiment in what words she could, she held her peace, being exercised by her growing sickness.

But I, considering Thy gifts, Thou unseen God, which Thou instillest into the hearts of Thy faithful ones, whence wondrous fruits do spring, did rejoice and give thanks to Thee, recalling what I before knew, how careful and anxious she had ever been, as to her place of burial, which she had provided and prepared for herself by the body of her husband. For because they had lived in great harmony together; she also wished (so little can the human mind embrace things divine) to have this addition to that happiness, and to have it remembered among men, that after her pilgrimage beyond the seas, what was earthly of this united pair had been permitted to be united beneath the same earth. But when this emptiness had through the fulness of Thy goodness begun to cease in her heart, I knew not, and rejoiced admiring what she had so disclosed to me; though indeed in that our discourse also in the window, when she said, "What do I here any longer?" there appeared no desire of dying in her own country. I heard afterwards also, that when we were now at Ostia, she with a mother's confidence, when I was absent, one day discoursed with certain of my friends about the contempt of this life, and the blessing of death: and when they were amazed at such courage which Thou hadst given to a woman, and asked, "Whether she were not afraid to leave her body so far from her own city?" she replied, "Nothing is far to God; nor was it to be feared lest at the end of the world, He should not recognize whence He were to raise me up." On the ninth day then of her sickness, and the fifty-sixth year of her age, and the three and thirtieth of mine, was that religious and holy soul freed from the body.

I closed her eyes; and there flowed a mighty sorrow into my heart, which was overflowing into tears; mine eyes at the same time, by the violent command of my mind, drank up their fountain wholly dry; and woe was me in such a strife! But when she breathed her last, the boy Adeodatus burst out into a loud lament; then, checked by us all, held his peace. In like manner also a childish feeling in me, which was, through my heart's youthful voice, finding its vent in weeping, was checked and silenced. For we thought it not fitting to solemnize that funeral with tearful lament, and groanings: for thereby do they for the most part express grief for the departed, as though unhappy, or altogether dead; whereas she was neither unhappy in her death, nor altogether dead. Of this, we were assured on good grounds, the testimony of her good conversation and her *faith unfeigned*.

What then was it which did grievously pain me within, but a fresh wound wrought through the sudden wrench of that most sweet and dear custom of living together? I joyed indeed in her testimony, when, in that her last sickness, mingling her endearments with my acts of duty, she called me "dutiful," and mentioned, with great affection of love, that she never had heard any harsh or reproachful sound uttered by my mouth against her. But yet, O my God, Who madest us, what comparison is there betwixt that honour that I paid to her, and her slavery for me? Being then forsaken of so great comfort in her, my soul was wounded, and that life rent asunder as it were, which, of hers and mine together, had been made but one.

The boy then being stilled from weeping, Euodius took up the Psalter, and began to sing, our whole house answering him, the Psalm, *I will sing of mercy and judgment to Thee, O Lord*.[18] But hearing what we were doing, many brethren and religious women came together; and whilst they (whose office it was) made ready for the burial, as the manner is, I (in a part of the house, where I might properly), together with those who thought not fit to leave me, discoursed upon something fitting the time; and by this balm of truth, assuaged that torment, known to Thee, they unknowing and listening intently, and conceiving me to be without all sense of sorrow. But in Thy ears, where none of them heard, I blamed the weakness of my feelings, and refrained my flood of grief, which gave way a little unto me; but again came, as with a tide, yet not so as to burst out into tears, nor to a change of countenance; still I knew what I was keeping down in my heart. And being very much displeased, that these human things had such power over me, which in the due order and appointment of our natural condition, must needs come to pass, with a new grief I grieved for my grief, and was thus worn by a double sorrow.

And behold, the corpse was carried to the burial; we went and returned without tears. For neither in those prayers which we

18. the opening words of Psalm 101.

poured forth unto Thee, when the sacrifice of our ransom[19] was offered for her, when now the corpse was by the grave's side, as the manner there is, previous to its being laid therein, did I weep even during those prayers; yet was I the whole day in secret heavily sad, and with troubled mind prayed Thee, as I could, to heal my sorrow, yet Thou didst not; impressing, I believe, upon my memory by this one instance, how strong is the bond of all habit, even upon a soul, which now feeds upon no deceiving Word. It seemed also good to me to go and bathe, having heard that the bath had its name (balneum) from the Greek βαλανεῖον, for that it drives sadness from the mind.[20] And this also I confess unto Thy mercy, *Father of the fatherless,* that I bathed, and was the same as before I bathed. For the bitterness of sorrow could not exsude out of my heart. Then I slept, and woke up again, and found my grief not a little softened; and as I was alone in my bed, I remembered those true verses of Thy Ambrose. For Thou art the

> Maker of all, the Lord,
>   And Ruler of the height,
> Who, robing day in light, hast poured
>   Soft slumbers o'er the night,
> That to our limbs the power
>   Of toil may be renew'd,
> And hearts be rais'd that sink and cower,
>   And sorrows be subdu'd;

And then by little and little I recovered my former thoughts of Thy handmaid, her holy conversation towards Thee, her holy tenderness and observance towards us, whereof I was suddenly deprived: and I was minded to weep in Thy sight, for her and for myself, in her behalf and in my own. And I gave way to the tears which I before restrained, to overflow as much as they desired; reposing my heart upon them; and it found rest in them, for it was in Thy ears, not in those of man, who would have scornfully interpreted my weeping. And now, Lord, in writing I confess it unto Thee. Read it, who will, and interpret it, how he will: and if he finds sin therein, that I wept my mother for a small portion of an hour, (the mother who for the time was dead to mine eyes, who had for many years wept for me, that I might live in Thine eyes,) let him not deride me; but rather, if he be one of large charity, let him weep himself for my sins unto Thee, the Father of all the brethren of Thy Christ.

But now, with a heart cured of that wound, wherein it might seem blameworthy for an earthly feeling, I pour out unto Thee, our

19. *the sacrifice of our ransom:* the Eucharist.

20. Augustine evidently derives the Greek word for "bath" from the words *ballo* and *ania,* which mean "cast away" and "sorrow" respectively.

God, in behalf of that Thy handmaid, a far different kind of tears, flowing from a spirit shaken by the thoughts of the dangers of every soul *that dieth in Adam.* And although she having been quickened in Christ, even before her release from the flesh, had lived to the praise of Thy name for her faith and conversation; yet dare I not say that from what time Thou regeneratedst her by baptism, no word issued from her mouth against Thy Commandment. Thy Son, the Truth, hath said, *Whosoever shall say unto his brother, Thou fool, shall be in danger of hell fire.* And woe be even unto the commendable life of men, if, laying aside mercy, Thou shouldest examine it. But because Thou art not extreme in inquiring after sins, we confidently hope to find some place with Thee. But whosoever reckons up his real merits to Thee, what reckons he up to Thee, but Thine own gifts? O that men would know themselves to be men; *and that he that glorieth, would glory in the Lord.*

I therefore, O my Praise and my Life, God of my heart, laying aside for a while her good deeds, for which I give thanks to Thee with joy, do now beseech Thee for the sins of my mother. Hearken unto me, I entreat Thee, by the Medicine of our wounds, Who hung upon the tree, and now *sitting at Thy right hand maketh intercession to Thee for us.* I know that she dealt mercifully, and from her heart *forgave her debtors their debts, do Thou also forgive her debts,* whatever she may have contracted in so many years, since the water of salvation. Forgive her, Lord, forgive, I beseech Thee; *enter not into judgment with her. Let Thy mercy be exalted above Thy justice,* since Thy words are true, and *Thou hast promised mercy unto the merciful;* which Thou gavest them to be, *who wilt have mercy on whom Thou wilt have mercy;* and wilt *have compassion, on whom Thou hast had compassion.*

And, I believe, Thou hast already done what I ask; but *accept, O Lord, the free-will offerings of my mouth.* For she, the day of her dissolution now at hand, took no thought to have her body sumptuously wound up, or embalmed with spices; nor desired she a choice monument, or to be buried in her own land. These things she enjoined us not; but desired only to have her name commemorated at Thy Altar, which she had served without intermission of one day: whence she knew that holy sacrifice to be dispensed, by which the *hand-writing that was against us, is blotted out;* through which the enemy was triumphed over, who summing up our offences, and seeking what to lay to our charge, *found nothing in Him,* in Whom we conquer. Who shall restore to Him the innocent blood? Who repay Him the price wherewith He bought us, and so take us from Him? Unto the Sacrament of which our ransom, Thy handmaid bound her soul by the bond of faith. Let none sever her from Thy protection: let neither *the lion nor the dragon* interpose himself by force or fraud. For she will not answer that she owes nothing, lest she be convicted and seized by the crafty accuser: but she will answer, that *her sins are forgiven* her by Him, to Whom none can repay that price, which He, Who owed nothing, paid for us.

May she rest then in peace with the husband, before and after whom she had never any; whom she obeyed, *with patience bringing forth fruit* unto Thee, that she might win him also unto Thee. And inspire, O Lord my God, inspire Thy servants my brethren, Thy sons my masters, whom with voice, and heart, and pen I serve, that so many as shall read these Confessions, may at Thy Altar remember Monnica Thy handmaid, with Patricius, her sometimes husband, by whose bodies Thou broughtest me into this life, how, I know not. May they with devout affection remember my parents in this transitory light, my brethren under Thee our Father in our Catholic Mother, and my fellow citizens in that eternal Jerusalem, which Thy pilgrim people sigheth after from their Exodus, even unto their return thither. That so, my mother's last request of me, may through my confessions, more than through my prayers, be, through the prayers of many, more abundantly fulfilled to her.

Masterpieces of the
Middle Ages

EDITED BY
JOHN C. McGALLIARD

Professor of English, The University of Iowa

The period of the Middle Ages —approximately 500–1500 A.D. —encompasses a thousand years of European history distinguished by the unique fusion of a Heroic-Age society with Greco-Roman culture and Christian religion. The era is fairly well marked off by the emergence and disappearance of certain massive forces. It begins with the collapse of the Roman Empire in Western Europe, a development coincident with and partly occasioned by the settlement of Germanic peoples within the territory of the empire. It ends with the discovery of the Western Hemisphere, the invention of the printing press, the consolidation of strong national states, the break in religious unity brought about by the Protestant Reformation, and the renewal—after a lapse of nearly a thousand years—of direct contact with Greek art, thought,

and literature. The medieval centuries created, or at least refashioned, and bequeathed to us such institutional patterns as the Christian church; the monarchical state; the town and village; the traditional European social order—the "lords spiritual," the "lords temporal," with the hierarchy of nobility and gentry ranging from duke to knight, and the third, or bourgeois, estate; the university; the system and logical method of Scholastic philosophy; Romanesque and Gothic architecture; and a rich variety of literary forms.

The literature of the earlier Middle Ages reflects directly and clearly the life and civilization of a Heroic Age. The dominant figure is the fighting king or chieftain; the favorite pursuit is war; the characteristic goals are power, wealth, and glory; and the primary virtues, accordingly, are valor and loyalty. The literary pattern is based on actuality, of which it presents a kind of idealization. In early Germanic and Celtic society the king ruled a small, essentially tribal nation; he and his companions in battle constituted a formal or informal noble class controlling the life of the people. The poems of such a society naturally tell chiefly of the fights of great champions, though also of the druids or other counselors who advised them and of the minstrels who entertained them.

The proportions and the emphasis are much the same in the literature of the Irish, the Scandinavians, the French of the twelfth century, the Germans of the thirteenth. To be sure, the Irish and Scandinavian stories were fashioned before the influence of Christianity was felt, or apart from it. They portray the old, pagan ethics and way of life. The Icelandic family sagas show the Heroic Age in its less spectacular aspects: the champion is still a fighter, like Hrafnkel, but he is also engaged in the more prosaic activity of farming or trading. And he does not stand alone, for there are many men with the same ambitions and not a few with equal powers, Thorgeir and Thorkel, for instance. In Iceland in the tenth century any free man might theoretically become a Heroic-Age figure. The hero of the *Song of Roland*, a twelfth-century French work, combines the fighting chieftain, serving his king, with the devout Crusader; and Archbishop Turpin is both spiritual adviser and fighting champion.

In the literature of the fourteenth century, the warrior plays a smaller rôle and is assimilated to the more extensive pattern of later medieval civilization. Thus in Dante's Heaven only one of the nine celestial spheres—Mars —is occupied by great men-at-arms, all devout Christians, of course. Chaucer's Knight and Squire are only two among twenty-nine pilgrims on their way to Canterbury. The Knight is devoted to truth and honor, generosity, and courteous conduct, while his son, along with other virtues appropriate to a young soldier, possesses those of a courtly lover. The fighting champion of the Heroic Age has become the "officer and gentleman" of the modern world.

This gradual assimilation of the Celtic and Germanic hero to a civilization in which Christianity ordered the Greco-Roman culture to new ends was made possible by the religious unity and authority of Western Europe. The medieval millennium was indeed an age of faith, though it was far from being an age of religious passivity or inertia. The first half of the period was occupied in winning the new peoples of Europe to Christianity. When this had been accomplished, the Crusades began —a series of holy wars intended to rescue Palestine from pagan occupation and, in general, to defeat and either destroy or convert the pagans, chiefly Mohammedans. But the Greek and Arabic learning and philosophy which these non-Christian people introduced into Europe in the twelfth and thirteenth centuries demanded an intellectual alertness. The sharpness of the Crusader's sword had to be matched by the acumen of the Scholastic philosopher; one of the chief works of St. Thomas Aquinas is a summation of principles in defense of Christianity "against the pagans" (his *Summa contra Gentiles*). Medieval Christianity could never afford to take itself for granted. For the first four centuries after Christ the new religion was aggressively on the defensive; thereafter it had to be actively on the offensive in both the practical and the ideological spheres. Nevertheless, in Western Europe itself the combination of theological unity and ecclesiastical authority was a phenomenon unmatched either before or after the Middle Ages. The Roman Empire had provided political unity, law, and order, to assure the success of secular pursuits. Beyond that, it had left moral and spiritual problems to be handled by the individual, singly or in voluntary or ethnic groups. In medieval Europe political disunity was at something like a maximum; but under the leadership and direction of the Church there was achieved a remarkable unanimity of spiritual, moral, and intellectual attitudes and ideals.

The community of European culture in this period was such that the productions of individual countries look like regional manifestations of a central nuclear force. Generally speaking, students and scholars moved freely from land to land; monks, abbots, and bishops might be sent from the country of their birth to serve or preside in distant places; artists and poets wandered widely either in the train of or in search of patrons. Besides his native tongue, the educated man might be expected to speak and write the common "standard" language of Europe —Latin. In an age when the political state was relatively weak, a man's strongest loyalties were to an individual, a feudal lord, for example; to a code, such as the code of chivalry; to an order—of monks or friars or knights; or simply to the Church itself, if, like so many medieval men of intellectual interests, he was a cleric of some sort.

These ties—except for the feudal, and sometimes including that also—were *international* in nature. In such a cultural atmosphere the themes and subjects and techniques of art and literature circulated freely throughout Europe. The *Gothic* architecture of a building is a more central aspect of it than the fact that it was designed and built by an English, a French, a German, or an Italian school of builders. Christianity itself furnished a common subject matter for painters, sculptors, and countless others skilled in the graphic and plastic arts; the biblical stories and scenes had the same meaning in every country. The stories of Charlemagne, Roland, and Arthur, of Aeneas, of Troy and Thebes, were European literary property. They were handled and rehandled, copied, translated, adapted, expanded, condensed, and in general appropriated by innumerable authors, writing in various languages, with no thought of property rights or misgivings about plagiarism. There were no copyright regulations and no author's royalties to motivate insistence on individuality of authorship; there was comparatively little concern about the identity of the artist. Many medieval poems and tales are anonymous, including some of the greatest.

The submergence of the artist in his work is accounted for in part, at least, by the medieval system of human values. The dominant hierarchy of values—we have seen that it did not dominate universally, especially in the literature of northern Europe—was based on the Christian view of man. Man, in this conception, is a creature of God, toward whom he is inevitably oriented but from whom he is separated by the world in which he must live his earthly, mortal life. Human civilization under Christian direction may be regarded as ideally designed—even if not actually so functioning—to assist man on his way to union with God. This is the criterion for the ultimate appraisal of all the institutions of society and all the patterns of culture. Hence derive the scale, the order, the hierarchical categories of medieval life and thought. Since the spiritual side of man transcends the material, the saint becomes the ideal. The saint is one whose life is most fully subdued, assimilated, and ordered to the spiritual. On earth he may be a hermit, like Cuthbert; a reformer of monasteries, like Bernard; a philosopher and a theologian, like Aquinas; a king, like Louis IX of France; or a humble man in private life. Since communion with God—the essential aspect of bliss in heaven—is an experience of the soul, the contempla-tive life, which prepares for the mystical communion, is superior to any form of the active life. Hence the monk—by virtue of his vocation—has an advantage over the secular priest, just as the priest is, other things being equal, in a position spiritually more desirable than that of the layman. As a whole, medieval literature is a study in human life judged according to this scale of values. The scale is represented clearly in Dante's *Divine Comedy*. Secular-value patterns are assimilated to it, for instance in the *Song of Roland*; or it may be taken for granted without much emphasis, as in Chaucer's works. But it is always there, whether below or above the surface. For the modern reader it supplies a focus for the adequate reading and understanding of most of the literature of the Middle Ages.

THE SAGA OF HRAFNKEL PRIEST OF FREY

Aside from the poems of the *Edda*, the greatest literary achievement of medieval Scandinavia was the prose saga. Taken as a whole, the sagas constitute one of the finest bodies of literature in Europe or in the world. *The Saga of Burnt Njal*, *The Laxdaela Saga*, and *The Grettir Saga* are worthy of comparison with the best novels of later centuries. The saga was originally a form of oral literature. Some, called *lying sagas*, were told and heard as candid pieces of fiction. Others, including most of the best, were founded to a considerable extent on fact; this was especially true of the *family sagas*. *The Saga of Hrafnkel*, which was for a long time regarded as one of these, is now considered as the work of a highly gifted writer of fiction. The events recounted in the best of the sagas occurred between the late ninth and the early eleventh century. The narratives deal primarily with the great families living in Iceland in the generations immediately following its discovery and settlement, chiefly by Norwegians. The date of the extant written texts may be anywhere from the late twelfth to the fourteenth century.

The story of Hrafnkel is a good example of the shorter saga. It is the straightforward account of a proud man who suffers an unexpected defeat, quietly rebuilds his strength, profiting incidentally by the lesson of experience, and then crushes his enemies by a sudden but well-calculated stroke. The tone is calm, deliberate, unpretentious. The incidents are related quietly, objectively, with no romantic playing up of "adventure." Necessary preliminary information is given economically and then the action begins without fanfare. Dialogue and description are always a functional part of the action. There is no moralizing or psychologizing; characterization, accomplished through action, is objective; villains and plumed knights are alike absent. The author gets his effect by rigorous omission—by concentration upon the essentials.

The best sagas tell us just enough about each character and each action to enable us to appraise the one correctly in the light of the other. Since there are no caricatures and no real scoundrels in *The Saga of Hrafnkel*, the story includes no

merely frivolous or unqualifiedly evil acts. The killing and other violent deeds which occur are not performed either by highway robbers or by psychopathic characters. The society in which they take place is different in some respects from any with which we are familiar. The teachings of Christianity played little or no part in tenth-century Iceland; the new religion was not adopted, even formally, until the year 1000. On the other hand, there was a very precise code of law (transmitted orally), mostly derived from Norway but elaborated somewhat in Iceland. Behind the letter of the law there was the unformulated tradition of ethics and mores. All of the people portrayed in the saga probably subscribed to this same traditional body of ethics and laws. They disagreed only about concrete cases; but that led to difficulties and conflicts, which are reflected in the events of the saga. For, though Iceland had adequate legislative machinery in the form of the annual Thing, it had no proper executive force with which to carry out its laws or to assure fair trial of cases in court. Thus, within the range of customary principles of conduct, every powerful man was obliged to be, to some degree, a law unto himself.

There is no little irony in the course of events related in the saga. At the outset Hrafnkel is arrogant and overbearing; Thorkel, an enterprising man from the other end of the country, is motivated by the wish to take him down a peg. But although Hrafnkel deserves his unfavorable reputation in general, in this particular instance he has acted with at least some degree of consideration for others. He has killed Einar reluctantly, out of a serious regard for his oath to Frey, his favorite god—and only after Einar violates his express order and disregards his solemn warning. Then, contrary to his habit, he offers a compensation regarded as decidedly generous by everyone, including Sám—by everyone, that is, except old Thorbjorn. Thorbjorn's insistence on a more formal settlement is not motivated by love or respect for his dead son; it is clearly the stubbornness of a man with an inferiority complex.

Sám is a man who has opportunities thrust upon him to which he is not quite equal. Not devoid of shrewdness, common sense, and ambition to a degree, he lacks the imagination and the daring of a great chief; given the chance, he cannot reach the level of a Hrafnkel, a Thorgeir, or a Thorkel. We respect his intelligence when he demurs at starting the suit, his final acceptance of it out of regard for Thorbjorn, and his perseverance —contrasted with Thorbjorn's desire to surrender—when the outlook is unfavorable. But he does not seem to realize the danger, as well as the futility, of winning an unexecuted verdict against Hrafnkel; Thorgeir and Thorkel point it out to him. When he spares the life of Hrafnkel we are tempted to approve his humanity. But he fails to see that such a middle course is dangerous. Lacking the ruthlessness to kill Hrafnkel, he also lacks the magnanimity to treat him with real generosity—admittedly something not to be

expected in that world—and the foresight to estimate the future strength of his foe. The judgment of the author, and of the saga age, is represented by the final contempt and pity with which Thorgeir and Thorkel regard him.

THE SONG OF ROLAND

With some literal inaccuracy, but with substantial truth, it has been said that French literature begins with the *Song of Roland* (*Chanson de Roland*). Certainly it is the first great narrative poem in that language. Of unknown authorship and date, it was apparently composed in the decade or decades after the year 1100. Imbued with the spirit of the First Crusade, it seems to reproduce some details of the campaigns and expeditions to capture and hold the Holy Land for Christendom. The story it tells was developed from a historical incident in the career of Charlemagne (Charles the Great). As the Emperor was returning from a successful war in northern Spain, the Gascons attacked his baggage train and rear guard in the mountain passes of the Pyrenees. The rear guard perished, including Roland, the prefect of the Breton March. These events occurred in the year 778. Our poet of the twelfth century has transformed them—somewhat as Geoffrey of Monmouth, Chrétien de Troyes, and Malory transformed incidents involving the probably also historical Arthur, his exploits, and the deeds of his warriors. The Charles of the *Roland*, a magnificent figure, is white-haired and venerable, and not without a touch of the miraculous: though still valiant in fight, he is reputed among the enemy to be two hundred years old, or more. He is served especially by a choice band of leaders, the twelve peers, of whom the chief is Roland, his nephew —a relationship that in Heroic narrative intensifies either loyalty or disloyalty. The enemy, too, has been changed. Not a few border Gascons or Basques, but enormous Saracen armies fight against Roland and the Emperor. Thus we have a holy war; all the motives of a Crusade are invoked in this struggle of Christians against Mohammedans. Keeping the Emperor as the central *background* figure, the poet has concentrated his efforts on Roland as the hero, the central *foreground* character. Close beside him stand Oliver, the wise and faithful friend, and Ganelon, whose hatred of Roland leads him to treason against Charles.

The world of the poem is an idealization of feudal society in the early twelfth century. This society was headed by proud barons—a hereditary nobility— whose independent spirit found liberal scope in valiant action, fierce devotion, and bitter personal antagonism. A man was esteemed for his prowess in battle, for his loyalty to his king or other feudal chief, and for his wisdom, as the portrait of Oliver reminds us. The action of the poem is infused with a warm glow of patriotic feeling—not the flag-waving variety, but a cherishing love of the homeland, "sweet France." It might be called regional rather than political patriotism, for in a feudal regime a man's binding obligations are to his lord rather than to the country as a whole. Yet the larger issue enters, in a special way: in the second half of the poem, Ganelon is finally condemned and punished because in compassing the destruction of Roland he has injured the king and the French nation: the poet denies Ganelon's claim that these are separable things.

The present volume includes only the first half of the poem. As it is unabridged, however, this portion has a satisfactory completeness. We see the anger of Ganelon at Roland, out of which grows his treachery and the attack of the Saracens; the valor of Roland, and the rest, in battle; and their heroic death. The second half of the poem relates the vengeance taken by Charles against the Saracens— in two separate battles—and the trial and execution of Ganelon. Although the *Song of Roland* was the work, and probably the *written* work, of a well-educated man, during the period immediately following its composition it was sung or chanted. It is divided into strophes averaging fourteen lines, each of ten (or eleven) syllables.

It is easy to see why modern French readers and critics assign the *Roland* a high place in their national literature. Inherent in its structure and texture are the qualities especially esteemed in the French literary tradition—clarity of focus, lucidity in exposition and narration, definite design, and mastery of technical detail. In the poem as a whole—even in our abridgment of a part—scale and proportion are evident. The succession of quarrels, treachery, and battles is only the raw material out of which the poet has built a highly wrought work of art. The emphasis on action—on what Roland, Ganelon, and Oliver do and say—has been recognized since Aristotle as the right method for a poet. But mere action is the formula of the adventure story. The great-literature standard requires that the action have significance. This significance the author of the *Roland* has provided in rich and ordered variety. The acts of the hero, of his friend, and of his foe are presented as part of the total character of each; they grow out of the whole man, including his temperament and personality. But they are also presented against an ethical and social background. Every act, every decision, bears a relation to the feudal code of conduct, of right and wrong, and hence is an indication of human good or evil. Courage rather than cowardice, loyalty rather than treachery, judgment rather than folly—a belief in these criteria is implicit or explicit in the presentation of each action. And they apply to the outermost frame within which the poet has placed the specific events of the narrative—the contest between Christianity and paganism. For to the author and his audience the Christian cause is just, the Saracen, unjust. Roland, fighting for the crusading Emperor, is *right*; Ganelon, aiding the heathen enemy against his brother-in-arms, is doubly *wrong*.

The man who brings about the death of Roland and twenty thousand Franks is no mean and petty villain. The husband of the Emperor's sister and the stepfather of Roland, he holds a very high place in Charles's council. Nor does he lack the ability or the personality to sustain this position. He has no hesitation in speaking against Roland in the first discussion of the Saracen proposals; his nomination as envoy to King Marsile is readily accepted by Charles; and his success in his treachery is a brilliant feat. For in order to accomplish it he must first provoke the now peacefully inclined Marsile to wrath and then turn this anger against Roland. To this end he takes a calculated risk for the sake of a calculated—but far from guaranteed—result. Insulting Marsile deliberately, in the name of the Emperor, he makes himself the first target of the Saracen king's fury and definitely endangers his own life. Luckily for him, the king's hand is stayed; and the Saracen nobles applaud Ganelon's magnificent courage. The rest is comparatively easy—though everything now depends on Ganelon's success in getting Roland placed in command of the rear guard. That he succeeds is the more credible because it was Roland who previously nominated Ganelon for the embassy: Roland and Charles may be expected to act, as in fact they do, on the principle that turn about is fair play.

To the twelfth-century poet and his audience of proud knights the question of motive in Ganelon's hatred of Roland doubtless presented little difficulty. Indeed, if Ganelon had not resorted to treason, a tenable defense of his attitude could be established. For it may well be that he is honestly opposed to the policy of relentless war against the Saracens. His speech at the first council, urging acceptance of Marsile's proposals, wins the support of the wise counselor Naimes, and carries the day. An advocate of peace would obviously regard the uncompromising spokesman of the war party—Roland—as his opponent. Later, talking with the Saracen envoy Blancandrin, Ganelon plausibly represents Roland as the chief obstacle to pacific relations between the two peoples. To be sure, Ganelon is now plotting against Roland; but that should not blind us to the possibility that he honestly differs with Roland about this question of the Emperor's foreign policy. When we have said this, and when we have recognized the faults in Roland's personality that might normally vex another powerful, but less powerful, courtier, we have said all that can be said in defense of Ganelon. His acts put him quite beyond the possibility of moral justification. But justifying him is one thing; understanding him is quite another, and this the author has enabled us to do.

In Roland the poet has created one of the great heroes of European literature. Like Achilles, Aeneas, and Hamlet, he is the embodiment of a definite ideal of humanity. The ideal that Roland incarnates is that of feudal chivalry. Roland exhibits in superlative degree the traits and attitudes which feudal society and institutions sought to produce in a whole class. He is a supremely valiant fighter, a completely faithful vassal, and a warmly affectionate friend; and, since his creator lived in the early twelfth century, his fervent Christianity bears the Crusader's stamp. His words to his friend Oliver before the battle epitomize his vocation as he sees it:

Men for their lords great
    hardship must abide,
Fierce heat and cold endure in
    every clime,
Lose for his sake, if need be, skin
    and hide.
Look to it now! Let each man
    stoutly smite!
No shameful songs be sung for
    our despite!
Paynims are wrong, Christians
    are in the right!
Ill tales of me shall no man tell,
    say I!

This is the code of a man of action, of one to whom action appears as duty. Neither here nor elsewhere in the poem is Roland touched by any sense of the *lacrimae rerum*, and of the "doubtful doom of human kind" that haunts Aeneas. Nor has he ever dreamt of most of the things in Hamlet's philosophy. In assurance and self-reliance he is much closer to Achilles, except that Achilles fought essentially for himself—certainly not for Agamemnon! In Roland the man is wholly assimilated to the vassal. The ceiling above him is lower, the pattern he follows is more limited, than those of Achilles, Aeneas, and Hamlet; yet within his pattern Roland achieves perfection, as they do in theirs.

Roland's feats in battle require no analysis; they are bright and glorious; they outshine the great deeds of his noble comrades. This superiority is no more than the poet has led us to expect. It is the hero's weakness—weakness counterpoised to his greatness—that gives the poem depth and produces the tension that commands our interest. Roland's defect has been called the excess of his special virtue—confidence, courage, bravery; if assurance outstrips prudence, then bravery becomes recklessness, which can bring disaster upon the hero and those for whom he is responsible. The author carefully shows us that Roland has no habit or instinct of caution to match his marvelous courage. Charles notes the vindictive manner in which Ganelon proposes Roland for the rear guard, and though at a loss to divine its meaning, is moved to assign half his entire army to Roland. But Roland either has not noticed the gleam of triumph in Ganelon's eye, or, if he has, loftily disregards it and firmly refuses to take more than twenty thousand men, a relatively small force.

So far Roland has done nothing definitely wrong, though he has revealed a certain lack of perception and of intuitive prudence. But he does do wrong when, surprised by an army of a hundred thousand Saracens, he refuses to blow the horn that would summon Charles to the rescue. The error is emphasized by the repetition in Oliver's effort to persuade him, and the relationship between Roland's refusal and his rashness of character is made apparent both through his answers and through the contrast with Oliver. Roland fears that asking for help would make him look foolish among the Franks—instead, he will slay the foe himself; he will not leave his kin at home open to reproach because of him; if, as Oliver says, the rear guard is hopelessly outnumbered, then death is better than disgrace. Actually, Roland is confident of victory despite the odds. His judgment is not equal to his daring. As the poet sums it up, "Roland is fierce and Oliver wise."

Hence catastrophe ensues. But it is catastrophe redeemed by glorious heroism, as well as self-sacrificing penitence. When, despite tremendous exploits by the Franks, especially by Roland, all but a handful of the rear guard have been slain, Roland wishes to sound the horn to let the Emperor know what has happened. But now Oliver dissents on the ground of honor: Roland had refused to summon Charles to a rescue, and it would be shameful to summon him now only to witness a disaster. The repetitions in this scene balance those of the earlier one. Though the question is decided by Archbishop Turpin, the argument has embittered Oliver against Roland. Hence it is that when, blinded by his own blood, Oliver later strikes Roland, his comrade has to ask whether the blow was intentional. Roland's humility here is a part of his penitence, a penitence never put into words but sublimely revealed in deeds. Exhausted by battle as he is, his superhuman and repeated blasts on the horn burst his temples. The angels and archangels who receive his soul in Paradise are functional symbols of his final triumph in defeat. The poet does not remit the penalty of Roland's error, which is paid by his death. But his victory combines an epic with a tragic conclusion; atonement and redemption, not merely death, is the end, as it is in another profoundly Christian poem of action, Milton's *Samson Agonistes*.

THE STORY OF AUCASSIN AND NICOLETTE

Aucassin and Nicolette (*Aucassin et Nicolete*) is perhaps the most charming literary work of the entire Middle Ages. Its author is unknown, but it is written in the language in use in northern France in the twelfth century or thereabouts. The alternation of prose and verse in *Aucassin* is somewhat unusual; perhaps the prose passages were intended to be read aloud or recited and the poems sung by an entertainer, amateur or professional. It has been suggested that the work belonged to the repertory of a company or pair of traveling minstrels, who performed or acted it much as a play. If this was the case, it must have been presented in places like the castle of Count Garin de Beaucaire in the story, for there was apparently no secular theater—or opera—during the Middle Ages.

The remarkable achievement of *Aucassin* is the masterly use of familiar elements of diverse kinds to produce a unique result. A wide variety of incidents, motifs, and themes has been woven into a unified pattern designed and sustained with precision. It *partly* resembles several of the recognized types of narrative: the folk tale, the romance, the adventure story; and it recalls a number of familiar themes: the love of prince and pauper, the child of royalty in disguise, the conversion of the heathen. The repetition of statements in nearly identical phrasing, especially in the dialogue of the early prose sections, offers the assurance and the emphasis that repetition provides in the fairy tale. And the beauty of Nicolette is so surpassing that we may be tempted to suspect that she is a supernatural creature—until we find the ignorant shepherds making exactly that mistake. The escapes, the traveling to strange lands, the separation by capture and shipwreck, the hardships, all these are the materials of the *romans d'aventure* (tales of adventure). But here they are handled with a brevity and deftness that make them incidental to the central theme; vivid or comic, strange or poignant, none of them delays us long. Nor do the other motifs, mentioned above, ever dominate the narrative or determine the real structure of the work.

Aucassin and Nicolette is, of course, a love story. But the treatment differs considerably from that customary in the *romans d'amour* (tales of love). In these the lady is often hostile, at least ostensibly, or, at best, unaware of her lover's pangs; she has to be won; frequently she is capricious and gives her knight a hard time—he must conquer the lady's affection as well as the numerous and wearying external obstacles that keep them apart. But Nicolette is as much in love as Aucassin, and more ingenious and enterprising; both are utterly candid, direct, and steadily devoted to each other. The specific dangers and the devices employed to elude them, the castles, dungeons, escapes by a window into a garden and through a moat—these are traditional. But the atmosphere in which they are related is not: the warm night of early summer, saturated with moonlight and nightingales, the lyric joy of the two lovers. The work is built, by rigid selection, from elements of the real life of the time, a time when there actually were moats, dungeons, sentinels, parental authority, chattel slaves, fierce counts carrying on private wars—not to insist on Saracens or uncouth shepherds in the woodland. Hence, perhaps, the freshness and spontaneity, the naturally springing gaiety and joy. Hence, too, the stress, without impairment of tone, on the picturesque and the humorous in a world from which the processes of moral judgment have been largely expunged. Action is straightforward and decisive. At one point Aucassin is taken prisoner by his father's enemies before he realizes what has happened; when he becomes aware of his situation, he lays about him manfully, captures the enemy count, and so puts an end to a twenty years' war! The same absoluteness and directness are expressed in Aucassin's famous reply to the viscount of the town, who warns him that he may be sent to hell for loving Nicolette. He wants to go there, says Aucassin, along with the lively knights, the gay, sweet ladies, and the musicians and poets; that is, he belongs with those who take delight in the joys and beauties of human life. A heaven filled with the ugly, the weak, the miserable, and those who deny nature in the name of religion would not suit him at all. This is exuberance, of course, not atheism; the extravagance of Aucassin's words is a part of his character and a feature of his world.

The work is a kind of gospel of the religion of love, a religion that exacts a complete devotion and bestows a complete happiness. Yet there is some question about the tone which the author intended to give it for *his* day and generation. Precisely because motivation and action are so absolute, so neat, and so pat, some modern students of medieval French literature believe that it is a parody or satire. They may well be right. But the modern reader, unburdened by lengthy metrical romances of chivalric adventure and courtly love conducted by means of stereotyped characters and formula situations, need not worry too much about the question. *Aucassin and Nicolette* is a delight whether regarded simply as a story or as a vehicle for literary satire.

DANTE, THE DIVINE COMEDY

The greatest poem of the Middle Ages, called by its author a comedy and designated by later centuries *The Divine Comedy* (*La divina commedia*), was written in the early fourteenth century. The poet, Dante

Alighieri, born in Florence in 1265, was exiled from his native city in 1302 for political reasons and died at Ravenna in 1321. The poem is in many ways both the supreme and the centrally representative expression of medieval man in imaginative literature. But to appreciate the poem adequately in this light a reader must know it in its entirety, since it is an organic whole designed with the utmost symmetry. The present volume contains the entire *Inferno* and several cantos from the other two divisions. It will be best to look rapidly at the general plan and then concentrate on the part included in this book.

The three great divisions of the poem, *Hell* (*Inferno*), *Purgatory* (*Purgatorio*), and *Paradise* (*Paradiso*), are of identical length; each of the last two has thirty-three cantos, and the first, the *Hell*, has thirty-four; but the opening canto is a prologue to the entire poem. The total, one hundred, is the square of ten, regarded in the thought of the time as a perfect number. The three divisions correspond in number to the Trinity. Nine, the square of three, figures centrally in the interior structure of each of the three divisions. In Hell, the lost souls are arranged in three main groups, and occupy nine circles. Most of the circles are themselves subdivided. Hell itself is a funnel-shaped opening in the earth extending from the surface to the center. Dante's journey thus takes him steadily downward through the nine concentric circles. The progression is from the least to the greatest types of evil; all the souls are irrevocably condemned, but all are not intrinsically equal in the degree or nature of their sinfulness. Thus, as we follow Dante in his descent, we find first an ante-Hell, the abode of those who refused to choose between right and wrong; then the boundary river, Acheron; then a circle for virtuous pagans who knew not Christ; and then a series of circles occupied by those guilty of sins of self-indulgence, or Incontinence, of all kinds. These include the illicit lovers, the gluttons, the hoarders and spendthrifts, and those of violent or sullen disposition. Comparable classes and subclasses are found within the other two main groups of sinners, those guilty respectively of Violence and of Fraud, the latter including treachery and treason. At the bottom is the fallen angel, Satan, or Lucifer.

Purgatory is situated on a lofty mountain rising on an island in the sea. It is divided into the ante-Purgatory, which is the lower half of the mountain; Purgatory proper, just above; and the Earthly Paradise, or Garden of Eden, at the summit. Purgatory proper is arranged in a series of seven ledges encircling the mountain, each devoted to the purification of souls from particular kinds of sinful disposition—Pride, Envy, Anger, Sloth, Avarice, Gluttony, and Illicit Love. These seven divisions, plus the ante-Purgatory and the Earthly Paradise, make a total of nine.

The *Paradise* takes us, in ascending order, through the circles of the seven planets of medieval astronomy, the moon,

Mercury, Venus, the sun, Mars, Jupiter, and Saturn; then through the circles of the fixed stars and the *primum mobile*, or outermost circle, which moves the others; and finally to the Empyrean, or Heaven itself, the abode of God, the angels, and the redeemed souls. Again we have nine circles, besides the Empyrean, inclusion of which would give a total of ten. Such is the vast design and scope of *The Divine Comedy* as a whole. Our partial reading can give us some representative and illustrative experience of its execution in some of its parts.

INFERNO

The poem itself begins with action, not outline; explanations come along in suitable places; they are part of the traveler's experience. We shall do well to follow the hint. The incidents recounted in Canto I of the *Inferno* are concrete and definite; their literal meaning is perfectly plain. As critics have often said, Dante is a highly visual poet; he gives us clear pictures or images. Beginning with a man lost in a wood, hindered by three beasts from escape by his own effort, the canto might well be the start of a tale of unusual but quite earthly adventures. But when the stranger Dante meets identifies himself as the shade of the poet Virgil and offers to conduct him through realms which, though not named, can only be Hell and Purgatory, we realize that there is a meaning beyond the one which appears on the surface. We recognize that the wood, the mountain, the sun, and the three beasts,

though casually introduced, are not casual features of the scene. They represent something other than themselves; they are symbols. In the light of the entire poem, it is usually possible to tell what these other things are, and in this volume the head-notes and footnotes identify them. Occasionally, however, there is doubt. What do the three beasts stand for? A lack of certainty is not a serious disadvantage to the reader; he should regard it as a challenge to reach a correct decision for himself. Indeed, if he goes on to read the entire poem, he may arrive at an identification that seems sounder and more consistent with the work as a whole than those proposed. Meanwhile, there is no ambiguity about the animals themselves; they are the satisfying and specific images of poetry.

The simple style of this first canto may surprise the reader who has been told that *The Divine Comedy* is one of the five or six great poems of European literature, especially if he assumes that it will sound like an epic. For Dante begins with neither the splendor of Homer nor the stateliness of Virgil nor the grandeur of Milton. Indeed, except for the use of verse, Canto I seems more like a narrative by Defoe or Swift, particularly at the outset. It is quiet, factual, economical; it convinces us by its air of serious simplicity. Dante called the poem a comedy, in accordance with the use of the term in his day, not only because it began in misery and ended in happiness, but also because in that literary form a sustained loftiness of style was not requisite. In other words, he is free to use the whole range of style, from the humblest, including the colloquial and the humorous, to the highest. There is, indeed, a great variety of tone in the poem. Yet the reader will doubtless eventually agree that Dante strikes the right note *for him* at the beginning. Variation will result chiefly from change in intensity, achieved by differing degrees of concentration and repetition—rather than from a shift to the "grand style." This unpretentious manner is, we see, most suitable to a prolonged work of serious fiction in which the author is the central character. For *The Divine Comedy* is not primarily a Cook's tour of the world of the dead; it is an account of the effect of such a journey on the man who takes it—Dante. It is a record of his moral and spiritual experience of illumination, regeneration, and beatitude. We are interested partly because of the unique and individual character of the traveler—Dante as the man he was, the man revealed in the poem—and partly because the experience of the author is imaginatively available and meaningful to all of us.

In Canto IV we come to the first of the nine concentric circles of Hell. Here are the noble heroes, wise philosophers, and inspired poets of the ancient—and medieval—pagan world. They are excluded from Heaven because they knew nothing of Christ and his religion. This fate may seem harsh to us, but the orthodox view recognized only one gate to Heaven. These spirits suffer no punishment, Virgil (who is one of them) tells Dante, only "cut off from hope, we live on in desire." Here Dante's fervent pity and sympathy at once nourish and mirror the reader's; but there is no rebellion against God's decree. Further explanation, and thereby justification, in Dante's view, will come as the poem progresses toward its goal.

With Canto V we reach the second circle, the first of those containing souls guilty of active sin unrepented at the time of death, and hence suffering a penalty in Hell. Here, therefore, is found the contemptuous and monstrous judge Minos, another figure taken from classical myth and freely adapted to Dante's purposes. The souls assigned to the second circle are those guilty of unlawful love. The poet's method here, as throughout the journey, is first to point out a number of prominent figures who would be familiar to his fourteenth-century readers, and then to concentrate attention on a very few, one or two in each circle, telling more about them and eliciting his own story from each. In general, Dante lets the place and condition in which the sinners are found serve as a minimum essential of information. For the penalties in the various circles are of many different kinds. Their fundamental characteristic is appropriateness to the particular sin; this is one of the principal differences between the punishments in Dante's Hell and the miscellaneous and arbitrary horrors of many accounts of the place. In Dante the penalties symbolize the sin. Thus the illicit lovers of the second circle are continually blown about by storm winds; their suffering is one aspect of the sin itself. For the sin consisted in the surrender of reason to lawless passions.

Here we find Paolo and Francesca, the best-known figures of the entire *Divine Comedy*. Like all the human beings presented in the poem, they actually existed. They lived in Italy about the time of Dante's childhood and early youth, and were slain by Francesca's husband, a brother of Paolo. Dante's method, it is hence clear, is not to build up an allegorical cast of personified abstractions. Instead of, say, Passion and Rebellion, he portrays Paolo and Francesca. They represent, or symbolize, sinful love by example. They show how an intrinsically noble emotion, love, if contrary to God's law, can bring two essentially fine persons to damnation and spiritual ruin. The tenderness and the sympathy with which the story is told are famous. But its pathos, and Dante's personal response of overwhelming pity, should not blind us to the *justice* of the penalty. The poet who describes himself as fainting at the end of Francesca's recital is the same man who consigned her to Hell. His purpose is partly to portray the attractiveness of sin, an especially congenial theme when *this* is the sin involved—both for Dante and for most readers. But although Dante allows the lovers the bitter sweetness of inseparability in Hell, the modern "romantic" idea that union any-

where is sufficient happiness for lovers does not even occur to him. Paolo and Francesca indeed have their love; but they have lost God and thus corrupted their personalities—their inmost selves—from order into anarchy; they are the reverse of happy. In a sense, they have what they wanted, they continue in the lawless condition which they chose on earth. But that condition, seen from the point of view of eternity, is not bliss; it is, in effect, Hell.

In Canto X we are among the heretics in their flaming tomb in the sixth circle. Situated within the walled city of Dis—the capital, as it were, of Hell—this circle is a kind of border between the upper Hell (devoted to punishments for Incontinence) and the lower (concerned with Violence and Fraud). Here Dante portrays the proud aristocrat Farinata and his associate, the elder Cavalcante, father of Dante's closest friend. Their crime is heresy, a flagrant aspect of intellectual pride. But there is a nobility in Farinata's pride; Dante, like the reader, admires the splendid self-sufficiency of a man who, in this situation, can look "proclaiming his disdain for all this Hell." And the essence of the aristocratic nature is distilled in his address to Dante as "half-contemptuously / he asked, 'And *who* would *your* ancestors be?' " and in his abrupt resumption of the conversation interrupted by Cavalcante. Alongside the haughtiness of Farinata, Dante sets the pathetic —and mistaken—grief of Cavalcante for his son; each portrait gains in effect by the extreme contrast.

Canto XIII shows us one group of those guilty of Violence; for the suicides have been violent against themselves. Here they are turned into monstrous trees, their misery finding expression when a bough is plucked. In the eyes of the Church, suicide was murder, in no way diminished by the fact that the slayer and the victim were the same. By representing in Pier delle Vigne a man who had every human motive to end his life, Dante achieves the deepest pathos and evokes our shuddering pity. As Francesca displays in her dramatic monologue the charm and the potential weakness of her character, as Farinata's manner of speech portrays his nature, so Pier delle Vigne by his exact and legal-sounding language lets us see the careful, methodical counselor whose sense of logic and sense of justice were so outraged that he saw no point in enduring life any longer. His judgment is still unimpaired; he does not reproach his king, only the jealous courtiers who misled him. The Wood of the Suicides is one of the greatest—among many admirable—examples of landscape in Hell assimilated to theme and situation.

Canto XV describes the meeting of Dante and his venerable teacher and adviser, the scholar Brunetto Latini. We are in another ring of the seventh circle, among more of those who have sinned through Violence. The impact of this scene results from the contrast between the dignity of the man and the in-dignity of his condition in Hell, and by the tact with which both he and Dante ignore it for the moment. Brunetto, with the others guilty of homosexual vice, must move continually along a sandy desert under a shower of fiery flakes. Dante accords him the utmost respect and expresses his gratitude in the warmest terms; and something like their earthly relationship of teacher and pupil is re-enacted, for Brunetto is keenly interested in Dante's prospects in life. In the final image of Brunetto running, not like the loser, but like the winner of a race, Dante extracts dignity and victory out of indignity itself.

The presence of people like those we have been reviewing will remind the reader that Hell is not reserved exclusively for arrant ruffians, hoodlums, and scoundrels. They are there, of course; but so are many "nice," many charming, and some noble and great, men and women. These are in Hell because they preferred something else—no matter what—to God; at the moment of death they were therefore in rebellion against Him. God and Heaven would not be congenial to them, *as they are and as He is*; and there is no acceptable repentance after death. Hence they go on unchanged—only now experiencing the harsher aspects of the sin in which they chose to live.

In Canto XVII the travelers are carried on the back of the flying monster Geryon down the deep descent from the seventh to the eighth circle. With the face of a just man and the body of a serpent, Geryon symbolizes

Fraud. He is one of the most exciting figures in Hell. In an age before ferris wheels and airplanes, he gives our poets a ride that anticipates some of the terrifying thrill which a young child may feel in an airplane journey. The eighth circle is subdivided into ten chasms or trenches (Malebolge), each with its own kind of sinners: seducers and panders; flatterers; simoniacs (buyers and sellers of appointments in the Church); sorcerers; grafters; hypocrites; thieves; evil counselors; troublemakers; forgers, and impostors.

Most readers will agree that the punishments here fit the crimes; indeed, reflection will usually intensify this conviction. It is a long catalogue of iniquity; much, but not all, is sordid. Dante has avoided monotony not only by the vividness and intensity of the separate scenes but also by their ingenious variety and by the frequent changes of pace in the narrative. The satirical situation and fierce denunciation of the simoniacs is followed by the quiet horror of the sorcerers with twisted necks. The hilarious episode of the grafters precedes the encounter with the solemn, slow-walking hypocrites; and these are succeeded by the macabre serpent-transformations of the thieves. Nevertheless, our steadily deepening descent in hell gradually produces a sense of oppressiveness. This is appropriate and deliberate; it is a part of Dante's total design. But he recognizes the need of momentary relief, a breath of fresh air, a reminder of the world above. These he provides, for example, in the long simile describing the shipyard in Venice (the opening of Canto XXI) or the picture of the peasant and his two sallies outside on a winter morning (the opening of Canto XXIV).

The episode of the grafters (Cantos XXI and XXII) probably has biographical relevance for Dante. During his absence from Florence on business of state, the opposing political party seized power and sentenced Dante to death if he should return to Florence. The quite unfounded charge against him was misappropriation of public funds. In these cantos Dante cuts a ludicrous figure: fearful, cowering, in constant danger from the demons. He escapes their clutches, first by a distraction and then by belated vigilance. The whole sequence affords an oblique and amusing view of an actual episode. It is worth noting also that here, and here only, in the poem, we find ourselves in the kind of hell known in popular lore and anecdote, with winged devils playing rough jokes on their human prey. Scenes, style, and language alike here show one extreme of the range of the poem—the "low" comic. Dante very unobtrusively indicates his awareness of this by the contrasting allusions found in Canto XX, line 113 and Canto XXI, line 2.

Cantos XXVI and XXVII take us among the wicked counselors, who occupy the eighth chasm, or subdivision, of the eighth circle. Appearing at a distance like fireflies in a summer valley, these souls are wrapped in individual, or occasionally twin, flames. Fire is a fit punishment for those who used the flame of intellect to accomplish evil. When the two poets approach more closely, Virgil identifies one flame as that of Ulysses (Odysseus) and Diomed, who burn together. Among the deceptions devised by Ulysses was the wooden horse, which made possible the capture of Troy. It will strike the reader as strange that a man should suffer for his powers as a military tactician. But the Greeks were enemies of the Trojans, whom the Romans and later most of the nations of Western Europe regarded as their ancestors. Ulysses was on the wrong side, and was responsible for his deeds; but Dante mingles with his condemnation an admiration of the man's mental powers. Ulysses remains aloof; he does not converse with Dante, like most of the souls we have met. Instead, as Dorothy Sayers puts it in the notes to her translation of the poem, Virgil conjures the flame into monologue. Thus we are told how Ulysses determined not to return home after the Trojan War but to explore the western ocean instead. In this narrative, apparently invented by Dante, Ulysses becomes the type of the adventuring and searching spirit of man; the voyage is an act of the mind and soul as well as the body. When he has sailed within sight of a mountainous island, his ship is wrecked by a storm and he perishes. Since, as other parts of the poem indicate, this is the island of Purgatory, the episode clearly has symbolic significance. On this island is the Earthly Paradise, or Garden of Eden, lost to man by the sin of Adam. Man, unassisted by divine grace—pagan man, represented by Ulysses—cannot regain it by his own intelligence, although the effort toward that end is noble in itself.

The other evil counselor, Guido da Montefeltro, talks fluently in Canto XXVII; he shows a quite earthly eagerness for news, crafty, garrulous old intriguer that he is. It is a neat irony that, in spite of his deserved reputation for cleverness, Dante shows him twice deceived: first on earth, as he himself relates, and now in Hell— he does not want his story known and is convinced that Dante will never return to earth to tell it. He sketches in detail, with recollective acidity, the steps by which the pope led him, an aging and reformed man, to return for a moment to his old ways. He even includes the contest of St. Francis and the devil for his soul at his death, along with the devil's bitter witticism: you didn't think I was a logician, perhaps!

In Cantos XXXII and XXXIII we have reached the ninth and last circle, where the traitors are immersed in ice that symbolizes their unfeeling hearts. At the end of one canto we are shown the horror of Ugolino gnawing the skull of his enemy Ruggieri, both partly fastened in the ice. Dante does not concentrate on the acts which have put either man in Hell. Instead he lets Ugolino tell us, in the next canto, why his hatred of Ruggieri is so implacable. The fearful pathos, the power, and at the same time the restraint and compression of this narrative make it one of the finest episodes in the poem.

The last canto, Canto XXXIV, shows us the enormous shape of the fallen angel, Satan, fixed at the bottom of Hell, where the motion of his wings freezes the ice in which we have found the traitors immersed. In one of his three mouths he holds Judas Iscariot, who betrayed Christ; in the other two are Brutus and Cassius, who plotted the assassination of Julius Caesar. Dante did not regard them, as we generally do today, as perhaps misguided patriots; to him they were the destroyers of a providentially ordained ruler. Readers who remember Milton's *Paradise Lost* may be surprised at the absence of any interior presentation of Satan. One critic regrets that his suffering is not shown as different from that of the other inhabitants of Hell. But the fact is that his suffering is not presented at all; he is not a person, to Dante, but an object, a part of the machinery and geography of Hell. For *The Divine Comedy* is occupied exclusively with human sin, human redemption, and human beatitude.

PURGATORY

At the beginning of the *Purgatory*, Dante and Virgil have once more reached the surface of the earth and can look up and see the sky and the stars. Their long climb from the bottom of Hell, where they left Satan, has brought them out on the shore of the mountain-island of Purgatory. The scene and the situation are presented by Dante with a bold and happy use of imaginative symbols. Guided by Reason in the person of Virgil, Dante, a man still in the earthly life, has looked closely at sin and evil—in Hell—and turned away from them, and is now in search of the means of self-correction and purification. He arrives on the island shore, just before dawn, to find the reverend figure of Cato acting as guardian of the mountain. The austerely glorious figure of Cato, his face illumined by rays from stars representing the pagan virtues of Prudence, Temperance, Fortitude, and Justice, embodies the highest moral and ethical ideal available to man without divine revelation, pre- or post-Christian. Dante meets him, appropriately, before dawn—before the sun of God's illumination has risen. These elements in the situation, together with the reference to his sojourn with Marcia, his wife, in the circle of virtuous pagans in Hell, make Cato a remarkable transition or border symbol, standing both between Hell and Purgatory and between Greco-Roman philosophy and ethics and the dispensation of the Old and New Testaments.

These opening cantos admirably set quite a new tone in the second great division of the poem. They show us joy and brightness, cheer and hope, contrasting totally with the darkness and misery of Hell. They show us an angel arriving with a cargo of souls, all joyfully singing. They accustom us to a different set of attitudes, a different kind of people, and especially, they portray the naïveté, the almost childlike lack of intellectual and moral sophistication. the need of orientation, which characterize the penitent soul at this point in its progress to perfection. As yet uninstructed and spiritually immature, it looks back, seeking to carry on the harmless but no longer suitable delights of earthly life. Dante— and Virgil—share this simplicity to the full.

Cantos III-XVIII, not included in this book, take the reader along the slopes of the lower half of the mountain—the ante-Purgatory, where some of the souls must wait for varying periods of time (and for different reasons) before entering Purgatory itself—and through four of the seven terraces, those devoted to purgation from Pride, Envy, Anger, and Sloth. In Canto XIX we go on to the fifth of the ledges encircling the mountain, that in which the souls are purified of Avarice. There we meet Pope Adrian, one of Dante's most vivid illustrations of the anguish of purification. Concisely he sketches for Dante the poignant story of his late conversion (to the reality of the Christian life), his repentance, and his present hard penance. Only when, after a life of self-seeking, he had attained the pinnacle of the papacy did disillusionment come—and spiritual discovery: "I saw that there the heart no peace could claim." Now he recognizes the equity of the reforming penalty:

Even as our eyes on high we would not send,

Which only upon earthly things. were cast,
So here to earth Justice hath forced them bend.

Dante, on learning from Adrian's words that he was a pope, has knelt down in respect. But Adrian, perceiving this without lifting his eyes from the ground, peremptorily corrects Dante: there are no popes here. All the hierarchies and social orders of earth are annihilated in Purgatory—and, we may add, the hierarchy of Heaven is. not that of earth. Having answered Dante's questions, Adrian bids him go on—he hinders the task of penitence. Finally, remembering that Dante had offered to carry news of him to those possibly dear to him on earth, which might lead to helpful prayers, the old man adds that he has only a niece there who, if not corrupted by the bad example of his family, could possibly help him. But for this soul, absorbed in his penance, the earth has receded far away, and Heaven is not yet attained; he is essentially alone with his suffering.

The remaining parts of the *Purgatory* included in this book, Cantos XXVII, XXX, and XXXI, add a dimension to Dante's role in the poem. He is, as has been said, the protagonist throughout; the journey and all its disclosures are carried out for his benefit. In Hell, to be sure, he could do little except look and learn; yet his emotional education through the revelation of perfected evil was a large and positive achievement. As a candidate for salvation, he has learned. to abhor sin more completely in proportion as he has been shown its real nature; while, as a man of flesh and blood, he has felt alternate pity and hate for the sinners. Along the penitential ledges of Purgatory he has partially assimilated himself to the penitents; he has felt humility while among those purging themselves of Pride, and generosity among those seeking to root out Envy from their natures. On the seventh terrace, he has recognized an even closer kinship with those engaged in refining their love by fire. But now this same fire, it develops, is the boundary between Purgatory and the Earthly Paradise at the top of the mountain. To reach that goal, Dante must go through the fire. Remembering "Men's bodies burning, once beheld," he is overcome by a terrible fear. The encouraging words of the angel guardian of the ledge, the assurances of Virgil, who reminds him of perils safely passed—neither avail to move him until he is told that Beatrice is beyond the wall of flame. Then his resistance melts and he perseveres through the frightful but harmless fire. It is now nearly sunset, when all ascent ceases, but next morning Dante takes the few last steps to the Earthly Paradise. Here Virgil, who has guided him through Hell and Purgatory, gives him a farewell benediction. Dante, says Virgil, has explored evil in its final effects (in Hell) and the means of correcting the human inclinations that produce it (in Purgatory). His regenerated will is now truly free, and he may fearlessly follow its direction. He no longer needs the guidance of a teacher of morality ("Virgil") nor a political structure ("crown") nor an ecclesiastical institution ("mitre"). In short, he has regained the condition of man before the Fall.

These words apply to Dante in his role as a kind of Everyman, representing whoever has fully discerned the nature of evil and wholly freed himself from the impulses to sin. They apply to every soul when it completes the experience of Purgatory; if they did not, the soul would not be ready to go to Heaven, to enter the presence of God. But obviously they cannot apply, actually and practically, to any man still living on earth. That they were not meant as a literal description of Dante the Italian poet and political exile from Florence is clear enough from the events of Cantos XXX and XXXI. For if Dante has already perfected himself by penance, why should he now, in the scenes with Beatrice, repeat the painful experience of rebuke, confession, and satisfaction? It is this latter series of incidents that constitutes Dante's personal, individual experience of correction and purification.

In the midst of the celestial pageant that moves before Dante in the Earthly Paradise appears a lady whom he instantly recognizes as one who was the object of his idealizing love when she lived as a woman on earth. Turning excitedly to confide this to Virgil, he cannot find him anywhere, and is stricken with grief. Presently the lady names herself as Beatrice— whom the reader will remember for two reasons: she sent Virgil to guide her endangered servant, Dante, through Hell and Purgatory; and to see her Dante forced himself to go through the barrier of fire. There is no cause to doubt that, like the other human beings in the poem, Beatrice is an actual person transformed by the shaping imagination of the poet. What she was to Dante in her earthly life he tells us in the *New Life* (*Vita nuova*), written not long after her death in 1290. She was an incarnation of beauty and virtue; simply by existing, she engrossed the young Dante's ardent but remote devotion; her smile or greeting left him in trembling rapture. This was the full extent of the relationship between them. But the poems in the *New Life* are mostly inspired by the thought of her, whether on earth or in heaven. In short, she was a real woman who, even in this world, was an ideal for Dante, and after death became an even more glorious image of goodness and divine wisdom. The last section of the *New Life* records Dante's resolution to devote a great work to her, when he shall be qualified to achieve it; *The Divine Comedy* is that work. We have seen that he makes her the instigator of the imaginary journey through two realms of the life after death and the motive for his endurance of the fire. Now, as successor to Virgil, she comes

to guide him herself through the heavenly paradise. In the same way that Virgil is Reason without ceasing to be Virgil, Beatrice fulfills the role of Divine Revelation without ceasing to be Beatrice.

It is in this dual character, part beloved woman and part the voice of divine wisdom, that Beatrice, in Canto XXXI, unsparingly rebukes Dante. He had loved her mortal beauty as an image of the immortal; when death destroyed it, his devotion ought thenceforth to have fixed itself on the immortal and indestructible virtue of which that beauty had been the image. Instead, he turned aside to the lure of material things. Dante accepts the reproach with the utmost contrition. It is quite probable that this episode is based on some actual lapse, in Dante's life, from his highest moral ideal. These passages, then, recount his own personal experience of purgation, the autobiographical analogue of the penitence and purification portrayed on the mountain as a whole.

PARADISE

Like the invocations of *Paradise Lost*, that with which Dante begins the third division of his poem expresses his sense of the loftiness of the theme. Like Milton, he is venturing things unattempted hitherto in prose or rhyme. The three invocations of *The Divine Comedy* are incremental; the first (in Canto II of the *Hell*) is brief and unobtrusive, the second (in Canto I of the *Purgatory*) more extended, and the third (in Canto I of the *Paradise*) by its earnestness and solemnity indicates the epic stature, though not epic form, which he expects the poem to attain. The *Paradise* offers us an imagined experience of the entire celestial universe as it was charted by medieval astronomy. In that cosmology, the sun, the moon, and the rest, though immensely distant, had not retreated from the earth according to the scale established by modern knowledge. Dante's world is geocentric; the planetary circles, including those of the sun and moon, revolve about the earth, as does the circle of the stars—as does, in fact, everything except the "real" Heaven, or Empyrean, the abode of God and the saints and angels. The *Paradise* is the chronicle of an ascent from planet to planet, until finally Dante is in the Empyrean itself. In each planet a group of redeemed and perfected souls, come from their proper dwelling in the Empyrean, are present to converse with Dante and his guide, Beatrice. Their successive discussions set forth the essentials of Christian doctrine, along with the fundamental scientific concepts of the time; and they themselves exemplify various kinds and degrees of beatitude. For Dante—and the reader— the experience is educational, morally edifying, and spiritually preparatory for the vision with which the poem ends. In Canto II Dante learns of the hierarchy of souls in Heaven; not all are equal, indeed, no two are identical in bliss; yet each is completely satisfied, fulfilled, and happy—"in His will is perfected our peace." Piccarda, the not wholly blameless nun who speaks these words, is among the souls encountered in the moon, the group of lowest rank in Heaven. From these we rise to higher and higher kinds of blessed souls, each rejoicing wholly in God in its predestined way and in accordance with its capacity.

When all the cycles of the cosmos have been traversed, we come, in Canto XXXI, to Heaven itself, the real home of the blessed. Here the souls are arranged in the form of a great white rose; God is at the center —an ineffable brightness—and the souls have the aspect of rows of petals. Here Beatrice, who has set forth the truths of Divine Revelation throughout the journey, goes back to her place in Heaven, and St. Bernard, the great mystic of the twelfth century, becomes Dante's guide, or rather sponsor. For what remains is that Dante should be vouchsafed a vision in which, for an instant, he may see God as He really is—in so far as his human capacity enables him to do so. The last canto, Canto XXXIII, opens with Bernard's prayer to the Virgin Mary for intercession in Dante's behalf. There is no religious lyric poetry of greater depth or simplicity or beauty than this prayer; its intimacy, tenderness, and humility are consummate.

To obtain, to endure, such a vision is just within the limit of

Dante's powers. It transports him into an utterly different kind of being; it leaves him with the memory of an overpowering but indescribable experience. For of course no mystic can ever reveal the content of his vision; it does not belong to the order of reportable things. Dante can only tell us that he discerned with direct but momentary certitude the identity of God as inclusive of man and of universal love, and that he knew himself to be at that instant one with Him.

The Divine Comedy thus ends both quietly and climactically. For this union with God was the purpose of the entire long and arduous journey. This is the good which St. Thomas Aquinas, and Boethius before him, pointed out as the goal of man, as of the entire creation. But what the philosophers prove, Dante experiences, imaginatively. And we reach both center and summit of the medieval structure of human life in proportion as we can follow the record of that experience.

BOCCACCIO, DECAMERON

The tales of Boccaccio's *Decameron* (completed about 1353) constitute the greatest achievement of prose fiction in a vernacular language of southern Europe during the medieval centuries. In his round hundred stories the Italian author presents a great variety of people and situations, aptly and often acutely characterized, and abundant dialogue of varying liveliness and realism. Like Chaucer, who wrote his *Canterbury Tales* several decades later, he provides a dramatic framework for his narrations. But his storytellers are not miscellaneous pilgrims traveling to a famous shrine; they are seven young ladies and three young gentlemen who have withdrawn from Florence to the countryside, to escape the Black Death, or plague, of 1348. They engage in gay banter and good-natured raillery; but, as they are all refined and cultivated young people with no occupational bias or ingrained prejudices, their relationships are polite rather than boisterous.

Each member of the company is to tell a tale each day; on some days a general topic is assigned, on others each narrator follows his own taste and judgment.

The story of Federigo and his falcon is told on a day devoted to accounts of love that turns out happily after difficulties on the way. It presents the courtly-love relationship—or one of the possible relationships—in a remarkable combination of realism and nobility. Federigo's conduct perfectly fulfills the code; he devotes himself completely to Monna Giovanna, and his failure to receive any return in no way disturbs the pattern of that devotion. He never repines or complains; his lady's married or widowed condition is all one to him; and, having spent his fortune in the futile effort to attract her, he lives with resignation on his tiny estate. But Federigo is genuinely high-minded and noble; he has absorbed the ideals and not merely the etiquette of courtly love. His declaration, when Giovanna comes to call, that he has gained and not lost by his service to her, might be politeness learned out of a book—a romance, for example. But his sacrifice of the falcon to provide her with a good meal is a splendid and magnificent folly that could come only from an almost unbelievably generous heart. His grief at the outcome is probably sharper than Giovanna's, despite the painful disappointment which it produces for her.

Giovanna's dignity and charm and sensitivity are as clear to us as they evidently are to Federigo. Unwilling, whether as wife or widow, to have a romance with Federigo, she does not encourage him. Yet she knows that he loves her and that he has squandered his wealth on her account. We see her distress at having to ask him for anything, let alone the falcon, his most cherished possession. But when love for her young son, mortally ill, forces her to it, she acts with grace and decorum. And with something more; for she has discerned the nobleness of temper in Federigo through his consistently courteous behavior. It is that to which she appeals, not to any obligation of a courtly lover to please his lady. Later, when her brothers convince her that she should remarry, she also shows both generosity and independence of character. She gives Federigo his reward by marrying him—and seeing that his new fortune is not wasted! The happy ending is agreeable; but the notable achievement of the story is the brief but complete and poignant depiction of the dilemmas faced by the two against a background of preliminary characterization which gives their decision full significance.

The tale of Biondello, Ciacco, and Filippo Argenti, very different in setting and tone from the story of Federigo, would nowadays make a good "short short" story of the anecdotal type. Like one whole group of tales in the *Decameron*, it tells of tricks and countertricks. Besides the interest which the narrative arouses in itself, this tale gives us another view of two characters we met in Dante's *Inferno*—Ciacco, the glutton, in Canto VI and Filippo Argenti, the unmannerly bully, in Canto VIII. Boccaccio's account of these two admirably sustains and supplements Dante's portrayal. (In fact, the correspondence is so close that some critics think Boccaccio may have been heavily influenced by Dante here.)

LIVES, WRITINGS, AND CRITICISM

In almost all instances, biographical and critical works are listed only if they are available in English.

THE MIDDLE AGES: GENERAL

Robert S. Hoyt, *Europe in the Middle Ages* (1957) is a good historical survey. For a view of medieval thought and culture as a whole, the standard older work is H. O. Taylor, *The Mediaeval Mind*, 2 vols., 4th ed. (1925). A more recent book is F. B. Artz, *The Mind of the Middle Ages*, 2d ed. (1954).

THE SAGA OF HRAFNKEL PRIEST OF FREY

The best recent introduction to the sagas is Peter Hallberg, *The Icelandic Saga*, translated by Paul Schach (1962). For an extremely interesting account of the relations between history and fiction, see Sigurthur Nordal, *The Saga of Hrafnkel Freys-gotha*, translated by R. George Thomas (1958).

THE SONG OF ROLAND

The best summary in English of information about the origin and nature of the poem is contained in the introduction to the edition by T. A. Jenkins, *La Chanson de Roland* (1924), pp. ixxcviii. For discussion against the background of the *chanson de geste* in general, see Urban Tigner Holmes, *A History of Old French Literature* (1938). For French estimates of the poem, see Gaston Paris, *La Littérature française au moyen-âge* (3d ed., 1903); and E. Faral, *La Chanson de Roland* (1933), in the series of volumes entitled *Les Classiques expliquées*.

P. le Gentil, *The "Chanson de Roland"* (1969), provides technical information in the first half and a more general reading in the second.

AUCASSIN AND NICOLETTE

For a statement of the little that is known about the background of *Aucassin and Nicolette (Aucassin et Nicolete)*, see the English introduction to the edition by F. W. Bourdillon (1919); and Urban Tigner Holmes, *A History of Old French Literature* (1938). Henry Adams devotes a chapter to it in *Mont-Saint-Michel and Chartres* (1913).

DANTE ALIGHIERI

LIFE. Born in late May, 1265, at Florence, Italy. He took part in the battle of Campaldino, 1289, on the Florentine side. In 1291 he married Gemma Donati, by whom he had two sons and one or two daughters. In 1295 he was a member of the "people's council" of Florence, and in 1300 served for two months, the usual term, as one of the six priors, or magistrates, of Florence. In 1302 the Blacks, opponents of the Whites (a political group with which Dante was affiliated), seized power in Florence, and he, with other White leaders, was exiled. Dante had gone to Rome on a mission to Pope Boniface in 1301, and as the decree of banishment was soon coupled with a condemnation to execution by fire (on false charges of corruption in office), he never returned to his native city. The last twenty years of his life, from 1301 to 1321, were spent in exile in various parts of Italy and possibly elsewhere. He died at Ravenna in September, 1321.

CHIEF WRITINGS. *The New Life (La vita nuova)*, probably written about 1292: sonnets and odes with a prose account and running commentary by the poet; the poems were mostly inspired by Beatrice. *The Banquet (Il convivio)*, of uncertain date, unfinished: a work of encyclopedic scope in the form of a prose commentary on a series of the poet's odes *(canzoni)*. *On the Vernacular Language (De vulgari eloquentia)*, in Latin prose, of uncertain date, unfinished: an essay on language and poetry, especially on the dialects of Italy and Provence; of great linguistic and literary interest. *On Single Government (De monarchia)*, in Latin prose, of uncertain date: a closely reasoned defense of world government, together with an attempt to demonstrate the independent status of the Holy Roman Empire and the Papacy. *The Divine Comedy (La divina commedia)*, date of beginning uncertain, apparently finished shortly before Dante's death in 1321.

BIOGRAPHY AND CRITICISM. C. H. Grandgent, *Dante* (1916), and the introduction to his edition of *The Divine Comedy* (revised, 1933); T. S. Eliot, "Dante," most easily available in his *Selected Essays* (1932); George Santayana, "Dante," in *Three Philosophical Poets* (1910). Some recent studies are E. Gilson, *Dante the Philosopher* (1948); Charles Williams, *The Figure of Beatrice* (1943); and the introduction and notes by Dorothy Sayers to her translation of the *Inferno* (1949). See also her *Introductory Papers on Dante* (1954) and *Further Papers on Dante* (1957). The more ambitious student will derive profit from Charles S. Singleton, *Dante Studies 1, Commedia: Elements of Structure* (1956) and *Dante Studies 2, Journey to Beatrice* (1958); Francis Fergusson, *Dante's Drama of the Mind: A Modern Reading of the Purgatorio* (1953, 1968); and Erich Auerbach, *Dante, Poet of the Secular World*, translated by Ralph Manheim (1961). Also helpful is Michele Barbi, *Life of Dante*, translated by Paul G. Ruggiers, 1954.

For background in medieval European history and literature see K. Vossler, *Medieval Culture: An Introduction to Dante and His Times*, translated from the German, 2 vols. (1929), and E. R. Curtius, *European Literature and the Latin Middle Ages*, translated by Willard R. Trask (1953).

Recent studies include R. Hollander, *Allegory in Dante's "Commedia"* (1969), and I. Brandeis, *The Ladder of Vision* (1960). Two collections of essays representative of modern Dante studies are: *Dante: A Collection of Critical Essays*, edited by J. Freccero (1965), and *American Critical Essays on Dante*, edited by R. J. Clements (1969).

GIOVANNI BOCCACCIO

LIFE. Born in 1313 in Paris, son of a Florentine businessman and a Frenchwoman. He was apparently taken to Italy in infancy, and in 1328 was sent to Naples to learn commerce in the office of his father's partner; but after six years, bored with business, he turned to the study of canon law. In 1336 Boccaccio saw Maria d'Aquino in a church at Naples; she is represented as Fiammetta in several of his works, including the *Decameron*. A romantic affair ended in Maria's desertion of her lover, and finally in her death in the plague of 1348. In 1341 Boccaccio returned to Florence. After 1351 he was greatly influenced by Petrarch, and turned in his writing from Italian poetry and prose fiction to Latin works of a scholarly nature. He sheltered Leon Pilatus, inducing him to make the first translation of Homer from Greek. Unlike Petrarch, Boccaccio was devoted to the study of Dante, of whom he wrote a biography; in 1373 he was appointed to a Dante chair or lectureship in Florence. He died in 1375.

CHIEF WRITINGS. Italian narrative verse: *Filostrato*, a source of Chaucer's *Troilus and Criseyde; Teseide*, a source of Chaucer's "Knight's Tale." *The Filostrato of Giovanni Boccaccio*, a translation with parallel text by Nathaniel Edward Griffin and Arthur Beckwith Myrick (1929) is convenient. Italian prose: *Decameron*, finished about 1353; *Vita di Dante*. Latin works: *De casibus virorum illustrium* and *De claris mulieribus*, compendiums of biographical sketches; *De genealogiis deorum*, a kind of dictionary of mythology and defense of poetry.

BIOGRAPHY AND CRITICISM. T. C. Chubb, *The Life of Giovanni Boccaccio* (1930); Edward Hutton, *Giovanni Boccaccio* (1910). Interesting and sensitive criticism is to be found in Charles G. Osgood, *Boccaccio on Poetry* (1930). John Addington Symond, *Giovanni Boccaccio* (1895), has been reissued (1968). A. D. Scaglione, *Nature and Love in the Middle Ages* (1963), a useful discussion of the *Decameron*.

The Saga of Hrafnkel Priest of Frey[*]

It was in the days of King Harald the Fairhaired,[1] son of Halfdane the Black, son of Gudrud the Hunting King, son of Halfdane the Mild and Food-stingy, son of Eysteinn Fart, son of Olaf Wood-ax, king of the Swedes, that a man named Hallfred[2] came with his ship to Broaddale in Iceland. This is below Fleetdale District. On the ship were his wife and son, whose name was Hrafnkel. The son was then fifteen years old, promising and capable. Hallfred set up housekeeping. A foreign slave woman whose name was Arnthrud died there during the winter, and hence the place has since been called Arnthrudstead. In the spring Hallfred moved his household north across the heath and built a dwelling there called Goatdale. One night he dreamed that a man came to him and said, "There you are lying, all unawares, Hallfred. Move your household away to the west, across Lakefleet; all your luck is there." After that he woke up. He moved his household out across the Crooked River to the Tongue, to a place which has since been called Hallfredstead, and he lived there till old age. He left behind a pair of goats. And the same day that Hallfred moved away a landslide struck the house and these animals perished, and hence it has since been called Goatdale.

Hrafnkel was in the habit of riding over the heath in the summer. At this time Glacierdale was settled as far up as the bridges. Hrafnkel rode up along Fleetdale District and saw where an unoccupied valley led off from Glacierdale. This valley seemed to Hrafnkel more habitable than the other valleys that he had seen before. When Hrafnkel came home he asked his father for his share of the property, and said that he wanted to build a homestead for himself. His father consented, and he set up his farm in that valley

---

[*] Translated by John C. McGalliard. This translation is based primarily on the edition of the original by Frank Stanton Cawley, *Hrafnkels Saga Freysgoda*, Harvard University Press, 1932.

1. a strong king who ruled in Norway from about 860 to 933 A.D. Nicknames based on personal traits are very common in Scandinavian stories of the Middle Ages.

2. Hallfred came to Iceland about 920 and settled on the east coast, where most of the events in the saga occur. Exceptions are the incidents at the national assembly, or Thing, and Sám's visit to Thorgeir and Thorkel, who live at Cod Firth, in the northwestern corner of Iceland.

and called it Adalbol. Hrafnkel married Oddbjorg Skjolf's daughter from Salmon River Dale. They had two sons; the elder was named Thorir and the younger Asbjorn. At the time when Hrafnkel took up land at Adalbol he held a great sacrifice; and thereafter he maintained a large temple.[3] Hrafnkel loved no other god more than Frey,[4] and gave him half of all his best possessions. Hrafnkel had the whole valley and gave land to men; but he wished to be their chief and took priestly authority over them. Because of this he was given a nickname and was called Frey's Priest; he was very headstrong, but very capable. He compelled the Glacierdale people to be his dependents; he was mild and easygoing with his own men but hard and strict with the Glacierdale men, and they got no equality from him. Hrafnkel often engaged in duels and compensated no one with money, so that no man got any recompense from him, no matter what Hrafnkel did. Fleetdale District is difficult to travel, very stony and swampy; nevertheless, father and son rode regularly to each other's places, for they were on good terms. The road seemed difficult to Hallfred and he sought a route over the peaks that rise in Fleetdale District; there he got a drier and a longer road, and it is called Hallfred's Way. Only those who are quite familiar with Fleetdale District take this road.

Bjarni was the name of a man who lived at the farm called Bathhouses. It is close to Hrafnkelsdale. He was married and had two sons by his wife; one was named Sám[5] and the other Eyvind, both fine and able men. Eyvind was at home with his father, but Sám was married and lived in the northern part of the valley at the farm called Playsheds; and he had a great deal of property. Sám was very fond of litigation and keen in the law, but Eyvind became a voyager and went off to Norway and was there a year. From there he went on out to Constantinople[6] and was honorably received by the king of the Greeks and was there for a time.

Among his possessions Hrafnkel had a treasure that seemed to him better than any other. This was a horse, dark gray with a black stripe down the back, whom he called Freyfaxi. To Frey, his friend, he gave half the horse. He had such great affection for that horse that he took an oath that he would slay the man who should ride it without his permission.

3. As the text indicates, the priest in the pagan period in Scandinavia had his own temple—a simple wooden building with statues of the principal god or gods—and offered sacrifice in behalf of those families who lived in his district. But the priesthood seems to have involved no moral or ethical responsibilities. Instead, the office was usually held by the leader in the secular affairs of the community; the priest exercised a quite mundane authority over those in his district.

4. The god of fertility, including agriculture; along with Odin and Thor, one of the three most prominent Scandinavian—and general Germanic —deities.

5. Not the biblical "Samuel," but an old Germanic name; the vowel was pronounced like the *a* in *father*.

6. the present Istanbul. The sagas tell of many Scandinavians who served for varying periods of time as members of the Varangian Guard, as the armed retinue of the emperor was called. Thorkel, who appears later in this saga, is one of these.

There was a man named Thorbjorn; he was a brother of Bjarni and lived at the farm in Hrafnkelsdale called Hill, opposite Adalbol to the east. Thorbjorn had little wealth, but many family dependents. His eldest son was named Einar; he was large and well built. It happened, one spring, that Thorbjorn told Einar that he should look for some kind of job, "because I do not need more workmen than the crowd that is here; but it will be easy for you to get a good post, for you are well built. Lack of affection is not the cause of this separation, for you are the most useful of my children; rather, my poverty and lack of means is the cause of it; my other children will become farm workers, but you will fare better in getting a job than they." Einar answered, "You have told me this too late, for all the best jobs are now filled, and I don't like to take the leavings." One day Einar took his horse and rode to Adalbol. Hrafnkel was sitting in the hall. He greeted Einar cheerfully. Einar asked Hrafnkel for work. He answered, "Why did you look for this so late? For I should have taken you first. But now I have engaged all my staff, except for the one job for which you will have no inclination." Einar asked what that was. Hrafnkel said that he had not employed a man for the sheep-herding but that he was in great need of one. Einar said that he did not care what he worked at, whether it was that or something else, but that he wanted food and lodging for two seasons. "I will make you a quick offer," said Hrafnkel; "you are to drive fifty ewes to the summer shed and bring home all the summer wood. You will do this for board and lodging for two seasons. But I wish to stipulate one thing with you as with my other shepherds. Freyfaxi goes about in the dales with his herd; you will look after him winter and summer. But I give you warning about one thing: I wish you never to get on his back, however strong the motive you have to do so, for I have taken a great oath to be the slayer of the man who rides him. Twelve mares trail after him; whichever of them you wish shall be yours to ride by night or day. Do now as I say; for there is an old proverb that 'he who warns another is not responsible.' Now you know what I have had to say." Einar said that he would not be so ill bent as to ride the horse that was forbidden him if there were many others available. Einar now went home for his clothes and took them to Adalbol. Later he moved up to the shed in Hrafnkelsdale which is called Rocky Strip Shed.

Einar got along nicely as the summer passed, so that no sheep were lost until midsummer. Then, one night, nearly thirty ewes were missing. Einar looked through all the pastures and did not find them. One morning, when they had been lost nearly a week, Einar went out early. The rain and mist from the south had cleared off. He took his staff, bridle, and saddle-blanket and went along across the Rocky Strip River, which ran directly in front of the shed.

There, on the gravelly banks, lay the sheep that had been at home the evening before. He drove them back to the shed and went to look for those that had been missing all along. Now he saw the herd of horses on the banks ahead of him and decided to catch one to ride, thinking that he would get on more swiftly if he rode than if he walked. But when he came up and approached the horses they were all shy—except only Freyfaxi—not being used to riders. Frey-faxi was as quiet as if he had been rooted to the ground. Einar knew that the morning was advancing, and he believed that Hrafnkel would not know it if he should ride the stallion. Now he took the horse, bridled him, put the saddle-blanket on his back and rode up by Rocky River Gorge, then up to the glacier and west along it to where the Glacier River descends, and down the river to Hot Spring Shed. He asked all the shepherds at the sheds whether anyone had seen the sheep, and no one had. Einar rode Freyfaxi steadily from dawn till midafternoon. The horse carried him swiftly and far, for he was a good mount. Then it occurred to Einar that it was time to go back and drive in the flock that was at home, though he should not find the others. He rode then east over the ridge into Hrafnkels-dale, and when he came down by Rocky Strip he heard a bleating of sheep ahead in the ravine, which he had ridden past earlier. He turned in that direction and saw thirty ewes in front of him—the same ones that he had lost a week ago. He drove them home with the rest of the flock.

The horse was all wet with sweat, so that it dripped from every hair; he was badly spattered with mud and completely worn out. He rolled over about twelve times and after that set up a loud neighing. Then he took off at high speed down the road. Einar started after him, trying to catch him and take him back to his herd, but he was so wild that Einar got nowhere near him. The horse ran down the valley and did not stop until he came to Adal-bol. At that moment Hrafnkel was sitting at the table. When the horse came to the door he neighed loudly. Hrafnkel told a woman who was serving the meal to go to the door, for a horse had neighed, "and it seemed to me like Freyfaxi's neigh." She went to the door and saw Freyfaxi in bad shape. She told Hrafnkel that Freyfaxi was outside the door, looking very filthy. "What does the fine fel-low want—why has he come home?" said Hrafnkel. "No good will come of this." Then he went out and saw Freyfaxi and said to him, "I don't like it at all that you are treated this way, my fosterling; but you had your wits about you, for you have told me about it, and it shall be avenged. Go now to your herd." And the horse went at once up the valley to his herd of mares. Hrafnkel went to bed in the evening and slept through the night. Then in the morning he had his horse saddled and rode up to the shed. He was dressed in blue clothes and had an ax in his hand, but no other weapons.

Einar had just finished driving the sheep into the milking pens. He was leaning on the railing, counting the sheep, and the women were busy milking. They all greeted Hrafnkel. He asked how things were going. Einar answered, "They haven't gone so well with me, for thirty ewes were missing for nearly a week; but they are found now." Hrafnkel said that he was not complaining about that, "but has there been nothing worse?—and in fact sheep have not been lost as often as was expected. But did you not ride Freyfaxi yesterday?" Einar said he could not deny it. Hrafnkel answered, "Why did you ride that horse, which was forbidden you, when there were enough others that you were allowed to ride? Yet I should have let you off the first time if I had not taken such an oath—though you have clearly admitted the act." And in the belief that no good comes to those who bring down a curse on their heads by breaking their oaths, he leaped from his horse's back to Einar and struck him a death blow. After this he rode home to Adalbol and reported the news. Then he sent another man to the shed to take care of the sheep. And he had Einar carried from the shed to the hillside and raised a beacon beside the burial mound. It is called Einar's Beacon, and marks midevening[7] as seen from the shed.

Thorbjorn, over at Hill, heard of the slaying of Einar, his son. He was much distressed at the news. Now he took his horse and rode over to Adalbol and asked Hrafnkel for legal compensation for his son's slaying.[8] Hrafnkel said that he had killed more men than this one: "It is not unknown to you that I am unwilling to pay compensation for any man, and people have to put up with that. Nevertheless, I grant that this deed appears among the worst of the slayings that I have committed. You have been my neighbor for a long time and you have pleased me well—indeed, each has pleased the other. No other small matter would have caused trouble between Einar and me, if he had not ridden the horse. But we often have this to regret, that we are too free-spoken; less often do we regret saying fewer words rather than more. I will now show you that this act of mine seems to me worse than the others that I have done. I will supply your household with milk cattle in the summer and with meat in the fall; I will do this for you every season, as long as you wish to keep up a house. We shall provide for your sons and daughters with my support and assist them so that they make good marriage settlements thereby; and as for anything that you know to

7. about six P.M. At that hour the sun is on a straight line drawn between the shed and the beacon.

8. When a homicide occurred, the slain man's relatives might (1) accept compensation in money or property, the amount being arranged either informally or, more formally, through arbiters; or (2) take vengeance against the slayer or a close kinsman; or (3) bring suit against the slayer in the law court—at this period, the national assembly, called the Thing. Without acknowledging an obligation to do so, Hrafnkel in his reply actually offers rather liberal compensation for Einar, but on his own terms; he refuses to submit the matter to intermediaries, as Thorbjorn wishes.

be in my possession and that you have need of, you shall tell me of it and not go without anything that you need. You shall maintain your household as long as it pleases you and move over here when you get tired of it, and I will take care of you till you die. Thus we shall be reconciled; and I will venture the boast that many would say that this man is very expensive." "I will not accept that offer," said Thorbjorn. "What terms do you want, then?" said Hrafnkel. Then Thorbjorn said, "I wish us to choose men to arbitrate between us." Hrafnkel answered, "Then you consider yourself my equal, and we shall never be reconciled on that basis."

Then Thorbjorn rode away and down through the district. He came to Bathhouses and found Bjarni, his brother, told him the news, and asked him to take some part in the case. Bjarni said that he was not dealing with his match when Hrafnkel was involved, "and even though we had a great deal of money, still we couldn't contest a suit with Hrafnkel; and it is true that he is strong who knows himself. Hrafnkel has won out in lawsuits over many who had more backing than we. It seems to me that you have shown little sense if you have refused such good terms, and I will have nothing to do with the matter." Thorbjorn spoke many hard words to his brother, saying that the more important a thing was, the less he could be counted on. Thorbjorn then rode away and they said good-bye with little cordiality. He did not stop till he came down to Playsheds and knocked on the door. Someone came to the door and Thorbjorn asked Sám to come out. Sám greeted his kinsman cheerfully and invited him to stay. Thorbjorn was slow in his responses. Sám saw the dejection in his face and asked the news, and Thorbjorn told him of the slaying of Einar, his son. "It is no great news," said Sám, "that Hrafnkel is killing men." Thorbjorn asked whether Sám was willing to offer him some assistance, adding that "this case is such that, although the slain man is closest to me, yet the blow has fallen not far from you." "Have you asked for any redress from Hrafnkel?" Thorbjorn told the truth about everything that had happened between him and Hrafnkel. "I have not been aware before," said Sám, "that Hrafnkel has made such offers to anyone as he has to you. Now I am willing to ride with you up to Adalbol, and then let us take up the matter politely with Hrafnkel and find out whether he will confirm the original offer; in any event, things will go well for him." "Two points," says Thorbjorn: "one is that Hrafnkel will not be willing to do it now; the other is that I am no more in favor of it now than when I rode away from there." Sám said, "I think it will be a hard job to oppose Hrafnkel in a lawsuit." Thorbjorn answered, "That is why you young men never get anywhere—everything looks too big to you. I think there can be nobody who has such shiftless fellows for kinsmen as I. It appears to me that men like you are in a bad way: you seem to be keen in law and active enough in petty suits, but you will not take over this case, which is so clear. It will be a disgrace to you, as is right, for you are the great braggart of our whole family. I see now how it will turn out." Sám answered, "How much better off are you if I should take over the case and then we should both be shamefully driven away from the court?" Thorbjorn answered, "Nevertheless, it is a great consolation to me that you should take over the suit; let it end as it may." Sám answered, "I go into this thing against my will; I am doing it more for the sake of our kinship than anything else. But you shall know that, in aiding you, I feel that I am helping a foolish man." Then Sám reached out his hand and formally took over the case from Thorbjorn.

Sám got his horse and rode up the valley to a farmstead and gave legal notice of the slaying. He got men to aid him against Hrafnkel. Hrafnkel heard of this, and it appeared laughable to him that Sám had started a suit against him. Winter came on now. Then, in the spring, when the summons-days[9] came along, Sám rode from his home up to Adalbol and summoned Hrafnkel in the case of the slaying of Einar. After this Sám rode down through the dales and summoned householders to go to the Thing. Then he let matters rest until the time when people got ready for the trip to the Thing. Hrafnkel then sent men down through the dales and summoned *his* jurors. With his company of seventy Thingmen he rode east across Fleetdale District and around the end of the lake, over the ridge to Screeddale, up through the valley and south at Ax Heath to She-Bear Firth, reaching Thingmen's Road at Side. South from Fleet-dale it is seventeen days' journey to Thingfield. Then after Hrafnkel had ridden out of the district Sám summoned men. For his company he got mostly men without land and those whom he had called up; he supplied these men with weapons and clothes and provisions. Sám took a different route from the valley; he went north to the bridge, across it, and thence over Madderdale Heath, stopping in Madderdale for the night. From there the company rode to Broadshoulder Tongue, then down Blue Fells and from there into Crookdale and on south to Sand. Then they came down to Sheepfells and went on from there to Thingfield.[10]

Hrafnkel had not yet arrived; the journey had been slower for him since he had a longer route. Sám set up a booth[11] for his men at a considerable distance from the place where the men of the East Firths were accustomed to lodge. Sometime afterward Hrafnkel

---

9. the fixed legal time when both defendants and witnesses were given notice by a plaintiff to appear at the next session of the assembly, the Thing.

10. Hrafnkel follows the usual, or southern, route from the east coast to Thingfield, the river valley where the assembly was held annually in the latter part of June. Sám takes a northern route, shorter but more difficult.

Thingfield was in southwestern Iceland, about thirty miles from the present city of Reykjavik.

11. Those who attended sessions of the Thing—lasting two weeks—lived in structures somewhat like the modern tent with a wooden platform. The assembly convened in the open at the Law Rock.

came to the Thing and set up his booth in his usual place. He heard that Sám was at the Thing and thought that amusing. This Thing was very well attended, most of the chiefs in Iceland being on hand. Sám looked up all the chiefs and asked for help and support, but all answered the same way: no one said he had such obligations to Sám that he would be willing to oppose Hrafnkel Priest and thus endanger his own position. They said, too, that matters had turned out in just one way for most men who had engaged in a contest with Hrafnkel at the Thing, namely, that he had driven them all from the court in disgrace.[12] Sám went back to his booth; he and his kinsman were heavyhearted, fearing that their suit would fail, so that they would get nothing from it but shame and humiliation. They were so worried that they could not sleep or eat, for all the chiefs had refused to help them, including those from whom they had really expected assistance.

Old Thorbjorn woke up early one morning. He awakened Sám and asked him to get up, saying, "I can't sleep." Sám got up and put on his clothes. They went out and down to the Ax River below the bridge, and washed themselves. Thorbjorn said to Sám, "My advice is that you have our horses rounded up and we get ready to go home; it is clear now that we shall get nothing but disgrace." Sám answered, "That's fine, in view of the fact that you insisted on a suit against Hrafnkel and refused terms that many a man seeking compensation for a relative would have accepted gladly. You accused me of cowardice—and all the rest who were unwilling to go into the suit with you. Now, I shall not give it up until it seems to me beyond all expectation that I can get anything done." Thorbjorn was so moved by this that he wept. In a moment they saw five men walking away from a booth a little distance below the point on the river where they were sitting. The man who walked in front was tall but not thick; he wore a leaf-green kirtle and carried a sword in his hand. He was a man with regular features, a ruddy complexion, good looks, and thick blond hair. This man was easily recognized, for he had a light-colored lock of hair on the left side. Sám said, "Let's get up and go west across the river and see these men." Then they walked down the river; and the man who was in front of the group greeted them before they spoke to him; and he asked who they were. They told him, and Sám asked the man his name; he said he was Thorkel Thjostason. Sám asked what family he came from and where he lived. He said that he was a West Firther by birth and breeding and lived at Cod Firth. Sám said, "Are you a man of priestly rank?" He said definitely that he was not. "Have you an estate of your own?" said Sám. He said he did not. Sám said, "What is your situation, then?" He answered, "I am unattached; I came out here a year ago; I had been abroad seven years, having gone to Constantinople and joined the household of the king of the Greeks; but now I am living with my brother, whose name is Thorgeir." "Is he a man of priestly status?" said Sám. Thorkel answered, "Certainly, he has priestly authority around Cod Firth and elsewhere in the West Firths." "Is he here at the Thing?" said Sám. "Certainly, he is here." "How large a company has he?" "He has seventy men," said Thorkel. "Are there more brothers?" said Sám. "There is a third," said Thorkel. "Who is he?" said Sám. "His name is Thormod," said Thorkel, "and he lives at Garths in Swansness; he is married to Thordis, daughter of Thorolf Skallagrimsson of Borg." "Will you give us some assistance?" said Sám. "What do you need?" said Thorkel. "The help and support of chiefs," said Sám, "for we have a suit to carry on against Hrafnkel Priest in connection with the slaying of Einar Thorbjarnsson, and with your backing we can be sure of an opportunity to present the case properly." Thorkel answered, "As I said, I have no priestly authority." "Why are you excluded that way, when you are a chief's son like your brothers?" Thorkel said, "I didn't tell you that I had not had the rank; but I turned over my chief's authority to my brother Thorgeir before I went abroad. I have not taken it back since because I am satisfied as long as he has it in charge. Go and see him, ask him for help; he is of energetic nature, a good fellow, well endowed in every way, and a young man eager for honor; such men are the most likely to give you assistance." Sám said, "We shall get nothing from him unless you join us in asking for it." Thorkel said, "This I will promise, to be for you rather than against you, inasmuch as I think you have good cause to bring suit for the slaying of a close relative. Go ahead now to the booth, and inside it; people are sleeping there. You will see two pallets on the far side of the booth; I got up from one, and Thorgeir, my brother, is resting on the other. He has had a big boil on his foot, since he came to the Thing, and hence has slept little at night; but it burst last night and now the core is out and he has been sleeping since. He has his foot stuck out from under the footboard on account of the fever in the foot. Let this old man [Thorbjorn] go on inside the booth; he looks very feeble, both in eyesight and from old age in general. Then, fellow," said Thorkel to Thorbjorn, "when you come to the pallet you must stumble heavily and fall on the pallet, then take hold of the toe that is bound up and give it a jerk—and see how he takes it." Sám said, "You mean to give us good counsel, but this does not seem advisable to me." Thorkel answered, "You can take your choice: either do as I propose or do not look to me for help." Sám said to Thorbjorn, "You must do as he advises." Thorkel said he would come along later, "for I am waiting for my men."

Then Sám and Thorbjorn went along to the booth. Everybody was asleep there, and they saw at once where Thorgeir was lying. Old Thorbjorn stumbled badly as he walked, and when he came to the pallet he fell against the footboard, grasped the toe that had been inflamed, and pulled it toward him. Thorgeir awakened, jumped from the pallet, and asked who was moving about there so clumsily that he ran into people's feet that were already sore. Thorbjorn and Sám could think of nothing to say. Just then Thorkel slipped into the booth and said to his brother Thorgeir, "Don't be hasty or excited about this, kinsman, for nothing is going to harm you; things turn out worse for many people than they intend, and men are not always careful about everything when they have much on their minds. So it is an excuse for you that your foot is sore and has been very painful—that you know best yourself. Now it may be that for an old man his son's death is no less painful than to get no compensation and be lacking in everything himself. He will know his own feelings best; and it is to be expected that a man who has a great deal to worry about will not be careful about everything." Thorgeir said, "I should not have thought that he could be offended with me for that, for I did not kill his son and he cannot avenge the deed on me." "He did not mean to avenge it on you," said Thorkel; "instead, he came up to you more roughly than he intended, for which his dimness of sight is responsible; but he was expecting some assistance from you. It is a noble act, now, to aid an old and needy man. Necessity, and not avarice, leads him to bring suit for the slaying of his son. But now all the chiefs refuse support to this man and thereby show themselves very unheroic." Thorgeir said, "Against whom are these men bringing suit?" Thorkel answered, "Hrafnkel Priest has slain Thorbjorn's son without cause. He commits all kinds of misdeeds against others and will give no man redress for them." Thorgeir said, "It will be with me as with others—I do not know that I have such obligations to these men as to be willing to engage in contests with Hrafnkel. As it appears to me, the same thing happens every summer to those men who take part in suits against him: most of them get little or no honor when it is all over. I see that it goes that way for everybody, and hence I think most men would be reluctant about it, unless they are compelled by necessity." Thorkel said, "It may be that, if I were a chief, I should think it bad to oppose Hrafnkel; but actually it does not look that way to me. For it would appear to me as if one were going up against the most powerful kind of opponent, by whom all had hitherto been routed; and I should think my reputation, or that of any chief who might get the better of Hrafnkel, would be greatly increased. On the other hand, it would not be diminished if things should turn out for me as they have for the rest, for 'that may happen to me which has happened to others'; and also, 'nothing ventured, nothing gained.' " "I see how you are inclined," said Thorgeir; "you want to help these men. Now I will turn over to you my priestly authority over men; you take it, as I have had it hitherto, and henceforth let us both have it equally, and you help those you wish to help." "It seems to me," said Thorkel, "that our authority would be best managed if you should keep it as long as possible. There is no one to whom I am so willing to give it, for you have many qualifications beyond your two brothers, whereas I am uncertain what I shall do with myself at present. And you know, kinsman, that I have taken little part in affairs since I came to Iceland. I can see now how my advice is rated; and now I have said my say for the time being. It may be that Thorkel Lock[13] will reach the point where his words are more highly valued." Thorgeir said, "Now I see what is happening, kinsman—you are displeased, and I cannot allow that; so let us go in with these men, however things turn out, if you wish it." Thorkel said, "I ask only for that which it seems to me best to grant." "How much of their suit do these men think they can handle effectively?" said Thorgeir. "As I told you to-day," said Sám, "we need backing from chiefs, but I will undertake the pleading of the case." Thorgeir said that would do well; "and now it is important to prepare the case as correctly as possible, and it seems to me, if Thorkel is willing, that you should go to see him before the court sits. In the end you will have some solace in return for your trouble, or else more humiliation than before, besides the worry and anxiety. Go along now and don't be downhearted, for if you are going to contest against Hrafnkel you will need to keep up your spirits in the meantime. But don't tell anyone that we have promised you assistance." Then they went back to their booth very cheerfully. Everybody wondered why they had had a change of mood so quickly, for they had been very gloomy when they left their booth. They remained there now until the court sat.

Then Sám called his men and went to the Law Rock, where the court was in session. Sám walked boldly up to the court. He began by naming his witnesses and then presented his case against Hrafnkel Priest without error and according to the correct statutes of the land, as well as with excellent delivery. Just then Thjosti's sons arrived with a great crowd of men. All the men from the western part of the country supported them, and it appeared that Thjosti's sons were fortunate in friends. Sám prosecuted his case to the point where Hrafnkel was invited to defend himself, unless there was someone present who wished to offer a defense in his

---

13. A nickname, from the lock of especially light hair mentioned earlier. Names of this kind were very common; see, for example, the list of kings at the opening of the saga.

behalf according to correct legal procedure. Great applause followed Sám's speech, and no one offered to speak for the defense. Men ran to Hrafnkel's booth and told him what was going on. He sprang up quickly, called his men, and went to the court, thinking there would be few to resist him. He intended to teach little men a lesson about bringing suits against him; he was going to break up the court in Sám's presence and thus force him to give up the case. But now there was no chance of that. There was such a crowd that Hrafnkel got nowhere near; he was pushed away by a much larger force, so that he did not hear the speeches of those who were suing him. Thus it was difficult for him to offer his defense. But Sám prosecuted the case to the limit of the law, with the result that Hrafnkel was declared a full outlaw at that Thing.

Hrafnkel went at once to his booth, had his horses brought up, and rode away from the Thing ill pleased with the ending of the case, for he had never had such a thing happen before. He rode east to Heatherdale Heath, then east to Side, and did not stop till he got back home to Hrafnkelsdale. There he settled down at Adalbol and acted as though nothing had happened. Sám remained at the Thing and went about with great self-confidence. Many men thought it good that the affair had turned out that way, so that Hrafnkel suffered disgrace; they remembered that he had shown unfairness to many. Sám stayed until the Thing closed and people prepared to go home. He thanked the brothers for their support, and Thorgeir laughingly asked Sám how things were going. When he said he was well pleased with the result, Thorgeir said, "Do you think you are any better off than before?" Sám said, "I think Hrafnkel has had a humiliation that will be talked about for a long time, and that is worth a great deal of money." "A man is not a full outlaw until a judgment of execution[14] is carried out; and that must be done at his home, fourteen days after the Taking Up of Weapons." The Taking Up of Weapons marks the time when everyone leaves the Thing. "But I think," said Thorgeir, "that Hrafnkel has gone home and expects to remain at Adalbol; I think he will keep his chief's authority in spite of you. You, however, may at best hope to ride home and settle down on your farm, if you can. I think you have this as the result of your suit: you can call him an outlaw. But I think he will keep most men as much intimidated as before unless you should take further steps." "I never had that in mind," said Sám. "You are a brave man," said Thorgeir, "and I believe my kinsman Thorkel is unwilling to let you down in the end. He wishes to stand by you until your quarrel with Hrafnkel is finally settled and you can live in peace. You will naturally think us the most suitable ones to assist you, since we have taken the most interest in the matter hitherto. We should go with you this

14. a legal term denoting action taken on the part of the successful plaintiff in a suit, to carry out the decision of the court.

once to the East Firths. Now, do you know any route to the East Firths other than the regular road?" Sám was delighted at this, and said that they would go by the same route that he had come on the way from the east.

Thorgeir chose his band of followers and took forty men with him; Sám also had forty. When they had been well equipped with weapons and horses, the whole company traveled by the same route till they reached Glacierdale one morning at dawn and crossed the bridge over the river. This was the day on which the judgment of execution had to be carried out. Thorgeir now asked Sám how they could approach in the least expected way, and Sám said that he would know how to manage that. Then he led them off the road, up to the knoll, and then along the ridge between Hrafnkelsdale and Glacierdale until they came to the lower slope of the mountain beneath which lies the farmstead of Adalbol. Grassy glens reached as far up as the heath, and there was a sharp descent into the dale; and there lay the farmstead below. Sám now dismounted and said, "Let us turn our horses loose, with twenty men to guard them; then sixty of us can make a dash for the house—and I think few people will be stirring." They did so, and the place has since been called Horse Glens. They ran quickly to the house; it was then six o'clock, and no one had got up. They broke in the door with a stick and rushed in. Hrafnkel was resting in his bed. They took him outside, along with all his armed servants; the women and children were driven into an outbuilding. In the yard was also a storehouse; a clothes beam reached from this to the wall of the main house. They led Hrafnkel and his men to this spot. He made many offers for himself and for his men, and when that did no good, he entreated for the lives of the men—"for they have done no harm to you; but it is no dishonor to me, though you kill me; I will not ask to escape that. I do ask to be spared insult; there is no honor to you in that." Thorkel said, "We have heard that you have not been gentle with your enemies, and it is well that you should feel it to-day for yourself." Then they took Hrafnkel and his men and bound their hands behind their backs. Next they broke open the storehouse and took ropes from the hooks, got out their knives, and cut holes in the tendons of the captives. They pulled the ropes through the holes, tossed the men up over the beam, and then tied the eight of them together. Then Thorgeir said, "That has now happened to you, Hrafnkel, which is just; and you must have thought it unlikely that you would ever receive such shame from any man as has now been done to you. Which do you wish to do now, Thorkel: stay here beside Hrafnkel and guard these men or go with Sám outside the yard and away, within distance of a bow-shot from the house, to carry out the judgment of execution on some stony cliff or other, where there is neither plowed field nor meadow?" At that time this had to be done when the sun was due south. Thorkel said, "I will stay here by Hrafnkel, it seems like less work." Thorgeir and Sám then went and carried out the judgment of execution. When they came back, they took down Hrafnkel and his men and placed them in the yard; their eyes were now bloodshot. Then Thorgeir told Sám that he should do with Hrafnkel as he wished, "for he does not look hard to deal with now." Sám then answered, "I give you a choice of two things, Hrafnkel: one, you and such of your men as I wish shall be led out of the yard and killed; but inasmuch as you have many family dependents to care for, I am willing to allow you to make provision for them. On the other hand, if you choose life, then leave Adalbol together with all the members of your household and take only those possessions which I assign you—which will be very little. I shall take over your homestead and all your chief's authority; neither you nor your heirs shall ever lay claim to them; and you shall come nowhere nearer than the east side of Fleetdale District. Now you can be reconciled with me if you are willing to accept these terms." Hrafnkel said, "To many a quick death would seem better than such insults; but it will go with me as with many others—I will take life, if there is a choice. I do it mostly for the sake of my sons, for their prospects will be slight if I die." Then Hrafnkel was untied, and he granted Sám the right to settle things as he wished. Sám assigned Hrafnkel such of the property as he pleased, and it was little, indeed. Hrafnkel had his spear with him, but no other weapons. That day Hrafnkel and all his people moved away from Adalbol. Thorkel then said to Sám, "I do not know why you are doing this; you yourself will regret it most that you grant him life." Sám said that was the way it was to be.

Hrafnkel now moved his household east across Fleetdale District and beyond Fleetdale to the east of Lakefleet. At the end of the lake stood a little farmstead called Lockhill. Hrafnkel bought this land on credit, for he had no more capital than he needed for farm equipment. People talked a great deal about how his pride had fallen, and many recalled an old proverb, "Arrogance is short-lived." This property was a large forest land, of wide extent and poor in buildings, and for this reason he bought the land for a small price. Not worrying about the expense, he cut down the forest, for it was large, and built a splendid house, which has since been called Hrafnkelsstead. It has always been known as a good farmstead. For the first season Hrafnkel lived on the place with great inconvenience, but he did well with the fishing. While the house was under construction he worked very hard. Hrafnkel kept calves and kids through the winter that first season and took good care of them, so that nearly every one of his animals lived. One could almost say there were two heads to every living creature. In the summer of this year there was a great run of fish in Lakefleet. This was a great advantage for householders in the district, and it continued every summer.

Sám established his home at Adalbol as successor to Hrafnkel; soon after he made preparations for a noble feast and invited all those who had been Hrafnkel's liegemen. Sám planned to be their chief in his place. The men consented to this, although they thought it rather dubious. Thjosti's sons advised him that he should be kind, generous, and helpful to his men—a benefactor of those in need—"then they are not men if they do not stand firmly by you whenever you need anything. We give you this advice because we should like you to succeed in everything, for we think you are a fine man. Be on your guard, now, and wary, for 'it is hard to watch out for the wicked.' " Thjosti's sons had Freyfaxi and his herd sent for, saying that they wished to see these prized possessions, about which there were such tales. The horses were brought to the house and the brothers looked them over. Thorgeir said, "These horses appear to me to be serviceable on the estate; my advice is that they do such useful work as they can until they are ready to die of old age. But this stallion looks no better to me than other stallions— worse, rather, in that much evil has come about because of him. I do not wish him to be the occasion of more slayings than have already occurred; it will be proper, now, that he who owns him should take charge of him." They then led the horse down through the valley. There was a cliff along the river there, directly above a deep place in the stream. They led the horse to this cliff, and Thjosti's sons pulled a bag over his head. They tied a stone around his neck, then took long sticks and pushed him off the cliff, and thus destroyed the horse. The place has since been called Frey-faxi's Cliff. Farther down the valley stood the temples which Hrafnkel had owned, and Thorkel wanted to go there. He gave directions to strip all the statues of the gods of their ornaments and then to set fire to the temples and burn up everything at once. Then the guests prepared to leave. Sám chose excellent presents for both brothers, and both parties promised each other loyal devotion, so they said good-bye in perfect friendship. The brothers then rode west by the regular route to the Firths and came home with honor to Cod Firth. Sám settled Thorbjorn down at Playsheds, where he was to live, and Sám and his wife moved to Adalbol and lived there for a time.

Hrafnkel, over in east Fleetdale, heard that Thjosti's sons had destroyed Freyfaxi and burned the temples. He remarked, "I think it foolishness to believe in gods," and said that henceforth he would never believe in them. He held to that, and never offered sacrifice afterward. Hrafnkel remained at Hrafnkelsstead and accumulated wealth. He soon got a great reputation in the district; everyone was eager to do as Hrafnkel wished. This was the time when the largest number of ships came from Norway to Iceland; people settled the largest part of the land in the district in Hrafnkel's day. No one could occupy land in peace unless he asked Hrafnkel's permission. They all had to promise him their support, and he promised them his protection; thus he got all the land east of Lakefleet under his control. This Thing-district soon became much bigger and more populous than the one which he had had earlier; it extended to Screeddale and all along Lakefleet. By now a change had come about in his nature; the man was much better liked than before. He had the same disposition to be useful and helpful, but he was more popular, as well as milder and more reasonable in everything. Often Sám and Hrafnkel encountered each other at public meetings, but they never brought up their previous relations. Thus seven years went by. Sám was well liked by his liegemen, for he was mild and quiet and ready in helping people—he remembered the advice those brothers had given him. Incidentally, he was a great dandy.

It was reported that a ship from abroad, whose captain was Eyvind Bjarnason, had arrived at Whalefirth. Eyvind had been away seven years and had enormously improved and developed, so that he had become a very gallant man. He was quickly told what had happened at home; but, being a man of great reserve, he had little to say about it. As soon as Sám learned of his arrival, he rode down to the ship and there was a very happy meeting of the brothers. Sám invited him to come west to his place and Eyvind agreed, but asked Sám to ride on ahead and send back horses to carry his goods. Meanwhile he hauled his ship on shore and took care of it, and Sám went home and rounded up horses to go and meet him. When Eyvind had his goods ready, he started on the journey to Hrafnkelsdale, going up along Whale Firth. There were five in Eyvind's party—and his servant made a sixth. This last was of Icelandic origin and related to Eyvind, who had rescued the boy from destitution and taken him abroad, looking out for him as carefully as for himself. This act was generally known, and it was universally agreed that there were few like Eyvind. The party rode up Thorisdale Heath, driving sixteen pack horses ahead. Two of the men were servants of Sám and three were from the ship; all were in bright clothes and had handsome shields. They rode across Screeddale and over the Ridge to the place called Bulungfields in Fleetdale, then down to Gorge River bank; this stream flows west to the lake between Hallormsstead and Hrafnkelsstead. They rode up along Lakefleet below the plain to Hrafnkelsstead, then around the end of the lake and across the Glacier River at Shed Ford. It was now about half past seven in the morning. There was a woman on the bank washing clothes, and she saw the travelers. This serving woman bundled up the laundry, ran home, threw the clothes down outside near a woodpile, and rushed inside. Hrafnkel had not yet got up, and some trusted men were lying in the hall. The working men, however, had gone to their tasks; it was the time of hay harvest. The woman began speaking as soon as she came in: "Very true it is, as was said long ago, that 'he gets slack who grows old.' The repute that was won early becomes little if a man shamefully lets himself get sluggish and has not the courage to set things right some time or other—and this is a great wonder in a man who was once brave. Now it is otherwise with those who grow up with their father and seem to you of no esteem in comparison with you. But then, when they are grown, they go from land to land and appear to be of great repute wherever they go—and so come home and look better than chiefs. Eyvind Bjarnason rode across the river here at Shed Forth with a shield so bright that the light shone from it. He is such a man that vengeance on him would be fitting." Hrafnkel got up and answered her: "Maybe what you say is all too true—not because you intend it to be agreeable. It is well now that you should have more to do: go in a hurry to Willow Plains for Hallstein's sons, Sigvat and Snorri. Ask them to come quickly to me with the men there who bear arms." He sent another serving woman out to Hrolfsstead for Hrolf's sons, Thord and Halla, and the men who bore arms there. All these were valiant and very capable men. Hrafnkel also sent for his own servants; and the entire company amounted to eighteen.

Eyvind's party had now come up to the heath. Eyvind rode west till he came to a place in the middle of the heath called Bessi's Way. Here there is a marsh, with no grass at all, and it was like riding through nothing but mud that always came up to the knee or the mid-leg, sometimes to the belly. Underneath it was as hard as a stony field. There is a rocky, broken stretch to the west, and when they came to it the boy looked back and said to Eyvind, "Men are riding behind us, not less than eighteen; there is a tall man on horseback in blue clothes and he looks to me like Hrafnkel Priest, though I have not seen him for a long time." Eyvind answered, "What does it matter to us? I know of nothing to fear from Hrafnkel's riding; I have not done anything against him. Doubtless he has an appointment to meet his friends west in the Dale." The boy answered, "I still think it is you that he wants to meet." Eyvind said, "I don't know of anything that has happened between him and my brother Sám since they were reconciled." The boy answered, "I wish you would ride away west to the Dale; then you will be safe. I know Hrafnkel's nature; he will do nothing to us if he cannot get you. Everything is taken care of if you are, for then there is no animal in the trap;[15] and it will be all right, whatever happens to us." Eyvind said he would not ride away in a hurry, "for I don't know who these men are, it would seem laughable to many a man if I ran away without finding out

15. a proverbial expression, like our "nothing is at stake"; Hrafnkel is interested only in Eyvind.

something." They rode west then from the rocky strip and there was another marsh in front of them, called Ox Marsh. It is covered with grass, but there are quicksands, so that it is almost impassable; that is why old Hallfred built the upper road, longer though it was. Eyvind rode west to the marsh, and the horses sank deep in the mire, which delayed them a good deal. Hrafnkel's party, without packs on their horses, followed rapidly and came along to the marsh. Eyvind's party had not got through the marsh; they could see Hrafnkel and both his sons. Eyvind's men then asked him to ride off: "All the bad spots are now passed; you can get to Adalbol while the marsh is between them and you." Eyvind answered, "I will not flee from these men, for I have done them no harm." His party rode then up to the ridge. Moderate-sized peaks rise from the ridge, and on one of the slopes is a bit of turf, bare and windblown, surrounded by high banks. Eyvind rode to the spot and dismounted to wait for the pursuers, remarking, "Now we will soon know their business." Then he and his men walked up to the turf and broke up some stones. Hrafnkel then turned south off the road toward the turf. He exchanged no words with Eyvind, but attacked at once. Eyvind defended himself well and bravely. His servant, thinking himself inadequate to the fight, got his horse, rode west over the ridge to Adalbol, and told Sám what was going on. Sám got up quickly and sent for men. This company numbered twenty men, well equipped. Sám rode east on the heath to the site of the battle, which was now finished—and Hrafnkel had ridden away east. Eyvind and all his men had fallen. First of all, Sám looked for signs of life in his brother; but he was done for, and all five lay dead together. Twelve of Hrafnkel's men had also fallen, but six survivors had left the scene. Sám tarried only a little, and told his men to follow at once. Hrafnkel's party had ridden away as fast as they could, and now their horses would be tired. Sám declared, "We can catch them, for they have tired horses but ours are all fresh; it will be a near thing whether we catch them before they get off the heath." Hrafnkel had now gone east across Ox Marsh, and both parties rode along until Sám came to the edge of the heath. Then he saw that Hrafnkel had gone farther down into the slopes and that he would make good his escape into the district below. Sám then said, "Here we will turn back, for it will be easy for Hrafnkel to get men." In this situation, then, Sám went back to the place where Eyvind lay and set to work heaping up a burial mound over him and his fellows. These sites are now called Eyvind's Knoll, Eyvind's Fells, and Eyvind's Dale. Sám then took all Eyvind's goods home to Adalbol. When he arrived, he sent for his liegemen to come there next morning about nine o'clock, planning to ride west across the heath—"let the journey turn out as it may." In the evening Sám went to bed, there being a number of men on hand.

Hrafnkel rode home and told the news. He ate a meal and then summoned men, so that he got together a company of seventy. With these he rode west across the heath, arrived unexpectedly at Adalbol, took Sám in his bed, and led him out. Then Hrafnkel said, "Now something has happened to you, Sám, that you must have thought unlikely for some time—I have your life in my power. I shall not treat you worse than you did me. I offer you a choice of two things: to be killed or to let me fix and settle the terms between us." Sám said that he would choose to live; but he said he thought either choice would be hard. Hrafnkel said that he could expect it—"for we have that to pay you back. I should treat you twice as well if you deserved it. You shall leave Adalbol and go down to Playsheds to live. You shall take with you the property that Eyvind owned. You shall not remove from here anything except that which you have brought—all of that you shall take with you. I will take over my chief's authority, as well as the house and homestead. I see there has been a great increase in my property, and you shall not have the benefit of that. No compensation shall be paid for your brother Eyvind, because you ruthlessly prosecuted the case of Einar, your earlier kinsman, and have had sufficient compensation in that you have had power and property for six years. The killing of Eyvind and his men does not appear to me worth more than the maiming of me and my men. You made me a fugitive from the district, but I shall be pleased to have you live at Playsheds; and that will do well, if you are not too arrogant for your own good. You shall be my subordinate as long as we both live. You may also expect to fare worse if there is any more trouble between us." Sám then left with his company for Playsheds and went to live there.

Hrafnkel then arranged the household at Adalbol with his own men. His son, Thorir, he established at Hrafnkelsstead. Hrafnkel now had chief's authority in all the settlements. His son Asbjorn remained with his father, for he was younger. Sám stayed at Playsheds that winter, glum and silent. Many discovered that he was little pleased with his lot. But in the course of the winter, when the days grew longer, Sám, with another man and three horses between them, went across the river, thence over Madderdale Heath, then across the Glacier River up on the mountain; then to Midge Lake, and from there across Fleet Heath and Clear Lake Pass. He did not stop till he reached Cod Firth in the west, where he was well received. Thorkel had just recently returned from his travels; he had been abroad four years. When Sám had rested for a week, he told the brothers of the affair with Hrafnkel and asked for their aid and support as before. This time Thorgeir did more of the talking for the brothers. He said it was out of the question—"we are far away.[16] We thought we had put you in good shape before we left,

---

16. Cod Firth, where Thorgeir and Thorkel live, is on the northwestern peninsula of Iceland; Sám and Hrafnkel live near the east coast.

so that it would be easy for you to maintain yourself. It has turned out as I anticipated at the time when you granted Hrafnkel life, namely, that you would regret it most. We urged you to take his life, but you wanted to have your way. It is easy to see now what difference in sense there has been between you and him—since he let you live in peace and waited for the time when he could dispose of the man that he thought bigger than you. We cannot meddle in this lucklessness of yours; and we have no incentive to oppose Hrafnkel great enough to make us risk our reputation a second time. But we will invite you to move here under our protection, with your entire household, if you think it less vexatious than living near Hrafnkel." Sám said he did not care for that, but wished to go back home. He asked them to swap horses with him, and this was readily arranged. The brothers wanted to give Sám good gifts, but he would accept none, saying that they were mean-spirited men. In this situation he rode home and lived on there till old age. He never got the advantage of Hrafnkel as long as he lived. Hrafnkel remained on his estate and kept up his repute. He died of illness, and his burial mound is in Hrafnkelsdale out from Adalbol; in the grave beside him was laid much money, along with all his armor and his good spear. His sons took over his chief's authority. Thorir lived at Hrafnkelsstead, Asbjorn at Adalbol; they held the priesthood together and both were considered important men. Thus ends the story of Hrafnkel.

The Song of Roland*

1

Carlon the King, our Emperor Charlemayn,
Full seven years long has been abroad in Spain,
He's won the highlands as far as to the main;
No castle more can stand before his face,
City nor wall is left for him to break,   5
Save Saragossa in its high mountain place;
Marsilion holds it, the king who hates God's name,
Mahound he serves, and to Apollyon prays:
He'll not escape the ruin that awaits.

AOI†

---

* Apparently composed in the twelfth century. Abridged. *The Song of Roland*, translated by Dorothy L. Sayers. Copyright 1957 by the Executors of Dorothy L. Sayers. Reprinted by permission of David Higham Associates, Ltd.

† AOI: appears here and with more than half of the laisses in the poem. No pattern has been found for their occurrence, nor do scholars agree on the meaning of the word. Most theories consider it a refrain, perhaps shouted, which marks some kind of climax in the action or mood of the poem. For a fuller discussion, see the edition of T. A. Jenkins (1924), pp. xxxviii, 4–5.

6. *Saragossa*: city in Aragon, on the Ebro River.

8. *Mahound*: Mohammed, prophet of the god Allah and founder of the Mohammedan religion. *Apollyon*: the Greek god Apollo; but the poet is mistaken, for the Mohammedans were monotheists, recognizing only the god Allah.

2

Marsilion sat in Saragossa town,   10
He sought an orchard where shade was to be found,
On a bright dais of marble he lies down;
By twenty thousand his vassals stand around.
He calls before him all his dukes and his counts:
"Listen, my lords, what affliction is ours!   15
The Emperor Charles that wears fair France's crown
Invades our country our fortunes to confound.
I have no host but before him gives ground,
I find no force his forces for to flout;
Wise men of wit, give counsel to me now,   20
Save me from death and loss of my renown."
There's ne'er a paynim utters a single sound,
Till Blancandrin, Valfonda's lord, speaks out.

3

Blancandrin's wise amid the paynim horde;
He was for valour a mighty knight withal,   25
And fit of wit for to counsel his lord.
He tells the king; "Be you afeared for naught,
But send to Charles in his pride and his wrath
Your faithful service and your friendship henceforth.
Promise him lions and bears and hounds galore,   30
Sev'n hundred camels and a thousand mewed hawks,
Four hundred pack-mules with gold and silver store,
And fifty wagons, a wagon-train to form,
Whence he may give his soldiers rich rewards.
Say, in this land he has made enough war;   35
To Aix in France let him go home once more;
At Michaelmas you'll follow to his court,
There you'll submit unto the Christian law,
And be his man by faith and fealty sworn.
Hostages too, if for sureties he call,   40
You'll let him have, ten maybe or a score;
'Twere good we send the sons our wives have borne:
I'll send mine own, though he should die therefor.
Better by far the heads of them should fall
Than we should lose honour, estate and all.   45
And be reduced to beggary and scorn."

4

Quoth Blancandrin: "I swear by my right hand
And beard that flutters about my girdle-span,
Straightway you'll see the Frenchman's host disband:

---

31. *mewed hawks:* hawks which have
got over their molt, and are consequently
in good condition.

34. *soldiers:* these are the mercenaries,
who received their pay (*solde*) directly
from the king in cash, as distinct from
the feudal vassalage, who were maintained by their respective lords. Many of
them were knights-errant, without terri-

torial attachment, who wandered about
offering their services to whoever would
employ them.

36. *Aix:* Aix-la-Chapelle was the imperial city of Charlemagne, who rebuilt
its palace and chapel and granted it many
special privileges. He was reputed to have
been born there and certainly died and
was buried there in 814.

They'll hurry home to France, their native land,   50
When each within his favourite haunt is back,
Charles in his chapel at Aix will take his stand,
And there he'll hold high feast at Michaelmas.
The time will pass, the trysted hour elapse:
No news of us, no message will he have.   55
Fierce is the king, a cruel-hearted man;
Our sureties' heads he'll smite off with the axe.
Better their heads should fall into their laps
Than that fair Spain should fall from out our hands,
And we should suffer grave losses and mishap."   60
The Paynims say: "There is some truth in that."

5

The King Marsile had ended the debate;
He calls before him Clarin of Balagate,
Estramarin, and Eudropin his mate;
And Garlon Longbeard and Priamon he names,   65
And Machiner and his uncle Matthay,
Johun of Outremer, and Malabayn,
And Blancandrin; these ten make up the tale,
Ten matchless villains, to whom he's said his say:
"Barons, my lords, get you to Charlemayn,   70
Who sits at siege, Cordova town to take.
Bear each in hand an olive-branch displayed;
Peace and submission are signified that way.
If you contrive this treaty to arrange,
Of gold and silver I'll give you goodly weight,   75
And lands and fiefs as much as heart can crave."
The Paynims answer: "That will be ample pay."

6

Marsile the king his conference had ceased.
He tells his men: "My barons, go with speed;
Bear in your hands boughs of the olive tree.   80
On my behalf King Charlemayn beseech,
For his God's sake to show me clemency.
Say, this month's end in truth he shall not see
Ere I shall seek him with thousand vassals leal.
The law of Christ I'll then and there receive,   85
In faith and love I will his liegeman be.
I'll send him sureties if thus he shall decree."
Quoth Blancandrin: "Be sure he'll grant your plea."

7

Marsilion sent for ten mules white as snow
(A gift that erst Suatilia's king bestowed),   90
Their saddles silver, their bridles all of gold.
Now are they mounted, the men who are to go;
All in their hands the olive-branches hold.
They came to Carlon that hath France in control;
They'll trap him somehow, for it is fated so.   95

8

The Emperor Charles is glad and full of cheer.
Cordova's taken, the outer walls are pierced,
His catapults have cast the towers down sheer;
Rich booty's gone to all his chevaliers,
Silver and gold and goodly battle-gear.   100
In all the city no paynim now appears
Who is not slain or turned to Christian fear.
The Emperor sits in a great orchard near,
Having about him Roland and Olivere,
Samson the duke, and Anseis the fierce,   105
Geoffrey d'Anjou the King's gonfalonier,
And Gerin too, and with him too Gerier;
And where these were was many another fere—
Full fifteen thousand of France the fair and dear.
Upon white carpets they sit, those noble peers,   110
For draughts and chess the chequer-boards are reared;
To entertain the elder lords revered;
Young bachelors disport with sword and spear.
Beneath a pine beside an eglantier
A faldstool stands all of the red gold clear;   115
Of fairest France there sits the king austere.
White are his locks, and silver is his beard,
His body noble, his countenance severe:
If any seek him, no need to say, "Lo, here!"
From off their steeds lit down the messengers,   120
Well did they greet him with shows of love sincere.

9

Before them all Blancandrin forward stood;
And hailed the King: "God give His grace to you,
The glorious God to whom worship is due.
Thus speaks the king, Marsilion, great in rule: 125
Much hath he studied the saving faith and true.
Now of his wealth he would send you in sooth
Lions and bears, leashed greyhounds not a few,
Sev'n hundred camels, a thousand falcons mewed,
And gold and silver borne on four hundred mules;   130
A wagon-train of fifty carts to boot,
And store enough of golden bezants good
Wherewith to pay your soldiers as you should.
Too long you've stayed in this land to our rue:
To Aix in France return you at our suit.   135
Thither my liege will surely follow you,
[And will become your man in faith and truth,
And at your hand hold all his realm in feu!"]
With lifted hands to God the Emperor sues;
Then bows his head and so begins to brood.   140

---

108. *fere*: companion.   114. *eglantier*: wild-rose bush.

10

The Emperor bode long time with downcast eyes;
He was a man not hasty in reply,
But wont to speak only when well advised.
When he looked up, his glance was stern and high.
He told the envoys: "Fair is your speech and fine;   145
Yet King Marsile is foe to me and mine.
In all these words and offers you recite
I find no warrant wherein I may confide."
"Sureties for this," the Saracen replies,
"Ten or fifteen or twenty we'll provide.   150
One of my sons I'll send, on pain to die;
Others, yet nobler, you'll have, as I divine.
When in your palace high feast you solemnize
To great St Michael of Peril-by-the-Tide,
He'll follow you, on that you may rely,   155
And in those baths God made you by His might
He would turn Christian and there would be baptized."
Quoth Charles: "He yet may save his soul alive."

11

Fair was the ev'ning and clearly the sun shone;
The ten white mules Charles sends to stall anon;   160
In the great orchard he bids men spread aloft
For the ten envoys a tent where they may lodge,
With sergeants twelve to wait on all their wants.
They pass the night there till the bright day draws on.
Early from bed the Emperor now is got;   165
At mass and matins he makes his orison.
Beneath a pine straightway the King is gone,
And calls his barons to council thereupon;
By French advice whate'er he does is done.

12

The Emperor goes beneath a tall pine-tree,   170
And to his council he calls his barony:
There Duke Ogier, Archbishop Turpin meet,
Richard the Old and his nephew Henri,
Count Acelin the brave of Gascony,

---

154. *St. Michael of Peril-by-the-Tide:*
("St. M. in periculo maris"). The name
was originally given to the monastery built
on the great island rock called Mont
St. Michel, off the coast of Normandy.
Later it came to be applied to the archangel himself. "St. Michel del Peril."
156. *baths:* the curative mineral springs
for which Aix is still celebrated, and
which were held to be of miraculous
origin.
163. *sergeants:* the word "sergeant,"
meaning primarily "servant," was applied generally to almost any man, under
the rank of knight, who exercised any
kind of office in a lord's household or on

his estate. In military use, it denoted a
tenant doing military service, especially
one who was in attendance on a knight
in the field. The sergeant marched and
fought on horseback, but was more lightly
armed than the chevalier.
172. *Ogier the Dane:* this semihistorical
hero boasts a *Chanson de Geste* devoted
to his exploits, and figures in many others.
173. *Richard the Old:* his historical
prototype is Richard I of Normandy, who
lived (943–996) later than Charlemagne's
time, but has been attracted into the
Carolingian cycle by the natural tendency
of epic to accumulate famous names regardless of chronology.

Miles, and his cousin the Lord Tibbald of Rheims,   175
Gerin likewise and Gerier are convened;
And County Roland, there with the rest came he,
And Oliver, noble and good at need;
All French of France, thousand and more, maybe;
And Ganelon that wrought the treachery.   180
So starts that council which came to such sore grief.

13

"Barons, my lords," began the Emperor Carlon,
"From King Marsile come envoys, seeking parley.
He makes me offers of treasure overpassing:
Of lions and bears and hounds to the leash mastered,   185
Sev'n hundred camels, and falcons mewed and hearty,
Four hundred mules with Arab gold all chargèd,
And fifty wagons well-laden in a cart-train.
But now to France he urges my departure,
And to my palace at Aix he'll follow after,   190
There change his faith for one of more advantage,
Become a Christian and of me hold his marches.
But his true purpose—for that I cannot answer."
The French all say: "We'd best be very guarded."

14

The Emperor Charles had finished all his speech.   195
The County Roland, who fiercely disagrees,
Swift to oppose springs up upon his feet:
He tells the King: "Nevermore trust Marsile!
Seven years long in land of Spain we've been.
I won for you both Noples and Commibles,   200
I took Valterna, the land of Pine I seized,
And Balagate, and Seville and Tudele.
Then wrought Marsile a very treacherous deed:
He sent his Paynims by number of fifteen,
All of them bearing boughs of the olive tree,   205
And with like words he sued to you for peace.
Then did you ask the French lords for their rede;
Foolish advice they gave to you indeed.
You sent the Paynim two counts of your meinie:
Basan was one, the other was Basile.   210
He smote their heads off in hills beneath Haltile.
This war you've started wage on, and make no cease;
To Saragossa lead your host in the field,
Spend all your life, if need be, in the siege,
Revenge the men this villain made to bleed!"   215

15

The Emperor Charles sat still with his head bended;
He stroked his beard and his moustaches gently;
Nor good nor ill he answers to his nephew.
The French are silent, Guènes alone excepted;

207. *rede:* counsel.

But he leaps up, strides into Carlon's presence,   220
And full of pride begins thus to address him.
He tells the King: "Trust not a brawling fellow,
Me nor another; seek only your own welfare.
If King Marsile informs you by this message
He'll set his hands in yours, and fealty pledge you,   225
And hold all Spain from you, at your good pleasure,
And to that faith we follow give acceptance,
The man who tells you this plea should be rejected
Cares nothing, Sire, to what death he condemns us.
Counsel of pride must not grow swollen-headed;   230
Let's hear wise men, turn deaf ears to the reckless."

16

Naimon at this stood forth before them all:
No better vassal was ever seen in hall.
He tells the King: "Well have you heard, my lord,
The arguments Count Ganelon sets forth.   235
There's weight in them, and you should give them thought.
The King Marsile is vanquished in the war,
You've taken from him his castles and his forts,
With catapults you've broken down his walls,
You've burned his cities and his armies outfought.   240
Now that he comes on your mercy to call
Foul sin it were to vex him any more.
Since he'll find sureties his good faith to support,
We should make haste to cut this great war short."
The French all say: "The Duke speaks as he ought."   245

17

"Barons, my lords, whom shall we send anon
To Saragossa, to King Marsilion?"
"I, by your leave," saith Naimon, "will begone,
Therefore on me bestow the glove and wand."
"You are my wisest," the King makes answer prompt: 250
"Now by the beard my cheek and chin upon,
You shall not go so far this twelvemonth long.
Hence! sit you down, for we summon you not!"

18

"Barons, my lords, whom shall we send of you
To Saragossa, the Sarsen king unto?"   255
"Myself," quoth Roland, "may well this errand do."
"That shall you not," Count Oliver let loose;
"You're high of heart and stubborn of your mood,
You'd land yourself, I warrant, in some feud.
By the King's leave this errand I will do."   260
The King replies: "Be silent there, you two!
Nor you nor he shall on that road set foot.
By this my beard that's silver to the view,
He that names any of the Twelve Peers shall rue!"
The French say nothing: they stand abashed and mute.   265

255. *Sarsen:* Saracen.

19

Then from their ranks arose Turpin of Rheims;
He tells the King: "Leave your French lords at ease;
Full sev'n long years in this land have you been,
Much have they suffered of perils and fatigue;
Pray you then, Sire, give wand and glove to me;   270
The Saracen of Spain I'll seek and see,
And in his looks his purpose will I read."
The Emperor answers with anger in his mien:
"On that white carpet sit down and hold your peace;
Be still, I say, until I bid you speak."   275

20

The Emperor said: "My free and knightly band,
Come choose me out some baron of my land
To bring my message to King Marsilion's hand."
Quoth Roland: "Guènes my step-sire is the man."
The French all say: "Indeed, he is most apt;   280
If he's passed over you will not find his match."
Count Ganelon is furious out of hand;
His great furred gown of marten he flings back
And stands before them in his silk bliaut clad.
Bright are his eyes, haughty his countenance,   285
Handsome his body, and broad his bosom's span;
The peers all gaze, his bearing is so grand.
He says to Roland: "Fool! what has made thee mad?
I am thy step-sire, and all these know I am,
And me thou namest to seek Marsilion's camp!   290
If God but grant I ever thence come back
I'll wreak on thee such ruin and such wrack
That thy life long my vengeance shall not slack."
Roland replies: "This is all boast and brag!
Threats cannot fright me, and all the world knows that   295
To bear this message we must have a good man;
I'll take your place if the King says I can."

21

Quoth Ganelon: "My place thou shalt not take:
Thou'rt not my vassal, nor I thy suzerain.
Charles for his service commands me to obey.   300
I'll seek Marsile in Saragossa's gates;
But rather there some deadly trick I'll play
Than not find vent for my unbounded rage."
When Roland heard him, then he laughed in his face.

22

When Ganelon sees Roland laugh outright   305
He's fit to burst for anger and despite,
And very nearly goes clean out of his mind.
He tells the Count: "I love you not, not I;
You've picked on me unfairly, out of spite.
Just Emperor, here I stand before your eyes,   310
Ready to do whatever you think right.

23

To Saragossa I see that I must shift me;
There's no return for him that journeys thither.
Bethink you well that my wife is your sister,
A son she bare me, fairest of goodly children,   315
"Baldwin" (quoth he) "and a champion he will be.
To him I leave all my lands and my living;
No more I'll see him; take care, Sir, of your kinsman."
Quoth Charles: "Your heart is too tender within you;
Go now you must, for even so I bid you."   320

24

Then said the King: "Stand forward, Ganelon,
Here at my hand receive the glove and wand;
You've heard the French—you are the man they want."
"Messire," said Guènes, "Roland hath done this wrong!
I'll never love him the whole of my life long,   325
Nor Oliver his friend and fellow fond,
Nor the Twelve Peers by whom he's doted on;
Sire, in your presence I defy the whole lot."
Then said the King: "Your passion is too hot;
I bid you go and so you must begone."   330
"Well may I go, but safeguard have I not,
Basile had none, nor Basan none, God wot."

25

The King holds out to him his right-hand glove;
Fain would Count Guènes be an hundred miles off!
When he would take it, it fell into the dust.   335
"God! what is this?" cry all the French at once;
"For sure this message will bring us great ill-luck."
"My lords," quoth Guènes, "you'll know it soon enough."

26

"Sire, give me leave" quoth Guènes, "hence to hie;
Since go I must, it boots not to abide."   340
"Go," said the King, "by Jesu's leave and mine."
With his right hand he's absolved him and signed,
And to his care letter and wand consigned.

27

Guènes the Count to his lodging makes speed,
Of his array he setteth him to seek   345
The best he has to serve him for this need.
His golden spurs he buckles on his heels,

---

342. *absolved him and signed*: i.e., pronounced the absolution over him, making
the sign of the cross. Some commentators
have seen here a relic of the very ancient
popular conception of the priest-emperor,
preserved in the legend of Prester John.
But there is, I think, nothing in the line
which necessarily ascribes sacerdotal status to Charlemagne, however sacred his
person and function. What is probably
intended is the prayer of absolution, frequently called simply the Absolution (as
in the Book of Common Prayer) which
can be pronounced by, for example, an
abbess, or indeed any other lay person.
It would be some such formula as "The
Lord bless you and keep you, deliver
you from all your sins, and bring you to
everlasting life."

Girds to his side Murgleys his brand of steel,
And mounts him up on Tachëbrun his steed;
His stirrup's held by Guinëmer his eme.   350
Then might you see full many a brave knight weep,
Saying to him: "Woe worth your valour's meed!
In the King's court these many years you've been,
A noble vassal by all were you esteemed.
He that named you for this gear by his rede   355
Charlemayn's self shall not save him nor shield:
No right had Roland to have contrived this scheme;
For you're a man sprung of a noble breed."
Then they said, "Sir, take us with you, we plead."
Guènes replied: "God forbid it should be!   360
Best die alone nor slay good knights with me.
Sirs, you'll return to fair France presently:
On my behalf my wife I bid you greet,
And Pinabel that is my friend and peer.
Baldwin my son, whom you know well, I ween,   365
Him shall you help and accept for your liege."
Then he sets forth and on his way goes he.

28

Under tall olives the County Guènes rides;
The Paynim envoys he's caught up in good time,
And Blancandrin drops back with him behind.   370
Now each to other begins to speak with guile.
Blancandrin says: "Charles is a wondrous wight!
Pulia he's ta'en, Calabria likewise,
And unto England passed over the salt tide
To win St Peter the tribute of the isle.   375
What seeks he here, warring in our confines?"
"Such is his pleasure," Count Ganelon replies;
"In all the world you will not find his like."

29

Quoth Blancandrin: "The French are men of worth,
Yet to their lord they do a scurvy turn,   380
These dukes and counts, when they counsel such work;
Both him and others they harry to their hurt."
"There's none," quoth Guènes, "who merits such ill words,
Save only Roland, for whom 'twill be the worse.
But now, the Emperor in the cool shade conversed;   385
Up came his nephew all in his byrny girt,
Fresh with his booty from Carcassone returned.
Roland in hand a golden apple nursed
And showed his uncle, saying, 'Take it, fair sir;
The crowns I give you of all the kings on earth.'   390
One day his pride will undo him for sure,

---

350. *eme:* uncle.
375. *the tribute of the isle:* The annual tribute known as Peter's Pence, paid by England to the See of Rome, was of Anglo-Saxon origin and instituted in the eighth or ninth century, though not in consequence of political or military pressure by Charlemagne.

Danger of death day by day he incurs.
If one should slay him some peace might be preserved."

30

Quoth Blancandrin: "Roland's a villain fell,
Presuming thus all folk on earth to quell,   395
And every land under his yoke compel!
Whom does he count on to lend his arms such strength?"
Ganelon answers: "He counts upon the French;
They'll never fail him, they love him far too well.
Silver and gold he gives them for largesse,   400
Horses and mules, silks and accoutrements.
And everything the Emperor wants, he gets—
He'll win for him all lands 'twixt east and west."

31

So long rides Guènes with Blancandrin that day
Till each to each has pledged his truth and faith   405
They will seek means Count Roland for to slay.
So long they ride, they come by road and way
To Saragossa, and by a yew draw rein.
A faldstool stood beneath a pine-tree's shade,
With silken cloth of Alexandria draped;   410
There sat the King that bore the rule in Spain.
Full twenty thousand Saracens stood arrayed.
Not one of them has any word to say,
So eagerly upon the news they wait.
And here come Guènes and Blancandrin apace!   415

32

Blancandrin came before Marsilion,
And by the hand held County Ganelon;
Saith to the King: "Save you, sir, by Mahond,
And by Apollyon, whose blest faith we extol!
To Charles we gave your message every jot;   420
Both of his hands he lifted up aloft
And praised his God; further, he answered not.
One of his nobles, you see, he's sent along—
A lord of France, of most illustrious stock;
From him you'll hear if peace is won or lost."   425
"We'll hear him," quoth Marsile; "let him say on."

33

Now Ganelon had giv'n this matter thought,
And with great cunning he now begins to talk,
Even as a man that's to the manner born.
He tells the King: "God have you in His ward,   430
The glorious God whom we ought to adore!
King Charlemayn, the Great, thus sends you word:
You must receive the faith of Christ Our Lord,
And as your fief half Spain he will award.
If you refuse to accept this accord,   435
You shall be taken and fettered by main force,

And haled away to Aix, into his court,
There to be doomed and done with once for all;
There shall you die in shamefulness and scorn."
On hearing this Marsile was quite distraught;   440
He held a dart with golden feathers wrought,
And would have struck him, but he was overborne.

34

The King Marsile has all his colour changed.
Grasping the shaft, his javelin he shakes.
When Guènes sees it he sets hand to his blade,   445
Two fingers' breadth forth of the scabbard hales,
And says to it: "Full bright you are and brave!
In the King's court I've borne you many a day!
Ne'er shall the Emperor of France have cause to say
I died alone in strange lands far away;   450
Before their bravest the price of you have paid!"
The Paynims cry: "We must prevent this fray."

35

The wiser Paynims remonstrate with him so
That King Marsile has sunk back on this throne.
Quoth the Caliph: "You put us to reproach,   455
Thinking to threaten this Frenchman with a blow!
It is your business to listen and take note."
Saith Ganelon: "All this, sir, must I thole.
For all the gold God made, I'll not forgo,
No, not for all the wealth your land can boast,   460
To speak the message—so I'm but given scope—
Which Charles the King, that mighty man of mould,
Has sent by me to this his mortal foe."
He had on him a sable-fur-lined cloak
Covered with silk which Alexandria wove;   465
He flings it down for Blancandrin to hold,
But of his sword he nowise will let go;
In his right hand he grasps the hilts of gold,
The Paynims say: "Lo there a baron bold!"

36

Guènes approached the King and thus addressed him: 470
He saith to him: "You do vainly to vex you.
Carlon thus bids you, that hath France in possession:
The Christian faith must of you be accepted,
And one half Spain he will give you in tenure;
The other half is for Roland his nephew;   475
A right proud partner you'll have there for co-tenant!
If these conditions should by you be rejected,
In Saragossa he'll besiege and invest you,
And by main force you shall be seized and fettered.
Thence to his city of Aix you'll go directly.   480
You shall not ride on palfrey nor on destrier,
Nor for the road shall you have mule nor jennet;

458. *thole:* endure.

On some poor screw of a pack-ass he'll set you;
And you will lose your head there by his sentence.
See now, the Emperor has written you this letter."   485
To the right hand of the Moor he presents it.

37

The King Marsile for very rage went white;
He breaks the seal and flings the wax aside,
Looks at the letter and reads what is inside.
"These words to me Carlon the French King writes: 490
I'm to remember his grief and his despite
For those two brothers, Basan and Basil hight,
Whom I beheaded in Haltoye-on-the-Height;
And if I value the purchase of my life,
Must send my uncle the Caliph as his prize;   495
Else nevermore will he be friend of mine."
Marsilion's son at this broke in and cried:
"Ganelon's words are madness out of mind!
This is too much—he shall not rest alive;
Give him to me and justice he shall find!"   500
When Guènes heard, he shook his blade on high,
And set his back to the trunk of the pine.

38

Unto the orchard the King Marsile repairs;
Of his best men he takes with him a share,
And thither came Blancandrin white of hair,   505
And Jurfaret, who is his son and heir,
And the Caliph, his eme and officer.
Quoth Blancandrin: "Call in that Frenchman there:
He'll serve our ends, to this I've heard him swear."
"Fetch him yourself, 'twere best," the King declares.   510
In his right hand Count Ganelon he bare
Into the orchard where king and council were.
So they begin to plot the treacherous snare.

39

"Guènes, fair sir," said Marsile, "I allow,
Something too lightly I treated you just now   515
When in my fury I would have struck you down;
But by these pelts of sable fur I vow,
Which of good gold are worth five hundred pounds,
Richly I'll quite you ere the next day be out."
"This I refuse not," said Ganelon the Count;   520
"God, if He please, shall balance the account."

40

"Truly, Count Guènes," then said the King Marsile.
"I have in mind your right good friend to be.
Of Charlemayn fain would I hear you speak.
He's very old, a hard life his has been;   525
Two hundred years and more I know he's seen;
In lands so many his body he's fatigued,
Hard strokes so many he's taken on his shield,

Rich kings so many he's brought to beggary—
When will he weary of fighting in the field?"   530
"That's not his way," said Guènes, "in the least.
None knows the Emperor, or looks upon his mien,
But says of him: 'A right great man is he.'
Howe'er I sounded his praise and his esteem,
His worth and honour would still outrun my theme.   535
His mighty valour who could proclaim in speech?
God kindled in him a courage so supreme,
He'd rather die than fail his knights at need."

41

The Paynim said: "I marvel in my thought,
At Charlemayn, that is so old and hoar!   540
I know he's lived two hundred years and more.
In lands so many his body he's forworn,
Sharp strokes so many of lance and spear has borne,
Rich kings so many beggared and brought to naught—
When will he weary of going to the wars?"   545
"Never," said Guènes, "while Roland still bears sword;
There's none so valiant beneath the heavens broad,
Oliver too, his friend, is a brave lord;
And the Twelve Peers whom Charles so much adores
Protect the vanward with knights a thousand score;   550
Charles is secure, he fears no man at all."

42

The Paynim said: "I marvel in my mind
At Charlemayn whose head is old and white.
Two hundred years, I know, have passed him by.
In lands so many he's conquered far and wide,   555
Lance-thrusts so many he's taken in the strife,
Rich kings so many brought to a beggar's plight—
When will he weary of going forth to fight?"
"Never," said Guènes, "while Roland sees the light;
'Twixt east and west his valour has no like,   560
Oliver too, his friend, is a brave knight;
And the twelve Peers, in whom the King delights,
With twenty thousand Frenchmen to vanward ride:
Charles is secure, he fears no man alive."

43

"Guènes, fair sir," then said the King directly,   565
"I have an army, you will not find a better,
Four hundred thousand good knights as I may reckon:
Can I give battle to Carlon and his Frenchmen?"
Guènes replies: "Not you, and so I tell you,
For of your Paynims the losses would be deadly.   570
Leave all this folly, come to your sober senses.
Send to the Emperor so huge a heap of treasure
That all the French will marvel at its splendour.
For twenty sureties, that you will likewise send him,
Back to fair France Charles will return contented,   575
Leaving behind a rear-guard to protect him.

With them, I warrant, will be Roland his nephew,
Oliver too, the valorous and gentle.
Dead are these Counts, if you will give me credit.
Carlon will see his great pride fall'n and ended;   580
He'll have no heart to fight with you from henceforth."

44

"Guènes, fair sir," [the King Marsilion cries,]
"What must I do to bring Roland to die?"
"I'll tell you that," Count Ganelon replies.
"At Sizer Gate the King will have arrived,   585
Leaving a rear-guard to keep the pass behind.
There'll be his nephew Count Roland, the great knight,
Oliver too, on whom he most relies.
With twenty thousand good Frenchmen at their side.
An hundred thousand send of your Paynim kind,   590
And these shall first engage the French in fight.
Of the French force the loss will not be light—
Yours will be slaughtered, and that I'll not disguise!
The like assault you'll launch a second time,
And, first or last, Roland will not get by.   595
You will have done a deed of arms full fine;
You'll ne'er again see war in all your life.

45

Whoso should smite the County Roland dead,
From Carlon's body then were the right hand reft;
The wondrous armies would dwindle off and melt,   600
Nor could Charles gather so great a host afresh;
Our fathers' land would thus find peace and rest."
When he heard this Marsile fell on his neck,
And straightway bad them unlock his treasure-chests.

46

Then said Marsile: "One thing alone remains: 605
There's no good bond where there is no good faith;
Give me your oath Count Roland to betray."
Guènes replies: "It shall be as you say."
Upon the relics of his good sword Murgleys
He sware the treason and sware his faith away.   610

47

There was a faldstool of ivory all wrought;
Marsile commands a volume to be brought
Of Termagant's and of Mahomet's law;
The Saracen of Spain thereon has sworn
That in the rear-guard Count Roland shall be sought;   615
If there he find him, he'll fight with his whole force,
And do his best to slay him once for all.
Guènes replies: "And may it so befall!"

---

585. *Sizer Gate: Port de Sizer*, or *Sizre* (the spelling varies): This is the pass now called the Col de Cize, which cuts through the Pyrenees on the road running from St.-Jean-Pied-de-Port by way of Roncevaux to Pampeluna, and forms the Gate of Spain.
602. *Our fathers' land:* France.
612. *a volume:* the Koran (?).

48

Lo, now! there comes a Paynim, Valdebron;
He stands before the King Marsilion,   620
And gaily laughing he says to Ganelon:
"Here, take my sword, a better blade is none.
A thousand mangons are in the hilt thereof;
'Tis yours, fair, sir, for pure affection,
For help against Roland the champion,   625
If in the rear-guard we find him as we want."
Quoth Ganelon to him: "It shall be done."
They kiss each other the cheek and chin upon.

49

Thereafter comes a Paynim, Climborin,
And laughing gaily to Ganelon begins: 630
"Come, take my helm, I ne'er saw none so rich:
[Above the nasal a carbuncle there is.
Out of pure friendship I offer you this gift]
If against Roland you'll aid us by your wit
That we may bring a shameful death on him."   635
"It shall be done," quoth Ganelon to this;
They kissed each other upon the mouth and chin.

50

Then to the Count Queen Bramimonda spoke:
"Dearly, fair sir, I love you, by my troth,
My king so lauds you, and his vassals also.   640
This pair of owches on your wife I bestow,
Heavy with jacinth and amethyst and gold;
More worth are they than all the wealth of Rome,
The like of them your Emperor never owned."
He takes the jewels and thrusts them in his poke.   645

51

The King calls Malduit, the keeper of his treasure:
"King Carlon's gifts, have you yet got them ready?"
And he replies, "Yea, sire, in ample measure:
Sev'n hundred camels laden with precious metal,
And twenty sureties, the noblest under heaven."   650

52

Marsilion's hand on Guènes' shoulder lies;
He says to him: "You are both bold and wise.
Now by that faith which seems good in your eyes
Let not your heart turn back from our design.
Treasure I'll give you, a great and goodly pile,   655
Ten mule-loads gold, digged from Arabian mines;
No year shall pass but you shall have the like.
Take now the keys of this great burg of mine,
Offer King Charles all its riches outright.
Make sure that Roland but in the rear-guard rides,   660
And if in pass or passage I him find

---

623. *mangons:* Saracen gold coins.   645. *poke:* pouch.
641. *owches:* brooches (?).

I'll give him battle right bitter to abide."
"I think," said Guènes, "that I am wasting time."
He mounts his horse and on his journey hies.

53

The Emperor now returns upon his way   665
And has arrived before the town of Gayne
(Count Roland took it and all its wall down-razed,
An hundred years thereafter it lay waste;)
And there the King for news of Guènes waits,
And for the tribute of the great land of Spain.   670
In the white dawn, at breaking of the day,
Into the camp the County Guènes came.

54

Early that day the Emperor leaves his bed.
Matins and mass the King has now heard said;
On the green grass he stood before his tent.   675
Roland was with him, brave Oliver as well,
Naimon the Duke and many another yet.
Then perjured Guènes the traitor comes to them
And starts to speak with cunning false pretence.
He tells the King: "To you (whom God defend!)   680
Of Saragossa the keys I here present.
I bring you also wealth to your heart's content,
And twenty sureties: see they be closely kept.
The valiant king, Marsile, this message sends:
The Caliph's absence he prays you'll not resent.   685
Mine own eyes saw four hundred thousand men
In hauberk armed, some having laced their helms,
And girt with swords whose hilts were richly gemmed,
Attend him forth; to the sea-shore they went.
The faith of Christ they'd keep not, nor accept,   690
And for this cause they from Marsilion fled.
But ere they'd sailed four leagues, maybe, or less,
Black wind and storm and tempest on them fell;
They were all drowned; they'll ne'er be seen again.
Had he been living I would have had him fetched.   695
Now, as regards the Paynim King himself:
Believe me, sire, before a month is sped
He'll follow you to France, to your own realm.
There he'll receive the faith that you profess,
There with joined hands to you his fealty pledge,   700
And hold from you in fief the Spanish realm."
Then said the King: "The name of God be blest!
Well have you done: I shall reward you well."
Throughout the host a thousand trumpets swell,
The French strike camp, their goods on sumpters set;   705
Home to fair France behold them all addressed.

· · ·

683. *twenty sureties:* This is the last
we hear of the hostages, whose ultimate
fate is not mentioned.

55

King Charlemayn has spoiled the Spanish borders,
He's taken castles, put cities to the slaughter;
Now the King says he has ended his warfare.
Home to fair France the Emperor turns his horses.   710
Pennon to lancehead Count Roland now has corded;
High on a hillock he displays it abroad there.
In fields all round the French set up their quarters.
Through the wide valleys the Paynim hosts go forward,
[All fully armed,] accoutred in their corslets,   715
Their helms laced on, and their swords in the sword-belt,
Shields on their necks, and their lances well ordered.
High on the mountains in a thicket they've halted:
Four hundred thousand they wait there for the morning;
God! it is grievous that the French have no warning!   720

56

The day goes down, dark follows on the day.
The Emperor sleeps, the mighty Charlemayn.
He dreamed he stood in Sizer's lofty gate,
Holding in hand his ashen lance full great.
Count Ganelon takes hold of it, and shakes,   725
And with such fury he wrenches it and breaks
That high as heaven the flinders fly away.
Carlon sleeps on, he sleeps and does not wake.

57

After this dream he had another dream:
That in his chapel at Aix in France was he;   730
In his right arm a fierce bear set its teeth.
Forth from Ardennes he saw a leopard speed,
That with rash rage his very body seized.
Then from the hall ran in a greyhound fleet,
And came to Carlon by gallops and by leaps.   735
From the first brute it bit the right ear clean,
And to the leopard gives battle with great heat.
The French all say the fight is good to see,
But none can guess which shall the victor be.
Carlon sleeps on; he wakes not from his sleep.   740

58

The night is past and the clear dawn is showing.
[A thousand trumpets] are sounded for the hosting.
The Emperor rides full lordly in his going.
"Barons, my lords," quoth Charlemayn, "behold now
These lofty passes, these narrows winding closely—   745
Say, who shall have the rearguard now to hold them?"
Quoth Ganelon: "I name my nephew Roland;
You have no baron who can beat him for boldness."

710–711: The scribe has perhaps omitted a line or two here, mentioning where
Charlemagne and his army have got to.
We learn from laisse 58 that they have
reached the entrance to the pass, at the
foot of the Pyrenees.
    731 ff. *a fierce bear*, etc.: The bear is
presumably Ganelon, as in laisse 186;
the leopard, Marsilion; the greyhound,
Roland.

When the King heard, a stern semblance he showed him:
"A fiend incarnate you are indeed," he told him;   750
"Malice hath ta'en possession of you wholly!
Who then should keep the vanguard of my progress?"
Quoth Ganelon: "Ogier the Dane I vote for;
You have no baron can do it with more prowess."

59

When Roland hears what he's appointed to,   755
He makes reply as knighthood bids him do:
"My noble stepsire, I owe you gratitude
That I'm assigned the rearguard at your suit.
Charles, King of France, the loss shall never rue
Of steed or palfrey thereby, I warrant you,   760
No saddle-beast, nor hinny neither mule,
Pack-horse nor sumpter thereby he shall not lose,
Save first the sword have paid the reckoning due."
Quoth Ganelon: "I know it; you speak truth."

60

When Roland hears that to the rearward guard   765
His stepsire names him, he speaks in wrath of heart:
"Ah! coward wretch, foul felon, baseborn carle,
Didst think the glove would fall from out my grasp
As did the wand from thine, before King Charles?"

61

"Just Emperor," then besought Count Roland bold,   770
"From your right hand deliver me your bow;
No man, I swear, shall utter the reproach
That I allowed it to slip from out my hold
As did the wand that Ganelon let go."
The Emperor sits with his head bended low,   775
On cheek and chin he plucks his beard for woe,
He cannot help but let the tears o'erflow.

62

Straightway thereon comes Naimon to the King—
No better vassal in court did ever sit.
He says to him: "You've listened to all this;   780
The County Roland is angered to the quick;
The rear-guard now has been adjudged to him
And you've no baron can ever make him quit.
Give him the bow now bended in your grip,
And find good men to aid him in this shift."   785
So the King gives it, and Roland seizes it.

---

752. *who then should keep the van-guard?:* i.e., in Roland's place, since he usually takes command there with the other peers (see ll. 549–550, 561–562).

769. *the wand:* the mention of the wand, here and in l. 774, seems to be a lapse of memory on the poet's part. Actually (333–335) it was the glove that Ganelon let fall.

771. *your bow:* the use of a bow as the token of an appointment does not seem to be very usual, nor is it clear why Charlemagne should have one in his hand, since the bow was not reckoned as a "noble" weapon, except for use in hunting. Later MSS substitute, or add, the more customary glove or standard.

63

To Roland then the King his uncle said:
"Nephew, fair sir, hear now and heed me well:
Half of my army I'll leave you for this stead;
Keep them with you and you'll be safe with them."   790
The Count said: "No; I never will consent;
May God confound me if I shame my descent!
A thousand score I'll keep of valiant French.
Safe through the passes go you with confidence;
Never fear man so long as I draw breath."   795

64

Roland the Count mounts on his destrier.
Comes then to him his comrade Oliver,
And Gerin comes and brave Count Gerier,
And Othon comes and so does Berenger,
Old Anseis, and Astor, great of worth,   800
And Gerard too, Roussillon's haughty earl;
And with them comes the rich Duke Gaïfer.
Quoth the Archbishop: "By Heav'n, I'm with you, sirs!"
"And so am I," Walter the Count affirms,
"I'm Roland's man, him am I bound to serve!"   805
Knights twenty thousand they choose for followers.

65

To Walter Hum Count Roland gives command:
"A thousand French take, of our own French land,
And hold the gorges and heights on either hand;
Nor let the Emperor lose from his side one man."   810
Quoth Walter: "Mine to do as you demand."
With thousand French of France their own dear land
On gorge and hill Count Walter holds the flanks;
Come what come may he'll never quit his stand
Till from the sheath have flashed sev'n hundred brands.   815
King Almeric, lord of Balferna's strand,
That day shall give hard battle to their band.

66

High are the hills, the valleys dark and deep,
Grisly the rocks, and wonderous grim the steeps.
The French pass through that day with pain and grief;   820
The bruit of them was heard full fifteen leagues.
But when at length their fathers' land they see,
Their own lord's land, the land of Gascony,
Then they remember their honours and their fiefs,

---

801. *Gerard of Roussillon:* not Roussillon in the Pyrenees, but a hill in Burgundy (now Mont Lassois), near the Abbey of Pothières, which was founded, together with the Abbey of Vèzelay by the historical Gerard. His exploits are celebrated in the *Chanson de Geste* which bears his name.

805. *man:* i.e., vassal.

816. The engagement between Almeric and Walter Hum is not described in the poem; its results are mentioned in laisse 152.

Sweethearts and wives whom they are fain to greet,   825
Not one there is for pity doth not weep.
Charles most of all a boding sorrow feels,
His nephew's left the Spanish gates to keep;
For very ruth he cannot choose but weep.

67

All the twelve peers in Spain are left behind,   830
Full twenty thousand stout Frenchmen at their side;
Valiant they are, and have no fear to die.
To land of France the Emperor homeward hies.
And still his face beneath his cloak he hides.
Close at his rein the good Duke Naimon rides;   835
He asks the King: "What troubles thus your mind?"
"This is ill done," quoth Charles, "to ask me why!
So much I grieve I cannot choose but sigh.
Through Ganelon fair France is ruined quite.
An angel showed me a vision in the night,   840
How in my hand he broke my lance outright,
He that my nephew to the rear-guard assigned.
In foreign marches abandoned, Roland bides—
God! if I lose him I shall not find his like."

68

King Charlemayn from tears cannot refrain;   845
Full hundred thousand, the French grieve for his sake,
And for Count Roland are wondrously afraid.
Him has the false lord Ganelon betrayed;
Vast the reward the paynim king has paid:
Silver and gold, and cloth of silk and saye,   850
Horses and mules, camels and beasts of prey.
Marsile has called the barony of Spain;
His viscounts, counts, almanzors stand arrayed,
Dukes and emirs, and youths of high estate;
Four hundred thousand he's summoned in three days.   855
In Saragossa he bids his tabors play;
Mahound their idol high on the tower they raise,
And every Paynim adores and gives it praise.
Then by forced marches their army hastes away,
Through Terracerta they ride by hill and dale.   860
Now have they seen French gonfalons displayed.
The twelve companions who in the rear-guard wait
Mean to give battle, and none shall say them nay.

69

Marsilion's nephew trips out before the throng,
Riding a mule which he whips with a wand;   865
He tells his uncle with laughter on his tongue:

843. *marches:* the frontier region of a
province; the province itself.
850. *saye:* a fine cloth of silk and wool.
860. *Terracerta:* Tere Certaine, possibly

Cerdagne, the region about Catalonia.
864. *Marsilion's nephew:* His name, as
we learn in l. 1192, is Adelroth.

"Fair sir and king, I've served you well and long;
Much have I suffered, much labour undergone,
Many fields fought, and many battles won!
First blow at Roland is the reward I want;   870
With my sharp sword I'll split him through the sconce!
Yea, if I find good favour with Mahond,
I'll set Spain free, unloosing of her bonds
From Gate of Spain to Durstant and beyond.
Charles will lose heart, the French will yield anon,   875
You shall be quit of wars your whole life long."
He gets the glove from King Marsilion.

70

Marsilion's nephew holds the glove in his fist:
Unto his uncle thus proudly he begins:
"Fair sire and king, you've made me a great gift.   880
Find me twelve lords, the best that you can pick.
'Gainst the twelve peers our valour for to pit."
The first that answers is Falsaron to wit,
He was own brother unto Marsile the king:
"You and I, nephew, will gladly go to it.   885
In very deed this battle will we give
To Carlon's rearward that guards his host for him:
The thing is done! by us they'll all be killed."

71

King Corsablis now springs from out the host,
Barbarian born, the magic art he knows.   890
Like a brave man thus valiantly he spoke:
"No coward I, no, not for all God's gold!"
.   .   .
Malprimis of Brigale comes spurring bold,
He'll run afoot swifter than steed can go;
With a loud voice before Marsile he boasts: 895
"I'll bear my body with you to Roncevaux:
If I find Roland I'll fight till he's laid low."

72

From Balaguet there cometh an Emir;
His form is noble, his eyes are bold and clear,
When on his horse he's mounted in career   900
He bears him bravely armed in his battle-gear,
And for his courage he's famous far and near;
Were he but Christian, right knightly he'd appear.
Before Marsile he cries for all to hear:
"To Roncevaux," saith he, "my course I'll steer;   905
If I find Roland, then death shall be his weird,

---

870. *first blow at Roland* (le colp de Roland): The privilege of striking the first blow in the battle was much sought after. In l. 3200 we find Malpramis, the son of the Emir Baligant, similarly demanding of his father the honor (le coup) in the battle with Charlemagne. The commander in chief bestows the honor by handing over his glove in token (l. 877).
892–893. A few lines seem to have been omitted here, completing Corsablis's speech of defiance.
906. *weird*: doom.

And Oliver's, and all of the Twelve Peers!
The French shall die the death in shame and tears.
King Charlemayn, the dotard old and blear,
Will soon be sick of waging warfare here!   910
Spain shall be ours in peace this many a year!"
The King Marsile pours thanks into his ears.

73

Comes an Almanzor, a lord of Moriane,
There's no worse villain in all the land of Spain.
Before Marsilion his bragging boast he makes: 915
"To Roncevaux I'll lead my people straight,
Full twenty thousand with spear and lance arrayed.
If I meet Roland I'll kill him, by my faith!
No day shall dawn but Carlon shall bewail."

74

And next there comes Turgis of Tortelosa;   920
A count he is, and the whole city owneth;
A right ill will to Christian men he showeth.
Before Marsile with the rest he enrolls him.
He tells the King: "Fear not for any foeman!
Mahound's worth more than St Peter the Roman;   925
Serve him; the field is ours and ours the trophy!
To Roncevaux I go to meet with Roland;
There shall he die; he shall have help of no man.
See here my sword, how long it is and noble;
'Gainst Durendal I'll measure it right boldly;   930
Which shall prevail you'll not be long in knowing.
The French shall die if they dare to oppose us;
Carlon the old shall be grieving and groaning;
Crown nevermore shall he wear from that moment."

75

And Escremiz of Valterne is the next;   935
He owns that fief, and he's a Saracen;
Before Marsile he shouts amid the press:
"To Ronceval I go to stoop their crests.
If I find Roland, there shall he lose his head,
And Oliver, who's captain of the rest;   940
The whole Twelve Peers are all marked out for death.
The French shall die and France shall be bereft.
Few men of worth to Carlon shall be left."

76

Next comes a Paynim, called Estorgan by name,
Estramarin his comrade with him came;   945
Foul felons both and knavish traitors they.
Then said Marsile: "My lords, draw near, I pray;
Through Roncevaux you mean to force your way,
And lead my troops, and lend us your best aid."
And they reply: "Command, and we obey.   950
Both Oliver and Roland we'll assail,

Of the Twelve Peers none shall survive the fray.
Sharp are our swords and goodly are the blades,
All in hot blood we'll dye them red this day;
The French shall die, and Carlon shall bewail.   955
A gift we'll make you of the home of their race;
Come with us, King, and see how goes the game,
And as a gift we'll give you Charlemayn."

77

Then comes at speed Margaris of Seville,
Who holds his land as far as Cazmarin.   960
Ladies all love him, so beautiful he is,
She that beholds him has a smile on her lips,
Will she or nill she, she laughs for very bliss,
And there's no Paynim his match for chivalry.
He joins the throng and cries unto the King   965
Loudest of all: "Never you fear a whit!
In Roncevaux this Roland I'll go kill,
Nor Oliver shall any longer live;
All the Twelve Peers we'll cut in little bits.
Lo! here my sword with golden pummel gilt!   970
Th' Emir of Primes gave it me for a gift,
I swear I'll dye it vermilion to the hilt.
The French shall die and France in shame shall sit.
Old greybeard Charles shall never live, I think,
One day but what he'll rage and weep for this.   975
France can be ours in a year if we will;
In Saint-Denis we'll eat and sleep our fill."
The Paynim King makes deep salaam to him.

78

And last there comes Chernubles of Munigre;
His unshorn hair hangs trailing to his feet.   980
He for his sport can shoulder if he please
More weight than four stout sumpter-mules can heave.
He dwells in regions wherein, so 'tis believed,
Sun never shines nor springs one blade of wheat,
No rain can fall, no dew is ever seen,   985
There, every stone is black as black can be,
And some folk say it's the abode of fiends.
Chernubles saith: "My sword's girt in the sheath;
In Roncevaux red blood shall dye it deep.
Should Roland cross my path, that doughty chief,   990
And I not smite him, never put faith in me!
To this my blade his Durendal shall yield,
The French shall die, and France be left bereaved."
This said, the whole Twelve Champions are convened;
One hundred thousand stout Saracens they lead.   995
Each one afire with zeal to do great deeds.
Beneath a pine-grove they arm them for the field.

---

977. *Saint Denis:* a town near Paris with a famous abbey, founded by Dago- bert in 626, the burial place of the kings of France.

79

Now are the Paynims in Sarsen hauberks dight
Whereof the most with triple mail are lined;
Good Saragossa helms they lace on tight,   1000
Swords of Viana steel gird on their thighs;
Spears of Valence they have, and shields full fine,
Their gonfalons are scarlet, blue, and white.
They leave their mules, their palfreys leave behind,
And mount their steeds; in serried ranks they ride.   1005
Fair was the day, the sun shone clear and bright,
No piece of harness but glittered in the light.
A thousand trumpets ring out for more delight.
Great is the noise; it reaches the French lines.
Quoth Oliver: "I think, companion mine,   1010
We'll need this day with Saracens to fight."
Roland replies: "I hope to God you're right!
Here must we stand to serve on the King's side.
Men for their lords great hardship must abide,
Fierce heat and cold endure in every clime,   1015
Lose for his sake, if need be, skin and hide.
Look to it now! Let each man stoutly smite!
No shameful songs be sung for our despite!
Paynims are wrong, Christians are in the right!
Ill tales of me shall no man tell, say I!"   1020

80

Oliver's climbed upon a hilly crest,
Looks to his right along a grassy cleft,
And sees the Paynims and how they ride addressed.
To his companion Roland he calls and says:
"I see from Spain a tumult and a press—   1025
Many bright hauberks, and many a shining helm!
A day of wrath, they'll make it for our French.
Ganelon knew it, false heart and traitor fell;
When to the Emperor he named us for this stead!"
Quoth Roland: "Silence, Count Oliver, my friend!   1030
He is my stepsire, I will have no word said."

81

Oliver's climbed a hill above the plain,
Whence he can look on all the land of Spain,
And see how vast the Saracen array;
All those bright helms with gold and jewels gay,   1035
And all those shields, those coats of burnished mail;
And all those lances from which the pennons wave;
Even their squadrons defy all estimate,
He cannot count them, their numbers are so great;
Stout as he is, he's mightily dismayed.   1040
He hastens down as swiftly as he may,
Comes to the French and tells them all his tale.

82

Quoth Oliver: "The Paynim strength I've seen;
Never on earth has such a hosting been:

A hundred thousand in van ride under shield 1045
Their helmets laced, their hauberks all agleam,
Their spears upright, with heads of shining steel.
You'll have such battle as ne'er was fought on field.
My lords of France, God give you strength at need!
Save you stand fast, this field we cannot keep." 1050
The French all say: "Foul shame it were to flee!
We're yours till death; no man of us will yield."

83

Quoth Oliver: "Huge are the Paynim hordes,
And of our French the numbers seem but small.
Companion Roland, I pray you sound your horn, 1055
That Charles may hear and fetch back all his force."
Roland replies: "Madman were I and more,
And in fair France my fame would suffer scorn.
I'll smite great strokes with Durendal my sword,
I'll dye it red high as the hilt with gore. 1060
This pass the Paynims reached on a luckless morn;
I swear to you death is their doom therefor."

84

"Companion Roland, your Olifant now sound!
King Charles will hear and turn his armies round;
He'll succour us with all his kingly power." 1065
Roland replies: "May never God allow
That I should cast dishonour on my house
Or on fair France bring any ill renown!
Rather will I with Durendal strike out,
With this good sword, here on my baldrick bound; 1070
From point to hilt you'll see the blood run down.
Woe worth the Paynims that e'er they made this rout!
I pledge my faith, we'll smite them dead on ground."

85

"Companion Roland, your Olifant now blow;
Charles in the passes will hear it as he goes, 1075
Trust me, the French will all return right so."
"Now God forbid," Roland makes answer wroth,
"That living man should say he saw me go
Blowing of horns for any Paynim foe!
Ne'er shall my kindred be put to such reproach. 1080
When I shall stand in this great clash of hosts
I'll strike a thousand and then sev'n hundred strokes,
Blood-red the steel of Durendal shall flow.
Stout are the French, they will do battle bold,
These men of Spain shall die and have no hope." 1085

1063. *Olifant:* The word (which is a form of "elephant") means (a) "ivory," (b) "a horn made of ivory," and is used specifically, almost as a proper name, to denote Roland's horn, made of an elephant's tusk, and aborned with gold and jewels about the rim.

86

Quoth Oliver: "Herein I see no blame:
I have beheld the Saracens of Spain;
They cover all the mountains and the vales,
They spread across the hillsides and the plains;
Great is the might these foreigners display,   1090
And ours appears a very small array."
"I thirst the more," quoth Roland, "for the fray.
God and His angels forbid it now, I pray,
That e'er by me fair France should be disfamed!
I'd rather die than thus be put to shame;   1095
If the King loves us it's for our valour's sake."

87

Roland is fierce and Oliver is wise
And both for valour may bear away the prize.
Once horsed and armed the quarrel to decide,
For dread of death the field they'll never fly.   1100
The counts are brave, their words are stern and high.
Now the false Paynims with wondrous fury ride.
Quoth Oliver: "Look, Roland, they're in sight.
Charles is far off, and these are very nigh;
You would not sound your Olifant for pride;   1105
Had we the Emperor we should have been all right.
To Gate of Spain turn now and lift your eyes,
See for yourself the rear-guard's woeful plight.
Who fights this day will never more see fight."
Roland replies: "Speak no such foul despite!   1110
Curst be the breast whose heart knows cowardice!
Here in our place we'll stand and here abide:
Buffets and blows be ours to take and strike!"

88

When Roland sees that battle there must be
Leopard nor lion ne'er grew so fierce as he.   1115
He calls the French, bids Oliver give heed:
"Sir friend and comrade, such words you shall not speak!
When the King gave us the French to serve this need
These twenty thousand he chose to do the deed;
And well he knew not one would flinch or flee.   1120
Men must endure much hardship for their liege,
And bear for him great cold and burning heat,
Suffer sharp wounds and let their bodies bleed.
Smite with your lance and I with my good steel,
My Durendal the Emperor gave to me: 1125
And if I die, who gets it may agree
That he who bore it, a right good knight was he."

89

Then to their side comes the Archbishop Turpin,
Riding his horse and up the hillside spurring.

He calls the French and preaches them a sermon: 1130
"Barons, my lords, Charles picked us for this purpose;
We must be ready to die in our King's service.
Christendom needs you, so help us to preserve it.
Battle you'll have, of that you may be certain,
Here come the Paynims—your own eyes have observed them. 1135
Now beat your breasts and ask God for His mercy:
I will absolve you and set your souls in surety.
If you should die, blest martyrdom's your guerdon;
You'll sit on high in Paradise eternal."
The French alight and all kneel down in worship;   1140
God's shrift and blessing the Archbishop conferreth,
And for their penance he bids them all strike firmly.

90

The French rise up and on their feet stand close;
All of their sins are shriven and made whole,
And the Archbishop God's blessing has bestowed.   1145
Then on swift steeds they leap to saddle-bow.
Armed with the arms prescribed by knightly code;
All are now ready into the field to go.
Count Roland said to Oliver right so:
"Sir my companion, too true the word you spoke,   1150
That all of us by Ganelon were sold.
He's ta'en his wage of wealth and goods and gold.
The Emperor's vengeance I think will not be slow!
Marsile the King has bargained for our bones:
He'll need the sword to fetch his purchase home."   1155

91

Through Gate of Spain Roland goes riding past
On Veillantif, his swiftly-running barb;
Well it becomes him to go equipped in arms,
Bravely he goes, and tosses up his lance,
High in the sky he lifts the lancehead far,   1160
A milk-white pennon is fixed above the shaft
Whose falling fringes whip his hands on the haft.
Nobly he bears him, with open face he laughs;
And his companion behind him follows hard;
The Frenchmen all acclaim him their strong guard. 1165
On Saracens he throws a haughty glance
But meek and mild looks on the men of France,
To whom he speaks out of a courteous heart:
"Now, my lord barons, at walking pace—advance!
Looking for trouble these Paynims ride at large— 1170
A fine rich booty we'll have ere this day's past;
Never French king beheld the like by half."
E'en as he speaks, their battles join and charge.

92

Quoth Oliver: "I have no more to say:
To sound your horn for help you would not deign,   1175

So here you are, you've not got Charlemayn;
Little he knows, brave heart! he's not to blame.
Nor those with him, nowise in fault are they.
Ride forward then and do the best you may!
Barons my lords, hold firm amid the fray!   1180
Now for God's sake be resolute, I pray,
To strike hard blows, to give them and to take.
King Carlon's war-cry forget not to proclaim!"
A mighty shout the Frenchmen give straightway;
Whoso had heard the cry "Mountjoy" they raise   1185
He would remember its valiance all his days.
They charge—Lord God, was ever sight so brave?
They spur their steeds to make the greater haste,
They fall afighting—there is no other way—
The Saracens join battle undismayed;   1190
Paynims and Franks are fighting face to face.

93

Now Adelroth, (he was King Marsile's nephew),
Before the host comes first of all his fellows;
With evil words the French he thus addresses:
"Villainous Franks, with us you have to reckon!   1195
You've been betrayed by him that should protect you,
Your king lacked wit who in the passes left you.
Fair France will lose her honour in this venture;
From Carlon's body the right arm will be severed."
When Roland hears him, God! but his rage is reckless!   1200
He spurs his horse, gives full rein to his mettle,
His blow he launches with all his mightiest effort;
The shield he shatters, and the hauberk he rendeth,
He splits the breast and batters in the breast bone,
Through the man's back drives out the backbone bended,   1205
And soul and all forth on the spear-point fetches;
Clean through he thrusts him, forth of the saddle wrenching,
And flings him dead a lance-length from his destrier;
Into two pieces he has broken his neckbone.
No less for that he speaks to him and tells him: 1210
"Out on thee, churl! no lack-wit is the Emperor,
He is none such, nor loved he treason ever;
Right well he did who in the passes left us,
Neither shall France lose honour by this venture.
First blood to us! Go to it, gallant Frenchmen!   1215
Right's on our side, and wrong is with these wretches!"

94

A duke was there, he was named Falsaron,
Brother was he to King Marsilion,

1185. *Mountjoy:* A mountjoy (mont-joie) was (according to Littré) a mound or cairn of stones set up to mark the site of a victory. The old French war cry, "Montjoie St.-Denis!" or, briefly, "Montjoie!" derived from the cairn set up at St.-Denis on the site of the saint's martyrdom (his spiritual victory). Others derive "Montjoie" from the Hill of Rama, called "Mons Gaudii," from which pilgrims obtained their first view of Jerusalem.

Abiram's land and Dathan's did he own;
Under the sky was no worse villain known; 1220
Between the eyes his brow was broad of bone,
A full half-foot is measured, I suppose.
His nephew's death he bitterly bemoans;
Forth of the press he gallops out alone,
The Paynim war-cry he utters as he goes, 1225
And on the French an evil taunt bestows:
"Fair France this day shall find her honour flown!"
Oliver's heard him, great wrath within him grows,
Into his horse he strikes his spurs of gold,
Right baronly he rides to smite the foe. 1230
He breaks the shield, he cleaves the hauberk close,
Clean through his breast drives lance and pennon both,
A spear's length flings him dead from the saddle-bow;
Looks down and sees the infidel lie low
And thus upbraids him in a right haughty tone: 1235
"Churl, for your threats I do not care a groat!
French lords, strike on! we'll have them all o'erthrown."
King Carlon's war-cry, "Mountjoy!" he shouts full bold.

95

A king was there, his name was Corsablis,
From a far land he came, from Barbary; 1240
The Saracens he calls, and thus he speaks:
"Well are we placed this field of arms to keep;
For of these Franks the number is but weak,
And we may well despise the few we see.
Charles cannot come to help them in their need, 1245
This is the day their deaths are all decreed!"
Archbishop Turpin has listened to his speech,
And hates him worse than any man that breathes.
His golden spurs he strikes into his steed,
And rides against him right valiant for the deed. 1250
He breaks the buckler, he's split the hauberk's steel,
Into his breast driven the lance head deep,
He spits him through, on high his body heaves,
And hurls him dead a spear's length o'er the lea.
Earthward he looks and sees him at his feet, 1255
But yet to chide him he none the less proceeds:
"Vile infidel, you lied between your teeth!
Charles my good lord to help us will not cease,
Nor have our French the least desire to flee.
These friends of yours stock-still we're like to leave; 1260
Here's news for you—you'll die, and there you'll be.
Frenchmen, strike home! forget not your high breed!
This first good stroke is ours, God's gramercy!"
He shouts "Mountjoy!" to hearten all the field.

96

And Gerin strikes Malprimis of Brigale; 1265
No penny-piece the stubborn shield avails;
The crystal boss he splinters all in twain,
That half the buckler falls down upon the plain:

Through to the flesh he cleaves the hauberk-mail,
Through to the heart he drives the good spear straight;   1270
The paynim falls flat down with all his weight.
Then Satan comes and hales his soul away.

97
Gerier his friend on the Emir runs in,
Shatters the shield and bursts the byrny-rings,
Clean through the guts the trusty spear he swings,   1275
Thrusts it well in, then out at back with it;
A whole spear's length on field the body flings:
Quoth Oliver: "We're doing well with this!"

98
Samson the Duke on the Almanzor runs:
Through gilded shield and painted flowers he thrusts;   1280
Nought for defence avails the hauberk tough,
He splits his heart, his liver, and his lung,
And strikes him dead, weep any or weep none.
Cries the Archbishop: "This feat was knightly done!"

99
And Anseïs gives rein to his good steed,   1285
He runs on Turgis of Tortelose at speed;
Under the boss of gold he cleaves the shield,
And of the hauberk the double mail unseams,
Into his body strikes home the head of steel,
Through to his back he drives the point out clean,   1290
A full spear's length he flings him dead on field.
Quoth Roland: "Lo! that was a valiant feat!"

100
And Engelier the Gascon of Bordeaux
Spurs his good steed, slacks rein and lets him go;
With Escrimiz, Valterna's lord, he's closed,   1295
Off from his neck the splintered buckler broke.
The hauberk's ventail he's shattered with the stroke.
He splits his throat between the collar-bones,
A full spear's length dead from the saddle throws;
Then says to him: "The devil take thy soul!"   1300

101
And Othon strikes a Paynim, Estorgant,
Full in mid-chief he smites the shield point-blank,
So that the white splits and the scarlet cracks;
The skirt of mail he's riven through and smashed,
Into his body the cleaving spear he rams;   1305
From his swift steed he hurls him dead on land,
"And now," says he, "find comfort if you can!"

102
Then Berenger drives at Estramarin,
He cleaves the shield, and the good hauberk splits,
On his stout spear the trunk of him he spits   1310

And flings him dead 'mid thousand Sarrasins.
Of the Twelve Peers ten are already killed,
Two and no more are left of them who live;
These are Chernubles and the Count Margaris.

103

Now Margaris is a right valiant peer,   1315
Buxom and strong, nimble and fleet and fierce.
He spurs his horse to strike at Olivere;
He splits the shield, the golden boss he sheers,
Along his ribs the glancing spear-point veers,
But by God's grace his body is not pierced;   1320
Nor is he thrown, though the shock breaks the spear.
Past him the Paynim is borne in full career,
Rallying his men he sounds his bugle clear.

104

Great is the battle and crowded the mellay,
Nor does Count Roland stint of his strokes this day;   1325
While the shaft holds he wields his spear amain—
Fifteen great blows ere it splinters and breaks.
Then his bare brand, his Durendal, he takes;
Against Chernubles he spurs his steed in haste,
Splits through the helm with carbuncles ablaze,   1330
Through the steel coif, and through scalp and through brain
'Twixt the two eyes he cleaves him through the face;
Through the bright byrny close-set with rings of mail,
Right through the body, through the fork and the reins,
Down through the saddle with its beaten gold plates,   1335
Through to the horse he drives the cleaving blade,
Seeking no joint through the chine carves his way,
Flings horse and man dead on the grassy plain.
"Foul befall, felon, that e'er you sought this fray!
Mahound," quoth he, "shall never bring you aid.   1340
Villains like you seek victory in vain."

105

The County Roland throughout the field goes riding;
With Durendal, good sword, he stabs and slices,
The toll he takes of Saracens is frightful.
Would you had seen him, dead man on dead man piling,   1345
Seen the bright blood about his pathway lying!
Bloody his hauberk and both his arms with fighting,
His good horse bloody from crest to withers likewise;
Oliver too doth never cease from striking,
And the Twelve Peers are not a whit behindhand,   1350
And all the French are hammering and smiting;
The Paynims fall, some dead and others dying.
Quoth the Archbishop: "Right blessèd be our knighthood";
He shouts "Mountjoy!" war-cry of Charles the mighty.

1312. *the Twelve Peers:* i.e., the Saracen Peers enumerated in ll. 882–994.

106

And Oliver goes riding through the press; 1355
His spear is broken, only the shaft is left.
Against a Paynim, Malun, he rides addrest,
Smashes the shield with flowers and gold bedecked,
Both of his eyes he smites out of his head,
So that his brains around his feet are spread, 1360
And flings the corpse amid sev'n hundred dead.
Turgis he's slain, and slain Esturgot next,
Till to the grips the spear-shaft splits in shreds.
Roland cries out: "What are you doing, friend?
I'd give no groat for sticks in such a stead! 1365
Here iron avails, and steel and nothing else.
Where is your sword that Hauteclaire is y-clept,
With its gold hilts and pummel crystal-gemmed?"
"I've had no time to draw," Oliver said,
"I've been so busy with striking right and left." 1370

107

Dan Oliver has drawn his goodly brand,
As his friend Roland so urgently demands;
Now will he prove him a stout knight of his hands!
He smites a Paynim, Justin of Val Ferrat;
Clean through the middle the skull of him he cracks, 1375
The saffron byrny splits, and his breast and back,
And saddle, brave with gems and golden bands,
And through the spine the horse in sunder hacks,
And dead on field flings all before him flat.
"I'll call you brother," quoth Roland, "after that! 1380
'Tis for such strokes our Emperor loves a man."
The shout "Mountjoy!" goes up on every hand.

108

Gerin the Count bestrides his steed Sorel,
Gerier his comrade on Passëcerf is set;
Eagerly both loose rein and spur ahead 1385
And go to strike a Paynim, Timozel,
One on the shield, the other on the chest.
Both spears at once are broken in his breast,
Flat in the fallow straightway they fling him dead—
I do not know, I never have heard tell, 1390
Which of the two was the more swift and snell.
[And Engelier, Knight of Bordeaux, he next
Slew Esprevere, that son was to Burel.]
Archbishop Turpin has o'erthrown Siglorel,
The sorcerer, who'd once been down to Hell, 1395

1367. *y-clept:* named.
1371. *Dan* (Dominus): lord.
1376. *saffron:* burnished with a yellow varnish made from bismuth oxide.

1391. *snell:* speedy.
1392–1393. These two lines have been telescoped in the text, and are thus emended by most editors.

With Jupiter for guide, by magic spells.
Quoth Turpin then: "Ear-marked was he for death!"
Roland replies: "The churl has made an end.
Oliver, brother, such strokes delight me well!"

109

Fiercer and still more fierce the battle grows;   1400
Both French and Paynims deal wondrous heavy strokes,
Some in attacking, and some in parrying blows.
How many spears are bloodied there and broke!
What gonfalons, what banners rent and strown!
How many French in flower of youth laid low,   1405
Whom wives and mothers shall never more behold,
Nor those of France who wait them on the road!
King Charlemayn must weep and wail for woe;
What help in that? he cannot save his folk.
Ill did Count Guènes serve Carlon, when he rode   1410
To Saragossa and all his people sold;
Thereby he lost life and limbs of his own
When at Aix after they judged him to the rope,
And of his kin thirty were hanged also,
Who ne'er had thought such death should be their dole.   1415

110

Fierce is the battle and wondrous grim the fight.
Both Oliver and Roland boldly smite,
Thousands of strokes the stout Archbishop strikes,
The whole Twelve Peers are not a whit behind,
And the French ranks lay on with all their might.   1420
Heaped by the hundred thousands of Paynims lie,
None can escape unless he turns and flies,
Will he or nill he, there must he leave his life.
There France must lose the noblest of her knights,
They'll see no more their kindred and their sires,   1425
Nor Charles, who scans the pass with anxious eyes.
Throughout all France terrific tempests rise,
Thunder is heard, the stormy winds blow high,
Unmeasured rain and hail fall from the sky,
While thick and fast flashes the levin bright,   1430
And true it is the earth quakes far and wide.
Far as from Saintes to Michael-of-the-Tide,
From Besançon to Wissant Port, you'd find
There's not a house but the walls crack and rive.
Right at high noon a darkness falls like night,   1435
Save for the lightning there's not a gleam of light;
None that beholds it but is dismayed for fright,
And many say: "This is the latter time,

1396. *Jupiter:* like Apollo, the classical Jove has been demoted to the status of demon.

The world is ending, and the Great Doom is nigh."
They speak not true, they cannot read the signs: 1440
'Tis Roland's death calls forth this mighty cry.

111

The French have fought with valour and success;
By scores and thousands lie Paynim corpses spread,
Of hundred thousand scarce two will fight again.
Quoth the Archbishop: "Right valiant are our men,   1445
The like of these hath no lord under heav'n.
Thus it is written in the Gestes of the French:
Our Emperor's power was never rivalled yet."
They search the field for their maimed and their dead,
With grief and sorrow the eyes of them are wet,   1450
With love and pity for their kindred and friends.
Now falls upon them Marsile with all his strength.

112

The King Marsile comes riding up a gorge
With all his army about him in great force;
He has assembled twenty huge battle-hordes.   1455
Such flash of helms with gems and gold adorned!
Such shields, such byrnies with burnished saffron wrought!
Sev'n hundred trumpets are sounding the assault;
Through all the country the noise of them goes forth.
"Brother," quoth Roland, "friend Oliver, sweet lord,   1460
It is our death false Ganelon has sworn;
The treason's plain, it can be hid no more;
A right great vengeance the Emperor will let fall.
But we must bide a fearful pass of war.
No man has ever beheld the like before.   1465
I shall lay on with Durendal my sword,
You, comrade, wield the great Hauteclaire of yours.
In lands how many have we those weapons borne!
Battles how many victoriously fought!
Ne'er shall base ballad be sung of them in hall!"   1470

113

Marsile beholds his slaughtered chivalry.
He bids his trumpets and horns sound instantly
And then sets forward with his great company.
Then first rides out a Saracen, Abisme,
In all that host was none more vile than he,   1475
With evil vice and crimes he's dyed full deep,
In Mary's Child, God's Son, he's no belief,
And black he is as melted pitch to see.
Better he loves murder and treachery
Than all the gold that is in Galicie   1480
None ever saw him in mirth or jollity;

1447. *the Gestes of the French:* the chronicle, to which the poet from time to time refers, and from which he claims to derive his information.

But bold he is and rash to a degree,
And for that reason he's loved by King Marsile.
He bears a dragon to rally his meinie.
The good Archbishop observes him, much displeased, 1485
He'd like to hit him on sight, that's how he feels,
And to himself he says quite quietly:
"This Sarsen looks right heretic to me.
'Twere best by far to go and kill the beast;
I never loved cowards nor coward deeds." 1490

114

Th'Archbishop opens the battle up anew;
He rides a charger that from Grossayle he took
(That was a king in Denmark, whom he slew).
A steed he is swiftly-running and smooth,
Flat in the knee and hollow in the hoof, 1495
Short in the thigh and ample in the croup,
Long in the flank and the back well set up,
White of his tail and yellow of his plume,
Small of his ears and his head tawny-hued;
Here is a horse no courser could outdo. 1500
Him the Archbishop, of his valour right good,
Spurs on Abisme, and none shall stay his mood.
He rides to strike him on his target of proof
Wondrous with topaz and amethyst to boot,
With carbuncle ablaze, and beryl blue 1505
(Emir Galafe gave it him for a boon
Whom in Val Metas a devil gave it to.)
Turpin lays on, nor spares; I tell you true,
After he hit it it was not worth a sou!
From flank to flank he spits his body through, 1510
And flings him dead wherever he finds room.
The French all cry. "A valiant blow and shrewd!
Right strong to save is our Archbishop's crook!"

115

Now can the French count up the Paynim might
They see it filling the plains from side to side. 1515
They urge on Roland and Oliver likewise
And the Twelve Peers to flee for all their lives;
To whom straightway the Prelate speaks his mind:
"Barons, my lords, these shameful thoughts put by;
By God I charge you, hold fast and do not fly, 1520
Lest brave men sing ill songs in your despite.
Better it were to perish in the fight.
Soon, very soon, we all are marked to die,
None of us here will see to-morrow's light;
One thing there is I promise you outright: 1525
To you stand open the gates of Paradise,
There with the holy sweet Innocents to bide."

1484. *meinie:* household.

His words so fill them with courage and delight
There's none among them but shouts "Mountjoy" on high.

116

A Saracen, of Saragossa Town   1530
Was there, the lord of half that city round—
Climborin namely, that traitor false and foul
Which took the oath of Ganelon the Count
And then for friendship kissed him upon the mouth
And with his helm and carbuncle endowed;   1535
Our Fatherland he swore he'd disrenown,
And from the Emperor would snatch away the crown.
Now he comes riding on Barbëmouche his mount—
Fleeter was never swallow nor falcon found—
Slacks rein, spurs hard its mettle to arouse,   1540
On Engelier the Gascon forward bounds.
Buckler nor byrny avails against him now,
Into the midriff lance-point and pennon plough,
From breast to back the shaft runs through and out,
A whole spear's length he hurls him dead on ground.   1545
"Fit for destruction is all this gear!" he shouts;
"Paynims, strike hard! carve your way through the rout!"
"God!" say the French, "one of our best is down!"

117

Count Roland calls to Oliver his friend:
"Fair sir, companion, see, Engelier is dead;   1550
No better man had we for knightliness."
The Count replies: "God give me fair revenge!"
In his steed's flanks the golden spurs he sets,
He grasps Hauteclaire, whose steel is all dyed red,
He deals the Paynim a mighty stroke and dread,   1555
Twists out the blade, down falls the Saracen;
The Adversary bears off his soul to Hell.
Then he goes on, slays Duke Alfayen next,
From Escababa he hews away the head,
And seven Arabs unhorses then pell-mell: 1560
That lot at least will never fight again.
"My friend is angry," the County Roland said:
"Fighter for fighter he matches me right well;
'Tis for such strokes King Carlon loves us best!"
Aloud he cries: "Strike on, my valiant men!"   1565

118

Elsewhere, behold a Paynim, Valdabron,
Was godfather to King Marsilion;
He owns a navy four hundred dromonds strong,
And to his service no seaman but is bond.
He captured Salem by fraud in times bygone,   1570

1557. *the Adversary:* Satan.
1568. *dromond(s):* a large and very   swift medieval sailing ship, used both for war and commerce.

And sacked the Temple of good King Solomon,
Murdering there the Patriarch by the font.
He took the oath of County Ganelon,
And sword and mangons gave him as pledge thereon.
He rides a horse that he calls Gramimond, 1575
Never of speed was peregrine more prompt.
With the sharp spur he urges it headlong;
The great Duke Samson straightway he falls upon.
He splits the shield, he bursts the habergeon,
Drives through his body spear-head and gonfalon, 1580
Flings him from saddle a full spear's length along:
"Paynims!" he cries, "we'll beat them yet! Lay on!"
"God!" say the French, "there's a brave baron gone!"

119

When the Count Roland sees Samson thus laid low
Well may you guess how he is grieved of soul. 1585
He spurs his horse and speeds to smite the foe
With Durendal, more worth than finest gold.
By might and main the Baron deals the stroke
Full on the helm that is all gemmed with gold;
The skull he splits, byrny and breast are broke, 1590
Cloven the saddle, that is all gemmed with gold;
Through the beast's back deep down the weapon goes;
Like it or leave it, he has destroyed them both.
The Paynims say: "This is a bitter blow!"
"I love you not," quoth Roland, "by my troth; 1595
Yours is the outrage, yours is the lying boast!"

120

An African there was of Afric, too,
Was called Malquiant, the son of King Malcude;
Harnessed he is in gold from head to foot,
None in the sun so glitters to the view, 1600
He rides a horse that he calls Saut-Perdu;
No steed could rival the swiftness of its hoofs.
He strikes Anseïs in mid-shield square and true,
He shears away the scarlet and the blue,
Rips the mailed skirt of the hauberk of proof, 1605
Into the body drives the steel and the wood.
The Count falls dead, his days have met their doom.
The French all say: "Brave lord, alack for you!"

121

Archbishop Turpin goes riding through the field;
Ne'er was mass sung by any tonsured priest 1610
That of his body could do such valiant deeds!
He hails the Paynim: "God send the worst to thee!
Thou hast slain one for whom my whole heart grieves."
Into a gallop he urges his good steed,
He strikes him hard on his Toledo shield, 1615
And lays him dead upon the grassy green.

122

There was a Paynim, and Grandoyne was he called,
King Capuel's son, from Cappadocia's shores,
Mounted on Marmor, for so he names his horse,
Swifter of speed than any bird that soars.　　　　　1620
He slacks the rein and he goes spurring forth,
And runs to strike Gerin with all his force.
From off his neck he splits the red shield shorn,
From off his body he rips the byrny torn,
Into his heart the pennon blue he's borne,　　　　　1625
And down he flings him dead on a rocky tor.
Gerin his comrade he smites down afterward,
Berenger next, Guy of St Antoine fall;
And then he strikes the mighty duke Astorge,
(Envers-on-Rhône and Valence called him lord),　　　1630
And lays him dead; for joy the Paynims roar;
The French all say: "What loss we have to mourn!"

123

The County Roland grips fast his blood-red blade;
Well has he heard how the French are dismayed;
His heart grieves so, 'tis like to split in twain.　　　1635
In hails the Paynim: "God send thee all His plagues!
Thou has slain one for whom I'll make thee pay!"
He spurs his horse that gladly runs apace;
Let win who may, they're at it, face to face.

124

The Prince Grandoyne was a good knight and gallant,　1640
Strong of his hands and valorous in battle;
Athwart him now comes Roland the great captain:
He'd never met him, but he knew him instanter.
By his proud aspect, and by his noble stature,
His haughty looks, and his bearing and manner.　　　1645
He cannot help it, a mortal fear unmans him;
Fain would he fly, but what's the good? he cannot.
The Count assails him with such ferocious valour
That to the nasal the whole helmet is shattered,
Cloven the nose and the teeth and the palate,　　　1650
The jaz'rain hauberk and the breastbone and backbone,
Both silver bows from off the golden saddle;
Horseman and horse clean asunder he slashes,
Lifeless he leaves them and the pieces past patching.
The men of Spain fall a-wailing for sadness:　　　1655
The French all cry: "What strokes! and what a champion!"

125

Fierce is the battle and marvellous and great.
The Frenchmen ply their burnished spears amain.
There had you seen how many men in pain,
How many wounded and bleeding there and slain!　　1660

1651. *jazerain:* a kind of chain mail made in Algiers.

Heaped up pell-mell they lie, on back or face.
The Saracens cannot endure the strain;
Will they or nill they they flee across the plain,
And the French forces with all their might give chase.

126

Wondrous the battle, and it grows faster yet;   1665
The French fight on with rage and fury fell,
They lop off wrists, hew ribs and spines to shreds,
They cleave the harness through to the living flesh;
On the green ground the blood runs clear and red.
[The Paynims say: "We cannot stand the stress,]   1670
French Fatherland, be curst of Máhomet!
Your sons are bravest of all the sons of men."
There's none of them but cries: "Marsile to help!
Ride, ride, O King, for we are hard bested."

127

Roland the Count calls out to Olivere: 1675
"Fair sir, companion, confess that for this gear
Our lord Archbishop quits him like any peer;
Earth cannot match him beneath the heavens' sphere,
Well does he know to handle lance and spear."
The Count replies: "Let's aid him now and here!"   1680
At this the French lay on the lustier,
Hard are their strokes, the fight is very fierce,
And for the Christians the losses are severe.
Who then had seen Roland and Olivere
Smite with their swords and through all the press pierce!   1685
And the Archbishop goes thrusting with his spear.
Of those they slew the numbers are writ clear
In many charters and tales of chroniclers:
More than four thousand as in the Geste appears.
Four great assaults they've borne with right good cheer;   1690
Then comes a fifth, doleful and dread and drear.
All the French knighthood has fallen in career;
Sixty alone by God's grace persevere;
These ere they die will sell their bodies dear.

128

When County Roland sees all his brave men down,   1695
To Oliver his friend he cries aloud:
"For God's sake, comrade, fair sir, what think you now?
See what good knights lie here upon the ground!
Well may we pity this fair sweet France of ours,
Thus left so barren of all her knighthood's flower.   1700
Why aren't you here, O friend and Emperour?
Oliver, brother, what way is to be found?
How send him news of what is come about?"
Oliver said: "And how should I know how?
I'd rather die than we should lose renown."   1705

129

"I'll sound," quoth Roland, "my Olifant straightway;
When Carlon hears, passing through Gate of Spain,
I pledge my word, the French will turn again."
Quoth Oliver: "It would be foul disdain,
And to your kindred the reproach would be great: 1710
All their lives long they'd not live down the shame.
When I desired you, why then you said me nay;
If now you do it, of men you'll get no praise.
Blow if you will—such conduct is not brave.
Nay, but how deep in blood your arms are bathed!"   1715
The Count replies: "I've struck good blows this day."

130

Said Roland then: "Full grievous is this fight.
I'll sound my horn, and Charles will hear the cry."
Quoth Oliver: " 'Twould ill beseem a knight.
I asked you, comrade, and you refused, for pride.   1720
Had Charles been here, then all would have gone right;
He's not to blame, nor the men at his side.
Now by my beard (quoth he) if e'er mine eyes
Again behold my sister Aude the bright,
Between her arms never you think to lie."   1725

131

Quoth Roland: "Why so angry with me, friend?"
And he: "Companion, you got us in this mess.
There is wise valour, and there is recklessness:
Prudence is worth more than fool hardiness.
Through your o'erweening you have destroyed the French;   1730
Ne'er shall we do service to Charles again.
Had you but given some heed to what I said,
My lord had come, the battle had gone well,
And King Marsile had been captured or dead.
Your prowess, Roland, is a curse on our heads.   1735
No more from us will Charlemayn have help,
Whose like till Doomsday shall not be seen of men.
Now you will die, and fair France will be shent;
Our loyal friendship is here brought to an end;
A bitter parting we'll have ere this sun set."   1740

132

When the Archbishop thus hears them in dispute,
With his gold spurs he pricks his steed anew,
Draws near to them and utters this rebuke:
"Lord Oliver, and you, Lord Roland, too,
Let's have no quarrel, o'God's name, 'twixt you two.   1745
It will not save us to sound the horn, that's true;
Nevertheless, 'twere better so to do.

1738. *shent:* put to shame.

Let the king come; his vengeance will be rude;
None shall to Spain ride home with merry news.
After, our French will light them down on foot,   1750
Seek out our bodies and limbs in sunder hewn,
Lay us on biers borne upon sumpter-mules,
And weep for us with grief right pitiful;
In the church-close we shall have burial due,
And not be food for dogs and swine and wolves."   1755
Quoth Roland, "Sir, your words are right and good."

133

Roland has set Olifant to his lips,
Firmly he holds it and blows it with a will.
High are the mountains, the blast is long and shrill,
Thirty great leagues the sound went echoing.   1760
King Carlon heard it and all who rode with him.
"Lo, now, our men are fighting," quoth the King.
Guènes retorts: "If any man said this
Except yourself, it were a lie, methinks."

134

The County Roland with pain and anguish winds   1765
His Olifant, and blows with all his might.
Blood from his mouth comes spurting scarlet-bright
He's burst the veins of his temples outright.
From hand and horn the call goes shrilling high:
King Carlon hears it who through the passes rides,   1770
Duke Naimon hears, and all the French beside.
Quoth Charles: "I hear the horn of Roland cry!
He'd never sound it but in the thick of fight."
"There is no battle," Count Ganelon replies;
"You're growing old, your hair is sere and white,   1775
When you speak thus, you're talking like a child.
Full well you know Roland's o'erweening pride;
'Tis strange that God endures him so long time!
Took he not Noples against your orders quite?
The Paynims made a sally from inside,   1780
And there gave battle to Roland the great knight;
So he swilled down the field—a brave device
To keep the bloodstains from coming to your eyes!
For one small hare he'll blow from morn till night;
Now to the Peers he's showing-off in style.   1785
Who dare attack him? No man beneath the sky!
Ride on, ride on! Why loiter here the while?
Our Fathers' land lies distant many a mile."

135

Count Roland's mouth with running blood is red;
He's burst asunder the temples of his head;   1790
He sounds his horn in anguish and distress.
King Carlon hears, and so do all the French.

Then said the King: "This horn is long of breath."
" 'Tis blown," quoth Naimon, "with all a brave man's strength;
Battle there is, and that I know full well.   1795
He that would stay you is but a traitor fell.
To arms! let sound your battle-cry to heav'n!
Make haste to bring your gallant household help!
You hear how Roland makes desperate lament!"

136

The Emperor Charles lets sound his horns aloft.   1800
The French light down and arm themselves anon
With helm and hauberk and gilded swords girt on;
Goodly their shields, their lances stiff and strong,
Scarlet and white and blue the gonfalons.
Straightway to horse the warrior lords have got;   1805
Swift through the passes they spur and never stop.
Each unto other they speak and make response:
"Might we reach Roland ere he were dead and gone,
We'ld strike good strokes beside him in the throng."
What use is that? They have delayed too long.   1810

137

Vespers draws on and shining is the day;
Against the sun glitters their armed array,
Hauberk and helm flash back a mighty blaze,
So many shields their painted flowers display,
Such store of spears with gilded pennons gay!   1815
The Emperor rides right wrathful on his way.
And all the French in anger and dismay;
There is not one but weeps for very rage;
For Roland's sake they're grievously afraid.
The King arrests Count Ganelon straightway;   1820
He's turned him over to the cooks in his train;
The master-cook he calls, Besgun by name:
"Guard me him well, as fits a man so base,
For all my house this villain has betrayed!"
Besgun takes charge, with five-score kitchen knaves,   1825
The best and worst that serve in that estate.
They pluck the beard from off his chin and face,
With four sound thumps each gives him a good baste,
With sticks and faggots they pound him and they paste,
And round his neck they fasten a strong chain,   1830
Right well they chain him like a bear in a cage;
Now on a pack-horse they've hoisted him in shame;
Till Carlon want him 'tis they will keep him safe.

138

Huge are the hills and shadowy and high,
Deep in the vales the living streams run by.   1835
The trumpets sound before them and behind,
All with one voice to Olifant reply.

In wrath of heart the Emperor Carlon rides,
And all the French in sorrow and in ire;
There's none but grieves and weeps from out his eyes;   1840
They all pray God to safeguard Roland's life
Till they may come to battle by his side;
Once they are with him they'll make it a great fight.
What use is that? their prayers are empty quite,
Too long they've lingered, they cannot come in time.   1845

139
King Charlemayn rides on in anger grim,
Over his byrny flows the white beard of him;
All the French barons beside him spur full swift;
There's none of them but is with fury filled
Not to be aiding Roland the Paladin   1850
Now that he's fighting the Spanish Sarrasins.
He's hurt so sore, I fear he cannot live.
God! and what men, those sixty with him still!
Better had never nor captain nor yet king.

140
Roland surveys the mountains and the fells;   1855
How many French he sees there lying dead!
Like a good knight he makes them this lament:
"Barons, my lords, may God of His largesse
Bring all your souls to Paradise the blest,
Amid bright flowers to make their hallowed beds!   1860
I never saw braver or truer men.
So long you served me unceasingly and well,
So many lands conquered for Carlon's realm!
The Emperor bred you alas! to what sad end!
O dearest land, fair nursery of the French,   1865
By what hard hap art thou this day bereft!
Barons of France, for me you go to death,
Nought can I give you of safeguard or defence;
Now aid you God, who ne'er failed any yet!
Oliver, brother, you shall not lack my help.   1870
Though none should slay me I'll die of grief no less;
Sweet sir, companion, let's go and fight afresh!"

141
The County Roland returns into the field
And like a warrior his Durendal he wields;
Faldron de Puy through the midriff he cleaves   1875
With four-and-twenty besides, of great esteem.
Never on vengeance was any man so keen.
E'en as the deer before the deerhound flees
So before Roland the Paynims show their heels.
Quoth the Archbishop: "Well done, well done indeed!   1880
Valour like this becomes a knight of breed
That bears his arms and sits a goodly steed;

Forward and fierce in battle should he be,
Else he's not worth a single penny-piece.
Best he turn monk in monastery meek   1885
And for our sins pray daily on his knees."
Quoth Roland: "Strike, spare none of them," saith he.
At this the French renew the fight with speed;
Therein the Christians endure great loss and grief.

142

When it is known no prisoners will be made   1890
Men fight back fiercely, and stubborn is the fray;
Therefore the French grow very lions for rage.
Here comes Marsile, e'en as a baron brave,
Riding a horse, and Gaignun is its name.
Full upon Bevon he rides and spurs amain,   1895
That held all Beaune and Dijon for domain.
The shield he shatters, and the hauberk he breaks,
And lays him dead, he need not strike again.
And Ivon next and Ivor too, his mate,
And Gerard too of Roussillon he slays.   1900
Roland the Count, who is not far away,
Cries to the Paynim: "God damn your soul, I say!
These my companions by treason you have slain!
Ere we go hence a bitter price you'll pay,
And you shall learn the name of my good blade!"   1905
He rides to strike him, e'en as a baron brave;
From his sword-arm he shears the hand away.
And Jurfaret the Fair he next waylays,
Marsilion's son, and slices off his pate.
The Paynims cry: "Mahound! Mahound to aid!   1910
Venge us on Carlon, all you gods of our faith!
Into our land he's sent this evil race!
Come life come death they'll never quit the place."
Then one to other cries: "Fly then! fly in haste!"
An hundred thousand have fled the field straightway;   1915
They'll not return, call after them who may.

143

What help is that? Marsile has taken flight,
Yet there remains his uncle Marganice,
That governs Carthage, Alfrere and Garamile,
And Éthiope, a land accursed and vile.   1920
In his command are all the Negro tribes;
Thick are their noses, their ears are very wide;
Full fifty thousand are gathered in their lines,
Boldly and fast and furiously they ride,
Yelling aloud the Paynim battle-cry.   1925
Then Roland said: "Here are we doomed to die;
Full well, I know we cannot long survive.
Fail not for shame, right dear to sell your lives.
Lift up, my lords, your burnished blades and fight!

Come life, come death, the foe shall pay the price,   1930
Lest we should bring fair France into despite!
When on this field Carlon my lord sets eyes
He'll see what toll we've taken of their might:
Fifteen dead Paynims for each of us he'll find;
Nor fail to bless us for this our great emprise."   1935

144

When Roland looks on these accursed tribesmen—
As black as ink from head to foot their hides are,
With nothing white about them but their grinders—
Then said the Count: " 'Tis true beyond denial,
Right well I know it, this day shall death betide us.   1940
I'll to the throng; Frenchmen, fight on beside me!"
Quoth Oliver: "The devil take the hindmost!"
The French hear this and once more fall a-fighting.

145

When Paynims see how few the French are grown
They plume themselves, puffed up with pride and hope: 1945
"Now to the Emperor," they say, "his crimes come home!"
Marganice comes, riding a sorrel colt;
He spurs him hard with rowels all of gold,
And from behind deals Oliver a blow;
Deep in his back the burnished mail is broke,   1950
That the spear's point stands forth at his breast bone.
He saith to him: "You've suffered a sore stroke;
Charlemayn sent you to the pass for your woe.
Foul wrong he did us, 'tis good he lose his boast:
I've well requited our loss on you alone."   1955

146

Oliver feels that he is hurt to death;
He grasps his sword Hauteclaire the keen of edge,
Smites Marganice on his high golden helm,
Shearing away the flowers and crystal gems,
Down to the teeth clean splits him through the head,   1960
Shakes loose the blade and flings him down and dead;
Then saith: "Foul fall you, accursèd Paynim wretch!
Charles has had losses, so much I will confess:
But ne'er shall you, back to the land you left,
To dame or damsel return to boast yourself   1965
That e'er you spoiled me to the tune of two pence,
Or made your profit of me or other men."
This done, to Roland he cries aloud for help.

147

Oliver feels he's wounded mortally;
His thirst for vengeance can never glutted be.   1970
Amid the press he strikes right valiantly;
He breaks asunder the spear-shaft and the shield,
Splits chines and saddles and lops off hands and feet.

1935. *emprise*: enterprise, feat of arms.

Whoso had seen him hew Paynims piece from piece,
Throw one on other their bodies down in heaps, 1975
Might well remember that flower of knightly deeds!
And Carlon's war-cry he fails not to repeat,
But still "Mountjoy!" goes shouting loud and clear.
He calls to Roland his comrade and his peer:
"Sir, my companion, draw nigh and stand with me; 1980
We must this day be parted to our grief."

148

Oliver's face, when Roland on him looks,
Is grey and ghastly, discoloured, wan with wounds,
His bright blood sprays his body head to foot;
Down to the ground it runs from him in pools. 1985
"God!" says the Count, "I know not what to do!
Fair sir, companion, woe worth your mighty mood!—
Ne'er shall be seen a man to equal you.
Alas, fair France! what valiant men and true
Must thou bewail this day, cast down and doomed! 1990
Bitter the loss the Emperor has to rue!"
So much he says, and in the saddle swoons.

149

See Roland now swooning in saddle laid,
And Oliver that unto death is maimed;
He's bled so much that his eyes are all glazed, 1995
Or far or near he can see nothing straight,
Nor recognize a single living shape;
So when he comes to where his comrade waits,
On the gold helm he smites at him amain,
Down to the nasal he splits the jewelled plates, 2000
Only his head is not touched by the blade.
Then Roland, stricken, lifts his eyes to his face,
Asking him low and mildly as he may:
"Sir, my companion, did you mean it that way?
Look, I am Roland, that loved you all my days; 2005
You never sent me challenge or battle-gage."
Quoth Oliver: "I cannot see you plain;
I know your voice; may God see you and save.
And I have struck you; pardon it me, I pray."
Roland replies: "I have taken no scathe; 2010
I pardon you, myself and in God's name."
Then each to other bows courteous in his place.
With such great love thus is their parting made.

150

Oliver feels the coming pangs of death;
Both of his eyes are turning in his head, 2015
Now he is blind wholly, and wholly deaf.

2005. *challenge or battle-gage:* Roland
wonders whether Oliver is still angry
with him, but cannot believe that he
would bear arms against him without
having sent him a formal challenge, accompanied by the usual token of defiance.

He lights from horse and to his knees he gets
And makes confession aloud, and beats his breast,
Then clasps his hands and lifts them up to Heav'n;
In Paradise he prays God give him rest,   2020
And France the Fair and Carlon prays Him bless,
And his companion Roland above all men.
His heart-strings crack, he stoops his knightly helm,
And sinks to earth, and lies there all his length.
Dead is the Count, his days have reached their end.   2025
The valiant Roland weeps for him and laments,
No man on earth felt ever such distress.

151

When Roland sees his friend and comrade die,
And on the ground face down beholds him lie,
With tender words he bids him thus goodbye: 2030
"Sir, my companion, woe worth your valiant might!
Long years and days have we lived side by side,
Ne'er didst thou wrong me nor suffer wrong of mine.
Now thou art dead I grieve to be alive."
Having thus said, the Marquis swoons outright   2035
On his steed's back, that Veillantif is hight;
He's kept from falling by the gold stirrups bright;
Go as he may, then hold him still upright.

152

Or ever Roland comes to himself again
And has recovered and rallied from his faint,   2040
Fearful disaster his fortunes have sustained;
All of the French are lost to him and slain;
Sole, the Archbishop and Walter Hum remain.
Walter has come down from the heights again;
Well has he striven against the men of Spain,   2045
His men are dead, mown down by Paynim blades;
Will he or nill he, he flees towards the vale,
And upon Roland he cries aloud for aid:
"Where art thou, where, great county, warrior brave?
While thou wast there I never was dismayed.   2050
Walter am I, who Maëlgut o'ercame,
Nephew am I to Droön white with age;
Thou for my valour wast wont to love me aye!
My lance is shattered, my shield is split in twain,
Battered and broken is my hauberk of mail,   2055
A spear has pierced me [through the midst of my reins;]
Death is upon me, yet dear I made them pay."
Lo! at that word Roland hears him and wakes;
He spurs his horse and comes to him in haste.

153

Roland is filled with grief and anger sore;   2060
In the thick press he now renews his war.

2035. *marquis:* The title means "lord of the marches" (see note on l. 843). Roland was Lord of the Marches of Brittany.

Of those of Spain he's overthrown a score,
And Walter six, the Archbishop five more.
The Paynims say: "These men are worst of all!
Let none escape alive; look to it, lords!   2065
Who fears the onset, let shame be his reward!
Who lets these go, may he be put to scorn!"
Then once again the hue and cry breaks forth;
From every side pour in the Paynim hordes.

154

The County Roland is mighty of his mood,   2070
Walter de Hum well-famed for knightlihood,
And the Archbishop a warrior tried and proved;
Betwixt their valours there's not a pin to choose.
In the thick press they smite the Moorish crew.
A thousand Paynims dismount to fight on foot,   2075
And forty thousand horsemen they have, to boot,
Yet 'gainst these three, my troth! they fear to move.
They hurl against them their lances from aloof,
Javelins, jereeds, darts, shafts and spears they loose.
In the first shock brave Walter meets his doom.   2080
Turpin of Rheims has his shield split in two,
His helm is broken, his head has ta'en a wound,
His hauberk's pierced, the mail-rings burst and strewn,
By four sharp spears his breast is stricken through,
Killed under him his horse rolls neck and croup;   2085
Th'Archbishop's down, woe worth the bitter dule.

155

Turpin of Rheims, finding himself o'erset,
With four sharp lance-heads stuck fast within his breast,
Quickly leaps up, brave lord, and stands erect.
He looks on Roland and runs to him and says   2090
Only one word: "I am not beaten yet!
True man failed never while life in him was left."
He draws Almace, his steel-bright brand keen-edged;
A thousand strokes he strikes amid the press.
Soon Charles shall see he spared no foe he met,   2095
For all about him he'll find four hundred men,
Some wounded, some clean through the body cleft,
And some of them made shorter by the head.
So tells the Geste; so he that fought there tells:
The worthy Giles, whom God with marvels blessed,   2100
In Laön minster thus-wise the charter penned;
Who knows not this knows nought of what befel.

156

The County Roland fights bravely as he may,
But his whole body in heat and sweat is bathed,
And all his head is racked with grievous pain   2105
From that great blast which brake his temples' veins.

2086. *dule:* grief.
2100. *the worthy Giles:* St. Giles, who
had a hermitage in Provence, and became
the hero of many legends.

Fain would he know if Charles is bringing aid;
His Olifant he grasps, and blows full faint.
The Emperor halts, hearing the feeble strain:
"My lords," quoth he, "this tells a woeful tale;   2110
Roland my nephew is lost to us this day,
That call proclaims his breath is nigh to fail.
Whoso would reach him must ride with desperate haste
Sound through the host! bid every trumpet play!"
Full sixty thousand so loud their clarions bray   2115
The hills resound, the valleys ring again.
The Paynims hear, no lust to laugh have they:
"We'll soon have Charles to reckon with," they say.

157

The Paynims say: "The Emperor's turned about;
Of those of France hark how the trumpets sound!   2120
If Carlon comes, we shall have rack and rout,
If Roland lives, once more he'll war us down,
We shall not keep one foot of Spanish ground."
Straightway four hundred helmed warriors rally round,
The finest fighters that in the field are found;   2125
A fearful onslaught they'll make upon the Count;
Truly Lord Roland has got his work cut out.

158

Whenas Count Roland sees their assault begin,
Right fierce he makes him, and strong and menacing;
While life is in him he'll never quail or quit.   2130
He sits his horse that is named Veillantif,
Into his flanks the golden spurs he pricks
And sets upon them where most the press is thick.
The Lord Archbishop, brave Turpin, rides with him.
Paynim to paynim cries: "Comrade, go to it!   2135
Have we not heard the Frankish trumpets ring?
Charles is returning, the great, the mighty king!"

159

The County Roland ne'er loved a recreant,
Nor a false heart, nor yet a braggart jack,
Nor knight that was not a good man of his hands.   2140
He cried to Turpin, the Churchman militant,
"Sir, you're on foot, I'm on my horse's back;
For love of you here will I make my stand,
And side by side we'll take both good and bad.
I'll not desert you for any mortal man.   2145
Go we together these Paynims to attack;
The mightiest blows are those of Durendal."
Quoth the Archbishop: " 'Twere shame our strokes to slack;
Carlon is coming, our vengeance shall not lack."

160

The Paynims say: "Why were we ever born?   2150
Woe worth the while! our day of doom has dawned.

Now have we lost our peerage and our lords,
The mighty Carlon comes on with all his force,
Of those of France we hear the shrilling horns,
The cry "Mountjoy!" sounds fearfully abroad.   2155
So grim of mood is Roland in his wrath
No man alive can put him to the sword.
Let fly at him, and then give up the war."
So they let fly; spears, lances they outpour,
Darts and jereeds and feathered shafts galore.   2160
The shield of Roland is pierced and split and scored,
The mail-rings riven, and all his hauberk torn,
Yet in his body he is not touched at all,
Though under him, with thirty wounds and more,
His Veillantif is stricken dead and falls.   2165
The Paynims flee, abandoning the war;
Count Roland's left amid the field, unhorsed.

161

In wrath and grief away the Paynims fly;
Backward to Spain with headlong haste they hie.
The County Roland cannot pursue their flight,   2170
Veillantif's lost, he has no steed to ride;
Will he or nill he, he must on foot abide,
He's turned to aid Archbishop Turpin's plight,
And from his head the gilded helm untied,
Stripped off the hauberk of subtle rings and bright,   2175
And all to pieces has cut the bliaut fine
Wherewith to bandage his wounds that gape so wide.
Then to his breast he clasps and lifts him light
And gently lays him upon the green hill-side,
With fair soft speech entreating on this wise: 2180
"Ah, noble sir, pray give me leave awhile;
These friends of ours, we loved so well in life,
We must not leave them thus lying where they died.
I will go seek them, find, and identify,
And lay them here together in your sight."   2185
"Go and return," the Bishop makes reply;
"Thanks be to God, this field is yours and mine."

162

Roland departs and through the field is gone;
Alone he searches the valleys and high rocks.
[And there he finds Ivor, and there Ivon],   2190
Gerier and Gerin, the good companions,
[And Engelier whom Gascony begot];
And he has found Berenger and Oton,
And after finds Anseïs and Samson,
And finds Gerard the Old, of Roussillon.   2195
He lifts them up, brave baron, one by one,
To the Archbishop he carries them anon,
And by his knees ranges them all along.
The Bishop weeps, he cannot stint thereof;

He lifts his hand and gives them benison,   2200
And after saith: "Alack, brave champions!
May your souls rest with the all-glorious God
In Paradise, amid the rose-blossoms.
I too am dying and sorrow for my lot,
Who the great Emperor no more may look upon."   2205

163

Roland once more unto the field repairs,
And has sought out his comrade Oliver.
Close to his breast he lifts him, and with care
As best he may to the Archbishop bears
And on his shield lays with the others there;   2210
The Bishop signs and shrives them all with prayer.
With tears renewed their sorrow is declared,
And Roland saith: "Fair fellow Oliver,
You were own son unto Duke Renier
That held the marches of the Vale of Runers.   2215
To shatter shield or break lance anywhere,
And from their seat proud men to overbear,
And cheer the brave with words of counsel fair,
And bring the cruel to ruin and despair,
No knight on earth was valiant as you were."   2220

164

The County Roland, seeing his peers lie dead,
And Oliver, who was his dearest friend,
Begins to weep for ruth and tenderness;
Out of his cheeks the colour all has fled,
He cannot stand, he is so deep distressed,   2225
He swoons to earth, he cannot help himself.
"Alas, for pity, sweet lord!" the Bishop saith.

165

When the Archbishop saw Roland faint and fallen,
So sad was he, he never had been more so;
He reaches out; he's taken Roland's horn up.   2230
In Ronceval there runs a stream of water;
Fain would he go there and fetch a little for him.
With feeble steps he turns him thither, falt'ring;
He is so weak, that he cannot go forward,
For loss of blood he has no strength to call on.   2235
Ere one might cover but a rood's length in walking
His heart has failed him, he has fallen face-foremost;
The pangs of death have seized him with great torment.

166

The County Roland has rallied from his faint,
Gets to his feet, though he's in grievous pain,   2240
And looks about him over hill, over vale.
Beyond his comrades, upon the grass-green plain,
There he beholds the noble baron laid,

The great Archbishop, vice-gerent of God's name.
He beats his breast with eyes devoutly raised,   2245
With folded hands lifted to Heaven he prays
That God will give him in Paradise a place.
Turpin is dead that fought for Charlemayn;
In mighty battles, and in preaching right brave,
Still against Paynims a champion of the Faith;   2250
Blest mote he be, the Lord God give him grace!

167

The County Roland sees the Archbishop lie;
He sees his bowels gush forth out of his side
And on his brow the brain laid bare to sight.
Midst of his breast where the key-bones divide,   2255
Crosswise he lays his comely hands and white,
And thus laments him as native use requires:
"Ah, debonair, thou good and noble knight!
Now I commend thee to the great Lord of might,
Servant more willing than thee He shall not find.   2260
Since the Apostles no prophet was thy like,
For to maintain the Faith, and win mankind.
May thy soul meet no hindrance in her flight!
May Heaven's gate to her stand open wide!"

168

Now Roland feels that he is at death's door;   2265
Out of his ears the brain is running forth.
Now for his peers he prays God call them all,
And for himself St Gabriel's aid implores;
Then in each hand he takes, lest shame befall,
His Olifant and Durendal his sword.   2270
Far as a quarrel flies from a cross-bow drawn,
Toward land of Spain he goes, to a wide lawn,
And climbs a mound where grows a fair tree tall,
And marble stones beneath it stand by four.
Face downward there on the green grass he falls,   2275
And swoons away, for he is at death's door.

169

High are the hills and very high the trees are;
Four stones there are set there, of marble gleaming.
The County Roland lies senseless on the greensward.
A Saracen is there, watching him keenly;   2280
He has feigned death, and lies among his people,
And has smeared blood upon his breast and features.
Now he gets up and runs towards him fleetly;
Strong was he, comely and of valour exceeding.
Now in his rage and in his overweening   2285
He falls on Roland, his arms and body seizing;
He saith one word: "Now Carlon's nephew's beaten.

2274. *marble stones:* probably posts such as were used to mark a frontier.

I'll take his sword, to Araby I'll reive it."
But as he draws it Roland comes to, and feels him.

170

Roland has felt his good sword being stol'n;   2290
Opens his eyes and speaks this word alone:
"Thou'rt none of ours, in so far as I know."
He takes his horn, of which he kept fast hold,
And smites the helm, which was all gemmed with gold;
He breaks the steel and the scalp and the bone,   2295
And from his head batters his eyes out both,
And dead on ground he lays the villain low;
Then saith: "False Paynim, and how wast thou so bold,
Foully or fairly, to seize upon me so?
A fool he'll think thee who hears this story told.   2300
Lo, now! the mouth of my Olifant's broke;
Fallen is all the crystal and the gold."

171

Now Roland feels his sight grow dim and weak;
With his last strength he struggles to his feet;
All the red blood has faded from his cheeks.   2305
A grey stone stands before him at his knee:
Ten strokes thereon he strikes, with rage and grief;
It grides, but yet nor breaks nor chips the steel.
"Ah!" cries the Count, "St Mary succour me!
Alack the Day, Durendal, good and keen!   2310
Now I am dying, I cannot fend for thee.
How many battles I've won with you in field!
With you I've conquered so many goodly fiefs
That Carlon holds, the lord with the white beard!
Let none e'er wield you that from the foe would flee—   2315
You that were wielded so long by a good liege!
The like of you blest France shall never see."

172

Count Roland smites the sardin stone amain.
The steel grides loud, but neither breaks nor bates.
Now when he sees that it will nowise break   2320
Thus to himself he maketh his complaint:
"Ah, Durendal! so bright, so brave, so gay!
How dost thou glitter and shine in the sun's rays!
When Charles was keeping the vales of Moriane,
God by an angel sent to him and ordained   2325
He should bestow thee on some count-capitayne.
On me he girt thee, the noble Charlemayn.
With this I won him Anjou and all Bretayn,
With this I won him Poitou, and conquered Maine;
With this I won him Normandy's fair terrain,   2330
And with it won Provence and Acquitaine,
And Lombardy and all the land Romayne,

2288. *reive*: steal away.

Bavaria too, and the whole Flemish state,
And Burgundy and all Apulia gained;
Constantinople in the King's hand I laid;   2335
In Saxony he speaks and is obeyed;
With this I won Scotland, [Ireland and Wales,]
And England, where he set up his domain;
What lands and countries I've conquered by its aid,
For Charles to keep whose beard is white as may!   2340
Now am I grieved and troubled for my blade;
Should Paynims get it, 'twere worse than all death's pains.
Dear God forbid it should put France to shame!"

173

Count Roland smites upon the marble stone;
I cannot tell you how he hewed it and smote;   2345
Yet the blade breaks not nor splinters, though it groans;
Upward to heaven it rebounds from the blow.
When the Count sees it never will be broke,
Then to himself right softly he makes moan:
"Ah, Durendal, fair, hallowed, and devote,   2350
What store of relics lie in thy hilt of gold!
St Peter's tooth, St Basil's blood, it holds,
Hair of my lord St Denis, there enclosed,
Likewise a piece of Blessed Mary's robe;
To Paynim hands 'twere sin to let you go;   2355
You should be served by Christian men alone,
Ne'er may you fall to any coward soul!
Many wide lands I conquered by your strokes
For Charles to keep whose beard is white as snow,
Whereby right rich and mighty is his throne."   2360

174

Now Roland feels death press upon him hard;
It's creeping down from his head to his heart.
Under a pine-tree he hastens him apart,
There stretches him face down on the green grass,
And lays beneath him his sword and Olifant.   2365
He's turned his head to where the Paynims are,
And this he doth for the French and for Charles,
Since fain is he that they should say, brave heart,
That he has died a conqueror at the last.
He beats his breast full many a time and fast,   2370
Gives, with his glove, his sins into God's charge.

175

Now Roland feels his time is at an end;
On the steep hill-side, toward Spain he's turned his head,
And with one hand he beats upon his breast;
Saith: "*Mea culpa*; Thy mercy, Lord, I beg   2375
For all the sins, both the great and the less,

2337. The text is corrupt; but either Ireland or Wales is certainly intended, and possibly both.

That e'er I did since first I drew my breath
Unto this day when I'm struck down by death."
His right-hand glove he unto God extends;
Angels from Heaven now to his side descend.   2380

176

The County Roland lay down beneath a pine;
To land of Spain he's turned him as he lies,
And many things begins to call to mind:
All the broad lands he conquered in his time,
And fairest France, and the men of his line,   2385
And Charles his lord, who bred him from a child;
He cannot help but weep for them and sigh.
Yet of himself he is mindful betimes;
He beats his breast and on God's mercy cries:
"Father most true, in whom there is no lie,   2390
Who didst from death St Lazarus make to rise,
And bring out Daniel safe from the lions' might,
Save Thou my soul from danger and despite
Of all the sins I did in all my life."
His right-hand glove he's tendered unto Christ,   2395
And from his hand Gabriel accepts the sign.
Straightway his head upon his arm declines;
With folded hands he makes an end and dies.
God sent to him His Angel Cherubine,
And great St Michael of Peril-by-the-Tide;   2400
St. Gabriel too was with them at his side;
The County's soul they bear to Paradise.

2396–97. *the sign:* the glove is offered and accepted in token of Roland's
surrender to God of the life which he
holds as a fief from Him.

2399. *Cherubine:* "Cherubin" seems to
be used by the poet as the name of an
individual angel.

Aucassin and Nicolette (Aucassin et Nicolete)*

I

He who wants to hear good rhyme
Of the sport in ancient time
Of two children, young and sweet,
Aucassin and Nicolette,
Of the pains that he endured,
Of the noble deeds he did
For his love with clearest face.
Lovely the song, sweet the tale,
Courteous and well-disposed.

* Translated by Edward Francis
Moyer and Carey DeWitt Eldridge.   Copyright, 1937, by Robert Linker. Reprinted by permission.

> No man can be so oppressed,
> So cast down and comfortless,
> Burdened down with heaviness,
> Who will not be, hearing this,
> Cured, restored to joyfulness,
>> It is so sweet.

II

Now they tell and relate and continue the tale

That Count Bougars de Valence was making war on Count Garin de Beaucaire, so great and so marvelous and so mortal, that not a single day dawned that he was not at the gates and at the walls and at the barriers of the town with a hundred knights and ten thousand soldiers on foot and on horse; and he burned his land and wasted his country and killed his men.

Count Garin de Beaucaire was old and frail and had outlived his time. He had no heir, neither son nor daughter, except a single boy, who was such as I shall tell you.

Aucassin was the name of the lad. Handsome he was and shapely and large and well formed in legs and feet and in body and in arms. His hair was blond and tightly curled, and his eyes were gray and laughing, and his face clear and slender, and his nose high and well placed. He was so endowed with good points that there was in him nothing bad, or that was not good. But he was so overtaken by love which conquers all, that he didn't want to be a knight, or to take arms, or go into the tourney, or do anything at all which he ought to have done.

His father and his mother used to say to him, "Son, take up your arms, get on your horse, defend your land, and aid your men. If they see you among them, they will defend better their bodies and their goods, and your land and mine."

"Father," said Aucassin, "what are you talking about now? Never may God give me anything I ask of him, if as a knight I mount my horse, or go into the fray or battle, there where I may strike a knight or others strike me, if you do not give me Nicolette, my sweet love, whom I love so much."

"Son," said the father, "that could not be. You let Nicolette alone since she is a slave-girl who was brought from a foreign land. The viscount of this town bought her from the Saracens and brought her to this town. And he has reared her and baptized her and has made her his god-daughter. So will he give her one of these days to some young man who will earn bread for her with honor. You have nothing to do with all this. If you wish to have a wife, I will give you the daughter of a king or of a count. There is no man in France so rich that if you wish for his daughter you shall not have her."

"Look here, Father," said Aucassin, "where is there such high honor on the earth that if Nicolette, my very sweet love, had it, it wouldn't be well placed in her? If she were Empress of Constantinople or of Germany, or Queen of France or of England, it would be little enough for her, so noble she is, and courtly, and of good manner, and the acme of all good qualities."

III

Now it is sung

> Aucassin lived in Beaucaire;
> Well-built was his castle there.
> Nicolette, of form so fair,
> From her no man could tear him;
> His father tried to scare him,
> And his mother threatened him,
> "Scamp, what do you want to do?
> Nicolette is trim and gay
> But from Carthage cast away;
> From the pagans she was bought.
> Since you want to take a wife,
> Take a wife of high degree."
> "Mother, those wives don't please me.
> Nicolette is debonair,
> Form so sweet and face so clear;
> My heart jumps when she is near.
> Why can't I enjoy her love?
> It is too sweet."

IV

Now they tell and relate and continue the tale

When Count Garin de Beaucaire saw that he would not be able to turn his son away from the love of Nicolette, he went to the viscount of the town, who was in his service; so did he speak to him.

"Sir Count, get rid of Nicolette, your god-daughter. Cursed be the land from which she was brought to this country! For because of her, I lose Aucassin, who does not want to become a knight, or do any of the things he ought to do. And know well that if I could have her, I would burn her in a fire, and you might well have great fear for yourself."

"Sire," said the Viscount, "much does it trouble me that he goes and comes and that he speaks to her. I bought her with my money; so have I reared her and baptized her and made her my god-daughter. And I would have given her to some young man who would have earned bread for her with honor. With this your son, Aucassin, would have had nothing to do. But since it is your will and your pleasure, I will send her to such a land and to such a country that never again will he set eyes upon her."

"Take care that you do it," said Count Garin, "for great evil may come to you from it."

Each went his own way. Now the Viscount was a very, very rich man, and he had a rich palace looking on a garden. In a room in it he had Nicolette placed, high in the tower, and an old woman with her for company and to take care of her. And he had bread and meat and wine brought there and whatever they might need. Then he had the door sealed up so that none might be able, in any way, to go in or come out, except that, opening on the garden, there was one window, quite small, through which there came to them a little fresh air.

v

Now it is sung

> Nicolette in prison put;
> She's in a vaulted chamber
> Fashioned with the greatest skill
> And marvelously painted.
> On the marble window frame
> There the wretched maiden leans.
> Now her hair was blond as grain,
> And her eyebrows were well shaped,
> Clear and slender was her face,
> Never was there fairer seen.
> Toward the forest she looked out
> And saw the roses swelling,
> Heard the birds which twittered there;
> Then the orphan maid cried out,
> "Wretched captive, woe is me!
> Why am I in prison put?
> Aucassin, my youthful lord,
> I am still your own sweetheart
> And by you I'm not abhorred.
> For you I'm a prisoner
> Within this vaulted chamber.
> Now my life is very hard;
> But, by God, sweet Mary's son,
> I will not stay longer here
> If I can get out."

vi

Now they tell and relate and continue the tale

Nicolette was in prison, just as you have heard and understood, in the chamber. The cry and the rumor went through all the land

and through all the country that Nicolette was lost. Some said that she had fled out of the country, and others said that Count Garin de Beaucaire had had her murdered. Whoever else had joy of it, Aucassin was not glad. He went to the viscount of the town, so did he address him:

"Sir Viscount, what have you done with Nicolette, my very sweet love, for there is nothing in all the world that I love more? Have you stolen her away from me? Know well that if I die of it, payment will be demanded of you; and that will be very right, for you will have slain me with your two hands, for you have taken from me the thing which I love most in this world."

"Fair lord," said the Viscount, "now stay out of this. Nicolette is a captive whom I brought from a strange land, so did I buy her with my wealth from the Saracens. And I have reared her and baptized her and made her my god-daughter; so have I nourished her. And I should have given her one of these days to a young man who should earn bread for her with honor. With this you have nothing to do. Instead, take the daughter of a king or a count. Moreover, what would you think to have gained if you had made her your mistress and put her in your bed? Little indeed would you have won, for all the days of the world your soul would be in Hell because of it, for into Paradise you could never enter."

"What would I be doing in Paradise? I don't want to enter there, but only to have Nicolette, my very sweet love, whom I love so much. For to Paradise go only such people as I shall tell you of: the old priests, the old cripples and maimed ones who, all night and all day, drag themselves before the altars and in the old crypts, and those who wear old worn-out clothes and are dressed in tattered rags, who are naked and without shoes and stockings, and dying of hunger and thirst and of cold and of misery. These go to Paradise. I have nothing to do with them. But to Hell I wish indeed to go; for to Hell go the handsome clerics, and the fine knights who have died in the tourneys and in great wars, and the good soldiers and the brave men; with them I do wish to go. There, also, go the fair and courteous ladies who have two or three lovers besides their husbands. And there go the gold and silver and miniver and gray furs. There, also, go the harpers and the jongleurs, and the kings of the world. With them do I wish to go—provided that I have Nicolette, my very sweet love, with me."

"Surely," said the Viscount, "your speaking gets you nowhere, for you shall never see her. And if you were to speak to her and your father knew it, he would burn both me and her in a fire, and you might well fear for yourself."

"That's what worries me," said Aucassin, and filled with grief he left the viscount.

Now it is sung

> Aucassin has turned away
> Very sad and all downcast;
> For his love with clearest face
> No one now can comfort him,
> Neither give him good advice.
> Toward the palace has he gone;
> He has mounted up the steps.
> In a chamber has he come,
> So did he begin to weep
> And to sigh in deepest grief,
> Lamenting his lost sweetheart.
> "Nicolette, how sweet you were,
> Sweet to come and sweet to go,
> Sweet to play and sweet to say,
> Sweet to tease and sweet to please,
> Sweet to kiss and sweet to squeeze.
> I for you am all cast down
> And am so badly treated
> That I think I'll leave this life,
> > Sister, sweet love."

Now they tell and relate and continue the tale

While Aucassin was in his chamber mourning for Nicolette his love, Count Bougars de Valence, who had his war to maintain, was in no way forgetting it. He had sent forward his horsemen and foot soldiers, and he then directed himself toward the castle to assail it. And a cry arose and a disturbance, and the knights and the soldiers armed themselves and ran to the gates and to the walls to defend the castle, and the bourgeois went up the passage-ways in the walls and threw down rocks and sharpened stakes. While the assault was great and in full swing, the Count Garin de Beaucaire came to the chamber where Aucassin was grieving and mourning Nicolette, his very sweet love, whom he loved so much.

"Ha! Son," said he, "how very weak and wretched you are, that you watch while they assault the best and strongest of all castles. And know that if you lose it, you are disinherited. Come on, Son, take up your arms, and mount your horse and defend your land, and aid your men, and go into the battle. You need never strike a man there, nor let another strike you; yet if they see you among them, they will defend better their goods and their bodies and your land and mine. You are so big and so strong that you can easily do it, and you ought to do it."

"Father," said Aucassin, "what are you talking about now? May God give me nothing of what I ask of him if I play the knight or mount on a horse or go into the battle, where I may strike some knights, or be struck by others, unless you give me Nicolette, my sweet love, whom I love so much."

"Son," said the father, "that can't be done; rather would I suffer that I should be entirely dispossessed and that I should lose all that I have than that you should ever have her for your wife or for your bride."

He turned away, and when Aucassin saw him about to go, he called him back.

"Father," said Aucassin, "come back, I will make a good bargain with you."

"Such as what, my fine son?"

"I will take up arms and go into the battle on your promise that, if God brings me back safe and sound, you will let me see Nicolette, my sweet love, long enough to have two or three words with her, and that I may kiss her one single time."

"I grant it," said the father.

He gave him his word, and Aucassin was glad.

IX

Now it is sung

Aucassin a kiss will have
If he should return alive;
For a hundred thousand marks
He would not be half so glad.
He demanded armor bright;
Servants clothed him as a knight.
Double hauberk he put on,
Laced his helmet on his head,
Girt his sword with golden hilt,
And on his charger mounted.
Then he took his shield and spear,
Cast a glance down at his feet.
In his stirrups well they sat;
High he holds his head aloft.
He remembers his sweet love.
Forward then he spurs his horse;
Willingly he takes his course.
Right up to the gate he goes
    To the battle.

X

Now they tell and relate

Aucassin was armed and on his horse, as you have heard and understood. God, how becoming the shield was at his neck and the helmet on his head and the belt of his sword on his left hip. The lad was big and strong and handsome and noble and well turned out, and the horse which he rode, quick and rapid; and the lad had ridden him straight through the middle of the gate.

Now don't you believe that he was thinking of taking oxen or cows or goats, or that he would strike some knight or another strike him. Nothing like that! Not once did it occur to him. But he thought so much of Nicolette, his sweet love, that he forgot the reins and all that he had to do. And the horse that had felt the spurs carried him into the thick of the battle and hurled him right into the midst of his enemies. They grabbed him from all sides; so did they take him. And they relieved him of his shield and lance; so did they quickly lead him away a prisoner. And they went along, already considering what death they would make him die.

And when Aucassin heard them:

"Ah, God," said he, "sweet creature! Are these my mortal enemies who are holding me here, and who now will cut off my head? And after my head is cut off, never will I speak to Nicolette, my sweet love, whom I love so much. Yet I have here a good sword, and I'm riding a good fresh war-horse. If now I don't defend myself for her sake, never may God help her if she loves me any more."

The lad was big and strong, and the horse on which he sat was lively. And he snatched his sword and began to strike right and left and cut through helmets and nose-pieces and fists and arms and made a slaughter round about him, like the wild boar when the dogs attack him in the forest. And so did he strike down ten knights and wound seven, and rode quickly out of the thick of things. So did he come galloping back, sword in hand.

The Count Bougars de Valence heard them say that they were going to hang Aucassin, his enemy, and he came to that place, and Aucassin did not mistake him. He took his sword in hand and whacked down on the helmet so that it went down over his head. He was so stunned that he fell onto the ground. And Aucassin put out his hand, took him and led him along by the nose-guard of his helmet, and handed him over to his father.

"Father," said Aucassin, "look, here is your enemy who for so long has made war on you and done harm; this war has lasted for twenty years and never could it be ended by anyone."

"Fair son," said the father, "you ought to do these youthful deeds and not chase after foolishness."

"Father," said Aucassin, "don't you go making sermons to me, but keep your promises to me."

"Bah! What promises, fair son?"

"What, Father, have you forgotten them? By my head, whoever else forgets them, I don't want to forget them, so close I hold them to my heart. Didn't you make an agreement with me that if I took up arms and went into battle and if God brought me back safe and sound, you would let me see Nicolette, my sweet love, long enough to have two or three words with her? And didn't you make an agreement that I might kiss her one time? I want you to keep this promise to me."

"I?" said the father. "May God never aid me if I keep faith with you in this. And if she were here now, I would burn her in a fire, and you, yourself, might well be afraid."

"Is this your last word?" asked Aucassin.

"So help me God," said the father, "yes!"

"Well," said Aucassin, "very, very much do I grieve when a man of your age is a liar."

"Count de Valence," said Aucassin, "I took you a prisoner."

"You surely did, sir," said the count.

"Give me your hand on it," said Aucassin.

"Willingly, sir." And he put his hand in his.

"Now swear to me," said Aucassin, "that, any day as long as you live, should you be able to do dishonor or destruction to my father, either in his person or his property, you won't fail to do it.

"Sir, for God's sake," said he, "don't mock me, but set a ransom on me. You will not be able to ask of me gold, or silver, horses or palfreys, miniver or gray fur, or hounds or birds, that I will not give you."

"What?" said Aucassin. "Don't you know that I have taken you prisoner?"

"Oh yes, sir," said the Count Bougars.

"If you do not swear it to me," said Aucassin, "may God never help me if I do not send your head flying now."

"In the name of God," he said, "I'll swear to whatever you please."

So he swore, and Aucassin made him mount on a horse, and he mounted another and led him back until he was in safety.

XI

Now it is sung

Now when sees the Count Garin
That his offspring Aucassin
Cannot tear himself away
From the clear-faced Nicolette,
In a cell he had him set,
In a prison underground,
Which was made of marble dark.
Now when Aucassin came there
He was sadder than before.

If you wish, you now may hear
What lamenting he began:
"Nicolette, sweet fleur-le-lis,
Sweet love with the clearest face,
Sweeter than a bunch of grapes,
Sweeter than the wine bowl's sop.
One time I saw a pilgrim
Who was born in Limousin,
With the palsy nearly dead;
Thus he lay upon his bed.
A sick man he was indeed,
Stricken with a dread disease.
When you passed before his bed,
Then you lifted up your skirt,
And your coat with ermine lined,
Your chemise of linen white,
Until he could see your leg.
Straightway was the pilgrim cured
More than he had ever been.
Then he jumped up from his bed;
To his country he returned,
Safe and sound, completely cured.
O sweet love, sweet fleur-de-lis,
Sweet to kiss, sweet to embrace,
Sweet to come and sweet to go,
Sweet to say and sweet to play,
Sweet to please and sweet to squeeze,
No man could ever hate you.
Yet for your sake I am here
In this prison underground
Where I make a dismal end.
Now I ought to kill myself
　　　For you, my love."

XII

Now they tell and relate and continue the tale

Aucassin was put in prison, as you have heard and understood, and Nicolette was elsewhere in her chamber. This was in the summertime, in the month of May, when the days are hot and long and clear and the nights still and serene.

Nicolette lay one night in her bed, and she saw the moon shine clear through a window, and she heard the nightingale singing in the garden; so did she recall Aucassin, her love whom she loved to much. She began to reflect about Count Garin de Beaucaire, who hated her to death. So did she think that she would remain there no longer; for, if she were discovered and Count Garin heard about it, he would make her die an evil death. She perceived that the old woman who was with her was sleeping. She got up and put on a good chemise of cloth of silk that she had, and she took her bed-clothes and towels, and tied them one to another and made a cord as long as she could. This she tied to the pillar of the window; so did she slide down into the garden. She took the front of her dress with one hand and the back with the other and raised it close about her, because of the dew which she saw heavy upon the grass, and so she made off down the garden.

She had blond hair tightly curled, and eyes gray and laughing, and a slender face, and a nose high and well placed, and lips redder than the cherry or the rose in the summertime, and teeth small and white. And she had firm little breasts which raised up her gown as if they were two walnuts, and she was so slender in the waist that you could have circled it with your two hands. And the blossoms of daisies which she broke with the toes of her feet and which were lying upon her instep were completely black beside her feet and legs, so very, very white was the maiden.

She came to the postern and unlocked it. So did she pass out into the streets of Beaucaire, under cover of the shadows, for the moon was shining very clear. And she wandered about until she came to the tower where her lover was. The tower was cracked from place to place. And Nicolette squatted down against one of the buttresses and wrapped her cloak about her. She stuck her head in through a crevice of the tower, which was old and ancient. So did she hear Aucassin, who, inside, was weeping and wailing loudly and regretting his sweet love, whom he loved so much. And when she had listened enough to him, she began to speak.

XIII

Now it is sung

> Nicolette with clearest face
> Was leaning on a buttress.
> Aucassin she heard to weep
> And lament his sweetheart lost.
> Now she speaks and says her thought.
> "Aucassin, my noble lord,
> Gentle, high-born, honored youth,
> What's the use of all these sighs,
> This weeping and lamenting?
> For you can never have me;
> Your father and your family
> All hate me and detest me.
> For you I'd sail the high seas

And go to other countries."
From her hair she cut a lock
And threw it in his dungeon.
Noble Aucassin took it
And did it a great homage.
He kissed it and embraced it
And stuck it in his bosom,
Then began again to weep
All for his love.

XIV

Now they tell and relate and continue the tale

When Aucassin heard Nicolette say that she wished to go away to another country, in him there was nothing but anger.

"Fair sweet love," said he, "you shall not go away, for then you would be the death of me. And the first one who saw you, and who would be able to do it, would take you immediately and put you into his bed, and so would he make you his mistress. And once you had lain in a man's bed—if it wasn't mine—don't think that I would wait until I had found a knife with which I could pierce my heart and kill myself. No, indeed, I wouldn't wait that long, but I would rush about until I saw a wall or a dark stone, and I would dash my head against it so hard that I would make my eyes pop out and brain myself completely. For I would much prefer to die such a death than to know that you were in a man's bed—if it wasn't mine."

"Ah!" said she. "I don't think that you love me as much as you say. But I love you more than you love me."

"Look here," said Aucassin, "fair sweet love, it couldn't be that you should love me as much as I love you. Woman can't love man as much as man loves woman, for the love of a woman is in her eye, and in the nipple of her breast, and in the toe of her foot, but the love of a man is planted in the heart where it can't escape."

While Aucassin and Nicolette were talking there, the guardsmen of the town were coming down the street. They had their swords drawn beneath their cloaks, for Count Garin had commanded them that if they were able to take her, they should kill her. And the watchman who was on the tower saw them coming and heard them going along talking about Nicolette and threatening to kill her.

"God," said he, "what a great pity for so fair a girl, if they should kill her. And it would be a very great charity if I could tell her, in some way they wouldn't perceive, that she should be on her guard. For if they kill her, then Aucassin, my young lord, will die, and that will be a great loss."

XV

Now it is sung

> The watchman was a gallant,
> Knowing, proud and courteous man.
> So did he begin a song
> Which was sweet and ran along.
> "Maiden of the noble heart,
> Body fair and full of grace,
> Thou hast blond and shining hair,
> Grayish eyes and smiling face.
> Well do I see by thy air,
> Thou hast spoken to thy love,
> Who now for thee dying is.
> Listen while I tell thee this:
> From seducers guard thyself;
> They are looking for thee here,
> Bearing swords beneath their cloaks.
> Terribly they'll threaten thee;
> Soon much evil will they do
> > If thou guard not well."

XVI

Now they tell and relate and continue the tale

"Ah," said Nicolette, "may the souls of your father and mother be in blessed repose, since so fairly and courteously you have told me about them. If it please God, I will guard myself well from them, and God help me do it."

She wrapped her cloak about her in the shadow of the buttress until they had passed beyond. Then she took leave of Aucassin and went on until she came to the wall of the castle. The wall was in pieces and had been boarded up, and she climbed up on this and made her way along until she was between the wall and the moat. And she looked down and saw that the moat was very deep and very steep, and she was very, very much afraid.

"Oh God," said she, "sweet creature! If I let myself fall, I'll break my neck, and if I remain here, they will take me tomorrow, and they will burn me in a fire. I would much prefer that I die here than that all the folk should stare at me tomorrow under marvelous circumstances."

She made the sign of the cross above her head and let herself slide down into the moat. And when she came to the bottom, her beautiful feet and her beautiful hands, which had never learned that things might wound them, were bruised and torn, and the blood flowed from them in at least a dozen places; but nevertheless she felt neither hurt nor pain because of the great fear which she had. And though getting in had been much trouble, getting out was even more. She thought to herself that it would never do any good to remain there. She found a sharpened stake which those within had thrown down in defense of the castle, and placing one foot before the other, she mounted up with great difficulty until she came to the top.

Now there was a forest, about two crossbow shots away, which stretched for at least thirty leagues in length and in breadth, and there were savage beasts in it—also serpents. She was afraid that if she entered there, these might kill her; and, on the other hand, she reflected, if they found her there, they would lead her back to the town to burn her.

XVII

Now it is sung

> Nicolette with clearest face
> Up the moat has made her way.
> Then began she to lament
> And in Jesus' name to pray:
> "Father, King of Majesty,
> I do not know where to go.
> If I go into the woods,
> There the wolves will eat me sure,
> The wild boars and the lions,
> Of which there are a-plenty.
> If I wait the daylight clear
> So that they could find me here,
> They will light their fires of wood
> And my body will be burned.
> But, by God of Majesty,
> I would very much prefer
> That even wolves should eat me,
> Or wild boars or the lions,
> Than go into the city.
> I *will* not go."

XVIII

Now they tell and relate and continue the tale

Nicolette lamented as you have heard. She commended herself to God and wandered on until she came into the forest. She didn't dare to enter very deep into it because of the savage beasts and because of the serpents; so she crawled into a thick bush. Sleep seized her, and she slept until the next morning at seven-thirty when the shepherds came out of the town and drove their beasts between the wood and the river. There they drew aside to a very beautiful spring which was at the edge of the forest, and spread out a cape and set their bread upon it. And while they were eating, Nicolette was awakened by the cries of the birds and of the shepherds; so did she hurry toward them.

"Fair children," said she, "may the Mother of God aid you."

"God bless *you!*" said the one of them who was more talkative than the others.

"Fair children," said she, "do you know Aucassin, the son of Count Garin de Beaucaire?"

"Yes, we know him well."

"So may God aid you, fair children," she said. "Tell him that there is a beast in this forest, and that he is to come to hunt for it; and if he could catch it, he would not give one leg of it for one hundred marks of gold, not for five hundred, nor for any amount."

And they looked at her, and so did they see her so beautiful that they were all astonished.

"I should tell him *that?*" said he who was more talkative than the others. "Damned be the one who would ever talk about it, or who would ever tell him! It's a phantom that you're talking about, for there is no beast in the forest so valuable, neither stag nor lion nor wild boar, that one of his legs would be worth more than a shilling or two at the most, and you speak of such a great value! Damned be the one who believes you, or whoever shall tell it to him! You are some fairy, and we have no desire for your company, so you keep on your way."

"Ah, fair children," she said, "you will do this. The beast has such medicine that Aucassin will be cured of his illness. And I have five sous here in my purse; take them—if you will tell him. And he ought to hunt it within three days; and if, within three days, he doesn't find it, he never will be cured of his illness."

"By faith," said he, "we will take the money, and if he comes here, we will tell him; but we'll never go to look for him."

"It's up to God," said she.

Then she took leave of the shepherds, and so did she go on her way.

XIX

Now it is sung

> Nicolette with clearest face
> Has parted from the shepherds.
> So she's taken up her way
> Right into the leafy wood,
> Following an abandoned path
> Until she met a highway
> Where seven roads divided
> Which went through the country-side.

Then the thought came to her head
How she could prove her lover,
If he loved her as he said.
So she took the iris-flower
And green grass from a thicket
And some branches thick with leaves.
So she made a leafy hut;
Prettier was there never seen.
By the truthful God she swore
That if Aucassin came there
And did not for love of her
Rest in it a little while
Never would he be her love
    Nor she be his.

xx

Now they tell and relate and continue the tale

Nicolette had made a hut, as you have heard and understood, very pretty and attractive, for she had decorated it well inside and outside with flowers and with leaves. Then she lay down close by the hut in a thick bush to know what Aucassin would do.

And the cry and rumor went through all the land and through all the country that Nicolette was lost. Some said that she had run away, and others said that Count Garin had had her murdered. Whoever may have had joy from it, Aucassin wasn't at all happy about it. And Count Garin, his father, had him taken out of prison. So did he send for the knights and the ladies, and he had made a great rich feast, with which he thought to comfort Aucassin, his son.

Although the feast was most complete, Aucassin stood leaning on a post all sad and all limp. Whoever had joy, Aucassin was in no mood for it; for he saw nothing at all there of the thing he loved. A knight looked at him and came up to him; so did he speak to him.

"Aucassin," said he, "I have been sick with the same illness that you have. I will give you some good advice, if you wish to believe me."

"Sir," said Aucassin, "many thanks. I would appreciate some good advice."

"Get on a horse," said he, "and ride along the forest to cheer yourself up. And you will see the flowers and the plants, and you will hear the little birds sing. By some chance you may hear some word for which you will be better."

"Sir," said Aucassin, "Thanks very much. That's what I'll do."

He slipped out of the hall and went down the stairs and came to the stable where his horse was. He had the saddle and bridle put

on. He put his foot in the stirrup and mounted and went out of
the castle. And he wandered until he came to the forest and rode
along until he reached the spring and found the shepherds just at
mid-afternoon. They had spread out a cape on the grass, and they
were eating their bread and making very merry.

XXI

Now it is sung

> Now the shepherds gather round,
> Little Martin and Esmy,
> Little Frulin and Johnny,
> Little Robin and Aubrey.
> "Little shepherd boys," said one,
> "God help little Aucassin;
> He is a fine young fellow.
> And the girl with form so small
> And curly hair so yellow.
> Bright her face, her eye so gray,
> She gave us little pennies
> With which we'll buy little cakes,
> Little knives and little sheaths,
> Little flutes and little horns,
> Little crooks and little pipes.
>   May God help her."

XXII

Now they tell and relate and continue the tale

When Aucassin heard the shepherds, he recalled Nicolette, his
very sweet love, whom he loved so much, and thought that she had
been there. He pricked his horse with the spurs, and so did he come
up to the shepherds.

"Fair children, may God aid you!"

"God bless *you*!" said the one who was more talkative than the
others.

"Fair children," said he, "repeat the song that you were singing
just now."

"We will not say it," said the one who was more talkative than
the others. "Damned now be the one who will sing it for you, fair
sir."

"Fair children," said Aucassin, "don't you know me?"

"Yes, we know very well that you are Aucassin, our young lord,
but we don't belong to you, but rather to the count."

"Fair children, you will do this, I pray you."

"Oh, for God's sake!" said he. "Why should I sing for you if it
doesn't suit me? When there is no man so rich in this country,
except Count Garin in person, who, if he found my oxen, or my

cows, or my sheep in his fields, or even in his grain, would risk having his eyes put out, for daring to chase them from it? And why should I sing for you if it doesn't suit me?"

"God aid you, fair children, if you will do it, and take ten sous which I have here in my purse."

"Sir, we will take the money, but I will not sing it for you, for I have sworn it, but I will tell it to you if you wish."

"It's up to God," said Aucassin, "I would rather have it told than nothing."

"Sir, we were here a little while ago, between six and nine this morning, eating our bread by this spring, as we are now, and a maiden came here, the most beautiful in the world, so that we believed her to be a fairy, and this whole wood was made bright by her. And she gave us so much of what she had that we made a promise to her, that if you came here, we would tell you that you should go and hunt in this forest, where there is a beast which, if you should be able to catch it, you would never give up one of its legs for five hundred marks of silver, or for any price. For the beast has such a medicine that, if you could catch it, you would be cured of your illness. And you must take it within three days, and if you haven't caught it, you will never see it again. Now hunt it, if you will; or if you will, leave it, for I have fully acquitted myself towards her."

"Fair children," said Aucassin, "you have told me enough about it, and God let me find it!"

XXIII

Now it is sung

> Aucassin has heard the words
> Of his love with form so fair.
> Much they struck him to the core.
> Soon he leaves the shepherd boys
> And in the deep woods enters.
> His war-horse ambled quickly,
> At a gallop carried him.
> Now he speaks and says three words:
> "Nicolette, of form so fair,
> In this woods for you I've come.
> I'm not hunting stag or boar;
> Your tracks I am following.
> Your gray eyes and your sweet form,
> Your soft speech and gentle laugh
> Unto death my heart do wound.
> If it please the Father, God.
> Then shall I see you again.
>   Sister, sweet love."

XXIV

Now they tell and relate and continue the tale

Aucassin went through the forest from path to path, and his war horse carried him along at a great speed. Don't think that the briars and thorns spared him. Nothing of the sort! Rather they ripped up his clothes so that one could scarcely have made a knot out of the biggest pieces. And blood ran from his arms and his sides and his legs in forty places—or thirty, so that after the lad one might follow the traces of blood which fell on the grass. But he thought so much about Nicolette, his sweet love, that he felt neither pain nor unhappiness. And he went all day through the forest in such a way that he never did get news of her. And when he saw evening approaching, he began to weep because he couldn't find her.

He was riding along an old path all covered with leaves, when he looked before him, in the middle of the path; so did he see a yokel such as I shall tell you. Great he was, and marvelous and ugly and hideous; and he had a great bushy head blacker than charcoal, and he had more than a hand's breath between his two eyes, and he had great cheeks and a huge flat nose, and wide nostrils and thick lips redder than roast beef, and big teeth, yellow and ugly. And he wore leggings and shoes of cow-hide, cross-laced with willow bark to above the knee. He was wearing a cape unfinished inside and out, and he was leaning on a big club.

Aucassin hurried toward him and was very frightened when he got a good look at him.

"Fair brother, God help you!"

"God help *you*," said he.

"God help *you*. What are you doing here?"

"What's it to you?" said he.

"Nothing," said Aucassin, "I don't ask you except with good reason."

"But why are you crying," said he, "and making such a to-do? Surely, if I were as rich a man as you are, all the world wouldn't make me cry."

"What! do you know me?" said Aucassin.

"Sure, I know well that you are Aucassin, the son of the count, and if you will tell me why you are crying, I will tell you what I am doing here."

"Surely," said Aucassin, "I will tell you very gladly. I came this morning to hunt in the forest, and I had a white greyhound, the most beautiful in the world, and I have lost it. That's why I'm crying."

"To hear," said he, "by the heart that the Lord had in his belly, that you were crying over a stinking dog? May he be badly damned who shall ever take any account of you, when there is no man in this land so rich, that if your father asked him for ten or fifteen or twenty, he would not have given them only too willingly and have been only too glad. But I ought to cry and wail."

"And for what reason, brother?"

"Sir, I'll tell you. I was in the hire of a rich farmer, and I drove his plough, a four-ox one. Now three days ago there came to me a great accident by which I lost the best one of my oxen, Roget, the best of my team. So now I am looking for him, and I haven't eaten or drunk for the last three days. And I don't dare go to the town, for they would put me in prison since I don't have the money to pay for it. Of all the wealth in the world, I have nothing more valuable than what you see on my body. I have a poor old mother, and she had nothing more valuable than an old mattress, and they have taken it right out from under her back, so that she lies on the bare straw now. I am much more worried about her than about myself, for money comes and goes. If I have lost now, I will gain it another time; so shall I pay for my ox when I can, nor will I ever cry about it. And you were crying over a filthy dog—may anyone who ever takes any account of you be damned forever!"

"You certainly are a good comfort, fair brother, and may you be blessed! And what was your ox worth?"

"Sir, twenty sous they are asking me for it, and I can't get a single sou knocked off."

"Now take," said Aucassin, "the twenty which I have in my purse, and pay for your ox."

"Sir," said he, "thanks very much, and may God let you find what you are seeking."

He parted from him, and Aucassin rode on. The night was fair and still, and he wandered along until he came to the place where the seven roads forked. So did he look before him, and he saw the hut that Nicolette had built, which was hung outside and inside and on top and in front with flowers and was so beautiful that it could not be more so. When Aucassin saw it, he stopped all of a sudden, and the rays of the moon were shining in it.

"Oh, God," said Aucassin, "Nicolette, my sweet love, was here, and she made this with her own beautiful hands. Because of her sweetness and for love of her, I will get down now and stretch out there for the rest of the night."

Now the horse was big and tall, and Aucassin took his foot out of the stirrup to get down. He was thinking so much about Nicolette, his very sweet love, that he fell so hard on a stone that his shoulder flew out of place. He felt himself badly hurt, but he forced himself along as best he could, and tied the horse with his other hand to a thornbush; then he turned on his side so that he crawled into the hut. He looked up through a hole in the hut, and he saw the stars in the sky. He saw one brighter than the others, and he began to say.

XXV

Now it is sung

> "I can see you, little star,
> Which the moon draws after her.
> Nicolette is with you there,
> My sweet love with golden hair.
> I think God wants to have her
> So that all the evening light
> Can by her be made more bright.
> At the risk of falling down
> Would that I were up with you;
> I would kiss you willingly.
> Though I were a monarch's son,
> You would worthy be of me.
>   Sister, sweet love."

XXVI

Now they tell and relate and continue the tale

When Nicolette heard Aucassin, she came to him, for she was not far off. She came into the hut; so did she throw her arms around his neck, kissed him, and embraced him.

"Fair sweet love, it's good to find you!"

"And you, fair sweet love, it's good to find *you*!"

They kissed each other and embraced; so was their joy beautiful.

"Ah, sweet love," said Aucassin, "just now I hurt my shoulder, and now I feel neither pain nor grief since I have you."

She felt him carefully and found that he had his shoulder out of place. She handled it and pulled it about so with her white hands that, as God who loves lovers willed it, it came back into place; and then she took some flowers and fresh grass and green leaves, and she bound it up with the tail of her chemise, and he was completely cured.

"Aucassin," said she, "fair sweet love, take counsel what you will do. If your father has this forest searched tomorrow, whatever may become of *you*, they will kill *me*."

"Surely, fair sweet love, I should be very sad over it; but if I am able, they shall never get hold of you."

He mounted on his horse, and took his love up in front of him, kissing and embracing her; so did they set off to the open fields.

XXVII

Now it is sung

> Aucassin, the fair, the blond,
> The gentle and the loving,
> Out of that deep woods has gone
> With his love between his arms,
> His saddle-bow before him.
> He kissed her eyes and forehead,
> Kissed her mouth and then her chin;
> Then did Nicolette begin,
> "Aucassin, sweet handsome love,
> To what country shall we go?"
> "My sweet love, how should I know?
> I do not care where we go
> In the woods or on the roads
> So long as I am with you."
> They passed the hills and valleys,
> The villages and cities,
> And at dawn they reached the sea
> And dismounted on the sand
> > Near the seashore.

XXVIII

Now they tell and relate and continue the tale

Aucassin had dismounted, both he and his love, as you have heard and understood. He held his horse by the reins, and his love by the hand, and so did they begin to go along the shore. And Aucassin looked toward the sea and saw a ship of merchants who were sailing near the coast.

He hailed them and they came to him, and he made such terms with them that they took them into their ship. And when they were on the high seas, a storm arose, great and marvelous, which drove them from land to land, until they arrived in a strange country and entered into the port of the Castle of Torelore. Then they asked whose land it was, and they told them that it was the land of the King of Torelore. Then they asked what sort of a man he was, and if he had a war, and they told him, "Yes, a great one."

He took leave of the merchants, and they commended him to God. He mounted on his horse, his sword girded on, and his love in front of him, and wandered until he came to the castle. He asked where the king was, and they told him that he was lying in bed with child.

"And where is his wife, then?"

And they told him that she was with the army, and that she had taken away with her everybody in the country. Aucassin heard it, and it seemed to him a great marvel. He came up to the palace and dismounted—both he and his love; and she held the horse, and he went up into the palace, his sword girded on, and wandered about until he came into the room where the king was lying.

XXIX

Now it is sung

> In the room came Aucassin
> The courteous and the noble.
> He came straight up to the bed
> On which the king was lying.
> Right in front of him he stopped
> And spoke; listen what he said:
> "Fool, what are you doing here?"
> Said the king, "I am with child.
> When my month shall be fulfilled
> And I shall be well again,
> I shall then be churched at mass
> As my ancestors have done;
> Then from carrying on great war
> With my enemies again,
>> I shall never stop."

XXX

Now they tell and relate and continue the tale

When Aucassin heard the king speak thus, he took all the bed clothes which were upon him and threw them around the room. He saw just in back of him a big stick. He took it, turned about, and he struck him and beat him so much that he almost killed him.

"Ah, fair sir," said the king, "what do you want of me? Have you gone crazy that you beat me in my own house?"

"By God's heart," said Aucassin, "evil son of a slut, I will kill you, if you do not swear to me that never again shall a man in your land be brought to bed with child."

He swore it, and when he had heard him swear it:

"Sir," said Aucassin, "now lead me there where your wife is with the army."

"Sir, willingly," said the king.

He mounted on his horse, and Aucassin mounted on his, and Nicolette remained in the chambers of the queen. And the king and Aucassin rode along until they came to the place where the queen was, and they found there a battle of rotted wild apples, and of eggs and of fresh cheeses; and Aucassin began to look at them, and he was very, very much astonished indeed.

XXXI

Now it is sung

   Aucassin had stopped and now,
   Elbow on his saddle-bow,
   He begins to marvel at
   This violent battlefield,
   For both sides had brought with them
   Cheeses quite fresh from the vats,
   With wood apples rotted soft,
   And some large field mushrooms too.
   He who most stirs up the fords
   Is proclaimed the lord of lords.
   Aucassin the valiant knight
   Stared at them with all his might
      And began to laugh.

XXXII

Now they tell and relate and continue the tale

When Aucassin saw this marvel, he came to the king; so did he speak to him.

"Sir," said Aucassin, "are these your enemies?"

"Yes, sir," said the king.

"And would you like me to avenge you on them?"

"Yes," said he, "if you like."

And Aucassin put his hand on his sword, so did he rush among them and began to strike right and left and killed many of them. When the king saw that he was killing them, he took him by the bridle and said:

"Ah, fair sir, don't kill them like this."

"What?" said Aucassin, "don't you want me to avenge you?"

"Sir," said the king, "you have done too much. It is not our custom to kill each other."

The enemy turned and fled, and the king and Aucassin returned to the castle of Torelore. And the people of the country told the king that he should cast Aucassin out of the land and detain Nicolette as a wife for his son since she seemed, indeed, to be a woman of high lineage. Nicolette heard it, and was not at all glad about it, and she began to say:

XXXIII

Now it is sung

   "O, sir king of Torelore,"
   Said the lovely Nicolette,
   "Your folk take me for a fool;

When my love embraces me
And feels me plump and tender,
Then am I in such a state
That neither songs nor dances,
Fiddle, harp, nor viol gay,
Nor the pleasures of the play
     Are worth a thing."

XXXIV
Now they tell and relate and continue the tale

Aucassin was in the castle of Torelore, and Nicolette, his love; and he had great delight and great ease that he had with him Nicolette, his sweet love, whom he loved so much. And while he was in such ease and in such delight, a fleet of the Saracens came by sea and assailed the castle; so did they take it by force. And they took all the treasure and led the men and women away captive. They took Nicolette and Aucassin, and they bound Aucassin's hands and his feet, and they threw him into one ship and Nicolette into another. And there arose a storm on the sea, which separated them.

The ship in which Aucassin was went skimming over the sea until it arrived at the Castle of Beaucaire. The people of the country ran to the wreckage, and they found Aucassin, and so did they recognize him. When those of Beaucaire saw their young lord, they made great joy over it, for Aucassin had lived in the castle of Torelore for three full years, and his father and mother were dead. They led him to the Castle of Beaucaire; so did they all become his men, and he held his land in peace.

XXXV
Now it is sung

Aucassin has gone away
To his city of Beaucaire.
All the country and the realm
He now held in greatest calm,
Swore by God of Majesty
That he much more regretted
Nicolette with clearest face
Than all of his relations
Though they all were dead and gone.
"Sweetheart with the clearest face,
I don't know where you may be.
God has never made that place
Either on the land or sea
Where if I thought to find you
     I would not look."

XXXVI

Now they tell and relate and continue the tale

Now we will leave off about Aucassin and talk of Nicolette. The ship in which Nicolette was belonged to the king of Carthage, and he was her father, and she had twelve brothers, all princes and kings. When they saw Nicolette so beautiful, they offered her very, very great honors and made a feast for her, and often did they ask her who she was, for indeed she seemed to be a very noble lady and of high lineage. But she didn't know how to tell them who she was, for she had been stolen away as a little child. They sailed along until they arrived below the city of Carthage; and when Nicolette saw the walls of the castle and the country, she recognized that she had been brought up there and stolen from there as a little child. But she was not so small a child that she didn't know very well that she had been the daughter of the king of Carthage, and that she had been brought up in the city.

XXXVII

Now it is sung

Nicolette, high-born and wise,
Now has landed on the shore,
Saw the buildings and the walls
And the castle and the halls.
Seeing which, she cried, "Alas,
I am of a high descent,
Daughter to the Carthage king
And cousin to the emir!
Savage people hold me here.
Aucassin, well-born and wise,
Honorable, noble lord,
Your sweet love so urges me,
Speaks to me and troubles me,
God the Spirit grant me this:
That you hold me in your arms,
Once again my forehead kiss,
Kiss my mouth and kiss my face,
    My sweet young lord."

Now they tell and relate and continue the tale

When the king of Carthage heard Nicolette speak in that way, he threw his arms around her neck.

"Fair sweet love," said he, "tell me who you are; don't you be afraid of me."

"Sir," said she, "I am the daughter of the king of Carthage, and I was stolen as a little child, fully fifteen years ago."

When he heard her speak thus, he knew well that she was speaking the truth; so did he make a very great holiday for her, and led her into the palace with great honor as the daughter of a king. For a husband he wished to give her a king of the pagans, but she had no desire to get married. She was there three or four full days. She reflected by what device she would be able to search for Aucassin. She bought herself a viol and learned to play it, until they wanted one day to marry her off to a rich pagan king. And she slipped out that night and came to the seaport; so did she take shelter with a poor woman on the shore. And she took an herb and smeared her head and face with it so that she was all black and stained. And she had a coat made and a cloak and a shirt and underbreeches, and rigged herself out in the guise of a jongleur. So she took her viol and came up to a sailor, and she made such terms with him that he took her aboard his ship. They raised their sails, and so did they sail away over the high seas until they arrived at the land of Provence. And Nicolette started out and took her viol; so did she go along playing through the country until she came to the Castle of Beaucaire, there where Aucassin was.

XXXIX

Now it is sung

> At Beaucaire beneath the tower
> There was Aucassin one day
> Seated on a stone stairway.
> Round him were his barons proud.
> He saw the grass and flowers
> And heard the small birds singing
> And remembered of his love,
> For the noble Nicolette,
> Whom he'd loved so many days.
> He gives way to sighs and tears.
> Look, below is Nicolette
> With her viol and her bow.
> Now she speaks and tells her tale,
> "Listen to me, noble lords,
> Those above and those below,
> Would you like to hear a song
> Of a proud lord, Aucassin,
> Of the noble Nicolette,
> How their love endured so long,
> How he sought her in the wood;
> At Torelore in prison
> The pagans one day put them.

Naught of Aucassin we know,
But the noble Nicolette
At Carthage is in prison.
Now her father loves her well
Who is lord of all that realm.
As bride they wish to give her
To a wretched pagan king.
Nicolette won't think of it,
For she loves a fair young lord
By the name of Aucassin.
Well she swears by God's own name
That she will never marry
If she cannot have the one
    Whom she so loves."

XL

Now they tell and relate and continue the tale

When Aucassin heard Nicolette speak thus, he was very glad, and he drew her aside and asked her:

"Fair sweet friend," said Aucassin, "do you know anything of this Nicolette of whom you have just sung?"

"Sir, yes," said she, "I know of her as the most noble creature, and the most gentle and the most wise that was ever born. She is the daughter of the King of Carthage, who took her when Aucassin was taken; so did he lead her into the city of Carthage until he had learned indeed that she was his daughter. He made a great festival; and he wished each day to give her for a husband one of the most exalted kings in all Spain, but she would rather let herself be hanged or burned than take any one of them, however rich he might be."

"Ah, fair sweet friend," said Count Aucassin, "if you would go back to that land and tell her to come here to speak to me, I would give you as much of my wealth as you would dare demand or take. And know that for love of her, I have no desire to take a wife however high her lineage may be, but only to wait for her. For I will have no wife if it isn't she. And if I had known where to find her, I would not be looking for her now."

"Sir," said she, "if you would do this, I would go and seek her for you and for her, whom I love very much."

He swore it to her, and then he had her given twenty pounds. She started to leave him, and he wept for the sweetness of Nicolette. When she saw him weeping:

"Sir," she said, "don't be dismayed, for in a little time I will have her brought into this town; so you will see her."

And when Aucassin heard her, he was very, very glad. And she went away from him; so did she go through the town to the house of the Viscountess, for the Viscount, her god-father, was dead.

There she stayed, and she talked to her until she had revealed her plan, and the Viscountess had recognized her and knew indeed that it was Nicolette whom she had reared. So did she have her washed and bathed, and she stayed there eight full days. Then she took an herb which is called Clarity and smeared herself with it. So was she as beautiful as she had ever been at any day. And she dressed herself in rich cloth of silk, of which the lady had much.

She sat in her chamber upon a quilt of stitched silk cloth, and she called the lady and told her that she should go for Aucassin, her love. She did it; and when she came to the palace, she found Aucassin who was weeping and regretting Nicolette his love because she delayed so long, and the lady called him and said to him:

"Aucassin, don't cry any more, but come along with me, and I will show you the thing that you love most in all the world, for it is Nicolette, your sweet love, who has come from distant lands to find you."

And Aucassin was overjoyed!

XLI

Now it is sung

Now when Aucassin had heard
Of his love with clearest face,
How she had come to this land,
Glad was he, never more so.
With the lady has he gone;
Straight to that house did he ride.
There they entered in a room
Where Nicolette was sitting.
When she saw her lover there,
Glad was she, never more so.
Up she jumped and ran to him.
And when Aucassin saw her,
With both arms stretched out to her,
He embraced her tenderly
While he kissed her eyes and face.
All that night they left them thus.
In the morning, the next day,
Aucassin made her his wife.
Lady of Beaucaire she was;
Then they lived for many days
And much pleasure did they have.
Now has Aucassin his joy
And Nicolette hers likewise.
Our *chantefable* takes its end.
I cannot tell you more.

DANTE ALIGHIERI
(1265–1321)
The Divine Comedy (La divina commedia)*

Hell (*Inferno*)

CANTO I

Halfway through his life, Dante the Pilgrim wakes to find himself lost in a dark wood. Terrified at being alone in so dismal a valley, he wanders until he comes to a hill bathed in sunlight, and his fear begins to leave him. But when he starts to climb the hill his path is blocked by three fierce beasts: first a Leopard, then a Lion, and finally a She-Wolf. They fill him with fear and drive him back down to the sunless wood. At that moment the figure of a man appears before him; it is the shade of Virgil, and the Pilgrim begs for help. Virgil tells him that he cannot overcome the beasts which obstruct his path; they must remain until a "Greyhound" comes who will drive them back to Hell. Rather by another path will the Pilgrim reach the sunlight, and Virgil promises to guide him on that path through Hell and Purgatory, at which time another spirit, more fit than Virgil, will lead him to Paradise. The Pilgrim begs Virgil to lead on, and the Guide starts ahead. The Pilgrim follows.

Midway along the journey of our life
   I woke to find myself in some dark woods,
   for I had wandered off from the straight path.
How hard it is to tell what it was like,
   this wood of wilderness, savage and stubborn   5
   (the thought of it brings back all my old fears),

* Abridged. Written in the early fourteenth century. *Inferno* (complete), from *Dante's Inferno*, translated with notes and commentary by Mark Musa, copyright, 1971, by Indiana University Press, Bloomington and London. Reprinted by permission of Indiana University Press. *Purgatorio* and *Paradiso* translated, with headnotes, by Lawrence Binyon; the footnotes are by C. H. Grandgent, from *La divina commedia di Dante Alighieri*, edited and annotated by C. H. Grandgent, copyright, 1933, by D. C. Heath and Company, Boston. Reprinted with the permission of the translator's wife and the Society of Authors, and by special permission of D. C. Heath and Company, Boston.

1-10. The reader must be careful from the beginning to distinguish between the two uses of the first person singular in the *Divine Comedy:* one designating Dante the Pilgrim, the other Dante the Poet. The first is a character in a story invented by the second. The events are represented as having taken place in the past; the writing of the poem and the memories of these events are represented as taking place in the poet's present. We find references to both past and present, and to both pilgrim and poet in line 10: "How *I entered* there *I cannot* truly say."

1. In the Middle Ages life was often thought of as a journey, a pilgrimage, the goal of which was God and Heaven; and in the first line of the *Divine Comedy* Dante establishes the central motif of his poem—it is the story of man's pilgrimage to God. That we are meant to think in terms not just of the Pilgrim but of Everyman is indicated by the phrase "the journey of *our* life" (*our* journey through sin to repentance and redemption).

The imaginary date of the poem's beginning is the night before Good Friday in 1300, the year of the papal jubilee proclaimed by Boniface VIII. Born in 1265, Dante was thirty-five years old, which is one half of man's biblical life span of seventy years.

Island of Purgatory

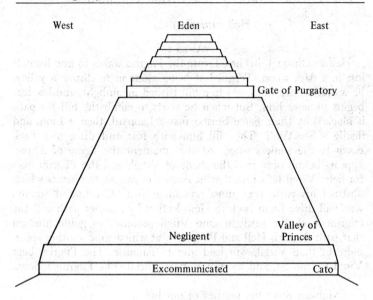

West · Eden · East

Gate of Purgatory

Valley of Princes

Negligent

Excommunicated · Cato

Eden and Purgatory

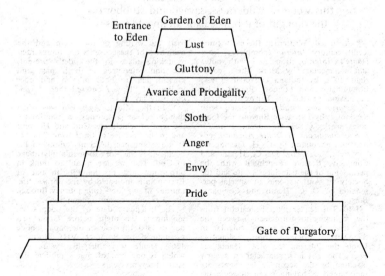

Entrance to Eden · Garden of Eden

Lust

Gluttony

Avarice and Prodigality

Sloth

Anger

Envy

Pride

Gate of Purgatory

The Slope of Hell

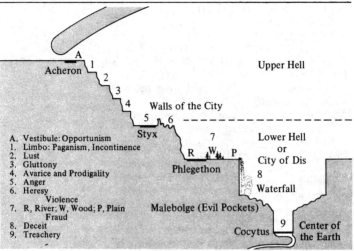

Upper Hell

Acheron

Walls of the City

Styx

A. Vestibule: Opportunism
1. Limbo: Paganism, Incontinence
2. Lust
3. Gluttony
4. Avarice and Prodigality
5. Anger
6. Heresy
　　　Violence
7. R, River; W, Wood; P, Plain
　　　Fraud
8. Deceit
9. Treachery

Lower Hell

or

City of Dis

Phlegethon

Waterfall

Malebolge (Evil Pockets)

Cocytus　Center of the Earth

The Heavenly Spheres

Empyrean
Ninth Sphere
Eighth Sphere
Seventh Sphere
Sixth Sphere
Fifth Sphere
Fourth Sphere
Third Sphere
Second Sphere
First Sphere
Fire
Air
Earth
Moon
Mercury
Venus
Sun
Mars
Jupiter
Saturn
Constellations
Primum Mobile
Empyrean

a bitter place! Death could scarce be bitterer.
  But if I would show the good that came of it
  I must talk about things other than the good.
How I entered there I cannot truly say,   10
  I had become so sleepy at the moment
  when I first strayed, leaving the path of truth;
but when I found myself at the foot of a hill,
  at the edge of the wood's beginning, down in the valley,
  where I first felt my heart plunged deep in fear,   15
I raised my head and saw the hilltop shawled
  in morning rays of light sent from the planet
  that leads men straight ahead on every road.
And then only did terror start subsiding
  in my heart's lake, which rose to heights of fear   20
  that night I spent in deepest desperation.
Just as a swimmer, still with panting breath,
  now safe upon the shore, out of the deep,
  might turn for one last look at the dangerous waters,
so I, although my mind was turned to flee,   25
  turned round to gaze once more upon the pass
  that never let a living soul escape.
I rested my tired body there awhile
  and then began to climb the barren slope
  (I dragged my stronger foot and limped along).   30
Beyond the point the slope begins to rise
  sprang up a leopard, trim and very swift!
  It was covered by a pelt of many spots.
And, everywhere I looked, the beast was there
  blocking my way, so time and time again   35
  I was about to turn and go back down.
The hour was early in the morning then,
  the sun was climbing up with those same stars
  that had accompanied it on the world's first day,
the day Divine Love set their beauty turning;   40
  so the hour and sweet season of creation
  encouraged me to think I could get past
that gaudy beast, wild in its spotted pelt,
  but then good hope gave way and fear returned
  when the figure of a lion loomed up before me,   45

13–15. Once we leave Canto I, which is the introduction to the whole of the *Divine Comedy*, the topography of the various regions of Hell will be described with elaborate carefulness. But in this canto all is vague and unprepared for; the scene is set in a "nowhere land"—the region of undifferentiated sin. Suddenly the Pilgrim awakes in a forest (which is not described except in terms that could apply to Sin itself: "wilderness, savage and stubborn"); suddenly, as he is wandering through it, there is a hill—whereupon the forest becomes a valley. Other suggestions of this dreamlike atmosphere (which, under the circumstances, must be that of a nightmare) will be found throughout this canto.

32–60. The early critics thought of the three beasts which block the Pilgrim's path as symbolizing three specific sins: lust, pride, and avarice; but I prefer to see in them the three major divisions of Hell. The spotted Leopard (l. 32) represents Fraud (cf. Canto XVI, ll. 106–108) and reigns over the Eighth and Ninth Circles where the Fraudulent are punished (Cantos XVIII–XXXIV). The Lion (l. 45) symbolizes all forms of Violence which are punished in the Seventh Circle (XII–XVII). The She-Wolf (l. 49) represents the different types of Concupiscence or Incontinence which are punished in Circles Two to Five (V–VIII).

and he was coming straight toward me, it seemed,
  with head raised high, and furious with hunger—
  the air around him seemed to fear his presence.
And now a she-wolf came, that in her leanness
  seemed racked with every kind of greediness   50
  (how many people she has brought to grief!).
This last beast brought my spirit down so low
  with fear that seized me at the sight of her,
  I lost all hope of going up the hill.
As a man who, rejoicing in his gains,   55
  suddenly seeing his gain turn into loss,
  will grieve as he compares his then and now,
so she made me do, that relentless beast;
  coming towards me, slowly, step by step,
  she forced me back to where the sun is mute.   60
While I was moving down to that low place,
  my eyes made out a figure coming toward me
  of one grown weak, perhaps from too much silence.
And when I saw him standing in this wasteland,
  "Have pity on my soul," I cried to him,   65
  "whichever you are, shade or living man!"
"No longer living man, though once I was,"
  he said, "and my parents were from Lombardy,
  both of them were Mantuans by birth.
I was born, though somewhat late, *sub Julio*,   70
  and lived in Rome when good Augustus reigned,
  when still the false and lying gods were worshipped.
I was a poet and sang of that just man,
  son of Anchises, who sailed off from Troy
  after the burning of proud Ilium.   75
But why retreat to so much misery?
  Why aren't you climbing up this joyous mountain,
  the beginning and the source of all man's bliss?"
"Are you then Virgil, are you then that fount
  from which pours forth so rich a stream of words?" 80
  I said to him bowing my head modestly.
"O light and honor of the other poets,
  may my long years of study, and that deep love
  that made me search your verses, help me now!
You are my teacher, the first of all my authors,   85

46–50. Note the triple use of the verb *seem* (which is a faithful reproduction of the original), intended to blur the figures of the Lion and the She-Wolf—in harmony with the "nowhereness" of the moral landscape.

62. The shade of Virgil miraculously appears before Dante. The Roman poet, who was born (70 B.C.) in the time of Julius Caesar (*sub Julio*), represents Reason, Natural Philosophy. The Pilgrim cannot proceed to the light of Divine Love (the mountain top) until he has overcome the three beasts of his sin; and because it is impossible for man to cope with the beasts unaided, Virgil, as Reason, has been summoned through the chain of divine command to guide the Pilgrim and help him overcome his sins by understanding and, later, repudiating them.

63. The voice of Reason has been silent in the Pilgrim's ear for a long time.

73–75. In the *Aeneid* Virgil relates the *post bellum* travels and deeds of Aeneas (son of Anchises) who, destined by the gods, founded on Italian soil the nation which, in the course of time, would become the Roman Empire.

and you alone the one from whom I took
   the beautiful style that was to bring me honor.
You see the beast that forced me to retreat;
   save me from her, I beg you, famous sage,
   she makes me tremble, the blood throbs in my veins."   90
"But your journey must be down another road,"
   he answered, when he saw me lost in tears,
   "if ever you hope to leave this wilderness;
this beast, the one you cry about in fear,
   allows no soul to succeed along her path,   95
   she blocks his way and puts an end to him.
She is by nature so perverse and vicious,
   her craving belly is never satisfied,
   still hungering for food the more she eats.
She mates with many creatures, and will go on   100
   mating with more until the greyhound comes
   and tracks her down to make her die in anguish.
He will not feed on either land or money:
   his wisdom, love, and virtue shall sustain him;
   he will be born between Feltro and Feltro.   105
He comes to save that fallen Italy
   for which the maid Camilla gave her life
   and Turnus, Nisus, Euryalus died of wounds.
And he will hunt for her through every city
   until he drives her back to Hell once more,   110
   whence Envy first unleashed her on mankind.
And so, I think it best you follow me
   for your own good, and I shall be your guide
   and lead you out through an eternal place
where you will hear desperate cries, and see   115
   tormented shades, some old as Hell itself,
   and know what second death is, from their screams.
And later you will see those who rejoice
   while they are burning, for they have hope of coming,
   whenever it may be, to join the blessèd—   120

87. The reasons for the poet's selection of Virgil as the Pilgrim's guide (instead of, shall we say, Aristotle, *the* philosopher of the time) are several: Virgil was a poet and an Italian; in the *Aeneid* is recounted the hero's descent into Hell. But the main reason surely lies in the fact that, in the Middle Ages, Virgil was considered a prophet, a judgment stemming from the interpretation of some obscure lines in the *Fourth Eclogue* as foretelling the coming of Christ.

91. Dante must choose another road because, in order to arrive at the Divine Light, it is necessary first to recognize the true nature of sin, renounce it, and pay penance for it.

101–111. The Greyhound has been identified with Henry VII, Charles Martel, and even Dante himself. It seems more plausible that the Greyhound represents Can Grande della Scala, the ruler of Verona from 1308 to 1329 whose "wisdom, love, and virtue" (l. 104) were certainly well-known to Dante. Whoever the Greyhound may be, the prophecy would seem to indicate in a larger sense the establishment of a spiritual kingdom on earth in which "wisdom, love, and virtue" will replace the bestial sins of the world.

107. "Camilla": the valiant daughter of King Metabus, who was slain while fighting against the Trojans (*Aeneid* XI).

108. "Turnus, Nisus, Euryalus": Turnus was the king of the Rutulians. Nisus and Euryalus were young Trojan warriors slain during a nocturnal raid on the camp of the Rutulians.

117. "second death": the death of the soul, which occurs when the soul is damned.

to whom, if you too wish to make the climb,
  a spirit, worthier than I, must take you;
  I shall go back, leaving you in her care,
because that Emperor dwelling on high
  will not let me lead any to his city,   125
  since I in life rebelled against his law.
Everywhere he reigns, and there he rules;
  there is his city, there is his high throne.
  Oh happy the one he makes his citizen!"
And I to him: "Poet, I beg of you,   130
  in the name of God, that God you never knew,
  save me from this evil place and worse,
lead me there to the place you spoke about
  that I may see the gate Saint Peter guards
  and those whose anguish you have told me of."   135
Then he moved on, and I moved close behind him.

CANTO II

But the Pilgrim begins to waver; he expresses to Virgil his misgivings about his ability to undertake the journey proposed by Virgil. His predecessors have been Aeneas and St. Paul, and he feels unworthy to take his place in their company. But Virgil rebukes his cowardice, and relates the chain of events which led him to come to Dante. The Virgin Mary took pity on the Pilgrim in his despair and instructed St. Lucia to aid him. The Saint turned to Beatrice because of Dante's great love for her, and Beatrice in turn went down to Hell, into Limbo, and asked Virgil to guide her friend until that time when she herself would become his guide. The Pilgrim takes heart at Virgil's explanation and agrees to follow him.

The day was fading and the darkening air
  was releasing all the creatures on our earth
  from their daily tasks, and I, one man, alone,
was making ready to endure the battle
  of the journey, and of the pity it involved,   5
  which my memory, unerring, shall now retrace.
O Muses! O high genius! Help me now!
  O memory that wrote down what I saw,
  here your true excellence shall be revealed!

122. Just as Virgil, the pagan Roman poet, cannot enter the Christian Paradise because he lived before the birth of Christ and lacks knowledge of Christian salvation, so Reason can only guide the Pilgrim to a certain point: in order to enter Paradise, the Pilgrim's guide must be Christian Grace or Revelation (Theology) in the figure of Beatrice.

124. Note the pagan terminology of Virgil's reference to God; it expresses, as best it can, his unenlightened conception of the Supreme Authority.

7–9. Dante links his own poem to the classical epic tradition by invoking the Muses.

Then I began: "O poet come to guide me,   10
    tell me if you think my worth sufficient
    before you trust me to this arduous road.
You wrote about young Sylvius' father
    who went beyond, with flesh corruptible,
    with all his senses, to the immortal realm;   15
but if the adversary of all evil
    was kind to him, considering who he was,
    and the consequence that was to come from him,
this cannot seem, to thoughtful men, unfitting,
    for in the highest heaven he was chosen   20
    father of glorious Rome and of her empire,
and both the city and her lands, in truth,
    were established as the place of holiness
    where the successors of great Peter sit.
And from this journey you celebrate in verse,   25
    Aeneas learned those things that were to bring
    victory for him, and for Rome, the Papal seat;
then later the Chosen Vessel, Paul, ascended
    to bring back confirmation of that faith
    which is the first step on salvation's road.   30
But, why am I to go? Who allows me to?
    I am not Aeneas, I am not Paul,
    neither I nor any man would think me worthy;
and so, if I should undertake the journey,
    I fear it might turn out an act of folly—   35
    you are wise, you see more than my words express."
As one who unwills what he willed, will change
    his purposes with some new second thought,
    completely quitting what he first had started,
so I did, standing there on that dark slope,   40
    thinking, ending the beginning of that venture
    I was so quick to take up at the start.
"If I have truly understood your words,"
    that shade of magnanimity replied,
    "your soul is burdened with that cowardice   45
which often weighs so heavily on man

10–48. Dante the Pilgrim expresses fear of a journey such as Virgil proposes, for he finds himself wholly unworthy beside the two who have been allowed to visit "eternal regions" before—Aeneas and St. Paul. The comparison between Dante the Pilgrim and Aeneas and Paul is significant. For Virgil, Aeneas's journey had but one consequence: empire; for Dante, however, it signified both empire and the establishment of the Holy Roman Church, the "City of God" where all popes reside and reign. The fundamental concepts of Church and State, their government, their conflicts and internal problems were very important to Dante, and form one of the central themes of the *Comedy*.

13–21. "Sylvius": the son of Aeneas by Lavinia, his second wife and daughter to Latinus.

In the *Aeneid* Virgil recounts the history of the founding of Rome. After the fall of Troy, Aeneas, the legendary hero of the epic, embarked on his divinely inspired journey that eventually led him to the shores of Italy, where he was to establish his city and nation.

28–30. "the Chosen Vessel, Paul": In his *Second Epistle to the Corinthians* (12:2–4) the Apostle Paul alludes to his mystical elevation to the third heaven and to the arcane messages pronounced there.

37–42. One of Dante's favorite poetic devices is to imitate the "action" stylistically. Here the Pilgrim's confused state of mind (his fear and lack of conviction) is reflected by the involved structure of the lines.

it turns him from a noble enterprise
   like a frightened beast that shies at its own shadow.
To free you from this fear, let me explain
   the reason I came here, the words I heard   50
   that first time I felt pity for your soul:
I was among those dead who are suspended,
   when a lady summoned me. She was so blessed
   and beautiful, I implored her to command me.
With eyes of light more bright than any star,   55
   in low, soft tones she started to address me
   in her own language, with an angel's voice:
'O noble soul, courteous Mantuan,
   whose fame the world continues to preserve
   and will preserve as long as world there is,   60
my friend, who is no friend of Fortune's, strays
   on desert slope; so many obstacles
   have crossed his path, his fright has turned him back.
   have crossed his path, his fright has turned him back.
I fear he may have gone so far astray,   65
   from what report has come to me in Heaven,
   that I may have started to his aid too late.
Now go, and with your elegance of speech,
   with whatever may be needed for his freedom,
   give him your help, and thereby bring me solace.   70
I am Beatrice, who urges you to go;
   I come from the place I am longing to return to;
   love moved me, as it moves me now to speak.
When I return to stand before my Lord,
   often I shall sing your praises to Him.'   75
   And then she spoke no more. And I began,
'O Lady of Grace, through whom alone mankind
   may go beyond all worldly things contained
   within the sphere that makes the smallest circle,
your plea fills me with happy eagerness—   80
   to have obeyed already would still seem late!
   You needed only to express your wish.
But tell me how you dared to make this journey

49–142. The second major movement in Canto II includes Virgil's explanation of his coming to the Pilgrim, and the subsequent restoration of the latter's courage. According to Virgil, the Virgin Mary, who traditionally signifies mercy and compassion in Christian thought, took pity on the Pilgrim in his predicament and set in motion the operation of Divine Grace. Lucia, whose name means "light," suggests the Illuminating Grace sent for by the Blessed Virgin; without Divine Grace the Pilgrim would be lost. Beatrice, whose name signifies blessedness or salvation, appears to Virgil in order to reveal to him the will of God who is the ultimate bestower of Divine Grace. The three heavenly ladies balance the three beasts of Canto I; they represent man's salvation from sin through Grace, as the beasts represent man's sins. The Pilgrim's journey, then, actually starts in Paradise when the Blessed Virgin Mary takes pity on him; thus the action of the *Divine Comedy* is in one sense a circle which begins in Heaven, as related here, and will ultimately end in Heaven with the Pilgrim's vision of God (*Paradiso*, Canto XXXIII).

52. In the *Inferno* Virgil is assigned to Limbo, the dwelling place of those virtuous shades not eligible for Heaven because they either lived before Christ's birth or remained heathen after the advent of Christianity (see Canto IV, note on l. 34).

all the way down to this point of spacelessness
away from your spacious home that calls you back.'   85
'Because your question searches for deep meaning,
     I shall explain in simple words,' she said,
     'just why I have no fear of coming here.
A man must stand in fear of just those things
     that truly have the power to do us harm,   90
     of nothing else, for nothing else is fearsome.
God gave me such a nature through His Grace,
     the torments you must bear cannot affect me,
     nor are the fires of Hell a threat to me.
A gracious lady sits in Heaven grieving   95
     for what happened to the one I send you to,
     and her compassion breaks Heaven's stern decree.
She called Lucia and making her request
     she said, "Your faithful one is now in need
     of you, and to you I now commend his soul."   100
Lucia, the enemy of cruelty,
     hastened to make her way to where I was,
     sitting by the side of ancient Rachel,
and said to me: "Beatrice, God's true praise,
     will you not help the one whose love was such   105
     it made him leave the vulgar crowd for you?
Do you not hear the pity of his weeping,
     do you not see what death it is that threatens him
     along that river the sea shall never conquer?"
There never was a worldly person living   110
     more anxious to promote his selfish gains
     than I was at the sound of words like these—
to leave my holy seat and come down here
     and place my trust in you, in your noble speech
     that honors you and all those hearing it.'   115
When she had finished reasoning, she turned
     her shining eyes away, and there were tears.
     How eager then I was to come to you!
And I have come to you just as she wished,
     and I have freed you from the beast that stood   120
     blocking the quick way up the mount of bliss.
So what is wrong? Why, why do you delay?
     why are you such a coward in your heart,
     why aren't you bold and free of all your fear,
when three such gracious ladies who are blessed   125
     watch out for you up there in Heaven's court,
     and my words, too, bring promise of such good?"
As little flowers from the evening chill
     are closed and limp, and when the sun shines down

94. The Virgin Mary.

102. In the Dantean Paradise Rachel is seated by Beatrice.

119–126. The Pilgrim's initial failure to climb the mountain (due to the presence of the She-Wolf, I, 49–60) and his subsequent state of desperation are recalled in these lines. Freed now, however, from this peril by Virgil, and assured of success by the "three gracious ladies," he should no longer be hindered from his journey by fear or any hesitation.

on them, they rise to open on their stem,   130
my wilted strength began to bloom within me,
  and such good zeal went flowing to my heart
  I began to speak as one free in the sun.
"O, she, compassionate, who moved to help me!
  And you, all kindness, in obeying quick   135
  those words of truth she brought with her for you—
you and the words you spoke have moved my heart
  with such desire to continue onward
  that now I have returned to my first purpose.
Let us start, for both our wills, joined now, are one.   140
  You are my guide, you are my lord and teacher."
  These were my words to him and, when he moved,
I entered on that deep and rugged road.

CANTO III

As the two poets enter the vestibule that leads to Hell itself,
Dante sees the inscription above the gate, and he hears the screams
of anguish from the damned souls. Rejected by God and not
accepted by the powers of Hell the first group of souls are
"nowhere," because of their cowardly refusal to make a choice in
life. Their punishment is to follow a banner at a furious pace forever, and to be tormented by flies and hornets. The Pilgrim recognizes several of these shades but mentions none by name. Next they
come to the River Acheron where they are greeted by the infernal
boatman Charon. Among those doomed souls who are to be ferried
across the river, Charon sees the living man and challenges him, but
Virgil lets it be known that his companion must pass. Then across
the landscape rushes a howling wind which blasts the Pilgrim out of
his senses, and he falls to the ground.

THROUGH ME THE WAY INTO THE DOLEFUL CITY,
  THROUGH ME THE WAY INTO ETERNAL GRIEF,
  THROUGH ME THE WAY AMONG A RACE FORSAKEN.
JUSTICE MOVED MY HEAVENLY CONSTRUCTOR;
  DIVINE OMNIPOTENCE CREATED ME,   5
  AND HIGHEST WISDOM JOINED WITH PRIMAL LOVE.
BEFORE ME NOTHING BUT ETERNAL THINGS
  WERE MADE, AND I SHALL LAST ETERNALLY.
  ABANDON HOPE, FOREVER, YOU WHO ENTER.
I saw these words spelled out in somber colors   10
  inscribed along the ledge above a gate;
  "Master," I said, "these words I see are cruel."
He answered me, speaking with experience:

5–6. "DIVINE OMNIPOTENCE . . . HIGH-
EST WISDOM . . . PRIMAL LOVE": the
Father, the Son, the Holy Ghost. Thus,
the gate of Hell was created by the Trinity moved by Justice.

"Now here you must leave all distrust behind;
    let all your cowardice die on this spot.   15
We are at the place where earlier I said
    you could expect to see the suffering race
    of souls who lost the good of intellect."
Placing his hand on mine, smiling at me
    in such a way that I was reassured,   20
    he led me in, into those mysteries.
Here sighs and cries and shrieks of lamentation
    echoed throughout the starless air of Hell;
    at first these sounds resounding made me weep:
tongues confused, a language strained in anguish   25
    with cadences of anger, shrill outcries
    and raucous groans in time to slapping hands,
raising a whirling storm that turns itself
    forever through that air of endless black,
    like grains of sand swirling when a whirlwind blows.   30
And I, in the midst of all this circling horror,
    began, "Teacher, what are these sounds I hear?
    What souls are these so overwhelmed by grief?"
And he to me: "This wretched state of being
    is the fate of those sad souls who lived a life   35
    but lived it with no blame and with no praise.
They are mixed with that repulsive choir of angels
    neither faithful nor unfaithful to their God,
    but undecided in neutrality.
Heaven, to keep its beauty, cast them out,   40
    but even Hell itself would not receive them
    for fear the wicked there might glory over them."
And I: "Master, what torments do they suffer
    that make such bitterness ring through their screams?"
He answered: "I will tell you in few words: 45
these wretches have no hope of truly dying,
    and this blind life they lead is so abject
    it makes them envy every other fate.
The world will not record their having been there;
    Heaven's mercy and its justice turn from them.   50
    Let's not discuss them; look and pass them by."
And so I looked and saw a kind of banner
    rushing ahead, whirling with aimless speed
    as though it would not ever take a stand;

---

18. Souls who have lost sight of God.

22–30. Entering the Vestibule of Hell, the Pilgrim is immediately stunned by the screams of the shades in the Vestibule, borne to him in the form of an awesome tempest. In this first encounter with eternal punishment, he receives, as it were, an acoustical impression of Hell in its entirety.

35–42. The first tormented souls whom the Pilgrim meets are not in Hell itself but in the Vestibule leading to it. In a sense they are the most loathsome sinners of all because in life they performed neither meritorious nor reprehensible acts. Heaven has damned them but Hell will not accept them.

52–69. In the *Inferno* divine retribution assumes the form of the *contrapasso*, i.e., the just punishment of sin, effected by a process either resembling or contrasting to the sin itself. In this Canto the *contrapasso* opposes the sin of neutrality, or inactivity: The souls who in their early lives had no banner, no leader to follow, now run forever after one.

behind it an interminable train   55
  of souls pressed on, so many that I wondered
  how death could have undone so great a number.
When I had recognized a few of them,
  I saw the shade of the one who must have been
  the coward who had made the great refusal.   60
At once I understood, and I was sure
  this was that sect of evil souls who were
  hateful to God and to His enemies.
These wretches, who had never truly lived,
  went naked, and were stung and stung again   65
  by the hornets and the wasps that circled them
and made their faces run with blood in streaks;
  their blood, mixed with their tears, dripped to their feet,
  and disgusting maggots collected in the pus.
And when I looked beyond this crowd I saw   70
  a throng upon the shore of a wide river,
  which made me ask, "Master, I would like to know:
who are these people, and what law is this
  that makes those souls so eager for the crossing—
  as I can see, even in this dim light?"   75
And he: "All this will be made plain to you
  as soon as we shall come to stop awhile
  upon the sorrowful shore of Acheron."
And I, with eyes cast down in shame, for fear
  that I perhaps had spoken out of turn,   80
  said no more until we reached the river.
And suddenly, coming towards us in a boat,
  a man of years whose ancient hair was white
  screamed at us, "Woe to you, perverted souls!
Give up all hope of ever seeing heaven: 85
  I come to lead you to the other shore,
  into eternal darkness, ice and fire.
And you, the living soul, you over there,
  get away from all these people who are dead."
But when he saw I did not move aside   90
he said, "Another way, by other ports,
  not here, shall you pass to reach the other shore;
  a lighter skiff than this must carry you."

60. Most critics say this is Celestine V who renounced the papacy in 1294 five months after having been elected. However, Celestine, considering himself inadequate to the task, resigned his office out of humility, not out of cowardice. And the fact that the ex-pope was canonized in 1313 indicates that his refusal might well have been interpreted as a pious act.

Perhaps it is most likely that this shade is Pontius Pilate who refused to pass sentence on Christ. His role, then, would be paralleled to that of the "neutral angels": as they stood by while Lucifer rebelled against God, so Pilate's neutral attitude at the trial of Christ resulted in the crucifixion of Christ.

78. "Acheron": one of the rivers of Hell whose origin is explained in Canto XIV, ll. 112–120; it serves as the outer boundary of Hell proper.

83. "a man of years": Charon, the boatman of classical mythology who transports the souls of the dead across the Acheron into Hades.

91–93. Charon, whose boat bears only the souls of the damned, recognizes the Pilgrim as a living man and refuses him passage. This tercet contains a prophecy of Dante's salvation: "by other ports" he will pass to "reach the other shore (of the Tiber)," and go to Purgatory and eventually to Paradise.

And my guide, "Charon, this is no time for anger!
   It is so willed, there where the power is   95
   for what is willed; that's all you need to know."
These words brought silence to the woolly cheeks
   of the ancient steersman of the livid marsh,
   whose eyes were set in glowing wheels of fire.
But all those souls there, naked, in despair,   100
   changed color and their teeth began to chatter
   at the sound of his announcement of their doom.
They were cursing God, cursing their mother and father,
   the human race, and the time, the place, the seed
   of their beginning, and their day of birth.   105
Then all together, weeping bitterly,
   they packed themselves along the wicked shore
   that waits for everyman who fears not God.
The devil, Charon, with eyes of glowing coals,
   summons them all together with a signal,   110
   and with an oar he strikes the laggard sinner.
As in autumn when the leaves begin to fall,
   one after the other (until the branch
   is witness to the spoils spread on the ground),
so did the evil seed of Adam's Fall   115
   drop from that shore to the boat, one at a time,
   at the signal, like the falcon to its lure.
Away they go across the darkened waters,
   and before they reach the other side to land,
   a new throng starts collecting on this side.   120
"My son," the gentle master said to me,
   "all those who perish in the wrath of God
   assemble here from all parts of the earth;
they want to cross the river, they are eager;
   it is Divine Justice that spurs them on,   125
   turning the fear they have into desire.
A good soul never comes to make this crossing,
   so, if Charon grumbles at the sight of you,
   you see now what his words are really saying."
He finished speaking, and the grim terrain   130
   shook violently; and the fright it gave me
   even now in recollection makes me sweat.
Out of the tear-drenched land a wind arose
   which blasted forth into a reddish light,
   knocking my senses out of me completely,   135
and I fell as one falls tired into sleep.

---

100. Though we must assume that all the damned in the *Inferno* are naked (except the Hypocrites, Canto XXIII), only occasionally is this fact pointed out.

124–126. It is perhaps a part of the punishment that the souls of all the damned are eager for their punishment to begin; those who were so willing to sin on earth, are in Hell damned with a willingness to go to their just retribution.

136. The swoon (or sleep) as a transitional device is used again at the end of Canto V. Note also the opening lines of Canto I where the Pilgrim's awaking from sleep serves an introductory purpose.

CANTO IV

Waking from his swoon, the Pilgrim is led by Virgil to the first Circle of Hell, known as Limbo, where the sad shades of the virtuous non-Christians dwell. The souls here, including Virgil, suffer no physical torment, but they must live, in desire, without hope of seeing God. Virgil tells about Christ's descent into Hell and His salvation of several Old Testament figures. The poets see a light glowing in the darkness, and as they proceed toward it, they are met by the four greatest (other than Virgil) pagan poets: Homer, Horace, Ovid, and Lucan, who take the Pilgrim into their group. As they come closer to the light, the Pilgrim perceives a splendid castle where the greatest non-Christian thinkers dwell together with other famous historical figures. Once within the castle, the Pilgrim sees, among others, Electra, Aeneas, Caesar, Saladin, Aristotle, Plato, Orpheus, Cicero, Avicenna, and Averroës. But soon they must leave; and the poets move from the radiance of the castle toward the fearful encompassing darkness.

A heavy clap of thunder! I awoke
    from the deep sleep that drugged my mind—startled,
    the way one is when shaken out of sleep.
I turned my rested eyes from side to side,
    already on my feet and, staring hard,   5
    I tried my best to find out where I was,
and this is what I saw: I found myself
    right on the brink of grief's abysmal valley
    that collects the thunderings of endless cries.
So dark and deep and nebulous it was,   10
    try as I might to force my sight below
    I could not see the shape of anything.
"Let us descend into the sightless world,"
    began the poet (his face was deathly pale):
    "I will go first, and you will follow me."   15
And I, aware of his changed color, said:
    "But how can I go on if you are frightened?
    You are my constant strength when I lose heart."
And he to me: "The anguish of the souls
    that are down here paints my face with pity—   20
    which you have wrongly taken to be fear.
Let us go on, the long road urges us."
    He entered then, leading the way for me
    down to the first circle of the abyss.
Down there, to judge only by what I heard,   25
    there were no wails but just the sounds of sighs
    rising and trembling through the timeless air,
The sounds of sighs of untormented grief
    burdening these groups, diverse and teeming,
    made up of men and women and of infants.   30

Then the good master said, "You do not ask
    what sort of souls are these you see around you.
    Now you should know before we go on farther,
they have not sinned. But their great worth alone
    was not enough, for they did not know Baptism   35
    which is the gateway to the faith you follow,
and if they came before the birth of Christ
    they did not worship God the way one should;
    I myself am a member of this group.
For this defect, and for no other guilt,   40
    we here are lost. In this alone we suffer:
    cut off from hope, we live on in desire."
The words I heard weighed heavy on my heart;
    to think that souls as virtuous as these
    were suspended in that limbo, and forever!   45
"Tell me, my teacher, tell me, O my master,"
    I began (wishing to have confirmed by him
    the teachings of unerring Christian doctrine),
"did any ever leave here, through his merit
    or with another's help, and go to bliss?"   50
And he who understood my hidden question,
    answered: "I was a novice in this place
    when I saw a mighty lord descend to us
    who wore the sign of victory as his crown.
He took from us the shade of our first parent,   55
    of Abel, his good son, of Noah, too,
    and of obedient Moses, who made the laws;
Abram, the Patriarch, David the King,
    Israel with his father and his children,
    with Rachel whom he worked so hard to win;   60
and many more he chose for blessedness;
    and you should know, before these souls were taken,
    no human soul had ever reached salvation."
We did not stop our journey while he spoke,
    but continued on our way along the woods—   65
    I say the woods, for souls were thick as trees.
We had not gone too far from where I woke
    when I made out a fire up ahead,

---

34. According to Christian doctrine no one outside the Church (i.e., without baptism, the first Sacrament and, thus, the "gateway to the faith") can be saved. The souls suspended in Limbo, the first circle of Hell, were on earth virtuous individuals who had no knowledge of Christ and His teachings (through no fault of their own since they preceded Him) or who, after His coming, died unbaptized. Here physical torment is absent; these shades suffer only mental anguish for, now cognizant of the Christian God, they have to "live on in desire" without any hope of beholding Him.

49–50. The Pilgrim, remembering the Church's teaching concerning Christ's Harrowing of Hell, attempts to verify it by questioning Virgil, who should have been there at the time. Note the cautious presentation of the question (especially on the phrase" with another's help"), by means of which the Pilgrim, more than reassuring himself about Church doctrine, is subtly testing his guide. Virgil responds to the Pilgrim's "hidden question" in the terms of his classical culture. Unable to understand Christ in Christian terms, Virgil can only refer to Him as a "mighty lord . . . who wore the sign of victory as his crown."

a hemisphere of light that lit the dark.
Though we were still some distance from that place,   70
  we were close enough for me to vaguely see
  that distinguished people occupied that spot.
"O glory of the sciences and arts,
  who are these souls enjoying special honor,
  dwelling apart from all the others here?"   75
And he to me: "The honored name they bear
  that still resounds above in your own world
  wins Heaven's favor for them in this place."
And as he spoke I heard a voice announce:
  "Now let us honor our illustrious poet,   80
  his shade that left is now returned to us."
And when the voice was silent and all was quiet
  I saw four mighty shades approaching us,
  their faces showing neither joy nor sorrow.
Then my good master started to explain: 85
  "Observe the one who comes with sword in hand,
  leading the three as if he were their master.
It is the shade of Homer, sovereign poet,
  and coming second, Horace, the satirist;
  Ovid is the third, and last comes Lucan.   90
Since they all share one name with me, the name
  you heard resounding in that single voice,
  they honor me and do well doing so."
So I saw gathered there the noble school
  of the master singer of sublimest verse   95
  who soars above all others like the eagle.
And after they had talked awhile together,
  they turned and with a gesture welcomed me,
  and at that sign I saw my master smile.
Greater honor still they deigned to grant me: 100
  they welcomed me as one of their own group,
  so that I numbered sixth among such minds.
We walked together towards the shining light,
  discussing things that here are best kept silent,
  as there they were most fitting for discussion.   105

69. The "hemisphere of light" emanates from a "splendid castle" (l. 106), the dwelling place of the virtuous men of wisdom in Limbo. The light is the illumination of human intellect which those who dwell there had in such high measure on earth.

86–88. Because his name was inseparably linked with the Trojan War, Homer is portrayed by Dante as a sword-bearing poet, one who sang of arms and martial heroes.

90. Ovid's major work, the *Metamorphoses*, was widely read and consulted as the principal source and authority for classical mythology during the Middle Ages. Lucan provided Dante with mythological material, and with much historical information on the civil war between Pompey and Caesar (*Pharsalia*).

100–102. In this passage Dante, equating himself with the famous poets of antiquity, acknowledges his art and talent. By this it should not be assumed that he is merely indulging in self-praise; rather, the reader should also interpret these lines as an indication of Dante's awareness of his role as a poet, of his purpose in writing, and of his unique position in the literary scene of his day.

We reached the boundaries of a splendid castle
  that seven times was circled by high walls
  defended by a sweetly flowing stream.
We walked right over it as on hard ground;
  through seven gates I passed with those wise spirits,   110
  and then we reached a meadow fresh in bloom.
There people were whose eyes were calm and grave,
  whose bearing told of great authority;
  seldom they spoke and always quietly.
Then moving to one side we reached a place   115
  spread out and luminous, higher than before,
  allowing us to view all who were there.
And right before us on the lustrous green
  the mighty shades were pointed out to me
  (my heart felt glory when I looked at them).   120
There was Electra standing with a group,
  among whom I saw Hector and Aeneas,
  and Caesar, falcon-eyed and fully armed.
I saw Camilla and Penthesilea;
  across the way I saw the Latian King,   125
  with Lavinia, his daughter, by his side.
I saw the Brutus who drove out the Tarquin;
  Lucretia, Julia, Marcia and Cornelia;
  off, by himself, I noticed Saladin,

106–111. The allegorical construction of the castle is open to question. It may represent natural philosophy unilluminated by divine wisdom, in which case the seven walls serving to protect the castle would be the seven moral and speculative virtues (prudence, justice, fortitude, temperance, intellect, science, and knowledge); and the seven gates which provide access to the castle would be the seven liberal arts which formed the medieval school curriculum (music, arithmetic, geometry, astronomy—the *quadrivium;* and grammar, logic, and rhetoric —the *trivium*). The symbolic value of the stream also remains uncertain; it could signify eloquence, a "stream" which the eloquent Virgil and Dante should have no trouble crossing—and indeed, they "walked right over it as on hard ground" (l. 109).
112–144. The inhabitants of the great castle are important pagan philosophers and poets, as well as famous writers. Three of the shades named (Saladin, Avicenna, Averroës) lived only one or two hundred years before Dante. Modern readers might wonder at the inclusion of medieval non-Christians among the virtuous Pagans of antiquity, but the three just mentioned were among the non-Christians whom the Middle Ages, particularly, respected.
121. "Electra": daughter of Atlas, the

mother of Dardanus, the founder of Troy. Thus, her followers include all members of the Trojan race. She should not be confused with Electra, daughter of Agamemnon, the character in plays by Aeschylus, Sophocles, and Euripides.
122. Among Electra's descendants are: "Hector," the eldest son of Priam, king of Troy, and "Aeneas" (cf. I, 73–75, and II, 13–24).
123. Julius Caesar proclaimed himself the first emperor of Rome after defeating numerous opponents in civil conflicts.
124–126. "Camilla": see Canto I, note on l. 107. "Penthesilea": the glamorous Queen of the Amazons who aided the Trojans against the Greeks and was slain by Achilles during the conflict. "King Latinus": commanded the central region of the Italian peninsula, the site where Aeneas founded Rome. He gave Lavinia to the Trojan conqueror in marriage.
127–129. Outraged by the murder of his brother and the rape (and subsequent suicide) of his sister (Lucretia), Lucius Brutus incited the Roman populace to expel the Tarquins, the perpetrators of the offences. This accomplished, he was elected first consul and consequently became the founder of the Roman Republic. The four women were famous Roman wives and mothers. "Lucretia": wife of Collatinus; "Julia": daughter of Julius Caesar and wife of Pompey; "Marcia":

and when I raised my eyes a little higher   130
    I saw the master sage of those who know
    sitting with his philosophic family.
All gaze at him, all pay their homage to him;
    and there I saw both Socrates and Plato,
    each closer to his side than any other;   135
Democritus, who said the world was chance,
    Diogenes, Thales, Anaxagoras,
    Empedocles, Zeno, and Heraclitus;
I saw the one who classified our herbs:
    Dioscorides I mean. And I saw Orpheus,   140
    Tully, Linus, Seneca the moralist,
Euclid the geometer and Ptolemy,
    Hippocrates, Galen, Avicenna,
    and Averroës who made the Commentary.
I cannot tell about them all in full;   145
    my theme is long and urges me ahead,
    often I must omit things I have seen.
The company of six becomes just two;
    my wise guide leads me by another way
    out of the quiet into tempestuous air.   150
I come into a place where no light is.

second wife of Cato of Utica (in the *Convivio* Dante makes her the symbol of the noble soul); "Cornelia": daughter of Scipio Africanus Major and mother of the Gracchi, the tribunes Tiberius and Caius. A distinguished soldier, Saladin became sultan of Egypt in 1174. Medieval opinion of Saladin was favorable; he was lauded for his generosity and his magnanimity.

131. To Dante, Aristotle represented the summit of human reason, that point which man could reach on his own without the benefit of Christian revelation.

137. "Diogenes": the Cynic Philosopher who believed that the only good lies in virtue secured through self-control and abstinence. "Anaxagoras": a Greek philosopher of the Ionian school (500–428 B.C.). Among his famous students were Pericles and Euripides. "Thales": (ca. 635–ca. 545 B.C.), an early Greek philosopher born at Miletus, founded the Ionian school of philosophy, and in his main doctrine maintained that water is the elemental principle of all things.

140. "Dioscorides": a Greek natural scientist and physician of the first century A.D. "Orpheus": a mythical Greek poet and musician whose lyrical talent was such that it moved rocks and trees and tamed wild beasts.

141. "Tully": Marcus Tullius Cicero, celebrated Roman orator, writer, and philosopher (106–43 B.C.). "Linus": a mythical Greek poet and musician who is

credited with inventing the dirge. Lucius Annaeus "Seneca" (4 B.C.–65 A.D.): followed the philosophy of the Stoics in his moral treatises. Dante calls him "the moralist" to distinguish him from Seneca the tragedian who was thought (erroneously) during the Middle Ages to be another person.

142. "Euclid": a Greek mathematician (ca. 300 B.C.) who wrote a treatise on geometry which was the first codification and exposition of mathematical principles. "Ptolemy": a Greek mathematician, astronomer, and geographer. The Ptolemaic system of the universe (which was accepted by the Middle Ages), so named although he did not invent it, presented the earth as its fixed center encircled by nine spheres (see illustration p. 837).

143. "Hippocrates": a Greek physician (ca. 460–ca. 377 B.C.), who founded the medical profession and introduced the scientific art of healing. "Galen": a celebrated physician (ca. 130–ca. 200 A.D.) who practiced his art in Greece, Egypt, and Rome. "Avicenna" (or Ibn-Sina): an Arabian philosopher and physician (980–1037 A.D.) who was a prolific writer.

144. "and Averroës who made the Commentary": Ibn-Rushd, called Averroës (ca. 1126–ca. 1198 A.D.), was a celebrated Arabian scholar born in Spain. He was widely known in the Middle Ages for his commentary on Aristotle, which served as the basis for the work of St. Thomas Aquinas.

CANTO V

From Limbo Virgil leads his ward down to the threshold of the
Second Circle of Hell where, for the first time, he will see the
damned in Hell being punished for their sins. There, barring their
way, is the hideous figure of Minòs, the bestial judge of Dante's
underworld; but after strong words from Virgil, the poets are
allowed to pass into the dark space of this circle, where can be
heard the wailing voices of the Lustful, whose punishment consists
of being forever whirled about in a dark, stormy wind. After seeing
a thousand or more famous lovers—including Semiramis, Dido,
Helen, Achilles, and Paris—the Pilgrim asks to speak to two figures
he sees together. They are Francesca da Rimini and her lover Paolo,
and the scene in which they appear is probably the most famous
episode of the *Inferno*. At the end of the scene, the Pilgrim, who
has been overcome by pity for the lovers, faints to the ground.

This way I went, descending from the first
    into the second circle, that holds less space
    but much more pain—stinging the soul to wailing.
There stands Minòs grotesquely, and he snarls,
    examining the guilty at the entrance;   5
    he judges and dispatches, tail in coils.
By this I mean that when the evil soul
    appears before him, it confesses all,
    and he who is the expert judge of sins
sees what place in Hell the soul belongs to;   10
    the times he wraps his tail around himself
    tells just how far the sinner must go down.
The damned keep crowding up in front of him:
    they pass along to judgment one by one;
    they speak, they hear, and then are hurled below.   15
"Oh you who come to the place where pain is host,"
    Minòs spoke out when he caught sight of me,
    putting aside the duties of his office,
"be careful how you enter and whom you trust:
    it is easy to get in, but don't be fooled!"   20
And my guide to him: "Why do you keep on shouting?
Do not attempt to stop his fated journey;
    it is so willed there where the power is
    for what is willed; that's all you need to know."
And now the notes of anguish start to play   25
    upon my ears; and now I find myself

4. "Minòs": the son of Zeus and
Europa. As king of Crete he was revered
for his wisdom and judicial gifts. For
these qualities he became chief magistrate of the underworld in classical literature:

    Quaesitor Minos urnam movet: ille si-
    lentum

    Conciliumque vocat, vitasque et crim-
    ina discit.

        (Virgil, *Aeneid* VI, 432–433)
Although Dante did not alter Minòs's
official function, he transformed him into
a demonic figure, both in his physical
characteristics and in his bestial activity.

where sounds on sounds of weeping pound at me.
I came to a place where no light shone at all,
  bellowing like the sea racked by a tempest,
  when warring winds attack it from both sides. 30
The infernal storm, eternal in its rage,
  sweeps and drives the spirits with its blast:
  it whirls them, lashing them with punishment.
When they are swept back past their place of judgment,
  then come the shrieks, laments and anguished cries; 35
  there they blaspheme the power of almighty God.
I learned that to this place of punishment
  all those who sin in lust have been condemned,
  those who make reason slave to appetite;
and as the wings of starlings in the winter 40
  bear them along in wide-spread, crowded flocks,
  so does that wind propel the evil spirits:
here, then there, and up and down, it sweeps them
  forever, without hope to comfort them
  (hope, not of taking rest, but of suffering less). 45
And just like cranes in flight, chanting their lays,
  stretching an endless line in their formation,
  I saw approaching, crying their laments,
spirits carried along by the battling winds.
And so I asked, "Teacher, tell me, what souls 50
  are these punished in the sweep of the black wind?"
"The first of those whose story you should know,"
  my master wasted no time answering,
  "was empress over lands of many tongues;
her vicious tastes had so corrupted her, 55
  she licensed every form of lust with laws
  to cleanse the stain of scandal she had spread;
she is Semiramis who, legend says,
  was Ninus' wife and successor to his throne;
  she governed all the land the Sultan rules. 60
The next is she who killed herself for love
  and broke faith with the ashes of Sichaeus;
  and there is Cleopatra who loved men's lusting.

31–32. The *contrapasso* or punishment suggests that lust (the "infernal storm") is pursued without the light of reason (in the darkness).

34. In Italian this line reads, "Quando giungon davanti a la ruina," literally, "When they come before the falling place." According to Busnelli (*Miscellanea dantesca*, Padova, 1922, pp. 51–53) the *ruina* refers to the tribunal of Minòs; that is, to the place where the condemned sinners "fall" before him at the entrance to the second circle to be judged. Therefore I have translated *ruina* as "their place of judgment"; the entire tercet means that every time the sinners in the windstorm are blown near Minòs they shriek, lament, and blaspheme.

58. "Semiramis": The legendary queen of Assyria who, although renowned for her military conquests and civic projects, fell prey to her passions and became dissolute to the extent of legalizing lust. Dante conceived her as the motivating force of the degenerate society that ultimately opposes God's divine order.

61–62. According to Virgil (*Aeneid* I and IV), Dido, the queen of Carthage, swore faithfulness to the memory of her dead husband, Sichaeus. However, when the Trojan survivors of the war arrived in port, she fell helplessly in love with their leader, Aeneas, and they lived together as man and wife until the gods reminded Aeneas of his higher destiny: the founding of Rome and the Roman Empire. Immediately he set sail for Italy, and Dido, deserted, committed suicide.

See Helen there, the root of evil woe
　　lasting long years, and see the great Achilles　　　65
　　who lost his life to love, in final combat;
see Paris, Tristan"—then, more than a thousand
　　he pointed out to me, and named them all,
　　those shades whom love cut off from life on earth.
After I heard my teacher call the names　　　70
　　of all these knights and ladies of ancient times,
　　pit confused my senses, and I was dazed.
I began: "Poet, I would like, with all my heart,
　　to speak to those two there who move together
　　and seem to be so light upon the winds."　　　75
And he: "You'll see for yourself when they are closer;
　　if you entreat them by that love of theirs
　　that carries them along, they will come to you."
When the winds bent their course in our direction
　　I raised my voice to them, "Oh, wearied souls,　　　80
　　come speak with us if it be not forbidden."
As doves, called by desire to return
　　to their sweet nest, with wings outstretched and poised,
　　float downward through the air, guided by their will,
so these two left the flock where Dido is　　　85
　　and came toward us through the malignant air,
　　such was the tender power of my call.
"O living creature, gracious and so kind,
　　who make your way here through this dingy air
　　to visit us who stained the world with blood,　　　90
if we could claim as friend, the King of Kings,
　　we would beseech him that he grant you peace,
　　you who show pity for our atrocious plight.
Whatever pleases you to hear or speak
　　we will hear and we will speak about with you　　　95

64. Helen of Troy.

65–66. Enticed by the beauty of Polyxena, a daughter of the Trojan king, Achilles desired her to be his wife, but Hecuba, Polyxena's mother, arranged a counterplot with Paris so that when Achilles entered the temple for his presumed marriage, he was treacherously slain by Paris.

67. "Paris": the son of Priam, king of Troy, whose abduction of Helen ignited the Trojan War. "Tristan": the central figure of numerous medieval French, German, and Italian romances. Sent as a messenger by his uncle, King Mark of Cornwall, to obtain Isolt for him in marriage, Tristan became enamored of her, and she of him. After Isolt's marriage to Mark, the lovers continued their love affair, and in order to maintain its secrecy they necessarily employed many deceits and ruses. According to one version, however, Mark, growing continuously more suspicious of their attachment, finally discovered them together and ended the incestuous relationship by mortally wounding Tristan with a lance.

74. "those two there who move together": Francesca, daughter of Guido Vecchio da Polenta, lord of Ravenna, and Paolo Malatesta, third son of Malatesta da Verrucchio, lord of Rimini. Around 1275 the aristocratic Francesca was married for political reasons to Gianciotto, the physically deformed second son of Malatesta da Verrucchio. In time a love affair developed between Francesca and Gianciotto's younger brother, Paolo. One day the betrayed husband discovered them in an amorous embrace and slew them both.

82–84. "As doves": Paolo and Francesca are compared to "doves, called by desire" who "float downward through the air, guided by their will." The use of the words "desire" and "will" is particularly interesting because it suggests the nature of lust as a sin: the subjugation of the will to desire.

as long as the wind, here where we are, is silent.
The place where I was born lies on the shore
  where the river Po with its attendant streams
  descends to seek its final resting place.
Love, that kindles quick in the gentle heart,   100
  seized this one for the beauty of my body,
  torn from me. (How it happened still offends me!)
Love, that excuses no one loved from loving,
  seized me so strongly with delight in him
  that, as you see, he never leaves my side.   105
Love led us straight to sudden death together.
  Caïna awaits the one who quenched our lives."
  These were the words that came from them to us.
When those offended souls had told their story,
  I bowed my head and kept it bowed until   110
  the poet said, "What are you thinking of?"
When finally I spoke, I sighed, "Alas,
  what sweet thoughts, and oh, how much desiring
  brought these two down into this agony."
And then I turned to them and tried to speak;   115
  I said, "Francesca, the torment that you suffer
  brings painful tears of pity to my eyes.
But tell me, in that time of your sweet sighing
  how, and by what signs, did love allow you
  to recognize your dubious desires?"   120
And she to me: "There is no greater pain
  than to remember, in our present grief,
  past happiness (as well your teacher knows)!
But if your great desire is to learn
  the very root of such a love as ours,   125
  I shall tell you, but in words of flowing tears.
One day we read, to pass the time away,
  of Lancelot, how he had fallen in love;
  we were alone, innocent of suspicion.
Time and again our eyes were brought together   130
  by the book we read; our faces flushed and paled.
To the moment of one line alone we yielded:
  it was when we read about those longed-for lips
  now being kissed by such a famous lover,
  that this one (who shall never leave my side)   135
then kissed my mouth, and trembled as he did.
  The book and its author was our galehot!

97–99. "The place where I was born": Ravenna, a city on the Adriatic coast.

100–108. "Love . . . Love . . . Love . . .": These three tercets, each beginning with the word "Love," are particularly important as revealing the deceptive nature of Francesca. In lines 100 and 103, Francesca deliberately employs the style of *stilnovisti* poets such as Guinizelli and Cavalcanti in order to ensure the Pilgrim's sympathy, but she follows each of those lines with sensual and most un-*stilnovistic* ideas. For in the idealistic world of the *dolce stil nuovo* love would never "seize" a man for the beauty of the woman's body alone, nor would the sensual delight which "seized" Francesca be appropriate to *stilnovistic* love, which was distant, nonsexual, and ideal.

107. "Caïna": one of the four divisions of Cocytus, the lowest part of Hell, wherein are tormented those souls who treacherously betrayed their kin.

That day we read no further." And all the while
the one of the two spirits spoke these words,
   the other wept, in such a way that pity   140
   blurred my senses; I swooned as though to die,
and fell to Hell's floor as a body, dead, falls.

CANTO VI

On recovering consciousness the Pilgrim finds himself with Virgil
in the Third Circle where the Gluttons are punished. These shades
are mired in filthy muck and are eternally battered by cold and dirty
hail, rain, and snow. Soon the travelers come upon Cerberus, the
three-headed, doglike beast who guards the Gluttons, but Virgil
pacifies him with fistfuls of slime and the two poets pass on. One of
the shades recognizes Dante the Pilgrim and hails him. It is Ciacco,
a Florentine who, before they leave, makes a prophecy concerning
the political future of Florence. As the poets move away, the Pilgrim questions Virgil about the Last Judgment and other matters
until the two arrive at the next circle.

When I regained my senses that had fainted
   at the sight of these two who were kinsmen lovers,
   a piteous sight confusing me to tears,
new suffering and new sinners suffering
   appeared to me, no matter where I moved   5
   or turned my eyes, no matter where I gazed.
I am in the third circle, in the round of rain
   eternal, cursèd, cold and falling heavy,
   unchanging beat, unchanging quality.
Thick hail and dirty water mixed with snow   10
   come down in torrents through the murky air,
   and the earth is stinking from this soaking rain.
Cerberus, a ruthless and fantastic beast,
   with all three throats howls out his dog-like sounds
   above the drowning sinners of this place.   15
His eyes are red, his beard is slobbered black,
   his belly swollen, and he has claws for hands;
   he rips the spirits, flays and mangles them.

7–21. The shades in this circle are the
Gluttons, and their punishment fits their
sin. Gluttony, like all the sins of Incontinence, subjects reason to desire; in this
case desire is a voracious appetite. Thus
the shades howl like dogs—in desire,
without reason; they are sunk in slime,
the image of their excess. The warm comfort their gluttony brought them in life
here has become cold, dirty rain and
hail.

13–22. "Cerberus": In classical mythology Cerberus is a fierce three-headed

dog which guards the entrance to the
Underworld, permitting admittance to all
and escape to none. He is the prototype
of the Gluttons, with his three howling,
voracious throats that gulp down huge
handfuls of muck. He has become Appetite and as such he flays and mangles the
spirits who reduced their lives to a satisfaction of appetite. With his three heads,
he appears to be a prefiguration of Lucifer and thus another infernal distortion
of the Trinity.

Under the rain they howl like dogs, lying
  now on one side with the other as a screen,   20
  now on the other turning, these wretched sinners.
When the slimy Cerberus caught sight of us,
  he opened up his mouths and showed his fangs;
  his body was one mass of twitching muscles.
My master stooped and, spreading wide his fingers,   25
  he grabbed up heaping fistfuls of the mud
  and flung it down into those greedy gullets.
As a howling cur, hungering to get fed,
  quiets down with the first mouthful of his food,
  busy with eating, wrestling with that alone,   30
so it was with all three filthy heads
  of the demon Cerberus, used to barking thunder
  on these dead souls, who wished that they were deaf.
We walked across this marsh of shades beaten
  down by the heavy rain, our feet pressing   35
  on their emptiness that looked like human form.
Each sinner there was stretched out on the ground
  except for one who quickly sat up straight,
  the moment that he saw us pass him by.
"O you there being led through this inferno,"   40
  he said, "try to remember who I am,
  for you had life before I gave up mine."
I said: "The pain you suffer here perhaps
  disfigures you beyond all recognition:
  I can't remember seeing you before.   45
But tell me who you are, assigned to grieve
  in this sad place, afflicted by such torture
  that—worse there well may be, but none more foul."
"Your own city," he said," so filled with envy
  its cup already overflows the brim,   50
  once held me in the brighter life above.
You citizens gave me the name of Ciacco;
  and for my sin of gluttony I am damned
  as you can see, to rain that beats me weak.
And my sad sunken soul is not alone,   55
  for all these sinners here share in my pain
  and in my sin." And that was his last word.

26–27. With this action, Virgil imitates the action of the Sibyl who, leading Aeneas through the Underworld, placates Cerberus by casting honeyed cakes into his three throats (*Aeneid* VI, 417–423). By substituting dirt for the Virgilian cakes, Dante emphasizes Cerberus's irrational gluttony.

36. The shades in Hell bear only the *appearance* of their corporeal forms, although they can be ripped and torn and otherwise suffer physical torture—just as here they are able to bear the Pilgrim's weight. Yet they themselves evidently are airy shapes without weight (cf. Canto VIII, l. 27) which will, after the Day of Judgment, be possessed of their actual bodies once more (see Canto XIII, l. 103).

52. "Ciacco": The only Glutton whom the Pilgrim actually talks to is Ciacco, one of his Florentine contemporaries, whose true identity has never been determined. Several commentators believe him to be Ciacco dell'Anguillaia, a minor poet of the time and presumably the Ciacco of one of Boccaccio's stories (*Decameron*, IX, 8). However, more than a proper name, *ciacco* is a derogatory Italian word for "pig," or "hog," and is also an adjective, "filthy," or "of a swinish nature."

"Ciacco," I said to him, "your grievous state
  weighs down on me, it makes me want to weep;
  but tell me what will happen, if you know,   60
to the citizens of that divided state?
  And are there any honest men among them?
  And tell me, why is it so plagued with strife?"
And he replied: "After much contention
  they will come to bloodshed; the rustic party   65
  will drive the other out by brutal means.
Then it will come to pass, this side will fall
  within three suns, and the other rise to power
  with the help of one now listing toward both sides.
For a long time they will keep their heads raised high,   70
  holding the others down with crushing weight,
  no matter how these weep or squirm for shame.
Two just men there are, but no one listens,
  for pride, envy, avarice are the three sparks
  that kindle in men's hearts and set them burning."   75
With this his mournful words came to an end.
  But I spoke back: "There's more I want to know;
  I beg you to provide me with more facts:
Farinata and Tegghiaio, who were so worthy,
  Jacopo Rusticucci, Arrigo, Mosca   80
  and all the rest so bent on doing good,
where are they? Tell me what's become of them;
  one great desire tortures me: to know
  whether they taste Heaven's sweetness or Hell's gall."
"They lie below with blacker souls," he said,   85
  "by different sins pushed down to different depths;
  if you keep going you may see them all.
But when you are once more in the sweet world
  I beg you to remind our friends of me.
  I speak no more; no more I answer you."   90
He twisted his straight gaze into a squint
  and stared awhile at me, then bent his head,

59. The Pilgrim, having learned very little from his experience in Canto V, feels pity again at the sight of Ciacco.
65–75. "they will come to bloodshed": Ciacco's political prophecy reveals the fact that the shades in Hell are able to see the future; they also know the past, but they know nothing of the present (see Canto X, ll. 100–108). The Guelph party, having gained complete control over Florence by defeating the Ghibellines (1289), was divided into factions: the Whites (the "rustic party," l. 65), headed by the Cerchi family, and the Blacks ("the other," l. 66), led by the Donatis. These two groups finally came into direct conflict on May 1, 1300, which resulted in the expulsion of the Blacks from the city (1301). However, they returned in 1302 ("within three suns," l. 68, i.e., within three years), and with the help of Pope Boniface VIII, sent the Whites (including Dante) into exile. Boniface VIII, the "one now listing toward both sides" (l. 69), for a time did not reveal his designs on Florence, but rather steered a wavering course between the two factions, planning to aid the ultimate victor.
91–93. The manner in which Ciacco takes leave is certainly odd: his eyes, fixed on the Pilgrim throughout their conversation, gradually lose their power to focus and can only stare blankly. The concentration required for the prophecy seems to have exhausted him.

falling to join his other sightless peers.
My guide then said to me: "He'll wake no more
    until the day the angel's trumpet blows,   95
    when the unfriendly Judge shall come down here;
each soul shall find again his wretched tomb,
    assume his flesh and take his human shape,
    and hear his fate resound eternally."
And so we made our way through the filthy mess   100
    of muddy shades and slush, moving slowly,
    talking a little about the afterlife.
I said, "Master, will these torments be increased,
    or lessened, on the final Judgment Day,
    or will the pain be just the same as now?"   105
And he: "Remember your philosophy:
    the closer a thing comes to its perfection,
    more keen will be its pleasure or its pain.
Although this cursèd race of punished souls
    shall never know the joy of true perfection,   110
    more perfect will their pain be then than now."
We circled round that curving road while talking
    of more than I shall mention at this time,
    and came to where the ledge begins descending;
there we found Plutus, mankind's arch-enemy.   115

CANTO VII

At the boundary of the Fourth Circle the two travelers confront clucking Plutus, the god of wealth, who collapses into emptiness at a word from Virgil. Descending farther, the Pilgrim sees two groups of angry, shouting souls who clash huge rolling weights against each other with their chests. They are the Prodigal and the Miserly. Their earthly concern with material goods prompts the Pilgrim to question Virgil about Fortune and her distribution of the worldly goods of men. After Virgil's explanation, they descend to the banks of the swamplike river Styx, which serves as the Fifth Circle. Mired in the bog are the Wrathful, who constantly tear and mangle each other. Beneath the slime of the Styx, Virgil explains, are the Slothful; the bubbles on the muddy surface indicate their presence beneath. The poets walk around the swampy area and soon come to the foot of a high tower.

106–111. "Remember your philosophy": In answer to the Pilgrim's question (ll. 103–105), Virgil reminds him of the popular doctrine which states that the more a thing is perfect, the more it knows what pleasure is and pain. The perfected state of man from a "technical" point of view will be attained on Judgment Day, when the soul is reunited with the body. Therefore, the damned will feel more torment later than now; similarly, the blessed in Paradise will enjoy God's beautitude more.

115. For Plutus see Canto VII, l. 2.

"Pape Satàn, pape Satàn aleppe!"
  the voice of Plutus clucked these words at us,
  and that kind sage, to whom all things were known,
said reassuringly: "Pay no attention
  to your fear, for no matter what his power be   5
  he cannot stop our journey down this rock."
Then he turned toward that swollen face of rage
  crying, "Be quiet, cursèd wolf of Hell:
  feed on the burning bile that rots your guts.
This journey to the depths does have a reason,   10
  for it is willed on high, where Michael wrought
  a just revenge for the bold assault on God."
As sails swollen by wind when the ship's mast breaks,
  collapse, deflated, tangled in a heap,
  just so the savage beast fell to the ground.   15
And then we started down a fourth abyss,
  making our way along the dismal slope
  where all the evil of the world is dumped.
Ah, God's avenging justice! Who could heap up
  suffering and pain as strange as I saw here?   20
  How can we let our guilt bring us to this?
As every wave Charybdis whirls to sea
  comes crashing against its counter-current wave,
  so these folk here must dance their roundelay.
More shades were here than anywhere above,   25
  and from both sides, to the sound of their own screams,
  straining their chests, they rolled enormous weights.
And when they met and clashed against each other
  they turned to push the other way, one side
  screaming, "Why hoard?", the other side, "Why waste?"   30
And so they moved back round the gloomy circle
  returning on both sides to opposite poles
  to scream their shameful tune another time;
again they came to clash and turn and roll
  forever in their semi-circle joust.   35
  And I, my heart pierced through by such a sight,

1. This line, while it has never been interpreted satisfactorily, has certainly been interpreted variously. Critics as early as Boccaccio have noted a relation of "pape" to "papa" (pope). Boccaccio implies that "pape" is a word expressive of great admiration, and Plutus applies it to Satan, "the prince of demons." Some think that the line is addressed by Plutus to Dante; "Satàn" then is seen as the traditional, biblical term for "enemy." But the main thrust of modern criticism is to accept the line as simple gibberish (cf. Nimrod's speech in Canto XXI, l. 67).

2–15. Plutus, the god of wealth in classical mythology, appropriately presides over the Miserly and the Prodigal, those who did not use their material goods with moderation. In this canto his collapse like inflated sails "when the ship's mast breaks" is interesting not only because it attests to the true, airy emptiness of wealth, but also because the simile prefigures an image Dante uses in describing Lucifer at the end of the *Inferno*.

11–12. The archangel Michael fought against and triumphed over the rebellious angels in Heaven.

22–66. The Miserly and the Prodigal, linked together as those who misused their wealth, suffer a joint punishment. Their material wealth has become a heavy weight which each group must shove against the other, since their attitudes toward wealth on earth were opposed to each other. Part of their punishment is to complete the turn of the Wheel (circle) of Fortune against which they had rebelled during their short space of life on earth.

spoke out, "My Master, please explain to me
  who are these people here? Were they all priests,
  these tonsured souls I see there to our left?"
He said, "In their first life all you see here   40
  had such myopic minds they could not judge
  with moderation when it came to spending;
their barking voices make this clear enough,
  when they arrive at the two points on the circle
  where opposing guilts divide them into two.   45
The ones who have the bald spot on their heads
  were priests and popes and cardinals, in whom
  avarice is most likely to prevail."
And I: "Master, in such a group as this
  I should be able to recognize a few   50
  who dirtied themselves by such crimes as these."
And he replied, "Yours is an empty hope:
  their undistinguished life that made them foul
  now makes it harder to distinguish them;
forever they will come to their two battles;   55
  then from the tomb they will be resurrected:
  these with tight fists, those without any hair.
It was squandering and hoarding that have robbed them
  of the lovely world, and got them in this brawl:
  I will not waste choice words describing it!   60
You see, my son, the short-lived mockery
  of all the wealth that is in Fortune's keep,
  over which the human race is bickering;
for all the gold that is or ever was
  beneath the moon won't buy a moment's rest   65
  for even one among these weary souls."
"Master, now tell me what this Fortune is
  you touched upon before. What is she like
  who holds all worldly wealth within her fists?"
And he to me, "Oh foolish race of man,   70
  how overwhelming is your ignorance!
  Now listen while I tell you what she means:
that One, whose wisdom knows infinity,
  made all the heavens and gave each one a guide,
  and each sphere shining shines on all the others,   75
so light is spread with equal distribution:
  for worldly splendors He decreed the same
  and ordained a guide and general ministress
who would at her discretion shift the world's
  vain wealth from nation to nation, house to house,   80
  with no chance of interference from mankind;

38–48. The fact that most of the avaricious are tonsured priests indicates a major abuse practiced by the priesthood in Dante's time.

73–96. Virgil's digression concerns Fortune, a major theme of medieval and Renaissance writers such as Boethius, Petrarch, Boccaccio, Chaucer, and Machiavelli. Usually it was visualized as a female figure with a wheel, the revolutions of which symbolized the rise and fall of fortune in a man's life, but Dante deviates somewhat from the standard concept of Fortune by assigning to her the role of an angel.

so while one nation rules, another falls
    according to whatever she decrees
    (her sentence hidden like a snake in grass).
Your knowledge has no influence on her;   85
    she provides for change, she judges, and she rules
    her domain as do the other gods their own.
Her changing changes never take a rest;
    necessity keeps her in constant motion,
    as men come and go to take their turn with her.   90
And this is she so crucified and cursed;
    even those in luck who should be praising her,
    instead, revile her and condemn her acts.
But she is blest and in her bliss hears nothing;
    with all God's joyful first-created creatures   95
    she turns her sphere and, blest, turns it with joy.
Now let's move down to greater wretchedness;
    the stars that rose when I set out for you
    are going down—we cannot stay too long."
We crossed the circle to its other bank,   100
    passing a spring that boils and overflows
    into a ditch the spring itself cut out.
The water was a deeper dark than perse,
    and we, with its grey waves for company,
    made our way down along a rough, strange path.   105
This dingy little stream, when it has reached
    the bottom of the grey malignant slopes,
    becomes a swamp that has the name of Styx.
And I, intent on looking as we passed,
    saw muddy people moving in that marsh,   110
    all naked, with their faces scarred by rage.
They fought each other, not with hands alone,
    but struck with head and chest and feet as well,
    with teeth they tore each other limb from limb.
And the good teacher said: "My son, now see   115
    the souls of those that anger overcame;
    and I ask you to believe me when I say
beneath the slimy top are sighing souls
    who make these waters bubble at the surface;
    your eyes will tell you this—just look around.   120
Bogged in this slime they say, 'Sluggish we were
    in the sweet air made happy by the sun,
    and the smoke of sloth was smoldering in our hearts;
now we lie sluggish here in this black muck!'

---

84. This simile may seem comic to the reader, but it is not comic in Italian. Furthermore, it must be retained in translation because it is the pre-Christian Virgil who is speaking, and even though he knows the divine nature of Fortune for Christians, he cannot help but think of it in pre-Christian terms—as a monstrous and cunning evil force, and *not* a minister of God.

98–99. The time is past midnight. The stars setting in the west were rising in the east when Virgil first met Dante on the evening of Good Friday in the "dark wood."

108. "Styx": The river Styx is the second of the rivers of Hell; Dante, following the *Aeneid*, refers to it here as a marsh or quagmire.

This is the hymn they gurgle in their throats   125
   but cannot sing in words that truly sound."
Then making a wide arc we walked around
   the pond between the dry bank and the slime,
   our eyes still fixed on those who gobbled mud.
We came, in time, to the foot of a high tower.   130

CANTO VIII

But before they had reached the foot of the tower, the Pilgrim
had noticed two signal flames at the tower's top, and another flame
answering from a distance; soon he realizes that the flames are signals to and from Phlegyas, the boatman of the Styx, who suddenly
appears in a small boat speeding across the river. Wrathful and irritated though he is, the steersman must grant the poets passage, but
during the crossing an angry shade rises from the slime to question
the Pilgrim. After a brief exchange of words, scornful on the part of
the Pilgrim, who has recognized this sinner, the spirit grabs hold of
the boat. Virgil pushes him away, praising his ward for his just
scorn, while a group of the wrathful attack the wretched soul whose
name is Filippo Argenti. At the far shore the poets debark and find
themselves before the gates of the infernal City of Dis where howling figures threaten them from the walls. Virgil speaks with them
privately, but they slam the gate shut in his face. His ward is terrified, and Virgil too is shaken, but he insists that help from Heaven
is already on the way.

I must explain, however, that before
   we finally reached the foot of that high tower,
   our eyes had been attracted to its summit
by two small flames we saw flare up just there;
   and, so far off the eye could hardly see,   5
   another burning torch flashed back a sign.
I turned to that vast sea of human knowledge:
   "What signal is this? And the other flame,
   what does it answer? And who's doing this?"
And he replied: "You should already see   10
   across the filthy waves what has been summoned,
   unless the marsh's vapors hide it from you."
A bowstring never shot an arrow off
   that cut the thin air any faster than
   a little boat I saw that very second   15
skimming along the water in our direction,
   with a solitary steersman, who was shouting,
   "Aha, I've got you now, you wretched soul!"

18. Phlegyas, the son of Mars, set fire
to Apollo's temple at Delphi, furiously
enraged because Apollo raped his daughter Coronis. For this Apollo killed him
and sent him to Tartarus. Dante makes
Phlegyas the demonic guardian of the
Styx. As a personification of great wrath

he is well-suited not only for guarding
the Fifth Circle where the Wrathful are,
but also for transporting the Pilgrim to
the inner division of Hell, the City of Dis
(l. 68), whose gates are guarded by the
rebellious angels (l. 82–83).

"Phlegyas, Phlegyas, this time you shout in vain,"
  my lord responded, "you will have us with you   20
  no longer than it takes to cross the muck."
As one who learns of some incredible trick
  just played on him, flares up resentfully—
  so, Phlegyas there, was seething in his anger.
My leader calmly stepped into the skiff   25
  and when he was inside, he had me enter,
  and only then it seemed to carry weight.
Soon as my guide and I were in the boat
  the ancient prow began to plough the water,
  more deeply, now, than anytime before.   30
And as we sailed the course of this dead channel,
  before me there rose up a slimy shape
  that said: "Who are you, who come before your time?"
And I spoke back, "Though I come, I do not stay;
  but who are you, in all your ugliness?"   35
  "You see that I am one who weeps," he answered.
And then I said to him: "May you weep and wail
  stuck here in this place forever, you damned soul,
  for, filthy as you are, I recognize you."
With that he stretched both hands out toward the boat   40
  but, on his guard, my teacher pushed him back:
  "Away, get down there with the other curs!"
And then he put his arms around my neck
  and kissed my face and said, "Indignant soul,
  blessèd is she in whose womb you were conceived.   45
In the world this man was filled with arrogance,
  and nothing good about him decks his memory;
  for this, his shade is filled with fury here.
Many in life esteem themselves great men
  who then will wallow here like pigs in mud,   50
  leaving behind them their repulsive fame."
"Master, it certainly would make me happy
  to see him dunked deep in this slop just once
  before we leave this lake—it truly would."
And he to me, "Before the other shore   55

---

32. Filippo Argenti (l. 61), a member of the Adimari family.

36–63. The scene with Filippo Argenti is one of the most dramatic in the *Inferno*. The Pilgrim who had shown such pity for Francesca, and had even felt compassion for Ciacco, the swinish glutton, bursts into rage as soon as he recognizes Argenti. The Pilgrim repulses Filippo with harsh words; later he expresses his wish to Virgil to see the sinner "dunked" in the mud; when he sees Filippo being attacked viciously he rejoices and thanks God for the sight. Many commentators believe his attitude can be explained as a personal reaction to a political adversary whom he hated. But if that had been the moti- vation for his outburst, this would surely not have won Virgil's encomium: "Indignant soul, / blessèd is she in whose womb you were conceived" (ll. 44–45). Virgil's words must mean that he has sensed a core of righteous wrath in the Pilgrim's outburst, he sees that the hatred he has expressed is primarily a hatred of the sin of wrath. But we must remember that this is only the beginning of a spiritual development in the right direction, away from pity of the sinner toward hatred of his sin. Dante the Pilgrim has not yet learned to hate and at the same time show self-control and mastery of the situation, as he will later on (Canto XIX).

comes into sight, you will be satisfied:
a wish like that is worthy of fulfillment."
Soon afterwards, I saw the wretch so mangled
  by a gang of muddy souls that, to this day,
  I thank my Lord and praise Him for that sight: 60
"Get Filippo Argenti!" they all cried.
  And at those shouts the Florentine, gone mad,
  turned on himself and bit his body fiercely.
We left him there, I'll say no more about him.
  A wailing noise began to pound my ears 65
  and made me strain my eyes to see ahead.
"And now, my son," the gentle teacher said,
  "coming closer is the city we call Dis,
  with its great walls and its fierce citizens."
And I, "Master, already I can see 70
  the clear glow of its mosques above the valley,
  burning bright red, as though just forged, and left
to smoulder." And he to me: "Eternal fire
  burns within, giving off the reddish glow
  you see diffused throughout this lower Hell." 75
And then at last we entered those deep moats
  that circled all of this unhappy city
  whose walls, it seemed to me, were made of iron.
For quite a while we sailed around, until
  we reached a place and heard our boatsman shout 80
  with all his might, "Get out! Here is the entrance."
I saw more than a thousand fiendish angels
  perching above the gates enraged, screaming:
  "Who is the one approaching? Who, without death,
dares walk into the kingdom of the dead?" 85
  And my wise teacher made some kind of signal
  announcing he would speak to them in secret.
They managed to suppress their great resentment
  enough to say: "You come, but he must go
  who thought to walk so boldly through this realm. 90
Let him retrace his foolish way alone,
  just let him try. And you who led him here
  through this dark land, you'll stay right where you are."
And now, my reader, consider how I felt
  when those foreboding words came to my ears! 95
  I thought I'd never see our world again!
"Oh my dear guide, who more than seven times
  restored my confidence, and rescued me
  from the many dangers that blocked my going on,

---

68. The walls of the City of Dis mark
the division between upper Hell and
"lower Hell" (l. 75), and between the
sins of Incontinence and those of Violence. In terms of the Seven Capital Sins,
we have passed through circles punishing
the five lesser ones (lust, gluttony, avarice,
sloth, and wrath); beyond are sins occas-
sioned specifically by envy and pride.

82–83. These are the rebellious angels
who, with their leader Lucifer, were cast
into Hell after their abortive attempt to
gain control of Heaven.

don't leave me, please," I cried in my distress,   100
 "and if the journey onward is denied us
 let's turn our footsteps back together quickly."
Then that lord who had brought me all this way
 said, "Do not fear, the journey we are making
 none can prevent: such power did decree it.   105
Wait here for me and feed your weary spirit
 with comfort and good hope; you can be sure
 I will not leave you in this underworld."
With this he walks away. He leaves me here,
 that gentle father, and I stay, doubting,   110
 and battling with my thoughts of "yes"—but "no."
I could not hear what he proposed to them,
 but they did not remain with him for long;
 I saw them race each other back for home.
Our adversaries slammed the heavy gates   115
 in my lord's face, and he stood there outside,
 then turned toward me and walked back very slowly
with eyes downcast, all self-assurance now
 erased from his forehead—sighing, "Who are these
 to forbid my entrance to the halls of grief!"   120
He spoke to me: "You need not be disturbed
 by my vexation, for I shall win the contest,
 no matter how they plot to keep us out!
This insolence of theirs is nothing new;
 theu used it once at a less secret gate   125
 which is, and will forever be, unlocked;
you saw the words of death inscribed above it:
 already passing through, and with no guide,
 descending, through the circles, down the slope
comes one by whom the city will be opened."   130

CANTO IX

The help from Heaven has not yet arrived; the Pilgrim is afraid
and Virgil is obviously worried. He reassures his ward by telling him
that, soon after his own death, he was forced by the Sorceress Erichtho to resume mortal shape and go to the very bottom of Hell in
order to bring up the soul of a traitor; thus Virgil knows the way
well. But no sooner is the Pilgrim comforted than the Three Furies
appear before him, on the top of the tower, shrieking and tearing
their breasts with their nails. They call for Medusa whose horrible
face has the power of turning anyone who looks on her to stone.
Virgil turns his ward around and covers his eyes. After an "address
to the reader" calling attention to the coming allegory, a strident
blast splits the air, and the poets perceive an Angel coming through

---

125–126. The rebellious angels tried to
deny Christ entry into Hell, by barring the
principal ("less secret") gate, but it was
forced open by Him and will remain open
for eternity.
127. See Canto III, ll. 1–9.
130. See Canto IX, ll. 61–105.

the murky darkness to open the gates of the City for them. Then the angel returns on the path whence he had come, and the two travelers enter the gate. Within are great open burning sarcophagi from which groans of torment issue. Virgil explains that these are Arch Heretics and their lesser counterparts.

The color of the coward on my face,
  when I realized my guide was turning back,
  made him quickly change the color of his own.
He stood alert, like one who strains to hear;
  his eyes could not see far enough ahead   5
  to cut the heavy fog of that black air.
"But surely we were meant to win this fight,"
  he began, "or else.... But, such help was promised!
  O how much time it's taking him to come!"
I saw too well how quickly he amended   10
  his opening words with what he added on!
  They were different from the ones he first pronounced;
but nonetheless his words made me afraid,
  perhaps because the phrase he left unfinished
  I finished with worse meaning than he meant.   15
"Has anyone before ever descended
  to this sad hollow's depths from that first circle
  whose pain is all in having hope cut off?"
I put this question to him. He replied,
  "It is not usual for one of us   20
  to make the journey I am making now.
But it happens I was down here once before,
  conjured by that heartless witch, Erichtho
  (who could recall the spirit to its body).
Soon after I had left my flesh in death   25
  she sent me through these walls, and down as far
  as the pit of Judas to bring a spirit out;
and that place is the lowest and the darkest
  and the farthest from the sphere that circles all;
  I know the road, and well, you can be sure.   30
This swamp that breathes with a prodigious stink
  lies in a circle round the doleful city
  that now we cannot enter without strife."
And he said other things, but I forget them,
  for suddenly my eyes were drawn above,   35
  up to the fiery top of that high tower
where in no time at all and all at once
  sprang up three hellish Furies stained with blood,

1. Extreme fear makes the Pilgrim pale.
17–18. See Canto IV, ll. 34–42.
22–30. In answer to the Pilgrim's question Virgil states that, although such a journey is rarely made, he himself accomplished it once before at the command of Erichtho, a Thessalian necromancer who conjured up dead spirits. Having no literary or legendary source, the story of Virgil's descent into Hell was probably Dante's invention.

their bodies and their gestures those of females;
their waists were bound in cords of wild green hydras,   40
   horned snakes and little serpents grew as hair,
   and twined themselves around the savage temples.
And he who had occasion to know well
   the handmaids of the queen of timeless woe
   cried out to me "Look there! The fierce Erinyes!   45
That is Megaera, the one there to the left,
   and that one raving on the right, Alecto,
   Tisiphone, in the middle." He said no more.
With flailing palms the three would beat their breasts,
   then tear them with their nails, shrieking so loud   50
   I drew close to the poet, confused with fear.
"Call Medusa: we'll turn him into stone,"
   they shouted all together glaring down,
   "how wrong we were to let off Theseus lightly!"
"Now turn your back and cover up your eyes,   55
   for if the Gorgon comes and you should see her,
   there would be no returning to the world!"
These were my master's words. He turned me round
   and did not trust my hands to hide my eyes
   but placed his own on mine and kept them covered.   60
O all of you whose intellects are sound,
   look now and see the meaning that is hidden
   beneath the veil that covers my strange verses:
and then, above the filthy swell, approaching,
   a blast of sound, shot through with fear, exploded,   65
   making both shores of Hell begin to tremble;
it sounded like one of those violent winds,
   born from the clash of counter-temperatures,
   that tear through forests; raging on unchecked
it splits and rips and carries off the branches   70
   and proudly whips the dust up in its path
   and makes the beasts and shepherds flee its course!
He freed my eyes and said, "Now turn around
   and set your sight along the ancient scum,
   there where the marsh's mist is hovering thickest."   75
As frogs before their enemy, the snake,
   all scatter through the pond and then dive down
   until each one is squatting on the bottom,
so I saw more than a thousand fear-shocked souls
   in flight, clearing the path of one who came   80

44. The Furies are "handmaids" to Persephone (Hecate), wife of Pluto, classical god of the Underworld.

52. "Medusa": in classical mythology one of the three Gorgons. Minerva, furious at Medusa for giving birth to two children in one of the former's temples, changed her beautiful hair into serpents, so that whoever gazed on her terrifying aspect was turned to stone.

54. "Theseus": the greatest Athenian hero, descended to Hades with his friend Pirithous, King of the Lapithae, in order to kidnap Proserpina for him. Pluto slew Pirithous, however, and kept Theseus a prisoner in Hades by having him sit on the Chair of Forgetfulness, which made his mind blank and thereby kept him from moving. Dante chooses a less common version of the myth which has Theseus set free by Hercules. See note on ll. 98–99.

walking the Styx, his feet dry on the water.
From time to time with his left hand he fanned
his pace to push the putrid air away,
and this was all that seemed to weary him.
I was certain now that he was sent from Heaven.   85
I turned to my guide, but he made me a sign
to keep my silence and bow low to this one.
Ah, the scorn that filled his holy presence!
He reached the gate and touched it with a wand;
it opened without resistance from inside.   90
"Oh Heaven's outcasts, despicable souls,"
he started, standing on the dreadful threshold,
"what insolence is this that breeds in you?
Why do you stubbornly resist that will
whose end can never be denied and which,   95
more than one time, increased your suffering?
What do you gain by locking horns with fate?
If you remember well, your Cerberus
still bears his chin and throat peeled for resisting!"
He turned then and retraced the squalid path   100
without one word to us, and on his face
the look of one concerned and spurred by things
that were not those he found surrounding him.
And then we started moving toward the city
in the safety of the holy words pronounced.   105
We entered there, and with no opposition.
And I, so anxious to investigate
the state of souls locked up in such a fortress,
once in the place, allowed my eyes to wander,
and saw, in all directions spreading out,   110
a countryside of pain and ugly anguish.
As at Arles where the Rhône turns to stagnant waters
or as at Pola near Quarnero's Gulf
that closes Italy and bathes her confines,
the sepulchers make all the land uneven,   115
so they did here, strewn in all directions,
except the graves here served a crueler purpose:
for scattered everywhere among the tombs
were flames that kept them glowing far more hot
than any iron an artisan might use.   120
Each tomb had its lid loose, pushed to one side,

94. The will of God.
98–99. When Hercules descended into Hell to rescue Theseus, he chained the three-headed dog Cerberus and dragged him around and outside Hell so that the skin around his neck was ripped away.
112–117. "Arles": a city in Provence near the delta of the Rhône, the site of the famous Roman (later Christian) cemetery of Aliscamps. There, as at Pola, a city in Istria (now Yugoslavia) on the Quarnero Bay also famous for its an-cient burying ground, great sarcophagi cover the landscape. Interestingly, according to tradition, Christ appeared to St. Trophimus when the latter consecrated Aliscamps as a Christian resting place, and promised that the souls of those buried there would be free from the sep-ulchral torments of the dead. Thus, Dante compares the sepulchers here to those at Pola and Arles, except that "the graves here served a crueler purpose" (l. 117).

and from within came forth such fierce laments
that I was sure inside were tortured souls.
I asked, "Master, what kind of shades are these
lying down here, buried in the graves of stone,   125
speaking their presence in such dolorous sighs?"
And he replied: "There lie arch-heretics
of every sect, with all of their disciples;
more than you think are packed within these tombs.
Like heretics lie buried with their like   130
and the graves burn more, or less, accordingly."
Then turning to the right, we moved ahead
between the torments there and those high walls.

CANTO X

They come to the tombs containing the Epicurean heretics, and
as they are walking by them, a shade suddenly rises to full height in
one tomb, having recognized the Pilgrim's Tuscan dialect. It is the
proud Farinata who, in life, opposed Dante's party; while he and
the Pilgrim are conversing, another figure suddenly rises out of the
same tomb. It is the shade of Cavalcante de' Cavalcanti who interrupts the conversation with questions about his son Guido. Misin-
terpreting the Pilgrim's confused silence as evidence of his son's
death, Cavalcante falls back into his sepulcher, and Farinata
resumes the conversation exactly where it had been broken off. He
defends his political actions in regard to Florence and prophesies
that Dante, like himself, will soon know the pain of exile. But the
Pilgrim is also interested to know how it is that the damned can see
the future but not the present. When his curiosity is satisfied, he
asks Farinata to tell Cavalcante that his son is still alive, and that
his silence was caused only by his confusion about the shade's ina-
bility to know the present.

Now onward down a narrow path, between
the city's ramparts and the suffering,
my master walks, I following close behind.
"O lofty power who through these impious gyres
lead me around as you see fit," I said,   5
"I want to know, I want to understand:
the people buried there in sepulchers,

127–131. The Heretics are in a circle
in Hell which is outside of the three main
divisions of Incontinence, Violence, and
Fraud. Heresy is not due to weaknesses
of the flesh or mind (Incontinence), nor
is it a form of violence or of fraud; it is
a clearly willed sin based on intellectual
pride, and because it denies the Christian
concept of reality, it is punished outside
of the area allocated to the Christian
categories of sin.

There is great irony in the fact that
those who believed that the death of the
body meant the death of the soul suffer
as their punishment the entombment of
their living souls.

132. Why Dante and Virgil, who have
been circling always to the left, suddenly move off to the right remains a
mystery; this will happen one other time
in the *Inferno*, Canto XVII, l. 31.

can they be seen? I mean, since all the lids
are off the tombs and no one stands on guard."
And he: "They will forever be locked up,   10
when they return here from Jehosaphat
with the bodies that they left up in the world
The private cemetery on this side
serves Epicurus and his followers,
who make the soul die when the body dies.   15
As for the question you just put to me,
it will be answered soon, while we are here;
and the wish you are keeping from me will be granted."
And I: "O my good guide, I do not hide
my heart; I'm trying not to talk too much,   20
as you have told me more than once to do."
"O Tuscan walking through our flaming city,
alive, and speaking with such elegance,
be kind enough to stop here for a while.
Your mode of speech identifies you clearly   25
as one whose birthplace is that noble city
with which in my time, perhaps, I was too harsh."
One of the vaults resounded suddenly
with these clear words, and I, intimidated,
drew up a little closer to my guide,   30
who said, "What are you doing? Turn around
and look at Farinata who has risen,
you will see him from the waist up standing straight."
I already had my eyes fixed on his face,
and there he stood out tall, with chest and brow 35
proclaiming his disdain for all this Hell.
My guide, with a gentle push, encouraged me
to move among the sepulchers toward him;
"Be sure you choose your words with care," he said.
And when I reached the margin of his tomb   40
he looked at me, and half-contemptuously
he asked, "And *who* would *your* ancestors be?"
And I who wanted only to oblige him
held nothing back but told him everything.
At this he lifted up his brows a little,   45
then said, "Bitter enemies of mine they were

11–12. According to the Old Testament
prophet Joel (3:2, 12), the valley of
Jehosaphat, situated between Jerusalem
and the Mount of Olives, would be the
site of the Last Judgment, when the soul
and the body would be reunited and thus
returned to Heaven or Hell for eternity.
14–15. "Epicurus": the Greek philosopher who in 306 B.C. organized in Athens
the philosophical school named after him.
The philosophy of the Epicureans taught
that the highest good is temporal happiness which is to be achieved by the
practice of the virtues. In Dante's time
Epicureans were considered heretics because they exalted temporal happiness,

and therefore denied the immortality of
the soul and the afterlife. Epicurus is
among the heretics even though he was
a pagan, because he denied the immortality of the soul, a truth known even to the
ancients.
22–27. Having recognized Dante as a
fellow Tuscan, Farinata bids him pause
a moment. Born of an old and respected
Florentine family, Farinata (Manente
di Jacopo degli Uberti) took an active
role in the political life of the Commune
on the side of the Ghibelline party, whose
head he became in 1239. He died in 1264,
one year before Dante's birth.

and of my ancestors and of my party;
  I had to scatter them not once but twice."
"They were expelled, but only to return
  from everywhere," I said, "not once but twice—   50
  an art your men, however, never mastered!"
Just then along that same tomb's open ledge
  a shade appeared, but just down to his chin,
  beside this other; I think he got up kneeling.
He looked around as though he hoped to see   55
  if someone else, perhaps, had come with me
  and, when his expectation was deceived,
he started weeping: "If it be great genius
  that carries you along through this blind jail,
  where is my son? Why is he not with you?"   60
"I do not come alone," I said to him,
  "that one waiting over there guides me through here,
  the one, perhaps, your Guido held in scorn."
(The place of pain assigned him, and what he asked,
  already had revealed his name to me   65
  and made my pointed answer possible).
Instantly, he sprang to his full height and cried,
  "What did you say? He *held*? Is he not living?
  The day's sweet light no longer strikes his eyes?"
And when he heard the silence of my delay   70
  responding to his question, he collapsed
  into his tomb, not to be seen again.
That other stately shade, at whose request
  I had first stopped to talk, showed no concern
  nor moved his head nor turned to see what happened; 75
he merely picked up where we had left off:
  "If that art they did not master," he went on,
  "that gives me greater pain than does this bed.
But the face of the queen who reigns down here will glow
  not more than fifty times before you learn   80
  how hard it is to master such an art;
and as I hope that you may once more know

48–51. It happens that the Pilgrim's ancestors (along with other Guelphs) were twice (in 1248 and 1260) driven from the city (note the Pilgrim's appraisal of the action, revealed by his correcting Farinata's term "scatter" to "expel") by Farinata and his kinsmen (along with other Ghibellines), but they returned after both defeats (in 1251 and 1267). Dante's jibe, "an art your men, however, never mastered," refers to the expulsion of the Uberti family and other Ghibellines who never returned to Florence. See below, note on l. 84.

53. The shade is Cavalcante de' Cavalcanti, a member of an important Florentine family and father of Guido Cavalcanti. Cavalcante's son Guido, born about 1255, was one of the major poets of the day and was Dante's "first friend," as he

says in the *Vita Nuova*.

63. Some commentators, offering a different interpretation of the syntax of these two lines (to make the line mean that Virgil was leading the Pilgrim "to her whom" Guido perhaps held in scorn) believe that it is Beatrice whom Guido scorned. Most believe, however, that the object of Guido's attitude is Virgil. Perhaps it could be said that Guido as a skeptic refused to allow Reason to fulfill its ultimate purpose (according to the teachings of the time): that of leading man to God.

79–81. Hecate or Proserpina, the moon goddess, queen of the Underworld (cf. Canto IX, l. 44). Farinata makes the prophecy that Dante will know how difficult is the art of returning from exile before fifty months have passed.

the sweet world, tell me, why should your party be
so harsh to my clan in every law they make?"
I answered: "The massacre and butchery   85
that stained the waters of the Arbia red
now cause such laws to issue from our councils."
He sighed, shaking his head. "It was not I
alone took part," he said, "nor certainly
would I have joined the rest without good cause.   90
But I alone stood up when all of them
were ready to have Florence razed. It was *I*
who openly stood up in her defense."
"And now, as I would have your seed find peace,"
I said, "I beg you to resolve a problem   95
that has kept my raason tangled in a knot:
if I have heard correctly, all of you
can see ahead to what the future holds
but your knowledge of the present is not clear."
"Down here we see like those with faulty vision   100
who only see," he said, "what's at a distance;
this much the sovereign lord still grants us here.
When events are close to us, or when they happen,
our mind is blank, and were it not for others
we would know nothing of your living state.   105
Thus you can understand how all our knowledge
will be completely dead at that time when
the door to future things is closed forever."
Then I, moved by regret for what I'd done,
said, "Now, will you please tell the fallen one   110
his son is still on earth among the living;
and if, when he asked, silence was my answer,
tell him: while he was speaking, all my thoughts
were struggling with that point you solved for me."
My teacher had begun to call me back,   115
so I quickly asked that spirit to reveal
the names of those who shared a tomb with him.

84. The Uberti, Farinata's family, were excluded, according to Villani, from all pardons conceded to the Ghibellines, including the pardon of 1280, when most of the Ghibellines were permitted to return to Florence.

85–86. The hill of Montaperti, on the left bank of the Arbia, a small stream near Siena, was the scene of the fierce battle between the Florentine Guelphs and Ghilbellines (September 4, 1260), in which the Guelphs were defeated. Farinata was a leader of the Ghibellines.

88–93. In rebuttal, Farinata states that he was not the only Ghibelline at the battle of Montaperti, and that he had good reason to fight; but that at the Council in Empoli after the victory at Montaperti, when the Ghibellines wanted to plan the destruction of Florence, Farinata was the only Ghibelline to oppose the plan. He proudly points out that the credit for the latter action is his alone, while, on the other hand, he is not willing to accept all the blame for the bloodshed at Montaperti.

100–108. In answer to the Pilgrim's wish (the "knot," l. 96) to know the shades' capacity for knowledge of the present, Farinata states that, while they have complete knowledge of things past and future, they are ignorant of the present (except, of course, for the news of current events brought them by the new arrivals in Hell, the "others," l. 104). Even this knowledge will be denied them after the Day of Judgment, when all will become absolute and eternal. The door of the future will be closed (l. 108) and their remembrance of the past will fade away since there will no longer be any past, present, or future.

He said, "More than a thousand lie with me,
  the Second Frederick is here and the Cardinal
  is with us. And the rest I shall not mention."   120
His figure disappeared. I made my way
  to the ancient poet, reflecting on those words,
  those words which were prophetic enemies.
He moved, and as we went along he said,
  "What troubles you? Why are you so distraught?"   125
And I told him all the thoughts that filled my mind.
"Be sure your mind retains," the sage commanded,
  "those words you heard pronounced against yourself,
  and listen carefully now." He raised a finger:
"When at last you stand in the glow of her sweet ray,   130
  the one whose splendid eyes see everything,
  from her you'll learn your life's itinerary."
Then to the left he turned. Leaving the walls,
  he headed toward the center by a path
  that strikes into a vale, whose stench arose   135
disgusting us as high up as were were.

CANTO XI

Continuing their way within the Sixth Circle where the heretics
are punished, the poets are assailed by a stench rising from the
abyss ahead of them which is so strong that they must stop in order
to accustom themselves to the odor. They pause beside a tomb
whose inscription declares that within is Pope Anastasius. When
the Pilgrim expresses his desire to pass the time of waiting profitably, Virgil proceeds to instruct him about the plan of punishments
in Hell. Then, seeing that dawn is only two hours away, he urges
the Pilgrim on.

We reached the curving brink of a steep bank
  constructed of enormous broken rocks;
  below us was a crueler den of pain.
And the disgusting overflow of stench
  the deep abyss was vomiting, forced us   5
  back from the edge. Crouched underneath the lid
of some great tomb, I saw it was inscribed:
  "Within lies Anastasius, the Pope

119–120. The Emperor Frederick II
(1194–1250) is in the circle of the Heretics
because of the commonly held belief that
he was an Epicurean.
  Cardinal Ottaviano degli Ubaldini, a
Ghibelline, was papal legate in Lombardy
and Romagna until his death in 1273. He
is reported to have once said, "If I have
a soul, I have lost it for the Ghibellines."
  131. Beatrice.
  8–9. "Anastasius, the Pope": Anastasius II, pope from 496 to 498, was popularly believed for many centuries to be

a heretic because, supposedly, he allowed
Photinus, a deacon of Thessalonica who
followed the heresy of Acacius, to take
communion. This heresy denied Christ's
divine birth, asserting that He was begotten by a mortal man; thus Anastasius
II supposedly revealed his belief in the
heretical doctrine. It has been proved,
however, that this pope was confused
with the Byzantine Emperor Anastasius I
(491–518) by Dante's probable sources.
Emperor Anastasius was convinced by
Photinus to accept the heretical doctrine.

Photinus lured away from the straight path."
"Our descent will have to be delayed somewhat   10
    so that our sense of smell may grow accustomed
    to these vile fumes; then we will not mind them,"
my master said. And I: "You will have to find
    some way to keep our time from being wasted."
"That is precisely what I had in mind,"   15
he said, and then began the lesson: "My son,
    within these boulders' bounds are three more circles,
    concentrically arranged like those above,
all tightly packed with souls; and so that, later,
    the sight of them alone will be enough,   20
    I'll tell you how and why they are imprisoned.
All malice has injustice as its end,
    an end achieved by violence or by fraud;
    while both are sins that earn the hate of Heaven,
since fraud belongs exclusively to man,   25
    God hates it more and, therefore, far below,
    the fraudulent are placed and suffer most.
In the first of the circles below are all the violent;
    since violence can be used against three persons,
    into three concentric rounds it is divided: 30
violence can be done to God, to self,
    or to one's neighbor—to him or to his goods,
    as my reasoned explanation will make clear.
By violent means a man can kill his neighbor
    or wound him grievously; he can violate   35
    his goods by arson, theft and devastation;
so, homicides and those who strike with malice,
    those who destroy and plunder, are all punished
    in the first round, but all in different groups.
Man can raise violent hands against himself   40
    and his own goods; so in the second round,
    paying the debt that never can be paid,
are suicides, self-robbers of your world,
    or those who gamble all their wealth away
    and weep up there when they should have rejoiced. 45
One can use violence against the deity
    by heartfelt disbelief and cursing Him,
    or by despising Nature and God's bounty;
therefore, the smallest round stamps with its seal
    both Sodom and Cahors and all those souls   50
    who hate God in their hearts and curse His name.
Fraud, that gnaws the conscience of its servants,
    can be used on one who puts his trust in you
    or else on one who has no trust invested.

---

50. "Sodom": the biblical city (Genesis 18–19) destroyed by God for its vicious sexual offenses. "Cahors": a city in the south of France which was widely known in the Middle Ages as a thriving seat of usury. Dante uses the city names to indicate the Sodomites and Usurers who are punished in the smallest round of Circle Seven.

This latter sort seems only to destroy   55
    the bond of love that Nature gives to man;
    so in the second circle there are nests
of hypocrites, flatterers, dabblers in sorcery,
    falsifiers, thieves and simonists,
    panders, seducers, grafters and like filth.   60
The former kind of fraud both disregards
    the love Nature enjoys and that extra bond
    between men which creates a special trust;
thus, it is in the smallest of the circles,
    at the earth's center, around the throne of Dis,   65
    that traitors suffer their eternal pain."
And I, "Master, your reasoning runs smooth,
    and your explanation certainly makes clear
    the nature of this pit and of its inmates,
but what about those in the slimy swamp,   70
    those driven by the wind, those beat by rain,
    and those who come to blows with harsh refrains?
Why are they, too, not punished here inside
    the city of flame, if they have earned God's wrath?
    If they have not, why are they suffering?"   75
And he to me, "Why do you let your thoughts
    stray from the path they are accustomed to?
    Or have I missed the point you have in mind?
Have you forgotten how your *Ethics* reads,
    those terms it explicates in such detail: 80
    the three conditions that the heavens hate,
incontinence, malice and bestiality?
    Do you not remember how incontinence
    offends God least, and merits the least blame?
If you will reconsider well this doctrine   85
    and then recall to mind who those souls were
    suffering pain above, outside the walls,
you will clearly see why they are separated
    from these malicious ones, and why God's vengeance
    beats down upon their souls less heavily."   90
"O sun that shines to clear a misty vision,
    such joy is mine when you resolve my doubts
    that doubting pleases me no less than knowing!
Go back a little bit once more," I said
    "to where you say that usury offends   95
    God's goodness, and untie that knot for me."

---

65. Here the name Dis refers to Lucifer.
70–75. The sinners are those guilty of
Incontinence. Virgil's answer (ll. 76–90)
is that the Incontinent suffer a lighter punishment because their sins, being without
malice, are less offensive to God.
79–84. Virgil says "your Ethics" in referring to Aristotle's *Ethica Nicoma-
chea* because he realizes how thoroughly
the Pilgrim studied this work.
    While the distinction here offered be-
tween Incontinence and Malice is based
on Aristotle it should be clear that the
overall classification of sins in the *Inferno*
is not. Dante's is a twofold system, the
main divisions of which may be illustrated as follows:

Sins of { Incontinence
        { Malice { through Violence
               { through Fraud

"Philosophy," he said, "and more than once,
    points out to one who reads with understanding
    how Nature takes her course from the Divine
Intellect, from its artistic workmanship;   100
    and if you have your *Physics* well in mind
    you will find, not many pages from the start,
how your art too, as best it can, imitates
    Nature, the way an apprentice does his master;
    so your art may be said to be God's grandchild.   105
From Art and Nature man was meant to take
    his daily bread to live—if you recall
    the book of Genesis near the beginning;
but the usurer, adopting other means,
    scorns Nature in herself and in her pupil,   110
    Art—he invests his hope in something else.
Now follow me, we should be getting on;
    the Fish are shimmering over the horizon,
    the Wain is now exactly over Caurus,
and the passage down the bank is farther on."   115

CANTO XII

They descend the steep slope into the Seventh Circle by means
of a great landslide which was caused when Christ descended into
Hell. At the edge of the abyss is the Minotaur, who presides over
the circle of the Violent and whose own bestial rage sends him into
such a paroxysm of violence that the two travelers are able to run
past him without his interference. At the base of the precipice, they
see a river of boiling blood which contains those who have inflicted
violence upon others. But before they can reach the river they are
intercepted by three fierce Centaurs whose task it is to keep those
who are in the river at their proper depth by shooting arrows at
them if they attempt to rise. Virgil explains to one of the centaurs
(Chiron) that this journey of Pilgrim and himself is ordained by
God; and he requests him to assign someone to guide the two of
them to the ford in the river and carry the Pilgrim across it to the
other bank. Chiron gives the task to Nessus, one of the centaurs,
who, as he leads them to the river's ford, points out many of the
sinners there in the boiling blood.

101–105. Aristotle's *Physics* (II, ii) concerns the doctrine that Art imitates Nature. Art, or human industry, is the child of Nature in the sense that it is the use to which man puts Nature, and thus is the grandchild of God. Usurers, who are in the third round of Circle Seven, by doing violence to human industry are, in effect, doing violence to God.

113–115. Virgil, as always, indicates the time by referring to the stars; how he knows of their position at any given mo-ment Dante does not explain (the stars are not visible from Hell). Pisces, the Fish, is just appearing on the horizon, while the Great Bear, the Wain, is lying completely in the northwest quadrant of the heavens (Caurus is the Northwest Wind). The next sign of the Zodiac after Pisces is Aries; from Canto I we know that the sun is currently rising in Aries. Each sign of the Zodiac covers about two hours, thus it must be nearly two hours before sunrise.

Not only was that place, where we had come
   to descend, craggy, but there was something there
   that made the scene appalling to the eye.
Like the ruins this side of Trent left by the landslide
   (an earthquake or erosion must have caused it)   5
   that hit the Adige on its left bank,
when, from the mountain's top where the slide began
   to the plain below, the shattered rocks slipped down,
   shaping a path for a difficult descent—
so was the slope of our ravine's formation.   10
   And at the edge, along the shattered chasm,
   there lay stretched out the infamy of Crete:
the son conceived in the pretended cow.
   When he saw us he bit into his flesh,
   gone crazy with the fever of his rage.   15
My wise guide cried to him: "Perhaps you think
   you see the Duke of Athens come again
   who came once in the world to bring your death?
Begone you beast, for this one is not led
   down here by means of clews your sister gave him;   20
   he comes here only to observe your torments."
The way a bull breaks loose the very moment
   he knows he has been dealt the mortal blow,
   and cannot run but jumps and twists and turns,
just so I saw the Minotaur perform,   25
   and my guide, alert, cried out: "Run to the pass!
   While he still writhes with rage, get started down."
And so we made our way down through the ruins
   of rocks, which often I felt shift and tilt
   beneath my feet from weight they were not used to.   30
I was deep in thought when he began: "Are you,
   perhaps, thinking about these ruins protected
   by the furious beast I quenched in its own rage?
Now let me tell you that the other time
   I came down to the lower part of Hell,   35
   this rock had not then fallen into ruins;
but certainly, if I remember well,

4–10. The way down the precipice to the Seventh Circle is here compared to a great landslide, the *Slavini di Marco*, located near Trent in northern Italy; the event which took place about 883 diverted the Adige River from its course (l. 6). In the *Inferno* the steep, shattered terrain was caused by the earthquake which shook Hell just before Christ descended there.

12–21. The Sins of Violence are also the Sins of Bestiality, and the perfect overseer of the circle is the half-man, half-bull known as the Minotaur. Called the "infamy of Crete," that creature was the result of an act of Violence against Nature (punished in the third round of this circle): Pasiphaë, wife of King Minos of Crete, conceived an unnatural desire for a bull, which she satisfied by creeping into a wooden cow and having intercourse with the bull. The Cretan labyrinth, designed by Daedalus, was the Minotaur's home. He was finally slain by Theseus (the duke of Athens, l. 17) with the help of Ariadne (Pasiphaë's human daughter and, as such, a half-sister to the beast, l. 20). Note the continued appearance of the half-human, half-animal monsters, begun in Canto IV with the Furies.

it was just before the coming of that One
who took from Hell's first circle the great spoil,
that this abyss of stench, from top to bottom   40
    began to shake, so I thought the universe
    felt love—whereby, some have maintained, the world
has more than once renewed itself in chaos.
    That was the moment when this ancient rock
    was split this way—here, and in other places.   45
But now look down the valley. Coming closer
    you will see the river of blood that boils the souls
    of those who through their violence injured others."
(Oh blind cupidity and insane wrath,
    spurring us on through our short life on earth   50
    to steep us then forever in such misery!)
I saw a river—wide, curved like a bow—
    that stretched embracing all the flatland there,
    just as my guide had told me to expect.
Between the river and the steep came centaurs   55
    galloping in single file equipped with arrows,
    off hunting as they used to in the world;
then, seeing us descend, they all stopped short
    and three of them departed from the ranks
    with bows and arrows ready from their quivers.   60
One of them cried from his distant post: "You there,
    on your way down here, what torture are you seeking?
    Speak where you stand, if not, I draw my bow."
And then my master shouted back: "Our answer
    we will give to Chiron when we're at his side;   65
    as for you, I see you are as rash as ever!"
He nudged me saying: "That one there is Nessus
    who died from loving lovely Dejanira,
    and made of himself, of his blood, his own revenge.
The middle one who contemplates his chest   70

38. "that One": Christ, who, in the Harrowing of Hell, removed to Heaven the souls of the Elect.

41–43. According to Empedoclean doctrine, Hate, by destroying pristine harmony (i.e., original chaos), occasions the creation of all things, and Love, by reunifying these disparate elements, re-establishes concord in the universe.

47–48. Phlegethon, the Virgilian river of fire, here one of boiling blood, in which are punished those shades who committed violence against their fellow men.

56. Like the Minotaur, the Centaurs who guard the murderers and tyrants are men-beasts (half-horse, half-man) and thus appropriate to the sins of violence or bestiality.

65. "Chiron": Represented by the ancient poets as chief of the Centaurs, he

was particularly noted for his wisdom. In mythology he was the son of Saturn (who temporarily changed himself into a horse to avoid the notice and anger of his wife) and Philyra.

67–69. "Nessus": The Centaur who is the first to speak to the two travelers. He is later appointed by Chiron (ll. 98–99) to accompany them; he does so, pointing out various sinners along the way. Virgil refers to Dejanira, Hercules' wife, whom Nessus desired. In attempting to rape her, Nessus was shot by Hercules, but as he died he gave Dejanira a robe soaked in his blood which he said would preserve Hercules' love. Dejanira took it to her husband, whose death it caused, whereupon the distraught woman hanged herself.

is great Chiron who reared and taught Achilles;
the last is Pholus, known for his drunken wrath.
They gallop, by the thousands round the ditch
 shooting at any daring soul emerging
 above the bloody level of his guilt." 75
When we came closer to those agile beasts,
 Chiron drew an arrow, and with its notch
 he parted his beard to both sides of his jaws,
and when he had uncovered his great mouth
 he spoke to his companions: "Have you noticed, 80
 how the one behind moves everything he touches?
This is not what a dead man's feet would do!"
 And my good guide, now standing by the torso
 at the point the beast's two natures joined, replied:
"He is indeed alive, and so alone 85
 that I must show him through this dismal valley;
 he travels by necessity, not pleasure.
A spirit came, from singing Alleluia,
 to give me this extraordinary mission;
 he is no rogue nor I a criminal spirit. 90
Now, in the name of that power by which I move
 my steps along so difficult a road,
 give us one of your troop to be our guide:
to lead us to the ford and, once we are there,
 to carry this one over on his back, 95
 for he is not a spirit who can fly."
Chiron looked over his right breast and said
 to Nessus, "You go, guide them as they ask,
 and if another troop protests, disperse them!"
So with this trusted escort we moved on 100
 along the boiling crimson river's bank
 where piercing shrieks rose from the boiling souls.
There I saw people sunken to their eyelids,
 and the huge centaur explained, "These are the tyrants
 who dealt in bloodshed and in plundered wealth. 105
Their tears are paying for their heartless crimes:
 here stand Alexander and fierce Dionysius
 who weighed down Sicily with years of pain;
and there, that forehead smeared with coal-black hair,
 is Azzolino; the other one, the blond, 110

---

72. During the wedding of Pirithous and Hippodamia, when the drunken Centaurs tried to rape the Lapithaen women, Pholus attempted to rape the bride herself.
88. Beatrice.
107–108. Possibly Alexander the Great (356–323 B.C.), who is constantly referred to as a cruel and violent man by Orosius, Dante's chief source of ancient history. But many modern scholars believe this figure to be Alexander, tyrant of Pherae

(368–359 B.C.), whose extreme cruelty is recorded by Cicero and Valerius Maximus. Both of these authors link Alexander of Pherae with the tyrant Dionysius of Syracuse, mentioned here.
110. "Azzolino": Ezzelino III da Romano (1194–1259), a Ghibelline chief and tyrant of the March of Treviso. He was notoriously cruel and committed such inhuman atrocities that he was called a "son of Satan."

Opizzo d'Esti who, and this is true,
was killed by his own stepson in your world."
With that I looked to Virgil, but he said
"Let him instruct you now, don't look to me."
A little farther on, the centaur stopped   115
above some people peering from the blood
that came up to their throats. He pointed out
a shade off to one side, alone, and said:
"There stands the one who, in God's keep, murdered
the heart still dripping blood above the Thames."   120
Then I saw other souls stuck in the river
who had their heads and chests above the blood,
and I knew the names of many who were there.
The river's blood began decreasing slowly
until it cooked the feet and nothing more,   125
and here we found the ford where we could cross.
"Just as you see the boiling river here
on this side getting shallow gradually,"
the centaur said, "I would also have you know
that on the other side the riverbed   130
sinks deeper more and more until it reaches
the deepest meeting place where tyrants moan:
it is there that Heaven's justice strikes its blow
against Attila known as the scourge of earth,
against Pyrrhus and Sextus; and forever   135
extracts the tears the scalding blood produces
from Rinier da Corneto and Rinier Pazzo
whose battlefields were highways where they robbed."
Then he turned round and crossed the ford again.

111–114. "Opizzo d'Esti": Obizzo d'Esti was Marquis of Ferrara and of the March of Ancona (1264–1293). He was a cruel tyrant.

120. In 1272 during Holy Mass at the church ("in God's keep") in Viterbo, Guy de Montfort (one of Charles d'Anjou's emissaries), in order to avenge his father's death at the hands of Edward I, king of England, stabbed to death the latter's cousin, Prince Henry, son of Richard, earl of Cornwall. According to Giovanni Villani, the thirteenth-century chronicler, Henry's heart was placed in "a golden cup . . . above a column at the head of London bridge" where it still drips blood above the Thames (*Cronica* VII, xxxix). The dripping blood signifies that the murder has not yet been avenged.

124–126. The sinners are sunk in the river to a degree commensurate with the gravity of their crimes; tyrants, whose crimes of violence are directed against both man and his possessions, are sunk deeper than murderers, whose crimes are against men alone. The river is at its shallowest at the point where the poets cross; from this ford, in both directions of its circle, it grows deeper.

134. "Attila": king of the Huns, called the "scourge of God."

135. "Pyrrhus and Sextus": The first named is probably Pyrrhus (318–272 B.C.), king of Epirus, who fought the Romans three times between 280 and 276 B.C. before they finally defeated him. Sextus is probably the younger son of Pompey the Great. After the murder of Caesar he turned to piracy, causing near famine in Rome by cutting off the grain supply from Africa. He is condemned by Lucan (*Pharsalia* VI, 420–422) as being unworthy of his father. A few commentators believe that Dante is referring to Sextus Tarquinius Superbus, who raped and caused the death of Lucretia, the wife of his cousin.

137–138. "Rinier da Corneto and Rinier Pazzo": Two highway robbers famous in Dante's day.

CANTO XIII

No sooner are the poets across the Phlegethon than they encounter a dense forest, from which come wails and moans, and which is presided over by the hideous harpies—half-woman, half-beast, birdlike creatures. Virgil tells his ward to break off a branch of one of the trees; when he does, the tree weeps blood and speaks. In life he was Pier Delle Vigne, chief counselor of Frederick II of Sicily; but he fell out of favor, was accused unjustly of treachery and was imprisoned, whereupon he killed himself. The Pilgrim is overwhelmed by pity. The sinner also explains how the souls of the suicides come to this punishment and what will happen to them after the Last Judgment. Suddenly they are interrupted by the wild sounds of the hunt, and two naked figures, Lano of Siena and Giacomo da Sant' Andrea, dash across the landscape shouting at each other until one of them hides himself in a thorny bush; immediately a pack of fierce, black dogs rush in, pounce on the hidden sinner, and rip his body, carrying away mouthfuls of flesh. The bush, which has been torn in the process, begins to lament. The two learn that the cries are those of a Florentine who had hanged himself in his own home.

Not yet had Nessus reached the other side
   when we were on our way into a forest
   that was not marked by any path at all.
No green leaves, but rather black in color,
   no smooth branches, but twisted and entangled,   5
   no fruit, but thorns of poison bloomed instead.
No thick, rough, scrubby home like this exists—
   not even between Cecina and Corneto—
   for those wild beasts that hate the run of farmlands.
Here the repulsive harpies twine their nests,   10
   who drove the Trojans from the Strophades
   with filthy forecasts of their close disaster.
Wide-winged they are, with human necks and faces,
   their feet are clawed, their bellies fat and feathered;
   perched in the trees they shriek their strange laments.   15
"Before we go on farther," my guide began,
   "remember, you are in the second round
   and shall be till we reach the dreadful sand;
now look around you carefully and see

1-9. The Wood of the Suicides is described in a series of negatives ("No green leaves . . . no smooth branches . . . no fruit), and in fact the first three tercets begin with a negative. This device anticipates the negation inherent in suicide and suggests the atmosphere in which the action of this canto will move: mistrust and incredulity.

8-9. The vast swampland known as the "Maremma toscana" lies between the towns of Cecina and Corneto, which mark its northern and southern boundaries.

10-15. The Harpies were the daughters of Thaumas and Electra. Because of their malicious deeds they were banished to the Strophades Islands, where, having encountered Aeneas and his followers from Troy, they defiled their table and forecast future hardships for them.

with your own eyes what I will not describe,   20
    for if I did, you wouldn't believe my words."
Around me wails of grief were echoing,
    and I saw no one there to make those sounds;
    bewildered by all this I had to stop.
I think perhaps he thought I might be thinking   25
    that all the voices coming from those stumps
    belonged to people hiding there from us,
and so my teacher said, "If you break off
    a little branch of any of these plants,
    what you are thinking now will break off too."   30
Then slowly raising up my hand a bit
    I snapped the tiny branch of a great thorn,
    and its trunk cried: "Why are you tearing me?"
And when its blood turned dark around the wound,
    it started saying more: "Why do you rip me?   35
    Have you no sense of pity whatsoever?
Men were we once, now we are changed to scrub;
    but even if we had been souls of serpents,
    your hand should have shown more pity than it did."
Like a green log burning at one end only,   40
    sputtering at the other, oozing sap,
    and hissing with the air it forces out,
so from that splintered trunk a mixture poured
    of words and blood. I let the branch I held
    fall from my hand and stood there stiff with fear.   45
"O wounded soul," my sage replied to him,
    "if he had only let himself believe
    what he had read in verses I once wrote,
he never would have raised his hand against you,
    but the truth itself was so incredible   50
    I urged him on to do the thing that grieves me.
But tell him who you were; he can make amends,
    and will, by making bloom again your fame
    in the world above, where his return is sure."
And the trunk: "So appealing are your lovely words,   55
    I must reply. Be not displeased if I
    am lured into a little conversation.
I am that one who held both of the keys

47–49. Virgil is referring to that section
of the *Aeneid* (III, 22–43), where Aeneas
breaks a branch from a shrub, which then
begins to pour forth blood; at the same
time a voice issues from the ground beneath the shrub where Polydorus is
buried. See Canto XXX, l. 18.

58–78. Born in the Southern Italian
town of Capua (ca. 1190), Pier delle
Vigne studied at Bologna and, having
attracted the attention of Frederick II,
became attached to his court at Palermo,
where he soon became the Emperor's most
trusted minister. Around 1248, however,
he fell from the emperor's grace and was

placed in jail, where he committed suicide.
Pier delle Vigne tells how Envy ("that
courtesan," l. 64), ever-present at Frederick's court ("Caesar's household," l.
65), inflamed everyone against him, Frederick ("Augustus," l. 68) becoming influenced by the attitude of others. The
dishonor of the imprisonment and the
envisaged self-justification through death
led him to take his own life by dashing
his head against the prison wall. He concludes by declaring his innocence and expressing the desire for re-evaluation of his
deeds, which will ensure his earthly fame.

that fitted Frederick's heart; I turned them both,
   locking and unlocking, with such finesse   60
that I let few into his confidence.
I was so faithful to my glorious office,
   I lost not only sleep but life itself.
That courtesan who constantly surveyed
   Caesar's household with her adulterous eyes,   65
   mankind's undoing, the special vice of courts,
inflamed the hearts of everyone against me,
   and these, inflamed, inflamed in turn Augustus,
   and my happy honors turned to sad laments.
My mind, moved by scornful satisfaction,   70
   believing death would free me from all scorn,
   made me unjust to me who was all just.
By these strange roots of my own tree I swear
   to you that never once did I break faith
   with my lord who was so worthy of all honor.   75
If one of you should go back to the world,
   restore the memory of me, who here
   remain cut down by the blow that Envy gave."
My poet paused awhile then said to me,
   "Since he is silent now, don't lose your chance,   80
   ask him, if there is more you wish to know."
"Why don't you keep on questioning," I said,
   "and ask him, for my part, what I would ask,
   for I cannot, such pity chokes my heart."
He began again: "That this man may fulfill   85
   generously what your words cry out for,
   imprisoned soul, may it please you to continue
by telling us just how a soul gets bound
   into these knots, and tell us, if you know,
   whether any soul might someday leave his branches."   90
At that the trunk breathed heavily, and then
   the breath changed to a voice that spoke these words:
   "Your question will be answered very briefly.
The moment that the violent soul departs
   the body it has torn itself away from,   95
   Minòs sends it down to the seventh hole;
it drops to the wood, not in a place allotted,
   but anywhere that fortune tosses it.
   There, like a grain of spelt, it germinates,
soon springs into a sapling, then a wild tree;   100
   at last the harpies, feasting on its leaves,
   create its pain, and for the pain an outlet.
Like the rest, we shall return to claim our bodies,
   but never again to wear them—wrong it is
   for a man to have again what he once cast off.   105

68–72. Pier was also a renowned poet of the Sicilian School which flourished under Frederick's patronage and which is noted for its love of complex conceits and convoluted word play.

95–108. Having denied the God-given sanctity of their bodies on earth, in Hell the Suicides are completely denied bodily form. It is only when part of the tree or bush is torn or broken that the shades can make sounds, thus the necessity for Dante to break a branch before Pier can speak.

We shall drag them here and, all along the mournful
  forest, our bodies shall hang forever more,
  each one on a thorn of its own alien shade."
We were standing still attentive to the trunk,
  thinking perhaps it might have more to say,   110
  when we were startled by a rushing sound,
such as the hunter hears from where he stands:
  first the boar, then all the chase approaching,
  the crash of hunting dogs and branches smashing,
then, to the left of us appeared two shapes   115
  naked and gashed, fleeing with such rough speed
  they tore away with them the bushes' branches.
The one ahead: "Come on, come quickly, Death!"
  The other, who could not keep up the pace,
  screamed, "Lano, your legs were not so nimble   120
when you jousted in the tournament of Toppo!"
  And then, from lack of breath perhaps, he slipped
  into a bush and wrapped himself in thorns.
Behind these two the wood was overrun
  by packs of black bitches ravenous and ready,   125
  like hunting dogs just broken from their chains;
they sank their fangs in that poor wretch who hid,
  they ripped him open piece by piece, and then
  ran off with mouthfuls of his wretched limbs.
Quickly my escort took me by the hand   130
  and led me over to the bush that wept
  its vain laments from every bleeding sore:
"O Giacomo da Sant' Andrea," it said,
  "what good was it for you to hide in me?
  What fault have I if you led an evil life?"   135
My master, standing over it, inquired:
  "Who were you once that now through many wounds
  breathes a grieving sermon with your blood?"
He answered us: "O souls who have just come
  in time to see this unjust mutilation   140
  that has separated me from all my leaves,
gather them round the foot of this sad bush.
  I was from the city that took the Baptist

115–121. The second group of souls
punished here are the Profligates, who did
violence to their earthly goods by not
valuing them as they should have, just as
the Suicides did not value their bodies.
They are represented by Lano (l. 120),
probably a member of the wealthy Maconi
family of Siena, and by Giacomo da
Sant'Andrea (l. 133) from Padua. Both
had the dubious honor of being incorrigi-
ble spendthrifts who squandered most of
their wealth and property. The "tournament of Toppo" (l. 121) recalls the disastrous defeat of the Sienese troops at the
hands of the Aretines in 1287 at a river
ford near Arezzo. Lano went into this
battle to die because he had squandered
his fortune; as legend has it, he remained
to fight rather than escape on foot (hence
Giacomo's reference to his "legs," (l.
120), and was killed.
143–150. The identity of this Florentine
Suicide remains unknown. The "first
patron" of Florence was Mars, the god of
war (thus his "art" [l. 145] is warfare);
a fragment of his statue was to be found
on the Ponte Vecchio ("the Arno's
bridge," l. 146) until 1333.
  The second patron of the city was John
the Baptist (l. 143), whose image appeared on the florin, the principal monetary unit of the time. It has been suggested that Florence's change of patron
indicates its transformation from a stronghold of martial excellence (under Mars)
to one of servile money making (under
the Baptist).

in exchange for her first patron, who, for this,
swears by his art she will have endless sorrow;   145
  and were it not that on the Arno's bridge
  some vestige of his image still remains,
those citizens who built anew the city
  on the ashes that Attila left behind
  would have accomplished such a task in vain;   150
I turned my home into my hanging place."

CANTO XIV

They come to the edge of the Wood of the Suicides where they
see before them a stretch of burning sand upon which flames rain
eternally and through which a stream of boiling blood is carried in a
raised channel formed of rock. There, many groups of tortured souls
are on the burning sand; Virgil explains that those lying supine on
the ground are the Blasphemers, those crouching are the Usurers,
and those wandering aimlessly, never stopping, are the Sodomites.
Representative of the blasphemers is Capaneus who died cursing his
god. The Pilgrim questions his guide about the source of the river
of boiling blood; Virgil's reply contains the most elaborate symbol
in the *Inferno*, that of the Old Man of Crete, whose tears are the
source of all rivers in Hell.

The love we both shared for our native city
  moved me to gather up the scattered leaves
  and give them back to the voice that now had faded.
We reached the confines of the woods that separate
  the second from the third round. There I saw   5
  God's justice in its dreadful operation.
Now to picture clearly these unheard-of things:
  we arrived to face an open stretch of flatland
  whose soil refused the roots of any plant;
the grieving forest made a wreath around it,   10
  as the sad river of blood enclosed the woods.
  We stopped right here, right at the border line.
This wasteland was a dry expanse of sand,
  thick, burning sand, no different from the kind
  that Cato's feet packed down in other times.   15
O just revenge of God! how awesomely
  you should be feared by everyone who reads
  these truths that were revealed to my own eyes!
Many separate herds of naked souls I saw,

151. The Florentine's anonymity cor-
roborates his symbolic value as a representative of his city. Like the suicides
condemned to this round, the city of Florence was killing itself, in Dante's opinion,
through its internecine struggles.
  15. 'Cato": sided with Pompey in the

Roman civil war. After Pompey was defeated at Pharsalia, and when it became
apparent that he was about to be captured
by Caesar, he killed himself (46 B.C.).
The year before his death he led a march
across the desert of Libya.

all weeping desperately; it seemed each group   20
 had been assigned a different penalty:
some were stretched out flat upon their backs,
 others were crouching there all tightly hunched,
 some wandered, never stopping, round and round.
Far more there were of those who roamed the sand   25
 and fewer were the souls stretched out to suffer,
 but their tongues were looser, for the pain was greater.
And over all that sandland, a fall of slowly-
 raining broad flakes of fire showered steadily
 (a mountain snowstorm on a windless day),   30
like those that Alexander saw descending
 on his troops while crossing India's torrid lands:
 flames falling, floating solid to the ground,
and he with all his men began to tread
 the sand so that the burning flames might be   35
 extinguished one by one before they joined.
Here too a never-ending blaze descended,
 kindling the sand like tinder under flint-sparks,
 and in this way the torment there was doubled.
Without a moment's rest the rhythmic dance   40
 of wretched hands went on, this side, that side,
 brushing away the freshly fallen flames.
And I: "My master, you who overcome
 all opposition (except for those tough demons
 who came to meet us at the gate of Dis),   45
who is that mighty one that seems unbothered
 by burning, stretched sullen and disdainful there,
 looking as if the rainfall could not tame him?"
And that very one, who was quick to notice me
 inquiring of my guide about him, answered: 50
"What I was once, alive, I still am, dead!
Let Jupiter wear out his smith, from whom
 he seized in anger that sharp thunderbolt
 he hurled, to strike me down, my final day;
let him wear out those others, one by one,   55
 who work the soot-black forge of Mongibello
 (as he shouts, "Help me good Vulcan, I need your help,"
the way he cried that time at Phlegra's battle),
 and with all his force let him hurl his bolts at me,
 no joy of satisfaction would I give him!"   60
My guide spoke back at him with cutting force,

22–24. The shades in this third round of the Seventh Circle are divided into three groups: the Blasphemers lie supine on the ground, the Usurers are "crouching", and the Sodomites wander "never stopping". The sand they lie on perhaps suggests the sterility of their acts.

44–45. "those tough demons": The rebel angels of Canto IX who barred the travelers' entrance to the city of Dis.

51–60. The representative of the Blasphemers is Capaneus, who, as Virgil will explain, was one of the seven kings who assaulted Thebes. Statius describes how Capaneus, when scaling the walls of Thebes, blasphemed against Jove, who then struck him with a thunderbolt. Capaneus died with blasphemy on his lips and now, even in Hell, he is able to defy Jove's thunderbolts.

(I never heard his voice so strong before):
"O Capaneus, since your blustering pride
will not be stilled, you are made to suffer more:
no torment other than your rage itself   65
could punish your gnawing pride more perfectly."
And then he turned a calmer face to me,
saying, "That was a king, one of the seven
besieging Thebes; he scorned, and would seem still
to go on scorning God and treat him lightly,   70
but, as I said to him, he decks his chest
with ornaments of lavish words that prick him.
Now follow me and also pay attention
not to put your feet upon the burning sand,
but to keep them well within the wooded line."   75
Without exchanging words we reached a place
where a narrow stream came gushing from the woods
(its reddish water still runs fear through me!);
like the one that issues from the Bulicame,
whose waters are shared by prostitutes downstream,   80
it wore its way across the desert sand.
This river's bed and banks were made of stone,
so were the tops on both its sides; and then
I understood this was our way across.
"Among the other marvels I have shown you,   85
from the time we made our entrance through the gate
whose threshold welcomes every evil soul,
your eyes have not discovered anything
as remarkable as this stream you see here
extinguishing the flames above its path."   90
These were my master's words, and I at once
implored him to provide me with the food
for which he had given me the appetite.
"In the middle of the sea there lies a wasteland,"

79–80. "the Bulicame": Near Viterbo there was a hot spring called the Bulicame, whose sulphurous waters transformed the area into a watering place. Among the inhabitants were many prostitutes who were required to live in a separate quarter. A special stream channeled the hot spring water through their section, since they were denied use of public baths.

94–119. The island of Crete is given as the source of Acheron, Styx, and Phlegethon, the joined rivers of Hell whose course eventually leads to the "pool," Cocytus, at the bottom of Hell. According to mythology, Mt. Ida on Crete was the place chosen by Rhea to protect her infant son, Jupiter, from his father, Saturn, who usually devoured his sons when they were born. Rhea, to keep him from finding Jupiter, "had her servants scream loud when he cried" (l. 102) to drown out the infant's screams.

Within Mt. Ida Dante places the statue of the "Old Man of Crete" (certainly one of the most elaborate symbols in the *Inferno*), with his back to Damietta and gazing toward Rome (ll. 104–105). Damietta, an important Egyptian seaport, represents the East, the pagan world; Rome of course, the modern, Christian world. The figure of the Old Man is drawn from the book of Daniel (2:32–35), but the symbolism is different, and more nearly (though not absolutely) reflects a poetic symbol utilized by Ovid (*Metamorphoses* I). The head of gold represents the Golden Age of man (that is, in Christian terms, before the Fall). The arms and breast of silver, the trunk of brass, and the legs of iron represent the three declining ages of man. The clay foot (the one made of terra cotta) may symbolize the Church, weakened and corrupted by temporal concerns and political power struggles.

he immediately began, "that is known as Crete,   95
under whose king the world knew innocence.
There is a mountain there that was called Ida;
then happy in its verdure and its streams,
now deserted like an old, discarded thing;
Rhea chose it once as a safe cradle   100
for her son, and, to conceal his presence better,
she had her servants scream loud when he cried.
In the mountain's core an ancient man stands tall;
he has his shoulders turned toward Damietta
and faces Rome as though it were his mirror.   105
His head is fashioned of the finest gold;
pure silver are his arms and hands and chest;
from there to where his legs spread, he is brass;
the rest of him is all of chosen iron,
except his right foot which is terra cotta;   110
he puts more weight on this foot than the other.
Every part of him, except the gold, is broken
by a fissure dripping tears down to his feet
where they collect to erode the cavern's rock;
from stone to stone they drain down here, becoming   115
rivers: the Acheron, Styx, the Phlegethon
then overflow down through this tight canal
until they fall to where all falling ends:
they form Cocytus. What that pool is like
I need not tell you. You will see, yourself."   120
And I to him: "If this small stream beside us
has its source, as you have told me, in our world,
why have we seen it only on this ledge?"
And he to me: "You know this place is round,
and though your journey has been long, circling   125
toward the bottom, turning only to the left,
you have not completed any circle's round;
so you should never look surprised, as now,
if you see something you have not seen before."
And I again: "Where, Master, shall we find   130
Lethe and Phlegethon? You omit the first
and say the other forms from the rain of tears."
"I am very happy when you question me,"
he said, "but that the blood-red water boiled
should answer certainly one of your questions.   135
And Lethe you shall see, but beyond this valley,
at a place where souls collect to wash themselves
when penitence has freed them of their guilt.
Now it is time to leave this edge of woods,"
he added. "Be sure you follow close behind me: 140
the margins are our road, they do not burn,
and all the flames above them are extinguished."

134–135. To the Pilgrim's naïve question (ll. 130–131) Virgil replies that he
should have been able to recognize Phlegethon by its extreme heat.

CANTO XV

They move out across the plain of burning sand, walking along the ditchlike edge of the conduit through which the Phlegethon flows, and after they have come some distance from the wood they see a group of souls running toward them. One, Brunetto Latini, a famous Florentine intellectual and Dante's former teacher, recognizes the Pilgrim and leaves his band to walk and talk with him. Brunetto learns the reason for the Pilgrim's journey and offers him a prophecy of the troubles lying in wait for him—an echo of Ciacco's words in Canto VI. Brunetto names some of the others being punished with him (Priscian, Francesco d'Accorso, Andrea de' Mozzi); but soon, in the distance, he sees a cloud of smoke approaching which presages a new group, and because he must not associate with them, like a foot racer Brunetto speeds away to catch up with his own band.

Now one of those stone margins bears us on
   and the river's vapors hover like a shade,
   sheltering the banks and water from the flames.
As the Flemings, living with the constant threat
   of flood tides rushing in between Wissant   5
   and Bruges, build their dikes to force the sea back;
as the Paduans build theirs on the shores of Brenta
   to protect their town and homes before warm weather
   turns Chiarentana's snow to rushing water—
so were these walls we walked upon constructed,   10
   though the engineer, whoever he may have been,
   did not make them as high or thick as those.
We had left the wood behind (so far behind,
   by now, that if I had stopped to turn around,
   I am sure it could no longer have been seen)   15
when we saw a troop of souls come hurrying
   toward us beside the bank, and each of them
   looked us up and down as some men look,
at other men, at night, when the moon is new.
   They strained their eye-brows, squinting hard at us,   20
   as an old tailor might at his needle's eye.
Eyed in such a way by this strange crew,
   I was recognized by one of them who grabbed
   my garment's hem and shouted: "How marvelous!"
And I, when he reached out his arm toward me,   25
   straining my eyes, saw through his face's crust,
   through this burned features that could not prevent

4–6. The cities of Wissant and Bruges were centers of trade during the thirteenth century. It is not inconceivable that cities such as these, which counted a considerable number of itinerant tradesmen and sailors among their population, might have had a reputation for sodomy during Dante's time.

7. In the Journals of William Lithgow, a seventeenth century traveler and writer, we find reference made to the propensity for sodomy he had noted among the Paduans.

9. "Chiarentana's": a mountainous district situated north of the Brenta River.

11. God.

my memory from bringing back his name;
 and bending my face down to meet with his,
  I said: "Is this really you, here, Ser Brunetto?"   30
And he: "O my son, may it not displease you
 if Brunetto Latini lets his troop file on
  while he walks at your side for a little while."
And I: "With all my heart I beg you to,
 and if you wish me to sit here with you,   35
  I will, if my companion does not mind."
"My son," he said, "a member of this herd
 who stops one moment lies one hundred years
  unable to brush off the wounding flames,
so, move on; I shall follow at your hem   40
 and then rejoin my family that moves
  along, lamenting their eternal pain."
I did not dare step off the margin-path
 to walk at his own level but, with head
  bent low in reverence, I moved along.   45
He began: "What fortune or what destiny
 leads you down here before your final hour?
  And who is this one showing you the way?"
"Up there above in the bright living life
 before I reached the end of all my years,   50
  I lost myself in a valley," I replied;
"just yesterday at dawn I turned from it.
 This spirit here appeared as I turned back,
  and by this road he guides me home again."
He said to me: "Follow your constellation   55
 and you cannot fail to reach your port of glory,
  not if I saw clearly in the happy life;
and if I had not died just when I did,
 I would have cheered you on in all your work,
  seeing how favorable Heaven was to you.   60
But that ungrateful and malignant race
 which descended from the Fiesole of old,
  and still have rock and mountain in their blood,
will become, for your good deeds, your enemy—
 and right they are: among the bitter berries   65
  there's no fit place for the sweet fig to bloom.
They have always had the fame of being blind,
 an envious race, proud and avaricious;
  you must not let their ways contaminate you.
Your destiny reserves such honors for you: 70
 both parties shall be hungry to devour you,

61–67. During a Roman power struggle, Cataline fled Rome and found sanctuary for himself and his troops in the originally Etruscan town of Fiesole. After Caesar's successful siege of that city, the survivors of both camps founded Florence, where those of the Roman camp were the elite.

The phophecy with its condemnation of the current state of Florence (and Italy) and its implied hope of a renascent empire continues the political theme, begun with the speech of the Anonymous Suicide in Canto XIII, and continued in the symbol of the Old Man of Crete in Canto XIV.

but the grass will not be growing where the goat is.
Let the wild beasts of Fiesole make fodder
    of each other, and let them leave the plant untouched
    (so rare it is that one grows in their dung-heap)   75
in which there lives again the holy seed
    of those remaining Romans who survived there
    when this new nest of malice was constructed."
"O, if all I wished for had been granted,"
    I answered him, "you certainly would not,   80
    not yet, be banished from our life on earth;
my mind is etched (and now my heart is pierced)
    with your kind image, loving and paternal,
    when, living in the world, hour after hour
you taught me how man makes himself eternal.   85
    And while I live my tongue shall always speak
    of my debt to you, and of my gratitude.
I will write down what you tell me of my future
    and save it, with another text, to show
    a lady who can interpret, if I can reach her.   90
This much, at least, let me make clear to you:
    if my conscience continues not to blame me,
    I am ready for whatever Fortune wants.
This prophecy is not new to my ears,
    and so let Fortune turn her wheel, spinning it   95
    as she pleases, and the peasant turn his spade."
My master hearing this looked to the right,
    then, turning round and facing me, he said:
    "He listens well who notes well what he hears."
But I did not answer him; I went on talking,   100
    walking with Ser Brunetto, asking him
    who of his company were the most distinguished.
And he: "It might be good to know who some are,
    about the rest I feel I should be silent,
    for the time would be too short, there are so many.   105
In brief, let me tell you, all here were clerics
    and respected men of letters of great fame,
    all befouled in the world by one same sin:
Priscian is travelling with that wretched crowd
    and Francesco d'Accorso too; and also there,   110
    if you could have stomached such repugnancy,
you might have seen the one the Servant of Servants

89–90. Again (as in Canto X, ll. 130–132), Beatrice is referred to as the one who will reveal to the Pilgrim his future course. However, in the *Paradiso* this role is given to Dante's ancestor, Cacciaguida.

95–96. It is as right for Fortune to spin her wheel as it is for the peasant to turn his spade; and the Pilgrim will be as indifferent to the first as to the second.

110. A celebrated Florentine lawyer (1225–1294) who taught law at the University of Bologna and later at Oxford at the request of King Edward I.

112–114. Andrea de' Mozzi was Bishop of Florence from 1287 to 1295, when, by order of Pope Boniface VIII (the "Servant of Servants," i.e., the servant of the servants of God), he was transferred to Vicenza (on the Bacchiglione River), where he died that same year or the next. The early commentators make reference to his naïve and inept preaching and to his general stupidity. Dante, by mentioning his "sinfully-erected nerves" calls attention to his major weakness: unnatural lust or sodomy.

transferred to the Bacchiglione from the Arno
    where his sinfully-erected nerves were buried.
I would say more, but my walk and conversation   115
    with you cannot go on, for over there
    I see a new smoke rising from the sand:
people approach with whom I must not mingle.
    Remember my *Trésor*, where I live on,
    this is the only thing I ask of you."   120
Then he turned back, and he seemed like one of those
    who run in Verona's race across its fields
    to win the green cloth prize, and he was like
the winner of the group, not the last one in.

CANTO XVI

Continuing through the third round of the Circle of Violence,
the Pilgrim hears the distant roar of a waterfall which grows louder
as he and his guide proceed. Suddenly three shades, having recognized him as a Florentine, break from their company and converse
with him, all the while circling like a turning wheel. Their spokesman, Jacopo Rusticucci, identifies himself and his companions
(Guido Guerra and Tegghiaio Aldobrandini) as well-known and
honored citizens of Florence, and begs for news of their native city.
The three ask to be remembered in the world and then rush off. By
this time the sound of the waterfall is so deafening that it almost
drowns out speech, and when the poets reach the edge of the precipice, Virgil takes a cord which had been bound around his pupil's
waist and tosses it into the abyss. It is a signal, and in response a
monstrous form looms up from below, swimming through the air.
On this note of suspense, the canto ends.

Already we were where I could hear the rumbling
    of the water plunging down to the next circle,
    something like the sound of beehives humming,
when three shades with one impulse broke away,
    running, from a group of spirits passing us   5
    beneath the rain of bitter suffering.
They were coming toward us shouting with one voice:
    "O, you there, stop! From the clothes you wear, you seem
    to be a man from our perverted city."
Ah, the wounds I saw covering their limbs,   10
    some old, some freshly branded by the flames!

119–120. "my *Trésor*." The *Livres dou Trésor*, Brunetto's most significant composition, was written during his exile in France, and is an encyclopedic work written in French prose.
123–124. "the green cloth prize": The first prize for the foot-race, which was one of the games held annually on the first Sunday of Lent in Verona during the thirteenth century, was a green cloth.
9. "our perverted city": Florence.

Even now, when I think back to them, I grieve.
Their shouts caught the attention of my guide,
   and then he turned to face me saying, "Wait,
   for these are shades that merit your respect. 15
And were it not the nature of this place
   to rain with piercing flames, I would suggest
   you run toward *them*, for it would be more fitting."
When we stopped, they resumed their normal pace
   and when they reached us, then they started circling; 20
   the three together formed a turning wheel,
just like professional wrestlers stripped and oiled
   eyeing one another for the first, best grip
   before the actual blows and thrusts begin.
And circling in this way each kept his face 25
   pointed up at me, so that their necks and feet
   moved constantly in opposite directions.
"And if the misery along these sterile sands,"
   one of them said, "and our charred and peeling flesh
   makes us, and what we ask, repulsive to you, 30
let our great worldly fame persuade your heart
   to tell us who you are, how you can walk
   safely with living feet through Hell itself.
This one in front whose footsteps I am treading,
   even though he runs his round naked and skinned, 35
   was of noble station, more than you may think:
he was the grandson of the good Gualdrada;
   his name was Guido Guerra, and in his life
   he accomplished much with counsel and with sword.
This other one who pounds the sand behind me 40
   is Tegghiaio Aldobrandi whose wise voice
   the world would have done well to listen to.
And I who share this post of pain with them
   was Jacopo Rusticucci, and for sure
   my reluctant wife first drove me to my sin." 45
If I could have been sheltered from the fire,
   I would have thrown myself below with them,
   and I think my guide would have allowed me to;
but, knowing well I would be burned and seared,
   my fear won over my first good intention 50
   that made me want to put my arms around them.

37–39. "Gualdrada": the daughter of Bellincione Berti of Florence. Her grandson was the Guido Guerra (1220–1272) mentioned here. This Guido was a Guelph leader in several battles, hence his nickname (*guerra*, "war"). His wisdom ("counsel," l. 39) is exemplified by his advice to the Florentine Guelphs not to undertake the campaign against Siena in 1260; they ignored his words, and that battle destroyed the Guelph party in Florence.

41–42. "Tegghiaio Aldobrandi": Like Guido Guerra, he was a leader of the Guelph party in Florence (died before 1266). He, too, tried to dissuade the Guelphs from attacking the Sienese in 1260; in fact, he was the spokesman for the group of Guelph soldiers headed by Guido Guerra. The fact that his advice was disregarded probably accounts for Dante's saying that "the world would have done well to listen to" his voice.

44–45. "Jacopo Rusticucci": Little is known of this spokesman for the three Sodomites. He is occasionally mentioned in Florentine records between 1235 and 1266 and was probably a rich merchant.

And then I spoke: "Repulsion, no, but grief
    for your condition spread throughout my heart
    (and years will pass before it fades away),
as soon as my lord here began to speak   55
    in terms that led me to believe a group
    of such men as yourselves might be approaching.
I am from your city, and your honored names
    and your accomplishments I have always heard
    rehearsed, and have rehearsed, myself, with fondness.   60
I leave the bitter gall, and journey toward
    those sweet fruits promised me by my true guide,
    but first I must go down to the very center."
"So may your soul remain to guide your body
    for years to come," that same one spoke again,   65
    "and your fame's light shine after you are gone,
tell us if courtesy and valor dwell
    within our city as they used to do,
    or have they both been banished from the place?
Guglielmo Borsiere, who joined our painful ranks   70
    of late, and travels there with our companions,
    has given us reports that make us grieve."
"A new breed of people with their sudden wealth
    have stimulated pride and unrestraint
    in you, O Florence, made to weep so soon."   75
These words I shouted with my head strained high,
    and the three below took this to be my answer
    and looked, as if on truth, at one another.
"If you always answer questions with such ease,"
    they all spoke up at once, "O happy you   80
    to have this gift of ready, open speech;
therefore, if you survive these unlit regions
    and return to gaze upon the lovely stars,
    when it pleases you to say 'I was down there,'
do not fail to speak of us to living men."   85
    They broke their man-made wheel and ran away,
    their nimble legs were more like wings in flight.
"Amen" could not have been pronounced as quick
    as they were off, and vanished from our sight;
    and then my teacher thought it time to leave.   90
I followed him, and we had not gone far
    before the sound of water was so close
    that if we spoke we hardly heard each other.
As that river on the Apennines' left slope
    first springing from its source at Monte Veso   95

70–72. "Guglielmo Borsiere": Little is known of him except that he must have died about 1300, as is evident from lines 70–71. Boccaccio says that he was a knight of the court, a matchmaker, and a peace-maker.

94–101. Dante compares the descent of the tributary of the Phlegethon River in Hell with the plummeting fall of the Montone River near the San Benedetto dell'Alpe monastery. Evidently, in Dante's time the river was called the Acquacheta as far as Forlì, where it became the Mon-tone. Today the entire river is known as the Montone.

then flowing eastward holding its own course
(called Acquacheta at its start above
  before descending to its lower bed
  where, at Forlì, it has another name),
reverberates there near San Benedetto   100
  dell'Alpe (plunging in a single bound)
  where at least a thousand vassals could be housed,
so down a single rocky precipice
  we found the tainted waters falling, roaring
  sound loud enough to deafen us in seconds.   105
I wore a cord that fastened round my waist
  with which I once had thought I might be able
  to catch the leopard with the gaudy skin.
As soon as I removed it from my body
  just as my guide commanded me to do,   110
  I gave it to him looped into a coil.
Then taking it and turning to the right,
  he flung it quite a distance past the bank
  and down into the deepness of the pit.
"Now surely something strange is going to happen,"   115
  I thought to myself, "to answer the strange signal
  whose course my master follows with his eyes."
How cautious a man must be in company
  with one who can not only see his actions
  but read his mind and understand his thoughts!   120
He spoke: "Soon will rise up what I expect;
  and what you are trying to imagine now
  soon must reveal itself before your eyes."
It is always better to hold one's tongue than speak
  a truth that seems a bold-face lie when uttered,   125
  since to tell this truth could be embarrassing;
but I shall not keep quiet; and by the verses
  of my *Comedy*—so may they be received
  with lasting favor, Reader—I swear to you
I saw a figure coming, it was swimming   130
  through the thick and murky air, up to the top
  (a thing to startle even stalwart hearts),
like one returning who has swum below
  to free the anchor that has caught its hooks
  on a reef or something else the sea conceals   135
spreading out his arms, and doubling up his legs.

---

102. According to Boccaccio, one of the Conti Guidi, who ruled over this region, had planned to construct, near the waterfall, lodgings for a large number of his vassals; he died, however, before his plan could be put into effect.

106–108. There are many interpretations for the cord which Virgil takes from the Pilgrim and throws over the edge of the steep. Some have seen in this passage evidence that Dante the Poet became a Franciscan friar, the cord being a sign of that order.

CANTO XVII

The beast which had been seen approaching at the end of the
last canto is the horrible monster Geryon; his face is appealing like
that of an honest man, but his body ends in a scorpionlike stinger.
He perches on the edge of the abyss and Virgil advises his ward,
who has noticed new groups of sinners squatting on the fiery sand,
to learn who they are, while he makes arrangements with Geryon
for the descent. The sinners are the Usurers, unrecognizable except
by the crests on the moneybags hanging about their necks which
identify them as members of the Gianfigliazzi, Ubriachi, and Scrovegni families. The Pilgrim listens to one of them briefly but soon
returns to find his master sitting on Geryon's back. After he conquers his fear and mounts, too, the monster begins the slow, spiral-
ing descent into the Eighth Circle.

"And now, behold the beast with pointed tail
    that passes mountains, annulling walls and weapons,
    behold the one that makes the whole world stink!"
These were the words I heard my master say
    as he signaled for the beast to come ashore,   5
    up close to where the rocky levee ends.
And that repulsive spectacle of fraud
    floated close, maneuvering head and chest
    on to the shore, but his tail he let hang free.
His face was the face of any honest man,   10
    it shone with such a look of benediction;
    and all the rest of him was serpentine;
his two clawed paws were hairy to the armpits,
    his back and all his belly and both flanks
    were painted arabesques and curlicues: 15
the Turks and Tartars never made a fabric
    with richer colors intricately woven,
    nor were such complex webs spun by Arachne.
As sometimes fishing boats are seen ashore,
    part fixed in sand and part still in the water;   20
    and as the beaver, living in the land
of drunken Germans, squats to catch his prey,
    just so that beast, the worst of beasts, hung waiting

1–27. In classical mythology Geryon
was a three-bodied giant who ruled Spain,
and was slain by Hercules in the course
of his Twelve Labors. Here in the *Inferno*
he is the personification of Fraud.

18. "Arachne": A legendary Lydian
maiden who was so skilled in the art of
weaving that she challenged the goddess
Minerva to a contest. Minerva, furious

because her opponent's cloth was perfect,
tore it to shreds; Arachne hanged herself,
but Minerva loosened the rope, turning it
into a web and Arachne into a spider.

21–22. "the beaver": According to medieval bestiaries the beaver, squatting on
the ground at the edge of the water
catches fish with its tail hanging in the
water. Geryon assumes a similar pose.

on the bank that bounds the stretch of sand in stone.
In the void beyond he exercised his tail,   25
twitching and twisting-up the venomed fork
that armed its tip just like a scorpion's stinger.
My leader said: "Now we must turn aside
a little from our path, in the direction
of that malignant beast that lies in wait."   30
Then we stepped off our path down to the right
and moved ten paces straight across the brink
to keep the sand and flames at a safe distance.
And when we stood by Geryon's side, I noticed,
a little farther on, some people crouched   35
in the sand quite close to the edge of emptiness.
Just then my master spoke: "So you may have
a knowledge of this round that is complete,"
he said, "go and see their torment for yourself.
But let your conversation there be brief;   40
while you are gone I shall speak to this one
and ask him for the loan of his strong back."
So I continued walking, all alone,
along the seventh circle's outer edge
to where the group of sufferers were sitting.   45
The pain was bursting from their eyes; their hands
went scurrying up and down to give protection
here from the flames, there from the burning sands.
They were, in fact, like a dog in summertime
busy, now with his paw, now with his snout,   50
tormented by the fleas and flies that bite him.
I carefully examined several faces
among this group caught in the raining flames
and did not know a soul, but I observed
that around each sinner's neck a pouch was hung   55
each of a different color, with a coat of arms,
and fixed on these they seemed to feast their eyes.
And while I looked about among the crowd,
I saw something in blue on a yellow purse
that had the face and bearing of a lion;   60
and while my eyes continued their inspection
I saw another purse as red as blood

35–36. The Usurers, described in Canto XI as those who scorn "Nature in herself and in her pupil / Art" (ll. 110–111), are the last group in the third round of the Seventh Circle. Having introduced Geryon, Dante the Poet then brings in these sinners who, crouching very close to the edge of the abyss, serve as the artistic and spatial connection between the sins of Violence and those of Fraud.

55–56. The identity (or rather the family connection) of the usurers, who "feast their eyes" (l. 57) on the purses dangling from their necks, is revealed to the Pilgrim by the different coats of arms visible on the pouches. Apparently the usurers are unrecognizable through facial characteristics because their total concern with their material goods has caused them to lose their individuality. The yellow purse with the blue lion (ll. 59–60) indicates the Gianfigliazzi family of Florence; the red purse with the "goose more white than butter" (ll. 62–63), the Ubriachi family, also of Florence; the one with the "blue sow, pregnant-looking" (ll. 64–65), the Scrovegni family of Padua.

exhibiting a goose more white than butter.
And one who had a blue sow, pregnant-looking,
    stamped on the whiteness of his moneybag   65
    asked me: "What are you doing in this pit?
Get out of here! And since you're still alive,
    I'll tell you that my neighbor Vitaliano
    will come to take his seat on my left side.
Among these Florentines I sit, one Paduan: 70
    time after time they fill my ears with blasts
    of shouting: 'Send us down the sovereign knight
who will come bearing three goats on his pouch;' "
    As final comment he stuck out his tongue—
    as far out as an ox licking its nose.   75
And I, afraid my staying there much longer
    might anger the one who warned me to be brief,
    turned my back on these frustrated sinners.
I found my guide already sitting high
    upon the back of that fierce animal;   80
    he said: "And now, take courage and be strong.
From now on we descend by stairs like these.
    Get on up front. I want to ride behind,
    to be between you and the dangerous tail."
A man who feels the shivers of a fever   85
    coming on, his nails already dead of color,
    will tremble at the mere sight of cool shade;
I was that man when I had heard his words.
    But then I felt those stabs of shame that make
    a servant brave before his valorous master.   90
As I squirmed around on those enormous shoulders,
    I wanted to cry out, "Hold on to me,"
    but I had no voice to second my desire.
Then he who once before had helped me out
    when I was threatened, put his arms around me   95
    as soon as I was settled, and held me tight;
and then he cried: "Now Geryon, start moving,
    descend with gentle motion, circling wide:
    remember you are carrying living weight."
Just as a boat slips back away from shore,   100
    back slowly, more and more, he left that pier;
    and when he felt himself all clear in space,
to where his breast had been he swung his tail
    and stretched it undulating like an eel,

68–69. Referred to as "my neighbor" by one of the Scrovegni family, the Vitaliano who will join the company of usurers is undoubtedly from Padua, but beyond this nothing certain is known.

70. The theme of the decadence and materialism of Florence is continued to the very edge of the circle of Violence.

72–73. "the sovereign knight": This is generally considered to be Giovanni Buiamonte, one of the Florentine Becchi family. He took part in public affairs and was honored with the title of "knight" in 1298. His business, moneylending, made his family one of the wealthiest in Florence; however, after going bankrupt he died in abject poverty in 1310.

as with his paws he gathered in the air.   105
I doubt if Phaëthon feared more—that time
  he dropped the sun-reins of his father's chariot
  and burned the streak of sky we see today—
or if poor Icarus did—feeling his sides
  unfeathering as the wax began to melt,   110
  his father shouting: "Wrong, your course is wrong"—
than I had when I felt myself in air
  and saw on every side nothing but air;
  only the beast I sat upon was there.
He moves along slowly, and swimming slowly,   115
  descends a spiral path—but I know this
  only from a breeze ahead and one below;
I hear now on my right the whirlpool roar
  with hideous sound beneath us on the ground;
  at this I stretch my neck to look below,   120
but leaning out soon made me more afraid,
  for I heard moaning there and saw the flames;
  trembling I cowered back, tightening my legs,
and I saw then what I had not before:
  the spiral path of our descent to torments   125
  closing in on us, it seemed, from every side.
As the falcon on the wing for many hours,
  having found no prey, and having seen no signal
  (so that his falconer sighs: "Oh, he falls already,")
descends, worn out, circling a hundred times   130
  (instead of swooping down), settling at some distance
  from his master, perched in anger and disdain,
so Geryon brought us down to the bottom
  at the foot of the jagged cliff, almost against it,
  and once he got our bodies off his back,   135
he shot off like a shaft shot from a bowstring.

CANTO XVIII

The Pilgrim describes the view he had of the Eighth Circle of
Hell while descending through the air on Geryon's back. It consists
of ten stone ravines called Malebolge (Evil Pockets), and across
each *bolgia* is an arching bridge. When the poets find themselves
on the edge of the first ravine they see two lines of naked sinners,
walking in opposite directions. In one are the Pimps or Panderers

106–108. "Phaëthon": son of Apollo
who was told by Epaphus that Apollo was
not his father. Thereupon the boy begged
Apollo to allow him to drive the Chariot
of the Sun for one day to prove himself
the offspring of the God of the Sun. The
request was granted, but Phaëthon,
unable to control the Chariot, let loose the
reins. The Chariot raced wildly through
the heavens, burning the "streak of sky"
which today we call the Milky Way, and
at one point dipping so close to the Earth
that it almost set the planet afire.

109–111. Daedalus, father of Icarus, in
order to escape from Crete, fashioned
wings for himself and his son. Because the
feathers were fastened with wax, Daedalus
warned his son not to fly too close to the
sun. But Icarus, ignoring his father's
words, flew too high, and when the sun
had melted the wax, he plunged to his
death in the Aegean Sea.

The stories of Phaëthon and Icarus
were often used in the Middle Ages as
examples of pride, thus giving more support to the theory that Pride and Envy
underlie the sins punished in Lower Hell.

and among them the Pilgrim recognizes Venedico Caccianemico; in
the other are the Seducers, among whom Virgil points out Jason. As
the two move toward the next *bolgia*, they are assailed by a terrible
stench, for here the Flatterers are immersed in excrement. Among
them are Alessio Interminei and Thaïs, the whore.

There is a place in Hell called Malebolge
   cut out of stone the color of iron ore,
   just like the circling cliff that walls it in.
Right at the center of this evil plain
   there yawns a very wide, deep well, whose structure   5
   I will talk of when the place itself is reached.
That belt of land remaining, then, runs round
   between the well and cliff, and all this space
   is divided into ten descending valleys,
just like a ground-plan for successive moats   10
   that in concentric circles bind their center
   and serve to protect the ramparts of the castle.
This was the surface image they presented;
   and as bridges from a castle's portal stretch
   from moat to moat to reach the farthest bank,   15
so, from the great cliff's base, jut spokes of rock
   crossing from bank to bank, intersecting ditches
   until the pit's hub cuts them off from meeting.
This is the place in which we found ourselves,
   once shaken from the back of Geryon.   20
   The poet turned to the left, I walked behind him.
There, on our right, I saw new suffering souls,
   new means of torture, and new torturers,
   crammed into the depths of the first ditch.
Two files of naked souls walked on the bottom,   25
   the ones on our side faced us as they passed,
   the others moved as we did but more quickly.
The Romans, too, in the year of the Jubilee
   took measures to accommodate the throngs
   that had to come and go across their bridge: 30
they fixed it so on one side all were looking
   at the castle, and were walking to St. Peter's;
   on the other, they were moving toward the mount.
On both sides, up along the deadly rock,
   I saw horned devils with enormous whips   35
   lashing backs of shades with cruel delight.

26–27. The first *bolgia* accommodates
two classes of sinners, each filing by rapidly, but in separate directions. The Pimps
are those walking toward the Pilgrim and
his guide; the Seducers go in the same
direction with them.
   28–33. Dante compares the movement
of the sinners in the first *bolgia* to that of

the many pilgrims who, having come to
Rome for the Jubilee in 1300, were herded
across the bridge, half going toward the
Castel Sant'Angelo and St. Peter's and
the other half going toward Monte Gior-
dano ("the mount," l. 33), a small knoll
on the opposite side of the Tiber River.

Ah, how they made them skip and lift their heels
   at the very first crack of the whip! Not one of them
   dared pause to take a second or a third!
As I walked on my eyes met with the glance   40
   of one down there; I murmured to myself:
   "I know this face from somewhere, I am sure."
And so I stopped to study him more closely;
   my leader also stopped, and was so kind
   as to allow me to retrace my steps;   45
and that whipped soul thought he would hide from me
   by lowering his face—which did no good.
I said, "O you, there, with your head bent low,
if the features of your shade do not deceive me,
   you are Venedico Caccianemico, I'm sure.   50
   How did you get yourself in such a pickle?"
"I'm not so keen on answering," he said,
   "but I feel I must; your plain talk is compelling,
   it makes me think of old times in the world.
I was the one who coaxed Ghisolabella   55
   to serve the lusty wishes of the Marquis,
   no matter how the sordid tale is told;
I'm not the only Bolognese who weeps here—
   hardly! This place is packed with us; in fact,
   there are more of us here than there are living tongues,   60
between Savena and Reno, saying 'Sipa';
   I call on your own memory as witness:
   remember we have avaricious hearts."
Just at that point a devil let him have
   the feel of his tailed whip and cried: "Move on,   65
   you pimp, you can't cash in on women here!"
I turned and hurried to rejoin my guide;
   we walked a few more steps and then we reached
   the rocky bridge that juts out from the bank.
We had no difficulty climbing up,   70
   and turning right, along the jagged ridge,
   we left those shades to their eternal circlings.
When we were where the ditch yawned wide below
   the ridge, to make a passage for the scourged,
   my guide said: "Stop and stand where you can see   75
these other misbegotten souls whose faces

50–57. "Venedico Caccianemico": Born ca. 1228, he was head of the Guelphs in Bologna from 1260 to 1297; he was at various times *podestà* ("mayor") of Pistolia, Modena, Imola, and Milan. He was accused, among other things, of murdering his cousin, but he is placed in this *bolgia* because, according to popular report, he acted as a procurer, turning his own sister, Ghisolabella, over to the Marquis of Este (either Obizzo II or his son, Azzo VIII) to curry favor.

51. Dante is undoubtedly punning on the word *salse* ("pickle") which characterizes the torments suffered in this *bolgia*, and also is the name of a certain ravine (a *bolgia*, if you will) near Bologna (Venedico's city) into which the bodies of criminals were thrown.

61. Venedico reveals that he is not the only Bolognese punished in this *bolgia* and further states that there are more pimps here from that city than there are present-day inhabitants of the region between the Savena and Reno rivers.

you could not see before, for they were moving
   in the same direction we were, over there."
So from the ancient bridge we viewed the train
   that hurried toward us along the other tract—   80
   kept moving, like the first, by stinging whips.
And the good master, without my asking him,
   said, "Look at that imposing one approaching,
   who does not shed a single tear of pain:
what majesty he still maintains down there!   85
   He is Jason, who by courage and sharp wits,
   fleeced the Colchians of their golden ram.
He later journeyed through the isle of Lemnos
   whose bold and heartless females, earlier,
   had slaughtered every male upon the island;   90
there with his words of love, and loving looks,
   he succeeded in deceiving young Hypsipyle
   who had in turn deceived the other women.
He left her there, with child, and all alone:
   such sin condemns him to such punishment,   95
   and Medea, too, gets her revenge on him.
With him go all deceivers of this type,
   and let this be enough to know concerning
   the first valley and the souls locked in its jaws."
We were already where the narrow ridge   100
   begins to cross the second bank, to make it
   an abutment for another ditch's arch.
Now we could hear the shades in the next *bolgia*
   whimpering, making snorting grunting sounds,
   and sounds of blows, slapping with open palms.   105
From a steaming stench below, the banks were coated
   with a slimy mould that stuck to them like glue,
   disgusting to behold and worse to smell,
The bottom was so hollowed out of sight,
   we saw it only when we climbed the arch   110
   and looked down from the ridge's highest point:
there we were, and from where I stood I saw

86–96. Jason: Leader of the Argonauts
who, when a child, had been deprived of
the throne of Iolcus by his half-brother
Pelias. When Jason grew up, Pelias promised him the kingdom if he could secure
the golden fleece of King Aeëtes of Colchis. Jason agreed to make the attempt,
and on the way to Colchis stopped at
Lemnos, where he seduced and abandoned
Hypsipyle (l. 92), the daughter of the
King of Lemnos. At Colchis King Aeëtes
agreed to give Jason the fleece if he would
yoke two fire-breathing oxen to a plow
and sow the teeth of the dragon that
guarded the fleece. Medea (l. 96), who
was a sorceress and the daughter of the
king, fell in love with Jason and with
magic helped him fulfill her father's conditions and obtain the fleece. The two
returned to Greece where Jason married
her, but later he fell in love with Creusa,
daughter of Creon, king of Corinth, and
deserted Medea to marry her. Medea,
mad with rage, killed Creusa by sending
her a poisoned coat as a wedding gift,
and then murdered her own children;
Jason himself died of grief.

Hypsipyle "deceived the other women"
(l. 93) of Lemnos by swearing that she
had slain her father Thoas, the king,
when the Lemnian women massacred all
the males on that island. Instead she hid
him, saving his life.

104–105. The sinners found in the excrement of the second *bolgia* are the
Flatterers. Note the teeming nature of the
language, different from that of the first
bolgia, a change indicative of the sin of
flattery and its punishment.

souls in the ditch plunged into excrement
that might well have been flushed from our latrines;
my eyes were searching hard along the bottom,   115
and I saw somebody's head so smirched with shit
you could not tell if he were priest or layman.
He shouted up: "Why do you feast your eyes
on me more than these other dirty beasts?"
And I replied: "Because, remembering well,   120
I've seen you with your hair dry once or twice.
You are Alessio Interminei from Lucca,
that's why I stare at you more than the rest."
He beat his slimy forehead as he answered:
"I am stuck down here by all those flatteries   125
that rolled unceasing off my tongue up there."
He finished speaking, and my guide began:
"Lean out a little more, look hard down there
so you can get a good look at the face
of that repulsive and dishevelled tramp   130
scratching herself with shitty finger-nails,
spreading her legs while squatting up and down:
it is Thaïs the whore who gave this answer
to her lover when he asked: 'Am I very worthy
of your thanks?': 'Very, nay, incredibly so!'   135
I think our eyes have had their fill of this."

CANTO XIX

From the bridge above the third *bolgia* can be seen a rocky landscape below filled with holes, from each of which protrude a sinner's legs and feet; flames dance across their soles. When the Pilgrim expresses curiosity about a particular pair of twitching legs,
Virgil carries him down into the *bolgia* so that the Pilgrim himself
may question the sinner. The legs belong to Pope Nicholas III, who
astounds the Pilgrim by mistaking him for Boniface VIII, the next
pope who, as soon as he dies, will fall to the same hole, thereby
pushing Nicholas farther down. He predicts that soon after Boniface, Pope Clement V will come, stuffing both himself and Boniface still deeper. To Nicholas's rather rhetoric-filled speech the Pilgrim responds with equally high language, inveighing against the
Simonists, the evil churchmen who are punished here. Virgil is
much pleased with his pupil and, lifting him in an affectionate
embrace, he carries him to the top of the arch above the next
bolgia.

122. "Alessio Interminei from Luca": The Interminei family was prominent in the White party at Lucca. But of Alessio almost nothing is known save that his name is recorded in several documents of the second half of the thirteenth century.

135. This Thaïs is not the historical person by the same name (the most famous courtesan of all time) but a character in Terence's *Eunuchus*.

O Simon Magus! O scum that followed him!
  Those things of God that rightly should be wed
  to holiness, you, rapacious creatures,
for the price of gold and silver, prostitute.
  Now, in your honor, I must sound my trumpet   5
  here in the third bolgia where you are packed.
We had already climbed to see this tomb,
  and were standing high above it on the bridge,
  exactly at the mid-point of the ditch.
O Highest Wisdom, how you demonstrate   10
  your art in Heaven, on earth, and here in Hell!
  How justly does your power make awards!
I saw along the sides and on the bottom
  the livid-colored rock all full of holes;
  all were the same in size, and each was round.   15
To me they seemed no wider and no deeper
  than those inside my lovely San Giovanni,
  made for priests to stand in or baptize from;
and one of these, not many years ago,
  I smashed for someone who was drowning in it: 20
  let this be mankind's picture of the truth!
From the mouth of every hole were sticking out
  a single sinner's feet, and then the legs
  up to the calf—the rest was stuffed inside.
The soles of every sinner's feet were flaming;   25
  their naked legs were twitching frenziedly—
  they would have broken any chain or rope.
Just as a flame will only move along
  an object's oily outer peel, so here
  the fire slid from heel to toe and back.   30
"Who is that one, Master, that angry wretch,
  who is writhing more than any of his comrades,"
  I asked, "the one licked by a redder flame?"
And he to me, "If you want to be carried down
  along that lower bank to where he is,   35
  you can ask him who he is and why he's here."
And I, "My pleasure is what pleases you:
  you are my lord, you know that from your will
  I would not swerve. You even know my thoughts."
When we reached the fourth bank, we began to turn   40

1–6. As related in Acts (8:9–24), Simon the magician, having observed the descent of the Holy Spirit upon the Apostles John and Peter, desired to purchase this power for himself. Whereupon Peter harshly admonished him for even thinking that the gift of God might be bought. Derived from this sorcerer's name, the word "simony" refers to those offences involving the sale or fraudulent possession of ecclesiastical offices.

5–6. Dante in announcing the nature of the sin being punished in the third *bolgia* is comparing himself to the medieval town crier whose announcements were preceded by a blast from his trumpet.

25. Just as the Simonists' perversion of the Church is symbolized by their "perverted" immersion in holes resembling baptismal fonts, so their "baptism" is perverted: instead of the head being moistened with water, the feet are "baptized" with oil and fire.

and, keeping to the left, made our way down
to the bottom of the holed and narrow ditch.
The good guide did not drop me from his side
    until he brought me to the broken rock
    of that one who was fretting with his shanks.   45
"O whatever you are, holding your upside down,
    wretched soul, stuck in the ground like a stake,
    make some sound," I said, "that is, if you can."
I stood there like a priest hearing confession
    from a vile assassin who, once fixed in his ditch,   50
    calls him back again to put off dying.
He cried: "Is that *you*, here, already, upright?
    Is that you here already upright, Boniface?
    By many years the book has lied to me!
Are you fed up so soon with all that wealth   55
    for which you did not fear to take by guile
    the beautiful lady, then tear her asunder?"
I stood there like a person just made fun of,
    dumbfounded by a question for an answer,
    not knowing how to answer the reply.   60
Then Virgil said: "Quick, hurry up and tell him:
    'I'm not the one, I'm not the one you think!' "
    And I answered just the way he told me to.
The spirit heard, and twisted both his feet,
    then, sighing with a grieving, tearful voice   65
    he said: "Well then, what do you want of me?
If it concerns you so to learn my name
    that for this reason you came down the bank,
    know that I once was dressed in the great mantle.
But actually I was the she-bear's son,   70
    so greedy to advance my cubs, that wealth
    I pocketed in life, and here, myself.
Beneath my head are pushed down all the others
    who came, sinning in simony, before me,
    squeezed tightly in the fissures of the rock.   75
I, in my turn, shall join the rest below

---

53. From the foreknowledge granted to the infernal shades, the speaker knows that Pope Boniface VIII, upon his death in 1303, will take his place in that very receptacle wherein he himself is now being tormented. The Pilgrim's voice, so close at hand, has caused the sinner to believe that his successor has arrived unexpectedly before his time (three years, in fact) and, consequently, that the Divine Plan of Events, the Book of Fate (1. 54), has lied to him.

Having obtained the abdication of Pope Celestine V, Boniface gained the support of Charles II of Naples and thus was assured of his election to the papacy (1294). In addition to misusing the Church's influence in his dealings with Charles, Boniface VIII freely distributed ecclesiastical offices among his family and confidants. As early as 1300 he was plotting the destruction of the Whites, the Florentine political faction to which Dante belonged.

57. "the beautiful lady": the Church.

67–72. Gian Gaetano degli Orsini (lit., "of the little bears," hence the designation "she-bear's son," and the reference to "my cubs") became Pope Nicholas III in 1277. As a Cardinal he won renown for his integrity; however, in the short three years between ascent to the papal throne and his death he became notorious for his simoniacal practices.

74. The Italian verb, *simoneggiare* (here used in the gerund by Nicholas III —"sinning in simony"), was invented by Dante, doubtless to anticipate the parallel form *puttaneggiando* ("playing whore"), l. 108, employed by the Pilgrim.

as soon as *he* comes, the one I thought you were
  when, all too quick, I put my question to you.
But already my feet have baked a longer time
  (and I have been stuck upside-down like this)   80
  than he will stay here planted with feet aflame:
soon after him shall come one from the West,
  a lawless shepherd, one whose fouler deeds
  make him a fitting cover for us both.
He shall be another Jason, like the one   85
  in Maccabees: just as his king was pliant,
  so France's king shall soften to this priest."
I do not know, perhaps I was too bold here,
  but I answered him in tune with his own words:
  "Well tell me now: what was the sum of money   90
that holy Peter had to pay our Lord
  before He gave the keys into his keeping?
  Certainly He asked no more than 'Follow me.'
Nor did Peter or the rest extort gold coins
  or silver from Matthias when he was picked   95
  to fill the place the evil one had lost.
So stay stuck there, for you are rightly punished,
  and guard with care the money wrongly gained
  that made you stand courageous against Charles.
And were it not for the reverence I have   100
  for those highest of all keys that you once held
  in the happy life—if this did not restrain me,
I would use even harsher words than these,
  for your avarice brings grief upon the world,
  crushing the good, exalting the depraved.   105
You shepherds it was the Evangelist had in mind
  when the vision came to him of her who sits
  upon the waters playing whore with kings:
that one who with the seven heads was born
  and from her ten horns managed to draw strength   110
  so long as virtue was her bridegroom's joy.
You have built yourselves a God of gold and silver!

77. Boniface VIII. See above, note on
l. 53.

82–84. Pope Clement V of Gascony,
upon his death in 1314, will join Nicholas
and Boniface in eternal torment.

85–87. Having obtained the high priest
hood of the Jews by bribing King Antiochus of Syria, Jason neglected the sacrifices and sanctuary of the temple and introduced Greek modes of life into his
community. As Jason had fraudulently
acquired his position, so had Menelaus,
who offered more money to the king, supplanted Jason (2 Maccabees 47:7–27). As
Jason obtained his office from King Antiochus fraudulently, so shall Clement acquire his from Philip.

94–96. After the treachery and subsequent expulsion of Judas, the Apostles
cast lots in order to replenish their number. Thus, by the will of God, not through
monetary payment, was Matthias elected
to the vacated post (Act 1:15–26).

98–99. The thirteenth-century Florentine chronicler, Giovanni Villani, alludes
to a plot against Charles d'Anjou, king of
Naples and Sicily, promoted by Nicholas
III and supported by the "money wrongly
gained" of Michael Palaeologus, emperor
of Greece.

106–111. St. John the Evangelist relates
his vision of the dissolute Imperial City
of Rome. To Dante, she "who sits / upon
the waters" represents the Church which
has been corrupted by the simoniacal activities of many popes (the "shepherds"
of the Church). The seven heads symbolize the seven Holy Sacraments; the
ten horns represent the Ten Commandments.

How do you differ from the idolator,
except he worships one, you worship hundreds?
Oh, Constantine, what evil did you sire,   115
not by your conversion, but by the dower
that the first wealthy Father got from you!"
And while I sang these very notes to him,
his big flat feet kicked fiercely out of anger,
—or perhaps it was his conscience gnawing him.   120
I think my master liked what I was saying,
for all the while he smiled and was intent
on hearing the ring of truly-spoken words.
Then he took hold of me with both his arms,
he climbed back up the path he had come down.   125
and when he had me firm against his breast,
He did not tire of the weight clasped tight to him,
but brought me to the top of the bridge's arch,
the one that joins the fourth bank to the fifth.
And here he gently set his burden down—   130
gently, for the ridge, so steep and rugged,
would have been hard even for goats to cross.
From here another valley opened up.

CANTO XX

In the fourth *bolgia* they see a group of shades weeping as they
walk slowly along the valley; they are the Soothsayers and their
heads are twisted completely around so that their hair flows down
their fronts and their tears flow down to their buttocks. Virgil
points out many of them including Amphiaraus, Tiresias, Aruns,
and Manto. It was Manto who first inhabited the site of Virgil's
home city of Mantua, and the poet gives a long description of the
city's founding, after which he names more of the condemned
soothsayers: Eurypylus, Michael Scot, Guido Bonatti, and Asdente.

Now I must turn strange torments into verse
to form the matter of the twentieth canto
of the first chant, the one about the damned.
Already I was where I could look down
into the depths of the ditch: I saw its floor   5

115–117. "Constantine": Constantine the Great, emperor of Rome (306–337), was converted to Christianity in the year 312. Having conquered the eastern Mediterranean lands, he transferred the capital of the Roman Empire to Constantinople (330). This move, according to tradition, stemmed from Constantine's decision to place the western part of the empire under the jurisdiction of the Church in order to repay Pope Sylvester ("the first wealthy Father") for healing him of leprosy. The so-called "Donation of Constantine," though it was proved in the fifteenth century to be a complete fabrication on the part of the clergy, was universally accepted as the truth in the Middle Ages. Dante the Pilgrim reflects this tradition in his sad apostrophe to the individual who first would have introduced wealth to the Church and who, unknowingly, would be ultimately responsible for its present corruption.

was wet with anguished tears shed by the sinners,
and I saw people in the valley's circle,
   silent, weeping, walking at a litany pace
   the way processions push along in our world.
And when my gaze moved down below their faces,   10
   I saw all were incredibly distorted,
   the chin was not above the chest, the neck
was twisted—their faces looked down on their backs;
   they had to move ahead by moving backwards,
   for they never saw what was ahead of them.   15
Perhaps there was a case of someone once
   in a palsy fit becoming so distorted,
   but none that I know of! I doubt there could be!
So may God grant you, Reader, benefit
   from reading of my poem, just ask yourself   20
   how I could keep my eyes dry when, close by,
I saw the image of our human form
   so twisted—the tears their eyes were shedding
   streamed down to wet their buttocks at the cleft.
Indeed I did weep, as I leaned my body   25
   against a jut of rugged rock. My guide:
   "So you are still like all the other fools?
In this place piety lives when pity is dead,
   for who could be more wicked than that man
   who tries to bend divine will to his own!   30
Lift your head up, lift it, see him for whom
   the earth split wide before the Thebans' eyes,
   while they all shouted, 'Where are you rushing off to,
Amphiaraus? Why do you quit the war?'
   He kept on rushing downwards through the gap   35
   until Minòs, who gets them all, got him
You see how he has made his back his chest:
   because he wished to see too far ahead,
   he sees behind and walks a backward track.
Behold Tiresias who changed his looks: 40
   from a man he turned himself into a woman,
   transforming all his body, part for part;

15. Note the appropriate nature of the punishment: The augurs who, when living, looked into the future are here in Hell denied any forward vision.

28. In the original there is a play on words: the word *"pietà"* means both "piety" and "pity." The Pilgrim has once again felt pity for the torments of the sinners, and Virgil rebukes him with some exasperation.

34–36. "Amphiaraus": a seer, and one of the seven kings who led the expedition against Thebes (see Canto XIV, ll. 68–69). He foresaw that he would die during the siege, and to avoid his fate he hid himself so that he would not have to fight. But his wife Eriphyle revealed his hiding place to Polynices, and Amphiaraus was forced to go to battle. He met his death when the earth opened up and swallowed him. Dante's source was Statius's *Thebaid*, VII and VIII.

40–45. "Tiresias": the famous soothsayer of Thebes referred to by Ovid (*Metamorphoses* III, 316–338). According to Ovid, Tiresias with his rod once separated two serpents which were coupled together, whereupon he was transformed into a woman. Seven years later he found the same two serpents, struck them again, and became a man once more. Later Jupiter and Juno asked Tiresias, who had had the experience of belonging to both sexes, which sex enjoyed love-making more. When Tiresias answered "woman," Juno struck him blind. However, Jupiter, in compensation, gave him the gift of prophecy.

then later on he had to take the wand
   and strike once more those two snakes making love
   before he could get back his virile parts.   45
Backing up to this one's chest comes Aruns
   who, in the hills of Luni, worked by peasants
   of Carrara dwelling in the valley's plain,
lived in white marble cut into a cave,
   and from this site where nothing blocked his view   50
   he could observe the sea and stars with ease.
And that one, with her hair loose, flowing back
   to cover both her breasts you cannot see,
   and with her hairy parts in front behind her,
was Manto who had searched through many lands   55
   before she came to dwell where I was born;
   now let me tell you something of her story.
When her father had departed from the living,
   and Bacchus' sacred city fell enslaved,
   she wandered through the world for many years.   60
High in fair Italy there spreads a lake,
   beneath the mountains bounding Germany
   beyond the Tyrol, known as Lake Benaco;
by a thousand streams and more, I think, the Alps
   are bathed from Garda to the Val Camonica   65
   with the waters flowing down into that lake;
at its center is a place where all three bishops
   of Trent and Brescia and Verona could,
   if they would ever visit there, say Mass;
Peschiera sits, a handsome well-built fortress,   70
   to ward off Brescians and the Bergamese,
   along the lowest point of that lake's shore
where all the water that Benaco's basin
   cannot hold must overflow to make a stream
   that winds its way through countrysides of green;   75
but when the water starts to flow, its name
   is not Benaco but Mencio, all the way
   to Governol where it falls into the Po;
but before its course is run it strikes a lowland
   on which it spreads and turns into a marsh   80

46–51. "Aruns": the Etruscan diviner who forecast the Roman civil war and its outcome. He made his home "in the hills of Luni" (l. 47), the area now known as Carrara and renowned for its white marble.

52–60. Manto, upon the death of her father Tiresias, fled Thebes ("Bacchus' sacred city," l. 59) and its tyrant Creon. She finally arrived in Italy and there founded the city of Mantua, Virgil's birthplace (l. 56).

63. "Lake Benaco": today Lake Garda, which lies in northern Italy at the center of the triangle formed by the cities of Trent, Brescia, and Verona.

64–66. Here, the "Alps" means that range between the Camonica valley, west of Lake Garda, and the city of Garda, on the lake's eastern shore, that is watered by many streams which ultimately flow into Lake Garda.

67–69. On an island in Lake Garda (Benaco) the boundaries of the dioceses of Trent, Brescia, and Verona met, thereby making it possible for all three bishops to hold services or "say Mass" there.

70–72. "Peschiera": The fortress of Peschiera and the town of the same name are on the southeast shore of Lake Garda.

78. "Governol": Now called Governolo, it is twelve miles from Mantua and situated at the junction of the Mincio and the Po rivers.

that can become unbearable in summer.
Passing this place one day the savage virgin
  saw land that lay in the center of the mire,
  untilled and empty of inhabitants.
There, to escape all human intercourse,   85
  she stopped to practice magic with her servants;
  there she lived, and there she left her corpse.
Later on, the men who lived around there gathered
  on that very spot, for it was well-protected
  by the bog that girded it on every side.   90
They built a city over her dead bones,
  and for her, the first to choose that place, they named it
  Mantua, without recourse to sorcery.
Once, there were far more people living there,
  before the foolish Casalodi listened   95
  to the fraudulent advice of Pinamonte.
And so, I warn you, should you ever hear
  my city's origin told otherwise,
  let no false tales adulterate the truth."
And I replied: "Master, your explanations   100
  are truth for me, winning my faith entirely;
  any others would be just like burned-out coals.
But speak to me of these shades passing by,
  if you see anyone that is worth noting;
  for now my mind is set on only that."   105
He said: "That one whose beard flows from his cheeks
  and settles on his back and makes it dark,
  was (when the war stripped Greece of all its males
so that the few there were still rocked in cradles)
  an augur who, with Calchas, called the moment   110
  to cut the first ship's cable free at Aulis:
he is Eurypylus. I sang his story
  this way, somewhere in my high tragedy;
  you should know where—you know it, every line.
That other one whose thighs are scarcely fleshed   115
  was Michael Scot, who most assuredly

93. The customs of ancient peoples dictated that the name of a newly founded city be obtained through sorcery. Such was not the case with Mantua.

95–96. "Casalodi": In 1272, Alberto da Casalodi, one of the Guelph counts of Brescia, was lord of Mantua. Having encountered public opposition, he was duped by the Ghibelline Pinamonte de' Bonaccolsi into thinking that he could remain in power only by exiling the nobles. Having faithfully followed Pinamonte's false counsel, he found himself bereft of his supporters and protectors, and consequently Pinamonte was able to take command; he banished the Guelphs, and ruled until 1291.

106–112. At the time of the Trojan War ("when the war stripped Greece of all its males," l. 108) Eurypylus, whom Dante thought to be a Greek augur (as was Calchas, l. 110), was asked to divine the most opportune time to launch the Greek fleet ("to cut the first ship's cable free," l. 111) from the port at Aulis.

113. "high tragedy": the *Aeneid* (II, 114–119). In this work, however, Eurypylus is not an augur, but a soldier sent to the oracle to discover Apollo's predictions as to the best time to set sail from Troy.

116–117. "Michael Scot": A Scottish philosopher attached to Frederick II's court at Palermo (see Canto X, l. 119) who translated the works of Aristotle from the Arabic of his commentator, Avicenna (see Canto IV, l. 143). By reputation he was a magician and augur. Cf. Boccaccio, *Decameron*, VIII, 9.

knew every trick of magic fraudulence.
See there Guido Bonatti; see Asdente,
    who wishes now he had been more devoted
    to making shoes—too late now for repentence.   120
And see those wretched hags who traded in
    needle, spindle, shuttle, for fortune-telling,
    and cast their spells with image-dolls and potions.
Now come along. Cain with his thorn-bush straddles
    the confines of both hemispheres already   125
    and dips into the waves below Seville;
and the moon last night already was at full;
    and you should well remember that at times
    when you were lost in the dark wood she helped you."
And we were moving all the time he spoke.   130

CANTO XXI

When the two reach the summit of the arch over the fifth *bolgia*,
they see in the ditch below the bubbling of boiling pitch. Virgil's
sudden warning of danger frightens the Pilgrim even before he sees
a black devil rushing toward them, with a sinner slung over his
shoulder. From the bridge the devil flings the sinner into the pitch
where he is poked at and tormented by the family of Malebranche
devils. Virgil, advising his ward to hide behind a rock, crosses the
bridge to face the devils alone. They threaten him with their
pitchforks, but when he announces to their leader, Malacoda, that
Heaven has willed that he lead another through Hell, the devil's
arrogance collapses. Virgil calls the Pilgrim back to him. Scarmiglione, who tries to take a poke at him is rebuked by his leader, who
tells the travelers that the sixth arch is broken here but farther on
they will find another bridge to cross. He chooses a squad of his
devils to escort them there: Alichino, Calcabrina, Cagnazzo, Barbariccia, Libicocco, Draghignazzo, Ciriatto, Graffiacane, Farfarello, and
Rubicante. The Pilgrim's suspicion about their unsavory escorts is
brushed aside by his guide, and the squad starts off giving an
obscene salute to their captain who returns their salute with a fart.

From this bridge to the next we walked and talked
    of things my Comedy does not care to tell;
    and when we reached the summit of the arch,

118–120. "Guido Bonatti": A native of
Forlì, he was a well-known astrologer and
diviner. Benvenuto (or Asdente, "toothless," as he was called) was a cobbler
from Parma who supposedly possessed
certain magical powers.
124–126. By some mysterious power
Virgil is able to reckon time in the depths
of Hell. The moon (referred to as "Cain
with his thorn-bush," l. 124, the medieval
Italian counterpart of our "Man in the
Moon") is directly over the line of de-

marcation between the Northern (land)
and the Southern (water) hemispheres
and is setting on the western horizon (the
"waves below Seville," l. 126). The time
is approximately six A.M.
129. See Canto I, l. 2. The literal significance of this line defies explanation,
since in the beginning of the *Inferno* describing the Pilgrim's wanderings in the
"dark woods" no mention is made of the
moon.

we stopped to see the next fosse of Malebolge
   and to hear more lamentation voiced in vain: 5
   I saw that it was very strangely dark!
In the vast and busy shipyard of the Venetians
   there boils all winter long a tough, thick pitch
   that is used to caulk the ribs of unsound ships.
Since winter will not let them sail, they toil: 10
   some build new ships, others repair the old ones,
   plugging the planks come loose from many sailings;
some hammer at the bow, some at the stern,
   one carves the oars while others twine the ropes,
   one mends the jib, one patches up the mainsail;   15
here, too, but heated by God's art, not fire,
   a sticky tar was boiling in the ditch
   that smeared the banks with viscous residue.
I saw it there, but I saw nothing in it,
   except the rising of the boiling bubbles   20
   breathing-in air to burst and sink again.
I stood intently gazing there below,
   my guide, shouting to me: "Watch out, watch out!"
   took hold of me and drew me to his side.
I turned my head like one who can't resist   25
   looking to see what makes him run away
   (his body's strength draining with sudden fear),
but, looking back, does not delay his flight;
   and I saw coming right behind our backs,
   rushing along the ridge, a devil, black!   30
His face, his look, how frightening it was!
   With outstretched wings he skimmed along the rock,
   and every single move he made was cruel;
on one of his high-hunched and pointed shoulders
   he had a sinner slung by both his thighs,   35
   held tightly clawed at the tendons of his heels.
He shouted from our bridge: "Hey, Malebranche,
   here's one of Santa Zita's elders for you!
   You stick him under—I'll go back for more;
I've got that city stocked with the likes of him,   40
   they're all a bunch of grafters, save Bonturo!
   You can change a 'no' to 'yes' for cash in Lucca."
He flung him in, then from the flinty cliff
   sprang off. No hound unleashed to chase a thief

7–15. During the Midde Ages the shipyard at Venice, built in 1104, was one of
the most active and productive in all
Europe. The image of the busy shipyard
with its activity revolving around a vat
of viscous pitch establishes the tone for
this canto (and the next) as one of tense
and excited movement.

37. The Malebranche ("Evil Claws")
are the overseer-devils of this *bolgia*
wherein are punished the Barrators (grafters, l. 41), those swindlers in public

office whose sin against the state is comparable to that of the Simonists against
the Church.

38–42. "Santa Zita": lived and was
canonized in the thirteenth century; the
patron saint of Lucca. The "elders" (l.
38) are the Luccan government officials;
an done of them, Bonturo Dati (l. 41), is
ironically referred to here as being guiltless when in reality he was the worst
barrator of them all.

could have taken off with greater speed than he.   45
That sinner plunged, then floated up stretched out,
   and the devils underneath the bridge all shouted:
   "You shouldn't imitate the Holy Face!
The swimming's different here from in the Serchio!
   We have our grappling-hooks along with us—   50
   don't show yourself above the pitch, or else!"
With a hundred prongs or more they pricked him, shrieking:
   "You've got to do your squirming under cover,
   try learning how to cheat beneath the surface."
They were like cooks who make their scullery boys   55
   poke down into the caldron with their forks
   to keep the meat from floating to the top.
My master said: "We'd best not let them know
   that you are here with me; crouch down behind
   some jutting rock so that they cannot see you;   60
whatever insults they may hurl at me,
   you must not fear, I know how things are run here;
   I have been caught in as bad a fix before."
He crossed the bridge and walked on past the end;
   as soon as he set foot on the sixth bank   65
   he forced himself to look as bold as possible.
With all the sound and fury that breaks loose
   when dogs rush out at some poor begging tramp,
   making him stop and beg from where he stands—
the ones who hid beneath the bridge sprang out   70
   and blocked him with a flourish of their pitchforks,
   but he shouted: "All of you behave yourselves!
Before you start to jab me with your forks,
   let one of you step forth to hear me out,
   and then decide if you still care to grapple."   75
They all cried out: "Let Malacoda go!"
   One stepped forward—the others stood their ground—
   and moving, said, "What good will this do him?"
"Do you think, Malacoda," said my master,
   "That you would see me here, come all this way,   80
   against all opposition, and still safe,
without propitious fate and God's permission?
   Now let us pass, for it is willed in Heaven
   that I lead another by this savage path."
With this the devil's arrogance collapsed,   85
   his pitchfork, too, dropped right down to his feet,
   as he announced to all: "Don't touch this man!"
"You, hiding over there," my guide called me,

46–51. "the Holy Face": a wooden crucifix at Lucca. The sinner surfaces
stretched out (l. 46) on his back with
arms flung wide like the figure on a crucifix—and this gives rise to the devil's remark that here in Hell one does not swim
the same way as in the Serchio (a river
near Lucca). In other words, in the Serchio people swim for pleasure, often floating on their backs (in the position of a
crucifix).

  76. "Malacoda": the leader of the
devils in this *bolgia*. It is significant that
a devil whose name means "Evil Tail"
ends this canto with a fart (l. 139).

"behind the bridge's rocks, curled up and quiet,
  come back to me, you may return in safety."   90
At his words I rose and then I ran to him
  and all the devils made a movement forward;
  I feared they would not really keep their pact.
(I remember seeing soldiers under truce,
  as they left the castle of Caprona, frightened   95
  to be passing in the midst of such an enemy.)
I drew up close to him, as close as possible,
  and did not take my eyes from all those faces
  that certainly had nothing good about them.
Their prongs were aimed at me, and one was saying: 100
  "Now do I let him have it in the rump?"
  They answered all for one: "Sure, stick him good!"
But the devil who had spoken with my guide
  was quick to spin around and scream an order:
  "At ease there, take it easy, Scarmiglione!"   105
Then he said to us: "You cannot travel straight
  across this string of bridges, for the sixth arch
  lies broken at the bottom of its ditch;
if you have made your mind up to proceed,
  you must continue on along this ridge;   110
  not far, you'll find a bridge that crosses it.
Five hours more and it will be one thousand,
  two hundred sixty-six years and a day
  since the bridge-way here fell crumbling to the ground.
I plan to send a squad of mine that way   115
  to see that no one airs himself down there;
  go along with them, they will not misbehave.
Front and center, Alichino, Calcabrina,"
  he shouted his commands, "you too, Cagnazzo;
  Barbariccia, you be captain of the squad.   120
Take Libicocco with you and Draghignazzo,
  toothy Ciriatto and Graffiacane,
  Farfarello and our crazy Rubicante.
Now tour the ditch, inspect the boiling tar;
  these two shall have safe passage to the bridge   125
  connecting den to den without a break."
"O master, I don't like the looks of this,"
  I said, "let's go, just you and me, no escort,
  you know the way. I want no part of them!
If you're observant as you usually are,   130
  why is it you don't see them grind their teeth

94–96. Dante's personal recollection concerns the siege of Caprona (a fortress on the Arno River near Pisa) by Guelph troops from Lucca and Florence in 1289.

112–114. Christ's death on Good Friday, 34 A.D., would in five hours, according to Malacoda, have occurred 1266 years ago yesterday—"today" being the morning of Holy Saturday, 1300. Al-

though the bridge across the next *bolgia* was shattered by the earthquake following Christ's crucifixion, Malacoda tells Virgil and the Pilgrim that there is another bridge that crosses this *bolgia*. This lie, carefully contrived by the spokesman for the devils, sets the trap for the overly confident, trusting Virgil and his wary charge.

and wink at one another?—we're in danger!"
And he to me: "I will not have you frightened;
    let them do all the grinding that they want,
    they do it for the boiling souls, not us."   135
Before they turned left-face along the bank
    each one gave their good captain a salute
    with farting tongue pressed tightly to his teeth,
and he blew back with his bugle of an ass-hole.

CANTO XXII

The note of grotesque comedy in the *bolgia* of the Malebranche
continues, with a comparison between Malacoda's salute to his soldiers and different kinds of military signals the Pilgrim has witnessed in his lifetime. He sees many Grafters squatting in the pitch,
but as soon as the Malebranche draw near, they dive below the surface. One unidentified Navarrese, however, fails to escape and is
hoisted up on Graffiacane's hooks; Rubicante and the other Malebranche start to tear into him, but Virgil, at his ward's request,
manages to question him between torments. The sinner briefly tells
his story, and then relates that he has left below in the pitch an
Italian, Fra Gomita, a particularly adept grafter, who spends his
time talking to Michele Zanche.

The Navarrese sinner promises to lure some of his colleagues to
the surface for the devils' amusement, if the tormentors will hide
themselves for a moment. Cagnazzo is skeptical but Alichino agrees,
and no sooner do the Malebranche turn away than the crafty grafter dives below the pitch. Alichino flies after him, but too late; now
Calcabrina rushes after Alichino and both struggle above the boiling
pitch, and then fall in. Barbariccia directs the rescue operation as
the two poets steal away.

I have seen troops of horsemen breaking camp,
    opening the attack, or passing in review,
    I have even seen them fleeing for their lives;
I have seen scouts ride exploring your terrain,
    O Aretines, and I have seen raiding-parties   5
    and the clash of tournaments, the run of jousts—
to the tune of trumpets, to the ring of clanging bells,
    to the roll of drums, to the flash of flares on ramparts,
    to the accompaniment of every known device;
but I never saw cavalry or infantry   10
    or ships that sail by landmarks or by stars
    signaled to set off by such strange bugling!

1–12. The reference to the Aretines (l. 5) recalls Dante's presence at their defeat in the battle of Campaldino (1289) at the hands of the Florentine and Luccan troops.

So, on our way we went with those ten fiends.
  What savage company! But—in church, with saints—
  with rowdy good-for-nothings, in the tavern!   15
My attention now was fixed upon the pitch
  to see the operations of this *bolgia*,
  and how the cooking souls got on down there.
Much like the dolphins that are said to surface
  with their backs arched warn all men at sea   20
  to rig their ships for stormy seas ahead,
so now and then a sinner's back would surface
  in order to alleviate his pain,
  then dive to hide as quick as lightning strikes.
Like squatting frogs along the ditch's edge,   25
  with just their muzzles sticking out of water,
  their legs and all the rest concealed below,
these sinners squatted all around their pond;
  but as soon as Barbariccia would approach
  they quickly ducked beneath the boiling pitch.   30
I saw (my heart still shudders at the thought)
  one lingering behind—as it sometimes happens,
  one frog remains while all the rest dive down—
and Graffiacan, standing in front of him,
  hooked and twirled him by his pitchy hair   35
  and hoisted him. He looked just like an otter!
By then I knew the names of all the fiends:
  I had listened carefully when they were chosen,
  each of them stepping forth to match his name.
"Hey, Rubicante, dig your claws down deep,   40
  into his back and peel the skin off him,"
  this fiendish chorus egged him on with screams.
I said: "Master, will you, if you can, find out
  the name of that poor wretch who has just fallen
  into the cruel hands of his adversaries?"   45
My guide walked right up to the sinner's side
  and asked where he was from, and he replied:
  "I was born and bred in the kingdom of Navarre;
my mother gave me to a lord to serve,
  for she had me by some dishonest spendthrift   50
  who ran through all he owned and killed himself.
Then I became a servant in the household
  of good King Thibault. There I learned my graft,
  and now I pay my bill by boiling here."

48–54. Early commentators have given the name of Ciampolo or Giampolo to this native of Navarre who, after being placed in the service of a Spanish nobleman, later served at the court of Thibault II. Exploiting the court duties with which he was entrusted, he took to barratry. One commentator suggests that were it not for the tradition which attributes the name of Ci-ampolo to this man, one might identify him with the seneschal Goffredo di Beaumont who took over the government of Navarre during Thibault's absence.

53. "good King Thibault": Thibault II, the son-in-law of Louis IX of France, was count of Champagne and later king of Navarre during the mid-thirteenth century.

Ciriatto who had two tusks sticking out   55
    on both sides of his mouth, just like a boar's,
    let him feel how just one tusk could rip him open.
The mouse had fallen prey to evil cats,
    but Barbariccia locked him with his arms
    shouting: "Get back while I've got hold of him!"   60
Then toward my guide he turned his face and said:
    "If you want more from him, keep questioning
    before he's torn to pieces by the others."
My guide went on: "Then tell me, do you know
    of some Italian stuck among these sinners   65
    beneath the pitch?" And he, "A second ago
I was with one who lived around those parts.
    Oh, I wish I were undercover with him now!
    I wouldn't have these hooks or claws to fear."
Libicocco cried: "We've waited long enough,"   70
    then with his fork he hooked the sinner's arm
    and, tearing at it, he pulled out a piece.
Draghignazzo, too, was anxious for some fun;
    he tried the wretch's leg, but their captain quickly
    spun around and gave them all a dirty look.   75
As soon as they calmed down a bit, my master
    began again to interrogate the wretch
    who still was contemplating his new wound:
"Who was it, you were saying, that unluckily
    you left behind you when you came ashore?"   80
    "Gomita," he said, "the friar from Gallura,
receptacle for every kind of fraud:
    when his lord's enemies were in his hands,
    the treatment they received delighted them:
he took their cash, and as he says, hushed up   85
    the case and let them off; none of his acts
    was petty grafting, all were of sovereign order.
He spends his time with don Michele Zanche
    of Logodoro, talking on and on
    about Sardinia—their tongues no worse for wear!   90
Oh, but look how that one grins and grinds his teeth;
    I could tell you so much more, but I am afraid
    he is going to grate my scabby hide for me."

81–87. "Gomita": Fra Gomita was a Sardinian friar, chancellor of Nino Visconti, governor of Pisa, whom Dante places in *Purgatory* (Canto VIII, l. 53). From 1275–1296 Nino Visconti was judge of Gallura, one of the four districts into which Sardinia, a Pisan possession during the thirteenth century, was divided. Profiting by his position and the good faith of Nino Visconti, who refused to listen to the complaints raised against him, Fra Gomita indulged in the sale of public offices. When Nino learned, however, that he had accepted bribes to let prisoners escape, he promptly had him hanged.

88–89. "Michele Zanche": Although no documents mentioning the name of Michele Zanche have been found, he is believed to have been the governor of Logodoro, another of the four districts into which Sardinia was divided in the thirteenth century during the period when King Enzo of Sardinia, the son of Frederick II, was engaged in war.

But their master-sergeant turned to Farfarello,
   whose wild eyes warned he was about to strike,   95
   shouting, "Get away, you filthy bird of prey."
"If you would like to see Tuscans or Lombards,"
   the frightened shade took up where he left off,
   "and have a talk with them, I'll bring some here;
but the Malebranche must back up a bit,   100
   or else those shades won't risk a surfacing;
   I, by myself, will bring you up a catch
of seven, without moving from this spot,
   just by whistling—that's our signal to the rest
   when one peers out and sees the coast is clear."   105
Cagnazzo raised his snout at such a story,
   then shook his head and said: "Listen to the trick
   he's cooked up to get off the hook by jumping!"
And he, full of tricks his trade had taught him,
   said: "Tricky, I surely am, especially   110
   when it comes to getting friends into worse trouble."
But Alichin could not resist the challenge,
   and in spite of what the others thought, cried out:
   "If you jump, I won't come galloping for you,
I've got my wings to beat you to the pitch.   115
   We'll clear this ledge and wait behind that slope.
   Let's see if one of you can outmatch us!"
Now listen, Reader, here's a game that's strange:
   they all turned toward the slope, and first to turn
   was the fiend who from the start opposed the game.   120
The Navarrese had perfect sense of timing:
   feet planted on the ground, in a flash he jumped,
   the devil's plan was foiled, and he was free.
The squad was stung with shame but most of all
   the one who brought this blunder to perfection;   125
   he swooped down howling, "Now I've got you caught!"
Little good it did, for wings could not outstrip
   the flight of terror: down the sinner dived
   and up the fiend was forced to strain his chest
like a falcon swooping down on a wild duck: 130
   the duck dives quickly out of sight, the falcon
   must fly back up dejected and defeated.
In the meantime, Calcabrina, furious,
   also took off, hoping the shade would make it,
   so he could pick a fight with his companion.   135
And when he saw the grafter hit the pitch
   he turned his claws to grapple with his brother,
   and they tangled in mid-air above the ditch;
but the other was a fullfledged hawk as well
   and used his claws on him, and both of them   140
   went plunging straight into the boiling tar.
The heat was quick to make them separate,

but there seemed no way of getting out of there;
    their wings were clogged and could not lift them up.
Barbariccia, no less peeved than all his men,   145
    sent four fiends flying to the other shore
    with their equipment at top speed; instantly,
some here, some there, they took the posts assigned them.
    They stretched their hooks to reach the pitch-dipped pair
    who were by now deep-fried within their crusts.   150
And we left them messed up in their occupation.

CANTO XXIII

The antics of Ciampolo, the Navarrese, and the Malebranche
bring to the Pilgrim's mind the fable of the frog, the mouse, and
the hawk—and that in turn reminds him of the immediate danger
he and Virgil are in from the angry Malebranche. Virgil senses the
danger too, and grabbing his ward as a mother would her child, he
dashes to the edge of the bank and slides down the rocky slope into
the sixth *bolgia*—not a moment too soon, for at the top of the
slope they see the angry Malebranche. When the Pilgrim looks
around him he sees weeping shades slowly marching in single file,
each one covered from head to foot with a golden cloak, lined with
lead that weights them down. These are the Hypocrites. Two in
this group identify themselves as Catalano de' Malavolti and Loderingo degli Andalò, two Jovial Friars. The Pilgrim is about to address
them when he sees the shade of Caiaphas (the evil counselor who
advised Pontius Pilate to crucify Christ) crucified and transfixed by
three stakes to the ground. Virgil discovers from the two friars that
in order to leave this *bolgia* they must climb up a rockslide; he also
learns that this is the only *bolgia* over which the bridge is broken.
Virgil is angry with himself for having believed Malacoda's lie about
the bridge over the sixth *bolgia* (Canto XXI, l. 111).

In silence, all alone, without an escort,
    we moved along, one behind the other,
    like minor friars bent upon a journey.
I was thinking over one of Aesop's fables
    that this recent skirmish had brought back to mind,   5
    where he tells the story of the frog and mouse;
for "yon" and "there" could not be more alike
    than the fable and the fact, if one compares
    the start and finish of both incidents.
As from one thought another often rises,   10
    so this thought gave quick birth to still another,

3. The image of the "minor friars"
(Franciscans) who walk in single file is
preparatory to the presentation of the
Hypocrites whose clothing is compared
to that of monks (ll. 61–66).

and then the fear I first had felt was doubled.
I was thinking: "Since these fiends, on our account,
   were tricked and mortified by mockery,
   they certainly will be more than resentful;   15
with rage now added to their evil instincts,
   they will hunt us down with all the savagery
   of dogs about to pounce upon the hare."
I felt my body's skin begin to tighten—
   I was so frightened!—and I kept looking back: 20
   "O master," I said, "if you do not hide
both of us, and very quick, I am afraid
   of the Malebranche—right now they're on our trail—
   I feel they're there, I think I hear them now."
And he replied: "Even if I were a mirror   25
   I could not reflect your outward image faster
   than your inner thoughts transmit themselves to me.
In fact, just now they joined themselves with mine,
   and since they were alike in birth and form,
   I decided to unite them toward one goal: 30
if the right-hand bank should slope in such a way
   as to allow us to descend to the next *bolgia,*
   we could escape that chase we have imagined."
He had hardly finished telling me his plan
   when I saw them coming with their wings wide-open   35
   not too far off, and now they meant to get us!
My guide instinctively caught hold of me,
   like a mother waking to some warning sound,
   who sees the rising flames are getting close
and grabs her son and runs—she does not wait   40
   the short time it would take to put on something;
   she cares not for herself, only for him.
And over the edge, then down the stony bank
   he slid, on his back, along the sloping rock
   that walls the higher side of the next *bolgia.*   45
Water that turns a mill wheel never ran
   the narrow sluice at greater speed, not even
   at the point before it hits the paddle-blades,
than down that sloping border my guide slid
   bearing me with him, clasping me to his chest   50
   as though I were his child, not his companion.
His feet had hardly touched rock bottom, when
   there they were, the ten of them, above us
   on the height; but now there was no need to fear:
High Providence that willed for them to be   55
   the ministers in charge of the fifth ditch
   also willed them powerless to leave their realm.
And now, down there, we found a painted people,
   slow-motioned: step by step, they walked their round
   in tears, and seeming wasted by fatigue.   60

All were wearing cloaks with hoods pulled low
   covering the eyes (the style was much the same
   as those the Benedictines wear at Cluny),
dazzling, gilded cloaks outside, but inside
   they were lined with lead, so heavy, that the capes   65
   King Frederick used, compared to these, were straw.
O cloak of everlasting weariness!
   We turned again, as usual, to the left
   and moved with them, those souls lost in their mourning;
but with their weight that tired-out race of shades   70
   paced on so slowly that we found ourselves
   in new company with every step we took;
and so I asked my guide: "Would you look around
   and see, as we keep walking, if you find
   someone here whose name or deeds are known."   75
And one who overheard me speaking Tuscan
   cried out somewhere behind us: "Not so fast,
   you there, rushing ahead through this heavy air,
perhaps from me you can obtain an answer."
   At this my guide turned toward me saying, "Stop,   80
   and wait for him, then match your pace with his."
I paused and saw two shades with straining faces
   revealing their mind's haste to join my side,
   but the weight they bore and the crowded road delayed them.
When they arrived, they looked at me sideways   85
   and for some time, without exchanging words;
   then they turned to one another and were saying:
"He seems alive, the way his throat is moving,
   and if both are dead, what privilege allows them
   to walk uncovered by the heavy cloak?"   90
Then they spoke to me: "O Tuscan who has come
   to visit the college of the sullen hypocrites,
   do not disdain to tell us who you are."
I answered them: "I was born and I grew up
   in the great city on the lovely Arno's shore,   95
   and I have the body I have always had.
But who are you, distilling tears of grief,
   so many I see running down your cheeks?
   And what kind of pain is this that it can glitter?"
One of them answered: "The orange-gilded cloaks   100
   are thick with lead so heavy that it makes us,
   who are the scales it hangs on, creak as we walk.

61–63. The vestments of the monks at Cluny were particularly famous for their fullness and elegance.

64–66. Dante's image of the gilded exterior concealing a leaden interior is perhaps drawn from Matthew 23:27, "Woe unto you, scribes and Pharisees, hypocrites! For ye are like unto whited sepulchers, which indeed appear beautiful outwardly but are within full of dead men's bones, and of all uncleanness." "capes / King Frederick used" (ll. 65–66): refers to a mode of punishment for traitors reportedly instituted by Frederick II, grandson of Frederick Barbarossa. The condemned were dressed in leaden capes which were then melted on their bodies.

Jovial Friars we were, both from Bologna.
  My name was Catalano, his, Loderingo,
  and both of us were chosen by your city, 105
that usually would choose one man alone,
  to keep the peace. Evidence of what we were
  may still be seen around Gardingo's parts."
I began: "O Friars, all your wretchedness . . ."
  but said no more; I couldn't, for I saw 110
  one crucified with three stakes on the ground.
And when he saw me all his body writhed,
  and through his beard he heaved out sighs of pain;
  then Friar Catalano, who watched the scene,
remarked: "That impaled figure you see there 115
  advised the Pharisees it was expedient
  to sacrifice one man for all the people.
Naked he lies stretched out across the road,
  as you can see, and he must feel the load
  of every weight that steps on him to cross. 120
His father-in-law and the other council members,
  who were the seed of evil for all Jews,
  are racked the same way all along this ditch."
And I saw Virgil staring down amazed
  at this body stretching out in crucifixion, 125
  so vilely punished in the eternal exile.
Then he looked up and asked one of the friars:
  "Could you please tell us, if your rule permits:
  is there a passage-way on the right, somewhere,
by which the two of us may leave this place 130
  without summoning one of those black angels

103–108. The Order of the *Cavalieri di Beata Santa Maria*, or "Jovial Friars" (*frati gaudenti*) as they were called, was founded at Bologna in 1261 and was dedicated to the maintenance of peace between political factions and families, and to the defense of the weak and poor. However, because of its rather liberal rules, this high-principled organization gained the nickname of "Jovial Friars"— which, no doubt, impaired its serious function to some degree. The Bolognese friars Catalano de' Malavolti (c. 1210–1285) and Loderingo degli Andalò (ca. 1210–1293) were elected jointly to the office of *Podestà* ("mayor") in Florence because it was thought that the combination of the former, a Guelph, and the latter, a Ghibelline, would ensure the peace of the city. In reality their tenure, short though it was, was characterized by strife, which culminated in the expulsion of the Ghibellines from Florence in 1266. Gardingo (l. 108) is the name of the section of Florence around the Palazzo Vecchio; in this area the Uberti family, the heads of the Florentine Ghibelline party, had their palace, which was razed during the uprisings of 1266. Modern historians have proved that Pope Clement IV controlled both the election and actions of Catalano and Loderingo, in order to overthrow the Ghibellines and establish the Guelphs in power.

115–124. Caiaphas, the high priest of the Jews, maintained that it was better that one man (Jesus) die than for the Hebrew nation to be lost (John 11:49–50). Annas, Caiaphas's father-in-law (l. 121), delivered Jesus to him for judgment. For their act against God these men and the other evil counselors who judged Christ were the "seed of evil for all Jews" (l. 122); in retaliation God caused Jerusalem to be destroyed and the Hebrew people dispersed to all parts of the world. It is, then, a fitting punishment for Caiaphas, Annas, and the rest to bear the weight of all the hypocrites for their crime, and to be crucified on the ground with "three stakes."

124–127. Most commentators seem to think that Virgil's amazement at seeing the crucified Caiaphas is due to the fact that he was not there when Virgil first descended into Hell.

to come down here and raise us from this pit?"
He answered: "Closer than you might expect,
    a ridge jutting out from the base of the great circle
    extends, and bridges every hideous ditch   135
except this one whose arch is totally smashed
    and crosses nowhere; but you can climb up
    its massive ruins that slope against this bank."
My guide stood there awhile, his head bent low,
    then said, "He told a lie about this business,   140
    that one who hooks the sinners over there."
And the friar: "Once, in Bologna, I heard discussed
    the devil's many vices; one of them is
    that he tells lies and is father of all lies."
In haste, taking great strides, my guide walked off,   145
    his face revealing traces of his anger.
I turned and left the heavy-weighted souls
to make my way behind those cherished footprints.

CANTO XXIV

After an elaborate simile describing Virgil's anger and the return
of his composure, the two begin the difficult, steep ascent up the
rocks of the fallen bridge. The Pilgrim can barely make it to the top
even with Virgil's help, and after the climb he sits down to catch
his breath; but his guide urges him on, and they make their way
back to the bridge over the seventh *bolgia*. From the bridge confused sounds can be heard rising from the darkness below. Virgil
agrees to take his pupil down into the *bolgia*, and once they are
below, the scene reveals a terrible confusion of serpents, and Thieves
madly running.

Suddenly a snake darts out and strikes a sinner's neck, whereupon
he flares up, turning into a heap of crumbling ashes; then the ashes
gather together into the shape of a man. The metamorphosed
sinner reveals himself to be Vanni Fucci, a Pistoiese condemned for
stealing the treasure of the sacristy of the church of San Zeno at
Pistoia. He makes a prophecy about the coming strife in Florence.

In the season of the newborn year, when the sun
    renews its rays beneath Aquarius
    and nights begin to last as long as days,
at the time the hoarfrost paints upon the ground
    the outward semblance of his snow-white sister   5
    (but the color from his brush soon fades away),
the peasant wakes, gets up, goes out and sees
    the fields all white. No fodder for his sheep!

146–148. Virgil is angry, of course, because he had trusted Malacoda and had
been deceived, and also because of the
friar's slightly taunting rebuke at his
naïveté (ll. 142–144).

He smites his thighs in anger and goes back
into his shack and, pacing up and down,   10
   complains, poor wretch, not knowing what to do;
   once more he goes outdoors, and hope fills him
again when he sees the world has changed its face
   in so little time, and he picks up his crook
   and out to pasture drives his sheep to graze—   15
just so I felt myself lose heart to see
   my master's face wearing a troubled look,
   and as quickly came the salve to heal my sore:
for when we reached the shattered heap of bridge,
   my leader turned to me with that sweet look   20
   of warmth I first saw at the mountain's foot;
he opened up his arms (but not before
   he had carefully studied how the ruins lay
   and found some sort of plan) to pick me up.
Like one who works and thinks things out ahead,   25
   always ready for the next move he will make,
   so while he raised me up toward one great rock,
he had already singled out another,
   saying, "Now get a grip on that rock there,
   but test it first to see it holds your weight."   30
It was no road for one who wore a cloak!
   Even though I had his help and he weighed nothing,
   we could hardly lift ourselves from crag to crag.
And had it not been that the bank we climbed
   was lower than the one we had slid down—   35
   I cannot speak for him—but I for one
surely would have quit. But since the Evil Pits
   slope toward the yawning well that is the lowest,
   each valley is laid out in such a way
that one bank rises higher than the next.   40
   We somehow finally reached the point above
   where the last of all that rock was shaken loose.
My lungs were so pumped out of breath by the time
   I reached the top, I could not go on farther,
   and instantly I sat down where I was.   45
"Come on, shake off the covers of this sloth,"
   the master said, "for sitting softly cushioned,
   or tucked in bed, is no way to win fame;
and without it man must waste his life away,
   leaving such traces of what he was on earth   50
   as smoke in wind and foam upon the water.
Stand up! Dominate this weariness of yours
   with the strength of soul that wins in every battle
   if it does not sink beneath the body's weight.
Much steeper stairs than these we'll have to climb;   55

21. "at the mountain's foot": The
mountain of Canto I, a reference which
reminds the reader of the entire journey.
   31. Such as the Hypocrites of the previous *bolgia*.
   55. Virgil is referring to the ascent up
Lucifer's legs and beyond. See Canto
XXXIV, ll. 82–84.

we have not seen enough of sinners yet!
  If you understand me, act, learn from my words."
At this I stood up straight and made it seem
  I had more breath than I began to breathe,
  and said: "Move on, for I am strong and ready."   60
We climbed and made our way along the bridge
  which was jagged, tight and difficult to cross,
  and steep—far more than any we had climbed.
Not to seem faint I spoke while I was climbing;
  then came a voice from the depths of the next chasm,   65
  a voice unable to articulate.
I don't know what it said, even though I stood
  at the very top of the arch that crosses there;
  to me it seemed whoever spoke, spoke running.
I was bending over, but no living eyes   70
  could penetrate the bottom of that darkness;
  therefore I said: "Master, why not go down
this bridge onto the next encircling bank,
  for I hear sounds I cannot understand,
  and I look down but cannot see a thing."   75
"No other answer," he replied, "I give you
  than doing what you ask, for a fit request
  is answered best in silence and in deed."
From the bridge's height we came down to the point
  where it ends and joins the edge of the eighth bank,   80
  and then the *bolgia* opened up to me:
down there I saw a terrible confusion
  of serpents, all of such a monstrous kind
  the thought of them still makes my blood run cold.
Let all the sands of Libya boast no longer,   85
  for though she breeds chelydri and jaculi,
  phareans, cenchres and head-tailed amphisbenes,
she never bred so great a plague of venom,
  not even if combined with Ethiopia
  or all the sands that lie by the Red Sea.   90
Within this cruel and bitterest abundance
  people ran terrified and naked, hopeless
  of finding hiding-holes or heliotrope.
Their hands were tied behind their backs with serpents
  which pushed their tails and heads around the loins   95
  and coiled themselves in knots around the front.
And then—at a sinner running by our bank
  a snake shot out and, striking, hit his mark:
  right where the neck attaches to the shoulder.
No *o* or *i* was ever quicker put   100
  by pen to paper than he flared up and burned,
  and turned into a heap of crumbled ash;

85–90. Libya and the other lands near the Red Sea (Ethiopia and Arabia) were renowned for producing several types of dreadful reptiles.
93. According to folk tradition, heliotrope was believed to be a stone of many virtues. It could cure snakebites and make the man who carried it on his person invisible.

and then, these ashes scattered on the ground
    began to come together on their own
    and quickly take the form they had before: 105
precisely so, philosophers declare
    the phoenix dies to be reborn again
    as she approaches her five-hundredth year;
alive she does not feed on herbs or grain,
    but on teardrops of frankincense and balm,   110
    and wraps herself to die in nard and myrrh.
As a man in a fit will fall, not knowing why
    (perhaps some hidden demon pulls him down,
    or some oppilation chokes his vital spirits),
then, struggling to his feet, will look around,   115
    confused and overwhelmed by the great anguish
    he has suffered, moaning as he stares about—
so did this sinner when he finally rose.
    Oh, how harsh the power of the Lord can be,
    raining in its vengeance blows like these!   120
My guide asked him to tell us who he was,
    and he replied: "It's not too long ago
    I rained from Tuscany to this fierce gullet.
I loved the bestial life more than the human,
    like the bastard that I was; I'm Vanni Fucci,   125
    the beast! Pistoia was my fitting den."
I told my guide: "Tell him not to run away;
    ask him what sin has driven him down here,
    for I knew him as a man of bloody rage."
The sinner heard and did not try to feign;   130
    directing straight at me his mind and face,
    he reddened with a look of ugly shame,
and said: "That you have caught me by surprise
    here in this wretched *bolgia*, makes me grieve
    more than the day I lost my other life.   135
Now I am forced to answer what you ask:
    I am stuck so far down here because of theft:
    I stole the treasure of the sacristy—
a crime falsely attributed to another.
    I don't want you to rejoice at having seen me,   140

108–111. Dante compares the complex metamorphosis of Vanni Fucci to that of the phoenix which, according to legend, consumes itself in flames every five hundred years.

112–117. It was a popular belief that during an epileptic fit, the victim was possessed by the devil; in addition to this, Dante presents a more rational explanation: that some blockage of his veins inhibits the proper functioning of a man's body.

125–129. "Vanni Fucci": the illegitimate son of Fuccio de' Lazzari, a militant leader of the Blacks in Pistoia. His notoriety "as a man of bloody rage" (l. 129) was widespread; in fact, the Pilgrim is surprised to find him here and not immersed in the Phlegethon together with the other shades of the Violent (Canto XII).

138–139. Around 1293 the treasury of San Iacopo in the church of San Zeno at Pistoia was robbed, The person unjustly accused (l. 139) of the theft (and almost executed for it) was Rampino Foresi. Later, the true facts came to light, and Vanni della Mona, one of the conspirators, was sentenced to death. Vanni Fucci, however, escaped, and although he received a sentence in 1295 for murder and other acts of violence, he managed to remain free until his death in 1300.

if ever you escape from these dark pits,
so open your ears and hear my prophecy:
   Pistoia first shall be stripped of all its Blacks,
   and Florence then shall change its men and laws;
from Valdimagra Mars shall thrust a bolt   145
   of lightning wrapped in thick, foreboding clouds,
   then bolt and clouds will battle bitterly
in a violent storm above Piceno's fields
   where rapidly the bolt will burst the cloud,
   and no White will escape without his wounds.   150
And I have told you this so you will suffer!"

CANTO XXV

The wrathful Vanni Fucci directs an obscene gesture to God, whereupon he is attacked by several snakes, which coil about him, tying him so tight that he can not move a muscle. As soon as he flees, the centaur Cacus gallops by with a fire-breathing dragon on his back, and following close behind are three shades, concerned because they cannot find Cianfa—who soon appears as a snake which attacks Agnèl; the two merge into one hideous monster which then steals off. Next, Guercio, in the form of a snake, strikes Buoso, and the two exchange shapes. Only Puccio Sciancato is left unchanged.

When he had finished saying this, the thief
   shaped his fists into figs and raised them high
   and cried: "Here, God, I've shaped them just for you!"
From then on all those snakes became my friends,
   for one of them at once coiled round his neck   5
   as if to say, "That's all you're going to say,"
while another twisted round his arms in front;
   it tied itself into so tight a knot,
   between the two he could not move a muscle.
Pistoia, ah Pistoia! why not resolve   10
   to burn yourself to ashes, ending all,
   since you have done more evil than your founders?
Throughout the circles of this dark inferno
   I saw no shade so haughty toward his God,
   not even he who fell from Thebes' high walls.   15
Without another word he fled, and then
   I saw a raging centaur gallop up

2. An obscene gesture still current in Italy. The gesture is made by closing the hand to form a fist with the thumb inserted between the first and second fingers.

10–12. "Pistoia": supposedly founded by the remnants of the defeated army of Catiline, composed primarily of evildoers and brigands.

15. Capaneus, whom Dante placed among the Blasphemers in the Seventh Circle.

roaring: "Where is he, where is that untamed beast?"
I think that all Maremma does not have
  as many snakes as he had on his back,   20
  right up to where his human form begins.
Upon his shoulders, just behind the nape,
  a dragon with its wings spread wide was crouching
  and spitting fire at whoever came its way.
My master said to me: "That one is Cacus,   25
  who more than once in the grotto far beneath
  Mount Aventine spilled blood to fill a lake.
He does not go the same road as his brothers
  because of the cunning way he committed theft
  when he stole his neighbor's famous cattle-herd;   30
and then his evil deeds came to an end
  beneath the club of Hercules, who struck
  a hundred blows, and he, perhaps, felt ten."
While he was speaking Cacus galloped off;
  at the same time three shades appeared below us;   35
  my guide and I would not have seen them there
if they had not cried out: "Who are you two?"
  At this we cut our conversation short
  to give our full attention to these three.
I didn't know who they were, but then it happened,   40
  as often it will happen just by chance,
  that one of them was forced to name another:
"Where did Cianfa go off to?" he asked. And then,
  to keep my guide from saying anything,
  I put my finger tight against my lips.   45
Now if, my reader, you should hesitate
  to believe what I shall say, there's little wonder,
  for I, the witness, scarcely can believe it.
While I was watching them, all of a sudden
  a serpent—and it had six feet—shot up   50
  and hooked one of these wretches with all six.
With the middle feet it hugged the sinner's stomach
  and, with the front ones, grabbed him by the arms,
  and bit him first through one cheek then the other;
the serpent spread its hind feet round both thighs   55
  then stuck its tail between the sinner's legs,
  and up against his back the tail slid stiff.
No ivy ever grew to any tree
  so tight entwined, as the way that hideous beast

19–20. "Maremma": a swampy area along the Tuscan coast which was infested with snakes.

25–33. "Cacus": a centaur, the son of Vulcan; he was a fire-belching monster who lived in a cave beneath Mt. Aventine and pillaged the inhabitants of the area. But when he stole several cattle of Hercules's, the latter went to Cacus's cave and killed him. "His brothers" (l. 28) are the centaurs who serve as guardians in the first round of the Seventh Circle.

43. "Cianfa": a member of the Florentine Donati family. He makes his appearance in line 50 in the form of a serpent.

had woven in and out its limbs with his;   60
and then both started melting like hot wax
    and, fusing, they began to mix their colors
    (so neither one seemed what he was before),
just as a brownish tint, ahead of flame,
    creeps up a burning page that is not black   65
    completely, even though the white is dying.
The other two who watched began to shout:
    "Oh Agnèl! If you could see how you are changing!
    You're not yourself, and you're not both of you!"
The two heads had already fused to one   70
    and features from each flowed and blended into
    one face where two were lost in one another;
two arms of each were four blurred strips of flesh;
    and thighs with legs, then stomach and the chest
    sprouted limbs that human eyes have never seen.   75
Each former likeness now was blotted out:
    both, and neither one it seemed—this picture
    of deformity. And then it sneaked off slowly.
Just as a lizard darting from hedge to hedge,
    under the stinging lash of the dog-days' heat,   80
    zips across the road, like a flash of lightning,
so, rushing toward the two remaining thieves,
    aiming at their guts, a little serpent,
    fiery with rage and black as pepper-corn,
shot up and sank its teeth in one of them   85
    right where the embryo receives its food,
    then back it fell and lay stretched out before him.
The wounded thief stared speechless at the beast,
    and standing motionless began to yawn
    as though he needed sleep, or had a fever.   90
The snake and he were staring at each other;
    one from his wound, the other from its mouth
    fumed violently, and smoke with smoke was mingling.
Let Lucan from this moment on be silent,
    who tells of poor Nasidius and Sabellus,   95
    and wait to hear what I still have in store;
and Ovid, too, with his Cadmus and Arethusa—
    though he metamorphosed one into a snake,
    the other to a fountain, I feel no envy,
for never did he interchange two beings   100
    face to face so that both forms were ready

---

68. Besides the indication that Agnèl is Florentine (except for Vanni Fucci, the thieves in this canto are all Florentines), and possibly is one of the Brunelleschi family, nothing more is known of him.

86. "right where the embryo receives its food": The navel.

94–102. In the *Pharsalia* Lucan tells of the physical transformations undergone by Sabellus and Nasidius, both soldiers in Cato's army who, being bitten by snakes, turned respectively into ashes and into a formless mass. Ovid relates how Cadmus took the form of a serpent and how Arethusa became a fountain.

to exchange their substance, each one for the other's,
an interchange of perfect symmetry:
the serpent split its tail into a fork,
and the wounded sinner drew his feet together;   105
the legs, with both the thighs, closed in to join
and in a short time fused, so that the juncture
didn't show signs of ever having been there,
the while the cloven tail assumed the features
that the other one was losing, and its skin   110
was growing soft, the other's getting scaly;
I saw his arms retreating to the armpits,
and the reptile's two front feet, that had been short,
began to stretch the length the man's had shortened;
the beast's hind feet then twisted round each other   115
and turned into the member man conceals,
while from the wretch's member grew two legs.
The smoke from each was swirling round the other,
exchanging colors, bringing out the hair
where there was none, and stripping off the other's.   120
The one rose up, the other sank, but neither
dissolved the bond between their evil stares,
fixed eye to eye, exchanging face for face;
the standing creature's face began receding
toward the temples; from the excess stuff pulled back,   125
the ears were growing out of flattened cheeks,
while from the excess flesh that did not flee
the front, a nose was fashioned for the face,
and lips puffed out to just the normal size.
The prostrate creature strains his face out long   130
and makes his ears withdraw into his head,
the way a snail pulls in its horns. The tongue,
that once had been one piece and capable
of forming words, divides into a fork,
while the other's fork heals up. The smoke subsides.   135
The soul that had been changed into a beast
went hissing off along the valley's floor,
the other close behind him, spitting words.
Then he turned his new-formed back on him and said
to the shade left standing there: "Let Buoso run   140
the valley on all fours, the way I did."
Thus I saw the cargo of the seventh hold
exchange and interchange; and let the strangeness
of it all excuse me, if my pen has failed.
And though this spectacle confused my eyes   145
and stunned my mind, the two thieves could not flee

140–141. "Buoso": The identity of
Buoso, the newly formed serpent, is uncertain; some commentators think him
to be Buoso degli Abati and others,
Buoso Donati (see Canto XXX, l. 44).

so secretly I did not recognize
    that one was certainly Puccio Sciancato
    (and he alone, of that company of three
    that first appeared, did not change to something else),   150
the other, he who made you mourn, Gaville.

CANTO XXVI

From the ridge high above the eighth *bolgia* can be perceived a
myriad of flames flickering far below, and Virgil explains that
within each flame is the suffering soul of a Deceiver. One flame,
divided at the top, catches the Pilgrim's eye and he is told that
within it are jointly punished Ulysses and Diomed. Virgil questions
the pair for the benefit of the Pilgrim. Ulysses responds with the
famous narrative of his last voyage, during which he passed the Pillars of Hercules and sailed the forbidden sea until he saw a mountain shape, from which came suddenly a whirlwind that spun his
ship around three times and sank it.

Be joyful, Florence, since you are so great
    that your outstretched wings beat over land and sea,
    and your name is spread throughout the realm of Hell!
I was ashamed to find among the thieves
    five of your most eminent citizens,   5
    a fact which does you very little honor.
But if early morning dreams have any truth,
    you will have the fate, in not too long a time,
    that Prato and the others crave for you.
And were this the day, it would not be too soon!   10
    Would it had come to pass, since pass it must!
    The longer the delay, the more my grief.
We started climbing up the stairs of boulders
    that had brought us to the place from where we watched;
    my guide went first and pulled me up behind him.   15
We went along our solitary way
    among the rocks, among the ridge's crags,
    where the foot could not advance without the hand.
I know that I grieved then, and now again
    I grieve when I remember what I saw,   20

148. "Puccio Sciancato": (the only one of the original three Florentine thieves who does not assume a new shape) a member of the Galigai family and a supporter of the Ghibellines. He was exiled from Florence in 1268.

151. Francesco Cavalcanti, known as Guercio, was slain by the inhabitants of Gaville, a small town near Florence in Valdarno (Arno Valley). The Cavalcanti family avenged his death by decimating the populace; thus, he was Gaville's rea-

son to mourn.

7. "But if early morning dreams have any truth": According to the ancient and medieval popular tradition, the dreams that men have in the early morning hours before daybreak will come true.

9. It seems most plausible, given the phrase "and the others" that Prato is to be interpreted here in a generic sense to indicate all the small Tuscan towns subjected to Florentine rule, which soon rebel against their master.

and more than ever I restrain my talent
lest it run a course that virtue has not set;
  for if a lucky star or something better
  has given me this good, I must not misuse it.
As many fireflies (in the season when 25
  the one who lights the world hides his face least,
  in the hour when the flies yield to mosquitoes)
as the peasant on the hillside at his ease
  sees, flickering in the valley down below,
  where perhaps he gathers grapes or tills the soil— 30
with just so many flames all the eighth *bolgia*
  shone brilliantly, as I became aware
  when at last I stood where the depths were visible.
As he who was avenged by bears beheld
  Elijah's chariot at its departure, 35
  when the rearing horses took to flight toward Heaven,
and though he tried to follow with his eyes,
  he could not see more than the flame alone
  like a small cloud once it had risen high—
so each flame moves itself along the throat 40
  of the abyss, none showing what it steals
  but each one stealing nonetheless a sinner.
I was on the bridge, leaning far over—so far
  that if I had not grabbed some jut of rock
  I could easily have fallen to the bottom. 45
And my guide who saw me so absorbed, explained:
  "There are souls concealed within these moving fires,
  each one swathed in his burning punishment."
"O master," I replied, "from what you say
  I know now I was right; I had guessed already 50
  it might be so, and I was about to ask you:
Who's in that flame with its tip split in two,
  like that one which once sprang up from the pyre
  where Eteocles was placed beside his brother?"
He said: "Within, Ulysses and Diomed
  are suffering in anger with each other, 55
  just vengeance makes them march together now.

34–39. The prophet Elisha saw Elijah transported to Heaven in a fiery chariot. When Elisha on another occasion cursed, in the name of the Lord, a group of children who were mocking him, two bears came out of the forest and devoured them. (4 Kings, 2:9–12, 23–24).

52–54. Dante compares this flame with that which rose from the funeral pyre of Eteocles and Polynices, twin sons of Oedipus and Jocasta, who, contesting the throne of Thebes, caused a major conflict known as the Seven against Thebes (see Canto XIV, ll. 68–69). The two brothers met in single combat and slew each other. They were placed together on the pyre, but because of their mutual hatred, the flame split.

55–57. "Ulysses"; the son of Laertes, a central figure in the Trojan War. Although his deeds are recounted by Homer, Dictys of Crete, and many others, the story of his last voyage presented here by Dante (ll. 90–142), has no literary or historical precedent. His story, being an invention of Dante's, is unique in the *Divine Comedy*.

"Diomed": the son of Tydeus and Deipyle, ruled Argos. He was a major Greek figure in the Trojan War and was frequently associated with Ulysses in his exploits.

And they lament inside one flame the ambush
   of the horse become the gateway that allowed
   the Romans' noble seed to issue forth.   60
Therein they mourn the trick that caused the grief
   of Deidamia who still weeps for Achilles;
   and there they pay for the Palladium."
"If it is possible for them to speak
   from within those flames," I said, "master, I pray   65
   and repray you—let my prayer be like a thousand—
that you do not forbid me to remain
   until the two-horned flame comes close to us;
   you see how I bend toward it with desire!"
"Your prayer indeed is worthy of highest praise,"   70
   he said to me, "and therefore I shall grant it;
   but see to it your tongue refrains from speaking.
Leave it to me to speak, for I know well
   what you would ask; perhaps since they were Greeks
   they might not pay attention to your words."   75
So when the flame had reached us, and my guide
   decided that the time and place were right,
   he addressed them and I listened to him speaking:
"O you who are two souls within one fire,
   if I have deserved from you when I was living,   80
   if I have deserved from you much praise or little,
when in the world I wrote my lofty verses,
   do not move on; let one of you tell where
   he lost himself through his own fault, and died."
The greater of the ancient flame's two horns   85
   began to sway and quiver, murmuring
   just like a flame that strains against the wind;
then, while its tip was moving back and forth,
   as if it were the tongue itself that spoke,
   the flame took on a voice and said: "When I   90
set sail from Circe who, more than a year,
   had kept me occupied close to Gaëta

58–60. The Trojans mistakenly believed the mammoth wooden horse, left outside the city's walls, to be a sign of Greek capitulation. They brought it through the gates of the city amid great rejoicing. Later that evening the Greek soldiers hidden in the horse emerged and sacked the city. The Fall of Troy occasioned the journey of Aeneas and his followers ("noble seed") to establish a new nation on the shores of Italy which would become the heart of the Roman Empire.

61–62. Thetis brought her son Achilles, disguised as a girl, to the court of King Lycomedes on the island of Scyros, so that he would not have to fight in the Trojan War. There Achilles seduced the king's daughter Deidamia, who bore him a child and whom he later abandoned, encouraged by Ulysses (who in company with Diomed had come in search of him) to join the war.

63. "the Palladium": The sacred Palladium, a statue of the goddess Pallas Athena, guaranteed the integrity of Troy as long as it remained in the citadel. Ulysses and Diomed stole it and carried it off to Argos, thereby securing victory for the Greeks over the Trojans.

90–92. On his return voyage to Ithaca from Troy Ulysses was detained by Circe, the daughter of the Sun, for more than a year. She was an enchantress who transformed Ulysses's men into swine.

92–93. "Gaëta": Along the coast of southern Italy above Naples there is a promontory (and now on it there is a city) then called Gaëta. Aeneas named it to honor his nurse who had died there.

(before Aeneas called it by that name),
not sweetness of a son, not reverence
   for an aging father, not the debt of love   95
   I owed Penelope to make her happy,
could quench deep in myself the burning wish
   to know the world and have experience
   of all man's vices, of all human worth.
So I set out on the deep and open sea   100
   with just one ship and with that group of men,
   not many, who had not deserted me.
I saw as far as Spain, far as Morocco,
   both shores; I had left behind Sardinia,
   and the other islands which that sea encloses.   105
I and my mates were old and tired men.
   Then finally we reached the narrow neck
   where Hercules put up his signal-pillars
to warn men not to go beyond that point.
   On my right I saw Seville, and passed beyond;   110
   on my left, Ceuta had already sunk behind me.
'Brothers,' I said, 'who through a hundred thousand
   perils have made your way to reach the West,
   during this so brief vigil of our senses
that is still reserved for us do not deny   115
   yourself experience of what there is beyond,
   behind the sun, in the world they call unpeopled.
Consider what you came from: you are Greeks!
   You were not born to live like mindless brutes
   but to follow paths of excellence and knowledge.'   120
With this brief exhortation I made my crew
   so anxious for the way that lay ahead,
   that then I hardly could have held them back;
and with our stern turned toward the morning light,
   we made our oars our wings for that mad flight,   125
   gaining distance, always sailing to the left.
The night already had surveyed the stars
   the other pole contains; it saw ours so low
   it did not show above the ocean floor.
Five times we saw the splendor of the moon   130
   grow full and five times wane away again

94–96. In his quest for knowledge of the world Ulysses puts aside his affection for his son, Telemachus, his duty toward his father, Laertes, and the love of his devoted wife Penelope; that is, he sinned against the classical notion of *pietas*.

108. The Strait of Gibraltar, referred to in ancient times as the Pillars of Hercules. The two pillars are Mt. Abyla on the North African coast and Mt. Calpe on the European side, which, originally one mountain, were separated by Hercules to designate the farthest reach of the inhabited world, beyond which no man was permitted to venture.

110–111. Ulysses has passed through the Strait of Gibraltar and is now in the Atlantic Ocean. Ceuta is a town on the North African coast opposite Gibraltar; in this passage Seville probably represents the Iberian peninsula and, as such, the boundary of the inhabited world.

130–131. Five months had passed since they began their voyage.

since we had entered through the narrow pass—
when there appeared a mountain shape, darkened
   by distance, that arose to endless heights.
I had never seen another mountain like it.   135
Our celebrations soon turned into grief:
   from the new land there rose a whirling wind
   that beat against the forepart of the ship
and whirled us round three times in churning waters;
   the fourth blast raised the stern up high, and sent   140
   the bow down deep, as pleased Another's will.
And then the sea was closed again, above us."

CANTO XXVII

As soon as Ulysses has finished his narrative, another flame—its soul within having recognized Virgil's Lombard accent—comes forward asking the travelers to pause and answer questions about the state of affairs in the region of Italy from which he came. The Pilgrim responds by outlining the strife in Romagna and ends by asking the flame who he is. The flame, although he insists he does not want his story to be known among the living, answers because he is supposedly convinced that the Pilgrim will never return to earth. He is another famous deceiver, Guido da Montefeltro, a soldier who became a friar in his old age; but he was untrue to his vows because, at the urging of Pope Boniface VIII, he counseled the use of fraud in the pope's campaign against the Colonna family. He was damned to Hell because he failed to repent his sins, trusting instead in the pope's fraudulent absolution.

By now the flame was standing straight and still,
   it said no more and had already turned
   from us, with sanction of the gentle poet,
when another, coming right behind it,
   attracted our attention to its tip,   5
   where a roaring of confusing sounds had started.
As the Sicilian bull—that bellowed first
   with cries of that one (and it served him right)
   who with his file had fashioned such a beast—
would bellow with the victim's voice inside   10
   so that, although the bull was only brass,

133. In Dante's time the Southern Hemisphere was believed to be composed entirely of water; the mountain that Ulysses and his men see from afar is the Mount of Purgatory which rises from the sea in the Southern Hemisphere, the polar opposite of Jerusalem. For the formation of the mountain see Canto XXXIV, ll. 122–126.

7–15. Phalaris, despotic ruler of Agrigentum in Sicily, commissioned Perillus to construct a bronze bull intended to be used as an instrument of torture; it was fashioned so that, once it was heated, the victim roasting within would emit cries which sounded without like those of a bellowing bull. To test the device, Phalaris made the artisan himself its first victim, and thus he received his just reward for creating such a cruel instrument.

the effigy itself seemed pierced with pain:
so, lacking any outlet to escape
  from the burning soul that was inside the flame,
  the suffering words became the fire's language.   15
But after they had made their journey upward
  to reach the tip, giving it that same quiver
  the sinner's tongue inside had given them,
we heard the words: "O you to whom I point
  my voice, who spoke just now in Lombard, saying: 20
  'you may move on, I won't ask more of you,'
although I have been slow in coming to you,
  be willing, please, to pause and speak with me.
  You see how willing I am—and I burn!
If you have just now fallen to this world   25
  of blindness, from that sweet Italian land
  where I took on the burden of my guilt,
tell me, are the Romagnols at war or peace?
  For I come from the hills between Urbino
  and the mountain chain that lets the Tiber loose."   30
I was still bending forward listening
  when my master touched my side and said to me:
  "*You* speak to him; *this* one is Italian."
And I, who was prepared to answer him,
  began without delaying my response: 35
  "O soul who stands concealed from me down there,
your Romagna is not now and never was
  without war in her tyrants' hearts, although
  there was no open warfare when I came here.
Ravenna's situation has not changed: 40
  the eagle of Polenta broods up there;
  covering all of Cervia with its pinions;
the land that stood the test of long endurance
  and left the French piled in a bloody heap
  is once again beneath the verdant claws.   45
Verrucchio's Old Mastiff and its New One,
  who both were bad custodians of Montagna,
  still sink their fangs into their people's flesh;

---

28. "the Romagnols": the inhabitants of Romagna, the area bounded by the Po and the Reno rivers, the Apennines, and the Adriatic Sea.

29–30. Between the town of Urbino and Mount Coronaro lies the region known as Montefeltro. The speaker is Guido da Montefeltro, the Ghibelline captain whose wisdom and skill in military strategy won him fame.

41–42. In 1300 Guido Vecchio, head of the Polenta family (whose coat of arms bears an eagle) and father of Francesca da Rimini, governed Ravenna and the surrounding territory which included Cervia, a small town on the Adriatic.

43–45. Besieged for many months by French and Guelph troops, the Ghibelline city of Forlì emerged victorious. In May, 1282, her inhabitants led by Guido da Montefeltro broke the siege and massacred the opposing army. However, in 1300 Forlì was dominated by the tyrannical Ordelaffi family whose insignia bore a green lion ("beneath the verdant claws," l. 45).

46–48. In return for their services, the city of Rimini gave her ruling family the castle of Verrucchio. Malatesta, lord of Rimini from 1295 to 1312, and his first born son, Malatestino, are respectively the "Old" and "New" Mastiffs. Having defeated the Ghibellines of Rimini in 1295, Malatesta captured Montagna de' Parcitati, the head of the party, who was subsequently murdered in prison by Malatestino.

the cities by Lamone and Santerno
   are governed by the Lion of the White Lair   50
   who changes parties every change of season.
As for the town whose side the Savio bathes:
   just as it lies between the hills and plains,
   it lives between freedom and tyranny.
And now I beg you tell us who you are—   55
   grant me my wish as yours was granted you—
   so that your fame may hold its own on earth."
And when the fire, in its own way, had roared
   a while, the flame's sharp tip began to sway
   to and fro, then released a blow of words: 60
"If I thought that I were speaking to a soul
   who someday might return to see the world,
   most certainly this flame would cease to flicker;
but since no one, if I have heard the truth,
   ever returns alive from this deep pit,   65
   with no fear of dishonor I answer you:
I was a man of arms and then a friar,
   believing with the cord to make amends;
   and surely my belief would have come true
were it not for that High Priest (his soul be damned!) 70
   who put me back among my early sins;
   I want to tell you why and how it happened.
While I still had the form of the bones and flesh
   my mother gave me, all my actions were
   not those of a lion, but those of a fox;   75
the wiles and covert paths, I knew them all,
   and so employed my art that rumor of me
   spread to the farthest limits of the earth.
When I saw that the time of life had come
   for me, as it must come for every man,   80
   to lower the sails and gather in the lines,
things I once found pleasure in then grieved me;
   repentant and confessed, I took the vows
   a monk takes. And, oh, to think it could have worked!
And then the Prince of the New Pharisees   85
   chose to wage war upon the Lateran

49–51. The cities of Faenza (situated
on the Lamone River) and Imola (near
the Santerno) were governed by Mag-
hinardo Pagani da Susinana whose coat
of arms bore a blue lion on a white field.
52–54. Unlike the other cities mentioned
by Guido, Cesena was not ruled by a
despot; rather, her government, although
not completely determined by the people,
was in the hands of an able ruler, Galasso
da Montefeltro, a cousin of Guido.
67–71. In 1296 Guido joined the Franciscan order. The reason for his harsh condemnation of Pope Boniface VIII ("that
High Priest") is found in lines 85–111.
85–90. In 1297 the struggle between

Boniface VIII ("the Prince of the New
Pharisees") and the Colonna family (who
lived near the Lateran palace, the pope's
residence, and who did not consider the
resignation of Celestine V valid) erupted
into open conflict. Boniface did not
launch his crusade against the traditional
rivals—Saracens and Jews (l. 87)—but
rather against his fellow Christians, faithful warriors of the Church who neither
aided the Saracens during the conquest of
Acre in 1291 (the last Christian stronghold in the Holy Land), nor disobeyed
the interdict on commerce with Mohammedan lands (ll. 89–90).

instead of fighting Saracens or Jews,
for all his enemies were Christian souls,
   (none among the ones who conquered Acri,
   none a trader in the Sultan's kingdom).   90
His lofty Papal Seat, his sacred vows
   were no concern to him, nor was the cord
   I wore (that once made those it girded leaner).
As Constantine once had Silvestro brought
   from Mount Soracte to cure his leprosy,   95
   so this one sought me out as his physician
to cure his burning fever caused by pride.
   He asked me to advise him. I was silent,
   for his words were drunken. Then he spoke again:
'Fear not, I tell you: the sin you will commit,   100
   it is forgiven. Now you will teach me how
   I can level Palestrina to the ground.
Mine is the power, as you cannot deny,
   to lock and unlock Heaven. Two keys I have,
   those keys my predecessor did not cherish.'   105
And when his weighty arguments had forced me
   to the point that silence seemed the poorer choice,
   I said: 'Father, since you grant me absolution
for the sin I find I must fall into now:
   ample promise with a scant fulfillment   110
   will bring you triumph on your lofty throne.'
Saint Francis came to get me when I died,
   but one of the black Cherubim cried out:
   'Don't touch him, don't cheat me of what is mine!
He must come down to join my other servants   115
   for the false counsel he gave. From then to now
   I have been ready at his hair, because
one cannot be absolved unless repentant,
   nor can one both repent and will a thing
   at once—the one is cancelled by the other!'   120
O wretched me! How I shook when he took me,
   saying: 'Perhaps you never stopped to think
   that I might be somewhat of a logician!'
He took me down to Minòs, who eight times
   twisted his tail around his hardened back,   125
   then in his rage he bit it, and announced:
'He goes with those the thievish fire burns.'

---

102. The Colonna family, excommunicated by Boniface, took refuge in their fortress at Palestrina (twenty-five miles east of Rome) which was able to withstand the onslaughts of papal troops. Acting on Guido's counsel (ll. 110–111), Boniface promised (but without serious intentions) to grant complete pardon to the Colonna family, who then surrendered and, consequently, lost everything.

104–105. Deceived by Boniface who was to be his successor, Celestine V renounced the papacy ("those two keys") in 1294.

108–109. Guido's principal error was self-deception: A man cannot be absolved from a sin before he commits it, and moreover, he cannot direct his will toward committing a sin and repent it at the same time (ll. 118–120).

113. Some of the Cherubim (the *eighth* order of angels) were transformed into demons for their rebellion against God; appropriately they appear in the *eighth* circle and the *eighth bolgia* of Hell.

And here you see me now, lost, wrapped this way,
    moving, as I do, with my resentment."
When he had brought his story to a close,   130
    the flame, in grievous pain, departed from us
    gnarling and flickering its pointed horn.
My guide and I moved farther on; we climbed
    the ridge until we stood on the next arch
    that spans the fosse where penalties are paid   135
by those who, sowing discord, earned Hell's wages.

CANTO XXVIII

In the ninth *bolgia* the Pilgrim is overwhelmed by the sight of mutilated, bloody shades, many of whom are ripped open with the entrails spilling out. They are the Sowers of Scandal and Schism, and among them are Mahomet, Ali, Pier da Medicina, Gaius Scribonius Curio, Mosca de' Lamberti, and Bertran de Born. All bemoan their painful lot, and Mahomet and Pier da Medicina relay warnings through the Pilgrim to certain living Italians who are soon to meet terrible ends. Bertran de Born, who comes carrying his head in his hand like a lantern, is a particularly arresting example of a Dantean *contrapasso*.

Who could, even in the simplest kind of prose
    describe in full the scene of blood and wounds
    that I saw now—no matter how he tries!
Certainly any tongue would have to fail:
    man's memory and man's vocabulary   5
    are not enough to comprehend such pain.
If one could bring together all the wounded
    who once upon the fateful soil of Puglia
    grieved for their life's-blood spilled by the Romans,
and spilled again in the long years of the war   10
    that ended in great spoils of golden rings
    (as Livy's history tells, that does not err),
and pile them with the ones who felt the blows
    when they stood up against great Robert Guiscard,

7–12. In order to introduce the great number of maimed and dismembered shades which will present themselves in the ninth *bolgia*, Dante "piles" together references to a number of bloody battles which took place in Puglia, the southeastern section of the Italian peninsula. The first of the series, in which the Pugliese "grieved for their life's-blood spilled by the Romans" (l. 9), is the long war between the Samnites and the Romans (343–290 B.C.). The next, "the long years of the war / that ended in great spoils of golden rings" (ll. 10–11), is the Second Punic War which Hannibal's legions fought against Rome (218–201 B.C.). Livy writes that after the battle of Cannae

(where Hannibal defeated the Romans, 216 B.C.), the Carthaginians gathered three bushels of rings from the fingers of dead Romans.

14. "Robert Guiscard": In the eleventh century Robert Guiscard (ca. 1015–1085), a noble Norman adventurer, gained control of most of southern Italy and became duke of Apulia and Calabria, as well as gonfalonier of the Church (1059). For the next two decades he battled the schismatic Greeks and the Saracens for the Church in the south of Italy. Later he fought for the Church in the east, raised a siege against Pope Gregory VII (1084), and died at the age of seventy, still engaged in warfare.

and with those others whose bones are still in heaps   15
at Ceprano (there where every Puglian
    turned traitor), and add those from Tagliacozzo
    where old Alardo conquered, weaponless—
if all these maimed with limbs lopped off or pierced
    were brought together, the scene would be nothing   20
    to compare with the foul ninth *bolgia*'s bloody sight.
No wine cask with its stave or cant-bar sprung
    was ever split the way I saw someone
    ripped open from his chin to where we fart.
Between his legs his guts spilled out, with the heart   25
    and other vital parts, and the dirty sack
    that turns to shit whatever the mouth gulps down.
While I stood staring into his misery,
    he looked at me and with both hands he opened
    his chest and said: "See how I tear myself!   30
See how Mahomet is deformed and torn!
    In front of me, and weeping, Ali walks,
    his face cleft from his chin up to the crown.
The souls that you see passing in this ditch
    were all sowers of scandal and schism in life,   35
    and so in death you see them torn asunder.
A devil stands back there who trims us all
    in this cruel way, and each one of this mob
    receives anew the blade of the devil's sword
each time we make one round of this sad road,   40
    because the wounds have all healed up again
    by the time each one presents himself once more.
But who are you there gawking from the bridge
    and trying to put off, perhaps, fulfillment
    of the sentence passed on you when you confessed?"   45
"Death does not have him yet, he is not here
    to suffer for his guilt," my master answered;
    "but that he may have full experience,
I, who am dead, must lead him through this Hell

15–18. A further comparison between bloody battles in Puglia and the ninth *bolgia*: In 1266 Charles of Anjou marched against the armies of Manfred, king of Sicily. Manfred blocked the passes leading to the south, but the pass at Ceprano was abandoned by its traitorous defenders. Charles then advanced unhindered and defeated the Sicilians at Benevento, killing Manfred. In reality, then, the battle did not take place at Ceprano, but at Benevento.

The final example in the lengthy series of battles was a continuation of the hostilities between Charles of Anjou and the followers of Manfred. In 1268 at the battle of Tagliacozzo Charles adopted the suggestions of his general Érard de Valéry ("Alardo") and won the encounter. Although Érard's strategy was one of wit rather than force (a "hidden" reserve troop entered the battle at the last minute when Manfred's nephew Conradin seemed to have won), it can hardly be said that "old Alardo" conquered without arms.

31. "Mahomet": founder of the Mohammedan religion, born at Mecca about 570 and died in 632. His punishment, to be split open from the crotch to the chin, together with the complementary punishment of Ali, represents Dante's belief that they were initiators of the great schism between the Christian Church and Mohammedanism. Many of Dante's contemporaries thought that Mahomet was originally a Christian and a cardinal who wanted to become pope.

32. "Ali": (ca. 600–661) the first of Mahomet's followers, who married the prophet's daughter Fatima. Mahomet died in 632, and Ali assumed the caliphate in 656.

from round to round, down to the very bottom,   50
and this is as true as my presence speaking here."
More than a hundred in that ditch stopped short
to look at me when they had heard his words,
forgetting in their stupor what they suffered.
"And you, who will behold the sun, perhaps   55
quite soon, tell Fra Dolcino that unless
he wants to follow me here quick, he'd better
stock up on food, or else the binding snows
will give the Novarese their victory,
a conquest not won easily otherwise."   60
With the heel of one foot raised to take a step
Mahomet said these words to me, and then
stretched out and down his foot and moved away.
Another, with his throat slit, and his nose
cut off as far as where the eyebrows start   65
(and he only had a single ear to show),
who had stopped like all the rest to stare in wonder,
stepped out from the group and opened up his throat
that ran with red from all sides of his wound,
and spoke: "O you whom guilt does not condemn,   70
whom I have seen in Italy up there,
unless I am deceived by similarity,
recall to mind Pier da Medicina,
should you return to see the gentle plain
declining from Vercelli to Marcabò,   75
and inform the two best citizens of Fano—
tell Messer Guido and tell Angiolello—
that, if our foresight here is no deception,
from their ship they shall be hurled bound in a sack
to drown in the water near Cattolica,   80
the victims of a tyrant's treachery;
between the isles of Cyprus and Mallorca

56–60. "Fra Dolcino": (died 1307)
though not a monk as his name would
seem to indicate, the leader of a religious
sect banned as heretical by Pope Clement
V in 1305. Dolcino's sect, the Apostolic
Brothers, preached the return of religion
to the simplicity of apostolic times, and
among their tenets was community of
property and sharing of women. When
Clement V ordered the eradication of the
Brothers, Dolcino and his followers retreated to the hills near Novara, where
they withstood the papal forces for over a
year until starvation conquered them. Dolcino and his companion, Margaret of
Trent, were burned at the stake in 1307.

73. "Pier da Medicina": Although nothing certain is known about the life of this
sinner, we do know that his home was in
Medicina, a town in the Po River Valley
("the gentle plain," which lies between
the towns of Vercelli and Marcabò, l. 74)
near Bologna. According to the early
commentator Benvenuto da Imola, Pier
da Medicina was the instigator of strife
between the Polenta and Malatesta families.

77–90. "tell Messer Guido and tell Angiolello": Guido del Cassero and Angiolello di Carignano, leading citizens of
Fano, a small town on the Adriatic, south
of Rimini, were invited by Malatestino
(the "traitor, who sees only with one
eye," l. 85) to meet on a ship off the
coastal city of Cattolica, which lies between Rimini and Fano. There Malatestino, lord of Rimini from 1312 to 1317,
ordered them thrown overboard in order
that he might gain control of Fano. Already dead, the two victims of Malatestino's treachery will not have to pray to
escape "Focara's wind," l. 90), the terribly destructive gale which preyed on
vessels passing by the promontory of
Focara near Cattolica.

so great a crime Neptune never witnessed
   among the deeds of pirates or the Argives.
That traitor, who sees only with one eye   85
   and rules the land that someone with me here
   wishes he'd never fed his eyes upon,
will have them come to join him in a parley,
   then see to it they do not waste their breath
   on vows or prayers to escape Focara's wind."   90
And I to him: "If you want me to bring back
   to those on earth your message—who is the one
   sated with the bitter sight? Show him to me."
At once he grabbed the jaws of a companion
   standing near by, and squeezed his mouth half-open,   95
   announcing, "Here he is, and he is mute.
This man, in exile, drowned all Caesar's doubts
   and helped him cast the die, when he insisted:
   'a man prepared, who hesitates, is lost.' "
How helpless and bewildered he appeared,   100
   his tongue hacked off as far down as the throat,
   this Curio, once so bold and quick to speak!
And one who had both arms but had no hands,
   raising the gory stumps in the filthy air
   so that the blood dripped down and smeared his face,   105
cried: "You, no doubt, also remember Mosca,
   who said, alas, 'What's done is over with,'
   and sowed the seed of discord for the Tuscans."
"And of death for all your clan," I quickly said,
   and he, this fresh wound added to his wound,   110
   turned and went off like one gone mad from pain.
But I remained to watch the multitude,
   and saw a thing that I would be afraid
   to tell about without more evidence,
were I not reassured by my own conscience—   115
   that good companion enheartening a man
   beneath the breastplate of its purity.
I saw it, I'm sure, and I seem to see it still:
   a body with no head that moved along,
   moving no differently from all the rest;   120
he held his severed head up by its hair,
   swinging it in one hand just like a lantern,
   and as it looked at us it said: "Alas!"
Of his own self he made himself a light

92–93. The Pilgrim refers to what Pier da Medicina said earlier about "someone" who "wishes he'd never fed his eyes upon" Rimini (ll. 86–87).

97–102. Caius Scribonius Curio wishes he had never seen Rimini, the city near which the Rubicon river empties into the Adriatic. Once a Roman tribune under Pompey, Curio defected to Caesar's side, and, when the Roman general hesitated to cross the Rubicon, Curio convinced him to cross and march on Rome. At that time the Rubicon formed the boundary between Gaul and the Roman Republic; Caesar's decision to cross it precipitated the Roman Civil War.

106–108. "Mosca": Mosca, about whom the Pilgrim earlier had asked Ciacco (Canto VI, l. 80), was a member of the Lamberti family of Florence. His counsel ("What's done is over with," l. 107) was the cause of the division of Florence into the feuding Guelph and Ghibelline parties.

and they were two in one and one in two.   125
How could this be? He who ordained it knows.
And when he had arrived below our bridge,
  he raised the arm that held the head up high
  to let it speak to us at closer range.
It spoke: "Now see the monstrous punishment,   130
  you there still breathing, looking at the dead,
  see if you find anything else like this;
and that you may report on me up there,
  know that I am Bertran de Born, the one
  who evilly encouraged the young king.   135
Father and son I set against each other:
  Achitophel with his wicked instigations
  did not do more with Absalom and David.
Because I cut the bonds of persons joined
  I bear my head cut off from its life-source   140
  which is back there, alas, within its trunk.
In me you see the perfect *contrapasso!*"

CANTO XXIX

When the Pilgrim is rebuked by his mentor for his inappropriate
interest in these wretched shades, he replies that he was looking for
someone. Virgil, who can read the Pilgrim's mind, knows that this
was Geri del Bello. They discuss Geri until they reach the edge of
the next *bolgia* where all types of Falsifiers are punished. There
miserable, shrieking shades are afflicted with diseases of various
kinds and are arranged in various positions. Sitting back to back,
madly scratching their leprous sores, are the shades of Griffolino da
Arezzo and one Capocchio, who talk to the Pilgrim, the latter shade
making wisecracks about the Sienese.

The crowds, the countless, different mutilations
  had stunned my eyes and left them so confused
  they wanted to keep looking and to weep,
but Virgil said: "What are you staring at?
  Why do your eyes insist on drowning there   5
  below, among those wretched, broken shades?
You did not act this way in other *bolge*.
  If you hope to count them one by one, remember
  the valley winds some twenty-two miles around;
and already the moon is underneath our feet;   10

134–136. "Bertran de Born": One of the
greatest of the Provençal troubadours,
Bertran de Born lived in the second half
of the twelfth century. He suffers here
in Hell for having caused the rebellion
of Prince Henry (the "young king,' l. 135)
against his father Henry II, king of England.

137–138. Dante compares Bertran de
Born's evil counsel with that of Achitophel. Once the aide of David, Achitophel
the Gilonite provoked Absalom's rebellion against David, his father and king.
See 2 Samuel, 15–17.

10. The sun, then, is directly overhead,
indicating that it is midday in Jerusalem.

the time remaining to us now is short—
and there is more to see than you see here."
"If you had taken time to find out what
I was looking for," I started telling him,
"perhaps you would have let me stay there longer."   15
My guide was moving on, with me behind him
answering as I did while we went on,
and adding: "Somewhere down along this ditch
that I was staring at a while ago,
I think there is a spirit of my family   20
mourning the guilt that's paid so dear down there."
And then my master said: "From this time on
you should not waste another thought on him;
think on ahead, and let him stay behind,
for I saw him standing underneath the bridge   25
pointing at you, and threatening with his gesture,
and I heard his name called out: Geri del Bello.
That was the moment you were so absorbed
with him who was the lord of Altaforte
that you did not look his way before he left."   30
"Alas, my guide," I answered him, "his death
by violence which has not yet been avenged
by anyone who shares in his disgrace,
made him resentful, and I suppose for this
he went away without a word to me,   35
and because he did I feel great piety."
We spoke of this until we reached the start
of the bridge across the next *bolgia*, from which
the bottom, with more light, might have been seen.
Having come to stand above the final cloister   40
of Malebolge, we saw it spreading out
revealing to our eyes its congregation.
Weird shrieks of lamentation pierced through me
like arrow-shafts whose tips are barbed with pity,
so that my hands were covering my ears.   45
Imagine all the sick in the hospitals
of Maremma, Valdichiana and Sardinia
between the months of July and September,
crammed altogether rotting in one ditch—
such was the misery here; and such a stench   50
was pouring out as comes from flesh decaying.
Still keeping to our left we made our way

27–35. "Geri del Bello": a first cousin of Dante's father. Little is known about him except that he was among those to whom reparation was made in 1269 for damages suffered at the hands of the Ghibellines in 1260, and that he was involved in a blood feud with the Sacchetti family. It was probably one of the Sacchetti who murdered him. Vengeance by kinsmen for a slaying was considered obligatory at the time, and apparently Geri's murder was still unavenged by the Alighieri in 1300.

29. "the lord of Altaforte": Bertran de Born. See Canto XXVIII, ll. 130–142.

47–49. "of Maremma, Valdichiana and Sardinia": Valdichiana and Maremma are swampy areas in Tuscany. Along with the swamps of Sardinia they were famous for breeding malaria and other diseases.

down the long bridge on to the final bank,
and now my sight was clear enough to find
the bottom where the High Lord's ministress,   55
    Justice infallible, metes out her punishment
    to falsifiers she registers on earth.
I doubt if all those dying in Aegina
    when the air was blowing sick with pestilence
    and the animals, down to the smallest worm,   60
all perished (later on this ancient race,
    according to what the poets tell as true,
    was born again from families of ants),
offered a scene of greater agony
    than was the sight spread out in that dark valley   65
    of heaped-up spirits languishing in clumps.
Some sprawled out on others' bellies, some
    on others' backs, and some, on hands and knees,
    dragged themselves along that squalid alley.
Slowly, in silence, slowly we moved along   70
    looking, listening to the words of all those sick
    who had no strength to raise their bodies up.
I saw two sitting, leaning against each other
    like pans propped back to back against a fire,
    and they were blotched from head to foot with scabs.   75
I never saw a curry-comb applied
    by a stable-boy who is harried by his master,
    or simply wants to finish and go to bed,
the way those two applied their nails and dug
    and dug into their flesh, crazy to ease   80
    the itching that can never find relief.
They worked their nails down, scraping off the scabs
    the way one works a knife to scale a bream
    or some other fish with larger, tougher scales.
"O you there scraping off your scabs of mail   85
    and even making pincers of your fingers,"
    my guide began to speak to one of them,
"so may your finger-nails eternally
    suffice their task, tell us: among the many
    packed in this place is anyone Italian?"   90
"Both of us whom you see disfigured here,"
    one answered through his tears, "we are Italians.
    But you, who ask about us, who are you?"
"I am one accompanying this living man
    descending bank from bank," my leader said,   95
    "and I intend to show him all of Hell."
With that each lost the other back's support
    and each one, shaky, turned to look at me,
    as others did who overheard these words.

58–66. This comparison with the sufferers of the tenth *bolgia* concerns the island
of Aegina in the Saronic Gulf. Juno sent a
plague to the island which killed all the
inhabitants except Aeacus. Aeacus prayed
to Jupiter to repopulate the island, and
Jupiter did so by turning ants into men.

My gentle master came up close to me   100
   and said: "Now ask them what you want to know,"
   and since he wanted me to speak, I started:
"So may the memory of you not fade
   from the minds of men up there in the first world,
   but rather live on under many suns,   105
tell me your names and where it was you lived;
   do not let your dreadful, loathsome punishment
   discourage you from speaking openly."
"I'm from Arezzo," one of them replied,
   "and Albert of Siena had me burned,   110
   but I'm not here for what I died for there;
it's true I told him, jokingly, of course:
   'I know the trick of flying through the air,'
   and he, eager to learn and not too bright,
asked me to demonstrate my art; and only   115
   just because I didn't make him Daedalus,
   he had me burned by one whose child he was.
But here, to the last *bolgia* of the ten,
   for the alchemy I practiced in the world
   I was condemned by Minòs, who cannot err."   120
I said to my poet: "Have you ever known
   people as silly as the Sienese?
   Even the French cannot compare with them!"
With that the other leper who was listening
   feigned exception to my quip: "Excluding,   125
   of course, Stricca, who lived so frugally,
and Niccolo, the first to introduce
   the luxury of the clove for condiment
   into that choice garden where the seed took root,
and surely not that fashionable club   130
   where Caccia squandered all his woods and vineyards
   and Abbagliato flaunted his great wit!
That you may know who this is backing you

109–117. Most of the commentators
identify this man as Griffolino da Arezzo.
The story was that Griffolino had led the
doltish Alberto da Siena to believe that
he could teach him how to fly. Alberto
paid him well but, upon discovering the
fraud, he denounced Griffolino to the
bishop of Siena as a magician, and the
bishop had him burned.

122. The Florentines made the citizens
of rival Siena the butt of many jokes.

124–126. Capocchio (see below, l. 136)
makes several ironic comments here about
the foolishness of the Sienese. Stricca
(probably Stricca di Giovanni dei Salim-
beni of Siena) was evidently renowned as
a spendthrift. The old commentators hold
that he was a member of the "Spendthrifts' Brigade" (see l. 130), a group of
young Sienese who wasted their fortunes
carelessly.

127–129. "Niccolò": Niccolò de' Salim-

beni was another member of the "Spendthrifts' Club" and possibly the brother of
Stricca. He introduced to Siena the use
of cloves, then a very expensive spice.
Some of the early commentators claim
that he roasted pheasants on beds of
flaming cloves. In any case Capocchio is
referring to Niccolò's careless extravagance as another example of the silliness
of the Sienese. The "choice garden" is
Siena itself, where any fashionable custom, no matter how foolish, could gain
acceptance.

131. "Caccia": Caccia d'Asciano was
another member of the "Spendthrifts'
Brigade" (that "fashionable club," l.
130), who squandered his inheritance.

132. "Abbagliato": Abbagliato has
been identified as one Bartolomeo dei
Folcacchieri, who held office in Siena up
to 1300. He was another member of this
"fashionable club."

against the Sienese, look sharply at me
   so that my face will give you its own answer,   135
and you will recognize Capocchio's shade,
   betrayer of metals with his alchemy;
   you'll surely recall—if you're the one I think—
how fine an ape of nature I once was."

CANTO XXX

Capocchio's remarks are interrupted by two mad, naked shades
who dash up, and one of them sinks his teeth into Capocchio's
neck and drags him off; he is Gianni Schicchi and the other is
Myrrha of Cyprus. When they have gone, the Pilgrim sees the ill-
proportioned and immobile shade of Master Adamo, a counterfei-
ter, who explains how members of the Guidi family had persuaded
him to practice his evil art in Romena. He points out the fever-
stricken shades of two infamous liars, Potiphar's Wife and Sinon,
the Greek, whereupon the latter engages Master Adamo in a verbal
battle. Virgil rebukes the Pilgrim for his absorption in such futile
wrangling, but his immediate shame wins Virgil's immediate forgiveness.

In ancient times when Juno was enraged
   against the Thebans because of Semele
   (she showed her wrath on more than one occasion)
she made King Athamas go raving mad:
   so mad that one day when he saw his wife   5
   coming with his two sons in either arm,
he cried: "Let's spread the nets, so I can catch
   the lioness with her lion-cubs at the pass!"
   Then he spread out his insane hands, like talons
and, seizing one of his two sons, Learchus,   10
   he whirled him round and smashed him on a rock.
   She drowned herself with the other in her arms.
And when the wheel of Fortune brought down low
   the immeasurable haughtiness of Trojans,
   destroying in their downfall king and kingdom,   15
Hecuba sad, in misery, a slave

---

136. "Capocchio's": Capocchio is the name (or nickname) of a man who in 1293 was burned alive in Siena for alchemy. Apparently Dante had known him; according to the early commentators, it was in their student days.

1–12. Jupiter's predilection for mortal women always enraged Juno, his wife. In this case her ire was provoked by her husband's dalliance with Semele, the daughter of Cadmus, king of Thebes, who bore him Bacchus. Having vowed to wreak revenge on her and her family, Juno not only had Semele struck by lightning, but also caused King Athamas, the husband of Ino (Semele's sister), to go insane. In his demented state he killed his son Learchus. Ino drowned herself and her other son, Melicertes.

16–21. Having triumphed over the Trojans, the Greeks returned to their homeland bearing with them as a slave Hecuba, wife of Priam, king of Troy. She was also to make some tragic discoveries: she saw Polyxena, her daughter, slain on the grave of Achilles (l. 17) and she discovered her son Polydorus dead and unburied on the coast of Thrace (ll. 18–19). So great was her grief that she became insane.

(after she saw Polyxena lie slain,
  after this grieving mother found her son
Polydorus left unburied on the shore),
  now gone quite mad, went barking like a dog—   20
  it was the weight of grief that snapped her mind.
But never in Thebes or Troy were madmen seen
  driven to acts of such ferocity
  against their victims, animal or human,
as two shades I saw white with rage and naked,   25
  running, snapping crazily at things in sight,
  like pigs, directionless, broken from their pen.
One, landing on Capocchio sank his teeth
  into his neck, and started dragging him
  along, scraping his belly on the rocky ground.   30
The Aretine spoke, shaking where he sat:
  "You see that batty shade? He's Gianni Schicchi!
  He's rabid and he treats us all that way."
"Oh," I answered, "so may that other shade
  never sink its teeth in you—if you don't mind,   35
  please tell me who it is before it's gone."
And he to me: "That is the ancient shade
  of Myrrha, the depraved one, who became,
  against love's laws, too much her father's friend.
She went to him, and there she sinned in love,   40
  pretending that her body was another's—
  just as the other there fleeing in the distance,
contrived to make his own the 'queen of studs',
  pretending that he was Buoso Donati,
  making his will and giving it due form."   45
Now that the rabid pair had come and gone
  (from whom I never took my eyes away),
  I turned to watch the other evil shades.
And there I saw a soul shaped like a lute,
  if only he'd been cut off from his legs   50
  below the belly, where they divide in two.
The bloating dropsy, disproportioning
  the body's parts with unconverted humors

31. "the Aretine": He is Griffolino d'Arezzo. See Canto XXIX, ll. 109–120.

32. "Gianni Schicchi!": A member of the Florentine Cavalcanti family, Gianni Schicchi was well known for his mimetic virtuosity. Simone Donati, keeping his father's death a secret in order that he might change the will to his advantage, engaged Gianni to impersonate his dead father (Buoso Donati, l. 44) and alter the latter's wil'. The plan was carried out to perfection, and in the process Gianni willed himself, among other things, a prize mare ("the 'queen of studs,' " l. 43).

33. Gianni Schicchi, then, is insane as must be also his companion in the mad fight through this *bolgia*. These are the only two sinners in the *Divine Comedy* who are mentally deranged, so that it is most fitting that the canto should open with a reminder of two famous cases of insanity in classical mythology.

37–41. The other self-falsifier darting about the *bolgia* with Gianni Schicchi is Myrrha, who, overpowered by an incestuous desire for her father, King Cinyras of Cyprus, went incognita to his bed where they made love. Discovering the deception, Cinyras vowed to kill her; however, Myrrha escaped and wandered about until the gods took pity on her and transformed her into a myrrh tree, from which Adonis, the child conceived in the incestuous union, was born.

so that the face, matched with the paunch, was puny,
forced him to keep his parched lips wide apart,   55
   as a man who suffers thirst from raging fever
   has one lip curling up, the other sagging.
"O you who bear no punishment at all
   (I can't think why) within this world of sorrow,"
he said to us, "pause here and look upon   60
the misery of one Master Adamo:
   in life I had all that I could desire,
   and now, alas, I crave a drop of water.
The little streams that flow from the green hills
   of Casentino, descending to the Arno   65
   keeping their banks so cool and soft with moisture
forever flow before me, haunting me;
   and the image of them leaves me far more parched
   than the sickness that has dried my shriveled face.
Relentless Justice, tantalizing me,   70
   exploits the countryside that knew my sin,
   to draw from me ever new sighs of pain:
I still can see Romena where I learned
   to falsify the coin stamped with the Baptist,
   for which I paid with my burned body there;   75
but if I could see down here the wretched souls
   of Guido or Alexander or their brother,
   I would not exchange the sight for Branda's fountain.
One is here already, if those maniacs
   running around this place have told the truth,   80
   but what good is it, with my useless legs?
If only I were lighter, just enough
   to move one inch in every hundred years,
   I would have started on my way by now
to find him somewhere in this gruesome lot,   85
   although this ditch winds round eleven miles
   and is at least a half a mile across.
It's their fault I am here with this choice family:
   they encouraged me to turn out florins
   whose gold contained three carats' worth of alloy."   90
And I to him: "Who are those two poor souls
   lying to the right, close to your body's boundary,
   steaming like wet hands in wintertime?"
"When I poured into this ditch, I found them here,"
   he answered, "and they haven't budged since then,   95
   and I doubt they'll move through all eternity.

64–66. "Casentino": a hilly region southeast of Florence where the headwaters of the Arno River spread out.

76–78. Master Adamo, as much as he craves a "drop of water" (l. 63), would forego that pleasure if only he could see here in Hell the Conti Guidi (Guido, Alexander, Aghinolfo, and Ildebrando), who encouraged him in crime. "Branda's fountain" (l. 78): the name of a spring which once flowed near Romena. Often confused with it is the still-functioning fountain of the same name at Siena.

79. Guido (died 1292) is the only one of the four Conti Guidi who died before 1300.

90. The florin was supposed to contain twenty-four carat gold; those of Master Adamo had twenty-one carats.

One is the false accuser of young Joseph;
    the other is false Sinon, the Greek in Troy:
    it's their burning fever makes them smell so bad."
And one of them, perhaps somewhat offended   100
    at the kind of introduction he received,
    with his fist struck out at the distended belly,
which responded like a drum reverberating;
    and Master Adam struck him in the face
    with an arm as strong as the fist he had received,   105
and he said to him: "Although I am not free
    to move around, with swollen legs like these,
    I have a ready arm for such occasions."
"*But* it was *not* as free and ready, was it,"
    the other answered, "when you went to the stake?   110
    Of course, when you were coining, it was readier!"
And he with the dropsy: "*Now* you tell the truth,
    but you were not as full of truth that time
    when you were asked to tell the truth at Troy!"
"My words were false—so were the coins you made,"   115
    said Sinon, "and *I* am here for one false act
    but *you* for more than any fiend in hell!"
"The horse, recall the horse, you falsifier,"
    the bloated paunch was quick to answer back,
    "may it burn your guts that all the world remembers!"   120
"May your guts burn with thirst that cracks your tongue,"
    the Greek said, "may they burn with rotting humors
    that swell your hedge of a paunch to block your eyes!"
And then the money-man: "So there you go,
    your evil mouth pours out its filth as usual;   125
    for if *I* thirst, and humors swell me up,
you burn more, and your head is fit to split,
    and it wouldn't take much coaxing to convince you
    to lap the mirror of Narcissus dry!"
I was listening, all absorbed in this debate,   130
    when the master said to me: "Keep right on looking,
    a little more, and I shall lose my patience."
I heard the note of anger in his voice
    and turned to him; I was so full of shame
    that it still haunts my memory today.   135
Like one asleep who dreams himself in trouble
    and in his dream he wishes he were dreaming,
    longing for that which is, as if it were not,
just so I found myself: unable to speak,
    longing to beg for pardon and already   140

---

97. Potiphar's wife falsely accused Joseph, son of Jacob and Rachel, of trying to seduce her, while in reality it was she who made improper amorous advances.

98. Sinon was left behind by his fellow Greek soldiers in accordance with the master plan for the capture of Troy. Taken prisoner by the Trojans, and misrepresenting his position with the Greeks, he persuaded them to bring the wooden horse into the city.

129. "the mirror of Narcissus": water. According to the myth, Narcissus, enamoured with his own reflection in a pond, continued to gaze at it until he died.

begging for pardon, not knowing that I did.
"Less shame than yours would wash away a fault
  greater than yours has been," my master said,
  "and so forget about it, do not be sad.
If ever again you should meet up with men   145
  engaging in this kind of futile wrangling,
  remember I am always at your side;
to have a taste for talk like this is vulgar!"

CANTO XXXI

Through the murky air they move, up across the bank which separates the Malebolge from the pit of Hell, the Ninth (and last)
Circle of the *Inferno*. From a distance is heard the blast of a
mighty horn which turns out to have been that of the giant
Nimrod. He and other giants, including Ephialtes, are fixed eternally in the pit of Hell; are all chained except Antaeus, who at Virgil's request, lifts the two poets in his monstrous hand and deposits
them below him, on the lake of ice known as Cocytus.

The very tongue that first spoke—stinging me,
  making the blood rush up to both my cheeks—
  then gave the remedy to ease the pain,
just as, so I have heard, Achilles' lance,
  belonging to his father, was the source   5
  of pain, and then of balm, to him it struck.
Turning our backs on that trench of misery,
  gaining the bank again that walls it in,
  we cut across, walking in dead silence.
Here it was less than night and less than day,   10
  so that my eyes could not see far ahead;
  but then I heard the blast of some high horn
which would have made a thunder-clap sound dim;
  it drew my eyes directly to one place,
  as they retraced the sound's path to its source.   15
After the tragic rout when Charlemagne
  lost all his faithful, holy paladins,
  the sound of Roland's horn was not as ominous.

4–6. Dante aptly compares the nature of
Virgil's words at the end of Canto XXX
(first rebuking then comforting) to the
spear of Achilles and his father, Peleus,
which reputedly could heal the wounds
it had inflicted.
16–18. In the medieval French epic *La
Chanson de Roland*, the title character,
one of Charlemagne's "holy paladins" (1.

17), was assigned to the rear guard on the
return from an expedition in Spain. At
Roncevalles in the Pyrenees the Saracens
attacked, and Roland, proud to the point
of foolishness, refused to sound his horn
until total extermination was imminent
[*The Song of Roland*, ll. 1695 ff., pp. 790
ff. in this volume.—J. C. McG.]

Keeping my eyes still turned that way, I soon
    made out what seemed to be high, clustered towers.   20
"Master," I said, "what city lies ahead?"
"Because you try to penetrate the shadows,"
    he said to me, "from much too far away,
    you confuse the truth with your imagination.
You will see clearly when you reach that place   25
    how much the eyes may be deceived by distance,
    and so, just push ahead a little more."
Then lovingly he took me by the hand
    and said: "But now, before we go on farther,
    to prepare you for the truth that could seem strange,   30
I'll tell you these aren't towers, they are giants;
    they're standing in the well around the bank—
    all of them hidden from their navels down."
As, when the fog begins to thin and clear,
    the sight can slowly make out more and more   35
    what is hidden in the mist that clogs the air,
so, as I pierced the thick and murky air,
    approaching slowly, closer to the well,
    confusion cleared and my fear took on more shape.
For just as Montereggion is crowned with towers   40
    soaring high above its curving ramparts,
    so, on the bank that runs around the well,
towering with only half their bodies out,
    stood the terrible giants, forever threatened
    by Jupiter in the heavens when he thunders.   45
And now I could make out one of the faces,
    the shoulders, the chest and a good part of the belly
    and, down along the sides, the two great arms.
Nature, when she cast away the mold
    for shaping beasts like these, without a doubt   50
    did well, depriving Mars of more such agents.

19–127. From afar, the Pilgrim, who has mistaken the great giants for towers, asks Virgil, "what city lies ahead?" a question which should recall the scene before the gates of the walled city of Dis in Cantos VIII and IX. By this device not only are we introduced to a new division of Hell (the Pit of the Giants and Cocytus: Complex Fraud), but also the unified nature of Lower Hell (i.e., from the City of Dis to Cocytus) is underscored. And the Fallen Angels perched on the wall who shut the gate to the City in Virgil's face (Canto VIII) are analogous to the Giants here, who stand at the boundary of the lowest part of Hell. The fact that the Giants—in terms of pagan mythology— the Fallen Angels—in terms of the Judeo-Christian tradition—both rebelled against their respective gods, not only links the parts of Lower Hell together, but also suggests that the bases for all the sins

punished in Lower Hell (Heresy, Violence, and Fraud) are Envy and Pride, the sins of both groups of rebels.

40–41. In 1213 the Sienese constructed Montereggioni, a fortress on the crest of a hill eight miles from their city. The specific allusion here is to the fourteen high towers which stood on its perimeter like giant sentries.

49–57. Dante praises the wisdom that Nature showed in discontinuing the race of giants, for Mars (l. 51), the god of war, with the help of the giants could have effectively destroyed mankind. A clear distinction is made between brute animals ("whales / and elephants," ll. 52–53), which Nature rightly allows to live, and giants, whom she made extinct, in that the former do not possess a rational faculty, and therefore are easily subjugated by man.

And if she never did repent of whales
    and elephants, we must consider her,
    on sober thought, all the more just and wary:
for when the faculty of intellect   55
    is joined with brute force and with evil will,
    no man can win against such an alliance.
His face, it seemed to me, was about as long
    and just as wide as St. Peter's cone in Rome,
    and all his body's bones were in proportion,   60
so that the bank which served to cover him
    from his waist down showed so much height above
    that three tall Frisians on each other's shoulders
could never boast of stretching to his hair,
    for downwards from the place men clasp their cloaks   65
    I saw a generous thirty hand-spans of him.
"Raphel may amech zabi almi!"
    He played these sputtering notes with prideful lips
    for which no sweeter psalm was suitable.
My guide called up to him: "Blathering idiot,   70
    stick to your horn and take it out on that
    when you feel a fit of anger coming on;
search round your neck and you will find the strap
    it's tied to, you poor muddle-headed soul,
    and there's the horn so pretty on your chest."   75
And then he turned to me: "His words accuse him.
    He is Nimrod, through whose infamous device
    the world no longer speaks a common language.
But let's leave him alone and not waste breath,
    for he can no more understand our words   80
    than anyone can understand his language."
We had to walk still farther than before,
    continuing to the left, a full bow's-shot,
    to find another giant, huger and more fierce.
What engineer it took to bind this brute   85
    I cannot say, but there he was, one arm
    pinned to his back, the other locked in front,
with a giant chain winding around him tight
    which, starting from his neck, made five great coils—
    and that was counting only to his waist.   90
"This beast of pride decided he would try
    to pit his strength against almighty Jove,"

59. This bronze pine cone measuring over seven feet in height, which now stands in an inner courtyard of the Vatican was, at Dante's time, in the courtyard of St. Peter's.

63. The inhabitants of Friesland, a northern province of the Netherlands, were renowned for their height.

67. Although there have been numerous attempts to interpret these words, I, along with most modern commentators, believe that they are gibberish—the perfect representation of Nimrod's role in the confusion of languages caused by his construction of the Tower of Babel (the "infamous device," l. 77).

77. Orosius, St. Augustine, and other early Christians believed Nimrod to be a giant; and his "infamous device," the Tower of Babel, through which he tried to ascend to Heaven, certainly equates him with the giants who besieged Jupiter.

78. Before the construction of the Tower of Babel all men spoke a common language.

my leader said, "and he has won this prize.
He's Ephialtes who made his great attempt,
   when the giants arose to fill the Gods with panic;   95
   the arms he lifted then, he moves no more."
And I to him: "If it were possible,
   I would really like to have the chance to see
   the fantastic figure of Briareus."
His answer was: "Not far from here you'll see   100
   Antaeus who can speak and is not chained;
   he will set us down in the very pit of sin.
The one you want to see is farther off;
   he too is bound and looks just like this one,
   except for his expression, which is fiercer."   105
No earthquake of the most outrageous force
   ever shook a tower with such violence
   as, suddenly, Ephialtes shook himself.
I never feared to die as much as then,
   and my fear might have been enough to kill me,   110
   if I had not already seen those chains.
We left him and continued moving on
   and came to where Antaeus stood, extending
   from the well a good five ells up to his head.
"O you who in the celebrated valley   115
   (that saw Scipio become the heir of glory,
   when Hannibal with all his men retreated)
once captured a thousand lions as your quarry
   (and with whose aid, had you chosen to take part
   in the great war with your brothers, the sons of earth   120
would, as many still think, have been the victors),
   do not disdain this modest wish: take us,
   and put us down where ice locks in Cocytus.
Don't make us go to Tityus or Typhon;
   this man can give you what all long for here,   125
   and so bend down, and do not scowl at us.
He still can spread your legend in the world,
   for he yet lives, and long life lies before him,
   unless Grace summons him before his time."
Thus spoke my master, and the giant in haste   130
   stretched out the hands whose formidable grip
   great Hercules once felt, and took my guide.
And Virgil, when he felt the grasping hands,
   called out: "Now come and I'll take hold of you."
   Clasped together, we made a single burden.   135
As the Garisenda looks from underneath

---

94. "Ephialtes": the son of Neptune and Iphimedia. At the age of nine, together with his brother Otus, he attempted to put Mt. Pelion on top of Ossa in order to ascend to the gods and make war on them. But Apollo slew the brothers.

99. "Briareus": Son of Uranus and Gaea (Earth), the Titan Briareus joined the rebellion against the Olympian deities.

124. "Tityus or Typhon": Also members of the race of Titans.

136–138. 'the Garisenda': Of the two leaning towers in Bologna, the Garisenda, built ca. 1110, is the shorter. The passage of a cloud "against the tower's slant" (l. 138) would make the tower appear to be falling.

its leaning side, at the moment when a cloud
   comes drifting over against the tower's slant,
just so the bending giant Antaeus seemed
   as I looked up, expecting him to topple.   140
   I wished then I had gone another way.
But he, most carefully, handed us down
   to the pit that swallows Lucifer with Judas.
   And then, the leaning giant immediately
drew himself up as tall as a ship's mast.   145

CANTO XXXII

They descend farther down into the darkness of the immense plain of ice in which shades of Traitors are frozen. In the outer region of the ice lake, Caina, are those who betrayed their kin in murder; among them, locked in a frozen embrace, are Napoleone and Alessandro of Mangona, and others are Mordred, Focaccia, Sassol Mascheroni, and Camicion de' pazzi. Then the two travelers enter the area of ice called Antenora, and suddenly the Pilgrim kicks one of the faces sticking out of the ice. He tries to force the sinner to reveal his name by pulling out his hair, and when another shade identifies him as Bocca degli Abati, the Pilgrim's fury mounts still higher. Bocca, himself furious, names several other sinners in Antenora, including Buoso da Duera, Tesauro dei Beccheria, Gianni de' Soldanier, Ganelon, and Tibbald. Going farther on, the Pilgrim sees two heads frozen in one hole, the mouth of one gnawing at the brain of the other.

If I had words grating and crude enough
   that really could describe this horrid hole
   supporting the converging weight of Hell,
I could squeeze out the juice of my memories
   to the last drop. But I don't have these words,   5
   and so I am reluctant to begin.
To talk about the bottom of the universe
   the way it truly is, is no child's play,
   no task for tongues that gurgle baby-talk.
But may those heavenly ladies aid my verse   10
   who aided Amphion to wall-in Thebes,
   that my words may tell exactly what I saw.
O misbegotten rabble of all rabble
   who crowd this realm, hard even to describe,
   it were better you had lived as sheep or goats!   15
When we reached a point of darkness in the well
   below the giant's feet, farther down the slope,

10–12. The Muses ("those heavenly ladies," l. 10) helped Amphion, the son of Jupiter and Antiope, construct a wall around Thebes. As the legend has it, Am- phion played upon his lyre and so charmed the stones on Mt. Cithaeron that they came of their own accord and formed the wall.

and I was gazing still at the high wall,
I heard somebody say: "Watch where you step!
   Be careful that you do not kick the heads 20
   of this brotherhood of miserable souls."
At that I turned around and saw before me
   a lake of ice stretching beneath my feet,
   more like a sheet of glass than frozen water.
In the depths of Austria's wintertime, the Danube 25
   never in all its course showed ice so thick,
   nor did the Don beneath its frigid sky,
as this crust here; for if Mount Tambernic
   or Pietrapana would crash down upon it
   not even at its edges would a crack creak. 30
The way the frogs (in the season when the harvest
   will often haunt the dreams of the peasant girl)
   sit croaking with their muzzles out of water,
so these frigid, livid shades were stuck in ice
   up to where a person's shame appears; 35
   their teeth clicked notes like storks' beaks snapping shut,
And each one kept his face bowed toward the ice:
   the mouth bore testimony to the cold,
   the eyes, to sadness welling in the heart.
I gazed around a while and then looked down, 40
   and by my feet I saw two figures clasped
   so tight that one's hair could have been the other's.
"Tell me, you two, pressing your chests together,"
   I asked them, "who are you?" Both stretched their necks
   and when they had their faces raised toward me, 45
their eyes, which had before been only glazed,
   dripped tears down to their lips and the cold froze
   the tears between them, locking the pair more tightly.
Wood to wood with iron was never clamped
   so firm! And the two of them like billy-goats 50
   were butting at each other, mad with anger.
Another one with both ears frozen off,
   and head still bowed over his icy mirror,
   cried out: "What makes you look at us so hard?
If you're interested to know who these two are: 55
   the valley where Bisenzio's waters flow
   belonged to them and to their father, Albert;
the same womb bore them both, and if you scour
   all of Caïna, you will not turn up one

---

27. The river Don which has its source in the heart of Russia would naturally be icebound in the frigid Russian winter.

28–30. "Tambernic": has never been successfully identified. The older commentators place it in the Balkans. "Pietrapana": probably a rocky peak in the northwest corner of Tuscany, today called Pania della Croce.

55–58. The two brothers were Napoleone and Alessandro, sons of Count Alberto of Mangona, who owned part of the valley of the Bisenzio near Florence. The two quarreled often and eventually killed each other in a fight concerning their inheritance.

59. "Caïna": The icy ring of Cocytus is named Caïna after Cain, who slew his brother Abel. Thus, in the first division of this, the Ninth Circle, are punished those treacherous shades who murderously violated family bonds.

who's more deserving of this frozen aspic—   60
not him who had his breast and shadow pierced
    with one thrust of the lance from Arthur's hand;
    not Focaccia; not even this one here
whose head gets in my way and blocks my view,
    known in the world as Sassol Mascheroni,   65
    and if you're Tuscan you must know who he was.
To save me from your asking for more news:
    I was Camicion de' Pazzi, and I await
    Carlin whose guilt will make my own seem less."
Farther on I saw a thousand dog-like faces   70
    purple from the cold. That's why I shudder,
    and always will, when I see a frozen pond.
While we were getting closer to the center
    of the universe where all weights must converge
    and I was shivering in the eternal chill—   75
by fate or chance or willfully perhaps,
    I do not know—but stepping among the heads,
    my foot kicked hard against one of those faces.
Weeping he screamed: "Why are you kicking me?
    You have not come to take revenge on me   80
    for Montaperti, have you? Why bother me?"
And I: "My master, please wait here for me,
    let me clear up a doubt concerning this one,
    then I shall be as rapid as you wish."
My leader stopped, and to that wretch who still   85
    had not let up in his barrage of curses,
    I said: "Who are you, insulting other people?"
"And you, who are *you* who march through Antenora
    kicking other people in their faces?
    No living man could kick as hard!" he answered.   90
"I am a living man," was my reply,
    "and it might serve you well, if you seek fame,

61–62. Mordred, the wicked nephew of King Arthur, tried to kill the king and take his kingdom. But Arthur pierced him with such a mighty blow that when the lance was pulled from the dying traitor a ray of sunlight traversed his body and interrupted Mordred's shadow. The story is told in the Old French romance *Lancelot du Lac*, the book which Francesca claims led her astray with Paolo in Canto V, l. 127.

63. "Focaccia": one of the Cancellieri family of Pistoia and a member of the White party. His treacherous murder of his cousin, Detto de' Cancellieri (a Black), was possibly the act which led to the Florentine intervention in Pistoian affairs.

65. "Sassol Mascheroni": The early commentators say that Sassol Mascheroni was a member of the Toschi family in Florence who murdered his nephew in order to gain his inheritance.

68–69. "Camicion de' Pazzi": Nothing is known of Camicion de' Pazzi except that he murdered one Umbertino, a relative. Another of Camicion's kin, Carlino de' Pazzi (l. 69) from Valdarno, was still alive when the Pilgrim's conversation with Camicion was taking place. But Camicion already knew that Carlino in July, 1302, would accept a bribe to surrender the castle of Piantravigne to the Blacks of Florence.

88. Dante and Virgil have passed into the second division of Cocytus, named Antenora after the Trojan warrior who, according to one legend, betrayed his city to the Greeks. In this round are tormented those who committed acts of treachery against country, city, or political party.

for me to put your name down in my notes."
And he said: "That's the last thing I would want!
   That's not the way to flatter in these lowlands!   95
   Stop pestering me like this—get out of here!"
At that I grabbed him by his hair in back
   and said: "You'd better tell me who you are
   or else I'll not leave one hair on your head."
And he to me: "Go on and strip me bald   100
   and pound and stamp my head a thousand times,
   you'll never hear my name or see my face."
I had my fingers twisted in his hair
   and already I'd pulled out more than one fistful,
   while he yelped like a cur with eyes shut tight,   105
when someone else yelled: "What's the matter, Bocca?
   It's bad enough to hear your shivering teeth;
   now you bark! What the devil's wrong with you?"
"There's no need now for you to speak," I said,
   "you vicious traitor! Now I know your name   110
   and I'll bring back the shameful truth about you."
"Go away!" he answered, "Tell them what you want;
   but if you do get out of here, be sure
   you also tell about that blabber-mouth
who's paying here what the French silver cost him: 115
   'I saw,' you can tell the world, 'the one from Duera
   stuck in with all the sinners keeping cool.'
And if you should be asked: 'Who else was there?'
   Right by your side is the one from Beccheria
   whose head was chopped off by the Florentines.   120
As for Gianni Soldanier I think you'll find him
   farther along with Ganelon and Tibbald
   who opened up Faenza while it slept."
Soon after leaving him I saw two souls
   frozen together in a single hole   125
   so that one head used the other for a cap.
As a man with hungry teeth tears into bread,

106. "Bocca": Bocca degli Abati was a Ghibelline who appeared to side with the Florentine Guelphs. However, while fighting on the side of the Guelphs at the battle of Montaperti in 1260, he is said to have cut off the hand of the standard bearer. The disappearance of the standard led to panic among the Florentine Guelphs, who were then decisively defeated by the Sienese Ghibellines and their German allies under Manfred.

116–117. "the one from Duera": Buoso da Duera, a chief of the Ghibelline party of Cremona, was a well-known traitor.

119–120. "is the one from Beccheria": Tesauro dei Beccheria of Pavia was an abbot of Vallombrosa and a papal legate to Alexander IV in Tuscany. He was tortured and finally beheaded in 1258 by the Guelphs of Florence for carrying on secret intercourse with Ghibellines who had been exiled.

121. "Gianni Soldanier": Gianni de' Soldanier was an important Ghibelline of Florence who, when the Florentines (mostly Guelph) began to chafe under Ghibelline rule, deserted his party and went over to the Guelphs.

122–123. "Ganelon": the treacherous knight who betrayed Roland (and the rear guard of Charlemagne's army) to the Saracens.

"Tibbald": one of the Zambrasi family of Faenza. In order to avenge himself on the Ghibelline Lambertazzi family (who had been exiled from Bologna in 1274 and had taken refuge in Faenza) he opened his city to their Bolognese Guelph enemies on the morning of November 13, 1280.

the soul with capping head had sunk his teeth
into the other's neck, just beneath the skull.
Tydeus in his fury did not gnaw   130
    the head of Menalippus with more relish
    than this one chewed that head of meat and bones.
"O you who show with every bestial bite
    your hatred for the head you are devouring,"
    I said, "tell me your reason, and I promise   135
if you are justified in your revenge,
    once I know who you are and this one's sin,
    I'll repay your confidence in the world above
unless my tongue dry up before I die."

CANTO XXXIII

Count Ugolino is the shade gnawing at the brain of his one-time
associate Archbishop Ruggieri, and Ugolino interrupts his gruesome
meal long enough to tell the story of his imprisonment and cruel
death, which his innocent offspring shared with him. Moving farther into the area of Cocytus known as Ptolomea, where those who
betrayed their guests and associates are condemned, the Pilgrim sees
sinners with their faces raised high above the ice, whose tears freeze
to lock their eyes. One of the shades agrees to identify himself on
condition that the ice be removed from his eyes. The Pilgrim
agrees, and learns that this sinner is Friar Alberigo and that his soul
is dead and damned even though his body is still alive on earth,
inhabited by a devil. Alberigo also names a fellow sinner with him
in the ice, Branca d'Oria, whose body is still functioning up on
earth. But the Pilgrim does not honor his promise to break the ice
from Alberigo's eyes.

Lifting his mouth from his horrendous meal,
    this sinner first wiped off his messy lips
    in the hair remaining on the chewed-up skull,
then spoke: "You want me to renew a grief
    so desperate that just the thought of it,   5
    much less the telling, grips my heart with pain;
but if my words can be the seed to bear
    the fruit of infamy for this betrayer
    who feeds my hunger, than I shall speak—in tears.
I do not know your name, nor do I know   10
    how you have come down here, but Florentine
    you surely seem to be, to hear you speak.

130–131. "Tydeus": one of the Seven
against Thebes, slew Menalippus in combat—who, however, managed to wound
him fatally. Tydeus called for his enemy's
head, which, when brought to him by
Amphiaraus, he proceeded to gnaw in
rage.

First you should know I was Count Ugolino
 and my neighbor here, Ruggieri the Archbishop;
 now I'll tell you why I'm so unneighborly.   15
That I, trusting in him, was put in prison
 through his evil machinations, where I died,
 this much I surely do not have to tell you.
What you could not have known, however, is
 the inhuman circumstances of my death.   20
 Now listen, then decide if he has wronged me!
Through a narrow slit of window high in that mew
 (which is called the tower of hunger, after me,
 and I'll not be the last to know that place)
I had watched moon after moon after moon go by,   25
 when finally I dreamed the evil dream
 which ripped away the veil that hid my future.
I dreamed of this one here as lord and huntsman,
 pursuing the wolf and the wolf-cubs up the mountain
 (which blocks the sight of Lucca from the Pisans)   30
with skinny bitches, well trained and obedient;
 he had out front as leaders of the pack
 Gualandi with Sismondi and Lanfranchi.
A short run, and the father with his sons
 seemed to grow tired, and then I thought I saw   35
 long fangs sunk deep into their sides, ripped open.
When I awoke before the light of dawn,
 I heard my children sobbing in their sleep
 (you see they, too, were there) asking for bread.
If the thought of what my heart was telling me   40
 does not fill you with grief, how cruel you are!
 If you are not weeping now—do you ever weep?
And then they awoke. It was around the time
 they usually brought our food to us. But now
 each one of us was full of dread from dreaming;   45
then from below I heard them driving nails
 into the dreadful tower's door; with that,
 I stared in silence at my flesh and blood.

13–14. "Count Ugolino": Ugolino della Gherardesca, the Count of Donoratico, belonged to a noble Tuscan family whose political affiliations were Ghibelline. In 1275 he conspired with his son-in-law, Giovanni Visconti, to raise the Guelphs to power in Pisa. Although exiled for this subversive activity, Ugolino (Nino) Visconti, took over the Guelph government of the city. Three years later (1288) he plotted with Archbishop Ruggieri degli Ubaldini to rid Pisa of the Visconti. Ruggieri, however, had other plans, and with the aid of the Ghibellines, he seized control cf the city and imprisoned Ugolino, together with his sons and grandsons, in the "tower of hunger" (l. 23). The two were evidently just at the boundary between Antenora and Ptolomea, for Ugolino is being punished for betraying his country (in Antenora), and Ruggieri for betraying his associate, Ugolino (in Ptolomea).

25. Imprisoned in June of 1288, they were finally starved to death in February 1289.

28–36. Ugolino's dream was indeed prophetic. The "lord and huntsman" (l. 28) is Archbishop Ruggieri, who, with the leading Ghibelline families of Pisa ("Gualandi . . . Sismondi and Lanfranchi," l. 33) and the populace ("Skinny bitches," l. 33), runs down Ugolino and his offspring ("the wolf and the wolf-cubs," l. 29) and finally kills them.

I did not weep, I turned to stone inside;
    they wept, and my little Anselmuccio spoke: 50
    'What is it, father? Why do you look that way?'
For them I held my tears back, saying nothing,
    all of that day, and then all of that night,
    until another sun shone on the world.
A meager ray of sunlight found its way 55
    to the misery of our cell, and I could see
    myself reflected four times in their faces;
I bit my hands in anguish. And my children,
    who thought that hunger made me bite my hands
    were quick to draw up closer to me, saying: 60
'O father, you would make us suffer less,
    if you would feed on us: you were the one
    who gave us this sad flesh; you take it from us!'
I calmed myself to make them less unhappy,
    That day we sat in silence, and the next day. 65
    O pitiless earth! You should have swallowed us!
The fourth day came, and it was on that day
    my Gaddo fell prostrate before my feet,
    crying: 'Why don't you help me? Why, my father?'
There he died. Just as you see me here, 70
    I saw the other three fall one by one,
    as the fifth day and the sixth day passed. And I,
by then gone blind, groped over their dead bodies.
    Though they were dead, two days I called their names.
    Then hunger proved more powerful than grief." 75
He spoke these words; then, glaring down in rage,
    attacked again the live skull with his teeth
    sharp as a dog's, and as fit for grinding bones.
O Pisa, blot of shame upon the people
    of that fair land where the sound of "sì" is heard! 80
    Since your neighbors hesitate to punish you,
let Capraia and Gorgona move and join,
    damming up the River Arno at its mouth,
    and let every Pisan perish in its flood!
For if Count Ugolino was accused 85
    of turning traitor, trading-in your castles,
    you had no right to make his children suffer.
Their new-born years (O new-born Thebes!) made them
    all innocents: Brigata, Uguiccione
    and the other two soft names my canto sings. 90

---

50. "Anselmuccio": the younger of Ugolino's grandsons who, according to official documents, must have been fifteen at the time.

68. "Gaddo": one of Ugolino's sons.

75. Whether in this line Ugolino is confessing to an act of cannibalism or whether it simply relates the cause of his death (hunger instead of grief)—Dante has left this to the reader's imagination.

80. Italy. It was customary in Dante's time to indicate a language area by the words signifying "yes."

89–90. "Brigata": Ugolino's second grandson; "Uguiccione": his fifth son.

We moved ahead to where the frozen water
   wraps in harsh wrinkles another sinful race,
   with faces not turned down but looking up.
Here, the weeping puts an end to weeping,
   and the grief that finds no outlet from the eyes   95
   turns inward to intensify the anguish:
for the tears they first wept knotted in a cluster
   and like a visor made for them in crystal,
   filled all the hollow part around their eyes.
Although the bitter coldness of the dark   100
   had driven all sensation from my face,
   as though it were not tender skin but callous,
I thought I felt the air begin to blow,
   and I: "What causes such a wind, my master?
   I thought no heat could reach into these depths."   105
And he to me: "Before long you will be
   where your own eyes can answer for themselves,
   when they will see what keeps this wind in motion."
And one of the wretches with the frozen crust
   screamed out at us: "O wicked souls, so wicked   110
   that you have been assigned the ultimate post,
break off these hard veils covering my eyes
   and give relief from the pain that swells my heart—
   at least until the new tears freeze again."
I answered him: "If this is what you want,   115
   tell me your name; and if I do not help you,
   may I be forced to drop beneath this ice!"
He answered then: "I am Friar Alberigo,
   I am he who offered fruit from the evil orchard:
   here dates are served me for the figs I gave."   120
"Oh, then!" I said, "Are you already dead?"
   And he to me: "Just how my body is

91–93. Virgil and the Pilgrim have now entered the third division of Cocytus, called Tolomea (l. 124) after Ptolemy, the captain of Jericho, who had Simon, his father-in-law, and two of his sons killed while dining (see 1 Macabees 16: 11–17). Or possibly this zone of Cocytus is named after Ptolemy XII: the Egyptian king, who, having welcomed Pompey to his realm, slew him. In Tolomea are punished those who have betrayed their guests.

105. Wind, according to the science of Dante's time, is produced by varying degrees of heat; thus, Cocytus, being completely icebound, lacks all heat, and should be free of winds. In the next canto the Pilgrim will see for himself that Lucifer's giant wings cause the wind.

115–117. The Pilgrim, fully aware that his journey will indeed take him below the ice, carefully phrases his treacherous promise to the treacherous shade, and successfully deceives him (ll. 149–150). The Pilgrim betrays a sinner in this circle, as the latter does one of his companions there with him in the ice (by naming him).

118–120. "Friar Alberigo": One of the Jovial Friars (see Canto XXIII, ll. 103–108), Alberigo di Ugolino dei Manfredi was a native of Faenza. In 1285, in the midst of a family feud, Alberigo invited his principal opponents, Manfred (close relative) and Alberghetto (Manfred's son), to dinner as a gesture of good will. During the course of the meal, Alberigo, using a prearranged signal, called for the fruit, at which his men murdered the dinner guests. Continuing the fruit imagery, Alberigo laments his present anguish by saying ironically that "here dates are served me for the figs I gave" (l. 120), which is to say that he is suffering more than his share (since a date is more valuable than a fig).

in the world above, I have no way of knowing.
This zone of Tolomea is very special,
    for it often happens that a soul falls here   125
    before the time that Atropos should send it.
And that you may more willingly scrape off
    my cluster of glass tears, let me tell you:
    whenever a soul betrays the way I did,
a demon takes possession of the body,   130
    controlling its maneuvers from then on,
    for all the years it has to live up there,
while the soul falls straight into this cistern here;
    and the shade in winter quarters just behind me
    may well have left his body up on earth.   135
But you should know, if you've just come from there:
    he is Ser Branca D'Oria; and many years
    have passed since he first joined us here, ice-bound."
"I think you're telling me a lie," I said,
    "for Branca D'Oria is not dead at all;   140
    he eats and drinks, he sleeps and wears out clothes."
"The ditch the Malebranche watch above,"
    he said, "the ditch of clinging, boiling pitch,
    had not yet caught the soul of Michel Zanche,
when Branca left a devil in his body   145
    to take his place, and so did his close kinsman,
    his accomplice in this act of treachery.
But now, at last, give me the hand you promised.
    Open my eyes." I did not open them.
    To be mean to him was a generous reward.   150
O all you Genovese, you men estranged
    from every good, at home with every vice,
    why can't the world be wiped clean of your race?
For in company with Romagna's rankest soul
    I found one of your men whose deeds were such   155
    that his soul bathes already in Cocytus
but his body seems alive and walks among you.

CANTO XXXIV

Far across the frozen ice can be seen the gigantic figure of Lucifer, who appears from this distance like a windmill seen through
fog; and as the two travelers walk on toward that terrifying sight,
they see the shades of sinners totally buried in the frozen water. At
the center of the earth Lucifer stands frozen from the chest down-

124–135. According to Church doctrine, under certain circumstances a living person may, through acts of treachery, lose possession of his soul before he dies ("before the time that Atropos [the Fate who cuts man's thread of life] should send it," l. 126). Then, on earth, a devil inhabits the body until its natural death.

137–147. "Ser Branca D'Oria": A prominent resident of Genoa, Branca D'Oria murdered his father-in-law, Michele Zanche (See Canto XXII, l. 88), after having invited him to dine with him.

154. Friar Alberigo. Faenza, his home town, was in the region of Romagna (now called Emilia).

155. Branca D'Oria.

ward and his horrible ugliness (he has three heads) is made more
fearful by the fact that in each of his three mouths he chews on one
of the three worst sinners of all mankind, the worst of those who
betrayed their benefactors: Judas Iscariot, Brutus, and Cassius.
Virgil with the Pilgrim on his back begins the descent down the
shaggy body of Lucifer. They climb down through a crack in the
ice, and when they reach the Evil One's thighs, Virgil turns and
begins to struggle upward (because they have passed the center of
the earth) still holding onto the hairy body of Lucifer until they
reach a cavern where they stop for a short rest. Then a winding
path brings them eventually to the earth's surface, where they see
the stars.

"*Vexilla regis prodeunt Inferni*,"
   my master said, "closer to us, so now
   look ahead and see if you can make him out."
A far-off windmill turning its huge sails
   when a thick fog begins to settle in,   5
   or when the light of day begins to fade,
that is what I thought I saw appearing.
   And the gusts of wind it stirred made me shrink back
   behind my guide, my only means of cover.
Down here, I stood on souls fixed under ice   10
   (I tremble as I put this into verse),
   to me they looked like straws worked into glass.
Some lying flat, some perpendicular,
   either with their heads up or their feet,
   and some bent head to foot, shaped like a bow.   15
When we had moved far enough along the way
   that my master thought time had come to show me
   the creature who was once so beautiful,
he stepped aside, and stopping me, announced:
   "This is he, this is Dis; this is the place   20
   that calls for all the courage you have in you."
How chilled and nerveless, Reader, I felt then;

1. "*Vexilla regis prodeunt Inferni*":
The opening lines of the hymn "Vexilla
regis prodeunt"—"The banners of the
King advance" (written by Venantius For-
tunatus, sixth-century bishop of Poitiers;
this hymn belongs to the liturgy of the
Church) are here parodied by the addition of the word *Inferni*, "of Hell," to the
word *regis*, "of the King." Sung on Good
Friday, the hymn anticipates the unveil-
ing of the Cross; Dante, who began his
journey on the evening of Good Friday,
is prepared by Virgil's words for the sight
of Lucifer, who will appear like a "windmill" in a "thick fog." The banners referred to are Lucifer's wings.
   10. These sinners in various positions
fixed rigidly in the ice present a picture

of complete immobility and incommuni-
cability, as though they have been entombed a second time. Silence reigns in
this fourth division of Cocytus (named
Judecca, l. 117, after the traitor Judas),
the gelid abode of those souls in whom
all warmth of love for God and for their
fellow man has been extinguished.
   18. Before his fall Lucifer was held by
God to be the fairest of the angels. Pride
caused Lucifer's rebellion against his
Maker and precipitated his expulsion from
Heaven. The arch traitor is, like the other
sinners, fixed and suffering in the ice. He
weeps.
   20. In antiquity Pluto, god of the
Underworld, was often referred to as
Dis, a name here applied to Lucifer.

do not ask me—I cannot write about it—
there are no words to tell you how I felt.
I did not die—I was not living either!   25
Try to imagine, if you can imagine,
me there, deprived of life and death at once.
The king of the vast kingdom of all grief
stuck out with half his chest above the ice;
my height is closer to the height of giants   30
than theirs is to the length of his great arms;
consider now how large all of him was:
this body in proportion to his arms.
If once he was as fair as now he's foul
and dared to raise his brows against his Maker,   35
it is fitting that all grief should spring from him.
Oh, how amazed I was when I looked up
and saw a head—one head wearing three faces!
One was in front (and that was a bright red),
the other two attached themselves to this one   40
just above the middle of each shoulder,
and at the crown all three were joined in one:
The right face was a blend of white and yellow,
the left the color of those people's skin
who live along the river Nile's descent.   45
Beneath each face two mighty wings stretched out,
the size you might expect of this huge bird
(I never saw a ship with larger sails):
not feathered wings but rather like the ones
a bat would have. He flapped them constantly,   50
keeping three winds continuously in motion
to lock Cocytus eternally in ice.
He wept from his six eyes, and down three chins
were dripping tears all mixed with bloody slaver.
In each of his three mouths he crunched a sinner   55
with teeth like those that rake the hemp and flax,
keeping three sinners constantly in pain;
the one in front—the biting he endured
was nothing like the clawing that he took:
sometimes his back was raked clean of its skin.   60
"That soul up there who suffers most of all,"
my guide explained, "is Judas Iscariot:
the one with head inside and legs out kicking.

38–45. Dante presents Lucifer's head as a perverted parallel of the Trinity. The symbolic value of the three single faces has been much debated. Although many commentators believe that the colors (red, yellow, black) represent the three known continents (Europe, Asia, Africa), it seems more logical that they should be antithetically analogous to the qualities attributed to the Trinity (see Canto III, ll. 5–6). Therefore, Highest Wisdom would be opposed by ignorance (black), Divine Omnipotence by impotence (yellow), Primal Love by hatred or envy (red).

46. The entire figure of Lucifer is a parody of the angelic. Originally belonging to the order of the Cherubim, he retains his six wings even in Hell, though here, devoid of their heavenly plumage, they appear as those of a bat (the standard depiction of the devil's wings in the Middle Ages).

61–63. Having betrayed Christ for thirty pieces of silver Judas endures greater punishment than the other two souls.

As for the other two whose heads stick out,
　　the one who hangs from that black face is Brutus—　65
　　see how he squirms in silent desperation,
the other one is Cassius, he still looks sturdy.
　　But soon it will be night. Now is the time
　　to leave this place, for we have seen it all."
I held on to his neck, as he told me to,　70
　　while he watched and waited for the time and place,
　　and when the wings were stretched out just enough,
he grabbed on to the shaggy sides of Satan;
　　then downward, tuft by tuft, he made his way
　　between the tangled hair and frozen crust.　75
When we had reached the point exactly where
　　the thigh begins, right at the haunch's curve,
　　my guide with strain and force of every muscle,
turned his head toward the shaggy shanks of Dis
　　and grabbed the hair as if about to climb—　80
　　I thought that we were heading back to Hell.
"Hold tight, there is no other way," he said,
　　panting, exhausted, "only by these stairs
　　can we leave behind the evil we have seen."
When he had got me through the rocky crevice,　85
　　he raised me to its edge and set me down,
　　then carefully he climbed and joined me there.
I raised my eyes expecting I would see
　　the half of Lucifer I saw before.
　　Instead I saw his two legs stretching upward.　90
If at that sight I found myself confused,
　　so will those simple-minded folk who still
　　don't see what point it was I must have passed.
"Get up," my master said, "get to your feet,
　　the way is long, the road a rough climb up,　95
　　already the sun approaches middle tierce!"

65. "Brutus": Marcus Brutus, who was deceitfully persuaded by Cassius (l. 67) to join the conspiracy, aided in the assassination of Julius Caesar. It is fitting that in his final vision of the Inferno the Pilgrim should see those shades who committed treacherous acts against Divine and worldly authorities: the Church and the Roman Empire. This provides the culmination, at least in this canticle, of these basic themes: Church and Empire.

67. "Cassius": Caius Cassius Longinus was another member of the conspiracy against Caesar. By describing Cassius as "still looking sturdy," Dante shows he has evidently confused him with Lucius Cassius, whom Cicero calls *adeps*, "corpulent."

79–81. Virgil, carrying the Pilgrim on his back, slowly makes his way down Lucifer's hairy body and, upon reaching a certain point (the center of the universe and, consequently, of terrestial gravity), where Lucifer's thighs begin, he must turn his head in the direction of Lucifer's legs and begin to climb "upward"—thus confusing the Pilgrim on his back. The way in which Virgil executed his own shift of position on Lucifer's body must have been as follows: when he reached the thigh he moved his head to the side and downward until (still holding on with one hand to the hair of the chest) he could reach with his other hand to grasp the hair on the thigh—then (aided now by the shift of gravitational pull) to free the first hand and complete the half circle he had initiated, proceeding henceforth as a man climbing.

96. The time is approximately halfway between the canonical hours of Prime and Tierce, i.e., 7:30 A.M. The rapid change from night ("But soon it will be night," l. 68) to day (l. 96) is the result of the travelers' having passed the earth's center, thus moving into the Southern Hemisphere which is twelve hours ahead of the Northern.

It was no palace promenade we came to,
   but rather like some dungeon Nature built:
   it was paved with broken stone and poorly lit.
"Before we start to struggle out of here,   100
   O master," I said when I was on my feet,
   "I wish you would explain some things to me.
Where is the ice? And how can he be lodged
   upside-down! And how, in so little time
   could the sun go all the way from night to day?"   105
"You think you're still on the center's other side,"
   he said, "where I first grabbed the hairy worm
   of rottenness that pierces the earth's core;
and you *were* there as long as I moved downward
   but, when I turned myself, you passed the point   110
   to which all weight from every part is drawn.
Now you are standing beneath the hemisphere
   which is opposite the side covered by land,
   where at the central point was sacrificed
the Man whose birth and life were free of sin.   115
   You have both feet upon a little sphere
   whose other side Judecca occupies;
when it is morning here, there it is evening.
   And he whose hairs were stairs for our descent
   has not changed his position since his fall.   120
When he fell from the heavens on this side,
   all of the land that once was spread out here,
   alarmed by his plunge, took cover beneath the sea
and moved to our hemisphere; with equal fear
   the mountain-land, piled up this side, fled   125
   and made this cavern here when it rushed upward.
Below somewhere there is a space, as far
   from Beelzebub as the limit of his tomb,
   known not by sight but only by the sound
of a little stream that makes its way down here   130
   through the hollow of a rock that it has worn
   gently winding in gradual descent."
My guide and I entered that hidden road
   to make our way back up to the bright world.
   We never thought of resting while we climbed.   135

112–115. Lucifer's body, falling head first from Heaven to the Southern Hemisphere, bored through to the earth's center where he remains imprisoned. Before he fell through the Southern Hemisphere ("this side," l. 121), it was covered with land, but the land, "alarmed by his plunge," sank beneath the sea and shifted to the Northern Hemisphere ("our hemisphere," l. 24). But the land at the center of the earth rushed upward, at once leaving the "cavern" above Lucifer's legs and forming the Mount of Purgatory, the only land in the Southern Hemisphere.

127–132. Somewhere below the land

which rushed upward to form the Mount of Purgatory "there is a space" (l. 127) through which a stream runs, and it is through this space that Virgil and Dante will climb to reach the base of the Mount. The "space" is "as far/from Beelzebub [Lucifer] as the limit of his tomb" (l. 127–128); that is, at the edge of the natural dungeon that constitutes Lucifer's "tomb," there is an opening, a "space," serving as the entrance to the passage from the earth's center to its circumference, created by Lucifer in his fall from Heaven to Hell.

We climbed, he first and I behind, until,
  through a small round opening ahead of us
  I saw the lovely things the heavens hold,
and we came out to see once more the stars.

Purgatory (*Purgatorio*)

CANTO I

[Having emerged from Hell, Virgil and Dante find themselves
on the eastern shores of the island-mountain of Purgatory, which
is at the antipodes of Jerusalem. It is the dawn of Easter Day, 1300.
Four stars, symbols of the cardinal virtues (perhaps suggested by
descriptions of the Southern Cross), blaze in the sky. Cato, the
Guardian of Purgatory, appears to the poets and questions them.
Being satisfied by Virgil, he tells them to wait·for the daylight; but
first Virgil is to wash Dante's face with dew and to gird him with a
reed.]

Now hoisteth sail the pinnace of my wit
  For better waters, and more smoothly flies
  Since of a sea so cruel she is quit,
And of that second realm, which purifies
  Man's spirit of its soilure, will I sing,   5
  Where it becometh worthy of Paradise.
Here let dead Poesy from her grave up-spring,
  O sacred Muses, whom I serve and haunt,
  And sound, Calliope, a louder string
To accompany my song with that high chant   10
  Which smote the Magpies' miserable choir
  That they despaired of pardon for their vaunt.
Tender colour of orient sapphire
  Which on the air's translucent aspect grew,
  From mid heaven to horizon deeply clear,   15
Made pleasure in mine eyes be born anew
  Soon as I issued forth from the dead air
  That had oppressed both eye and heart with rue.
The planet that promoteth Love was there,
  Making all the East to laugh and be joyful,   20
  And veiled the Fishes that escorted her.

139. The Pilgrim, denied sight of the celestial bodies in Hell, now looks up at them again. The direction his journey will now take is upward, toward that Divine Realm of which the stars are the signal for us on earth. That all three canticles end with the word "stars," symmetrically reinforces the concept of movement upward toward God, the central theme and motive force of the *Divine Comedy*.

9–11. The Magpies were the nine daughters of King Pieros; they challenged the Muses to a contest and, being worsted by one of them, Calliope, became so insolent that they were turned into birds.

21. Venus was dimming, by her brighter light, the constellation of the Fishes; the time indicated is an hour or more before sunrise.

I turned to the right and contemplated all
    The other pole; and four stars o'er me came,
    Never yet seen save by the first people.
All the heavens seemed exulting in their flame.   25
    O widowed Northern clime, from which is ta'en
    The happy fortune of beholding them!
When from my gaze I had severed them again,
    Turned somewhat to the other pole, whose law
    By now had sunken out of sight the Wain,   30
Near me an old man solitary I saw,
    In his aspect so much to be revered
    That no son owes a father more of awe.
Long and with white hairs brindled was his beard,
    Like to his locks, of which a double list   35
    Down on his shoulders and his breast appeared.
The beams of the four sacred splendours kist
    His countenance, and they glorified it so
    That in its light the sun's light was not missed.
"Who are ye, that against the blind stream go,"   40
    Shaking those venerable plumes, he said,
    "And flee from the eternal walls of woe?
Who hath guided you? what lamp your footsteps led,
    Issuing from that night without fathom
    Which makes a blackness of the vale of dread?   45
Is the law of the abyss thus broken from?
    Or is there some new change in Heaven's decrees,
    That, being damned, unto my crags ye come?"
Then did my leader on my shoulder seize
    And with admonishing hand and word and sign   50
    Make reverent my forehead and my knees;
Then spoke: "I come not of my own design.
    From Heaven came down a Lady, at whose prayer,
    To help this man, I made his pathway mine.
But since it is thy will that we declare   55
    More of our state, needs must that I obey
    And tell thee all: deny thee I would not dare.
He hath never yet seen darken his last day,
    Yet so near thereto through his folly went
    That short time was there to re-shape his way.   60

23–24. Dante invents here a constellation of four bright lights, corresponding to the Great Bear of the north. These luminaries symbolize the four cardinal virtues: Prudence, Temperance, Fortitude, and Justice. Adam and Eve before the fall ("the first people"), dwelling at the top of the mountain of Purgatory, beheld these stars.

31. This custodian of Purgatory (an example of that free will which the souls in his domain are striving, by purification, to regain) is Cato the Younger, who on earth killed himself in Utica rather than submit to Caesar.

Even as I said, to his rescue I was sent,
    Nor other way appeared that was not vain
    But this on which our footsteps now are bent.
I have shown him all the sinners in their pain,
    And now intend to show him those who dwell   65
    Under thy charge and cleanse themselves of stain.
How I have brought him were too long to tell.
    Our steps a Virtue, helping from on high,
    That he might see thee and hear thee, did impel.
Now on his coming look with gracious eye.   70
    He seeketh freedom, that so precious thing,
    How precious, he knows who for her will die.
Thou knowest: for her sake, death had no sting
    In Utica, where thou didst leave what yet
    The great day shall for thy bright raiment bring. 75
The eternal laws are still inviolate;
    For he doth live, nor me doth Minos bind.
    But I am of the circle where the chaste eyes wait
Of Marcia, visibly praying that thy mind,
    O sainted breast, still hold her for thine own.   80
    For love of her, then, be to us inclined.
Suffer that thy seven realms to us be shown;
    And thanks of thee shall unto her be brought,
    If there below thou deign still to be known."
"Marcia was so pleasing to my thought   85
    Yonder," he answered, "and myself so fond,
    Whate'er she willed, I could refuse her naught.
Now no more may she move me, since beyond
    The evil stream she dwells, by the decree
    Made when I was delivered from that bond.   90
But if a heavenly lady hath missioned thee,
    As thou hast said, of flattery is no need.
    Enough, that in her name thou askest me.
Go then; first gird this man with a smooth reed,
    And see thou bathe his features in such wise   95
    That from all filthiness they may be freed.
It were not meet that mist clouded his eyes
    To dim their vision, when he goes before
    The first of those that serve in Paradise.
This little isle, there where for evermore   100
    The waters beat all round about its foot,

77–79. Minos, the Judge of Hell, does not bind Virgil, who dwells in the Limbus. "Marcia" was Cato's wife. 88–90. When Cato was released from Limbus by Christ, he became subject to the law forbidding the blessed to be moved by the fate of the damned.

Bears rushes on the soft and oozy shore.
No other plant that would put forth a shoot
    Or harden, but from life there is debarred,
    Since to the surf it yields not from its root.   105
And then return not this way afterward.
    The sun, at point to rise now, shall reveal
    Where the mount yieldeth an ascent less hard."
So he vanished; and I rose up on my heel
    Without word spoken, and all of me drew back   110
    Toward my guide, making with mine eyes appeal.
He began: "Son, follow thou in my track.
    Turn we on our footsteps, for this way the lea
    Slopes down, where the low banks its boundary make."
The dawn was moving the dark hours to flee   115
    Before her, and far off amid their wane
    I could perceive the trembling of the sea.
We paced along the solitary plain,
    Like one who seeks to his lost road a clue,
    And till he reach it deems he walks in vain.   120
When we had come there where the melting dew
    Contends against the sun, being in a place
    Where the cool air but little of it updrew,
My Lord laid both hands out on the lank grass
    Gently, amid the drops that it retained: 125
    Wherefore I, conscious what his purpose was,
Lifted to him my cheeks that tears had stained;
    And at his touch the colour they had worn,
    Ere Hell had overcast it, they regained.
Then came we down to the land's desert bourne,   130
    Which never yet saw man that had essayed
    Voyage upon that water and knew return.
There did he gird me as that other bade.
    O miracle! even as it was before,
    The little plant put forth a perfect blade   135
On the instant in the place his fingers tore.

CANTO II

[The sun rises. A boat, steered by an angel, swiftly approaches
the shore; it contains a company of spirits brought to Purgatory.
These landed, the angel with the boat departs to collect other spirits
at the mouth of the Tiber. Among the newcomers Dante recognizes
a friend; it is Casella the musician. Casella is persuaded to sing,
and the spirits gather round to listen, when Cato appears and rebukes them for loitering, and they scatter up the slopes of the mountain.]

Now the sun touched the horizon with his flame,
   The circle of whose meridian, at the height
   It reaches most, covers Jerusalem;
And opposite to him in her circling, Night
   Came up from Ganges, and the Scales with her   5
   That from her hand fall as she grows in might;
So that the fair cheeks of Aurora, there
   Where I was, gave their red and white away,
   Sallowing, as if old age had turned them sere.
We lingered yet by the ocean-marge, as they   10
   Who think upon the road that lies before
   And in their mind go, but in body stay;
And lo! as at the approach of morning frore
   Mars through the mist glimmers a fiery red
   Down in the West over the ocean-floor,   15
(May mine eyes yet upon that sight be fed!)
   Appeared, moving across the water, a light
   So swift, all earthly motion it outsped.
From which when for a space I had drawn my sight
   Away, and of my Guide the meaning sought,   20
   I saw it now grown bigger and more bright.
On either side of it I knew not what
   Of white appeared to gleam out; and below
   Another whiteness by degrees it got.
My master spoke not yet a word, till lo!   25
   When those first whitenesses as wings shone free
   And his eyes now could well the Pilot know,
He exclaimed: "Bend, see that thou bend the knee.
   Behold the Angel of God! Lay hand to hand!
   Such ministers henceforth thou art to see.   30
Look, how he scorneth aid that man hath planned,
   And wills not oar nor other sail to ply,
   But only his own wings from far land to land.
See how he has them stretcht up toward the sky,
   Sweeping the air with that eternal plume   35
   Which moulteth not as the hair of things that die."
Such an exceeding brightness did allume
   The Bird of God, who near and nearer bore,

1–6. This is one of the astronomical riddles to which our poet was addicted. According to medieval cosmology, Jerusalem and Purgatory are on opposite sides of the earth, 180° from each other: when Jerusalem sees the sun rise, Purgatory sees it set. The river Ganges, which flowed on the eastern confines of the inhabited world, stands for the "east." What we are told, in a devious and ingenious way, is that for the spectators on the island of Purgatory the sun was rising.

7–9. The poet transfers to the face of the goddess of dawn (Aurora) the changing colors of the morning sky.

16. "May mine eyes . . .": after death, when my soul shall be wafted to Purgatory.

Mine eyes to endure him might not now presume,
But bent them down; and he came on to shore   40
Upon a barque so swift and light and keen
As scarcely a ripple from the water tore.
On the heavenly Steersman at the stern was seen
Inscribed that blissfulness whereof he knew;
And more than a hundred spirits sat within.   45
Together all were singing *In exitu*
Israel de Egypto as one host
With what of that psalm doth those words ensue.
With the holy sign their company he crossed;
Whereat themselves forth on the strand they threw: 50
Swift as he came, he sped, and straight was lost.
They that remained seemed without any clue
To the strange place, casting a wondering eye
Round them, like one assaying hazards new.
On every side the arrowing sun shot high   55
Into the day, and with his bright arrows
Had hunted Capricorn from the mid sky,
When the new people lifted up their brows
Towards us, and spoke to us: "If ye know it, show
What path to us the mountain-side allows."   60
And Virgil answered: "Peradventure you
Suppose we have experience of the way;
But we are pilgrims, even as ye are too.
We came but now, a little before you, nay,
By another road than yours, so steep and rude   65
That the climb now will seem to us but play."
The spirits, who by my breathing understood
That I was still among the living things,
Marvelling, became death-pale where they stood.
As round a messenger, who the olive brings,   70
Folk, to hear news, each on the other tread,
And none is backward with his elbowings,
So on my face their gaze intently fed
Those spirits, all so fortunate, and forgot
Almost to go up and be perfected.   75
One of them now advanced, as if he sought
To embrace me, with a love so fond and fain,
That upon me to do the like he wrought.
O Shades, in all but aspect, void and vain!

57. At dawn the constellation of
Capricorn was on the meridian; it is
effaced by the rays of the rising sun.
70. Bearers of good tidings used to
carry an olive branch.

79–81. Throughout Hell the souls,
though without weight, are not only
visible but tangible. On the lower slopes
of the mountain of Purgatory, however,
Dante cannot touch a shade, although
two spirits can still embrace.

Behind it thrice my hands did I enlace,   80
   And thrice they came back to my breast again.
Wonder, I think, was painted on my face;
   At which the spirit smiled and backward drew,
   And, following it, I sprang forward a pace.
Gently it bade me pause: and then I knew   85
   Who it was, and prayed him pity on me to show
   And talk with me as he was used to do.
"As in the mortal body I loved thee, so
   In my release I love thee," he answered me.
   "Therefore I stay: but thou, why dost thou go?"   90
"Casella mine, that this place I may see
   Hereafter," I said, "have I this journey made.
   But how hath so much time been stolen from thee?"
And he to me: "None have I to upbraid
   If he who takes when he chooses, and whom,   95
   This passage many times to me forbade.
For in a just will hath his will its home.
   Truly he has taken now these three months past
   Whoso hath wished to enter, in all welcome.
So I, whose eyes on the sea-shore were cast   100
   Where Tiber's water by the salt is won,
   By him was gathered in benignly at last.
To that mouth now his wings he urgeth on
   Because for ever assemble in that spot
   They who are not to sink towards Acheron."   105
And I: "If a new law forbid thee not
   Memory and usage of the enamoured song
   Which used to soothe all wishes of my thought,
May it please thee awhile to solace with thy tongue
   My spirit that, in its mortal mask confined,   110
   The journey hither bitterly hath wrung."
"Love that discourseth to me in my mind"
   Began he then so sweetly, that the sound
   Still in my heart with sweetness is entwined.
My Master and I, and all that people around   115
   Who were with him, had faces so content
   As if all else out of their thoughts were drowned.

91. Of Casella we know only that he was a musician of Florence and a close friend of the poet and, perhaps, that he set to music Dante's canzone, "Love that discourseth to me in my mind" (see line 112).

92–93. Dante's present experience is intended to fit him to return to Purgatory after death. Casella evidently had died some time before, and Dante is astonished to see him just arrived in the other world.

95–97. "He who takes . . .": the angelic boatman. "In a just will . . .": the will of God.

101. The "Tiber's water" signifies allegorically the Church of Rome. There congregate the souls of those who die in its bosom. The souls of the unrepentant descend to Acheron.

We to his notes, entranced, our senses lent:
    And lo! the old man whom all the rest revere
    Crying, "What is this, ye laggard spirits faint?   120
What truancy, what loitering is here?
    Haste to the Mount and from the slough be freed
    Which lets not God unto your eyes appear."
As doves, when picking corn or darnel seed,
    All quiet and close-crowding to that fare,   125
    Their strut of pride forgotten in their greed,
If anything appear their hearts to scare
    On the instant leave the food there, where it lies,
    Because they are assailed by greater care,
So saw I that new company arise,   130
    And leave the song, and the steep slope essay,
    Like one who goes, knowing not of where he hies:
Nor with less haste went we upon our way.

. . .

CANTO XIX

[In a dream Dante has a vision of the Siren (symbolizing worldly enticements). A lady from heaven appears in this dream; and Virgil, at her bidding, exposes the Siren's real foulness. Dante is roused by Virgil, the sun having now risen, and an angel speeds them up the passage to the fifth terrace, where are the souls of the avaricious and the prodigal, lying prone on the ground. Virgil asks the way, and is answered by one who proves to be Pope Adrian V. He tells them that he was possessed by avarice till he reached the highest office, and then turned to God. Dante kneels, to show his reverence, but is told by the spirit to rise.]

In that hour when the heat of day no more
    Can warm the Moon's cold influence, and it dies
    O'ercome by the earth or whiles by Saturn's power;
When geomancers see in the East arise
    Their Greater Fortune, ere the dawn be come,   5
    By a path which not long dark before it lies,
In dream came to me a woman stuttering dumb,
    With squinting eyes and twisted on her feet,
    With deformed hands and cheeks of pallor numb.
I gazed on her; and as the sun's good heat   10
    Comforteth cold limbs weighed down by the night,
    So did my look make her tongue nimbly feat,
And straightened her and set her all upright

4. "Geomancers" foretold the future by means of figures constructed on points that were distributed by chance. One of their figures, called "Greater Fortune," resembled a constellation.

In short time, and her ruined countenance made
Into the colour which is love's delight.   15
Soon as her loosened tongue came to her aid,
    She began singing, so that for its sake
    From her voice hardly had my hearing strayed.
"I am," she said, "the sweet Siren, who make
    Mariners helpless, charmed in the mid-sea;   20
    Such pleasure in my music do men take.
I turned Ulysses from his wandering, he
    So loved my song; and who with me hath found
    Home, seldom quits, so glad is he of me."
Her lips were not yet closed upon the sound   25
    When came a lady in whom was holiness
    Prompt to my side, that other to confound.
"O Virgil, Virgil, tell me who is this?"
    Indignantly she said; and straight he went
    With eyes fixt on that honest one, to seize   30
The other, and when her garments he had rent,
    He laid her open and showed her belly creased,
    That waked me with the stench that forth it sent.
I turned my eyes, and Virgil said: "At least
    Thrice have I called thee; up, let us begone!   35
    Find we the opening where thou enterest."
I raised me up; high day now overshone
    The holy mount and filled each winding ledge.
    We went, and at our back was the new sun.
I followed him, like one who is the siege   40
    Of heavy thought that droops his forehead, when
    He makes himself the half-arch of a bridge.
And I heard: "Come! Here is the pass"; spoken
    With so much loving kindness in the tone
    As is not heard in this our mortal pen.   45
With outspread wings that shone white as a swan
    He who thus spoke guided our journeying
    Upward between the two walls of hard stone.
Stirring his plumes, he fanned us with his wing
    And named *qui lugent* blessed, for that they   50
    Shall dispense consolation, like a king.
We both had passed the angel a little way
    When, "What now ails thee that thine eyes are so
    Fixt on the ground?" my Guide began to say.
And I: "In such misgiving do I go   55
    From a strange dream which doth my mind possess
    So that the thought I cannot from me throw."

50. *"Qui lugent"*: those who mourn.

"Sawest thou," he said, "that ancient sorceress
For whom alone the mount above us wails?
Sawest thou how man obtains from her release?   60
Let that suffice: beat the earth down with thy heels;
Turn thine eyes toward the lure which from his seat
The Eternal King spins round with the great wheels."
As a falcon, that first gazes at his feet,
Turns at the cry and stretches him beyond   65
Where desire draws him thither to his meat,
Such I became; and far as, for one bound
Upwards, a path is cloven through the stone,
Such went I up to where one must go round.
Soon as I was enlarged on the fifth zone   70
I saw on it a weeping multitude
With faces to the ground all lying prone.
My spirit clave unto the dust, I could
Hear them cry out, with sighings and laments
So that the words hardly were understood.   75
"O ye chosen of God, whose punishments
Both hope and justice make less hard to bear,
Direct our footsteps to the high ascents."
"If from the lying prone exempt ye are,
And wish the speediest way to be revealed,   80
Keep your right hands to the outside as ye fare."
This answer to the poet, who thus appealed,
Was made a little in front of us; therefore
I noted, as each spoke, what was concealed.
My Lord then with my eyes I turned to implore,   85
Whereat his glad sign of assent I caught
To what my eager look was craving for.
Then, free to do according to my thought,
I passed forward above that creature there
Whose words before had made me of him take note,   90
Saying: "Spirit, in whom weeping ripens fair
That without which one cannot turn to God,
Suspend for me awhile thy greater care.
Who thou wast, tell me, and why to earth ye are bowed,
Face down, and if thou would'st that I should win   95
Aught for thee yonder, whence I tread this road."
And he: "Why turned to Heaven our backs have been
Thou shalt learn; but first *scias quod ego
Fui successor Petri*. Down between.

59. "Above us": in the three upper
circles.
62. "The lure . . .": the uplifting influence of the revolving heavens.

70. This is the circle of avarice and
prodigality.
92. The fruit of repentance.
98. "Know that I was a successor of
Peter." The speaker is Pope Adrian V.

Sestri and Chiaveri waters flow   100
   Of a fair stream, wherefrom our old estate
   Nameth the title it vaunts most to bestow.
One month, scarce more, taught me how weighs the great
   Mantle on him who keeps it from the dirt,
   So that all others seem a feather's weight.   105
Late came the day that could my soul convert,
   But when the Roman Pastor I became,
   Thus found I life to be with lies begirt.
I saw that there the heart no peace could claim,
   Nor in that life could one mount higher: of this   110
   Therefore the love sprang in me to a flame.
Up to that hour I, lost in avarice,
   Was miserable, being a soul in want
   Of God; thou seëst here what my forfeit is.
Here of what avarice works is made the account,   115
   In purge of souls converted ere the end;
   And no more bitter penalty hath the mount.
Even as our eyes on high we would not send,
   Which only upon earthly things were cast,
   So here to earth Justice hath forced them bend.   120
As avarice turned all our works to waste
   Because it quenched our love of all goodness,
   Even so Justice here doth hold us fast,
Both hands and feet, in seizure and duress;
   And so long as the just Lord hath assigned,   125
   So long we lie stretched-out and motionless."
I had knelt down; to speak was in my mind;
   But he, by the mere hearing, in that pause
   Being aware that I my back inclined,
Said, "Dost thou bow thy knees?,and for what cause?"   130
   And I to him: " 'Tis for your dignity:
   My conscience pricked me, standing as I was."
"Make straight thy legs and rise up from thy knee,
   Brother," he answered: "err not; of one Lord
   I am fellow-servant with the rest and thee.   135
If thou hast understood that holy chord
   The Gospel sounds which *Neque nubent* saith,
   Thou mayest perceive well why I spoke that word.
Go now, and no more tarry upon thy path,
   For thou disturb'st the tears wherewith I crave   140
   To ripen what thyself didst say of faith.

101. "A fair stream": the Lavagna river. Adrian belonged to the Fieschi family, who were counts of Lavagna.

103. "One month": Adrian V held the papal office only for 38 days.

137. If thou hast interpreted *Neque nubent* ("They neither marry") in the broader sense, as meaning that earthly relations are not preserved in the spiritual world.

A niece yonder, Alagia named, I have,
    Good in herself, so only that our house
    Her nature by example not deprave.
She only is there to assist me with her vows."   145

. . .

CANTO XXVII

[Night is coming on, when the Angel of Chastity appears and tells Dante that he cannot go further without passing through the fire. He is terrified, remembering deaths by burning that he had witnessed on earth; and even Virgil's encouragement cannot overcome his fears till he is reminded that Beatrice awaits him beyond. The three pass through the fire and emerge at the place of ascent. Another angel warns them to hasten, as the sun is setting. Each now makes a bed for himself on a step of the stair. Dante sleeps, and dreams of Leah and Rachel, types of the active and contemplative life, foreshadowing the meeting with Matilda and Beatrice which is to come. He wakes with morning, and at the summit Virgil tells him that his mission is ended and that Dante now needs no guide or instructor.]

As when his first beams tremble in the sky
    There, where his own Creator shed his blood,
    While Ebro is beneath the Scales on high,
And noon scorches the wave on Ganges' flood,
    Such was the sun's height; day was soon to pass;   5
    When the angel of God joyful before us stood.
Outside the flames, above the bank, he was.
    Beati mundo corde we heard him sing
    In a voice more living far than comes from us.
Then "None goes further, if first the fire not sting.   10
    O hallowed spirits, enter unafraid
    And to the chant beyond let your ears cling."
When we were near him, this to us he said.
    Wherefore I, when I knew what his words meant,
    Became as one who in the grave is laid.   15
Over my clasping hands forward I leant,
    Eyeing the fire, and vivid to my mind
    Men's bodies burning, once beheld, it sent.
Then toward me turned them both my escorts kind;
    And Virgil said to me: "O my son, here   20
    Torment, may-be, but death thou shalt not find.

142. "Alagia" de' Fieschi was the daughter of Adrian's brother Niccolò. 1-5. The time described is the approach of sunset.
8. Matt. 5:8: "Blessed are the pure in heart."

Remember, O remember . . . and if thy fear
  On Geryon into safety I recalled,
  What shall I do now, being to God more near?
If thou within this womb of flames wert walled   25
  Full thousand years, for certainty believe
  That not of one hair could they make thee bald.
And if perchance thou think'st that I deceive,
  Go forward into them, and thy faith prove,
  With hands put in the edges of thy sleeve.   30
Out of thy heart all fear remove, remove!
  Turn hither and come confidently on!"
  And I stood fixed and with my conscience strove.
When he beheld me still and hard as stone,
  Troubled a little, he said: "Look now, this same   35
  Wall is 'twixt Beatrice and thee, my son."
As Pyramus at the sound of Thisbe's name
  Opened his dying eyes and gazed at her
  Then, when the crimson on the mulberry came,
So did I turn unto my wise Leader,   40
  My hardness melted, hearing the name told
  Which like a well-spring in my mind I bear.
Whereon he shook his head, saying: "Do we hold
  Our wish to stay on this side?" He smiled then
  As on a child by an apple's bribe cajoled.   45
Before me then the fire he entered in,
  Praying Statius that he follow at his heel
  Who for a long stretch now had walked between.
When I was in, I had been glad to reel,
  Therefrom to cool me, into boiling glass,   50
  Such burning beyond measure did I feel.
My sweet Father, to give me heart of grace,
  Continued only on Beatrice to descant,
  Saying: "Already I seem to see her face."
On the other side, to guide us, rose a chant,   55
  And we, intent on that alone to dwell,
  Came forth there, where the ascent began to slant.
And there we heard a voice *Venite* hail
  Benedicti patris mei out of light
  So strong, it mastered me and made me quail.   60
"The sun departs," it added; "comes the night.
  Tarry not; study at good pace to go

---

39. The mulberry turned red on being spattered with the blood of Pyramus, who stabbed himself when he thought Thisbe slain by a lion (Ovid, *Met.*, IV, 55–166).

58–59. Matt. 25:34: "Come, ye blessed of my Father . . ."

Before the west has darkened on your sight."
Straight rose the path within the rock, and so
    Directed onward, that I robbed the ray   65
    Before me from the sun, already low.
I and my sages few steps did assay
    When by the extinguished shadow we perceived
    That now behind us had sunk down the day.
And ere the horizon had one hue received   70
    In all the unmeasured regions of the air,
    And night her whole expansion had achieved,
Each of us made his bed upon a stair,
    Seeing that the nature of the mount o'ercame
    Alike the power to ascend and the desire.   75
As goats, now ruminating, though the same
    That, before feeding, brisk and wanton played
    On the high places of the hills, grow tame,
Silent, while the sun scorches, in the shade,
    Watched by the herd that props him hour by hour   80
    Upon his staff and, propt so, tends his trade;
And as the shepherd, lodging out-of-door,
    Watches night-long in quiet by his flock,
    Wary lest wild beast scatter it or devour;
Such were we then, all three, within that nook,   85
    I as a goat, they as a shepherd, there,
    On this and that side hemmed by the high rock.
Little could there of the outside things appear;
    But through that little I saw the stars to glow
    Bigger than ordinary and shine more clear.   90
Ruminating and gazing on them so
    Sleep took me; sleep which often will apprize
    Of things to come, and ere the event foreknow.
In the hour, I think, when first from Eastern skies
    Upon the mountain Cytherea beamed   95
    Whom fire of love forever glorifies,
A lady young and beautiful I seemed
    To see move through a plain and flower on flower
    To gather; singing, she was saying (I dreamed),
"Let them know, whoso of my name inquire,   100
    That I am Leah, and move my fingers fair
    Around, to make me a garland for a tire.

[80. *herd:* herdsman.—J. C. McG.]
95. "Cytherea" is Venus, whose star shines before sunrise.
100. Dante is about to visit the Garden of Eden, the abode of innocence and harmless activity. Consequently the active and the contemplative life are revealed to him in the form of Laban's daughters, Leah and Rachel.

To glad me at the glass I deck me here;
    But never to her mirror is untrue
    My sister Rachel, and sits all day there.   105
She is fain to hold her beauteous eyes in view
    As me with these hands I am fain to adorn:
    To see contenteth her, and me to do."
Already, through the splendour ere the morn,
    Which to wayfarers the more grateful shows,   110
    Lodging less far from home, where they return,
The shadows on all sides were fleeing, and close
    On them my sleep fled; wherefore, having seen
    The great masters risen already, I rose.
"That apple whose sweetness in their craving keen   115
    Mortals go seeking on so many boughs
    This day shall peace to all thy hungers mean."
Words such as these to me did Virgil use;
    And no propitious gifts did man acquire
    For pleasure matching these, to have or choose.   120
So came on me desire upon desire
    To be above, that now with every tread
    I felt wings on me growing to waft me higher.
When under us the whole high stair was sped
    And we unto the topmost step had won,   125
    Virgil, fixing his eyes upon me, said:
"The temporal and the eternal fire, my son,
    Thou hast beheld: thou art come now to a part
    Where of myself I see no farther on.
I have brought thee hither both by wit and art.   130
    Take for thy guide thine own heart's pleasure now.
    Forth from the narrows, from the steeps, thou art.
See there the sun that shines upon thy brow;
    See the young grass, the flowers and coppices
    Which this soil, of itself alone, makes grow.   135
While the fair eyes are coming, full of bliss,
    Which weeping made me come to thee before,
    Amongst them thou canst go or sit at ease.
Expect from me no word or signal more.
    Thy will is upright, sound of tissue, free: 140
    To disobey it were a fault; wherefore
Over thyself I crown thee and mitre thee."

. . .

115. "That apple . . .": earthly happiness.

142. I make thee thine own Emperor and Pope.

CANTO XXX

[Like the stars of Ursa Minor which guide sailors to port, the
Seven Candlesticks, stars of the Empyrean, control the movements
of those in the procession; and the elders who preceded the car now
turn toward it, and one (who represents the Song of Solomon) calls
on Beatrice to appear. Angels are seen scattering flowers, and in the
midst of them a veiled lady clad in the colors of Faith, Hope, and
Charity. It is Beatrice; and Dante experiences the same agitation
in her presence, though her face is not revealed, as when he first
saw her. Overcome, he turns for comfort to Virgil; but Virgil has
now disappeared; and Beatrice addresses Dante by name, severe in
look and in speech. Frozen by her reproaches, he is melted by the
compassion of the angels, to whom Beatrice tells of Dante's life
and disloyalty to her.]

Now when those Seven of the First Heaven stood still
    Which rising and declension never knew
    Nor veil of other mist than the evil will,
And which apprized each there what he should do,
    Even as the starry Seven in lower air   5
    Guide him to port who steereth by them true,
The people in whom truth doth itself declare,
    Who first between it and the Gryphon came,
    Turned to the car, as if their peace were there.
And one, as if Heaven prompted that acclaim,   10
    Veni, sponsa, de Libano chanted thrice,
    And after him all the others cried the same.
As at the last trump shall the saints arise,
    Crying alleluias to be re-attired
    In flesh, up from the cavern where each lies,   15
Upon the heavenly chariot so inspired
    A hundred sprang *ad vocem tanti senis,*
    Messengers of eternal life, who quired
Singing together *Benedictus qui venis,*
    While from their hands flowers up and down were
        thrown,   20
    And *Manibus O date lilia plenis.*
I have seen ere now at the beginning dawn
    The region of the East all coloured rose,

1–4. "The First Heaven": the
Empyrean.—"The evil will": man's
sinfulness.—"There": in the procession
of the Church.
5–6. As the Ursa Minor guides the
helmsman.
11. "Come with me from Lebanon,
my spouse." [Song of Solomon 4:8.—

J. C. McG.]
    17. "At the voice of so great an
elder."
    19. "Blessed is he that cometh" (in
the name of the Lord). [Matthew 21:9.
—J. C. McG.]
    21. "Oh, give lilies with full hands!"
[*Aeneid*, Book VI, l. 883.—J. C. McG.]

(The pure sky else in beauty of peace withdrawn)
When shadowed the sun's face uprising shows,   25
  So that the mists, attempering his powers,
  Let the eye linger upon him in repose;
So now for me amid a cloud of flowers
  That from the angels' hands up-floated light
  And fell, withinside and without, in showers,   30
A lady, olive-crowned o'er veil of white,
  Clothed in the colour of a living flame,
  Under a mantle green, stole on my sight.
My spirit that a time too long to name
  Had passed, since, at her presence coming nigh,   35
  A trembling thing and broken it became,
Now by no recognition of the eye
  But virtue invisible that went out from her
  Felt old love seize me in all its mastery.
When smote my sight the high virtue that, ere   40
  The years of boyhood were behind me laid,
  Already had pierced me through, as with a spear,
With such trust as a child that is afraid
  Or hurt, runs to his mother with his pains,
  I turned me to the left, to seek me aid   45
And say to Virgil: "Scarce one drop remains
  Of blood in me that trembles not: by this
  I recognize the old flame within my veins."
But Virgil had from us his company's
  Sweet solace taken, Virgil, father kind,   50
  Virgil, who for my soul's weal made me his.
Nor all that our first mother had resigned
  Availed to keep my cheeks, washed with the dew,
  From tears that once more stained them, welling blind.
"Dante, that Virgil leaves thee, and from thy view   55
  Is vanished, O not yet weep; weep not yet,
  For thou must weep, another stab to rue."
Like the Admiral who on poop or prow is set,
  To eye his men, in the other ships dispersed,
  And comes, each heart to embolden and abet,   60
So on the left side of the car, when first
  I turned, hearing my own name in my ear
  (Which of necessity is here rehearsed)
I found the gaze of her I had seen appear
  Erewhile, veiled, in the angelic festival,   65
  Toward me, this side the stream, directed clear;
Howbeit the veil she had from her head let fall,

52. Not all Eden.

With grey leaf of Minerva chapleted,
  Disclosing her, did not disclose her all.
Still severe, standing in her queenlihead,   70
  She spoke on, as one speaks whose purpose is
  To keep the hottest word awhile unsaid.
"Look on me well: I am, I am Beatrice.
  How, then, didst thou deign to ascend the Mount?
  Knewest thou not that, here, man is in bliss?"   75
I dropt mine eyes down to the lucent fount,
  But seeing myself there, drew them back in haste
  To the grass, heavy upon my shame's account.
As to a child a mother looks stern-faced,
  So to me seemed she: pity austere in thought   80
  Hath in its savour a so bitter taste.
She ceased then, and from every angel throat
  Straightway *In te, Domine, speravi* rose
  But beyond *pedes meos* they passed not.
As on the chine of Italy the snows   85
  Lodged in the living rafters harden oft
  To freezing, when the North-East on them blows,
Then, inly melted, trickle from aloft,
  If from the shadeless countries a breath stirs,
  Like in the flame a candle melting soft,   90
So was I, without sighs and without tears,
  In presence of their singing who accord
  Their notes to music of the eternal spheres;
But when I was aware of the sweet chord
  Of their compassion, more than if they spoke   95
  Saying, "Lady, why this shame upon him poured?"
The ice that round my heart had hardened woke
  Warm into breath and water, and from my breast
  In anguish, through mouth and through eyes, outbroke.
She, standing ever in her still'd arrest   100
  Upon the car's same side, to the array
  Of those compassionate beings these words addrest:
"Ye so keep watch in the everlasting day
  That neither night stealeth from you, nor sleep,
  One step that the world takes upon its way;   105
Therefore my answer shall the more care keep
  That he, there, understand me amid those tears,
  So that transgression equal sorrow reap.

83–84. Ps. 31: "In thee, O Lord, do
I put my trust." Verse 8 ends with:
"Thou hast set my feet in a large
room."

85. "The chine of Italy" is the
Apennine range.
89. "The shadeless countries": the
African desert.

Not only by operation of great spheres
    Which to some certain end each seed uptrain   110
    According as the starry voice it hears,
But bounty of heavenly graces, which for rain
    Have exhalations born in place so high
    That our eyes may not near to them attain,
This man was such in natural potency,   115
    In his new life, that all the ingrained good
    Looked in him to have fruited wondrously.
But so much groweth the more rank and rude
    The soil with bad seed and unhusbanded,
    The more it hath from earth of hardihood.   120
His spirit some time my countenance comforted
    With look of my young eyes for its support,
    Drawing him, the right path with me to tread.
Soon as the threshold I had passed, athwart
    The second period, and life changed its home,   125
    Me he forsook, with others to consort.
When from the flesh to spirit I had clomb
    And beauty and virtue greater in me grew,
    Less dear to him, more strange did I become;
And with perverted steps on ways untrue   130
    He sought false images of good, that ne'er
    Perform entire the promise that was due.
Nor helped me the inspiration won by prayer
    Whereby through dream or other hidden accost
    I called him back; so little had he care.   135
So low he sank, all means must I exhaust,
    Till naught for his salvation profited
    Save to be shown the people that are lost.
For this I broached the gateway of the dead,
    For this with tears was my entreaty brought   140
    To him, by whom his feet were hither led.
The ordinance of high God were set at naught
    If Lethe were passed over into peace,
    And such viand enjoyed, without some scot
Of penitence that may the tears release."   145

CANTO XXXI

[Dante, accused by Beatrice, confesses his sin and is filled with
penitence. Overwhelmed by the severity of Beatrice's words, and by

109–112. The "great spheres" are
the revolving heavens, which determine
the disposition of every human being.
God also bestows upon every individual
a special degree of grace.

116. "New life": young life.
125. "The second period": begins at
25. Her "life changed" the temporal
home for the eternal.

his own remorse, he falls senseless. When he recovers from his faint,
he finds that Matilda is drawing him across Lethe stream, in which
she immerses him. The four dancers (the four cardinal virtues)
lead him up to the Gryphon [who represents Christ, the second
person of the Trinity—J. C. McG.], where Beatrice is standing; in
her eyes the Gryphon is mirrored, now in one form now in the other.
The other three (the Theological Virtues) then come forward,
dancing, and implore Beatrice to smile upon her faithful servant.]

"O thou who art yon-side the sacred stream,"
   Turning her speech to point at me the blade
   Which even the edge had made so sharp to seem,
She spoke again, continuing undelayed.
   "Say, say if this be true; for, thus accused,   5
   Confession must thereto by thee be made"
Whereat my faculties were so confused
   That the voice stirred and faltered and was dead
   Ere it came free of the organs that it used.
Short time she endured; "What think'st thou?" then she
     said.   10
   "Answer, for in thee the sad memories
   By the water are not yet discomfited."
Fear and confusion's mingled miseries
   Constrained out of my mouth a "Yes" so low
   That to understand it there was need of eyes.   15
As the arbalast that snaps both string and bow,
   When to a too great tautness it is forced,
   And shooting hits the mark with feebler blow,
So under this so heavy charge I burst,
   Out of me letting gush the sighs and tears;   20
   And in its vent my voice failed as from thirst.
Wherefore she questioned: "Within those desires
   I stirred in thee, to make thee love the Good
   Beyond which nought is, whereto man aspires,
What moats or what strong chains athwart thy road   25
   Didst thou encounter, that of hope to pass
   Onward, thou needs must strip thee as of a load?
And what solace or profit in the face
   Of the others was displayed unto thine eye
   That thou before them up and down must pace?"   30
After the drawing of a bitter sigh
   Scarce had I voice an answer to essay,
   And lips with difficulty shaped reply.
Weeping I said: "Things of the passing day,

12. "The water": of Lethe.

Soon as your face no longer on me shone,   35
　　With their false pleasure turned my steps away."
And she: "If thou wert silent, nor didst own
　　What thou avowest, not less were record
　　Of thy fault made: by such a judge 'tis known.
But when the sinner's own mouth has outpoured   40
　　The accusation, in our court the wheel
　　Against the edge is turned back on the sword.
Howbeit, that now the shame thou carry still
　　For thine error, and at the Siren's plea
　　Another time thou be of stronger will,   45
Lay aside the seed of weeping; hark to me.
　　Hear how my buried body should have spurred
　　And on the opposite path have furthered thee.
Nature or art never to thee assured
　　Such pleasure as the fair limbs that did house   50
　　My spirit, and now are scattered and interred.
And if the highest pleasure failed thee thus
　　By my death, at such time what mortal thing
　　Ought to have drawn thee toward it amorous?
Truly oughtest thou at the first arrow's sting   55
　　Of those lures, to rise after me on high,
　　Who was no more made in such fashioning.
Nay, nor should girl or other vanity
　　Of such brief usage have thy wings down-weighed
　　To wait for other coming shafts to fly.   60
The young bird waiteth two or three indeed;
　　But in the eyes of the full-fledged in vain
　　The net is spread and the arrows vainly speed."
As boys that dumb with shamefastness remain,
　　Eyes to ground, listening to their faults rehearsed,   65
　　Knowing themselves in penitence and pain,
So stood I; and she said: "From what thou hear'st
　　If thou art grieving, lift thy beard and look,
　　And thou shalt by a greater grief be pierced."
With less resistance is a stubborn oak   70
　　Torn up by wind (whether 'twas ours that blew
　　Or wind that from Iarbas' land awoke)
Than at her bidding I my chin up-drew;
　　And when by "beard" she asked me for my face,
　　The venom in the meaning well I knew.   75

41–42. The sword of justice is blunted, i.e., tempered with mercy.

58. Is the "girl" to be taken literally, or does she symbolize some intellectual pursuit inconsistent with the spiritual ideal? The question remains open.

68. "Beard": chin.

72. "Iarbas" was king of Libya.

75. The implication that the beard is inconsistent with Dante's youthful vagaries.

And when to expose my features I could brace
  My spirit, I saw those primal Essences
  Reposing from their strewings in their place.
And mine eyes, hardly as yet assured of these,
  Were 'ware of Beatrice, turned toward that beast   80
  Which in two natures one sole person is.
Under her veil beyond the stream I wist
  That she surpassed her ancient self yet more
  Than when amongst us she surpassed the rest.
The nettle of penitence pricked me now so sore   85
  That, of all things, that which did most pervert
  To love of it, I had most hatred for.
The recognition gnawed so at my heart
  That I fell conquered, and what then of me
  Became, she knows who had devised the smart.   90
Then when my heart restored the faculty
  Of sense, the lady I had found alone
  I saw above me, and "Hold," she said, "hold me."
To the neck into the stream she had led me on
  And, drawing me behind her, went as light   95
  Over the water as a shuttle thrown.
When I was near the bank of blessed sight
  Asperges me my ears so sweetly graced
  I cannot recollect it, far less write.
The fair lady opened her arms, embraced   100
  My head, and plunged me underneath the flow,
  Where swallowing I must needs the water taste,
Then raised me and presented me, bathed so,
  Within the dancing of the beauteous Four;
  And each an arm about me came to throw.   105
"Here we are nymphs, in the sky stars: before
  Beatrice descended to the world, we were
  Ordained to be her handmaids evermore.
We'll lead thee to her eyes; but the Three there,
  Whose gaze is deeper, in the blissful light   110
  That is within, shall make thine own more clear."
Thus singing they began, and me then right
  Up to the Gryphon's breast with them they led
  Where Beatrice was standing opposite.
"See that thou spare not of thy gaze," they said.   115
  "We have set thee afore the emeralds to stand

---

77. "Primal Essences": the angels.
80. "That beast": the Gryphon.
92. "The lady": Matilda.
98. "Purge me": Ps. 51:7.
104. "The beauteous Four": the cardinal virtues.
109. "The Three": the theological virtues.
116. "The emeralds": the eyes of Beatrice.

Wherefrom for thee Love once his armoury fed."
Thousand desires, hotter than flame, constrained
   The gaze of mine eyes to the shining eyes
   Which on the Gryphon only fixed remained.   120
As in the glass the sun, not otherwise
   The two-fold creature had its mirroring
   Within them, now in one, now the other guise.
Think, Reader, if I marvelled at this thing,
   When I beheld it unchanged as at first   125
   Itself, and in its image altering.
While in deep astonishment immersed
   My happy soul was tasting of that food
   Which, itself sating, of itself makes thirst,
Showing themselves as if of loftiest blood   130
   In their demeanour, the other three came then
   Dancing to the angelic air they trod.
"Turn, Beatrice, turn thy sainted eyes again,"
   So were they singing, "to thy servant leal
   Who to see thee so many steps hath ta'en.   135
Of thy grace do us this grace, to unveil
   To him thy mouth, so that he may discern
   The second beauty which thou dost conceal."
O splendour of the living light eterne,
   Who is there that beneath Parnassus' shade   140
   Has grown pale or has drunk of that cistern
That would not seem to have his mind o'er-weighed
   Striving to paint thee as thou appeared'st where
   To figure thee, heaven's harmonies are made,
When thou didst unveil to the open air?   145

Paradise (*Paradiso*)

CANTO I

[The poet invokes the aid of Apollo in attempting the hardest part of his theme, the description of Paradise.

On earth, in Italy, it is evening; but at the summit of the Mount of Purgatory it is near noon about the time of the vernal equinox; the sun being in Aries, a propitious conjunction. Dante and Beatrice are suddenly transported to the sphere of fire, between the earth and the moon. Dante is so "transhumanized" that he is now able to hear the music of the spheres; but at first he is bewildered, not understanding, till Beatrice explains that he has left the earth behind. He is still puzzled to know how it is that he has risen, more swiftly

123. Now with its human, now with its divine, bearing—the two component parts of the nature of Christ.

138. "The second beauty" is the mouth, the first beauty being the eyes.

than air or fire, against the laws of gravitation. Beatrice tells him
that the instinct implanted in the soul is to rise, as fire rises, towards
heaven; this belongs to the order of the universe, in which each
part has its own function. Dante has been liberated from the dis-
tractions which, through man's possession of free will, sometimes
cause the soul to be diverted from its aim.]

The glory of Him who moveth all that is
    Pervades the universe, and glows more bright
    In the one region, and in another less.
In that heaven which partakes most of His light
    I have been, and have beheld such things as who   5
    Comes down thence has no wit nor power to write;
Such depth our understanding deepens to
    When it draws near unto its longing's home
    That memory cannot backward with it go.
Nevertheless what of the blest kingdom   10
    Could in my memory, for its treasure, stay
    Shall now the matter of my song become.
For the last labour, good Apollo, I pray,
    Make me so apt a vessel of thy power
    As is required for gift of thy loved bay.   15
One of Parnassus' peaks hath heretofore
    Sufficed me; both now shall I need forthwith
    For entering on the last arena-floor.
Enter into my bosom, and in-breathe
    Such force as filled thee to out-sing the strain   20
    Of Marsyas when thou didst his limbs unsheathe.
O divine power, if thou so far sustain,
    That I may show the image visibly
    Of the holy realm imprinted on my brain,
Thou'lt see me come to thy beloved tree   25
    And there the leaves upon my temples fit
    Which I shall earn both through the theme and thee.
So few times, Father, is there plucked of it
    For Caesar or for poet triumphing
    (Fault and reproach of human will and wit),   30
That in the joyous Delphic god must spring
    A joy new-born, when the Peneian frond
    With longing for itself doth any sting.
A small spark kindles a great flame beyond:
    Haply after me with better voice than mine   35

15. "Loved bay": Daphne, loved and
pursued by Apollo, was changed to a
laurel.
  21. "Marsyas": a satyr, who was defeated and then flayed by Apollo.
  25. "Thy beloved tree": the laurel.
  31–32. "The joyous Delphic god":
Apollo. "The Peneian frond": the laurel.

Such prayer shall plead, that Cirrha may respond.
The world's lamp rises upon men to shine
  By divers gates, but from that gate which makes
  Four circles with three crosses to conjoin,
With happier star joined, happier course it takes,   40
  And more to its own example can persuade,
  Moulding and stamping it, the mundane wax.
Almost this gate had morning yonder made
  And evening here; and there that hemisphere
  Was all white, and the other part in shade,   45
When, turned on her left side, I was aware
  Of Beatrice, fixing on the sun her eyes:
  Never on it so fixed was eagle's stare.
And as a second ray will always rise
  Where the first struck, and backward seek ascent,   50
  Like pilgrim hastening when he homeward hies,
So into my imagination went
  Through the eyes her gesture; and my own complied,
  And on the sun, past wont, my eyes were bent.
Much is permitted there which is denied   55
  Here to our faculties, thanks to the place
  Made for mankind to own, and there abide.
Not long I endured him, yet not so brief space
  But that I saw what sparkles round him shone
  Like molten ore fresh from the fierce furnace;   60
And, on a sudden, day seemed added on
  To day, as if He, who such things can do,
  Had glorified heaven with a second sun.
Beatrice was standing and held full in view
  The eternal wheels, and I fixed on her keen   65
  My eyes, that from above their gaze withdrew.
And at her aspect I became within
  As Glaucus after the herb's tasting, whence
  To the other sea-gods he was made akin.
The passing beyond bounds of human sense   70
  Words cannot tell; let then the examples sate
  Him for whom grace reserves the experience.

36. "Cirrha" stands for Delphi, Apollo's abode.

37–44. In these lines Dante describes the season. [The "gate" is the point of the horizon from which the sun rises on a particular day. On this day (Wednesday, April 13, 1300) it was still in the zodiacal sign Aries (March 21–April 21). On the day the sun enters Aries, three circles—the celestial equator, the ecliptic, and the colure of the equinoxes—intersect the horizon (itself a circle); hence, four circles and three crosses. It was believed that the sun's influence was most favorable when it was in Aries.—J. C. McG.]

44–45. Here Dante tells the hour: it was noon in Eden, midnight in Jerusalem.

56. "Thanks to the place": Eden.

65. "The eternal wheels": the revolving heavens.

68. The fisherman Glaucus, tasting of a certain herb, became a sea-god.

If I was only what thou didst create
    Last in me, O Love whose rule the heavens attest,
    Thus know'st, who with thy light didst lift my state.   75
When that the wheel which thou eternizest
    In longing, held me with the harmony
    Which thou attunest and distinguishest,
So much of heaven was fired, it seemed to me,
    With the sun's blaze that never river or rain   80
    Widened the waters to so great a sea.
The new sound and the great light made me fain
    With craving keener than had ever been
    Before in me, their cause to ascertain.
She then, who saw me as I myself within,   85
    My mind's disturbance eager to remit,
    Opened her lips before I could begin,
And spoke: "Thou makest thyself dense of wit
    With false fancy, so that thou dost not see
    What thou would'st see, wert thou but rid of it.   90
Thou'rt not on earth, as thou supposest thee:
    But lightning from its own place rushing out
    Ne'er sped as thou, who to thy home dost flee."
If I was stript of my first teasing doubt
    By the brief smiling little words, yet freed   95
    I was not, but enmeshed in a new thought.
And I replied: "I am released indeed
    From much amazement; yet am still amazed
    That those light bodies I transcend in speed."
She, sighing in pity, gave me as she gazed   100
    The look that by a mother is bestowed
    Upon her child in its delirium crazed,
And said: "All things, whatever their abode,
    Have order among themselves; this Form it is
    That makes the universe like unto God.   105
Here the high beings see the imprint of His
    Eternal power, which is the goal divine
    Whereto the rule aforesaid testifies.
In the order I speak of, all natures incline
    Either more near or less near to their source   110
    According as their diverse lots assign.
To diverse harbours thus they move perforce
    O'er the great ocean of being, and each one

73. Dante is not sure whether he took his body with him to Heaven, or left it behind.

77. The swift motion of the Primum Mobile, the outermost sphere of the material universe, is due to the eagerness of every one of its parts to come into contact with every part of God's own Heaven, the Empyrean.

93. "Thy home": the Empyrean.

110. "Their source": God.

With instinct given it to maintain its course.
This bears the fiery element to the moon;   115
   This makes the heart of mortal things to move;
   This knits the earth together into one.
Not only creatures that are empty of
   Intelligence this bow shoots towards the goal,
   But those that have both intellect and love.   120
The Providence, that rules this wondrous whole,
   With its own light makes the heaven still to stay
   Wherein whirls that which doth the swiftest roll.
And thither now upon the appointed way
   We are borne on by virtue of that cord still   125
   Which means a joyful mark, shoot what it may.
True it is that as the form oftentimes ill
   Accordeth with the intention of the art,
   The matter being slow to serve the will,
So aside sometimes may the creature start;   130
   For it has power, though on this course impelled,
   To swerve in purpose toward some other part
(And so the fire from cloud may be beheld
   To fall), if the first impulse of its flight
   To earth be wrested, by false pleasure held.   135
Thou should'st not marvel, if I esteem aright,
   More at thy rising than at streams we see
   Fall to the base down from a mountain's height;
Marvel it were if thou, from hindrance free,
   Had'st sat below, resolved there to remain,   140
   As stillness in live flame on earth would be."
Thereon toward heaven she turned her gaze again.

· · ·

CANTO III

[Dante becomes aware of faces appearing eager to speak to him.
At first he supposes them to be reflections (unlike Narcissus, who
supposed his reflection to be real). One of these spirits is Piccarda,
about whom Dante had asked her brother Forese in Purgatory
(Canto XXIV). She is with those placed in the sphere of the Moon
because of vows broken or imperfectly performed. Dante asks if
those who are in this lowest sphere ever crave for a more exalted
place in Paradise. She tells him that this is impossible; it is of the
essence of their bliss merely to fulfill the divine will: "In His will is
our peace." And she goes on to tell how she took the veil in the
Order of Saint Clare, but was forcibly taken from her convent (to

122–125. "The heaven": the Empyrean, within which the swift Primum Mobile revolves. "That cord": the bowstring of instinct.

131. "For it has power": the free will.

be married to a noble). Among these spirits is the Empress Constance, who also was torn from her convent and married to Henry VI, the second of the three "whirlwinds" from Suabia (line 119); the first being Frederick Barbarossa, and the third Frederick II; all these emperors were men of tempestuous energy.]

That Sun which fired my bosom of old with love
    Had thus bared for me in beauty the aspect sweet
    Of truth, expert to prove as to disprove;
And I, to avow me of all error quit,
    Confident and assured, lifted my head   5
    More upright, in such measure as was fit.
But now appeared a sight that riveted
    Me to itself with such compulsion keen
    That my confession from my memory fled.
As from transparent glasses polished clean,   10
    Or water shining smooth up to its rim,
    Yet not so that the bottom is unseen,
Our faces' lineaments return so dim
    That pearl upon white forehead not more slow
    Would on our pupils its pale image limn;   15
So I beheld faces that seemed aglow
    To speak, and fell into the counter-snare
    From what made love 'twixt man and pool to grow.
No sooner had I marked those faces there,
    Than, thinking them reflections, with swift eyes   20
    I turned about to see of whom they were,
And saw nothing: again, in my surprise,
    I turned straight to the light of my sweet Guide,
    Who smiling, burned within her sainted eyes.
"Marvel not at my smiling," she replied,   25
    "To contemplate thy childlike thought revealed
    Which cannot yet its foot to truth confide,
But moves thee, as ever, on emptiness to build.
    True substances are these thine eyes perceive,
    Remitted here for vows not all fulfilled.   30
Speak with them therefore, hearken and believe,
    For the true light which is their happiness
    Lets them not swerve, but to it they must cleave."
And I to the shade that seemed most near to press
    For converse, turned me and began, as one   35
    Who is overwrought through longing in excess:
"O spirit made for bliss, who from the sun
    Of life eternal feelest the sweet ray

1. "That Sun": Beatrice.   18. "Man": Narcissus.

Which, save 'tis tasted, is conceived by none,
It will be gracious to me, if I may   40
   Be gladdened with thy name and all your fate."
   And she, with laughing eyes and no delay:
"Our charity no more locks up the gate
   Against a just wish than that Charity
   Which would have all its court in like estate.   45
On earth I was a Virgin Sister: see
   What memory yields thee, and my being now
   More beautiful will hide me not from thee,
But that I am Piccarda thou wilt know,
   Who with these other blessed ones placed here   50
   Am blessed in the sphere that moves most slow;
For our desires, which kindle and flame clear
   Only in the pleasure of the Holy Ghost,
   To what he appointeth joyfully adhere;
And this which seems to thee so lowly a post   55
   Is given to us because the vows we made
   Were broken, or complete observance lost."
Then I to her: "Something divinely glad
   Shines in your marvellous aspect, to replace
   In you the old conceptions that I had;   60
I was slow therefore to recall thy face:
   But what thou tell'st me helpeth now to clear
   My sight, and thee more easily to retrace.
But tell me: you that are made happy here,
   Do ye to a more exalted place aspire,   65
   To see more, or to make yourselves more dear?"
She smiled a little, and with her smiled that choir
   Of spirits; then so joyous she replied
   That she appeared to burn in love's first fire:
"Brother, the virtue of love hath pacified   70
   Our will; we long for what we have alone,
   Nor any craving stirs in us beside.
If we desired to reach a loftier zone,
   Our longings would be all out of accord
   With His will who disposeth here His own.   75
For that, these circles, thou wilt see, afford
   No room, if love be our whole being's root
   And thou ponder the meaning of that word.
Nay, 'tis of the essence of our blessed lot
   In the divine will to be cloistered still   80
   Through which our own wills into one are wrought,

44. "That Charity": of God.   company; *thy* refers to Piccarda alone.
[59–61. *Your* refers to the whole   —J. C. McG.]

As we from step to step our stations fill
    Throughout this realm, to all the realm 'tis bliss
    As to its King, who wills us into His will;
And in His will is perfected our peace.   85
    It is the sea whereunto moveth all
    That it creates and nature makes increase."
Then saw I how each heaven for every soul
    Is paradise, though from the Supreme Good
    The dews of grace not in one measure fall.   90
But as may hap, when sated with one food
    Still for another we have appetite,
    We ask for this, and that with thanks elude,
Such words and gesture used I that I might
    Learn from her what that web was where she plied   95
    The shuttle and yet drew not the head outright.
"Perfect life and high merit have enskied
    A Lady above," she said, "whose rule they take
    In your world who in robe and veil abide,
That they till death may, sleeping and awake,   100
    Be with that Spouse who giveth welcome free
    To all vows love may for His pleasure make.
To follow her, a young girl, did I flee
    The world and, closed within her habit, vowed
    Myself to the pathway of her company.   105
Afterwards men, used to evil more than good,
    Tore me away, out of the sweet cloister;
    And God knows then what way of life I trod.
This other splendour whom thou see'st appear
    To thee on my right side, who, glowing pale,   110
    Kindles with all the radiance of our sphere,
Can of herself tell also the same tale.
    She was a Sister; from her head they tore
    Likewise the shadow of the sacred veil.
She was turned back into the world once more   115
    Against her will, against good usage too;
    Yet still upon her heart the veil she wore.
This is the light of the great Constance, who
    From Suabia's second whirlwind was to bring
    To birth the third Power, and the last ye knew."   120
Thus spoke she to me, and then began to sing
    Ave Maria, and singing disappeared,
    As through deep water sinks a heavy thing.
My sight, which followed far as it was powered,

98. "A Lady above": St. Clare, the friend of St. Francis; she founded the order that bears her name.

106. "Men": her brother Corso Donati and his followers.

When it had lost her, turned and straightway shot   125
    To the other mark, more ardently desired,
And Beatrice, only Beatrice, it sought.
    But she upon my look was flaming so
    That at the first my sight endured it not;
And this made me for questioning more slow.   130

. . .

CANTO XXXI

[Further description of the Rose of Paradise, into and out of which the angels flit like bees about a flower. Dante, having taken in its general form, turns to Beatrice to inquire more particularly about it. But Beatrice has disappeared, and in her place is an old man, who proves to be St. Bernard, and who points out Beatrice, now in her appointed seat above. Next, he bids Dante contemplate the beauty of the Virgin.]

In form, then, of a radiant white rose
    That sacred soldiery before mine eyes
    Appeared, which in His blood Christ made His spouse.
But the other host which seëth and, as it flies,
    Singeth His glory who enamours it   5
    And the goodness which its greatness magnifies,
Like bees, which deep into the flowers retreat
    One while, and at another winging come
    Back thither where their toil is turned to sweet,
Descended into the great flower, a-bloom   10
    With petal on petal, and re-ascended thence
    To where its love forever hath its home.
Their faces all were as a flame intense,
    Their wings of gold, the rest so pure a white
    That never snow could dazzle so the sense.   15
Into the flower descending from the height
    Through rank on rank they breathed the peace, the glow,
    They gathered as they fanned their sides in flight.
And, spite of the interposing to and fro
    Of such a throng 'twixt high heaven and the flower,   20
    Vision and splendour none had to forgo;
For the divine light pierceth with such power
    The world, in measure of its complement
    Of worth, that naught against it may endure.
This realm of unimperilled ravishment   25
    With spirits thronged from near times and from far

2–4. "That sacred soldiery": the Redeemed.—"The other host": the angels.

Had look and love all on the one mark bent.
O triple Light, which in a single star
   Shining on them their joy can so expand,
   Look down upon this storm wherein we are!   30
If the barbarian, coming from such land
   As every day by wheeling Helice
   And her belovèd son with her, is spanned,
Seeing Rome and her stupendous works,—if he
   Was dazed, in that age when the Lateran   35
   Rose, builded to outsoar mortality,
I, who was come to the divine from man,
   To the eternal out of time, and from
   Florence unto a people just and sane,
How dazed past measure must I needs become!   40
   Between this and my joy I found it good,
   Truly, to hear naught and myself be dumb.
And as the pilgrim quickens in his blood
   Within the temple of his vow at gaze,
   Already in hope to re-tell how it stood,   45
So traversing the light of living rays
   My eyes along the ranks, now up I led,
   Now down, and now wandered in circling ways.
I saw faces, such as to love persuade,
   Adorned by their own smile and Other's light   50
   And gestures that all dignity displayed.
The general form of Paradise my sight
   Had apprehended in its ambience,
   But upon no part had it rested quite;
I turned then with a wish re-kindled thence   55
   To ask my Lady and to be satisfied
   Concerning things which held me in suspense.
One thing I thought, another one replied:
   I thought to have seen Beatrice, and behold!
   An elder, robed like to those glorified.   60
His eyes and cheeks of benign gladness told,
   And in his bearing was a kindliness
   Such as befits a father tender-souled:
"Where is she?" I cried on a sudden in my distress.
   "To end thy longing, Beatrice was stirred,"   65.
   He answered then, "to bring me from my place.
Her shalt thou see, if to the circle third

31–33. "Such land": the North.
"Helice" and "her . . . son" Arcas
are the Great and the Little Bear.

35. "The Lateran": the old Papal
palace in Rome.

60. "An elder": St. Bernard, a
great mystic of the twelfth century,
famous for his devotion to the Blessed
Virgin.

67. The first circle is that of Mary,

From the highest rank thine eyes thou wilt up-raise,
   There on the throne whereto she hath been preferred."
Without reply I lifted up my gaze   70
   And saw her making for herself a crown
   Of the reflection from the eternal rays.
From the highest sky which rolls the thunder down
   No mortal eye is stationed so remote,
   Though in the deepest of the seas it drown,   75
As then from Beatrice was my sight; but naught
   It was to me; for without any veil
   Her image down to me undimmed was brought.
"O Lady, in whom my hopes all prosper well,
   And who for my salvation didst endure   80
   To leave the printing of thy feet in Hell,
Of all that I have seen, now and before,
   By virtue of what thy might and goodness gave,
   I recognize the grace and sovereign power.
Thou hast drawn me up to freedom from a slave   85
   By all those paths, all those ways known to thee
   Through which thou had'st such potency to save.
Continue thy magnificence in me,
   So that my soul, which thou hast healed of scar,
   May please thy sight when from the body free."   90
So did I pray; and she, removed so far
   As she appeared, looked on me smiling-faced;
   Then to the eternal fountain turned her there.
Whereon the holy Elder: "That thou may'st
   Consummate this thy journey, whereunto   95
   Prayer and a holy love made me to haste,
Fly with thine eyes this heavenly garden through!
   Gazing on it shall better qualify
   Thy vision, the light upward to pursue.
The Queen of Heaven, for whom continually   100
   I burn with love, will grant us every grace
   Since Bernard, her own faithful one, am I."
Like one, some Croat perhaps, who comes to gaze
   On our Veronica with eyes devout,
   Nor states the inveterate hunger that he has,   105
So long as it is shown, but says in thought,
   "My Lord Christ Jesus, very God, is this
   Indeed Thy likeness in such fashion wrought?"

the second that of Eve, the third that
of Rachel, beside whom Beatrice sits.
  96. The "prayer and a holy love" are
Beatrice's.

104. The "Veronica" is the true image of the Savior, left on a kerchief. It was shown at St. Peter's in Rome.

Such was I, gazing on the impassioned bliss
  Of love in him who even in this world's woe   110
  By contemplation tasted of that peace.
"Child of Grace," he began, "thou wilt not know
  This joyous being in its felicity
  If thine eyes rest but on the base below.
Look on the farthest circles thou can'st see,   115
  Till thou perceive enthroned the Queen, to whom
  This realm devoteth its whole fealty."
I raised my eyes; and as in morning bloom
  The horizon's eastern part becometh bright
  And that where the sun sinks is overcome,   120
So with my eyes climbing a mountain's height,
  As from a valley, I saw on the utmost verge
  What outshone all else fronting me in light.
As that point where the car is to emerge,
  Which Phaëthon drove ill, glows fieriest   125
  And softens down its flame on either marge,
So did that oriflamme of peace attest
  The midmost glory, and on either side
  In equal measure did its rays arrest.
And at that mid-point, with wings opened wide,   130
  A myriad angels moved in festive play,
  In brilliance and in art diversified.
There, smiling upon dance and roundelay,
  I saw a Beauty, that was happiness
  In the eyes of all the other saints' array.   135
And if in speaking I had wealth not less
  Than in imagining, I would not dare
  To attempt the least part of her loveliness.
When of my fixt look Bernard was aware,
  So fastened on his own devotion's flame,   140
  He turned his eyes with so much love to her
That mine more ardent and absorbed became.

CANTO XXXII

[Bernard explains the conformation of the Celestial Rose. It is
divided down the middle, and across; on one side are male, on the
other female, saints. Below the horizontal division are the souls
of beatified children. That Dante may be vouchsafed a vision of
Deity itself, Bernard makes supplication to the Virgin, and bids
Dante accompany him in his prayer.]

111. St. Bernard in his meditations
had a foretaste of the peace of Heaven.
124. "The car": of the sun.

127. "That oriflamme," i.e., golden
pennant, is the streak of light on Mary's
side.
141. "To her": on Mary.

Rapt in love's bliss, that contemplative saint
  Nevertheless took up the instructor's part,
  Uttering these sacred words with no constraint:
"The wound that Mary closed, and soothed its smart,
  She, who so beautiful sits at her feet,   5
  Opened, and yet more deeply pressed the dart.
In the order making the third rank complete
  Rachel thou can'st distinguish next below
  With Beatrice in her appointed seat.
Sara, Rebecca, Judith, and her too,   10
  Ancestress of the singer, whose cry rose
  Miserere mei for his fault and rue,—
These thou beholdest tier by tier disclose,
  Descending, as I name them each by name,
  From petal after petal down the Rose.   15
And from the seventh grade downward, following them,
  Even as above them, Hebrew women bide,
  Parting the tresses on the Rose's stem;
Because, according as faith made confide
  In Christ, these serve as for a party-wall   20
  At which the stairs of sanctity divide.
On this side, where the flower is filled in all
  Its numbered petals, sit in order they
  Who waiting on Christ Coming heard His call;
On the other side, where certain gaps betray   25
  Seats empty, in semicircle, thou look'st on
  Such as in Christ Come had their only stay.
And as on the one side the glorious throne
  Of the Lady of Heaven and the other thrones as well
  Below it make partition, so great John   30
Sits over against her, ever there to dwell,
  Who, ever holy, endured the desert's fare,
  And martyrdom, and then two years in Hell.
Beneath him, chosen to mark the boundary there
  Francis and Benedict and Augustine shine   35
  And others, round by round, down even to here.
Now marvel at the deep foresight divine!
  For the faith's either aspect, equal made,
  Shall consummate this garden's full design.
And know that downward from the midmost grade   40

4-5. "The wound": of original sin. "She": Eve.

11. "Ancestress": Ruth; "the singer": David.

12. *Miserere mei*: "Have mercy upon me."

19. On one side of the partition are the Hebrews (line 24), on the other the Christians (line 27).

[30. *John:* John the Baptist—J. C. McG.]

33. "In Hell": the Limbus.

38. "Either aspect": the Old Church and the New.

Which runneth the two companies betwixt
  They sit there by no merit that they had
But by another's, on conditions fixt;
  For these are spirits that were all released
  Ere they had made a true choice, unperplext.   45
And by their faces this is manifest
  And also by their voices' childish note,
  If looking heedfully thou listenest.
Now thou art doubting, and doubt makes thee mute;
  But for thy sake will I the coil undo   50
  Wherein thou art bound by subtlety of thought.
Within this kingdom's compass thou must know
  Chance hath no single point's determining,
  No more than thirst, or hunger, or sorrow;
Because eternal law, in everything   55
  Thou see'st, it stablisht with such close consent
  As close upon the finger fits the ring:
Wherefore these children, hastened as they went
  Into the true life, are not without cause
  Within themselves more and less excellent.   60
The King, through whom this realm hath its repose
  In so great love and such felicities,
  That no rash will on further venture goes,
Creating all minds in His own eyes' bliss,
  At His own pleasure dowers them with grace   65
  Diversely; on this point let the fact suffice.
This is made known to you, clear and express,
  In Holy Writ, by those twins who, ere birth,
  In the womb wrestled in their wrathfulness.
According to the colour figuring forth   70
  In the hair such grace, the sublime Light must needs
  Chaplet their heads according to their worth.
Wherefore without reward for any deeds
  Their places are to different ranks assigned,
  Differing only in what from gift proceeds.   75
In the early ages parents' faith, combined
  With innocence, sufficed and nothing more
  To wing them upward and salvation find.
The first age being completed, other power
  Was needed for the innocent males to attain   80
  By virtue of circumcision, Heaven's door.

43–45. "But by another's": one's parents. "Released": from the flesh. These are the spirits of children who died before the age of moral responsibility.

49. Dante is wondering why some have higher seats than others. He learns that the degree of beatitude is determined by predestination.

68. "Those twins": Jacob and Esau

70–72. Our halo in Heaven is proportionate to the grace bestowed on us at birth.

But when the time of grace began its reign,
  Having not perfect baptism of Christ,
  Such innocence below there must remain.
Look now upon the face most like to Christ!　　85
  For only its radiance can so fortify
  Thy gaze as fitteth for beholding Christ."
I saw rain over her such ecstasy
  Brought in the sacred minds that with it glowed—
  Created through the heavenly height to fly—　　90
That all I had seen on all the way I had trod
  Held me not in such breathless marvelling
  Nor so great likeness vouched to me of God.
And that Love which at its first down-coming
  Sang to her: "Hail, O Mary, full of grace!"　　95
  Now over her extended either wing.
The divine song echoed through all the space,
  Answered from all sides of the Blessed Court
  So that serener joy filled every face.
"O holy father, who for my comfort　　100
  Hast deigned thy sweet allotted place to quit,
  With me in this low station to consort,
What is that angel who with such delight
  Looketh our Queen in the eyes, lost in love there
  So that he seems one flame of living light?"　　105
To his instruction thus did I repair
  Once more, who drew from Mary increasingly
  Beauty, as from the sun the morning star.
"Blitheness and buoyant confidence," said he,
  "As much as angel or a soul may own,　　110
  Are all in him; so would we have it be.
For he it is who brought the palm-leaf down
  To Mary, when the burden of our woe
  In flesh was undertaken by God's Son.
Now with thine eyes come with me, as I go　　115
  Discoursing, and the great patricians note
  Of the empire that the just and pious know.
Those two above, most blessed in their lot
  By being nearest to the august Empress,
  Are of our rose as 'twere the double root.　　120
He on the left who has the nearest place
  Is that father, through whose presumptuous taste
  The human tribe tasteth such bitterness.
That ancient Father of Holy Church thou may'st

See on the right, to whom Christ gave in trust   125
   The keys of this, of all flowers loveliest.
And he who, ere he died, saw all the host
   Of grievous days prepared for that fair spouse
   Won by the nails and by the lance's thrust,
Sits by him; by the other, see repose   130
   That leader under whom was fed by manna
   The ungrateful people, fickle and mutinous.
And, sitting over against Peter, Anna
   Looks on her daughter, so content of soul,
   She moveth not her eyes, singing Hosanna;   135
And opposite the greatest father of all
   Sits Lucy, who stirred the lady of thy troth,
   When, eyes down, thou wert running to thy fall.
But stop we here as the good tailor doth
   (Since of thy sleeping vision the time flies),   140
   Cutting the gown according to the cloth;
And turn we to the Primal Love our eyes,
   So that, still gazing toward Him, thou may'st pierce
   Into His splendour, far as in thee lies.
Yet, lest it happen that thou should'st reverse,   145
   Thinking to advance, the motion of thy wing,
   A prayer for grace needs must we now rehearse,
Grace from her bounty who can the succour bring.
   And do thou with thy feeling follow on
   My words, that close to them thy heart may cling."   150
And he began this holy orison.

CANTO XXXIII

[The prayer of St. Bernard to the Virgin Mary. The prayer is
granted; and then Dante prays to God that some trace of the dazzling glimpse of the divine mystery of Trinity in Unity may be
communicated to men through his verse.]

"Maiden and Mother, daughter of thine own Son,
   Beyond all creatures lowly and lifted high,
   Of the Eternal Design the corner-stone!
Thou art she who did man's substance glorify
   So that its own Maker did not eschew   5

127–129. St. John, the author of
the Apocalypse. "Spouse": the Church.
"The nails and . . . the lance": of
Christ's Passion.
   130–131. "By him": Peter. "By the
other": Adam. "That leader": Moses.
   133. "Anna": St. Anna, mother of
Mary.

137. [*Lucy:* St. Lucia; see Canto II
of the *Inferno.*—J. C. McG.] "The lady
of thy troth": Beatrice.
   148. "From her bounty": the Blessed Virgin's.
   1. A great part of this beautiful
prayer was copied by Chaucer in the
Second Nun's Tale, 29–84.

Even to be made of its mortality.
   Within thy womb the Love was kindled new
   By generation of whose warmth supreme
   This flower to bloom in peace eternal grew.
Here thou to us art the full noonday beam   10
   Of love revealed: below, to mortal sight,
   Hope, that forever springs in living stream.
Lady, thou art so great and hast such might
   That whoso crave grace, nor to thee repair,
   Their longing even without wing seeketh flight.   15
Thy charity doth not only him up-bear
   Who prays, but in thy bounty's large excess
   Thou oftentimes dost even forerun the prayer.
In thee is pity, in thee is tenderness,
   In thee magnificence, in thee the sum   20
   Of all that in creation most can bless.
Now he that from the deepest pit hath come
   Of the universe, and seen, each after each,
   The spirits as they live and have their home,
He of thy grace so much power doth beseech   25
   That he be enabled to uplift even higher
   His eyes, and to the Final Goodness reach.
And I who never burned with more desire
   For my own vision than for his, persist
   In prayer to thee—my prayers go forth in choir,   30
May they not fail!—that thou disperse all mist
   Of his mortality with prayers of thine,
   Till joy be his of that supreme acquist.
Also I implore thee, Queen who can'st incline
   All to thy will, let his affections stand   35
   Whole and pure after vision so divine.
The throbbings of the heart do thou command!
   See, Beatrice with how many of the blest,
   To second this my prayer, lays hand to hand."
Those eyes, of God loved and revered, confest,   40
   Still fixt upon him speaking, the delight
   She hath in prayer from a devoted breast.
Then were they lifted to the eternal light,
   Whereinto it may not be believed that eye
   So clear in any creature sendeth sight.   45
And I, who to the goal was drawing nigh
   Of all my longings, now, as it behoved,

9. "This flower": the Rose of the   22. "He that . . .": Dante.
Blessed.

Felt the ardour of them in contentment die.
Bernard signed, smiling, as a hand he moved,
  That I should lift my gaze up; but I knew   50
  Myself already such as he approved,
Because my sight, becoming purged anew,
  Deeper and deeper entered through the beam
  Of sublime light, which in itself is true.
Thenceforth my vision was too great for theme   55
  Of our speech, that such glory overbears,
  And memory faints at such assault extreme.
As he who dreams sees, and when disappears
  The dream, the passion of its print remains,
  And naught else to the memory adheres,   60
Even such am I; for almost wholly wanes
  My vision now, yet still the drops I feel
  Of sweetness it distilled into my veins.
Even so the sunbeam doth the snow unseal;
  So was the Sibyl's saying lost inert   65
  Upon the thin leaves for the wind to steal.
O supreme Light, who dost thy glory assert
  High over our imagining, lend again
  Memory a little of what to me thou wert.
Vouchsafe unto my tongue such power to attain   70
  That but one sparkle it may leave behind
  Of thy magnificence to future men.
For by returning somewhat to my mind
  And by a little sounding in this verse
  More of thy triumph shall be thence divined.   75
So keenly did the living radiance pierce
  Into me, that I think I had been undone
  Had mine eyes faltered, from the light averse.
And I recall that with the more passion
  I clove to it, till my gaze, thereat illumed,   80
  With the Infinite Good tasted communion.
O Grace abounding, whereby I presumed
  To fix upon the eternal light my gaze
  So deep, that in it I my sight consumed!
I beheld leaves within the unfathomed blaze   85
  Into one volume bound by love, the same
  That the universe holds scattered through its maze.
Substance and accidents, and their modes, became
  As if together fused, all in such wise

---

65. The Cumean "Sibyl" was accustomed to write her prophecies on loose tree-leaves.
84. I became blind to all else.

86. God is the Book of the Universe.
89. God, containing all things, is a perfect unit.

That what I speak of is one simple flame.   90
Verily I think I saw with mine own eyes
 The form that knits the whole world, since I taste,
 In telling of it, more abounding bliss.
One moment more oblivion has amassed
 Than five-and-twenty centuries have wrought   95
 Since Argo's shadow o'er wondering Neptune passed.
Thus did my mind in the suspense of thought
 Gaze fixedly, all immovable and intent,
 And ever fresh fire from its gazing caught.
Man at that light becometh so content   100
 That to choose other sight and this reject,
 It is impossible that he consent,
Because the good which is the will's object
 Dwells wholly in it, and that within its pale
 Is perfect, which, without, hath some defect.   105
Even for my remembrance now must fail
 My words, and less than could an infant's store
 Of speech, who at the pap yet sucks, avail;
Not that within the living light was more
 Than one sole aspect of divine essence,   110
 Being still forever as it was before,
But the one semblance, seen with more intense
 A faculty, even as over me there stole
 Change, was itself transfigured to my sense.
Within the clear profound Light's aureole   115
 Three circles from its substance now appeared,
 Of three colours, and each an equal whole.
One its reflection on the next conferred
 As rainbow upon rainbow, and the two
 Breathed equally the fire that was the third.   120
To my conception O how frail and few
 My words! and that, to what I looked upon,
 Is such that "little" is more than is its due.
O Light Eternal, who in thyself alone
 Dwell'st and thyself know'st, and self-understood, 125
 Self-understanding, smilest on thine own!
That circle which, as I conceived it, glowed
 Within thee like reflection of a flame,
 Being by mine eyes a little longer wooed,

[94–96. One moment caused Dante to forget more of his vision than Neptune, god of the sea, has forgotten—in the 2500 years that have elapsed since the first sea voyage—of his initial shock.—J. C. McG.]

115. The threefold oneness is disclosed by the symbol of three mysterious rings occupying exactly the same place.

120. "The third": the Holy Ghost, who emanates equally from Father and Son.

Deep in itself, with colour still the same,   130
   Seemed with our human effigy to fill,
   Wherefore absorbed in it my sight became.
As the geometer who bends all his will
   To measure the circle, and howsoe'er he try
   Fails, for the principle escapes him still,   135
Such at this mystery new-disclosed was I,
   Fain to understand how the image doth alight
   Upon the circle, and with its form comply.
But these my wings were fledged not for that flight,
   Save that my mind a sudden glory assailed   140
   And its wish came revealed to it in that light.
To the high imagination force now failed;
   But like to a wheel whose circling nothing jars
   Already on my desire and will prevailed
The Love that moves the sun and the other stars.   145

134. The problem is the squaring of the circle.
143–145. Circular motion symbolizes faultless activity. Dante's individual will is merged in the World-Will of the Creator.

GIOVANNI BOCCACCIO

(1313–1375)

The Decameron[*]

The First Day

In the year 1348 after the fruitful incarnation of the Son of God, that most beautiful of Italian cities, noble Florence, was attacked by deadly plague. It started in the East either through the influence of the heavenly bodies or because God's just anger with our wicked deeds sent it as a punishment to mortal men; and in a few years killed an innumerable quantity of people. Ceaselessly passing from place to place, it extended its miserable length over the West. Against this plague all human wisdom and foresight were vain. Orders had been given to cleanse the city of filth, the entry of any sick person was forbidden, much advice was given for keeping healthy; at the same time humble supplications were made to God by pious persons in processions and otherwise. And yet, in the beginning of the spring of the year mentioned, its horrible results began to appear, and in a miraculous manner. The symptoms were not the same as in the East, where a gush of blood from the nose was the plain sign of inevitable death; but it began both in men

* Completed about 1353. The selections reprinted here are from the translation by Richard Aldington, in *The Decameron of Giovanni Boccaccio*, copyright, 1930, by Garden City Publishing Company, Inc. Reprinted by permission.

and women with certain swellings in the groin or under the arm-pit. They grew to the size of a small apple or an egg, more or less, and were vulgarly called tumours. In a short space of time these tumours spread from the two parts named all over the body. Soon after this the symptoms changed and black or purple spots appeared on the arms or thighs or any other part of the body, sometimes a few large ones, sometimes many little ones. These spots were a certain sign of death, just as the original tumour had been and still remained.

No doctor's advice, no medicine could overcome or alleviate this disease. An enormous number of ignorant men and women set up as doctors in addition to those who were trained. Either the disease was such that no treatment was possible or the doctors were so ignorant that they did not know what caused it, and consequently could not administer the proper remedy. In any case very few recovered; most people died within about three days of the appearance of the tumours described above, most of them without any fever or any other symptoms.

The violence of this disease was such that the sick communicated it to the healthy who came near them, just as fire catches anything dry or oily near it. And it even went further. To speak to or go near the sick brought infection and a common death to the living; and moreover, to touch the clothes or anything else the sick had touched or worn gave the disease to the person touching.

What I am about to tell now is a marvelous thing to hear; and if I and others had not seen it with our own eyes I would not dare to write it, however much I was willing to believe and whatever the good faith of the person from whom I heard it. So violent was the malignancy of this plague that it was communicated, not only from one man to another, but from the garments of a sick or dead man to animals of another species, which caught the disease in that way and very quickly died of it. One day among other occasions I saw with my own eyes (as I said just now) the rags left lying in the street of a poor man who had died of the plague; two pigs came along and, as their habit is, turned the clothes over with their snouts and then munched at them, with the result that they both fell dead almost at once on the rags, as if they had been poisoned.

From these and similar or greater occurrences, such fear and fanciful notions took possession of the living that almost all of them adopted the same cruel policy, which was entirely to avoid the sick and everything belonging to them. By so doing, each one thought he would secure his own safety.

Some thought that moderate living and the avoidance of super-fluity would preserve them from the epidemic. They formed small communities, living entirely separate from everybody else. They shut themselves up in houses where there were no sick, eating the finest food and drinking the best wine very temperately, avoiding all excess, allowing no news or discussion of death and sickness, and passing the time in music and suchlike pleasures. Others thought just the opposite. They thought the sure cure for the plague was to drink and to be merry, to go about singing and amusing themselves, satisfying every appetite they could, laughing and jesting at what happened. They put their words into practise, spent day and night going from tavern to tavern, drinking immoderately, or went into other people's houses, doing only those things which pleased them. This they could easily do because everyone felt doomed and had abandoned his property, so that most houses became common property and any stranger who went in made use of them as if he had owned them. And with all this bestial behavior, they avoided the sick as much as possible.

In this suffering and misery of our city, the authority of human and divine laws almost disappeared, for, like other men, the ministers and the executors of the laws were all dead or sick or shut up with their families, so that no duties were carried out. Every man was therefore able to do as he pleased.

Many others adopted a course of life midway between the two just described. They did not restrict their victuals so much as the former, nor allow themselves to be drunken or dissolute like the latter, but satisfied their appetites moderately. They did not shut themselves up, but went about, carrying flowers or scented herbs or perfumes in their hands, in the belief that it was an excellent thing to comfort the brain with such odours; for the whole air was infected with the smell of dead bodies, of sick persons and medicines.

Others again held a still more cruel opinion, which they thought would keep them safe. They said that the only medicine against the plague-stricken was to go right away from them. Men and women, convinced of this and caring about nothing but themselves, abandoned their own city, their own houses, their dwellings, their relatives, their property, and went abroad or at least to the country round Florence, as if God's wrath in punishing men's wickedness with this plague would not follow them but strike only those who remained within the walls of the city, or as if they thought nobody in the city would remain alive and that its last hour had come.

Not everyone who adopted any of these various opinions died, nor did all escape. Some when they were still healthy had set the example of avoiding the sick, and, falling ill themselves, died untended.

One citizen avoided another, hardly any neighbour troubled about others, relatives never or hardly ever visited each other. Moreover, such terror was struck into the hearts of men and women by this calamity, that brother abandoned brother, and the uncle his nephew, and the sister her brother, and very often the wife her husband. What is even worse and nearly incredible is that fathers and mothers refused to see and tend their children, as if they had not been theirs.

Thus, a multitude of sick men and women were left without any care except from the charity of friends (but these were few), or the greed of servants, though not many of these could be had even for high wages. Moreover, most of them were coarse-minded men and women, who did little more than bring the sick what they asked for or watch over them when they were dying. And very often these servants lost their lives and their earnings. Since the sick were thus abandoned by neighbours, relatives and friends, while servants were scarce, a habit sprang up which had never been heard of before. Beautiful and noble women, when they fell sick, did not scruple to take a young or old manservant, whoever he might be, and with no sort of shame, expose every part of their bodies to these men as if they had been women, for they were compelled by the necessity of their sickness to do so. This, perhaps, was a cause of looser morals in those women who survived.

In this way many people died who might have been saved if they had been looked after. Owing to the lack of attendants for the sick and the violence of the plague, such a multitude of people in the city died day and night that it was stupefying to hear of, let alone to see. From sheer necessity, then, several ancient customs were quite altered among the survivors.

The custom had been (as we still see it today), that women relatives and neighbours should gather at the house of the deceased, and there lament with the family. At the same time the men would gather at the door with the male neighbours and other citizens. Then came the clergy, few or many according to the dead person's rank; the coffin was placed on the shoulders of his friends and carried with funeral pomp of lighted candles and dirges to the church which the deceased had chosen before dying. But as the fury of the plague increased, this custom wholly or nearly disappeared, and new customs arose. Thus, people died, not only without having a number of women near them, but without a single witness. Very few indeed were honoured with the piteous laments and bitter tears of their relatives, who, on the contrary, spent their time in mirth, feasting and jesting. Even the women abandoned womanly pity and adopted this custom for their own safety. Few were they whose bodies were accompanied to church by more than ten or a dozen neighbours. Nor were these grave and honourable citizens but grave-diggers from the lowest of the people who got themselves called sextons, and performed the task for money. They took up the bier and hurried it off, not to the church chosen by the deceased but to the church nearest, preceded by four or six of the clergy with few candles and often none at all. With the aid of the grave-diggers, the clergy huddled the bodies away in any grave they could find, without giving themselves the trouble of a long or solemn burial service.

The plight of the lower and most of the middle classes was even more pitiful to behold. Most of them remained in their houses, either through poverty or in hopes of safety, and fell sick by thousands. Since they received no care and attention, almost all of them died. Many ended their lives in the streets both at night and during the day; and many others who died in their houses were only known to be dead because the neighbours smelled their decaying bodies. Dead bodies filled every corner. Most of them were treated in the same manner by the survivors, who were more concerned to get rid of their rotting bodies than moved by charity towards the dead. With the aid of porters, if they could get them, they carried the bodies out of the houses and laid them at the doors, where every morning quantities of the dead might be seen. They then were laid on biers, or, as these were often lacking, on tables.

Often a single bier carried two or three bodies, and it happened frequently that a husband and wife, two or three brothers, or father and son were taken off on the same bier. It frequently happened that two priests, each carrying a cross, would go out followed by three or four biers carried by porters; and where the priests thought there was one person to bury, there would be six or eight, and often, even more. Nor were these dead honoured by tears and lighted candles and mourners, for things had reached such a pass that people cared no more for dead men than we care for dead goats. Thus it plainly appeared that what the wise had not learned to endure with patience through the few calamities of ordinary life, became a matter of indifference even to the most ignorant people through the greatness of this misfortune.

Such was the multitude of corpses brought to the churches every day and almost every hour that there was not enough consecrated ground to give them burial, especially since they wanted to bury each person in the family grave, according to the old custom. Although the cemeteries were full they were forced to dig huge trenches, where they buried the bodies by hundreds. Here they stowed them away like bales in the hold of a ship and covered them with a little earth, until the whole trench was full.

Not to pry any further into all the details of the miseries which afflicted our city, I shall add that the surrounding country was spared nothing of what befell Florence. The villages on a smaller scale were like the city; in the fields and isolated farms the poor wretched peasants and their families were without doctors and any assistance, and perished in the highways, in their fields and houses, night and day, more like beasts than men. Just as the townsmen became dissolute and indifferent to their work and property, so the peasants, when they saw that death was upon them, entirely neglected the future fruits of their past labours both from the earth and from cattle, and thought only of enjoying what they had. Thus it happened that cows, asses, sheep, goats, pigs, fowls and even dogs, those faithful companions of man, left the farms and wandered at their will through the fields, where the wheat crops stood abandoned, unreaped and ungarnered. Many of these animals seemed endowed with reason, for, after they had pastured all day, they returned to the farms for the night of their own free will, without being driven.

Returning from the country to the city, it may be said that such was the cruelty of Heaven, and perhaps in part of men, that between March and July more than one hundred thousand persons died within the walls of Florence, what between the violence of the plague and the abandonment in which the sick were left by the cowardice of the healthy. And before the plague it was not thought that the whole city held so many people.

Oh, what great palaces, how many fair houses and noble dwellings, once filled with attendants and nobles and ladies, were emptied to the meanest servant! How many famous names and vast possessions and renowned estates were left without an heir! How many gallant men and fair ladies and handsome youths, whom Galen, Hippocrates and Aesculapius themselves would have said were in perfect health, at noon dined with their relatives and friends, and at night supped with their ancestors in the next world!

But it fills me with sorrow to go over so many miseries. Therefore, since I want to pass over all I can leave out, I shall go on to say that when our city was in this condition and almost emptied of inhabitants, one Tuesday morning the venerable church of Santa Maria Novella had scarcely any congregation for divine service except (as I have heard from a person worthy of belief) seven young women in the mourning garments suitable to the times, who were all related by ties of blood, friendship or neighbourship. None of them was older than twenty-eight or younger than eighteen; all were educated and of noble blood, fair to look upon, well-mannered and of graceful modesty.

I should tell you their real names if I had not a good reason for not doing so, which is that I would not have any of them blush in the future for the things they say and hearken to in the following pages. The laws are now strict again, whereas then, for the reasons already shown, they were very lax, not only for persons of their age but for those much older. Nor would I give an opportunity to the envious (always ready to sneer at every praiseworthy life) to attack the virtue of these modest ladies with vulgar speech. But so that you may understand without confusion what each one says, I intend to give them names wholly or partly suitable to the qualities of each.

The first and eldest I shall call Pampinea, the second Fiammetta, the third Filomena, the fourth Emilia, the fifth Lauretta, the sixth Neifile, and the last Elisa (or "the virgin") for a very good reason. They met, not by arrangement, but by chance, in the same part of the church, and sat down in a circle. After many sighs they ceased to pray and began to talk about the state of affairs and other things After a short space of silence, Pampinea said:

"Dear ladies, you must often have heard, as I have, that to make a sensible use of one's reason harms nobody. It is natural for everybody to aid, preserve and defend his life as far as possible. And this is so far admitted that to save their own lives men often kill others who have done no harm. If this is permitted by the laws which are concerned with the general good, it must certainly be lawful for us to take any reasonable means for the preservation of our lives. When I think of what we have been doing this morning and still more on former days, when I remember what we have been saying, I perceive and you must perceive that each of us goes in fear of her life. I do not wonder at this, but, since each of us has a woman's judgement, I do wonder that we do not seek some remedy against what we dread.

"In my opinion we remain here for no other purpose than to witness how many bodies are buried, or listen whether the friars here (themselves reduced almost to nothing) sing their offices at the canonical hours, or to display by our clothes the quantity and quality of our miseries to anyone who comes here. If we leave this church we see the bodies of the dead and the sick being carried about. Or we see those who had been exiled from the city by the authority of the laws for their crimes, deriding this authority because they know the guardians of the law are sick or dead, and running loose about the place. Or we see the dregs of the city battening on our blood and calling themselves sextons, riding about on horseback in every direction and insulting our calamities with vile songs. On every side we hear nothing but 'So-and-so is dead' or 'So-and-so is dying.' And if there were anyone left to weep we should hear nothing but piteous lamentations. I do not know if it is the same in your homes as in mine. But if I go home there is nobody left there but one of my maids, which fills me with such horror that the hair stands upon my head. Wherever I go or sit at home I seem to see the ghosts of the departed, not with the faces as I knew them but with dreadful looks which terrify me.

"I am ill at ease here and outside of here and at home; the more so since nobody who has the strength and ability to go away (as we have) now remains here, except ourselves. The few that remain (if there are any), according to what I see and hear, do anything which gives them pleasure or pleases their appetites, both by day and night, whether they are alone or in company, making no distinction between right and wrong. Not only laymen, but those cloistered in convents have broken their oaths and given themselves up to the delights of the flesh, and thus in trying to escape the plague by doing what they please, they have become lascivious and dissolute.

"If this is so (and we may plainly see it is) what are we doing here? What are we waiting for? What are we dreaming about? Are we less eager and active than other citizens in saving our lives? Are they less dear to us than to others? Or do we think that our lives are bound to our bodies with stronger chains than to other people's, and so believe that we need fear nothing which might harm us? We were and are deceived. How stupid we should be to believe such a thing! We may see the plainest proofs from the number of young men and women who have died of this cruel plague.

"I do not know if you think as I do, but in my opinion if we, through carelessness, do not want to fall into this calamity when we can escape it, I think we should do well to leave this town, just as many others have done and are doing. Let us avoid the wicked examples of others like death itself, and go and live virtuously in our country houses, of which each of us possesses several. There let us take what happiness and pleasure we can, without ever breaking the rules of reason in any manner.

"There we shall hear the birds sing, we shall see the green hills and valleys, the wheat-fields rolling like a sea, and all kinds of trees. We shall see the open Heavens which, although now angered against man, do not withhold from us their eternal beauties that are so much fairer to look upon than the empty walls of our city. The air will be fresher there, we shall find a greater plenty of those things necessary to life at this time, and fewer troubles. Although the peasants are dying like the townsmen, still, since the houses and inhabitants are fewer, we shall see less of them and feel less misery. On the other hand I believe we are not abandoning anybody here Indeed we can truthfully say that we are abandoned, since our relatives have either died or fled from death and have left us alone in this calamity as if we were nothing to them.

"If we do what I suggest, no blame can fall upon us; if we fail to do it, the result may be pain, trouble and perhaps death. Therefore I think that we should do well to take our servants and all things necessary, and go from one house to another, enjoying whatever merriment and pleasure these times allow. Let us live in this way (unless death comes upon us) until we see what end Heaven decrees to this plague. And remember that going away virtuously will not harm us so much as staying here in wickedness will harm others."

The other ladies listened to what Pampinea said, praised her advice, and in their eagerness to follow it began to discuss details, as if they were going to leave at once. But Filomena, who was a most prudent young woman, said:

"Ladies, although what Pampinea says is excellent advice, we must not rush off at once, as you seem to wish. Remember we are all women; and any girl can tell you how women behave together and conduct themselves without the direction of some man. We are fickle, wayward, suspicious, faint-hearted and cowardly. So if we have no guide but ourselves I greatly suspect that this company will very soon break up, without much honour to ourselves. Let us settle this matter before we start."

Elisa than broke in:

"Indeed men are a woman's head and we can rarely succeed in anything without their help; but how can we find any men? Each of us knows that most of her menfolk are dead, while the others are away, we know not where, flying with their companions from the end we wish to escape. To ask strangers would be unbecoming; for, if we mean to go away to save our lives we must take care that scandal and annoyance do not follow us where we are seeking rest and amusement."

While the ladies were thus arguing, three young men came into the church, the youngest of whom was not less than twenty-five. They were lovers whose love could not be quenched or even cooled by the horror of the times, the loss of relatives and friends, or even fear for themselves. The first was named Pamfilo, the second Filostrato, the third Dioneo. They were pleasant, well-mannered men, and in this public calamity they sought the consolation of looking upon the ladies they loved. These ladies happened to be among our seven, while some of the others were related to one or other of the three men. They no sooner came into sight than the ladies saw them; whereupon Pampinea said with a smile:

"See how Fortune favours our plan at once by sending us these valiant and discreet young men, who will gladly act as our guides and servants if we do not refuse to accept them for such duties."

Neifile then became crimson, for she was one of the ladies beloved by one of the young men, and said:

"For God's sake, Pampinea, be careful what you are saying. I know quite well that nothing but good can be said of any of them and I am sure they could achieve greater things than this. I also think that their company would be fitting and pleasant, not only to us, but to ladies far more beautiful and charming than we are. But it is known to everyone that they are in love with some of us women here; and so, if we take them with us, I am afraid that blame and infamy will fall upon us, through no fault of ours or theirs."

Then said Filomena:

"What does that matter? If I live virtuously, my conscience never pricks me, whatever people may say. God and the truth will fight for me. If these men would come with us, then indeed, as Pampinea said, fortune would be favourable to our plan of going away."

The others not only refrained from censuring what she said, but agreed by common consent that the men should be spoken to, told their plan, and asked if they would accompany the ladies on their expedition. Without more ado, Pampinea, who was related to one of them, arose and went towards them where they stood looking at the ladies, saluted them cheerfully, told them the plan, and begged them in the name of all the ladies to accompany them out of pure and fraternal affection.

At first the young men thought this was a jest. But when they saw the lady was speaking seriously, they said they were willing to go. And in order to start without delay they at once gave the orders necessary for departure. Everything necessary was made ready, and word was sent on ahead to the place they were going. At dawn next morning, which was Wednesday, the ladies with some of their servants, and the young men with a manservant each, left the city and set out. They had not gone more than two miles when they came to the first place where they were going to stay.

This estate was on slightly raised ground, at some distance from any main road, with many trees and plants, fair to look upon. At the top of the rise was a country mansion with a large inner court-yard. It had open colonnades, galleries and rooms, all beautiful in themselves and ornamented with gay paintings. Roundabout were lawns and marvelous gardens and wells of cool water. There were cellars of fine wines, more suitable to wine connoisseurs than to sober and virtuous ladies. The whole house had been cleaned, the beds were prepared in the rooms, and every corner was strewn with the flowers of the season and fresh rushes. All of which the company beheld with no little pleasure.

They all sat down to discuss plans, and Dioneo, who was a most amusing young man and full of witticisms, remarked:

"Ladies, your good sense, rather than our foresight, has brought us here. I do not know what you are thinking of doing with your troubles here, but I dropped mine inside the gates of the city when I left it with you a little time ago. Therefore, either you must make up your minds to laugh and sing and amuse yourselves with me (that is, to the extent your dignity allows), or you must let me go back to my troubles and stay in the afflicted city."

Pampinea, who had driven away her woes in the same way, cheerfully replied:

"Dioneo, you speak well; let us amuse ourselves, for that was the reason why we fled from our sorrows. But when things are not organized they cannot long continue. And, since I began the discussion which brought this fair company together and since I wish our happiness to continue, I think it necessary that one of us should be made chief, whom the others will honour and obey, and whose duty shall be to regulate our pleasures. Now, so that everyone—both man and woman—may experience the cares as well as the pleasures of ruling and no one feel any envy at not sharing them, I think the weight and honour should be given to each of us in turn for one day. The first shall be elected by all of us. At vespers he or she shall choose the ruler for the next day, and so on. While their reigns last these rulers shall arrange where and how we are to spend our time."

These words pleased them all and they unanimously elected her for the first day. Filomena ran to a laurel bush, whose leaves she had always heard were most honourable in themselves and did great honour to anyone crowned with them, plucked off a few small branches and wove them into a fair garland of honour. When this was placed on the head of any one of them, it was a symbol of rule and authority over the rest so long as the party remained together.

Pampinea, thus elected queen, ordered silence. She then sent for the three servants of the young men and the four young women servants the ladies had brought, and said:

"To set a first example to you all (which may be bettered) and thus allow our gathering to live pleasantly and orderly and without shame and to last as long as we desire, I appoint Dioneo's servant Parmeno as my steward, and hand over to him the care of the whole family and of everything connected with the dining hall. Pamfilo's servant Sirisco shall be our treasurer and buyer, and carry out Parmeno's instructions. Tindaro shall wait on Filostrato and Dioneo and Pamfilo in their rooms, when the other two servants are occupied with their new duties. Filomena's servant Licisca and my own servant Misia shall remain permanently in the kitchen and carefully prepare the food which Parmeno sends them. Lauretta's Chimera and Fiametta's Stratilia shall take care of the ladies' rooms and see that the whole house is clean. Moreover we will and command that everyone who values our good grace shall bring back only cheerful news, wherever he may go or return from, and whatever he may hear or see."

Having given these orders, which were approved by everyone, she jumped gaily to her feet and said:

"Here are gardens and lawns and other delicious places, where each of us can wander and enjoy them at will. But let everyone be here at the hour of Tierce[1] so that we can eat together while it is still cool."

The company of gay young men and women, thus given the queen's permission, went off together slowly through the gardens, talking of pleasant matters, weaving garlands of different leaves, and singing love songs. After the time allotted by the queen had elapsed they returned to the house and found that Parmeno had carefully carried out the duties of his office. Entering a ground-floor room decorated everywhere with broom blossoms, they found tables covered with white cloths and set with glasses which shone like silver. They washed their hands and, at the queen's command, all sat down in the places allotted them by Parmeno. Delicately cooked food was brought, exquisite wines were at hand, and the three men-servants waited at table. Everyone was delighted to see things so handsome and well arranged, and they ate merrily with much happy talk.

All the ladies and young men could dance and many of them could play and sing; so, when the tables were cleared, the queen called for musical instruments. At her command Dioneo took a lute and Fiammetta a viol, and began to play a dance tune. The queen sent the servants to their meal, and then with slow steps danced with the two young men and the other ladies. After that, they began to sing gay and charming songs.

In this way they amused themselves until the queen thought it was time for the siesta. So, at the queen's bidding, the three young men went off to their rooms (which were separated from the ladies') and found them filled with flowers as the dining hall had been. And similarly with the women. So they all undressed and went to sleep.

Not long after the hour of Nones[2] the queen arose and made the other women and the young men also get up, saying that it was harmful to sleep too long during the daytime. Then they went out to a lawn of thick green grass entirely shaded from the sun. A soft breeze came to them there. The queen made them sit down in a circle on the grass, and said:

"As you see, the sun is high and the heat great, and nothing can be heard but the cicadas in the olive trees. To walk about at

1. the third canonical hour, 9 A.M.   2. the fifth canonical hour, 3 P.M.

this hour would be foolish. Here it is cool and lovely, and, as you see, there are games of chess and draughts which everyone can amuse himself with, as he chooses. But, if my opinion is followed, we shall not play games, because in games the mind of one of the players must necessarily be distressed without any great pleasure to the other player or the onlookers. Let us rather spend this hot part of the day in telling tales, for thus one person can give pleasure to the whole company. When each of us has told a story, the sun will be going down and the heat less, and we can then go walking anywhere we choose for our amusement. If this pleases you (for here I am ready to follow your pleasure) let us do it. If it does not please you, let everyone do as he likes until evening."

The women and men all favoured the telling of stories.

"Then if it pleases you," said the queen, "on this first day I order that everyone shall tell his tale about any subject he likes."

She then turned to Pamfilo, who was seated on her right, and ordered him to begin with a tale. Hearing this command, Pamfilo at once began as follows, while all listened.[3]

The Ninth Tale of the Fifth Day

Filomena had ceased speaking, and the queen, seeing that nobody was left to speak except Dioneo (who had his privilege) and herself, began cheerfully as follows:

It is now my turn to speak, dearest ladies, and I shall gladly do so with a tale similar in part to the one before, not only that you may know the power of your beauty over the gentle heart, but because you may learn yourselves to be givers of rewards when fitting, without allowing Fortune always to dispense them, since Fortune most often bestows them, not discreetly but lavishly.

You must know then that Coppo di Borghese Domenichi, who was and perhaps still is one of our fellow citizens, a man of great and revered authority in our days both from his manners and his virtues (far more than from nobility of blood), a most excellent person worthy of eternal fame, and in the fullness of his years, delighted often to speak of past matters with his neighbours and other men. And this he could do better and more orderly and with a better memory and more ornate speech than anyone else.

Among other excellent things, he was wont to say that in the past there was in Florence a young man named Federigo, the son of Messer Filippo Alberighi, renowned above all other young gentlemen of Tuscany for his prowess in arms and his courtesy. Now, as most often happens to gentlemen, he fell in love with a lady named Monna

---

3. This introduction is succeeded by the first of the hundred tales. The remainder of the *Decameron* consists of the tales told by each member of the group on this and nine subsequent days, along with short connecting passages.

Giovanna, in her time held to be one of the gayest and most beautiful women ever known in Florence. To win her love, he went to jousts and tourneys, made and gave feasts, and spent his money without stint. But she, no less chaste than beautiful, cared nothing for the things he did for her nor for him who did them.

Now as Federigo was spending far beyond his means and getting nothing in, as easily happens, his wealth failed, and he remained poor with nothing but a little farm, on whose produce he lived very penuriously, and one falcon which was among the best in the world. More in love than ever, but thinking he would never be able to live in the town any more as he desired, he went to Campi where his farm was. There he spent his time hawking, asked nothing of anybody, and patiently endured his poverty.

Now while Federigo was in this extremity it happened one day that Monna Giovanna's husband fell ill, and seeing death come upon him, made his will. He was a very rich man and left his estate to a son who was already growing up. And then, since he had greatly loved Monna Giovanna, he made her his heir in case his son should die without legitimate children; and so died.

Monna Giovanna was now a widow, and as is customary with our women, she went with her son to spend the year in a country house she had near Federigo's farm. Now the boy happened to strike up a friendship with Federigo, and delighted in dogs and hawks. He often saw Federigo's falcon fly, and took such great delight in it that he very much wanted to have it, but did not dare ask for it, since he saw how much Federigo prized it.

While matters were in this state, the boy fell ill. His mother was very much grieved, as he was her only child and she loved him extremely. She spent the day beside him, trying to help him, and often asked him if there was anything he wanted, begging him to say so, for if it were possible to have it, she would try to get it for him. After she had many times made this offer, the boy said:

"Mother, if you can get me Federigo's falcon, I think I should soon be better."

The lady paused a little at this, and began to think what she should do. She knew that Federigo had loved her for a long time, and yet had never had one glance from her, and she said to herself:

"How can I send or go and ask for this falcon, which is, from what I hear, the best that ever flew, and moreover his support in life? How can I be so thoughtless as to take this away from a gentleman who has no other pleasure left in life?"

Although she knew she was certain to have the bird for the asking, she remained in embarrassed thought, not knowing what to say, and did not answer her son. But at length love for her child got the upper hand and she determined that to please him in whatever way it might be, she would not send, but go herself for it and bring it back to him. So she replied:

"Be comforted, my child, and try to get better somehow. I promise you that tomorrow morning I will go for it, and bring it to you."

The child was so delighted that he became a little better that same day. And on the morrow the lady took another woman to accompany her, and as if walking for exercise went to Federigo's cottage, and asked for him. Since it was not the weather for it, he had not been hawking for some days, and was in his garden employed in certain work there. When he heard that Monna Giovanna was asking for him at the door, he was greatly astonished, and ran there happily. When she saw him coming, she got up to greet him with womanly charm, and when Federigo had courteously saluted her, she said:

"How do you do, Federigo? I have come here to make amends for the damage you have suffered through me by loving me more than was needed. And in token of this, I intend to dine today familiarly with you and my companion here."

"Madonna,"[4] replied Federigo humbly, "I do not remember ever to have suffered any damage through you, but received so much good that if I was ever worth anything it was owing to your worth and the love I bore it. Your generous visit to me is so precious to me that I could spend again all that I have spent; but you have come to a poor host."

So saying, he modestly took her into his house, and from there to his garden. Since there was nobody else to remain in her company, he said:

"Madonna, since there is nobody else, this good woman, the wife of this workman, will keep you company, while I go to set the table."

Now, although his poverty was extreme, he had never before realized what necessity he had fallen into by his foolish extravagance in spending his wealth. But he repented of it that morning when he could find nothing with which to do honour to the lady, for love of whom he had entertained vast numbers of men in the past. In his anguish he cursed himself and his fortune and ran up and down like a man out of his senses, unable to find money or anything to pawn. The hour was late and his desire to honour the lady extreme, yet he would not apply to anyone else, even to his own workman; when suddenly his eye fell upon his falcon, perched on a bar in the sitting room. Having no one to whom he could appeal, he took the bird, and finding it plump, decided it would be food worthy such a lady. So, without further thought, he wrung its neck, made his little maidservant quickly pluck and prepare it, and put

4. my lady.

it on a spit to roast. He spread the table with the whitest napery, of which he had some left, and returned to the lady in the garden with a cheerful face, saying that the meal he had been able to prepare for her was ready.

The lady and her companion arose and went to the table, and there together with Federigo, who served it with the greatest devotion, they ate the good falcon, not knowing what it was. They left the table and spent some time in cheerful conversation, and the lady, thinking the time had now come to say what she had come for, spoke fairly to Federigo as follows:

"Federigo, when you remember your former life and my chastity, which no doubt you considered harshness and cruelty, I have no doubt that you will be surprised at my presumption when you hear what I have come here for chiefly. But if you had children, through whom you could know the power of parental love, I am certain that you would to some extent excuse me.

"But, though you have no child, I have one, and I cannot escape the common laws of mothers. Compelled by their power, I have come to ask you—against my will, and against all good manners and duty—for a gift, which I know is something especially dear to you, and reasonably so, because I know your straitened fortune has left you no other pleasure, no other recreation, no other consolation. This gift is your falcon, which has so fascinated my child that if I do not take it to him, I am afraid his present illness will grow so much worse that I may lose him. Therefore I beg you, not by the love you bear me (which holds you to nothing), but by your own nobleness, which has shown itself so much greater in all courteous usage than is wont in other men, that you will be pleased to give it to me, so that through this gift I may be able to say that I have saved my child's life, and thus be ever under an obligation to you."

When Federigo heard the lady's request and knew that he could not serve her, because he had given her the bird to eat, he began to weep in her presence, for he could not speak a word. The lady at first thought that his grief came from having to part with his good falcon, rather than from anything else, and she was almost on the point of retraction. But she remained firm and waited for Federigo's reply after his lamentation. And he said:

"Madonna, ever since it has pleased God that I should set my love upon you, I have felt that Fortune has been contrary to me in many things, and have grieved for it. But they are all light in comparison with what she has done to me now, and I shall never be at peace with her again when I reflect that you came to my poor house, which you never deigned to visit when it was rich, and asked me for a little gift, and Fortune has so acted that I cannot give it to you. Why this cannot be, I will briefly tell you.

"When I heard that you in your graciousness desired to dine with me and I thought of your excellence and your worthiness, I thought it right and fitting to honour you with the best food I could obtain; so, remembering the falcon you ask me for and its value, I thought it a meal worthy of you, and today you had it roasted on the dish and set forth as best I could. But now I see that you wanted the bird in another form, it is such a grief to me that I cannot serve you that I think I shall never be at peace again."

And after saying this, he showed her the feathers and the feet and the beak of the bird in proof. When the lady heard and saw all this, she first blamed him for having killed such a falcon to make a meal for a woman; and then she inwardly commended his greatness of soul which no poverty could or would be able to abate. But, having lost all hope of obtaining the falcon, and thus perhaps the health of her son, she departed sadly and returned to the child. Now, either from disappointment at not having the falcon or because his sickness must inevitably have led to it, the child died not many days later, to the mother's extreme grief.

Although she spent some time in tears and bitterness, yet, since she had been left very rich and was still very young, her brothers often urged her to marry again. She did not want to do so, but as they kept on pressing her, she remembered the worthiness of Federigo and his last act of generosity, in killing such a falcon to do her honour.

"I will gladly submit to a marriage when you please," she said to her brothers, "but if you want me to take a husband, I will take no man but Federigo degli Alberighi."

At this her brothers laughed at her, saying:

"Why, what are you talking about, you fool? Why do you want a man who hasn't a penny in the world?"

But she replied:

"Brothers, I know it is as you say, but I would rather have a man who needs money than money which needs a man."

Seeing her determination, the brothers, who knew Federigo's good qualities, did as she wanted, and gave her with all her wealth to him, in spite of his poverty. Federigo, finding that he had such a woman, whom he loved so much, with all her wealth to boot, as his wife, was more prudent with his money in the future. and ended his days happily with her.

The Eighth Tale of the Ninth Day

Everyone in the merry band said that what Talano had seen in his sleep was not a dream but a vision, since it had all happened exactly as he dreamed it. When everyone was silent, the queen ordered Lauretta to follow next, and she said:

Most wise ladies, those who have spoken before me today have almost all been inspired by something we have talked of formerly. I myself am now moved by Pampinea's tale of yesterday about the savage revenge of the scholar, to tell you of a vengeance which was serious enough to the person who suffered it, although not so savage as that.

I must therefore tell you that among the Florentines was a very gluttonous man, named Ciacco. His income was not sufficient to meet the expense of his gluttony, and since he was well mannered and full of witty jokes and sayings, he made himself, not a courtier, but a sarcastic buffoon. He frequented the rich and delighted to eat good food; so he dined and supped with the wealthy, although he was not always invited.

At the same time in Florence there was a man called Biondello, who had the same parasitical occupation as Ciacco. He was a pleasant little man, as neat as a fly, with his cap on his head, and a mass of yellow hair with never a single hair out of place. One morning in Lent he went to the fish market and bought two very large lampreys for Messer Vieri de' Cerchi. Ciacco saw him, and going up to him, said:

"What is the meaning of this?"

"Yesterday," replied Biondello, "three lampreys much larger than these and a sturgeon were sent to Messer Corso Donati. They are not sufficient to entertain the gentlemen he has invited, and so he sent me to buy two more. Won't you come along?"

"Indeed I'll come," replied Ciacco.

So at the right time he went to Messer Corso's house, and found him with several of his neighbours waiting for dinner. When he was asked why he had come there, he replied:

"Messer, I have come to dine with you and your friends."

"You are welcome," replied Messer Corso, "and since it is dinner time, let us sit down to it."

So they sat down to table, and were served with peas and tunny fish, and then fried fish from the Arno, and nothing more. Ciacco then saw through Biondello's trick, and, being very angry at it, made up his mind to pay him back. Biondello made a lot of people laugh by telling them the trick; and not many days later he met Ciacco. Biondello greeted him, and laughingly asked him how he liked Messer Corso's lampreys.

"Before a week has passed," said Ciacco, "you'll be able to tell much better than I."

He then left Biondello and at once put his plan into action. He promised some money to a market-man and, handing him a glass bottle, took him to the Loggia de' Cavicciuli. There he pointed to a knight, named Messer Filippo Argenti, a tall, strong, sinewy man, haughty, irascible and hasty; and said to the market-man:

"Take this bottle to him, and speak these words: 'Messer, I am sent to you by Biondello, who begs that you will redden this bottle with your good ruby wine, because he wants to treat some of his friends.' Be careful that he doesn't get his hands on you, because he would give you a bad time and it would spoil my plan."

"Am I to say anything else?" asked the market-man.

"No," said Ciacco, "go along; when you have said this to him, come back to me with the bottle, and I'll pay you."

So the market-man went off, and delivered the message to Messer Filippo. When Messer Filippo heard it, he went red in the face, for he was very prone to wrath and thought that Biondello, whom he knew, was making a jest of him. He started to his feet, saying: "What 'reddening' and what 'friends' does he mean? God curse him and you!" And he stretched out his arm to grasp the market-man; but he was on the alert and fled away at once. He returned to Ciacco, who had watched everything from a safe distance, and told him what Messer Filippo had said. Ciacco in delight at once paid the market-man, and did not rest until he found Biondello, to whom he said:

"Were you in the Loggia de' Cavicciuli just now?"

"No," replied Biondello. "Why do you ask?"

"Because," replied Ciacco, "I know that Messer Filippo is looking for you—I don't know why."

"Good," said Biondello, "I'll go to him and make a joke."

Biondello went off, followed at a distance by Ciacco who wanted to see what would happen. Messer Filippo, who had not been able to catch the market-man, was in a great rage and chafed inwardly, for he could make nothing of the market-man's words except that Biondello, at someone's instigation, was making fun of him. And while he was chafing in this way, up came Biondello. As soon as Messer Filippo saw him, he went up and gave him a punch in the face.

"Oh! Messer!" exclaimed Biondello. "What does this mean?"

Messer Filippo took him by the hair, tore off his cap and threw his hood on the ground, still punching him hard, and saying:

"Traitor! You'll soon see what it means! What do you mean by sending me messages about 'reddening' and 'friends'? Do you think I am a boy to be hoodwinked?"

So saying, he kept smashing at his face with a fist which seemed like iron, tore out his hair, and dragging him through the mud made rags of his clothes. And he went at it so violently that Biondello had not time to say a word or to ask him why he was attacking him. He had certainly heard the "reddening" and the "friends," but did not know what they meant.

Finally, after Messer Filippo had given him a sound thrashing, a number of people gathered round and with great difficulty rescued Biondello, who was all buffeted and bruised, from his hands. They told him why Messer Filippo had done this, and reprehended him for having sent such a message, telling him that he ought to know the sort of man Messer Filippo was, and that he was not a man to be jested with. Biondello in tears tried to clear himself, and said that he had never sent to Messer Filippo for wine. And when he had collected himself a little, he went home sadly and painfully, suspecting that this was Ciacco's work. Several days later, when the marks of the bruises had left his face, he began to go about again. He happened to meet Ciacco, who said to him:

"Well, Biondello, how did you like Messer Filippo's wine?"

"I wish you had found Messer. Corso's lampreys like it!" replied Biondello.

"Right!" said Ciacco. "Next time you give me such a dinner as that I'll give you another drink like the one you had!"

Biondello realized that he was more able to feel ill will towards Ciacco than he had power to hurt him, and prayed God to make his peace with him. Thereafter he was very careful not to play such tricks.

Masterpieces of the
Renaissance

EDITED BY

P. M. PASINETTI

Professor of Italian and Comparative Literature,
University of California, Los Angeles

THE RENAISSANCE
AND ANTIQUITY

The term *Renaissance* describes a period of proverbially great intellectual and artistic achievements. The literal meaning of the word—"rebirth"—suggests that one impulse toward these achievements came from the example of ancient culture, or even better, from a certain vision which the artists and intellectuals of the Renaissance possessed of the world of antiquity which was "reborn" through their work. Especially in the more mature phase of the Renaissance, men were aware of having brought about in many fields a vigorous renewal, which they openly associated with the cult of antiquity. The restoration of ancient canons was regarded as a glorious achievement to be set beside the thrilling discoveries of their own age. "To-

day," Rabelais writes through his Gargantua,

the old sciences are revived, knowledge is systematized, discipline reëstablished. The learned languages are restored: Greek, without which a man would be ashamed to consider himself educated; Hebrew, Chaldean and Latin. Printing is now in use, an art so accurate and elegant that it betrays the divine inspiration of its discovery, which I have lived to witness. Alas! Conversely, I was not spared the horror of such diabolic works as gunpowder and artillery.

Machiavelli, whose infatuation with antiquity is as typical a trait as his better-advertised political realism, in the opening of his *Discourses on the First Ten Books of Livy* (*Discorsi sopra la prima deca di Tito Livio,* 1513–1521) suggests that rulers should be as keen on the imitation of ancient "virtues" as are artists, lawyers, and the scientists: "The

1033

civil laws are nothing but decisions given by the ancient juris-
consults. . . . And what is the
science of medicine, but the experience of ancient physicians,
which their successors have
taken for their guide?"

The vogue of the term *Renaissance* is relatively recent, and
its wide popularization stems in
part from the success of Jakob
Burckhardt's famous book, *The
Civilization of the Renaissance
in Italy* (1860). As with other
terms which have currency in
the history of culture (for instance, *romanticism*), its usefulness depends on its keeping a
certain degree of elasticity. Thus
the Renaissance as a "movement" can be regarded as extending through varying periods of
years, and also as including
phases and traits of what is
otherwise known as the Middle
Ages (and vice versa). The peak
of the Renaissance can be shown
to have occurred at different
times in different countries, the
movement having had its incep-
tion in Italy, where its impact
was at first most visible in the
fine arts, while in England, for
instance, it developed later and
its main achievements were in
literature, particularly the drama.
The meaning of the term has
also, in the course of time, wid-
ened considerably: nowadays it
conveys, to say the least, a general notion of artistic creativity,
of extraordinary zest for life and
knowledge, of sensory delight in
opulence and magnificence, of
spectacular individual achievement, thus extending beyond
the literal meaning of rebirth
and the strict idea of a revival

and imitation of antiquity.

Even in the stricter sense the
term continues to have its function. The degree to which European intellectuals of the period
were steeped in the vision of antiquity is difficult for the average modern reader to realize
fully. Even at first sight the
student will discover that for
these writers references to classical mythology, philosophy, and
literature are not ornaments or
affectations; along with references to the Scriptures they are
part, and a major part, of their
mental equipment and way
of thinking. When Erasmus
through his "Folly" speaks in a
cluster of classical allusions, or
Machiavelli writes to a friend:
"I get up before daylight, prepare my birdlime, and go out
with a bundle of cages on my
back, so that I look like Geta
when he came back from the
harbor with the books of Amphitryo," the words have by no
means the sound of erudite self-
gratification which might attend
them nowadays; they are wholly
natural, familiar, unassuming.

When we are overcome by
sudden emotion, our first exclamations are likely to be in the
language most familiar to us—
our dialect, if we happen to have
one. Montaigne thus relates of
himself that when once his
father unexpectedly fell back in
his arms in a swoon, the first
words he uttered under the emotion of that experience were in
Latin. Similarly Cellini in expressing his admiration of a
Greek statue establishes with the
ancient artist an immediate contact, a proud familiarity:

I cried to the Duke: "My lord, this is a statue in Greek marble, and it is a miracle of beauty. . . . If your Excellency permits, I should like to restore it—head and arms and feet. . . . It is certainly not my business to patch up statues, that being the trade of botchers, who do it in all conscience villainously ill; yet the art displayed by this great master of antiquity cries out to me to help him."

The men who, starting at about the middle of the fourteenth century, gave new impulse to this taste for the classics are often referred to as Humanists. The word in that sense is related to what we call the humanities, and the humanities at that time were Latin and Greek. Every cultivated person wrote and spoke Latin, with the result that a Western community of intellectuals could exist, a spiritual "republic of letters" above individual nations. The archetype of the modern "man of letters" is often said to be Petrarch (Francesco Petrarca), a fourteenth-century Italian poet and diplomat who anticipated certain ideals cherished later by the men of the Renaissance: a strong sense of the glories of antiquity, a high conception of the literary art, a taste for the good life, a basic pacifism.

On the other hand, in any mention of the Renaissance as a revival of antiquity, we should never forget the imaginative quality, the visionary impulse, with which the men of letters of the period looked at those memories—the same vision and imagination with which they regarded such contemporary heroes as the great navigators

and astronomers. The Renaissance view of the cultural monuments of antiquity was far from being merely that of the philologist and the antiquarian; indeed, familiarity may have been facilitated by the very lack of a scientific sense of history. We find the visionary and imaginative element not only in the creations of poets and dramatists (Shakespeare's Romans, to give an obvious example) but also in the works of political writers: as when Machiavelli describes himself entering, through his reading, the

ancient courts of ancient men, where, being lovingly received, I feed on that food which alone is mine, and which I was born for; I am not ashamed to speak with them and to ask the reasons for their actions, and they courteously answer me. For . . . hours I feel no boredom and forget every worry; I do not fear poverty, and death does not terrify me. I give myself completely over to the ancients.

Imitation of antiquity (a standard modern description of certain Renaissance ideals) acquires, in Machiavelli and many others, a special aspect; between schoolroom imitation and that of the Renaissance there is as much difference as between the impulse to *learn* and the impulse to *be*.

THE RENAISSANCE AND THE MIDDLE AGES: "THE DIGNITY OF MAN"

Inaccurate as the hackneyed notion may be that the "light" of the Renaissance broke through a long "night" of the Middle Ages, it is necessary to remember that this view was not devised by subsequent "enlightened" centuries but held by the men of the Renaissance themselves. In his genealogy of giants from Grangousier to Gargantua to Pantagruel Rabelais conveniently represents the generations of modern learning with their varying degrees of enlightenment; this is what Gargantua writes to his son:

My late father Grangousier, of blessed memory, made every effort that I might achieve mental, moral and technical excellence. . . . But you can realize that conditions were not as favorable to learning as they are to-day. Nor had I such gifted teachers as you. We were still in the dark ages; we still walked in the shadow of the dark clouds of ignorance; we suffered the calamitous consequences of the destruction of good literature by the Goths. Now, by God's grace, light and dignity have been restored to letters, and I have lived to see it.

Definitions of the Renaissance must also in one way or another include the idea that the period was characterized by preoccupation with this life rather than with the life beyond. The contrast of an ideal Medieval Man, whose mode of action is basically oriented toward the thought of the afterlife, and who therefore conceives of his days on earth as transient and preparatory, with an ideal Renaissance Man, possessing and cherishing earthly interests so concrete and self-sufficient that the very realization of the ephemeral quality of life is to him nothing but an added spur to its immediate enjoyment—this is a useful contrast even though it represents an enormous oversimplification of the facts.

This same emphasis on the immediate is reflected in the earthly, amoral, and esthetic character of the Renaissance code of conduct. According to this code, human action is judged not in terms of right and wrong, of good and evil (as it is judged when life is viewed as a moral "test," with reward or punishment in the afterlife), but in terms of its present concrete validity and effectiveness, of the delight it affords, of its memorability, its *beauty*. In that sense a good deal that is typical of the Renaissance, from architecture to poetry, from sculpture to rhetoric, may be related to a taste for the harmonious and the memorable, for the spectacular effect, for the successful striking of a pose. Individual human action, seeking as it were in itself its own reward, finds justification in its *formal* appropriateness; in its being a well-rounded achievement, perfect of its kind; in the zest and gusto with which it is, here and now, performed; and, finally, in its proving worthy of remaining as a testimony to the performer's power on earth.

A convenient way of grasping this emphasis is to consider certain words which are often especially expressive of the interests of the period—"virtue," "fame," "glory." "Virtue," particularly in its Italian form, *virtù*, is to be understood in a wide sense. As we may see even now in some relics of its older meanings, the word (from the Latin *vir*, "man") connotes active power —the intrinsic force and ability of a person or thing (the "virtue" of a law, or of a medicament)—and hence, also, technical skill (the capacity of the "virtuoso"). The Machiavellian prince's "virtues," therefore, are not necessarily goodness, temperance, clemency, and the like; they are whatever forces and skills may help him in the efficient management and preservation of his princely powers. The idealistic, intangible part of his success is consigned to such concepts as "fame" and "glory," and here the dimension within which human action is considered is still an earthly one: they connote the hero's success and reputation with his contemporaries, or look forward to splendid recognition from posterity, on earth.

In this sense (though completely pure examples of such an attitude are rare) the purpose of life is the unrestrained and self-sufficient practice of one's "virtue," the competent and delighted exercise of one's skill. At the same time, there is no reason to forget that such virtues and skills are God's gift to man. The world-view of even some of the most clearly earth-bound Renaissance men was hardly godless; Machiavelli, Cellini, Rabelais, take for granted the presence of God in their own and their heroes' lives:

. . . we have before our eyes extraordinary and unexampled means prepared by God. The sea has been divided. A cloud has guided you on your way. The rock has given forth water. Manna has fallen. Everything has united to make you great. The rest is for you to do. God does not intend to do everything, lest he deprive us of our free will and the share of glory that belongs to us. [Machiavelli.]

According to the Pythagorean system, Gargantua would, with his tutor, recapitulate briefly all that he had read, seen, learned, done and assimilated in the course of the day. Then they prayed to God the Creator, doing Him worship and confirming their faith in Him, glorifying Him for His immense goodness, vouchsafing thanks for all the mighty past and imploring His divine clemency for all the future. And so they retired to rest. [Rabelais.]

I found that all the bronze my furnace contained had been exhausted in the head of this figure [of the statue of Perseus]. It was a miracle to observe that not one fragment remained in the orifice of the channel, and that nothing was wanting to the statue. In my great astonishment I seemed to see in this the hand of God arranging and controlling all. [Cellini.]

Yet there is no doubt that if we compare the attitudes of these authors with the view of the world and of the value of human action which emerges from the major literary work of the Middle Ages, the *Divine Comedy,* and with the manner in which human action is there seen within a grand extratemporal design, the presence of God in the Renaissance writers cited above cannot help appearing marginal and perfunctory. Castiglione in the first pages of the *Courtier* pays homage to the memory of the former duke of Montefeltro, in whose palace at Urbino the book's personages hold their lofty debate on the idea of a perfect gentleman (an earlier member of the same family appears in Dante's *Hell,* another in Dante's *Purgatory*); but he praises him only for his achievements as a man of arms and a promoter of the arts. There is no thought of either the salvation or the damnation of his soul (though the general tone of the work would seem to imply his salvation), and he is exalted instead for victories in battle and, even more warmly, for having built a splendid palace—the tangible symbol of his earthly glory, for it is both the mark of political and social power, and a work of art.

Thus the popular view which associates the idea of the Renaissance especially with the flourishing of the arts is correct. The leaders of the period saw in a work of art the clearest instance of beautiful, harmonious, and self-justified performance. To create such a work became the valuable occupation *par excellence,* the most satisfactory display of *virtù.* The Renaissance view of antiquity exemplifies this attitude: the artists and intellectuals of the period not only drew on antiquity for certain practices and forms but found there as well a recognition of the place of the arts among outstanding modes of human action. In this way, the concepts of "fame" and "glory" became particularly associated with the art of poetry because the Renaissance drew from antiquity the idea of the poet as celebrator of high deeds, the "dispenser of glory."

There is, then, an important phase of Renaissance psychology in which terrestrial life is seen as positive fulfillment. This is clear in all fields of endeavor, and especially where there is a close association between the practical and the intellectual, as in the exercise of political power, the act of scientific discovery, the creation of works of art. The Renaissance assumption is that there are things highly worth doing, within a simply temporal pattern. By doing them, man proves his privileged position in Creation and therefore incidentally follows God's intent. The often cited phrase "the dignity of man" describes this positive, strongly affirmed awareness of the intellectual and physical "virtues" of the human being, and of his place in Creation.

It is important, however, to see this fact about the Renaissance in the light of another: where there is a singularly high capacity for feeling the delight of earthly achievement, there is a possibility that its ultimate worth will also be questioned profoundly. What (the Renaissance mind usually asks at some point) is the purpose of all this activity? What meaningful relation does it bear to any all-inclusive, cosmic pattern? The Renaissance coincided with, and perhaps to some extent occasioned, a loss of firm belief in the final unity and the final intelligibility of the universe, such belief as underlies, for example, the *Divine Comedy,* enabling Dante to say in the *Paradise:*

I beheld leaves within the
  unfathomed blaze
Into one volume bound by
  love, the same
That the universe holds scattered through its maze.
Substance and accidents, and
  their modes, became
As if together fused, all in
  such wise

That what I speak of is one
simple flame.

Once the notion of this grand
unity of design has lost its authority, certainty about the final
value of human actions is no
longer to be found. For some
minds, indeed, the sense of void
becomes so strong as to paralyze
all aspiration to power or thirst
for knowledge or delight in
beauty; the attitude resulting
when this happens, we call Renaissance melancholy, whether
it be openly shown (as by
some characters in Elizabethan
drama) or provide an undercur-
rent of sadness, or incite to ironical forms of compromise, to
some sort of wise adjustment
(as in Erasmus or Montaigne.)
The legend of Faust—"Doctor"
Faustus—a great amasser of
knowledge doomed to frustration by his perception of the
vanity of science, for which he
finds at one point desperate substitutes in pseudo science and
the devil's arts, is one illustration of this sense of void. Shakespeare's *Hamlet* is another, a
play in which the very word
"thought" seems to acquire a
troubled connotation: "the pale
cast of thought"; "thought and
affliction, passion, hell itself."
In these instances, the intellectual excitement of understanding, the zest and pride of
achievement through what chiefly constitutes man's dignity,"
his intellect seem not so much
lost as directly inverted.

Thus while on one, and perhaps the better-known, side of
the picture man's intellect in
Renaissance literature enthusias-
tically expatiates over the realms
of knowledge and unveils the
mysteries of the universe, on the
other it is beset by puzzling
doubts and a profound mistrust
of its own powers. Man's moral
nature is seen as only little
lower than the angels, but also
scarcely above the beasts. Earthly power—a favorite theme because Renaissance literature was
so largely produced in the courts
or with a vivid sense of courtly
ideas—is the crown of human
aspirations ("How sweet a thing
it is to wear a crown, / Within
whose circuit is Elysium") but
it is also the death's head ("Im-
perious Caesar, dead and turn'd
to clay, / Might stop a hole to
keep the wind away").

From the tensions generated
by this simultaneous exaltation
and pessimism about the human
situation, much of Renaissance
literature takes its character and
strength.

PETRARCH

The trait which first strikes us
as new in Petrarch, if we compare him to the standard image
of "medieval man," is the self-
centered quality of his work. A
comparison between him and
Dante, who was about forty
years older, points to this quality, and the contrast is made
sharper by certain analogies in
their situations. Both pursued
the same basic motif, the quest
for salvation. But while Dante
as hero of the quest focused
dramatically on himself only on
a few enormously effective and
severe occasions (his first exchange with Beatrice in the
Purgatory, XXX, for example).
Petrarch was continuously at
work on his personal drama, on

its lights and shades, on all of its subtle modulations of feeling. In *canzone* 50, he describes an old woman, a woodsman, a shepherd, and some sailors, in beautifully musical verse, for the sole purpose of comparing their happiness with his suffering. All of this takes place in a portentously cosmic setting—a vision of the setting sun, richly presented and lovingly worked upon with poetic mastery at every stanza.

A different way of getting at the same distinction between Renaissance and medieval man may be found in Petrarch's conception of the literary profession and the poet's status. His attitude toward classical antiquity makes him "the first writer of the Renaissance," rather than a writer of the Middle Ages. As a self-conscious man of letters he modeled his work on classical examples, those texts which, as a humanistic scholar, he had helped to rediscover and bring back to life. For example, in 1333 at Liège, he discovered Cicero's oration *Pro Archia*, a Roman "defense of poetry." It would be difficult to overestimate the importance, for European culture, of Petrarch and his friend Boccaccio in establishing the Renaissance model of poet, scholar, and member of the "republic of letters," which even today is an ideal of Western civilization.

Petrarch was a prominent figure of his time. He was a courtier and a diplomat, living for a time near the papal court at Avignon and traveling widely through Europe on diplomatic missions for such families as the Visconti of Milan. But his greatest importance is as a man of letters and learning. Many of Petrarch's travels were devoted to his search for ancient texts, and his literary gifts were fully recognized in his lifetime; he was "crowned" poet laureate in Rome in 1340. As a writer, Petrarch self-consciously attended to the creation of his own image, defining, ordering, and polishing with exquisite care his poems and letters (the letter was then an established literary form). Even accidental events in his life seem to have been inspired by his taste for the harmonious and well-rounded gesture. He came within a few hours of reaching the "perfect" life-span, three score and ten. On April 6, 1327, in the Church of St. Clare, he saw Laura for the first time; she was to become the object and image of his poetic love. Twenty-one years later, Laura died on that very day, the day of Christ's passion. Petrarch frequently used April 6th, as in sonnet 3, to symbolize his own drama of passion.

There would be no drama, of course, in Petrarch's love of Laura without an element of the tragic—his sense of its sinfulness and vanity. Thus he sounds a "medieval" note, but in a new context: that of a great literary artist keenly aware of the ever-changing and ambiguous attractions of mortal beauty and earthly values. One even surmises that these values might have been less attractive to him had they not contained the suspicion of vanity, for without it, they would have afforded a less rich and less complex life. Thus he sings in sonnet 61, "Blest Be the Day" of his first encounter with Laura, the source of his torment. Even though calling Petrarch a romantic may stretch the meaning of that term to the point where it loses its usefulness, we can say that his definition of love as sorrow has had a much wider influence than his relatively superficial traits, such as his self-conscious imagery, which degenerated into the artifices of "Petrarchism."

Another essential part of Petrarch's drama is the death of the lady and her role in death as the mediator between the penitent poet and Divine Grace. Here again the inevitable comparison with Dante makes the differences only more evident. The shift in tone between the poems for Laura alive and those for her "in death" is less relevant than the similarity of the two groups. A sensuous quality pervades both groups, suggesting that even when she is dead, there is an earthly relationship. Thus the poet, in sonnet 300, envies the earth "folding her in invisible embrace" and in sonnet 292, also written after her death, the larger part of the octave is devoted to the living lady's physical appearance. In other sonnets Laura herself, in heaven, refers to her mortal body as her "beautiful veil." In sonnet 333 the poet implores her to come to him the moment of his death and guide him to "the blessed place." His poetry has made the world know and love her, and the implication is that he has thus become worthy of her succor.

The prose selection is the let-ter to Dionisio da Borgo San Sepolcro describing the poet's ascent of Mount Ventoux. While there can be no doubt about his profound moral tension and the passionate seriousness of his contrition, the tone of this famous letter is established by the way in which reality is turned into symbol, experience ordered into form. As in many of the poems, here is not only a repentant sinner but also a literary master turning autobiography and confession into art. However strong his sense of the vanity and fallaciousness of human attachments, he seems to have no doubt about the validity of one particular manifestation of *virtù*: the sensuous and expert handling of words, the poetic art itself, which knows how to make beauty yield meaning and meaning yield beauty.

ERASMUS, *THE PRAISE OF FOLLY*

Keeping in mind some of the contrasts indicated above, we realize at once that in Erasmus' *Praise of Folly* (*Moriae encomium*, 1509) easy and one-sided conclusions about the power of the human intellect, the worth and extent of knowledge, and above all the wisdom of man's behavior and the purpose of life are discarded.

To present the issues concretely, Erasmus uses a dramatic setting; he takes for his speaker a feminine figure, Folly, placing her in front of an audience of which she herself makes us aware: "as soon as I began to speak to this great audience, all faces suddenly brightened." One can almost visualize Folly gesturing, pointing to the public, attracting attention: "I am almost out of breath." "But why not speak to you more openly . . . ?" "You applaud! I was sure that you were not so wise, or rather so foolish—no, so wise."

The general tone of her speech is an elegant balance between the jocose and the serious, the erudite and the foolish. This attitude also throws light upon the audience—a congenial one, we feel, made up of people to whom the cultured allusions with which Folly's speech is studded are so familiar that they will appreciate the comic twists performed upon them, as they will, more generally, appreciate the mild satire on conventional oratory which the monologue contains. "I see that you are expecting a peroration, but," she admits in the end, "you are certainly foolish if you think that I can remember any part of such a hodgepodge of words as I have poured out." Folly's attitude toward her audience is not polemic but convivial. The butts of her polemic (the passionless Stoics) constitute a third party, and rather than address such people, Folly enlists her audience's support in rejecting them: "I ask you, if it were put to a vote, what city would choose such a person as mayor?"

This is the "play" as it is presented to us. But of course it is actually a "play within a play"; it is performed within the larger framework consisting of Erasmus and *his* audience, Erasmus and ourselves. From his advantageous position backstage, he uses Folly as an ambiguous mouth-piece. In fact, by presenting his mouthpiece as foolish, lightheaded, and rambling, he throws into sharper focus the truths which she expresses; he has secured the advantages of her directness and "innocence" while he grants her the full support of his own erudition and wit. Thus in spite of apparent frivolity, we cannot help continuously suspecting in the book a depth and complexity of meaning between the lines, as it were, for the expression of which Folly is used as a convenient instrument. We shall perhaps best gauge that complexity and come nearest to the ideal center of Erasmus' meaning by asking ourselves, What does Folly stand for? Does she stand for carefree living? For a way of life not hostile to the passions? For foolishness? For self-abandonment? For naïveté? For imagination? Is she simply the lighthearted creation of a great scholar in a frivolous moment, deploring the vanity of intellectual knowledge, and the scholar's austere and solitary life, in favor of instinct, intuition, good fellowship, "innocence"? Or does she embody a paradoxical "wisdom" to be found at the end of a long and perhaps finally frustrating accumulation of learning? Our answer to such questions must be at least as equivocal as the attitude of the work itself.

Clearly the issue of knowledge versus ignorance underlies this writing; Folly's talk may often look like a debunking of the former in favor of the latter, but—and this is the function of the "play"—the attitude ultimately suggested is one of neither "barbaric" rebellion nor unrelieved satiety and desperation. Erasmus' position, whether overtly or between the lines, is rather that of noble and wise compromise: a serene acceptance of the limitations of knowledge rather than a "melancholic" rejection of its value followed by a desperate gesture of rebellion. In other words, Erasmus' attitude toward Folly is not at all the polemical reaction of a dissatisfied intellectual who finds that the mind has not given him satisfactory answers and who therefore embraces folly in the same way as Faust embraces the devil's arts. On the other hand, the author's "praise" of Folly is certainly not feigned or *mainly* ironical. His point of view is not that of the sophisticate who takes a frivolous delight in masquerading, let us say, as a shepherd. When a man like Erasmus implies that possibly fools are really wiser than we are (an implication that underlies many a passage in the book), his attitude toward the "fool" includes understanding, affection, and a real question about value. The balance of irony is kept just in both directions; the wisdom of compromise and the sage's sense of limits are guiding, from backstage, the performance.

What has been said about the value of knowledge can be extended to the value of life: the world is a stage, and the forces ruling its actors may be irrational or ununderstandable, but it is in accordance with nature that we should go on playing our roles. Folly is imagination, inventiveness, and therefore pretense and make-believe; "everything is pretense." But at the same time, "this play is performed in no other way"; "true prudence . . . consists in not desiring more wisdom than is proper to mortals." This is "to act the play of life."

The acceptance of life as a play, as a pageant, opens a vision of true human reality, Erasmus feels, whereas the wisdom of the Stoics (who stand for pure intellectualism) produces "a marble imitation of a man" from which one shudders away "as from a ghost." Thus Folly regulates life by "a timely mixture of ignorance, thoughtlessness, forgetfulness of evil, hope of good, and a dash of delight."

CASTIGLIONE, *THE BOOK OF THE COURTIER*

In reading selections from Baldesar Castiglione's treatise on the ideal courtly gentleman, *The Book of the Courtier* (Il libro del cortegiano, published in 1528), it is helpful to consider the background description with which the book opens as a "setting," because this approach serves to suggest the vaguely theatrical and "artificial" atmosphere which pervades the composition. It is important to observe, however, that the characters whose highly mannered conversation the book purports to record were all actual members (presented with their own names) of a courtly milieu of which the author himself was a part. These people, then, were known to him not as objects of adulation or satire (the two extremes with which we are perhaps more accustomed to associate literary pictures of aristocracies) but rather as equals and companions whose standards were also his own. Hence Castiglione's attitude is one neither of conventional adulation nor of mockery; the theatrical way in which the scene is set and his characters talk (the traditional form of the Platonic dialogue acquires here the tone of what in the Renaissance was called "civil conversation") does not suggest either official courtly pomp or, conversely, a comedy of manners; it is simply the expression of a style, "artificial" in no derogatory sense, which both the characters and the author considered ideally appropriate to people of their kind and station. The speakers appear somewhat like ladies and gentlemen who have kindly consented, on some courtly occasion, to take roles in a play, except that it happens that the play is their own; they enact, so to speak, themselves. The strong element of stylization (the elaborate phrasings, the manner of the repartee, and the like) is not forced by the writer on his material; we feel rather that in his formalizing process he has followed, and emphasized, qualities that were inherent in the world he pictures. He presents a theatrical and stylized view of a world which was theatrical and stylized to begin with. In this sense the book is the best expression of Renaissance court society at its most refined and self-conscious; of that society which had a taste, as was observed in the general remarks earlier in this introduction, for the well-finished gesture, the act formally perfect of its kind—a taste which applied to all modes and norms of activity, conversation or dueling, art, courtship, etiquette.

Our selections are from the first of the four books (or evening conversations) into which the *Courtier* is divided. The purpose of this first book is to arrive, through the contributions of the obviously experienced speakers, at a description of the perfect courtly gentleman. Though Machiavelli too, in his description of the prince, presents something of an idealization of a type, his explicit intention is to come down to reality and practical motives, in contrast with the abstractions of preceding authors. Castiglione's attitude is different from the start. He has what we may call a Platonic turn of mind, in the sense that he intentionally and openly seeks the ideal and permanent form behind the transient and fragmentary examples. This point of view in the *Courtier* suggests, among other things, the sense of rule, of adjustment to correct norms, within which Castiglione's mentality characteristically moves. The aim of the book is positive acceptance of certain standards: the assumption is that codes of behavior exist and can be defined, and man can educate himself to comply with them. Relations between individuals, and particularly between members of the ruling portion of society, can be correctly and pleasantly regulated; there is even, as the famous passage on "nonchalance" (*sprezzatura*) at the end of our second selection suggests, a sort of formalization of informality.

Considered against the background of the period with which

we are here concerned, the book presents the face opposite to those views of the Renaissance court, especially popularized by drama, in which that institution is the typical scene of intrigue, corruption, violence. In such instances the discrepancy between the reality presented and the idea of "courtesy" is total; the balance is lost, and the eventual consequence is a sense of void, of the purposelessness of actions unsustained by norms, of Hamlet-like melancholy. In Castiglione the balance is still fully kept; in fact, the *Courtier* registers the clearest moment of perfect and gentle equilibrium.

MACHIAVELLI, THE PRINCE

The Prince (*Il principe*, 1513) consists of twenty-six chapters of various lengths. The first eleven chapters deal with the different types of states and dominions and the ways in which they are acquired and preserved—the early title of the whole book, in Latin, was *De principatibus* (*Of Princedoms*) —and the twelfth to fourteenth chapters focus particularly on the problems of military power. But the book's astounding fame is based mainly on the final part (from the fifteenth chapter to the end), which deals primarily with the personal attributes and "virtues" of the prince himself. In other words, a work which is generally associated with cold and precise realism presents what is after all a hypothetical type, a portrait of an ideal man.

Books of this sort may be classified, in one sense, as pedagogical literature. While for their merits of form and of vivid, if stylized, characterization they can be considered works of art, their overt purpose is to codify a certain set of manners and rules of conduct; the author presents himself therefore as especially wise, an expert in the field. His position is quite different from that of another prominent type of Renaissance writer, the court poet, with his more or less perfunctory panegyric on the patron. The relation between the patron and the pedagogical writer is, at least in appearance, more purposeful. The latter's wisdom concerns something more immediately practical than, say, the poet's vague celebration of his lord's or his lord's ancestors' virtues; he poses ideally at least, as the "mind" behind the lord's "arm."

Machiavelli is a clear example of the pedagogical writer. His pedagogical fervor, the dramatic and oratorical way in which he confronts his listener, the wealth and promptness of his pertinent illustrations are characteristic: "Either you are already prince, or you are on the way to become one. In the first case liberality is dangerous; in the second it is very necessary to be thought liberal. Caesar was one of those. . . . Somebody may answer . . . I answer. . . ." Having a direct knowledge of politics, he is quick to use examples with which he is personally acquainted:

Men are so simple and so subject to present needs that he who deceives in this way will always find those who will let themselves be deceived. I do not wish to keep still about one of the recent instances. Alexander VI did nothing else than deceive

...en, and had no other intention....

The implied tone of I *know, I have seen such things myself* adds a special immediacy to the writing. Machiavelli's view of the practical world may have been an especially startling one; but the sensation caused by his work would have been far less without the rhetorical force, the drama of argumentation, which makes *The Prince* a unique piece of persuasive art.

The view of man in Machiavelli is not at all cheerful. Indeed, the pessimistic notion that man is evil is not so much his conclusion about human nature as his premise; it is the starting point of all subsequent reasoning upon the course for a ruler to follow. The very fact of its being given as a premise, however, tends to qualify it; it is not a firm philosophical judgment but a stratagem, dictated by the facts as they are seen by a lucid observer here and now. The author is committed to his view of mankind not as a philosopher or as a religious man but as a practical politician. He indicates the rules of the game as his experience shows that the game must, under the circumstances, be played.

A prudent ... ruler cannot and should not observe faith when such observance is to his disadvantage and the causes that made him give his promise have vanished. If men were all good, this advice would not be good, but since men are wicked and do not keep their promises to you, you likewise do not have to keep yours to them.

A basic question in the study of Machiavelli, therefore, is:

How much of a realist is he? His picture of the perfectly efficient ruler has something of the character of an abstraction and idealization; it shows, though much less clearly than Castiglione's picture of the courtier, the well-known Renaissance tendency toward idealized, "perfect" form. Machiavelli's abandonment of specific and immediate realities in favor of the ideal is shown most clearly at the conclusion of the book, particularly in the last chapter. He offers there what amounts to the greatest of his illustrations as the prince's preceptor and counselor: the ideal ruler, technically equipped now by his pedagogue, is to undertake a mission—the liberation of Machiavelli's Italy. If we regard the last chapter as a culmination of his discussion rather than a dissonant addition to it, we are likely to feel at that point not only that Machiavelli's realistic method is finally directed toward an ideal task but that his conception of that task, far from being based on immediate realities, is founded on cultural and poetic myths. Machiavelli's method here becomes imaginative rather than scientific. His exhortation to liberate Italy, and his final prophecy, belong to the tradition of poetic visions in which a present state of decay is lamented, and a hope of future redemption is expressed (as in Dante, *Purgatory*, Canto VI). And a very significant part of this hope is presented not in terms of technical political considerations (choice of the opportune moment, evaluation of military power) but in terms of a sort of poetic justice for which precedents are sought in religious and ancient history and in mythology:

... if it was necessary to make clear the ability of Moses that the people of Israel should be enslaved in Egypt, and to reveal Cyrus's greatness of mind that the Persians should be oppressed by the Medes, and to demonstrate the excellence of Theseus that the Athenians should be scattered, so at the present time.... Everything is now fully disposed for the work . . . if only your House adopts the methods of those I have set forth as examples. Moreover, we have before our eyes extraordinary and unexampled means prepared by God. The sea has been divided. . . . Manna has fallen.

His Italy, as he observed in the previous chapter, is now a country "without dykes and without any wall of defence." It has suffered from "deluges," and its present rule, a "barbarian" one, "stinks in every nostril." Something is rotten in it, in short, as in Hamlet's Denmark. And we become more and more detached even from the particular example, Italy, as we recognize in the situation a pattern frequently exemplified in tragedy: the desire for communal regeneration, for the cleansing of the *polis*. Of this cleansing, Italy on one side and the imaginary prince and redeemer on the other may be taken as symbols. The envisaged redemption is identified with antiquity and Roman virtue, while the realism of the political observer is here drowned out by the cry of the humanist dreaming of ancient glories.

RABELAIS, GARGANTUA AND PANTAGRUEL

The life of François Rabelais, a man of wide humanistic education in the Renaissance tradition, typifies the variety of interests of the period, for he was at various points a law student, a monk, and a practicing physician; and he knew the life of people in cities and on country estates, in monasteries and at court. He was not by any means exclusively a professional writer; and his story of giants, written piecemeal through the years of his maturity, in the second quarter of the sixteenth century, is not so much a unified work of fiction as a summation of his wide knowledge, his diverse notions of the world, and his fantasies.

Its peculiar quality may be described in terms of contrasts: the supernatural and the realistic in the characters and in the action; the solemn and the comic, the lofty and the bawdy, in the themes; the erudite and the colloquial in the style. His heroes, as giants, move in a dimension which is entirely out of proportion with ordinary reality. They belong—with their extraordinary size, power, and longevity —to a tradition known to us from myth, from folk tale, and from biblical narrative. Yet these same characters express the feelings and attitudes of ordinary men. In fact they seem to be present as epitomes of what man, according to Rabelais, ought to be in a reasonable and enjoyable world. Rabelais' view of the world, we soon realize, is also well reflected in his literary style. High and low, pedantic and farcical, ponderous and mocking, it is the sign of a broad intellectual and moral inclusiveness, an enthusiastic open-mindedness and gusto. As we come across the learned allusion, the solemn Ciceronian phrasing, and the scholastic pedantry, all mingled with the familiar and the folksy, we notice that the presence of the colloquial quality by no means destroys the impact of the erudition or necessarily gives it the tone of parody. For the author attends to both with equal delight and mixes them completely; the blending results in an inseparable whole, sustained everywhere by the same rich manipulation of words and the same exuberant vitality. Thus Rabelais' style concretely embodies his view of the world and of man. His message, as even the new reader soon feels, his view of the human condition, is basically a cheerful one; his work is usually considered a major monument of the Renaissance at its most satisfied and affirmative. The basic theme of drinking, the vast thirst of his giant protagonists, is conveniently taken to symbolize the healthy and all-embracing sensual and intellectual appetites of the period.

As we shall see below, Benvenuto Cellini, in another of our selections, can also be regarded as an instance of the affirmative Renaissance spirit little hampered by doubt and melancholy. In fact, Cellini is even too pure and thoughtless, too "innocent" an example. In his fully adjusted way of living, that somewhat bombastic extrovert does not ask himself about value and meaning. Rabelais, at least implicitly, does take an interest in questions of value; and he seems assured, on what may appear to some of us relatively scant evidence, of the basic goodness and perfectibility of man. The selections given here emphasize that aspect, showing, among other things, Rabelais' faith in a certain type of physical and mental education. They reveal, therefore, his conception of the ideal man fit to live in what he considered a new age. It will be observed in this connection that although Rabelais was, among Europeans of the period, as responsible as anyone for the popular notion of an intellectual Renaissance following the aridity and bondage of medieval scholasticism and the barbarism of the "Gothic night," his ideal man also presents certain qualities which seem to us survivals of medieval codes. His ideal man remains a kind of knight-at-arms, even with the added emphasis on the intellectual ornaments of humanism. And this is true of other Renaissance writers. For example, in the works of Castiglione, Cervantes, Ariosto, and Shakespeare the knightly ideal continues to appear, though variously twisted through irony or in other ways distorted. Rabelais' approach is very direct and hopeful; from his pages we gather the impression that a healthy, wise, gallant, and happy type of man is a concrete possibility. Give the young the right tutoring (his implication is), do away with hampering scholasticism, let them take proper care of their bodily functions, and certain values of tolerance, *bonhommie*, and substantial well-being will finally and inevitably triumph. The sophistic, the arrogant, the hypocritical will be exposed and defeated in the most reasonable and enjoyable of worlds.

Nowhere is this pleasant view expressed more clearly than in the conception of Thélème, the supremely good place on earth, the "abbey" according to Rabelais' heart. All restrictions are banned here, not because total anarchy and license are advocated but rather because for such supremely civilized "nuns" and "monks" as those of the Thélèmite order instinctive inclinations will coincide with virtue: "The only rule of the house was: DO AS THOU WILT because men that are free, of gentle birth, well-bred and at home in civilized company possess a natural instinct that inclines them to virtue and saves them from vice. This instinct they name their honor."

Rabelais' broad optimism is qualified, of course, by the very premises of his story. For all its realism, and in spite of the fact that some episodes are mock-heroic versions of actual and even provincial and domestic events (the Picrochole war that precedes the establishment of the abbey of Thélème), this is still a fable, with giants as its main heroes and fantasy as its frequent method.

Much war, horror, intrigue, and injustice existed in the world as Rabelais knew it. In practical life, he muddled through by his tolerance, wisdom, and capacity for compromise (his temporary sympathy for the Reformation, in a time of raging religious conflict, stopped "this side of the stake"). But he survived also because he invented through his literature a world fashioned according to his own aspirations. In that world, for example, the heroes on the side of good and of justice not only win wars but also get a chance to display toward the vanquished an effective and nobly magniloquent clemency. The utopian quality of this world illustrates again the tendency of the Renaissance mind to seek the perfect model, the exemplary, ideal form. Some important passages of the book, especially the famous letter (reprinted here) of Gargantua to Pantagruel, dated from Sir Thomas More's ideal land, Utopia, make clear that this chronicle of giants, biblical in its magnitude and in its patriarchal qualities, with its Renaissance aspiration to "achieve mental, moral and technical excellence," in its serious moments symbolizes the urge to perpetuate, from father to son, the true and noble form of man and thus idealistically confirm his divine origin, his "dignity."

And, as a matter of fact, Gargantua hardly dwells in Utopia. Even less so from the moment he meets the man who will become his most important companion, Panurge. Our view of the Pantagruelian mode of life would be considerably slanted if, after the loftier images offered in previous selections, we had not at least a sampling of that side of the Rabelaisian world which is most aptly summarized in Panurge.

Our last selection, therefore, has him as the central character and describes one of his ingenious and bawdy exploits.

It will be noticed that Rabelais, when writing fiction of this sort, is second to none of the more modern so-called bawdy writers in his use of language and in his presentation of action. Yet the naturalness and spontaneity with which he practices the genre exclude any duplicity, any conscious desire to titillate or scandalize the reader. And his narrative always presents the typical mixture of folksy and cultured elements, of vulgarity and refinement, of crass realism and odd imagination. In the finale of the episode, we have an excellent example of geographic and historical realities being illuminated by fantasy and legend.

CELLINI, AUTOBIOGRAPHY

Like many other writers of autobiographical literature, the Italian sculptor and goldsmith Benvenuto Cellini offers an idealized, highly colorful picture of himself, almost a poetic mask. Consequently his *Autobiography (La vita di Benvenuto Cellini*, written between 1558 and 1562), though historically unreliable (as in the famous description of the sacking of Rome and particularly of his own rôle on that occasion), is interesting less as the portrait of a particular individual than as a representation of the "virtues" and codes of behavior which a man of Cellini's time and quality considered desirable and worthy of spirited record. The more we read, the more he seems intent upon inventing a character, a favorite hero, to whom he gives his own name.

Cellini offers the purest case we know of the wholly positive, affirmative side of the Renaissance psychology, which is discussed in its various aspects earlier in this introduction. He is, indeed, unaware of being ruled by any "philosophy"; he is wholly immersed in the particular action at hand, in the part he plays, fully persuaded of its validity. He comes closest to placing himself in a large perspective, and to thinking in terms of the condition and destiny of man, when he shows a sort of superstitious reliance on his own good fortune and pluck: the teller of the tale is regarded as a hero singled out by Providence for high and lucky deeds. A sense of the exceptional and the miraculous is pressed upon the reader from the very start. There are prodigious omens when he is a little child; his father is himself a man of fabulous skills; his grandfather has passed his hundredth year; and *Benvenuto*, of course, means "welcome."

Cellini's life was the life of a Renaissance artist, and therefore it involved, practically, two main sorts of relationships: the relationship to his work and the relationship to his patrons—in his case a pope, a king of France, and a member of the Medici family. The accounts of his work provide some of the most serious and moving sections of the book; the description of the casting of the statue of Perseus is deservedly a classic. The contemporary milieu—the background of the courts that offered him patronage and, generally, of the society, high and low, in which he moved—provides among other things an element necessary in narratives where the central hero is prodigiously endowed and privileged: the "enemies," those who seek to destroy him by turning the patron's grace away from him, as in the Charlemagne stories the villain, the treacherous Ganelon of Mayence, acts against the privileged paladins. In the intrigue-filled Renaissance courts, this situation was characteristic, and we possess few documents which give us so vivid a notion of that world and of the peculiar position of the artist in it as Cellini does. Cellini is lawless because he considers himself, as an artist, above the law. Whatever stands in the way of a full display of his particular *virtù*, whether natural impediments (casting metal) or human ones (the "enemies"), must be eliminated. With his aggressive spirit and his taste for the dramatic, he always has a special "enemy" singled out; the Pompeo of our selection is one. In disposing of Pompeo the hero illustrates what has sometimes been called the amoralism of the Renaissance; he gives to killing the same sort of clean and athletic competence which he gives to art: "Then I aimed to strike him in the face; but fright made him turn his head round; and I stabbed him just beneath the ear. I only gave two blows, for he fell stone dead at the second." Nor would the picture be complete if, a little later, he did not have the Pope declare that

"men like Benevenuto . . . stand above the law."

The very unreliability of certain sections of this account, as well as the histrionic tone which generally pervades it, call to mind one of the favorite images of Renaissance literature: the image of the world as a stage, of life as a pageant, in which men are more or less consciously playing their roles. The exuberant gusto with which Cellini performs suggests that he is perfectly adjusted to the situation. The world is a stage on which he is "welcome" and where no higher "truth" concerns him. In other, more sensitive writers this same fictitious quality which the mystery of life and the fragmentariness of knowledge bestow on the human condition was to prompt, instead, a sense of ghastly vanity, and to conduce to melancholy or even folly.

ARETINO, *LETTERS*

Aretino is convenient to have in a selection of Renaissance writings for two main reasons: the blatant, "excessive" way in which he embodies some of the characteristics of the period; and the fact that his most significant literary products are his *Letters*. A selection from these, however limited, will exemplify this important literary genre and implicitly illustrate what the relationship between the man of intellect and the man of power can be like when the former is at least as self-assured and as far above "ordinary morals" as the latter.

Renaissance literature, as we know, acquires much of its richness from a concomitance of opposite tendencies, from an exceptional awareness of the highest and the lowest in man. Hence, a popular conception of Renaissance life, by no means unwarranted, implies a mixture of splendor and turpitude in private and public conduct, of loyalty and treachery in human relations. Aretino in his writings could go all the way from scurrilous invective and calumny to the offering of the wise counsel and to the expression of noble feeling and emotion. And there seems to be little doubt that quite a few among the very powerful feared his invective and listened to his counsel. In an age of low morals some people bought him off, some hated him and tried to destroy him, some simply valued and cherished his intellect and his wit. He was known as "divine Aretino," "the scourge of princes," and prided himself on being "secretary to the world."

There is hyperbole and bombast in all that, but there is also an essential core of truth. Aretino's house in Venice, where he spent the larger part of his life, was frequented by kings and princes, high prelates, great artists, along with scores of less splendid figures and a more or less permanent retinue of courtesans; it is one of the standard images in any picture of European Renaissance society. If he said that the steps of his staircase were worn out by the feet of the great "as the pavement of the Capitol by the wheels of triumphal chariots," he only testifies to that sense of theatricality, typical of his age, which he possessed to the highest degree. Like many others he attended to the

formation of his own legend and was as successful at it as anybody in his time. His effigy appeared on gold and silver medals and on other memento objects. Michelangelo, whose drawings for the *Last Judgment* were disapproved by Aretino, painted him there as St. Bartholomew. His commerce with the great and powerful permitted him to magnify himself on the one side, and on the other to exercise a rewarding form of adulation or to cash in on threat and blackmail. He called money "the breath blown into the trumpets of virtue." The fact that a man of this sort wielded considerable power would be significant in itself; more significant, of course, is the fact that this power was achieved through the written word.

The letter as a genre was not necessarily a simple communication from person to person. Aretino's letters to the great of this world were not only addressed to their individual recipients but also printed and sold to the public. It has been said that the genre constitutes an early form of journalism. Of course, some of his motivations for writing them were exhibitionism and hope for recognition and reward. In the pursuit of these aims he could be proud and humble, caressing and threatening; he loudly enjoys his standing with the powerful, ready to spite them if he is not recognized and to beam with self-applause if he is. In one of our selections, writing to Titian who was then painting portraits at the court of Charles V, he warns: "You know that I could make even the Emperor a laughing stock if he should make a jest of me," but on a following occasion he is delighted to be informed that the Emperor upon receiving Titian had asked him whether he brought letters from Aretino, and that such a sign of special consideration was given by that monarch in the presence of a highly prominent courtier.

Underlying these fairly negative qualities, we find at least two positive ones in Aretino's letters: definite moral courage, and a fundamental soundness of judgment. Three of his most famous letters, which will be found in our selections (to Francis I, to Charles V, and to Pope Clement VII), are hardly dictated by mere ostentation and opportunism. Aretino, who once wrote that "all princes are creatures of violence," will be found to advocate conciliation, temperance, justice. His manner is both solemn and familiar, his rhetoric a blend of shrewd adulation and political common sense. More than once his judgment in public affairs proved to be sound.

In private relationships, though more than once he was ferocious in covering his adversaries with obloquy of the lowest kind, on other occasions he was equally warm in expressing affection and praise, exemplified in our selections by his letter to a Venetian courtesan and by several letters to Titian. The great painter was not only his closest friend but certainly taught the writer Aretino (who in turn acted as agent and promoter to the painter) how to look at beauty with an artist's eye. Finally, the letters to Titian are also significant since they clearly imply a scale of values that is typical of the age:

particularly, the superiority of the creative genius over the man of action, of the artist over the prince.

MONTAIGNE, *ESSAYS*

If one accepts the common view that in the Renaissance the individual human being was exalted, and therefore a special emphasis was placed on the study of man in his "virtues" and singularities, it is natural to think of Montaigne as representative. As the father of the modern genre of the personal essay, in the last quarter of the sixteenth century, he obviously felt that the characteristics of his individual mind and heart—all their minute aspects, variations, and even whims—were worthy of being carefully recorded. The student will soon notice that of the writers presented in this book Montaigne is the one who most openly speaks in his own right, clearly and unabashedly as himself. While Erasmus takes for the expression of certain views the ambiguous mouthpiece of his "Folly" and, to choose a totally different example, Cellini, although writing an autobiography, seems obviously intent on building himself into a colorful protagonist, Montaigne's characteristic and somewhat rambling speech is in the simplest and most quintessential first person. Perhaps at no other time in literature—certainly not in the nineteenth-century age of romanticism, where in spite of the widespread notions about "free" expression of individual feelings writers so often showed themselves through an alter ego or a heroic mask—has a writer so thoroughly attempted to present himself without in the least assuming a pose, or falling into a type. "Had my intention been to court the world's favor," Montaigne writes in the foreword to his *Essays* (*Essais*), "I should have trimmed myself more bravely, and stood before it in a studied attitude. I desire to be seen in my simple, natural, and everyday dress, without artifice or constraint; for it is myself I portray." And elsewhere he affirms:

Authors communicate themselves to the world by some special and extrinsic mark; I am the first to do so by my general being, as Michel de Montaigne, not as a grammarian or a poet or a lawyer. If the world finds fault with me for speaking too much of myself, I find fault with the world for not even thinking of itself.

But nothing would be more erroneous than to suppose that Montaigne's focusing on his individual self implies a sense of the extraordinary importance of man, of his central place in the world, or of the special power of his understanding. The contrary is true. In the first place, in temperament Montaigne is singularly opposed to assuming an attitude of importance: one of the keynotes of his writing, and one of his premises in undertaking it, is that the subject is average, "mediocre." In describing himself he is presenting an example of the ordinary human being, for the benefit of a few intimates. He declares that he has "but a private and family end in view," and in that sense, in fact, his way of introducing himself to the reader shows a

nobly elegant and perhaps vaguely ironical humbleness: "So, Reader, I am myself the subject of my book; it is not reasonable to expect you to waste your leisure on a matter so frivolous and empty." And then there is an even more fundamental reason why Montaigne's presentation of himself is free from any heroic posturing or intellectual pride—a reason which involves his whole view of man's place in the world. In his deciding to write about himself and to probe, to "essay," his own nature, the implication is that this is the only subject on which a man can speak with any degree of certainty. Actually, then, this writer whose work is the most acute exposure of an individual personality in the literature of the Renaissance, is at the same time one of the highest illustrations of man's ironical consciousness of his intellectual limits.

It would be a mistake to forget, however, that his work remains an outstanding assertion of an individuality, even though it is an assertion of doubt, contradiction, change. Here as in other instances the student will do well to examine the quality and novelty of the work in the actual text in terms of realized writing, of "style." A solid classical manner, reflected in certain elements of the syntactical structure and in the continuous support of classical quotations, is combined in Montaigne's style with the variety, the apparent disconnectedness, and the dramatic assertiveness of a man who is continuously analyzing a fluid and, his modesty notwithstanding, singularly attractive subject.

Others form man; I describe him, and portray a particular, very ill-made one, who, if I had to fashion him anew, should indeed be very different from what he is. But now it is done.... The world is but a perennial see-saw. All things in it are incessantly on the swing, the earth, the rocks of the Caucasus, the Egyptian pyramids.... Even fixedness is nothing but a more sluggish motion. I cannot fix my object; it is befogged, and reels with a natural intoxication.... I do not portray the thing in itself. I portray the passage....

In spite of what may often seem a leisurely gait, the writer is continuously on the alert, listening to the promptings of his thought, his sensibility, his imagination, and registering them. The affirmation of the fluidity of the human personality, of the universality of the flux, is therefore both the premise of his writing and the sum of his study of man; it is both his method and his result.

Thus, although he writes in terms of one individual, and with a fairly obvious abhorrence of any sort of classification or description of types in the manner of conventional moralists, a powerfully keen observation of man in general emerges from his writings—an observation of man's nature, intellectual power, and capacity for coherent action; of his place on earth among other beings; of his place in Creation. Our selections offer instances of Montaigne's remarks on these matters.

If we keep in mind the large pattern of Renaissance literature, poised betwen positive and negative, enthusiasm and melancholy, we shall probably find that the general temper of his assertions of doubt and his consciousness of vanity, by no means suggests an attitude of despair and gloom. His attitude seems positive and negative in the same breath; it could be called a rich and fruitful sense of the relativity of everything. Thus if he examines and "essays" man's capacity to act purposefully and coherently (see the essay "Of the Inconsistency of Our Actions" among our selections), his implicit verdict is not that man's action is absolutely vain. Rather, observing the usual example—his own self—and seeing that there is nothing he can say of himself "absolutely, simply, and steadily," he refuses to attribute to the human personality a coherence which it does not possess and which, we may be tempted to surmise, would rather impoverish it. "Our actions are but a patchwork. . . . We are all made up of bits. . . . There is as much difference between us and ourselves, as between us and others." And he sustains his arguments, as usual, with a wealth of examples and anecdotes which are at once evidence of his vital curiosity about human nature and, in many cases, of his man-to-man familiarity with antiquity: Emperor Augustus, to mention one, pleases him because his character successfully escapes an all-of-a-piece description; he has "slipped through the fingers of even the most daring critics."

A sense of relativity and a balanced outlook, rather than a negative and desperate reversal of the optimistic view of the human situation, are apparent also from Montaigne's observation of man—and particularly of the civilized Renaissance man whom he exemplifies—in relation to his fellow human beings. In the famous essay "Of Cannibals," where a comparison is made between the codes of primitive tribes and those of "ourselves," the basic idea is not a disparagement of our civilization but a relativistic warning, for "we all call barbarism that which does not fit in with our usages." The cannibals' acts of barbarity are recognized, but the writer is "not so much concerned that we should remark on the horrible barbarity of such acts, as that, whilst rightly judging their errors, we should be so blind to our own." We do much worse, adds Montaigne, who wrote in times of horrible religious strife, and we do it under the guise of piety. The enlightening sense of relativity —rather than a more extreme and totally paradoxical view of the "nobility" of savages—permits him to see and admire what he considers superior elements in the customs of the cannibals (for instance, their conception of valor and their conduct of warfare). Here, in fact, Montaigne describes and admires a code of unrewarded gallantry, of valor for valor's sake, which was not uncommonly cherished by writers of the Renaissance (Castiglione, for example). ". . . the acquisition of the victor," writes Montaigne, "is the glory and advantage of having proved himself the superior in valour and virtue. . . . The honour of virtue consists in combating, not in beating." We may incidentally add that acceptance of this notion of pure "virtue," practiced for no material purposes and as self-rewarding as a beautiful object, appears to have been, for a writer like Montaigne, the way to preserve an admiration for the warrior's code of manly courage and valor in spite of the basically pacifist tendencies of his temperament and his bitter disinclination for the spectacles of conflict and bloodshed witnessed in his own time.

Naturally, an even larger sense of relativity emerges from Montaigne's writing when he examines man's place in the universal frame of things, as he does, in an outstanding instance, in some famous passages of the "Apology for Raimond Sebond" (a selection from which is included in this volume). Man's notion of his privileged position in Creation is eloquently questioned: "What has induced him to believe that that wonderful motion of the heavenly vault, the eternal light of those torches rolling so proudly over his head, the awe-inspiring agitations of that infinite sea, were established, and endure through so many centuries for his service and convenience?" The tone of the whole section is revealing. In many writers a similar anxiety about man's smallness and ignorance casts upon the human condition a light of tragic vanity. Montaigne's acceptance of the situation is to use some of our other examples as convenient points of reference—more Erasmian than Hamletlike. If he asks questions which involve, to say the very least, the whole Renaissance conception of man's "dignity," the impression, as we listen to his voice, is never really one of dark negation and melancholy. While man's advantages over other beings are quietly evaluated and discredited ("this licence of thought . . . is an advantage sold to him very dearly . . . For from it springs the principal source of . . . sin, sickness, irresolution, affliction, despair"), he maintains a balanced and often humorous tone in which even the frivolous aside of the personal essayist is not dissonant, but characteristic: "When I play with my cat, who knows but that she regards me more as a plaything than I do her?" Thus without raising his voice too much he achieves a point of view which suggests broadness and inclusiveness rather than gloom and despair. For, while his view of the "mediocrity" of man among other beings debunks any form of intellectual conceit, on the other hand an encompassing sense of natural fellowship in Creation is envisaged: "I have said all this to establish the resemblance to human conditions, and to bring us back and join us to the majority."

This sense of a "natural" fellowship seems to characterize not only Montaigne's view of the position of man in Creation but also his conception of man as a moral individual in relation to other men. The student may see this at the end of our final selection, where good is envisaged, elsewhere as valor, as a beautiful and self-rewarding act of "virtue":

There is . . . no goodness in which a well-born nature does not delight. . . . There is no small pleasure in feeling oneself preserved from the contagion of so corrupt an age, and saying to oneself, "Should any one look into my very soul, he would

yet not find me guilty of the affliction or ruin of any man. . . ." These testimonies of a good conscience please; and this natural satisfaction is a great boon to us, and the only payment that will never fail us.

Difficult as it is to reduce Montaigne's views to short and abstract statements, the reader will probably be left with the impression that here his vision of man, and of the possibility of a good life, is nearer to hopefulness than to despair. Though his attitude is far from Rabelais' optimism and exuberance, it too is based on a balance between the "natural" and the intellectual, between instinct and reason. He belittles, at times even scornfully, the power of the human intellect, and like Erasmus he points to instinctive simplicity of mind as being more conducive to happiness and even to true knowledge; but on the other hand the whole tone of his work, its intellectual sophistication, its very bulk, and the loving manner with which he attended to it, show that his own thought was not something that "sicklied o'er" his life, but something that gave it sustenance and delight. Thus we see in him some of the basic contrasts of the Renaissance mind —the acceptance and the rejection of the intellectual dignity of man—conducing not to disruption but to temperately positive results. Though his work offers anything but the abstract scheme of an ideal man, and he is not proposing a model or a recipe, yet in passages like the one cited in the preceding paragraph, some norm of the pattern of a truly virtuous man—in the sense expressed later by the

French as "honest" (as in the phrase *honnête homme*)—seems unobtrusively to emerge. And though it is not imposed upon the audience, any reader is free to think that acceptance of this norm would result in better spiritual balance in the individual and a more harmonious and sensible fellowship in society. The author does not preach ("Others form man; I describe him . . .") because his pattern of conduct is one which cannot be taught but only experienced. He limits himself to exemplifying it in his own wise and unheroic self.

CERVANTES, DON QUIXOTE

Although *Don Quixote* was a popular success from the time Part I was published in 1605, it was only later recognized as important literature. This delay was due partly to the fact that in a period of established and well-defined genres like the epic, the tragedy, and the pastoral romance (Cervantes himself tried his hand frequently at some of these forms), the unconventional combination of elements in *Don Quixote* resulted in a work of considerable novelty, with the serious aspects hidden under a mocking surface.

The initial and overt purpose of the book was to satirize a very popular type of literature, the romances of chivalry. In those long yarns, which had to do with the Carolingian and Arthurian legends and were full of supernatural deeds of valor, implausible and complicated adventures, duels, and enchantments, the literature which had expressed the medieval spirit of chivalry and romance had degenerated to the same extent to which, in our day, certain conventions of romantic literature have degenerated in "pulp" fiction and film melodrama. Up to a point, then, what Cervantes set out to do was to produce a parody, the caricature of a literary type. But neither the nature of his genius nor the particular method he chose allowed him to limit himself to such a relatively simple and direct undertaking. The actual method he followed in order to expose the silliness of the romances of chivalry was to show to what extraordinary consequences they would lead a man insanely infatuated with them, once this man set out to live "now" according to their patterns of action and belief. So what we have is not mere parody or caricature, for there is a great deal of difference between simply presenting a grotesque version of a story dealing with a remote and more or less imaginary world, and presenting a modern man deciding to live by the standards of that world in a modern and realistic context. The first consequence is a mingling of two different genres. On the one hand, as even the beginning reader of *Don Quixote* soon recognizes, much of the language and material of the book turns out to have the color and intonation of the glamorous world of chivalry. The fact that that world and that tone depend for their existence in the book on the powers of evocation and self-deception of the hero himself makes them no less operative artistically, and adds, in fact, an important element of idealization. On the other hand, the chivalric world is continuously combined with the elements of contemporary life evoked by the narrator—the realities of landscape and talk, peasants and nobles, inns and highways. So the author can draw on two sources, roughly the realistic and the romantic, truth and imagination, practical facts and metaphysical values. In this respect, in his having found a way to bring together concrete actuality and highly ideal values, Cervantes can be said to have fathered the modern novel.

The consequences of Cervantes' invention are more apparent when the reader begins to analyze a little more closely the nature of those two worlds, the romantic and the realistic, or the kind of impact which the first exercises on the second. The hero embodying the world of the romances is not, as we know, a cavalier of old; he is an impoverished country gentleman, adopting that code in the "modern" world. The code of chivalry is not simply and directly satirized; it is placed in a context different from its native one. The result of that new association is a new whole, a new unity. The "code" is renovated; it is put into a different perspective, given another chance.

We should remember in this connection that in the process of deterioration which the romances of chivalry had undergone, certain basically attractive ideals had become empty conventions—for instance, the ideals of love as devoted "service," of adventurousness, of loyalty to high concepts of valor and generosity. In the new context those values are re-examined. Incidentally, Cervantes may well have gained a practical sense of them in his own life, at the time of his early youth, when he was a warrior at Lepanto (the great victory of the European coalition against the "infidels"), and a pirate's captive. Since he began writing *Don Quixote* in his late fifties, a vantage point from which his adventurous youth must have appeared impossibly remote, a factor of nostalgia—which could hardly have been present in a pure satire—may well have entered into his composition of the work. Furthermore, had Cervantes undertaken a direct caricature of the romance genre, the serious and noble values of chivalry could not have been made apparent except negatively, but in the context devised by him in *Don Quixote* they find a way to assert themselves positively also.

The book in its development is, to a considerable extent, the story of that assertion—of the impact that Don Quixote's revitalization of the chivalric code has on a contemporary world. We must remember, of course, that there is ambiguity in the way that assertion is made; it works slowly on the reader, as his own discovery rather than as the narrator's open suggestion. Actually, whatever attraction the chivalric world of his hero's vision may have had for Cervantes, he does not openly support Don Quixote at all. He even seems at times to go further in repudiating him than he needs to, for the hero is officially insane, and the narrator never tires of reminding us of this. One critic has described the attitude he affects toward his creature as "animosity." Nevertheless, by the very magniloquence and, often, the extraordinary coherence and beauty which the narrator allows his hero to display in his speeches in defense of his vision and of his code, we are gradually led to discover for ourselves the serious and important elements these contain; in fact, we suspect that the "animosity" ultimately does nothing but intensify our interest in Don Quixote and our sympathy for him. And in that process we are, as audience, simply repeating the experiences which many characters are having on the "stage" of the book, in their relationships with him.

Generally speaking, the encounters between the ordinary world and Don Quixote are encounters betwen the world of reality and that of illusion, between reason and imagination, ultimately between the world in which action is prompted by material considerations and interests and a world in which action is prompted by ideal motives. Our selections exemplify these aspects of the experience. Among the first adventures are some which have most contributed to popularize the Don Quixote legend: he sees windmills and decides they are giants; country inns become castles; flocks of sheep, armies. Though the conclusions of such episodes often have the ludicrousness of slapstick comedy,

there is a powerfully imposing quality about Don Quixote's insanity: his madness always has method, a commanding persistence and coherence. And there is perhaps an inevitable sense of moral grandeur in the spectacle of anyone remaining so unflinchingly faithful to his own vision. The world of "reason" may win in point of fact, but a residue of moral superiority is left with Quixote.

Besides, we increasingly realize that his own manner of action has greatness in itself, and not only the greatness of persistence: his purpose is to redress wrongs, to come to the aid of the afflicted, to offer generous help, to challenge danger and practice valor. And we finally feel the impact of the arguments which sustain his action—for example, in the section from Part II (the episode of the lions) in which he expounds "the meaning of valor." The ridiculousness of the situation is counterbalanced by the basic seriousness of Quixote's motives; his notion of courage for the sake of courage appears, and is recognized, as singularly noble, a sort of generous display of integrity in a world usually run on a lower plane. Thus the distinction between "reason" and "madness," truth and illusion, becomes, to say the least, ambiguous. Don Quixote's delusions are indeed exposed, once they are checked against hard facts, but the authority of such facts is, morally, questionable.

The effectiveness of Don Quixote's conduct and vision is seen most clearly in his relation with Sancho Panza. An attempt to define that relation will be the best way for the student to come to grips with the book. It would be rather crude oversimplification to say that Don Quixote and Sancho represent illusion and reality, the world of the abstract and insane code of knight-errantry in contrast with the present world of down-to-earth practicalities. Actually Sancho, though his nature is strongly defined by such elements as his common sense, his earthy speech, his simple phrases studded with proverbs set against the hero's magniloquence, is mainly characterized in his development by the degree to which he believes in his master. He is caught in the snare of Don Quixote's vision; the seeds of·the imaginative life are successfully implanted in him.

The impact on Sancho of Quixote's view of life serves therefore to illustrate one of the important aspects of the hero and, we may finally say, one of the important aspects of Renaissance literature: the attempt, finally frustrated but extremely attractive as long as it lasts, of the individual mind to produce a vision and a system of its own, in a world which often seems to have lost a universal frame of reference and an ultimately satisfactory sense of the value and meaning of action. What Don Quixote presents is a vision of a world which, for all its aberrant qualities, appears generally to be more colorful and more thrilling, and also, incidentally, to be inspired by more honorable rules of conduct, than the world of ordinary people, "real-

ism," current affairs, private interests, easy jibes, and petty pranks. It is a world in which actions are performed out of a sense of their beauty and excitement, not for the sake of their utility or, as we would say now, of their practicality. It is, again, the world as stage, animated by "folly"; in this case the lights go out at the end, an end which is "reasonable" and therefore gloomy. Sancho provides the major example of one who is exposed to that vision and absorbs that light while it lasts. How successfully he has done so is seen during the hero's death scene, in which he begs of his master not to die but to continue the play, as has been suggested, in a new dress. But at that final point the hero is "cured" and killed, and Sancho is restored to the petty interests of the world as he can see it by his own lights, after the cord connecting him to his imaginative master is cut by the latter's "repentance" and death.

CALDERÓN, *LIFE IS A DREAM*

It is appropriate to read *Life Is a Dream* at this point since it presents, albeit in new and extreme versions, some of the motifs we have already encountered. *Life Is a Dream* (*La vida es sueño*, 1636?) was written as a comedy by Pedro Calderón de la Barca while he was in his early thirties; yet the play has tragic overtones and its leading characters meditate on such serious questions as the nature of life. In the play, the notion that the world is a stage and life an apparition, a dream, is not sim-

ply a poetic image or a metaphor; it is presented as the basic
orientation of life, a design for
living, the norm. Granted that
it is possible and useful to reduce the theme of a play, especially a play as varied and exuberant as this one, to a brief
and convenient statement, the
formula here would go something like this: Life is a dream.
Even if one should occasionally
suspect that life is real and substantial, one must still think of
it as a dream so that one may
live it properly and achieve
moral salvation.

The place of the action is a
kingdom which, without even
the remotest trace of historical
justification, is called Poland.
There is a king, that character so
important in traditional dramas
and fairy tales. Superficially the
plot involves a kingdom and dy-
nastic succession, a familiar
theme in classical and Renaissance drama. King Basil is, as
kings ought to be, a sage, but
his sagacity is peculiar and somewhat sinister: he regulates his
life according to the revelations
of the fabulous and degenerate
"science" of astrology. He has
confined his son and heir apparent, Segismund, to a remote
tower dungeon because before
and during his birth, the stars
and heavens showed awful portents. These portents suggest
some of the cosmic aspects of
the play:

The whole earth overflowed with
    conflagrations
So that it seemed the final paroxysm
Of existence. The skies grew dark.
    Buildings shook.
The clouds rained stones. The riv-
    ers ran with blood.

But King Basil is sufficiently
reasonable to pay at least lip
service to the notion of man's
free will. He knows that

Violent inclination, the most im-
    pious
Planet—all can but influence, not
    force,
The free will which man holds
    direct from God.

Consequently Calderón's play
is a wonderful mixture of odd
frenzied activity and subtle abstract discussion, which is one
of its most attractive traits. The
main plot gets underway as
Basil, in an elaborate explanation, decides to "test" Segismund, allowing him to be
brought to the palace in a trance
and there to be given courtly
homage and royal powers. His
conduct will show whether he is
of royal timber or a dangerous
monster, as the stars predicted.

The experiment fails: Segismund behaves like an unruly tyrant. The beast prevails. For
example, after a brief exchange
with a servant of the household
concerning what amounts to a
point of courtly etiquette (the
impropriety of wooing a lady as
boldly as Segismund does Stella), he throws the man out of
a window into "the sea" to prove
that it is he who decides what
is "just." Basil does not take his
share of the blame for the
prince's bestiality and considers
the experiment a failure and a
confirmation of his dire forecast.
Nevertheless he plants in Segismund's mind the first seeds of
his redemption by warning him
that *all* royal splendor and power
may be a dream. Clotaldo, the
hero's guardian-mentor, draws
the moral of the lesson more

precisely: "even in dreams, I warn you/Nothing is lost by trying to do good." This prompts Segismund's most celebrated speech at the end of Act II, and anticipates his full enlightenment in the last act.

The subplot, which interlocks with the main plot from the very first scene, is filled with the typical coincidences and implausibilities of a comedy of intrigue. The main character of the subplot is Rosaura. In terms of literary conventions, she lies somewhere between the stock characters of the lady in distress and the woman warrior. She has come to "Poland" disguised as a man to look for her seducer, Astolfo. There she finds not only her faithless lover—he has already taken up with his cousin, Stella, a possible heir to Basil's throne—but her father as well, and *he* turns out to have been the seducer of her mother. The subplot proceeds with the help of crude devices and props (the sword and the portrait) and elaborate debates on points of honor, so typical of Spanish plays of the period. What, for example, is the point of honor for Clotaldo when he is caught between two facts: that Astolfo, who saved his life during Segismund's tyrannical phase, is the seducer of his daughter?

The dénouement is, of course, happy; Astolfo will marry Rosaura and Segismund will marry Stella. The only casualty, oddly enough, is the talkative clown, Clarion. The central issue, as the final knots are tied, is Segismund's development; the happy ending of the subplot parallels Segismund's successful execu-tion of the second "test." This test of Segismund's royal fitness is brought about by the action of insurgents against King Basil. They liberate Segismund from his renewed confinement and recognize him as their leader. He discourses upon his predicament at some length and then decides to act, equipped as he now is with new wisdom. For Segismund now accepts not only the principle that life is a dream —and an incomprehensible one to boot, as he suggested in the closing speech of Act II—but also the idea, earlier expressed by Clotaldo and now paraphrased by the hero, that "good actions,/Even in a dream, are not entirely lost." Segismund promises to lead the rebels "bravely and skillfully," even though he knows that life is an illusion. The implication is that in spite of the purposelessness of life, or perhaps *because* of it, life should be lived with dignity, courage, and a sense of purpose.

It would be easy to superimpose a strictly orthodox interpretation of Calderón's theme: life is an illusion and a test and is followed by revelation and a just reward. But the language and impact of the play hardly warrant it. After all, Calderón wrote this as a comedy, not as an *auto sacramental*, the religious allegories of which he was to become a master later in life. This play is about human conduct and carries a twofold "message": life is a dream, yet it must not be lived irresponsibly. Each of us must discover his own idea of virtue and honor and practice it, as it were, gratuitously. This interpretation has a lingering flavor of Quixotism and at the same time a haunting suggestion of modernity.

With all this, *Life Is a Dream* is difficult to summarize in terms of abstract philosophies. Its tone is particularly hard to describe. It has elements of the fairy tale, with its happy ending, but it is set against the dark background of a tragic awareness of reality. There are cloak-and-dagger routines and debates on points of honor which, for all their conventions, suddenly seem authentic and strangely relevant to real life. The plot is a mechanical comedy, full of disguises and surprise recognitions; yet it is carried on by characters whose main purpose seems to be to meditate on human destiny and contemplate death, while their speech, at once formal and exuberant, full of rich imagery, expresses their vitality and earthly attachment. The general truth that no commentary can replace or even approach the impact of direct immersion in a literary text applies to this play with particular force. The play is its own haunting "meaning," and so confirms in a splendid manner the nature of literary art.

LIVES, WRITINGS, AND CRITICISM
Biographical and critical works are listed only if they are available in English.

FRANCIS PETRARCH

LIFE AND WRITINGS. Francesco Petrarca was born at Arezzo on July 13, 1304. His father, like Dante, was exiled from Florence and in 1312 moved with his family to Avignon. Following his father's wish, Petrarch studied law at Montpellier and Bologna, but he abandoned these studies by 1326 when he took minor orders, which brought him certain financial benefits. Back in Avignon, he was well received by the brilliant and refined society that moved around the papal court. On April 6, 1327, in the Church of St. Clare, he saw, for the first time, Laura, who was to become the object and image of his love poetry. Soon after, Petrarch began a series of wide travels, to France, Flanders, and Germany, as a humanist searching for ancient texts, as a man of letters, and as a diplomat. In 1337 he paid his first visit to Rome, to him as a restorer of antiquity and a Christian a twofold spiritual capital. Later in the same year, at Vaucluse near Avignon he tried to revive the ancient ideal of spiritually active relaxation, or *otium*, and began his major Latin work, the epic poem *Africa*.

In 1340 Petrarch received from both Paris and Rome an invitation to be crowned poet laureate; he chose Rome, receiving the crown in the Capitol. Later he visited Parma and nearby Selvapiana, then again Avignon, where his natural daughter Francesca was born in 1343. His natural son was then six years old. Petrarch's spiritual conflicts of the period, enlivened by his brother Gherardo's decision to enter a monastery, are reflected in the autobiographical treatise *Secretum*. In 1348, while traveling in Italy, he received news of Laura's death by plague. She died on April 6, the same day that he had first seen her and the day of Christ's passion.

In 1350 on his way to Rome for the Jubilee, Petrarch stopped at Florence as a guest of Boccaccio. The friendship of these two poets and humanists was an important event for European culture. After another period at Vaucluse, Petrarch spent most of 1353-1361 in Milan, entrusted by the Visconti rulers with various diplomatic missions (to Venice, to Prague, to the king of France). Such occupations he alternated with intense study and work, attending during this period to a complete edition of his lyric poetry in Italian, to letters and treatises in Latin, and to work on his great unfinished *terza rima* allegory, *The Triumphs (I Trionfi)*. Escaping from the danger of the plague, he moved to Padua in 1361 and the next year to Venice, where his daughter Francesca lived and where Boccaccio visited him in 1362. He began at this time the definitive ordering of the *rime* (his Italian lyric poetry), his most influential work. In 1367 he moved back to Padua, spending much of his time in a nearby country house at Arquà in the Euganean

Hills. There he died in 1374, on the eve of his seventieth birthday.

BIOGRAPHY AND CRITICISM: Ugo Foscolo, *Essays on Petrarch* (1823); Maud F. Jerrold, *Francis Petrarch, Poet and Humanist* (1909); Pierre de Nolhac, *Petrarch and the Ancient World* (1907); J. H. Whitfield, *Petrarch and the Renascence* (1943); and E. H. Wilkins, *Studies in the Life and Works of Petrarch* (1955) and *Life of Petrarch* (1961).

DESIDERIUS ERASMUS

LIFE AND WRITINGS. Born out of wedlock to a physician's daughter and a father who later became a priest, in 1466?, apparently at Rotterdam, for he later referred to himself as Desiderius Erasmus Roterodamus. He was schooled at Gouda, then at Deventer, where humanistic masters fostered his love of good letters. After both parents died, his guardians sent him, with an older brother, to Hertogenbosch and later to the Augustinian Canons at Steyn, although his desire had been to enter a university. He was ordained a priest on April 25, 1492. His humanistic aspirations found an outlet in 1494 when he became Latin secretary to Henry of Bergen, bishop of Cambrai, through whose help, in 1495, he entered the college of Montaigu at the University of Paris. College discipline was very strict, but in the following year Erasmus had lodgings in town and received pupils. With a pupil, William Blount, Baron Mountjoy, he paid a first visit to England in 1499-1500 and met Thomas More and John Colet, the latter encouraging him toward serious theological study and a direct scholarly approach to the early Church Fathers. In the following years he traveled on the Continent, stopping for an interval at Louvain; his first collection of *Adages* (*Adagia*, short sayings from classical authors) appeared in Paris in 1500, and his *Handbook of the Christian Knight* (*Enchiridion militis christiani*), a plea for the return to primitive Christian simplicity, was published at Antwerp in 1504. After a second visit to England in 1505–1506, during which he met Warham, the archbishop of Canterbury, a chance to act as tutor to the son of Henry VII's physician, Boeri, enabled him to fulfill the humanist's aspiration to visit Italy. There he spent some time at the universities of Turin (where he received a doctorate of theology) and Bologna, visited Padua and Florence, and conversed with high church dignitaries in Rome; in Venice, Aldo Manuzio, the great Humanistic printer, became a friend and published the enlarged *Adages*. In 1509 he returned to England; he wrote there in that year the *Praise of Folly* (*Moriae encomium*) During this third and longest residence (until 1514) he lectured in Greek and divinity at Cambridge and completed his work on the Greek New Testament. After leaving England, Erasmus, whose life offers the highest illustration of the type of the cosmopolitan humanist, particularly in his wish to unite humanistic learning and religious piety, continued to travel on the Continent, finally making his most permanent home in Basel, a center whose cultural importance cannot be overestimated, especially as the seat of the printing house of Frobenius, whose general editor Erasmus became. In 1529 religious disturbances and the victories of the Swiss reformers caused him to move to Freiburg in the Breisgau, the German university town in the Black Forest. Erasmus' attitude toward the reformers (Luther in Germany, Zwingli in Switzerland) was typical: after having tried to promote an impartial arbitration of the question between Luther and the Roman church, he was alienated by excesses on both sides. The shattering news of More's execution in England reached him in Freiburg. He returned to Basel in 1535 and died there in July, 1536. Besides his literary works and pamphlets, his editions of the Church Fathers, and the like, his letters (about three thousand) are an important document of the cultural life of the period.

BIOGRAPHY AND CRITICISM. P. S. Allen, *The Age of Erasmus* (1914), and *Erasmus, Lectures and Wayfaring Sketches* (1934); *The Praise of Folly by Desiderius Erasmus*, edited by Leonard F. Dean, a new translation, with introduction and notes (1946); Christopher Hollis, *Erasmus* (1933); Johan Huizinga, *Erasmus* (1924); Joseph Mangan, *The Life, Character and Influence of Desiderius Erasmus* (1926); Preserved Smith, *Erasmus* (1923); Stefan Zweig, *Erasmus* (1934).

BALDESAR CASTIGLIONE

LIFE AND WRITINGS. Born at Casatico, near Mantua, in 1487. His father, Cristoforo, was a courtier and his mother was a Gonzaga, related to the lords of Mantua. He received a humanistic education in Milan. From 1499 to 1503 he was in the service of Francesco Gonzaga, lord of Mantua, and from 1504 to 1513 he was at Urbino in the service (diplomatic and military) of Guidobaldo da Montefeltro (whose wife was a Gonzaga) and of Francesco Maria della Rovere, by whom he was made a count. In 1506 he went to England on an embassy to the court of Henry VII, from whom he received, on behalf of his lord, the Order of the Garter and to whom he presented a painting by Raphael. In 1515 he was again with the Gonzagas, who made him their ambassador to Pope Leo X (Giovanni de' Medici). In Rome his friends included Raphael and Michelangelo, and he saw Renaissance social and intellectual life at its most brilliant; he thus not only codified the ideal of the refined and "virtuous" courtier but also embodied it. In 1525 Pope Clement VII made him his ambassador to the court of Emperor Charles V in Spain. Castiglione's premature death there, at Toledo in 1529, was probably caused in part by sorrow at his failure to foresee the emperor's designs as they most dramatically took shape in the "sack of Rome" in 1527. *The Book of the Courtier (Il libro del cortegiano)*, in which the court of Urbino is idealized, was written between 1508 and 1516 and published after constant revisions, in 1528 in Venice.

BIOGRAPHY AND CRITICISM. Julia Cartwright Ady, *Baldassare Castiglione, the Perfect Courtier: His Life and Letters* (1908); Ralph Roeder, *The Man of the Renaissance; Four Lawgivers: Savonarola, Machiavelli, Castiglione, Aretino* (1933); Wilhelm Schenk, "The *Cortegiano* and the Civilization of the Renaissance," *Scrutiny, XVI* (Summer 1949), 93-103.

NICCOLÒ MACHIAVELLI

LIFE AND WRITINGS. Born in Florence on May 3, 1469. His father was a jurist and owned some land. Little is known of his schooling; it is obvious from his work that he knew the Latin and Italian writers well. He entered public life in 1494 as a clerk and from 1498 to 1512 was secretary to the second chancery of the commune of Florence, whose magistrates were in charge of internal and war affairs. In connection with the duties of this post, during the war against Pisa he dealt with military problems firsthand, at this time forming his aversion to mercenary troops. He went on many diplomatic missions—among others, to King Louis XII of France in 1500 and in 1502 to Cesare Borgia, whose ruthless conquest of the Romagna he described in a booklet showing direct insight into the type of the amoral and technically efficient "prince." In 1506 he went on a mission to Pope Julius II, whose expedition into the Romagna he followed closely. From his missions to Emperor Maximilian (1508) and again to the king of France (1509) he drew his two books of observations or *Portraits (Ritratti)* of the affairs of those countries—*Ritratto delle cose della Magna*, written in 1508; and *Ritratto di cose di Francia*, written in 1510. Pre-eminently a student of politics and an observer, he endeavored to apply his experience

of other states to the strengthening of his own, the Florentine Republic, and busied himself in 1507 with the establishment of a Florentine militia, encountering great difficulties. When the republican regime came to an end, Machiavelli lost his post and was banned from the city though forbidden to leave Florentine territory; the new regime under the Medici accused him unjustly of conspiracy, and he was released only after a period of imprisonment and torture. To the time of his exile spent near San Casciano, a few miles from Florence, where he retired with his wife, Marietta Corsini, and five children, we owe the major works: the *Discourses on the First Ten Books of Livy (Discorsi sopra la prima deca di Tito Livio, 1513–1521)* and *The Prince (Il principe)*, which was written in 1513, with the hope of obtaining public office from the Medici. In 1520 he was employed on an insignificant commercial mission to Lucca; in the same year he was commissioned to write a history of Florence, which he presented in 1525 to the pope, Clement VII (Giulio de' Medici). He was sent on a mission to the papal president of the Romagna, who happened to be the great historian Francesco Guicciardini; and in 1526, conscious of imminent dangers, he was employed in the work for the military fortifications of Florence. The fate of the Medici at that point was connected with the larger struggle between King Francis I of France and the Holy Roman emperor, Charles V. Pope Clement's siding with the king of France led to the disastrous "sack of Rome"; the repercussion in Florence was the collapse of Medici domination. With the re-establishment of the republic Machiavelli's hopes rose, but they came to naught because he now was regarded as a Medici sympathizer. This last disappointment may have accelerated his end. He died on June 22, 1527, and was buried in the church of Santa Croce. He has a place in literature also for a short novel and two plays, one of which, *The Mandrake (La mandragola)*, first performed in the early 1520's, is among the most outstanding Italian comedies.

BIOGRAPHY AND CRITICISM. Ernst Cassirer, *The Myth of the State* (1946); Allan H. Gilbert, *Machiavelli's Prince and Its Forerunners* (1938); Ettore Janni, *Machiavelli* (1930); Giuseppe Prezzolini, *Niccolò Machiavelli the Florentine* (1928); Ralph Roeder, *The Man of the Renaissance: Four Lawgivers: Savonarola, Machiavelli, Castiglione, Aretino* (1933); Pasquale Villari, *The Life and Times of Niccolò Machiavelli* (1929).

FRANÇOIS RABELAIS

LIFE AND WRITINGS. Born probably about 1494-1495 into a middle-class landowning family at La Devinière, near Chinon in the province of Touraine. The father was a successful lawyer. Rabelais apparently saw in a monastic career an opportunity for study; he was trained as a novice in the Franciscan order in the monastery of La Baumette at Angers. Later, as a monk in the Franciscan monastery of Puy-Saint-Martin at Fontenay-le-Comte, he busied himself especially with the "new learning" (Greek and other Humanistic studies), which was suspect to conventional theologians. In 1524 he obtained authorization from Pope Clement VII to transfer to the less strict Benedictine order. He had close and continuous contacts, both personal and epistolary, with prominent Humanists and jurists. He probably studied law at Poitiers. Between 1527 and 1530 he seems to have traveled considerably, and probably to have studied medicine at the University of Paris, a supposition warranted by the fact that when in 1530 he entered the University of Montpellier as a medical student, he received the degree of bachelor of medicine in two months. In 1532 he was a physician in the important hospital of the Pont-du-Rhône, at Lyon, and practiced medicine with success. In the same year he published, under the name of Alcofribas Nasier, an anagram of his own name, the volume of *Pantagruel* which now constitutes Book II of *Gargantua and Pantagruel*. The story of *Gargantua*, the present Book I, appeared in 1534. In that year Rabelais traveled to Rome as personal physician to Jean du Bellay, then bishop of Paris and later a cardinal. In Rome in 1536 Rabelais obtained papal absolution for having discarded the monk's robe without authorization; later in the same year, back in France, his status became that of a secular priest. In 1537 he received his doctorate of medicine at Montpellier and held lectures there, using the Greek physicians' texts in the original. In the following years he traveled widely, and also acquired some standing at court, holding a minor post in the retinue of King Francis I. In 1538 he witnessed the historic meeting between Francis and Charles V at Aigues-Mortes. Court contacts helped him counteract the condemnations of his literary work by the theologians of the Sorbonne. The seriousness of his difficulties—arising out of accusations of heresy and leanings toward the Reformation—varied according to the protection that the court could grant him, and his own success in compromising. After Book III of *Gargantua and Pantagruel* (1546) was banned, he resided for two years in voluntary exile at Metz. He was in Rome again in 1548,

and in 1551 he was appointed to the two curacies of Saint-Martin-de-Meudon and Saint-Cristophe-de-Jambet, both of which he resigned early in 1553 because of ill health. The tradition is that he died in Paris, in the Rue des Jardins, probably in April of that year. Book IV of *Gargantua and Pantagruel*, which had appeared in 1552, had also been banned; a fifth book, of doubtful authenticity, appeared in 1562-1564.

BIOGRAPHY AND CRITICISM. Anatole France, *François Rabelais* (1929); A. J. Nock and C. R. Wilson, *François Rabelais: The Man and His Work* (1929); Jean Plattard, *The Life of Rabelais* (1930); Samuel Putnam, *Rabelais, Man of the Renaissance* (1930); Francis Watson, *Laughter for Pluto: A Book about Rabelais* (1933).

BENVENUTO CELLINI

LIFE AND WRITINGS. Born in Florence on November 1, 1500; his father, Giovanni, a musician and architect, wished the son to be a musician, but Benvenuto trained himself as a goldsmith and silversmith. An extraordinary craftsman and a very temperamental man, he early showed his inclination to produce refined objects of art and to indulge in violent quarrels; it was his involvement in a brawl in 1523 that compelled him to escape from Florence (dressed as a monk) and find refuge in Rome. His Roman residence, interrupted by several journeys, covered the years 1521-1540. Here he was a participant in the historical events (including the "sack of Rome," 1527) of which he gives a colorful account in his autobiography, while the most outstanding private event was his killing of his bitter enemy Pompeo de' Capitaneis. Both Pope Clement VII and his successor, Paul III (Alessandro Farnese), were his patrons. Pier Luigi Farnese, the son of Paul III, was his enemy and successfully accused him of theft. Consequently Cellini was imprisoned in Castel Sant'Angelo, whence he once escaped; he was caught again and placed in a particularly horrible cell, where he claims to have received supernatural visions and where he composed religious poems and drew an effigy of Christ in coal on a wall. During a journey some time before, he had become acquainted with the king of France, Francis I, who was now instrumental in his liberation. Cellini spent the years 1540-1545 in France, working with his apprentices in the castle of the Petit Nesle. In 1545 he moved back to Florence, where his patron was the duke of Florence, Cosimo de' Medici, and where he stayed until his death. The major achievements of this long last period were in the arts; his culminating triumph was at the dedication, in April, 1554, in the

Piazza della Signoria, of the statue of Perseus, to the casting of which he had devoted heroic efforts. As thanksgiving for that great success he went on a week's pilgrimage. One of his last works was the white crucifix on a black cross which is now at the Escorial. He was long ill and died poor in February, 1571; he is buried in the church of the Santissima Annunziata in Florence. The *Autobiography* (*La vita di Benvenuto Cellini*), mainly dictated to an apprentice, was begun in 1558 and reaches only the year 1562. It was first printed in 1728 and soon became famous. It was translated into German by Goethe.

BIOGRAPHY AND CRITICISM. Cellini's best biography is, of course, the one written by himself. See also Royal Cortissoz, *Benvenuto Cellini, Artist and Writer* (1906).

PIETRO ARETINO

LIFE AND WRITINGS. A literal translation of the name is "Peter of Arezzo"; Aretino was born in that Tuscan town on April 19, 1492, the son of a cobbler. In early youth he studied painting at Perugia and worked in a bookshop where he acquired an education through reading. At twenty he went to Rome where he first received employment at the court of Agostino Chigi, a prince and a wealthy banker, and later in the Pope's court (Leo X). He made and cultivated important friendships while his ferocious satires made him numerous enemies. His period at the papal court was interrupted when he entered the household of Cardinal Giulio de' Medici and later when he became a brilliant member of the court of Federigo Gonzaga at Mantua. During this period he also spent some time on the battlefield as a close friend and counselor to Giovanni de' Medici, leader of the "Black Bands" (Giovanni delle Bande Nere) whose death he witnessed and reported on. When his former protector Giulio de' Medici became Pope (Clement VII) Aretino was again at the papal court but soon found himself in disgrace and even under threat of assassination. He left Rome and settled in Venice where the Doge (Andrea Gritti) received him with favor; his house became one of the most famous and picturesque gathering points for high and low society in Renaissance Europe. He died there on October 21, 1556.

Besides his *Letters*, printed and collected also during his lifetime, some of his main works are *I Ragionamenti* (1532–1534), *Dialoghi delle corti* (1538), *Orazia*, a tragedy (1546), and a half-dozen comedies (1526-1546) which are considered among the most outstanding in Italian Renaissance theater.

BIBLIOGRAPHY AND CRITICISM. T. C. Chubb, *Aretino, Scourge of Princes* (1940); James Cleugh, *The Divine Aretino: A Biography* (1966); Edward Hutton, *Pietro Aretino, the Scourge of Princes* (1922); Ralph Roeder, *The Man of the Renaissance; Four Lawgivers: Savonarola, Machiavelli, Castiglione, Aretino* (1933).

MICHEL DE MONTAIGNE

LIFE AND WRITINGS. Michel Eyquem de Montaigne was born on February 28, 1533, in the castle of Montaigne (in the Bordeaux region), which had been bought by his great-grandfather and from which his family of traders derived their surname. His father, Pierre Eyquem, was for two terms mayor of Bordeaux and had fought in Italy under King Francis I. The writer's inclination to tolerance and naturalness may have had its origin in certain aspects of his background and early training: his mother, of Spanish-Jewish descent, was a Protestant, as were his brother Beauregard and his sister Jeanne; the third of nine children, Michel himself, like his other brothers and sisters, was raised a Catholic. His father, though no man of learning, had unconventional ideas of upbringing: Michel, who had a peasant nurse and peasant godparents, was awakened in the morning by the sound of music and had Latin taught him as his mother tongue by a German tutor. At six he went to the famous Collège de Guienne at Bordeaux; later he studied law, probably at Toulouse. In his youth he already knew court life firsthand. (At the court celebrations at Rouen for the majority of Charles IX in 1560, he saw among other things the cannibals, brought from Brazil, who became the subject of the famous essay.) In 1557 he was a member of the Bordeaux parliament; during that period he formed the deepest friendship of his life, with the young nobleman and fellow lawyer Étienne de la Boétie, who was to die a few years later. During his friend's last illness, Montaigne assisted him day and night despite the contagiousness of the disease. In 1565 he married Françoise de la Chassaigne, daughter of a colleague in the Bordeaux parliament, to whom he was temperately attached. It is difficult to say whether disappointed political ambitions contributed in any relevant measure to Montaigne's decision to "retire" at thirty-eight to his castle of Montaigne and devote himself to meditation and writing. At any rate, his residence there had various interruptions. The country was split between the Protestants, led by Henry of Navarre, and two Catholic factions: those faithful to the reigning Valois kings (first Charles IX and then Henry III) and the "leaguers" or followers of the house of Guise. In the midst of such conflicts Montaigne's attitude was balanced and conservative (both Henry III of Valois and Henry of Navarre bestowed honors upon him), though his sympathies went to the unfanatical Navarre, the future founder of the Bourbon dynasty as Henry IV. In 1574 Montaigne attempted to mediate an agreement between him and the Duke of Guise. In 1580 he undertook a journey through Switzerland, Germany, and Italy (partly to cure his gallstones); while in Italy he received news that he had been appointed mayor of Bordeaux. He held that office competently for two terms (1581-1585). Toward the end of his life he began an important friendship with the intelligent and ardently devoted Marie de Gournay, who became a kind of adopted daughter and was his literary executrix. When his favorite, Henry of Navarre, who had visited him twice in his castle, became king, Montaigne expressed his joy, though he refused Henry's offers of money; he did not live to witness in Paris, as he probably would have, the entry of the king turned Catholic ("Paris is well worth a Mass") for he died on September 13, 1592; he was buried in a church in Bordeaux. The *Essays* (*Essais*), which Montaigne started as a collection of interesting quotations, observations, remarkable events, and the like, and slowly developed to their large form and bulk, are divided into three books: Books I and II were first published in 1580; Book III (together with Books I and II revised and amplified) appeared in 1588. A posthumous edition prepared by Mlle. de Gournay, and containing some further additions, appeared in 1595. A noteworthy early English translation by John Florio was published in 1603.

BIOGRAPHY AND CRITICISM. Edward Dowden, *Michel de Montaigne* (1906); Ralph Waldo Emerson, "Montaigne, or The Skeptic," in *Representative Men* (1850); Donald M. Frame, introduction to Montaigne's *Selected Essays* (1943); André Gide, *Montaigne, An Essay in Two Parts* (1929); André Lamandé, *Montaigne, Grave and Gay* (1928); John Middleton Murry, "Montaigne," in *Heroes of Thought* (1938); Grace Norton, *The Spirit of Montaigne* (1908); J. M. Robertson, *Montaigne and Shakespeare* (2d ed., 1909); Samuel A. Tannenbaum, *Michel Eyquem de Montaigne, A Concise Biography* (1942); George C. Taylor, *Shakespeare's Debt to Montaigne* (1925); Irene C. Willis, *Montaigne* (1927).

MIGUEL DE CERVANTES

LIFE AND WRITINGS. Son of an apothecary, Miguel de Cervantes Saavedra was born in 1547 in Alcalá de Henares, a university town near Madrid. Almost nothing is known of his early life and education. In a work published in 1569 he is mentioned as a favorite pupil by a Madrid Humanist, Juan López. Records indicate that by the end of that year he had left Spain and was living in Rome, for a while in the service of Giulio Acquaviva, later a cardinal. Enlisting in the Spanish fleet under the command of Don John of Austria, Cervantes engaged in the struggle of the allied forces of Christendom against the Turks. He was at the crucial battle of Lepanto (1571), where he fought valiantly in spite of fever and received three gunshot wounds, one of which permanently impaired the use of his left hand, "for the greater glory of the right." After further military engagements and garrison duty at Palermo and Naples, with his brother Rodrigo, and carrying testimonials from Don John and the viceroy of Sicily, he began the journey back to Spain, where he hoped to obtain a captaincy. In September, 1575, their boat was captured near the Marseilles coast by Barbary pirates, and the two brothers, taken prisoner, were brought to Algiers. Cervantes' captors, considering him a person of some consequence, held him as a slave for a good ransom. He repeatedly attempted to escape, and his daring and fortitude excited the admiration of Hassan Pasha, the viceroy of Algiers, who at length bought Cervantes for five hundred crowns. Nevertheless, Rodrigo was ransomed after two years of captivity, while Cervantes' own liberation took five.

He was freed on September 15, 1580, and reached Madrid in December of that year. Here his literary career started rather unauspiciously; he wrote twenty or thirty plays, with little success, and in 1585 published his pastoral romance *Galatea*. At about this time he had a natural daughter by Ana Franca de Rojas, and during the same period he married Catalina de Salazar, eighteen years his junior. Seeking non-literary employment, he obtained a position in the navy, requisitioning and collecting supplies for the Invincible Armada. There seem to have been irregularities in his administration, for which he was held responsible if not directly guilty; he spent several intervals in prison. In 1590 he tried unsuccessfully to obtain colonial employment in the New World. Later he had a post as tax collector in the Granada province. He was dismissed from government service in 1597. The following years are most obscure; there is a tradition that *Don Quixote* was first conceived and planned in prison at Seville. In 1604 he was at Valladolid, then the temporary capital, living in sordid surroundings with the numerous women of his family (his wife, daughter, niece, and two sisters). There he obtained in late 1604 the official license for publication of *Don Quixote*

(Part I). The book appeared in 1605 and was a popular success. Cervantes followed the court's return to Madrid, where he still lived poorly in spite of a vogue with readers which quickly made his heroes proverbial figures. A false continuation of the story soon appeared, and Cervantes' own continuation (*Don Quixote*, Part II) was published in 1615. His *Exemplary Tales* (*Novelas ejemplares*) had appeared in 1613. He died on April 23, 1616, and was buried in the convent of the Barefooted Trinitarian nuns. *Persiles and Sigismunda* (*Persiles y Sigismunda*), his last novel, was published posthumously in 1617.

BIOGRAPHY AND CRITICISM. W. H. Auden, "Ironic Hero: Some Reflections on Don Quixote," *Horizon*, XX (August 1949), 86-94; A. F. G. Bell, *Cervantes* (1947); Gerald Brenan, "Novelist-Philosophers: Cervantes," *Horizon*, XVIII (July 1948), 25-46; J. Fitzmaurice-Kelly, *Miguel de Cervantes Saavedra* (1913); Joseph Wood Krutch, "Cervantes," in *Five Masters* (1930); Salvador de Madariaga, *Don Quixote: An Introductory Essay in Psychology* (1935); Rudolph Schevill, *Cervantes* (1919); Miguel de Unamuno, *The Life of Don Quixote and Sancho.* (1927).

PEDRO CALDERÓN DE LA BARCA

LIFE AND WRITINGS. Born at Madrid in 1600. Calderón spent his early childhood at Valladolid where the court then was, his father being a secretary to the Council of the Treasury. He studied from 1609 to 1614 at a Jesuit college and later at the universities of Alcalá de Henares and Salamanca. His earliest known literary work came from his participation in 1620 in a poetic competition to celebrate the canonization of St. Isidore; Lope de Vega was the principal judge. In the following year, Calderón and one of his brothers were accused of having killed a servant of the duke of Frias and both were fined. Between 1623 and 1625 he may have served in the army in Italy or Flanders. In 1626 he was again in Madrid. King Philip IV assembled around the court a small number of playwrights and Calderón soon became the most prominent among them. His first play was performed in 1623. In 1635, when Lope de Vega died, he became the leading dramatist in Spain. In 1636 he was knighted; 1640 he enlisted in a cavalry company in the Order of Santiago. At the outbreak of the Catalonian rebellion in of knights supplied by the military orders and served until 1642. From 1644 to 1649 his theatrical production practically ceased, as the theaters were closed from the queen's death until the king's remarriage. In 1645 he entered the service of the duke of Alba. In 1648 or 1649 his mistress died, possibly in bearing his natural son, whom he recognized. His sorrow at her death may have contributed to his decision to enter the priesthood. He was appointed to a Toledo parish but could not serve because his superior objected to his being a playwright. For several years he was chaplain to the Brotherhood of the Refugio at Toledo, an order dedicated to charity work among the sick. Throughout this period and to the end of his life, he wrote *autos sacramentales* (theological one-act allegories) for the court. In 1663 he was appointed honorary chaplain to the king. Thereafter he lived a retired life of writing, study, and meditation in Madrid, gathering in his house a rare collection of religious works of art and devotional objects. He died on May 25, 1681.

Calderón theatrical output was immense and varied. The major subdivision is between secular and religious plays. Among the secular plays, there are dramas of honor and jealousy like *The Physician of His Own Honor* (*El médico de su honra*) and *Secret Offense, Secret Revenge* (*A secreto agravio, secreta venganza*); of cloak-and-sword intrigue like *A House with Two Doors Is Hard to Guard* (*Una casa con dos puertas mala es de guardar*) and *The Phantom Lady* (*La dama duende*); and on classical and mythological themes like *The Daughter of the Air* (*La hija del aire*), and on historical and legendary themes like *The Mayor of Zalamea* (*El alcade de Zalamea*). Calderón's deep preoccupation with religious themes shows itself in such complex melodramas as *The Devotion of the Cross* (*La Devoción de la Cruz*) and such strictly religious plays as the 70 *autos sacramentales*, the most famous of which is *The Great Theatre of the World* (*El gran teatro del mundo*). One of them has the same title, though hardly the same content and meaning, of the selection here, *Life Is a Dream.*

BIOGRAPHY AND CRITICISM. Gerald Brenan, "Calderón and the Late Drama," Chapter XII of *The Literature of the Spanish People* (1957); M. A. Buchanan, "Calderón's *Life Is a Dream*," *PMLA*, XLVIII (1932); A. A. Parker, *The Allegorical Drama of Calderón*, (1943) on the theological allegories, and "The Approach to the Spanish Drama of the Golden Age" in *The Tulane Drama Review* (Autumn 1959); and W. W. Whitby, "Rosaura's Role in the Structure of *La vida es sueño*," *Hispanic Review*, XXVIII (1960).

FRANCIS PETRARCH

(1304–1374)

It Is the Evening Hour*

It is the evening hour; the rapid sky
Bends westward; and the hasty daylight flees
To some new land, some strange expectant race.
An old and weary pilgrim-woman sees
The lonely foreign desert-dark drawn nigh.   5
Fearful, she urges on her stumbling pace.
And to her resting-place
At length she comes, and knows
The sweetness of repose;
The pains of pilgrimage, the road's duress   10
Fade in enveloping forgetfulness.
But oh, alas, my hurts that ache by day
Are but more pitiless
When the light sinks into the west away.

When the sun's burning wheels have sped along,   15
And night pursues, rolling its deepest black
From highest peaks into the sheltered plain,
The sober woodsman slings upon his back
His tools, and sings his artless mountain-song,
Discharging on the air his load of pain.   20
And yet his only gain
Is, on his humble board,
The food the woods afford,
Acorns, which poets honor, yet abjure.
Let him be happy, let him sleep secure,   25
Though I no happiness have ever won,
No rest, no ease, no cure,
For all the turning of the stars and sun.

And when the shepherd sees the evening shade
Rising and graying o'er the eastward land,   30

* *Ne la stagion che 'l ciel rapido inchina*, canon 50. Translated by Morris Bishop.
  In the traditional numbering of the collected poems (known as *canzoniere* or *rime sparse*, "scattered rhymes"), this *canzone* is number 50. The varied and relatively loose pattern of a *canzone's* stanzas, line lengths, and rhyme schemes permits, in the best examples, a tone which is both discursive and very musical.
  17. *From . . . plain:* The original line echoes Virgil (*Eclogues*, I, 83), and interestingly enough, it is a literary rather than a realistic view of sunset. Actually the setting sun still hits high peaks while the plain is already in the shadow.
  24. *Acorns:* People in general (the translator restricts the idea to "poets") pay lip service to the idea of simple living, symbolized by acorns. Possibly there is also allusion to the simple nourishment of the primitive Golden Age.

And the sun dropping to its nightly nest,
He rises; takes his well-worn crook in hand;
And leaves the grass, the spring, the beechen glade,
And quietly leads the tired flock to its rest.
He finds a cave, recessed   35
In crags, wherein to spread
Green branches for his bed,
And there he sleeps, untroubled, solitary.
But then, O cruel Love, the more you harry
My breaking strength to that most hopeless chase   40
Of her who flees apace,
And Love will never aid to noose the quarry.

In the sea's vales the sailors on their bark
Throw down their limbs on the hard board to sleep
When the sun dips beneath the western main.   45
Oh, though he hide within the farthest deep,
And leave Morocco's mountains to the dark,
Granada and the Pillars and all Spain,
And though the worldwide pain
Of suffering man and beast   50
In the first night have ceased.
There comes no night with mercy to conclude
My ardor, ever in suffering renewed.
My love grows old; soon shall my captor see me
Ten years in servitude.   55
And still no savior comes with strength to free me!

And as I seek with words my wounds to numb,
I watch at eve the unyoked oxen turning
In from the fields, down from the furrowed hill.
My yoke, alas, is never lifted from   60
My shoulders, and my hurts are ever burning,
And in my eyes the tears are springing still.
Alas, it was my will
To carve the unearthly grace
Of her most lovely face   65
In the immutable matter of my heart.
Now it is carved so deep that strength nor art
May rub it thence until that final day
When soul and body part.
Even then, perhaps, it will not pass away.   70

48. *Pillars:* the Pillars of Hercules, now called the Straits of Gibraltar, traditional limit to man's navigation in antiquity. (*Cf.* Ulysses' last voyage in Dante, *Inferno,* XXVI, esp. lines 103-109.)

54. *Captor:* the woman he vainly loves.

55. *Ten years in servitude:* This dates the poem at some time close to April 6, 1347. (*Cf.* below, the sonnet *It Was the Morning.*)

O my unhappy song,
My grief has made you grieve,
You will not dare to leave
My heart, to show your sorrows anywhere;
And yet, for others' praise you shall not care,   75
For all your burden is the weight of pain
Left by the flames that flare
From the cold rock to which I cling, in vain.

71. *my unhappy song:* Traditionally a *canzone* is concluded by a shorter, send-off stanza in which the poet addresses the poem itself.

It Was the Morning*

It was the morning of that blessèd day
Whereon the Sun in pity veiled his glare
For the Lord's agony, that, unaware,
I fell a captive, Lady, to the sway

Of your swift eyes: that seemed no time to stay   5
The strokes of Love: I stepped into the snare
Secure, with no suspicion: then and there
I found my cue in man's most tragic play.

Love caught me naked to his shaft, his sheaf,
The entrance for his ambush and surprise   10
Against the heart wide open through the eyes,

The constant gate and fountain of my grief:
How craven so to strike me stricken so,
Yet from you fully armed conceal his bow!

* *Era 'l giorno ch'al sol si scoloraro,* sonnet 3. Translated by Joseph Auslander.
1. *day:* Elsewhere (sonnet 211) Petrarch gives the date as April 6, 1327, a Monday. Here too the day is apparently intended to be the day of Christ's death (April 6) rather than Good Friday, 1327.
11. *heart . . . eyes:* The image of the eyes as the gateway to the heart had been a poetic commonplace since pre-Dante days.
13. *stricken:* with grief on commemorating Christ's Passion.

Blest Be the Day*

Blest be the day, and blest the month and year,
Season and hour and very moment blest,
The lovely land and place where first possessed
By two pure eyes I found me prisoner;

* *Benedetto sia 'l giorno e 'l mese e l'anno,* sonnet 61. Translated by Joseph Auslander.
2. *Season:* spring; *hour:* "upon the first hour" (sonnet 211), sunrise.
3. *place:* the Church of Saint Clare at Avignon.

And blest the first sweet pain, the first most dear,   5
Which burnt my heart when Love came in as guest;
And blest the bow, the shafts which shook my breast,
And even the wounds which Love delivered there.

Blest be the words and voices which filled grove
And glen with echoes of my lady's name;   10
The sighs, the tears, the fierce despair of love;

And blest the sonnet-sources of my fame;
And blest that thought of thoughts which is her own,
Of her, her only, of herself alone!

Father in Heaven*

Father in heaven, after each lost day,
Each night spent raving with that fierce desire
Which in my heart has kindled into fire
Seeing your acts adorned for my dismay;

Grant henceforth that I turn, within your light   5
To another life and deeds more truly fair,
So having spread to no avail the snare
My bitter foe might hold it in despite.

The eleventh year, my Lord, has now come round
Since I was yoked beneath the heavy trace   10
That on the meekest weighs most cruelly.

Pity the abject plight where I am found;
Return my straying thoughts to a nobler place;
Show them this day you were on Calvary.

* *Padre del ciel, dopo i perduti giorni,*
sonnet 62. Translated by Vernard Ber-
gonzi.
  5. *light:* the light of grace.

8. *bitter foe:* the Devil, not Love as
some commentators have thought.
  9. *Cf.* note to 1.1, *It Was the Morning.*

She Used to Let Her Golden Hair Fly Free*

She used to let her golden hair fly free
For the wind to toy and tangle and molest;
Her eyes were brighter than the radiant west.
(Seldom they shine so now.) I used to see

Pity look out of those deep eyes on me.   5
("It was false pity," you would now protest.)
I had love's tinder heaped within my breast;
What wonder that the flame burned furiously?

* *Erano i capei d'oro a l'aura sparsi,* sonnet 90. Translated by Morris Bishop.

She did not walk in any mortal way,
But with angelic progress; when she spoke,   10
Unearthly voices sang in unison.

She seemed divine among the dreary folk
Of earth. You say she is not so today?
Well, though the bow's unbent, the wound bleeds on.

The Eyes That Drew from Me*

The eyes that drew from me such fervent praise,
The arms and hands and feet and countenance
Which made me a stranger in my own romance
And set me apart from the well-trodden ways;

The gleaming golden curly hair, the rays   5
Flashing from a smiling angel's glance
Which moved the world in paradisal dance,
Are grains of dust, insensibilities.

And I live on, but in grief and self-contempt,
Left here without the light I loved so much,   10
In a great tempest and with shrouds unkempt.

No more love songs, then, I have done with such;
My old skill now runs thin at each attempt,
And ears are heard within the harp I touch.

   * *Gli occhi di ch'io parlai si calda-* commemorate Laura. She died at Avig-
mente, sonnet 292. Translated by Edwin non on April 6, 1348.
Morgan. All the poems in the canon 14. *Cf. Job* 30:31.
from number 267 on were written to

Great Is My Envy of You*

Great is my envy of you, earth, in your greed
Folding her in invisible embrace,
Denying me the look of the sweet face
Where I found peace from all my strife at need!

Great is my envy of heaven which can lead   5
And lock within itself in avarice
That spirit from its lovely biding-place
And leave so many others here to bleed!

Great is my envy of those souls whose reward
Is the gentle heaven of her company,   10
Which I so fiercely sought beneath these skies!

Great is my envy of death whose curt hard sword
Carried her whom I called my life away;
Me he disdains, and mocks me from her eyes!

   * *Quanta invidia io ti porto, avara terra,* sonnet 300. Translated by Edwin
Morgan.

Go, Grieving Rimes of Mine [*]

Go, grieving rimes of mine, to that hard stone
Whereunder lies my darling, lies my dear,
And cry to her to speak from heaven's sphere.
Her mortal part with grass is overgrown.

Tell her, I'm sick of living; that I'm blown   5
By winds of grief from the course I ought to steer,
That praise of her is all my purpose here
And all my business; that of her alone

Do I go telling, that how she lived and died
And lives again in immortality,   10
All men may know, and love my Laura's grace.

Oh, may she deign to stand at my bedside
When I come to die; and may she call to me
And draw me to her in the blessèd place!

* *Ite, rime dolenti, al duro sasso*, sonnet 333. Translated by Morris Bishop.

Letter to Dionisio da Borgo San Sepolcro*

[*The Ascent of Mount Ventoux*]

To-day[1] I made the ascent of the hightest mountain in the region, which is not improperly called Ventosum.[2] My only motive was the wish to see what so great an elevation had to offer. I have had the expedition in mind for many years; for as you know, I have lived in this region from infancy, having been cast here by that fate[3] which determines the affairs of men. Consequently the mountain, which is visible from a great distance, was ever before my eyes, and I conceived the plan of some time doing what I have at last accomplished to-day. The idea took hold upon me with especial force when, in re-reading Livy's *History of Rome*, yesterday, I happened upon the place where Philip of Macedon, the same who waged war against the Romans, ascended Mount Haemus in Thessaly, from whose summit he was able, it is said, to see two seas,

* Letter IV, i, from a group of letters entitled *De Rebus Familiaribus*. From *Petrarch, the First Modern Scholar and Man of Letters*, by James Harvey Robinson and Henry Winchester Rolfe (New York: G. P. Putnam's Sons, 1914), 2nd ed., and translated by the authors.

Dionisio, or Dionigi, da Borgo San Sepolcro was an Augustinian monk whom Petrarch had probably met in Paris in 1333. A learned theologian, he taught at Paris and in 1339 was appointed bishop of Monopoli. He spent the last part of his life in Naples at the court of the learned king Robert d'Anjou and died there in 1342 (Petrarch wrote a verse epistle on his death).

1. April 26. From internal evidence the year should be 1336, ten years after Petrarch left Bologna, but the letter was probably revised and made into an "allegory" at a later date (*cf.* note 8 below).

2. *Ventosum:* windy. Mount Ventoux (*ca.* 6,000 feet) is near Malaucène, not far from Petrarch's place of retirement in Vaucluse.

3. *Cf.* Biographical Note on Petrarch, p. 1064.

the Adriatic and the Euxine.[4] Whether this be true or false I have not been able to determine, for the mountain is too far away, and writers disagree. Pomponius Mela, the cosmographer—not to mention others who have spoken of this occurrence—admits its truth without hesitation[5]; Titus Livius, on the other hand, considers it false. I, assuredly, should not have left the question long in doubt, had that mountain been as easy to explore as this one. Let us leave this matter to one side, however, and return to my mountain here,—it seems to me that a young man in private life may well be excused for attempting what an aged king could undertake without arousing criticism.

When I came to look about for a companion I found, strangely enough, that hardly one among my friends seemed suitable, so rarely do we meet with just the right combination of personal tastes and characteristics, even among those who are dearest to us. This one was too apathetic, that one over-anxious; this one too slow, that one too hasty; one was too sad, another over-cheerful; one more simple, another more sagacious, than I desired. I feared this one's taciturnity and that one's loquacity. The heavy deliberation of some repelled me as much as the lean incapacity of others. I rejected those who were likely to irritate me by a cold want of interest, as well as those who might weary me by their excessive enthusiasm. Such defects, however grave, could be borne with at home, for charity suffereth all things, and friendship accepts any burden; but it is quite otherwise on a journey, where every weakness becomes much more serious. So, as I was bent upon pleasure and anxious that my enjoyment should be unalloyed, I looked about me with unusual care, balanced against one another the various characteristics of my friends, and without committing any breach of friendship I silently condemned every trait which might prove disagreeable on the way. And—would you believe it?—I finally turned homeward for aid, and proposed the ascent to my only brother, who is younger than I, and with whom you are well acquainted.[6] He was delighted and gratified beyond measure by the thought of holding the place of a friend as well as of a brother.

At the time fixed we left the house, and by evening reached Malaucène, which lies at the foot of the mountain, to the north. Having rested there a day, we finally made the ascent this morning, with no companions except two servants; and a most difficult task it was. The mountain is a very steep and almost inaccessible mass of stony soil. But, as the poet[7] has well said, "Remorseless toil conquers all." It was a long day, the air fine. We enjoyed the advantages of vigour

4. *Cf.* Livy, *Roman History*, XL, 21, 2.

5. Pomponius Mela, Roman geographer of Spanish birth, wrote toward the middle of the first century A.D.; the passage referred to in his *Corographia* is II, 17.

6. Gherardo, probably about three years younger than the poet.

7. Virgil, in *Georgics*, I, 145-146.

of mind and strength and agility of body, and everything else essential to those engaged in such an undertaking, and so had no other difficulties to face than those of the region itself. We found an old shepherd in one of the mountain dales, who tried, at great length, to dissuade us from the ascent, saying that some fifty years before he had, in the same ardour of youth, reached the summit, but had gotten for his pains nothing except fatigue and regret, and clothes and body torn by the rocks and briars. No one, so far as he or his companions knew, had ever tried the ascent before or after him. But his counsels increased rather than diminished our desire to proceed, since youth is suspicious of warnings. So the old man, finding that his efforts were in vain, went a little way with us, and pointed out a rough path among the rocks, uttering many admonitions, which he continued to send after us even after we had left him behind. Surrendering to him all such garments or other possessions as might prove burdensome to us, we made ready for the ascent, and started off at a good pace. But, as usually happens, fatigue quickly followed upon our excessive exertion, and we soon came to a halt at the top of a certain cliff. Upon starting on again we went more slowly, and I especially advanced along the rocky way with a more deliberate step. While my brother chose a direct path straight up the ridge,[8] I weakly took an easier one which really descended. When I was called back, and the right road was shown me, I replied that I hoped to find a better way round on the other side, and that I did not mind going farther if the path were only less steep. This was just an excuse for my laziness; and when the others had already reached a considerable height I was still wandering in the valleys. I had failed to find an easier path, and had only increased the distance and difficulty of the ascent. At last I became disgusted with the intricate way I had chosen, and resolved to ascend without more ado. When I reached my brother, who, while waiting for me, had had ample opportunity for rest, I was tired and irritated. We walked along together for a time, but hardly had we passed the first spur when I forgot about the circuitous route which I had just tried, and took a lower one again. Once more I followed an easy, roundabout path through winding valleys, only to find myself soon in my old difficulty. I was simply trying to avoid the exertion of the ascent; but no human ingenuity can alter the nature of things, or cause anything to reach a height by going down. Suffice it to say that, much to my vexation and my brother's amusement, I made this same mistake three times or more during a few hours.

After being frequently misled in this way, I finally sat down in a valley and transferred my winged thoughts from things corporeal to the immaterial, addressing myself as follows:—"What thou hast re-

8. In the allegorical reading of the letter, this could be an allusion to Gherardo achieving God and salvation more directly (he became a monk in 1342, retiring into the monastery of Montrieux).

peatedly experienced to-day in the ascent of this mountain, happens to thee, as to many, in the journey toward the blessed life. But this is not so readily perceived by men, since the motions of the body are obvious and external while those of the soul are invisible and hidden. Yes, the life which we call blessed is to be sought for on a high eminence, and strait is the way that leads to it. Many, also, are the hills that lie between, and we must ascend, by a glorious stairway, from strength to strength. At the top is at once the end of our struggles and the goal for which we are bound. All wish to reach this goal, but, as Ovid says, 'To wish is little; we must long with the utmost eagerness to gain our end.'[9] Thou certainly dost ardently desire, as well as simply wish, unless thou deceivest thyself in this matter, as in so many others. What, then, doth hold thee back? Nothing, assuredly, except that thou wouldst take a path which seems, at first thought, more easy, leading through low and worldly pleasures. But nevertheless in the end, after long wanderings, thou must perforce either climb the steeper path, under the burden of tasks foolishly deferred, to its blessed culmination, or lie down in the valley of thy sins, and (I shudder to think of it!), if the shadow of death overtake thee, spend an eternal night amid constant torments." These thoughts stimulated both body and mind in a wonderful degree for facing the difficulties which yet remained. Oh, that I might traverse in spirit that other road for which I long day and night, even as to-day I overcame material obstacles by my bodily exertions! And I know not why it should not be far easier, since the swift immortal soul can reach its goal in the twinkling of an eye, without passing through space, while my progress to-day was necessarily slow, dependent as I was upon a failing body weighed down by heavy members.

One peak of the mountain, the highest of all, the country people call "Sonny," why, I do not know, unless by antiphrasis,[10] as I have sometimes suspected in other instances; for the peak in question would seem to be the father of all the surrounding ones. On its top is a little level place, and here we could at least rest our tired bodies.

Now, my father, since you have followed the thoughts that spurred me on in my ascent, listen to the rest of the story, and devote one hour, I pray you, to reviewing the experiences of my entire day. At first, owing to the unaccustomed quality of the air and the effect of the great sweep of view spread out before me, I stood like one dazed. I beheld the clouds under our feet, and what I had read of Athos and Olympus seemed less incredible as I myself witnessed the same things from a mountain of less fame. I turned my eyes toward Italy, wither my heart most inclined. The Alps, rugged and

9. Ovid, *Ex Ponto*, III, i, 35.
10. the rhetorical use of a word in a   sense opposite to its actual meaning.

snow-capped, seemed to rise close by, although they were really at a great distance; the very same Alps through which that fierce enemy of the Roman name once made his way, bursting the rocks, if we may believe the report, by the application of vinegar. I sighed, I must confess, for the skies of Italy, which I beheld rather with my mind than with my eyes. An inexpressible longing came over me to see once more my friend and my country. At the same time I reproached myself for this double weakness, springing, as it did, from a soul not yet steeled to manly resistance. And yet there were excuses for both of these cravings, and a number of distinguished writers might be summoned to support me.

Then a new idea took possession of me, and I shifted my thoughts to a consideration of time rather than place. "To-day it is ten years since, having completed thy youthful studies, thou didst leave Bologna.[11] Eternal God! In the name of immutable wisdom, think what alterations in thy character this intervening period has beheld! I pass over a thousand instances. I am not yet in a safe harbour where I can calmly recall past storms. The time may come when I can review in due order all the experiences of the past, saying with St. Augustine, 'I desire to recall my foul actions and the carnal corruption of my soul, not because I love them, but that I may the more love thee, O my God.'[12] Much that is doubtful and evil still clings to me, but what I once loved, that I love no longer. And yet what am I saying? I still love it, but with shame, but with heaviness of heart. Now, at last, I have confessed the truth. So it is. I love, but love what I would not love, what I would that I might hate. Though loath to do so, though constrained, though sad and sorrowing, still I do love, and I feel in my miserable self the truth of the well known words, 'I will hate if I can; if not, I will love against my will.'[13] Three years have not yet passed since that perverse and wicked passion which had a firm grasp upon me and held undisputed sway in my heart began to discover a rebellious opponent, who was unwilling longer to yield obedience. These two adversaries have joined in close combat for the supremacy, and for a long time now a harassing and doubtful war has been waged in the field of my thoughts."

Thus I turned over the last ten years in my mind, and then, fixing my anxious gaze on the future, I asked myself, "If, perchance, thou shouldst prolong this uncertain life of thine for yet two lustres, and shouldst make an advance toward virtue proportionate to the distance to which thou hast departed from thine original infatuation during the past two years, since the new longing first encountered the old, couldst thou, on reaching thy fortieth year, face death, if not with complete assurance, at least with hopefulness, calmly dismissing from thy thoughts the residuum of life as it faded into old age?"

11. *Cf.* Biographical Note, p. 1064, and note 3 above.

12. St. Augustine, *Confessions*, II, i, 1.
13. Ovid, *Amores*, III, ii, 35.

These and similar reflections occurred to me, my father. I rejoiced in my progress, mourned my weaknesses, and commiserated the universal instability of human conduct. I had well-nigh forgotten where I was and our object in coming; but at last I dismissed my anxieties, which were better suited to other surroundings, and resolved to look about me and see what we had come to see. The sinking sun and the lengthening shadows of the mountain were already warning us that the time was near at hand when we must go. As if suddenly wakened from sleep, I turned about and gazed toward the west. I was unable to discern the summits of the Pyrenees, which form the barrier between France and Spain; not because of any intervening obstacle that I know of but owing simply to the insufficiency of our mortal vision. But I could see with the utmost clearness, off to the right, the mountains of the region about Lyons, and to the left the bay of Marseilles and the waters that lash the shores of Aigues Mortes, altho' all these places were so distant that it would require a journey of several days to reach them. Under our very eyes flowed the Rhone.

While I was thus dividing my thoughts, now turning my attention to some terrestial object that lay before me, now raising my soul, as I had done my body, to higher planes, it occurred to me to look into my copy of St. Augustine's *Confessions*, a gift that I owe to your love, and that I always have about me, in memory of both the author and the giver. I opened the compact little volume, small indeed in size, but of infinite charm, with the intention of reading whatever came to hand, for I could happen upon nothing that would be otherwise than edifying and devout. Now it chanced that the tenth book presented itself. My brother, waiting to hear something of St. Augustine's from my lips, stood attentively by. I call him, and God too, to witness that where I first fixed my eyes it was written: "And men go about to wonder at the heights of the mountains, and the mighty waves of the sea, and the wide sweep of rivers, and the circuit of the ocean, and the revolution of the stars, but themselves they consider not."[14] I was abashed, and, asking my brother (who was anxious to hear more), not to annoy me, I closed the book, angry with myself that I should still be admiring earthly things who might long ago have learned from even the pagan philosophers that nothing is wonderful but the soul, which, when great itself, finds nothing great outside itself. Then, in truth, I was satisfied that I had seen enough of the mountain; I turned my inward eye upon myself, and from that time not a syllable fell from my lips until we had reached the bottom again. Those words had given me occupation enough, for I could not believe that it was by a mere accident that I happened upon them. What I had there read I believed to be addressed to me and to no other, remembering that St. Augustine had once suspected the same thing in his own case, when, on opening the

14. St. Augustine, *Confessions*, X, viii, 15.

book of the Apostle, as he himself tells us,[15] the first words that he saw there were, "Not in rioting and drunkenness, not in chambering and wantonness, not in strife and envying. But put ye on the Lord Jesus Christ, and make not provision for the flesh, to fulfil the lusts thereof."[16]

The same thing happened earlier to St. Anthony, when he was listening to the Gospel where it is written, "If thou wilt be perfect, go and sell that thou hast, and give to the poor, and thou shalt have treasure in heaven: and come and follow me."[17] Believing this scripture to have been read for his especial benefit, as his biographer Athanasius says,[18] he guided himself by its aid to the Kingdom of Heaven. And as Anthony on hearing these words waited for nothing more, and as Augustine upon reading the Apostle's admonition sought no farther, so I concluded my reading in the few words which I have given. I thought in silence of the lack of good counsel in us mortals, who neglect what is noblest in ourselves, scatter our energies in all directions, and waste ourselves in a vain show, because we look about us for what is to be found only within. I wondered at the natural nobility of our soul, save when it debases itself of its own free will, and deserts its original estate, turning what God has given it for its honour into dishonour. How many times, think you, did I turn back that day, to glance at the summit of the mountain, which seemed scarcely a cubit high compared with the range of human contemplation,—when it is not immersed in the foul mire of earth? With every downward step I asked myself this: If we are ready to endure a little nearer heaven, how can a soul struggling toward God, up the steeps of human pride and human destiny, fear any cross or prison or sting of fortune? How few, I thought, but are diverted from their path by the fear of difficulties or the love of ease! How happy the lot of those few, if any such there be! It is to them, assuredly, that the poet was thinking, when he wrote:

> Happy the man who is skilled to understand
> Nature's hid causes; who beneath his feet
> All terrors casts, and death's relentless doom,
> And the loud roar of greedy Acheron.[19]

How earnestly should we strive, not to stand on mountain-tops, but to trample beneath us those appetites which spring from earthly impulses.

With no consciousness of the difficulties of the way, amidst these preoccupations which I have so frankly revealed, we came, long after dark, but with the full moon lending us its friendly light, to the little inn which we had left that morning before dawn. The time during which the servants have been occupied in preparing our supper,

15. *Ibid.*, VIII, xii, 29.
16. *Romans* 13:13-14.
17. *Matthew*, 19:21.
18. Saint Athanasius, Doctor of the

Church (*ca.* 295-373), in his *Vita Antonii*, II.
19. Virgil, *Georgics*, II, 490-492.

I have spent in a secluded part of the house, hurriedly jotting down these experiences on the spur of the moment, lest, in case my task were postponed, my mood should change on leaving the place, and so my interest in writing flag.

You will see, my dearest father, that I wish nothing to be concealed from you, for I am careful to describe to you not only my life in general but even my individual reflections. And I beseech you, in turn, to pray that these vague and wandering thoughts of mine may some time become firmly fixed, and, after having been vainly tossed about from one interest to another, may direct themselves at last toward the single, true, certain, and everlasting good.

MALAUCÈNE, April 26.

DESIDERIUS ERASMUS
(1466?–1536)
The Praise of Folly (Moriae encomium)*

I. Folly Herself

Folly Speaks:

No matter what is ordinarily said about me (and I am not ignorant of how bad the name of Folly sounds, even to the biggest fools), I am still the one, the only one I may say, whose influence makes Gods and men cheerful. A convincing proof of this is that as soon as I began to speak to this great audience, all faces suddenly brightened with a new and unusual gaiety, all frowns disappeared, and you applauded hilariously. Now you seem intoxicated with nectar, and also with nepenthe,[1] like the gods of Homer; whereas a moment ago you were sad and careworn, as if you had just come out of the cave of Trophonius.[2] Just as a new and youthful color reappears everywhere when the sun first shows its beautiful, golden face to the earth, or when spring breathes softly after a hard winter, so your faces changed at the sight of me. And thus what great orators can hardly accomplish with long and elaborate speeches, namely the banishment of care, I have done with my appearance alone.

. . . Since my ancestry is not known to many, I will undertake to describe it, with the Muses' kind assistance. My father was neither Chaos, Orcus, Saturn, Japetus, nor any other of that obsolete and senile set of gods; on the contrary he was Plutus,[3] the real father of

---

* Abridged. Written in 1509. Our text is from *Erasmus: In Praise of Folly*, a new translation by Leonard F. Dean. Hendricks House Farrar Straus, 1946.
1. legendary drug causing oblivion.
2. seat of a particularly awesome oracle.

3. god of wealth and abundance. In Aristophanes' play by that name, to which Erasmus refers later in the paragraph, he is shown in decrepit age; ordinarily he is represented as a boy with a cornucopia.

men and gods, despite the opinion of Hesiod,[4] Homer, and Jove himself. Now, as always, one nod from Plutus turns everything sacred or profane upside down. By his decision wars, peace, empires, plans, judgments, assemblies, marriages, treaties, pacts, laws, arts, sports, solemnities (I am almost out of breath)—in short, all public and private affairs are governed. Without his help, all the poets' multitude of gods, even, I may boldly say, the chief ones, either would not exist or would have to live leanly at home. Not even Pallas can help the person who arouses Plutus' anger, but with his favor one can laugh at Jove's thunderbolts. What a magnificent father! He did not beget me out of his head, as Jupiter did that grim and gloomy Pallas, but from Youth, the best-looking as well as the gayest of all the nymphs. Nor was this done dully in wedlock, in the way that lame blacksmith[5] was conceived, but more pleasantly in passion, as old Homer puts it. It should also be clearly understood that I was not born of Aristophanes' worn-out and weak-eyed Plutus, but of the unimpaired Plutus, hot with youth and still hotter with nectar which by chance he had drunk straight and freely at a party of the gods.

Next, if you want to know the place of my birth (since the place where one first squalled is nowadays considered a mark of nobility), I was born neither in wandering Delos,[6] nor on the foaming sea,[7] nor "in deep caves,"[8] but in the Fortunate Isles[9] themselves, where all things grow "without plowing or planting." There where there is no labor, no old age, and no sickness; where not a daffodil, mallow, onion, bean, or any other ordinary thing is to be seen; but where nose and eyes are equally delighted by moly, panacea, nepenthes, sweet marjoram, ambrosia, lotus, rose, violet, hyacinth, and the gardens of Adonis. Being born amidst these pleasant things, I did not begin life crying, but from the first laughed good-naturedly at my mother. I certainly need not envy Jove for being suckled by a she-goat, for I was nursed at the breasts of two charming nymphs—Drunkenness, offspring of Bacchus, and Ignorance, daughter of Pan. Both of them you see here with my other attendants and followers. If you ask the names of the others, I must answer in Greek. The haughty one over there is Philantia (Self-love). The one with laughing eyes who is clapping her hands is Kolakia (Flattery). This drowsy one is Lethe (Forgetfulness). She leaning on her elbows with folded hands is Misoponia (Laziness). She with the perfume and wreath of roses is Hedone (Pleasure.) This wild-eyed one is Anoia (Madness). The smooth-skinned and shapely one is Tryphe (Sensuality). And you see those two gods playing with the girls; well, one is Comus (Intemperance) and the other is

4. Greek didactic poet of the eighth century B.C., cited here because he was author of the *Theogony* (about the generation and genealogy of the gods).
5. Hephaestus (Vulcan).

6. birthplace of Apollo.
7. from which Venus emerged.
8. a Homeric expression.
9. the mythical and remote islands

Negretos Hypnos (Sound Sleep). With the help of these faithful servants I gain control of all things, even dictating to dictators.

II. *The Powers and Pleasures of Folly*

. . . Now, that it may not seem that I call myself a goddess without good cause, let me tell you of the range of my influence and of my benefits to men and gods. If to be a god is simply to aid men, as someone has wisely said, and if they have been deservedly deified who have shown mankind the uses of wine or grain, why am I not justly called the Alpha[10] of gods, I who have all alone given all things to all men.

First, what is more dear and precious than life itself? And by whose aid but mine is life conceived? It is not the spear of "potently-sired" Pallas nor the shield of "cloud-controlling" Jove that propagates and multiplies mankind. Even the father of gods and the king of men, he who shakes Olympus with a nod, must lay aside the three-pronged thunderer and that Titanic manner with which when he pleases he terrifies the gods, and like a poor actor assume another character, if he wishes to do what he is forever doing, namely, begetting children. The Stoics[11] assert that they are almost god-like. But give me one who is three, four, or six hundred times a Stoic, and if on this occasion he does not remove his beard, the sign of wisdom (in common with goats), at least he will shed his gravity, stop frowning, abandon his rock-bound principles and for a while be a silly fool. In short, the wise man must send for me if he wants to be a father. But why not speak to you more openly, as I usually do? I ask whether the head, the face, the breast, the hand, or the ear—each an honorable part—creates gods and men? I think not, but instead the job is done by that foolish, even ridiculous part which cannot be named without laughter. This is the sacred fountain from which all things rise, more certainly than from the Pythagorean tetrad.[12]

What man, I ask you, would stick his head into the halter of marriage if, following the practice of the wise, he first weighed the inconveniences of that life? Or what woman would ever embrace her husband if she foresaw or considered the dangers of childbirth and the drudgery of motherhood? Now since you owe your life to the marriage-bed, and marriage itself to my follower Madness, you

where, according to a Greek tradition, some favorites of the gods dwelt in immortality and bliss.

10. first letter of the Greek alphabet; hence, "beginning," "origin."

11. Stoicism originated in the Stoa Poikile ("painted porch"), a building in the market place in Athens where the philosopher Zeno lectured in the fourth century B.C., and later was perhaps the main type of philosophy of the Roman elite. It became known during the Renaissance especially through Seneca. Erasmus here makes the Stoics the butts of Folly's irony on account of their supposedly godlike disregard of the passions.

12. According to the numerical conception of the universe of Pythagoras (sixth century B.C.) and his followers, the first four numbers (the "tetrad"—one, two, three, and four, adding up to the ideal number, ten) signified the root of all being.

can see how completely indebted you are to me. Moreover, would a woman who had experienced that travail once ever repeat it without the influence of my Forgetfulness? And Venus herself, no matter what Lucretius says,[13] cannot deny that her work would be weak and inconclusive without my help. Hence from my ridiculous and crazy game are produced supercilious philosophers, their present-day successors, vulgarly called monks, kings in purple robes, pious priests, thrice-holy popes, and finally all the gods invented by the poets, so numerous that spacious Olympus is crowded.

That the conception of life is due to me is a small matter when I can show you that I am responsible for everything agreeable. Would life without pleasure be life at all? You applaud! I was sure that you were not so wise, or rather so foolish—no, so wise, as to think otherwise. As a matter of fact, even the Stoics do not really dislike pleasure; they carefully pretend to and they loudly denounce it in public, but only in order to deter others and thus have it all to themselves. Just let them explain to me what part of life is not sad, troublesome, graceless, flat, and distressing without a dash of pleasure, or in other words, folly. This is very adequately proved by Sophocles,[14] a person insufficiently appreciated, who has left this pretty eulogy of me: "Ignorance is bliss." . . .

If someone should unmask the actors in the middle of a scene on the stage and show their real faces to the audience, would he not spoil the whole play? And would not everyone think he deserved to be driven out of the theater with brickbats as a crazy man? For at once a new order of things would suddenly arise. He who played the woman is now seen to be a man; the juvenile is revealed to be old; he who a little before was a king is suddenly a slave; and he who was a god now appears as a little man. Truly, to destroy the illusion is to upset the whole play. The masks and costumes are precisely what hold the eyes of the spectators. Now what else is our whole life but a kind of stage play through which men pass in various disguises, each one going on to play his part until he is led off by the director? And often the same actor is ordered back in a different costume, so that he who played the king in purple, now acts the slave in rags. Thus everything is pretense; yet this play is performed in no other way.

What if some wise man, dropped from heaven, should suddenly confront me at this point and exclaim that the person whom everyone has looked up to as a god and ruler is not even a man, because he is led sheeplike by his passions; that he is the meanest slave because he voluntarily serves so many and such foul masters? Or what if this wise man should instruct someone mourning his parent's

---

13. In the opening lines of his poem *On the Nature of Things*, Lucretius (99?–55 B.C.) invokes Venus because "all living things" are conceived through her.

14. See his *Ajax*, ll. 554–555: ". . . life is sweetest before the feelings are awake—until one learns to know joy and pain."

death to laugh, on the grounds that the parent had at last really begun to live—our life here being in one way nothing but a kind of death? And what if he should entitle another who was glorying in ancestry, ignoble and illegitimate, because he was so far from virtue, the only source of nobility? And what if he should speak of all others in the same way? What, I ask, would he gain by it except to be regarded as dangerously insane by everyone? Just as nothing is more foolish than unseasonable wisdom, so nothing is more imprudent than bull-headed prudence. And he is indeed perverse who does not accommodate himself to the way of the world, who will not follow the crowd, who does not at least remember the rule of good fellowship, drink or begone, and who demands that the play shall no longer be a play. True prudence, on the contrary, consists in not desiring more wisdom than is proper to mortals, and in being willing to wink at the doings of the crowd or to go along with it sociably. But that, they say, is folly itself. I shall certainly not deny it; yet they must in turn admit that it is also to act the play of life.

I hesitate to speak about the next point. But why should I be silent about what is truer than truth? For so great an undertaking, however, it would probably be wise to call the Muses from Helicon;[15] the poets usually invoke them on the slightest pretext. Therefore, stand by for a moment, daughters of Jove, while I show that one cannot acquire that widely advertised wisdom, which the wise call the secret of happiness, unless one follows the leadership of Folly. First, everyone admits that all the emotions belong to folly. Indeed a fool and a wise man are distinguished by the fact that emotions control the former, and reason the latter. Now the Stoics would purge the wise man of all strong emotions, as if they were diseases; yet these emotions serve not only as a guide and teacher to those who are hastening toward the portal of wisdom, but also as a stimulus in all virtuous actions, as exhorters to good deeds. Of course that superstoic, Seneca, strongly denies this and strips the wise of absolutely every emotion; yet in so doing he leaves something that is not a man at all, but rather a new kind of god or sub-god who never existed and never will. To put it bluntly, he makes a marble imitation of a man, stupid, and altogether alien to every human feeling.

If this is the way they want it, let them keep their wise man. They can love him without any rivals and live with him in Plato's republic or, if they prefer, in the realm of Ideas, or in the gardens of Tantalus.[16] Who would not shudder at such a man and flee from him as from a ghost? He would be insensible to every natural feeling, no more moved by love or pity than if he were solid flint or Mar-

---

15. mythical mountain, home of the Muses.

16. Plato's republic, his celestial realm of pure ideas, and the mythical garden of Tantalus in Hades (where rich fruit always evades Tantalus' grasp) are all mentioned because they are characterized by the presence of abstractions and figments.

pesian[17] stone. Nothing escapes him; he never makes a mistake; like another Lynceus[18] he sees all; he evaluates everything rigidly; he excuses nothing; he alone is satisfied with himself as the only one who is really rich, sane, royal, free—in short, unique in everything, but only so in his own opinion. Desiring no friend, he is himself the friend of none. He does not hesitate to bid the gods go hang themselves. All that life holds he condemns and scorns as folly. And this animal is the perfect wise man. I ask you, if it were put to a vote, what city would choose such a person as mayor? What army would want such a general? What woman such a husband? What host such a guest? What servant such a master? Who would not rather have any man at all from the rank and file of fools? Now such a choice, being a fool, would be able to command or obey fools. He would be able to please those like himself—or nearly everyone; he would be kind to his wife, a jolly friend, a gay companion, a polished guest; finally, he would consider nothing human to be alien to him.[19] But this wise man has been boring me for some time; let us turn to other instructive topics.

Imagine, then, that a man should look down from a great height, as the poets say that Jove does. What calamities would he see in man's life. How miserable, how vile, man's birth. How laborious his education. His childhood is subject to injuries; his youth is painful; his age a burden; his death a hard necessity. He is attacked by a host of diseases, threatened by accidents, and assaulted by misfortunes; there is nothing without some gall. There are also the multitude of evils that man does to man. Here are poverty, imprisonment, infamy, shame, tortures, plots, treachery, slander, lawsuits fraud. But this is plainly to count the grains of sand. It is not proper for me at the moment to suggest for what offenses men have deserved these misfortunes, nor what angry god caused them to be born to such miseries. Yet will not anyone who considers these things approve the example of the Milesian virgins,[20] pitiable as it is? Recall, however, what kind of people have committed suicide because they were tired of life. Have they not been the wise or near-wise? Among them, besides Diogenes, Xenocrates, Cato, Cassius, and Brutus, there was Chiron,[21] who chose death rather than immortality. Now you begin to see, I believe, what would happen if all men became wise: there would be need for new clay and another potter like Prometheus.[22]

---

17. from Marpessos, a mountain on the island of Paros famous for its marble.

18. a mythical figure whose eyesight was proverbially supposed to penetrate even solid objects.

19. from a proverbial phrase in Terence's *Self-Tormentor*, l. 77: "I am a man; nothing human do I consider alien to me."

20. of the city of Miletus, in Asia Minor. There is an ancient tale that most of them, seemingly gone insane, hanged themselves.

21. the centaur (half man, half horse); incurably wounded and suffering great pain, he asked Zeus for relief from his own immortality.

22. He supposedly molded man out of clay.

But by a timely mixture of ignorance, thoughtlessness, forgetfulness of evil, hope of good, and a dash of delight, I bring relief from troubles; so that men are unwilling to relinquish their lives even when their lives are ready to relinquish them. They are so far from being weary of existence, that the less reason they have for living, the more they enjoy life. Clearly it is because of my good work that you everywhere see old fellows of Nestor's[23] age, scarcely recognizable as members of the human race, babbling, silly, toothless, whitehaired, bald—or better let me describe them in the words of Aristophanes: "dirty, stooped, wrinkled, bald, toothless, and toolless."[24] And yet they are so in love with life and so eager to be young that one of them dyes his white hair, another hides his baldness with a wig, another obtains false teeth from heaven knowns where, another is infatuated with some young girl and is a sillier lover than any adolescent. Nowadays for one of these old sticks, these drybones, to marry a juicy young wife, and one without a dowry and sure to be enjoyed by others, is becoming the usual and proper thing. But it is even more entertaining to observe the old women, long since halfdead with age, so cadaverous that they seem to have returned from the grave; yet always saying, "It's good to be alive." They, too, are always in heat, and hire young men at a handsome fee. They carefully paint their faces, and constantly inspect themselves in the mirror; they pluck out hairs from the strangest places; they display their withered and flabby breasts; with a quavering love-song they stir a worn-out desire; they drink and go around with girls; they write love-letters. Everyone laughs at all this, and very properly, since it is the greatest folly in the world; yet the old ladies are well pleased with themselves. They are perfectly happy solely because of me. Moreover, those who scorn this kind of behavior might consider whether it is not better to lead a life of pleasant folly than to look for a rafter and a rope. Anyway, it is nothing to my fools that their actions are scorned; they either feel no shame, or shrug it off easily. If a rock falls on your head, that is clearly painful; but shame, disgrace, and curses hurt only so far as they are felt. What isn't noticed isn't troublesome. So long as you applaud yourself, what harm are the hisses of the world? And folly is the only key to this happiness.

I seem to hear the philosophers disagreeing. This is really unhappiness, they say, this life of folly, error, and ignorance. No, indeed; this is to be human. I cannot see why they should call this unhappiness when it is the common lot of all to be thus born, brought up, and constituted. Nothing can be unhappy if it expresses its true nature. Or do you argue that man is to be pitied because he cannot fly with the birds, and cannot run on four legs with the animals,

---

23. the old, eloquent sage in the Homeric epic.

24. See Aristophanes, *Plutus*, ll. 266–267.

and is not armed with horns like a bull? It can be argued equally well that the finest horse is unhappy because it is not a grammarian and a gourmet, or that a bull is miserable because it is found wanting at the minuet. A foolish man is no more unhappy than an illiterate horse: both are true to themselves.

The casuists argue next that men are naturally imperfect, and support and strengthen themselves by the peculiarly human device of study. As if it were possible that nature should be so careful in making a midge, a flower, or an herb, and then should have dozed in making man! And with the result that the sciences are needed! They were really invented by Theuth,[25] the evil genius of the human race, for the hurt of mankind. Instead of promoting man's happiness, they hinder it. They were probably even discovered for that purpose, just as letters were, according to the admirable argument of Plato's wise king.[26] In this way, studies crept in with the other trials of life, and from the same devilish source. This is shown by their name: "daemons," which means "those who know."

The people of the golden age lived without the advantages of learning, being guided by instinct and nature alone. What was the need of grammar when all spoke the same language, and spoke only to be understood? What use for dialectic when there was no conflict of opinion? What place for rhetoric when no one wished to get the better of another? What need for legal skill before the time of those evil acts which called forth our good laws? Furthermore, they were then too religious to pry impiously into nature's secrets, to measure the size, motion, and influence of the stars, or to seek the hidden causes of things. They considered it a sacrilege for man to know more than he should. They were free from the insane desire to discover what may lie beyond the stars. But as men fell slowly from the innocence of the golden age, the arts were invented, and by evil spirits, as I have said. At first they were few in number and were accepted by a few people. Later, hundreds more were added by the superstition of the Chaldeans and by the idle speculation of the Greeks. This was a needless vexation of the spirit, when one considers that a single grammatical system is perfectly adequate for a lifetime of torture.

Of course the arts which are nearest to common sense, that is, to folly, are most highly esteemed. Theologians are starved, scientists are given the cold shoulder, astrologers are laughed at, and logicians are ignored. The doctor alone, as they say, is worth all the rest put together. And a doctor is honored, especially among nobles, to the degree that he is ignorant and impudent. Medicine, as now generally practiced, is a branch of the art of flattery just as much as rhetoric is. Lawyers rank next to doctors. Perhaps they should be placed

25. in Plato's *Phaedrus*, the name of an Egyptian god who brought the art of writing to King Thamus.

26. King Thamus argued that the invention of writing would produce only false wisdom and destroy the power of man's memory.

first, but I hesitate to join the philosophers, who unanimously laugh at lawyers as being so many asses. Nevertheless, all affairs, both great and small, are arbitrated by these asses. Their lands increase; while the theologian, who has mastered a trunkful of manuscripts, lives on beans, and wages a gallant war against lice and fleas. As those arts are more successful which have the greatest proportion of folly, so those people are happiest who have nothing to do with learning and follow nature as their only guide. She is in no way wanting, except as a man wishes to go beyond what is proper for him. Nature hates counterfeits; the less the art, the greater the happiness.

Isn't it true that the happiest creatures are those which are least artificial and most natural? What could be happier than the bees, or more wonderful? They lack some of the senses, but what architect has equalled their constructive skill, or what philosopher has framed a republic to match theirs? Now the horse, who does have some of the human senses and who travels around with men, suffers also from human ills. He feels ashamed if he loses a race. While seeking military glory, he is run through and bites the dust along with his rider. Think, too, of the hard bit, the sharp spurs, the prison-like stable, the whips, sticks, and straps, the rider himself—in short, all the tragedy of servitude to which he exposes himself when he imitates men of honor and zealously seeks vengeance against the enemy. How much more desirable except for the interference of men, is the lot of flies and birds, who live for the moment and by the light of nature. Everyone has noticed how a bird loses its natural beauty when it is shut up in a cage and taught to speak. In every sphere, what is natural is happier than what is falsified by art.

For these reasons I can never sufficiently praise that cock (really Pythagoras)[27] who had been all things—philosopher, man, woman, king, subject, fish, horse, frog, perhaps even a sponge—and who concluded that none is as miserable as man. All the others are content with their natural limitations; man alone is vainly ambitious. Among men, furthermore, the fools are in many respects superior to the learned and the great. Gryllus,[28] for example, proved to be considerably wiser than wise Ulysses when he chose to grunt in a sty rather than to expose himself to the dangers of a further odyssey. Homer, the father of fiction, seems to agree with this: he often observes that men are wretched, and he still oftener describes Ulysses, the pattern of wisdom, as miserable, but he never speaks in this way of Paris, Ajax, or Achilles. Obviously Ulysses was unhappy because that tricky and artful fellow never did anything without consulting the goddess of wisdom. Wouldn't you say that he

27. In the dialogue *The Dream, or the Cock*, written in the second century A.D. by the Greek satirist Lucian, the cock upholds the Pythagorean notion of transmigration of souls from one body to another by claiming that he is Pythagoras.

28. character in a dialogue by Plutarch, changed into a pig by Circe.

was over-educated, and that he had got too far away from nature? The seekers after wisdom are the farthest from happiness. They are fools twice over: forgetting the human station to which they were born, they grasp at divinity, and imitating the Giants,[29] they use their arts as engines with which to attack nature. It follows that the least unhappy are those who approximate the naivete of the beasts and who never attempt what is beyond men.

There is no need to argue this like a Stoic logician, however, when we can prove it with a plain example. Is anyone happier than those we commonly call morons, fools, nitwits, and naturals—the most beautiful of names? This may sound absurd at first, but it is profoundly true. In the first place, these fools are free from the fear of death—and that fear is not an insignificant evil. They are free from the pangs of conscience. They are not terrified by ghosts and hobgoblins. They are not filled with vain worries and hopes. In short, they are not troubled by the thousand cares to which this life is subject. Shame, fear, ambition, envy, and love are not for them. If they were just a little dumber and more animal-like, they would not even sin—or so the theologians say. Count your cares, you stupid intellectuals, and then you will begin to appreciate what I do for my followers. Remember also that they are always merry; wherever they go they bring pleasure, as if they were mercifully created by the gods to lighten the sadness of human life.

In a world where men are mostly at odds, all are as one in their attitude toward these innocents. They are sought out and sheltered; everyone permits them to do and say what they wish with impunity. Even the wild beasts perceive their harmlessness and do not attack them. They are sacred to the gods, and especially to me; therefore do all men properly honor them. Kings cannot eat or travel or spend an hour without their fools, in whom they take the greatest delight.[30] In fact they rather prefer them to their crabbed counsellors, whom they nevertheless support for the sake of appearances. This royal preference is easily explained, I think. Counsellors, confident in their wisdom and forced to speak the unpleasant truth, bring only problems to princes; but fools bring what rulers are always looking for—jokes and laughter.

Fools have another not insignificant virtue: they alone are candid and truthful. What is more admirable than truth? I know that Alcibiades[31] thought that only drunkards and children speak the truth; nevertheless, the merit is really mine, as is proved by a line from Euripides: A fool speaks folly.[32] Whatever a fool has in his heart is all over his face and in his speech. Now wise men have two

29. following the example of the Giants, or Titans, of Greek mythology who, inspired by their wronged mother Gaea (Earth), fought the Olympian gods and were defeated.

30. The fool, or professional jester, was of course a common feature at Medieval and Renaissance courts.

31. See Plato's *Symposium*.

32. *The Bacchanals* (*Bacchae*), l. 369.

tongues, as Euripides also remarks,[33] one for speaking the truth, and the other for saying whatever is expedient at the moment. They turn black into white, and blow hot and cold with the same breath; their words are far from what is in their hearts. Kings are unhappiest at this point it seems to me, since in the midst of their prosperity they can find no one to tell them the truth, and are obliged to have flatterers for friends. You may say that kings hate to hear the truth and avoid wise counsellors for fear that one more daring than the others will speak what is true rather than what is pleasant. By and large this is so. It is remarkable, therefore, that kings will take the truth, and a sharp truth too, from my fools. A statement which would cost a wise man his head is received from a fool with the greatest delight. Truth that is free from offensiveness does give genuine pleasure, and only fools have the power to speak it. It is for these reasons, too, that fools are taken up by women, who are naturally inclined to pleasure and frivolity. Moreover, they can explain away whatever games they indulge in with fools, even when the sport becomes serious, as good clean fun—for the sex is ingenious, especially at covering up its own lapses.

Now let's return to the subject of the happiness of fools. After a life of jollity, and with no fear of death, or sense of it, they go straight to the Elysian fields, where they entertain the pious and leisurely shades. Compare the life of a wise man with that of a fool. Put up against a fool some model of wisdom, one who lost his boyhood and youth in the classroom, who dissipated the best part of his life in continual worry and study, and who never tasted a particle of pleasure thereafter. He is always abstemious, poor, unhappy, and crabbed; he is harsh and unjust to himself, grim and mean to others; he is pale, emaciated, sickly, sore-eyed, prematurely old and white-haired, dying before his time. Of course it really makes little difference when such a man dies. He has never lived. Well, there is your wise man for you.

Here the Stoics croak at me again. Nothing, they say, is more lamentable than madness, and pure folly is either very near madness, or more likely is the same thing. What is madness but a wandering of the wits? (But the Stoics wander the whole way.) With the Muses' help we will explode this line of reasoning. The argument is plausible, but our opponents should remember the practice of Socrates in splitting Cupids and Venuses,[34] and distinguish one kind of madness from another—at least they should if they wish to be considered sane themselves. To begin with, not every kind of madness is a calamity. Otherwise Horace would not have said, "A pleasant madness inspires me."[35] Nor would Plato have ranked the frenzy of poets, prophets, and lovers among the chief blessings

33. The source of this reference is uncertain.
34. distinguishing different types of love.
35. Horace, *Odes*, Book III, Ode iv, ll. 5–6.

of life. And the oracle would not have called the labors of Aeneas, insane.[36] Madness is really of two kinds. The first is sent up from hell by the vengeful Furies. Unloosing their snaky locks, they assault the hearts of men with hot desire for war, with insatiable greed and shameful lust, with parricide, incest, sacrilege, or any other evil of that sort. At other times the Furies pursue the guilty and conscience-stricken soul with terror and the fire of wrath. The second kind of madness is far different from this. It comes from me and is to be desired above all things. It arises whenever a cheerful confusion of the mind frees the spirit from care and at the same time anoints it with many-sided delight. It is the state of mind that Cicero desired as a defense against the evils of his age. The Greek in Horace[37] also had the right idea. He was just sufficiently mad to sit alone in the theater all day, laughing and applauding at a bare stage, because he thought that tragedies were being enacted there. Otherwise he was sane enough—pleasant with his friends, kind to his wife, and indulgent to his servants, who could uncork a bottle without his getting angry. When the care of family and physician had freed him of his disease, he protested that he had been killed rather than cured, that they had taken away his pleasures and destroyed his delightful delusions. And he was perfectly right. They were the mad ones themselves, and needed the medicine more than he did. What sense is there in regarding a fortunate delusion like his as a disease to be purged with drugs?

It is not certain that every delusion and vagary ought to be called madness. A short-sighted man who thinks a mule is an ass is not commonly considered insane, nor is one who judges popular music to be great poetry. However, we must grant that a man is pretty nearly mad if he is continually and extraordinarily deluded by both his senses and his judgment. Take, for example, a person who thinks he is listening to a symphony orchestra whenever an ass brays, or a beggar who believes himself to be Croesus. Nevertheless, when this extreme madness gives pleasure, as it usually does, it is remarkably delightful both to those who are possessed by it, and to those who look on and are not mad in exactly the same way. Indeed this kind of madness is much more common than the ordinary person realizes. One madman laughs at another; they take turns entertaining each other. And the maddest one gets the biggest laugh.

If Folly is any judge, the happiest man is the one who is the most thoroughly deluded. May he maintain that ecstasy. It comes only from me, and is so widespread that I doubt if there is one man anywhere who is consistently wise and untouched by some madness. It may be only a tendency to think a gourd is a woman; but since very few see eye to eye with him on this, he will be called mad.

---

36. *Aeneid*, Book VI, l. 135.
37. What follows is a paraphrase of a passage in Horace's *Epistles*, Book II, Epistle ii, ll. 128–140.

When a man foolishly maintains that his wife (whom he shares with many others) is a pluperfect Penelope, however, nobody calls him mad, because they see that this is a plight common to other husbands.

To this latter class belong those who sacrifice everything for hunting. They swear that the sound of the horn and the baying of the hounds fill them with indescribable joy. I understand that even the dung of the dogs smells like cinnamon to them. And what is so delightful as an animal being butchered? Bulls and oxen are of course slaughtered by commoners, but it is a crime for anyone except a gentleman to touch wild game. Bareheaded and kneeling, he performs the ceremony with a special knife (no other can be used), cutting certain parts in approved order. The silent company stands as if spellbound by some novelty, although it has seen the spectacle a thousand times. If one of them is given a piece to taste, he feels that he has risen somewhat in the ranks of nobility. They think they are living royally, whereas they are really gaining nothing from this butchering and eating of animals, except to degenerate into animals themselves.

A similar class is those who are afire with a tremendous enthusiasm for building. They change round structures into square ones, and then back into round ones again. There is no end to this, until, having built themselves into poverty, they have no house to live in, and nothing to eat. What of it? In the meantime, they have been happy.

Next to these, I believe, are those who with new and secret arts labor to transmute the forms of things and who ransack earth and sea for a fifth essence.[38] Lured on by hope, and begrudging neither pain nor cost, they contrive, with marvelous ingenuity, their own delightful deception. Finally, they have spent all their money and can't afford another furnace. Even then, however, they dream on pleasantly, urging others to experience the same happiness. When absolutely all hope is gone, they find much comfort in this last thought, "In great things, it is enough to have tried." They complain that life is too short for the magnitude of their undertaking.

I am not sure that gamblers should be admitted to our fellowship, and yet some of these addicts are a foolish and ridiculous sight. At the sound of the dice their hearts beat faster. The hope of winning always lures them on, until their means are gone, until their ship is split on the gaming table, which is a more deadly promontory than Malea.[39] Now, when they have lost their shirt, they will cheat anyone except the winner, in order to preserve their word and honor. Think, also, of the old and half-blind fellows, who have to wear glasses to play. When well-earned gout has tied their joints in knots,

---

38. a substance (in addition to the four traditional elements—earth, water, air, and fire) of which the heavenly bodies were believed to be composed.

39. a proverbially dangerous promontory in Greece.

they hire a proxy to put the dice in the box for them. A delightful affair, were it not that the game usually degenerates into a brawl, and so belongs to the Furies rather than to me.

A group that does belong with us beyond any doubt is made up of those who enjoy telling and hearing monstrous lies and tall tales. They never get enough of ghosts and goblins and the like. They are most pleased by stories that are farthest from the truth. Such wonders are a diversion from boredom, and they may also be very profitable, especially for priests and pardoners.

Closely related are those who have reached the foolish but comforting belief that if they gaze on a picture of Polyphemus-Christopher,[40] they will not die that day; or that whoever speaks the right words to an image of Barbara[41] will return unharmed from battle; or that a novena[42] to Erasmus, with proper prayers and candles, will shortly make one rich. In St. George they have turned up another Hercules or Hippolytus.[43] They all but adore his horse, which is piously studded and ornamented, and they ingratiate themselves by small gifts. To swear by St. George's brass helmets is an oath for a king. Then, what shall I say of those who happily delude themselves with forged pardons for their sins? They calculate the time to be spent in Purgatory down to the year, month, day, and hour, as if from a fool-proof mathematical table. There are also those who propose to get everything they desire by relying on magical charms and prayers devised by some pious impostor for the sake of his soul, or for profit. They will have wealth, honor, pleasure, plenty, good health, long life, a vigorous old age, and at last, a place next to Christ in heaven. However they don't want that seat of honor until the very last minute; celestial pleasures may come only when worldly pleasures, hung on to with tooth and nail, finally depart.

I picture a business man, a soldier, or a judge taking from all his loot one small coin as a proper expiation for the infinite evil of his life. He thinks it possible to buy up, like notes, so many perjuries, rapes, debauches, fights, murders, frauds, lies and treacheries. Having done this, he feels free to start with a clean slate on a new round of sin. How foolish also—and how happy—are those who expect something more than the highest happiness if they repeat daily the seven verses of the Psalms. These are the verses believed to have been pointed out to St. Bernard by the devil. He was a merry fellow but not very shrewd, since his tongue was loosened by the saint's trick.[44] Things like that are so foolish that I am almost

40. Polyphemus is the Cyclops (one-eyed giant) in Homer's *Odyssey;* St. Christopher is also represented with only one eye.

41. St. Barbara, supposed to protect her worshipers against fire and artillery.

42. a nine days' devotion.

43. In Greco-Roman mythology, both fought against monsters.

44. A devil had told St. Bernard that repeating seven particular verses of the Psalms would bring him the certainty of salvation; "the saint's trick" was that of proposing to recite all of the Psalms.

ashamed of them myself; yet they are accepted not only by the laity but by the professors of theology themselves. The same thing on a larger scale occurs when sections of the country set up regional saints, and assign peculiar rites and powers to each one. One gives relief from toothache, another aids women in labor, a third recovers stolen goods, a fourth succors the shipwrecked, and still another watches over the sheep—the list is too long to finish. Some are helpful in a number of difficulties, especially the Virgin Mother, whom the common people honor more than they do the Son.

Do men ask anything but folly from these saints? Among all the gifts hanging from the walls and even from the ceilings of churches, have you ever seen one in payment for an escape from folly, or for making the giver wiser? One person has escaped from drowning. Another has lived after being run through. This fellow had the good luck or the nerve to leave the battlefield, allowing the others to fight. Another was delivered from the shadow of the gallows by the patron saint of thieves so that he could continue to relieve those who are burdened with too much wealth. This one escaped from jail. That one crossed up his doctor by surviving a fever. This man was saved by a poisoned drink, which loosened his bowels instead of killing him. His wife was not exactly pleased, since she lost both her labor and expense. Another's wagon was overturned, but he drove his horses home unharmed. That fellow's house fell on him and he lived. This one sneaked out safely when he was surprised by a husband. No one, however, gives thanks for warding off folly. It is so pleasant not to be wise that men will seek to avoid anything rather than folly.

Why should I go farther on this sea of superstition? "If I had a hundred tongues, a hundred mouths, a voice of brass, I could not describe all the forms of folly, or list all its names."[45] The life of Christians everywhere runs over with such nonsense. Superstitions are allowed and even promoted by the priests; they do not regret anything so profitable. Imagine, in the midst of this, some insolent wise men speaking the real truth: "You will not die badly if you live well. Your sins are redeemed if to the payment of money you add tears, vigils, prayers, fastings, and hatred of evil, and if you change your whole way of living. The saints will favor you if you imitate them." A wise man who snarled out things like that would throw the world into turmoil and deprive it of happiness!

Also of our fellowship are those who while still living make elaborate funeral arrangements, even prescribing the number of candles, mourners, singers, and hired pall-bearers. They must think that their

---

45. a variation on a passage in the *Aeneid*, Book VI, ll. 625–627, in which, however, Virgil is talking of "forms of crime" rather than of "folly."

sight will be returned to them after they are dead, or that their
corpses will feel ashamed at not being buried grandly. They labor
as if they were planning a civic entertainment.

I must not pass over those nobodies who take enormous pride in
empty titles of nobility. One will trace his family back to Aeneas,
another to Brutus,[46] and a third to King Arthur. They are surrounded by busts and portraits of their ancestors. They name over
their grandfathers and great-grandfathers, and have the old titles
by heart. At the same time, they are not far from being senseless
statues themselves, and are probably worth less than the ones they
show off. My follower, Self-love, enables them to live happily,
however; and there are always other fools who regard monsters like
these as gods.

Of course Self-love brings joy to others too. This ape-like fellow
here seems handsome enough to himself. That one drawing circles
over there thinks he is another Euclid. The man with the rooster's
voice considers himself a great musician. The happiest fool, however, is the dolt who glories in some talent which is really made possible by his followers. Seneca tells[47] of that doubly-happy rich man,
for example, who had servants on hand to refresh his memory whenever he told stories. He was so weak he could hardly stand, but he
was a great fighter—with the support of hired thugs.

Artists are notoriously conceited. They would rather lose the
family homestead than any part of their talent. This is especially
true of actors, singers, orators, and poets. The worse they are, the
more insolent, pushing, and conceited they become. And the more
applause they receive. The worst always please the most, because
the majority of people, as I have remarked, are fools. If the poorer
artist is most pleased with himself and is admired by the largest
number, why should he wish to have true skill? It will cost him more;
it will make him self-conscious and critical; and it will please far
fewer of his audience.

I observe that races and cities are also attended by self-love. The
English pride themselves on their good looks, their music, and their
fine food, among other things. Noble or royal lineage is the claim
of all Scots, together with argumentative skill. The French are the
masters of courtesy; and the Parisians,[48] in addition, are the only
ones who understand theology. The Italians have a monopoly on
literature and eloquence, and they are pleased to admit that they
alone are not barbarians. Happiest in this delusion are the Romans,
who dream pleasantly of their ancient glories.[49] The Venetians
are content with their own nobility. The Greeks, of course, discovered the arts and possess the heroes of antiquity. Christian

46. the legendary founder of Britain.
47. The reference has not been traced.
48. The Sorbonne, the theological faculty in Paris, was the center of theological studies in Europe. See our first selection from Rabelais.
49. In connection with this passage see the closing paragraphs of Machiavelli's *Prince* (reprinted in this volume).

superstitions entertain the Turks and the other actual barbarians, who boast of their own religions. Better yet, the Jews steadfastly await the Messiah, and still hold grimly to Moses. The Spaniards scorn all other soldiers; and the Germans pride themselves on their great size and their knowledge of magic. I believe this is sufficient to convince you that the happiness of men, individually and collectively, springs from self-love.

Another source of pleasure is flattery, an extension of self-love. Instead of admiring yourself, you simply admire someone else. Nowadays flattery is condemned, but only among those who confuse the names of things with the things themselves. They think that flattery is necessarily insincere. The example of dumb animals should show them how wrong they are. What is more fawning than a dog? And yet, what is more faithful and a better friend to man? Or perhaps you prefer fierce lions, tigers, and leopards? Of course there is a harmful kind of flattery, the kind with which traitors and mockers destroy their victims; but my kind springs from kindliness and candor. It is much closer to virtue than is its opposite, surliness —or what Horace calls a heavy and awkward rudeness.[50] It raises the spirits and dispels grief; it stimulates the faint, enlivens the dull, and eases the suffering; it brings lovers together and keeps them together. It entices boys to study literature; it inspires the old. Disguised as praise, it warns and instructs princes without offense. In short, it makes everyone more pleased with himself— which is the chief part of happiness. What is more courteous than the way two mules scratch each other? There is no need to point out that flattery is important in the admired art of oratory, that it is a great part of medicine, and that it is a still greater part of poetry. It is nothing less than the sugar and spice of all human intercourse.

Still, it is a sad thing, they say, to be deceived. No; the saddest thing is not to be deceived. The notion that happiness comes from a knowledge of things as they really are is wrong. Happiness resides in opinion. Human affairs are so obscure and various that nothing can be clearly known. This was the sound conclusion of the Academics,[51] who were the least surly of the philosophers. At least if something can be truly known, it is rarely anything that adds to the pleasure of life. Anyway, man's mind is much more taken with appearances than with reality. This can be easily and surely tested by going to church. When anything serious is being said, the congregation dozes or squirms. But if the ranter—I mean the reverend —begins some old wives' tale, as often happens, everyone wakes up and strains to hear. You will also see more devotion being paid to such fabulous and poetic saints as George, Christopher, or Barbara

50. Horace, *Epistles*, Book I, Epistle xviii, ll. 508.

51. philosophers of Plato's school, the Academy, which later became a school of skeptics.

than to Peter or Paul or even to Christ Himself. But these examples belong elsewhere.

The price of this kind of happiness is very low. Much more must be paid for substantial things, even for the least of them—grammar, for instance. It is easy enough to acquire mere opinions; nevertheless they bring greater happiness than knowledge does. The satisfaction of a man who thinks rotten kippers taste and smell like ambrosia is not affected by the fact that his neighbor cannot abide their odor. On the other hand, if the finest fish turn your stomach, their quality has no bearing on your happiness. A man who thinks his extremely ugly wife is another Venus is as well off as if she really were beautiful. Here's a person who gazes admiringly at a picture made of red lead and mud which he believes is by Apelles or Zeuxis. Isn't he happier than someone who has paid a high price for an authentic masterpiece, but who gets little pleasure from it? I know a man by my name;[52] a practical joker, who gave his new wife some imitation jewels and persuaded her that they were genuine and very valuable. Now what difference did it make to the girl? She was delighted with the glass trinkets and kept them locked in a secret place. In the meantime, the husband had saved money, had enjoyed fooling his wife, and had won her devotion as well as he would have by a more expensive present.

What difference do you see between the self-satisfied inhabitants of Plato's cave[53] who contentedly admire the shadows of things, and the wise man who emerges from the cave and sees reality? If Lucian's Micyllus[54] could have dreamed forever his rich and golden dream, there would have been no reason for him to desire any other kind of happiness. Evidently, then, there is either no difference between a fool and a wise man, or if there is a difference, a fool has the better of it. A fool's happiness costs least—no more than a bit of illusion. In addition, it is enjoyed in the company of a great many others. The good things of life must be shared to be delightful; and who has not heard of the scarcity of wise men, if indeed any exist at all. The Greeks listed seven all told;[55] a more accurate census would do well to turn up one-half or one-third of a wise man.

Of course drink will drown your sorrows, but only for a time. The next morning they come galloping back, riding four white horses, as the saying is. Folly, on the other hand, is a spree that never ends. Its effect is complete and immediate. Without requiring any bothersome preparations, it fills the heart with joy. It is available to all, rather than to a chosen few, as with other gifts of the gods.

52. Sir Thomas More, who was a close friend of Erasmus', and on whose name Erasmus puns with *moria* (Latin for "folly").

53. The reference is to Plato's allegory in the *Republic*, Book VII, where he compares the soul in the body to a prisoner chained in a cave,

his back against the light, able to see only the shadows of things outside.

54. a character in Lucian's *The Dream, or the Cock* who dreams that he has taken the place of a rich man.

55. The Seven Sages listed were philosophers of the sixth century B.C., among them Thales and Solon.

Vintage wine is not made everywhere; beauty comes to few, and eloquence to fewer still. Not many are rich, and not many can be kings. Mars often favors neither side; Neptune drowns more than he saves. The majority are turned away from wisdom. Jove himself thunders, and the anti-Joves—Pluto, Ate, Poena, Febris,[56] and the others—are executioners rather than gods. Only I, great-hearted Folly, embrace all men equally. Nor do I come only when prayed for. If some devotion is neglected, I don't grow testy and demand expiation. I don't upset heaven and earth if I have been left at home and not invited along with the other gods to smell the sacrifices. In fact, the other gods are so hard to please that it is safer and wiser not to try to worship them, but rather to avoid them altogether. Men are sometimes like that; so thin-skinned and irritable that hands off is the best policy.

Even though all this is so, I understand that no one sacrifices to Folly or builds a temple for her. Such ingratitude, I repeat, is amazing. At the same time, I good-naturedly persuade myself that respect is not really lacking. What need have I for incense, meal, a he-goat, or a she-hog, so long as men everywhere whole-heartedly worship me in the way that preachers tell us is best? Let Diana have her human sacrifices! I am not envious when I consider that all men honor me in the truest way, that is, by taking me to their hearts and manifesting me in their lives and actions. This kind of worship of the saints is not exactly customary among Christians. Plenty of them burn little candles to the Virgin, and in the middle of the day, when it does no good; but how few of them burn with zeal to imitate her in chastity, temperance, and love of heavenly things! That, after all, is the true worship, and it is by far the most pleasing to those above. Besides, why should I desire a temple, when the whole world, if I am not mistaken, is a handsome shrine to me? Nor are priests lacking—except where men are lacking. As for stone and painted images, I am not so foolish as to demand what stands in the way of worship. The stupid adore such substitutes in place of the saints themselves, who are finally crowded out altogether. The same thing would happen to me. One might say, of course, that there are as many statues to me as there are people who look foolish, even unintentionally so. What do I care if other gods are worshipped in certain places on stated days—Phoebus at Rhodes, Venus at Cyprus, Juno at Argos, Minerva at Athens, Jupiter at Olympus, Neptune at Tarentum, Priapus[57] at Lampsacus? Why should I envy them when all men eagerly offer greater sacrifices to me?

[The third section deals with "The Followers of Folly," and includes among them, in lively and paradoxical descriptions, all cate-

---

56. Pluto was god of the underworld; *Ate*, goddess of revenge and discord; *Poena*, goddess of punishment; *Febris*, goddess of fever.

57. a god of procreation, son of Dionysus and Aphrodite.

gorics of people, from merchants to poets, from scholars to popes and cardinals; in fact, Folly concludes: "My real point has been that no man can live happily unless he has been admitted into my mysteries and enjoys my favor."]

IV. The Christian Fool

. . . There is really no need for me to marshal proof[58] with so much care, when in the mystical psalms Christ himself, speaking to the Father, says perfectly plainly, "Thou knowest my foolishness."[59] It is not hard to see why fools are greatly pleasing to God. We know that great princes look with suspicion on men who are too clever, and hate them. Julius Caesar, for instance, suspected and hated Brutus and Cassius, while he did not fear the drunken Antony at all. Nero, likewise, was suspicious of Seneca, and Dionysius[60] of Plato; but all princes take pleasure in duller and simpler souls. In the same way, Christ always hates and condemns those who rely on their own wisdom. Paul testifies to this clearly enough when he says, "God has chosen the foolish things of the world,"[61] and when he says, "It has pleased God to save the world by foolishness,"[62] since it could never be redeemed by wisdom. God himself indicates this plainly when he proclaims through the mouth of the prophet, "I will destroy the wisdom of the wise and I will reject the prudence of the prudent."[63] Christ also gave thanks that God had concealed the mystery of salvation from the wise, but had revealed it to babes, that is, to fools.[64] The Greek for "babes" is νηπίοις, which is the opposite of σοφοῖς, "the wise." Equally pertinent is the fact that in the Gospels Christ often attacks the scribes and Pharisees and doctors of laws, whereas he faithfully defends the ignorant multitude. What is "Woe unto you, scribes and Pharisees,"[65] except "Woe unto you that are wise"? Little children, women, and fishermen seem to delight Him most. Even among animals, those pleased Christ best which had the least slyness. He preferred to ride upon a donkey, though had He chosen He could safely have ridden upon a lion. The Holy Spirit descended in the likeness of a dove, not of an eagle or a hawk; and the Gospels frequently mention harts, fawns, and lambs. Those who are chosen

---

58. of the relationship between "Folly" and Christianity.

59. The quotation is from Psalm 69:5, where the speaker is not Christ, but the Psalmist.

60. Dionysius the Younger, tyrant of Syracuse, in Sicily, in the fourth century B.C.

61. "But God hath chosen the foolish things of the world to confound the wise." (I Corinthians 1:27.)

62. "For after that in the wisdom of God the world by wisdom knew not God, it pleased God by the foolishness of preaching to save them that believe."

63. ". . . for the wisdom of their wise men shall perish, and the understanding of their prudent men shall be hid."

64. "I thank thee, O Father, Lord of heaven and earth, because thou hast hid these things from the wise and prudent, and hast revealed them unto babes." (Matthew 11:25.)

65. Luke 11:44.

for eternal life are called "sheep." No animal is more foolish, as is shown by the proverbial phrase in Aristotle, "sheepish character," which was suggested by the stupidity of the animal and is commonly used as a taunt against dull and foolish men. Nevertheless, Christ declares himself the shepherd of his flock, and even takes delight in the name of "the Lamb," as when John pointed Him out, "Behold the Lamb of God."[66] The expression also appears frequently in the book of *Revelations*.

What do these things declare except that all men, even the pious, are fools? And that Christ himself, although He possessed the wisdom of the Father,[67] became something like a fool in order to cure the folly of mankind, when He assumed the nature and being of a mortal? And that He was made "to be sin"[68] in order to redeem sinners? He did not wish to redeem them by any way except by the foolishness of the Cross,[69] and by weak and simple apostles. These He taught to practice folly and to avoid wisdom. He incited them by the example of children, lilies, mustard-seed, and sparrows,[70] all of them foolish things, living without art or care, by the light of nature alone. Furthermore, He forbade the apostles to be concerned about how they should answer the charges of the magistrates, and He forbade them to pry into the times and seasons. They should not rely on their own wisdom, but should wholly depend upon Him. We know, likewise, that the Creator commanded men not to eat of the Tree of Knowledge, just as if knowledge were the destroyer of happiness. Paul roundly condemns knowledge as that which puffs up[71] and works harm. St. Bernard is following him, I believe, when he explains that the mountain wherein Lucifer established his headquarters was "the Mount of Knowledge."

Surely we should not overlook this argument, that folly is so pleasing to the heavenly powers that forgiveness of its errors is certain; whereas nothing is forgiven to wisdom. And so it comes about that when the prudent pray to be forgiven, although they were clever enough when they sinned, they use the excuse and defense of having acted foolishly. This was the argument that Aaron used in the book of *Numbers*, if I remember correctly, to excuse his sister from punishment: "I beseech, my master, that you lay not this sin, which we have committed foolishly, to our charge."[72] Saul asked forgiveness of David by saying, "It is apparent that I have

---

66. John 1:29, 36.
67. "But unto them which are called, both Jews and Greeks, Christ the power of God, and the wisdom of God." (I Corinthians 1:24.)
68. "For he hath made him to be sin for us, who knew no sin." (II Corinthians 5:21.)
69. The source of this allusion is uncertain.
70. For the reference to *children*, see

Luke 18:17; for *lilies*, see Matthew 6:28; for *mustard-seed*, see Luke 17:6; for *sparrows*, see Matthew 10:29.
71. "Knowledge puffeth up, but charity edifieth." (I Corinthians 8:1.)
72. "And Aaron said unto Moses, Alas, my lord, I beseech thee, lay not the sin upon us, wherein we have done foolishly, and wherein we have sinned." (Numbers 12:11.)

done foolishly."[73] David, in turn, speaks placatingly to the Lord: "I beseech Thee, do away the iniquity of thy servant, for I have done very foolishly."[74] It is as if he could not obtain grace by praying unless he pleaded folly and ignorance. Much stronger proof is the fact that Christ when he prayed on the Cross for His enemies, "Father, forgive them," pleaded no other excuse than ignorance, saying, "for they know not what they do."[75] In the same manner, Paul wrote to Timothy: "But therefore I have obtained the mercy of the Lord, because I acted ignorantly in unbelief."[76] What is "I acted ignorantly" except "I acted foolishly, not maliciously"? What is "But therefore I have obtained the mercy of the Lord" except "I should not have obtained it if I had not been supported by the excuse of folly"? The mystical psalmist, whom I failed to recall at the proper place, aids us: "Remember not the sins of my youth and my ignorances."[77]

Let me stop pursuing the infinite and try to summarize. The Christian religion on the whole seems to have some kinship with folly, while it has none at all with wisdom. If you want proof of this, observe first that children, old people, women, and fools take more delight than anyone else in holy and religious things; and that they are therefore ever nearest the altars, led no doubt solely by instinct. Next, you will notice that the founders of religion have prized simplicity exceedingly, and have been the bitterest foes of learning. Finally, no people seem to act more foolishly than those who have been truly possessed with Christian piety. They give away whatever is theirs; they overlook injuries, allow themselves to be cheated, make no distinction between friends and enemies, shun pleasure, and feast on hunger, vigils, tears, labors, and scorn. They disdain life, and utterly prefer death; in short, they seem to have become altogether indifferent to ordinary interests, quite as if their souls lived elsewhere and not in their bodies. What is this, if not to be mad? Considering this, we should not find it very strange that the apostles appeared to be drunk on new wine, and that Paul, in the eyes of Festus,[78] his judge, looked as if he had gone mad.

. . . Since the pious and the vulgar are so radically different, it comes about that each appears to the other to be mad. It is obvious to me, however, that the word is more correctly applied to the pious rather than to the others. This will become clearer if I briefly demonstrate, as I promised to do, that their *summum bonum* is nothing but a kind of insanity. First, let us assume that Plato was

---

73. ". . . behold, I have played the fool, and have erred exceedingly." (I Samuel 26:21.)
74. I Chronicles 21:8.
75. Luke 23:34.
76. ". . . but I obtained mercy, because I did it ignorantly in unbelief." (I Timothy 1:13.)

77. "Remember not the sins of my youth, nor my transgressions." (Psalms 25:7.)
78. a Roman official. ". . . Festus said with a loud voice, Paul, thou art beside thyself; much learning doth make thee mad." (Acts 26:24.)

dreaming of approximately the same thing when he wrote that "the madness of lovers is the highest kind of happiness."[79] He who loves intensely no longer lives in himself but in whatever he loves, and the more he can leave himself and enter into the other, the happier he is. Now when a soul is eager to leave the body, and does not use its bodily organs normally, you call it madness and rightly so. Isn't this what is meant by the common sayings: "there's nobody home," and "to come to," and "he is himself again"? Furthermore, as the love becomes more nearly complete, the madness is greater and more delightful. What is that heavenly life, then, towards which the truly religious aspire with such devotion? Very certainly the stronger and victorious spirit will absorb the body, and it will do this the more easily because now it is in its own realm, and also because during life it has cleansed and contracted the body in preparation for this change. Then the soul will itself be marvellously absorbed by that supreme spirit, which is greater than its infinite parts. And so at last the whole man will be outside of himself; nor will he be happy for any other reason than that, being outside of himself, he shall have some ineffable portion of that supreme good which draws all things unto itself. Although this happiness becomes complete only when the soul has recovered its original body by being clothed with immortality; yet since the life of pious folk is a contemplation and a shadowing forth of that other life, they feel a glow and a foretaste of the reward to come. This is only a drop, of course, in comparison with the fountain of eternal happiness, but it far surpasses all physical pleasures, even all mortal delights rolled into one. By so much does the spiritual exceed the bodily, the invisible exceed the visible. This surely is what the prophet has promised: "Eye hath not seen, nor ear heard, neither have entered into the heart of man, the things which God hath prepared for them that love Him."[80] And this is that portion of folly which will not be taken away by the transformation of life, but will be perfected.

Those who are permitted to have a foretaste of this—and it comes to very few—experience something very like madness. They say things that are not quite coherent or conventional, sounds without meaning, and their expressions change suddenly. They are exuberant and melancholy, crying, laughing, and sighing by turns; in brief, they are truly beside themselves. When presently they return to themselves, they say that they do not know where they have been, whether in the body or out of it, waking or sleeping. They do not remember what they have heard, seen, said, or done; and yet mistily as in a dream, they know that they were happiest when they were out of their minds. So they are sorry to come to themselves again, and they desire nothing more than to be mad always with this kind

---

79. See Plato, *Phaedrus.*   80. I Corinthians 2:9.

of madness. And this is only the slightest taste of the happiness hereafter.

But indeed I have long since forgotten who I am and have run out of bounds. If anything I have said seems sharp or gossipy, remember that it is Folly and a woman who has spoken. At the same time remember the Greek proverb, "Even a foolish man will often speak a word in season." Or perhaps you think that does not hold for women? I see that you are expecting a peroration, but you are certainly foolish if you think that I can remember any part of such a hodgepodge of words as I have poured out. There is an old saying, "I hate a drinking companion with a memory." Here is a new one, "I hate an audience that remembers anything."

And so farewell. Applaud, live, drink, most distinguished worshippers of Folly.

BALDESAR CASTIGLIONE
(1478–1529)
The Book of the Courtier (Il libro del cortegiano)*

[The Setting]†

On the slopes of the Apennines towards the Adriatic sea, almost in the centre of Italy, there lies (as everyone knows) the little city of Urbino. Although amid mountains, and less pleasing ones than perhaps some others that we see in many places, it has yet enjoyed such favour of heaven that the country round about is very fertile and rich in crops; so that besides the wholesomeness of the air, there is great abundance of everything needful for human life. But among the greatest blessings that can be attributed to it, this I believe to be the chief, that for a long time it has ever been ruled by the best of lords; although in the calamities of the universal wars of Italy, it was for a season[1] deprived of them. But without seeking further, we can give good proof of this by the glorious memory of Duke Federico,[2] who in his day was the light of Italy; nor is there lack of credible and abundant witnesses, who are still living, to his prudence, humanity, justice, liberality, unconquered courage,—and to his military discipline, which is conspicuously attested by his numerous victories, his capture of impregnable places, the sudden

---

* Written between 1508 and 1516; first published in 1528. Reprinted from *Book of the Courtier* by Count Baldesar Castiglione; copyright 1901 by Charles Scribner's Sons; 1929 by Leonard E. Opdycke; translated by Leonard E. Opdycke; used by permission of the publishers.

† Book I, Chapters 2–4.

1. for a certain period of time, until Duke Guidobaldo, described below, had to relinquish the duchy of Urbino to Cesare Borgia, who occupied it by force.

2. Federico II (1422–1482), of the house of Montefeltro, duke of Urbino.

swiftness of his expeditions, the frequency with which he put to flight large and formidable armies by means of a very small force, and by his loss of no single battle whatever; so that we may not unreasonably compare him to many famous men of old.

Among his other praiseworthy deeds, he built on the rugged site of Urbino a palace regarded by many as the most beautiful to be found in all Italy; and he so well furnished it with everything suitable that it seemed not a palace but a city in the form of a palace; and not merely with what is ordinarily used,—such as silver vases, hangings of richest cloth-of-gold and silk, and other similar things,—but for ornament he added countless antique statues in marble and bronze, pictures most choice, and musical instruments of every sort, nor would he admit anything there that was not very rare and excellent. Then at very great cost he collected a goodly number of most excellent and rare books in Greek, Latin and Hebrew, all of which he adorned with gold and with silver, esteeming this to be the chiefest excellence of his great palace.

Following then the course of nature, and already sixty-five[3] years old, he died gloriously, as he had lived; and he left as his successor a motherless little boy of ten years, his only son Guidobaldo. Heir to the State, he seemed to be heir also to all his father's virtues, and soon his noble nature gave such promise as seemed not permissible to hope for from mortal man; so that men esteemed none among the notable deeds of Duke Federico to be greater than to have begotten such a son. But envious of so much virtue, fortune thwarted this glorious beginning with all her power; so that before Duke Guido reached the age of twenty years, he fell ill of the gout, which grew upon him with grievous pain, and in a short space of time so crippled all his members that he could neither stand upon his feet nor move; and thus one of the fairest and most promising forms in the world was distorted and spoiled in tender youth.

And not content even with this, fortune was so contrary to him in all his purposes, that he could seldom carry into effect anything that he desired; and although he was very wise of counsel and unconquered in spirit, it seemed that what he undertook, both in war and in everything else whether small or great, always ended ill for him. And proof of this is found in his many and diverse calamities, which he ever bore with such strength of mind, that his spirit was never vanquished by fortune; nay, scorning her assaults with unbroken courage, he lived in illness as if in health and in adversity as if fortunate, with perfect dignity and universal esteem; so that although he was thus infirm in body, he fought with most honourable rank[4] in the service of their Serene Highnesses the Kings of Naples,

---

3. actually only sixty.

4. as a mercenary captain or *condottiere*.

Alfonso and Ferdinand the Younger;[5] later with Pope Alexander VI,[6] and with the Venetian and Florentine signories.

Upon the accession of Julius II[7] to the pontificate, he was made Captain of the Church;[8] at which time, following his accustomed habit, above all else he took care to fill his household with very noble and valiant gentlemen, with whom he lived most familiarly, delighting in their intercourse: wherein the pleasure he gave to others was not less than that he received from others, he being well versed in both the [learned] languages, and uniting affability and pleasantness to a knowledge of things without number. And besides this, the greatness of his spirit so set him on, that although he could not practise in person the exercises of chivalry, as he once had done, yet he took the utmost pleasure in witnessing them in others; and by his words, now correcting now praising every man according to desert, he clearly showed his judgment in those matters; wherefore, in jousts and tournaments, in riding, in the handling of every sort of weapon, as well as in pastimes, games, music,—in short, in all the exercises proper to noble cavaliers,—everyone strove so to show himself, as to merit being deemed worthy of such noble fellowship.

Thus all the hours of the day were assigned to honourable and pleasant exercises as well for the body as for the mind; but since my lord Duke was always wont by reason of his infirmity to retire to sleep very early after supper, everyone usually betook himself at that hour to the presence of my lady Duchess, Elisabetta Gonzaga;[9] where also was ever to be found my lady Emilia Pia,[10] who was endowed with such lively wit and judgment that, as you know, it seemed as if she were the Mistress of us all, and as if everyone gained wisdom and worth from her. Here then, gentle discussions and innocent pleasantries were heard, and on the face of everyone a jocund gaiety was seen depicted, so that the house could truly be called the very abode of mirth: nor ever elsewhere, I think, was so relished, as once was here, how great sweetness may flow from dear and cherished companionship; for not to speak of the honour it was to each of us to serve such a lord as he of whom I have just spoken, there was born in the hearts of all a supreme contentment every time we came into the presence of my lady Duchess; and it seemed as if this were a chain that held us all linked in love, so that

5. Alfonso II and Ferdinand II (both of the house of Aragon), kings of Naples in the late fifteenth century.

6. Rodrigo Borgia, pope from 1492 to 1503.

7. in 1503; for further information about Pope Alexander VI (mentioned above) and Pope Julius II, see in our Machiavelli selection "Princely Virtues" footnote 2, the corresponding text, and the other passages in Machiavelli mentioned in the note.

8. captain in the pontiff's army.

9. Of the ruling family of Mantua, she had married Duke Guidobaldo in 1488. She is the one who presides over this courtly scene.

10. Sister-in-law and companion of the duchess, widow of an illegitimate son of the old duke, Federico, she wittily directs much of the conversation.

never was concord of will or cordial love between brothers greater than that which here was between us all.

The same was it among the ladies, with whom there was intercourse most free and honourable; for everyone was permitted to talk, sit, jest and laugh with whom he pleased; but such was the reverence paid to the wish of my lady Duchess, that this same liberty was a very great check; nor was there anyone who did not esteem it the utmost pleasure he could have in the world, to please her, and the utmost pain to displease her. And thus, most decorous manners were here joined with greatest liberty, and games and laughter in her presence were seasoned not only with witty jests, but with gracious and sober dignity; for that modesty and loftiness which governed all the acts, words and gestures of my lady Duchess, bantering and laughing, were such that she would have been known for a lady of noblest rank by anyone who saw her even but once. And impressing herself thus upon those about her, she seemed to attune us all to her own quality and tone; accordingly every man strove to follow this pattern, taking as it were a rule of beautiful behaviour from the presence of so great and virtuous a lady; whose highest qualities I do not now purpose to recount, they not being my theme and being well known to all the world, and far more because I could not express them with either tongue or pen; and those that perhaps might have been somewhat hid, fortune, as if wondering at such rare virtue, chose to reveal through many adversities and stings of calamity, so as to give proof that in the tender breast of woman, in company with singular beauty, there may abide prudence and strength of soul, and all those virtues that even among stern men are very rare.

[*"Everything He May Do or Say Shall Be Stamped with Grace"*]*

"I am of opinion[11] that the principal and true profession of the Courtier ought to be that of arms; which I would have him follow actively above all else, and be known among others as bold and strong, and loyal to whomsoever he serves. And he will win a reputation for these good qualities by exercising them at all times and in all places, since one may never fail in this without severest censure. And just as among women, their fair fame once sullied never recovers its first lustre, so that reputation of a gentleman who bears arms, if once it be in the least tarnished with cowardice or other disgrace, remains forever infamous before the world and

---

* From Book I, Chapters 17–26.

11. The conversational "game" through which the courtiers at Urbino are attempting to achieve a description of the perfect courtly gentleman, is in progress. The speaker at this point is Count Ludovico da Canossa (1476–1532). A relative of the writer and a friend of the painter Raphael, he was later a bishop and held many important offices, such as that of papal ambassador to England.

full of ignominy. Therefore the more our Courtier excels in this art, the more he will be worthy of praise; and yet I do not deem essential in him that perfect knowledge of things and those other qualities that befit a commander; since this would be too wide a sea, let us be content, as we have said, with perfect loyalty and unconquered courage, and that he be always seen to possess them. For the courageous are often recognized even more in small things than in great; and frequently in perils of importance and where there are many spectators, some men are to be found, who, although their hearts be dead within them, yet, moved by shame or by the presence of others, press forward almost with their eyes shut, and do their duty God knows how. While on occasions of little moment, when they think they can avoid putting themselves in danger without being detected, they are glad to keep safe. But those who, even when they do not expect to be observed or seen or recognized by anyone, show their ardour and neglect nothing, however paltry, that may be laid to their charge,—they have that strength of mind which we seek in our Courtier.

"Not that we would have him look so fierce, or go about blustering, or say that he has taken his cuirass to wife, or threaten with those grim scowls that we have often seen in Berto; because to such men as this, one might justly say that which a brave lady jestingly said in gentle company to one whom I will not name at present; who, being invited by her out of compliment to dance, refused not only that, but to listen to the music, and many other entertainments proposed to him,—saying always that such silly trifles were not his business; so that at last the lady said, 'What is your business, then?' He replied with a sour look, 'To fight.' Then the lady at once said, 'Now that you are in no war and out of fighting trim, I should think it were a good thing to have yourself well oiled, and to stow yourself with all your battle harness in a closet until you be needed, lest you grow more rusty than you are'; and so, amid much laughter from the bystanders, she left the discomfited fellow to his silly presumption.

"Therefore let the man we are seeking, be very bold, stern, and always among the first, where the enemy are to be seen; and in every other place, gentle, modest, reserved, above all things avoiding ostentation and that impudent self-praise by which men ever excite hatred and disgust in all who hear them."

Then my lord Gaspar[12] replied:

"As for me, I have known few men excellent in anything whatever, who do not praise themselves; and it seems to me that this may well be permitted them; for when anyone who feels himself

---

12. Count Gaspar Pallavicino (1486–1511), a very young member of the court, who died only a few years afterward.

to be of worth, sees that he is not known to the ignorant by his works, he is offended that his worth should lie buried, and needs must in some way hold it up to view, in order that he may not be cheated of the fame that is the true reward of worthy effort. Thus among the ancient authors, whoever carries weight seldom fails to praise himself. They indeed are insufferable who do this without desert, but such we do not presume our Courtier to be."

The Count then said:

"If you heard what I said, it was impudent and indiscriminate self-praise that I censured: and as you say, we surely ought not to form a bad opinion of a brave man who praises himself modestly, nay we ought rather to regard such praise as better evidence than if it came from the mouth of others. I say, however, that he, who in praising himself runs into no error and incurs no annoyance or envy at the hands of those that hear him, is a very discreet man indeed and merits praise from others in addition to that which he bestows upon himself; because it is a very difficult matter."

Then my lord Gaspar said:

"You must teach us that."

The Count replied:

"Among the ancient authors there is no lack of those who have taught it; but to my thinking, the whole art consists in saying things in such a way that they shall not seem to be said to that end, but let fall so naturally that it was impossible not to say them, and while seeming always to avoid self-praise, yet to achieve it; but not after the manner of those boasters, who open their mouths and let the words come forth haphazard. Like one of our friends a few days ago, who, being quite run through the thigh with a spear at Pisa, said he thought it was a fly that had stung him; and another man said he kept no mirror in his room because, when angry, he became so terrible to look at, that the sight of himself would have frightened him too much."

Everyone laughed at this, but Messer Cesare Gonzaga [13] added:

"Why do you laugh? Do you not know that Alexander the Great, on hearing the opinion of a philosopher to be that there was an infinite number of worlds, began to weep, and being asked why he wept, replied, 'Because I have not yet conquered one of them;' as if he would fain have vanquished all? Does not this seem to you a greater boast than that about the fly-sting?"

Then the Count said:

"Yes, and Alexander was a greater man than he who made the other speech. But extraordinary men are surely to be pardoned when they assume much; for he who has great things to do must

13. considered by some the "first gentleman" at the court of Urbino. A cousin of the writer, he was a warrior, a diplomat, and a pastoral poet; he died in 1512, at thirty-seven.

needs have daring to do them, and confidence in himself, and must not be abject or mean in spirit, yet very modest in speech, showing less confidence in himself than he has, lest his self-confidence lead to rashness."

The Count now paused a little, and messer Bernardo Bibbiena[14] said, laughing:

"I remember what you said earlier, that this Courtier of ours must be endowed by nature with beauty of countenance and person, and with a grace that shall make him so agreeable. Grace and beauty of countenance I think I certainly possess, and this is the reason why so many ladies are ardently in love with me, as you know; but I am rather doubtful as to the beauty of my person, especially as regards these legs of mine, which seem to me decidedly less well proportioned than I should wish: as to my bust and other members, however, I am quite content. Pray, now, describe a little more in particular the sort of body that the Courtier is to have, so that I may dismiss this doubt and set my mind at rest."

After some laughter at this, the Count continued:

"Of a certainty that grace of countenance can be truly said to be yours, nor need I cite further example than this to show what manner of thing it is, for we unquestionably perceive your aspect to be most agreeable and pleasing to everyone, albeit the lineaments of it are not very delicate. Still it is of a manly cast and at the same time full of grace; and this characteristic is to be found in many different types of countenance. And of such sort I would have our Courtier's aspect; not so soft and effeminate as is sought by many, who not only curl their hair and pluck their brows, but gloss their faces with all those arts employed by the most wanton and unchaste women in the world; and in their walk, posture and every act, they seem so limp and languid that their limbs are like to fall apart; and they pronounce their words so mournfully that they appear about to expire upon the spot: and the more they find themselves with men of rank, the more they affect such tricks. Since nature has not made them women, as they seem to wish to appear and be, they should be treated not as good women but as public harlots, and driven not merely from the courts of great lords but from the society of honest men.

"Then coming to the bodily frame, I say it is enough if this be neither extremely short nor tall, for both of these conditions excite a certain contemptuous surprise, and men of either sort are gazed upon in much the same way that we gaze on monsters. Yet if we must offend in one of the two extremes, it is preferable to fall a little short of the just measure of height than to exceed it, for

14. Bernardo Dovizi da Bibbiena (1470–1520), author of a play performed at the court of Urbino, patron and friend of the painter Raphael, and later a cardinal.

besides often being dull of intellect, men thus huge of body are also unfit for every exercise of agility, which thing I should much wish in the Courtier. And so I would have him well built and shapely of limb, and would have him show strength and lightness and suppleness, and know all bodily exercises that befit a man of war: whereof I think the first should be to handle every sort of weapon well on foot and on horse, to understand the advantages of each, and especially to be familiar with those weapons that are ordinarily used among gentlemen; for besides the use of them in war, where such subtlety in contrivance is perhaps not needful, there frequently arise differences between one gentleman and another, which afterwards result in duels often fought with such weapons as happen at the moment to be within reach: thus knowledge of this kind is a very safe thing. Nor am I one of those who say that skill is forgotten in the hour of need; for he whose skill forsakes him at such a time, indeed gives token that he has already lost heart and head through fear.

"Moreover I deem it very important to know how to wrestle, for it is a great help in the use of all kinds of weapons on foot. Then, both for his own sake and for that of his friends, he must understand the quarrels and differences that may arise, and must be quick to seize an advantage, always showing courage and prudence in all things. Nor should he be too ready to fight except when honour demands it; for besides the great danger that the uncertainty of fate entails, he who rushes into such affairs recklessly and without urgent cause, merits the severest censure even though he be successful. But when he finds himself so far engaged that he cannot withdraw without reproach, he ought to be most deliberate, both in the preliminaries to the duel and in the duel itself, and always show readiness and daring. Nor must he act like some, who fritter the affair away in disputes and controversies, and who, having the choice of weapons, select those that neither cut nor pierce, and arm themselves as if they were expecting a cannonade; and thinking it enough not to be defeated, stand ever on the defensive and retreat,—showing therein their utter cowardice. And thus they make themselves a laughing-stock for boys, like those two men of Ancona who fought at Perugia not long since, and made everyone laugh who saw them."

"And who were they?" asked my lord Gaspar Pallavicino.

"Two cousins," replied messer Cesare.

Then the Count said:

"In their fighting they were as like as two brothers"; and soon continued: "Even in time of peace weapons are often used in various exercises, and gentlemen appear in public shows before the people and ladies and great lords. For this reason I would have our

Courtier a perfect horseman in every kind of seat; and besides understanding horses and what pertains to riding, I would have him use all possible care and diligence to lift himself a little beyond the rest in everything, so that he may be ever recognized as eminent above all others. And as we read of Alcibiades that he surpassed all the nations with whom he lived, each in their particular province, so I would have this Courtier of ours excel all others, and each in that which is most their profession. And as it is the especial pride of the Italians to ride well with the rein, to govern wild horses with consummate skill, and to play at tilting and jousting,—in these things let him be among the best of the Italians. In tourneys and in the arts of defence and attack, let him shine among the best in France. In stick-throwing, bull-fighting, and in casting spears and darts, let him excel among the Spaniards. But above everything he should temper all his movements with a certain good judgment and grace, if he wishes to merit that universal favour which is so greatly prized.

"There are also many other exercises, which although not immediately dependent upon arms, yet are closely connected therewith, and greatly foster manly sturdiness; and one of the chief among these seems to me to be the chase, because it bears a certain likeness to war; and truly it is an amusement for great lords and befitting a man at court, and furthermore it is seen to have been much cultivated among the ancients. It is fitting also to know how to swim, to leap, to run, to throw stones, for besides the use that may be made of this in war, a man often has occasion to show what he can do in such matters; whence good esteem is to be won, especially with the multitude, who must be taken into account withal. Another admirable exercise, and one very befitting a man at court, is the game of tennis, in which are well shown the disposition of the body, the quickness and suppleness of every member, and all those qualities that are seen in nearly every other exercise. Nor less highly do I esteem vaulting on horse, which although it be fatiguing and difficult, makes a man very light and dexterous more than any other thing; and besides its utility, if this lightness is accompanied by grace, it is to my thinking a finer show than any of the others.

"Our Courtier having once become more than fairly expert in these exercises, I think he should leave the others on one side: such as turning summersaults, rope-walking, and the like, which savour of the mountebank and little befit a gentleman.

"But since one cannot devote himself to such fatiguing exercises continually, and since repetition becomes very tiresome and abates the admiration felt for what is rare, we must always diversify our life with various occupations. For this reason I would have our

Courtier sometimes descend to quieter and more tranquil exercises, and in order to escape envy and to entertain himself agreeably with everyone, let him do whatever others do, yet never departing from praiseworthy deeds, and governing himself with that good judgment which will keep him from all folly; but let him laugh, jest, banter, frolic and dance, yet in such fashion that he shall always appear genial and discreet, and that everything he may do or say shall be stamped with grace."

Then messer Cesare Gonzaga said:

"We certainly ought on no account to hinder the course of this discussion; but if I were to keep silence, I should be neglected both of the right I have to speak and of my desire to know one thing: and let me be pardoned if I ask a question instead of contradicting; for this I think may be permitted me, after the precedent of messer Bernardo here, who in his over desire to be held comely, broke the rules of our game by asking a question instead of contradicting."[15]

Then my lady Duchess said:

"You see how one error begets many. Therefore he who transgresses and sets a bad example, like messer Bernardo, deserves to be punished not only for his own transgression but also for the others'."

Then messer Cesare replied:

"In that case, my Lady, I shall be exempt from penalty, since messer Bernardo is to be punished for his own fault as well as mine."

"Nay," said my lady Duchess, "you both ought to have double punishment: he for his own transgression and for leading you to transgress; you for your own transgression and for imitating him."

"My Lady," replied messer Cesare, "as yet I have not transgressed; so, to leave all this punishment to messer Bernardo alone, I will keep silence."

And indeed he remained silent; when my lady Emilia laughed and said:

"Say whatever you like, for under leave of my lady Duchess I pardon him that has transgressed and him that shall transgress, in so small a degree."

"I consent," continued my lady Duchess. "But take care lest perchance you fall into the mistake of thinking to gain more by being merciful than by being just; for to pardon him too easily that has transgressed is to wrong him that transgresses not. Yet I would not have my severity reproach your indulgence, and thus be the cause of our not hearing this question of messer Cesare."

15. According to the plan agreed upon at the start, one of the company began a description of the perfect courtier, and the others made their contributions by contradicting the preceding speaker.

And so, being given the signal by my lady Duchess and by my lady Emilia, he at once said:

"If I remember rightly, Sir Count, I think you have repeated several times this evening that the Courtier must accompany his actions, gestures, habits, in short his every movement, with grace; and this you seem to regard as an universal seasoning, without which all other properties and good qualities are of little worth. And indeed I think that in this everyone would allow himself to be persuaded easily, since from the very force of the word, it may be said that he who has grace finds grace. But since you said that this is oftentimes the gift of nature and of heaven and, even when not thus perfect, can with care and pains be made much greater,—those men who are born so fortunate and so rich in this treasure as are some we see, seem to me in this to have little need of other master; because that benign favour of heaven almost in despite of themselves leads them higher than they will, and makes them not only pleasing but admirable to all the world. Therefore I do not discuss this, it not being in our power to acquire it of ourselves. But they who have received from nature only so much, that they are capable of becoming graceful by pains, industry and care,—I long to know by what art, by what training, by what method, they can acquire this grace, as well in bodily exercises (in which you esteem it to be so necessary) as also in everything else that they may do or say. Therefore, since by much praise of this quality you have aroused in all of us, I think, an ardent thirst to pursue it, you are further bound, by the charge that my lady Emilia laid upon you, to satisfy that thirst by teaching us how to attain it."

"I am not bound," said the Count, "to teach you how to become graceful, or anything else; but only to show you what manner of man a perfect Courtier ought to be. Nor would I in any case undertake the task of teaching you this perfection; especially having said a little while ago that the Courtier must know how to wrestle, vault, and do many other things, which I am sure you all know quite as well as if I, who have never learned them, were to teach you. For just as a good soldier knows how to tell the smith what fashion, shape and quality his armour ought to have, but cannot show how it is to be made or forged or tempered; so I perhaps may be able to tell you what manner of man a perfect Courtier ought to be, but cannot teach you what you must do to become one.

"Yet to comply with your request as far as is within my power,—although it is almost a proverb that grace is not to be learned,—I say that whoever would acquire grace in bodily exercises (assuming first that he be by nature not incapable), ought to begin early and learn the rudiments from the best masters. And how important this seemed to King Philip of Macedon, may be seen from the fact that he chose Aristotle, the famous philosopher and perhaps the greatest that has ever been in the world, to teach his son Alexander the first elements of letters. And of the men whom we know at the present day, consider how well and how gracefully my lord Galeazzo Sanseverino,[16] Grand Equerry of France, performs all bodily exercises; and this because in addition to the natural aptitude of person that he possesses, he has taken the utmost pains to study with good masters, and always to have about him men who excel and to select from each the best of what they know: for just as in wrestling, vaulting and in the use of many sorts of weapons, he has taken for his guide our friend messer Pietro Monte,[17] who (as you know) is the true and only master of every form of trained strength and ability,—so in riding, jousting and all else, he has ever had before his eyes the most proficient men that were known in those matters.

"Therefore he who wishes to be a good pupil, besides performing his tasks well, must put forth every effort to resemble his master, and, if it were possible, to transform himself into his master. And when he feels that he has made some progress, it will be very profitable to observe different men of the same calling, and governing himself with that good judgment which must ever be his guide, to go about selecting now this thing from one and that thing from another. And as the bee in the green meadows is ever wont to rob the flowers among the grass, so our Courtier must steal this grace from all who seem to possess it, taking from each that part which shall most be worthy praise; and not act like a friend of ours whom you all know, who thought he greatly resembled King Ferdinand the Younger of Aragon,[18] and made it his care to imitate the latter in nothing but a certain trick of continually raising the head and twisting one side of the mouth, which the king had contracted from some infirmity. And there are many such, who think they gain a point if only they be like a great man in some thing; and frequently they devote themselves to that which is his only fault.

"But having before now often considered whence this grace springs, laying aside those men who have it by nature, I find one universal rule concerning it, which seems to me worth more in this matter than any other in all things human that are done or said: and that is to avoid affectation to the uttermost and as it were a very sharp and dangerous rock; and, to use possibly a new word,[19]

16. Of a famous Neapolitan family, he fought for Louis XII and Francis I of France, and died at the battle of Pavia (1525).

17. fencing master at the court of Urbino.

18. Ferdinand II, king of Naples from 1495 to 1496.

19. *Sprezzatura*, here translated as "nonchalance," is indeed Castiglione's own word, epitomizing the important concept of gentlemanly behavior discussed in this passage.

to practise in everything a certain nonchalance that shall conceal design and show that what is done and said is done without effort and almost without thought. From this I believe grace is in large measure derived, because everyone knows the difficulty of those things that are rare and well done, and therefore facility in them excites the highest admiration; while on the other hand, to strive and as the saying is to drag by the hair, is extremely ungraceful, and makes us esteem everything slightly, however great it be.

"Accordingly we may affirm that to be true art which does not appear to be art; nor to anything must we give greater care than to conceal art, for if it is discovered, it quite destroys our credit and brings us into small esteem. And I remember having once read that there were several very excellent orators of antiquity, who among their other devices strove to make everyone believe that they had no knowledge of letters; and hiding their knowledge they pretended that their orations were composed very simply and as if springing rather from nature and truth than from study and art; the which, if it had been detected, would have made men wary of being duped by it.

"Thus you see how the exhibition of art and study so intense destroys the grace in everything. Which of you is there who does not laugh when our friend messer Pierpaolo[20] dances in his peculiar way, with those capers of his,—legs stiff to the toe and head motionless, as if he were a stick, and with such intentness that he actually seems to be counting the steps? What eye so blind as not to see in this the ungracefulness of affectation,—and in many men and women who are here present, the grace of that nonchalant ease (for in the case of bodily movements many call it thus), showing by word or laugh or gesture that they have no care and are thinking more of everything else than of that, to make the onlooker think they can hardly go amiss?"

20. an otherwise unidentified character.

NICCOLÒ MACHIAVELLI

(1469–1527)

["That Food Which Alone Is Mine"]*

I am living on my farm, and since my last troubles[1] I have not been in Florence twenty days, putting them all together. Up to now

* From a letter of December 10, 1513, to Francesco Vettori, Florentine Ambassador at Rome. Our text is from *Machiavelli, The Prince and Other Works*, new translation by Allan H. Gilbert, copyright, by Hendricks House, Farrar Straus.

1. Machiavelli had been suspected of participation in a conspiracy led by two young friends of his, and had been imprisoned and subjected to torture before his innocence was recognized.

I have been setting snares for thrushes with my own hands; I get up before daylight, prepare my birdlime, and go out with a bundle of cages on my back, so that I look like Geta when he came back from the harbor with the books of Amphitryo,[2] and catch at the least two thrushes and at the most six. So I did all of September; then this trifling diversion, despicable and strange as it is, to my regret failed. What my life is now I shall tell you.

In the morning I get up with the sun and go out into a grove that I am having cut; there I remain a couple of hours to look over the work of the past day and kill some time with the woodmen, who always have on hand some dispute either among themselves or among their neighbors. . . .

When I leave the grove, I go to a spring, and from there into my aviary. I have a book in my pocket, either Dante or Petrarch or one of the minor poets, as Tibullus,[3] Ovid, and the like. I read about their tender passions and their loves, remember mine, and take pleasure for a while in thinking about them. Then I go along the road to the inn, talk with those who pass by, ask the news of their villages, learn various things, and note the varied tastes and different fancies of men. It gets to be dinner time, and with my troop I eat what food my poor farm and my little property permit. After dinner, I return to the inn; there I usually find the host, a butcher, a miller, and two furnace-tenders. With these fellows I sink into vulgarity for the rest of the day, playing at *cricca* and *tricche-trach*;[4] from these games come a thousand quarrels and numberless offensive and insulting words; we often dispute over a penny, and all the same are heard shouting as far as San Casciano.[5] So, involved in these trifles, I keep my brain from getting mouldy, and express the perversity of Fate, for I am willing to have her drive me along this path, to see if she will be ashamed of it.

In the evening, I return to my house, and go into my study. At the door I take off the clothes I have worn all day, mud spotted and dirty, and put on regal and courtly garments. Thus appropriately clothed, I enter into the ancient courts of ancient men,[6] where, being lovingly received, I feed on that food which alone is mine, and which I was born for; I am not ashamed to speak with them and to ask the reasons for their actions, and they courteously answer me. For four hours I feel no boredom and forget every worry; I do not fear poverty, and death does not terrify me. I give myself completely over to the ancients. And because Dante says that there

2. allusion to a popular tale in which Amphitryo, returning to Thebes after having studied at Athens, sends forward from the harbor his servant Geta to announce his arrival to his wife Alcmene, and loads him with his books.
3. Albius Tibullus, Roman elegiac poet of the first century B.C.

4. two popular games, the first played with cards, the second with dice thrown to regulate the movements of pawns on a chessboard.
5. nearby village; in the region around Florence.
6. Machiavelli here refers figuratively to his study of ancient history.

is no knowledge unless one retains what one has read,[7] I have written down the profit I have gained from their conversation, and composed a little book *De principatibus*,[8] in which I go as deep as I can into reflections on this subject, debating what a principate is, what the species are, how they are gained, how they are kept, and why they are lost. If ever any of my trifles can please you, this one should not displease you; and to a prince, and especially a new prince, it ought to be welcome.

7. ". . . for knowledge none can vaunt / Who retains not, although he have understood." (*Paradise*, Canto V, ll. 41–42.)

8. *Of Princedoms;* the Latin title of *The Prince.* All chapter headings are also in Latin in the original.

The Prince (Il principe)*
[Princely Virtues]†

ON THE THINGS FOR WHICH MEN, AND ESPECIALLY PRINCES, ARE PRAISED OR CENSURED

. . . Because I know that many have written on this topic, I fear that when I too write I shall be thought presumptuous, because, in discussing it, I break away completely from the principles laid down by my predecessors. But since it is my purpose to write something useful to an attentive reader, I think it more effective to go back to the practical truth of the subject than to depend on my fancies about it. And many have imagined republics and principalities that never have been seen or known to exist in reality. For there is such a difference between the way men live and the way they ought to live, that anybody who abandons what is for what ought to be will learn something that will ruin rather than preserve him, because anyone who determines to act in all circumstances the part of a good man must come to ruin among so many who are not good. Hence, if a prince wishes to maintain himself, he must learn how to be not good, and to use that ability or not as is required.

Leaving out of account, then, things about an imaginary prince, and considering things that are true, I say that all men, when they are spoken of, and especially princes, because they are set higher, are marked with some of the qualities that bring them either blame or praise. To wit, one man is thought liberal, another stingy (using a Tuscan word, because *avaricious* in our language is still applied to one who desires to get things through violence, but *stingy* we apply to him who refrains too much from using his own property);

* Written in 1513. Our text is from *Machiavelli, The Prince and Other Works*, new translation by Allan H. Gilbert, copyright, by Hendricks House Farrar Straus.
† From Chapters 15–18.

one is thought open-handed, another grasping; one cruel, the other compassionate; one is a breaker of faith, the other reliable; one is effeminate and cowardly, the other vigorous and spirited; one is philanthropic, the other egotistic; one is lascivious, the other chaste; one is straight-forward, the other crafty; one hard, the other easy to deal with; one is firm, the other unsettled; one is religious, the other unbelieving; and so on.

And I know that everybody will admit that it would be very praiseworthy for a prince to possess all of the above-mentioned qualities that are considered good. But since he is not able to have them or to observe them completely, because human conditions do not allow him to, it is necessary that he be prudent enough to understand how to avoid getting a bad name because he is given to those vices that will deprive him of his position. He should also, if he can, guard himself from those vices that will not take his place away from him, but if he cannot do it, he can with less anxiety let them go. Moreover, he should not be troubled if he gets a bad name because of vices without which it will be difficult for him to preserve his position. I say this because, if everything is considered, it will be seen that some things seem to be virtuous, but if they are put into practice will be ruinous to him; other things seem to be vices, yet if put into practice will bring the prince security and well-being.

ON LIBERALITY AND PARSIMONY

Beginning, then, with the first of the above-mentioned qualities, I assert that it is good to be thought liberal.[1] Yet liberality, practiced in such a way that you get a reputation for it, is damaging to you, for the following reasons: If you use it wisely and as it ought to be used, it will not become known, and you will not escape being censured for the opposite vice. Hence, if you wish to have men call you liberal, it is necessary not to omit any sort of lavishness. A prince who does this will always be obliged to use up all his property in lavish actions; he will then, if he wishes to keep the name of liberal, be forced to lay heavy taxes on his people and exact money from them, and do everything he can to raise money. This will begin to make his subjects hate him, and as he grows poor he will be little esteemed by anybody. So it comes about that because of this liberality of his, with which he has damaged a large number and been of advantage to but a few, he is affected by every petty annoyance and is in peril from every slight danger. If he recognizes this and wishes to draw back, he quickly gets a bad name for stinginess.

Since, then, a prince cannot without harming himself practice

1. generous, openhanded.

this virtue of liberality to such an extent that it will be recognized, he will, if he is prudent, not care about being called stingy. As time goes on he will be thought more and more liberal, for the people will see that because of his economy his income is enough for him, that he can defend himself from those who make war against him, and that he can enter upon undertakings without burdening his people. Such a prince is in the end liberal to all those from whom he takes nothing, and they are numerous; he is stingy to those to whom he does not give, and they are few. In our times we have seen big things done only by those who have been looked on as stingy; the others have utterly failed. Pope Julius II,[2] though he made use of a reputation for liberality to attain the papacy, did not then try to maintain it, because he wished to be able to make war. The present King of France[3] has carried on great wars without laying unusually heavy taxes on his people, merely because his long economy has made provision for heavy expenditures. The present King of Spain,[4] if he had continued liberal, would not have carried on or completed so many undertakings.

Therefore a prince ought to care little about getting called stingy, if as a result he does not have to rob his subjects, is able to defend himself, does not become poor and contemptible, and is not obliged to become grasping. For this vice of stinginess is one of those that enables him to rule. Somebody may say: Caesar, by means of his liberality became emperor, and many others have come to high positions because they have been liberal and have been thought so. I answer: Either you are already prince, or you are on the way to become one. In the first case liberality is dangerous; in the second it is very necessary to be thought liberal. Caesar was one of those who wished to attain dominion over Rome. But if, when he had attained it, he had lived for a long time and had not moderated his expenses, he would have destroyed his authority. Somebody may answer: Many who have been thought very liberal have been princes and done great things with their armies. I answer: The prince spends either his own property and that of his subjects or that of others. In the first case he ought to be frugal; in the second he ought to abstain from no sort of liberality. When he marches with his army and lives on plunder, loot, and ransom, a prince controls the property of others. To him liberality is essential, for without it his soldiers would not follow him. You can be a free giver of what does not belong to you or your subjects, as were Cyrus, Caesar, and Alexander, because to spend the money of others does

2. Giuliano della Rovere, elected to the papacy in 1503 at the death of Pius III, who had been successor to Alexander VI (Rodrigo Borgia). Alexander VI is discussed in the chapter "In What Way Faith Should Be Kept by Princes"; for Machiavelli's view of the character of Julius II, see the chapter "The Power of Fortune in Human Affairs . . ."

3. Louis XII.

4. Ferdinand II, "the Catholic."

not decrease your reputation but adds to it. It is only the spending of your own money that hurts you.

There is nothing that eats itself up as fast as does liberality, for when you practice it you lose the power to practice it, and become poor and contemptible, or else to escape poverty you become rapacious and therefore are hated. And of all the things against which a prince must guard himself, the first is being an object of contempt and hatred. Liberality leads you to both of these. Hence there is more wisdom in keeping a name for stinginess, which produces a bad reputation without hatred, than in striving for the name of liberal, only to be forced to get the name of rapacious, which brings forth both bad reputation and hatred.

ON CRUELTY AND PITY, AND WHETHER IT IS BETTER TO BE LOVED OR TO BE FEARED, AND VICE VERSA

Coming then to the other qualities already mentioned, I say that every prince should wish to be thought compassionate and not cruel; still, he should be careful not to make a bad use of the pity he feels. Cesare Borgia[5] was considered cruel, yet this cruelty of his pacified the Romagna, united it, and changed its condition to that of peace and loyalty. If the matter is well considered, it will be seen that Cesare was much more compassionate than the people of Florence, for in order to escape the name of cruel they allowed Pistoia to be destroyed.[6] Hence a prince ought not to be troubled by the stigma of cruelty, acquired in keeping his subjects united and faithful. By giving a very few examples of cruelty he can be more truly compassionate than those who through too much compassion allow disturbances to continue, from which arise murders or acts of plunder. Lawless acts are injurious to a large group, but the executions ordered by the prince injure a single person. The new prince, above all other princes, cannot possibly avoid the name of cruel, because new states are full of perils. Dido in Vergil puts it thus: "Hard circumstances and the newness of my realm force me to do such things, and to keep watch and ward over all my lands."[7]

All the same, he should be slow in believing and acting, and should make no one afraid of him, his procedure should be so tempered with prudence and humanity that too much confidence does not make him incautious, and too much suspicion does not make him unbearable.

All this gives rise to a question for debate: Is it better to be loved than to be feared, or the reverse? I answer that a prince should

5. son of Pope Alexander VI, and duke of Valentinois and Romagna. His skillful and merciless subjugation of the local lords of Romagna occurred during the years between 1499 and 1502.

6. by internal dissensions because the Florentines, Machiavelli contends, failed to treat the leaders of the dissenting parties with an iron hand.

7. *Aeneid*, Book I, ll. 563–564.

wish for both. But because it is difficult to reconcile them, I hold that it is much more secure to be feared than to be loved, if one of them must be given up. The reason for my answer is that one must say of men generally that they are ungrateful, mutable, pretenders and dissemblers, prone to avoid danger, thirsty for gain. So long as you benefit them they are all yours; as I said above, they offer you their blood, their property, their lives, their children, when the need for such things is remote. But when need comes upon you, they turn around. So if a prince has relied wholly on their words, and is lacking in other preparations, he falls. For friendships that are gained with money, and not with greatness and nobility of spirit, are deserved but not possessed, and in the nick of time one cannot avail himself of them. Men hesitate less to injure a man who makes himself loved than to injure one who makes himself feared, for their love is held by a chain of obligation, which, because of men's wickedness, is broken on every occasion for the sake of selfish profit; but their fear is secured by a dread of punishment which never fails you.

Nevertheless the prince should make himself feared in such a way that, if he does not win love, he escapes hatred. This is possible, for to be feared and not to be hated can easily coexist. In fact it is always possible, if the ruler abstains from the property of his citizens and subjects, and from their women. And if, as sometimes happens, he finds that he must inflict the penalty of death, he should do it when he has proper justification and evident reason. But above all he must refrain from taking property, for men forget the death of a father more quickly than the loss of their patrimony. Further, causes for taking property are never lacking, and he who begins to live on plunder is always finding cause to seize what belongs to others. But on the contrary, reasons for taking life are rare and fail sooner.

But when a prince is with his army and has a great number of soldiers under his command, then above all he must pay no heed to being called cruel, because if he does not have that name he cannot keep his army united or ready for duty. It should be numbered among the wonderful feats of Hannibal that he led to war in foreign lands a large army, made up of countless types of men, yet never suffered from dissension, either among the soldiers of against the general, in either bad or good fortune. His success resulted from nothing else than his inhuman cruelty, which, when added to his numerous other strong qualities, made him respected and terrible in the sight of his soldiers. Yet without his cruelty his other qualities would not have been adequate. So it seems that those writers have not thought very deeply who on one side admire his accomplishment and on the other condemn the chief cause for it.

The truth that his other qualities alone would not have been adequate may be learned from Scipio,[8] a man of the most unusual powers not only in his own times but in all ages we know of. When he was in Spain his armies mutinied. This resulted from nothing other than his compassion, which had allowed his soldiers more license than befits military discipline. This fault was censured before the Senate by Fabius Maximus, and Scipio was called by him the corruptor of the Roman soldiery. The Locrians[9] were destroyed by a lieutenant of Scipio's, yet he did not avenge them or punish the disobedience of that lieutenant. This all came from his easy nature, which was so well understood that one who wished to excuse him in the Senate said there were many men who knew better how not to err than how to punish errors. This easy nature would in time have overthrown the fame and glory of Scipio if, in spite of this weakness, he had kept on in independent command. But since he was under the orders of the Senate, this bad quality was not merely concealed but was a glory to him.

Returning, then, to the debate on being loved and feared, I conclude that since men love as they please and fear as the prince pleases, a wise prince will evidently rely on what is in his own power and not on what is in the power of another. As I have said, he need only take pains to avoid hatred.

IN WHAT WAY FAITH SHOULD BE KEPT BY PRINCES

Everybody knows how laudable it is in a prince to keep this faith and to be an honest man and not a trickster. Nevertheless, the experience of our times shows that the princes who have done great things are the ones who have taken little account of their promises and who have known how to addle the brains of men with craft. In the end they have conquered those who have put their reliance on good faith.

You must realize, then, that there are two ways to fight. In one kind the laws are used, in the other, force. The first is suitable to man, the second to animals. But because the first often falls short, one has to turn to the second. Hence a prince must know perfectly how to act like a beast and like a man. This truth was covertly taught to princes by ancient authors, who write that Achilles and many other ancient princes were turned over for their up-bringing to Chiron the centaur,[10] that he might keep them under his tuition.

---

8. Publius Cornelius Scipio Africanus the Elder (235–183 B.C.). The episode of the mutiny occurred in 206 B.C.
9. citizens of Locri, in Sicily.

10. reputed in myth to be the educator of many heroes, among them Achilles, Theseus, Jason, and Hercules.

To have as teacher one who is half beast and half man means nothing else than that a prince needs to know how to use the qualities of both creatures. The one without the other will not last long.

Since, then, it is necessary for a prince to understand how to make good use of the conduct of the animals, he should select among them the fox and the lion, because the lion cannot protect himself from traps, and the fox cannot protect himself from the wolves. So the prince needs to be a fox that he may know how to deal with traps, and a lion that he may frighten the wolves. Those who act like the lion alone do not understand their business. A prudent ruler, therefore, cannot and should not observe faith when such observance is to his disadvantage and the causes that made him give his promise have vanished. If men were all good, this advice would not be good, but since men are wicked and do not keep their promises to you, you likewise do not have to keep yours to them. Lawful reasons to excuse his failure to keep them will never be lacking to a prince. It would be possible to give innumerable modern examples of this and to show many treaties and promises that have been made null and void by the faithlessness of princes. And the prince who has best known how to act as a fox has come out best. But one who has this capacity must understand how to keep it covered, and be a skilful pretender and dissembler. Men are so simple and so subject to present needs that he who deceives in this way will always find those who will let themselves be deceived.

I do not wish to keep still about one of the recent instances. Alexander VI[11] did nothing else than deceive men, and had no other intention; yet he always found a subject to work on. There never was a man more effective in swearing that things were true, and the greater the oaths with which he made a promise, the less he observed it. Nonetheless his deceptions always succeeded to his wish, because he thoroughly understood this aspect of the world.

It is not necessary, then, for a prince really to have all the virtues mentioned above, but it is very necessary to seem to have them. I will even venture to say that they damage a prince who possesses them and always observes them, but if he seems to have them they are useful. I mean that he should seem compassionate, trustworthy, humane, honest, and religious, and actually be so; but yet he should have his mind so trained that, when it is necessary not to practice these virtues, he can change to the opposite, and do it skilfully. It is to be understood that a prince, especially a new prince, cannot observe all the things because of which men are considered good, because he is often obliged, if he wishes to maintain his govern-

---

11. **Rodrigo Borgia**, father of Cesare Borgia; he was pope from 1492 to 1503. (See footnote 2.)

ment, to act contrary to faith, contrary to charity, contrary to humanity, contrary to religion. It is therefore necessary that he have a mind capable of turning in whatever direction the winds of Fortune and the variations of affairs require, and, as I said above, that he should not depart from what is morally right, if he can observe it, but should know how to adopt what is bad, when he is obliged to.

A prince, then, should be very careful that there does not issue from his mouth anything that is not full of the above-mentioned five qualities. To those who see and hear him he should seem all compassion, all faith, all honesty, all humanity, all religion. There is nothing more necessary to make a show of possessing than this last quality. For men in general judge more by their eyes than by their hands; everybody is fitted to see, few to understand. Everybody sees what you appear to be; few make out what you really are. And these few do not dare to oppose the opinion of the many, who have the majesty of the state to confirm their view. In the actions of all men, and especially those of princes, where there is no court to which to appeal, people think of the outcome. A prince needs only to conquer and to maintain his position. The means he has used will always be judged honorable and will be praised by everybody, because the crowd is always caught by appearance and by the outcome of events, and the crowd is all there is in the world; there is no place for the few when the many have room enough. A certain prince of the present day,[12] whom it is not good to name, preaches nothing else than peace and faith, and is wholly opposed to both of them, and both of them, if he had observed them, would many times have taken from him either his reputation or his throne.

[*"Fortune Is a Woman"*]*

THE POWER OF FORTUNE IN HUMAN AFFAIRS, AND TO WHAT EXTENT SHE SHOULD BE RELIED ON

It is not unknown to me that many have been and still are of the opinion that the affairs of this world are so under the direction of Fortune and of God that man's prudence cannot control them; in fact, that man has no resource against them. For this reason many think there is no use in sweating much over such matters, but that one might as well let Chance take control. This opinion has been the more accepted in our times, because of the great changes in the state of the world that have been and now are seen every day, beyond all human surmise. And I myself, when thinking on these things, have now and then in some measure inclined to

12. Ferdinand II, "the Catholic," king of Spain. In refraining from mentioning him, Machiavelli apparently had in mind the good relations existing between Spain and the house of Medici.
* Chapter 25.

their view. Nevertheless, because the freedom of the will should not be wholly annulled, I think it may be true that Fortune is arbiter of half of our actions, but that she still leaves the control of the other half, or about that, to us.

I liken her to one of those raging streams that, when they go mad, flood the plains, ruin the trees and the buildings, and take away the fields from one bank and put them down on the other. Everybody flees before them; everybody yields to their onrush without being able to resist anywhere. And though this is their nature, it does not cease to be true that, in calm weather, men can make some provisions against them with walls and dykes, so that, when the streams swell, their waters will go off through a canal, or their currents will not be so wild and do so much damage. The same is true of Fortune. She shows her power where there is no wise preparation for resisting her, and turns her fury where she knows that no walls and dykes have been made to hold her in. And if you consider Italy—the place where these variations occur and the cause that has set them in motion—you will see that she is a country without dykes and without any wall of defence. If, like Germany, Spain, and France, she had had a sufficient bulwark of military vigor, this flood would not have made the great changes it has, or would not have come at all.

And this, I think, is all I need to say on opposing oneself to Fortune, in general. But limiting myself more to particulars, I say that a prince may be seen prospering today and falling in ruin tomorrow, though it does not appear that he has changed in his nature or any of his qualities. I believe this comes, in the first place, from the causes that have been discussed at length in preceding chapters. That is, if a prince bases himself entirely on Fortune, he will fall when she varies. I also believe that a ruler will be successful who adapts his mode of procedure to the quality of the times, and likewise that he will be unsuccessful if the times are out of accord with his procedure. Because it may be seen that in things leading to the end each has before him, namely glory and riches, men proceed differently. One acts with caution, another rashly; one with violence, another with skill; one with patience, another with its opposite; yet with these different methods each one attains his end. Still further, two cautious men will be seen, of whom one comes to his goal, the other does not. Likewise you will see two who succeed with two different methods, one of them being cautious and the other rash. These results are caused by nothing else than the nature of the times, which is or is not in harmony with the procedure of men. It also accounts for what I have mentioned, namely, that two persons, working differently, chance to arrive at the same result; and that of two who work in the same way, one attains his end, but the other does not.

On the nature of the times also depends the variability of the best method. If a man conducts himself with caution and patience, times and affairs may come around in such a way that his procedure is good, and he goes on successfully. But if times and circumstances change, he is ruined, because he does not change his method of action. There is no man so prudent as to understand how to fit himself to this condition, either because he is unable to deviate from the course to which nature inclines him, or because, having always prospered by walking in one path, he cannot persuade himself to leave it. So the cautious man, when the time comes to go at a reckless pace, does not know how to do it. Hence he comes to ruin. Yet if he could change his nature with the times and with circumstances, his fortune would not be altered.

Pope Julius II proceeded rashly in all his actions, and found the times and circumstances so harmonious with his mode of procedure that he was always so lucky as to succeed. Consider the first enterprise he engaged in, that of Bologna, while Messer Giovanni Bentivogli[13] was still alive. The Venetians were not pleased with it; the King of Spain felt the same way; the Pope was debating such an enterprise with the King of France. Nevertheless, in his courage and rashness Julius personally undertook that expedition. This movement made the King of Spain and the Venetians stand irresolute and motionless, the latter for fear, and the King because of his wish to recover the entire kingdom of Naples. On the other side, the King of France was dragged behind Julius, because the King, seeing that the Pope had moved and wishing to make him a friend in order to put down the Venetians, judged he could not refuse him soldiers without doing him open injury. Julius, then, with his rash movement, attained what no other pontiff, with the utmost human prudence, would have attained. If he had waited to leave Rome until the agreements were fixed and everything arranged, as any other pontiff would have done, he would never have succeeded, for the King of France would have had a thousand excuses, and the others would have raised a thousand fears. I wish to omit his other acts, which are all of the same sort, and all succeeded perfectly. The brevity of his life did not allow him to know anything different. Yet if times had come in which it was necessary to act with caution, they would have ruined him, for he would never have deviated from the methods to which nature inclined him.

---

13. of the ruling family Bentivogli (the prefix *Messer* means "my lord"); the Pope undertook to dislodge him from Bologna, in 1506.

I conclude, then, that since Fortune is variable and men are set in their ways, they are successful when they are in harmony with Fortune and unsuccessful when they disagree with her. Yet I am of the opinion that it is better to be rash than over-cautious, because Fortune is a woman and, if you wish to keep her down, you must beat her and pound her. It is evident that she allows herself to be overcome by men who treat her in that way rather than by those who proceed coldly. For that reason, like a woman, she is always the friend of young men, because they are less cautious, and more courageous, and command her with more boldness.

[The Roman Dream]*

AN EXHORTATION TO TAKE HOLD OF ITALY AND RESTORE HER TO LIBERTY FROM THE BARBARIANS

Having considered all the things discussed above, I have been turning over in my own mind whether at present in Italy the time is ripe for a new prince to win prestige, and whether conditions there give a wise and vigorous ruler occasion to introduce methods that will do him honor, and bring good to the mass of the people of the land. It appears to me that so many things unite for the advantage of a new prince, that I do not know of any time that has ever been more suited for this. And, as I said, if it was necessary to make clear the ability of Moses that the people of Israel should be enslaved in Egypt, and to reveal Cyrus's greatness of mind that the Persians should be oppressed by the Medes, and to demonstrate the excellence of Theseus that the Athenians should be scattered, so at the present time, in order to make known the greatness of an Italian soul, Italy had to be brought down to her present position, to be more a slave than the Hebrews, more a servant than the Persians, more scattered than the Athenians; without head, without government; defeated, plundered, torn asunder, overrun; subject to every sort of disaster.

And though before this, certain persons[14] have showed signs from which it could be inferred that they were chosen by God for the redemption of Italy, nevertheless it has afterwards been seen that in the full current of action they have been cast off by Fortune. So Italy remains without life and awaits the man, whoever he may be, who is to heal her wounds, put an end to the plundering of Lombardy and the tribute laid on Tuscany and the kingdom of Naples, and cure her of those sores that have long been suppurating. She may be seen praying God to send some one to redeem her from these cruel and barbarous insults. She is evidently ready and

---

* Chapter 26.
14. possibly Cesare Borgia and Fran- cesco Sforza, discussed in an earlier chapter of the book.

willing to follow a banner, if only some one will raise it. Nor is there at present anyone to be seen in whom she can put more hope than in your illustrious House,[15] because its fortune and vigor, and the favor of God and of the Church, which it now governs,[16] enable it to be the leader in such a redemption. This will not be very difficult, as you will see if you will bring to mind the actions and lives of those I have named above.[17] And though these men were striking exceptions, yet they were men, and each of them had less opportunity than the present gives; their enterprises were not more just than this, nor easier, nor was God their friend more than he is yours. Here justice is complete. "A way is just to those to whom it is necessary, and arms are holy to him who has no hope save in arms."[18] Everything is now fully disposed for the work, and when that is true an undertaking cannot be difficult, if only your House adopts the methods of those I have set forth as examples. Moreover, we have before our eyes extraordinary and unexampled means prepared by God. The sea has been divided. A cloud has guided you on your way. The rock has given forth water. Manna has fallen.[19] Everything has united to make you great. The rest is for you to do. God does not intend to do everything, lest he deprive us of our free will and the share of glory that belongs to us.

It is no wonder if no one of the above-named Italians[20] has been able to do what we hope your illustrious House can. Nor is it strange if in the many revolutions and military enterprises of Italy, the martial vigor of the land always appears to be exhausted. This is because the old military customs were not good, and there has been nobody able to find new ones. Yet nothing brings so much honor to a man who rises to new power, as the new laws and new methods he discovers. These things, when they are well founded and have greatness in them, make him revered and worthy of admiration. And in Italy matter is not lacking on which to impress forms of every sort. There is great vigor in the limbs if only it is not lacking in the heads. You may see that in duels and combats between small numbers, the Italians have been much superior in force, skill, and intelligence. But when it is a matter of armies, Italians cannot be compared with foreigners. All this comes from the weakness of the heads, because those who know are not obeyed, and each man thinks he knows. Nor up to this time has there been a man able to raise himself so high, through both ability

15. the house of Medici. The *Prince* was first meant for Giuliano de' Medici; after Giuliano's death it was dedicated to his nephew, Lorenzo, later duke of Urbino.

16. Pope Leo X was a Medici (Giovanni de' Medici).

17. in the preceding paragraph.

18. Livy, *History*, Book IX, Chapter 1, paragraph 10.

19. See the allusion to Moses in the preceding paragraph.

20. Possibly a further allusion to Cesare Borgia and Francesco Sforza.

and fortune, that the others would yield to him. The result is that for the past twenty years, in all the wars that have been fought when there has been an army entirely Italian, it has always made a bad showing. Proof of this was given first at the Taro, and then at Alessandria, Capua, Genoa, Vailà, Bologna, and Mestri.[21]

If your illustrious House, then, wishes to imitate those excellent men who redeemed their countries, it is necessary, before everything else, to furnish yourself with your own army, as the true foundation of every enterprise. You cannot have more faithful, nor truer, nor better soldiers. And though every individual of these may be good, they become better as a body when they see that they are commanded by their prince, and honored and trusted by him. It is necessary, therefore, that your House should be prepared with such forces, in order that it may be able to defend itself against the foreigners with Italian courage.

And though the Swiss and the Spanish infantry are properly estimated as terribly effective, yet both have defects. Hence a third type would be able not merely to oppose them but to feel sure of overcoming them. The fact is that the Spaniards are not able to resist cavalry, and the Swiss have reason to fear infantry, when they meet any as determined in battle as themselves. For this reason it has been seen and will be seen in experience that the Spaniards are unable to resist the French cavalry, and the Swiss are overthrown by Spanish infantry. And though of this last a clear instance has not been observed, yet an approach to it appeared in the battle of Ravenna,[22] when the Spanish infantry met the German battalions, who use the same methods as the Swiss. There the Spanish, through their ability and the assistance given by their shields, got within the points of the spears from below, and slew their enemies in security, while the Germans could find no means of resistance. If the cavalry had not charged the Spanish, they would have annihilated the Germans. It is possible, then, for one who realizes the defects of these two types, to equip infantry in a new manner, so that it can resist cavalry and not be afraid of foot-soldiers; but to gain this end they must have weapons of the right sorts, and adopt varied methods of combat. These are some of the things which, when they are put into service as novelties, give reputation and greatness to a new ruler.[23]

This opportunity, then, should not be allowed to pass, in order that after so long a time Italy may see her redeemer. I am unable to express with what love he would be received in all the provinces that have suffered from these foreign deluges; with what thirst for

21. sites of battles occurring between the end of the fifteenth century and the year 1513.

22. between Spaniards and French in April, 1512.

23. Machiavelli was subsequently the author of a treatise on the *Art of War* (*Arte della guerra*, 1521).

vengeance, what firm faith, what piety, what tears! What gates would be shut against him? what peoples would deny him obedience? what envy would oppose itself to him? what Italian would refuse to follow him? This barbarian rule stinks in every nostril. May your illustrious House, then, undertake this charge with the spirit and the hope with which all just enterprises are taken up, in order that, beneath its ensign, our native land may be ennobled, and, under its auspices, that saying of Petrarch may come true: "Manhood[24] will take arms against fury, and the combat will be short, because in Italian hearts the ancient valor is not yet dead."

24. an etymological translation of the original *virtù* (from the Latin *vir*, "man"; see the introductory discussion, pp. 1036–37). The quotation is from Petrarch's *canzone* "My Italy" ("Italia mia").

FRANÇOIS RABELAIS
(1494?–1553)
Gargantua and Pantagruel, Book I*

[*Education of a Giant Humanist*]

CHAPTER 14

How Gargantua was taught Latin by a Theologian and Sophist.

The excellent Grangousier was rapt with admiration as he listened to his son[1] talking. Truly this lad was marvellously gifted! What a vast intelligence, what cogent understanding! Turning to the governesses:

"Philip, King of Macedon," he declared, "recognized the sound judgment of Alexander, his son, when he saw how skilfully the lad managed his horse. This beast Bucephalus was so fierce and unruly that it threw all its riders. It cracked one man's neck, smashed another's legs, brained a third, and crushed the jawbone of a fourth. No one, then, dared mount it. Alexander happened to be in the hippodrome watching them breaking in and training the horses; he noticed at once that the beast's frenzy came from fright at its own shadow. He therefore made short shrift of vaulting upon its back and heading it towards the sun. There, its shadow falling behind it, he easily mastered it. Philip, by this token, realized the divine insight rooted in his son's intelligence and had him most carefully reared by Aristotle, then the most renowned philosopher in Greece.

* Book I was published in 1534; Book II, in 1532; Book III, in 1546; Book IV, in 1552. Book V, of doubtful authenticity, appeared in 1562–1564. Translated by Jacques Le Clercq. From *Gargantua and Pantagruel*, copyright 1936 by The Limited Editions Club, 1942, by The Heritage Press. Used by permission of The Cardavon Press, Avon, Conn.

1. Gargantua.

"For my part, the brief conversation I have just had with Gargantua in your presence suffices to convince me that his mind is illumined by the divine spark. How else, pray, could he have proved so acute, so subtle, so profound and withal so serene? Give the boy proper schooling, say I, and he will attain a supreme degree of wisdom! Accordingly, I intend to trust him to some scholar who will instruct him to his capacity. What is more, I shall spare no cost."

The name of Master Tubal Holofernes, a great sophist and Doctor of Theology, was proposed to Grangousier. Subsequently this savant taught Gargantua his A B C so thoroughly that he could say it by heart backwards. This took five years and three months. A succession of standard texts[2] followed; the *Facet* (a treatise of puerile moral precepts), the *Ars Grammatica* of Actius Donatus, the fourth-century grammarian; the *Theodolet* (in which Theodulus, Bishop of Syria in the fifth century, exposed in Latin the falsity of mythology and the truth of Holy Scripture) and the *Alanus in Parabolis* (a series of moral quatrains by Alanus of Lille, a thirteenth-century worthy). It took Gargantua thirteen years, six months and two weeks to master these authorities.

It is only fair to add, however, that Gargantua, in the process, learned to write in Gothic characters. (Printing had not yet been invented and the young student had to write out his own texts.)

He had, therefore, to carry in front of him a tremendous writing apparatus that weighed more than seven hundred thousand pounds. The pencase was as large and as tall as the great columns of the Church of St. Martin of Ainay in Lyons; the inkhorn was suspended to it by great iron chains wide enough to hold five cubic yards of merchandise.

Another book, *De Modis Significandi*—a work of speculative grammar by Thomas Aquinas, or Albert of Saxony or probably Duns Scotus—was Gargantua's next reading, together with comments by Hurtebize or Windjammer, by Fasquin or Roadheaver, by Tropditeux or Toomanysuch, by Gualchault or Galahad, by Jean Le Veau or John Calf, by Billonio or Lickspittle, by Brelinguandus or Timeserver, and by a rabble of others. This took more than eighteen years and eleven months, but Gargantua knew the texts so well that at examinations he could recite them by heart backwards. And he could prove to his mother on his fingers' ends that *de modis significandi non erat scientia*, grammar was no science.

Next he read the *Compost* or *Popular Calendar*, and had spent sixteen years and two months at it, when suddenly, in 1420, his tutor died of the pox.

---

2. The books mentioned in this chapter were actually part of the educational curriculum which Rabelais is here satirizing.

Holofernes' successor was another wheezy old pedant named Master Jobelin Bridé or Jolter Clotpoll, who read him the *Liber Derivationum* or *Latin Vocabulary* of Hugutio of Pisa, thirteenth-century Bishop of Ferrara . . . the *Grecism* by Everard de Béthune, a philological lexicon illustrating the Latin words derived from the Greek . . . *De Octo Partibus Orationis* or *Of the Eight Parts of Speech* . . . the *Quid Est?* or *What is it?* a school manual in the form of questions and answers . . . the *Supplementum*, a collection of commentaries . . . the *Mammotreptus*, a monkish or monkeyish commentary on the Psalter and the Saints . . . the *Libellus de Moribus in Mensa Servandis* or *Essay on Manners in Serving at Table*, a rhymed treatise on youthful propriety and morals by Sulpizio de Veroli . . . Seneca's *De Quatuor Virtutibus Cardinalibus* or *Of the Four Cardinal Virtues*, a moral work by Martin de Braga, Bishop of Mondonedo in the sixth century . . . the *Specchio della vera Penitenza* or *Mirror of True Penitence* by Jacopo Passavanti, the Florentine monk of the sixteenth century—with its inevitable commentary! . . . a book of sermons, *Dormi Secure* or *Sleep in Peace*, a collection designed to save the preacher the pains of composing his sermons . . . and finally, other stuff of the same ilk, feather, kidney and broth. . . .

Indeed, Gargantua grew as even as any down ever smoothed, as full of matter as any goose liver ever crammed!

CHAPTER 15

How Gargantua was put under other professors.

At last his father realized that though Gargantua was studying most industriously and spending all his time at it, he was profiting not at all. Worse, this training had actually made the lad over into a fool, a dunce, a booby and a nincompoop.

One day Grangousier happened to complain of it to Don Philippe des Marais, Viceroy of Papeligosse, a kingdom of Cockaigne.[3] That monarch assured Grangousier that Gargantua would be better off learning nothing than studying books of the sort with pedagogues of that school. Their knowledge, said Don Philippe, was but rubbish, this wisdom flapdoodle; they succeeded merely in bastardizing noble spirits and corrupting the flower of youth.

"Upon my word, I'll prove it!" Don Philippe declared. "Take any lad of to-day with but two years' schooling. If he is not superior to your son in judgment, speech, bearing and personality, then I'm the greatest loggerhead and shallowpate from here to Brenne."[4]

3. Rabelais probably alludes to some existing person; his method is to take real people and introduce them into his fantastic world. The kingdom of Cockaigne is the traditional imaginary land of luck and plenty.

4. an actual locality. What was said of Rabelais' characters in footnote 3 applies also to his geography, his local lore, and the like.

This challenge pleased Grangousier mightily; he at once gave orders that a match of wits take place.

That evening, at supper, Don Philippe brought in a young page of his named Eudemon, which means "the fortunate." The lad hailed from Villegongis near St. Genou in Touraine. He was so neat, so spruce, so handsome and his hair was so beautifully combed that he looked more like an angel than like a man.

Don Philippe turned to Grangousier:

"Do you see this lad? He's not twelve years old. Let us prove, if you will, the difference between the pedantic balderdash of yesterday's wiseacres and the intelligence of our modern boys."

Grangousier was agreeable to such a test and bade the page begin the debate. Whereupon Eudemon, asking leave of the Viceroy, his master, to do so, rose, hat in hand. His face was open and frank, his lips red, his glance confident. Looking at Gargantua with youthful modesty, he proceeded to praise and commend the boy—first for his virtues and good manners, next for his knowledge, thirdly for his nobility, fourthly for his bodily excellences and, in the fifth place, exhorted him most gracefully to reverence his father in all respects, because his father was so careful to have him well brought up. Finally, Eudemon prayed Gargantua to admit him among the least of his bondsmen. He added that the only boon he craved from Heaven, at present, was to serve Gargantua in some agreeable manner. Eudemon accompanied the whole speech with gestures so appropriate, his delivery was so distinct, his voice rang so eloquent, his idiom was so elegant and he couched his phrases in such perfect Latin that he seemed rather a Tiberius Gracchus, a Cicero or an Aemilius Lepidus of old, than a youth of our own day.

Gargantua's only reaction was to burst into tears. He bawled like a sick cow, hung his head and hid his face in his cap, until there was about as much possibility of drawing a word from him as a salvo of farts from the rump of a dead donkey.

This so incensed his father that Grangousier vowed to slay Master Jobelin Clotpoll, but Don Philippe remonstrated with him and, by fair persuasions, soothed his ire. Grangousier thereupon ordered them to pay the pedagogue off and to get him as properly fuddled up as your finest scholar of the Sorbonne. This accomplished, let him go to the devil!

"There is this consolation!" cried Grangousier. "To-day at least, he will not cost his host much if by chance he dies in his cups like an Englishman."

When Master Jobelin Clotpoll had gone away, Grangousier asked Don Philippe's advice about a tutor for Gargantua. They finally decided to appoint Ponocrates, Eudemon's teacher, to the position; auspiciously enough, in Greek the name means "vigorous." And soon, the three were to go to Paris in order to find out what studies young men were at this period pursuing in France.

CHAPTER 16

How Gargantua went to Paris upon an enormous mare which destroyed the oxflies of the Beauce.

In the same season, Fayolles, fourth king of Numidia, sent Grangousier a mare from Africa. It was the hugest and most enormous mare ever seen, the strangest monster in the world; for Africa, as the saying goes, may always be relied upon to produce something wonderfully new. The beast was as big as six elephants; like Julius Caesar's charger, her feet were cloven into human toes; her ears hung down like those of the goats of Languedoc; and a little horn grew out of one buttock. Save for a few dapple-gray spots as overlay, her coat was the color of burnt sorrel, which shows that she partook of the four elements, earth, water, air and fire. Above all, she had a horrible tail. It was more or less as tall as the tower of St. Mars near Langeais; and just as square, with tufts of hair as tightly spun and woven as the beards on ears of corn.

Do you marvel at this? You have greater cause to marvel at the tails of the rams of Scythia, which weighed more than thirty pounds each, or—if Jean Thenaud speaks truthfully in his *Voyage from Angoulême to Cairo*—at those of the Syrian sheep which are so long and heavy that, to hold them up, the natives have to hitch a small cart to the beast's rump. Ha! my lusty country wenchthumpers, you've no such tails as these!

The mare Fayolles sent Grangousier was brought overseas in three Genoese carracks and a brigantine; she landed at Les Sables d'Olonne in Talmondais.

When Grangousier laid eyes upon her:

"Ah!" he exclaimed. "Here is just what my son needs to bear him to Paris! So now, in God's name, all will go well: Gargantua shall be a great scholar one of these days! Were it not for dumb brutes we should all be scholars!"

Next day, having drunk liberally, as you may imagine, Gargantua set out on his journey, accompanied by his tutor Ponocrates, the young page Eudemon and his train. And, because the weather was serene and temperate, Grangousier had a pair of dun-colored boots made for him. According to Babin and the Chinon cobblers, these are technically known as buskins.

So they travelled along the highway very merrily, living on the fat of the land and making the best of cheer, until a little beyond Orléans they came to a huge forest, about thirty-five leagues long and seventeen wide. Alas! the woods were aswarm with oxflies and hornets of all varieties, so the wretched mares, asses and horses suffered a veritable massacre. But, by means of a trick they never suspected, Gargantua's mare handsomely avenged all the outrages visited upon her kind. For suddenly, when in the heart of the forest the wasps attacked her, she swished her tail and, sweeping all about her, not only felled the stingers but uprooted all the trees. Up and down, right and left, lengthwise and athwart, here and there, over and under, before her and aback, this way and that, she mowed down the woods like so much grass. And this region, which she thus turned into fallow land, has never known tree or wasp since.

Gargantua, delighted by the spectacle, forebore to boast, merely commenting to his followers:

"*Je trouve beau ce!* I find this pleasant!"

Whence this pleasant land has been known as Beauce ever since.

However, when it came to breakfasting, they had to content themselves with their yawns; in memory of which the gentlemen of the Beauce, proverbially poor, still subsist on a diet of yawns and gaping, and find it very nourishing. Indeed, they spit all the better for it.

At last they reached Paris, where Gargantua rested two or three days, making merry with his followers and inquiring about what scholars were then in the city and what wines people drank.

· · ·

CHAPTER 21

Gargantua's education and social life under the direction of his preceptors at the Sorbonne.

. . . Gargantua resolved with all his heart to study under the direction of Ponocrates. But the latter, wishing to learn how the lad's former teachers had wasted so much time making a crack-brained, addlepated dunce of him, decided he should do exactly as he had in the past.

Gargantua therefore arranged his schedule so as to awake usually between eight and nine o'clock, rain or shine, dark or daylight, simply because his preceptors had decided this on the strength of the Psalmist's saw: "*Vanum est vobis ante lucem surgere*, it is vain for you to rise up betimes."[5]

Then he wriggled and writhed, wallowing in his bed and tossing about like a parched pea, the better to stimulate his vital spirits. Next, he would dress, according to the season, but he was always happy to don a long, hanging gown of heavy wool lined with fox. Next, he combed out his hair with the comb of Jacques Almain, the Sorbonne theologian, known in English as John Handy—a comb

---

5. "It is vain for you to rise up early, to sit up late, to eat the bread of sorrows: for so he giveth his beloved sleep." (Psalm 127:2.)

consisting of four fingers and a thumb—for his mentors maintained that to brush one's hair, wash one's face and make oneself clean were, in this world, a pure waste of time.

Next Gargantua dunged, piddled, vomited, belched, broke wind, yawned, spat, coughed, hiccoughed, sneezed and snotted himself as majestically and bountifully as an archdeacon. Next he proceeded to breakfast in order to fortify himself against the morning mist and cold. His menu consisted of splendid fried tripe, choice meats grilled on charcoal, rich hams, succulent roast venison and numerous soups and brews, with toast, cheese, parsley and chopped meat floating on the surface.

Ponocrates objected that he should not eat so soon after rising without having taken any exercise. To which he replied:

"Exercise? Good God, didn't I tumble and jounce in bed six or seven times before I got up? Surely, that is exercise enough? Pope Alexander VI did this on the advice of his Jew physician, Bonnet de Lates, and lived till the day of his death in spite of his enemies. My first masters taught me this habit, for breakfast, they said, gave man a good mind. So they started the day by drinking, It suits me perfectly and I manage to dine the better for it. Master Tubal Holofernes, who was graduated Licentiate in Paris at the head of his class, used to tell me that hasten was not enough, one must set out betimes. By the same token, the total health of mankind does not consist in drinking down and lapping up, *glub, glub, glub,* like so many ducks, but rather in falling to, early in the morning. *Unde versus;* so runs the rune:

> Lever matin n'est point bonheur
> Boire matin est le meilleur.
>
> To rise betimes is not enough,
> To drink at morning, that's the stuff!"

After an abundant breakfast, Gargantua repaired to church, with, in his train, a varlet bearing a basket. The latter contained a huge breviary swaddled in velvet and weighing about twelve hundred and six pounds including the filth of thumbmarks, dogeared corners, golden clasps and nonpareil parchment. Twenty-six, if not thirty, masses ensued for the benefit of Gargantua and his chaplain. Under his tall hood, this chaplain looked for all the world like a peewit . . . and had very thoroughly antidoted his breath against possible poisons with much syrup of the vine! Chaplain and pupil babbled the mumbo jumbo of the litany, thumbing their rosaries so carefully that not one single bead fell to the ground.

As he left the church, they brought him an oxcart laden with a huge heap of paternosters, chaplets and relics from St. Claude in the Jura, each bigger than a hatblock. Gargantua and his chaplain then strolled in the cloisters, galleries or garden, saying more aves than sixteen hermits.

After, Gargantua would study for a short half-hour, his eyes glued to his book but his mind, to quote Terence's *Eunuch*, wool-gathering in the kitchen.[6] Then he proceeded to make water, filling a large urinal to capacity, after which he sat down at table, and, being naturally phlegmatic, began his meal with a few dozen hams, smoked tongues of beef, caviar, sausages and other like forerunners of wine.

Then four servants in turn shovelled mustard into his mouth by the spadeful, thus preparing him to drain a horrific draught of white wine to relieve his kidneys. Then the meal proper began with viands to his liking, according to the season; Gargantua ceasing to eat only when his belly had reached bursting point.

When it came to drinking, he acknowledged neither end nor rule; for, he said, there were no limits and boundaries to swilling until the tosspot felt the cork soles of his shoes swell up a half-foot from the ground.

. . .

CHAPTER 23

How Ponocrates gave Gargantua such instruction that not an hour of the day was wasted.

When Ponocrates saw Gargantua's vicious mode of life, he determined to bring him up otherwise. But for the first few days he bore with him, for he realized that nature cannot endure sudden and violent changes.

To begin his work the better, Ponocrates requested a learned physician of the times, Master Theodore—the name means "God-given"—to examine Gargantua thoroughly with a view to steering him on the right course. The scholar purged Gargantua canonically with Anticyrian hellebore, an herb indicated for cerebral disorders and insanity, thus cleansing his brain of its unnatural, perverse condition. Ponocrates, by the same aperient means, made the lad forget all he had learned under his former teachers, just as Timotheus[7] of old treated pupils who had already studied under other musicians. Timotheus, incidentally, used to charge this class of students double!

For Gargantua's further edification, Ponocrates made him mingle among learned men whose company fired him with a desire to emulate them, to study more profitably and to make his mark. Next,

6. See Terence's play *The Eunuch*, l. 816.

7. Timotheus of Miletus, famous musician of the time of Alexander the Great.

Ponocrates so arranged the lad's schedule that not a moment of the day was wasted; all his time was spent in the pursuit of learning and honest knowledge.

By this new dispensation, Gargantua awoke at about four in the morning. While the servants massaged him, he would listen to some page of Holy Scripture, read aloud in clear tones and pronounced with fitting respect for the text. A young page, a native of Basché, near Chinon, was appointed reader, as his name, Anagnostes,[8] shows. According to the purpose and argument of this lesson, Gargantua frequently turned to worship, adore, pray and reverence Almighty God, Whose majesty and wondrous wisdom were made manifest in the reading.

Next, he would repair to secret places to make excretion of his natural digestions; here his tutor repeated what had been read, expounding its more obscure and difficult features. Returning to the house, they would study the heavens. Was it the same sky they had observed the night before? Into what signs was the sun entering that day? and the moon?

After this astronomical survey, Gargantua was dressed, combed, curled, trimmed and perfumed, and, while this was being done, he heard the lessons of the day before. Then, having recited them by heart, he would argue certain practical, human and utilitarian cases based upon the principles enunciated. This part of the program sometimes took two or three hours, though usually he had exhausted it by the time he was fully clad.

Then, for three good hours, he was read or lectured to, after which they went to the Tennis Court at the Grande Bracque in the Place de l'Estrapade or to the playing fields.

On the way, they discussed various aspects of the subject previously treated. Then they would play tennis, handball and three-cornered catch, exercising their bodies as vigorously as they had exercised their minds before.

All their play was free for they left off when they pleased, which was usually when they had sweated a good bit or were otherwise tired. They were thoroughly wiped and rubbed down, after which they changed their shirts and walked quietly home to see if dinner were ready. As they waited, they would go over certain points they had retained of the lectures.

Meanwhile My Lord Appetite put in an appearance and they sat down most opportunely to table.

At the beginning of the meal, they listened to the reading of some agreeable chronicle of chivalry in ancient times, until Gargantua gave the signal for wine to be served. Then, if they wished, the reading went on or they could talk merrily together. Often they dis-

8. in Greek meaning "reader."

cussed the virtues, property, efficacy and nature of what was served at table: bread, wine, water, salt, meat, fish, fruit, herbs, roots and their preparation. Thus Gargantua soon knew all the relevant passages of Pliny's *Natural History* . . . in the grammarian Athenæus' *Deipnosophistes* or *The Banquet of the Sages*, which treats of flowers, fruits and their various uses . . . in Dioscorides' famous medical treatise, the bible of apothecaries . . . in the *Vocabularium* by Julius Pollux, a grammarian and sophist of Marcus Aurelius' day, who wrote of hunting and fishing . . . in Galen's numerous dissertations upon alimentation . . . in the works of Porphyrius, the third-century Greek author of a *Treatise upon Abstinence from Meat* . . . in Oppian's two poems, *Cynegetica* which deals with venery and *Halieutica* with angling . . . in *Of Healthy Diet* by Polybius of Cos, disciple and son-in-law of Hippocrates . . . in Heliodorus of Emesa, Syrian Bishop of Tricca and a celebrated novelist of the fourth century . . . in Aristotle's essays on natural history . . . in the Greek works upon animals by Claudius Ælianus, a Roman contemporary of Heliogabalus . . . and in various other tomes. . . .[9] Often for surer authority as they argued, they would have the book in question brought to the table. Gargantua so thoroughly and cogently learned and assimilated all he heard that no physician of his times knew one-half so much as he.

They discussed the lessons they had learned that morning and topped their meal off with quiddany, a sort of quince marmalade and an excellent digestive. After which Gargantua picked his teeth with a fragment of mastic,[10] washed his hands and daubed his eyes with cool clear water, and, instead of saying grace, sang the glory of God in noble hymns, composed in praise of divine bounty and munificence.

Presently cards were brought them and they played, not for the sake of the pastime itself but to learn a thousand new tricks and inventions all based on arithmetic.

Thus Gargantua developed a keen enthusiasm for mathematics, spending his leisure after dinner and supper every evening as pleasantly as once he had, dicing and gaming. As a result, he knew so much about its theory and practice that Cuthbert Tunstal, Bishop of Durham and secretary to King Henry VIII, a voluminous writer on the subject,[11] confessed that, beside Gargantua, he knew no more about arithmetic than he did about Old High Gothic. Nor was it arithmetic alone our hero learned, but also such sister sciences as geometry, astronomy and music.

9. Some of the most famous scientific treatises of antiquity are listed in Gargantua's new curriculum, which, exacting as it is, reflects a less "medieval" type of learning than was embodied in his earlier course of study. See also the enumeration of authors on p. 1146.

10. Wood from the mastic tree.

11. Tunstal was the author of the treatise *The Art of Computation* (*De arte supputandi*, 1522).

Now the digestion of foods is a most important matter. There is the first stage which occurs in the stomach, where the viands are changed into chyle; the second, in the liver, where the chyle is transformed into blood; the third, in the habit of the body, where the blood is finally converted into the substance of each part. So, whilst Gargantua awaited the first stage of digestion, they made a thousand delightful instruments, drew geometrical figures and even applied the principles of astronomy.

After, they amused themselves singing a five-part score or improvising on a theme chosen at random. As for musical instruments, Gargantua learned to play the lute, the spinet, the harp, the nine-holed transverse or German flute, the viol and the sackbut or trombone.

Having spent an hour thus and completed his digestion, he discharged his natural excrements and then settled down again to work three hours or more at his principal study. Either he revised the morning reading, or proceeded in the text at hand or practised penmanship in the most carefully formed characters of modern Roman and ancient Gothic script.

Next, they went out with a young gentleman of Touraine, the esquire Gymnastes, who instructed Gargantua in the art of horsemanship. Having changed his clothes, he proceeded to mount a fiery Italian charger, a Flemish dray horse, a Spanish jennet, an Arab thoroughbred and a hackney. These he would put vigorously through their paces, letting them "career" or gallop a short distance at full speed, making them leap high in the air, jump ditches, clear stiles, and turn short in a ring both to the right and to the left. Next he wielded but did not break his lance, for it is arrant stupidity to boast: "I have broken ten lances in a tilt or fight." A wretched carpenter can do the same. On the contrary, the whole glory of such combat lies in besting ten enemies with one and the same lance. So with strong, stiff, steel-tipped lance, Gargantua would force the outer door of some house, pierce an adversary's armor, beat down a tree, pick up a ring, carry off a cuirassier saddle, a hauberk[12] or a gauntlet. And he performed these feats armed cap-à-pie.[13]

In the technique of parading his horse with prances and flourishes to a fanfare of trumpets—the ceremonial of knights as they enter the lists—he had no equal. As for the divers terms of the equine vocabulary from *giddy-up* and *cluck* to *whoa* and *grrr*, no horseman could hold a candle to him. Indeed Cesare Fieschi, the celebrated jockey of Ferrara, was a mere monkey in comparison.

He learned, too, to leap hastily and with singular dexterity from one horse to another without setting foot to the ground (the nags were circus horses or, to be technical, "desultories"). Further, lance

---

12. coat of mail.   13. from head to foot.

in hand, he could leap on horseback from either side without stirrups and rule the beast at will without a bridle, for such accomplishments are highly useful in military engagements.

Another day he would practise wielding the battle-axe, which he managed so skilfully, in the nimblest thrusts, the most powerful lunges and the vast encircling sweeps of the art, that he passed knight-at-arms in the field and at all tests. Sometimes unarmed, sometimes carrying a buckler or a rolled cape of mail over his arm or a small shield over his wrist, Gargantua brandished the pike, plied the double-edged, two-handed sword, the bastard claymore used by archers, the Spanish rapier, the dagger and the poniard.

He hunted, too: stag, roebuck, bear, fallow deer, wild boar, hare, partridge, pheasant and otter . . . he played at ball, ever ready with well-aimed foot or powerful fist to send the great sphere whizzing through the air . . . he learned to wrestle and to run. . . . As for jumping, he did not go in for the various forms of running jumps, such as the three-steps-and-a-leap, the hop-step-and-jump or the German high-jump. As Gymnastes pointed out, these were quite useless in warfare. Instead, he practised the standing jumps. Starting from scratch, he could in one leap top a hedge, clear a ditch, mount six paces upon a wall and thus reach a window-ledge one lance's height from the ground.

Gargantua could swim in the deepest water, breaststroke, back and sidestroke, using his whole body or his feet alone. He could cross the breadth of the Seine or the Loire at Montsoreau, dragging his cloak along in his teeth and holding a book high and dry over the waters—thus renewing the exploit with which Plutarch credits Julius Cæsar during the Alexandrian War. Then, using one hand only, he could, with a single great pull, climb into a boat, whence a moment later he would dive headlong into the water again, sound its utmost depths, touch bottom, explore the hollows of rocks and plunge into any pits and abysses he fancied. He would turn the boat about, managing it perfectly, bringing it swiftly or slowly upstream or down and arresting its course at a milldam. He could guide it with one hand while he plied hard about him with a great oar; he could run up a sail, hoist himself up a mast by the shrouds, dance along the yards, operate the compass, tackle the bowlines to sail close to the wind and steer the helm.

His water sports done, he would dash full speed up a mountain, then down quite as fast. He climbed trees like a cat, hopping from one to the next like a squirrel and pulling down great boughs—like the celebrated Milo of Crotona who, Pausanias[14] tells us, met his death devoured by wolves, his hands caught in the cleft of an oak he had sought to split. With two well-steeled daggers and a pair of

---

14. Greek geographer and traveler of the second century A.D.

well-tried mason's punches, he could scurry up the side of a house like a rat, then leap down again, from roof to ground, so expertly that he landed without hurt. Gargantua also cast the dart, threw the iron bar, put the stone, tossed the boar-spear, hurled the javelin, shied the halberd. He drew the bow to breaking point; he could shoulder a harquebuss—a great siege piece weighing fifty pounds— and fire it off like a crossbow. He could set a huge cannon on its carriage, hit buttmarks and other targets for horizontal shooting, or, point-blank, bring down papgays (stuffed figures of parrots on poles), clay pigeons and other vertical marks, facing them on a level or upwards, or downwards or sidewise. Like the ancient Parthians, he could even hit them as he retreated.

They would tie a cable to a high tower and let it dangle to the ground. Gargantua hoisted himself up with both hands, then slipped down again as evenly, surely and plumb as a man running along a flat meadow. Or they would set a great pole across two trees for Gargantua to hang from by his hands. He moved along the pole from tree to tree so swiftly, without setting foot on *terra firma*, that a man, running on the ground below, could not have caught him. To expand his chest and exercise his lungs, he would roar like all the devils in hell. Once indeed, I heard him call Eudemon across all Paris, from the Porte St. Victor, the gate by the University, all the way to Montmartre, a village on a hill two miles beyond the walls of the city. Stentor,[15] who cried louder than forty men, displayed no such vocal power, even at the siege of Troy.

To develop his sinews, they made him two great pigs of lead, each weighing eight hundred and five tons. These pigs (called salmons in France because the metal is shaped like this fish) Gargantua named *alteres*, an ancient Greek term for the weights used to give jumpers their initial spring—our modern dumb-bells. Taking one in each hand, Gargantua then performed an inimitable feat. He would raise them high above his head and, never turning a hair, stock-still as a statue, hold them aloft for three-quarters of an hour. He played at Barriers or Tug-of-War with the stoutest champions. When his turn came he took root so firmly as to defy the sturdiest to budge him. Nor was it thus alone he emulated Milo of Crotona. Like the ancient athlete, he could hold a pomegranate so fast in his hand that none could wrest it from him, yet so adroitly that he did not crush it.

Having spent his time in such manly sports, he had himself washed, rubbed down and given a change of clothes. Then he returned home at a leisurely pace, passing through some meadow or grassy space to examine the trees and plants. These he would compare with what the authorities wrote of them in their books: among

15. the loud-voiced herald in the *Iliad*, Book V.

the Ancients, Theophrastus, the successor of Aristotle and teacher of Menander . . . or Palladius, whose poem *De re rustica* was trans-lated by Pietro Marini . . . or Dioscorides Pedanius, the Greek physician of the first century . . . or Pliny or Nicander or Aemi-lius Macer, the Roman, or Galen himself. . . . Gargantua and his companions picked specimens by the handful and took them home to a young page named Rhizotome or Rootcutter, who watched over them and the various small mattocks, pickaxes, hooks, hoes, pruning-knives, shears and other botanical instruments.

At home, whilst the servants prepared dinner, our young men re-peated certain passages of what had been read. Then they sat down to table. Here I would have you note that their dinner was simple and frugal; they ate no more than necessary to quiet the baying of the belly. Supper, on the contrary, was a large and copious meal; they ate what they needed for their sustenance and nourishment. Such indeed is the true system prescribed by the art of sound, self-respecting physicians though a rabble of dunderhead quacks, wran-gling eternally in the claptrap routine of the Arab nostrum shop of Avicenna,[16] recommend the exact opposite. During supper, they continued the lesson given at dinner as long as they saw fit; the rest of the meal was spent in earnest and profitable discussion.

Having said grace, they applied their voices to sing tunefully or they played upon harmonious instruments. Or they amused them-selves with such minor pastimes as cards, dice cups and dice af-forded. Sometimes they tarried here enjoying themselves and mak-ing merry until bedtime; they would visit learned men or such as had travelled in foreign lands. Well into the night, before retiring, they would go to the most exposed spot in the house, whence they examined the face of the sky, noting the comets, if any were visible, and the various figures, positions, aspects, oppositions and con-junctions of the heavenly bodies.

According to the Pythagorean system, Gargantua would, with his tutor, recapitulate briefly all that he had read, seen, learned, done and assimilated in the course of the day.

Then they prayed to God the Creator, doing Him worship and confirming their faith in Him, glorifying Him for His immense goodness, vouchsafing thanks for all the mighty past and imploring His divine clemency for all the future.

And so they retired to rest.

CHAPTER 24

How Gargantua spent his time in rainy weather.

In intemperate or rainy weather, things went on much the same as usual before dinner except that Gargantua had a fine bright fire

16. Arab physician and philosopher (980–1037).

lighted to correct the inclemency of the air. But after dinner, instead of gymnastics, they stayed indoors and, by way of apotherapy[17] or exercise amused themselves by bundling hay, splitting logs, sawing wood and threshing sheaves in the barn. Then they studied the arts of painting and sculpture. Or they revived the ancient Roman game of *Tali,* dicing as the Italian humanist Nicolaus Leonicus Thomaeus[18] wrote of it in his dialogue *Sannutus, Of the Game of Dice,* and as our good friend Janus Lascaris,[19] librarian to our sovereign king, plays at the game. In their sport, they reviewed such passages of ancient authors as mention or quote some metaphor drawn from this play.

In much the same way, they might go to watch workmen forging metals or casting pieces of ordnance. Or they might visit the lapidaries, goldsmiths and cutters of precious stones in their ateliers, the alchemists in their laboratories, the coiners at the mint, the tapestry-workers, velvet-workers and weavers at their looms, the watchmakers, looking-glass framers, printers, lutemakers, dyers and other such artisans in their workships. Wherever they went, they would distribute gratuities, invariably investigating and learning the various inventions and industry of the trade.

Or they might attend public lectures, official convocations, oratorical performances, speeches, pleadings by eloquent attorneys and sermons by evangelical preachers—that is, such priests as wished to restore Christianity to the primitive tradition of the Gospel. Gargantua also frequented fencing halls and tested his skill at all weapons against the masters, proving to them by experience that he knew as much as they and, indeed, even more.

Instead of herborizing,[20] they would inspect the shops of druggists, herbalists and apothecaries, studiously examining the sundry fruits, roots, leaves, gums, seeds and exotic unguents and learning how they could be diluted or adulterated. He viewed jugglers, mountebanks and medicasters—who sold Venice treacle, a cure for all ills—carefully observing their tricks and gestures, their agile capers and smooth oratory. His favorites were those from Chauny in Picardy who are born jabberers and the readiest expounders of mealymouthed flimflam concerning their ability to weave ropes of sand, extract sunbeams from cucumbers and milk a he-goat into a sieve.

Returning home to supper, they would eat more sparingly than on fine days. Their meats would, by the same token, be more desiccative and extenuating so as to counteract the humidity communicated to their bodies by the necessary contiguity of the atmosphere

---

17. physical exercise as a regime to maintain health. The terminology is from Galen (the outstanding Greek physician of the second century A.D.).
18. a Venetian, professor at Padua

(died 1531).
19. André Jean de Lascaris, librarian to King Francis I and a friend of Rabelais'.
20. gathering herbs.

and to nullify what harm might arise from lack of their customary exercise.

Such was Gargantua's program and so he continued from day to day, benefiting as you would expect a young man of his age and intelligence to benefit under such a system faithfully applied. To be sure, the whole thing may have seemed incredibly difficult to him at the outset, but it soon proved so light, so easy and so pleasant as to appear more like a king's pastime than the study of a schoolboy.

However, Ponocrates was careful to supply relaxation from this violent bodily and mental tension. Once a month, on some very bright serene day, they would clear out of town early in the morning, bound for the near-by villages of Gentilly, Boulogne, Montrouge, Pont-de-Charenton, Vanves or St. Cloud. There they spent the whole day enjoying themselves to their heart's content, sporting and merrymaking, drinking toast for proffered toast, playing, singing, dancing, tumbling about or loafing in some fair meadow, turning sparrows out of their nests, bagging quail and fishing for frogs and crayfish.

But though this holiday was free of books and reading, it was not spent unprofitably. Lying in the green meadow, they usually recited certain delightful lines from Virgil's *Georgics*, from Hesiod's *Works and Days* or from Politian's *Husbandry*.[21] Or they broached some savory epigram in Latin, then turned it into a French roundelay or ballade.

In their feasting, they would sometimes separate the twin elements, isolating the wine and the water in their drink by pouring the latter into a cup of ivy-wood, as Cato teaches in his *De re rustica*, and Pliny elsewhere.[22] Then they would wash the wine in a basin full of water and draw it out with a funnel, as pure as ever. And they pumped the water with a syphon from one glass to another, manufacturing several sorts of automatic or self-operating devices.

[The Abbey of Thélème]

CHAPTER 52

How Gargantua had the Abbey of Thélème built for the monk.

There remained only the monk[23] to provide for. Gargantua offered him the Abbey of Seuilly: he refused. What about the Bene-

---

21. a poem, *Rusticus*, in the manner of Virgil's *Georgics*, by the Italian fifteenth-century poet Politian.

22. Both Cato in his book *On Farming* (*De re rustica*), CIX, and Pliny in his *Natural History* (*Historia naturalis*), Book XVI, Chapter 63, suggest an ivy-wood cup as a means to detect water in wine.

23. Friar John of the Funnels, the muscular and highly unconventional monk who has had a major part in helping the party of Gargantua's father win the mock-heroic war against the arrogant Picrochole.

dictine abbeys of Bourgueil or St. Florent, among the richest in France: he might have either or both?[24] Again, the offer met with a flat refusal: Friar John of the Funnels answered peremptorily that he did not seek the charge or government of monks.

"For," he explained, "how shall I govern others when I cannot possibly govern myself?" There was a pause. "But—" he hesitated. "But if you believe I have given and can give you good service, let me found an abbey after my own heart."

The notion delighted Gargantua: he forthwith offered his estate of Thélème, by the Loire, two leagues away from Port Huault. Thélème in Greek means free will, an auspicious name for Friar John's abbey. Here indeed he could institute a religious order contrary to all others.

"First," said Gargantua, "you must not build a wall around it, for all other abbeys are solidly enclosed."

"Quite so," agreed the monk, "for where there are *mures*, walls, before, and *mures*, walls, behind, we have *murmures*, murmurs of envy and plotting."

Now in certain monasteries it is a rule that if any women enter (I mean honest and chaste ones) the ground they tread upon must be swept over. Therefore it was decreed that if a monk or nun should by any chance enter Thélème, every place that religious passed through should be thoroughly disinfected.

Similarly because all monasteries and convents on earth are compassed, limited and regulated by hours, at Thélème no clock or dial of any sort should be tolerated. On the contrary, their time here would be governed by what occasions and opportunities might arise. As Gargantua sagaciously commented:

"I can conceive of no greater waste of time than to count the hours. What good comes of it? To order your life by the toll of a bell instead of by reason or common sense is the veriest piece of asininity imaginable."

By the same token, they established the qualifications for entrance into their order. Was it not true that at present women took the veil only if they were wall-eyed, lame, hunchbacked, ill-favored, misshapen, half-witted, unreasonable or somewhat damaged? That only such men entered monasteries as were cankered, ill-bred idiots or plain nuisances?

("Incidentally," said Friar John, "if the woman is neither fair nor good, of what use is the cloth?"

"Let the clot hump her," Gargantua replied.

"I said 'cloth' not 'clot.' "

"Well, what's the answer?"

"To cover her face or her arse with!")

24. a satiric allusion to the custom of accumulating church livings.

Accordingly, they decided to admit into the new order only such women as were beautiful, shapely, pleasing of form and nature, and such men as were handsome, athletic and personable.

Again, because men entered the convents of this world only by guile and stealth, it was decreed that no women would be in Thélème unless men were there also, and vice-versa.

Moreover, since both men in monasteries and women in convents were forced after their year of noviciate to stay there perpetually, Gargantua and Friar John decided that the Thélèmites, men or women, might come and go whenever they saw fit.

Further, since the religious usually made the triple vow of chastity, poverty and obedience, at Thélème all had full leave to marry honestly, to enjoy wealth and to live in perfect freedom.

As for the age of initiation, they stipulated that women were admissible between the ages of ten and fifteen, men between twelve and eighteen.

CHAPTER 53

How the Abbey of Thélème was built and endowed.

To build and furnish the abbey, Gargantua paid in cash twenty-seven hundred thousand eight hundred and thirty-one crowns in current coin of the realm, fresh from the mint, with a sheep on the obverse and the king's head on the reverse. He undertook to pay yearly, until the project was completed, sixteen hundred and sixty-nine thousand crowns, with the sum on the obverse, and as many again with the seven stars, the whole to be levied upon custom receipts.

For the foundation and maintenance of Thélème, he settled in perpetuity twenty-three hundred and sixty-nine thousand, five hundred and fourteen nobles (a coin stamped by the English kings with the rose of York), free of all tax, burden or fealty, payable yearly at the abbey gate. These privileges were all corroborated by letters patent.

The building was hexagonal; in each corner rose a great, circular tower, each identical, sixty yards in diameter. To the north, the river Loire flowed past the first tower which was named *Arctice* or Northern. East of it rose *Calaer* which means "situated in the balmy air"; then, successively, *Anatole* or Eastern; *Mesembrine* or Southern; *Hesperia* or Occidental; and the last, *Cryere* or Glacial. The distance between each tower was three hundred and twelve yards. The building was throughout six storeys high, counting the underground cellar for one. The ground floor was vaulted like a basket handle; the others, covered with Flanders mistletoe, jutting out like brackets and pendants. The roof, of finest slate, was lined with lead and bore little figures of mannikins and animals well assorted and gilt. The gutters jutted out from the walls between the casement arches; they were painted diagonally gold and blue down to the ground, where they ended in pipes which carried the water into the river below.

This building was a hundred times more magnificent than Bonnivet, Chambord or Chantilly.[25] There were nine thousand three hundred and thirty-two suites, each with a salon, a study, a dressing room, an oratory and an exit into a great hall. In the wing between each tower was a winding stairway. The steps, grouped in units of twelve between each landing, were of porphyry, of Numidian stone, of serpentine marble; they were twenty-two feet long and three fingers thick. At each landing, two splendid round antique archways admitted the light and led to an open loggia of the same dimensions. The stairway, rising to the roof, ended in a pavilion; on either side lay a great hall which in turn led to the apartments.

The wing between the towers called *Arctice* and *Cryere* contained rich libraries of Greek, Latin, Hebrew, French, Italian and Spanish volumes, grouped in their respective sections. In the centre rose a marvellous winding ramp conceived in such ample proportions that six soldiers with their lances at rest could ride up it abreast to the top of the palace. Its entry, outside the house, was an archway six fathoms wide.

Between *Anatole* and *Mesembrine* were spacious galleries with murals representing heroic feats of olden times, scenes from history and pictures of the earth. Here again were a stairway and gate as described upon the river side. On this gate, couched in great antique letters, ran the following legend.

CHAPTER 54

Inscription engraved on the main gate at Thélème.

Here enter not, smug hypocrites or holy loons,
Bigots, sham-Abrahams, impostors of the cloth,
Mealy-mouthed humbugs, holier-than-thou baboons,
Lip-service lubbers, smell-feast picaroons.[26]
Else had we to admit the Goth and Ostrogoth
Precursors of the ape and others of that broth.
Hence, sneaks and mischief-makers, colporteurs of lies,
Be off to other parts to sell your merchandise.

Being foul you would befoul
Man, woman, beast or fowl.

25. châteaux built in the early and middle years of the sixteenth century. By referring to actual buildings, building materials, and architectural elements, Rabelais as usual mixes realism with his fantasy.

26. various ways of saying "hypocritical bigots."

The vileness of your ways
Would sully my sweet lays,
Owls—And your own black cowl,
Being foul, you would befoul.

Here enter not, defenders of dishonest pleas,
Clerks, barristers, attorneys who make freemen slaves,
Canon Law pettifoggers, censors, Pharisees,
Judges, assessors, arbitrators, referees
Who blithely doom good people to untimely graves,
The gibbet is your destination, legal knaves!
Be off: indict the rope if you should find it short,
Here there is no abuse; we do not need your court.

Tangle, wrangle, brangle
We loathe, from any angle.
Our aim is joy and sport,
Time's swift, youth's fleet, life's short.
You, go and disentangle
Tangle, wrangle, brangle!

Here enter not, curmudgeon, loan shark, muckworm, hunks,
Bloodsucking usurer, extortioner, pennystint, . . .
Hence, lawsuit-chasing crimps, greedy as starving punks
Tracking a patron; lickgolds, hiding cash in trunks,
Harpyclaws, crunchfists, jaundiced zealots of the mint,
Your crackling, sallow palms are itching. Skin a flint!
Heap up your hoard, O scrub-faced curs, heap up afresh,
And as you grudge and gripe and screw, God rot your flesh!

Those grim and grisly faces
Bear all the ravaged traces
Of hidebound avarice;
We cannot stomach this.
Banish from all blithe places
Those grim and grisly faces.

Here enter not, you churls, sour boors, invidious fools,
Old, jealous brabblers, scolds, neither by night nor day,
Nor grumblers, soreheads, sulkers, badgers bred in schools
Of hate; nor ghosts of malaperts; nor firebrands' ghouls
From Rhineland, Greece or Rome, fiercer than wolves at bay;
Nor you, riddled with pox, your face a Milky Way
Of scars not stars; nor you, clapstricken to the bone:
Enjoy your shameless crusts and blemishes alone.

Honor, praise and pleasure
Are here in goodly measure:

> Health reigns supreme because
> We follow Nature's laws.
> Ours is a triple treasure:
> Honor, praise and pleasure.

But enter here thrice welcome, men of goodly parts,
Gallants and noble gentlemen, thrice welcome be!
Here you will find an abbey after your own hearts,
Where living is esteemed the highest of the arts.
Come in your tens and hundreds, come in thousands, we
Shall clasp you to our bosoms in fond amity:
Come wise, come proud, come gay, come courteous, come mellow,
Come true sophisticate, come worldling, come, good fellow!

> Comrades, companions, friends,
> Assemble from the ends
> Of earth in this fair place
> Where all is mirth and grace.
> Felicity here blends
> Comrades, companions, friends.

Here enter, all ye loyal scholars who expound
Novel interpretations of the Holy Writ.
Here is a fort and refuge; from this favored ground
You may confound the error that is elsewhere found,
You may found a profound new faith instead of it,
Sweeping away false teachings, bit by fallacious bit.
Come unto us and make your cogent meanings heard:
Destroy the foes of God and of his Holy Word.

> The Holy Word of God
> Shall never be downtrod
> Here in this holy place,
> If all deem reason grace,
> And use for staff and rod
> The Holy Word of God.

Here enter, ladies fair of eminent degree,
Come soon with starry eyes, lips smiling, comely face,
Flowers of loveliness, angels of harmony,
Resplendent, proud yet of the rarest modesty,
Sprightly of flesh, lithe-waisted and compact of grace,
Here is your home. A gallant lord designed this place
For you, that beauty, charm and virtue might find room
Deliciously to breathe, exquisitely to bloom.

> Who makes a priceless gift
> Wins pardon without shrift.

Donor, recipient
Alike find rich content.
To him your voices lift
Who makes a priceless gift.

CHAPTER 55

How the monks and nuns lived at Thélème.

In the middle of the lower court stood a magnificent alabaster fountain, surmounted by the Three Graces holding cornucopias and spouting water through their breasts, mouths, ears, eyes and other orifices. The buildings above this court stood upon great pillars of chalcedony and porphyry, forming classical arches about lengthy wide galleries adorned with paintings and trophies of various animals: the horns of bucks, unicorns and hippopotami, elephants' tusks and sundry other curiosities.

The ladies' quarters ran from *Arctice* all the way to the *Mesembrine* Gate; the rest of the abbey was reserved for men. In front of this part, between the outer two towers, lay the recreational facilities: the tilting yard, the riding school, the theatre and the natatorium which included wonderful swimming pools on three different levels, with every sort of equipment and myrtle water aplenty.

Near the river was the fine pleasure garden, with, in the middle, a maze. Tennis courts and football fields spread out between the next two towers. Close to *Cryere*, an orchard offered a mass of fruit trees laid out in quincunxes, with, at its end, a sizy park abounding in venison.

The space between the third pair of towers was reserved for the shooting ranges: here were targets and butts for harquebuss, long bow and crossbow. The servants' quarters, one storey high, were situated outside *Hesperia*. Beyond was the falconry, managed by expert falconers and hawk trainers and annually supplied by the Cretans, Venetians and Sarmatian Poles with all manner of birds. There were priceless eagles for hunting hares, foxes and cranes. There were gerfalcons, goshawks, sakers for hunting wild geese, herons and bitterns. There were falcons, lanners, sparhawks and merlins for hunting larks and partridges. Other birds there were, too, in great quantities, so well trained that when they flew afield for their own sport they never failed to catch every bird they encountered. . . . The venery with its hounds and beagles stood a little further along towards the park.

All the halls, apartments and chambers were richly hung with tapestries varying with the season; the floors were covered with green cloth, the beds all embroidered. Each rear chamber boasted a pierglass set in a heavy gold frame adorned with pearls. Near the exits of the ladies' halls were the perfumers and hairdressers who ministered to the gentlemen before the latter visited the ladies. These attendants furnished the ladies' rooms with rose water, orange-flower water and angelica, supplying a precious small atomizer to give forth the most exquisite aromatic perfumes.

CHAPTER 56

How the monks and nuns of Thélème were apparelled.

When first the abbey was founded, the ladies dressed according to their taste and pleasure. Subsequently of their own free will they modified their costume as follows.

They wore hose, of scarlet or kermes-red, reaching some three inches above the knee, the edge being exquisitely embroidered or slashed. Their garters, which matched their bracelets, came both a whit over and under the knee. Their shoes, pumps and slippers were of red, violet or crimson velvet and jagged as a lobster's claws.

Over their slips, they put on a tight tunic of pure silk camlet, and over that a taffeta farthingale or petticoat, red, white, beige, gray or of any other color. Above this farthingale went a skirt of silver taffeta, with fine gold embroidery and delicate cross-stitch work. According to the temperature, the season or the ladies' whim, these skirts might be satin, damask or velvet and, in color, orange, green, cendré, blue, canary yellow, scarlet, crimson or white, or of cloth-of-gold, cloth-of-silver, or any other choice material variously embroidered, stitched, brocaded or spangled according to the occasion for which they were worn.

Their gowns, or over-garments, were also governed by timely considerations. They might be cloth-of-gold with silver embossing or red satin with gold brocade or taffeta, white, blue, black or tawny. Or they might be silk rep, silk camlet, velvet, cloth-of-silver, cloth-of-gold or satin variously figured with gold and silver thread.

In summer, instead of these gowns, they wore lovely light smocks made of the same material, or capes, Moorish-fashion, with hoods to protect and shade their faces from the sun. These Moresco capes were of violet velvet, having raised gold stitching over silver purl or gold piping and cording, with small Indian pearls at their ends. And ever a gay colored plume, the color of their sleeves, bravely garnished with gold! In winter, their gowns were of taffeta in all the colors mentioned above, but lined with lynx, weasel, Calabrian marten, sable and other rare fur. Their beads, rings, chains and necklaces were of precious stones: carbuncles, rubies, balas rubies, diamonds, sapphires, emeralds, turquoises, garnets, agates, beryls and priceless pearls.

Their headgear also varied with the season. In winter, it was in

the French fashion with a cap over the temples covered by a velvet
hood with hanging veil. In spring it was in the Spanish, with laces
and veils. In summer it was in the Tuscan, the hair elaborately entwined with gold chains and jewels. On Sundays and holidays, however, they followed the French mode which is more seemly and
modest.

The men, too, dressed according to their personal taste. Their
hose were of light wool or serge cloth, white, black, scarlet or
kermes-red. Their velvet breeches were of the same hue or almost;
they were embroidered or slashed to their taste. The doublet was
of cloth-of-gold, cloth-of-silver, velvet, satin or damask, embroidered,
panelled or slashed on one model, the points silk to match and
the ornaments of fine enamelled gold.

Their cloaks and jerkins were of cloth-of-gold, cloth-of-silver,
gold tissue or velvet, purfled or brocaded at pleasure; their over-
garments were every whit as costly as the ladies'. Their girdles were
silk, matching their doublets. Each wore on his side a handsome
sword with gilt hilt and pommel; the scabbard velvet, matching his
breeches, and the ferrule a wondrous example of the goldsmith's
art. So too the dagger. Their caps were of black velvet, trimmed
with jewels and rings and buttons of gold, with a white plume set
in jauntily and parted by many rows of spangles from which hung
splendid emeralds and various other stones.

Such was the sympathy between the gallants and their ladies that
they matched one another's costumes every day. And in order to be
sure of it, certain gentlemen were appointed to report every morning to the youths what garments their ladies planned to wear on
that occasion. All here was done for the pleasure of the fair.

Handsome though the clothes were and rich the accoutrements,
lads or girls wasted no time in dressing. The wardrobe masters had
everything ready before their gentlemen arose and the maids were
so nimble that in a trice their mistresses were apparelled from head
to toe.

To facilitate matters, over a distance of half-a-league, a row of
light, well-appointed cottages housed the goldsmiths, lapidaries,
embroiderers, tailors, gold drawers, velvet weavers, tapestry makers
and upholsterers. Here each worked at his trade, and all for the
jolly friars and comely nuns of the new abbey. They received
materials and stuffs from My Lord Nausiclete, famous for his ships,
as the name indicates. Each year brought them seven vessels from
the Pearl and Cannibal Islands or Antilles, laden with ingots of
gold, raw silk, pearls and precious stones.

If pearls through age tended to lose their lustre, the jewellers,
following the method of Avicenna,[27] fed them to the roosters, and
they regained their native sparkle.

27. See footnote 16.

CHAPTER 57

How those of Thélème were governed in their manner of living.

Their whole life was ordered not by law, statute or rule, but according to their free will and pleasure. They arose when they pleased. They ate, drank, worked and slept when the spirit moved them. No one awoke them, forced food or drink upon them or *made* them do anything else. Gargantua's plan called for perfect liberty. The only rule of the house was:

DO AS THOU WILT

because men that are free, of gentle birth, well-bred and at home in civilized company possess a natural instinct that inclines them to virtue and saves them from vice. This instinct they name their honor. Sometimes they may be depressed or enslaved by subjection or constraint; for we all long for forbidden fruit and covet what is denied us. But they usually apply the fine forces that tend to virtue in such a way as to shake off the yoke of servitude.

The Thélèmites, thanks to their liberty, knew the virtues of emulation. All wished to do what they saw pleased one of their number. Let some lad or maid say "Let us drink" and all of them drank, "Let us play" and all of them played, "Let us frolic in the fields" and all of them frolicked. When falconry or hawking were in order, the ladies sat high upon their saddles on fine nags, a sparhawk, lanner or merlin on one daintily gloved wrist, while the men bore other kinds of hawks.

They were so well-bred that none, man or woman, but could read, write, sing, play several instruments, speak five or six languages and readily compose verse and prose in any of them. Never had earth known knights so proud, so gallant, so adroit on horseback and on foot, so athletic, so lively, so well-trained in arms as these. Never were ladies seen so dainty, so comely, so winsome, so deft at handwork and needlework, so skilful in feminine arts, so frank and so free as these.

Thus when the time came for a man to leave the abbey (either at his parents' request or for some other reason) he took with him one of the ladies—the particular one who had chosen him for her knight—and they were married. And though they had lived in devotion and friendship at Thélème, their marriage relations proved even more tender and agreeable. Indeed to the end of their lives they loved one another as they had on the day of their wedding. . . .

Gargantua and Pantagruel, Book II

[*Pantagruel: Birth and Education*]

CHAPTER 2

Of the nativity of the most redoubtable Pantagruel.

At the age of four hundred fourscore and forty-four years, Gargantua begat his son Pantagruel upon his wife named Badebec, daughter to the king of the dimly-seen Amaurotes in Utopia.[28] She died in the throes of childbirth. Alas! Pantagruel was so extraordinarily large and heavy that he could not possibly come to light without suffocating his mother.

If you would fully understand how he came to be christened Pantagruel, you must remember that a terrible drought raged that year throughout the land of Africa. For thirty-six months, three weeks, four days, thirteen hours and even longer, there was no drop of rain. And the sun blazed so fiercely that the whole earth was parched.

Even in the days of Elijah, the soil was no drier, for now no tree on earth bore leaf or flower. The grass had no verdure; rivers and springs ran dry; the luckless fishes, abandoned by their element, crawled on solid earth, crying and screaming most horribly. Birds fell from the air for want of moisture; wolves, foxes, harts, wild boars, fallow deer, hares, rabbits, weasels, martens, badgers and other beasts were found dead in the fields, their mouths agape.

As for the men, their state was very piteous. You should have seen them with their tongues dangling like a hound's after a run of six hours. Not a few threw themselves into the wells. Others lay under a cow's belly to enjoy the shade—these it is whom Homer calls *Alibantes,* the desiccated.[29] The whole country was at a standstill. The strenuous efforts of mortals against the vehemence of this drought was a horrible spectacle. It was hard enough, God knows, to save the holy water in the churches from being wasted; but My Lords the Cardinals and our Holy Father laid down such strict rules that no man dared take more than a lick of it. In the churches, scores of parched, unhappy wretches followed the priest who distributed it, their jaws yawning for one tiny driblet. Like the rich man in *Luke,* who cried for Lazarus to dip his fingers in water, they were tormented by a flame,[30] and would not suffer the slightest

28. names taken from Sir Thomas More's *Utopia.* Literally, "no place," the word *Utopia* has become synonymous with "ideal country."

29. The allusion to Homer is apparently mistaken, but "Alibantes"—possibly derived from the name of Alibas, a dry river in hell—is used by other ancient writers with reference to the dead or the very old.

30. "And he cried and said, Father Abraham, have mercy on me, and send Lazarus, that he may dip the tip of his finger in water, and cool my tongue; for I am tormented in this flame." (Luke 16:24.)

drop to be wasted. Ah! thrice happy that year the man who had a cool, well-plenished wine cellar underground!

In discussing the question: "Why is sea water salty?" the philosopher Aristotle, after Empedocles, supplies the following reason. When Phœbus gave the reins of his luminous chariot[31] to Phaëton, his son, the latter, unskilled in the art of driving, was incapable of following the ecliptic lines between the two tropics of the sun's sphere. Accordingly, he strayed from the appointed path and came so close to earth that he dried up all the countries under his course. He also burnished that great portion of heaven which philosophers call *Via Lactea* or the Milky Way, and good drinkers St. James' Way, since it is the starry line that guides pilgrims to Santiago de Compostella. (On the other hand, poets declare that it is here Juno's milk dropped while she was suckling Hercules.)

Earth at that time was so excessively heated that it broke into an enormous sweat which ran over the sea, making the latter salty, since all sweat is salt. If you do not admit this last statement, then taste of your own sweat. Or savor the perspiration of your pox-stricken friends when they are put in sweatboxes for treatment. It is all one to me.

Practically the same thing happened the year I am speaking of. On a certain Friday, all the people were intent upon their devotions. A noble procession was in progress with plenty of litanies and fine preachings. Supplications arose toward Almighty God beseeching Him to cast His eye of mercy upon them in their affliction. Suddenly they clearly saw some great drops of water stand out upon the ground, exactly as from a person sweating copiously.

The wretched populace began to rejoice as though here were a great blessing. Some declared that, since the air lacked all moisture, earth was supplying the deficiency. Other scientists asseverated that it was a shower of the Antipodes, as described by Seneca in *Quaestiones Naturales*, Book IV, where he treats of the Nile's source, attributing its floods to distant rains washed underground into the river. But they were thoroughly deceived. For, the procession done, when each sought to gather up this dew and drink it up by the bowlful, they found it was only pickle, far saltier than the saltiest water of the sea.

Another great mishap befell Gargantua that week. A dungchafing lout, bearing two great bags of salt and a hambone in his game-pouch, walked into poor Gargantua's mouth as the giant lay snoring. The clod spilled a quantity of salt in Gargantua's throat. Gargantua, crazy with a thirst he could not slake, angrily snapped his mouth shut. He gnashed his teeth fiercely; they ground like mill-stones. Later the rascal told me he was so terrified you could have

31. the chariot of the sun.

stopped up his nose with a bale of hay. He fell flat on his face like a dead man, dropping the two saltbags that had tormented Gargantua. They were at once swallowed up and entombed.

My rogue vowed vengeance. Thrusting his hand in his game-pouch, he drew out a great hambone, highly salted, still covered with hair, and twenty-eight inches long. Ragefully he rammed it down Gargantua's throat. The giant, drier than ever, felt the pig's hair tickling his belly and, willy-nilly, spewed up all he had. Eighteen tumbrils could not have drawn away the rich nauseous yield. My dungchafer, hidden in the cavity of one of his teeth, was forced to take French leave in such pitiful condition that all who saw him were horrified. Gargantua, looking down, noticed this jackpudding whirling about in a great puddle.

"Here is some worm that sought to sting me in the belly," he mused, happy to have expelled him from his body.

Because he was born that very day, his father called him Pantagruel or All-Athirst, a name derived from the Greek *panta* meaning all, and the Hagarene or Saracen *gruel* meaning athirst. Gargantua inferred thereby that at his son's birth the entire universe was wholly parched. Prophetically, too, he realized that some day Pantagruel would become Supreme Lord of the Thirsty, a fact indicated even more surely by a further portent.

For while his mother Badebec was bringing him forth and the midwives stood by ready to receive him, there first issued from her belly seventy-eight salt-vendors, each leading a salt-laden mule by the halter. They were followed by nine dromedaries, bearing hams and smoked oxtongues; seven camels bearing chitterlings; twenty-five cartloads of leeks, garlic, onions and chives. This terrified some midwives, but others said:

"Here is good provision! As it is, we drink but lazily, instead of vigorously. This must be a good omen, since these victuals are spurs to bibbing wine!"

As they were tattling away, out pops Pantagruel, hairy as a bear! At which, prophetically, one of them exclaimed:

"God help us, he is born hair and all, straight from the arse of Satan in flight. He will do terrible wonders. If he lives, he will grow to a lusty age!"

Of Pantagruel's race are those who drink so heavily in the evening that they must rise at night to drink again, quenching the coals of fire and blistering thirst in their throats. This form of thirst is called Pantagruel, in memory of the giant.

[*Father's Letter from Home*]

CHAPTER 8

How Pantagruel in Paris received a letter from his father Gargantua.

As you may suppose, Pantagruel studied very hard and profited much by his study, for his intelligence was naturally active and his memory as full as twelve casks of olives. While in Paris,[32] he received the following letter from his father:

MY BELOVED SON,

Among the gifts, graces and prerogatives with which our sovereign Creator, God Almighty, blessed and enriched humanity from the beginning, there is one that I deem supreme. By its means, though we be mortal, we can yet achieve a sort of immortality; through it, we may, in the course of our transitory lives, yet perpetuate our name and race.

To be sure, what we gain by a progeny born of lawful wedlock cannot make up for what we lost through the sin of our first parents. Adam and Eve disobeyed the commandments of the Lord their God: mortality was their punishment. By death the magnificent mould in which Man was fashioned vanished into the dust of oblivion.

However, thanks to seminal propagation, what a man loses his children revive and, where they fail, their children prevail. So it has gone, and so it shall be, from generation to generation, until the Day of Judgment, when Christ shall restore to God the Father His kingdom pacified, secured and cleansed of all sin. Then all generations and corruption shall cease, for the elements will have completed their continuous transmutations. The peace humanity has craved so anxiously will have been attained; all things will have been reduced to their appointed end and period.

I therefore have reason to give thanks to God, my Saviour, for having granted me the joy of beholding my old age blossom anew in your youth. When, by His pleasure, which rules and orders everything, my soul must abandon this human habitation, I shall not believe I am dying utterly, but rather passing from one place to another. For in you my visible image will continue to live on earth; by you, I shall go on frequenting honorable men and true friends, as I was wont to do.

My associations have not been without sin, I confess. We all transgress and must continually beseech God to forgive us our

---

32. Like his father before him, Pantagruel has been sent to Paris to study. The following letter, patterned after Ciceronian models of eloquence, summarizes Rabelais' view of an ideal education, and generally illustrates the attitude of the Renaissance intellectual elite toward culture.

trespasses. But they have been without reproach in the eyes of men.

That is why if, beside my bodily image, my soul did not likewise shine in you, you would not be accounted worthy of guarding the precious immortality of my name. In that case, the least part of me (my body) would endure. Scant satisfaction, that, when the best part (my soul, which should keep my name blessed among men) had degenerated and been bastardized. I say this not through any doubt as to your virtue, which I have already often tested, but to encourage you to go on doing ever better and profiting by your constant improvement.

My purpose is not so much to keep you absolutely on your present virtuous course as to make you rejoice that you have kept and are keeping on it. I seek to quicken your heart with resolutions for the future. To help you make and carry these out, remember that I have spared nothing. I have helped you as though my sole treasure on earth were once in my lifetime to see you well-bred and accomplished in honesty and valor as well as in knowledge and civility. Ay, I have longed to leave you after my death as a mirror of your father's personality. The reflection may not prove perfect in practice, but certainly I could not more studiously wish for its perfection.

My late father Grangousier, of blessed memory, made every effort that I might achieve mental, moral and technical excellence. The fruit of my studies and labors matched, indeed surpassed, his dearest wish. But you can realize that conditions were not as favorable to learning as they are to-day. Nor had I such gifted teachers as you. We were still in the dark ages; we still walked in the shadow of the dark clouds of ignorance; we suffered the calamitous consequences of the destruction of good literature by the Goths. Now, by God's grace, light and dignity have been restored to letters, and I have lived to see it. Indeed, I have watched such a revolution in learning that I, not erroneously reputed in my manhood the leading scholar of the century, would find it difficult to enter the bottom class in a grammar school.

I tell you all this not through boastfulness, though in writing to you I might be proud with impunity. Does not Marcus Tullius[33] authorize it in his book *Of Old Age,* and Plutarch in *How a Man May Praise Himself without Envy?* Both authors recognize that such pride is useful in fostering the spirit of emulation. No—I do it simply to give you a proof of my love and affection.

To-day, the old sciences are revived, knowledge is systematized, discipline reëstablished. The learned languages are restored: Greek, without which a man would be ashamed to consider himself educated; Hebrew, Chaldean and Latin.[34] Printing is now in use, an

33. Cicero.   34. The languages which are the in-

art so accurate and elegant that it betrays the divine inspiration of its discovery,[35] which I have lived to witness. Alas! Conversely, I was not spared the horror of such diabolic works as gunpowder[36] and artillery.

To-day, the world is full of learned men, brilliant teachers and vast libraries: I do not believe that the ages of Plato, Cicero or Papinian[37] afforded such facilities for culture. From now on, it is unthinkable to come before the public or move in polite circles without having worshipped at Minerva's shrine. Why, the robbers, hangmen, adventurers and jockeys of to-day are infinitely better educated than the doctors and preachers of my time. More, even women and girls aspire to the glory, the heavenly manna of learning. Thus, at my advanced age, I have been forced to take up Greek. Not that I had despised it, like Cato;[38] I never had the opportunity to learn it. Now I delight in reading Plutarch's *Morals*, Plato's noble *Dialogues*, the *Monuments* of Pausanias and the *Antiquities* of Athenæus,[39] as I await the hour when it shall please God, my Creator, to call me back to His bosom.

That is why, my dear son, I urge you to spend your youth making the most of your studies and developing your moral sense. You are in Paris, which abounds in noble men upon whom to pattern yourself; you have Epistemon, an admirable tutor, who can inspire you by direct oral teaching. But I demand more of you. I insist you learn languages perfectly! Greek first, as old Quintilian[40] prescribes; then Latin; then Hebrew for the sake of the Holy Scripture; then Chaldee and Arabic, too. Model your Greek style on Plato, your Latin on Cicero. Let no history slip your memory; cultivate cosmography, for you will find its texts helpful.

As for the liberal arts of geometry, arithmetic and music, I gave you a taste of them when you were a little lad of five or six. Proceed further in them yourself, learning as much as you can. Be sure to master all the rules of astronomy; but dismiss astrology and the divinatory art of Lullius[41] as but vanity and imposture. Of civil law, I would have you know the texts of the Code by heart, then compare them with philosophy.

A knowledge of nature is indispensable; devote yourself to this

struments of classical learning are listed along with those useful for the study of the Old Testament.

35. Printing from movable type was independently invented in Europe about the middle of the fifteenth century; the idea of its divine origin was commonplace during the Renaissance.

36. probably introduced into Europe through the Arabs, rather than invented, in the fourteenth century.

37. jurisconsult of the time of Emperor Septimius Severus (reigned A.D. 193–211).

38. Plutarch's life of Cato is the source of the notion that he despised Greek.

39. The works of Pausanias and Athenaeus were standard sources of information on ancient geography, art, and everyday life.

40. In his *Institutio oratoria*, Book I, Chapter 1, paragraph 12, he recommends studying Greek before Latin.

41. Raymond Lully, Spanish philosopher of the thirteenth century, who dabbled in magic.

study with unflagging curiosity. Let there be no sea, river or fountain but you know the fish that dwell in it. Be familiar with all the
shrubs, bushes and trees in forest or orchard, all the plants, herbs
and flowers that grow on the ground, all the birds of the air, all the
metals in the bowels of earth, all the precious stones in the orient
and the south. In a word, be well informed in everything that concerns the physical world we live in.

Then carefully consult the works of Greek, Arabian and Latin
physicians, without slighting the Jewish doctors, Talmudists and
Cabbalists. By frequent exercises in dissection, acquire a perfect
knowledge of that other world, which is man.

Devote a few hours a day to the study of Holy Writ. Take up
the New Testament and the Epistles in Greek; then, the Old
Testament in Hebrew. Strive to make your mind an inexhaustible
storehouse of knowledge. For you are growing to manhood now:
soon you will have to give up your studious repose to lead a life of
action. You will have to learn to bear arms, to achieve knighthood,
so as to defend my house and help our allies frustrate the attacks
of evildoers.

Further, I wish you soon to test what profit you have gained
from your education. This you can best do by public discussion and
debate on all subjects against all comers, and by frequenting learned
men both in Paris and elsewhere.

But remember this. As Solomon says, wisdom entereth not into
a malicious soul, and science without conscience spells but destruction of the spirit. Therefore serve, love and fear God, on Him pin
all your thoughts and hopes; by faith built of charity, cling to Him
so closely that never a sin come between you. Hold the abuses of
the world in just suspicion. Set not your heart upon vanity, for this
life is a transitory thing, but the Word of God endureth forever.
Be serviceable to your neighbor, love him as you do yourself. Honor
your teachers. Shun the company of all men you would not wish to
resemble; receive not in vain the favors God has bestowed upon you.

When you realize that you have acquired all the knowledge Paris
has to offer, come back so I may see you and give you my blessing
before I die.

My son, the peace and grace of Our Lord be with you. Amen.

Your father,
GARGANTUA

From Utopia, the seventeenth day of September.

Having read this letter, Pantagruel, greatly encouraged, strove
more ardently than ever to profit in his work. Had you seen him
studying vigorously, practically and tirelessly, you would have com-

pared his spirit moving among his books to flames blazing through a bonfire of dry branches.

CHAPTER 16

Of the character and condition of Panurge.[42]

Panurge was then about thirty-five years old and as fine to gild as a dagger of lead. Of medium height, neither too tall nor too short, he had an aquiline nose, shaped like the handle of a razor. He cut a very gallant figure though he was a trifle lewd by nature, and subject to a disease at that time called impecunitis, an incomparable malady.

Yet when he needed money, he knew thirty-three methods of acquiring it, the most ordinary and honorable of which was filching. He was a quarrelsome fellow, a sharper, a toper, a roisterer and a profligate, if ever there was one in the city of Paris. In every other respect, he was the best fellow in the world.

He was constantly plotting against the sergeants and the watch. Sometimes he assembled three or four sportsmen, plied them with drink until they were boozy as Knights Templars,[43] then took them up the hill to Ste. Geneviève or near the Collège de Navarre. Placing his sword on the pavement and his ear to his sword, he waited till he heard the blade shake—an infallible sign that the watch was not far off. Then he and his companions took a dung cart and rolled it down hill. Ere it was halfway down, they had fled in the opposite direction, for in less than two days Panurge knew every street and alley in Paris as well as his postprandial grace: *Deus det nobis pacem suam,* God grant us His peace.

Another time he laid down a train of gunpowder where the watch was due to pass. Just as the troop debouched, he set fire to it, vastly delighted in observing how gracefully they took to their heels, in mortal terror that St. Anthony's fire had caught them by the legs.

The luckless Masters of Arts and theologians he persecuted more than any other class of men. When he met one, he never failed to do him some harm, either slipping a turd into his hood or pinning little foxtails or hares' ears to his back.

One day when all the theologians had been summoned to the

<hr>

42. Panurge (*Pan-ourgos* in Greek, the "all-doer") is the major character in *Gargantua and Pantagruel* except for the heroes themselves: a magnification of the perennial-student type. Panurge is an imaginative and scandalous pauper, erudite and bawdy, a lover of outrageous pranks. On first meeting Pantagruel he addressed him in thirteen different languages, a couple of them invented, before discovering that they both spoke French. He has since become a permanent fixture of the young lord's retinue.

43. a medieval religious and medical order, suppressed in 1312. The original *templiers,* not capitalized, suggests a current proverbial expression.

Sorbonne to examine the articles of the faith, he made a tart of garlic, asafoetida, galbanum, castoreum[44] and steaming excrement, which he steeped and tempered in the corrupt manner of chancres and pockbiles. Very early in the morning he so theologically greased and anointed the lattices and grates of the trellised gallery of the Hall of Records that not even the devil himself had dared stay there. The worthy pedagogues pewked in public as abundantly as though they had flayed the fox. Ten or twelve died of the plague, fourteen contracted leprosy, eight came down with pestiferous ulcers, and more than twenty-eight caught the pox. But Panurge was jubilant.

Usually he carried a whip under his gown with which he mercilessly belabored such pages as he met bearing wine for their masters, in order to speed them on their way.

In his coat he had more than twenty-six little pockets and pouches which were always full. One held a pair of loaded dice and a small knife like a glover's awl to cut purses with. Another, verjuice to throw in the eyes of those who annoyed him. A third, burrs, penned with gosling or capon feathers, to stick on to the robes and bonnets of honest people. He often gave married men a fine pair of horns which they bore through the city sometimes all their lives long. To the back of the women's hoods, he liked to affix various knickknacks shaped like the sexual organ of man.

Another pocket held a lot of little packages filled with fleas and lice which he recruited from the tramps at St. Innocent's graveyard and cast with small sticks or quills down the backs of the smartest gentlewomen he could find. He did this even in church, for he never sat up in the choir, preferring to stand in the nave among the women during mass, vespers or sermon. Another pocket held a large supply of bent nails with which he would couple men and women together where they sat. This was particularly amusing when the victims wore gowns of costly sarsenet taffeta, because they ripped them to shreds as they sought to separate. Still another pocket held a squib with tinder, flints, matches, vesuvians, sulphur and other combustibles. Another, two or three burning-glasses with which he tortured and disconcerted men and women at church. For he said there was only an antistrophe between *femme folle à la messe* and *molle à la fesse* or working a cunning stunt and a stunning cunt. Another pouch held needles, threads and pins for all manner of minor deviltries.

Once at the door of the Great Hall in the Palais de Justice, Panurge saw a Cordelier father getting ready to say mass before the proceedings of the day. Immediately he ran up to help the holy man

44. Asafoetida and galbanum are resins extracted from Persian plants; castoreum is a substance obtained from the inguinal region of the beaver; all three produce nauseous smells.

don his vestments and, in the process, managed to sew his alb to his robe and shirt. Then, as the magistrates arrived for mass, Panurge withdrew. Mass done, as he reached the formula *Ite, missa est,* the wretched friar tried to take off his alb. But, at the same time, off came the robe and shirt solidly sewn to it. Our Cordelier, thus stripped to the shoulders, revealed his dangledingus to all the world —and it was no small crosier, as you may imagine. The harder he tugged, the more he exposed himself. So much so, indeed, that one of the counsellors cried:

"What is the matter? Is this good friar making an offering of his tail for us to kiss? No, by heaven, let St. Anthony's fire kiss it for us!"

From then on, an ordinance forbade the poor good fathers to disrobe before the world, the vestry-room being indicated as the only fit place for this. They were especially warned against doing so in the presence of women, lest it tempt the latter to sin through longing. When people wondered why the fathers were genitally so well-equipped, Panurge solved the problem.

"What makes the ears of asses so long?" he asked, and answering his own question: "Their dams put no caps on their ears. Alliacus,[45] Chancellor of the University and Chaplain to Charles VI, proves this in his *Suppositiones.* Similarly, what makes the whangle-tools of our holy fathers hang so low? Well, they never wear dark breeches, so their lusty organs, dangling down at liberty like a horse given head, knock against their knees like women's beads. Why are they correspondingly large? Because, with all this waggling to and fro, the humors of the body sink down into these parts. Do not the legists point out that continual agitation and continual motion are the cause of attraction?"

Another of Panurge's pouches held stone-alum, an itching-powder which he poured down the backs of those he considered the proudest and most stately ladies. Some would at once strip off their clothes then and there before the public . . . others danced like cats on hot coals or a drumstick on a tabor . . . others again rushed madly into the street and he at their heels. . . . Those inclined to disrobe, he assisted by sheltering them under his cape, as any courteous and gallant gentleman would have done.,

In another pocket he had a small leather bottle full of old oil. If he saw a man or woman in a handsome costume, he would grease and stain it in the most conspicuous places. His technique here was an art. Pretending to admire the material, he would finger it.

"Rare cloth, this, sir," or "Fine satin, upon my word!" or "Oh, what lovely taffeta, Madame!" he would exclaim. "God give you all your noble heart desires. You have a new suit, My Lord! And you a

45. Latinized name of Pierre d'Ailly (1350–1425).

new dress, My Lady. Well, you know the saying: New clothes, new friends. God give you joy in them!"

As he spoke, his hands passed lightly over the shoulders and a long ugly smear remained

> So indelible a spot
> Stamped on body, soul and fame
> That the devil could not blot
> Out its testament of shame.

As he took his leave of the ladies, he would say:

"Madame, take care not to fall. You've a huge filthy hole out of sight in front of you, there!"

In another pocket he kept euphorbium, very finely pulverized and spread over a dainty handkerchief he had stolen from a pretty sales-girl in the Galleries of the Sainte-Chapelle,[46] hard by the law courts and frequented by the gallants of the day. (He filched it while removing from between her breasts a louse he had dropped there.)

When he happened to be in gentle company, he would steer the conversation on to the subject of lace and lingerie. Then, thrusting his hands into some lady's bosom:

"Glorious work, this. Is it Flanders or Hainault?"

Then, drawing his handkerchief:

"Just look at this kerchief, Madame. Would you say it was Frontignan or Fontarabia?"

Shaking it hard under her nose, he would make her sneeze for hours at a time. Then he would fart like a dray horse.

"Tut, tut," the lady would say. "Are you whiffling, Panurge?"

"No, Madame," he would reply gallantly, "I am merely tuning my tail to the plain song you make with your nose."

Panurge was never without pincers, a picklock, a pelican, a jimmy, a crook or other tools against which no chest or door could avail. Finally, in another pocket he kept a whole battery of small goblets which he worked with amazing skill, for his fingers were nimble and adroit as those of Minerva or Arachne.[47] He had indeed once been an itinerant quack, barking antidotes for poison. When he presented a sum of money and asked for change, the changer had to be spry as Argus[48] to catch Panurge spiriting away five, six or seven coins at a time, visibly, openly, manifestly, without lesion or hurt, whilst all the changer noticed was a slight draught.

---

46. a shopping center in old Paris.

47. In Greek mythology the goddess Athena, being enraged at the Lydian maid Arachne's irreverence and weaving skill, transformed her into a spider.

48. the Greek mythological figure with a hundred eyes.

CHAPTER 21

How Panurge fell in love with a Parisienne of high degree.

As a result of his debate with the English scholar,[49] Panurge had acquired quite a reputation in Paris. The activity of his codpiece was proportionally greater, and, to that effect, he had it pinked and slashed with ornate embroidery, after the Roman fashion. His praises became a topic of general conversation. There was even a song written to celebrate his exploits; the little children sang it as they went to fetch mustard. Best of all, he was made welcome in the most elegant circles. But it went to his head; he actually had the presumption to beleaguer one of the great ladies of the city.

Scorning the rigmarole of prefaces and preliminaries dear to such languishing, dreamy lovers as never touch meat in Lent, Panurge popped the question outright.

"Madame," he told this lofty lady, "it would prove beneficent to the commonwealth, pleasurable to your person, honorable to your progeny and necessary to me that I cover you for the propagation of my race. You may take my word for this, Madame; experience will prove it to you conclusively."

The lady, indignant, thrust him a thousand leagues away.

"You crazy knave, how dare you talk like that? Who do you think I am? Get out of here at once and never let me lay eyes upon you again. For two pins, I'd have your arms and legs sawed off!"

"Madame," he protested, "I would not care two pins if my arms and legs were sawed off, providing you and I had first fought a merry bout of spermary-snuggery. For," he showed her his long codpiece, "here is Master Johnny Inigo, a master instrumentalist who begs to fiddle and thrum, sweep the *viola d'amore,* play the mani-chord, tweedle the gittern, strike the lyre, beat the drum, wind the horn and grind the organ until you feel his music throbbing in the marrow of your bones. A wily gallant, Master Johnny: he will not fail to find all the cranks, winches, wedges, pullies, nippers, clutches, teeth, springs and rigging stored in your delicate cockpit. You'll be needing no scouring or brushing up after *him.*"

"Go to, scoundrel, and away! One more word out of you and I'll shout for help; I'll have my servants beat you to death."

"No, Madame," Panurge protested. "You are not as cruel as you pretend. You cannot be or else your face is a living lie. Let earth soar upward into the firmament, let high heaven sink into the bot-

49. Thaumastes, who in the previous chapters has long argued with Panurge, using both words and signs, and has been "nonplussed" by the latter's knowledge a hundred eyes.

tomless pit, let the whole concert of nature be annihilated ere your beauty and grace secrete one drop of gall or malice. They say that it is virtually impossible for man:

> To find in women beauty unallied
> With arrogance or cruelty or pride

but that holds only for vulgar beauties. Your own is so priceless, so unique, so heavenly that I vow Nature has bestowed it on you as a paragon to prove what she can do when she cares to muster all her power and science. Everything in you is honey, sugar, celestial manna. To you Paris should have awarded the golden apple, not to Venus or Juno or Minerva. For Juno possessed no such nobility, Minerva no such wisdom, Venus no such comeliness.

"O ye heavenly gods and goddesses! how happy the man whom you allow to kiss and fondle you, to cosset, nuzzle and cockle you, to thrust his prolific engine of pleasure into the pod of your quivering quim. By God, I am that man, I plainly feel it. Already she loves me her bellyful I swear; ay, Panurge is predestined to it by the nixies and fairies. Let us lose no time: come, slap-dash, helter-skelter, holus-bolus, to horse and fair riding, tantivy, hoicks!"

Whereupon he sought to embrace her; but she moved towards the window as if to call for help, so Panurge made off hastily. Yet ere retreating:

"Madame," he said, "wait for me here; I'll call your friends, don't bother!"

And he withdrew, unfeased and no less cheerful despite the rebuff.

Next day, as she arrived at church, Panurge stood waiting at the door, offered her holy water, bowed deep as she passed, then kneeled familiarly beside her:

"Madame," he declared, "you must know how madly in love with you I am. Why, I can neither piddle nor cack for love of you! I don't know how *you* feel, but, Madame, suppose I took ill from it, wouldn't you be responsible?"

"Go away, I don't care anything about it. Leave me alone to my prayers."

"One moment!" Panurge begged. "Please equivocate on '*à Beaumont le Viconte?*' or on 'Runt and Codger are fellow-muckers!' "

"I don't know what you mean!"

"Quite easy! '*A beau con le vit monte*,' 'Cunt and Rodger are mellow fuckers!' Now, pray to God that He grant whatever your noble heart desires. And oh, Madame, I beg you: give me those beads a moment."

"Here you are, stop bothering me."

She was about to take off her rosary—it was of cestrin wood with gold ornamentation—when Panurge promptly drew one of his knives and neatly cut it. Before carrying it off to pawn:

"Would you like my knife?" he asked.

"No, certainly not!"

"It's yours to grind or sheathe, Madame, body and soul, bag and baggage, tripe and guts."

But the lady was worried over the loss of her beads, so many implements to help her keep her countenance in church:

"This chattering scoundrel must be some eccentric foreigner," she mused. "He will never return my rosary. What will my dear husband say? He'll be furious! But I'll tell him a sneak thief cut it off me at church. He must believe me: I've still the end fastened on my girdle."

After dinner, Panurge went to call on her with, in his sleeve, a purse full of tokens specially struck for use in the law courts.

"Which of us is the better lover, Madame, you or I?"

"For my part I cannot hate you," she said magnanimously. "God commands us to love our neighbors."

"Aren't you in love with me?"

"I've told you repeatedly not to talk to me like that!" she insisted. "If you mention it again, I'll show you I'm not to be trifled with. Go away, I tell you. But give me back my rosary; my husband might ask me for it."

"Give you back your rosary? No, by heaven, I shall do nothing of the sort. But I'll tell you what I *will* do: I'll gladly give you another. Would you like one in beautifully enamelled gold with beads shaped like great pendulous knockers? Or like loveknots or ingots, heavy in the hand? Or ebony or broad zircons or square-cut garnets with mountings of rare turquoises, or costly topazes or priceless sapphires or precious rubies set with glittering diamonds of twenty-eight facets? No, no, that is a trumpery gift. I know of a marvellous rosary: it's made of exquisite emeralds with a mounting of speckled gray amber; at the buckle there's a Persian pearl fat as an orange . . . and the bauble costs but a paltry five-and-twenty thousand ducats. I will make you a present of it; I've heaps of cash!"

He made his tokens ring as though they were genuine, authentic golden crowns with the shining sun of France stamped upon them.

"Do you fancy a piece of violet or crimson velure, dyed in grain, or a piece of scarlet or brocaded satin? Is it your pleasure to accept chains, brooches, tiaras or rings? You have but to say the word: fifty thousand is a trifle!"

His offer made her mouth water. Yet she stood her ground.

"No, thank you, I want nothing to do with you."

"By God, I certainly want to do something with *you*! What I want will cost you nothing; you'll be out nothing when you've given it. Look, Madame," and he showed her his long codpiece. "Here is Master Johnny Scramblecunney who craves lodging."

He was about to strike root there, when she started to cry out, though none too loud. The mask of courtesy fell from Panurge's face.

"So you won't let me have a little harmless fun, eh? Not even a morsel for me, eh? A bucket of turds to you! you don't deserve the honor or pleasure of it. But by God! I'll make the dogs ride you!"

With which he beat a hasty retreat in dread of blows. (He was by nature fearful of them.)

CHAPTER 22

How Panurge played a none too pleasant trick on the Parisienne of high degree.

Next day was Corpus Christi, a feast on which the ladies of Paris put on their stateliest apparel. Panurge's charmer was decked out in a rich gown of crimson velvet, with a skirt of costly white velure.

The day before, Panurge scoured the town for a bitch in heat. Having found one, he tied his belt around her neck and took her home. All that day and through the night, he fed her abundantly; in the morning he killed her, plucked out that part the Greek geomancians[50] know, cut it as fine as he could, tucked it away in one of his innumerable pockets and went to the church. He was sure his lady would soon arrive to take part in the procession always held on that day.

When she entered, Panurge bowed courteously, offered her some holy water and, shortly after she had finished her petty devotions, sat down on the bench beside her. As she looked up, he passed her a paper on which he had written the following rondeau:

> Sweet lady, once, once only I expressed
> My admiration; you denied my quest,
> You drove me irremediably away
> Although I never harmed you (welladay!)
> In act or word or libel or the rest. . . .
> Granted my wooing stirred no answering zest,
> You could have been more honest, and confessed:
> "I do not wish it, friend. Leave me, I pray!"
>   Sweet lady, once,
> Once more and never again I shall protest
> Ere love's flame utterly consume my breast,
> One boon alone I languish for: to lay
> My peacock, shoveller, cockerel, popinjay
> Deep in the shelter of your downy nest.
>   Sweet lady, once!

While she was unfolding the paper to see what was inside, Pan-

50. a species of magicians.

urge deftly sprinkled his drug all over her, spilling it impartially in the folds of her sleeves and skirt.

"Madame," he said before taking his leave, "a lover's life is not always a bed of roses. In my case I can only hope the anguished nights, the sorrows and tribulation I undergo for love of you will be deducted from my trials in purgatory. At least pray God He give me patience to bear my affliction."

Panurge had scarcely spoken when all the dogs in the church, attracted by the odor of the drug, scurried over to the lady. Big and little, large and small, one and all came up, sniffed, raised their legs, cocked their members and let fly on her dress. It was the most horrible sight imaginable.

Panurge pretended to chase them off, then bowed and retired to watch the sport from the vantage point of a chapel. Those wretched curs were squirting all over her clothes. One huge greyhound placed a paw on her shoulder to aim at her head ... other dogs pumped in her sleeves ... still others drenched her backside, while the puppies piddled in her shoes.... The women close to her sought to keep the beasts off, but with scant success. Meanwhile, holding his sides, Panurge, between guffaws of laughter, told certain lords who were next to him:

"I think that lady's in heat. Or some wolfhound covered her recently."

Seeing the dogs crowded as thick about her as about a bitch in heat, he ran off to fetch Pantagruel. On the way, he stopped to kick every dog he met, crying:

"To church with you! To your genuflexions! Follow the odor of sanctity! Be off and join your fellows at the urinarian baptism! Forward, by all the devils, be off, devil take you!"

"Master," he said breathlessly to Pantagruel, "please come and see all the dogs of the country gathered about the loveliest lady in town, and every one of them agog to scrounge her!"

Pantagruel, delighted at the novelty of it, accompanied Panurge back to church and enjoyed the fun immensely. By the time the procession began, matters had reached a crisis. There were more than six hundred thousand and fourteen dogs thronging about her and finding one thousand and one means of harassing her. Whichever way she turned, the newcomers followed the scent, dogged her heels and flooded whatever spot her dress touched. The only course left her was to go home. As she fled through the streets, every one stopped to watch the dogs leaping high as her neck, turning her elegant toilette into a very toilet, as she ran on, helpless and steaming. It was impossible to give them the slip, the trail was too pungent. So they followed her to her residence.

While she hid in her room and her chambermaids burst into laughter behind politely raised aprons, all the dogs within a radius of a half-league came rushing up and showered so hard against the gate as to form a stream in which ducks might very well have swum. To-day this same current, now called the creek of Bièvre, flows through the grounds of the Abbey of St. Victor and past the Gobelin dye-works.[51] Materials steeped in its waters turn a rare scarlet thanks to some special virtue of these pissdogs, as our learned Master Doribus recently pointed out in a brilliant sermon. God help us, a mill could have ground corn there, though not so much as the famous Bazacle in Toulouse on the Garonne.

51. The geography is correct. At the time of Rabelais' writing the celebrated dye-works were still run by the Gobelin family. Mysterious qualities were attributed to the water of the small river Bièvre, and urine was actually used in the industry on account of its ammonia contents.

BENVENUTO CELLINI

(1500–1571)

Autobiography (La vita di Benvenuto Cellini)*

[*World War*]†

The whole world was now in warfare.[1] Pope Clement had sent to get some troops from Giovanni de' Medici, and when they came, they made such disturbances in Rome, that it was ill living in open shops. On this account I retired to a good snug house behind the Banchi, where I worked for all the friends I had acquired. Since I produced few things of much importance at that period, I need not waste time in talking about them. I took much pleasure in music and amusements of the kind. On the death of Giovanni de' Medici in Lombardy, the Pope, at the advice of Messer Jacopo Salviati, dismissed the five bands he had engaged; and when the Constable of Bourbon[2] knew there were no troops in Rome, he pushed his army with the utmost energy up to the city. The whole of Rome upon this flew to arms. I happened to be intimate with Alessandro, the son of Piero del Bene, who, at the time when the Colonnesi entered Rome, had requested me to guard his palace. On this more serious occasion, therefore, he prayed me to enlist fifty comrades for the protection of the said house, appointing me their captain, as I had been when the Colonnesi[3] came. So I col-

* Written between 1558 and 1562. The selections reprinted here are from the translation by John Addington Symonds.

† Book I, Chapters 34–37.

1. The year is 1527; Benvenuto is now in Rome. The war between Charles V, the Holy Roman emperor, and the king of France, Francis I, which had been going on for six years, had important implications in Italy. A league of Italian states, including the Holy See, at this point was backing Francis I. The invasion described in this selection is generally referred to as the sack of Rome.

2. a cousin of the king of France who had gone over to the opposite side. Benvenuto's statement, in the following paragraph, that it was he who killed the Constable is considered wholly unreliable.

3. the troops of the house of Colonna, the Pope's enemies.

lected fifty young men of the highest courage, and we took up our quarters in his palace, with good pay and excellent appointments.

Bourbon's army had now arrived before the walls of Rome, and Alessandro begged me to go with him to reconnoitre. So we went with one of the stoutest fellows in our company; and on the way a youth called Cecchino della Casa joined himself to us. On reaching the walls by the Campo Santo, we could see that famous army, which was making every effort to enter the town. Upon the ramparts where we took our station, several young men were lying killed by the besiegers; the battle raged there desperately, and there was the densest fog imaginable. I turned to Alessandro and said: "Let us go home as soon as we can, for there is nothing to be done here; you see the enemies are mounting, and our men are in flight." Alessandro, in a panic, cried: "Would God that we had never come here!" and turned in maddest haste to fly. I took him up somewhat sharply with these words: "Since you have brought me here, I must perform some action worthy of a man"; and directing my arquebuse where I saw the thickest and most serried troop of fighting men, I aimed exactly at one whom I remarked to be higher than the rest: the fog prevented me from being certain whether he was on horseback or on foot. Then I turned to Alessandro and Cecchino, and bade them discharge their arquebuses, showing them how to avoid being hit by the besiegers. When we had fired two rounds apiece, I crept cautiously up to the wall, and observing among the enemy a most extraordinary confusion, I discovered afterwards that one of our shots had killed the Constable of Bourbon; and from what I subsequently learned, he was the man whom I had first noticed above the heads of the rest.

Quitting our position on the ramparts, we crossed the Campo Santo, and and entered the city of St. Peter's; then coming out exactly at the church of Santo Agnolo, we got with greatest difficulty to the great gate of the castle: for the generals Renzo di Ceri and Orazio Baglioni were wounding and slaughtering everybody who abandoned the defence of the walls. By the time we had reached the great gate, part of the foemen had already entered Rome, and we had them in our rear. The castellan had ordered the portcullis to be lowered, in order to do which they cleared a little space, and this enabled us four to get inside. On the instant that I entered, the captain Pallone de' Medici claimed me as being of the Papal household, and forced me to abandon Alessandro, which I had to do, much against my will. I ascended to the keep, and at the same instant Pope Clement came in through the corridors into the castle; he had refused to leave the palace of St. Peter earlier, being unable to believe that his enemies would effect their entrance into Rome. Having got into the castle in this way, I attached myself to certain pieces of artillery, which were under the command of a bombardier called Giuliano Fiorentino. Leaning there against the battlements, the unhappy man could see his poor house being sacked, and his wife and children outraged; fearing to strike his own folk, he dared not discharge the cannon, and flinging the burning fuse upon the ground, he wept as though his heart would break, and tore his cheeks with both his hands. Some of the other bombardiers were behaving in like manner; seeing which, I took one of the matches, and got the assistance of a few men who were not overcome by their emotions. I aimed some swivels and falconets at points where I saw it would be useful, and killed with them a good number of the enemy. Had it not been for this, the troops who poured into Rome that morning, and were marching straight upon the castle, might possibly have entered it with ease, because the artillery was doing them no damage. I went on firing under the eyes of several cardinals and lords, who kept blessing me and giving me the heartiest encouragement. In my enthusiasm I strove to achieve the impossible; let it suffice that it was I who saved the castle that morning, and brought the other bombardiers back to their duty. I worked hard the whole of that day; and when the evening came, while the army was marching into Rome through the Trastevere, Pope Clement appointed a great Roman nobleman named Antonio Santacroce to be captain of all the gunners. The first thing this man did was to come to me, and having greeted me with the utmost kindness, he stationed me with five fine pieces of artillery on the highest point of the castle, to which the name of the Angel[4] specially belongs. This circular eminence goes round the castle, and surveys both Prati and the town of Rome. The captain put under my orders enough men to help in managing my guns, and having seen me paid in advance, he gave me rations of bread and a little wine, and begged me to go forward as I had begun. I was perhaps more inclined by nature to the profession of arms than to the one I had adopted, and I took such pleasure in its duties that I discharged them better than those of my own art. Night came, the enemy had entered Rome, and we who were in the castle (especially myself, who have always taken pleasure in extraordinary sights) stayed gazing on the indescribable scene of tumult and conflagration in the streets below. People who were anywhere else but where we were, could not have formed the least imagination of what it was. I will not, however, set myself to describe that tragedy, but will content myself with continuing the history of my own life and the circumstances which properly belong to it.

During the course of my artillery practice, which I never intermitted through the whole month passed by us beleaguered in the castle, I met with a great many very striking accidents, all of them worthy to be related. But since I do not care to be too prolix, or to exhibit myself outside the sphere of my profession, I will omit the larger part of them, only touching upon those I cannot well neglect,

4. from the marble angel on top of the castle.

which shall be the fewest in number and the most remarkable. The first which comes to hand is this: Messer Antonio Santacroce had made me come down from the Angel, in order to fire on some houses in the neighbourhood, where certain of our besiegers had been seen to enter. While I was firing, a cannon shot reached me, which hit the angle of a battlement, and carried off enough of it to be the cause why I sustained no injury. The whole mass struck me in the chest and took my breath away. I lay stretched upon the ground like a dead man, and could hear what the bystanders were saying. Among them all, Messer Antonio Santacroce lamented greatly, exclaiming: "Alas, alas! we have lost the best defender that we had." Attracted by the uproar, one of my comrades ran up; he was called Gianfrancesco, and was a bandsman, but was far more naturally given to medicine than to music. On the spot he flew off, crying for a stoop of the very best Greek wine. Then he made a tile red-hot, and cast upon it a good handful of wormwood; after which he sprinkled the Greek wine; and when the wormwood was well soaked, he laid it on my breast, just where the bruise was visible to all. Such was the virtue of the wormwood that I immediately regained my scattered faculties. I wanted to begin to speak, but could not; for some stupid soldiers had filled my mouth with earth, imagining that by so doing they were giving me the sacrament; and indeed they were more like to have excommunicated me, since I could with difficulty come to myself again, the earth doing me more mischief than the blow. However, I escaped that danger, and returned to the rage and fury of the guns, pursuing my work there with all the ability and eagerness that I could summon.

Pope Clement, by this, had sent to demand assistance from the Duke of Urbino, who was with the troops of Venice; he commissioned the envoy to tell his Excellency that the Castle of St. Angelo would send up every evening three beacons from its summit, accompanied by three discharges of the cannon thrice repeated, and that so long as this signal was continued, he might take for granted that the castle had not yielded. I was charged with lighting the beacons and firing the guns for this purpose; and all this while I pointed my artillery by day upon the places where mischief could be done. The Pope, in consequence, began to regard me with still greater favour, because he saw that I discharged my functions as intelligently as the task demanded. Aid from the Duke of Urbino never came; on which, as it is not my business, I will make no further comment.

While I was at work upon that diabolical task of mine, there came from time to time to watch me some of the cardinals who were invested in the castle; and most frequently the Cardinal of Ravenna and the Cardinal de' Gaddi. I often told them not to show themselves, since their nasty red caps gave a fair mark to our enemies. From neighbouring buildings, such as the Torre de' Bini, we ran great peril when they were there; and at last I had them locked off, and gained thereby their deep ill-will. I frequently received visits also from the general, Orazio Baglioni, who was very well affected toward me. One day while he was talking with me, he noticed something going forward in a drinking-place outside the Porta di Castello, which bore the name of Baccanello. This tavern had for a sign a sun painted between two windows, of a bright red colour. The windows being closed, Signor Orazio concluded that a band of soldiers were carousing at table just between them and behind the sun. So he said to me: "Benvenuto, if you think that you could hit that wall an ell's breadth from the sun with your demi-cannon here, I believe you would be doing a good stroke of business, for there is a great commotion there, and men of much importance must probably be inside the house." I answered that I felt quite capable of hitting the sun in its centre, but that a barrel full of stones, which was standing close to the muzzle of the gun, might be knocked down by the shock of the discharge and the blast of the artillery. He rejoined: "Don't waste time, Benvenuto. In the first place, it is not possible, where it is standing, that the cannon's blast should bring it down; and even if it were to fall, and the Pope himself was underneath, the mischief would not be so great as you imagine. Fire, then, only fire!" Taking no more thought about it, I struck the sun in the centre, exactly as I said I should. The cask was dislodged, as I predicted, and fell precisely between Cardinal Farnese[5] and Messer Jacopo Salviati. It might very well have dashed out the brains of both of them, except that just at that very moment Farnese was reproaching Salviati with having caused the sack of Rome, and while they stood apart from one another to exchange opprobrious remarks, my gabion fell without destroying them. When he heard the uproar in the court below, good Signor Orazio dashed off in a hurry; and I, thrusting my neck forward where the cask had fallen, heard some people saying: "It would not be a bad job to kill that gunner!" Upon this I turned two falconets toward the staircase, with mind resolved to let blaze on the first man who attempted to come up. The household of Cardinal Farnese must have received orders to go and do me some injury; accordingly I prepared to receive them, with a lighted match in hand. Recognising some who were approaching, I called out: "You lazy lubbers, if you don't pack off from there, and if but a man's child among you dares to touch the staircase, I have got two cannon loaded, which will blow you into powder. Go and tell the Cardinal that I was acting at the order of superior officers, and that what we have done and are doing is in defence of them priests, and not to hurt them." They made away; and then came Signor Orazio Baglioni, running. I bade him stand back, else I'd murder him; for I knew very well who he was. He

5. already high in the Vatican hierarchy, later to become Pope Paul III.

drew back a little, not without a certain show of fear, and called out: "Benvenuto, I am your friend!" To this I answered: "Sir, come up, but come alone, and then come as you like." The general, who was a man of mighty pride, stood still a moment, and then said angrily: "I have a good mind not to come up again, and to do quite the opposite of that which I intended toward you." I replied that just as I was put there to defend my neighbours, I was equally well able to defend myself too. He said that he was coming alone; and when he arrived at the top of the stairs, his features were more discomposed than I thought reasonable. So I kept my hand upon my sword, and stood eyeing him askance. Upon this he began to laugh, and the colour coming back into his face, he said to me with the most pleasant manner: "Friend Benvenuto, I bear you as great love as I have in my heart to give; and in God's good time I will render you proof of this. Would to God that you had killed those two rascals; for one of them is the cause of all this trouble, and the day perchance will come when the other will be found the cause of something even worse." He then begged me, if I should be asked, not to say that he was with me when I fired the gun; and for the rest bade me be of good cheer. The commotion which the affair made was enormous, and lasted a long while. However, I will not enlarge upon it further, only adding that I was within an inch of revenging my father on Messer Jacopo Salviati, who had grievously injured him, according to my father's frequent complaints.[6] As it was, unwittingly I gave the fellow a great fright. Of Farnese I shall say nothing here, because it will appear in its proper place how well it would have been if I had killed him.

I pursued my business of artilleryman, and every day performed some extraordinary feat, whereby the credit and the favour I acquired with the Pope was something indescribable. There never passed a day but what I killed one or another of our enemies in the besieging army. On one occasion the Pope was walking round the circular keep, when he observed a Spanish Colonel in the Prati; he recognised the man by certain indications, seeing that this officer had formerly been in his service; and while he fixed his eyes on him, he kept talking about him. I, above by the Angel, knew nothing of all this, but spied a fellow down there, busying himself about the trenches with a javelin in his hand; he was dressed entirely in rose-colour; and so, studying the worst that I could do against him, I selected a gerfalcon which I had at hand; it is a piece of ordnance larger and longer than a swivel, and about the size of a demi-culverin. This I emptied, and loaded it again with a good charge of fine powder mixed with the coarser sort; then I aimed it exactly at the man in red, elevating prodigiously, because a piece of that

6. Benvenuto has a grudge against Salviati for depriving his father of his position with the Medici.

calibre could hardly be expected to carry true at such a distance. I fired, and hit my man exactly in the middle. He had trussed his sword in front, for swagger, after a way those Spaniards have; and my ball, when it struck him, broke upon the blade, and one could see the fellow cut in two fair halves. The Pope, who was expecting nothing of this kind, derived great pleasure and amazement from the sight, both because it seemed to him impossible that one should aim and hit the mark at such a distance, and also because the man was cut in two, and he could not comprehend how this should happen. He sent for me, and asked about it. I explained all the devices I had used in firing; but told him that why the man was cut in halves, neither he nor I could know. Upon my bended knees I then besought him to give me the pardon of his blessing for that homicide; and for all the others I had committed in the castle in the service of the Church. Thereat the Pope, raising his hand, and making a large open sign of the cross upon my face, told me that he blessed me, and that he gave me pardon for all murders I had ever perpetrated, or should ever perpetrate, in the service of the Apostolic Church. When I left him, I went aloft, and never stayed from firing to the utmost of my power; and few were the shots of mine that missed their mark. My drawing, and my fine studies in my craft, and my charming art of music, all were swallowed up in the din of that artillery; and if I were to relate in detail all the splendid things I did in that infernal work of cruelty, I should make the world stand by and wonder. But, not to be too prolix, I will pass them over. Only I must tell a few of the most remarkable, which are, as it were, forced in upon me.

To begin then: pondering day and night what I could render for my own part in defence of Holy Church, and having noticed that the enemy changed guard and marched past through the great gate of Santo Spirito, which was within a reasonable range, I thereupon directed my attention to that spot; but, having to shoot sideways, I could not do the damage that I wished, although I killed a fair percentage every day. This induced our adversaries, when they saw their passage covered by my guns, to load the roof of a certain house one night with thirty gabions, which obstructed the view I formerly enjoyed. Taking better thought than I had done of the whole situation, I now turned all my five pieces of artillery directly on the gabions, and waited till the evening hour, when they changed guard. Our enemies, thinking they were safe, came on at greater ease and in a closer body than usual; whereupon I set fire to my blow-pipes.[7] Not merely did I dash to pieces the gabions which stood in my way; but, what was better, by that one blast I slaughtered more than thirty men. In consequence of this manœuvre, which I repeated

7. artillery pieces in general.

twice, the soldiers were thrown into such disorder, that being, moreover, encumbered with the spoils of that great sack, and some of them desirous of enjoying the fruits of their labour, they oftentimes showed a mind to mutiny and take themselves away from Rome. However, after coming to terms with their valiant captain, Gian di Urbino, they were ultimately compelled, at their excessive inconvenience, to take another road when they changed guard. It cost them three miles of march, whereas before they had but half a mile. Having achieved this feat, I was entreated with prodigious favours by all the men of quality who were invested in the castle. This incident was so important that I thought it well to relate it, before finishing the history of things outside my art, the which is the real object of my writing: forsooth, if I wanted to ornament my biography with such matters, I should have far too much to tell.

["Men Like Benvenuto . . . Stand Above the Law"]*

. . . The Pope[8] was taken ill, and his physicians thought the case was dangerous. Accordingly my enemy[9] began to be afraid of me, and engaged some Neapolitan soldiers to do to me what he was dreading I might do to him. I had therefore much trouble to defend my poor life. In course of time, however, I completed the reverse; and when I took it to the Pope, I found him in bed in a most deplorable condition. Nevertheless, he received me with the greatest kindness, and wished to inspect the medals and the dies. He sent for spectacles and lights, but was unable to see anything clearly. Then he began to fumble with his fingers at them, and having felt them a short while, he fetched a deep sigh, and said to his attendants that he was much concerned about me, but that if God gave him back his health he would make it all right.

Three days afterwards the Pope died, and I was left with all my labour lost; yet I plucked up courage, and told myself that these medals had won me so much celebrity, that any Pope who was elected would give me work to do, and peradventure bring me better fortune. Thus I encouraged and put heart into myself, and buried in oblivion all the injuries which Pompeo had done me. Then putting on my arms and girding my sword, I went to San Piero, and kissed the feet of the dead Pope, not without shedding tears. Afterwards I returned to the Banchi to look on at the great commotion which always happens on such occasions.

While I was sitting in the street with several of my friends, Pompeo went by, attended by ten men very well armed; and when he came just opposite, he stopped, as though about to pick a quar-

* From Book I, Chapters 72–74.
  8. still Clement VII. The year is 1534.
  9. Benvenuto's great enemy and rival is Pompeo de' Capitaneis, a jeweler from Milan who tried several times, and with some success, to ruin his position with the Pope.

rel with myself. My companions, brave and adventurous young men, made signs to me to draw my sword; but it flashed through my mind that if I drew, some terrible mischief might result for persons who were wholly innocent. Therefore I considered that it would be better if I put my life to risk alone. When Pompeo had stood there time enough to say two Ave Maries, he laughed derisively in my direction; and going off, his fellows also laughed and wagged their heads, with many other insolent gestures. My companions wanted to begin the fray at once; but I told them hotly that I was quite able to conduct my quarrels to an end by myself, and that I had no need of stouter fighters than I was; so that each of them might mind his business. My friends were angry and went off muttering. Now there was among them my dearest comrade, named Albertaccio del Bene, own brother to Alessandro and Albizzo, who is now a very rich man in Lyons. He was the most redoubtable young man I ever knew, and the most high-spirited, and loved me like himself; and insomuch as he was well aware that my forbearance had not been inspired by want of courage, but by the most daring bravery, for he knew me down to the bottom of my nature, he took my words up and begged me to favour him so far as to associate him with myself in all I meant to do. I replied: "Dear Albertaccio, dearest to me above all men that live, the time will very likely come when you shall give me aid; but in this case, if you love me, do not attend to me, but look to your own business, and go at once like our other friends, for now there is no time to lose." These words were spoken in one breath.

In the meanwhile my enemies had proceeded slowly toward Chiavica, as the place was called, and had arrived at the crossing of several roads, going in different directions; but the street in which Pompeo's house stood was the one which leads straight to the Campo di Fiore. Some business or other made him enter the apothecary's shop which stood at the corner of Chiavica, and there he stayed a while transacting it. I had just been told that he had boasted of the insult which he fancied he had put upon me; but be that as it may, it was to his misfortune; for precisely when I came up to the corner, he was leaving the shop, and his bravi had opened their ranks and received him in their midst. I drew a little dagger with a sharpened edge, and breaking the line of his defenders, laid my hands upon his breast so quickly and coolly, that none of them were able to prevent me. Then I aimed to strike him in the face; but fright made him turn his head round; and I stabbed him just beneath the ear. I only gave two blows, for he fell stone dead at the second. I had not meant to kill him; but as the saying goes, knocks are not dealt by measure. With my left hand I plucked back the dagger, and with my right hand drew my sword to defend my life.

However, all those bravi ran up to the corpse and took no action against me; so I went back alone through Strada Giulia, considering how best to put myself in safety.

I had walked about three hundred paces, when Piloto the goldsmith, my very good friend, came up and said: "Brother, now that the mischief's done, we must see to saving you." I replied: "Let us go to Albertaccio del Bene's house; it is only a few minutes since I told him I should soon have need of him." When we arrived there, Albertaccio and I embraced with measureless affection; and soon the whole flower of the young men of the Banchi, of all nations except the Milanese,[10] came crowding in; and each and all made proffer of their own life to save mine. Messer Luigi Rucellai also sent with marvellous promptitude and courtesy to put his services at my disposal, as did many other great folk of his station; for they all agreed in blessing my hands, judging that Pompeo had done me too great and unforgivable an injury, and marvelling that I had put up with him so long.

Cardinal Cornaro, on hearing of the affair, despatched thirty soldiers, with as many partisans, pikes, and arquebuses, to bring me with all due respect to his quarters. This he did unasked; whereupon I accepted the invitation, and went off with them, while more than as many of the young men bore me company. Meanwhile, Messer Traiano, Pompeo's relative and first chamberlain to the Pope, sent a Milanese of high rank to Cardinal de' Medici, giving him news of the great crime I had committed, and calling on his most reverend lordship to chastise me. The Cardinal retorted on the spot: "His crime would indeed have been great if he had not committed this lesser one; thank Messer Traiano from me for giving me this information of a fact of which I had not heard before." Then he turned and in presence of the nobleman said to the Bishop of Frullì, his gentleman and intimate acquaintance: "Search diligently after my friend Benvenuto; I want to help and defend him; and whoso acts against him acts against myself." The Milanese nobleman went back, much disconcerted, while the Bishop of Frullì came to visit me at Cardinal Cornaro's palace. Presenting himself to the Cardinal, he related how Cardinal de' Medici had sent for Benvenuto, and wanted to be his protector. Now Cardinal Cornaro, who had the touchy temper of a bear, flew into a rage, and told the Bishop he was quite as well able to defend me as Cardinal de' Medici. The Bishop, in reply, entreated to be allowed to speak with me on some matters of his patron which had nothing to do with the affair. Cornaro bade him for that day make as though he had already talked with me.

Cardinal de' Medici was very angry. However, I went the follow-

10. men from all the states of Italy except Pompeo's own.

ing night, without Cornaro's knowledge, and under good escort, to pay him my respects. Then I begged him to grant me the favour of leaving me where I was, and told him of the great courtesy which Cornaro had shown me; adding that if his most reverend lordship suffered me to stay, I should gain one friend the more in my hour of need; otherwise his lordship might dispose of me exactly as he thought best. He told me to do as I liked; so I returned to Cornaro's palace, and a few days afterwards the Cardinal Farnese was elected Pope.

After he had put affairs of greater consequence in order, the new Pope sent for me, saying that he did not wish any one else to strike his coins. To these words of his Holiness a gentleman very privately acquainted with him, named Messer Latino Juvinale, made answer that I was in hiding for a murder committed on the person of one Pompeo of Milan, and set forth what could be argued for my justi-fication in the most favourable terms. The Pope replied: "I knew nothing of Pompeo's death, but plenty of Benvenuto's provocation; so let a safe-conduct be at once made out for him, in order that he may be placed in perfect security." A great friend of Pompeo's, who was also intimate with the Pope, happened to be there; he was a Milanese, called Messer Ambrogio. This man said: "In the first days of your papacy it were not well to grant pardons of this kind." The Pope turned to him and answered: "You know less about such matters than I do. Know then that men like Benvenuto, unique in their profession, stand above the law; and how far more he, then, who received the provocation I have heard of?" When my safe-conduct had been drawn out, I began at once to serve him, and was treated with the utmost favour.

["*I . . . Grew Somewhat Glorious*"]*

It happened on one feast-day that I went to the palace after dinner, and when I reached the clockroom, I saw the door of the wardrobe standing open. As I drew nigh it, the Duke[11] called me, and after a friendly greeting said: "You are welcome! Look at that box which has been sent me by my lord Stefano of Palestrina. Open it, and let us see what it contains." When I had opened the box, I cried to the Duke: "My lord, this is a statue in Greek marble, and it is a miracle of beauty. I must say that I have never seen a boy's figure so excellently wrought and in so fine a style among all the antiques I have inspected. If your Excellency permits, I should like to restore it—head and arms and feet. I will add an eagle, in order that we may christen the lad Ganymede. It is certainly not my business to patch up statues, that being the trade of botchers,

---

* From Book II, Chapters 69–78.   duke of Tuscany. Benvenuto now works
11. Cosimo de' Medici, the grand   for him in Florence.

who do it in all conscience villainously ill; yet the art displayed by this great master of antiquity cries out to me to help him." The Duke was highly delighted to find the statue so beautiful, and put me a multitude of questions, saying: "Tell me, Benvenuto, minutely, in what consists the skill of this old master, which so excites your admiration." I then attempted, as well as I was able, to explain the beauty of workmanship, the consummate science, and the rare manner displayed by the fragment. I spoke long upon these topics, and with the greater pleasure because I saw that his Excellency was deeply interested.

While I was thus pleasantly engaged in entertaining the Duke, a page happened to leave the wardrobe, and at the same moment Bandinello[12] entered. When the Duke saw him, his countenance contracted, and he asked him drily: "What are you about here?" Bandinello, without answering, cast a glance upon the box, where the statue lay uncovered. Then breaking into one of his malignant laughs and wagging his head, he turned to the Duke and said: "My lord, this exactly illustrates the truth of what I have so often told your Excellency. You must know that the ancients were wholly ignorant of anatomy, and therefore their works abound in mistakes." I kept silence, and paid no heed to what he was saying; nay, indeed, I had turned my back on him. But when the brute had brought his disagreeable babble to an end, the Duke exclaimed: "O Benvenuto, this is the exact opposite of what you were just now demonstrating with so many excellent arguments. Come and speak a word in defence of the statue." In reply to this appeal, so kindly made me by the Duke, I spoke as follows: "My lord, your most illustrious Excellency must please to know that Baccio Bandinello is made up of everything bad, and thus has he ever been; therefore, whatever he looks at, be the thing superlatively excellent, becomes in his ungracious eyes as bad as can be. I, who incline to the good only, discern the truth with purer senses. Consequently, what I told your Excellency about this lovely statue is mere simple truth; whereas what Bandinello said is but a portion of the evil out of which he is composed." The Duke listened with much amusement; but Bandinello writhed and made the most ugly faces —his face itself being by nature hideous beyond measure—which could be imagined by the mind of man.

The Duke at this point moved away, and proceeded through some ground-floor rooms, while Bandinello followed. The chamberlains twitched me by the mantle, and sent me after; so we all attended the Duke until he reached a certain chamber, where he seated himself, with Bandinello and me standing at his right hand and his left. I kept silence, and the gentlemen of his Excellency's

12. a mediocre artist, Cellini's rival.

suite looked hard at Bandinello, tittering among themselves about the speech I had made in the room above. So then Bandinello began again to chatter, and cried out: "Prince, when I uncovered my Hercules and Cacus,[13] I verily believe a hundred sonnets were written on me, full of the worst abuse which could be invented by the ignorant rabble." I rejoined: "Prince, when Michel Angelo Buonarroti displayed his Sacristy[14] to view, with so many fine statues in it, the men of talent in our admirable school of Florence, always appreciative of truth and goodness, published more than a hundred sonnets, each vying with his neighbour to extol these masterpieces to the skies. So then, just as Bandinello's work deserved all the evil which, he tells us, was then said about it, Buonarroti's deserved the enthusiastic praise which was bestowed upon it." These words of mine made Bandinello burst with fury; he turned on me, and cried: "And you, what have you got to say against my work?" "I will tell you if you have the patience to hear me out." "Go along then," he replied. The Duke and his attendants prepared themselves to listen. I began and opened my oration thus: "You must know that it pains me to point out the faults of your statue; I shall not, however, utter my own sentiments, but shall recapitulate what our most virtuous school of Florence says about it." The brutal fellow kept making disagreeable remarks and gesticulating with his hands and feet, until he enraged me so that I began again, and spoke far more rudely than I should otherwise have done, if he had behaved with decency. "Well, then, this virtuous school says that if one were to shave the hair of your Hercules, there would not be skull enough left to hold his brain; it says that it is impossible to distinguish whether his features are those of a man or of something between a lion and an ox; the face too is turned away from the action of the figure, and is so badly set upon the neck, with such poverty of art and so ill a grace, that nothing worse was ever seen; his sprawling shoulders are like the two pommels of an ass's packsaddle; his breasts and all the muscles of the body are not portrayed from a man, but from a big sack full of melons set upright against a wall. The loins seem to be modelled from a bag of lanky pumpkins; nobody can tell how his two legs are attached to that vile trunk; it is impossible to say on which leg he stands, or which he uses to exert his strength; nor does he seem to be resting upon both, as sculptors who know something of their art have occasionally set the figure. It is obvious that the body is leaning forward more than one-third of a cubit, which alone is the greatest and most insupportable fault committed by vulgar commonplace pretenders. Concerning the arms, they say that these are

13. a marble group, still in the Piazza della Signoria in Florence.

14. the sacristy of San Lorenzo, with the Medici tombs; commonly referred to as the Medici chapel.

both stretched out without one touch of grace or one real spark of artistic talents, just as if you had never seen a naked model. Again, the right leg of Hercules and that of Cacus have got one mass of flesh between them, so that if they were to be separated, not only one of them, but both together, would be left without a calf at the point where they are touching. They say, too, that Hercules has one of his feet underground, while the other seems to be resting on hot coals."

The fellow could not stand quiet to hear the damning errors of his Cacus in their turn enumerated. For one thing, I was telling the truth; for another, I was unmasking him to the Duke and all the people present, who showed by face and gesture first their surprise, and next their conviction that what I said was true. All at once he burst out: "Ah, you slanderous tongue! why don't you speak about my design?" I retorted: "A good draughtsman can never produce bad works; therefore I am inclined to believe that your drawing is no better than your statues." When he saw the amused expression on the Duke's face and the cutting gestures of the bystanders, he let his insolence get the better of him, and turned to me with that most hideous face of his, screaming aloud: "Oh, hold your tongue, you ugly sodomite." At these words the Duke frowned, and the others pursed their lips up and looked with knitted brows toward him. The horrible affront half maddened me with fury; but in a moment I recovered presence of mind enough to turn it off with a jest: "You madman! you exceed the bounds of decency. Yet would to God that I understood so noble an art as you allude to; they say that Jove used it with Ganymede in paradise, and here upon this earth it is practised by some of the greatest emperors and kings. I, however, am but a poor humble creature, who neither have the power nor the intelligence to perplex my wits with anything so admirable." When I had finished this speech, the Duke and his attendants could control themselves no longer, but broke into such shouts of laughter that one never heard the like. You must know, gentle readers, that though I put on this appearance of pleasantry, my heart was bursting in my body to think that a fellow, the foulest villain who ever breathed, should have dared in the presence of so great a prince to cast an insult of that atrocious nature in my teeth; but you must also know that he insulted the Duke, and not me; for had I not stood in that august presence, I should have felled him dead to earth. When the dirty stupid scoundrel observed that those gentlemen kept on laughing, he tried to change the subject, and divert them from deriding him; so he began as follows: "This fellow Benvenuto goes about boasting that I have promised him a piece of marble." I took him up at once. "What! did you not send to tell me by your journeyman, Francesco, that if I wished to work in marble you would give me a block? I accepted it, and mean to have it." He retorted: "Be very well assured that you will never get it." Still smarting as I was under the calumnious insults he had flung at me, I lost my self-control, forgot I was in the presence of the Duke, and called out in a storm of fury: "I swear to you that if you do not send the marble to my house, you had better look out for another world, for if you stay upon this earth I will most certainly rip the wind out of your carcass." Then suddenly awaking to the fact that I was standing in the presence of so great a duke, I turned submissively to his Excellency and said: "My lord, one fool makes a hundred; the follies of this man have blinded me for a moment to the glory of your most illustrious Excellency and to myself. I humbly crave your pardon." Then the Duke said to Bandinello: "Is it true that you promised him the marble?" He replied that it was true. Upon this the Duke addressed me: "Go to the Opera,[15] and choose a piece according to your taste." I demurred that the man had promised to send it home to me. The words that passed between us were awful, and I refused to take the stone in any other way. Next morning a piece of marble was brought to my house. On asking who had sent it, they told me it was Bandinello, and that this was the very block which he had promised.

I had it brought at once into my studio, and began to chisel it. While I was rough-hewing the block, I made a model. But my eagerness to work in marble was so strong, that I had not patience to finish the model as correctly as this art demands. I soon noticed that the stone rang false beneath my strokes, which made me oftentimes repent commencing on it. Yet I got what I could out of the piece—that is, the Apollo and Hyacinth, which may still be seen unfinished in my workshop. While I was thus engaged, the Duke came to my house, and often said to me: "Leave your bronze awhile, and let me watch you working on the marble." Then I took chisel and mallet, and went at it blithely. He asked about the model I had made for my statue; to which I answered: "Duke, this marble is all cracked, but I shall carve something from it in spite of that; therefore I have not been able to settle the model, but shall go on doing the best I can."

His Excellency sent to Rome post-haste for a block of Greek marble, in order that I might restore his antique Ganymede, which was the cause of that dispute with Bandinello. When it arrived, I thought it a sin to cut it up for the head and arms and other bits wanting in the Ganymede; so I provided myself with another piece of stone, and reserved the Greek marble for a Narcissus which I modelled on a small scale in wax. I found that the block had two

15. the workshop annexed to the cathedral of Santa Maria del Fiore.

holes, penetrating to the depth of a quarter of a cubit, and two good inches wide. This led me to choose the attitude which may be noticed in my statue, avoiding the holes and keeping my figure free from them. But rain had fallen scores of years upon the stone, filtering so deeply from the holes into its substance that the marble was decayed. Of this I had full proof at the time of a great inundation of the Arno, when the river rose to the height of more than a cubit and a half in my workshop. Now the Narcissus stood upon a square of wood, and the water overturned it, causing the statue to break in two above the breasts. I had to join the pieces; and in order that the line of breakage might not be observed, I wreathed that garland of flowers round it which may still be seen upon the bosom. I went on working at the surface, employing some hours before sunrise, or now and then on feast-days, so as not to lose the time I needed for my Perseus.[16]

It so happened on one of those mornings, while I was getting some little chisels into trim to work on the Narcissus, that a very fine splinter of steel flew into my right eye, and embedded itself so deeply in the pupil that it could not be extracted. I thought for certain I must lose the sight of that eye. After some days I sent for Maestro Raffaello de' Pilli, the surgeon, who obtained a couple of live pigeons, and placing me upon my back across a table, took the birds and opened a large vein they have beneath the wing, so that the blood gushed out into my eye. I felt immediately relieved, and in the space of two days the splinter came away, and I remained with eyesight greatly improved. Against the feast of S. Lucia,[17] which came round in three days, I made a golden eye out of a French crown, and had it presented at her shrine by one of my six nieces, daughters of my sister Liperata; the girl was ten years of age, and in her company I returned thanks to God and S. Lucia. For some while afterwards I did not work at the Narcissus, but pushed my Perseus forward under all the difficulties I have described. It was my purpose to finish it, and then to bid farewell to Florence.

Having succeeded so well with the cast of the Medusa, I had great hope of bringing my Perseus through; for I had laid the wax on, and felt confident that it would come out in bronze as perfectly as the Medusa. The waxen model produced so fine an effect, that when the Duke saw it and was struck with its beauty—whether somebody had persuaded him it could not be carried out with the same finish in metal, or whether he thought so for himself—he came to visit me more frequently than usual, and on one occasion said: "Benvenuto, this figure cannot succeed in bronze; the laws of

16. the statue of Perseus holding the head of Medusa, commissioned by Duke Cosimo as a symbol of victory.
17. patroness of eyesight.

art do not admit of it." These words of his Excellency stung me
so sharply that I answered: "My lord, I know how very little confidence you have in me; and I believe the reason of this is that
your most illustrious Excellency lends too ready an ear to my
calumniators, or else indeed that you do not understand my art."
He hardly let me close the sentence when he broke in: "I profess
myself a connoisseur, and understand it very well indeed." I replied: "Yes, like a prince, not like an artist; for if your Excellency
understood my trade as well as you imagine, you would trust me
on the proofs I have already given. These are, first, the colossal
bronze bust of your Excellency, which is now in Elba; secondly, the
restoration of the Ganymede in marble, which offered so many
difficulties and cost me so much trouble, that I would rather have
made the whole statue new from the beginning; thirdly, the
Medusa, cast by me in bronze, here now before your Excellency's
eyes, the execution of which was a greater triumph of strength and
skill than any of my predecessors in this fiendish art have yet
achieved. Look you, my lord! I constructed that furnace anew on
principles quite different from those of other founders; in addition
to many technical improvements and ingenious devices, I supplied
it with two issues for the metal, because this difficult and twisted
figure could not otherwise have come out perfect. It is only owing
to my intelligent insight into means and appliances that the statue
turned out as it did; a triumph judged impossible by all the practitioners of this art. I should like you furthermore to be aware, my
lord, for certain, that the sole reason why I succeeded with all
those great and arduous works in France under his most admirable
Majesty King Francis, was the high courage which that good
monarch put into my heart by the liberal allowances he made me,
and the multitude of work-people he left at my disposal. I could
have as many as I asked for, and employed at times above forty,
all chosen by myself. These were the causes of my having there
produced so many masterpieces in so short a space of time. Now
then, my lord, put trust in me; supply me with the aid I need. I am
confident of being able to complete a work which will delight your
soul. But if your Excellency goes on disheartening me, and does
not advance me the assistance which is absolutely required, neither
I nor any man alive upon this earth can hope to achieve the
slightest thing of value."

It was as much as the Duke could do to stand by and listen to
my pleadings. He kept turning first this way and then that; while
I, in despair, poor wretched I, was calling up remembrance of the
noble state I held in France, to the great sorrow of my soul. All at
once he cried: "Come, tell me, Benvenuto, how is it possible that
yonder splendid head of Medusa, so high up there in the grasp of

Perseus, should ever come out perfect?" I replied upon the instant: "Look you now, my lord! If your Excellency possessed that knowledge of the craft which you affirm you have, you would not fear one moment for the splendid head you speak of. There is good reason, on the other hand, to feel uneasy about this right foot, so far below and at a distance from the rest." When he heard these words, the Duke turned, half in anger, to some gentlemen in waiting, and exclaimed: "I verily believe that this Benvenuto prides himself on contradicting everything one says." Then he faced round to me with a touch of mockery, upon which his attendants did the like, and began to speak as follows: "I will listen patiently to any argument you can possibly produce in explanation of your statement, which may convince me of its probability." I said in answer: "I will adduce so sound an argument that your Excellency shall perceive the full force of it." So I began: "You must know, my lord, that the nature of fire is to ascend, and therefore I promise you that Medusa's head will come out famously; but since it is not in the nature of fire to descend, and I must force it downwards six cubits[18] by artificial means, I assure your Excellency upon this most convincing ground of proof that the foot cannot possibly come out. It will, however, be quite easy for me to restore it." "Why, then," said the Duke, "did you not devise it so that the foot should come out as well as you affirm the head will?" I answered: "I must have made a much larger furnace, with a conduit as thick as my leg; and so I might have forced the molten metal by its own weight to descend so far. Now, my pipe, which runs six cubits to the statue's foot, as I have said, is not thicker than two fingers. However, it was not worth the trouble and expense to make a larger; for I shall easily be able to mend what is lacking. But when my mould is more than half full, as I expect, from this middle point upwards, the fire ascending by its natural property, then the heads of Perseus and Medusa will come out admirably; you may be quite sure of it." After I had thus expounded these convincing arguments, together with many more of the same kind, which it would be tedious to set down here, the Duke shook his head and departed without further ceremony.

Abandoned thus to my own resources, I took new courage, and banished the sad thoughts which kept recurring to my mind, making me often weep bitter tears of repentance for having left France; for though I did so only to revisit Florence, my sweet birthplace, in order that I might charitably succour my six nieces, this good action, as I well perceived, had been the beginning of my great misfortune. Nevertheless, I felt convinced that when my Perseus

18. A *cubit* is a measure of length equaling a foot and a half.

was accomplished, all these trials would be turned to high felicity and glorious well-being.

Accordingly I strengthened my heart, and with all the forces of my body and my purse, employing what little money still remained to me, I set to work. First I provided myself with several loads of pinewood from the forests of Serristori, in the neighbourhood of Montelupo. While these were on their way, I clothed my Perseus with the clay which I had prepared many months beforehand, in order that it might be duly seasoned. After making its clay tunic (for that is the term used in this art) and properly arming it and fencing it with iron girders, I began to draw the wax out by means of a slow fire. This melted and issued through numerous air-vents I had made; for the more there are of these, the better will the mould fill. When I had finished drawing off the wax, I constructed a funnel-shaped furnace all round the model of my Perseus. It was built of bricks, so interlaced, the one above the other, that numerous apertures were left for the fire to exhale at. Then I began to lay on wood by degrees, and kept it burning two whole days and nights. At length, when all the wax was gone, and the mould was well baked, I set to work at digging the pit in which to sink it. This I performed with scrupulous regard to all the rules of art. When I had finished that part of my work, I raised the mould by windlasses and stout ropes to a perpendicular position, and suspending it with the greatest care one cubit above the level of the furnace, so that it hung exactly above the middle of the pit, I next lowered it gently down into the very bottom of the furnace, and had it firmly placed with every possible precaution for its safety. When this delicate operation was accomplished, I began to bank it up with the earth I had excavated; and, ever as the earth grew higher, I introduced its proper air-vents, which were little tubes of earthenware, such as folk use for drains and such-like purposes. At length, I felt sure that it was admirably fixed, and that the filling-in of the pit and the placing of the air-vents had been properly performed. I also could see that my work-people understood my method, which differed very considerably from that of all the other masters in the trade. Feeling confident, then, that I could rely upon them, I next turned to my furnace, which I had filled with numerous pigs of copper and other bronze stuff. The pieces were piled according to the laws of art, that is to say, so resting one upon the other that the flames could play freely through them, in order that the metal might heat and liquefy the sooner. At last I called out heartily to set the furnace going. The logs of pine were heaped in, and, what with the unctuous resin of the wood and the good draught I had given, my furnace worked so well that I was obliged to rush from side to side to keep it going. The labour was more than I could stand; yet I forced myself to strain every nerve and muscle. To increase my anxieties, the workshop took fire, and we were afraid lest the roof should fall upon our heads; while, from the garden, such a storm of wind and rain kept blowing in, that it perceptibly cooled the furnace.

Battling thus with all these untoward circumstances for several hours, and exerting myself beyond even the measure of my powerful constitution, I could at last bear up no longer, and a sudden fever, of the utmost possible intensity, attacked me. I felt absolutely obliged to go and fling myself upon my bed. Sorely against my will having to drag myself away from the spot, I turned to my assistants, about ten or more in all, what with master-founders, hand-workers, country-fellows, and my own special journeymen, among whom was Bernardino Mannellini of Mugello, my apprentice through several years. To him in particular I spoke: "Look, my dear Bernardino, that you observe the rules which I have taught you; do your best with all despatch, for the metal will soon be fused. You cannot go wrong; these honest men will get the channels ready; you will easily be able to drive back the two plugs with this pair of iron crooks; and I am sure that my mould will fill miraculously.[19] I feel more ill than I ever did in all my life, and verily believe that it will kill me before a few hours are over." Thus, with despair at heart, I left them, and betook myself to bed.

No sooner had I got to bed, than I ordered my servingmaids to carry food and wine for all the men into the workshop; at the same time I cried: "I shall not be alive to-morrow." They tried to encourage me, arguing that my illness would pass over, since it came from excessive fatigue. In this way I spent two hours battling with the fever, which steadily increased, and calling out continually, "I feel that I am dying." My housekeeper, who was named Mona Fiore da Castel del Rio, a very notable manager and no less warm-hearted, kept chiding me for my discouragement; but, on the other hand, she paid me every kind attention which was possible. However, the sight of my physical pain and moral dejection so affected her, that, in spite of that brave heart of hers, she could not refrain from shedding tears; and yet, so far as she was able, she took good

19. The translator, John Addington Symonds, explains in his gloss: "The *canali* or channels were sluices for carrying the molten metal from the furnace into the mould. The *mandriani*, which I have translated by iron crooks, were poles fitted at the end with curved irons, by which the openings of the furnace, plugs, or in Italian *spine*, could be partially or wholly driven back, so as to let the molten metal flow through the channels into the mould. When the metal reached the mould, it entered in a red-hot stream between the *tonaca*, or outside mould, and the *anima*, or inner block, filling up exactly the space which had previously been occupied by the wax extracted by a method of slow burning alluded to above."

care I should not see them. While I was thus terribly afflicted, I beheld the figure of a man enter my chamber, twisted in his body
into the form of a capital S. He raised a lamentable, doleful voice,
like one who announces their last hour to men condemned to die
upon the scaffold, and spoke these words: "O Benvenuto! your
statue is spoiled, and there is no hope whatever of saving it." No
sooner had I heard the shriek of that wretch than I gave a howl
which might have been heard from the sphere of flame. Jumping
from my bed, I seized my clothes and began to dress. The maids,
and my lad, and every one who came around to help me, got kicks
or blows of the fist, while I kept crying out in lamentation "Ah!
traitors! enviers! This is an act of treason, done by malice prepense!
But I swear by God that I will sift it to the bottom, and before I
die will leave such witness to the world of what I can do as shall
make a score of mortals marvel."

When I had got my clothes on, I strode with soul bent on mischief toward the workshop; there I beheld the men, whom I had
left erewhile in such high spirits, standing stupefied and downcast.
I began at once and spoke: "Up with you! Attend to me! Since you
have not been able or willing to obey the directions I gave you,
obey me now that I am with you to conduct my work in person.
Let no one contradict me, for in cases like this we need the aid of
hand and hearing, not of advice." When I had uttered these words,
a certain Maestro Alessandro Lastricati broke silence and said:
"Look you, Benvenuto, you are going to attempt an enterprise
which the laws of art do not sanction, and which cannot succeed."
I turned upon him with such fury and so full of mischief, that he
and all the rest of them exclaimed with one voice: "On then! Give
orders! We will obey your least commands, so long as life is left in
us." I believe they spoke thus feelingly because they thought I must
fall shortly dead upon the ground. I went immediately to inspect
the furnace, and found that the metal was all curdled; an accident
which we express by "being caked." I told two of the hands to cross
the road, and fetch from the house of the butcher Capretta, a load
of young oak-wood, which had lain dry for above a year; this wood
had been previously offered me by Madame Ginevra, wife of the
said Capretta. So soon as the first armfuls arrived, I began to fill
the grate beneath the furnace. Now oak-wood of that kind heats
more powerfully than any other sort of tree; and for this reason,
where a slow fire is wanted, as in the case of gun-foundry, alder or
pine is preferred. Accordingly, when the logs took fire, oh! how the
cake began to stir beneath that awful heat, to glow and sparkle in a
blaze! At the same time I kept stirring up the channels, and sent
men upon the roof to stop the conflagration, which had gathered
force from the increased combustion in the furnace; also I caused

boards, carpets, and other hangings to be set up against the garden, in order to protect us from the violence of the rain.

When I had thus provided against these several disasters, I roared out first to one man and then to another: "Bring this thing here! Take that thing there!" At this crisis, when the whole gang saw the cake was on the point of melting, they did my bidding, each fellow working with the strength of three. I then ordered half a pig of pewter to be brought, which weighed about sixty pounds, and flung it into the middle of the cake inside the furnace. By this means, and by piling on wood and stirring now with pokers and now with iron rods, the curdled mass rapidly began to liquefy. Then, knowing I had brought the dead to life again, against the firm opinion of those ignoramuses, I felt such vigour fill my veins, that all those pains of fever, all those fears of death, were quite forgotten.

All of a sudden an explosion took place, attended by a tremendous flash of flame, as though a thunderbolt had formed and been discharged amongst us. Unwonted and appalling terror astonied every one, and me more even than the rest. When the din was over and the dazzling light extinguished, we began to look each other in the face. Then I discovered that the cap of the furnace had blown up, and the bronze was bubbling over from its source beneath. So I had the mouths of my mould immediately opened, and at the same time drove in the two plugs which kept back the molten metal. But I noticed that it did not flow as rapidly as usual, the reason being probably that the fierce heat of the fire we kindled had consumed its base alloy. Accordingly I sent for all my pewter platters, porringers, and dishes, to the number of some two hundred pieces, and had a portion of them cast, one by one, into the channels, the rest into the furnace. This expedient succeeded, and every one could now perceive that my bronze was in most perfect liquefaction, and my mould was filling; whereupon they all with heartiness and happy cheer assisted and obeyed my bidding, while I, now here, now there, gave orders, helped with my own hands, and cried aloud: "O God! Thou that by Thy immeasurable power didst rise from the dead, and in Thy glory didst ascend to heaven!" . . . even thus in a moment my mould was filled; and seeing my work finished, I fell upon my knees, and with all my heart gave thanks to God.

After all was over, I turned to a plate of salad on a bench there, and ate with hearty appetite, and drank together with the whole crew. Afterwards I retired to bed, healthy and happy, for it was now two hours before morning, and slept as sweetly as though I had never felt a touch of illness. My good housekeeper, without my giving any orders, had prepared a fat capon for my repast. So that, when I rose, about the hour for breaking fast, she presented herself with a smiling countenance, and said: "Oh! is that the man who felt that he was dying? Upon my word, I think the blows and kicks you dealt us last night, when you were so enraged, and had that demon in your body as it seemed, must have frightened away your mortal fever! The fever feared that it might catch it too, as we did!" All my poor household, relieved in like measure from anxiety and overwhelming labour, went at once to buy earthen vessels in order to replace the pewter I had cast away. Then we dined together joyfully; nay, I cannot remember a day in my whole life when I dined with greater gladness or a better appetite.

After our meal I received visits from the several men who had assisted me. They exchanged congratulations, and thanked God for our success, saying they had learned and seen things done which other masters judged impossible. I too grew somewhat glorious; and deeming I had shown myself a man of talent, indulged a boastful humour. So I thrust my hand into my purse, and paid them all to their full satisfaction.

That evil fellow, my mortal foe, Messer Pier Francesco Ricci, majordomo of the Duke, took great pains to find out how the affair had gone. In answer to his questions, the two men whom I suspected of having caked my metal for me, said I was no man, but of a certainty some powerful devil, since I had accomplished what no craft of the art could do; indeed they did not believe a mere ordinary fiend could work such miracles as I in other ways had shown. They exaggerated the whole affair so much, possibly in order to excuse their own part in it, that the majordomo wrote an account to the Duke, who was then in Pisa, far more marvellous and full of thrilling incidents than what they had narrated.

After I had let my statue cool for two whole days, I began to uncover it by slow degrees. The first thing I found was that the head of Medusa had come out most admirably, thanks to the air-vents; for, as I had told the Duke, it is the nature of fire to ascend. Upon advancing farther, I discovered that the other head, that, namely, of Perseus, had succeeded no less admirably; and this astonished me far more, because it is at a considerably lower level than that of the Medusa. Now the mouths of the mould were placed above the head of Perseus and behind his shoulders; and I found that all the bronze my furnace contained had been exhausted in the head of this figure. It was a miracle to observe that not one fragment remained in the orifice of the channel, and that nothing was wanting to the statue. In my great astonishment I seemed to see in this the hand of God arranging and controlling all.

I went on uncovering the statue with success, and ascertained that everything had come out in perfect order, until I reached the foot of the right leg on which the statue rests. There the heel itself was formed, and going farther, I found the foot apparently complete. This gave me great joy on the one side, but was half un-welcome to me on the other, merely because I had told the Duke that it could not come out. However, when I reached the end, it appeared that the toes and a little piece above them were unfin-ished, so that about half the foot was wanting. Although I knew that this would add a trifle to my labour, I was very well pleased, because I could now prove to the Duke how well I understood my business. It is true that far more of the foot than I expected had been perfectly formed; the reason of this was that, from causes I have recently described, the bronze was hotter than our rules of art prescribe; also that I had been obliged to supplement the alloy with my pewter cups and platters, which no one else, I think, had ever done before.

Having now ascertained how successfully my work had been ac-complished, I lost no time in hurrying to Pisa, where I found the Duke. He gave me a most gracious reception, as did also the Duchess; and although the majordomo had informed them of the whole proceedings, their Excellencies deemed my performance far more stupendous and astonishing when they heard the tale from my own mouth. . . .

PIETRO ARETINO

(1492–1556)

Letters (Lettere)*

["*Certainly you must feel free now . . .*"]

To the King of France

Although your loss has been another man's gain, I do not know, Most Christian Sire, who deserves the greatest congratulations, the conquered or the conqueror.[1] For after the treacherous trick played upon you by Fate, you, Francis, can now free your mind from any doubt that she can take a king prisoner, whereas Charles, as he thinks over the prize which Chance has given him, must find his mind a prey to the realization that she could do the same thing to an emperor.

Certainly you must feel free now that you are aware how fickle good fortune is, and therefore, how greatly to be scorned. Charles, by the same token, must now be the bondsman, knowing how fair-spoken she is, and therefore to be feared. Yes, His Majesty must

* Reprinted from *The Letters of Pietro Aretino* by Thomas C. Chubb. Archon Books, 1971. Reprinted by permission.
1. The King of France, Francis I, had been defeated by the Emperor, Charles V, at the batle of Pavia on February 25, 1525, and was now the Emperor's captive. Aretino, who had in Francis one of his major supporters and patrons, received the news in Rome and wrote him this self-consciously noble and paradoxically wise letter, not without having copies of it printed, to be sold in the streets and in bookshops.

now be robed in cares, but your cares have been taken from you.

Do not complain, then, of Lady Luck. She cannot do you any more harm, since she has already done her worst to you by bringing you to the state in which you now are. Having done this, she has made all your good qualities shine forth resplendently. You glitter with your long-suffering forebearance, and because you have shown the firmest constancy in the world. By allowing virtues of this sort to rule over your heart and mind, you have turned Fortune into a woman. If you can believe the complaints of most men, she is usually a goddess.

Indeed, for my part I believe that Fortune, who now perceives that, although some lose by winning, you have won by losing, already holds that it was shabby to triumph over you, who now triumph over her. She realizes that the dire plight which she prepared for you has lifted you up to heaven, when it was meant to plunge you into the abyss.

She has learned this from the way you bear Adversity. You have learned to look her in the face, and to know that her reverses are like lamps of life to anyone who can still believe in himself.

For, behold, victory does not make Caesar[2] happy, as one might expect it to, for what men see and what they think has happened is not necessarily the end of the story. It is but the shadow of good fortune's countenance. And not only he may end up unhappy, but those stars and virtues to which he owes his success may fail him if it turn out that he has flouted God's will.

I assert, therefore that you are much more than the equal of any conqueror, since with your wisdom you now triumph over the very one who beat you with his strength. It is worth considering, too, that Augustus,[3] in whose power you now are, has only one way of showing you that he is generous, whereas you have many ways of showing yourself magnanimous to him.

His one way is clemency. If he fails in that, you can conquer him by bearing bravely his failure to be clement. You will prevail over him by being patient. Patience is always victorious, since it is the most sterling of all virtues and none other more worthy can be found in any man. In fact if a king like yourself—a king who is the handiwork of heaven—decks himself in patience, does he not become like God? They merit more praise who know how to suffer misfortune, than those who are moderate in success. A high heart must stand up under disaster. To run away from it, is low and vile.

And where else too, did one ever see so great a king, amid the shifts and changes of a day of battle, redden his own sword with the blood of his enemies? When you did this you compelled Fortune to confess that she took a man who fought himself and not one who had others fight for him.[4] You bore witness that human destiny is

---

2. the Emperor, Charles V.
3. same as above.
4. Francis himself fought on the battle-field while the Emperor rather entrusted the conduct of war campaigns to his generals.

not governed blindly, but by an intricate interplay of causes which still remain hidden to us. But indeed victory is the downfall of the man who wins it and the salvation of the loser, for the conqueror, made blind with insolence and pride, forgets God and remembers himself, but the vanquished, his mind lighted with modesty and humility, forgets himself, and thinks about the Deity. And who does not know that Fortune never favors those who sleep in her lap? Indeed, she takes their wits away.

Therefore, do not be ashamed of the buffet which she has given you. You will be worthy of every evil if your cheeks crimson at your sad fate. Remember, instead, all the things which your mind teaches you about Fate's annoyances. Lean, with all the endowment of strength your soul has given you, against the column of your fortitude. Stand up boldly and with that high spirit which burns always in your valiant, kingly heart. Remember that your worth makes men afraid as much when you are bound, as when you are free.

And let whatever misfortune you have found to be a bridle which keeps you from never even contemplating, not to say essaying any rash adventure. Then, in truth, a day will come when remembering your present plight will be both sweet and useful to you.

It is my opinion that it pleased Christ to let you fall into the power of your adversary for no other reason than to show you that you were a man and that Charles was also. And if you measure the shadow cast by your body, you will find it neither greater nor less than it was before you became the vanquished and your rival the victor.

Rome, April 24, 1525

["*. . . you conduct yourself*
as one who is aware that he is mortal"]

To the Emperor

It is a truism, O Caesar,[1] that good luck grows by leaps and bounds, and always far outstrips its modest beginnings.

This is manifest in the case of Your Majesty. For scarcely were those prison gates closed from which you had released a king[2] so as to conquer him with your clemency as you had already with your arms, than fate and your might placed the freedom of the Pope[3] in your hands.

---

1. Charles V. He held Aretino in considerably high esteem, to the point of bestowing a yearly pension upon him.
2. Francis I.
3. After the "sack of Rome" (cf. our first Cellini selection, p. 1174, n. 1), Pope Clement was the Emperor's captive. Aretino boasted of having predicted the Roman disaster, and he entertained no friendly feelings toward the Roman court; but he was repelled by atrocities perpetrated by the Emperor's army, and besides, as this and the following letter show, he was supporting a reunion between Pope and Emperor.

It is now plain to all that you have some of God's own qualities Whose goodness it is that has made you be so merciful, for there is no other person who would have held firm in playing this difficult role. You alone have a soul which is capable of emulating the greatness of His forgiving nature which is the scourge with which He humbles the pride of the contumaceous who are punished by His acts of loving kindness.

For who else but yourself would let his mind, heart, nay inmost thoughts dwell upon the idea of setting free an enemy? Who except you would have tempted fate by trusting in the promises—and the fickleness and pride—of a conquered prince? Is it not a well-known characteristic of the vanquished, not merely to give over soul and body to the pursuit of vengeance but their treasures and their people too?

Because you did this, the world has been able to see what power the generosity of mercy has in Caesar's heart. He can let it have this power since it is protected by his military might. The world has been able to see too that it can take hope from the former and must respect the latter, but that it must face the consequences of one or the other.

Besides this, who ever heard of any man except Charles who in the hour of triumph tried both to acknowledge God and know himself?

Yet that you acknowledge God is apparent in the generous actions by which you pay tribute to Him, and that you know yourself is made manifest by the fact that you conduct yourself as one who is aware that he is mortal. A great many bright lamps should be lighted in honor of this, since to acknowledge God in the hour of triumph is to make certain of eternal blessings, while he who is aware of his limitations when Fate favors him, knows God and is known of Him, and hence takes on some of His attributes.

This being so, once again put into practice that benign clemency of yours, without which, I insist, fame has her wing-feathers plucked, and glory is burned out. For since generosity to the enemy is the triumphal crown of the victor, to practice mercy will bring you greater honor than any conquest, and indeed you might call that victory lost which does not bring mercy in its train.

Mercy is the shadow of the arm of God and it is truly in your heart. Who doubts then, that you will set free the Shepherd of the Church? He was not led into captivity by the contumely of arrogant war, but by Heaven itself which turned the winds of adversity against the head of the wicked Papal court, and thus permitted Rome to suffer.

It would not do for the justice of your contempt to turn into cruelty. Let it please you, therefore, to bid the destruction to proceed no further. In your hands are two things—religious devotion and the Pope. Keep your devotion and set the Pope free. Give back to Christ His Vicar. It was His favor who brought you victory. Last of all, do not permit the exultation of triumph to deter you from acting as you always have. If you act thus, no other crown of glory which you have won, or which God and good fortune owe to the remaining years of your illustrious life, will be more worthy of admiration.

But who would not place his hopes in the goodness, piety and courtesy of His Majesty Charles V? He is always Caesar and he is always august.

Venice, May 20, 1527

["... *it was God's will*
that delivered you into Caesar's hands"]

To Pope Clement VII

My lord, although Fate rules the affairs of men in such a manner that no foresight upon their part can alter its decrees, yet when God intervenes, even Fate must bow to Him. Therefore, a man who has fallen as Your Holiness has should turn to Jesus in his prayers and not blame it upon Fate.

It was inevitable that the Vicar of Christ should pay off, with his own woe and downfall, the debts which had been piled up by others in his name.[1] If he had not been taken prisoner, that Justice which chastises error could not have been made known to all the world. You should console yourself with that thought amid your tribulations, for it was God's will that delivered you into Caesar's hands. He willed that you should know divine mercy and human clemency at the same time.

And since it ever brings honor to a brave and thoughtful ruler who has always girded himself against the outrages of misfortune to bear with dignity whatsoever evils this same fortune wishes to bestow upon him, think of the glory that will be yours if, now that you have come to the end of all that zeal and might and counsel could accomplish, you comfort yourself with patience and resolve to bear all that God has set before you! Look into His supreme mind, and when you have thought deeply upon His goodness, tell me if you would be worthy of Him if you did not hope that He would then permit you to mount higher than you have ever before! Or do you doubt that He will stand always at the right hand of His holy church? Do you doubt that He will guide you? And do you think that if He does guide you, your downfall will be a reality and not merely an illusion?

But one thing must be real, and not just seeming: Your Holiness must turn your mind to forgiveness and not to revenge,[2] for only by truly wishing to pardon and not to avenge, can you fit yourself for a role which is worthy of the high office which you hold. And, anyway, what deed would make you more worthy of the title of

---

1. Aretino blamed the Pope's misfortunes mainly on the bad counsel of his court.

2. against Charles V.

"most holy" or "most blessed" than to conquer hate with piety and enmity with being generous? Does not the grindstone whet steel and make it all the sharper? So, too, adversity tempers a generous soul and makes it able to laugh at its calamity. You would have to curse Fate if you did not realize the large implications of the misfortune which took away your liberty.

I do not deny that you have been assailed by every kind of cruel misfortune. Nor do I deny that because of this you have discovered that patriotism has been corrupted, that there is treachery among your friends, that your soldiers can tremble, your benefactors be ungrateful, and the temporal lords faithless and scornful. But even if God did not come to your aid, your conduct in adversity could at least teach them that you know how to serve as well as rule.

Therefore, to Him who hath power over all things, yield all things, and yielding them, give thanks that He has permitted you to fall into the hands of the Emperor.[3] He is the cornerstone of the church just as you are its father, and you can now make the Papal wishes and the Imperial plans agree. If you do this, your renown will be greater than ever. It will shine in every part of the known world.

For behold the good Charles courteously restoring you to your former state. Behold him kneeling before you with that reverence which we owe to the man who sits in Christ's seat and is fitting for the one who wears the crown of Caesar.[4]

His Majesty has no false pride. Embrace him, therefore, in the arms of that power which comes from above, and turning his Catholic sword against the haughty East,[5] make him do the thing you ought to want him to do.

Then from the sorry state in which you have been placed by the lewd doings of your priests, you will arise to reap the reward of your long suffering. For truly, and with constancy, Your Holiness has suffered.

Venice, the last of May, 1527

3. Aretino's rhetoric subtly tends to show that a policy of conciliation with the Emperor is dictated by Providence.
4. The alliance between Pope and Emperor had indeed its consecration in 1529 when Pope Clement in Bologna placed the imperial crown on Charles' head.
5. The threat from the Turks, apart from more general considerations, was strongly felt by Aretino whose adopted country was the Venetian Republic.

[*"Your womanly wisdom moves . . . in a royal manner . . ."*]

To Signora Angela Zaffetta[1]

Even though Rumor, pretending that she really knows something, has gone about Italy spreading the report that in your person

1. Angela del Moro, known as La Zaffetta. In the long printed roll of Venetian courtesans (Venice, 1535) which lists their names and prices, she was No. 3. A leading beauty, she was one of Titian's models and had Cardinal Ippolito de' Medici among her lovers.

and by your doings, Love has done me wrong, the truth is that I have always held your favor to be a fine thing since there is no fraud in anything which you do.

Indeed, I give you the palm among all those of your kind there ever were. More than anyone else you know how to put the mask of decency upon the face of lust, gaining by your wisdom and discretion both riches and praise.

You do not use your wiles—which are the essence of a harlot's trade—to betray men, but rather with such skill that he who spends his money on you, swears he is the gainer. It would not be possible to describe the charms with which you win new friends, nor the means you employ to draw to your house those who are doubtful and hesitate between a *yes* and a *no*. It would be difficult even to imagine the effort you make to keep the affection of those who have become your servants.

You distribute so well your kisses, your caresses, your laughter and your bed sharings that no one ever hears anyone quarrel nor curse at you nor complain. Modest in your demands, you take what is given you without trying to appropriate what is not. Your anger only comes at the right time, yet you are not anxious to become known as "the mistress of flatteries", nor, either, to keep people dancing on a string. You hold in contempt all those who study the devices of Nanna and of Pippa.[2]

You are not suspicious when there is no need to be suspicious, thus making people jealous who never even thought of it. You do not pull woes and consolations from your pocket, nor, pretending that you are in love, do you die and come to life again whenever you wish.

You do not rowel the flanks of gullible suitors with the spurs of your serving maids whom you have taught to swear that you do not eat, drink, sleep or find any peace on their account, and whom you make assert that you had come near to hanging yourself because your lover visited another lady. By God no, you are not one of those who are always ready with tears, and who, when they do weep, mingle their weeping with certain little sighs and sobs which come all too easily from the heart, the while they scratch their heads and bite their fingers with an "Alas! So be it!" in a hoarse and scarce-heard voice. Nor do you busy yourself with keeping those who want to go, while sending off the ones who long to stay. There is no place in your soul for such niggling deceits.

Your womanly wisdom moves, rather, in a royal manner, nor is feminine gossip to your taste, nor do you gather around you frivolous ladies and conceited men. Those who deal honorably rejoice in your gentle beauty which makes you shine in a most rare fashion.

2. mother and daughter in Aretino's celebrated *Ragionamenti* (conversations among courtesans).

Your hopes remain unshaken that you will attain a position in which you can triumph over the things which you must do.

Lying, envy, and slander—once again the innate characteristics of a harlot—do not keep your mind and your tongue in a constant turmoil. You caress virtue and adore the virtuous. This is something which is usually a stranger to the habits and the nature of those who, for a price, yield to the desires of others.

And so I give myself to your ladyship, feeling that your ladyship is worthy.

Venice, December 15, 1537

[*Five letters to a "unique friend"*]

To Titian[1]

[1]

O unique friend of mine, my lady Fame takes such great pleasure in proclaiming the miracle wrought by your brushes when you painted a portrait of the Pope,[2] that even if she did not also have an obligation to make known to the whole world the largeness of soul which you demonstrated in refusing the office of *piombatore*[3] which His Holiness thought to give you in reward for this painting, she would still never come to the end of trumpeting how living it was, and how animated, and how true to life.

But every masterpiece of yours, even though it be divine, has to take second place to what you did in scorning to accept something that any other painter would have called himself happy to have obtained. You alone demonstrated, by not being willing to take it, how much inferior Rome is to Venice both in worth and in beauty, and how much more secular garb was worth than the vile habits of a priest.

Over and above all this, the goodness of your heart should be praised with lip and pen, for you were too straightforward to want to make yourself rich if, so doing, you made two other persons poor. For if they made you an associate of the two who hold the office, needs must you would take part of the earnings of both one and the other.

In that way your lofty efforts would have been rewarded without any cost to the man who is under obligation to reward them.

But long live Vecelli who esteems a good name more than ample revenues!

Verona, July, 1543

1. Titian (Tiziano Vecellio, 1477–1576) was Aretino's constant companion in Venice. His splendid portrait of Aretino was painted in the same year this letter was written.
2. Paul III (Alessandro Farnese).
3. a sealer of papal bulls.

[2]

Having eaten alone, my good friend, although it is not my usual habit, or to put it better, having eaten in the company of an unpleasant quartan fever which did not even permit me to enjoy my food, I arise from the table consumed by the same despondency with which I had sat down, and in this mood I leaned my arm against the window sill, and on my arm my chest, and indeed almost my whole body. Then I began to look upon the marvelous scene outside.

Infinite boats, some laden with foreigners and others with the people of our own city, were moving about on the water. They diverted not only the onlookers, but the Grand Canal itself which diverts all those who plough its waves. In front of my eyes, two gondolas were having a race. Each was guided by a famous boatman and their contest gave great sport to a crowd of spectators, which thronged the Rialto Bridge, the fish markets, the Santa Sofia ferry landing, and the Casa da Mosto to see the regatta.

But while this group and that one seethed here and there applauding joyously, I, who was almost a man who was so revolting to himself that he does not know what to do either with his mind or with his thoughts, suddenly turned my eyes toward the sky. Since God created it, it had never been so beautiful with its subtle pattern of lights and shades. Indeed, anyone who had wished to record it would have been consumed with envy because he was not you. You will see this when I try to tell you about it.

To begin with, although the houses were of real stone, they seemed to be some unreal fabric. Next you must visualize the atmosphere. In some places, it was transparent and living, in other places turgid and dead. Think, too, of how I marvelled at the clouds, although in reality they were nothing but condensed humidity. In the center of the scene, half of them seemed to touch the very roofs of the houses, while the other receded into distance. On the right hand, they were like a poised mass of gray-black smoke.

Certainly, I was astonished at the various colors which they showed. Those near at hand burned with the flames of the sun's fire, while those in the distance had the dull glow of half-molten lead. Oh, with what clever strokes the paint brushes of nature gave perspective to the very air, withdrawing it skillfully from the palaces just as you, Titian, make it draw backward in your landscapes. In certain places, there appeared a green-blue, and in other a blue-green, which were truly composed by the errant fancy of nature, the master of all great masters. With lights and shadows, she brought forth or subdued in manner that which she thought ought to be brought forth or subdued.

And so I, who know that your brushes are the very soul of her soul, cried out three or four times: "O Titian, where are you now?"

By my faith, if you had painted what I describe to you, you would have turned men stock-still with the same astonishment that confounded me when I looked upon the scene that I am telling about, and realized that its wonder would not last.

Venice, May, 1544

[3]

Neither Apelles, nor Praxiteles, nor any of the others who of old carved statues or painted pictures of whatsoever Prince or King, can boast of having received rewards of gold or gems that even partly approached the reward that you have received from His Most High Majesty[1] when he deemed that you alone were worthy to be summoned to him in the midst of such disordered times. He thus showed that he attached more importance to you than he does to all the leagues and the alliances which he is organizing throughout the world.

For behold it has come to pass that he who swore in envy's name that he did not want to set himself upon the plane of the gods by means of paintings or of marble, and who is content merely to be carven and painted in the souls of the wise and of the good, now allows himself to be portrayed by your inimitable brush for the sole reason that it will please your unique genius.

So go to him, and when you are at his feet revere him with your whole being—and in my name also.

Venice, December, 1547

1. Charles V. Titian was the Emperor's   official painter.

[4]

Although I have had only one letter from you since you arrived at court,[1] I cannot yet persuade myself that the favors of His Majesty have so inflated your ego that you no longer deign to notice your friends. But if that were true which cannot be true, I would lament Caesar's grace toward you instead of congratulating you. Unfortunate is that fortune which makes a man overbearing!

But even if ambition had seized you by the hair with the hands of her pride, I know that you would deal with me with your accustomed modesty. You know that I could make even the Emperor a laughing stock if he should make a jest of me.

But now purge yourself from even the appearance of fault by writing me just two words, for Messer Giovanni[2] has told me that within four days you will follow the greeting which you sent me by him with a letter.

1. the Emperor's court at Augsburg. During this prolonged stay at court, Titian produced, among many others, one of his most famous portraits, *Charles V at the Battle of Mühlberg.*
2. possibly a sculptor friend.

In the meanwhile Sansovino[3] kisses you on the face and I kiss you on the forehead.

Venice, April, 1548

3. Jacopo Sansovino (1486–1570), the famous sculptor and architect, had left Rome after the "sack" of that city and did the most important part of his work in Venice. He sculpted Aretino's head as one of the Evangelists on the door of the sacristy of St. Mark's.

[5]

My honorable gossip, your letter of the 4th instant which Messer Aeneas[1] brought me, was much appreciated, because it assured me that I need no longer doubt that you had arrived at Augsburg[2] safe and sound. But the second letter I received—that of the 11th—made me leap for joy.

Why not? Who would not rejoice in his heart, when he heard with what affectionate benignity of grace His Majesty, as soon as he saw you, asked how I was, and whether you brought letters from me, and then added (after he had read first to himself and then aloud what I had humbly written him) that although he had not yet exerted his good offices with the Pope on my behalf,[3] he would answer my letter immediately?

He said this in the presence of His Highness, of the Duke of Alva and of Davila[4] with such honest pleasure that I must thank God for it all. It comes from His mercy and not from any worth that is now in me, or that you will ever see.

To you, divine man, I will say no more. Since we two are really one, to thank you would be superfluous.

Venice, November, 1550

1. Enea Parmigiano, a painter and engraver.
2. cf. Letter 4, page 1206, note 1.
3. Aretino was hoping, with some foundation, to obtain a cardinalate.
4. Francisco Alvarez de Toledo (1515–1584), who commanded the Emperor's armies in Italy.

[" . . . *the fury of my pen*"]

To Vassallo[1]

My lord Abbot, those people who curse me because they have come to the conclusion that the princes pay me tribute for fear that I will libel them, and not because they want my praises, are certainly bereft of that kind of judgment that can tell good from evil. The greater part of the world's mighty do not fear the anger of the Lord, yet they do fear the fury of my pen. That is because it praises the virtuous every day and heaps scorn upon the unrighteous.

Venice, December, 1552

1. a churchman not further identified.

MICHEL DE MONTAIGNE

(1533–1592)

Essays (Essais)*

Of Cannibals†

When King Pyrrhus[1] passed over into Italy, after acknowledging the good order that prevailed in the army that the Romans had sent to meet him, he said, 'I know not what barbarians are these (for so the Greeks called all foreign nations), but the disposition of this army I see is by no means barbarous'. The Greeks said the same of the army which Flaminius brought into their country, as did also Philip, on viewing from an eminence the orderly distribution of the Roman camp, in his kingdom, under Publius Sulpicius Galba.[2] Thereby we may see how we should be on our guard against clinging to vulgar opinions, and how we should judge things by the light of reason, and not from common rumour.

I had living with me for a long time a man who had lived for ten or twelve years in that other world which was discovered in our century, in that place where Villegaignon landed, which he called *Antarctic France*.[3] This discovery of an unbounded country seems to me worthy of consideration. I do not know that I could pledge myself that some other discovery may not be made in the future, so many persons greater than we having been mistaken about this one. I fear our eyes are greater than our bellies, and that we have more curiosity than capacity. We embrace all, but we clasp only wind.

Plato[4] introduces Solon, telling how he had learned of the priests of the city of Saïs in Egypt that, in days of old and before the Deluge, there was a large island named Atlantis, directly at the mouth of the Strait of Gibraltar, which contained more countries than all Asia and Africa together; and that the kings of that region, who not only possessed that island, but had extended their dominion so far into the mainland, that of the breadth of Africa they

---

* Books I and II were published in 1580; Book II, together with Books I and II revised and amplified, in 1588; a posthumous edition, with further additions, in 1595. Our text is from *The Essays of Montaigne*, translated by E. J. Trechmann, published by the Oxford University Press.

† *Essays*, Book I, Chapter 31.

1. king of Epirus, in Greece, fought the Romans in Italy in 280 B.C.

2. Both Titus Quinctius Flaminius (mentioned earlier in this sentence) and Publius Sulpicius Galba were Roman statesmen and generals who fought Philip V of Macedon in the early years of the second century B.C.

3. in Brazil. Villegaignon landed there in 1557.

4. in his *Timaeus*.

held as far as Egypt, and of the length of Europe as far as Tuscany, attempted to stride even into Asia, and to subjugate all the nations that border on the Mediterranean Sea as far as the gulf of the Greater Sea,[5] and to that end traversed the Spains, Gaul, Italy, as far as Greece, where the Athenians stood up against them; but that some time after both the Athenians and they and their island were swallowed up by the Flood.

It is most likely that that extreme watery devastation has caused some wonderful alterations in the habitations of the earth, as it is thought that the sea cut off Sicily from Italy,

These lands, 'tis said, one continent of yore
(Such change can ages work) an earthquake tore
Asunder; in with havoc rushed the main,
And far Sicilia from Hesperia bore,
And now, where leapt the parted lands in twain,
The narrow tide pours through, 'twixt severed town and plain;

(Virgil.)[6]

Cyprus from Syria, the island of Negropont from the mainland of Boeotia; and elsewhere joined lands which were divided, by filling up the channels between them with sand and mud:

Swamps, sterile long, all plashy, rank and drear,
Groan 'neath the plough, and feed whole cities near.

(Horace.)[7]

But it does not appear very likely that that great island was the new world that we have lately discovered, for it almost touched Spain, and it would have been an incredible result of an inundation to have removed it as far back as it is, more than twelve hundred leagues; besides that our modern navigators have already almost discovered it to be no island, but a firm land holding together with the East Indies on the one hand, and on the other with the lands which lie under the two poles; or, if it is separated from them, it is by so narrow a strait and interval, that it does not on that account deserve to be called an island.

It would seem that there are movements, some natural, others diseased, in those great bodies as well as in our own. When I consider the inroads that my river, the Dordogne, is making even in my time, upon the right bank in its descent, and that in twenty years it has gained so much ground, and robbed many buildings of their

5. the Black Sea.
6. *Aeneid*, Book III, ll. 414 ff.

7. *Art of Poetry*, ll. 65 f.

foundations, I plainly see that an extraordinary disturbance is going on; for if it had always been going on at this rate, or were to do so in the future, the face of the world would be entirely altered. But rivers are subject to changes: now they overflow in one direction, now in another, now they keep within their beds. I do not speak of the sudden inundations whose causes are manifest. In Médoc, along the sea-shore, my brother the Sieur d'Arsac sees an estate of his buried beneath the sands that the sea vomits before it; the tops of several buildings are still visible; his rents and domains have been converted into very poor pasturage. The inhabitants say that the sea has been for some time pushing so strongly towards them, that they have lost four leagues of land. These sands are its harbingers, and we see great dunes of moving sand, that march half a league before it, and are gaining ground.

The other testimony from antiquity, from which some infer this discovery, is in Aristotle, if at least that little book *Of Unheard-of Marvels* be his. He there relates how certain Carthaginians, having ventured across the Atlantic Sea, outside the Strait of Gibraltar, and navigated a long time, had at last discovered a large fertile island, all clothed in woods, and watered by broad and deep rivers, far remote from any mainland; and that they, and others after them, attracted by the goodness and fertility of the soil, had gone thither with their wives and children and begun to settle there. The lords of Carthage, seeing that their country was gradually becoming depopulated, expressly forbade any more to go there, on pain of death, and drove out those new settlers, fearing, it is said, lest in course of time they might multiply to such an extent as to supplant themselves and ruin their state. This narration of Aristotle no more agrees with our new-found lands than the other.

This man[8] I had was a simple and ignorant fellow: hence the more fit to give true evidence; for your sophisticated men are more curious observers, and take in more things, but they glose them; to lend weight to their interpretations and induce your belief, they cannot help altering their story a little. They never describe things as they really are, but bend them and mask them according to the point of view from which they see things, and, to make their judgements the more credible and attractive, they are not loath to add a little to their matter, and to spin out and amplify their tale. Now we need either a very truthful man, or one so simple that he has not the art of building up and giving an air of probability to fictions, and is wedded to no theory. Such was my man; and he has besides at different times brought several sailors and traders to see

8. Montaigne goes back to the man referred to in the second paragraph of this essay.

me, whom he had known on that voyage. So I shall content myself with his information, without troubling myself about what the cosmographers may say about it.

We need topographers who would give us an exact account of the places which they have visited. But because they have this advantage over us that they have seen Palestine, they claim to enjoy the privilege of telling us new things of all the rest of the world. I would have every man write about what he knows, and no more than he knows, not only in this but on all other subjects. For a man may have some particular knowledge or experience of the nature of a river or a fountain, who otherwise knows no more than what everybody knows. Yet he will undertake, in order to circulate this little scrap of knowledge, to write a book on the whole science of physics. From this fault spring many great abuses.

Now, to return to my subject, from what I have heard of that nation, I can see nothing barbarous or uncivilized about it, except that we all call barbarism that which does not fit in with our usages. And indeed we have no other level of truth and reason but the example and model of the opinions and usages of the country we live in. There we always see the perfect religion, the perfect government, the perfect and accomplished manner of doing all things. Those people are wild in the sense in which we call wild the fruits that Nature has produced by herself and in her ordinary progress; whereas in truth it is those we have altered artificially and diverted from the common order, that we should rather call wild. In the first we still see, in full life and vigour, the genuine and most natural and useful virtues and properties, which we have bastardized in the latter, and only adapted to please our corrupt taste. And yet in some of the uncultivated fruits of those countries there is a delicacy of flavour that is excellent even to our taste, and rivals even our own. It is not reasonable that art should gain the point of honour over our great and powerful mother Nature. We have so overburdened the beauty and richness of her works with our inventions, that we have quite smothered her. And yet, wherever she shines in her purity, she marvellously puts to shame our vain and trivial efforts,

> Uncared, unmarked the ivy blossoms best;
> Midst desert rocks the ilex clusters still;
> And sweet the wild bird's untaught melody.
> (Propertius.)[9]

With all our efforts we are unable even to copy the nest of the

9. *Elegies*, Book I, Elegy ii, ll. 10 ff.

smallest of little birds, its contexture, its beauty and convenience; not so much as the web of the poor spider.

All things, says Plato,[10] are produced either by Nature, or by chance, or by art: the greatest and most beautiful by one or other of the two first; the least and most imperfect by the latter.

Those nations, then, appear to me so far barbarous in this sense, that their minds have been formed to a very slight degree, and that they are still very close to their original simplicity. They are still ruled by the laws of Nature, and very little corrupted by ours; but they are still in such a state of purity, that I am sometimes vexed that they were not known earlier, at a time when there were men who could have appreciated them better than we do.

I am sorry that Lycurgus[11] and Plato had no knowledge of them, for it seems to me that what we have learned by contact with those nations surpasses not only all the beautiful colours in which the poets have depicted the golden age, and all their ingenuity in inventing a happy state of man, but also the conceptions and desires of Philosophy herself. They were incapable of imagining so pure and native a simplicity, as that which we see by experience; nor could they have believed that human society could have been maintained with so little human artifice and solder. This is a nation,[12] I should say to Plato, which has no manner of traffic; no knowledge of letters; no science of numbers; no name of magistrate or statesman; no use for slaves; neither wealth nor poverty; no contracts; no successions; no partitions; no occupation but that of idleness; only a general respect of parents; no clothing; no agriculture; no metals; no use of wine or corn. The very words denoting falsehood, treachery, dissimulation, avarice, envy, detraction, pardon, unheard of. How far removed from this perfection would he find the ideal republic he imagined! *Men newly come from the hands of the gods* (Seneca).[13]

These manners first by nature taught. (Virgil.)[14]

For the rest, they live in a region with a very agreeable and very temperate climate, so that, according to my witnesses, a sick man is rarely seen; and they assured me that they had never seen any man shaking with palsy, or with dripping eyes, toothless or bent with age. They are settled along the sea-coast, and closed in on the land side by large and high mountains, the land between them and the sea extending for a hundred leagues or thereabouts. They have great

10. See his *Laws*.
11. the half-legendary Spartan lawgiver (ninth century B.C.).
12. The passage beginning here is always compared with Shakespeare, *The Tempest*, Act II, Scene 1, ll. 154 ff.
13. *Epistles*, Epistle xc.
14. *Georgics*, Book II, l. 20.

abundance of fish and flesh, which bear no resemblance to ours, and they eat them roasted without any other preparation. The first man who brought a horse thither, although he had associated with them on several previous voyages, so horrified them in the riding posture, that they shot him dead with arrows before recognizing him.

Their buildings are very long, capable of holding two or three hundred souls, covered with the bark of tall trees, the strips resting by one end on the ground, and leaning to and supporting one another at the top, after the manner of some of our barns, the coverings of which slope down to the ground and serve as sidewalls. They have a wood so hard that they can cut with it, of which they make their swords, and gridirons to roast their meat. Their beds are made of cotton tissue, suspended from the roof like those in our ships, each one having his own: for the women sleep apart from their husbands.

They rise with the sun and eat immediately after rising, for the whole day: for they have no other meal. They drink nothing with that meal, like some other Eastern peoples of whom Suidas[15] tells us, who drank apart from eating; but they drink several times a day, and to excess. Their drink is made of some root, and is of the colour of our claret wines, and they only drink it warm. This beverage will keep only two or three days; it has a slightly pungent taste, is anything but heady, good for the stomach, and laxative for such as are not used to it, but a very pleasant drink for those who are. For bread they use a certain white material resembling preserved coriander. I have tried some of it: it is sweet but rather tasteless.

The whole day is spent in dancing. The younger men hunt animals with bows. Some of the women meanwhile spend their time warming their drink, which is their chief duty. One of their old men, in the morning before they begin to eat, preaches to the whole barnful of people in common, walking from one end to the other, repeating the same words several times, until he has finished the round (for the buildings are quite a hundred paces in length). He recommends only two things, valour against the enemy and love to their wives. And they never fail to stress this obligation, which forms their refrain, 'that it is they who keep their wine warm and seasoned'.

In several places, among others in my house, may be seen the formation of their beds, of their ropes, their wooden swords and bracelets, with which they cover their wrists in battle, and large canes open at one end, by the sound of which they keep the time and rhythm of their dances. They are close shaven all over, and

15. a Byzantine lexicographer.

remove the hair much more neatly than we do although their razors are only made of wood or stone. They believe the soul to be immortal, and that those who have deserved well of the gods are lodged in that part of the heaven where the sun rises, and those who are damned in the west.

They have some kind of priest and prophet, who very seldom appears among the people, having his dwelling in the mountains. On his arrival there is a great feast and a solemn assembly of several villages (each barn, as I have described it, forms a village, and they are about a French league[16] distant one from the other). This prophet speaks to them in public, exhorting them to virtue and their duty; but their whole ethical science comprises only these two articles: an unfaltering courage in war and affection to their women. This man foretells things to come, and the issue they are to expect from their enterprises; urges them to war, or holds them back; but he does so on the understanding that, where he fails to prophesy correctly, and if things turn out otherwise than he has predicted, he is cut into a thousand pieces if he is caught, and condemned for a false prophet. For that reason he who has once miscalculated is seen no more.

Divination is a gift of God, wherefore to abuse it ought to be regarded as a punishable imposture. Among the Scythians, when the prophets failed to hit the mark, they were laid, shackled hand and foot, on a little cart filled with heather and drawn by oxen, on which they were burned. They who take in hand such matters as depend on the conduct of human capacity are to be excused if they do their best. But those others who come and delude us with assurances of an extraordinary faculty that is beyond our ken, should they not be punished when they fail to carry out what they promise, and for the temerity of their imposture?

They have their wars with the nations beyond their mountains, further back on the mainland, to which they go quite naked, with no other weapons but bows or wooden swords pointed at one end, after the fashion of the tongues of our boar-spears. It is marvellous with what obstinacy they fight their battles, which never end but in massacre and bloodshed: for of routs and terrors they know not even the meaning. Each man brings back as a trophy the head of the enemy he has slain, and fixes it over the entrance to his dwelling. After treating his prisoner well for a considerable time, and giving him all that hospitality can devise, his captor convokes a great gathering of his acquaintance. He ties a cord to one of his prisoner's arms, holding him at some distance for fear of being hurt, and gives the other arm to be held in the same way by his best friend;

16. about 2.49 miles.

and these two, in presence of the whole assembly, dispatch him with their swords. This done, they roast and eat him in common, and send bits of him to their absent friends. Not, as one might suppose, for nourishment, as the ancient Scythians used to do, but to signify an extreme revenge.

And that it is so, may be seen from this: having perceived that the Portuguese, who had allied themselves with their adversaries, inflicted a different kind of death on their prisoners, which was to bury them up to the waist, shoot the upper part of the bodies full of arrows, and afterwards to hang them; they imagined that these people of another world (seeing that they had sown the knowledge of a great many vices among their neighbours, and were much greater masters than themselves in every kind of wickedness) had some reason for adopting this kind of vengeance, and that it must be more painful than their own; wherefore they began to give up their old method, and followed this one.

I am not so much concerned that we should remark on the horrible barbarity of such acts, as that, whilst rightly judging their errors, we should be so blind to our own. I think there is more barbarity in eating a live than a dead man, in tearing on the rack and torturing the body of a man still full of feeling, in roasting him piecemeal and giving him to be bitten and mangled by dogs and swine (as we have not only read, but seen within fresh memory, not between old enemies, but between neighbours and fellow citizens, and, what is worse, under the cloak of piety and religion),[17] than in roasting and eating him after he is dead.

Chrysippus and Zeno, the leaders of the Stoic sect, thought indeed that there was no harm in making use of our carrion for any purpose in case of necessity, and of extracting nourishment from it. And our ancestors,[18] when besieged by Caesar in the city of Alexia, decided to relieve the famine during the siege by eating the bodies of the old men, women, and other persons incapable of fighting;

> Time was, the Gascons, as old tales relate,
> Thus fed, contended long with cruel fate.
> (Juvenal.)[19]

And physicians are not afraid of using it in all sorts of ways as cures, either for inward or outward application. But no man's brain was ever so disordered that he would excuse treachery, disloyalty, cruelty, tyranny, which are our ordinary vices.

17. The allusion is to the spectacles of religious warfare which Montaigne himself had witnessed in his time and country.
18. the Gauls.
19. *Satires.* Satire xv, ll. 93 f.

We may therefore well call those people barbarians in respect to the rules of reason, but not in respect to ourselves, who surpass them in every kind of barbarity.

Their warfare is entirely noble and generous, and is as fair and excusable as can be expected in that human disease: their only motive being a zeal for valour. They do not strive to conquer new territory, for they still enjoy that luxuriance of nature which provides them, without labour and pains, with all necessary things in such abundance, that they have no need to enlarge their borders. They are still in that happy state of not desiring more than their natural needs demand: all that is over and above it is for them superfluity.

They generally call each other, if of the same age, brothers; if younger, children; and the old men are fathers to all the others. These latter leave to their heirs in common the full and undivided possession of their property, without any but that pure title that Nature gives to her creatures, by bringing them into the world. If their neighbours cross the mountains to attack them, and gain the victory over them, the acquisition of the victor is the glory and advantage of having proved himself the superior in valour and virtue, for otherwise they have no need for the spoils of the vanquished; and so they return to their own country, where they have no want of any necessaries, nor even of that great portion, which is to know how to enjoy happily their condition, and be content with it. These do the same in their turn. They ask of their prisoners no other ransom but a confession and acknowledgement of being vanquished. But you will not find one in a whole century who would not rather die than yield, either by word or look, one tittle of an invincible greatness of courage; not one who would not rather be killed and eaten than even pray to be spared. They are very liberal in their treatment of their prisoners, in order to make life the more dear to them, and usually entertain them with threats of their impending death, the torments they will suffer, the preparations made to that end, the cutting up of their limbs, and the banquet that will be made at their expense. All this is done with the sole purpose of extorting from them a weak or spiritless word, or to give them a desire to escape, in order to gain the advantage of having terrified them and shaken their firmness. For indeed, if rightly taken, therein alone lies the real victory:

> The victor's wreath no triumphs more attest
> Than when the foe's subjection is confest.
>
> (Claudian.) [20]

---

20. *Of the Sixth Consulate of Honorius*, ll. 248 f.

The Hungarians, very bellicose fighters, did not formerly pursue their advantage further than making their enemy cry for mercy. For, after forcing from them that confession, they let them go without hurt or ransom, except, at the most, making them pledge their word not again to take up arms against them.

We often enough gain an advantage over our enemy which is a borrowed advantage, and to which we have no real claim. To have more muscular arms and legs is the quality of a porter, not a sign of valour; skill is a dead and corporal quality: it is a stroke of fortune that causes our adversary to stumble or to be dazzled by the glare of the sun; it is a trick of art and science that makes an able fencer, who may easily be a coward and an insignificant fellow.

A man's value and estimation consists in heart and will: there lies his true honour. Valour is strength, not of legs and arms, but of heart and soul; it lies not in the goodness of our horse, or our weapons, but in our own. He who falls fighting with obstinate courage, *if his legs fail him, he fights on his knees* (Seneca).[21] He who, in spite of being in danger of imminent death, abates nothing of his assurance, who, in yielding up his soul, still fixes on his enemy a firm and scornful glance, is vanquished, not by us, but by Fortune: he is slain but not conquered.

The most valiant are sometimes the most unfortunate. Hence there are triumphant defeats that vie in glory with victories. Neither did those four sister victories, the most glorious that the sun has ever beheld with its eyes, of Salamis, Plataea, Mycale, and Sicily,[22] ever dare to oppose their combined glories to the glory of the discomfiture of King Leonidas and his comrades at the pass of Thermopylae.[23]

What man ever hastened with a more glorious and ambitious desire to the winning, than Captain Ischolas did to the losing, of a battle? What man ever used more care and ingenuity to secure his own safety than he did to ensure his destruction? He was charged to defend a certain pass in the Peloponnesus against the Arcadians. But knowing that he was wholly unable to do so, on account of the nature of the place and the inequality of the forces, and being sure that every man who confronted the enemy must needs remain on the spot; on the other hand, deeming it unworthy both of his own virtue and magnanimity, and of the name of a Spartan, to fail in his charge, he adopted a middle course between these two extremes, which was in this manner: the youngest

21. *Of Providence*, Book II.
22. Montaigne here refers to the famous Greek victories against the Persians and (at Himera, Sicily) against the Carthaginians in or about 480 B.C.

23. The Spartan king Leonidas' defense of the pass at Thermopylae also took place in 480 B.C., during the war against the Persians.

and most active of his band he reserved for the service and defence
of their country, and sent them home; and with those whose loss
would be of less account he decided to hold the pass, and with
their death make the enemy purchase their entry as dear as possible. And so it fell out: for, being presently surrounded on every
side by the Arcadians, after a great butchery of them he and his
comrades were all put to the sword. Was ever a trophy raised to a
victor that was not rather due to these vanquished men? The part
that true victory plays is the struggle, not the coming off safe; and
the honour of virtue consists in combating, not in beating.

To return to our narrative. Far from giving in, in spite of all
they suffer, these prisoners, on the contrary, during the two or three
months that they are held in captivity, bear a cheerful countenance;
they urge their captors to hasten to put them to the proof, defy
them, insult them, reproach them with their cowardice and the
number of battles lost against their own countrymen.

I have a song composed by a prisoner, which contains this outburst: 'Come boldly, every one of you, and assemble together to
dine off me, for you shall at the same time eat your fathers and
grandfathers, whose flesh has served to feed and nourish this body.
These muscles, this flesh and these veins are yours, poor fools that
you are! can you not see that they still contain the substance of
your ancestors' limbs? Relish them well, you will find that they
have the flavour of your own flesh.' A fiction that by no means
savours of barbarity. On the pictures which represent these prisoners
being executed or at the point of death, they are seen spitting in
the face of their slayers or making mouths at them. Indeed they
never cease to challenge and defy them by word and look until the
breath is out of their body. Verily here we see men who are indeed
savages if we compare them with ourselves: for either they must be
so in good sooth, or we; there is a wonderful distance between their
character and ours.

The men there have several wives, and the higher their reputation for valour the greater is the number of their wives. It is a remarkably beautiful feature in their marriages, that the same jealousy
that our wives have to keep us from the love and favors of other
women, they have to an equal degree to procure it. Being more
solicitous for their husbands' honour than for anything else, they
use their best endeavours to have as many companions as they can,
seeing that that is a proof of their husbands' worth.

Ours will cry 'miracle', but it is not so. It is after all a proper
matrimonial virtue, but of the highest order. And in the Bible,
Leah, Rachel, Sarah and Jacob's wives accommodated their husbands with their fair handmaids; and Livia gratified Augustus' ap-

petites to her own detriment; and Stratonice, the wife of King Deiotarus,[24] not only lent her husband the use of a very beautiful young chambermaid in her service, but carefully brought up her children, and gave them a shoulder in succeeding to their father's estates.

And, that it may not be supposed that all this is done through a simple and slavish obligation to follow usage, and under the weight of authority of their ancient customs, without reasoning or judgement, and because their minds are too dull to imagine any other, I must give a few proofs of their intellectual capacity. Besides the warlike song I have just cited I have another, of an amorous nature, which begins thus: 'Adder, stay; stay, adder, that thy colours may serve as a pattern for my sister to work a rich girdle to give to my love: thus shall thy beauty and disposition of thy spots be preferred for all time to all other serpents.' This first verse is the burden of the song. Now, I have enough knowledge of poetry to judge this much: that not only is there nothing barbarous in this idea, but that it is altogether Anacreontic.[25] Their language, by the way, is a soft language, with an agreeable tone, and their terminations resemble the Greek.

Three men of this nation, not knowing how dear, in tranquillity and happiness, it will one day cost them to know the corruptions of this side of the world, and that this intercourse will be the cause of their ruin, which indeed I imagine is already advanced (poor wretches, to be allured by the desire to see new things and to leave their own serene sky to come and see ours!), were at Rouen at a time when the late King Charles the Ninth was there. The King had a long talk with them. They were shown our ways, our pomp, the form of a fine city. After that somebody asked their opinion, desiring to know what they most wondered at. They mentioned three things, the third of which I am sorry to have forgotten, but I still remember two. They said that in the first place they thought it very strange that so many big men with beards, strong and armed, who were about the King (they were probably thinking of the Swiss who formed his guard) should submit to obey a child, and that they did not rather choose one of their own number to command them. Secondly (they have a way of speaking of men as if they were halves of one another), that they had observed that there were men amongst us, full and gorged with all kinds of good things, and that their halves were begging at their doors, emaciated with hunger and poverty; and they thought it strange how these necessitous

24. tetrarch of Galatia, in Asia Minor.

25. worthy of Anacreon (572?–488? B.C.) major Greek writer of amatory lyrics.

halves could suffer such injustice, and that they did not seize the others by the throat, or set fire to their houses.

I had a long talk with one of them; but I had an interpreter who followed my meaning so badly, and was at such a loss, in his stupidity, to take in my ideas, that I could get little satisfaction out of him. When I asked the native, 'What he gained from his superior position among his people?' (for he was a captain, and our sailors called him a king), he said it was 'to march foremost in war'. How many men did he lead? He pointed to a piece of ground, to signify as many as that space could hold: it might be four or five thousand men. Did all his authority lapse with the war? He said 'that this remained, that, when he visited the villages that were dependent on him, they made paths through their thickets, by which he might pass at his ease.' All this does not sound too ill; but hold! they don't wear trousers.

Of the Inconsistency of Our Actions*

They who make a practice of comparing human actions are never so perplexed as when they try to piece them together and place them in the same light, for they commonly contradict one another so strangely that it seems impossible they should have come out of the same shop. Marius the younger[26] is now a son of Mars, now a son of Venus.[27] Some one said that Pope Boniface the Eighth entered upon his charge like a fox, behaved therein like a lion, and died like a dog. And who could believe that it was Nero, the very image of cruelty, who, when the sentence of a condemned criminal was brought to him to be signed in the usual way, exclaimed, 'Would to God that I had never learned to write!' So grieved was he in his heart to doom a man to death!

The world is full of such examples, nay, any man may provide such an abundance of them out of his own experience, that I sometimes wonder to see intelligent men at pains to sort the pieces, seeing that irresolution is, in my view, the most common and conspicuous defect of our nature: witness that famous line of Publilius the writer of low comedies,

> Poor is the plan that never can be changed.
> (Publilius Syrus.)[28]

---

* *Essays*, Book II, Chapter 1.
26. nephew of the older and better known Marius. Montaigne's source is Plutarch's *Life of Marius.*
27. *Mars . . . Venus:* war and love
28. *Apothegms (Sententiae)*, l. 362.

It seems reasonable to judge a man by the most ordinary acts of his life, but in view of the natural instability of our habits and opinions, I have often thought that even good authors are wrong in obstinately attributing to us a steadfast and consistent character. They hit upon a general feature in a man and arrange and interpret all his actions in accordance with this fanciful conception; and if they are unable to twist them sufficiently, set them down to dissimulation. Augustus has escaped them, for we see in this man, throughout the course of his life, so manifest, abrupt, and continual a variety of actions, that he has slipped through the fingers of even the most daring critics, and been left undecided. I find nothing more difficult to believe than man's consistency, and nothing more easy than his inconsistency. If we examine him in detail and judge of his actions separately, bit by bit, we shall most often find this true.

Throughout ancient history it would be difficult to choose a dozen men who have steered their lives in one certain and constant course, which is the principal aim of wisdom. For, to comprise it all in one word, as an ancient writer[29] says, and to embrace all the rules of life in one, is 'to wish and not to wish always the same thing. I will not vouchsafe to add, he says, provided the wish be right; for if it be not right, it is impossible it should be always the same'. I once learned indeed that vice is no more than want of rule and moderation, and that it is consequently impossible to associate it with consistency. It is a saying attributed to Demosthenes, 'that the beginning of all virtue is consultation and deliberation; and the end and perfection, constancy'. If reason directed our course we should choose the fairest; but no one has thought of that:

He scorns that which he sought, seeks what he scorned of late;
He flows and ebbs, his whole life contradiction.   (Horace.)[30]

Our ordinary practice is to follow the inclinations of our appetite, to right, to left, up hill, down dale, as we are borne along by the wind of opportunity. We do not consider what we wish except at the moment of wishing it, and we change like that animal which takes its colour from what it is laid upon. What we have but now determined we presently alter, and soon again we retrace our steps: it is nothing but wavering and uncertainty;

We are led as a puppet is moved by the strings.
(Horace.)[31]

29. Seneca, in *Epistles*, Epistle xx.   31. *Satires*, Book II, Satire vii, l.
30. *Epistles*, Book I, Epistle i, ll.   82.
98 f.

We do not go, we are carried along, like things floating, now smoothly, now perturbedly, according as the water is angry or calm;

> We see them, knowing not
> What 'tis they want, and seeking ever and ever
> A change of place, as if to drop the burden.
> (Lucretius.)[32]

Every day a new fancy; and our humours move with the changes of weather:

> So change the minds of men, like days
> That Father Jove sends down to earth,
> To alternate 'twixt wet and fine. (Homer.)[33]

We waver between different minds; we wish nothing freely, nothing absolutely, nothing constantly. Should any man prescribe and establish definite laws and a definite policy in his own head, he would present throughout his life a shining example of even habits, an order and an unfailing relation of one action to another.

(Empedocles remarked in the inhabitants of Agrigentum this discrepancy, that they abandoned themselves to their pleasures as if they were to die on the morrow, and that they built as if they were never to die.)[34]

The reason will be easily found, as we see in the case of the younger Cato;[35] he who touches one note of the keyboard touches all: there is a harmony of sounds, all in perfect tune with each other, which is not to be mistaken. With us, on the other hand, the rule is: so many actions, so many particular judgements to be passed. The surest, in my opinion, would be to refer them to the nearest circumstances, without seeking any farther, and without drawing from them any other inferences.

It was told me, during the tumultuous times[36] our poor State had to go through, that a young woman who lived quite near to where I then was, had thrown herself from a high window to avoid the forcible caresses of a poor knave of a soldier who was quartered in her house; the fall did not kill her, and, repeating the attempt on her life, she would have cut her throat with a knife, but was prevented; not however without inflicting a serious wound. She herself then confessed that the soldier had done no more than importune her with gifts, entreaties, and solicitations, but that she feared he would in the end proceed to violence. And all this, her words, her

---

32. *On the Nature of Things*, Book III, ll. 1057 ff.

33. *Odyssey*, Book XVIII, l. 135.

34. from the life of the fifth-century Greek philosopher Empedocles, by Diogenes Laertius.

35. the philosopher, Cato "Uticensis" (first century B.C.); to Montaigne, and also traditionally, he is an epitome of moral and intellectual integrity.

36. See footnote 17 and the corresponding passage in the text of "Of Cannibals."

mien, and the blood which testified to her virtue, in the true manner of a second Lucretia![37]

Now I have heard, as a fact, that, both before and after, she was a wench not very difficult to come by. As the tale[38] has it, 'Be as handsome and as fine a gentleman as you will, when you have failed in your pursuit, do not immediately conclude an inviolable chastity in your mistress; it does not follow that the muleteer will not find his opportunity.'

Antigonus,[39] having taken a liking to one of his soldiers, on account of his virtue and valour, ordered his physicians to attend him for a persistent internal malady which had long tormented him, and perceiving that after his cure he went much more coldly to work than before, asked him what it was that had so altered and cowed him. 'You yourself, Sire, he replied, by delivering me from the ill which made me indifferent to life.' A soldier of Lucullus,[40] having been plundered by enemies, devised a bold stroke for his revenge; when he had retrieved his loss with interest, Lucullus, whose good opinion he had gained, tried to induce him, with the best persuasions he could think of, to undertake some risky business;

> With words that might have stirred a coward's heart.
> (Horace.)[41]

'Employ, he replied, some wretched soldier who has been plundered;'

> Though but a rustic clown, he'll go
> Who's lost his money-belt,' he said;   (Horace.)[42]

and resolutely refused to go.

When we read that Mahomet having furiously rated Chasan, chief of his Janissaries, for allowing his line of troops to be broken by the Hungarians, and bearing himself like a coward in the battle; and that Chasan made no reply but, alone and just as he was with his weapon in his hand, rushed furiously into the first body of enemies that he met with, and was immediately overwhelmed; it was not so much a justification of his conduct as a change of mood, not so much natural prowess as a new spite.

Do not think it strange that the man who was so venturesome yesterday should prove such a poltroon on the morrow; either anger, or necessity, or company, or wine, or the sound of the trumpet had put his heart into his belly; it was not a courage thus formed by

37. the legendary, virtuous Roman who stabbed herself after being raped by King Tarquinius' son.
38. a common folk tale.
39. Macedonian king.

40. Roman general of the first century B.C.
41. *Epistles*, Book II, Epistle ii, L 36.
42. *Epistles*, Book II, Epistle ii, ll. 39 f.

reason, but a courage stiffened by those circumstances; it was no marvel if other contrary circumstances made a new man of him.

These so supple changes and contradictions which we manifest have made some to imagine that we have two souls, others, that we have two powers which, each in its own way, accompany and stir us, the one to good, the other to evil, since so abrupt a diversity is not to be reconciled with a single subject.

Not only does the wind of accidents stir me according to its blowing, but I am also stirred and troubled by the instability of my attitude; and he who examines himself closely will seldom find himself twice in the same state. I give to my soul now one face, now another, according to the side to which I turn it. If I speak differently of myself, it is because I regard myself differently. All the contradictions are to be found in me, according as the wind turns and changes. Bashful, insolent; chaste, lascivious; talkative, taciturn; clumsy, gentle; witty, dull; peevish, sweet-tempered; mendacious, truthful; knowing, ignorant; and liberal and avaricious and prodigal: all this I see in myself in some degree, according as I veer about; and whoever will study himself very attentively will find in himself, yea, in his judgement, this discordance and unsteadiness. I can say nothing of myself absolutely, simply, and steadily, without confusion and mixture, nor in one word. *Distinguo*[43] is the most universal member of my logic.

Though I am ever inclined to speak well of what is good, and rather to interpret favourably the things that are capable of such interpretation, yet such is the strangeness of our nature that we are often driven to do good, even by vice; if it were not that well-doing is judged by the intention alone.

Therefore a courageous deed ought not to imply a valiant man: the man who is really brave will be always so, and on all occasions. If valour were a habit, and not a sudden eruption, it would make a man equally resolute for all emergencies, the same alone as in company, the same in single combat as in a battle; for let them say what they will, there is not one valour for the pavement and another for the field. As bravely would he bear sickness in his bed as a wound in camp, nor would he fear death in his own home any more than in an assault. We should not see the same man charge with brave assurance into the breach, and afterwards worrying like a woman, over the loss of a law-suit or a son. When, though afraid of infamy, he bears up against poverty; when, though wincing at a surgeon's lancet, he stiffly faces the enemy's sword, the action is praiseworthy. but not the man.

Many Greeks, says Cicero, cannot look upon an enemy, and are brave in sickness. The Cimbrians and the Celtiberians, quite the

43. I distinguish; I separate into its components.

contrary: *For nothing can be consistent that has not reason for its foundation* (Cicero).[44]

No valour could be more extreme in its kind than Alexander's; but it is of one kind only, and is not complete enough, nor universal on all occasions. Incomparable though it be, it has its blemishes. So it is that we see him so desperately disturbed by the slightest suspicions that his subjects may be plotting against his life, and carried away in his investigations to such violent and indiscriminate acts of injustice, and haunted by a fear that upsets his natural good sense. The superstition too with which he was so strongly tainted bears some likeness to pusillanimity. And the excess of his penitence for the murder of Clytus[45] is also evidence of uneven temper.

Our actions are but a patchwork (*they despise pleasure, but are cowardly in pain; they are indifferent to fame, but infamy breaks their spirit*[46]), and we try to gain honour by false pretences. Virtue will not be wooed but for her own sake, and if we sometimes borrow her mask for some other purpose, she will very soon snatch it from our face. When the soul is once steeped in it, the dye is strong and vivid, and will not go without taking the skin with it. Wherefore, to judge a man, we must long and carefully follow his traces. If constancy does not stand firm and wholly on its own foundation, *if the path of life has not been well considered and preconcerted* (Cicero);[47] if changing circumstances make him alter his pace (I should say his route, for the pace may be accelerated or retarded by them), let him go: that man will go *A vau le vent* (down the wind), as the motto of our Talebot[48] has it.

It is no wonder, says an ancient writer,[49] that chance has so great a hold over us, since we live by chance. Unless a man has directed his life as a whole to a certain fixed goal, he cannot possibly dispose his particular actions. Unless he have an image of the whole in his mind, he cannot possibly arrange the pieces. How can a painter lay in a stock of colours, if he knows not what he is going to paint? No man draws a definite outline of his life, and we only think it out in details. The archer must first know at what he is aiming, and then accommodate his hand, his bow, the string, the arrow, and his movements, accordingly. Our plans go wrong because they have neither aim nor direction. No wind serves the ship that has no port of destination.

I cannot agree with those judges who, on the strength of seeing one of his tragedies, declared in favour of Sophocles, when accused

44. *Tusculan Disputations*, Book II, Chapter 27.

45. Clytus, a commander in Alexander's army, was killed by him during an argument, an act which Alexander immediately and bitterly regretted, as related by Plutarch in his *Life of Alexander*, Chapters 50–52.

46. Cicero, *Of Duties* (*De officiis*), Book I, Chapter 21.

47. *Paradoxes* (*Paradoxa*), Paradox v.

48. Talbot, an English captain who fought in France and died there in 1453.

49. Seneca, in *Epistles*, Epistle lxxi.

by his son of being incapable of managing his domestic affairs. Nor do I hold with the conclusions arrived at by the Parians who were sent to reform the Milesians. Visiting the island, they remarked the best-cultivated lands and the best-kept country-houses, and made a note of their owners; and then, having called an assembly of the citizens in the town, they appointed these owners the new governors and magistrates, concluding that, being careful of their private affairs, they would be equally careful of those of the public.

We are all made up of bits, and so shapelessly and diversely put together, that every piece, at every moment, plays its own game. And there is as much difference between us and ourselves, as between us and others. *Be sure that it is very difficult to be always the same man* (Seneca).[50] Since ambition can teach a man valour, temperance, and liberality, yea and justice too; since greed can implant in the heart of a shop-apprentice, bred up in obscurity and neglect, the confidence to entrust himself, so far from the domestic hearth, to the mercy of the waves and angry Neptune in a frail bark; since it teaches also discretion and prudence; and since Venus herself can put resolution and temerity into the boy who is still under the discipline of the rod, and embolden the heart of the tender virgin in her mother's arms,

> With Love for guide,
> Alone the maid steps o'er her prostrate guards,
> And steals by night into the young man's arms;
> (Tibullus.)[51]

it is not enough for a sober understanding to judge us simply by our external actions: we must sound the innermost recesses, and observe the springs which give the swing. But since it is a high and hazardous undertaking, I would rather that fewer people meddled with it.

Apology for Raimond Sebond*

[MAN'S PRESUMPTION AND LITTLENESS]

What does Truth[52] preach to us, when she preaches to us to fly worldly philosophy,[53] when she so often impresses upon us, That our wisdom is but folly in the sight of God;[54] That of all vain things the most vain is man; That man, who presumes on his learning, does not yet know what it is to know;[55] and That if man, who is nothing, thinks himself something, he deceives and beguiles himself?[56] These sayings of the Holy Spirit so clearly and vividly express

---

50. *Epistles*, Epistle cxx.
51. *Elegies*, Book II, Elegy i, ll. 75 ff.
   * *Essays*, Book II, Chapter 12. A small but significant section of the very long "Apology" is reprinted here.
52. revealed truth, the Scriptures.

53. Colossians 2:8.
54. I Corinthians 3:19.
55. I Corinthians 8:2.
56. Galatians 6:3. This and the previous passages from St. Paul were among those inscribed on the walls of Montaigne's library.

what I wish to maintain, that I should need no other proof against men who would bow with all submission and obedience to its authority. But the others[57] would rather be whipped to their own cost, and will not suffer their reason to be combated except by itself.

Let us then for the nonce consider man alone, without outside assistance, armed only with his own weapons, and destitute of the divine grace and knowledge, which comprise all his honour, his strength and the foundation of his being. Let us see how he will hold out in this fine equipment. Let him explain to me, by the force of his reason, on what foundation he has built those great advantages he thinks he has over the other creatures. What has induced him to believe that that wonderful motion of the heavenly vault, the eternal light of those torches rolling so proudly over his head, the awe-inspiring agitations of that infinite sea, were established, and endure through so many centuries for his service and convenience?

Is it possible to imagine anything more ridiculous than that this miserable and puny creature, who is not so much as master of himself, exposed to shocks on all sides should call himself Master and Emperor of the universe, of which it is not in his power to know the smallest part, much less to command it? And that privilege which he assumes of being the only creature in this great edifice that has the capacity to know the beauty and the several parts of it, the only one who is able to give thanks to the architect, and to keep an account of the receipts and outlay of the world: who has sealed him this privilege? Let him show us his letters-patent for this great and noble charge.

Have they been granted in favour of the wise only? Then few people would be concerned. Are the fools and the wicked deserving of so extraordinary a favour, and, being the worst lot in the world, of being preferred to all the rest?

Shall we believe the man who says this, *For whose sake shall we then say that the world has been made? Undoubtedly for those creatures that have the use of reason: these are gods and men, to whom assuredly nothing is superior?* (Balbus the Stoic, according to Cicero).[58] We could never sufficiently deride the impudence of this coupling of gods and men.

But, poor devil, what is there in him deserving of such a privilege? When we consider the incorruptible life of the heavenly bodies, their beauty, their grandeur, their continual motion by so exact a rule:

> When we gaze aloft
> Upon the skiey vaults of yon great world

---

57. those who pretend to arrive at certainty through their human means, their reason, alone.

58. quoted in Cicero's *Of the Nature of the Gods*, Book II, Chapter 53.

The ether, fixt high over twinkling stars,
And into our thought there come the journeyings
Of sun and moon;   (Lucretius.)[59]

when we consider the dominion and power those bodies have, not
only over our lives and the conditions of our fortune,

Our lives and actions on the stars depend,
(Manilius.)[60]

but even over our dispositions, our judgement, our will, which they
govern, impel and stir at the mercy of their influence, as our reason
discovers and tells us:

This we learn: the far, far distant stars
Govern by silent laws; the world is ruled
By periodic causes, and the turns of destiny
Observed by certain signs;   (Manilius.)[61]

when we see that not only a man, not only a king, but kingdoms,
empires, and all this world here below are moved according to the
lightest swing of the heavenly motions:

How great a change each little motion brings!
So great this kingdom that it governs kings;
(Manilius.)[62]

if our virtue, our vices, our talents and our knowledge, if even this
dissertation of mine on the power of the stars, this comparison between them and ourselves, comes, as our reason supposes, by their
means and their favour;

Maddened by love, Leander swims the strait,
A Grecian king o'erturns the walls of Troy.
'Tis this man's lot to give his country laws.
Sons kill their fathers, fathers kill their sons,
And brothers arm themselves in mutual strife.
Not we have made these wars; 'tis Fate compels
To bear such pains with lacerated limbs.
And Fate it is that makes me ponder Fate;   (Manilius.)[63]

if this little portion of reason we possess has been allotted to us by
heaven, how can reason make us the equal of heaven? How can it
subject its essence and conditions to our knowledge? All that we see
in those bodies fills us with amazement. *What apparatus, what in-*

---

59. *On the Nature of Things*, Book
V, ll. 1204 ff.
60. *Astronomicon*, Book III, l. 58.
61. *Astronomicon*, Book I, ll. 60 ff.

62. *Astronomicon*, Book I, l. 57, and
Book IV, l. 93.
63. *Astronomicon*, Book IV, ll. 79
ff., and l. 118.

struments, what levers, what engines, what craftsmen were employed about so mighty a work? (Cicero).[64]

Why do we deny them a soul, and life and reason? Have we discovered in them any stubborn, senseless stupidity, we who have no concern with them but to obey them? Shall we say that we have seen no other creature but man in possession of a reasoning mind? Why! have we seen anything comparable to the sun? Does it exist the less for our not having seen its like? Does it move the less because no other movement is to be compared with it? If what we have not seen does not exist, our knowledge is marvellously short-sighted: *How close the confines of our mind!* (Cicero).[65]

Is it not a delusion of human vanity to make the moon a celestial earth, and to imagine that there are mountains and valleys upon it, as did Anaxagoras;[66] to set up human habitations and dwellings and establish colonies upon it for our convenience, as do Plato and Plutarch,[67] and to make our earth a bright and shining star? *Amongst other infirmities of human nature is that mental blindness which not only forces man to err, but makes him hug his errors* (Seneca).[68] *The corruptible body weighs down the soul, and this earthly habitation prevents it from pondering on many things* (The Book of Wisdom, quoted by Saint Augustine).[69]

Presumption is our natural and original infirmity. The frailest and most vulnerable of all creatures is man, and at the same time the most arrogant.[70] He sees and feels himself lodged here in the mud and filth of the world, nailed and riveted to the worst, the deadest and most stagnant part of the universe, at the lowest story of the house and the most remote from the vault of heaven, with the animals of the worst condition of the three; and he goes and sets himself in imagination above the circle of the moon, and brings heaven under his feet.

With this same vanity of imagination he makes himself the equal of God, assumes to himself divine qualities, selects and separates himself from among the multitude of other creatures, carves out their shares to each of his fellows and comrades, the animals, and allots to them their portion of faculties and powers according as it seems good to him. How can he know, by the force of his understanding, the secret and internal motions of the animals? By what comparison between them and himself does he suppose them to be as stupid as he thinks?

64. *Of the Nature of the Gods,* Book I, Chapter 8.

65. *Of the Nature of the Gods,* Book I, Chapter 31.

66. according to Diogenes Laertius, *Life of Anaxagoras,* Book II, Chapter 8.

67. For the notion that the moon is inhabited, Montaigne refers to Plu-

tarch's *Of the Face of the Moon.*

68. *Of Wrath,* Book II, Chapter 9.

69. *City of God,* Book XII, Section 15.

70. The phrase, originally Pliny's, is another of those engraved on the walls of Montaigne's library.

When I play with my cat, who knows but that she regards me more as a plaything than I do her? [We amuse each other with our respective monkey-tricks; if I have my moments for beginning and refusing, so she has hers.]

Plato,[71] in his picture of the golden age under Saturn, numbers, among the chief advantages of the man of that time, his communion with the beasts, of whom inquiring and learning he knew the real attributes and differences of each of them; whereby he acquired a very perfect understanding and wisdom, and in consequence passed his life very much more happily than we are able to do. Do we need a better proof of the impudence of man where the beasts are concerned? That great author[72] opined that, in giving them their bodily shape, Nature for the most part only considered the use they could be put to in the prognostications which were drawn from them in his time.

That defect which hinders communication between us and them, why may it not as well be in ourselves as in them? It is a matter of conjecture with whom the fault lies that we do not understand one another; for we understand them no more than they do us. By the same reasoning they may regard us as beasts, as we do them.

It is no great wonder if we do not understand them for neither do we understand the Basques[73] and the Troglodytes.[74] Yet some have boasted of understanding them, as Apollonius of Tyana, Melampus, Tiresias, Thales, and others.[75] And since it is the case that, as the cosmographers tell, there are nations that receive a dog for their king, they must needs in some way interpret its voice and actions.

We must observe the parity there is between us. We have some halfway understanding of their meaning, as the animals have of ours, in about the same degree. They cajole us, they threaten us, they entreat us, as we do them. Moreover, it is very evident to us that they are able fully and completely to communicate with one another, that they understand one another, and not only those of the same species, but also those of different species.

> Since even the speechless herds, aye, since
> The very generations of wild beasts
> Are wont dissimilar and diverse sounds
> To rouse from in them, when there's fear or pain,
> And when they burst with joys. (Lucretius.)[76]

A horse knows that a dog is angry when it barks in a certain way,

---

71. in his *Statesman*.
72. Plato, in the *Timaeus*.
73. inhabitants of the Pyrenees region on the Bay of Biscay, known for the difficulty and peculiarity of their language.
74. cavedwellers.
75. A mixture of mythical and historical figures: Apollonius of Tyana,

Greek neo-Pythagorean philosopher and magician (first century A.D.); Melampus, mythical physician and sage; Tiresias, mythical blind prophet of Thebes; Thales, regarded as the first Greek philosopher (sixth century B.C.), one of the Seven Sages of Greece.
76. *On the Nature of Things*, Book V, ll. 1058 ff.

but is not afraid when it gives voice in another way. Even in those creatures that have no voice we may easily infer, from the mutual services we see them rendering each other, that they have some other means of communication; their movements speak and negotiate:

> In much the same way as the lack-speech years
> Compel young children into gesturings. (Lucretius.)[77]

Why not? just as well as our deaf-mutes dispute, argue and tell stories by means of signs? I have seen some so skilful and practised in that language, that in truth they did not fall short of perfection in making themselves understood. Lovers use their eyes to express anger, reconciliation, entreaty, thanks, to make appointments, in short for every purpose;

> Silence too our thought and wish betrays.
> (Tasso.)[78]

What of the hands? We beg, we promise, we call, we send away, threaten, pray, entreat, deny, refuse, question, wonder, count, confess, repent, we express fear and shame, we doubt, inform, command, incite, encourage, swear, testify, accuse, condemn, absolve, insult, despise, challenge, we show vexation, we flatter, applaud, bless, humiliate, mock, reconcile, recommend, exalt, welcome, rejoice, complain, we express grief, dejection, despair, astonishment, protestation, silence, and what not, in such varied and numerous ways, in rivalry with the tongue.

With the head we invite, we dismiss, admit, disclaim, give the lie, welcome, honour, reverence, disdain, demand, show the door, we cheer, lament, caress, chide, submit, defy, exhort, threaten, assure, and inquire. What of the eye-brows? What of the shoulders? There is no movement that does not speak an intelligible, untaught language, that is understood by all. Which shows that, seeing the variety that distinguishes the spoken languages in use, this one must rather be considered the proper and natural speech of humankind. I pass over that which a particular necessity teaches one who is taken unawares; and the finger-alphabet; and grammar and the sciences which are only practised and expressed by gestures; and the nations that Pliny tells of, who have no other language.

An ambassador of the city of Abdera, after speaking at great length to King Agis of Sparta, said to him, 'Well, Sire, what answer do you wish me to carry back to our citizens?' 'That I allowed you to say all that you would and as much as you would, without ever a word.'[79] Was not that a very speaking and intelligible silence?

After all, which of our arts do we not see in the activities of ani-

77. *On the Nature of Things*, Book V, ll. 1029 f.
78. Torquato Tasso, in the pastoral drama *Aminta*, Act II, Scene 3, ll. 35–

36.
79. The story is told by Plutarch in *Apothegms of the Lacedaemonians*.

mals? Is there any organization regulated with more order, with a
better distribution of charges and functions, and more consistently
maintained, than that of the bees? Can we imagine that so well-
ordered a disposition of activities and occupations could be carried
on without reason and foresight?

> Following signs and instances like these,
> Some testify that bees possess a share
> Of the world-spirit and the mind divine. (Virgil.)[80]

Do the swallows that we see at the return of spring, ferreting out
all the corners of the houses, conduct their search without judgement? Do they choose without discrimination, out of a thousand
places, that which is most commodious for their lodging? Are the
birds, when they weave those beautiful and wonderful habitations
of theirs, able to use a square figure rather than a round, an obtuse
rather than a right angle, without knowing their properties and
effects? Do they fetch, now water, now clay, without having concluded that hardness is softened by moisture? Do they line the floors
of their palaces with moss or down unless they have foreseen that
the tender limbs of their young will lie more softly and comfortably?
Do they shelter themselves from the rainy wind and build their
cabins to the east, without knowing the different properties of the
winds, and without considering that one is more healthy for them
than the other?

Why does the spider thicken her web in one place and slacken it
in another? Why does she use now one kind of knot, now another,
unless she possesses thought, deliberation and the power of inference?

We may see well enough, in most of their works, how much the
animals surpass us, and how much we fall short in the art of imitating them. And yet, in our ruder performances, we are sensible
of what faculties we employ, and we know that our mind applies
to them its utmost powers; why do we not conclude the same of the
animals? Why do we ascribe to I know not what slavish instinct of
nature those works that excel anything we can do by nature or art?
Herein we unconsciously give them a very great advantage over ourselves, in making Nature, with a maternal kindness, to accompany
and lead them as it were by the hand, to all the activities and con-
veniences of their life; whilst us she abandons to chance and fortune, and forces us to seek by art the things necessary for our preservation, at the same time denying us the means of attaining, by
any education or mental effort, to the natural skill of the animals.
So that their brutish stupidity surpasses in all their contrivances
everything we are able to do with our divine intelligence.

Truly, by this reckoning, we might with great reason call her a very unjust stepmother; but that is not so. Our organization is not so formless and unregulated. Nature has been universally kind to all her creatures, and there is none that she has not very amply furnished with all the means necessary for the preservation of its being. For those common complaints that I hear men uttering (as the licence of their opinions now lifts them up above the clouds, now brings them down to the antipodes), that we are the only out-cast animal, bare on the bare earth, bound and tied down, with no means of arming or covering ourselves but with others' spoils; whereas all the other creatures have been clothed by Nature with shells, husks, bark, hair, wool, spikes, leather, down, feathers, scales, fleece, bristles, according to the need of their being; armed with claws, teeth, horns for attack and defence, and has herself in-structed them in what is requisite to each, to swim, run, fly, sing, whilst man cannot even walk or speak, nor eat, nor do anything but weep, without an apprenticeship:

> Then again the babe,
> Like to the castaway of the raging surf,
> Lies naked on the ground, speechless, in want
> Of every help for life, when Nature first
> Hath poured him forth upon the shores of light
> With birth-pangs from within the mother's womb,
> And with a plaintive wail he fills the place,—
> As well befitting one for whom remains
> In life a journey through so many ills.
> But all the flocks and herds and all wild beasts
> Come forth and grow, nor need the little rattles,
> Nor must be treated to the humouring nurse's
> Dear broken chatter; nor seek they divers clothes
> To suit the changing skies; nor need, in fine,
> Nor arms, nor lofty ramparts, wherewithal
> Their own to guard—because the earth herself
> And Nature, artificer of the world, bring forth
> Aboundingly all things for all.   (Lucretius.)[81]

These complaints are unfounded; there is in the governance of the world a much greater equality and a more uniform relationship. Our skin is provided as abundantly as theirs with power to resist the inclemency of the weather. Witness the many nations that have not yet tried the use of clothes. Our ancient Gauls wore hardly any clothes, like our neighbours the Irish of the present day, in spite of their cold climate.

But we may judge better by ourselves: for all those parts of our person which we are pleased to expose to the wind and air are

81. *On the Nature of Things*, Book V, ll. 222 ff.

adapted to endure it, the feet, the face, the hands, the legs, the shoulders, the head, according to the demands of usage. For if there is in us a tender spot, in which we should seem to fear the cold, it should be the stomach, where digestion takes place; our fathers used to leave it uncovered, and our ladies, soft and delicate as they are, sometimes go half-covered down to the navel.

Nor are the bindings and swaddlings of infants any more necessary. The Lacedemonian mothers reared their children in all freedom to move their limbs, without any wrappings or fastenings.

Our weeping we have in common with most of the other animals; there are hardly any that do not wail and whine long after their birth, seeing that it is a natural effect of their helplessness at that age. As to the habit of eating, it is natural to us as well as to them, and comes without instruction:

> For each creature feels
> By instinct to what use to put its powers.
> (Lucretius.)[82]

Who doubts but that a child, having acquired the strength to feed himself, is able to seek his food? And the earth yields and offers him enough for his needs, without any cultivation and artifice; and if not at all times, no more does she do it for the animals. Witness the provision we see made by the ants and other creatures, in view of the barren season of the year. Those nations we have lately discovered, so abundantly provided with meat and a natural drink, without care or trouble on their part, have now made us realize that bread is not our only sustenance, and that, without any tilling, our Mother Nature has plentifully provided us with all that we need. Nay, as seems very probable, more amply and richly than she does now that we have taken to meddling with it by our contrivances:

> She first, the Earth, of own accord
> The shining grains and vineyards of all joy
> Created for mortality; herself
> Gave the sweet fruitage and the pastures glad,
> Which now to-day yet scarcely wax in size,
> Even when, aided by our toiling arms,
> We break the ox, and wear away the strength
> Of sturdy farm-hands; (Lucretius.)[83]

the excess and unruliness of our appetite outstripping all the inventions wherewith we seek to satisfy it.

With regard to weapons, we are better provided by Nature than most other animals; we are more able to move our limbs about and to extract service from them, naturally and without being taught.

82. *On the Nature of Things,* Book V. ll. 1033 f.

83. *On the Nature of Things,* Book II, ll. 1157 ff.

Those who are trained to fight naked are seen to rush into dangers just like our own soldiers. If some of the beasts surpass us in this advantage, we surpass many others in the same. We possess by a natural instinct and teaching the skill to fortify our bodies and protect them by acquired means. That this is so is proved by the example of the elephant who sharpens and grinds the teeth which he makes use of in warfare (for he has special teeth which he saves and employs for this purpose only). When bulls go to battle they throw up and scatter the dust around them; the boars whet their tusks; the ichneumon, when it is about to grapple with the crocodile, fortifies its body by coating it all over with a crust of mud, well kneaded and compressed, as with a cuirass. Why shall we not say that it is as natural to us to arm ourselves with wood and iron?

As to speech, it is certain that, if it is not natural neither is it necessary. Nevertheless I believe that a child brought up in complete solitude, far from all intercourse (which would be a difficult experiment to make), would have some kind of speech to express his ideas. And it is not to be believed that Nature has denied us this power which she has given to many other animals; for what else but speech is that faculty we observe in them of complaining, rejoicing, calling to one another for succour, inviting to love, which they do by the use of their voice?

Why should they not speak with one another? They speak to us, and we to them: in how many different tones do we not speak to our dogs? and they answer us. We use another language with them, than we do in talking to birds, pigs, oxen and horses, and give them other names; we change the idiom according to the kind.

> So ants amidst their sable-coloured band
> One with another mouth to mouth confer,
> Haply their way or state to understand.   (Dante.)[84]

Lactantius seems to attribute to beasts not only the power of speech but also of laughter. And the same difference of tongues which, according to the differences of countries, is found in human beings, is also found in animals of the same species. Aristotle, writing on this subject, instances the various calls of partridges, according to locality:

> The dappled birds
> Utter at other times far other cries
> Than when they fight for food, or with their prey
> Struggle and strain. And birds there are which change
> With changing weather their own raucous songs.
>
> (Lucretius.)[85]

---

84. *Purgatory,* Canto XXVI, ll. 34 ff.   85. *On the Nature of Things,* Book V, ll. 1078 ff.

But it is yet to be known what language the supposed child would speak; and what has been conjectured about it has no great probability. If any one declares to me, in opposition to this belief, that those deaf by nature do not speak, I reply that it is not only because they have not been taught to speak by ear, but more because the sense of hearing, of which they are deprived, is related to that of speech, and that they hold together by a natural tie; in such a way that the words we speak must in the first place be spoken to ourselves, and be made to strike upon our own inward ears, before being sent out to others' ears.

I have said all this to establish the resemblance to human conditions, and to bring us back and join us to the majority. We are neither superior nor inferior to the rest. All that is under heaven, says the sage, is subject to one law and one fate:

> Enshackled in the gruesome bonds of doom.
> (Lucretius.) [86]

Some difference there is; there are orders and degrees, but under the aspect of one same Nature:

> But each sole thing
> Proceeds according to its proper wont,
> And all conserve their own distinctions, based
> In Nature's fixed decree. (Lucretius.) [87]

Man must be forced and lined up within the barriers of this organization. The poor wretch has no mind really to step over them. He is shackled and entangled, he is subjected to the same obligation as the other creatures of his order, and is of a very mediocre condition, without any real and essential prerogative and preeminence. That which he thinks and imagines himself to possess, neither has body nor can it be perceived. And if it be so that he alone of all the animals has this freedom of imagination, this licence of thought, which represents to him that which is, that which is not, that which he wills, the false and the true; it is an advantage sold to him very dearly, and of which he has very little cause to boast. For from it springs the principal source of all the ills that press upon him, sin, sickness, irresolution, affliction, despair.

Of Repentance*

["THESE TESTIMONIES OF A GOOD CONSCIENCE"]

Others form man; I describe him, and portray a particular, very ill-made one, who, if I had to fashion him anew, should indeed

86. *On the Nature of Things*, Book V, l. 874.
87. *On the Nature of Things*, Book V, ll. 921 ff.

* *Essays*, Book III, Chapter 2. The opening part of the essay is reprinted here.

be very different from what he is. But now it is done.

Now the features of my painting do not err, although they change and vary. The world is but a perennial see-saw. All things in it are incessantly on the swing, the earth, the rocks of the Caucasus, the Egyptian pyramids, both with the common movement and their own particular movement. Even fixedness is nothing but a more sluggish motion.

I cannot fix my object; it is befogged, and reels with a natural intoxication. I seize it at this point, as it is at the moment when I beguile myself with it. I do not portray the thing in itself. I portray the passage; not a passing from one age to another, or, as the people put it, from seven years to seven years,[88] but from day to day, from minute to minute. I must adapt my history to the moment. I may presently change, not only by chance, but also by intention. It is a record of diverse and changeable events, of undecided, and when the occasion arises, contradictory ideas; whether it be that I am another self, or that I grasp a subject in different circumstances and see it from a different point of view. So it may be that I contradict myself, but, as Demades[89] said, the truth I never contradict. If my mind could find a firm footing, I should not speak tentatively, I should decide; it is always in a state of apprenticeship, and on trial.

I am holding up to view a humble and lustreless life; that is all one. Moral philosophy, in any degree, may apply to an ordinary and secluded life as well as to one of richer stuff; every man carries within him the entire form of the human constitution.

Authors communicate themselves to the world by some special and extrinsic mark; I am the first to do so by my general being, as Michel de Montaigne, not as a grammarian or a poet or a lawyer. If the world finds fault with me for speaking too much of myself, I find fault with the world for not even thinking of itself.

But is it reasonable that I, who am so retired in actual life, should aspire to make myself known to the public? And is it reasonable that I should show up to the world, where artifice and ceremony enjoy so much credit and authority, the crude and simple results of nature, and of a nature besides very feeble? Is it not like making a wall without stone or a similar material, thus to build a book without learning or art? The ideas of music are guided by art, mine by chance. This I have at least in conformity with rules, that no man ever treated of a subject that he knew and understood better than I do this that I have taken up; and that in this I am the most learned man alive. Secondly, that no man ever penetrated more deeply into his matter, nor more minutely analysed its parts and consequences, nor more fully and exactly reached the goal he had

---

88. an allusion to the popular notion that the human body is completely renewed every seven years.

89. Greek orator and politician of the fourth century B.C.

made it his business to set up. To accomplish it I need only bring fidelity to it; and that is here, as pure and sincere as may be found.

I speak the truth, not enough to satisfy myself, but as much as I dare to speak. And I become a little more daring as I grow older; for it would seem that custom allows this age more freedom to prate, and more indiscretion in speaking of oneself. It cannot be the case here, as I often see elsewhere, that the craftsman and his work contradict each other. 'How could a man who shows to such advantage in company write so foolish a book?' or, 'Are these learned writings the work of a man of such feeble conversation?'

When a man of ordinary conversation writes uncommon things, it means that his talent lies in the place from which he borrows them, and not in himself. A learned man is not learned at all things; but the accomplished man is accomplished in all things, even in ignorance.

Here, my book and I go hand in hand together, and keep one pace. In other cases we may commend or censure the work apart from the workman; not so here. Who touches the one touches the other. He who judges the one without knowing the other will wrong himself more than he does me; he who has come to know the work will completely satisfy me. Happy beyond my deserts if I have only this share of public approval, that intelligent persons will be made to feel that I was capable of profiting by learning, if I had any; and that I deserved more assistance from my memory!

In this place let me offer an excuse for what I often repeat, that I seldom repent, and that my conscience is satisfied with itself, not as the conscience of an angel or a horse, but as the conscience of a man; always with the addition of this refrain, not a formal or conventional refrain, but prompted by a real and natural modesty, 'that I speak as an inquirer and an ignoramus, leaving the decision purely and simply to the common and authorized beliefs.' I do not teach, I relate.

There is no vice, that is really a vice, which is not hurtful and which a sound judgement does not condemn; for its ugliness and evil consequences are so apparent that they are perhaps right who say that it is chiefly begotten of stupidity and ignorance. So hard it is to imagine that a man may know it and not hate it!

Wickedness sucks in the greater part of its own venom, and poisons itself with it.

Vice, like an ulcer in the flesh, leaves a repentance in the soul, which is always scratching itself and drawing blood. For Reason blots out all other grief and sorrow, but begets that of repentance, which is the more hard to bear since it is born from within; as the chill and heat of a fever are more acutely felt than those which are external. I regard as vices (but each according to its measure), not only those which are condemned by reason and Nature, but those too which have been created by human opinion, even false and erroneous opinion, if it is authorized by laws and custom.

There is likewise no goodness in which a well-born nature does not delight. We feel indeed a certain self-congratulation when we do a good deed, which gives us inward satisfaction, and that generous pride which accompanies a good conscience. A boldly wicked soul may perhaps arm itself with assurance; but with that complacency and satisfaction it cannot provide itself.

There is no small pleasure in feeling oneself preserved from the contagion of so corrupt an age, and saying to oneself, 'Should any one look into my very soul, he would yet not find me guilty of the affliction or ruin of any man, or of revenge or envy, of publicly offending against the laws, of innovation or disturbance, or of failing to keep my word. And whatever the licence of the times may permit or suggest to any man, I have laid hands on no Frenchman's property nor dived into his purse. I have never lived but on what is my own, either in war or peace time; and have never used another man's labour without hire.' These testimonies of a good conscience please; and this natural satisfaction is a great boon to us, and the only payment that will never fail us.

MIGUEL DE CERVANTES
(1547–1616)
Don Quixote, Part I*
["*I Know Who I Am, and Who I May Be, If I Choose*"]

CHAPTER 1

Which treats of the station in life and the pursuits of the famous gentleman, Don Quixote de la Mancha.

In a village of La Mancha[1] the name of which I have no desire to recall, there lived not so long ago one of those gentlemen who always have a lance in the rack, an ancient buckler, a skinny nag, and a greyhound for the chase. A stew with more beef than mutton in it, chopped meat for his evening meal, scraps for a Saturday, lentils on Friday, and a young pigeon as a special delicacy for Sunday, went to account for three-quarters of his income. The rest of it he laid out on a broadcloth greatcoat and velvet stockings for feast

* From *The Ingenious Gentleman Don Quixote de la Mancha* by Miguel de Cervantes Saavedra, translated by Samuel Putnam. Copyright 1949 by The Viking Press, Inc. Reprinted by permission of The Viking Press, Inc., New York. Part I was published in 1605; Part II, in 1615.

1. Efforts at identifying the village have proved inconclusive; La Mancha is a section of Spain south of Madrid.

days, with slippers to match, while the other days of the week he cut a figure in a suit of the finest homespun. Living with him were a housekeeper in her forties, a niece who was not yet twenty, and a lad of the field and market place who saddled his horse for him and wielded the pruning knife.

This gentleman of ours was close on to fifty, of a robust constitution but with little flesh on his bones and a face that was lean and gaunt. He was noted for his early rising, being very fond of the hunt. They will try to tell you that his surname was Quijada or Quesada—there is some difference of opinion among those who have written on the subject—but according to the most likely conjectures we are to understand that it was really Quejana. But all this means very little so far as our story is concerned, providing that in the telling of it we do not depart one iota from the truth.

You may know, then, that the aforesaid gentleman, on those occasions when he was at leisure, which was most of the year around, was in the habit of reading books of chivalry with such pleasure and devotion as to lead him almost wholly to forget the life of a hunter and even the administration of his estate. So great was his curiosity and infatuation in this regard that he even sold many acres of tillable land in order to be able to buy and read the books that he loved, and he would carry home with him as many of them as he could obtain.

Of all those that he thus devoured none pleased him so well as the ones that had been composed by the famous Feliciano de Silva,[2] whose lucid prose style and involved conceits were as precious to him as pearls; especially when he came to read those tales of love and amorous challenges that are to be met with in many places, such a passage as the following, for example: "The reason of the unreason that afflicts my reason, in such a manner weakens my reason that I with reason lament me of your comeliness." And he was similarly affected when his eyes fell upon such lines as these: ". . . the high Heaven of your divinity divinely fortifies you with the stars and renders you deserving of that desert your greatness doth deserve."

The poor fellow used to lie awake nights in an effort to disentangle the meaning and make sense out of passages such as these, although Aristotle himself would not have been able to understand them, even if he had been resurrected for that sole purpose. He was not at ease in his mind over those wounds that Don Belianís[3] gave and received; for no matter how great the surgeons who treated him, the poor fellow must have been left with his face and his entire body covered with marks and scars. Nevertheless, he

2. a sixteenth-century author of romances; the quotation which follows is from his *Don Florisel de Niquea*.

3. The allusion is to a romance by Jerónimo Fernández.

was grateful to the author for closing the book with the promise of an interminable adventure to come; many a time he was tempted to take up his pen and literally finish the tale as had been promised, and he undoubtedly would have done so, and would have succeeded at it very well, if his thoughts had not been constantly occupied with other things of greater moment.

He often talked it over with the village curate,[4] who was a learned[5] man, a graduate of Sigüenza, and they would hold long discussions as to who had been the better knight, Palmerin of England or Amadis of Gaul;[6] but Master Nicholas, the barber of the same village, was in the habit of saying that no one could come up to the Knight of Phoebus,[7] and that if anyone *could* compare with him it was Don Galaor, brother of Amadis of Gaul, for Galaor was ready for anything—he was none of your finical knights, who went around whimpering as his brother did, and in point of valor he did not lag behind him.

In short, our gentleman became so immersed in his reading that he spent whole nights from sundown to sunup and his days from dawn to dusk in poring over his books, until, finally, from so little sleeping and so much reading, his brain dried up and he went completely out of his mind. He had filled his imagination with everything that he had read, with enchantments, knightly encounters, battles, challenges, wounds, with tales of love and its torments, and all sorts of impossible things, and as a result had come to believe that all these fictitious happenings were true; they were more real to him than anything else in the world. He would remark that the Cid Ruy Díaz had been a very good knight, but there was no comparison between him and the Knight of the Flaming Sword, who with a single backward stroke had cut in half two fierce and monstrous giants. He preferred Bernardo del Carpio, who at Roncesvalles had slain Roland despite the charm[8] the latter bore, availing himself of the stratagem which Hercules employed when he strangled Antaeus, the son of Earth, in his arms.[9]

He had much good to say for Morgante[10] who, though he belonged to the haughty, overbearing race of giants, was of an affable disposition and well brought up. But, above all, he cherished an admiration for Rinaldo of Montalbán,[11] especially as he beheld him

4. parish priest.
5. ironical, for Sigüenza was the seat of a minor and discredited university.
6. heroes of two very famous romances of chivalry.
7. or Knight of the Sun. Heroes of romances customarily adopted emblematic names and also changed them according to circumstances. See in the following paragraph the reference to the Knight of the Flaming Sword.

8. the magic gift of invulnerability.
9. The mythological Antaeus was invulnerable as long as he maintained contact with his mother, Earth; Hercules killed him while holding him raised in his arms.
10. in Pulci's *Morgante maggiore*, a comic-epic poem of the Italian Renaissance.
11. in Bojardo's *Roland in Love* (*Orlando innamorato*) and Ariosto's *Roland Mad* (*Orlando furioso*), roman-

sallying forth from his castle to rob all those that crossed his path, or when he thought of him overseas stealing the image of Mohammed which, so the story has it, was all of gold. And he would have liked very well to have had his fill of kicking that traitor Galalón,[12] a privilege for which he would have given his housekeeper with his niece thrown into the bargain.

At last, when his wits were gone beyond repair, he came to conceive the strangest idea that ever occurred to any madman in this world. It now appeared to him fitting and necessary, in order to win a greater amount of honor for himself and serve his country at the same time, to become a knight-errant and roam the world on horseback, in a suit of armor; he would go in quest of adventures, by way of putting into practice all that he had read in his books; he would right every manner of wrong, placing himself in situations of the greatest peril such as would redound to the eternal glory of his name. As a reward for his valor and the might of his arm, the poor fellow could already see himself crowned Emperor of Trebizond at the very least; and so, carried away by the strange pleasure that he found in such thoughts as these, he at once set about putting his plan into effect.

The first thing he did was to burnish up some old pieces of armor, left him by his great-grandfather, which for ages had lain in a corner, moldering and forgotten. He polished and adjusted them as best he could, and then he noticed that one very important thing was lacking: there was no closed helmet, but only a morion, or visorless headpiece, with turned up brim of the kind foot soldiers wore. His ingenuity, however, enabled him to remedy this, and he proceeded to fashion out of cardboard a kind of half-helmet, which, when attached to the morion, gave the appearance of a whole one. True, when he went to see if it was strong enough to withstand a good slashing blow, he was somewhat disappointed; for when he drew his sword and gave it a couple of thrusts, he succeeded only in undoing a whole week's labor. The ease with which he had hewed it to bits disturbed him no little, and he decided to make it over. This time he placed a few strips of iron on the inside, and then, convinced that it was strong enough, refrained from putting it to any further test; instead, he adopted it then and there as the finest helmet ever made.

After this, he went out to have a look at his nag; and although the animal had more *cuartos*, or cracks, in its hoof than there are quarters in a real,[13] and more blemishes than Gonela's steed[14]

---

tic and comic-epic poems of the Italian Renaissance. Rinaldo is Roland's cousin.

12. Ganelon, the villain in the Charlemagne legend who betrayed the French at Roncesvalles.

13. a coin (about five cents); a *cuarto* was one eighth of a *real*.

14. Gonela ("il Gonnella") was a jester at the court of Ferrara, seat of the house of Este.

which *tantum pellis et ossa fuit*,[15] it nonetheless looked to its master like a far better horse than Alexander's Bucephalus or the Babieca of the Cid.[16] He spent all of four days in trying to think up a name for his mount; for—so he told himself—seeing that it belonged to so famous and worthy a knight, there was no reason why it should not have a name of equal renown. The kind of name he wanted was one that would at once indicate what the nag had been before it came to belong to a knight-errant and what its present status was; for it stood to reason that, when the master's worldly condition changed, his horse also ought to have a famous, high-sounding appellation, one suited to the new order of things and the new profession that it was to follow.

After he in his memory and imagination had made up, struck out, and discarded many names, now adding to and now subtracting from the list, he finally hit upon "Rocinante," a name that impressed him as being sonorous and at the same time indicative of what the steed had been when it was but a hack, whereas now it was nothing other than the first and foremost of all the hacks[17] in the world.

Having found a name for his horse that pleased his fancy, he then desired to do as much for himself, and this required another week, and by the end of that period he had made up his mind that he was henceforth to be known as Don Quixote, which, as has been stated, has led the authors of this veracious history to assume that his real name must undoubtedly have been Quijada, and not Quesada as others would have it. But remembering that the valiant Amadis was not content to call himself that and nothing more, but added the name of his kingdom and fatherland that he might make it famous also, and thus came to take the name Amadis of Gaul, so our good knight chose to add his place of origin and become "Don Quixote de la Mancha"; for by this means, as he saw it, he was making very plain his lineage and was conferring honor upon his country by taking its name as his own.

And so, having polished up his armor and made the morion over into a closed helmet, and having given himself and his horse a name, he naturally found but one thing lacking still: he must seek out a lady of whom he could become enamored; for a knight-errant without a lady-love was like a tree without leaves or fruit, a body without a soul.

"If," he said to himself, "as a punishment for my sins or by a stroke of fortune I should come upon some giant hereabouts, a thing that very commonly happens to knights-errant, and if I should slay him in a hand-to-hand encounter or perhaps cut him in two,

15. was so much skin and bones.
16. "the chief," Ruy Díaz (see reference on p. 1241), celebrated hero of the twelfth-century *Poema del Cid*.
17. in Spanish, *rocín*.

or, finally, if I should vanquish and subdue him, would it not be well to have someone to whom I may send him as a present, in order that he, if he is living, may come in, fall upon his knees in front of my sweet lady, and say in a humble and submissive tone of voice, 'I, lady, am the giant Caraculiambro, lord of the island Malindrania, who has been overcome in single combat by that knight who never can be praised enough, Don Quixote de la Mancha, the same who sent me to present myself before your Grace that your Highness may dispose of me as you see fit'?"

Oh, how our good knight reveled in this speech, and more than ever when he came to think of the name that he should give his lady! As the story goes, there was a very good-looking farm girl who lived near by, with whom he had once been smitten, although it is generally believed that she never knew or suspected it. Her name was Aldonza Lorenzo, and it seemed to him that she was the one upon whom he should bestow the title of mistress of his thoughts. For her he wished a name that should not be incongruous with his own and that would convey the suggestion of a princess or a great lady; and, accordingly, he resolved to call her "Dulcinea del Toboso," she being a native of that place. A musical name to his ears, out of the ordinary and significant, like the others he had chosen for himself and his appurtenances.

CHAPTER 2

Which treats of the first sally that the ingenious Don Quixote made from his native heath.

Having, then, made all these preparations, he did not wish to lose any time in putting his plan into effect, for he could not but blame himself for what the world was losing by his delay, so many were the wrongs that were to be righted, the grievances to be redressed, the abuses to be done away with, and the duties to be performed. Accordingly, without informing anyone of his intention and without letting anyone see him, he set out one morning before daybreak on one of those very hot days in July. Donning all his armor, mounting Rocinante, adjusting his ill-contrived helmet, bracing his shield on his arm, and taking up his lance, he sallied forth by the back gate of his stable yard into the open countryside. It was with great contentment and joy that he saw how easily he had made a beginning toward the fulfillment of his desire.

No sooner was he out on the plain, however, than a terrible thought assailed him, one that all but caused him to abandon the enterprise he had undertaken. This occurred when he suddenly remembered that he had never formally been dubbed a knight, and so, in accordance with the law of knighthood, was not permitted to bear arms against one who had a right to that title. And even if he had been, as a novice knight he would have had to wear white armor, without any device on his shield, until he should have earned one by his exploits. These thoughts led him to waver in his purpose, but, madness prevailing over reason, he resolved to have himself knighted by the first person he met, as many others had done if what he had read in those books that he had at home was true. And so far as white armor was concerned, he would scour his own the first chance that offered until it shone whiter than any ermine. With this he became more tranquil and continued on his way, letting his horse take whatever path it chose, for he believed that therein lay the very essence of adventures.

And so we find our newly fledged adventurer jogging along and talking to himself. "Undoubtedly," he is saying, "in the days to come, when the true history of my famous deeds is published, the learned chronicler who records them, when he comes to describe my first sally so early in the morning, will put down something like this: 'No sooner had the rubicund Apollo spread over the face of the broad and spacious earth the gilded filaments of his beauteous locks, and no sooner had the little singing birds of painted plumage greeted with their sweet and mellifluous harmony the coming of the Dawn, who, leaving the soft couch of her jealous spouse, now showed herself to mortals at all the doors and balconies of the horizon that bounds La Mancha—no sooner had this happened than the famous knight, Don Quixote de la Mancha, forsaking his own downy bed and mounting his famous steed, Rocinante, fared forth and began riding over the ancient and famous Campo de Montiel.' "[18]

And this was the truth, for he was indeed riding over that stretch of plain.

"O happy age and happy century," he went on, "in which my famous exploits shall be published, exploits worthy of being engraved in bronze, sculptured in marble, and depicted in paintings for the benefit of posterity. O wise magician, whoever you be, to whom shall fall the task of chronicling this extraordinary history of mine! I beg of you not to forget my good Rocinante, eternal companion of my wayfarings and my wanderings."

Then, as though he really had been in love: "O Princess Dulcinea, lady of this captive heart! Much wrong have you done me in thus sending me forth with your reproaches and sternly commanding me not to appear in your beauteous presence. O lady, deign to be mindful of this your subject who endures so many woes for the love of you."

And so he went on, stringing together absurdities, all of a kind

18. famous because it had been the scene of a battle in 1369.

that his books had taught him, imitating insofar as he was able the language of their authors. He rode slowly, and the sun came up so swiftly and with so much heat that it would have been sufficient to melt his brains if he had had any. He had been on the road almost the entire day without anything happening that is worthy of being set down here; and he was on the verge of despair, for he wished to meet someone at once with whom he might try the valor of his good right arm. Certain authors say that his first adventure was that of Puerto Lápice, while others state that it was that of the windmills; but in this particular instance I am in a position to affirm what I have read in the annals of La Mancha; and that is to the effect that he went all that day until nightfall, when he and his hack found themselves tired to death and famished. Gazing all around him to see if he could discover some castle or shepherd's hut where he might take shelter and attend to his pressing needs, he caught sight of an inn not far off the road along which they were traveling, and this to him was like a star guiding him not merely to the gates, but rather, let us say, to the palace of redemption. Quickening his pace, he came up to it just as night was falling.

By chance there stood in the doorway two lasses of the sort known as "of the district"; they were on their way to Seville in the company of some mule drivers who were spending the night in the inn. Now, everything that this adventurer of ours thought, saw, or imagined seemed to him to be directly out of one of the storybooks he had read, and so, when he caught sight of the inn, it at once became a castle with its four turrets and its pinnacles of gleaming silver, not to speak of the drawbridge and moat and all the other things that are commonly supposed to go with a castle. As he rode up to it, he accordingly reined in Rocinante and sat there waiting for a dwarf to appear upon the battlements and blow his trumpet by way of announcing the arrival of a knight. The dwarf, however, was slow in coming, and as Rocinante was anxious to reach the stable, Don Quixote drew up to the door of the hostelry and surveyed the two merry maidens, who to him were a pair of beauteous damsels or gracious ladies taking their ease at the castle gate.

And then a swineherd came along, engaged in rounding up his drove of hogs—for, without any apology, that is what they were. He gave a blast on his horn to bring them together, and this at once became for Don Quixote just what he wished it to be: some dwarf who was heralding his coming; and so it was with a vast deal of satisfaction that he presented himself before the ladies in question, who, upon beholding a man in full armor like this, with lance and buckler, were filled with fright and made as if to flee indoors. Realizing that they were afraid, Don Quixote raised his pasteboard visor and revealed his withered, dust-covered face.

"Do not flee, your Ladyships," he said to them in a courteous manner and gentle voice. "You need not fear that any wrong will be done you, for it is not in accordance with the order of knighthood which I profess to wrong anyone, much less such highborn damsels as your appearance shows you to be."

The girls looked at him, endeavoring to scan his face, which was half hidden by his ill-made visor. Never having heard women of their profession called damsels before, they were unable to restrain their laughter, at which Don Quixote took offense.

"Modesty," he observed, "well becomes those with the dower of beauty, and, moreover, laughter that has not good cause is a very foolish thing. But I do not say this to be discourteous or to hurt your feelings; my only desire is to serve you."

The ladies did not understand what he was talking about, but felt more than ever like laughing at our knight's unprepossessing figure. This increased his annoyance, and there is no telling what would have happened if at that moment the innkeeper had not come out. He was very fat and very peaceably inclined; but upon sighting this grotesque personage clad in bits of armor that were quite as oddly matched as were his bridle, lance, buckler, and corselet, mine host was not at all indisposed to join the lasses in their merriment. He was suspicious, however, of all this paraphernalia and decided that it would be better to keep a civil tongue in his head.

"If, Sir Knight," he said, "your Grace desires a lodging, aside from a bed—for there is none to be had in this inn—you will find all else that you may want in great abundance."

When Don Quixote saw how humble the governor of the castle was—for he took the innkeeper and his inn to be no less than that —he replied, "For me, Sir Castellan,[19] anything will do, since

> Arms are my only ornament,
> My only rest the fight, etc."

The landlord thought that the knight had called him a castellan because he took him for one of those worthies of Castile, whereas the truth was, he was an Andalusian from the beach of Sanlúcar, no less a thief than Cacus[20] himself, and as full of tricks as a student or a page boy.

19. The original, *castellano*, means both "castellan" and "Castilian."

20. In Roman mythology he stole some of the cattle of Hercules, conceal-ing the theft by having them walk backward into his cave, but was finally discovered and slain.

"In that case," he said,

> "Your bed will be the solid rock,
> Your sleep: to watch all night.

This being so, you may be assured of finding beneath this roof enough to keep you awake for a whole year, to say nothing of a single night."

With this, he went up to hold the stirrup for Don Quixote, who encountered much difficulty in dismounting, not having broken his fast all day long. The knight then directed his host to take good care of his steed, as it was the best piece of horseflesh in all the world. The innkeeper looked it over, and it did not impress him as being half as good as Don Quixote had said it was. Having stabled the animal, he came back to see what his guest would have and found the latter being relieved of his armor by the damsels, who by now had made their peace with the new arrival. They had already removed his breastplate and backpiece but had no idea how they were going to open his gorget or get his improvised helmet off. That piece of armor had been tied on with green ribbons which it would be necessary to cut, since the knots could not be undone, but he would not hear of this, and so spent all the rest of that night with his headpiece in place, which gave him the weirdest, most laughable appearance that could be imagined.

Don Quixote fancied that these wenches who were assisting him must surely be the chatelaine and other ladies of the castle, and so proceeded to address them very gracefully and with much wit:

> "Never was knight so served
> By any noble dame
> As was Don Quixote
> When from his village he came,
> With damsels to wait on his every need
> While princesses cared for his hack . . .

"By hack," he explained, "is meant my steed Rocinante, for that is his name, and mine is Don Quixote de la Mancha. I had no intention of revealing my identity until my exploits done in your service should have made me known to you; but the necessity of adapting to present circumstances that old ballad of Lancelot has led to your becoming acquainted with it prematurely. However, the time will come when your Ladyships shall command and I will obey and with the valor of my good right arm show you how eager I am to serve you."

The young women were not used to listening to speeches like this and had not a word to say, but merely asked him if he desired to eat anything.

"I could eat a bite of something, yes," replied Don Quixote. "Indeed, I feel that a little food would go very nicely just now."

He thereupon learned that, since it was Friday, there was nothing to be had in all the inn except a few portions of codfish, which in Castile is called *abadejo*, in Andalusia *bacalao*, in some places *curadillo*, and elsewhere *truchuella* or small trout. Would his Grace, then, have some small trout, seeing that was all there was that they could offer him?

"If there are enough of them," said Don Quixote, "they will take the place of a trout, for it is all one to me whether I am given in change eight reales or one piece of eight. What is more, those small trout may be like veal, which is better than beef, or like kid, which is better than goat. But however that may be, bring them on at once, for the weight and burden of arms is not to be borne without inner sustenance."

Placing the table at the door of the hostelry, in the open air, they brought the guest a portion of badly soaked and worse cooked codfish and a piece of bread as black and moldy as the suit of armor that he wore. It was a mirth-provoking sight to see him eat, for he still had his helmet on with his visor fastened, which made it impossible for him to put anything into his mouth with his hands, and so it was necessary for one of the girls to feed him. As for giving him anything to drink, that would have been out of the question if the innkeeper had not hollowed out a reed, placing one end in Don Quixote's mouth while through the other end he poured the wine. All this the knight bore very patiently rather than have them cut the ribbons of his helmet.

At this point a gelder of pigs approached the inn, announcing his arrival with four or five blasts on his horn, all of which confirmed Don Quixote in the belief that this was indeed a famous castle, for what was this if not music that they were playing for him? The fish was trout, the bread was of the finest, the wenches were ladies, and the innkeeper was the castellan. He was convinced that he had been right in his resolve to sally forth and roam the world at large, but there was one thing that still distressed him greatly, and that was the fact that he had not as yet been dubbed a knight; as he saw it, he could not legitimately engage in any adventure until he had received the order of knighthood.

CHAPTER 3

Of the amusing manner in which Don Quixote had himself dubbed a knight.

Wearied of his thoughts, Don Quixote lost no time over the scanty repast which the inn afforded him. When he had finished, he summoned the landlord and, taking him out to the stable, closed the doors and fell on his knees in front of him.

"Never, valiant knight," he said, "shall I arise from here until you have courteously granted me the boon I seek, one which will redound to your praise and to the good of the human race."

Seeing his guest at his feet and hearing him utter such words as these, the innkeeper could only stare at him in bewilderment, not knowing what to say or do. It was in vain that he entreated him to rise, for Don Quixote refused to do so until his request had been granted.

"I expected nothing less of your great magnificence, my lord," the latter then continued, "and so I may tell you that the boon I asked and which you have so generously conceded me is that to-morrow morning you dub me a knight. Until that time, in the chapel of this your castle, I will watch over my armor, and when morning comes, as I have said, that which I so desire shall then be done, in order that I may lawfully go to the four corners of the earth in quest of adventures and to succor the needy, which is the chivalrous duty of all knights-errant such as I who long to engage in deeds of high emprise."

The innkeeper, as we have said, was a sharp fellow. He already had a suspicion that his guest was not quite right in the head, and he was now convinced of it as he listened to such remarks as these. However, just for the sport of it, he determined to humor him; and so he went on to assure Don Quixote that he was fully justified in his request and that such a desire and purpose was only natural on the part of so distinguished a knight as his gallant bearing plainly showed him to be.

He himself, the landlord added, when he was a young man, had followed the same honorable calling. He had gone through various parts of the world seeking adventures, among the places he had visited being the Percheles of Málaga, the Isles of Riarán, the District of Seville, the Little Market Place of Segovia, the Olivera of Valencia, the Rondilla of Granada, the beach of Sanlúcar, the Horse Fountain of Cordova, the Small Taverns of Toledo, and numerous other localities[21] where his nimble feet and light fingers had found much exercise. He had done many wrongs, cheated many widows, ruined many maidens, and swindled not a few minors until he had finally come to be known in almost all the courts and tribunals that are to be found in the whole of Spain.

At last he had retired to his castle here, where he lived upon his own income and the property of others; and here it was that he received all knights-errant of whatever quality and condition, simply

---

21. All the places mentioned were reputed to be haunts of robbers and rogues.

out of the great affection that he bore them and that they might share with him their possessions in payment of his good will. Unfortunately, in this castle there was no chapel where Don Quixote might keep watch over his arms, for the old chapel had been torn down to make way for a new one; but in case of necessity, he felt quite sure that such a vigil could be maintained anywhere, and for the present occasion the courtyard of the castle would do; and then in the morning, please God, the requisite ceremony could be performed and his guest be duly dubbed a knight, as much a knight as anyone ever was.

He then inquired if Don Quixote had any money on his person, and the latter replied that he had not a cent, for in all the storybooks he had never read of knights-errant carrying any. But the innkeeper told him he was mistaken on this point: supposing the authors of those stories had not set down the fact in black and white, that was because they did not deem it necessary to speak of things as indispensable as money and a clean shirt, and one was not to assume for that reason that those knights-errant of whom the books were so full did not have any. He looked upon it as an absolute certainty that they all had well-stuffed purses, that they might be prepared for any emergency; and they also carried shirts and a little box of ointment for healing the wounds that they received.

For when they had been wounded in combat on the plains and in desert places, there was not always someone at hand to treat them, unless they had some skilled enchanter for a friend who then would succor them, bringing to them through the air, upon a cloud, some damsel or dwarf bearing a vial of water of such virtue that one had but to taste a drop of it and at once his wounds were healed and he was as sound as if he had never received any.

But even if this was not the case, knights in times past saw to it that their squires were well provided with money and other necessities, such as lint and ointment for healing purposes; and if they had no squires—which happened very rarely—they themselves carried these objects in a pair of saddlebags very cleverly attached to their horses' croups in such a manner as to be scarcely noticeable, as if they held something of greater importance than that, for among the knights-errant saddlebags as a rule were not favored. Accordingly, he would advise the novice before him, and inasmuch as the latter was soon to be his godson, he might even command him, that henceforth he should not go without money and a supply of those things that have been mentioned, as he would find that they came in useful at a time when he least expected it.

Don Quixote promised to follow his host's advice punctiliously; and so it was arranged that he should watch his armor in a large barnyard at one side of the inn. He gathered up all the pieces, placed them in a horse trough that stood near the well, and, bracing his shield on his arm, took up his lance and with stately demeanor began pacing up and down in front of the trough even as night was closing in.

The innkeeper informed his other guests of what was going on, of Don Quixote's vigil and his expectation of being dubbed a knight; and, marveling greatly at so extraordinary a variety of madness, they all went out to see for themselves and stood there watching from a distance. For a while the knight-to-be, with tranquil mien, would merely walk up and down; then, leaning on his lance, he would pause to survey his armor, gazing fixedly at it for a considerable length of time. As has been said, it was night now, but the brightness of the moon, which well might rival that of Him who lent it, was such that everything the novice knight did was plainly visible to all.

At this point one of the mule drivers who were stopping at the inn came out to water his drove, and in order to do this it was necessary to remove the armor from the trough.

As he saw the man approaching, Don Quixote cried out to him, "O bold knight, whoever you may be, who thus would dare to lay hands upon the accouterments of the most valiant man of arms that ever girded on a sword, look well what you do and desist if you do not wish to pay with your life for your insolence!"

The muleteer gave no heed to these words—it would have been better for his own sake had he done so—but, taking it up by the straps, tossed the armor some distance from him. When he beheld this, Don Quixote rolled his eyes heavenward and with his thoughts apparently upon his Dulcinea exclaimed, "Succor, O lady mine, this vassal heart in this my first encounter; let not your favor and protection fail me in the peril in which for the first time I now find myself."

With these and other similar words, he loosed his buckler, grasped his lance in both his hands, and let the mule driver have such a blow on the head that the man fell to the ground stunned; and had it been followed by another one, he would have had no need of a surgeon to treat him. Having done this, Don Quixote gathered up his armor and resumed his pacing up and down with the same calm manner as before. Not long afterward, without knowing what had happened—for the first muleteer was still lying there unconscious—another came out with the same intention of watering his mules, and he too was about to remove the armor from the trough when the knight, without saying a word or asking favor of anyone, once more adjusted his buckler and raised his lance, and if he did not break the second mule driver's head to bits, he made more than three pieces of it by dividing it into quarters. At the sound of the fracas everybody in the inn came running out, among them the innkeeper; whereupon Don Quixote again lifted his buckler and laid his hand on his sword.

"O lady of beauty," he said, "strength and vigor of this fainting heart of mine! Now is the time to turn the eyes of your greatness upon this captive knight of yours who must face so formidable an adventure."

By this time he had worked himself up to such a pitch of anger that if all the mule drivers in the world had attacked him he would not have taken one step backward. The comrades of the wounded men, seeing the plight those two were in, now began showering stones on Don Quixote, who shielded himself as best he could with his buckler, although he did not dare stir from the trough for fear of leaving his armor unprotected. The landlord, meanwhile, kept calling for them to stop, for he had told them that this was a madman who would be sure to go free even though he killed them all. The knight was shouting louder than ever, calling them knaves and traitors. As for the lord of the castle, who allowed knights-errant to be treated in this fashion, he was a lowborn villain, and if he, Don Quixote, had but received the order of knighthood, he would make him pay for his treachery.

"As for you others, vile and filthy rabble, I take no account of you; you may stone me or come forward and attack me all you like; you shall see what the reward of your folly and insolence will be."

He spoke so vigorously and was so undaunted in bearing as to strike terror in those who would assail him; and for this reason, and owing also to the persuasions of the inkeeper, they ceased stoning him. He then permitted them to carry away the wounded, and went back to watching his armor with the same tranquil, unconcerned air that he had previously displayed.

The landlord was none too well pleased with these mad pranks on the part of his guest and determined to confer upon him that accursed order of knighthood before something else happened. Going up to him, he begged Don Quixote's pardon for the insolence which, without his knowledge, had been shown the knight by those of low degree. They, however, had been well punished for their impudence. As he had said, there was no chapel in this castle, but for that which remained to be done there was no need of any. According to what he had read of the ceremonial of the order, there was nothing to this business of being dubbed a knight except a slap on the neck and one across the shoulder, and that could be performed in the middle of a field as well as anywhere else. All that was required was for the knight-to-be to keep watch over his armor for a couple of hours, and Don Quixote had been at it more than four. The latter believed all this and announced that he was ready to obey and get the matter over with as speedily as possible. Once dubbed a knight, if he were attacked one more time, he did not think that he would leave a single person in the castle alive, save such as he might command be spared, at the bidding of his host and out of respect to him.

Thus warned, and fearful that it might occur, the castellan brought out the book in which he had jotted down the hay and barley for which the mule drivers owed him, and, accompanied by a lad bearing the butt of a candle and the two aforesaid damsels, he came up to where Don Quixote stood and commanded him to kneel. Reading from the account book—as if he had been saying a prayer—he raised his hand and, with the knight's own sword, gave him a good thwack upon the neck and another lusty one upon the shoulder, muttering all the while between his teeth. He then directed one of the ladies to gird on Don Quixote's sword, which she did with much gravity and composure; for it was all they could do to keep from laughing at every point of the ceremony, but the thought of the knight's prowess which they had already witnessed was sufficient to restrain their mirth.

"May God give your Grace much good fortune," said the worthy lady as she attached the blade, "and prosper you in battle."

Don Quixote thereupon inquired her name, for he desired to know to whom it was he was indebted for the favor he had just received, that he might share with her some of the honor which his strong right arm was sure to bring him. She replied very humbly that her name was Tolosa and that she was the daughter of a shoemaker, a native of Toledo who lived in the stalls of Sancho Bienaya.[22] To this the knight replied that she would do him a very great favor if from then on she would call herself Doña Tolosa, and she promised to do so. The other girl then helped him on with his spurs, and practically the same conversation was repeated. When asked her name, she stated that it was La Molinera and added that she was the daughter of a respectable miller of Antequera. Don Quixote likewise requested her to assume the "don" and become Doña Molinera and offered to render her further services and favors.

These unheard-of ceremonies having been dispatched in great haste, Don Quixote could scarcely wait to be astride his horse and sally forth on his quest for adventures. Saddling and mounting Rocinante, he embraced his host, thanking him for the favor of having dubbed him a knight and saying such strange things that it would be quite impossible to record them here. The innkeeper, who was only too glad to be rid of him, answered with a speech that was no less flowery, though somewhat shorter, and he did not so much as ask him for the price of a lodging, so glad was he to see him go.

22. an old square in Toledo.

CHAPTER 4

Of what happened to our knight when he sallied forth from the inn.

Day was dawning when Don Quixote left the inn, so well satisfied with himself, so gay, so exhilarated, that the very girths of his steed all but burst with joy. But remembering the advice which his host had given him concerning the stock of necessary provisions that he should carry with him, especially money and shirts, he decided to turn back home and supply himself with whatever he needed, and with a squire as well; he had in mind a farmer who was a neighbor of his, a poor man and the father of a family but very well suited to fulfill the duties to squire to a man of arms. With this thought in mind he guided Rocinante toward the village once more, and that animal, realizing that he was homeward bound, began stepping out at so lively a gait that it seemed as if his feet barely touched the ground.

The knight had not gone far when from a hedge on his right hand he heard the sound of faint moans as of someone in distress.

"Thanks be to Heaven," he at once exclaimed, "for the favor it has shown me by providing me so soon with an opportunity to fulfill the obligations that I owe to my profession, a chance to pluck the fruit of my worthy desires. Those, undoubtedly, are the cries of someone in distress, who stands in need of my favor and assistance."

Turning Rocinante's head, he rode back to the place from which the cries appeared to be coming. Entering the wood, he had gone but a few paces when he saw a mare attached to an oak, while bound to another tree was a lad of fifteen or thereabouts, naked from the waist up. It was he who was uttering the cries, and not without reason, for there in front of him was a lusty farmer with a girdle who was giving him many lashes, each one accompanied by a reproof and a command, "Hold your tongue and keep your eyes open"; and the lad was saying, "I won't do it again, sir; by God's Passion, I won't do it again. I promise you that after this I'll take better care of the flock."

When he saw what was going on, Don Quixote was very angry. "Discourteous knight," he said, "it ill becomes you to strike one who is powerless to defend himself. Mount your steed and take your lance in hand"—for there was a lance leaning against the oak to which the mare was tied—"and I will show you what a coward you are."

The farmer, seeing before him this figure all clad in armor and brandishing a lance, decided that he was as good as done for. "Sir

Knight," he said, speaking very mildly, "this lad that I am punishing here is my servant; he tends a flock of sheep which I have in these parts and he is so careless that every day one of them shows up missing. And when I punish him for his carelessness or his roguery, he says it is just because I am a miser and do not want to pay him the wages that I owe him, but I swear to God and upon my soul that he lies."

"It is you who lie, base lout," said Don Quixote, "and in my presence; and by the sun that gives us light, I am minded to run you through with this lance. Pay him and say no more about it, or else, by the God who rules us, I will make an end of you and annihilate you here and now. Release him at once."

The farmer hung his head and without a word untied his servant. Don Quixote then asked the boy how much his master owed him. For nine months' work, the lad told him, at seven reales the month. The knight did a little reckoning and found that this came to sixty-three reales; whereupon he ordered the farmer to pay over the money immediately, as he valued his life. The cowardly bumpkin replied that, facing death as he was and by the oath that he had sworn—he had not sworn any oath as yet—it did not amount to as much as that; for there were three pairs of shoes which he had given the lad that were to be deducted and taken into account, and a real for two blood-lettings when his servant was ill.

"That," said Don Quixote, "is all very well; but let the shoes and the blood-lettings go for the undeserved lashings which you have given him; if he has worn out the leather of the shoes that you paid for, you have taken the hide off his body, and if the barber[23] let a little blood for him when he was sick, you have done the same when he was well; and so far as that goes, he owes you nothing."

"But the trouble is, Sir Knight, that I have no money with me. Come along home with me, Andrés, and I will pay you real for real."[24]

"I go home with him!" cried the lad. "Never in the world! No, sir, I would not even think of it; for once he has me alone he'll flay me like a St. Bartholomew."

"He will do nothing of the sort," said Don Quixote. "It is sufficient for me to command, and he out of respect will obey. Since he has sworn to me by the order of knighthood which he has received, I shall let him go free and I will guarantee that you will be paid."

"But look, your Grace," the lad remonstrated, "my master is no knight; he has never received any order of knighthood whatsoever. He is Juan Haldudo, a rich man and a resident of Quintanar."

23. Barbers were also surgeons.   24. See footnote 13.

"That makes little difference," declared Don Quixote, "for there may well be knights among the Haldudos, all the more so in view of the fact that every man is the son of his works."

"That is true enough," said Andrés, "but this master of mine— of what works is he the son, seeing that he refuses me the pay for my sweat and labor?"

"I do not refuse you, brother Andrés," said the farmer. "Do me the favor of coming with me, and I swear to you by all the orders of knighthood that there are in this world to pay you, as I have said, real for real, and perfumed at that."

"You can dispense with the perfume," said Don Quixote; "just give him the reales and I shall be satisfied. And see to it that you keep your oath, or by the one that I myself have sworn I shall return to seek you out and chastise you, and I shall find you though you be as well hidden as a lizard. In case you would like to know who it is that is giving you this command in order that you may feel the more obliged to comply with it, I may tell you that I am the valorous Don Quixote de la Mancha, righter of wrongs and injustices; and so, God be with you, and do not fail to do as you have promised, under that penalty that I have pronounced."

As he said this, he put spurs to Rocinante and was off. The farmer watched him go, and when he saw that Don Quixote was out of the wood and out of sight, he turned to his servant, Andrés.

"Come here, my son," he said. "I want to pay you what I owe you as that righter of wrongs has commanded me."

"Take my word for it," replied Andrés, "your Grace would do well to observe the command of that good knight—may he live a thousand years; for as he is valorous and a righteous judge, if you don't pay me then, by Roque,[25] he will come back and do just what he said!"

"And I will give you my word as well," said the farmer; "but seeing that I am so fond of you, I wish to increase the debt, that I may owe you all the more." And with this he seized the lad's arm and bound him to the tree again and flogged him within an inch of his life. "There, Master Andrés, you may call on that righter of wrongs if you like and you will see whether or not he rights this one. I do not think I have quite finished with you yet, for I have a good mind to flay you alive as you feared."

Finally, however, he unbound him and told him he might go look for that judge of his to carry out the sentence that had been pronounced. Andrés left, rather down in the mouth, swearing that he would indeed go look for the brave Don Quixote de la Mancha; he would relate to him everything that had happened, point by

25. The origin of the oath is unknown.

point, and the farmer would have to pay for it seven times over. But for all that, he went away weeping, and his master stood laughing at him.

Such was the manner in which the valorous knight righted this particular wrong. Don Quixote was quite content with the way everything had turned out; it seemed to him that he had made a very fortunate and noble beginning with his deeds of chivalry, and he was very well satisfied with himself as he jogged along in the direction of his native village, talking to himself in a low voice all the while.

"Well may'st thou call thyself fortunate today, above all other women on earth, O fairest of the fair, Dulcinea del Toboso! Seeing that it has fallen to thy lot to hold subject and submissive to thine every wish and pleasure so valiant and renowned a knight as Don Quixote de la Mancha is and shall be, who, as everyone knows, yesterday received the order of knighthood and this day has righted the greatest wrong and grievance that injustice ever conceived or cruelty ever perpetrated, by snatching the lash from the hand of the merciless foeman who was so unreasonably flogging that tender child."

At this point he came to a road that forked off in four directions, and at once he thought of those crossroads where knights-errant would pause to consider which path they should take. By way of imitating them, he halted there for a while; and when he had given the subject much thought, he slackened Rocinante's rein and let the hack follow its inclination. The animal's first impulse was to make straight for its own stable. After they had gone a couple of miles or so Don Quixote caught sight of what appeared to be a great throng of people, who, as was afterward learned, were certain merchants of Toledo on their way to purchase silk at Murcia. There were six of them altogether with their sunshades, accompanied by four attendants on horseback and three mule drivers on foot.

No sooner had he sighted them than Don Quixote imagined that he was on the brink of some fresh adventure. He was eager to imitate those passages at arms of which he had read in his books, and here, so it seemed to him, was one made to order. And so, with bold and knightly bearing, he settled himself firmly in the stirrups, couched his lance, covered himself with his shield, and took up a position in the middle of the road, where he paused to wait for those other knights-errant (for such he took them to be) to come up to him. When they were near enough to see and hear plainly, Don Quixote raised his voice and made a haughty gesture.

"Let everyone," he cried, "stand where he is, unless everyone will confess that there is not in all the world a more beauteous damsel than the Empress of La Mancha, the peerless Dulcinea del Toboso."

Upon hearing these words and beholding the weird figure who uttered them, the merchants stopped short. From the knight's appearance and his speech they knew at once that they had to deal with a madman; but they were curious to know what was meant by that confession that was demanded of them, and one of their number who was somewhat of a jester and a very clever fellow raised his voice.

"Sir Knight," he said, "we do not know who this beauteous lady is of whom you speak. Show her to us, and if she is as beautiful as you say, then we will right willingly and without any compulsion confess the truth as you have asked of us."

"If I were to show her to you," replied Don Quixote, "what merit would there be in your confessing a truth so self-evident? The important thing is for you, without seeing her, to believe, confess, affirm, swear, and defend that truth. Otherwise, monstrous and arrogant creatures that you are, you shall do battle with me. Come on, then, one by one, as the order of knighthood prescribes; or all of you together, if you will have it so, as is the sorry custom of those of your breed. Come on, and I will await you here, for I am confident that my cause is just."

"Sir Knight," responded the merchant, "I beg your Grace, in the name of all the princes here present, in order that we may not have upon our consciences the burden of confessing a thing which we have never seen nor heard, and one, moreover, so prejudicial to the empresses and queens of Alcarria and Estremadura,[26] that your Grace will show us some portrait of this lady, even though it be no larger than a grain of wheat, for by the thread one comes to the ball of yarn; and with this we shall remain satisfied and assured, and your Grace will likewise be content and satisfied. The truth is, I believe that we are already so much of your way of thinking that though it should show her to be blind of one eye and distilling vermilion and brimstone from the other, nevertheless, to please your Grace, we would say in her behalf all that you desire."

"She distills nothing of the sort, infamous rabble!" shouted Don Quixote, for his wrath was kindling now. "I tell you, she does not distill what you say at all, but amber and civet wrapped in cotton;[27] and she is neither one-eyed nor hunchbacked but straighter than a spindle that comes from Guadarrama. You shall pay for the great blasphemy which you have uttered against such a beauty as is my lady!"

26. ironical, since both were known as particularly backward regions.

27. a musky substance used as perfume, imported from Africa in cotton packings.

Saying this, he came on with lowered lance against the one who had spoken, charging with such wrath and fury that if fortune had not caused Rocinante to stumble and fall in mid-career, things would have gone badly with the merchant and he would have paid for his insolent gibe. As it was, Don Quixote went rolling over the plain for some little distance, and when he tried to get to his feet, found that he was unable to do so, being too encumbered with his lance, shield, spurs, helmet, and the weight of that ancient suit of armor.

"Do not flee, cowardly ones," he cried even as he struggled to rise. "Stay, cravens, for it is not my fault but that of my steed that I am stretched out here."

One of the muleteers, who must have been an ill-natured lad, upon hearing the poor fallen knight speak so arrogantly, could not refrain from giving him an answer in the ribs. Going up to him, he took the knight's lance and broke it into bits, and then with a companion proceeded to belabor him so mercilessly that in spite of his armor they milled him like a hopper of wheat. The merchants called to them not to lay on so hard, saying that was enough and they should desist, but the mule driver by this time had warmed up to the sport and would not stop until he had vented his wrath, and, snatching up the broken pieces of the lance, he began hurling them at the wretched victim as he lay there on the ground. And through all this tempest of sticks that rained upon him Don Quixote never once closed his mouth nor ceased threatening Heaven and earth and these ruffians, for such he took them to be, who were thus mishandling him.

Finally the lad grew tired, and the merchants went their way with a good story to tell about the poor fellow who had had such a cudgeling. Finding himself alone, the knight endeavored to see if he could rise; but if this was a feat that he could not accomplish when he was sound and whole, how was he to achieve it when he had been thrashed and pounded to a pulp? Yet nonetheless he considered himself fortunate; for as he saw it, misfortunes such as this were common to knights-errant, and he put all the blame upon his horse; and if he was unable to rise, that was because his body was so bruised and battered all over.

CHAPTER 5

In which is continued the narrative of the misfortune that befell our knight.

Seeing, then, that he was indeed unable to stir, he decided to fall back upon a favorite remedy of his, which was to think of some passage or other in his books; and as it happened, the one that he

in his madness now recalled was the story of Baldwin and the
Marquis of Mantua, when Carloto left the former wounded upon
the mountainside,[28] a tale that is known to children, not unknown
to young men, celebrated and believed in by the old, and, for all
of that, not any truer than the miracles of Mohammed. Moreover,
it impressed him as being especially suited to the straits in which
he found himself; and, accordingly, with a great show of feeling, he
began rolling and tossing on the ground as he feebly gasped out the
lines which the wounded knight of the wood is supposed to have
uttered:

> "Where art thou, lady mine,
> That thou dost not grieve for my woe?
> Either thou art disloyal,
> Or my grief thou dost not know."

He went on reciting the old ballad until he came to the following
verses:

> "O noble Marquis of Mantua,
> My uncle and liege lord true!"

He had reached this point when down the road came a farmer of
the same village, a neighbor of his, who had been to the mill with
a load of wheat. Seeing a man lying there stretched out like that, he
went up to him and inquired who he was and what was the trouble
that caused him to utter such mournful complaints. Thinking that
this must undoubtedly be his uncle, the Marquis of Mantua, Don
Quixote did not answer but went on with his recitation of the ballad, giving an account of the Marquis' misfortunes and the amours
of his wife and the emperor's son, exactly as the ballad has it.

The farmer was astounded at hearing all these absurdities, and
after removing the knight's visor which had been battered to pieces
by the blows it had received, the good man bathed the victim's face,
only to discover, once the dust was off, that he knew him very well.

"Señor Quijana," he said (for such must have been Don Quixote's
real name when he was in his right senses and before he had given
up the life of a quiet country gentleman to become a knight-errant),
"who is responsible for your Grace's being in such a plight as this?"

But the knight merely went on with his ballad in response to all
the questions asked of him. Perceiving that it was impossible to obtain any information from him, the farmer as best he could relieved
him of his breastplate and backpiece to see if he had any wounds,
but there was no blood and no mark of any sort. He then tried to
lift him from the ground, and with a great deal of effort finally

---

28. The allusion is to an old ballad
about Charlemagne's son Charlot (Carloto) wounding Baldwin, nephew of the
Marquis of Mantua.

managed to get him astride the ass, which appeared to be the easier mount for him. Gathering up the armor, including even the splinters from the lance, he made a bundle and tied it on Rocinante's back, and, taking the horse by the reins and the ass by the halter, he started out for the village. He was worried in his mind at hearing all the foolish things that Don Quixote said, and that individual himself was far from being at ease. Unable by reason of his bruises and his soreness to sit upright on the donkey, our knight-errant kept sighing to Heaven, which led the farmer to ask him once more what it was that ailed him.

It must have been the devil himself who caused him to remember those tales that seemed to fit his own case; for at this point he forgot all about Baldwin and recalled Abindarráez, and how the governor of Antequera, Rodrigo de Narváez, had taken him prisoner and carried him off captive to his castle. Accordingly, when the countryman turned to inquire how he was and what was troubling him, Don Quixote replied with the very same words and phrases that the captive Abindarráez used in answering Rodrigo, just as he had read in the story *Diana* of Jorge de Montemayor,[29] where it is all written down, applying them very aptly to the present circumstances as the farmer went along cursing his luck for having to listen to such a lot of nonsense. Realizing that his neighbor was quite mad, he made haste to reach the village that he might not have to be annoyed any longer by Don Quixote's tiresome harangue.

"Señor Don Rodrigo de Narváez," the knight was saying, "I may inform your Grace that this beautiful Jarifa of whom I speak is not the lovely Dulcinea del Toboso, in whose behalf I have done, am doing, and shall do the most famous deeds of chivalry that ever have been or will be seen in all the world."

"But, sir," replied the farmer, "sinner that I am, cannot your Grace see that I am not Don Rodrigo de Narváez nor the Marquis of Mantua, but Pedro Alonso, your neighbor? And your Grace is neither Baldwin nor Abindarráez but a respectable gentleman by the name of Señor Quijana."

"I know who I am," said Don Quixote, "and who I may be, if I choose: not only those I have mentioned but all the Twelve Peers of France and the Nine Worthies[30] as well; for the exploits of all of them together, or separately, cannot compare with mine."

With such talk as this they reached their destination just as night was falling; but the farmer decided to wait until it was a little darker

---

29. The reference is to the tale of the love of Abindarráez, a captive Moor, for the beautiful Jarifa (mentioned in the following paragraph), contained in the second edition of *Diana*, the pastoral romance by Jorge de Montemayor.

30. In the French medieval epics the Twelve Peers (Roland, Olivier, and so on) were warriors all equal in rank forming a sort of guard of honor around Charlemagne. The Nine Worthies, in a tradition originating in France, were nine famous figures, three biblical, three classical, and three Christian (David, Hector, Alexander, Charlemagne, and so on).

in order that the badly battered gentleman might not be seen arriving in such a condition and mounted on an ass. When he thought the proper time had come, they entered the village and proceeded to Don Quixote's house, where they found everything in confusion. The curate and the barber were there, for they were great friends of the knight, and the housekeeper was speaking to them.

"Señor Licentiate Pero Pérez," she was saying, for that was the manner in which she addressed the curate, "what does your Grace think could have happened to my master? Three days now, and not a word of him, nor the hack, nor the buckler, nor the lance, nor the suit of armor. Ah, poor me! I am as certain as I am that I was born to die that it is those cursed books of chivalry he is always reading that have turned his head; for now that I recall, I have often heard him muttering to himself that he must become a knight-errant and go through the world in search of adventures. May such books as those be consigned to Satan and Barabbas,[31] for they have sent to perdition the finest mind in all La Mancha."

The niece was of the same opinion. "I may tell you, Señor Master Nicholas," she said, for that was the barber's name, "that many times my uncle would sit reading those impious tales of misadventure for two whole days and nights at a stretch; and when he was through, he would toss the book aside, lay his hand on his sword, and begin slashing at the walls. When he was completely exhausted, he would tell us that he had just killed four giants as big as castle towers, while the sweat that poured off him was blood from the wounds that he had received in battle. He would then drink a big jug of cold water, after which he would be very calm and peaceful, saying that the water was the most precious liquid which the wise Esquife, a great magician and his friend, had brought to him. But I blame myself for everything. I should have advised your Worships of my uncle's nonsensical actions so that you could have done something about it by burning those damnable books of his before things came to such a pass; for he has many that ought to be burned as if they were heretics."

"I agree with you," said the curate, "and before tomorrow's sun has set there shall be a public *auto de fe*, and those works shall be condemned to the flames that they may not lead some other who reads them to follow the example of my good friend."

Don Quixote and the farmer overheard all this, and it was then that the latter came to understand the nature of his neighbor's affliction.

"Open the door, your Worships," the good man cried. "Open for Sir Baldwin and the Marquis of Mantua, who comes badly

---

31. the thief whose release, rather than that of Jesus Christ, the crowd requested when Pilate, conforming to Passover custom, was ready to have one prisoner set free.

wounded, and for Señor Abindarráez the Moor whom the valiant Rodrigo de Narváez, governor of Antequera, brings captive."

At the sound of his voice they all ran out, recognizing at once friend, master, and uncle, who as yet was unable to get down off the donkey's back. They all ran up to embrace him.

"Wait, all of you," said Don Quixote, "for I am sorely wounded through fault of my steed. Bear me to my couch and summon, if it be possible, the wise Urganda to treat and care for my wounds."

"There!" exclaimed the housekeeper. "Plague take it! Did not my heart tell me right as to which foot my master limped on? To bed with your Grace at once, and we will take care of you without sending for that Urganda of yours. A curse, I say, and a hundred other curses, on those books of chivalry that have brought your Grace to this."

And so they carried him off to bed, but when they went to look for his wounds, they found none at all. He told them it was all the result of a great fall he had taken with Rocinante, his horse, while engaged in combating ten giants, the hugest and most insolent that were ever heard of in all the world.

"Tut, tut," said the curate. "So there are giants in the dance now, are there? Then, by the sign of the cross, I'll have them burned before nightfall tomorrow."

They had a thousand questions to put to Don Quixote, but his only answer was that they should give him something to eat and let him sleep, for that was the most important thing of all; so they humored him in this. The curate then interrogated the farmer at great length concerning the conversation he had had with his neighbor. The peasant told him everything, all the absurd things their friend had said when he found him lying there and afterward on the way home, all of which made the licentiate more anxious than ever to do what he did the following day,[32] when he summoned Master Nicholas and went with him to Don Quixote's house.

[*Fighting the Windmills*]

CHAPTER 7

Of the second sally of our good knight, Don Quixote de la Mancha.

. . . After that he remained at home very tranquilly for a couple of weeks, without giving sign of any desire to repeat his former madness. During that time he had the most pleasant conversations with his two old friends, the curate and the barber, on the point he had raised to the effect that what the world needed most was knights-errant and a revival of chivalry. The curate would occasionally contradict him and again would give in, for it was only by means

---

32. What he and the barber did was to burn most of Don Quixote's library.

of this artifice that he could carry on a conversation with him at
all.

In the meanwhile Don Quixote was bringing his powers of persuasion to bear upon a farmer who lived near by, a good man—
if this title may be applied to one who is poor—but with very few
wits in his head. The short of it is, by pleas and promises, he got
the hapless rustic to agree to ride forth with him and serve him as
his squire. Among other things, Don Quixote told him that he
ought to be more than willing to go, because no telling what adventure might occur which would win them an island, and then he
(the farmer) would be left to be the governor of it. As a result
of these and other similar assurances, Sancho Panza forsook his
wife and children and consented to take upon himself the duties
of squire to his neighbor.

Next, Don Quixote set out to raise some money, and by selling
this thing and pawning that and getting the worst of the bargain
always, he finally scraped together a reasonable amount. He also
asked a friend of his for the loan of a buckler and patched up his
broken helmet as well as he could. He advised his squire, Sancho,
of the day and hour when they were to take the road and told him
to see to laying in a supply of those things that were most necessary,
and, above all, not to forget the saddlebags. Sancho replied that he
would see to all this and added that he was also thinking of taking
along with him a very good ass that he had, as he was not much
used to going on foot.

With regard to the ass, Don Quixote had to do a little thinking,
trying to recall if any knight-errant had ever had a squire thus
asininely mounted. He could not think of any, but nevertheless he
decided to take Sancho with the intention of providing him with a
nobler steed as soon as occasion offered; he had but to appropriate
the horse of the first discourteous knight he met. Having furnished
himself with shirts and all the other things that the innkeeper had
recommended, he and Panza rode forth one night unseen by anyone and without taking leave of wife and children, housekeeper
or niece. They went so far that by the time morning came they
were safe from discovery had a hunt been started for them.

Mounted on his ass, Sancho Panza rode along like a patriarch,
with saddlebags and flask, his mind set upon becoming governor
of that island that his master had promised him. Don Quixote
determined to take the same route and road over the Campo de
Montiel that he had followed on his first journey; but he was not
so uncomfortable this time, for it was early morning and the sun's
rays fell upon them slantingly and accordingly did not tire them
too much.

"Look, Sir Knight-errant," said Sancho, "your Grace should not forget that island you promised me; for no matter how big it is, I'll be able to govern it right enough."

"I would have you know, friend Sancho Panza," replied Don Quixote, "that among the knights-errant of old it was a very common custom to make their squires governors of the islands or the kingdoms that they won, and I am resolved that in my case so pleasing a usage shall not fall into desuetude. I even mean to go them one better; for they very often, perhaps most of the time, waited until their squires were old men who had had their fill of serving their masters during bad days and worse nights, whereupon they would give them the title of count, or marquis at most, of some valley or province more or less. But if you live and I live, it well may be that within a week I shall win some kingdom with others dependent upon it, and it will be the easiest thing in the world to crown you king of one of them. You need not marvel at this, for all sorts of unforeseen things happen to knights like me, and I may readily be able to give you even more than I have promised."

"In that case," said Sancho Panza, "if by one of those miracles of which your Grace was speaking I should become king, I would certainly send for Juana Gutiérrez, my old lady, to come and be my queen, and the young ones could be infantes."

"There is no doubt about it," Don Quixote assured him.

"Well, I doubt it," said Sancho, "for I think that even if God were to rain kingdoms upon the earth, no crown would sit well on the head of Mari Gutiérrez,[33] for I am telling you, sir, as a queen she is not worth two maravedis. She would do better as a countess, God help her."

"Leave everything to God, Sancho," said Don Quixote, "and he will give you whatever is most fitting; but I trust you will not be so pusillanimous as to be content with anything less than the title of viceroy."

"That I will not," said Sancho Panza, "especially seeing that I have in your Grace so illustrious a master who can give me all that is suitable to me and all that I can manage."

CHAPTER 8

Of the good fortune which the valorous Don Quixote had in the terrifying and never-before-imagined adventure of the windmills, along with other events that deserve to be suitably recorded.

At this point they caught sight of thirty or forty windmills which were standing on the plain there, and no sooner had Don Quixote laid eyes upon them than he turned to his squire and said, "Fortune

33. Sancho's wife; she is called Juana Gutiérrez a few lines earlier.

is guiding our affairs better than we could have wished; for you see there before you, friend Sancho Panza, some thirty or more lawless giants with whom I mean to do battle. I shall deprive them of their lives, and with the spoils from this encounter we shall begin to enrich ourselves; for this is righteous warfare, and it is a great service to God to remove so accursed a breed from the face of the earth."

"What giants?" said Sancho Panza.

"Those that you see there," replied his master, "those with the long arms some of which are as much as two leagues in length."

"But look, your Grace, those are not giants but windmills, and what appear to be arms are their wings which, when whirled in the breeze, cause the millstone to go."

"It is plain to be seen," said Don Quixote, "that you have had little experience in this matter of adventures. If you are afraid, go off to one side and say your prayers while I am engaging them in fierce, unequal combat."

Saying this, he gave spurs to his steed Rocinante, without paying any heed to Sancho's warning that these were truly windmills and not giants that he was riding forth to attack. Nor even when he was close upon them did he perceive what they really were, but shouted at the top of his lungs, "Do not seek to flee, cowards and vile creatures that you are, for it is but a single knight with whom you have to deal!"

At that moment a little wind came up and the big wings began turning.

"Though you flourish as many arms as did the giant Briareus,"[34] said Don Quixote when he perceived this, "you still shall have to answer to me."

He thereupon commended himself with all his heart to his lady Dulcinea, beseeching her to succor him in this peril; and, being well covered with his shield and with his lance at rest, he bore down upon them at a full gallop and fell upon the first mill that stood in his way, giving a thrust at the wing, which was whirling at such a speed that his lance was broken into bits and both horse and horseman went rolling over the plain, very much battered indeed. Sancho upon his donkey came hurrying to his master's assistance as fast as he could, but when he reached the spot, the knight was unable to move, so great was the shock with which he and Rocinante had hit the ground.

"God help us!" exclaimed Sancho, "did I not tell your Grace to look well, that those were nothing but windmills, a fact which no one could fail to see unless he had other mills of the same sort in his head?"

34. mythological giant with a hundred arms.

"Be quiet, friend Sancho," said Don Quixote. "Such are the fortunes of war, which more than any other are subject to constant change. What is more, when I come to think of it, I am sure that this must be the work of that magician Frestón, the one who robbed me of my study and my books,[35] and who has thus changed the giants into windmills in order to deprive me of the glory of overcoming them, so great is the enmity that he bears me; but in the end his evil arts shall not prevail against this trusty sword of mine."

"May God's will be done," was Sancho Panza's response. And with the aid of his squire the knight was once more mounted on Rocinante, who stood there with one shoulder half out of joint. And so, speaking of the adventure that had just befallen them, they continued along the Puerto Lápice highway; for there, Don Quixote said, they could not fail to find many and varied adventures, this being a much traveled thoroughfare. . . .

[*Fighting the Sheep*]

CHAPTER 18

In which is set fort the conversation that Sancho Panza had with his master, Don Quixote, along with other adventures deserving of record.

. . . Don Quixote caught sight down the road of a large cloud of dust that was drawing nearer.

"This, O Sancho," he said, turning to his squire, "is the day when you shall see the boon that fate has in store for me; this, I repeat, is the day when, as well as on any other, shall be displayed the valor of my good right arm. On this day I shall perform deeds that will be written down in the book of fame for all centuries to come. Do you see that dust cloud rising there, Sancho? That is the dust stirred up by a vast army marching in this direction and composed of many nations."

"At that rate," said Sancho, "there must be two of them, for there is another one just like it on the other side."

Don Quixote turned to look and saw that this was so. He was overjoyed by the thought that these were indeed two armies about to meet and clash in the middle of the broad plain; for at every hour and every moment his imagination was filled with battles, enchantments, nonsensical adventures, tales of love, amorous challenges, and the like, such as he had read of in the books of chivalry, and every word he uttered, every thought that crossed his mind, every act he performed, had to do with such things as these. The dust clouds he had sighted were raised by two larges droves of sheep

---

35. Don Quixote had promptly attributed the ruin of his library, performed by the curate and the barber, to magical intervention.

coming along the road in opposite directions, which by reason of the dust were not visible until they were close at hand, but Don Quixote insisted so earnestly that they were armies that Sancho came to believe it.

"Sir," he said, "what are we to do?"

"What are we to do?" echoed his master. "Favor and aid the weak and needy. I would inform you, Sancho, that the one coming toward us is led and commanded by the great emperor Alifanfarón, lord of the great isle of Trapobana. This other one at my back is that of his enemy, the king of the Garamantas, Pentapolín of the Rolled-up Sleeve, for he always goes into battle with his right arm bare."

"But why are they such enemies?" Sancho asked.

"Because," said Don Quixote, "this Alifanfarón is a terrible pagan and in love with Pentapolín's daughter, who is a very beautiful and gracious lady and a Christian, for which reason her father does not wish to give her to the pagan king unless the latter first abjures the law of the false prophet, Mohammed, and adopts the faith that is Pentapolín's own."

"Then, by my beard," said Sancho, "if Pentapolín isn't right, and I am going to aid him all I can."

"In that," said Don Quixote, "you will only be doing your duty; for to engage in battles of this sort you need not have been dubbed a knight."

"I can understand that," said Sancho, "but where are we going to put this ass so that we will be certain of finding him after the fray is over? As for going into battle on such a mount, I do not think that has been done up to now."

"That is true enough," said Don Quixote. "What you had best do with him is to turn him loose and run the risk of losing him; for after we emerge the victors we shall have so many horses that even Rocinante will be in danger of being exchanged for another. But listen closely to what I am about to tell you, for I wish to give you an account of the principal knights that are accompanying these two armies; and in order that you may be the better able to see and take note of them, let us retire to that hillock over there which will afford us a very good view."

They then stationed themselves upon a slight elevation from which they would have been able to see very well the two droves of sheep that Don Quixote took to be armies if it had not been for the blinding clouds of dust. In spite of this, however, the worthy gentleman contrived to behold in his imagination what he did not see and what did not exist in reality.

Raising his voice, he went on to explain, "That knight in the gilded armor that you see there, bearing upon his shield a crowned lion crouched at the feet of a damsel, is the valiant Laurcalco, lord of the Silver Bridge; the other with the golden flowers on his armor, and on his shield three crowns argent on 'an azure field, is the dread Micocolembo, grand duke of Quirocia. And that one on Micocolembo's right hand, with the limbs of a giant, is the ever undaunted Brandabarbarán de Boliche, lord of the three Arabias. He goes armored in a serpent's skin and has for shield a door which, so report has it, is one of those from the temple that Samson pulled down, that time when he avenged himself on his enemies with his own death.

"But turn your eyes in this direction, and you will behold at the head of the other army the ever victorious, never vanquished Timonel de Carcajona, prince of New Biscay, who comes with quartered arms—azure, vert, argent, and or—and who has upon his shield a cat or on a field tawny, with the inscription *Miau*, which is the beginning of his lady's name; for she, so it is said, is the peerless Miulina, daughter of Alfeñquén, duke of Algarve. And that one over there, who weights down and presses the loins of that powerful charger, in a suit of snow-white armor with a white shield that bears no device whatever—he is a novice knight of the French nation, called Pierres Papin, lord of the baronies of Utrique. As for him you see digging his iron spurs into the flanks of that fleet-footed zebra courser and whose arms are vairs azure, he is the mighty duke of Nervia, Espartafilardo of the Wood, who has for device upon his shield an asparagus plant with a motto in Castilian that says 'Rastrea mi suerte.' "[36]

In this manner he went on naming any number of imaginary knights on either side, describing on the spur of the moment their arms, colors, devices, and mottoes; for he was completely carried away by his imagination and by this unheard-of madness that had laid hold of him.

Without pausing, he went on, "This squadron in front of us is composed of men of various nations. There are those who drink the sweet waters of the famous Xanthus; woodsmen who tread the Massilian plain; those that sift the fine gold nuggets of Arabia Felix; those that are so fortunate as to dwell on the banks of the clear-running Thermodon, famed for their coolness; those who in many and diverse ways drain the golden Pactolus; Numidians, whose word is never to be trusted; Persians, with their famous bows and arrows; Medes and Parthians, who fight as they flee; Scythians, as cruel as they are fair of skin; Ethiopians, with their pierced lips; and an infinite number of other nationalities whose visages I see and recognize although I cannot recall their names.

36. probably a pun on *rastrear:* the meaning of the motto may be either "On Fortune's track" or "My Fortune creeps."

"In this other squadron come those that drink from the crystal currents of the olive-bearing Betis; those that smooth and polish their faces with the liquid of the ever rich and gilded Tagus; those that enjoy the beneficial waters of the divine Genil; those that roam the Tartessian plains with their abundant pasturage; those that disport themselves in the Elysian meadows of Jerez; the men of La Mancha, rich and crowned with golden ears of corn; others clad in iron garments, ancient relics of the Gothic race; those that bathe in the Pisuerga, noted for the mildness of its current; those that feed their herds in the wide-spreading pasture lands along the banks of the winding Guadiana, celebrated for its underground course;[37] those that shiver from the cold of the wooded Pyrenees or dwell amid the white peaks of the lofty Apennines—in short, all those whom Europe holds within its girth."

So help me God! How many provinces, how many nations did he not mention by name, giving to each one with marvelous readiness its proper attributes; for he was wholly absorbed and filled to the brim with what he had read in those lying books of his! Sancho Panza hung on his words, saying nothing, merely turning his head from time to time to have a look at those knights and giants that his master was pointing out to him; but he was unable to discover any of them.

"Sir," he said, "may I go to the devil if I see a single man, giant, or knight of all those that your Grace is talking about. Who knows? Maybe it is another spell, like last night."[38]

"How can you say that?" replied Don Quixote. "Can you not hear the neighing of the horses, the sound of trumpets, the roll of drums?"

"I hear nothing," said Sancho, "except the bleating of sheep."

And this, of course, was the truth; for the flocks were drawing near.

"The trouble is, Sancho," said Don Quixote, "you are so afraid that you cannot see or hear properly; for one of the effects of fear is to disturb the senses and cause things to appear other than what they are. If you are so craven as all that, go off to one side and leave me alone, and I without your help will assure the victory to that side to which I lend my aid."

Saying this, he put spurs to Rocinante and, with his lance at rest, darted down the hillside like a flash of lightning.

As he did so, Sancho called after him, "Come back, your Grace, Señor Don Quixote; I vow to God those are sheep that you are charging. Come back! O wretched father that bore me! What madness is this? Look you, there are no giants, nor knights, nor cats, nor shields either quartered or whole, nor vairs azure or bedeviled.

37. The Guadiana does run underground part of the way through La Mancha.

38. The inn where they had spent the previous night had been pronounced by Don Quixote an enchanted castle.

What is this you are doing, O sinner that I am in God's sight?"

But all this did not cause Don Quixote to turn back. Instead, he rode on, crying out at the top of his voice, "Ho, knights, those of you who follow and fight under the banners of the valiant Pentapolín of the Rolled-up Sleeves; follow me, all of you, and you shall see how easily I give you revenge on your enemy, Alifanfarón of Trapobana."

With these words he charged into the middle of the flock of sheep and began spearing at them with as much courage and boldness as if they had been his mortal enemies. The shepherds and herdsmen who were with the animals called to him to stop; but seeing it was no use, they unloosed their slings and saluted his ears with stones as big as your first.

Don Quixote paid no attention to the missiles and, dashing about here and there, kept crying, "Where are you, haughty Alifanfarón? Come out to me; for here is a solitary knight who desires in single combat to test your strength and deprive you of your life, as a punishment for that which you have done to the valorous Pentapolín Garamanta."

At that instant a pebble from the brook struck him in the side and buried a couple of ribs in his body. Believing himself dead or badly wounded, and remembering his potion, he took out his vial, placed it to his mouth, and began to swallow the balm; but before he had had what he thought was enough, there came another almond, which struck him in the hand, crushing the tin vial and carrying away with it a couple of grinders from his mouth, as well as badly mashing two of his fingers. As a result of these blows the poor knight tumbled from his horse. Believing that they had killed him, the shepherds hastily collected their flock and, picking up the dead beasts, of which there were more than seven, they went off down the road without more ado.

Sancho all this time was standing on the slope observing the insane things that his master was doing; and as he plucked savagely at his beard he cursed the hour and minute when luck had brought them together. But when he saw him lying there on the ground and perceived that the shepherds were gone, he went down the hill and came up to him, finding him in very bad shape though not unconscious.

"Didn't I tell you, Señor Don Quixote," he said, "that you should come back, that those were not armies you were charging but flocks of sheep?"

"This," said Don Quixote, "is the work of that thieving magician, my enemy, who thus counterfeits things and causes them to disappear. You must know, Sancho, that it is very easy for them to make us assume any appearance that they choose; and so it is that malign one who persecutes me, envious of the glory he saw me about to achieve in this battle, changed the squadrons of the foe into flocks of sheep. If you do not believe me, I beseech you on my life to do one thing for me, that you may be undeceived and discover for yourself that what I say is true. Mount your ass and follow them quietly, and when you have gone a short way from here, you will see them become their former selves once more; they will no longer be sheep but men exactly as I described them to you in the first place. But do not go now, for I need your kind assistance; come over here and have a look and tell me how many grinders are missing, for it feels as if I did not have a single one left."

["To Right Wrongs and Come to the Aid
of the Wretched"]

CHAPTER 22

*Of how Don Quixote freed many unfortunate ones who, much
against their will, were being taken where they did not wish to go.*

Cid Hamete Benengeli, the Arabic and Manchegan[39] author, in the course of this most grave, high-sounding, minute, delightful, and imaginative history,[40] informs us that, following the remarks that were exchanged between Don Quixote de la Mancha and Sancho Panza, his squire, . . . the knight looked up and saw coming toward them down the road which they were following a dozen or so men on foot, strung together by their necks like beads on an iron chain and all of them wearing handcuffs. They were accompanied by two men on horseback and two on foot, the former carrying wheel-lock muskets while the other two were armed with swords and javelins.

"That," said Sancho as soon as he saw them, "is a chain of galley slaves, people on their way to the galleys where by order of the king they are forced to labor."

"What do you mean by 'forced'?" asked Don Quixote. "Is it possible that the king uses force on anyone?"

"I did not say that," replied Sancho. "What I did say was that these are folks who have been condemned for their crimes to forced labor in the galleys for his Majesty the King."

"The short of it is," said the knight, "whichever way you put it, these people are being taken there by force and not of their own free will."

"That is the way it is," said Sancho.

39. of La Mancha.
40. In the tradition of the romances,   Cervantes pretends that he is taking his story from an earlier chronicle.

"Well, in that case," said his master, "now is the time for me to fulfill the duties of my calling, which is to right wrongs and come to the aid of the wretched."

"But take note, your Grace," said Sancho, "that justice, that is to say, the king himself, is not using any force upon, or doing any wrong to, people like these, but is merely punishing them for the crimes they have committed."

The chain of galley slaves had come up to them by this time, whereupon Don Quixote very courteously requested the guards to inform him of the reason or reasons why they were conducting these people in such a manner as this. One of the men on horseback then replied that the men were prisoners who had been condemned by his Majesty to serve in the galleys, whither they were bound, and that was all there was to be said about it and all that he, Don Quixote, need know.

"Nevertheless," said the latter, "I should like to inquire of each one of them, individually, the cause of his misfortune." And he went on speaking so very politely in an effort to persuade them to tell him what he wanted to know that the other mounted guard finally said, "Although we have here the record and certificate of sentence of each one of these wretches, we have not the time to get them out and read them to you; and so your Grace may come over and ask the prisoners themselves, and they will tell you if they choose, and you may be sure that they will, for these fellows take a delight in their knavish exploits and in boasting of them afterward."

With this permission, even though he would have done so if it had not been granted him, Don Quixote went up to the chain of prisoners and asked the first whom he encountered what sins had brought him to so sorry a plight. The man replied that it was for being a lover that he found himself in that line.

"For that and nothing more?" said Don Quixote. "And do they, then, send lovers to the galleys? If so, I should have been rowing there long ago."

"But it was not the kind of love that your Grace has in mind," the prisoner went on. "I loved a wash basket full of white linen so well and hugged it so tightly that, if they had not taken it away from me by force, I would never of my own choice have let go of it to this very minute. I was caught in the act, there was no need to torture me, the case was soon disposed of, and they supplied me with a hundred lashes across the shoulders and, in addition, a three-year stretch in the *gurapas*, and that's all there is to tell."

"What are *gurapas*?" asked Don Quixote.

"*Gurapas* are the galleys," replied the prisoner. He was a lad of around twenty-four and stated that he was a native of Piedrahita.

The knight then put the same question to a second man, who

appeared to be very downcast and melancholy and did not have a word to say. The first man answered for him.

"This one, sir," he said, "is going as a canary—I mean, as a musician and singer."

"How is that?" Don Quixote wanted to know. "Do musicians and singers go to the galleys too?"

"Yes, sir; and there is nothing worse than singing when you're in trouble."

"On the contrary," said Don Quixote, "I have heard it said that he who sings frightens away his sorrows."

"It is just the opposite," said the prisoner; "for he who sings once weeps all his life long."

"I do not understand," said the knight.

One of the guards then explained. "Sir Knight, with this *non sancta*[41] tribe, to sing when you're in trouble means to confess under torture. This singer was put to the torture and confessed his crime, which was that of being a *cuatrero*, or cattle thief, and as a result of his confession he was condemned to six years in the galleys in addition to two hundred lashes which he took on his shoulders; and so it is he is always downcast and moody, for the other thieves, those back where he came from and the ones here, mistreat, snub, ridicule, and despise him for having confessed and for not having had the courage to deny his guilt. They are in the habit of saying that the word *no* has the same number of letters as the word *sí*,[42] and that a culprit is in luck when his life or death depends on his own tongue and not that of witnesses or upon evidence; and, in my opinion, they are not very far wrong."

"And I," said Don Quixote, "feel the same way about it." He then went on to a third prisoner and repeated his question.

The fellow answered at once, quite unconcernedly. "I'm going to my ladies, the *gurapas*, for five years, for the lack of five ducats."

"I would gladly give twenty," said Don Quixote, "to get you out of this."

"That," said the prisoner, "reminds me of the man in the middle of the ocean who has money and is dying of hunger because there is no place to buy what he needs. I say this for the reason that if I had had, at the right time, those twenty ducats your Grace is now offering me, I'd have greased the notary's quill and freshened up the attorney's wit with them, and I'd now be living in the middle of Zocodover Square in Toledo instead of being here on this highway coupled like a greyhound. But God is great; patience, and that's enough of it."

Don Quixote went on to a fourth prisoner, a venerable-looking old fellow with a white beard that fell over his bosom. When asked

41. unholy.   42. yes.

how he came to be there, this one began weeping and made no reply, but a fifth comrade spoke up in his behalf.

"This worthy man," he said, "is on his way to the galleys after having made the usual rounds clad in a robe of state and on horseback."[43]

"That means, I take it," said Sancho, "that he has been put to shame in public."

"That is it," said the prisoner, "and the offense for which he is being punished is that of having been an ear broker, or, better, a body broker. By that I mean to say, in short, that the gentleman is a pimp, and besides, he has his points as a sorcerer."

"If that point had not been thrown in," said Don Quixote, "he would not deserve, for merely being a pimp, to have to row in the galleys, but rather should be the general and give orders there. For the office of pimp is not an indifferent one; it is a function to be performed by persons of discretion and is most necessary in a well-ordered state; it is a profession that should be followed only by the wellborn, and there should, moreover, be a superviser or examiner as in the case of other offices, and the number of practitioners should be fixed by law as is done with brokers on the exchange. In that way many evils would be averted that arise when this office is filled and this calling practiced by stupid folk and those with little sense, such as silly women and pages or mountebanks with few years and less experience to their credit, who, on the most pressing occasions, when it is necessary to use one's wits, let the crumbs freeze between their hand and their mouth[44] and do not know which is their right hand and which is the left.

"I would go on and give reasons why it is fitting to choose carefully those who are to fulfill so necessary a state function, but this is not the place for it. One of these days I will speak of the matter to someone who is able to do something about it. I will say here only that the pain I felt at seeing those white hairs and this venerable countenance in such a plight, and all for his having been a pimp, has been offset for me by the additional information you have given me, to the effect that he is a sorcerer as well; for I am convinced that there are no sorcerers in the world who can move and compel the will, as some simple-minded persons think, but that our will is free and no herb or charm can force it.[45] All that certain foolish women and cunning tricksters do is to compound a few mixtures and poisons with which they deprive men of their senses while pretending that they have the power to make them loved,

---

43. after having been flogged in public, with all the ceremony that accompanied that punishment.
44. are too startled to act.
45. Here Don Quixote despises charms and love potions though often elsewhere, in his own vision of himself as a knight-errant, he accepts enchantments and spells as part of his world of fantasy.

although, as I have just said, one cannot affect another's will in that manner."

"That is so," said the worthy old man; "but the truth is, sir, I am not guilty on the sorcery charge. As for being a pimp, that is something I cannot deny. I never thought there was any harm in it, however, my only desire being that everyone should enjoy himself and live in peace and quiet, without any quarrels or troubles. But these good intentions on my part cannot prevent me from going where I do not want to go, to a place from which I do not expect to return; for my years are heavy upon me and an affection of the urine that I have will not give me a moment's rest."

With this, he began weeping once more, and Sancho was so touched by it that he took a four-real piece from his bosom and gave it to him as an act of charity.

Don Quixote then went on and asked another what his offense was. The fellow answered him, not with less, but with much more, briskness than the preceding one had shown.

"I am here," he said, "for the reason that I carried a joke too far with a couple of cousins-german of mine and a couple of others who were not mine, and I ended by jesting with all of them to such an extent that the devil himself would never be able to straighten out the relationship. They proved everything on me, there was no one to show me favor, I had no money, I came near swinging for it, they sentenced me to the galleys for six years, and I accepted the sentence as the punishment that was due me. I am young yet, and if I live long enough, everything will come out all right. If, Sir Knight, your Grace has anything with which to aid these poor creatures that you see before you, God will reward you in Heaven, and we here on earth will make it a point to ask God in our prayers to grant you long life and good health, as long and as good as your amiable presence deserves."

This man was dressed as a student, and one of the guards told Don Quixote that he was a great talker and a very fine Latinist.

Back of these came a man around thirty years of age and of very good appearance, except that when he looked at you his eyes were seen to be a little crossed. He was shackled in a different manner from the others, for he dragged behind a chain so huge that it was wrapped all around his body, with two rings at the throat, one of which was attached to the chain while the other was fastened to what is known as a keep-friend or friend's foot, from which two irons hung down to his waist, ending in handcuffs secured by a heavy padlock in such a manner that he could neither raise his hands to his mouth nor lower his head to reach his hands.

When Don Quixote asked why this man was so much more heavily chained than the others, the guard replied that it was be-

cause he had more crimes against him than all the others put together, and he was so bold and cunning that, even though they
had him chained like this, they were by no means sure of him but
feared that he might escape from them.

"What crimes could he have committed," asked the knight, "if
he has merited a punishment no greater than that of being sent to
the galleys?"

"He is being sent there for ten years," replied the guard, "and
that is equivalent to civil death. I need tell you no more than that
this good man is the famous Ginés de Pasamonte, otherwise known
as Ginesillo de Parapilla."

"Señor Commissary," spoke up the prisoner at this point, "go
easy there and let us not be so free with names and surnames. My
just name is Ginés and not Ginesillo; and Pasamonte, not Parapilla
as you make it out to be, is my family name. Let each one mind
his own affairs and he will have his hands full."

"Speak a little more respectfully, you big thief, you," said the
commissary, "unless you want me to make you be quiet in a way
you won't like."

"Man goes as God pleases, that is plain to be seen," replied the
galley slave, "but someday someone will know whether my name is
Ginesillo de Parapilla or not."

"But, you liar, isn't that what they call you?"

"Yes," said Ginés, "they do call me that; but I'll put a stop to it,
or else I'll skin their you-know-what. And you, sir, if you have anything to give us, give it and may God go with you, for I am tired
of all this prying into other people's lives. If you want to know
anything about my life, know that I am Ginés de Pasamonte whose
life story has been written down by these fingers that you see here."

"He speaks the truth," said the commissary, "for he has himself
written his story, as big as you please, and has left the book in
the prison, having pawned it for two hundred reales."

"And I mean to redeem it," said Ginés, "even if it costs me two
hundred ducats."

"Is it as good as that?" inquired Don Quixote.

"It is so good," replied Ginés, "that it will cast into the shade
Lazarillo de Tormes[46] and all others of that sort that have been or
will be written. What I would tell you is that it deals with facts,
and facts so interesting and amusing that no lies could equal them."

"And what is the title of the book?" asked Don Quixote.

"*The Life of Ginés de Pasamonte.*"

"Is it finished?"

"How could it be finished," said Ginés, "when my life is not

46. a picaresque or rogue novel, published anonymously about the middle of the
fifteenth century.

finished as yet? What I have written thus far is an account of what happened to me from the time I was born up to the last time that they sent me to the galleys."

"Then you have been there before?"

"In the service of God and the king I was there four years, and I know what the biscuit and the cowhide are like. I don't mind going very much, for there I will have a chance to finish my book. I still have many things to say, and in the Spanish galleys I shall have all the leisure that I need, though I don't need much, since I know by heart what it is I want to write."

"You seem to be a clever fellow," said Don Quixote.

"And an unfortunate one," said Ginés; "for misfortunes always pursue men of genius."

"They pursue rogues," said the commissary.

"I have told you to go easy, Señor Commissary," said Pasamonte, "for their Lordships did not give you that staff in order that you might mistreat us poor devils with it, but they intended that you should guide and conduct us in accordance with his Majesty's command. Otherwise, by the life of— But enough. It may be that someday the stains made in the inn will come out in the wash. Meanwhile, let everyone hold his tongue, behave well, and speak better, and let us be on our way. We've had enough of this foolishness."

At this point the commissary raised his staff as if to let Pasamonte have it in answer to his threats, but Don Quixote placed himself between them and begged the officer not to abuse the man; for it was not to be wondered at if one who had his hands so bound should be a trifle free with his tongue. With this, he turned and addressed them all.

"From all that you have told me, my dearest brothers," he said, "one thing stands out clearly for me, and that is the fact that, even though it is a punishment for offenses which you have committed, the penalty you are about to pay is not greatly to your liking and you are going to the galleys very much against your own will and desire. It may be that the lack of spirit which one of you displayed under torture, the lack of money on the part of another, the lack of influential friends, or, finally, warped judgment on the part of the magistrate, was the thing that led to your downfall; and, as a result, justice was not done you. All of which presents itself to my mind in such a fashion that I am at this moment engaged in trying to persuade and even force myself to show you what the purpose was for which Heaven sent me into this world, why it was it led me to adopt the calling of knighthood which I profess and take the knightly vow to favor the needy and aid those who are oppressed by the powerful.

"However, knowing as I do that it is not the part of prudence to do by foul means what can be accomplished by fair ones, I propose to ask these gentlemen, your guards, and the commissary to be so good as to unshackle you and permit you to go in peace. There will be no dearth of others to serve his Majesty under more propitious circumstances; and it does not appear to me to be just to make slaves of those whom God created as free men. What is more, gentlemen of the guard, these poor fellows have committed no offense against you. Up there, each of us will have to answer for his own sins; for God in Heaven will not fail to punish the evil and reward the good; and it is not good for self-respecting men to be executioners of their fellow-men in something that does not concern them. And so, I ask this of you, gently and quietly, in order that, if you comply with my request, I shall have reason to thank you; and if you do not do so of your own accord, then this lance and this sword and the valor of my arm shall compel you to do it by force."

"A fine lot of foolishness!" exclaimed the commissary. "So he comes out at last with this nonsense! He would have us let the prisoners of the king go free, as if we had any authority to do so or he any right to command it! Be on your way, sir, at once; straighten that basin that you have on your head, and do not go looking for three feet on a cat."[47]

"You," replied Don Quixote, "are the cat and the rat and the rascal!" And, saying this, he charged the commissary so quickly that the latter had no chance to defend himself but fell to the ground badly wounded by the lance blow. The other guards were astounded by this unexpected occurrence; but, recovering their self-possession, those on horseback drew their swords, those on foot leveled their javelins, and all bore down on Don Quixote, who stood waiting for them very calmly. Things undoubtedly would have gone badly for him if the galley slaves, seeing an opportunity to gain their freedom, had not succeeded in breaking the chain that linked them together. Such was the confusion that the guards, now running to fall upon the prisoners and now attacking Don Quixote, who in turn was attacking them, accomplished nothing that was of any use.

Sancho for his part aided Ginés de Pasamonte to free himself, and that individual was the first to drop his chains and leap out onto the field, where, attacking the fallen commissary, he took away that officer's sword and musket; and as he stood there, aiming first at one and then at another, though without firing, the plain was soon cleared of guards, for they had taken to their heels, fleeing at once Pasamonte's weapon and the stones which the galley slaves,

---

47. looking for the impossible ("five feet" in the more usual form of the proverb).

freed now, were hurling at them. Sancho, meanwhile, was very much disturbed over this unfortunate event, as he felt sure that the fugitives would report the matter to the Holy Brotherhood,[48] which, to the ringing of the alarm bell, would come out to search for the guilty parties. He said as much to his master, telling him that they should leave at once and go into hiding in the near-by mountains.

"That is all very well," said Don Quixote, "but I know what had best be done now." He then summoned all the prisoners, who, running riot, had by this time despoiled the commissary of every-thing that he had, down to his skin, and as they gathered around to hear what he had to say, he addressed them as follows:

"It is fitting that those who are wellborn should give thanks for the benefits they have received, and one of the sins with which God is most offended is that of ingratitude. I say this, gentlemen, for the reason that you have seen and had manifest proof of what you owe to me; and now that you are free of the yoke which I have removed from about your necks, it is my will and desire that you should set out and proceed to the city of El Toboso and there present yourselves before the lady Dulcinea del Toboso and say to her that her champion, the Knight of the Mournful Countenance, has sent you; and then you will relate to her, point by point, the whole of this famous adventure which has won you your longed-for freedom. Having done that, you may go where you like, and may good luck go with you."

To this Ginés de Pasamonte replied in behalf of all of them, "It is absolutely impossible, your Grace, our liberator, for us to do what you have commanded. We cannot go down the highway all together but must separate and go singly, each in his own direction, endeavoring to hide ourselves in the bowels of the earth in order not to be found by the Holy Brotherhood, which undoubtedly will come out to search for us. What your Grace can do, and it is right that you should do so, is to change this service and toll that you require of us in connection with the lady Dulcinea del Toboso into a certain number of Credos and Hail Marys which we will say for your Grace's intention, as this is something that can be accomplished by day or night, fleeing or resting, in peace or in war. To imagine, on the other hand, that we are going to return to the fleshpots of Egypt, by which I mean, take up our chains again by setting out along the highway for El Toboso, is to believe that it is night now instead of ten o'clock in the morning and is to ask of us something that is the same as asking pears of the elm tree."

"Then by all that's holy!" exclaimed Don Quixote, whose wrath

48. a tribunal instituted by Ferdi-nand and Isabella at the end of the fifteenth century to punish highway robberies.

was now aroused, "you, Don Son of a Whore, Don Ginesillo de Parapilla, or whatever your name is, you shall go alone, your tail between your legs and the whole chain on your back."

Pasamonte, who was by no means a long-suffering individual, was by this time convinced that Don Quixote was not quite right in the head, seeing that he had been guilty of such a folly as that of desiring to free them; and so, when he heard himself insulted in this manner, he merely gave the wink to his companions and, going off to one side, began raining so many stones upon the knight that the latter was wholly unable to protect himself with his buckler, while poor Rocinante paid no more attention to the spur than if he had been made of brass. As for Sancho, he took refuge behind his donkey as a protection against the cloud and shower of rocks that was falling on both of them, but Don Quixote was not able to shield himself so well, and there is no telling how many struck his body, with such force as to unhorse and bring him to the ground.

No sooner had he fallen than the student was upon him. Seizing the basin from the knight's head, he struck him three or four blows with it across the shoulders and banged it against the ground an equal number of times until it was fairly shattered to bits. They then stripped Don Quixote of the doublet which he wore over his armor, and would have taken his hose as well, if his greaves had not prevented them from doing so, and made off with Sancho's great-coat, leaving him naked; after which, dividing the rest of the battle spoils amongst themselves, each of them went his own way, being a good deal more concerned with eluding the dreaded Holy Brotherhood than they were with burdening themselves with a chain or going to present themselves before the lady Dulcinea del Toboso.

They were left alone now—the ass and Rocinante, Sancho and Don Quixote: the ass, crestfallen and pensive, wagging its ears now and then, being under the impression that the hurricane of stones that had raged about them was not yet over; Rocinante, stretched alongside his master, for the hack also had been felled by a stone; Sancho, naked and fearful of the Holy Brotherhood; and Don Quixote, making wry faces at seeing himself so mishandled by those to whom he had done so much good.

CHAPTER 52[49]

Of the quarrel that Don Quixote had with the goatherd, together with the rare adventure of the penitents, which the knight by the sweat of his brow brought to a happy conclusion.

All those who had listened to it were greatly pleased with the goatherd's story,[50] especially the canon,[51] who was more than usually interested in noting the manner in which it had been told. Far from being a mere rustic herdsman, the narrator seemed rather a cultured city dweller; and the canon accordingly remarked that the curate had been quite right in saying that the mountain groves bred men of learning. They all now offered their services to Eugenio, and Don Quixote was the most generous of any in this regard.

"Most assuredly, brother goatherd," he said, "if it were possible for me to undertake any adventure just now, I would set out at once to aid you and would take Leandra out of that convent, where she is undoubtedly being held against her will, in spite of the abbess and all the others who might try to prevent me, after which I would place her in your hands to do with as you liked, with due respect, however, for the laws of chivalry, which command that no violence be offered to any damsel. But I trust in God, Our Lord, that the power of one malicious enchanter is not so great that another magician may not prove still more powerful, and then I promise you my favor and my aid, as my calling obliges me to do, since it is none other than that of succoring the weak and those who are in distress."

The goatherd stared at him, observing in some astonishment the knight's unprepossessing appearance.

"Sir," he said, turning to the barber who sat beside him, "who is this man who looks so strange and talks in this way?"

"Who should it be," the barber replied, "if not the famous Don Quixote de la Mancha, righter of wrongs, avenger of injustices, protector of damsels, terror of giants, and champion of battles?"

"That," said the goatherd, "sounds to me like the sort of thing you read of in books of chivalry, where they do all those things that your Grace has mentioned in connection with this man. But if you

49. last chapter of Part I. Through various devices, including the use of Don Quixote's own belief in enchantments and spells, the curate and the barber have persuaded the knight to let himself be taken home in an ox cart.

50. Eugenio, a very literate goatherd met on the way, has just told them the story of his unhappy love for Leandra: the girl, instead of choosing one of her local suitors, had eloped with a flashy and crooked soldier; robbed and abandoned by him, she had been put by her father in a convent.

51. a canon from Toledo who has joined Don Quixote and his guardians on the way; conversing about chivalry with the knight, he has had cause to be "astonished at Don Quixote's well-reasoned nonsense."

ask me, either your Grace is joking or this worthy gentleman must have a number of rooms to let inside his head."

"You are the greatest villain that ever was!" cried Don Quixote when he heard this. "It is you who are the empty one; I am fuller than the bitch that bore you ever was." Saying this, he snatched up a loaf of bread that was lying beside him and hurled it straight in the goatherd's face with such force as to flatten the man's nose. Upon finding himself thus mistreated in earnest, Eugenio, who did not understand this kind of joke, forgot all about the carpet, the tablecloth, and the other diners and leaped upon Don Quixote. Seizing him by the throat with both hands, he would no doubt have strangled him if Sancho Panza, who now came running up, had not grasped him by the shoulders and flung him backward over the table, smashing plates and cups and spilling and scattering all the food and drink that was there. Thus freed of his assailant, Don Quixote then threw himself upon the shepherd, who, with bleeding face and very much battered by Sancho's feet, was creeping about on his hands and knees in search of a table knife with which to exact a sanguinary vengeance, a purpose which the canon and the curate prevented him from carrying out. The barber, however, so contrived it that the goatherd came down on top of his opponent, upon whom he now showered so many blows that the poor knight's countenance was soon as bloody as his own.

As all this went on, the canon and the curate were laughing fit to burst, the troopers[52] were dancing with glee, and they all hissed on the pair as men do at a dog fight. Sancho Panza alone was in despair, being unable to free himself of one of the canon's servants who held him back from going to his master's aid. And then, just as they were all enjoying themselves hugely, with the exception of the two who were mauling each other, the note of a trumpet fell upon their ears, a sound so mournful that it caused them all to turn their heads in the direction from which it came. The one who was most excited by it was Don Quixote; who, very much against his will and more than a little bruised, was lying pinned beneath the goatherd.

"Brother Demon," he now said to the shepherd, "for you could not possibly be anything but a demon, seeing that you have shown a strength and valor greater than mine, I request you to call a truce for no more than an hour; for the doleful sound of that trumpet that we hear seems to me to be some new adventure that is calling me."

Tired of mauling and being mauled, the goatherd let him up at once. As he rose to his feet and turned his head in the direction of the sound, Don Quixote then saw, coming down the slope of a hill, a large number of persons clad in white after the fashion of peni-

52. law officers from the Holy Brotherhood (cf. n. 48). They had wanted to arrest Don Quixote on account of his having attempted the liberation of the galley slaves but had been persuaded not to do so, considering the knight's state of insanity.

tents; for, as it happened, the clouds that year had denied their moisture to the earth, and in all the villages of that district processions for prayer and penance were being organized with the purpose of beseeching God to have mercy and send rain. With this object in view, the good folk from a near-by town were making a pilgrimage to a devout hermit who dwelt on these slopes. Upon beholding the strange costumes that the penitents wore, without pausing to think how many times he had seen them before, Don Quixote imagined that this must be some adventure or other, and that it was for him alone as a knight-errant to undertake it. He was strengthened in this belief by the sight of a covered image that they bore, as it seemed to him this must be some highborn lady whom these scoundrelly and discourteous brigands were forcibly carrying off; and no sooner did this idea occur to him than he made for Rocinante, who was grazing not far away.

Taking the bridle and his buckler from off the saddletree, he had the bridle adjusted in no time, and then, asking Sancho for his sword, he climbed into the saddle, braced his shield upon his arm, and cried out to those present, "And now, valorous company, you shall see how important it is to have in the world those who follow the profession of knight-errantry. You have but to watch how I shall set at liberty that worthy lady who there goes captive, and then you may tell me whether or not such knights are to be esteemed."

As he said this, he dug his legs into Rocinante's flanks, since he had no spurs, and at a fast trot (for nowhere in this veracious history are we ever told that the hack ran full speed) he bore down on the penitents in spite of all that the canon, the curate, and the barber could do to restrain him—their efforts were as vain as were the pleadings of his squire.

"Where are you bound for, Señor Don Quixote?" Sancho called after him. "What evil spirits in your bosom spur you on to go against our Catholic faith? Plague take me, can't you see that's a procession of penitents and that lady they're carrying on the litter is the most blessed image of the Immaculate Virgin? Look well what you're doing, my master, for this time it may be said that you really do not know."

His exertions were in vain, however, for his master was so bent upon having it out with the sheeted figures and freeing the lady clad in mourning that he did not hear a word, nor would he have turned back if he had, though the king himself might have commanded it. Having reached the procession, he reined in Rocinante, who by this time was wanting a little rest, and in a hoarse, excited voice he shouted, "You who go there with your faces covered, out of shame, it may be, listen well to what I have to say to you."

The first to come to a halt were those who carried the image; and then one of the four clerics who were intoning the litanies, upon beholding Don Quixote's weird figure, his bony nag, and other amusing appurtenances, spoke up in reply.

"Brother, if you have something to say to us, say it quickly, for these brethren are engaged in macerating their flesh, and we cannot stop to hear anything, nor is it fitting that we should, unless it is capable of being said in a couple of words."

"I will say it to you in one word," Don Quixote answered, "and that word is the following: 'Set free at once that lovely lady whose tears and mournful countenance show plainly that you are carrying her away against her will and that you have done her some shameful wrong. I will not consent to your going one step farther until you shall have given her the freedom that should be hers.'"

Hearing these words, they all thought that Don Quixote must be some madman or other and began laughing heartily; but their laughter proved to be gunpowder to his wrath, and without saying another word he drew his sword and fell upon the litter. One of those who bore the image, leaving his share of the burden to his companions, then sallied forth to meet the knight, flourishing a forked stick that he used to support the Virgin while he was resting; and upon this stick he now received a mighty slash that Don Quixote dealt him, one that shattered it in two, but with the piece about a third long that remained in his hand he came down on the shoulder of his opponent's sword arm, left unprotected by the buckler, with so much force that the poor fellow sank to the ground sorely battered and bruised.

Sancho Panza, who was puffing along close behind his master, upon seeing him fall cried out to the attacker not to deal another blow, as this was an unfortunate knight who was under a magic spell but who had never in all the days of his life done any harm to anyone. But the thing that stopped the rustic was not Sancho's words; it was, rather, the sight of Don Quixote lying there without moving hand or foot. And so, thinking that he had killed him, he hastily girded up his tunic and took to his heels across the countryside like a deer.

By this time all of Don Quixote's companions had come running up to where he lay; and the penitents, when they observed this, and especially when they caught sight of the officers of the Brotherhood with their crossbows, at once rallied around the image, where they raised their hoods and grasped their whips as the priests raised their tapers aloft in expectation of an assault; for they were resolved to defend themselves and even, if possible, to take the offensive against their assailants, but, as luck would have it, things turned out better than they had hoped. Sancho, meanwhile, believing Don Quixote to be dead, had flung himself across his master's body and was weeping and wailing in the most lugubrious and, at the same time, the most laughable fashion that could be imagined; and the curate had discovered among those who marched in the procession another curate whom he knew, their recognition of each other serving to allay the fears of all parties concerned. The first curate then gave the second a very brief account of who Don Quixote was, whereupon all the penitents came up to see if the poor knight was dead. And as they did so, they heard Sancho Panza speaking with tears in his eyes.

"O flower of chivalry,"[53] he was saying, "the course of whose well-spent years has been brought to an end by a single blow of a club! O honor of your line, honor and glory of all La Mancha and of all the world, which, with you absent from it, will be full of evildoers who will not fear being punished for their deeds! O master more generous than all the Alexanders, who after only eight months of service presented me with the best island that the sea washes and surrounds! Humble with the proud, haughty with the humble, brave in facing dangers, long-suffering under outrages, in love without reason, imitator of the good, scourge of the wicked, enemy of the mean—in a word, a knight-errant, which is all there is to say."

At the sound of Sancho's cries and moans, Don Quixote revived, and the first thing he said was, "He who lives apart from thee, O fairest Dulcinea, is subject to greater woes than those I now endure. Friend Sancho, help me onto that enchanted cart, as I am in no condition to sit in Rocinante's saddle with this shoulder of mine knocked to pieces the way it is."

"That I will gladly do, my master," replied Sancho, "and we will go back to my village in the company of these gentlemen who are concerned for your welfare, and there we will arrange for another sally and one, let us hope, that will bring us more profit and fame than this one has."

"Well spoken, Sancho," said Don Quixote, "for it will be an act of great prudence to wait until the present evil influence of the stars has passed."

The canon, the curate, and the barber all assured him that he would be wise in doing this; and so, much amused by Sancho Panza's simplicity, they placed Don Quixote upon the cart as before, while the procession of penitents re-formed and continued on its way. The goatherd took leave of all of them, and the curate paid the troopers what was coming to them, since they did not wish to go any farther. The canon requested the priest to inform him of the outcome of Don Quixote's madness, as to whether it yielded to treatment or not; and with this he begged permission to resume his journey. In short, the party broke up and separated, leaving only the curate and the barber, Don Quixote and Panza, and the good Rocinante, who looked upon everything that he had seen with the same resignation as his master. Yoking his oxen, the carter made the knight comfortable upon a bale of hay, and then at his customary slow pace proceeded to follow the road that the curate directed him to take. At the end of the six days they reached Don Quixote's village, making their entrance at noon of a Sunday, when the square

53. Note how Sancho has absorbed some of his master's speech mannerisms.

was filled with a crowd of people through which the cart had to pass.

They all came running to see who it was, and when they recognized their townsman, they were vastly astonished. One lad sped to bring the news to the knight's housekeeper and his niece, telling them that their master had returned lean and jaundiced and lying stretched out upon a bale of hay on an ox-cart. It was pitiful to hear the good ladies' screams, to behold the way in which they beat their breasts, and to listen to the curses which they once more heaped upon those damnable books of chivalry, and this demonstration increased as they saw Don Quixote coming through the doorway.

At news of the knight's return, Sancho Panza's wife had hurried to the scene, for she had some while since learned that her husband had accompanied him as his squire; and now, as soon as she laid eyes upon her man, the first question she asked was if all was well with the ass, to which Sancho replied that the beast was better off then his master.

"Thank God," she exclaimed, "for all his blessings! But tell me now, my dear, what have you brought me from all your squirings? A new cloak to wear? Or shoes for the young ones?"

"I've brought you nothing of the sort, good wife," said Sancho, "but other things of greater value and importance."

"I'm glad to hear that," she replied. "Show me those things of greater value and importance, my dear. I'd like a sight of them just to cheer this heart of mine which has been so sad and unhappy all the centuries that you've been gone."

"I will show them to you at home, wife," said Sancho. "For the present be satisfied that if, God willing, we set out on another journey in search of adventures, you will see me in no time a count or the governor of an island, and not one of those around here, but the best that is to be had."

"I hope to Heaven it's true, my husband, for we certainly need it. But tell me, what is all this about islands? I don't understand."

"Honey," replied Sancho, "is not for the mouth of an ass. You will find out in good time, woman; and you're going to be surprised to hear yourself called 'my Ladyship' by all your vassals."

"What's this you are saying, Sancho, about ladyships, islands, and vassals?" Juana Panza insisted on knowing—for such was the name of Sancho's wife, although they were not blood relatives, it being the custom in La Mancha for wives to take their husbands' surnames.

"Do not be in such a hurry to know all this, Juana," he said. "It is enough that I am telling you the truth. Sew up your mouth, then; for all I will say, in passing, is that there is nothing in the world that is more pleasant than being a respected man, squire to a knight-errant who goes in search of adventures. It is true that most of the adventures you meet with do not come out the way you'd like them to, for ninety-nine out of a hundred will prove to be all twisted and crosswise. I know that from experience, for I've come out of some of them blanketed and out of others beaten to a pulp. But, all the same, it's a fine thing to go along waiting for what will happen next, crossing mountains, making your way through woods, climbing over cliffs, visiting castles, and putting up at inns free of charge, and the devil take the maravedi that is to pay."

Such was the conversation that took place between Sancho Panza and Juana Panza, his wife, as Don Quixote's housekeeper and niece were taking him in, stripping him, and stretching him out on his old-time bed. He gazed at them blankly, being unable to make out where he was. The curate charged the niece to take great care to see that her uncle was comfortable and to keep close watch over him so that he would not slip away from them another time. He then told them of what it had been necessary to do in order to get him home, at which they once more screamed to Heaven and began cursing the books of chivalry all over again, praying God to plunge the authors of such lying nonsense into the center of the bottomless pit. In short, they scarcely knew what to do, for they were very much afraid that their master and uncle would give them the slip once more, the moment he was a little better, and it turned out just the way they feared it might.

Don Quixote, Part II
["Put into a Book"]

CHAPTER 3

Of the laughable conversation that took place between Don Quixote, Sancho Panza, and the bachelor Sansón Carrasco.

Don Quixote remained in a thoughtful mood as he waited for the bachelor Carrasco,[54] from whom he hoped to hear the news as to how he had been put into a book, as Sancho had said. He could not bring himself to believe that any such history existed, since the blood of the enemies he had slain was not yet dry on the blade of his sword; and here they were trying to tell him that his high deeds of chivalry were already circulating in printed form. But, for that matter, he imagined that some sage, either friend or enemy, must have seen to the printing of them through the art of magic. If the chronicler was a friend, he must have undertaken the task in order

---

54. the bachelor of arts Sansón Carrasco, an important new character who appears at the beginning of Part II and will play a considerable role in the story with his attempts at "curing" the Don (the first one a failure, the second one a success; see our following selections). Just now he has been telling Sancho about a book relating the adventures of Don Quixote and his squire, by which the two have been made famous; the book is, of course, *Don Quixote*, Part I.

to magnify and exalt Don Quixote's exploits above the most notable ones achieved by knights-errant of old. If an enemy, his purpose would have been to make them out as nothing at all, by debasing them below the meanest acts ever recorded of any mean squire. The only thing was, the knight reflected, the exploits of squires never were set down in writing. If it was true that such a history existed, being about a knight-errant, then it must be eloquent and lofty in tone, a splendid and distinguished piece of work and veracious in its details.

This consoled him somewhat, although he was a bit put out at the thought that the author was a Moor, if the appellation "Cid" was to be taken as an indication,[55] and from the Moors you could never hope for any word of truth, seeing that they are all of them cheats, forgers, and schemers. He feared lest his love should not have been treated with becoming modesty but rather in a way that would reflect upon the virtue of his lady Dulcinea del Toboso. He hoped that his fidelity had been made clear, and the respect he had always shown her, and that something had been said as to how he had spurned queens, empresses, and damsels of every rank while keeping a rein upon those impulses that are natural to a man. He was still wrapped up in these and many other similar thoughts when Sancho returned with Carrasco.

Don Quixote received the bachelor very amiably. The latter, although his name was Sansón, or Samson, was not very big so far as bodily size went, but he was a great joker, with a sallow complexion and a ready wit. He was going on twenty-four and had a round face, a snub nose, and a large mouth, all of which showed him to be of a mischievous disposition and fond of jests and witticisms. This became apparent when, as soon as he saw Don Quixote, he fell upon his knees and addressed the knight as follows:

"O mighty Don Quixote de la Mancha, give me your hands; for by the habit of St. Peter that I wear[56]—though I have received but the first four orders—your Grace is one of the most famous knights-errant that ever have been or ever will be anywhere on this earth. Blessings upon Cid Hamete Benengeli who wrote down the history of your great achievements, and upon that curious-minded one who was at pains to have it translated from the Arabic into our Castilian vulgate for the universal entertainment of the people."

Don Quixote bade him rise. "Is it true, then," he asked, "that there is a book about me and that it was some Moorish sage who composed it?"

"By way of showing you how true it is," replied Sansón, "I may

55. The allusion is to Cid Hamete Benengeli (see footnote 40 and the corresponding passage in the text); the word

cid, "chief," is of Arabic derivation.

56. the dress of one of the minor clerical orders.

tell you that it is my belief that there are in existence today more than twelve thousand copies of that history. If you do not believe me, you have but to make inquiries in Portugal, Barcelona, and Valencia, where editions have been brought out, and there is even a report to the effect that one edition was printed at Antwerp. In short, I feel certain that there will soon not be a nation that does not know it or a language into which it has not been translated."

"One of the things," remarked Don Quixote, "that should give most satisfaction to a virtuous and eminent man is to see his good name spread abroad during his own lifetime, by means of the printing press, through translations into the languages of the various peoples. I have said 'good name,' for if he has any other kind, his fate is worse than death."

"If it is a matter of good name and good reputation," said the bachelor, "your Grace bears off the palm from all the knights-errant in the world; for the Moor in his tongue and the Christian in his have most vividly depicted your Grace's gallantry, your courage in facing dangers, your patience in adversity and suffering, whether the suffering be due to wounds or to misfortunes of another sort, and your virtue and continence in love, in connection with that platonic relationship that exists between your Grace and my lady Doña Dulcinea del Toboso."

At this point Sancho spoke up. "Never in my life," he said, "have I heard my lady Dulcinea called 'Doña,' but only 'la Señora Dulcinea del Toboso'; so on that point, already, the history is wrong."

"That is not important," said Carrasco.

"No, certainly not," Don Quixote agreed. "But tell me, Señor Bachelor, what adventures of mine as set down in this book have made the deepest impression?"

"As to that," the bachelor answered, "opinions differ, for it is a matter of individual taste. There are some who are very fond of the adventure of the windmills—those windmills which to your Grace appeared to be so many Briareuses and giants. Others like the episode at the fulling mill. One relishes the story of the two armies which took on the appearance of droves of sheep, while another fancies the tale of the dead man whom they were taking to Segovia for burial. One will assert that the freeing of the galley slaves is the best of all, and yet another will maintain that nothing can come up to the Benedictine giants and the encounter with the valiant Biscayan."

Again Sancho interrupted him. "Tell me, Señor Bachelor," he said, "does the book say anything about the adventure with the Yanguesans, that time our good Rocinante took it into his head to go looking for tidbits in the sea?"

"The sage," replied Sansón, "has left nothing in the inkwell. He has told everything and to the point, even to the capers which the worthy Sancho cut as they tossed him in the blanket."

"I cut no capers in the blanket," objected Sancho, "but I did in the air, and more than I liked."

"I imagine," said Don Quixote, "that there is no history in the world, dealing with humankind, that does not have its ups and downs, and this is particularly true of those that have to do with deeds of chivalry, for they can never be filled with happy incidents alone."

"Nevertheless," the bachelor went on, "there are some who have read the book who say that they would have been glad if the authors had forgotten a few of the innumerable cudgelings which Señor Don Quixote received in the course of his various encounters."

"But that is where the truth of the story comes in," Sancho protested.

"For all of that," observed Don Quixote, "they might well have said nothing about them; for there is no need of recording those events that do not alter the veracity of the chronicle, when they tend only to lessen the reader's respect for the hero. You may be sure that Aeneas was not as pious as Vergil would have us believe, nor was Ulysses as wise as Homer depicts him."

"That is true enough," replied Sansón, "but it is one thing to write as a poet and another as a historian. The former may narrate or sing of things not as they were but as they should have been; the latter must describe them not as they should have been but as they were, without adding to or detracting from the truth in any degree whatsoever."

"Well," said Sancho, "if this Moorish gentleman is bent upon telling the truth, I have no doubt that among my master's thrashings my own will be found; for they never took the measure of his Grace's shoulders without measuring my whole body. But I don't wonder at that; for as my master himself says, when there's an ache in the head the members have to share it."

"You are a sly fox, Sancho," said Don Quixote. "My word, but you can remember things well enough when you choose to do so!"

"Even if I wanted to forget the whacks they gave me," Sancho answered him, "the welts on my ribs wouldn't let me, for they are still fresh."

"Be quiet, Sancho," his master admonished him, "and do not interrupt the bachelor. I beg him to go on and tell me what is said of me in this book."

"And what it says about me, too," put in Sancho, "for I have heard that I am one of the main presonages in it—"

"*Personages*, not *presonages*, Sancho my friend," said Sansón.

"So we have another one who catches you up on everything you say," was Sancho's retort. "If we go on at this rate, we'll never be through in a lifetime."

"May God put a curse on *my* life," the bachelor told him, "if you are not the second most important person in the story; and there are some who would rather listen to you talk than to anyone else in the book. It is true, there are those who say that you are too gullible in believing it to be the truth that you could become the governor of that island that was offered you by Señor Don Quixote, here present."

"There is still sun on the top of the wall," said Don Quixote, "and when Sancho is a little older, with the experience that the years bring, he will be wiser and better fitted to be a governor than he is at the present time."

"By God, master," said Sancho, "the island that I couldn't govern right now I'd never be able to govern if I lived to be as old as Methuselah. The trouble is, I don't know where that island we are talking about is located; it is not due to any lack of noddle on my part."

"Leave it to God, Sancho," was Don Quixote's advice, "and everything will come out all right, perhaps even better than you think; for not a leaf on the tree stirs except by His will."

"Yes," said Sansón, "if it be God's will, Sancho will not lack a thousand islands to govern, not to speak of one island alone."

"I have seen governors around here," said Sancho, "that are not to be compared to the sole of my shoe, and yet they call them 'your Lordship' and serve them on silver plate."

"Those are not the same kind of governors," Sansón informed him. "Their task is a good deal easier. The ones that govern islands must at least know grammar."

"I could make out well enough with the *gram*," replied Sancho, "but with the *mar* I want nothing to do, for I don't understand it at all. But leaving this business of the governorship in God's hands —for He will send me wherever I can best serve Him—I will tell you, Señor Bachelor Sansón Carrasco, that I am very much pleased that the author of the history should have spoken of me in such a way as does not offend me; for, upon the word of a faithful squire, if he had said anything about me that was not becoming to an old Christian, the deaf would have heard of it."

"That would be to work miracles," said Sansón.

"Miracles or no miracles," was the answer, "let everyone take care as to what he says or writes about people and not be setting down the first thing that pops into his head."

"One of the faults that is found with the book," continued the bachelor, "is that the author has inserted in it a story entitled *The*

One Who Was Too Curious for His Own Good. It is not that the story in itself is a bad one or badly written; it is simply that it is out of place there, having nothing to do with the story of his Grace, Señor Don Quixote."[57]

"I will bet you," said Sancho, "that the son of a dog has mixed the cabbages with the baskets."[58]

"And I will say right now," declared Don Quixote, "that the author of this book was not a sage but some ignorant prattler who at haphazard and without any method set about the writing of it, being content to let things turn out as they might. In the same manner, Orbaneja,[59] the painter of Ubeda, when asked what he was painting would reply, 'Whatever it turns out to be.' Sometimes it would be a cock, in which case he would have to write alongside it, in Gothic letters, 'This is a cock.' And so it must be with my story, which will need a commentary to make it understandable."

"No," replied Sansón, "that it will not; for it is so clearly written that none can fail to understand it. Little children leaf through it, young people read it, adults appreciate it, and the aged sing its praises. In short, it is so thumbed and read and so well known to persons of every walk in life that no sooner do folks see some skinny nag than they at once cry, 'There goes Rocinante!' Those that like it best of all are the pages; for there is no lord's antechamber where a *Don Quixote* is not to be found. If one lays it down, another will pick it up; one will pounce upon it, and another will beg for it. It affords the pleasantest and least harmful reading of any book that has been published up to now. In the whole of it there is not to be found an indecent word or a thought that is other than Catholic."

"To write in any other manner," observed Don Quixote, "would be to write lies and not the truth. Those historians who make use of falsehoods ought to be burned like the makers of counterfeit money. I do not know what could have led the author to introduce stories and episodes that are foreign to the subject matter when he had so much to write about in describing my adventures. He must undoubtedly, have been inspired by the old saying, 'With straw or with hay . . .'[60] For, in truth, all he had to do was to record my thoughts, my sighs, my tears, my lofty purposes, and my undertakings, and he would have had a volume bigger or at least as big as that which the works of El Tostado[61] would make. To sum the matter up, Señor Bachelor, it is my opinion that, in composing histories or books of any sort, a great deal of judgment and ripe understanding is called for. To say and write witty and amusing things is the mark of great genius. The cleverest character in a comedy is the clown, since he who would make himself out to be

57. The story, a tragic tale about a jealousy-ridden husband, occupies several chapters of Part I. Here, as elsewhere in this chapter, Cervantes echoes criticism currently aimed at his book.

58. has jumped together things of different kinds.

59. This painter is known only through the present allusion in *Don Quixote*.

60. The proverb concludes either "the mattress is filled" or "I fill my belly."

61. Alonso de Madrigal, bishop of Avila, a prolific author of devotional works.

a simpleton cannot be one. History is a near-sacred thing, for it must be true, and where the truth is, there is God. And yet there are those who compose books and toss them out into the world as if they were no more than fritters."

"There is no book so bad," opined the bachelor, "that there is not some good in it."

"Doubtless that is so," replied Don Quixote, "but it very often happens that those who have won in advance a great and well-deserved reputation for their writings, lose it in whole or in part when they give their works to the printer."

"The reason for it," said Sansón, "is that, printed works being read at leisure, their faults are the more readily apparent, and the greater the reputation of the author the more closely are they scrutinized. Men famous for their genius, great poets, illustrious historians, are almost always envied by those who take a special delight in criticizing the writings of others without having produced anything of their own."

"That is not to be wondered at," said Don Quixote, "for there are many theologians who are not good enough for the pulpit but who are very good indeed when it comes to detecting the faults or excesses of those who preach."

"All of this is very true, Señor Don Quixote," replied Carrasco, "but, all the same, I could wish that these self-appointed censors were a bit more forbearing and less hypercritical; I wish they would pay a little less attention to the spots on the bright sun of the work that occasions their fault-finding. For if *aliquando bonus dormitat Homerus*,[62] let them consider how much of his time he spent awake, shedding the light of his genius with a minimum of shade. It well may be that what to them seems a flaw is but one of those moles which sometimes add to the beauty of a face. In any event, I insist that he who has a book printed runs a very great risk, inasmuch as it is an utter impossibility to write it in such a manner that it will please all who read it."

"This book about me must have pleased very few," remarked Don Quixote.

"Quite the contrary," said Sansón, "for just as *stultorum infinitus est numerus*,[63] so the number of those who have enjoyed this history is likewise infinite. Some, to be sure, have complained of the author's forgetfulness, seeing that he neglected to make it plain who the thief was who stole Sancho's gray;[64] for it is not stated there, but merely implied, that the ass was stolen; and, a little further on, we find the knight mounted on the same beast, although it has not made its reappearance in the story. They also say that the author forgot to tell us what Sancho did with those hundred crowns that he

---

62. "Good Homer sometimes nods   (Ecclesiasticus 1:15.)
too." (Horace, *Art of Poetry*, l. 359.)   64. in Part I, Chapter 23.
63. "Infinite is the number of fools."

found in the valise on the Sierra Morena, as nothing more is said of them and there are many who would like to know how he disposed of the money or how he spent it. This is one of the serious omissions to be found in the work."

To this Sancho replied, "I, Señor Sansón, do not feel like giving any account or accounting just now; for I feel a little weak in my stomach, and if I don't do something about it by taking a few swigs of the old stuff, I'll be sitting on St. Lucy's thorn.[65] I have some of it at home, and my old woman is waiting for me. After I've had my dinner, I'll come back and answer any questions your Grace or anybody else wants to ask me, whether it's about the loss of the ass or the spending of the hundred crowns."

And without waiting for a reply or saying another word, he went on home. Don Quixote urged the bachelor to stay and take potluck with him, and Sansón accepted the invitation and remained. In addition to the knight's ordinary fare, they had a couple of pigeons, and at table their talk was of chivalry and feats of arms.

65. I shall be weak and exhausted.

[A Victorious Duel]

CHAPTER 12

Of the strange adventure that befell the valiant Don Quixote with the fearless Knight of the Mirrors.[66]

The night following the encounter with Death[67] was spent by Don Quixote and his squire beneath some tall and shady trees, the knight having been persuaded to eat a little from the stock of provisions carried by the gray.

"Sir, said Sancho, in the course of their repast, "how foolish I'd have been if I had chosen the spoils from your Grace's first adventure rather than the foals from the three mares.[68] Truly, truly, a sparrow in the hand is worth more than a vulture on the wing."[69]

"And yet, Sancho," replied Don Quixote, "if you had but let me attack them as I wished to do, you would at least have had as spoils

66. He will duly earn this title only in Chapter 15. In between, the author will be referring to him as the Knight of the Wood.

67. Don Quixote and his squire are now in the woody region around El Toboso, Dulcinea's town. Sancho has been sent to look for his knight's lady and has saved the day by pretending to see the beautiful damsel in a "village wench, and not a pretty one at that, for she was round-faced and snub-nosed." But by his imaginative lie he has succeeded, as he had planned, in setting in motion Don Quixote's belief in spells and enchant-

ments: enemy magicians, envious of him, have hidden his lady's splendor only from his sight. While the knight was still under the shock of this experience, further along their way he and his squire have met a group of itinerant players dressed in their proper costumes for a religious play, *The Parliament of Death.*

68. Don Quixote has promised them to Sancho as a reward for bringing news of Dulcinea.

69. a proverb roughly corresponding to "a bird in the hand is worth two in the bush."

the Empress's gold crown and Cupid's painted wings;[70] for I should have taken them whether or no and placed them in your hands."

"The crowns and scepters of stage emperors," remarked Sancho, "were never known to be of pure gold; they are always of tinsel or tinplate."

"That is the truth," said Don Quixote, "for it is only right that the accessories of a drama should be fictitious and not real, like the play itself. Speaking of that, Sancho, I would have you look kindly upon the art of the theater and, as a consequence, upon those who write the pieces and perform in them, for they all render a service of great value to the State by holding up a mirror for us at each step that we take, wherein we may observe, vividly depicted, all the varied aspects of human life; and I may add that there is nothing that shows us more clearly, by similitude, what we are and what we ought to be than do plays and players.

"Tell me, have you not seen some comedy in which kings, emperors, pontiffs, knights, ladies, and numerous other characters are introduced? One plays the ruffian, another the cheat, this one a merchant and that one a soldier, while yet another is the fool who is not so foolish as he appears, and still another the one of whom love has made a fool. Yet when the play is over and they have taken off their players' garments, all the actors are once more equal."

"Yes," replied Sancho, "I have seen all that."

"Well," continued Don Quixote, "the same thing happens in the comedy that we call life, where some play the part of emperors, others that of pontiffs—in short, all the characters that a drama may have—but when it is all over, that is to say, when life is done, death takes from each the garb that differentiates him, and all at last are equal in the grave."

"It is a fine comparison," Sancho admitted, "though not so new but that I have heard it many times before. It reminds me of that other one, about the game of chess. So long as the game lasts, each piece has its special qualities, but when it is over they are all mixed and jumbled together and put into a bag, which is to the chess pieces what the grave is to life."

"Every day, Sancho," said Don Quixote, "you are becoming less stupid and more sensible."[71]

"It must be that some of your Grace's good sense is sticking to me," was Sancho's answer. "I am like a piece of land that of itself is dry and barren, but if you scatter manure over it and cultivate it, it will bear good fruit. By this I mean to say that your Grace's conversation is the manure that has been cast upon the barren land of my dry wit; the time that I spend in your service, associating with you,

---

70. The Empress and Cupid were among the characters in *The Parliament of Death* (see n. 67).

71. This and Sancho's following ac-
knowledgment very well indicate the author's awareness of the development in Sancho's character under the influence of his master.

does the cultivating; and as a result of it all, I hope to bring forth blessed fruits by not departing, slipping, or sliding, from those paths of good breeding which your Grace has marked out for me in my parched understanding."

Don Quixote had to laugh at this affected speech of Sancho's, but he could not help perceiving that what the squire had said about his improvement was true enough; for every now and then the servant would speak in a manner that astonished his master. It must be admitted, however, that most of the time when he tried to use fine language, he would tumble from the mountain of his simple-mindedness into the abyss of his ignorance. It was when he was quoting old saws and sayings, whether or not they had anything to do with the subject under discussion, that he was at his best, displaying upon such occasions a prodigious memory, as will already have been seen and noted in the course of this history.

With such talk as this they spent a good part of the night. Then Sancho felt a desire to draw down the curtains of his eyes, as he was in the habit of saying when he wished to sleep, and, unsaddling his mount, he turned him loose to graze at will on the abundant grass. If he did not remove Rocinante's saddle, this was due to his master's express command; for when they had taken the field and were not sleeping under a roof, the hack was under no circumstances to be stripped. This was in accordance with an old and established custom which knights-errant faithfully observed: the bridle and saddlebow might be removed, but beware of touching the saddle itself! Guided by this precept, Sancho now gave Rocinante the same freedom that the ass enjoyed.

The close friendship that existed between the two animals was a most unusual one, so remarkable indeed that it has become a tradition handed down from father to son, and the author of this veracious chronicle even wrote a number of special chapters on the subject, although, in order to preserve the decency and decorum that are fitting in so heroic an account, he chose to omit them in the final version. But he forgets himself once in a while and goes on to tell us how the two beasts when they were together would hasten to scratch each other, and how, when they were tired and their bellies were full, Rocinante would lay his long neck over that of the ass—it extended more than a half a yard on the other side—and the pair would then stand there gazing pensively at the ground for as much as three whole days at a time, or at least until someone came for them or hunger compelled them to seek nourishment.

I may tell you that I have heard it said that the author of this history, in one of his writings, has compared the friendship of Rocinante and the gray to that of Nisus and Euryalus and that of Pylades and Orestes;[72] and if this be true, it shows for the edifica-

---

72. famous examples of friendship in Virgil's *Aeneid* and in Greek tradition and drama.

tion of all what great friends these two peace-loving animals were, and should be enough to make men ashamed, who are so inept at preserving friendship with one another. For this reason it has been said:

> There is no friend for friend,
> Reeds to lances turn . . .[73]

And there was the other poet who sang:

> Between friend and friend the bug . . .[74]

Let no one think that the author has gone out of his way in comparing the friendship of animals with that of men; for human beings have received valuable lessons from the beasts and have learned many important things from them. From the stork they have learned the use of clysters; the dog has taught them the salutary effects of vomiting as well as a lesson in gratitude; the cranes have taught them vigilance, the ants foresight, the elephants modesty, and the horse loyalty.[75]

Sancho had at last fallen asleep at the foot of a cork tree, while Don Quixote was slumbering beneath a sturdy oak. Very little time had passed when the knight was awakened by a noise behind him, and, starting up, he began looking about him and listening to see if he could make out where it came from. Then he caught sight of two men on horseback, one of whom, slipping down from the saddle, said to the other, "Dismount, my friend, and unbridle the horses; for there seems to be plenty of grass around here for them and sufficient silence and solitude for my amorous thoughts."

Saying this, he stretched himself out on the ground, and as he flung himself down the armor that he wore made such a noise that Don Quixote knew at once, for a certainty, that he must be a knight-errant. Going over to Sancho, who was still sleeping, he shook him by the arm and with no little effort managed to get him awake.

"Brother Sancho," he said to him in a low voice, "we have an adventure on our hands."

"God give us a good one," said Sancho. "And where, my master, may her Ladyship, Mistress Adventure, be?"

"Where, Sancho?" replied Don Quixote. "Turn your eyes and look, and you will see stretched out over there a knight-errant who, so far as I can make out, is not any too happy; for I saw him fling himself from his horse to the ground with a certain show of despondency, and as he fell his armor rattled."

"Well," said Sancho, "and how does your Grace make this out to be an adventure?"

---

73. from a popular ballad.
74. The Spanish "a bug in the eye" implies keeping a watchful eye on somebody.

75. all folkloristic beliefs about the "virtues" of animals.

"I would not say," the knight answered him, "that this is an adventure in itself, but rather the beginning of one, for that is the way they start. But listen; he seems to be tuning a lute or guitar, and from the way he is spitting and clearing his throat he must be getting ready to sing something."

"Faith, so he is," said Sancho. "He must be some lovesick knight."

"There are no knights-errant that are not lovesick," Don Quixote informed him. "Let us listen to him, and the thread of his song will lead us to the yarn-ball of his thoughts; for out of the abundance of the heart the mouth speaketh."

Sancho would have liked to reply to his master, but the voice of the Knight of the Wood,[76] which was neither very good nor very bad, kept him from it; and as the two of them listened attentively, they heard the following:

Sonnet

Show me, O lady, the pattern of thy will,
That mine may take that very form and shape;
For my will in thine own I fain would drape,
Each slightest wish of thine I would fulfill.
If thou wouldst have me silence this dread ill
Of which I'm dying now, prepare the crape!
Or if I must another manner ape,
Then let Love's self display his rhyming skill.
Of opposites I am made, that's manifest:
In part soft wax, in part hard-diamond fire;
Yet to Love's laws my heart I do adjust,
And, hard or soft, I offer thee this breast:
Print or engrave there what thou may'st desire,
And I'll preserve it in eternal trust.[77]

With an *Ay!* that appeared to be wrung from the very depths of his heart, the Knight of the Wood brought his song to a close, and then after a brief pause began speaking in a grief-stricken voice that was piteous to hear.

"O most beautiful and most ungrateful woman in all the world!" he cried, "how is it possible, O most serene Casildea de Vandalia,[78] for you to permit this captive knight of yours to waste away and perish in constant wanderings, amid rude toils and bitter hardships? Is it not enough that I have compelled all the knights of Navarre, all those of León, all the Tartessians and Castilians, and, finally, all those of La Mancha, to confess that there is no beauty anywhere that can rival yours?"

---

76. Cf. note 66.
77. The poem intentionally follows affected conventions of the time.

78. the Knight of the Wood's counterpart to Don Quixote's Dulcinea del Toboso.

"That is not so!" cried Don Quixote at this point. "I am of La Mancha, and I have never confessed, I never could nor would confess a thing so prejudicial to the beauty of my lady. The knight whom you see there, Sancho, is raving; but let us listen and perhaps he will tell us more."

"That he will," replied Sancho, "for at the rate he is carrying on, he is good for a month at a stretch."

This did not prove to be the case, however; for when the Knight of the Wood heard voices near him, he cut short his lamentations and rose to his feet.

"Who goes there?" he called in a loud but courteous tone. "What kind of people are you? Are you, perchance, numbered among the happy or among the afflicted?"

"Among the afflicted," was Don Quixote's response.

"Then come to me," said the one of the Wood, "and, in doing so, know that you come to sorrow's self and the very essence of affliction."

Upon receiving so gentle and courteous an answer, Don Quixote and Sancho as well went over to him, whereupon the sorrowing one took the Manchegan's arm.

"Sit down here, Sir Knight," he continued, "for in order to know that you are one of those who follow the profession of knight-errantry, it is enough for me to have found you in this place where solitude and serenity keep you company, such a spot being the natural bed and proper dwelling of wandering men of arms."

"A knight I am," replied Don Quixote, "and of the profession that you mention; and though sorrows, troubles, and misfortunes have made my heart their abode, this does not mean that compassion for the woes of others has been banished from it. From your song a while ago I gather that your misfortunes are due to love— the love you bear that ungrateful fair one whom you named in your lamentations."

As they conversed in this manner, they sat together upon the hard earth, very peaceably and companionably, as if at daybreak they were not going to break each other's heads.

"Sir Knight," inquired the one of the Wood, "are you by any chance in love?"

"By mischance I am," said Don Quixote, "although the ills that come from well-placed affection should be looked upon as favors rather than as misfortunes."

"That is the truth," the Knight of the Wood agreed, "if it were not that the loved one's scorn disturbs our reason and understanding; for when it is excessive scorn appears as vengeance."

"I was never scorned by my lady," said Don Quixote.

"No, certainly not," said Sancho, who was standing near by, "for my lady is gentle as a ewe lamb and soft as butter."

"Is he your squire?" asked the one of the Wood.

"He is," replied Don Quixote.

"I never saw a squire," said the one of the Wood, "who dared to speak while his master was talking. At least, there is mine over there; he is as big as your father, and it cannot be proved that he has ever opened his lips while I was conversing."

"Well, upon my word," said Sancho, "I have spoken, and I will speak in front of any other as good—but never mind; it only makes it worse to stir it."

The Knight of the Wood's squire now seized Sancho's arm. "Come along," he said, "let the two of us go where we can talk all we like, squire fashion, and leave these gentlemen our masters to come to lance blows as they tell each other the story of their loves; for you may rest assured, daybreak will find them still at it."

"Let us, by all means," said Sancho, "and I will tell your Grace who I am, so that you may be able to see for yourself whether or not I am to be numbered among the dozen most talkative squires."

With this, the pair went off to one side, and there then took place between them a conversation that was as droll as the one between their masters was solemn.

CHAPTER 13

In which is continued the adventure of the Knight of the Wood, together with the shrewd, highly original, and amicable conversation that took place between the two squires.

The knights and the squires had now separated, the latter to tell their life stories, the former to talk of their loves; but the history first relates the conversation of the servants and then goes on to report that of the masters. We are told that, after they had gone some little distance from where the others were, the one who served the Knight of the Wood began speaking to Sancho as follows:

"It is a hard life that we lead and live, *Señor mio*, those of us who are squires to knights-errant. It is certainly true that we eat our bread in the sweat of our faces, which is one of the curses that God put upon our first parents."[79]

"It might also be said," added Sancho, "that we eat it in the chill of our bodies, for who endures more heat and cold than we wretched ones who wait upon these wandering men of arms? It would not be so bad if we did eat once in a while, for troubles are less where there is bread; but as it is, we sometimes go for a day or two without breaking our fast, unless we feed on the wind that blows."

"But all this," said the other, "may very well be put up with, by reason of the hope we have of being rewarded; for if a knight is not

79. cf. Genesis 3:19.

too unlucky, his squire after a little while will find himself the governor of some fine island or prosperous earldom."

"I," replied Sancho, "have told my master that I would be satisfied with the governorship of an island, and he is so noble and so generous that he has promised it to me on many different occasions."

"In return for my services," said the Squire of the Wood, "I'd be content with a canonry. My master has already appointed me to one—and what a canonry!"

"Then he must be a churchly knight," said Sancho, "and in a position to grant favors of that sort to his faithful squire; but mine is a layman, pure and simple, although, as I recall, certain shrewd and, as I see it, scheming persons did advise him to try to become an archbishop. However, he did not want to be anything but an emperor. And there I was, all the time trembling for fear he would take it into his head to enter the Church, since I was not educated enough to hold any benefices. For I may as well tell your Grace that, though I look like a man, I am no more than a beast where holy orders are concerned."

"That is where you are making a mistake," the Squire of the Wood assured him. "Not all island governments are desirable. Some of them are misshapen bits of land, some are poor, others are gloomy, and, in short, the best of them lays a heavy burden of care and trouble upon the shoulders of the unfortunate one to whose lot it falls. It would be far better if we who follow this cursed trade were to go back to our homes and there engage in pleasanter occupations, such as hunting or fishing, for example; for where is there in this world a squire so poor that he does not have a hack, a couple of greyhounds, and a fishing rod to provide him with sport in his own village?"

"I don't lack any of those," replied Sancho. "It is true, I have no hack, but I do have an ass that is worth twice as much as my master's horse. God sent me a bad Easter, and let it be the next one that comes, if I would make a trade, even though he gave me four fanegas[80] of barley to boot. Your Grace will laugh at the price I put on my gray—for that is the color of the beast. As to greyhounds, I shan't want for them, as there are plenty and to spare in my village. And, anyway, there is more pleasure in hunting when someone else pays for it."

"Really and truly, Sir Squire," said the one of the Wood, "I have made up my mind and resolved to have no more to do with the mad whims of these knights; I intend to retire to my village and bring up my little ones—I have three of them, and they are like oriental pearls."

"I have two of them," said Sancho, "that might be presented to the Pope in person, especially one of my girls that I am bringing up to be a countess, God willing, in spite of what her mother says."

80. about 1.6 bushels.

"And how old is this young lady that is destined to be a countess?"

"Fifteen," replied Sancho, "or a couple of years more or less. But she is tall as a lance, fresh as an April morning, and strong as a porter."

"Those," remarked the one of the Wood, "are qualifications that fit her to be not merely a countess but a nymph of the verdant wildwood. O whore's daughter of a whore! What strength the she-rogue must have!"

Sancho was a bit put out by this. "She is not a whore," he said, "nor was her mother before her, nor will either of them ever be, please God, so long as I live. And you might speak more courteously. For one who has been brought up among knights-errant, who are the soul of courtesy, those words are not very becoming."

"Oh, how little your Grace knows about compliments, Sir Squire!" the one of the Wood exclaimed. "Are you not aware that when some knight gives a good lance thrust to the bull in the plaza, or when a person does anything remarkably well, it is the custom for the crowd to cry out, 'Well done, whoreson rascal!' and that what appears to be vituperation in such a case is in reality high praise? Sir, I would bid you disown those sons or daughters who do nothing to cause such praise to be bestowed upon their parents."

"I would indeed disown them if they didn't," replied Sancho, "and so your Grace may go ahead and call me, my children, and my wife all the whores in the world if you like, for everything that they say and do deserves the very highest praise. And in order that I may see them all again, I pray God to deliver me from mortal sin, or, what amounts to the same thing, from this dangerous calling of squire, seeing that I have fallen into it a second time, decoyed and deceived by a purse of a hundred ducats that I found one day in the heart of the Sierra Morena.[81] The devil is always holding up a bag full of doubloons in front of my eyes, here, there—no, not here, but there—everywhere, until it seems to me at every step I take that I am touching it with my hand, hugging it, carrying it off home with me, investing it, drawing an income from it, and living on it like a prince. And while I am thinking such thoughts, all the hardships I have to put up with serving this crackbrained master of mine, who is more of a madman than a knight, seem to me light and easy to bear."

"That," observed the Squire of the Wood, "is why it is they say that avarice bursts the bag. But, speaking of madmen, there is no greater one in all this world than my master; for he is one of those of whom it is said, 'The cares of others kill the ass.' Because another knight has lost his senses, he has to play mad too[82] and go

---

81. when Don Quixote retired there in Part I, Chapter 23.

82. In the Sierra Morena, Don Quixote had decided to imitate Amadis de Gaul and Ariosto's Roland "by playing the part of a desperate and raving madman" as a consequence of love (Part I, Chapter 25).

hunting for that which, when he finds it, may fly up in his snout."

"Is he in love, maybe?"

"Yes, with a certain Casildea de Vandalia, the rawest[83] and best-roasted lady to be found anywhere on earth; but her rawness is not the foot he limps on, for he has other and greater schemes rumbling in his bowels, as you will hear tell before many hours have gone by."

"There is no road so smooth," said Sancho, "that it does not have some hole or rut to make you stumble. In other houses they cook horse beans, in mine they boil them by the kettleful.[84] Madness has more companions and attendants than good sense does. But if it is true what they say, that company in trouble brings relief, I may take comfort from your Grace, since you serve a master as foolish as my own."

"Foolish but brave," the one of the Wood corrected him, "and more of a rogue than anything else."

"That is not true of my master," replied Sancho. "I can assure you there is nothing of the rogue about him; he is as open and aboveboard as a wine pitcher and would not harm anyone but does good to all. There is no malice in his make-up, and a child could make him believe it was night at midday. For that very reason I love him with all my heart and cannot bring myself to leave him, no matter how many foolish things he does."

"But, nevertheless, good sir and brother," said the Squire of the Wood, "with the blind leading the blind, both are in danger of falling into the pit. It would be better for us to get out of all this as quickly as we can and return to our old haunts; for those that go seeking adventures do not always find good ones."

Sancho kept clearing his throat from time to time, and his saliva seemed rather viscous and dry; seeing which, the woodland squire said to him, "It looks to me as if we have been talking so much that our tongues are cleaving to our palates, but I have a loosener over there, hanging from the bow of my saddle, and a pretty good one it is." With this, he got up and went over to his horse and came back a moment later with a big flask of wine and a meat pie half a yard in diameter. This is no exaggeration, for the pasty in question was made of a hutch-rabbit of such a size that Sancho took it to be a goat, or at the very least a kid.

"And are you in the habit of carrying this with you, Señor?" he asked.

"What do you think?" replied the other. "Am I by any chance one of your wood-and-water[85] squires? I carry better rations on the flanks of my horse than a general does when he takes the field."

Sancho ate without any urging, gulping down mouthfuls that were like the knots on a tether, as they sat there in the dark.

83. The original has a pun on *crudo*, meaning both "raw" and "cruel."
84. meaning that his misfortunes always come in large quantities.
85. of low quality.

"You are a squire of the right sort," he said, "loyal and true, and you live in grand style as shown by this feast, which I would almost say was produced by magic. You are not like me, poor wretch, who have in my saddlebags only a morsel of cheese so hard you could crack a giant's skull with it, three or four dozen carob beans, and a few nuts. For this I have my master to thank, who believes in observing the rule that knights-errant should nourish and sustain themselves on nothing but dried fruits and the herbs of the field."

"Upon my word, brother," said the other squire, "my stomach was not made for thistles, wild pears, and woodland herbs. Let our masters observe those knightly laws and traditions and eat what their rules prescribe; I carry a hamper of food and a flask on my saddlebow, whether they like it or not. And speaking of that flask, how I love it! There is scarcely a minute in the day that I'm not hugging and kissing it, over and over again."

As he said this, he placed the wine bag in Sancho's hands, who put it to his mouth, threw his head back, and sat there gazing up at the stars for a quarter of an hour. Then, when he had finished drinking, he let his head loll on one side and heaved a deep sigh.

"The whoreson rascal!" he exclaimed, "that's a fine vintage for you!"

"There!" cried the Squire of the Wood, as he heard the epithet Sancho had used, "do you see how you have praised this wine by calling it 'whoreson'?"

"I grant you," replied Sancho, "that it is no insult to call anyone a son of a whore so long as you really do mean to praise him. But tell me, sir, in the name of what you love most, is this the wine of Ciudad Real?"[86]

"What a winetaster you are! It comes from nowhere else, and it's a few years old, at that."

"Leave it to me," said Sancho, "and never fear, I'll show you how much I know about it. Would you believe me, Sir Squire, I have such a great natural instinct in this matter of wines that I have but to smell a vintage and I will tell you the country where it was grown, from what kind of grapes, what it tastes like, and how good it is, and everything that has to do with it. There is nothing so unusual about this, however, seeing that on my father's side were two of the best winetasters La Mancha has known in many a year, in proof of which, listen to the story of what happened to them.

"The two were given a sample of wine from a certain vat and asked to state its condition and quality and determine whether it was good or bad. One of them tasted it with the tip of his tongue while the other merely brought it up to his nose. The first man said that it tasted of iron, the second that it smelled of Cordovan leather. The owner insisted that the vat was clean and that there could be nothing in the wine to give it a flavor of leather or of iron,

---

86. the main town in La Mancha and the center of a wine region.

but, nevertheless, the two famous winetasters stood their ground. Time went by, and when they came to clean out the vat they found in it a small key attached to a leather strap. And so your Grace may see for yourself whether or not one who comes of that kind of stock has a right to give his opinion in such cases."

"And for that very reason," said the Squire of the Wood, "I maintain that we ought to stop going about in search of adventures. Seeing that we have loaves, let us not go looking for cakes, but return to our cottages, for God will find us there if He so wills."

"I mean to stay with my master," Sancho replied, "until he reaches Saragossa, but after that we will come to an understanding."

The short of the matter is, the two worthy squires talked so much and drank so much that sleep had to tie their tongues and moderate their thirst, since to quench the latter was impossible. Clinging to the wine flask, which was almost empty by now, and with half-chewed morsels of food in their mouths, they both slept peacefully; and we shall leave them there as we go on to relate what took place between the Knight of the Wood and the Knight of the Mournful Countenance.

CHAPTER 14

Wherein is continued the adventure of the Knight of the Wood.

In the course of the long conversation that took place between Don Quixote and the Knight of the Wood, the history informs us that the latter addressed the following remarks to the Manchegan:

"In short, Sir Knight, I would have you know that my destiny, or, more properly speaking, my own free choice, has led me to fall in love with the peerless Casildea de Vandalia. I call her peerless for the reason that she has no equal as regards either her bodily proportions or her very great beauty. This Casildea, then, of whom I am telling you, repaid my worthy affections and honorable intentions by forcing me, as Hercules was forced by his stepmother, to incur many and diverse perils;[87] and each time as I overcame one of them she would promise me that with the next one I should have that which I desired; but instead my labors have continued, forming a chain whose links I am no longer able to count, nor can I say which will be the last one, that shall mark the beginning of the realization of my hopes.

"One time she sent me forth to challenge that famous giantess of Seville, known as La Giralda,[88] who is as strong and brave as if made of brass, and who without moving from the spot where she stands is the most changeable and fickle woman in the world. I came, I saw, I conquered her. I made her stand still and point in

87. Son of Zeus and Alcmena, Hercules was persecuted by Zeus' wife Hera.

88. actually a statue on the Moorish belfry of the cathedral at Seville.

one direction only, and for more than a week nothing but north winds blew. Then, there was that other time when Casildea sent me to lift those ancient stones, the mighty Bulls of Guisando,[89] an enterprise that had better have been entrusted to porters than to knights. On another occasion she commanded me to hurl myself down into the Cabra chasm [90]—an unheard-of and terribly dangerous undertaking—and bring her back a detailed account of what lay concealed in that deep and gloomy pit. I rendered La Giralda motionless, I lifted the Bulls of Guisando, and I threw myself into the abyss and brought to light what was hidden in its depths; yet my hopes are dead—how dead!—while her commands and her scorn are as lively as can be.

"Finally, she commanded me to ride through all the provinces of Spain and compel all the knights-errant whom I met with to confess that she is the most beautiful woman now living and that I am the most enamored man of arms that is to be found anywhere in the world. In fulfillment of this behest I have already traveled over the greater part of these realms and have vanquished many knights who have dared to contradict me. But the one whom I am proudest to have overcome in single combat is that famous gentleman, Don Quixote de la Mancha; for I made him confess that my Casildea is more beautiful than his Dulcinea, and by achieving such a conquest I reckon that I have conquered all the others on the face of the earth, seeing that this same Don Quixote had himself routed them. Accordingly, when I vanquished him, his fame, glory, and honor passed over and were transferred to my person.

> The brighter is the conquered one's lost crown,
> The greater is the conqueror's renown.[91]

Thus, the innumerable exploits of the said Don Quixote are now set down to my account and are indeed my own."

Don Quixote was astounded as he listened to the Knight of the Wood, and was about to tell him any number of times that he lied; the words were on the tip of his tongue, but he held them back as best he could, thinking that he would bring the other to confess with his own lips that what he had said was a lie. And so it was quite calmly that he now replied to him.

"Sir Knight," he began, "as to the assertion that your Grace has conquered most of the knights-errant in Spain and even in all the world, I have nothing to say, but that you have vanquished Don Quixote de la Mancha, I am inclined to doubt. It may be that it was someone else who resembled him, although there are very few that do."

89. statues representing animals and supposedly marking a place where Caesar defeated Pompey. (Cf. the use of Caesar's famous words a few lines above.)

90. Possibly an ancient mine in the Sierra de Cobra near Cordova.

91. from the *Araucana*, a poem by Alonso de Ercilla y Zúñiga on the Spanish struggle against the Araucanian Indians of Chile.

"What do you mean?" replied the one of the Wood. "I swear by the heavens above that I did fight with Don Quixote and that I overcame him and forced him to yield. He is a tall man, with a dried-up face, long, lean legs, graying hair, an eagle-like nose somewhat hooked, and a big, black, drooping mustache. He takes the field under the name of the Knight of the Mournful Countenance, he has for squire a peasant named Sancho Panza, and he rides a famous steed called Rocinante. Lastly, the lady of his heart is a certain Dulcinea del Toboso, once upon a time known as Aldonza Lorenzo, just as my own lady, whose name is Casildea and who is an Andalusian by birth, is called by me Casildea de Vandalia. If all this is not sufficient to show that I speak the truth, here is my sword which shall make incredulity itself believe."

"Calm yourself, Sir Knight," replied Don Quixote, "and listen to what I have to say to you. You must know that this Don Quixote of whom you speak is the best friend that I have in the world, so great a friend that I may say that I feel toward him as I do toward my own self; and from all that you have told me, the very definite and accurate details that you have given me, I cannot doubt that he is the one whom you have conquered. On the other hand, the sight of my eyes and the touch of my hands assure me that he could not possibly be the one, unless some enchanter who is his enemy—for he has many, and one in particular who delights in persecuting him —may have assumed the knight's form and then permitted himself to be routed, by way of defrauding Don Quixote of the fame which his high deeds of chivalry have earned for him throughout the known world. To show you how true this may be, I will inform you that not more than a couple of days ago those same enemy magicians transformed the figure and person of the beauteous Dulcinea del Toboso into a low and mean village lass,[92] and it is possible that they have done something of the same sort to the knight who is her lover. And if all this does not suffice to convince you of the truth of what I say, here is Don Quixote himself who will maintain it by force of arms, on foot or on horseback, or in any way you like."

Saying this, he rose and laid hold of his sword, and waited to see what the Knight of the Wood's decision would be. That worthy now replied in a voice as calm as the one Don Quixote had used.

"Pledges," he said, "do not distress one who is sure of his ability to pay. He who was able to overcome you when you were transformed, Señor Don Quixote, may hope to bring you to your knees when you are your own proper self. But inasmuch as it is not fitting that knights should perform their feats of arms in the darkness, like ruffians and highwaymen, let us wait until it is day in order that the sun may behold what we do. And the condition governing our encounter shall be that the one who is vanquished must submit to the will of his conqueror and perform all those things that are com-

92. See note 67.

manded of him, provided they are such as are in keeping with the state of knighthood."

"With that condition and understanding," said Don Quixote, "I shall be satisfied."

With this, they went off to where their squires were, only to find them snoring away as hard as when sleep had first overtaken them. Awakening the pair, they ordered them to look to the horses; for as soon as the sun was up the two knights meant to stage an arduous and bloody single-handed combat. At this news Sancho was astonished and terrified, since, as a result of what the other squire had told him of the Knight of the Wood's prowess, he was led to fear for his master's safety. Nevertheless, he and his friend now went to seek the mounts without saying a word, and they found the animals all together, for by this time the two horses and the ass had smelled one another out. On the way the Squire of the Wood turned to Sancho and addressed him as follows:

"I must inform you, brother, that it is the custom of the fighters of Andalusia, when they are godfathers in any combat, not to remain idly by, with folded hands, while their godsons fight it out. I tell you this by way of warning you that while our masters are settling matters, we, too, shall have to come to blows and hack each other to bits."

"The custom, Sir Squire," replied Sancho, "may be all very well among the fighters and ruffians that you mention, but with the squires of knights-errant it is not to be thought of. At least, I have never heard my master speak of any such custom, and he knows all the laws of chivalry by heart. But granting that it is true and that there is a law which states in so many words that squires must fight while their masters do, I have no intention of obeying it but rather will pay whatever penalty is laid on peaceable-minded ones like myself, for I am sure it cannot be more than a couple of pounds of wax,[93] and that would be less expensive than the lint which it would take to heal my head—I can already see it split in two. What's more, it's out of the question for me to fight since I have no sword nor did I ever in my life carry one."

"That," said the one of the Wood, "is something that is easily remedied. I have here two linen bags of the same size. You take one and I'll take the other and we will fight that way, on equal terms."

"So be it, by all means," said Sancho, "for that will simply knock the dust out of us without wounding us."

"But that's not the way it's to be," said the other squire. "Inside the bags, to keep the wind from blowing them away, we will put a half-dozen nice smooth pebbles of the same weight, and so we'll be able to give each other a good pounding without doing ourselves any real harm or damage."

---

93. In some confraternities, penalties were paid in wax, presumably to make church candles.

"Body of my father!" cried Sancho, "just look, will you, at the marten and sable and wads of carded cotton that he's stuffing into those bags so that we won't get our heads cracked or our bones crushed to a pulp. But I am telling you, *Señor mio*, that even though you fill them with silken pellets, I don't mean to fight. Let our masters fight and make the best of it, but as for us, let us drink and live; for time will see to ending our lives without any help on our part by way of bringing them to a close before they have reached their proper season and fall from ripeness."

"Nevertheless," replied the Squire of the Wood, "fight we must, if only for half an hour."

"No," Sancho insisted, "that I will not do. I will not be so impolite or so ungrateful as to pick any quarrel however slight with one whose food and drink I've shared. And, moreover, who in the devil could bring himself to fight in cold blood, when he's not angry or vexed in any way?"

"I can take care of that, right enough," said the one of the Wood. "Before we begin, I will come up to your Grace as nicely as you please and give you three or four punches that will stretch you out at my feet; and that will surely be enough to awaken your anger, even though it's sleeping sounder than a dormouse."

"And I," said Sancho, "have another idea that's every bit as good as yours. I will take a big club, and before your Grace has had a chance to awaken my anger I will put yours to sleep with such mighty whacks that if it wakes at all it will be in the other world; for it is known there that I am not the man to let my face be mussed by anyone, and let each look out for the arrow.[94] But the best thing to do would be to leave one's anger to its slumbers, for no one knows the heart of any other, he who comes for wool may go back shorn, and God bless peace and curse all strife. If a hunted cat when surrounded and cornered turns into a lion, God knows what I who am a man might not become. And so from this time forth I am warning you, Sir Squire, that all the harm and damage that may result from our quarrel will be upon your head."

"Very well," the one of the Wood replied, "God will send the dawn and we shall make out somehow."

At that moment gay-colored birds of all sorts began warbling in the trees and with their merry and varied songs appeared to be greeting and welcoming the fresh-dawning day, which already at the gates and on the balconies of the east was revealing its beautiful face as it shook out from its hair an infinite number of liquid pearls. Bathed in this gentle moisture, the grass seemed to shed a pearly spray, the willows distilled a savory manna, the fountains laughed, the brooks murmured, the woods were glad, and the meadows put

94. a proverbial expression from archery: let each one take care of his own arrow. Other obviously proverbial expressions follow, as is typical of Sancho's speech.

on their finest raiment. The first thing that Sancho Panza beheld, as soon as it was light enough to tell one object from another, was the Squire of the Wood's nose, which was so big as to cast into the shade all the rest of his body. In addition to being of enormous size, it is said to have been hooked in the middle and all covered with warts of a mulberry hue, like eggplant; it hung down for a couple of inches below his mouth, and the size, color, warts, and shape of this organ gave his face so ugly an appearance that Sancho began trembling hand and foot like a child with convulsions and made up his mind then and there that he would take a couple of hundred punches before he would let his anger be awakened to a point where he would fight with this monster.

Don Quixote in the meanwhile was surveying his opponent, who had already adjusted and closed his helmet so that it was impossible to make out what he looked like. It was apparent, however, that he was not very tall and was stockily built. Over his armor he wore a coat of some kind or other made of what appeared to be the finest cloth of gold, all bespangled with glittering mirrors that resembled little moons and that gave him a most gallant and festive air, while above his helmet were a large number of waving plumes, green, white, and yellow in color. His lance, which was leaning against a tree, was very long and stout and had a steel point of more than a palm in length. Don Quixote took all this in, and from what he observed concluded that his opponent must be of tremendous strength, but he was not for this reason filled with fear as Sancho Panza was. Rather, he proceeded to address the Knight of the Mirrors,[95] quite boldly and in a highbred manner.

"Sir Knight," he said, "if in your eagerness to fight you have not lost your courtesy, I would beg you to be so good as to raise your visor a little in order that I may see if your face is as handsome as your trappings."

"Whether you come out of this emprise the victor or the vanquished, Sir Knight," he of the Mirrors replied, "there will be ample time and opportunity for you to have a sight of me. If I do not now gratify your desire, it is because it seems to me that I should be doing a very great wrong to the beauteous Casildea de Vandalia by wasting the time it would take me to raise my visor before having forced you to confess that I am right in my contention, with which you are well acquainted."

"Well, then," said Don Quixote, "while we are mounting our steeds you might at least inform me if I am that knight of La Mancha whom you say you conquered."

"To that our[96] answer," said he of the Mirrors, "is that you are

---

95. see above, note 66.

96. Note the dignified, "majestic" plural form.

as like the knight I overcame as one egg is like another; but since you assert that you are persecuted by enchanters, I should not venture to state positively that you are the one in question."

"All of which," said Don Quixote, "is sufficient to convince me that you are laboring under a misapprehension; but in order to relieve you of it once and for all, let them bring our steeds, and in less time than you would spend in lifting your visor, if God, my lady, and my arm give me strength, I will see your face and you shall see that I am not the vanquished knight you take me to be."

With this, they cut short their conversation and mounted, and, turning Rocinante around, Don Quixote began measuring off the proper length of field for a run against his opponent as he of the Mirrors did the same. But the Knight of La Mancha had not gone twenty paces when he heard his adversary calling to him, whereupon each of them turned halfway and he of the Mirrors spoke.

"I must remind you, Sir Knight," he said, "of the condition under which we fight, which is that the vanquished, as I have said before, shall place himself wholly at the disposition of the victor."

"I am aware of that," replied Don Quixote, "not forgetting the provision that the behest laid upon the vanquished shall not exceed the bounds of chivalry."

"Agreed," said the Knight of the Mirrors.

At that moment Don Quixote caught sight of the other squire's weird nose and was as greatly astonished by it as Sancho had been. Indeed, he took the fellow for some monster, or some new kind of human being wholly unlike those that people this world. As he saw his master riding away down the field preparatory to the tilt, Sancho was alarmed; for he did not like to be left alone with the big-nosed individual, fearing that one powerful swipe of that protuberance against his own nose would end the battle so far as he was concerned and he would be lying stretched out on the ground, from fear if not from the force of the blow.

He accordingly ran after the knight, clinging to one of Rocinante's stirrup straps, and when he thought it was time for Don Quixote to whirl about and bear down upon his opponent, he called to him and said, "*Señor mio*, I beg your Grace, before you turn for the charge, to help me up into that cork tree yonder where I can watch the encounter which your Grace is going to have with this knight better than I can from the ground and in a way that is much more to my liking."

"I rather think, Sancho," said Don Quixote, "that what you wish to do is to mount a platform where you can see the bulls without any danger to yourself."

"The truth of the matter is," Sancho admitted, "the monstrous nose on that squire has given me such a fright that I don't dare stay near him."

"It is indeed of such a sort," his master assured him, "that if I were not the person I am, I myself should be frightened. And so, come, I will help you up."

While Don Quixote tarried to see Sancho ensconced in the cork tree, the Knight of the Mirrors measured as much ground as seemed to him necessary and then, assuming that his adversary had done the same, without waiting for sound of trumpet or any other signal, he wheeled his horse, which was no swifter nor any more impressive-looking than Rocinante, and bore down upon his enemy at a mild trot; but when he saw that the Manchegan was busy helping his squire, he reined in his mount and came to a stop midway in his course, for which his horse was extremely grateful, being no longer able to stir a single step. To Don Quixote, on the other hand, it seemed as if his enemy was flying, and digging his spurs with all his might into Rocinante's lean flanks he caused that animal to run a bit for the first and only time, according to the history, for on all other occasions a simple trot had represented his utmost speed. And so it was that, with an unheard-of fury, the Knight of the Mournful Countenance came down upon the Knight of the Mirrors as the latter sat there sinking his spurs all the way up to the buttons without being able to persuade his horse to budge a single inch from the spot where he had come to a sudden standstill.

It was at this fortunate moment, while his adversary was in such a predicament, that Don Quixote fell upon him, quite unmindful of the fact that the other knight was having trouble with his mount and either was unable or did not have time to put his lance at rest. The upshot of it was, he encountered him with such force that, much against his will, the Knight of the Mirrors went rolling over his horse's flanks and tumbled to the ground, where as a result of his terrific fall he lay as if dead, without moving hand or foot.

No sooner did Sancho perceive what had happened than he slipped down from the cork tree and ran up as fast as he could to where his master was. Dismounting from Rocinante, Don Quixote now stood over the Knight of the Mirrors, and undoing the helmet straps to see if the man was dead, or to give him air in case he was alive, he beheld—who can say what he beheld without creating astonishment, wonder, and amazement in those who hear the tale? The history tells us that it was the very countenance, form, aspect, physiognomy, effigy, and image of the bachelor Sansón Carrasco!

"Come, Sancho," he cried in a loud voice, "and see what is to be seen but is not to be believed. Hasten, my son, and learn what magic can do and how great is the power of wizards and enchanters."

Sancho came, and the moment his eyes fell on the bachelor Carrasco's face he began crossing and blessing himself a countless number of times. Meanwhile, the overthrown knight gave no signs of life.

"If you ask me, master," said Sancho, "I would say that the best thing for your Grace to do is to run his sword down the mouth of this one who appears to be the bachelor Carrasco; maybe by so doing you would be killing one of your enemies, the enchanters."

"That is not a bad idea," replied Don Quixote, "for the fewer enemies the better." And, drawing his sword, he was about to act upon Sancho's advice and counsel when the Knight of the Mirrors' squire came up to them, now minus the nose which had made him so ugly.

"Look well what you are doing, Don Quixote!" he cried. "The one who lies there at your feet is your Grace's friend, the bachelor Sansón Carrasco, and I am his squire."

"And where is your nose?" inquired Sancho, who was surprised to see him without that deformity.

"Here in my pocket," was the reply. And, thrusting his hand into his coat, he drew out a nose of varnished pasteboard of the make that has been described. Studying him more and more closely, Sancho finally exclaimed, in a voice that was filled with amazement, "Holy Mary preserve me! And is this not my neighbor and crony, Tomé Cecial?"

"That is who I am!" replied the de-nosed squire, "your good friend Tomé Cecial, Sancho Panza. I will tell you presently of the means and snares and falsehoods that brought me here. But, for the present, I beg and entreat your master not to lay hands on, mistreat, wound, or slay the Knight of the Mirrors whom he now has at his feet; for without any doubt it is the rash and ill-advised bachelor Sansón Carrasco, our fellow villager."

The Knight of the Mirrors now recovered consciousness, and, seeing this, Don Quixote at once placed the naked point of his sword above the face of the vanquished one.

"Dead you are, knight," he said, "unless you confess that the peerless Dulcinea del Toboso is more beautiful than your Casildea de Vandalia. And what is more, you will have to promise that, should you survive this encounter and the fall you have had, you will go to the city of El Toboso and present yourself to her in my behalf, that she may do with you as she may see fit. And in case she leaves you free to follow your own will, you are to return to seek me out—the trail of my exploits will serve as a guide to bring you wherever I may be—and tell me all that has taken place between you and her. These conditions are in conformity with those that we arranged before our combat and they do not go beyond the bounds of knight-errantry."

"I confess," said the fallen knight, "that the tattered and filthy shoe of the lady Dulcinea del Toboso is of greater worth than the badly combed if clean beard of Casildea, and I promise to go to her presence and return to yours and to give you a complete and detailed account concerning anything you may wish to know."

"Another thing," added Don Quixote, "that you will have to confess and believe is that the knight you conquered was not and could not have been Don Quixote de la Mancha, but was some other that resembled him, just as I am convinced that you, though you appear to be the bachelor Sansón Carrasco, are another person in his form and likeness who has been put here by my enemies to induce me to restrain and moderate the impetuosity of my wrath and make a gentle use of my glorious victory."

"I confess, think, and feel as you feel, think, and believe," replied the lamed knight. "Permit me to rise, I beg of you, if the jolt I received in my fall will let me do so, for I am in very bad shape."

Don Quixote and Tomé Cecial the squire now helped him to his feet. As for Sancho, he could not take his eyes off Tomé but kept asking him one question after another, and although the answers he received afforded clear enough proof that the man was really his fellow townsman, the fear that had been aroused in him by his master's words—about the enchanters' having transformed the Knight of the Mirrors into the bachelor Sansón Carrasco—prevented him from believing the truth that was apparent to his eyes. The short of it is, both master and servant were left with this delusion as the other ill-errant knight and his squire, in no pleasant state of mind, took their departure with the object of looking for some village where they might be able to apply poultices and splints to the bachelor's battered ribs.

Don Quixote and Sancho then resumed their journey along the road to Saragossa, and here for the time being the history leaves them in order to give an account of who the Knight of the Mirrors and his long-nosed squire really were.

CHAPTER 15

Wherein is told and revealed who the Knight of the Mirrors and his squire were.

Don Quixote went off very happy, self-satisfied, and vainglorious at having achieved a victory over so valiant a knight as he imagined the one of the Mirrors to be, from whose knightly word he hoped to learn whether or not the spell which had been put upon his lady was still in effect; for, unless he chose to forfeit his honor, the vanquished contender must of necessity return and give an account of what had happened in the course of his interview with her. But Don Quixote was of one mind, the Knight of the Mirrors of another, for, as has been stated, the latter's only thought at the moment was to find some village where plasters were available.

The history goes on to state that when the bachelor Sansón Carrasco advised Don Quixote to resume his feats of chivalry, after having desisted from them for a while, this action was taken as the result of a conference which he had held with the curate and the barber as to the means to be adopted in persuading the knight to remain quietly at home and cease agitating himself over his unfortunate adventures. It had been Carrasco's suggestion, to which they had unanimously agreed, that they let Don Quixote sally forth, since it appeared to be impossible to prevent his doing so, and that Sansón should then take to the road as a knight-errant and pick a quarrel and do battle with him. There would be no difficulty about finding a pretext, and then the bachelor knight would overcome him (which was looked upon as easy of accomplishment), having first entered into a pact to the effect that the vanquished should remain at the mercy and bidding of his conqueror. The behest in this case was to be that the fallen one should return to his village and home and not leave it for the space of two years or until further orders were given him, it being a certainty that, once having been overcome, Don Quixote would fulfill the agreement, in order not to contravene or fail to obey the laws of chivalry. And it was possible that in the course of his seclusion he would forget his fancies, or they would at least have an opportunity to seek some suitable cure for his madness.

Sansón agreed to undertake this, and Tomé Cecial, Sancho's friend and neighbor, a merry but featherbrained chap, offered to go along as squire. Sansón then proceeded to arm himself in the manner that has been described, while Tomé disguised his nose with the aforementioned mask so that his crony would not recognize him when they met. Thus equipped, they followed the same route as Don Quixote and had almost caught up with him by the time he had the adventure with the Cart of Death.[97] They finally overtook him in the wood, where those events occurred with which the attentive reader is already familiar; and if it had not been for the knight's extraordinary fancies, which led him to believe that the bachelor was not the bachelor, the said bachelor might have been prevented from ever attaining his degree of licentiate, as a result of having found no nests where he thought to find birds.

Seeing how ill they had succeeded in their undertaking and what an end they had reached, Tomé Cecial now addressed his master.

"Surely, Señor Sansón Carrasco," he said, "we have had our deserts. It is easy enough to plan and embark upon an enterprise, but most of the time it's hard to get out of it. Don Quixote is a madman and we are sane, yet he goes away sound and laughing while your Grace is left here, battered and sorrowful. I wish you would tell me now who is the crazier: the one who is so because he cannot help it, or he who turns crazy of his own free will?"

"The difference between the two," replied Sansón, "lies in this:

97. cf. note 67.

that the one who cannot help being crazy will be so always, whereas the one who is a madman by choice can leave off being one whenever he so desires."

"Well," said Tomé Cecial, "since that is the way it is, and since I chose to be crazy when I became your Grace's squire, by the same reasoning I now choose to stop being insane and to return to my home."

"That is your affair," said Sansón, "but to imagine that I am going back before I have given Don Quixote a good thrashing is senseless; and what will urge me on now is not any desire to see him recover his wits, but rather a thirst for vengeance; for with the terrible pain that I have in my ribs, you can't expect me to feel very charitable."

Conversing in this manner they kept on until they reached a village where it was their luck to find a bonesetter to take care of poor Sansón. Tomé Cecial then left him and returned home, while the bachelor meditated plans for revenge. The history has more to say of him in due time, but for the present it goes on to make merry with Don Quixote.

CHAPTER 16

Of what happened to Don Quixote upon his meeting with a prudent gentleman of La Mancha.

With that feeling of happiness and vainglorious self-satisfaction that has been mentioned, Don Quixote continued on his way, imagining himself to be, as a result of the victory he had just achieved, the most valiant knight-errant of the age. Whatever adventures might befall him from then on he regarded as already accomplished and brought to a fortunate conclusion. He thought little now of enchanters and enchantments and was unmindful of the innumerable beatings he had received in the course of his knightly wanderings, of the volley of pebbles that had knocked out half his teeth, of the ungratefulness of the galley slaves and the audacity of the Yanguesans whose poles had fallen upon his body like rain. In short, he told himself, if he could but find the means, manner, or way of freeing his lady Dulcinea of the spell that had been put upon her, he would not envy the greatest good fortune that the most fortunate of knights-errant in ages past had ever by any possibility attained.

He was still wholly wrapped up in these thoughts when Sancho spoke to him.

"Isn't it strange, sir, that I can still see in front of my eyes the huge and monstrous nose of my old crony, Tomé Cecial?"

"And do you by any chance believe, Sancho, that the Knight of the Mirrors was the bachelor Sansón Carrasco and that his squire was your friend Tomé?"

"I don't know what to say to that," replied Sancho. "All I know is that the things he told me about my home, my wife and young ones, could not have come from anybody else; and the face, too, once you took the nose away, was the same as Tomé Cecial's, which I have seen many times in our village, right next door to my own house, and the tone of voice was the same also."

"Let us reason the matter out, Sancho," said Don Quixote. "Look at it this way: how can it be thought that the bachelor Sansón Carrasco would come as a knight-errant, equipped with offensive and defensive armor, to contend with me? Am I, perchance, his enemy? Have I given him any occasion to cherish a grudge against me? Am I a rival of his? Or can it be jealousy of the fame I have acquired that has led him to take up the profession of arms?"

"Well, then, sir," Sancho answered him, "how are we to explain the fact that the knight was so like the bachelor and his squire like my friend? And if this was a magic spell, as your Grace has said, was there no other pair in the world whose likeness they might have taken?"

"It is all a scheme and a plot," replied Don Quixote, "on the part of those wicked magicians who are persecuting me and who, foreseeing that I would be the victor in the combat, saw to it that the conquered knight should display the face of my friend the bachelor, so that the affection which I bear him would come between my fallen enemy and the edge of my sword and might of my arm, to temper the righteous indignation of my heart. In that way, he who had sought by falsehood and deceits to take my life, would be left to go on living. As proof of all this, Sancho, experience, which neither lies nor deceives, has already taught you how easy it is for enchanters to change one countenance into another, making the beautiful ugly and the ugly beautiful. It was not two days ago that you beheld the peerless Dulcinea's beauty and elegance in its entirety and natural form, while I saw only the repulsive features of a low and ignorant peasant girl with cataracts over her eyes and a foul smell in her mouth. And if the perverse enchanter was bold enough to effect so vile a transformation as this, there is certainly no cause for wonderment at what he has done in the case of Sansón Carrasco and your friend, all by way of snatching my glorious victory out of my hands. But in spite of it all, I find consolation in the fact that, whatever the shape he may have chosen to assume, I have laid my enemy low."

"God knows what the truth of it all may be," was Sancho's comment. Knowing as he did that Dulcinea's transformation had been due to his own scheming and plotting, he was not taken in by his master's delusions. He was at a loss for a reply, however, lest he say something that would reveal his own trickery.

As they were carrying on this conversation, they were overtaken by a man who, following the same road, was coming along behind them. He was mounted on a handsome flea-bitten mare and wore a hooded greatcoat of fine green cloth trimmed in tawny velvet and a cap of the same material, while the trappings of his steed, which was accoutered for the field, were green and mulberry in hue, his saddle being of the *jineta* mode.[98] From his broad green and gold shoulder strap there dangled a Moorish cutlass, and his half-boots were of the same make as the baldric. His spurs were not gilded but were covered with highly polished green lacquer, so that, harmonizing as they did with the rest of his apparel, they seemed more appropriate than if they had been of purest gold. As he came up, he greeted the pair courteously and, spurring his mare, was about to ride on past when Don Quixote called to him.

"Gallant sir," he said, "If your Grace is going our way and is not in a hurry, it would be a favor to us if we might travel together."

"The truth is," replied the stranger, "I should not have ridden past you if I had not been afraid that the company of my mare would excite your horse."

"In that case, sir," Sancho spoke up, "you may as well rein in, for this horse of ours is the most virtuous and well mannered of any that there is. Never on such an occasion has he done anything that was not right—the only time he did misbehave, my master and I suffered for it aplenty. And so, I say again, your Grace may slow up if you like; for even if you offered him your mare on a couple of platters, he'd never try to mount her."

With this, the other traveler drew rein, being greatly astonished at Don Quixote's face and figure. For the knight was now riding along without his helmet, which was carried by Sancho like a piece of luggage on the back of his gray, in front of the packsaddle. If the green-clad gentleman stared hard at his new-found companion, the latter returned his gaze with an even greater intensity. He impressed Don Quixote as being a man of good judgment, around fifty years of age, with hair that was slightly graying and an aquiline nose, while the expression of his countenance was half humorous, half serious. In short, both his person and his accouterments indicated that he was an individual of some worth.

As for the man in green's impression of Don Quixote de la Mancha, he was thinking that he had never before seen any human being that resembled this one. He could not but marvel at the knight's long neck, his tall frame, and the leanness and the sallowness of his face, as well as his armor and his grave bearing, the whole

98. a saddle with a high pummel and short stirrups.

constituting a sight such as had not been seen for many a day in those parts. Don Quixote in turn was quite conscious of the attentiveness with which the traveler was studying him and could tell from the man's astonished look how curious he was; and so, being very courteous and fond of pleasing everyone, he proceeded to anticipate any questions that might be asked him.

"I am aware," he said, "that my appearance must strike your Grace as being very strange and out of the ordinary, and for that reason I am not surprised at your wonderment. But your Grace will cease to wonder when I tell you, as I am telling you now, that I am a knight, one of those

> Of whom it is folks say,
> They to adventures go.

I have left my native heath, mortgaged my estate, given up my comfortable life, and cast myself into fortune's arms for her to do with me what she will. It has been my desire to revive a knight-errantry that is now dead, and for some time past, stumbling here and falling there, now throwing myself down headlong and then rising up once more, I have been able in good part to carry out my design by succoring widows, protecting damsels, and aiding the fallen, the orphans, and the young, all of which is the proper and natural duty of knights-errant. As a result, owing to my many valiant and Christian exploits, I have been deemed worthy of visiting in printed form nearly all the nations of the world. Thirty thousand copies of my history have been published, and, unless Heaven forbid, they will print thirty million of them.

"In short, to put it all into a few words, or even one, I will tell you that I am Don Quixote de la Mancha, otherwise known as the Knight of the Mournful Countenance. Granted that self-praise is degrading, there still are times when I must praise myself, that is to say, when there is no one else present to speak in my behalf. And so, good sir, neither this steed nor this lance nor this buckler nor this squire of mine, nor all the armor that I wear and arms I carry, nor the sallowness of my complexion, nor my leanness and gauntness, should any longer astonish you, now that you know who I am and what the profession is that I follow."

Having thus spoken, Don Quixote fell silent, and the man in green was so slow in replying that it seemed as if he was at a loss for words. Finally, however, after a considerable while, he brought himself to the point of speaking.

"You were correct, Sir Knight," he said, "about my astonishment and my curiosity, but you have not succeeded in removing the wonderment that the sight of you has aroused in me. You say that, knowing who you are, I should not wonder any more, but such is not the case, for I am now more amazed than ever. How can it be that there are knights-errant in the world today and that histories of them are actually printed? I find it hard to convince myself that at the present time there is anyone on earth who goes about aiding widows, protecting damsels, defending the honor of wives, and succoring orphans, and I should never have believed it had I not beheld your Grace with my own eyes. Thank Heaven for that book that your Grace tells me has been published concerning your true and exalted deeds of chivalry, as it should cast into oblivion all the innumerable stories of fictitious knights-errant with which the world is filled, greatly to the detriment of good morals and the prejudice and discredit of legitimate histories."

"As to whether the stories of knights-errant are fictitious or not," observed Don Quixote, "there is much that remains to be said."

"Why," replied the gentleman in green, "is there anyone who can doubt that such tales are false?"

"I doubt it," was the knight's answer, "but let the matter rest there. If our journey lasts long enough, I trust with God's help to be able to show your Grace that you are wrong in going along with those who hold it to be a certainty that they are not true."

From this last remark the traveler was led to suspect that Don Quixote must be some kind of crackbrain, and he was waiting for him to confirm the impression by further observations of the same sort; but before they could get off on another subject, the knight, seeing that he had given an account of his own station in life, turned to the stranger and politely inquired who his companion might be.

"I, Sir Knight of the Mournful Countenance," replied the one in the green-colored greatcoat, "am a gentleman, and a native of the village where, please God, we are going to dine today. I am more than moderately rich, and my name is Don Diego de Miranda. I spend my life with my wife and children and with my friends. My occupations are hunting and fishing, though I keep neither falcon nor hounds but only a tame partridge[99] and a bold ferret or two. I am the owner of about six dozen books, some of them in Spanish, others in Latin, including both histories and devotional works. As for books of chivalry, they have not as yet crossed the threshold of my door. My own preference is for profane rather than devotional

99. used as decoy.

writings, such as afford an innocent amusement, charming us by their style and arousing and holding our interest by their inventiveness, although I must say there are very few of that sort to be found in Spain.

"Sometimes," the man in green continued, "I dine with my friends and neighbors, and I often invite them to my house. My meals are wholesome and well prepared and there is always plenty to eat. I do not care for gossip, nor will I permit it in my presence. I am not lynx-eyed and do not pry into the lives and doings of others. I hear mass every day and share my substance with the poor, but make no parade of my good works lest hypocrisy and vainglory, those enemies that so imperceptibly take possession of the most modest heart, should find their way into mine. I try to make peace between those who are at strife. I am the devoted servant of Our Lady, and my trust is in the infinite mercy of God Our Savior."

Sancho had listened most attentively to the gentleman's account of his mode of life, and inasmuch as it seemed to him that this was a good and holy way to live and that the one who followed such a pattern ought to be able to work miracles, he now jumped down from his gray's back and, running over to seize the stranger's right stirrup, began kissing the feet of the man in green with a show of devotion that bordered on tears.

"Why are you doing that, brother?" the gentleman asked him. "What is the meaning of these kisses?"

"Let me kiss your feet," Sancho insisted, "for if I am not mistaken, your Grace is the first saint riding *jineta* fashion[100] that I have seen in all the days of my life."

"I am not a saint," the gentleman assured him, "but a great sinner. It is you, brother, who are the saint; for you must be a good man, judging by the simplicity of heart that you show."

Sancho then went back to his packsaddle, having evoked a laugh from the depths of his master's melancholy and given Don Diego fresh cause for astonishment.

Don Quixote thereupon inquired of the newcomer how many children he had, remarking as he did so that the ancient philosophers, who were without a true knowledge of God, believed that mankind's greatest good lay in the gifts of nature, in those of fortune, and in having many friends and many and worthy sons.

100. See note 98.

"I, Señor Don Quixote," replied the gentleman, "have a son without whom I should, perhaps, be happier than I am. It is not that he is bad, but rather that he is not as good as I should like him to be. He is eighteen years old, and for six of those years he has been at Salamanca studying the Greek and Latin languages. When I desired him to pass on to other branches of learning, I found him so immersed in the science of Poetry (if it can be called such) that it was not possible to interest him in the Law, which I wanted him to study, nor in Theology, the queen of them all. My wish was that he might be an honor to his family; for in this age in which we are living our monarchs are in the habit of highly rewarding those forms of learning that are good and virtuous, since learning without virtue is like pearls on a dunghill. But he spends the whole day trying to decide whether such and such a verse of Homer's *Iliad* is well conceived or not, whether or not Martial is immodest in a certain epigram, whether certain lines of Vergil are to be understood in this way or in that. In short, he spends all of his time with the books written by those poets whom I have mentioned and with those of Horace, Persius, Juvenal, and Tibullus. As for our own moderns, he sets little store by them, and yet, for all his disdain of Spanish poetry, he is at this moment racking his brains in an effort to compose a gloss on a quatrain that was sent him from Salamanca and which, I fancy, is for some literary tournament."

To all this Don Quixote made the following answer:

"Children, sir, are out of their parents' bowels and so are to be loved whether they be good or bad, just as we love those that gave us life. It is for parents to bring up their offspring, from the time they are infants, in the paths of virtue, good breeding, proper conduct, and Christian morality, in order that, when they are grown, they may be a staff to the old age of the ones that bore them and an honor to their own posterity. As to compelling them to study a particular branch of learning, I am not so sure as to that, though there may be no harm in trying to persuade them to do so. But where there is no need to study *pane lucrando*[101]—where Heaven has provided them with parents that can supply their daily bread—I should be in favor of permitting them to follow that course to which they are most inclined; and although poetry may be more pleasurable than useful, it is not one of those pursuits that bring dishonor upon those who engage in them.

"Poetry in my opinion, my dear sir," he went on, "is a young and tender maid of surpassing beauty, who has many other damsels (that is to say, the other disciplines) whose duty it is to bedeck, embellish, and adorn her. She may call upon all of them for service, and all of them in turn depend upon her nod. She is not one to be

101. earning one's bread.

rudely handled, nor dragged through the streets, nor exposed at street corners, in the market place, or in the private nooks of palaces. She is fashioned through an alchemy of such power that he who knows how to make use of it will be able to convert her into the purest gold of inestimable price. Possessing her, he must keep her within bounds and not permit her to run wild in bawdy satires or soulless sonnets. She is not to be put up for sale in any manner, unless it be in the form of heroic poems, pity-inspiring tragedies, or pleasing and ingenious comedies. Let mountebanks keep hands off her, and the ignorant mob as well, which is incapable of recognizing or appreciating the treasures that are locked within her. And do not think, sir, that I apply that term 'mob' solely to plebeians and those of low estate; for anyone who is ignorant, whether he be lord or prince, may, and should, be included in the vulgar herd.

"But," Don Quixote continued, "he who possesses the gift of poetry and who makes the use of it that I have indicated, shall become famous and his name shall be honored among all the civilized nations of the world. You have stated, sir, that your son does not greatly care for poetry written in our Spanish tongue, and in that I am inclined to think he is somewhat mistaken. My reason for saying so is this: the great Homer did not write in Latin, for the reason that he was a Greek, and Vergil did not write in Greek since he was a Latin. In a word, all the poets of antiquity wrote in the language which they had imbibed with their mother's milk and did not go searching after foreign ones to express their loftiest conceptions. This being so, it would be well if the same custom were to be adopted by all nations, the German poet being no longer looked down upon because he writes in German, nor the Castilian or the Basque for employing his native speech.

"As for your son, I fancy, sir, that his quarrel is not so much with Spanish poetry as with those poets who have no other tongue or discipline at their command such as would help to awaken their natural gift; and yet, here, too, he may be wrong. There is an opinion, and a true one, to the effect that 'the poet is born,' that is to say, it is as a poet that he comes forth from his mother's womb, and with the propensity that has been bestowed upon him by Heaven, without study or artifice, he produces those compositions that attest the truth of the line: '*Est deus in nobis*,' etc.[102] I further maintain that the born poet who is aided by art will have a great advantage over the one who by art alone would become a poet, the reason being that art does not go beyond, but merely perfects, nature; and so it is that, by combining nature with art and art with nature, the finished poet is produced.

"In conclusion, then, my dear sir, my advice to you would be to

102. "There is a god in us." (Ovid, *Fasti*, VI, 5.)

let your son go where his star beckons him; for being a good student as he must be, and having already successfully mounted the first step on the stairway of learning, which is that of languages, he will be able to continue of his own accord to the very peak of humane letters, an accomplishment that is altogether becoming in a gentleman, one that adorns, honors, and distinguishes him as much as the miter does the bishop or his flowing robe the learned jurisconsult. Your Grace well may reprove your son, should he compose satires that reflect upon the honor of other persons; in that case, punish him and tear them up. But should he compose discourses in the manner of Horace, in which he reprehends vice in general as that poet so elegantly does, then praise him by all means; for it is permitted the poet to write verses in which he inveighs against envy and the other vices as well, and to lash out at the vicious without, however, designating any particular individual. On the other hand, there are poets who for the sake of uttering something malicious would run the risk of being banished to the shores of Pontus.[103]

"If the poet be chaste where his own manners are concerned, he will likewise be modest in his verses, for the pen is the tongue of the mind, and whatever thoughts are engendered there are bound to appear in this writings. When kings and princes behold the marvelous art of poetry as practiced by prudent, virtuous, and serious-minded subjects of their realm, they honor, esteem, and reward those persons and crown them with the leaves of the tree that is never struck by lightning[104]—as if to show that those who are crowned and adorned with such wreaths are not to be assailed by anyone."

The gentleman in the green-colored greatcoat was vastly astonished by this speech of Don Quixote's and was rapidly altering the opinion he had previously held, to the effect that his companion was but a crackbrain. In the middle of the long discourse, which was not greatly to his liking, Sancho had left the highway to go seek a little milk from some shepherds who were draining the udders of their ewes near by. Extremely well pleased with the knight's sound sense and excellent reasoning, the gentleman was about to resume the conversation when, raising his head, Don Quixote caught sight of a cart flying royal flags that was coming toward them down the road and, thinking it must be a fresh adventure, began calling to Sancho in a loud voice to bring him his helmet. Whereupon Sancho hastily left the shepherds and spurred his gray until he was once more alongside his master, who was now about to encounter a dreadful and bewildering ordeal.

103. as Ovid was by Augustus in A.D. 8.   104. the laurel tree.

["For I Well Know the Meaning of Valor"]

CHAPTER 17

Wherein Don Quixote's unimaginable courage reaches its highest point, together with the adventure of the lions and its happy ending.

The history relates that, when Don Quixote called to Sancho to bring him his helmet,[105] the squire was busy buying some curds from the shepherds and, flustered by his master's great haste, did not know what to do with them or how to carry them. Having already paid for the curds, he did not care to lose them, and so he decided to put them into the headpiece, and, acting upon this happy inspiration, he returned to see what was wanted of him.

"Give me that helmet," said the knight; "for either I know little about adventures or here is one where I am going to need my armor."

Upon hearing this, the gentleman in the green-colored greatcoat[106] looked around in all directions but could see nothing except the cart that was approaching them, decked out with two or three flags which indicated that the vehicle in question must be conveying his Majesty's property. He remarked as much to Don Quixote, but the latter paid no attention, for he was always convinced that whatever happened to him meant adventures and more adventures.

"Forewarned is forearmed," he said. "I lose nothing by being prepared, knowing as I do that I have enemies both visible and invisible and cannot tell when or where or in what form they will attack me."

Turning to Sancho, he asked for his helmet again, and as there was no time to shake out the curds, the squire had to hand it to him as it was. Don Quixote took it and, without noticing what was in it, hastily clapped it on his head; and forthwith, as a result of the pressure on the curds, the whey began running down all over his face and beard, at which he was very much startled.

"What is this, Sancho?" he cried. "I think my head must be softening or my brains melting, or else I am sweating from head to foot. If sweat it be, I assure you it is not from fear, though I can well believe that the adventure which now awaits me is a terrible one indeed. Give me something with which to wipe my face, if you have anything, for this perspiration is so abundant that it blinds me."

Sancho said nothing but gave him a cloth and at the same time

---

105. Don Quixote has been deep in talk with "a prudent gentleman of La Mancha" met on the road, Don Diego de Miranda. Sancho has left the two for a moment to go and buy milk from some shepherds.

106. Don Diego de Miranda, whom Don Quixote later dubs the Knight of the Green-colored Greatcoat.

gave thanks to God that his master had not discovered what the trouble was. Don Quixote wiped his face and then took off his helmet to see what it was that made his head feel so cool. Catching sight of that watery white mass, he lifted it to his nose and smelled it.

"By the life of my lady Dulcinea del Toboso!" he exclaimed. "Those are curds that you have put there, you treacherous, brazen, ill-mannered squire!"

To this Sancho replied, very calmly and with a straight face, "If they are curds, give them to me, your Grace, so that I can eat them. But no, let the devil eat them, for he must be the one who did it. Do you think I would be so bold as to soil your Grace's helmet? Upon my word, master, by the understanding that God has given me, I, too, must have enchanters who are persecuting me as your Grace's creature and one of his members, and they are the ones who put that filthy mess there to make you lose your patience and your temper and cause you to whack my ribs as you are in the habit of doing. Well, this time, I must say, they have missed the mark; for I trust my master's good sense to tell him that I have neither curds nor milk nor anything of the kind, and if I did have, I'd put it in my stomach and not in that helmet."

"That may very well be," said Don Quixote.

Don Diego was observing all this and was more astonished than ever, especially when, after he had wiped his head, face, beard, and helmet, Don Quixote once more donned the piece of armor and, settling himself in the stirrups, proceeded to adjust his sword and fix his lance.

"Come what may, here I stand, ready to take on Satan himself in person!" shouted the knight.

The cart with the flags had come up to them by this time, accompanied only by a driver riding one of the mules and a man seated up in front.

"Where are you going, brothers?" Don Quixote called out as he placed himself in the path of the cart. "What conveyance is this, what do you carry in it, and what is the meaning of those flags?"

"The cart is mine," replied the driver, "and in it are two fierce lions in cages which the governor of Oran is sending to court as a present for his Majesty. The flags are those of our lord the King, as a sign that his property goes here."

"And are the lions large?" inquired Don Quixote.

It was the man sitting at the door of the cage who answered him. "The largest," he said, "that ever were sent from Africa to Spain. I am the lionkeeper and I have brought back others, but never any like these. They are male and female. The male is in this first cage, the female in the one behind. They are hungry right now, for they have had nothing to eat today; and so we'd be obliged if your Grace would get out of the way, for we must hasten on to the place where we are to feed them."

"Lion whelps against me?" said Don Quixote with a slight smile. "Lion whelps against me? And at such an hour? Then, by God, those gentlemen who sent them shall see whether I am the man to be frightened by lions. Get down, my good fellow, and since you are the lionkeeper, open the cages and turn those beasts out for me; and in the middle of this plain I will teach them who Don Quixote de la Mancha is, notwithstanding and in spite of the enchanters who are responsible for their being here."

"So," said the gentleman to himself as he heard this, "our worthy knight has revealed himself. It must indeed be true that the curds have softened his skull and mellowed his brains."

At this point Sancho approached him. "For God's sake, sir," he said, "do something to keep my master from fighting those lions. For if he does, they're going to tear us all to bits."

"Is your master, then, so insane," the gentleman asked, "that you fear and believe he means to tackle those fierce animals?"

"It is not that he is insane," replied Sancho, "but, rather, fool-hardy."

"Very well," said the gentleman, "I will put a stop to it." And going up to Don Quixote, who was still urging the lionkeeper to open the cages, he said, "Sir Knight, knights-errant should undertake only those adventures that afford some hope of a successful outcome, not those that are utterly hopeless to begin with; for valor when it turns to temerity has in it more of madness than of bravery. Moreover, these lions have no thought of attacking your Grace but are a present to his Majesty, and it would not be well to detain them or interfere with their journey."

"My dear sir," answered Don Quixote, "you had best go mind your tame partridge and that bold ferret of yours and let each one attend to his own business. This is my affair, and I know whether these gentlemen, the lions, have come to attack me or not." He then turned to the lionkeeper. "I swear, Sir Rascal, if you do not open those cages at once, I'll pin you to the cart with this lance!"

Perceiving how determined the armed phantom was, the driver now spoke up. "Good sir," he said, "will your Grace please be so kind as to let me unhitch the mules and take them to a safe place before you turn those lions loose? For if they kill them for me, I am ruined for life, since the mules and cart are all the property I own."

"O man of little faith!" said Don Quixote. "Get down and un-hitch your mules if you like, but you will soon see that it was quite unnecessary and that you might have spared yourself the trouble."

The driver did so, in great haste, as the lionkeeper began shouting, "I want you all to witness that I am being compelled against my will to open the cages and turn the lions out, and I further warn this gentleman that he will be responsible for all the harm and damage the beasts may do, plus my wages and my fees. You other gentlemen take cover before I open the doors; I am sure they will not do any harm to me."

Once more Don Diego sought to persuade his companion not to commit such an act of madness, as it was tempting God to undertake anything so foolish as that; but Don Quixote's only answer was that he knew what he was doing. And when the gentleman in green insisted that he was sure the knight was laboring under a delusion and ought to consider the matter well, the latter cut him short.

"Well, then, sir," he said, "if your Grace does not care to be a spectator at what you believe is going to turn out to be a tragedy, all you have to do is to spur your flea-bitten mare and seek safety."

Hearing this, Sancho with tears in his eyes again begged him to give up the undertaking, in comparison with which the adventure of the windmills and the dreadful one at the fulling mills—indeed, all the exploits his master had ever in the course of his life undertaken—were but bread and cakes.

"Look, sir," Sancho went on, "there is no enchantment here nor anything of the sort. Through the bars and chinks of that cage I have seen a real lion's claw, and judging by the size of it, the lion that it belongs to is bigger than a mountain."

"Fear, at any rate," said Don Quixote, "will make him look bigger to you than half the world. Retire, Sancho, and leave me, and if I die here, you know our ancient pact: you are to repair to Dulcinea—I say no more."

To this he added other remarks that took away any hope they had that he might not go through with his insane plan. The gentleman in the green-colored greatcoat was of a mind to resist him but saw that he was no match for the knight in the matter of arms. Then, too, it did not seem to him the part of wisdom to fight it out with a madman; for Don Quixote now impressed him as being quite mad in every way. Accordingly, while the knight was repeating his threats to the lionkeeper, Don Diego spurred his mare, Sancho his gray, and the driver his mules, all of them seeking to put as great a distance as possible between themselves and the cart before the lions broke loose.

Sancho already was bewailing his master's death, which he was convinced was bound to come from the lions' claws, and at the same time he cursed his fate and called it an unlucky hour in which he had taken it into his head to serve such a one. But despite his tears and lamentations, he did not leave off thrashing his gray in an effort to leave the cart behind them. When the lionkeeper saw that those who had fled were a good distance away, he once more entreated and warned Don Quixote as he had warned and entreated him before, but the answer he received was that he might save his breath as it would do him no good and he had best hurry and obey. In the space of time that it took the keeper to open the first cage, Don Quixote considered the question as to whether it would be well to give battle on foot or on horseback. He finally decided that he would do better on foot, as he feared that Rocinante would become frightened at sight of the lions; and so, leaping down from his horse, he fixed his lance, braced his buckler, and drew his sword, and then advanced with marvelous daring and great resoluteness until he stood directly in front of the cart, meanwhile commending himself to God with all his heart and then to his lady Dulcinea.

Upon reaching this point, the reader should know, the author of our veracious history indulges in the following exclamatory passage:

"O great-souled Don Quixote de la Mancha, thou whose courage is beyond all praise, mirror wherein all the valiant of the world may behold themselves, a new and second Don Manuel de León,[107] once the glory and the honor of Spanish knighthood! With what words shall I relate thy terrifying exploit, how render it credible to the ages that are to come? What eulogies do not belong to thee of right, even though they consist of hyperbole piled upon hyperbole? On foot and singlehanded, intrepid and with greathearted valor, armed but with a sword, and not one of the keen-edged Little Dog[108] make, and with a shield that was not of gleaming and polished steel, thou didst stand and wait for the two fiercest lions that ever the African forests bred! Thy deeds shall be thy praise, O valorous Manchegan; I leave them to speak for thee, since words fail me with which to extol them."

Here the author leaves off his exclamations and resumes the thread of the story.

Seeing Don Quixote posed there before him and perceiving that, unless he wished to incur the bold knight's indignation there was nothing for him to do but release the male lion, the keeper now opened the first cage, and it could be seen at once how extraordinarily big and horribly ugly the beast was. The first thing the recumbent animal did was to turn round, put out a claw, and stretch himself all over. Then he opened his mouth and yawned very slowly, after which he put out a tongue that was nearly two palms in length and with it licked the dust out of his eyes and washed his face. Having done this, he stuck his head outside the cage and gazed about him in all directions. His eyes were now like

---

107. **Don Manuel Ponce de León**, a paragon of gallantry and courtesy, belonging to the time of Ferdinand and Isabella.

108. the trademark of a famous armorer of Toledo and Saragossa.

live coals and his appearance and demeanor were such as to strike terror in temerity itself. But Don Quixote merely stared at him attentively, waiting for him to descend from the cart so that they could come to grips, for the knight was determined to hack the brute to pieces, such was the extent of his unheard-of madness.

The lion, however, proved to be courteous rather than arrogant and was in no mood for childish bravado. After having gazed first in one direction and then in another, as has been said, he turned his back and presented his hind parts to Don Quixote and then very calmly and peaceably lay down and stretched himself out once more in his cage. At this, Don Quixote ordered the keeper to stir him up with a stick in order to irritate him and drive him out.

"That I will not do," the keeper replied, "for if I stir him, I will be the first one he will tear to bits. Be satisfied with what you have already accomplished, Sir Knight, which leaves nothing more to be said on the score of valor, and do not go tempting your fortune a second time. The door was open and the lion could have gone out if he had chosen; since he has not done so up to now, that means he will stay where he is all day long. Your Grace's stoutheartedness has been well established; for no brave fighter, as I see it, is obliged to do more than challenge his enemy and wait for him in the field; his adversary, if he does not come, is the one who is disgraced and the one who awaits him gains the crown of victory."

"That is the truth," said Don Quixote. "Shut the door, my friend, and bear me witness as best you can with regard to what you have seen me do here. I would have you certify: that you opened the door for the lion, that I waited for him and he did not come out, that I continued to wait and still he stayed there, and finally went back and lay down. I am under no further obligation. Away with enchantments, and God uphold the right, the truth, and true chivalry! So close the door, as I have told you, while I signal to the fugitives in order that they who were not present may hear of this exploit from your lips."

The keeper did as he was commanded, and Don Quixote, taking the cloth with which he had dried his face after the rain of curds, fastened it to the point of his lance and began summoning the runaways, who, all in a body with the gentleman in green bringing up the rear, were still fleeing and turning around to look back at every step. Sancho was the first to see the white cloth.

"May they slay me," he said, "if my master hasn't conquered those fierce beasts, for he's calling to us."

They all stopped and made sure that the one who was doing the signaling was indeed Don Quixote, and then, losing some of their fear, they little by little made their way back to a point where they could distinctly hear what the knight was saying. At last they returned to the cart, and as they drew near Don Quixote spoke to the driver.

"You may come back, brother, hitch your mules, and continue your journey. And you, Sancho, may give each of them two gold crowns to recompense them for the delay they have suffered on my account."

"That I will, right enough," said Sancho. "But what has become of the lions? Are they dead or alive?"

The keeper thereupon, in leisurely fashion and in full detail, proceeded to tell them how the encounter had ended, taking pains to stress to the best of his ability the valor displayed by Don Quixote, at sight of whom the lion had been so cowed that he was unwilling to leave his cage, though the door had been left open quite a while. The fellow went on to state that the knight had wanted him to stir the lion up and force him out, but had finally been convinced that this would be tempting God and so, much to his displeasure and against his will, had permitted the door to be closed.

"What do you think of that, Sancho?" asked Don Quixote. "Are there any spells that can withstand true gallantry? The enchanters may take my luck away, but to deprive me of my strength and courage is an impossibility."

Sancho then bestowed the crowns, the driver hitched his mules, and the lionkeeper kissed Don Quixote's hands for the favor received, promising that, when he reached the court, he would relate this brave exploit to the king himself.

"In that case," replied Don Quixote, "if his Majesty by any chance should inquire who it was that performed it, you are to say that it was the Knight of the Lions; for that is the name by which I wish to be known from now on, thus changing, exchanging, altering, and converting the one I have previously borne, that of Knight of the Mournful Countenance; in which respect I am but following the old custom of knights-errant, who changed their names whenever they liked or found it convenient to do so."

With this, the cart continued on its way, and Don Quixote, Sancho, and the gentleman in the green-colored greatcoat likewise resumed their journey. During all this time Don Diego de Miranda had not uttered a word but was wholly taken up with observing what Don Quixote did and listening to what he had to say. The knight impressed him as being a crazy sane man and an insane one on the verge of sanity. The gentleman did not happen to be familiar with the first part of our history, but if he had read it he would have ceased to wonder at such talk and conduct, for he would then have known what kind of madness this was. Remaining as he did in ignorance of his companion's malady, he took him now for a sensible individual and now for a madman, since what Don Quixote said was coherent, elegantly phrased, and to the point, whereas his actions were nonsensical, foolhardy, and downright silly. What greater madness could there be, Don Diego asked himself, than to don a helmet filled with curds and then persuade oneself that enchanters were softening one's cranium? What could be more rashly absurd than to wish to fight lions by sheer strength alone? He was roused from these thoughts, this inward soliloquy, by the sound of Don Quixote's voice.

"Undoubtedly, Señor Don Diego de Miranda, your Grace must take me for a fool and a madman, am I not right? And it would be small wonder if such were the case, seeing that my deeds give evidence of nothing else. But, nevertheless, I would advise your Grace that I am neither so mad nor so lacking in wit as I must appear to you to be. A gaily caparisoned knight giving a fortunate lance thrust to a fierce bull in the middle of a great square makes a pleasing appearance in the eyes of his king. The same is true of a knight clad in shining armor as he paces the lists in front of the ladies in some joyous tournament. It is true of all those knights who, by means of military exercises or what appear to be such, divert and entertain and, if one may say so, honor the courts of princes. But the best showing of all is made by a knight-errant who, traversing deserts and solitudes, crossroads, forests, and mountains, goes seeking dangerous adventures with the intention of bringing them to a happy and successful conclusion, and solely for the purpose of winning a glorious and enduring renown.

"More impressive, I repeat, is the knight-errant succoring a widow in some unpopulated place than a courtly man of arms making love to a damsel in the city. All knights have their special callings: let the courtier wait upon the ladies and lend luster by his liveries to his sovereign's palace; let him nourish impoverished gentlemen with the splendid fare of his table; let him give tourneys and show himself truly great, generous, and magnificent and a good Christian above all, thus fulfilling his particular obligations. But the knight-errant's case is different.

"Let the latter seek out the nooks and corners of the world; let him enter into the most intricate of labyrinths; let him attempt the impossible at every step; let him endure on desolate highlands the burning rays of the midsummer sun and in winter the harsh inclemencies of wind and frost; let no lions inspire him with fear, no monsters frighten him, no dragons terrify him, for to seek them out, attack them, and conquer them all is his chief and legitimate occupation. Accordingly, I whose lot it is to be numbered among the knights errant cannot fail to attempt anything that appears to me to fall within the scope of my duties, just as I attacked those lions a while ago even though I knew it to be an exceedingly rash thing to do, for that was a matter that directly concerned me.

"For I well know the meaning of valor: namely, a virtue that lies between the two extremes of cowardice on the one hand and temerity on the other. It is, nonetheless, better for the brave man to carry his bravery to the point of rashness than for him to sink into cowardice. Even as it is easier for the prodigal to become a generous man than it is for the miser, so is it easier for the fool-hardy to become truly brave than it is for the coward to attain valor. And in this matter of adventures, you may believe me, Señor Don Diego, it is better to lose by a card too many than a card too few, and 'Such and such a knight is temerarious and overbold' sounds better to the ear than 'That knight is timid and a coward.' "

"I must assure you, Señor Don Quixote," replied Don Diego, "that everything your Grace has said and done will stand the test of reason; and it is my opinion that if the laws and ordinances of knight-errantry were to be lost, they would be found again in your Grace's bosom, which is their depository and storehouse. But it is growing late; let us hasten to my village and my home, where your Grace shall rest from your recent exertions; for if the body is not tired the spirit may be, and that sometimes results in bodily fatigue."

"I accept your offer as a great favor and an honor, Señor Don Diego," was the knight's reply. And, by spurring their mounts more than they had up to then, they arrived at the village around two in the afternoon and came to the house that was occupied by Don Diego, whom Don Quixote had dubbed the Knight of the Green-colored Greatcoat.

[*Last Duel*]

CHAPTER 64

Which treats of the adventure that caused Don Quixote the most sorrow of all those that have thus far befallen him.

. . . One morning, as Don Quixote went for a ride along the beach,[109] clad in full armor—for, as he was fond of saying, that was his only ornament, his only rest the fight, and, accordingly, he was never without it for a moment—he saw approaching him a horseman similarly arrayed from head to foot and with a brightly shining moon blazoned upon his shield.

As soon as he had come within earshot the stranger cried out to Don Quixote in a loud voice, "O illustrious knight, the never to be

109. Don Quixote and Sancho, after numberless encounters and experiences (of which the most prominent have been the Don's descent into the cave of Montesinos, and the residence at the castle of the playful ducal couple who give Sancho the "governorship of an island" for ten days), are now in Barcelona. Famous as they are, they meet the viceroy and the nobles; their host is Don Antonio Moreno, "a gentleman of wealth and discernment who was fond of amusing himself in an innocent and kindly way."

sufficiently praised Don Quixote de la Mancha, I am the Knight of the White Moon whose incomparable exploits you will perhaps recall. I come to contend with you and try the might of my arm, with the purpose of having you acknowledge and confess that my lady, whoever she may be, is beyond comparison more beautiful than your own Dulcinea del Toboso. If you will admit the truth of this fully and freely, you will escape death and I shall be spared the trouble of inflicting it upon you. On the other hand, if you choose to fight and I should overcome you, I ask no other satisfaction than that, laying down your arms and seeking no further adventures, you retire to your own village for the space of a year, during which time you are not to lay hand to sword but are to dwell peacefully and tranquilly, enjoying a beneficial rest that shall redound to the betterment of your worldly fortunes and the salvation of your soul. But if you are the victor, then my head shall be at your disposal, my arms and steed shall be the spoils, and the fame of my exploits shall go to increase your own renown. Consider well which is the better course and let me have your answer at once, for today is all the time I have for the dispatching of this business."

Don Quixote was amazed at the knight's arrogance as well as at the nature of the challenge, but it was with a calm and stern demeanor that he replied to him.

"Knight of the White Moon," he said, "of whose exploits up to now I have never heard, I will venture to take an oath that you have not once laid eyes upon the illustrious Dulcinea; for I am quite certain that if you had beheld her you would not be staking your all upon such an issue, since the sight of her would have convinced you that there never has been, and never can be, any beauty to compare with hers. I do not say that you lie, I simply say that you are mistaken; and so I accept your challenge with the conditions you have laid down, and at once, before this day you have fixed upon shall have ended. The only exception I make is with regard to the fame of your deeds being added to my renown, since I do not know what the character of your exploits has been and am quite content with my own, such as they are. Take, then, whichever side of the field you like, and I will take up my position, and may St. Peter bless what God may give."

Now, as it happened, the Knight of the White Moon was seen by some of the townspeople, who informed the viceroy that he was there, talking to Don Quixote de la Mancha. Believing this to be a new adventure arranged by Don Antonio Moreno or some other gentleman of the place, the viceroy at once hastened down to the beach, accompanied by a large retinue, including Don Antonio, and they arrived just as Don Quixote was wheeling Rocinante to measure off the necessary stretch of field. When the viceroy perceived that they were about to engage in combat, he at once interposed and inquired of them what it was that impelled them thus to do battle all of a sudden.

The Knight of the White Moon replied that it was a matter of beauty and precedence and briefly repeated what he had said to Don Quixote, explaining the terms to which both parties had agreed. The viceroy then went up to Don Antonio and asked him if he knew any such knight as this or if it was some joke that they were playing, but the answer that he received left him more puzzled than ever; for Don Antonio did not know who the knight was, nor could he say as to whether this was a real encounter or not. The viceroy, accordingly, was doutbful about letting them proceed, but inasmuch as he could not bring himself to believe that it was anything more than a jest, he withdrew to one side, saying, "Sir Knights, if there is nothing for it but to confess[110] or die, and if Señor Don Quixote's mind is made up and your Grace, the Knight of the White Moon, is even more firmly resolved, then fall to it in the name of God and may He bestow the victory."

The Knight of the White Moon thanked the viceroy most courteously and in well-chosen words for the permission which had been granted them, and Don Quixote did the same, whereupon the latter, commending himself with all his heart to Heaven and to his lady Dulcinea, as was his custom at the beginning of a fray, fell back a little farther down the field as he saw his adversary doing the same. And then, without blare of trumpet or other warlike instrument to give them the signal for the attack, both at the same instant wheeled their steeds about and returned for the charge. Being mounted upon the swifter horse, the Knight of the White Moon met Don Quixote two-thirds of the way and with such tremendous force that, without touching his opponent with his lance (which, it seemed, he deliberately held aloft) he brought both Rocinante and his rider to the ground in an exceedingly perilous fall. At once the victor leaped down and placed his lance at Don Quixote's visor.

"You are vanquished, O knight! Nay, more, you are dead unless you make confession in accordance with the conditions governing our encounter."

Stunned and battered, Don Quixote did not so much as raise his visor but in a faint, wan voice, as if speaking from the grave, he said, "Dulcinea del Toboso is the most beautiful woman in the world and I the most unhappy knight upon the face of this earth. It is not right that my weakness should serve to defraud the truth. Drive

110. admit one's error.

home your lance, O knight, and take my life since you already have deprived me of my honor."

"That I most certainly shall not do," said the one of the White Moon. "Let the fame of my lady Dulcinea del Toboso's beauty live on undiminished. As for me, I shall be content if the great Don Quixote will retire to his village for a year or until such a time as I may specify, as was agreed upon between us before joining battle."

The viceroy, Don Antonio, and all the many others who were present heard this, and they also heard Don Quixote's response, which was to the effect that, seeing nothing was asked of him that was prejudicial to Dulcinea, he would fulfill all the other conditions like a true and punctilious knight. The one of the White Moon thereupon turned and with a bow to the viceroy rode back to the city at a mild canter. The viceroy promptly dispatched Don Antonio to follow him and make every effort to find out who he was; and, in the meanwhile, they lifted Don Quixote up and uncovered his face, which held no sign of color and was bathed in perspiration. Rocinante, however, was in so sorry a state that he was unable to stir for the present.

Brokenhearted over the turn that events had taken, Sancho did not know what to say or do. It seemed to him that all this was something that was happening in a dream and that everything was the result of magic. He saw his master surrender, heard him consent not to take up arms again for a year to come as the light of his glorious exploits faded into darkness. At the same time his own hopes, based upon the fresh promises that had been made him, were whirled away like smoke before the wind. He feared that Rocinante was maimed for life, his master's bones permanently dislocated—it would have been a bit of luck if his madness also had been jolted out of him.[111]

Finally, in a hand litter which the viceroy had them bring, they bore the knight back to town. The viceroy himself then returned, for he was very anxious to ascertain who the Knight of the White Moon was who had left Don Quixote in so lamentable a condition.

CHAPTER 65

Wherein is revealed who the Knight of the White Moon was.

The Knight of the White Moon was followed not only by Don Antonio Moreno, but by a throng of small boys as well, who kept after him until the doors of one of the city's hostelries had closed behind him. A squire came out to meet him and remove his armor,

---

111. The original has an untranslatable pun on *deslocado,* which means "out of joint" ("dislocated") and also "cured of madness" (from *loco,* "mad").

for which purpose the victor proceeded to shut himself up in a lower room, in the company of Don Antonio, who had also entered the inn and whose bread would not bake until he had learned the knight's identity. Perceiving that the gentleman had no intention of leaving him, he of the White Moon then spoke.

"Sir," he said, "I am well aware that you have come to find out who I am; and, seeing that there is no denying you the information that you seek, while my servant here is removing my armor I will tell you the exact truth of the matter. I would have you know, sir, that I am the bachelor Sansón Carrasco from the same village as Don Quixote de la Mancha, whose madness and absurdities inspire pity in all of us who know him and in none more than me. And so, being convinced that his salvation lay in his returning home for a period of rest in his own house, I formed a plan for bringing him back.

"It was three months ago that I took to the road as a knight-errant, calling myself the Knight of the Mirrors, with the object of fighting and overcoming him without doing him any harm, intending first to lay down the condition that the vanquished was to yield to the victor's will. What I meant to ask of him—for I looked upon him as conquered from the start—was that he should return to his village and not leave it for a whole year, in the course of which time he might be cured. Fate, however, ordained things otherwise; for he was the one who conquered me and overthrew me from my horse, and thus my plan came to naught. He continued on his wanderings, and I went home, defeated, humiliated, and bruised from my fall, which was quite a dangerous one. But I did not for this reason give up the idea of hunting him up once more and vanquishing him as you have seen me do today.

"Since he is the soul of honor when it comes to observing the ordinances of knight-errantry, there is not the slightest doubt that he will keep the promise he has given me and fulfill his obligations. And that, sir, is all that I need to tell you concerning what has happened. I beg you not to disclose my secret or reveal my identity to Don Quixote, in order that my well-intentioned scheme may be carried out and a man of excellent judgment be brought back to his senses—for a sensible man he would be, once rid of the follies of chivalry."

"My dear sir," exclaimed Don Antonio, "may God forgive you for the wrong you have done the world by seeking to deprive it of its most charming madman! Do you not see that the benefit accomplished by restoring Don Quixote to his senses can never equal the pleasure which others derive from his vagaries? But it is my opinion that all the trouble to which the Señor Bachelor has put himself will not suffice to cure a man who is so hopelessly insane; and if it were not uncharitable, I would say let Don Quixote never be cured, since with his return to health we lose not only his own drolleries but also those of his squire, Sancho Panza, for either of the two is capable of turning melancholy itself into joy and merriment. Nevertheless, I will keep silent and tell him nothing, that I may see whether or not I am right in my suspicion that Señor Carrasco's efforts will prove to have been of no avail."

The bachelor replied that, all in all, things looked very favorable and he hoped for a fortunate outcome. With this, he took his leave of Don Antonio, after offering to render him any service that he could; and, having had his armor tied up and placed upon a mule's back, he rode out of the city that same day on the same horse on which he had gone into battle, returning to his native province without anything happening to him that is worthy of being set down in this veracious chronicle.

[*Homecoming and Death*]

CHAPTER 73

Of the omens that Don Quixote encountered upon entering his village, with other incidents that embellish and lend credence to this great history.

As they entered the village, Cid Hamete informs us, Don Quixote caught sight of two lads on the communal threshing floor who were engaged in a dispute.

"Don't let it worry you, Periquillo," one of them was saying to the other; "you'll never lay eyes on it again as long as you live."

Hearing this, Don Quixote turned to Sancho. "Did you mark what that boy said, my friend?" he asked. " 'You'll never lay eyes on it[112] again . . .' "

"Well," replied Sancho, "what difference does it make what he said?"

"What difference?" said Don Quixote. "Don't you see that, applied to the one I love, it means I shall never again see Dulcinea."

Sancho was about to answer him when his attention was distracted by a hare that came flying across the fields pursued by a large number of hunters with their greyhounds. The frightened animal took refuge by huddling down beneath the donkey, whereupon Sancho reached out his hand and caught it and presented it to his master.

"*Malum signum, malum signum*,"[113] the knight was muttering to himself. "A hare flees, the hounds pursue it, Dulcinea appears not,"

112. the same as "her" in the original, since the reference is to a cricket cage, denoted in Spanish by a feminine noun; hence the Don's inference concerning Dulcinea.
113. a bad sign. Meeting a hare is considered an ill omen.

"It is very strange to hear your Grace talk like that," said Sancho. "Let us suppose that this hare *is* Dulcinea del Toboso and the hounds pursuing it are those wicked enchanters that transformed her into a peasant lass; she flees, I catch her and turn her over to your Grace, you hold her in your arms and caress her. Is that a bad sign? What ill omen can you find in it?"

The two lads who had been quarreling now came up to have a look at the hare, and Sancho asked them what their dispute was about. To this the one who had uttered the words "You'll never lay eyes on it again as long as you live," replied that he had taken a cricket cage from the other boy and had no intention of returning it ever. Sancho then brought out from his pocket four curatos and gave them to the lad in exchange for the cage, which he placed in Don Quixote's hands.

"There, master," he said, "these omens are broken and destroyed, and to my way of thinking, even though I may be a dunce, they have no more to do with what is going to happen to us than the clouds of yesteryear. If I am not mistaken, I have heard our curate say that sensible persons of the Christian faith should pay no heed to such foolish things, and you yourself in the past have given me to understand that all those Christians who are guided by omens are fools. But there is no need to waste a lot of words on the subject; come, let us go on and enter our village."

The hunters at this point came up and asked for the hare, and Don Quixote gave it to them. Continuing on their way, the returning pair encountered the curate and the bachelor Carrasco, who were strolling in a small meadow on the outskirts of the town as they read their breviaries. And here it should be mentioned that Sancho Panza, by way of sumpter cloth, had thrown over his gray and the bundle of armor it bore the flame-covered buckram robe in which they had dressed the squire at the duke's castle, on the night that witnessed Altisidora's[114] resurrection; and he had also fitted the miter over the donkey's head, the result being the weirdest transformation and the most bizarrely appareled ass that ever were seen in this world. The curate and the bachelor recognized the pair at once and came forward to receive them with open arms. Don Quixote dismounted and gave them both a warm embrace; meanwhile, the small boys (boys are like lynxes in that nothing escapes them), having spied the ass's miter, ran up for a closer view.

"Come, lads," they cried, "and see Sancho Panza's ass trigged out finer than Mingo,[115] and Don Quixote's beast is skinnier than ever!"

Finally, surrounded by the urchins and accompanied by the

114. Altisidora was a girl in the duke's castle where Quixote and Sancho were guests for a time; she dramatically pretended to be in love with the Don.

115. The allusion is to the opening lines of a fifteenth-century satire, *Mingo Revulgo*.

curate and the bachelor, they entered the village and made their way to Don Quixote's house, where they found the housekeeper and the niece standing in the doorway, for the news of their return had preceded them. Teresa Panza, Sancho's wife, had also heard of it, and, half naked and disheveled, dragging her daughter Sanchica by the hand, she hastened to greet her husband and was disappointed when she saw him, for he did not look to her as well fitted out as a governor ought to be.

"How does it come, my husband," she said, "that you return like this, tramping and footsore? You look more like a vagabond than you do like a governor."

"Be quiet, Teresa," Sancho admonished her, "for very often there are stakes where there is no bacon. Come on home with me and you will hear marvels. I am bringing money with me, which is the thing that matters, money earned by my own efforts and without harm to anyone."

"You just bring along the money, my good husband," said Teresa, "and whether you got it here or there, or by whatever means, you will not be introducing any new custom into the world."

Sanchica then embraced her father and asked him if he had brought her anything, for she had been looking forward to his coming as to the showers in May. And so, with his wife holding him by the hand while his daughter kept one arm about his waist and at the same time led the gray, Sancho went home, leaving Don Quixote under his own roof in the company of niece and housekeeper, the curate and the barber.

Without regard to time or season, the knight at once drew his guests to one side and in a few words informed them of how he had been overcome in battle and had given his promise not to leave his village for a year, a promise that he meant to observe most scrupulously, without violating it in the slightest degree, as every knight-errant was obliged to do by the laws of chivalry. He accordingly meant to spend that year as a shepherd,[116] he said, amid the solitude of the fields, where he might give free rein to his amorous fancies as he practiced the virtues of the pastoral life; and he further begged them, if they were not too greatly occupied and more urgent matters did not prevent their doing so, to consent to be his companions. He would purchase a flock sufficiently large to justify their calling themselves shepherds; and, moreover, he would have them know, the most important thing of all had been taken care of, for he had hit upon names that would suit them marvelously well. When

---

116. Since the knight-errant's life has been forbidden him by his defeat, Don Quixote for a time plans to live according to another and no less "literary" code, that of the pastoral. In the following para-graphs the author, especially through the bachelor Carrasco, refers humorously to some of the conventions of pastoral literature.

the curate asked him what these names were, Don Quixote replied that he himself would be known as "the shepherd Quixotiz," the bachelor as "the shepherd Carrascón," the curate as "the shepherd Curiambro," and Sancho Panza as "the shepherd Pancino."

Both his listeners were dismayed at the new form which his madness had assumed. However, in order that he might not go faring forth from the village on another of his expeditions (for they hoped that in the course of the year he would be cured), they decided to fall in with his new plan and approve it as being a wise one, and they even agreed to be his companions in the calling he proposed to adopt.

"What's more," remarked Sansón Carrasco, "I am a very famous poet, as everyone knows, and at every turn I will be composing pastoral or courtly verses or whatever may come to mind, by way of a diversion for us as we wander in those lonely places; but what is most necessary of all, my dear sirs, is that each one of us should choose the name of the shepherd lass to whom he means to dedicate his songs, so that we may not leave a tree, however hard its bark may be, where their names are not inscribed and engraved as is the custom with lovelorn shepherds."

"That is exactly what we should do," replied Don Quixote, "although, for my part, I am relieved of the necessity of looking for an imaginary shepherdess, seeing that I have the peerless Dulcinea del Toboso, glory of these brookside regions, adornment of these meadows, beauty's mainstay, cream of the Graces—in short, one to whom all praise is well becoming however hyperbolical it may be."

"That is right," said the curate, "but we will seek out some shepherd maids that are easily handled, who if they do not square with us will fit in the corners."

"And," added Sansón Carrasco, "if we run out of names we will give them those that we find printed in books the world over: such as Fílida, Amarilis, Diana, Flérida, Galatea, and Belisarda; for since these are for sale in the market place, we can buy them and make them our own. If my lady, or, rather, my shepherdess, should by chance be called Ana, I will celebrate her charms under the name of Anarda; if she is Francisca, she will become Francenia; if Lucía, Luscinda; for it all amounts to the same thing. And Sancho Panza, if he enters this confraternity, may compose verses to his wife, Teresa Panza, under the name of Teresaina."

Don Quixote had to laugh at this, and the curate then went on to heap extravagant praise upon him for his noble resolution which did him so much credit, and once again he offered to keep the knight company whenever he could spare the time from the duties of his office. With this, they took their leave of him, advising and beseeching him to take care of his health and to eat plentifully of the proper food.

As fate would have it, the niece and the housekeeper had overheard the conversation of the three men, and as soon as the visitors had left they both descended upon Don Quixote.

"What is the meaning of this, my uncle? Here we were thinking your Grace had come home to lead a quiet and respectable life, and do you mean to tell us you are going to get yourself involved in fresh complications—

> Young shepherd, thou who comest here,
> Young shepherd, thou who goest there ... [117]

For, to tell the truth, the barley is too hard now to make shepherds' pipes of it."[118]

"And how," said the housekeeper, "is your Grace going to stand the midday heat in summer, the winter cold, the howling of the wolves out there in the fields? You certainly cannot endure it. That is an occupation for robust men, cut out and bred for such a calling almost from their swaddling clothes. Setting one evil over against another, it is better to be a knight-errant than a shepherd. Look, sir, take my advice, for I am not stuffed with bread and wine when I give it to you but am fasting and am going on fifty years of age: stay at home, attend to your affairs, go often to confession, be charitable to the poor, and let it be upon my soul if any harm comes to you as a result of it."

"Be quiet, daughters," said Don Quixote. "I know very well what I must do. Take me up to bed, for I do not feel very well; and you may be sure of one thing: whether I am a knight-errant now or a shepherd to be, I never will fail to look after your needs as you will see when the time comes."

And good daughters that they unquestionably were, the housekeeper and the niece helped him up to bed, where they gave him something to eat and made him as comfortable as they could.

CHAPTER 74

Of how Don Quixote fell sick, of the will that he made, and of the manner of his death.

Inasmuch as nothing that is human is eternal but is ever declining from its beginning to its close, this being especially true of the lives of men, and since Don Quixote was not endowed by Heaven with the privilege of staying the downward course of things, his own end came when he was least expecting it. Whether it was owing to

117. from a ballad. 118. a proverb.

melancholy occasioned by the defeat he had suffered, or was, simply, the will of Heaven which had so ordained it, he was taken with a fever that kept him in bed for a week, during which time his friends, the curate, the bachelor, and the barber, visited him frequently, while Sancho Panza, his faithful squire, never left his bedside.

Believing that the knight's condition was due to sorrow over his downfall and disappointment at not having been able to accomplish the disenchantment and liberation of Dulcinea, Sancho and the others endeavored to cheer him up in every possible way. The bachelor urged him to take heart and get up from bed that he might begin his pastoral life, adding that he himself had already composed an ecologue that would cast in the shade all that Sannazaro[119] had ever written, and had purchased with his own money from a herdsman of Quintanar two fine dogs to guard the flock, one of them named Barcino and the other Butrón. All this, however, did not serve to relieve Don Quixote's sadness; whereupon his friends called in the doctor, who took his pulse and was not very well satisfied with it. In any case, the physician told them, they should attend to the health of his soul as that of his body was in grave danger.

Don Quixote received this news calmly enough, but not so his housekeeper, niece, and squire, who began weeping bitterly, as if he were already lying dead in front of them. It was the doctor's opinion that melancholy and depression were putting an end to his patient's life. The knight then requested them to leave him alone as he wished to sleep a little, and they complied. He slept for more than six hours at a stretch, as the saying is, and so soundly that the housekeeper and niece thought he would never wake.

At last he did, however, and at once cried out in a loud voice, "Blessed be Almighty God who has given me so many blessings! Truly His mercy is boundless and is not limited or restrained by the sins of men."

The niece listened carefully to what her uncle said, and it seemed to her that he was speaking more rationally than was his wont, at least during his illness.

"Sir," she said to him, "what does your Grace mean? Has something occurred that we know nothing about? What is this talk of mercy and sins?"

"The mercy that I speak of," replied Don Quixote, "is that which God is showing me at this moment—in spite of my sins, as I have said. My mind now is clear, unencumbered by those misty shadows of ignorance that were cast over it by my bitter and continual reading of those hateful books of chivalry. I see through all the

---

119. the Italian poet Jacopo Sannazaro (1456?–1530), whose *Arcadia* is one of   the milestones in the pastoral tradition.

nonsense and fraud contained in them, and my only regret is that my disillusionment has come so late, leaving me no time to make any sort of amends by reading those that are the light of the soul. I find myself, niece, at the point of death, and I would die in such a way as not to leave the impression of a life so bad that I shall be remembered as a madman; for even though I have been one, I do not wish to confirm it on my deathbed. And so, my dear, call in my good friends: the curate, the bachelor Sansón Carrasco, and Master Nicholas the barber; for I want to confess my sins and make my last will and testament."

The niece, however, was relieved of this errand, for the three of them came in just then.

"I have good news for you, kind sirs," said Don Quixote the moment he saw them. "I am no longer Don Quixote de la Mancha but Alonso Quijano, whose mode of life won for him the name of 'Good.' I am the enemy of Amadis of Gaul and all his innumerable progeny; for those profane stories dealing with knight-errantry are odious to me, and I realize how foolish I was and the danger I courted in reading them; but I am in my right senses now and I abominate them."

Hearing this, they all three were convinced that some new kind of madness must have laid hold of him.

"Why, Señor Don Quixote!" exclaimed Sansón. "What makes you talk like that, just when we have received news that my lady Dulcinea is disenchanted?[120] And just when we are on the verge of becoming shepherds so that we may spend the rest of our lives in singing like a lot of princes, why does your Grace choose to turn hermit? Say no more, in Heaven's name, but be sensible and forget these idle tales."

"Tales of that kind," said Don Quixote, "have been the truth for me in the past, and to my detriment, but with Heaven's aid I trust to turn them to my profit now that I am dying. For I feel, gentlemen, that death is very near; so, leave all jesting aside and bring me a confessor for my sins and a notary to draw up my will. In such straits as these a man cannot trifle with his soul. Accordingly, while the Señor Curate is hearing my confession, let the notary be summoned."

Amazed at his words, they gazed at one another in some perplexity, yet they could not but believe him. One of the signs that led them to think he was dying was this quick return from madness to sanity and all the additional things he had to say, so well reasoned and well put and so becoming in a Christian that none of them could any longer doubt that he was in full possession of his

120. Sancho had imagined for the sake of his master that Dulcinea had been transformed into a country wench by enchanters, but ended up by believing his own invention.

faculties. Sending the others out of the room, the curate stayed behind to confess him, and before long the bachelor returned with the notary and Sancho Panza, who had been informed of his master's condition, and who, finding the housekeeper and the niece in tears, began weeping with them. When the confession was over, the curate came out.

"It is true enough," he said, "that Alonso Quijano the Good is dying, and it is also true that he is a sane man. It would be well for us to go in now while he makes his will."

At this news the housekeeper, niece, and the good squire Sancho Panza were so overcome with emotion that the tears burst forth from their eyes and their bosoms heaved with sobs; for, as has been stated more than once, whether Don Quixote was plain Alonso Quijano the Good or Don Quixote de la Mancha, he was always of a kindly and pleasant disposition and for this reason was beloved not only by the members of his household but by all who knew him.

The notary had entered along with the others, and as soon as the preamble had been attended to and the dying man had commended his soul to his Maker with all those Christian formalities that are called for in such a case, they came to the matter of bequests, with Don Quixote dictating as follows:

"ITEM. With regard to Sancho Panza, whom, in my madness, I appointed to be my squire, and who has in his possession a certain sum of money belonging to me: inasmuch as there has been a standing account between us, of debits and credits, it is my will that he shall not be asked to give any accounting whatsoever of this sum, but if any be left over after he has had payment for what I owe him, the balance, which will amount to very little, shall be his, and much good may it do him. If when I was mad I was responsible for his being given the governorship of an island, now that I am of sound mind I would present him with a kingdom if it were in my power, for his simplicity of mind and loyal conduct merit no less."

At this point he turned to Sancho. "Forgive me, my friend," he said, "for having caused you to appear as mad as I by leading you to fall into the same error, that of believing that there are still knights-errant in the world."

"Ah, master," cried Sancho through his tears, "don't die, your Grace, but take my advice and go on living for many years to come; for the greatest madness that a man can be guilty of in this life is to die without good reason, without anyone's killing him, slain only by the hands of melancholy. Look you, don't be lazy but get up from this bed and let us go out into the fields clad as shepherds as we agreed to do. Who knows but behind some bush we may come upon the lady Dulcinea, as disenchanted as you could wish. If it is because of worry over your defeat that you are dying, put the blame on me by saying that the reason for your being overthrown was that I had not properly fastened Rocinante's girth. For the matter of that, your Grace knows from reading your books of chivalry that it is a common thing for certain knights to overthrow others, and he who is vanquished today will be the victor tomorrow."

"That is right," said Sansón, "the worthy Sancho speaks the truth."

"Not so fast, gentlemen," said Don Quixote. "In last year's nests there are no birds this year. I was mad and now I am sane; I was Don Quixote de la Mancha, and now I am, as I have said, Alonso Quijano the Good. May my repentance and the truth I now speak restore to me the place I once held in your esteem. And now, let the notary proceed:

"ITEM. I bequeath my entire estate, without reservation, to my niece Antonia Quijana, here present, after the necessary deductions shall have been made from the most available portion of it to satisfy the bequests that I have stipulated. The first payment shall be to my housekeeper for the wages due her, with twenty ducats over to buy her a dress. And I hereby appoint the Señor Curate and the Señor Bachelor Sansón Carrasco to be my executors.

"ITEM. It is my will that if my niece Antonia Quijana should see fit to marry, it shall be to a man who does not know what books of chivalry are; and if it shall be established that he is acquainted with such books and my niece still insists on marrying him, then she shall lose all that I have bequeathed her and my executors shall apply her portion to works of charity as they may see fit.

"ITEM. I entreat the aforementioned gentlemen, my executors, if by good fortune they should come to know the author who is said to have composed a history now going the rounds under the title of *Second Part of the Exploits of Don Quixote de la Mancha*, to beg his forgiveness in my behalf, as earnestly as they can, since it was I who unthinkingly led him to set down so many and such great absurdities as are to be found in it; for I leave this life with a feeling of remorse at having provided him with the occasion for putting them into writing."

The will ended here, and Don Quixote, stretching himself at length in the bed, fainted away. They all were alarmed at this and hastened to aid him. The same thing happened very frequently in the course of the three days of life that remained to him after he had made his will. The household was in a state of excitement, but with it all the niece continued to eat her meals, the housekeeper had her drink, and Sancho Panza was in good spirits; for this business of inheriting property effaces or mitigates the sorrow which the heir ought to feel and causes him to forget.

Death came at last for Don Quixote, after he had received all the sacraments and once more, with many forceful arguments, had expressed his abomination of books of chivalry. The notary who was present remarked that in none of those books had he read of any knight-errant dying in his own bed so peacefully and in so Christian a manner. And thus, amid the tears and lamentations of those present, he gave up the ghost; that is to say, he died. Perceiving that their friend was no more, the curate asked the notary to be a witness to the fact that Alonso Quijano the Good, commonly known as Don Quixote, was truly dead, this being necessary in order that some author other than Cid Hamete Benengeli might not have the opportunity of falsely resurrecting him and writing endless histories of his exploits.

Such was the end of the Ingenious Gentleman of La Mancha, whose birthplace Cid Hamete was unwilling to designate exactly in order that all the towns and villages of La Mancha might contend among themselves for the right to adopt him and claim him as their own, just as the seven cities of Greece did in the case of Homer. The lamentations of Sancho and those of Don Quixote's niece and his housekeeper, as well as the original epitaphs that were composed for his tomb, will not be recorded here, but mention may be made of the verses by Sansón Carrasco:

> Here lies a gentleman bold
> Who was so very brave
> He went to lengths untold,
> And on the brink of the grave
> Death had on him no hold.
> By the world he set small store—
> He frightened it to the core—
> Yet somehow, by Fate's plan,
> Though he'd lived a crazy man,
> When he died he was sane once more.

CALDERÓN DE LA BARCA
(1600–1681)

Life Is a Dream*

Dramatis Personae

BASIL, *King of Poland*
SEGISMUND, *Prince*
ASTOLFO, *Duke of Muscovy*
CLOTALDO, *old man*
CLARION. *a comical servant*
ROSAURA, *a lady*
STELLA, *a princess*
Soldiers, guards, musicians, servants, retinues, women

The scene is laid in the court of Poland, a nearby fortress, and the open country.

Act I

On one side a craggy mountain: on the other a rude tower whose base serves as a prison for SEGISMUND. *The door facing the spectators is open. The action begins at nightfall.*

[ROSAURA, *dressed as a man, appears on the rocks climbing down to the plain: behind her comes* CLARION.]

ROSAURA. You headlong hippogriff who match the gale
  In rushing to and fro, you lightning-flicker
  Who give no light, you scaleless fish, you bird
  Who have no coloured plumes, you animal
  Who have no natural instinct, tell me whither   5
  You lead me stumbling through this labyrinth
  Of naked crags! Stay here upon this peak
  And be a Phaëthon to the brute-creation!
  For I, pathless save only for the track
  The laws of destiny dictate for me,   10
  Shall, blind and desperate, descend this height
  Whose furrowed brows are frowning at the sun.
  How rudely, Poland, you receive a stranger

---

* *La vida es sueño*, 1636? The English version by Roy Campbell. Reprinted from *Six Spanish Plays*, Vol. 3 in *The Classic Theatre*, edited by Eric Bentley (New York: Doubleday Anchor). Copyright © 1959 by Eric Bentley and reprinted by his permission.
1. *hippogriff:* a fantastic creature (a winged horse with an eagle's head and a lion's forelegs) invented by Italian Renaissance poets. Its most famous use was for Astolfo's flight to the moon in Ariosto's *Orlando Furioso*.
8. *Phaëthon:* in Greek mythology, the driver of the chariot of his father, the Sun; he came too close to earth and nearly burned it up.

(Hardly arrived, but to be treated hardly)
And write her entry down in blood with thorns.   15
My plight attests this well, but after all,
Where did the wretchèd ever pity find?

CLARION. Say *two* so wretchèd. Don't you leave me out
When you complain! If we two sallied out
From our own country, questing high adventure,   20
And after so much madness and misfortune
Are still two here, and were two when we fell
Down those rough crags—shall I not be offended
To share the trouble yet forego the credit?

ROSAURA. I did not give you shares in my complaint   25
So as not to rob you of the right to sorrow
Upon your own account. There's such relief
In venting grief that a philosopher
Once said that sorrows should not be bemoaned
But sought for pleasure.

CLARION.   Philosopher?   30
I call him a long-bearded, drunken sot
And would they'd cudgelled him a thousand blows
To give him something worth his while lamenting!
But, madam, what should we do, by ourselves,
On foot and lost at this late hour of day,   35
Here on this desert mountain far away—
The sun departing after fresh horizons?

ROSAURA. Clarion, how can I answer, being both
The partner of your plight and your dilemma?

CLARION. Would anyone believe such strange events?   40

ROSAURA. If there my sight is not deceived by fancy,
In the last timid light that yet remains
I seem to see a building.

CLARION.   Either my hopes
Are lying or I see the signs myself.

ROSAURA. Between the towering crags, there stands so small   45
A royal palace that the lynx-eyed sun
Could scare perceive it at midday, so rude
In architecture that it seems but one
Rock more down-toppled from the sun-kissed crags
That form the jaggèd crest.

CLARION.   Let's go closer,   50
For we have stared enough: it would be better

---

24. *trouble:* plays on words are not infrequent in Calderón, or, for that matter, in Shakespeare. Here, for example, the untranslatable pun is on the double meaning of *pesar* ("trouble" and "to weigh").

To let the inmates make us welcome.

ROSAURA.   See:
The door, or, rather, that funereal gap,
Is yawning wide—whence night itself seems born,
Flowing out from its black, rugged centre.   55

[*A sound of chains is heard.*]

CLARION. Heavens! What's that I hear?

ROSAURA.   I have become
A block immovable of ice and fire.

CLARION. Was that a little chain? Why, I'll be hanged
If that is not the clanking ghost of some
Past galley-slave—my terror proves it is!   60

SEGISMUND. Oh, miserable me! Unhappy me!

ROSAURA. How sad a cry that is! I fear new trials
And torments.

CLARION.   It's a fearful sound.

ROSAURA.   Oh, come,
My Clarion, let us fly from suffering!

CLARION. I'm in such sorry trim, I've not the spirit   65
Even to run away.

ROSAURA.   And if you had,
You'd not have seen that door, not known of it.
When one's in doubt, the common saying goes
One walks between two lights.

CLARION.   I'm the reverse.
It's not that way with me.

ROSAURA.   What then disturbs you?   70

CLARION. I walk in doubt between two darknesses.

ROSAURA. Is not that feeble exhalation there
A light? That pallid star whose fainting tremors,
Pulsing a doubtful warmth of glimmering rays,
Make even darker with its spectral glow   75
That gloomy habitation? Yes! because
By its reflection (though so far away)
I recognise a prison, grim and sombre,
The sepulchre of some poor living carcase.
And, more to wonder at, a man lies there   80
Clothed in the hides of savage beasts, with limbs
Loaded with fetters, and a single lamp
For company. So, since we cannot flee,
Let us stay here and listen to his plaint
And what his sorrows are.

SEGISMUND.   Unhappy me!   85

62. Notice how the interlocking of
the two major plots of the play (Segismund's and Rosaura's) begins almost
with the opening scene.

Oh, miserable me! You heavens above,
I try to think what crime I've done against you
By being born. Although to have been born,
I know, is an offence, and with just cause
I bear the rigours of your punishment: 90
Since to be born is man's worst crime. But yet
I long to know (to clarify my doubts)
What greater crime, apart from being born,
Can thus have earned my greater chastisement.
Aren't others born like me? And yet they seem   95
To boast a freedom that I've never known.
The bird is born, and in the hues of beauty
Clothed with its plumes, yet scarce has it become
A feathered posy—or a flower with wings—
When through ethereal halls it cuts its way,   100
Refusing the kind shelter of its nest.
And I, who have more soul than any bird,
Must have less liberty?
The beast is born, and with its hide bright-painted,
In lovely tints, has scarce become a spangled   105
And starry constellation (thanks to the skilful
Brush of the Painter) than its earthly needs
Teach it the cruelty to prowl and kill,
The monster of its labyrinth of flowers.
Yet I, with better instincts than a beast,   110
Must have less liberty?
The fish is born, the birth of spawn and slime,
That does not even live by breathing air.
No sooner does it feel itself a skiff
Of silver scales upon the wave than swiftly   115
It roves about in all directions taking
The measure of immensity as far
As its cold blood's capacity allows.
Yet I, with greater freedom of the will,
Must have less liberty?   120
The brook is born, and like a snake unwinds
Among the flowers. No sooner, silver serpent,
Does it break through the blooms than it regales
And thanks them with its music for their kindness,
Which opens to its course the majesty   125
Of the wide plain. Yet I, with far more life,
Must have less liberty?
This fills me with such passion, I become

106. *constellation:* the spots on the   109. *monster:* the Minotaur, kept by
beast's hide are compared to stars.   King Minos in the Cretan Labyrinth.

Like the volcano Etna, and could tear
Pieces of my own heart out of my breast! 130
What law, justice, or reason can decree
That man alone should never know the joys
And be alone excepted from the rights
God grants a fish, a bird, a beast, a brook?

ROSAURA. His words have filled me full of fear and pity. 135

SEGISMUND. Who is it overheard my speech? Clotaldo?

CLARION. Say "yes!"

ROSAURA.   It's only a poor wretch, alas,
Who in these cold ravines has overheard
Your sorrows.

SEGISMUND.   Then I'll kill you   [*Seizes her.*]
So as to leave no witness of my frailty. 140
I'll tear you into bits with these strong arms!

CLARION. I'm deaf. I wasn't able to hear that.

ROSAURA. If you were human born, it is enough
That I should kneel to you for you to spare me. 144

SEGISMUND. Your voice has softened me, your presence halted me,
And now, confusingly, I feel respect
For you. Who are you? Though here I have learned
So little of the world, since this grim tower
Has been my cradle and my sepulchre;
And though since I was born (if you can say 150
I really have been born) I've only seen
This rustic desert where in misery
I dwell alone, a living skeleton,
An animated corpse; and though till now,
I never spoke, save to one man who hears 155
My griefs and through whose converse I have heard
News of the earth and of the sky; and though,
To astound you more, and make you call me
A human monster, I dwell here, and am
A man of the wild animals, a beast 160
Among the race of men; and though in such
Misfortune, I have studied human laws,
Instructed by the birds, and learned to measure
The circles of the gentle stars, you only
Have curbed my furious rage, amazed my vision, 165
And filled with wonderment my sense of hearing.
Each time I look at you, I feel new wonder!
The more I see of you, the more I long
To go on seeing more of you. I think
My eyes are dropsical, to go on drinking 170
What it is death for them to drink, because

They go on drinking that which I am dying
To see and that which, seen, will deal me death.
Yet let me gaze on you and die, since I
Am so bewitched I can no longer think   175
What not seeing you would do to me—the sight
Itself being fatal! that would be more hard
Than dying, madness, rage, and fiercest grief:
It would be life—worst fate of all because
The gift of life to such a wretchèd man   180
Would be the gift of death to happiness!

ROSAURA. Astonished as I look, amazed to hear,
I know not what to say nor what to ask.
All I can say is that heaven guided me
Here to be comforted, if it is comfort   185
To see another sadder than oneself.
They say a sage philosopher of old,
Being so poor and miserable that he
Lived on the few plain herbs he could collect,
One day exclaimed: "Could any man be poorer   190
Or sadder than myself?"—when, turning round,
He saw the very answer to his words.
For there another sage philosopher
Was picking up the scraps he'd thrown away.
I lived cursing my fortune in this world   195
And asked within me: "Is there any other
Suffers so hard a fate?" Now out of pity
You've given me the answer. For within me
I find upon reflection that my griefs
Would be as joys to you and you'd receive them   200
To give you pleasure. So if they perchance
In any measure may afford relief,
Listen attentively to my misfortune
And take what is left over for yourself.
I am . . .

CLOTALDO. [*Within*] Guards of the tower! You sluggards   205
Or cowards, you have let two people pass
Into the prison bounds . . .

ROSAURA.   Here's more confusion!

SEGISMUND. That is Clotaldo, keeper of my prison.
Are my misfortunes still not at an end?

CLOTALDO. Come. Be alert, and either seize or slay them   210
Before they can resist!

VOICES. [*Within*]   Treason! Betrayal!

---

181. *The gift . . . happiness:* the gift of life, to a wretched man like himself, is
like giving death to a happy one.

CLARION. Guards of the tower who let us pass unhindered.
Since there's a choice, to seize us would be simpler.
  [*Enter* CLOTALDO *with soldiers. He holds a pistol and they all wear masks.*]
CLOTALDO. [*Aside to the soldiers*] Cover your faces, all! It's a precaution
Imperative that nobody should know us   215
While we are here.
CLARION.   What's this? A masquerade?
CLOTALDO. O you, who ignorantly passed the bounds
And limits of this region, banned to all—
Against the king's decree which has forbidden
That any should find out the prodigy   220
Hidden in these ravines—yield up your weapons
Or else this pistol, like a snake of metal,
Will spit the piercing venom of two shots
With scandalous assault upon the air.
SEGISMUND. Tyrannic master, ere you harm these people   225
Let my life be the spoil of these sad bonds
In which (I swear it by Almighty God)
I'll sooner rend myself with hands and teeth
Amid these rocks than see them harmed and mourn
Their suffering.
CLOTALDO.   Since you know, Segismund,   230
That your misfortunes are so huge that, even
Before your birth, you died by heaven's decree,
And since you know these walls and binding chains
Are but the brakes and curbs to your proud frenzies,
What use is it to bluster?
[*To the guards*]   Shut the door   235
Of this close prison! Hide him in its depths!
SEGISMUND. Ah, heavens, how justly you denied me freedom!
For like a Titan I would rise against you,
Pile jasper mountains high on stone foundations
And climb to burst the windows of the sun!   240
CLOTALDO. Perhaps you suffer so much pain today
Just to forestall that feat.
ROSAURA.   Now that I see
How angry pride offends you, I'd be foolish
Not to plead humbly at your feet for life.
Be moved by me to pity. It would be   245
Notoriously harsh that neither pride
Nor humbleness found favour in your eyes!
CLARION. And if neither Humility nor Pride
Impress you (characters of note who act

And motivate a thousand mystery plays)   250
Let me, here, who am neither proud nor humble,
But merely something halfway in between,
Plead to you both for shelter and for aid.
CLOTALDO. Ho, there!
SOLDIER.   Sir?
CLOTALDO.   Take their weapons. Bind their eyes
So that they cannot see the way they're led.   255
ROSAURA. This is my sword. To nobody but you
I yield it, since you're, after all, the chief.
I cannot yield to one of meaner rank.
CLARION. My sword is such that I will freely give it
To the most mean and wretched.
     [*To one soldier*]   Take it, you!   260
ROSAURA. And if I have to die, I'll leave it to you
In witness of your mercy. It's a pledge
Of great worth and may justly be esteemed
For someone's sake who wore it long ago.   264
CLOTALDO. [*Apart*] Each moment seems to bring me new misfortune!
ROSAURA. Because of that, I ask you to preserve
This sword with care. Since if inconstant Fate
Consents to the remission of my sentence,
It has to win me honour. Though I know not
The secret that it carries, I do know   270
It has got one—unless I trick myself—
And prize it just as the sole legacy
My father left me.
CLOTALDO.   Who then was your father?
ROSAURA. I never knew.
CLOTALDO.   And why have you come here?
ROSAURA. I came to Poland to avenge a wrong.   275
CLOTALDO. [*Apart*] Sacred heavens!
     [*On taking the sword he becomes very perturbed.*]
                              What's this? Still worse and worse.
I am perplexed and troubled with more fears.
     [*Aloud*] Tell me: who gave that sword to you?
ROSAURA.   A woman.
CLOTALDO. Her name?
ROSAURA.   A secret I am forced to keep.   280
CLOTALDO. What makes you think this sword contains a secret?
ROSAURA. That she who gave it to me said: "Depart
To Poland. There with subtlety and art
Display it so that all the leading people
And noblemen can see you wearing it,   285
And I know well that there's a lord among them

Who will both shelter you and grant you favour."
But, lest he should be dead, she did not name him.
CLOTALDO. [*Aside*] Protect me, heavens! What is this I hear?
  I cannot say if real or imagined   290
But here's the sword I gave fair Violante
In token that, whoever in the future
Should come from her to me wearing this sword,
Would find in me a tender father's love.
Alas, what can I do in such a pass,   295
When he who brings the sword to win my favour
Brings it to find his own red death instead
Arriving at my feet condemned already?
What strange perplexity! How hard a fate!
What an inconstant fortune to be plagued with!   300
This is my son not only by all signs
But also by the promptings of my heart,
Since; seeing him, my heart seems to cry out
To him, and beat its wings, and, though unable
To break the locks, behaves as one shut in,   305
Who, hearing noises in the street outside,
Cranes from the window-ledge. Just so, not knowing
What's really happening, but hearing sounds,
My heart runs to my eyes which are its windows
And out of them flows into bitter tears.   310
Protect me, heaven! What am I to do?
To take him to the king is certain death.
To hide him is to break my sacred oath
And the strong law of homage. From one side
Love of one's own, and from the other loyalty—   315
Call me to yield. Loyalty to my king
(Why do I doubt?) comes before life and honour.
Then live my loyalty, and let him die!
When I remember, furthermore, he came
To avenge an injury—a man insulted   320
And unavenged is in disgrace. My son
Therefore he is not, nor of noble blood.
But if some danger has mischanced, from which
No one escapes, since honour is so fragile
That any act can smash it, and it takes   325
A stain from any breath of air, what more
Could any nobleman have done than he,
Who, at the cost of so much risk and danger,
Comes to avenge his honour? Since he's so brave

---

291. *Violante:* whom he, Clotaldo,
has seduced.

301. *my son:* Rosaura, of course, is
disguised as a man.

He is my son, and my blood's in his veins.   330
And so betwixt the one doubt and the other,
The most important mean between extremes
Is to go to the king and tell the truth—
That he's my son, to kill, if so he wishes.
Perhaps my loyalty thus will move his mercy   335
And if I thus can merit a live son.
I'll help him to avenge his injury.
But if the king prove constant in his rigour
And deal him death, he'll die in ignorance
That I'm his father.
          [*Aloud to* ROSAURA *and* CLARION.]
                              Come then, strangers, come!   340
And do not fear that you have no companions
In your misfortunes, since, in equal doubt,
Tossed between life and death, I cannot guess
Which is the greater evil or the less.

          A hall at the royal palace, in court
          [*Enter* ASTOLFO *and soldiers at one side: from the other
          side* PRINCESS STELLA *and ladies. Military music and salvos.*]
ASTOLFO. To greet your excellent bright beams   345
     As brilliant as a comet's rays,
     The drums and brasses mix their praise
     With those of fountains, birds, and streams.
     With sounds alike, in like amaze,
     Your heavenly face each voice salutes,   350
     Which puts them in such lively fettle,
     The trumpets sound like birds of metal,
     The songbirds play like feathered flutes.
     And thus they greet you, fair señora—
     The salvos, as their queen, the brasses,   355
     As to Minerva when she passes,
     The songbirds to the bright Aurora,
     And all the flowers and leaves and grasses
     As doing homage unto Flora,
     Because you come to cheat the day   360
     Which now the night has covered o'er—
     Aurora in your spruce array,
     Flora in peace, Pallas in war,
     But in my heart the queen of May.
STELLA. If human voice could match with acts   365
     You would have been unwise to say

356. *Minerva:* the Roman Pallas
Athena.
357. *Aurora:* the Roman goddess of

Dawn.
     359. *Flora:* the Roman goddess of
flowers and fruitfulness.

Hyperboles that a few facts
May well refute some other day
Confounding all this martial fuss
With which I struggle daringly,   370
Since flatteries you proffer thus
Do not accord with what I see.
Take heed that it's an evil thing
And worthy of a brute accursed,
Loud praises with your mouth to sing   375
When in your heart you wish the worst.

ASTOLFO. Stella, you have been badly misinformed
If you doubt my good faith. Here let me beg you
To listen to my plea and hear me out.
The third Eugtorgius died, the King of Poland.   380
Basil, his heir, had two fair sisters who
Bore you, my cousin, and myself. I would not
Tire you with all that happened here. You know
Clorilene was your mother who enjoys,
Under a better reign, her starry throne.   385
She was the elder. Lovely Recisunda
(Whom may God cherish for a thousand years!)
The younger one, my mother and your aunt,
Was wed in Muscovy. Now to return:
Basil has yielded to the feebleness   390
Of age, loves learnèd study more than women,
Has lost his wife, is childless, will not marry.
And so it comes that you and I both claim
The heirdom of the realm. You claim that you
Were daughter to the elder daughter. I   395
Say that my being born a man, although
Son of the younger daughter, gives me title
To be preferred. We've told the king, our uncle,
Of both of our intentions. And he answered
That he would judge between our rival claims,   400
For which the time and place appointed was
Today and here. For that same reason I
Have left my native Muscovy. With that
Intent I come—not seeking to wage war
But so that you might thus wage war on me!   405
May Love, wise god, make true what people say
(Your "people" is a wise astrologer)
By settling this through your being chosen queen—
Queen and my consort, sovereign of my will;
My uncle crowning you, for greater honour;   410

385. *a better reign:* Heaven.

Your courage conquering, as it deserves;
My love applauding you, its emperor!
STELLA. To such chivalrous gallantry, my breast
Cannot hold out. The imperial monarchy
I wish were mine only to make it yours—   415
Although my love is not quite satisfied
That you are to be trusted since your speech
Is somewhat contradicted by that portrait
You carry in the locket round your neck.
ASTOFLO. I'll give you satisfaction as to that.   420
[*Drums*] But these loud instruments will not permit it
That sound the arrival of the king and council.
         [*Enter* KING BASIL *with his following.*]
STELLA. Wise Thales ...
ASTOLFO.   Learned Euclid ...
STELLA. Among the signs ...
ASTOLFO.   Among the stars ...   424
STELLA. Where you preside in power ...
ASTOLFO.   Where you reside ...
STELLA. And plot their paths ...
ASTOLFO.   And trace their fiery trails ...
STELLA. Describing ...
ASTOLFO.   ... Measuring and judging them ...
STELLA. Please read my stars that I, in humble bonds ...
ASTOLFO. Please read them, so that I in soft embraces ...
STELLA. May twine as ivy to this tree!
ASTOLFO.   May find   430
Myself upon my knees before these feet!
BASIL. Come and embrace me, niece and nephew. Trust me,
Since you're both loyal to my loving precepts,
And come here so affectionately both—
In nothing shall I leave you cause to cavil,   435
And both of you as equals will be treated.
The gravity of what I have to tell
Oppresses me, and all I ask of you
Is silence: the event itself will claim
Your wonderment. So be attentive now,   440
Belovèd niece and nephew, illustrious courtiers,
Relatives, friends, and subjects! You all know
That for my learning I have merited
The surname of The Learnèd, since the brush
Of great Timanthes, and Lisippus' marbles—   445

---

418. *that portrait:* a picture of Rosaura.
423. *Thales:* an early Greek philosopher. *Euclid:* the great Alexandrian geometer. The speech that follows is a long
flattering salutation to the king, shared
by Stella and Astolfo.
445. *Timanthes:* a Greek painter of

Stemming oblivion (consequence of time)—
Proclaimed me to mankind Basil the Great.
You know the science that I most affect
And most esteem is subtle mathematics
(By which I forestall time, cheat fame itself)   450
Whose office is to show things gradually.
For when I look my tables up and see,
Present before me, all the news and actions
Of centuries to come, I gain on Time—
Since Time recounts whatever I have said   455
After I say it. Those snowflaking haloes,
Those canopies of crystal spread on high,
Lit by the sun, cut by the circling moon,
Those diamond orbs, those globes of radiant crystal
Which the bright stars adorn, on which the signs   460
Parade in blazing excellence, have been
My chiefest study all through my long years.
They are the volumes on whose adamantine
Pages, bound up in sapphire, heaven writes,
In lines of burnished gold and vivid letters,   465
All that is due to happen, whether adverse
Or else benign. I read them in a flash,
So quickly that my spirit tracks their movements—
Whatever road they take, whatever goal
They aim at. Would to heaven that before   470
My genius had been the commentary
Writ in their margins, or the index to
Their pages, that my life had been the rubble,
The ruin, and destruction of their wrath,
And that my tragedy in them had ended,   475
Because, to the unlucky, even their merit
Is like a hostile knife, and he whom knowledge
Injures is but a murderer to himself.
And this I say myself, though my misfortunes
Say it far better, which, to marvel at,   480
I beg once more for silence from you all.
With my late wife, the queen, I had a son,
Unhappy son, to greet whose birth the heavens
Wore themselves out in prodigies and portents.
Ere the sun's light brought him live burial   485

the fourth century B.C. *Lisippus:* a
Greek sculptor of the same period. The
names are used symbolically to mean
great artists in general.
    473. *Their pages:* the image of the
heavens as a book that the king-astrolo-
ger reads is carried through here.
    476-478. *even their merit ... to him-
self:* the stars in the book of heaven portend death to the unlucky, and he who
can read it himself is like a self-murder-
er.

Out of the womb (for birth resembles death)
His mother many times, in the delirium
And fancies of her sleep, saw a fierce monster
Bursting her entrails in a human form,
Born spattered with her lifeblood, dealing death,   490
The human viper of this century!
The day came for his birth, and every presage
Was then fulfilled, for tardily or never
Do the more cruel ones prove false. At birth
His horoscope was such that the bright sun,   495
Stained in its blood, entered ferociously
Into a duel with the moon above.
The whole earth seemed a rampart for the strife
Of heaven's two lights, who—though not hand-to-hand—
Fought light-to-light to gain the mastery!   500
The worst eclipse the sun has ever suffered
Since Christ's own death horrified earth and sky.
The whole earth overflowed with conflagrations
So that it seemed the final paroxysm
Of existence. The skies grew dark. Buildings shook.   505
The clouds rained stones. The rivers ran with blood.
In this delirious frenzy of the sun,
Thus, Segismund was born into the world,
Giving a foretaste of his character
By killing his own mother, seeming to speak thus   510
By his ferocity: "I am a man,
Because I have begun now to repay
All kindnesses with evil." To my studies
I went forthwith, and saw in all I studied
That Segismund would be the most outrageous   515
Of all men, the most cruel of all princes,
And impious of all monarchs, by whose acts
The kingdom would be torn up and divided
So as to be a school of treachery
And an academy of vices. He,   520
Risen in fury, amidst crimes and horrors,
Was born to trample me (with shame I say it)
And make of my grey hairs his very carpet.
Who is there but believes an evil Fate?
And more if he discovers it himself,   525
For self-love lends its credit to our studies.
So I, believing in the Fates, and in
The havoc that their prophecies predestined,
Determined to cage up this newborn tiger

---

491. *viper:* reputedly the viper is killed and devoured by its offspring.

To see if on the stars we sages have   530
Some power. I gave out that the prince had died
Stillborn, and, well-forewarned, I built a tower
Amidst the cliffs and boulders of yon mountains
Over whose tops the light scarce finds its way,
So stubbornly their obelisks and crags   535
Defend the entry to them. The strict laws
And edicts that I published then (declaring
That nobody might enter the forbidden
Part of the range) were passed on that account.
There Segismund lives to this day, a captive,   540
Poor and in misery, where, save Clotaldo,
His guardian, none have seen or talked to him.
The latter has instructed him in all
Branches of knowledge and in the Catholic faith,
Alone the witness of his misery.   545
There are three things to be considered now:
Firstly Poland, that I love you greatly,
So much that I would free you from the oppression
And servitude of such a tyrant king.
He would not be a kindly ruler who   550
Would put his realm and homeland in such danger.
The second fact that I must bear in mind
Is this: that to deny my flesh and blood
The rights which law, both human and divine,
Concedes, would not accord with Christian charity,   555
For no law says that, to prevent another
Being a tyrant, I may be one myself,
And if my son's a tyrant, to prevent him
From doing outrage, I myself should do it.
Now here's the third and last point I would speak of,   560
Namely, how great an error it has been
To give too much belief to things predicted,
Because, even if his inclination should
Dictate some headlong, rash precipitancies,
They may perhaps not conquer him entirely,   565
For the most accursèd destiny, the most
Violent inclination, the most impious
Planet—all can but influence, not force,
The free will which man holds direct from God.
And so, between one motive and another   570
Vacillating discursively, I hit
On a solution that will stun you all.
I shall tomorrow, but without his knowing
He is my son—your king—place Segismund

(For that's the name with which he was baptised)   575
Here on my throne, beneath my canopy,
Yes, in my very place, that he may govern you
And take command. And you must all be here
To swear him fealty as his loyal subjects.
Three things may follow from this test, and these   580
I'll set against the three which I proposed.
The first is that should the prince prove prudent,
Stable, and benign—thus giving the lie
To all that prophecy reports of him—
Then you'll enjoy in him your rightful ruler   585
Who was so long a courtier of the mountains
And neighbour to the beasts. Here is the second:
If he prove proud, rash, cruel, and outrageous,
And with a loosened rein gallop unheeding
Across the plains of vice, I shall have done   590
My duty, and fulfilled my obligation
Of mercy. If I then re-imprison him,
That's incontestably a kingly deed—
Not cruelty but merited chastisement.
The third thing's this: that if the prince should be   595
As I've described him, then—by the love I feel
For you, my vassals—I shall give you worthier
Rulers to wear the sceptre and the crown;
Because your king and queen will be my nephew
And niece, each with an equal right to rule,   600
Each gaining the inheritance he merits,
And joined in faith of holy matrimony.
This I command you as a king, I ask you
As a kind father, as a sage I pray you,
As an experienced old man I tell you,   605
And (if it's true, as Spanish Seneca
Says, that the king is slave unto his nation)
This, as a humble slave, I beg of you.

ASTOLFO. If it behoves me to reply (being
The person most involved in this affair)   610
Then in the name of all, let Segismund
Appear! It is enough that he's your son!

ALL. Give us our prince: we want him for our king!

BASIL. Subjects, I thank you for your kindly favour.
Accompany these, my two Atlases,   615
Back to their rooms. Tomorrow you shall see him.

---

606. *Seneca:* the Roman dramatist and philosopher (4 B.C.?–A.D. 65) was born at Córdoba in Spain. The thought mentioned here is in his book *De cle-* *mentia,* I, 19.

615. *my two Atlases:* Astolfo and Stella, supporting him as the mythological Atlas supports the earth.

ALL. Long live the great King Basil! Long live Basil!
> [*Exeunt all, accompanying* STELLA *and* ASTOLFO. *The* KING
> *remains. Enter* CLOTALDO *with* ROSAURA *and* CLARION.]

CLOTALDO. May I have leave to speak, sire?

BASIL.   Oh, Clotaldo!
You're very welcome.

CLOTALDO.   Thus to kneel before you
Is always welcome, sire—yet not today   620
When sad and evil Fate destroys the joy
Your presence normally concedes.

BASIL.   What's wrong?

CLOTALDO. A great misfortune, sire, has come upon me
Just when I should have met it with rejoicing.

BASIL. Continue.

CLOTALDO.   Sire, this beautiful young man   625
Who inadvertently and daringly
Came to the tower, wherein he saw the prince,
Is my . . .

BASIL.   Do not afflict yourself, Clotaldo.
Had it not been just now, I should have minded,
I must confess. But I've revealed the secret,   630
And now it does not matter if he knows it.
Attend me afterwards. I've many things
To tell you. You in turn have many things
To do for me. You'll be my minister,
I warn you, in the most momentous action   635
The world has ever seen. These prisoners, lest you
Should think I blame your oversight, I'll pardon.
> [*Exit.*]

CLOTALDO. Long may you live, great sire! A thousand years!
> [*Aside*] Heaven improves our fates. I shall not tell him
Now that he is my son, since it's not needed   640
Till he's avenged.
> [*Aloud*] Strangers, you may go free.

ROSAURA. Humbly I kiss your feet.

CLARION.   Whilst I'll just *miss* them—
Old friends will hardly quibble at one letter.

ROSAURA. You've granted me my life, sir. I remain   645
Your servant and eternally your debtor.

CLOTALDO. No! It was not your life I gave you. No!
Since any wellborn man who, unavenged,
Nurses an insult does not live at all.
And seeing you have told me that you came   650
For that sole reason, it was not life I spared—
Life in disgrace is not a life at all.

[*Aside*] I see this spurs him.
ROSAURA.   Freely I confess it—
   Although you spared my life, it was no life.
   But I will wipe my honour's stain so spotless   655
   That after I have vanquished all my dangers
   Life well may seem a shining gift from you.
CLOTALDO. Take here your burnished steel: 'twill be enough,
   Bathed in your enemies' red blood, to right you.
   For steel that once was mine (I mean of course   660
   Just for the time I've had it in my keeping)
   Should know how to avenge you.
ROSAURA. Now, in your name I gird it on once more
   And on it I will swear to take revenge
   Although my foe were even mightier.   665
CLOTALDO. Is he so powerful?
ROSAURA.   So much so that . . .
   Although I have no doubt in your discretion . . .
   I say no more because I'd not estrange
   Your clemency.
CLOTALDO. You would have won me had you told me, since   670
   That would prevent me helping him.
   [*Aside*] If only I could discover who he is!
ROSAURA. So that you'll not think that I value lightly
   Such confidence, know that my adversary
   Is no less than Astolfo, Duke of Muscovy.   675
CLOTALDO. [*Aside*] (I hardly can withstand the grief it gives me
   For it is worse than aught I could imagine!
   Let us inquire of him some further facts.)
   [*Aloud*] If you were born a Muscovite, your ruler
   Could never have affronted you. Go back   680
   Home to your country. Leave this headstrong valour.
   It will destroy you.
ROSAURA.   Though he's been my prince,
   I know that he has done me an affront.
CLOTALDO. Even though he slapped your face, that's no affront.
   [*Aside*] O heavens!
ROSAURA.   My insult was far deeper!
CLOTALDO.   Tell it: 685
   Since nothing I imagine could be deeper.
ROSAURA. Yes. I will tell it, yet, I know not why,
   With such respect I look upon your face,
   I venerate you with such true affection,
   With such high estimation do I weigh you,   690

   661. With the words in parentheses, Clotaldo is trying to correct the impression
of his preceding slip of the tongue.

That I scarce dare to tell you—these men's clothes
Are an enigma, not what they appear.
So now you know. Judge if it's no affront
That here Astolfo comes to wed with Stella
Although betrothed to me. I've said enough.   695
    [*Exeunt* ROSAURA *and* CLARION.]
CLOTALDO. Here! Listen! Wait! What mazed confusion!
It is a labyrinth wherein the reason
Can find no clue. My family honour's injured.
The enemy's all powerful. I'm a vassal
And she's a woman. Heavens! Show a path   700
Although I don't believe there is a way!
There's nought but evil bodings in the sky.
The whole world is a prodigy, say I.

Act II

A Hall in the Royal Palace

    [*Enter* BASIL *and* CLOTALDO.]
CLOTALDO. All has been done according to your orders.
BASIL. Tell me, Clotaldo, how it went?
CLOTALDO.   Why, thus:
I took to Segismund a calming drug
Wherein are mixed herbs of especial virtue,
Tyrannous in their overpowering strength,   5
Which seize and steal and alienate man's gift
Of reasoning, thus making a live corpse
Of him. His violence evaporated
With all his faculties and senses too.
There is no need to prove it's possible   10
Because experience teaches us that medicine
Is full of natural secrets, that there is no
Animal, plant, or stone that has not got
Appointed properties. If human malice
Explores a thousand poisons which deal death,   15
Who then can doubt, that being so, that other
Poisons less violent, cause only sleep?
But (leaving that doubt aside as proven false
By every evidence) hear then the sequel:
I went down into Segismund's close prison   20
Bearing the drink wherein, with opium,
Henbane and poppies had been mixed. With him
I talked a little while of the humanities,

699-700. *I'm a vassal ... woman:*
hence, loyalty in his case and feminine
weakness in hers will make it difficult
to face the enemy and restore family
honor.

In which dumb Nature has instructed him,
The mountains and the heavens and the stars,   25
In whose divine academies he learned
Rhetoric from the birds and the wild creatures.
To lift his spirit to the enterprise
Which you require of him I choose for subject
The swiftness of a stalwart eagle, who,   30
Deriding the base region of the wind,
Rises into the sphere reserved for fire,
A feathered lightning, an untethered comet.
Then I extolled such lofty flight and said:
"After all, he's the king of birds, and so   35
Takes precedence, by right, over the rest."
No more was needful for, in taking up
Majesty for his subject, he discoursed
With pride and high ambition, as his blood
Naturally moves, incites, and spurs him on   40
To grand and lofty things, and so he said
That in the restless kingdom of the birds
There should be those who swear obedience, too!
"In this, my miseries console me greatly,
Because if I'm a vassal here, it's only   45
By force, and not by choice. Of my own will
I would not yield in rank to any man."
Seeing that he grew furious—since this touched
The theme of his own griefs—I gave the potion
And scarcely had it passed from cup to breast   50
Before he yielded all his strength to slumber.
A chill sweat ran through all his limbs and veins.
Had I not known that this was mere feigned death
I would have thought him dead. Then came the men
To whom you're trusted this experiment,   55
Who placed him in a coach and brought him here
To your own rooms, where all things were prepared
In royalty and grandeur as befitting
His person. In your own bed they have laid him
Where, when the torpor wanes, they'll do him service 60
As if he were Your Majesty himself.
All has been done as you have ordered it,
And if I have obeyed you well, my lord,
I'd beg a favour (pardon me this freedom)—
To know what your intention is in thus   65
Transporting Segismund here to the palace.
BASIL. Your curiosity is just, Clotaldo,
And yours alone I'll satisfy. The star

Which governs Segismund, my son, in life,
Threatens a thousand tragedies and woes. 70
And now I wish to see whether the stars
(Which never lie—and having shown to us
So many cruel signs seem yet more certain)
May yet be brought to moderate their sentence,
Whether by prudence charmed or valour won, 75
For man does have the power to rule his stars.
I would examine this, bringing him here
Where he may know he is my son, and make
Trial of his talent. If magnanimously
He conquers and controls himself, he'll reign, 80
But if he proves a tyrant and is cruel,
Back to his chains he'll go. Now, you will ask,
Why did we bring him sleeping in this manner
For the experiment? I'll satisfy you,
Down to the smallest detail, with my answer. 85
If he knows that he is my son today,
And if tomorrow he should find himself
Once more reduced to prison, to misery,
He would despair entirely, knowing truly
Who, and whose son, he is. What consolation 90
Could he derive, then, from his lot? So I
Contrive to leave an exit for such grief,
By making him believe it was a dream.
By these means we may learn two things at once:
First, his character—for he will really be 95
Awake in all he thinks and all his actions;
Second, his consolation—which would be
(If he should wake in prison on the morrow,
Although he saw himself obeyed today)
That he might understand he had been dreaming, 100
And he will not be wrong, for in this world,
Clotaldo, all who live are only dreaming.
CLOTALDO. I've proofs enough to doubt of your success,
But now it is too late to remedy it.
From what I can make out, I think he's wakened 105
And that he's coming this way, by the sound.
BASIL. I shall withdraw. You, as his tutor, go
And guide him through his new bewilderments
By answering his queries with the truth.
CLOTALDO. You give me leave to tell the truth of it? 110
BASIL. Yes, because knowing all things, he may find
Known perils are the easiest to conquer.
  [*Exit* BASIL. *Enter* CLARION.]

CLARION. It cost me four whacks to get here so quickly.
I caught them from a red-haired halberdier
Sprouting a ginger beard over his livery,   115
And I've come to see what's going on.
No windows give a better view than those
A man brings with him in his head, not asking
For tickets of admission or paid seats,
Since at all functions, festivals, or feasts   120
He looks out with the same nice self-composure.

CLOTALDO. [*Aside*] Here's Clarion who's the servant of that person—
That trader in woes, importer from Poland
Of my disgrace.
[*Aloud*]   Come, Clarion what news?

CLARION. Item the first: encouraged by the fact   125
Your clemency's disposed to venge her insult,
Rosaura has resumed her proper clothing.

CLOTALDO. That's right: it's less indecorous and bold.

CLARION. Item: she's changed her name, and given out
That she's your niece. And now they've made so much   130
Of her that she's been raised to maid of honour
To the unique and only princess, Stella.

CLOTALDO. That's right: her honour stands to my account.

CLARION. Indeed she merely bides the time till you
Will settle all accounts about her honour.   135

CLOTALDO. Biding the time is wise, for in the end
It's Time that's going to settle all accounts!

CLARION. Item: that she's attended like a queen,
Because they take her for your niece. Item:
That I, who trudged along with her, am dying   140
Of hunger. Nobody remembers me,
Nor yet remembers that I'm like my name
And (should I sound my Clarion) could tell
All to the king and Stella and Astolfo.
For I am both a Clarion and a servant—   145
Two things which ill-accord with secrecy.
If silence should, by chance, let slip my hand,
Then there's a chorus which would fit me well:
"Dawn-breaking Clarion plays no better tune!"

CLOTALDO. You've reason for complaint. I'll satisfy it   150
If you'll but serve me . . .

CLARION.   Hush, here's Segismund!
[*Enter musicians, singing, and servants arraying* SEGISMUND,
who seems amazed.]

141. The stock character of the clownish servant is distinguished by loquacity and perennial hunger (*cf.* Harle-
quin).

SEGISMUND. Heavens above! What's this that I am seeing?
　　I wonder at it all, with naught of fear!
　　But with a mighty doubt, I disbelieve it!
　　I?—in a sumptuous palace? I—encircled　　　　　　155
　　With rich brocades and silks? I—overwhelmed
　　With servants in such brilliant liveries?
　　I—to awake in such a gorgeous bed?
　　I—in the middle of so many footmen
　　Who clothe me in rich garments? I'm awake:　　　160
　　It would be false to take this for a dream.
　　Am I not Segismund? Heavens! disabuse me
　　If I'm mistaken. Say, what could have happened
　　In my imagination while I slept—
　　That I should find myself in such a place?　　　165
　　But why should I worry, whatever it was?
　　I'll let myself be served and entertained—
　　Befall what may.
FIRST SERVANT. [*Aside to* SECOND SERVANT *and* CLARION]
　　　　　　　　He's very melancholy!
SECOND SERVANT. Who would not be, considering all that's happened
　　To him?
CLARION.　I would not be!
SECOND SERVANT.　　　　You, speak to him.　　　　170
FIRST SERVANT. Shall they begin to sing again?
SEGISMUND.　　　　　　　　　　Why, no,
　　I would not have them sing.
SECOND SERVANT.　　　　　You're so distraught,
　　I wish you entertained.
SEGISMUND.　　　　My griefs are such
　　That no mere voices can amuse me now—
　　Only the martial music pleased my mind.　　　175
CLOTALDO. Your Highness, mighty prince, give me your hand
　　To kiss. I'm glad to be the first to offer
　　Obedience at your feet.
SEGISMUND. [*Aside*]　　　This is Clotaldo.
　　How is it he, that tyrannised my thralldom,
　　Should now be treating me with such respect?　　180
　　[*Aloud*] Tell me what's happening all round me here.
CLOTALDO. With the perplexities of your new state,
　　Your reason will encounter many doubts,
　　But I shall try to free you from them all
　　(If that may be) because you now must know　　185
　　You are hereditary Prince of Poland.
　　If you have been withdrawn from public sight
　　Under restraint, it was in strict obedience

To Fate's inclemency, which will permit
A thousand woes to fall upon this empire   190
The moment that you wear the sovereign's crown.
But trusting that you'll prudently defeat
Your own malignant stars (since they can be
Controlled by magnanimity) you've been
Brought to this palace from the tower you knew   195
Even while your soul was yielded up to sleep.
My lord the king, your father, will be coming
To see you, and from him you'll learn the rest.

SEGISMUND. Then, vile, infamous traitor, what have I
    To know more than this fact of who I am,   200
How have you played your country such a treason
As to deny me, against law and right,
The rank which is my own?

CLOTALDO.   Unhappy me!

SEGISMUND. You were a traitor to the law, a flattering liar   205
    To your own king, and cruel to myself.
And so the king, the law, and I condemn you,
After such fierce misfortunes as I've borne,
To die here by my hands.

SECOND SERVANT.   My lord!

SEGISMUND.   Let none
    Get in the way. It is in vain. By God!   210
If you intrude, I'll throw you through the window.

SECOND SERVANT. Clotaldo, fly!

CLOTALDO.   Alas, poor Segismund!
    That you should show such pride, all unaware
That you are dreaming this.
       [*Exit.*]

SECOND SERVANT.   Take care! Take care!

SEGISMUND. Get out!

SECOND SERVANT.   He was obeying the king's orders.   215

SEGISMUND. In an injustice, no one should obey
    The king, and I'm his prince.

SECOND SERVANT.   He had no right
    To look into the rights and wrongs of it.

SEGISMUND. You must be mad to answer back at me.

CLARION. The prince is right. It's you who're in the wrong!   220

SECOND SERVANT. Who gave you right to speak?

CLARION.   I simply took it.

SEGISMUND. And who are you?

CLARION.   I am the go-between,
    And in this art I think I am a master—

Since I'm the greatest jackanapes alive.

SEGISMUND. [*To* CLARION] In all this new world, you're the only one
Of the whole crowd who pleases me.

CLARION.   Why, my lord,   226
I am the best pleaser of Segismunds
That ever was: ask anybody here!
        [*Enter* ASTOLFO.]

ASTOLFO. Blessèd the day, a thousand times, my prince,
On which you landed here on Polish soil   230
To fill with so much splendour and delight
Our wide horizons, like the break of day!
For you arise as does the rising sun
Out of the rugged mountains, far away.
Shine forth then! And although so tardily   235
You bind the glittering laurels on your brows,
The longer may they last you still unwithered.

SEGISMUND. God save you.

ASTOLFO.   That you do not know me, sir,
Is some excuse for greeting me without
The honour due to me. I am Astolfo   240
The Duke of Muscovy. You are my cousin.
We are of equal rank.

SEGISMUND.   Then if I say,
"God save you," do I not display good feeling?
But since you take such note of who you are,
The next time that I see you, I shall say   245
"God save you *not*," if you would like that better.

SECOND SERVANT. [*To* ASTOLFO] Your Highness, make allowance for
    his breeding
Amongst the mountains. So he deals with all.
[*To* SEGISMUND] Astolfo does take precedence, Your Highness—

SEGISMUND. I have no patience with the way he came   250
To make his solemn speech, then put his hat on!

SECOND SERVANT. He's a grandee!

SEGISMUND.   I'm grander than grandees!

SECOND SERVANT. For all that, there should be respect between you,
More than among the rest.

SEGISMUND.   And who told you
To mix in my affairs?   255
        [*Enter* STELLA.]

STELLA. Many times welcome to Your Royal Highness,
Now come to grace the dais that receives him

227. *Segismunds:* There had been
three kings of Poland by that name between the early sixteenth century and
the time of this play.

252. *a grandee:* etiquette allowed a
grandee to keep his hat on in the king's
presence.

With gratitude and love. Long may you live
August and eminent, despite all snares,
And count your life by centuries, not years!   260

SEGISMUND. [*Aside to* CLARION] Now tell me, who's this sovereign
    deity
At whose divinest feet Heaven lays down
The fleece of its aurora in the east?

CLARION. Sir, it's your cousin Stella.

SEGISMUND.   She were better
Named "sun" than "star"!
[*To* STELLA]   Though your speech was fair,   265
Just to have seen you and been conquered by you
Suffices for a welcome in itself.
To find myself so blessed beyond my merit
What can I do but thank you, lovely Stella,
For you could add more brilliance and delight   270
To the most blazing star? When you get up
What work is left the sun to do? O give me
Your hand to kiss, from out whose cup of snow
The solar horses drink the fires of day!

STELLA. Be a more gentle courtier.

ASTOLFO.   I am lost.   275

SECOND SERVANT. I know Astolfo's hurt. I must divert him.
[*To* SEGISMUND] Sir, you should know that thus to woo so boldly
Is most improper. And, besides, Astolfo . . .

SEGISMUND. Did I not tell you not to meddle with me?

SECOND SERVANT. I only say what's just.

SEGISMUND.   All this annoys me.   280
Nothing seems just to me but what I want.

SECOND SERVANT. Why, sir, I heard you say that no obedience
Or service should be lent to what's unjust.

SEGISMUND. You also heard me say that I would throw
Anyone who annoys me from that balcony.   285

SECOND SERVANT. With men like me you cannot do such things.

SEGISMUND. No? Well, by God, I'll have to prove it then!
    [*He takes him in his arms and rushes out, followed by many,
    to return soon after.*]

ASTOLFO. What on earth have I seen? Can it be true?

STELLA. Go, all, and stop him!

SEGISMUND. [*Returning*]   From the balcony
He's fallen in the sea. How strange it seems!   290

ASTOLFO. Measure your acts of violence, my lord:
From crags to palaces, the distance is
As great as that between man and the beasts.

SEGISMUND. Well, since you are for speaking out so boldly,

Perhaps one day you'll find that on your shoulders   295
You have no head to place your hat upon.
    [*Exit* ASTOLFO. *Enter* BASIL]
BASIL. What's happened here?
SEGISMUND.   Nothing at all. A man
    Wearied me, so I threw him in the sea.
CLARION. [*To* SEGISMUND] Be warned. That is the king.
BASIL.   On the first day,
    So soon, your coming here has cost a life?   300
SEGISMUND. He said I couldn't: so I won the bet.
BASIL. It grieves me, Prince, that, when I hoped to see you
    Forewarned, and overriding Fate, in triumph
    Over your stars, the first thing I should see
    Should be such rigour—that your first deed here   305
    Should be a grievous homicide. Alas!
    With what love, now, can I offer my arms,
    Knowing your own have learned to kill already?
    Who sees a dirk, red from a mortal wound,
    But does not fear it? Who can see the place   310
    Soaking in blood, where late a man was murdered,
    But even the strongest must respond to nature?
    So in your arms seeing the instrument
    Of death, and looking on a blood-soaked place,
    I must withdraw myself from your embrace,   315
    And though I thought in loving bonds to bind
    Your neck, yet fear withholds me from your arms.
SEGISMUND. Without your loving arms I can sustain
    Myself as usual. That such a loving father
    Could treat me with such cruelty, could thrust me   320
    From his side ungratefully, could rear me
    As a wild beast, could hold me for a monster,
    And pray that I were dead, that such a father
    Wihholds his arms from winding round my neck,
    Seems unimportant, seeing that he deprives   325
    Me of my very being as a man.
BASIL. Would to heaven I had never granted it,
    For then I never would have heard your voice,
    Nor seen your outrages.
SEGISMUND.   Had you denied
    Me being, then I would not have complained,   330
    But that you took it from me when you gave it—
    That is my quarrel with you. Though to give
    Is the most singular and noble action,
    It is the basest action if one gives
    Only to take away.

BASIL. How well you thank me 335
For being raised from pauper to a prince!
SEGISMUND. In this what is there I should thank you for?
You tyrant of my will! If you are old
And feeble, and you die, what can you give me
More than what is my own by right of birth? 340
You are my father and my king, therefore
This grandeur comes to me by natural law.
Therefore, despite my present state, I'm not
Indebted to you, rather can I claim
Account of all those years in which you robbed me 345
Of life and being, liberty, and honour.
You ought to thank me that I press no claim
Since you're my debtor, even to bankruptcy.
BASIL. Barbarous and outrageous brute! The heavens
Have now fulfilled their prophecy: I call 350
Them to bear witness to your pride. Although
You know now, disillusioned, who you are,
And see yourself where you take precedence,
Take heed of this I say: be kind and humble
Since it may be that you are only dreaming, 355
Although it seems to you you're wide-awake. [*Exit.*]
SEGISMUND. Can I perhaps be dreaming, though I seem
So wide-awake? No: I am not asleep.
Since I can touch, and realise what I
Have been before, and what I am today. 360
And if you even now relented, Father,
There'd be no cure since I know who I am
And you cannot, for all your sighs and groans,
Cheat me of my hereditary crown.
And if I was submissive in my chains 365
Before, then I was ignorant of what I am,
Which I now know (and likewise know that I
Am partly man but partly beast as well).
   [*Enter* ROSAURA *in woman's clothing.*]
ROSAURA. [*Aside*] I came in Stella's train. I am afraid
Of meeting with Astolfo, since Clotaldo 370
Says he must not know who I am, not see me,
Because (he says) it touches on my honour.
And well I trust Clotaldo since I owe him
The safety of my life and honour both.

---

368. Notice how philosophical medita- "barbarous and outrageous brute" of
tion on the nature of man accompanies his father's description, Segismund
and underscores the developments of the knows that he is "partly man but part-
drama; at this stage in his enlighten- ly beast as well" (*un compuesto de*
ment, although he does not feel like the *hombre y fiera*).

CLARION. What pleases you, and what do you admire   375
　　Most, of the things you've seen here in the world?
SEGISMUND. Why, nothing that I could not have foreseen—
　　Except the loveliness of women! Once,
　　I read among the books I had out there
　　That who owes God most grateful contemplation   380
　　Is Man: who is himself a tiny world.
　　But I think who owes God more grateful study
　　Is Woman—since she is a tiny heaven,
　　Having as much more beauty than a man
　　As heaven than earth. And even more, I say,   385
　　If she's the one that I am looking at.
ROSAURA. [*Aside*] That is the prince. I'll go.
SEGISMUND.　　　　　　　　　　　Stop! Woman! Wait!
　　Don't join the sunset with the breaking day
　　By fading out so fast. If east and west
　　Should clash like that, the day would surely suffer   390
　　A syncope. But what is this I see?
ROSAURA. What I am looking at I doubt, and yet
　　Believe.
SEGISMUND. [*Aside*] This beauty I have seen before.
ROSAURA. [*Aside*] This pomp and grandeur I have seen before
　　Cooped in a narrow dungeon.
SEGISMUND. [*Aside*]　　　　　　　I have found   395
　　My life at last.
　　[*Aloud*]　　　　Woman (for that sole word
　　Outsoars all wooing flattery of speech
　　From one that is a man), woman, who are you?
　　If even long before I ever saw you
　　You owed me adoration as your prince,   400
　　How much the more should you be conquered by me
　　Now I recall I've seen you once before!
　　Who are you, beauteous woman?
ROSAURA. [*Aside*]　　　　　　　　I'll pretend.
　　[*Aloud*] In Stella's train, I am a luckless lady.
SEGISMUND. Say no such thing. You are the sun from which   405
　　The minor star that's Stella draws its life,
　　Since she receives the splendour of your rays.
　　I've seen how in the kingdom of sweet odours,
　　Commander of the squadrons of the flowers,
　　The rose's deity presides, and is   410
　　Their empress by divine right of her beauty.
　　Among the precious stones which can be listed
　　In the academy of mines, I've seen
　　The diamond much preferred above the rest,

And crowned their emperor, for shining brightest.   415
In the revolving empire of the stars
The morning star takes pride among the others.
In their perfected spheres, when the sun calls
The planets to his council, he presides
And is the very oracle of day.   420
Then if among stars, gems, planet, and flowers
The fairest are exalted, why do you
Wait on a lesser beauty than yourself
Who are, in greater excellence and beauty,
The sun, the morning star, the diamond, and the rose!   425

[*Enter* CLOTALDO, *who remains by the stage-curtain.*]

CLOTALDO. [*Aside*] I wish to curb him, since I brought him up.
  But, what is this?
ROSAURA.   I reverence your favour,
  And yet reply, rhetorical, with silence,
  For when one's mind is clumsy and untaught,
  He answers best who does not speak at all.   430
SEGISMUND. Stay! Do not go! How can you wish to go
  And leave me darkened by my doubts?
ROSAURA.   Your Highness,
  I beg your leave to go.
SEGISMUND.   To go so rudely
  Is not to beg my leave but just to take it.
ROSAURA. But if you will not grant it, I must take it.   435
SEGISMUND. That were to change my courtesy to rudeness.
  Resistance is like venom to my patience.
ROSAURA. But even if this deadly, raging venom
  Should overcome your patience, yet you dare not
  And could not treat me with dishonour, sir.   440
SEGISMUND. Why, just to see then if I can, and dare to—
  You'll make me lose the fear I bear your beauty,
  Since the impossible is always tempting
  To me. Why, only now I threw a man
  Over this balcony who said I couldn't: 445
  And so to find out if I can or not
  I'll throw your honour through the window too.
CLOTALDO. [*Aside*] He seems determined in this course. Oh, heavens!
  What's to be done that for a second time
  My honour's threatened by a mad desire?   450
ROSAURA. Then with good reason it was prophesied
  Your tyranny would wreak this kingdom

425. Like Segismund's very first
speech in Act I, this is a beautiful and
well-ordered piece of lyric poetry; here
too the main threads of the imagery
are elegantly brought together in the
last line.

Outrageous scandals, treasons, crimes, and deaths.
But what can such a creature do as you
Who are not even a man, save in the name—   455
Inhuman, barbarous, cruel, and unbending
As the wild beasts amongst whom you were nursed?

SEGISMUND. That you should not insult me in this way
I spoke to you most courteously, and thought
I'd thereby get my way; but if you curse me thus   460
Even when I am speaking gently, why,
By the living God, I'll really give you cause.
Ho there! Clear out, the lot of you, at once!
Leave her to me! Close all the doors upon us.
Let no one enter!   [*Exeunt* CLARION *and other attendants.*]

ROSAURA.   I am lost . . . I warn you . . .   465

SEGISMUND. I am a tyrant and you plead in vain.

CLOTALDO. [*Aside*] Oh, what a monstrous thing! I must restrain him
Even if I die for it.
[*Aloud*]   Sir! Wait! Look here!

SEGISMUND. A second time you have provoked my anger,
You feeble, mad old man! Do you prize lightly   470
My wrath and rigour that you've gone so far?

CLOTALDO. Brought by the accents of her voice, I came
To tell you you must be more peaceful
If still you hope to reign, and warn you that
You should not be so cruel, though you rule—   475
Since this, perhaps, is nothing but a dream.

SEGISMUND. When you refer to disillusionment
You rouse me near to madness. Now you'll see,
Here as I kill you, if it's truth or dreaming!
[*As he tries to pull out his dagger,* CLOTALDO *restrains him
and throws himself on his knees before him.*]

CLOTALDO. It's thus I'd save my life: and hope to do so—   480

SEGISMUND. Take your presumptuous hand from off this steel.

CLOTALDO. Till people come to hold your rage and fury
I shall not let you go.

ROSAURA.   O heavens!

SEGISMUND.   Loose it,
[*They struggle.*] I say, or else—you interfering fool—
I'll crush you to your death in my strong arms!   485

ROSAURA. Come quickly! Here's Clotaldo being killed!   [*Exit.*]
[ASTOLFO *appears as* CLOTALDO *falls on the floor, and the
former stands between* SEGISMUND *and* CLOTALDO.]

---

476. . . . *a dream:* the main theme and lesson of the drama; but Segismund is not
yet ripe for it.

ASTOLFO. Why, what is this, most valiant prince? What? Staining
   Your doughty steel in such old, frozen blood?
   For shame! For shame! Sheathe your illustrious weapon!
SEGISMUND. When it is stained in his infamous blood!   490
ASTOLFO. At my feet here he has found sanctuary
   And there he's safe, for it will serve him well.
SEGISMUND. Then serve me well by dying, for like this
   I will avenge myself for your behaviour
   In trying to annoy me first of all.   495
ASTOLFO. To draw in self-defense offends no king,
   Though in his palace. [ASTOLFO *draws his sword and they fight.*]
CLOTALDO. [*To* ASTOLFO] Do not anger him!
   [*Enter* BASIL, STELLA, *and attendants.*]
BASIL. Hold! Hold! What's this? Fighting with naked swords?
STELLA. [*Aside*] It is Astolfo! How my heart misgives me!
BASIL. Why, what has happened here?
ASTOLFO.   Nothing, my Lord,   500
   Since you've arrived.
   [*Both sheathe their swords.*]
SEGISMUND.   Much, though you *have* arrived.
   I tried to kill the old man.
BASIL.   Had you no
   Respect for those white hairs?
CLOTALDO.   Sire, since they're only
   Mine, as you well can see, it does not matter!
SEGISMUND. It is in vain you'd have me hold white hairs   505
   In such respect, since one day you may find
   Your own white locks prostrated at my feet
   For still I have not taken vengeance on you
   For the foul way in which you had me reared.   [*Exit.*]
BASIL. Before that happens you will sleep once more   510
   Where you were reared, and where what's happened may
   Seem just a dream (being mere earthly glory).
   [*All save* ASTOLFO *and* STELLA *leave.*]
ASTOLFO. How seldom does prediction fail, when evil!
   How oft, foretelling good! Exact in harm,
   Doubtful in benefit! Oh, what a great   515
   Astrologer would be one who foretold
   Nothing but harms, since there's no doubt at all
   That they are always due! In Segismund

___

497. Even in the most dramatic situations, these characters are sticklers for etiquette. The point implied here is that it is normally against the rules for courtiers to draw swords in the presence of their sovereign: hence Basil's surprise and alarm a few lines below.

And me the case is illustrated clearly.
In him, crimes, cruelties, deaths, and disasters   520
Were well predicted, since they all came true.
But in my own case, to predict for me
(As I foresaw beholding rays which cast
The sun into the shade and outface heaven)
Triumphs and trophies, happiness and praise,   525
Was false—and yet was true: it's only just
That when predictions start with promised favours
They should end in disdain.

STELLA.   I do not doubt
Your protestations are most heartfelt; only
They're not for me, but for another lady   530
Whose portrait you were wearing round your neck
Slung in a locket when you first arrived.
Since it is so, she only can deserve
These wooing flatteries. Let her repay you
For in affairs of love, flatteries and vows   535
Made for another are mere forged credentials.

[ROSAURA *enters but waits by the curtain.*]

ROSAURA. [*Aside*] Thanks be to God, my troubles are near ended!
To judge from what I see, I've naught to fear.

ASTOLFO. I will expel that portrait from my breast
To make room for the image of your beauty   540
And keep it there. For there where Stella is
Can be no room for shade, and where the sun is
No place for any star. I'll fetch the portrait.
[*Aside*] Forgive me, beautiful Rosaura, that,
When absent, men and women seldom keep   545
More faith than this.   [*Exit.*]

[ROSAURA *comes forward.*]

ROSAURA. [*Aside*] I could not hear a word. I was afraid
That they would see me.

STELLA.   Oh, Astrea!

ROSAURA.   My lady!

STELLA. I am delighted that you came. Because
To you alone would I confide a secret.   550

ROSAURA. Thereby you greatly honour me, your servant.

STELLA. Astrea, in the brief time I have known you

---

528. Judging by Stella's reply, Astolfo's uselessly involved speech seems to convey the notion that astrology proves safely right when it predicts harm, for when successes are foretold, they prove false, as witness the "promised favours" of his love for Stella now ending in "disdain."

531. *portrait:* of Rosaura (*cf.* p. 1653 and note 418), who had come to Poland to seek her unfaithful lover.

548. *Astrea:* a name assumed by Rosaura.

I've given you the latchkey of my will.
For that, and being who you are, I'll tell you
A secret which I've very often hidden   555
Even from myself.

ROSAURA.   I am your slave.

STELLA.   Then, briefly:
Astolfo, who's my cousin (the word cousin
Suffices, since some things are plainly said
Even by thinking them), is to wed me
If Fortune thus can wipe so many cares   560
Away with one great joy. But I am troubled
In that, the day he first came here, he carried
A portrait of a lady round his neck.
I spoke to him about it courteously.
He was most amiable, he loves me well,   565
And now he's gone for it. I am embarrassed
That he should give it me himself. Wait here,
And tell him to deliver it to you.
Do not say more. Since you're discreet and fair:
You'll surely know just what love is.   [*Exit.*]

ROSAURA.   Great heavens!   570
How I wish that I did not! For who could be
So prudent or so skilful as would know
What to advise herself in such a case?
Lives there a person on this earth today
Who's more beset by the inclement stars,   575
Who has more cares besieging him, or fights
So many dire calamities at once?
What can I do in such bewilderment
Wherein it seems impossible to find
Relief or comfort? Since my first misfortune   580
No other thing has chanced or happened to me
But was a new misfortune. In succession
Inheritors and heirs of their own selves
(Just like the Phoenix, his own son and father)
Misfortunes reproduce themselves, are born,   585
And live by dying. In their sepulchre
The ashes they consume are hot forever.
A sage once said misfortunes must be cowards
Because they never dare to walk alone
But come in crowds. I say they are most valiant   590
Because they always charge so bravely on
And never turn their backs. Who charges with them

584. *Phoenix:* the mythical bird which every 500 years is consumed by fire and
then rises from its own ashes.

May dare all things because there is no fear
That they'll ever desert him; and I say it
Because in all my life I never once   595
Knew them to leave me, nor will they grow tired
Of me till, wounded and shot through and through
By Fate, I fall into the arms of death.
Alas, what can I do in this dilemma?
If I reveal myself, then old Clotaldo,   600
To whom I owe my life, may take offence,
Because he told me to await the cure
And mending of my honour in concealment.
If I don't tell Astolfo who I am
And he detects me, how can I dissimulate?   605
Since even if I say I am not I,
The voice, the language, and the eyes will falter,
Because the soul will tell them that they lie.
What shall I do? It is in vain to study
What I should do, when I know very well   610
That, whatsoever way I choose to act,
When the time comes I'll do as sorrow bids,
For no one has control over his sorrows.
Then since my soul dares not decide its actions
Let sorrow fill my cup and let my grief   615
Reach its extremity and, out of doubts
And vain appearances, once and for all
Come out into the light—and Heaven shield me!
　　　[*Enter* ASTOLFO.]

ASTOLFO. Here, lady, is the portrait . . . but . . . great God!
ROSAURA. Why does Your Highness halt, and stare astonished?
ASTOLFO. Rosaura! Why, to see you here!
ROSAURA.　　　　　　　　　　　　　Rosaura?   621
Sir, you mistake me for some other lady.
I am Astrea, and my humble station
Deserves no perturbation such as yours.
ASTOLFO. Enough of this pretence, Rosaura, since   625
The soul can never lie. Though as Astrea
I see you now, I love you as Rosaura.
ROSAURA. Not having understood Your Highness' meaning
I can make no reply except to say
That Stella (who might be the star of Venus)   630
Told me to wait here and to tell you from her
To give to me the portrait you were fetching
(Which seems a very logical request)
And I myself will take it to my lady.
Thus Stella bids: even the slightest things   635

Which do me harm are governed by some star.

ASTOLFO. Even if you could make a greater effort
How poorly you dissimulate, Rosaura!
Tell your poor eyes they do not harmonise
With your own voice, because they needs must jangle   640
When the whole instrument is out of tune.
You cannot match the falsehood of your words
With the sincerity of what you're feeling.

ROSAURA. All I can say is—that I want the portrait.

ASTOLFO. As you require a fiction, with a fiction   645
I shall reply. Go and tell Stella this:
That I esteem her so, it seems unworthy
Only to send the counterfeit to her
And that I'm sending her the original.
And you, take the original along with you,   650
Taking yourself to her.

ROSAURA.   When a man starts
Forth on a definite task, resolved and valiant,
Though he be offered a far greater prize
Than what he seeks, yet he returns with failure
If he returns without his task performed.   655
I came to get that portrait. Though I bear
The original with me, of greater value,
I would return in failure and contempt
Without the copy. Give it me, Your Highness,
Since I cannot return without it.

ASTOLFO.   But   660
If I don't give it you, how can you do so?

ROSAURA. Like this, ungrateful man! I'll take it from you.
        [*She tries to wrest it from him.*]

ASTOLFO. It is in vain.

ROSAURA.   By God, it shall not come
Into another woman's hands!

ASTOLFO.   You're terrifying!

ROSAURA. And you're perfidious!

ASTOLFO.   Enough, my dear   665
Rosaura!

ROSAURA.   I, your dear? You lie, you villain!
        [*They are both clutching the portrait. Enter* STELLA.]

STELLA. Astrea and Astolfo, what does this mean?

ASTOLFO. [*Aside*] Here's Stella.

ROSAURA. [*Aside*]   Love, grant me the strength to win
My portrait.
        [*To* STELLA]   If you want to know, my lady,

636. *star:* the usual play on Stella = star.

What this is all about, I will explain.   670
ASTOLFO. [*To* ROSAURA, *aside*] What do you mean?
ROSAURA.   You told me to await
  Astolfo here and ask him for a portrait
  On your behalf. I waited here alone
  And as one thought suggests another thought,
  Thinking of portraits, I recalled my own   675
  Was here inside my sleeve. When one's alone,
  One is diverted by a foolish trifle
  And so I took it out to look at it.
  It slipped and fell, just as Astolfo here,
  Bringing the portrait of the other lady,   680
  Came to deliver it to you as promised.
  He picked my portrait up, and so unwilling
  Is he to give away the one you asked for,
  Instead of doing so, he seized upon
  The other portrait which is mine alone   685
  And will not give it back though I entreated
  And begged him to return it. I was angry
  And tried to snatch it back. That's it he's holding,
  And you can see yourself if it's not mine.
STELLA. Let go the portrait.   [*She snatches it from him.*]
ASTOLFO.   Madam!
STELLA.   The draughtsman   690
  Was not unkind to truth.
ROSAURA.   Is it not mine?
STELLA. Why, who could doubt it?
ROSAURA.   Ask him for the other.
STELLA. Here, take your own, Astrea. You may leave us.
ROSAURA. [*Aside*] Now I have got my portrait, come what will.
                                                  [*Exit.*]

STELLA. Now give me up the portrait that I asked for   695
  Although I'll see and speak to you no more.
  I do not wish to leave it in your power
  Having been once so foolish as to beg it.
ASTOLFO. [*Aside*] Now how can I get out of this foul trap?
  [*To* STELLA] Beautiful Stella, though I would obey you,   700
  And serve you in all ways, I cannot give you
  The portrait, since . . .
STELLA.   You are a crude, coarse villain
  And ruffian of a wooer. For the portrait—
  I do not want it now, since, if I had it,   704
  It would remind me I had asked you for it.   [*Exit.*]
ASTOLFO. Listen! Look! Wait! Let me explain!
  [*Aside*]   Oh, damn

Rosaura! How the devil did she get
To Poland for my ruin and her own?

The prison of Segismund in the tower

[SEGISMUND *lying on the ground loaded with fetters and clothed in skins as before.* CLOTALDO, *two attendants, and* CLARION.]

CLOTALDO. Here you must leave him—since his reckless pride
Ends here today where it began.

ATTENDANT.   His chain   710
I'll rivet as it used to be before.

CLARION. O Prince, you'd better not awake too soon
To find how lost you are, how changed your fate,
And that your fancied glory of an hour
Was but a shade of life, a flame of death!   715

CLOTALDO. For one who knows so well to wield his tongue
It's fit a worthy place should be provided
With lots of room and lots of time to argue.
This is the fellow that you have to seize   719
[*To the attendants*] And that's the room in which you are to lock
   him. [*Points to the nearest cell.*]

CLARION. Why me?

CLOTALDO.   Because a Clarion who knows
Too many secrets must be kept in gaol—
A place where even clarions are silent.

CLARION. Have I, by chance, wanted to kill my father
Or thrown an Icarus from a balcony?   725
Am I asleep or dreaming? To what end
Do you imprison me?

CLOTALDO.   You're Clarion.

CLARION. Well, say I swear to be a cornet now,
A silent one, a wretched instrument . . . ?
      [*They hustle him off.* CLOTALDO *remains. Enter* BASIL,
      wearing a mask.]

BASIL. Clotaldo.

CLOTALDO.   Sire . . . and is it thus alone   730
Your Majesty has come?

BASIL.   Vain curiosity
To see what happens here to Segismund.

CLOTALDO. See where he lies, reduced to misery!

BASIL. Unhappy prince! Born at a fatal moment!
Come waken him, now he has lost his strength   735

725. *Icarus:* a comic reference to the mythological flight of Icarus who came so close to the sun that his wax wings melted and he fell into the sea.

    With all the opium he's drunk.

CLOTALDO.   He's stirring
    And talking to himself.

BASIL.   What is he dreaming?
    Let's listen now.

SEGISMUND.   He who chastises tyrants
    Is a most pious prince . . . Now let Clotaldo
    Die by my hand . . . my father kiss my feet . . .   740

CLOTALDO. He threatens me with death!

BASIL   And me with insult
    And cruelty.

CLOTALDO.   He'd take my life away.

BASIL. And he'd humiliate me at his feet.

SEGISMUND. [*Still in a dream*]
    Throughout the expanse of this world's theatre
    I'll show my peerless valour, let my vengeance   745
    Be wreaked, and the Prince Segismund be seen
    To triumph—over his father . . . but, alas!
    [*Awakening*] Where am I?

BASIL. [*To* CLOTALDO] Since he must not see me here,   749
    I'll listen further off. You know your cue. [*Retires to one side.*]

SEGISMUND. Can this be I? Am I the same who, chained
    And long imprisoned, rose to such a state?
    Are you not still my sepulchre and grave,
    You dismal tower? God! What things I have dreamed!

CLOTALDO. [*Aside*] Now I must go to him to disenchant him. 755
    [*Aloud*] Awake already?

SEGISMUND.   Yes: it was high time.

CLOTALDO. What? Do you have to spend all day asleep?
    Since I was following the eagle's flight
    With tardy discourse, have you still lain here
    Without awaking?

SEGISMUND.   No. Nor even now   760
    Am I awake. It seems I've always slept,
    Since, if I've dreamed what I've just seen and heard
    Palpably and for certain, then I am dreaming
    What I see now—nor is it strange I'm tired,
    Since what I, sleeping, see, tells me that I   765
    Was dreaming when I thought I was awake.

CLOTALDO. Tell me your dream.

SEGISMUND.   That's if it *was* a dream!
    No, I'll not tell you what I dreamed, but what
    I lived and saw, Clotaldo, I *will* tell you.
    I woke up in a bed that might have been   770

758. *the eagle's flight:* cf. Clotaldo's long speech at the opening of this act.

The cradle of the flowers, woven by Spring.
A thousand nobles, bowing, called me Prince,
Attiring me in jewels, pomp, and splendour.
My equanimity you turned to rapture
Telling me that I was the Prince of Poland.   775
CLOTALDO. I must have got a fine reward!
SEGISMUND.   Not so:
For as a traitor, twice, with rage and fury,
I tried to kill you.
CLOTALDO.   Such cruelty to me?
SEGISMUND. I was the lord of all, on all I took revenge,
Except I loved one woman . . . I believe   780
That *that* was true, though all the rest has faded. [*Exit* BASIL.]
CLOTALDO. [*Aside*] I see the king was moved, to hear him speak.
[*Aloud*] Talking of eagles made you dream of empires,
But even in your dreams it's good to honour
Those who have cared for you and brought you up.   785
For Segismund, even in dreams, I warn you
Nothing is lost by trying to do good.   [*Exit*.]
SEGISMUND. That's true, and therefore let us subjugate
The bestial side, this fury and ambition,
Against the time when we may dream once more,   790
As certainly we shall, for this strange world
Is such that but to live here is to dream.
And now experience shows me that each man
Dreams what he is until he is awakened.
The king dreams he's a king and in this fiction   795
Lives, rules, administers with royal pomp.
Yet all the borrowed praises that he earns
Are written in the wind, and he is changed
(How sad a fate!) by death to dust and ashes.
What man is there alive who'd seek to reign   800
Since he must wake into the dream that's death.
The rich man dreams his wealth which is his care
And woe. The poor man dreams his sufferings.
He dreams who thrives and prospers in this life.
He dreams who toils and strives. He dreams who injures,   805
Offends, and insults. So that in this world
Everyone dreams the thing he is, though no one
Can understand it. I dream I am here,
Chained in these fetters. Yet I dreamed just now
I was in a more flattering, lofty station.   810
What is this life? A frenzy, an illusion,
A shadow, a delirium, a fiction.
The greatest good's but little, and this life

Is but a dream, and dreams are only dreams.

Act III

The tower

[*Enter* CLARION.]

CLARION. I'm held in an enchanted tower, because
    Of all I know. What would they do to me
    For all I don't know, since—for all I know—
    They're killing me by starving me to death.
    O that a man so hungry as myself   5
    Should live to die of hunger while alive!
    I am so sorry for myself that others
    May well say "I can well believe it," since
    This silence ill accords with my name "Clarion,"
    And I just can't shut up. My fellows here?   10
    Spiders and rats—fine feathered songsters those!
    My head's still ringing with a dream of fifes
    And trumpets and a lot of noisy humbug
    And long processions as of penitents
    With crosses, winding up and down, while some   15
    Faint at the sight of blood besmirching others.
    But now to tell the truth, I am in prison.
    For knowing secrets, I am kept shut in,
    Strictly observed as if I were a Sunday,
    And feeling sadder than a Tuesday, where   20
    I neither eat nor drink. They say a secret
    Is sacred and should be as strictly kept
    As any saint's day on the calendar.
    Saint Secret's Day for me's a working day
    Because I'm never idle then. The penance   25
    I suffer here is merited, I say:
    Because being a lackey, I was silent,
    Which, in a servant, is a sacrilege.
    [*A noise of drums and trumpets*]

FIRST SOLDIER. [*Within*] Here is the tower in which he is
    imprisoned.

    Smash in the door and enter, everybody!   30

CLARION. Great God! They've come to seek me. That is certain
    Because they say I'm here. What can they want?
    [*Enter several soldiers.*]

FIRST SOLDIER. Go in.

SECOND SOLDIER.   He's here!

---

2. *Cf.* note to line 141 above. This speech is played on the two themes of the clownish servant's hunger and loquacity.

CLARION. No, he's not here!

ALL THE SOLDIERS. Our lord!

CLARION. What, are they drunk?

FIRST SOLDIER. You are our rightful prince.
We do not want and never shall allow 35
A stranger to supplant our trueborn prince.
Give us your feet to kiss!

ALL THE SOLDIERS. Long live the prince!

CLARION. Bless me, if it's not real! In this strange kingdom
It seems the custom, everyday, to take
Some fellow and to make him prince and then 40
Shut him back in this tower. That *must* be it!
So I must play my role.

ALL THE SOLDIERS. Give us your feet.

CLARION. I can't. They're necessary. After all
What sort of use would be a footless prince?

SECOND SOLDIER. All of us told your father, as one man, 45
We want no prince of Muscovy but you!

CLARION. You weren't respectful to my father? Shame!

FIRST SOLDIER. It was our loyalty that made us tell him.

CLARION. If it was loyalty, you have my pardon. 49

SECOND SOLDIER. Restore your empire. Long live Segismund!

CLARION. [*Aside*] That is the name they seem to give to all
These counterfeited princes.
      [*Enter* SEGISMUND.]

SEGISMUND. Who called Segismund?

CLARION. [*Aside*] I seem to be a hollow sort of prince.

FIRST SOLDIER. Which of you's Segismund?

SEGISMUND. I am.

SECOND SOLDIER. [*To* CLARION] Then, why,
Rash fool, did you impersonate the prince 55
Segismund?

CLARION. What? I, Segismund? Yourselves
Be-Segismunded me without request.
All yours was both the rashness and the folly.

FIRST SOLDIER. Prince Segismund, whom we acclaim our lord,
Your father, great King Basil, in his fear 60
That heaven would fulfill a prophecy
That one day he would kneel before your feet
Wishes now to deprive you of the throne
And give it to the Duke of Muscovy.
For this he called a council, but the people 65
Discovered his design and knowing, now,
They have a native king, will have no stranger.

64. *Duke of Muscovy:* Astolfo.

So scorning the fierce threats of destiny,
We've come to seek you in your very prison,
That aided by the arms of the whole people,   70
We may restore you to the crown and sceptre,
Taking them from the tyrant's grasp. Come, then:
Assembling here, in this wide desert region,
Hosts of plebeians, bandits, and freebooters,
Acclaim you king. Your liberty awaits you!   75
Hark to its voice!
[*Shouts within*]   Long life to Segismund!
SEGISMUND. Once more, you heavens will that I should dream
Of grandeur, once again, 'twixt doubts and shades,
Behold the majesty of pomp and power
Vanish into the wind, once more you wish   80
That I should taste the disillusion and
The risk by which all human power is humbled,
Of which all human power should live aware.
It must not be. I'll not be once again
Put through my paces by my fortune's stars.   85
And since I know this life is all a dream,
Depart, vain shades, who feign, to my dead senses,
That you have voice and body, having neither!
I want no more feigned majesty, fantastic
Display, nor void illusions, that one gust   90
Can scatter like the almond tree in flower,
Whose rosy buds, without advice or warning,
Dawn in the air too soon and then, as one,
Are all extinguished, fade, and fall, and wither
In the first gust of wind that comes along!   95
I know you well. I know you well by now.
I know that all that happens in yourselves
Happens as in a sleeping man. For me
There are no more delusions and deceptions
Since I well know this life is all a dream.   100
SECOND SOLDIER. If you think we are cheating, just sweep
Your gaze along these towering peaks, and see
The hosts that wait to welcome and obey you.
SEGISMUND. Already once before I've seen such crowds
Distinctly, quite as vividly as these: 105
And yet it was a dream.
SECOND SOLDIER.   No great event
Can come without forerunners to announce it
And this is the real meaning of your dream.
SEGISMUND. Yes, you say well. It was the fore-announcement
And just in case it was correct, my soul,   110

(Since life's so short) let's dream the dream anew!
But it must be attentively, aware
That we'll awake from pleasure in the end.
Forewarned of that, the shock's not so abrupt,
The disillusion's less. Evils anticipated   115
Lose half their sting. And armed with this precaution—
That power, even when we're sure of it, is borrowed
And must be given back to its true owner—
We can risk anything and dare the worst.
Subjects, I thank you for your loyalty.   120
In me you have a leader who will free you,
Bravely and skilfully, from foreign rule.
Sound now to arms, you'll soon behold my valour.
Against my father I must march and bring
Truth from the stars. Yes: he must kneel to me.   125
[*Aside*] But yet, since I may wake before he kneels,
Perhaps I'd better not proclaim what may not happen.
ALL. Long live Segismund!
          [*Enter* CLOTALDO.]
CLOTALDO.   Gracious heavens! What is
This riot here?
SEGISMUND.   Clotaldo!
CLOTALDO.   Sir!
    [*Aside*]   He'll prove
His cruelty on me.
CLARION.   I bet he throws him   130
Over the mountain.
CLOTALDO.   At your royal feet
I kneel, knowing my penalty is death.
SEGISMUND. Rise, rise, my foster father, from the ground,
For you must be the compass and the guide
In which I trust. You brought me up, and I   135
Know what I owe your loyalty. Embrace me!
CLOTALDO. What's that you say?
SEGISMUND.   I know I'm in a dream,
But I would like to act well, since good actions,
Even in a dream, are not entirely lost.
CLOTALDO. Since doing good is now to be your glory,   140
You will not be offended that I too
Should do what's right. You march against your father!
I cannot give you help against my king.
Here at your feet, my lord, I plead for death.
SEGISMUND. [*Aloud*] Villain!

125. *Truth from the stars:* proof
that their predictions were truthful.

139. *Cf.* Clotaldo's own warning to
him in his last talk at the end of Act II.

[*Aside*]   But let us suffer this annoyance.
Though my rage would slay him, yet he's loyal.   146
A man does not deserve to die for that.
How many angry passions does this leash
Restrain in me, this curb of knowing well
That I must wake and find myself alone!   150

SECOND SOLDIER. All this fine talk, Clotaldo, is a cruel
    Spurn of the public welfare. We are loyal
    Who wish our own prince to reign over us.

CLOTALDO. Such loyalty, after the king were dead,
    Would honour you. But while the king is living   155
    He is our absolute, unquestioned lord.
    There's no excuse for subjects who oppose
    His sovereignty in arms.

FIRST SOLDIER.   We'll soon see well
    Enough, Clotaldo, what this loyalty
    Is worth.

CLOTALDO.   You would be better if you had some.   160
    It is the greatest prize.

SEGISMUND.   Peace, peace, I pray you.

CLOTALDO. My lord!

SEGISMUND   Clotaldo, if your feelings
    Are truly thus, go you, and serve the king;
    That's prudence, loyalty, and common sense.
    But do not argue here with anyone   165
    Whether it's right or wrong, for every man
    Has his own honour.

CLOTALDO.   Humbly I take my leave.   [*Exit.*]

SEGISMUND Now sound the drums and march in rank and order
    Straight to the palace.

ALL.   Long live Segismund!

SEGISMUND. Fortune, we go to reign! Do not awake me   170
    If I am dreaming! Do not let me fall
    Asleep if it is true! To act with virtue
    Is what matters, since if this proves true,
    That truth's sufficient reason in itself;
    If not, we win us friends against the time   175
    When we at last awake.

A room in the royal palace

[*Enter* BASIL *and* ASTOLFO.]

BASIL. Whose prudence can rein in a bolting horse?
    Who can restrain a river's pride, in spate?
    Whose valour can withstand a crag dislodged
    And hurtling downwards from a mountain peak?   180
    All these are easier by far than to hold back
    A crowd's proud fury, once it has been roused.

It has two voices, both proclaiming war,
And you can hear them echoing through the mountains,
Some shouting "Segismund," others "Astolfo."   185
The scene I set for swearing of allegiance
Lends but an added horror to this strife:
It has become the back cloth to a stage
Where Fortune plays out tragedies in blood.

ASTOLFO. My lord, forget the happiness and wealth   190
You promised me from your most blessèd hand.
If Poland, which I hope to rule, refuses
Obedience to my right, grudging me honour,
It is because I've got to earn it first.
Give me a horse, that I with angry pride   195
May match the thunder in my voice and ride
To strike, like lightning, terror far and wide.   [*Exit.*]

BASIL. No remedy for what's infallible!
What is foreseen is perilous indeed!
If something has to be, there's no way out;   200
In trying to evade it, you but court it.
This law is pitiless and horrible.
Thinking one can evade the risk, one meets it:
My own precautions have been my undoing,
And I myself have quite destroyed my kingdom.   205
   [*Enter* STELLA.]

STELLA. If you, my lord, in person do not try
To curb the vast commotion that has started
In all the streets between the rival factions,
You'll see your kingdom, swamped in waves of crimson,
Swimming in its own blood, with nothing left   210
But havoc, dire calamity, and woe.
So frightful is the damage to your empire
That, seen, it strikes amazement; heard, despair.
The sun's obscured, the very winds are hindered.
Each stone is a memorial to the dead.   215
Each flower springs from a grave while every building
Appears a mausoleum, and each soldier
A premature and walking skeleton.
   [*Enter* CLOTALDO.]

CLOTALDO. Praise be to God, I reach your feet alive!
BASIL. Clotaldo! What's the news of Segismund?   220
CLOTALDO. The crowd, a headstrong monster blind with rage,
Entered his dungeon tower and set him free.
He, now exalted for the second time,
Conducts himself with valour, boasting how
He will bring down the truth out of the stars.   225
BASIL. Give me a horse, that I myself, in person,
May vanquish such a base, ungrateful son!

For I, in the defence of my own crown,
Shall do by steel what science failed to do.   [*Exit.*]
STELLA. I'll be Bellona to your Sun, and try   230
To write my name next yours in history.
I'll ride as though I flew on outstretched wings
That I may vie with Pallas.   [*Exit.*]

[*Enter* ROSAURA, *holding back* CLOTALDO.]

ROSAURA. I know that all is war, Clotaldo, yet
Although your valour calls you to the front,   235
First hear me out. You know quite well that I
Arrived in Poland poor and miserable,
Where, shielded by your valour, I found mercy.
You told me to conceal myself, and stay
Here in the palace, hiding from Astolfo.   240
He saw me in the end, and so insulted
My honour that (although he saw me clearly)
He nightly speaks with Stella in the garden.
I have the key to it and I will show you
How you can enter there and end my cares.   245
Thus bold, resolved, and strong, you can recover
My honour, since you're ready to avenge me
By killing him.
CLOTALDO.   It's true that I intended,
Since first I saw you (having heard your tale)
With my own life to rectify your wrongs.   250
The first step that I took was bid you dress
According to your sex, for fear Astolfo
Might see you as you were, and deem you wanton.
I was devising how we could recover
Your honour (so much did it weigh on me)   255
Even though we had to kill him. (A wild plan—
Though since he's not my king, I would not flinch
From killing him.) But then, when suddenly
Segismund tried to kill me, it was he
Who saved my life with his surpassing valour.   260
Consider: how can I requite Astolfo
With death for giving me my life so bravely,
And when my soul is full of gratitude?
So torn between the two of you I stand—
Rosaura, whose life I saved, and Astolfo,   265
Who saved my life. What's to be done? Which side
To take, and whom to help, I cannot judge.

230. *Bellona:* the Roman war goddess.
234ff. Calderón, and generally dramatists and audiences of the period, had
a distinct taste for debate on points of
honor, valor, loyalty, retribution, of
which the following dialogue between
Rosaura and Clotaldo is an excellent
example. Notice how subtle theoretical
debate develops more and more into
high-sounding passion.

What I owe you in that I gave you life
I owe to him in that he gave me life.
And so there is no course that I can take   270
To satisfy my love. I am a person
Who has to act, yet suffer either way.
ROSAURA. I should not have to tell so brave a man
That if it is nobility to give,
It's baseness to receive. That being so   275
You owe no gratitude to him, admitting
That it was he who gave you life, and you
Who gave me life, since he forced you to take
A meaner role, and through me you assumed
A generous role. So you should side with me: 280
My cause is so far worthier than his own
As giving is than taking.
CLOTALDO.   Though nobility
Is with the giver, it is gratitude
That dwells with the receiver. As a giver
I have the name of being generous: 285
Then grant me that of being grateful too
And let me earn the title and be grateful,
As I am liberal, giving or receiving.
ROSAURA. You granted me my life, at the same time
Telling me it was worthless, since dishonoured,   290
And therefore was no life. Therefore from you
I have received no life at all. And since
You should be liberal first and grateful after
(Since so you said yourself) I now entreat you
Give me the life, the life you never gave me!   295
As giving magnifies the most, give first
And then be grateful after, if you will!
CLOTALDO. Won by your argument, I will be liberal.
Rosaura, I shall give you my estate
And you shall seek a convent, there to live.   300
This measure is a happy thought, for, see,
Fleeing a crime, you find a sanctuary.
For when the empire's threatened with disasters
And is divided thus, I, born a noble,
Am not the man who would augment its woes.   305
So with this remedy which I have chosen
I remain loyal to the kingdom, generous
To you, and also grateful to Astolfo.
And thus I choose the course that suits you best.
Were I your father, what could I do more?   310
ROSAURA. Were you my father, then I would accept
The insult. Since you are not, I refuse.
CLOTALDO. What do you hope to do then?

ROSAURA.   Kill the duke!

CLOTALDO. A girl who never even knew her father
  Armed with such courage?

ROSAURA.   Yes.

CLOTALDO.   What spurs you on?   315

ROSAURA. My good name.

CLOTALDO.   In Astolfo you will find . . .

ROSAURA. My honour rides on him and strikes him down!

CLOTALDO. Your king, too, Stella's husband!

ROSAURA.   Never, never
  Shall that be, by almighty God, I swear!

CLOTALDO. Why, this is madness!

ROSAURA.   Yes it is!

CLOTALDO.   Restrain it.   320

ROSAURA. That I cannot.

CLOTALDO.   Then you are lost forever!

ROSAURA. I know it!

CLOTALDO.   Life and honour both together!

ROSAURA. I well believe it!

CLOTALDO.   What do you intend?

ROSAURA. My death.

CLOTALDO.   This is despair and desperation.

ROSAURA. It's honour.

CLOTALDO.   It is nonsense.

ROSAURA.   It is valour.   325

CLOTALDO. It's frenzy.

ROSAURA.   Yes, it's anger! Yes, it's fury!

CLOTALDO. In short you cannot moderate your passion?

ROSAURA. No.

CLOTALDO.   Who is there to help you?

ROSAURA.   I, myself.

CLOTALDO. There is no cure?

ROSAURA.   There is no cure!

CLOTALDO.   Think well
  If there's not some way out . . .

ROSAURA.   Some other way   330
  To do away with me . . .   [*Exit.*]

CLOTALDO.   If you are lost,
  My daughter, let us both be lost together!

In the country

[*Enter* SEGISMUND *clothed in skins. Soldiers marching.*
  CLARION. *Drums beating.*]

SEGISMUND. If Rome, today, could see me here, renewing
  Her olden triumphs, she might laugh to see
  A wild beast in command of mighty armies,   335

A wild beast, to whose fiery aspirations
The firmament were all too slight a conquest!
But stoop your flight, my spirit. Do not thus
Be puffed to pride by these uncertain plaudits
Which, when I wake, will turn to bitterness   340
In that I won them only to be lost.
The less I value them, the less I'll miss them.
    [*A trumpet sounds.*]

CLARION. Upon a rapid courser (pray excuse me,
    Since if it comes to mind I must describe it)
    In which it seems an atlas was designed   345
    Since if its body is earth, its soul is fire
    Within its breast, its foam appears the sea,
    The wind its breath, and chaos its condition,
    Since in its soul, its foam, its breath and flesh,
    It seems a monster of fire, earth, sea, and wind,   350
    Upon the horse, all of a patchwork colour,
    Dappled, and rushing forward at the will
    Of one who plies the spur, so that it flies
    Rather than runs—see how a woman rides
    Boldly into your presence.

SEGISMUND.   Her light blinds me.   355

CLARION. Good God! Why, here's Rosaura!

SEGISMUND.   It is heaven
    That has restored her to my sight once more.
    [*Enter* ROSAURA *with sword and dagger in riding costume.*]

ROSAURA. Generous Segismund, whose majesty
    Heroically rises in the lustre
    Of his great deeds out of his night of shadows,   360
    And as the greatest planet, in the arms
    Of his aurora, lustrously returns
    To plants and roses, over hills and seas,
    When, crowned with gold, he looks abroad, dispersing
    Radiance, flashing his rays, bathing the summits,   365
    And broidering the fringes of the foam.
    So may you dawn upon the world, bright sun
    Of Poland, that a poor unhappy woman
    May fall before your feet and beg protection
    Both as a woman and unfortunate—   370
    Two things that must oblige you, sire, as one
    Who prize yourself as valiant, each of them
    More than suffices for your chivalry.
    Three times you have beheld me now, three times
    Been ignorant of who I am, because   375
    Three times you saw me in a different clothing.

343. "Clarion's speech is a parody of exaggerated style—including Calder-ón's." [Translator's note]
361. *the greatest planet:* the sun.

The first time you mistook me for a man,
Within that rigorous prison, where your hardships
Made mine seem pleasure. Next time, as a woman,
You saw me, when your pomp and majesty   380
Were as a dream, a phantasm, a shade.
The third time is today when, as a monster
Of both the sexes, in a woman's costume
I bear a soldier's arms. But to dispose you
The better to compassion, hear my story.   385
My mother was a noble in the court
Of Moscow, who, since most unfortunate,
Must have been beautiful. Then came a traitor
And cast his eyes on her (I do not name him,
Not knowing who he is). Yet I deduce   390
That he was valiant too from my own valour,
Since he gave form to me—and I could wish
I had been born in pagan times, that I might
Persuade myself he was some god of those
Who rain in showers of gold, turn into swans   395
Or bulls, for Danaës, Ledas, or Europas.
That's strange: I thought I was just rambling on
By telling old perfidious myths, yet find
I've told you how my mother was cajoled.
Oh, she was beautiful as no one else   400
Has been, but was unfortunate like all.
He swore to wed her (that's an old excuse)
And this trick reached so nearly to her heart
That thought must weep, recalling it today.
The tyrant left her only with his sword   405
As Aeneas left Troy. I sheathed its blade here
Upon my thigh, and I will bare it too
Before the ending of this history.
Out of this union, this poor link which neither
Could bind the marriage nor handcuff the crime,   410
Myself was born, her image and her portrait,
Not in her beauty, but in her misfortune,
For mine's the same. That's all I need to say.
The most that I can tell you of myself
Is that the man who robbed me of the spoils   415
And trophies of my honour is Astolfo.
Alas! to name him my heart rages so

---

396. *for Danaës, Ledas, or Europas:*
To seduce them, Zeus assumed the
shapes, respectively, of a gold shower,
a swan, and a bull.
    406. Probably Calderón was thinking

of Carthage rather than Troy. Aeneas
departed from Carthage in haste, leaving behind the sword which queen Dido
would use for her suicide.

(As hearts will do when men name enemies).
Astolfo was my faithless and ungrateful
Lord, who (quite forgetful of our happiness,   420
Since of a past love even the memory fades)
Came here to claim the throne and marry Stella
For she's the star who rises as I set.
It's hard to credit that a star should sunder
Lovers the stars had made conformable!   425
So hurt was I, so villainously cheated,
That I became mad, brokenhearted, sick,
Half wild with grief, and like to die, with all
Hell's own confusion ciphered on my mind
Like Babel's incoherence. Mutely I told   430
My griefs (since woes and griefs declare themselves
Better than can the mouth, by their effects),
When, with my mother (we were by ourselves),
She broke the prison of my pent-up sorrows
And from my breast they all rushed forth in troops.   435
I felt no shyness, for in knowing surely
That one to whom one's errors are recounted
Has also been an ally in her own,
One finds relief and rest, since bad example
Can sometimes serve for a good purpose too.   440
She heard my plaint with pity, and she tried
To palliate my sorrows with her own.
How easily do judges pardon error
When they've offended too! An example,
A warning, in herself, she did not trust   445
To idleness, or the slow cure of time,
Nor try to find a remedy for her honour
In my misfortunes, but, with better counsel,
She bade me follow him to Poland here
And with prodigious gallantry persuade him   450
To pay the debt to honour that he owes me.
So that it would be easier to travel,
She bade me don male clothing, and took down
This ancient sword which I am wearing now.
Now it is time that I unsheathe the blade   455
As I was bid, for, trusting in its sign,
She said: "Depart to Poland, show this sword
That all the nobles may behold it well,
And it may be that one of them will take
Pity on you, and counsel you, and shield you."   460
I came to Poland and, you will remember,

423. *the star*: Stella = star.

Entered your cave. You looked at me in wonder.
Clotaldo passionately took my part
To plead for mercy to the king, who spared me,
Then, when he heard my story, bade me change   465
Into my own clothes and attend on Stella,
There to disturb Astolfo's love and stop
Their marriage. Again you saw me in woman's dress
And were confused by the discrepancy.
But let's pass to what's new: Clotaldo, now   470
Persuaded that Astolfo must, with Stella,
Come to the throne, dissuades me from my purpose,
Against the interests of my name and honour.
But seeing you, O valiant Segismund,
Are claiming your revenge, now that the heavens   475
Have burst the prison of your rustic tower,
(Wherein you were the tiger of your sorrows,
The rock of sufferings and direful pains)
And sent you forth against your sire and country,
I come to aid you, mingling Dian's silks   480
With the hard steel of Pallas. Now, strong Captain,
It well behoves us both to stop this marriage—
Me, lest my promised husband should be wed,
You, lest, when their estates are joined, they weigh
More powerfully against your victory.   485
I come, as a mere woman, to persuade you
To right my shame; but, as a man, I come
To help you battle for your crown. As woman,
To melt your heart, here at your feet I fall;
But, as a man, I come to serve you bravely   490
Both with my person and my steel, and thus,
If you today should woo me as a woman,
Then I should have to kill you as a man would
In honourable service of my honour;
Since I must be three things today at once—   495
Passionate, to persuade you: womanly,
To ply you with my woes: manly, to gain
Honour in battle.

SEGISMUND.   Heavens! If it is true I'm dreaming,
Suspend my memory, for in a dream
So many things could not occur. Great heavens!   500
If I could only come free of them all!
Or never think of any! Who ever felt
Such grievous doubts? If I but dreamed that triumph
In which I found myself, how can this woman
Refer me to such sure and certain facts?   505
Then all of it was true and not a dream.

But if it be the truth, why does my past life
Call it a dream? This breeds the same confusion.
Are dreams and glories so alike, that fictions
Are held for truths, realities for lies?   510
Is there so little difference in them both
That one should question whether what one sees
And tastes is true or false? What? Is the copy
So near to the original that doubt
Exists between them? Then if that is so,   515
And grandeur, power, majesty, and pomp,
Must all evaporate like shades at morning,
Let's profit by it, this time, to enjoy
That which we only can enjoy in dreams.
Rosaura's in my power: my soul adores her beauty.   520
Let's take the chance. Let love break every law
On which she has relied in coming here
And kneeling, trustful, prostrate at my feet.
This is a dream. If so, dream pleasures now
Since they must turn to sorrows in the end!   525
But with my own opinions, I begin
Once again to convince myself. Let's think.
If it is but vainglory and a dream,
Who for mere human vainglory would lose
True glory? What past blessing is not merely   530
A dream? Who has known heroic glories,
That deep within himself, as he recalls them,
Has never doubted that they might be dreams?
But if this all should end in disenchantment,
Seeing that pleasure is a lovely flame   535
That's soon converted into dust and ashes
By any wind that blows, then let us seek
That which endures in thrifty, lasting fame
In which no pleasures sleep, nor grandeurs dream.
Rosaura's without honour. In a prince   540
It's worthier to restore it than to steal it.
I shall restore it, by the living God,
Before I win my throne! Let's shun the danger
And fly from the temptation which is strong!
Then sound to arms!   545
[*To a soldier*] Today I must give battle before darkness
Buries the rays of gold in green-black waves!

ROSAURA. My lord! Alas, you stand apart, and offer
  No word of pity for my plight. How is it
  You neither hear nor see me nor even yet   550
  Have turned your face on me?

SEGISMUND.   Rosaura, for your honour's sake

I must be cruel to you, to be kind.
My voice must not reply to you because
My honour must reply to you. I am silent
Because my deeds must speak to you alone.   555
I do not look at you since, in such straits,
Having to see your honour is requited,
I must not see your beauty.
    [Exit with soldiers.]

ROSAURA. What strange enigma's this? After such trouble
Still to be treated with more doubtful riddles!   560
    [Enter CLARION.]

CLARION. Madam, may you be visited just now?

ROSAURA. Why, Clarion, where have you been all this time?

CLARION. Shut in the tower, consulting cards
About my death: "to be or not to be."
And it was a near thing.

ROSAURA.   Why?

CLARION.   Because I know   565
The secret who you are: in fact, Clotaldo . . .
[Drums.] But hush what noise is that?

ROSAURA.   What can it be?

CLARION. From the beleaguered palace a whole squadron
Is charging forth to harry and defeat
That of fierce Segismund.

ROSAURA.   Why, what a coward   570
Am I, not to be at his side, the terror
And scandal of the world, while such fierce strife
Presses all round in lawless anarchy.   *[Exit.]*

VOICES OF SOME. Long live our king!

VOICES OF OTHERS.   Long live our liberty!

CLARION. Long live both king and liberty. Yes, live!   575
And welcome to them both! I do not worry
In all this pother, I behave like Nero
Who never grieved at what was going on.
If I had anything to grieve about
It would be me, myself. Well hidden here,   580
Now, I can watch the sport that's going on.
This place is safe and hidden between crags,
And since death cannot find me here, two figs for death!
    [He hides. Drums and the clash of arms are heard. Enter
    BASIL, CLOTALDO, *and* ASTOLFO, *fleeing.]*

BASIL. Was ever king so hapless as myself
Or father more ill used?

CLOTALDO.   Your beaten army   585
Rush down, in all directions, in disorder.

ASTOLFO. The traitors win!

BASIL   In battles such as these

Those on the winning side are ever "loyal,"
And traitors the defeated. Come, Clotaldo,
Let's flee from the inhuman cruelty   590
Of my fierce son!
        [*Shots are fired within.* CLARION *falls wounded.*]
CLARION.   Heavens, save me!
ASTOLFO.   Who is this
    Unhappy soldier bleeding at our feet?
CLARION. I am a most unlucky man who, wishing
    To guard myself from death, have sought it out
    By fleeing from it. Shunning it, I found it,   595
    Because, to death, no hiding-place is secret.
    So you can argue that whoever shuns it
    Most carefully runs into it the quickest.
    Turn, then, once more into the thick of battle:
    There is more safety there amidst the fire   600
    And clash of arms than here on this secluded
    Mountain, because no hidden path is safe
    From the inclemency of Fate; and so,
    Although you flee from death, yet you may find it   604
    Quicker than you expect, if God so wills. [*He falls dead.*]
BASIL. "If God so wills" . . . With what strange eloquence
    This corpse persuades our ignorance and error
    To better knowledge, speaking from the mouth
    Of its fell wound, where the red liquid flowing
    Seems like a bloody tongue which teaches us   610
    That the activities of man are vain
    When they are pitted against higher powers.
    For I, who wished to liberate my country
    From murder and sedition, gave it up
    To the same ills from which I would have saved it.   615
CLOTALDO. Though Fate, my lord, knows every path, and finds
    Him whom it seeks even in the midst of crags
    And thickets, it is not a Christian judgment
    To say there is no refuge from its fury.
    A prudent man can conquer Fate itself.   620
    Though you are not exempted from misfortune,
    Take action to escape it while you can!
ASTOLFO. Clotaldo speaks as one mature in prudence,
    And I as one in valour's youthful prime.
    Among the thickets of this mount is hidden   625
    A horse, the very birth of the swift wind.
    Flee on him, and I'll guard you in the rear.
BASIL. If it is God's will I should die, or if
    Death waits here for my coming, I will seek
    Him out today, and meet him face to face.   630
        [*Enter* SEGISMUND, STELLA, ROSAURA, *soldiers, and their*

train.]

A SOLDIER. Amongst the thickets of this mountain
  The king is hiding.
SEGISMUND.   Seek him out at once!
  Leave no foot of the summit unexplored
  But search from stem to stem and branch to branch!
CLOTALDO. Fly, sir!
BASIL.   What for?
ASTOLFO.   What do you mean to do?   635
BASIL. Astolfo, stand aside!
CLOTALDO.   What is your wish?
BASIL. To take a cure I've needed for sometime.
  [*To* SEGISMUND] If you have come to seek me, here I am.
  [*Kneeling*] Your father, prince, kneels humbly at your feet.
  The white snow of my hair is now your carpet.   640
  Tread on my neck and trample on my crown!
  Lay low and drag my dignity in dust!
  Take vengeance on my honour! Make a slave
  Of me and, after all I've done to thwart them,
  Let Fate fulfil its edict and claim homage   645
  And Heaven fulfil its oracles at last!
SEGISMUND. Illustrious court of Poland, who have been
  The witness of such unwonted wonders,
  Attend to me, and hear your prince speak out.
  What Heaven decrees and God writes with his finger   650
  (Whose prints and ciphers are the azure leaves
  Adorned with golden lettering of the stars)
  Never deceives nor lies. They only lie
  Who seek to penetrate the mystery
  And, having reached it, use it to ill purpose.   655
  My father, who is here to evade the fury
  Of my proud nature, made me a wild beast:
  So, when I, by my birth of gallant stock,
  My generous blood, and inbred grace and valour,
  Might well have proved both gentle and forbearing,   660
  The very mode of life to which he forced me,
  The sort of bringing up I had to bear
  Sufficed to make me savage in my passions.
  What a strange method of restraining them!
  If one were to tell any man: "One day   665
  You will be killed by an inhuman monster,"
  Would it be the best method he could choose
  To wake that monster when it was asleep?
  Or if they told him: "That sword which you're wearing
  Will be your death," what sort of cure were it   670
  To draw it forth and aim it at his breast?

Or if they told him: "Deep blue gulfs of water
Will one day be your sepulchre and grave
Beneath a silver monument of foam,"
He would be mad to hurl himself in headlong   675
When the sea highest heaved its showy mountains
And crystalline sierras plumed with spray.
The same has happened to the king as to him
Who wakes a beast which threatens death, to him
Who draws a naked sword because he fears it,   680
To him who dives into the stormy breakers.
Though my ferocious nature (hear me now)
Was like a sleeping beast, my inborn rage
A sheathèd sword, my wrath a quiet ripple,
Fate should not be coerced by man's injustice—   685
This rouses more resentment. So it is
That he who seeks to tame his fortune must
Resort to moderation and to measure.
He who foresees an evil cannot conquer it
Thus in advance, for though humility   690
Can overcome it, this it can do only
When the occasion's there, for there's no way
To dodge one's fate and thus evade the issue.
Let this strange spectacle serve as example—
This prodigy, this horror, and this wonder,   695
Because it is no less than one, to see,
After such measures and precautions taken
To thwart it, that a father thus should kneel
At his son's feet, a kingdom thus be shattered.
This was the sentence of the heavens above,   700
Which he could not evade, much though he tried.
Can I, younger in age, less brave, and less
In science than the king, conquer that fate?
[*To the* KING] Sire, rise, give me your hand, now that the heavens
Have shown you that you erred as to the method   705
To vanquish them. Humbly I kneel before you
And offer you my neck to tread upon.
BASIL. Son, such a great and noble act restores you
    Straight to my heart. Oh, true and worthy prince!
    You have won both the laurel and the palm.   710
    Crown yourself with your deeds! For you *have* conquered!
ALL. Long live Segismund! Long live Segismund!
SEGISMUND. Since I have other victories to win,
    The greatest of them all awaits me now:
    To conquer my own self. Astolfo, give   715
    Your hand here to Rosaura, for you know
    It is a debt of honour and must be paid.

ASTOLFO. Although, it's true, I owe some obligations—
  She does not know her name or who she is,
  It would be base to wed a woman who . . .   720
CLOTALDO. Hold! Wait! Rosaura's of as noble stock
  As yours, Astolfo. In the open field
  I'll prove it with my sword. She is my daughter,
  And that should be enough.
ASTOLFO.   What do you say?
CLOTALDO. Until I saw her married, righted, honoured,   725
  I did not wish for it to be discovered.
  It's a long story but she is my daughter.
ASTOLFO. That being so, I'm glad to keep my word.
SEGISMUND. And now, so that the princess Stella here
  Will not remain disconsolate to lose   730
  A prince of so much valour, here I offer
  My hand to her, no less in birth and rank.
  Give me your hand.
STELLA.   I gain by meriting
  So great a happiness.
SEGISMUND.   And now, Clotaldo,
  So long so loyal to my father come   735
  To my arms. Ask me anything you wish.
FIRST SOLDIER. If thus you treat a man who never served you,
  What about me who led the revolution
  And brought you from your dungeon in the tower?
  What will you give me?
SEGISMUND.   That same tower and dungeon   740
  From which you never shall emerge till death.
  No traitor is of use after his treason.
BASIL. All wonder at your wisdom!
ASTOLFO.   What a change
  Of character!
ROSAURA.   How wise and prudent!
SEGISMUND.   Why
  Do you wonder? Why do you marvel, since   745
  It was a dream that taught me and I still
  Fear to wake up once more in my close dungeon?
  Though that may never happen, it's enough
  To dream it might, for thus I came to learn
  That all our human happiness must pass   750
  Away like any dream, and I would here
  Enjoy it fully ere it glide away,
  Asking (for noble hearts are prone to pardon)
  Pardon for faults in the actors or the play.

---

754. This form of close, addressed to the audience and begging for its favor, is a well-established Renaissance convention.

A Note on Translation

Reading literature in translation is a pleasure on which it is fruitless to frown. The purist may insist that we ought always read in the original languages, and we know ideally that he is right. But his counsel is a counsel of perfection, quite impractical even for him, since no man in one lifetime can master all the languages whose literatures he might wish to explore. Master languages as fast as we may, we shall always have to read to some extent in translation, and this means we must be alert to what we are about: if in reading a work of literature in translation we are not reading the "original," what precisely are we reading? This is a question of great complexity, to which justice cannot be done in a brief note. Nevertheless, the following sketch of some of the considerations that a mature answer would involve may be helpful to those who are coming into a self-conscious relation with literature in translation for the first time.

One of the memorable scenes of ancient literature is the meeting of Hector and Andromache in Book VI of Homer's *Iliad*. Hector, leader and mainstay of the armies defending Troy, is implored by his wife Andromache to withdraw within the city walls and carry on the defense from there, where his life will not be constantly at hazard. In Homer's text her opening words to him are these: δαιμόνιε, φθίσει σε τὸ σὸν μένος. How should they be translated into English?

Here is how they have actually been translated into English by capable translators, at various periods, in verse and prose.

1. George Chapman, 1598

> O noblest in desire,
> Thy mind, inflamed with others' good, will set thy self on fire.

2. John Dryden, 1693

> Thy dauntless heart (which I foresee too late),
> Too daring man, will urge thee to thy fate.

3. Alexander Pope, 1715

> Too daring Prince! ...
> For sure such courage length of life denies,
> And thou must fall, thy virtue's sacrifice.

4. William Cowper, 1791

> Thy own great courage will cut short thy days,
> My noble Hector....

5. Lang, Leaf, and Myers, 1883 (prose)

> Dear my lord, this thy hardihood will undo thee....

6. A. T. Murray, 1924 (prose, Loeb Library)

> Ah, my husband, this prowess of thine will be thy doom....

7. E. V. Rieu, 1950 (prose)

> "Hector," she said, "you are possessed. This bravery of yours will be your end."

8. I. A. Richards, 1950 (prose)

> "Strange man," she said, "your courage will be your destruction."

9. Richmond Lattimore, 1951

> Dearest,
> Your own great strength will be your death....

From these strikingly different renderings of the same six words, certain facts about the nature of translation begin to emerge. We notice, for one thing, that Homer's word μένος is diversified by the translators into "mind," "dauntless heart," "such courage," "great courage," "hardihood," "prowess," "bravery," "courage," "great strength." The word has in fact all these possibilities. Used of things, it normally means "force"; of animals, "fierceness" or "brute strength" or (in the case of horses) "mettle"; of men, "passion" or "spirit" or even "purpose." Homer's application of it in the present case points our attention equally—whatever particular sense we may imagine Andromache to have uppermost—to Hector's force, strength, fierceness in battle, spirited heart and mind. But since English has no matching term of like inclusiveness, the passage as the translators give it to us reflects this lack and we find one attribute singled out to the exclusion of the rest.

Here then is the first and most crucial fact about any work of literature read in translation. It cannot escape the linguistic characteristics of the language into which it is turned: the grammatical, syntactical, lexical, and phonetic boundaries which constitute collectively the individuality or "genius" of that language. A Greek play or a Russian novel in English will be governed first of all by the resources of the English language, resources which are certain to be in every instance very different, as the efforts with μένος show, from those of the original.

Turning from μένος to δαιμόνιε in Homer's clause, we encounter a second crucial fact about translations. Nobody knows exactly what shade of meaning δαιμόνιε had for Homer. In later writers the word normally suggests divinity, something miraculous, wondrous; but in Homer it appears as a vocative of address for both chieftain and commoner, man and wife. The coloring one gives it must therefore be determined either by the way one thinks a Greek wife of Homer's era might actually address her husband (a subject on which we have no information whatever), or in the way one thinks it suitable for a hero's wife to address her husband in an epic poem, that is to say, a highly stylized and formal work. In general, the translators of our century will be seen to have eschewed formality in order to stress the intimacy, the wifeliness, and, especially in Lattimore's case, the tenderness of Andromache's appeal: (6) "Ah, my husband," (7) "Hector" (with perhaps a hint, in "you are possessed," of the alarmed distaste with which wives have so often viewed their husbands' bellicose moods), (8) "Strange man," (9) "Dearest." On the other hand, the older translators have obviously removed Andromache to a certain epic or heroic distance from her beloved, whence she sees and kindles to his selfless courage, acknowledging, even in the moment of pleading with him to be otherwise, his moral grandeur and the tragic destiny this too certainly implies: (1) "O noblest in desire, . . . inflamed by others' good"; (2) "Thy dauntless heart (which I foresee too late), / Too daring man"; (3) "Too daring Prince! . . . / And thou must fall, thy virtue's sacrifice"; (4) "My noble Hector." Even the less specific "Dear my lord" of Lang, Leaf, and Myers looks in the same direction because of its echo of the speech of countless Shakespearean men and women who have shared this powerful moral sense: "Dear my lord, make me acquainted with your cause of grief"; "Perseverance, dear my lord, keeps honor bright"; etc.

The fact about translation which emerges from all this is that just as the translated work reflects the individuality of the language it is turned into, so it reflects the individuality of the age in which it is done, and the age will permeate it everywhere like yeast in dough. We think of one kind of permeation when we think of the governing verse forms and attitudes toward verse at a given epoch. In Chapman's time, experiments seeking an "heroic" verse form for English were widespread, and accordingly he tries a "fourteener" couplet (two rhymed lines of seven stresses each) in his *Iliad* and a pentameter couplet in his *Odyssey*. When Dryden and Pope wrote, a closed pentameter couplet had become established as the heroic form *par excellence*. By Cowper's day, thanks largely to the prestige of *Paradise Lost*, the couplet had gone out of fashion for narrative poetry in favor of blank verse. Our age, inclining to prose and in verse to proselike informalities and relaxations, has predictably produced half a dozen excellent prose translations of the *Iliad*, but only one in verse, and that one in swirling loose hexameters which are much of the time closer to the verse of William Carlos Williams and some of the prose of novelists like Faulkner than to the swift firm tread of Homer's Greek. For if it is true that what we translate from a given work is what, wearing the spectacles of our time, we see in it, it is also true that we see in it what we have the power to translate.

Of course there are other effects of the translator's epoch on his translation besides those exercised by contemporary taste in verse and verse forms. Chapman writes in a great age of poetic metaphor and therefore almost instinctively translates his understanding of Homer's verb φθίσει ("to cause to wane, consume, waste, pine") into metaphorical terms of flame, presenting his Hector to us as a man of burning generosity who will be consumed by this very ardor. This is a conception rooted in large part in the psychology of the Elizabethans, who had the habit of speaking of the soul as "fire," of one of the four temperaments as "fiery," of even the more material bodily processes, like digestion, as if they were carried on by the heat of fire ("concoction," "decoction"). It is rooted too in that characteristic Renaissance élan so unforgettably expressed in characters like Tamburlaine and Dr. Faustus, the former of whom exclaims to the stars above:

> ... I, the chiefest lamp of all the earth,
> First rising in the East with mild aspect,
> But fixèd now in the meridian line,
> Will send up fire to your turning spheres,
> And cause the sun to borrow light of you....

Pope and Dryden, by contrast, write to audiences for whom strong metaphor has become suspect. They therefore reject the fire image (which we must recall is not present in the Greek) in favor of a form of speech more congenial to their age, the *sententia* or aphorism, and give it extra vitality by making it the scene of a miniature drama: in Dryden's case, the hero's dauntless heart "urges" him (in the double sense of physical as well as moral pressure) to his fate; in Pope's, the hero's courage, like a judge, "denies" continuance of life, with the consequence that he "falls"—and here Pope's second line suggests analogy to the sacrificial animal—the victim of his own essential nature, of what he is.

To pose even more graphically the pressures that a translator's period brings, consider the following lines from Hector's reply to Andromache's appeal that he withdraw, first in Chapman's Elizabethan version, then in Lattimore's twentieth-century one:

Chapman, 1598:

> The spirit I did first breathe
> Did never teach me that—much less since the contempt of death
> Was settled in me, and my mind knew what a Worthy was,
> Whose office is to lead in fight and give no danger pass
> Without improvement. In this fire must Hector's trial shine.
> Here must his country, father, friends be in him made divine.

Lattimore, 1951:

> ...the spirit would not let me, since I have learned to be valiant
> and to fight always among the foremost rank of the Trojans,
> winning for myself great glory, and for my father.

If one may exaggerate to make a necessary point, the world of Henry V and Othello suddenly gives way here to the world of Willie Loman; we are still reading the *Iliad*, but we have obviously come home.

Besides the two factors so far mentioned, language and period, as affecting the character of a translation, there is inevitably a third— the translator himself, with his particular degree of talent, his personal way of regarding the work to be translated, his own special hierarchy of values, moral, esthetic, metaphysical (which may or may not be summed up in a "world view"), his unique style or lack of it. But this influence all readers are likely to bear in mind, and it needs no laboring here. That, for example, two translators of Hamlet, one a Freudian, the other an Existentialist, will produce impressively different translations is obvious from the fact that when Freudian and Existentialist argue about the play in English they often seem to have different plays in mind.

We can now return to the question from which we started. After all allowances have been made for language, age, and individual translator, is anything of the original left? What, in short, does the reader of translations read? Let it be said at once that in utility prose —prose whose function is mainly referential—he reads everything that matters. "*Nicht Rauchen,*" "*Défense de Fumer,*" and "*No Smoking,*" posted in a railway car, make their point, and the differences between them in sound and form have no significance for us in that context. Since the prose of a treatise and of most fiction is preponderantly referential, we rightly feel, when we have paid close attention to Cervantes or Montaigne or Machiavelli or Tolstoy in a good English translation, that we have had roughly the same experience as a native Spaniard, Frenchman, Italian, or Russian. But "roughly" is the correct word; for good prose points iconically *to* itself as well as referentially beyond itself, and everything that it points to in itself in the original (rhythms, sounds, idioms, word play, etc.) must alter radically in being translated. The best analogy is to imagine a Van Gogh painting reproduced in the medium of tempera, etching, or engraving: the "picture" remains, but the intricate interanimation of volumes with colorings with brushstrokes has disappeared.

When we move on to poetry, even in its longer narrative and dramatic forms—plays like *Oedipus*, poems like the *Iliad* or the *Divine Comedy*—our situation as English readers worsens appreciably, as the many unlike versions of Andromache's appeal to Hector make very clear. But, again, only appreciably. True, this is the point at which the fact that a translation is *always* an interpretation explodes irresistibly on our attention; but if it is a good translation, the result will be a sensitive interpretation and also a work with intrinsic interest in its own right—at very best, a true work of art, a new poem. It is only when the shorter, primarily lyrical forms of poetry are presented that the reader of translations faces insuperable disadvantage. In these forms, the referential aspect of language has a tendency to disappear into, or, more often, draw its real meaning and accreditation from, the iconic aspect. Let us look for just a moment at a brief poem by Federico García Lorca and its English translation (by Stephen Spender and J. L. Gili):

> .*Alto pinar!*
> ¹ *Cuatro palomas por el aire van.*
>
> *Cuatro palomas*
> *vuelan y tornan.*
> *Llevan heridas*
> *sus cuatro sombras.*
>
> .*Bajo pinar!*
> ¹ *Cuatro palomas en la tierra están.*

> Above the pine trees:
> Four pigeons go through the air.
>
> Four pigeons
> fly and turn round.
> They carry wounded
> their four shadows.
>
> Below the pine trees:
> Four pigeons lie on the earth.

In this translation the referential sense of the English words follows with remarkable exactness the referential sense of the Spanish words they replace. But the life of Lorca's poem does not lie in that sense. It lies in such matters as the abruptness, like an intake of breath at a sudden revelation, of the two exclamatory lines (1 and 5), which then exhale musically in images of flight and death; or as the

echoings of *palomas* in *heridas* and *sombras*, bringing together (as
in fact the hunter's gun has done) these unrelated nouns and the
unrelated experiences they stand for in a sequence that seems, mo-
mentarily, to have all the logic of a tragic action, in which *doves*
become *wounds* become *shadows;* or as the external and internal
rhyming among the five verbs, as though all motion must (as in fact
it must) end with *están.*

 Since none of this can be brought over into another tongue (least
of all Lorca's rhythms), the translator must decide between leaving
his reader to wonder why Lorca is a poet to be bothered about at all,
and making a new but true poem of his own, whose merit will almost
certainly be in inverse ratio to its likeness to the original. Samuel
Johnson made such a poem in translating Horace's famous *Diffugere
nives,* and so did A. E. Housman. If we juxtapose the last two stanzas
of each translation, and the corresponding Latin, we can see at a
glance that each has the consistency and inner life of a genuine
poem, and that neither of them (even if we consider only what is
obvious to the eye, the line-lengths) is very close to Horace.

> *Cum semel occideris, et de te splendida Minos*
> * fecerit arbitria,*
> *non, Torquate, genus, non te facundia, non te*
> * restituet pietas.*
>
> *Infernis neque enim tenebris Diana pudicum*
> * liberat Hippolytum*
> *nec Lethaea valet Theseus abrumpere caro*
> * vincula Pirithoo.*

Johnson:

> Not you, Torquatus, boast of Rome,
> When Minos once has fixed your doom,
> Or eloquence, or splendid birth,
> Or virtue, shall restore to earth.
> Hippolytus, unjustly slain,
> Diana calls to life in vain;
> Nor can the might of Theseus rend
> The chains of hell that hold his friend.

Housman:

> When thou descendest once the shades among,
>   The stern assize and equal judgment o'er,
> Not thy long lineage nor thy golden tongue,
>   No, nor thy righteousness, shall friend thee more.
>
> Night holds Hippolytus the pure of stain,
>   Diana steads him nothing, he must stay;
> And Theseus leaves Pirithous in the chain
>   The love of comrades cannot take away.

The truth of the matter is that when the translator of short poems chooses to be literal, he loses most or all of the poetry; and when he chooses to make his own poetry, he loses most or all of the author. There is no way out of this dilemma, and in our own selection of short poems for this edition we have acknowledged the problem by excluding translations in favor of short poems written originally in English.[1]

We may assure ourselves, then, that the reading of literature in translation is not the disaster it has sometimes been represented. It is true that, however good the translation, we remain at a remove from the original, the remove becoming closest to impassable in the genre of the lyric poem. But with this exception, it is obvious that translation brings us closer by far to the work than we could be if we did not read it at all, or read it with a defective knowledge of the language. "To a thousand cavils," said Samuel Johnson, "one answer is sufficient; the purpose of a writer is to be read, and the criticism which would destroy the power of pleasing must be blown aside." Johnson was defending Pope's Homer for those marks of its own time and place that make it the great interpretation it is; but Johnson's exhilarating common sense applies equally to the problem we are considering here. Literature is to be read, and the criticism that would destroy the reader's power to make some form of contact with much of the world's great writing must indeed be blown aside.

MAYNARD MACK

1. So in the first two editions. In this edition we have been less exclusive for the reasons given in the Preface.

Index